# Fundamentals of Corporate Finance

## European Edition

# Fundamentals of Corporate Finance

## European Edition

David Hillier, Iain Clacher,
Stephen Ross, Randolph Westerfield,
Bradford Jordon

**London** Boston Burr Ridge, IL Dubuque, IA Madison, WI New York San Francisco
St. Louis Bangkok Bogotá Caracas Kuala Lumpur Lisbon Madrid Mexico City Milan
Montreal New Delhi Santiago Seoul Singapore Sydney Taipei Toronto

*Fundamentals of Corporate Finance: European Edition*
David Hillier, Iain Clacher, Stephen Ross, Randolph Westerfield, Bradford Jordan
ISBN-13 978-0-07-712525-7
ISBN-10 0-07-712525-8

**McGraw-Hill
Higher Education**

Published by McGraw-Hill Education
Shoppenhangers Road
Maidenhead
Berkshire
SL6 2QL
Telephone: 44 (0) 1628 502 500
Fax: 44 (0) 1628 770 224
Website: www.mcgraw-hill.co.uk

**British Library Cataloguing in Publication Data**
A catalogue record for this book is available from the British Library

**Library of Congress Cataloguing in Publication Data**
The Library of Congress data for this book has been applied for from the Library
of Congress

Acquisitions Editor: Mark Kavanagh
Development Editor: Tom Hill
Marketing Manager: Vanessa Boddington
Senior Production Editor: James Bishop

Cover design by Adam Renvoize
Printed and bound in Singapore by Markono Print Media Pte Ltd

# Brief Table of Contents

# Detailed Table of Contents

> *Available on the Online Learning Centre*: www.mcgraw-hill.co.uk/textbooks/hillier
> Appendix 6A: The Term Structure of Interest Rates, Spot Rates, and Yield to Maturity

# Preface

*Fundamentals of Corporate Finance* is my third and final adaptation of quality finance textbooks for the international readers. In a way, it completes the trilogy of texts from *Financial Markets and Corporate Strategy* through *Corporate Finance* to the present text. All three books will take a student from having virtually no knowledge of corporate finance to a doctoral level of understanding.

As a lecturer of 16 years, I fully understand the need for textbooks to be targeted to different reader groups and *Fundamentals* is no different in that regard. When asked to do the European adaptation by McGraw-Hill I was determined that the book would be significantly more relevant to the students that I teach in the UK, Europe, Africa and South East Asia. The original US version of *Fundamentals* is an excellent textbook that clearly introduces non-specialists to the concepts underlying modern corporate finance. However, it is clearly written with a North American readership in mind and although the United States is the largest economy in the world, it is not representative of the corporate environment in most other countries.

In this regard, I have endeavoured to maintain the theoretical and conceptual foundations of the original text but extend and focus the discussion to the European (and international) context. Drawing from comprehensive reviewer feedback, focus sessions, as well as earlier innovations in *Corporate Finance* and *Financial Markets and Corporate Strategy*, I have extensively revised *Fundamentals* to be at the forefront of European corporate finance thought and practice.

Important improvements include:

- **Rewritten for an Environment that Follows Fair Value Accounting and International Financial Reporting Standards** Accounting standards are very different in the US from the rest of the world and the material in nearly every chapter is rewritten to acknowledge this difference.

- **International Tax System** Taxation affects the main sections of the book (Capital Budgeting and Capital Structure) and this is reflected in the examples and end of chapter questions of every chapter.

- **Bankruptcy Laws** Bankruptcy regulations have significant differences across countries.

- **International Corporate Governance** There is now a recognition of different governance systems across countries and their effect on corporate behaviour and decision making.

- **Business Practice across Countries** Companies in the US have quite different operational methods and strategies from Europe and the rest of the world. This is now reflected in the text and supported by research references.

- **Capital Raising** Similarly, the US capital-raising environment is quite different to that of Europe and the rest of the world. Pre-emptive rights and other regulatory constraints introduce important differences in corporate financing.

- **Regulatory Differences** There is a range of regulatory differences that affect business decision-making. For example, illegality of poison pills in Europe has affected merger and acquisition activity. Moreover, there have been a number of harmonization laws within the European Union that have changed corporate finance practice. Examples are the Single Euro Payments Area for cash transactions and the Common Consolidated Tax Base (affects all cross-border business within Europe).

I also recognise that the readership and teaching styles are different across the world. As a result, the book is now broader in its approach:

- **Online Support** A major part of McGraw-Hill's strategy is to provide considerable online backup to the text. The online resources are substantial and are being continually revised and upgraded. More information on this follows.

- **End of Chapter Questions** The questions have now been completely overhauled for an international readership.

The field of Corporate Finance is always changing and the book has been updated to reflect the newest developments in the field:

- **New Theories and Fields** The text benefits from recent developments in corporate finance including corporate governance and behavioural finance.

- **Full Integration of the Global Financial Crisis of 2008** Corporate finance has fundamentally changed as a result of the seismic effects of the credit crunch and resulting shift in economic power across the world. This has changed the way that financial managers think about business and the financial markets. The text reflects these changes and deals with many current issues in the area.

*Fundamentals of Corporate Finance* captures current thinking in corporate finance and expresses it in a highly intuitive and accessible way. I've thoroughly enjoyed writing the chapters and sincerely hope you have the same enjoyment reading them.

David Hillier
January 2011

# Guided Tour

In addition to illustrating pertinent concepts and presenting up-to-date coverage, *Fundamentals of Corporate Finance* strives to present the material in a way that makes it coherent and easy to understand. To meet the varied needs of its intended audience, *Fundamentals of Corporate Finance* is rich in valuable learning tools and support:

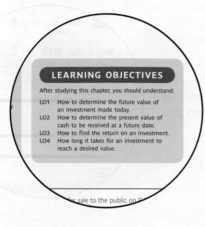

## Learning Objectives

Each chapter opens with a set of learning objectives, summarizing what knowledge, skills or understanding you should acquire from each chapter.

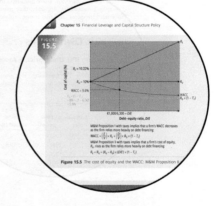

## Figures and Tables

Each chapter provides a number of figures and tables to help you visualize the material being covered.

## Examples

Boxed examples using both real and hypothetical companies are integrated throughout the chapters. Each example illustrates an intuitive or mathematical application in a step-by-step format.

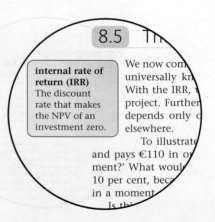

## Key Terms

These are printed in bold type and defined within the margin for easy location and identification.

## Spreadsheet Strategies

This feature introduces you to Microsoft Excel and helps you brush up your Excel spreadsheet skills. This feature appears in self-contained sections and shows you how to set up spreadsheets and analyse common financial problems.

## Work the Web

This boxed feature shows you how to research financial issues using the internet and how to use information you find to make business decisions.

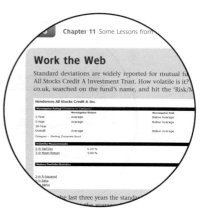

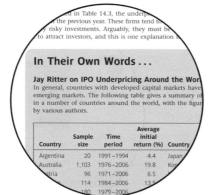

## In Their Own Words

This series of boxes are popular articles written by a distinguished scholar or practitioner on key topics in the text.

## Summary and Conclusions

This briefly reviews and reinforces the main topics you will have covered in each chapter to ensure you have acquired a solid understanding of the key topics.

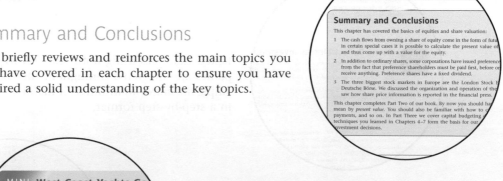

## Mini Cases

Most chapters end with a mini case that focuses on common company situations. Each case presents a new scenario, data, and a dilemma. Several questions at the end of each case reinforce the material learned in that chapter.

We find that many students learn better when they have plenty of opportunity to practise: therefore we have provided extensive questions and problems to test your knowledge throughout the book.

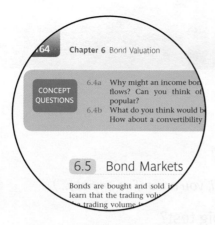

## Concept Questions

Chapter sections are intentionally kept short to promote a step-by-step, building-block approach to learning. Most sections are then followed by a series of short concept questions that highlight the key ideas just presented.

## Chapter Review and Self-Test Problems

These questions and answers allow you to test your abilities in solving key problems related to the chapter content, and provide instant reinforcement.

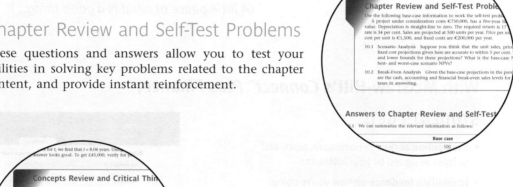

## Concepts Review and Critical Thinking Questions

This end-of-chapter section facilitates your knowledge of key principles, as well as intuitive understanding of the chapter concepts.

## Questions and Problems

Each chapter ends with up to 70 questions, graded by difficulty to fully test your knowledge of the chapter.

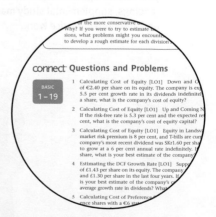

Minus the Concept Questions all of these questions are integrated into our online assignment and assessment platform **Connect**. For more information on Connect see overleaf.

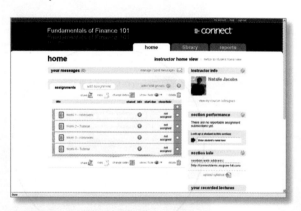
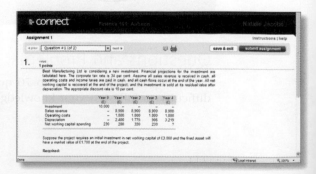

*Less managing. More teaching. Greater learning.*

# INSTRUCTORS...

Would you like your **students** to show up for class **more prepared**?
*(Let's face it, class is much more fun if everyone is engaged and prepared...)*

Want an **easy way to assign** homework online and track student **progress**?
*(Less time grading means more time teaching...)*

Want an **instant view** of student or class performance? *(No more wondering if students understand...)*

Need to **collect data and generate reports** required for administration or accreditation? *(Say goodbye to manually tracking student learning outcomes...)*

Want to **record and post your lectures** for students to view online?

## With **McGraw-Hill's *Connect*™ *Plus Finance*,**

### INSTRUCTORS GET:

- Simple **assignment management**, allowing you to spend more time teaching.

- **Auto-graded** assignments, quizzes, and tests.

- **Detailed Visual Reporting** where student and section results can be viewed and analyzed.

- Sophisticated **online testing** capability.

- A **filtering and reporting** function that allows you to easily assign and report on materials that are correlated to accreditation standards, learning outcomes, and Bloom's taxonomy.

- An easy-to-use **lecture capture** tool.

- The option to **upload course documents** for student access.

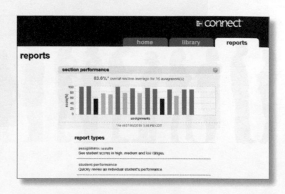

Want an online, **searchable version** of your textbook?

Wish your textbook could be **available online** while you're doing your assignments?

 ## *Connect™ Plus Finance* eBook

If you choose to use *Connect™ Plus Finance*, you have an affordable and searchable online version of your book integrated with your other online tools.

### *Connect™ Plus Finance* eBook offers features like:

- Topic search
- Direct links from assignments
- Adjustable text size
- Jump to page number
- Print by section

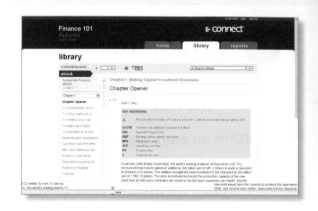

 Want to get more **value** from your textbook purchase?

Think learning finance should be a bit more **interesting**?

 ## Check out the STUDENT RESOURCES section under the *Connect™* Library tab.

Here you'll find a wealth of resources designed to help you achieve your goals in the course. Every student has different needs, so explore the STUDENT RESOURCES to find the materials best suited to you.

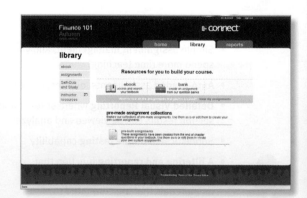

# Technology to enhance learning and teaching

## Visit www.mcgraw-hill.co.uk/textbooks/hillier today!

After completing each chapter, log on to the supporting Online Learning Centre website. Take advantage of the study tools offered to reinforce the material you have read in the text, and to develop your knowledge of finance in a fun and effective way.

**For students:**
The Online Learning Centre (OLC) is your gateway to the following resources designed to accompany the book:

- Mini cases
- Additional chapters
- Appendices
- Videos
- Chapter Objectives

**For lecturers:**
This collection of resources has been put together to help lecturers adopting this text save time when preparing their teaching, and to help them engage and challenge their students so that they get more out of their course:

- PowerPoint slides
- Instructor manual
- Solutions to all the end of chapter questions and case studies
- Artwork from the book

Plus lecturers get access to a **Test Bank** (see overleaf for more details).

**Test Bank available in McGraw-Hill EZ Test Online**

A test bank of over 2000 questions is available to lecturers adopting this book for their module. A range of questions is provided for each chapter, including multiple choice, true or false, and short answer or essay questions. The questions are identified by type, difficulty, learning objective and topic to help you to select questions that best suit your needs, and are accessible through an easy-to-use online testing tool, **McGraw-Hill EZ Test Online**.

**McGraw-Hill EZ Test Online** is accessible to busy academics virtually anywhere – in their office, at home or while travelling – and eliminates the need for software installation. Lecturers can choose from question banks associated with their adopted textbook or easily create their own questions. They also have access to hundreds of banks and thousands of questions created for other McGraw-Hill titles. Multiple versions of tests can be saved for delivery on paper or online through WebCT, Blackboard and other course management systems. When created and delivered though EZ Test Online, students' tests can be immediately marked, saving lecturers time and providing prompt results to students.

To register for this FREE resource, visit www.eztestonline.com

# Custom Publishing Solutions: Let us help make our *content* your *solution*

At McGraw-Hill Education our aim is to help lecturers find the most suitable content for their needs delivered to their students in the most appropriate way. Our **custom publishing solutions** offer the ideal combination of content delivered in the way that best suits lecturer and students.

Our custom publishing programme offers lecturers the opportunity to select just the chapters or sections of material they wish to deliver to their students from a database called CREATE™ at **www.mcgrawhillcreate.co.uk**

CREATE™ contains over two million pages of content from:

- textbooks
- professional books
- case books – Harvard Articles, Insead, Ivey, Darden, Thunderbird and BusinessWeek
- Taking Sides – debate materials

across the following imprints:

- McGraw-Hill Education
- Open University Press
- Harvard Business Publishing
- US and European material

There is also the option to include additional material authored by lecturers in the custom product – this does not necessarily have to be in English.

We will take care of everything from start to finish in the process of developing and delivering a custom product to ensure that lecturers and students receive exactly the material needed in the most suitable way.

With a **Custom Publishing Solution**, students enjoy the best selection of material deemed to be the most suitable for learning everything they need for their courses – something of real value to support their learning. Teachers are able to use exactly the material they want, in the way they want, to support their teaching on the course.

Please contact your **local McGraw-Hill representative** with any questions, or alternatively contact Warren Eels **e:** warren_eels@mcgraw-hill.com.

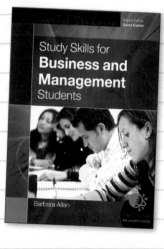

# Acknowledgements

A project as large as *Fundamentals* involves more than just writing and before I started working with McGraw-Hill, I never truly understood just how much goes into getting a book off the ground. As a result, I would like to thank the following (large) group of individuals who have all contributed in some way to the book.

First, I would like to thank my long-suffering friend, colleague, and co-author, Iain Clacher, who has been an integral part of this project and most other things over the past year. Thanks for everything, Iain! You can take the man out of Glasgow…

Second, I would like to thank Mark Kavanagh and Tom Hill of McGraw-Hill who have been absolutely crucial to every stage of development. Holding hand on heart, I know that *Fundamentals* would not be anywhere near as polished if it wasn't for Tom getting on my back every second day. Alas, Mark Kavanagh has now moved on to his next career position and I wish him all the best for the future. Mark, this project is as much about you as it is about me. Many thanks for everything and I'm sure our paths will cross again in time.

I would also like to thank all the people at McGraw-Hill who have worked on *Fundamentals* behind the scenes and who rarely ever get a mention in a textbook. I would like to thank Shona Mullen, General Manager for Content and Digital Development; Vanessa Boddington for all her work on the online Connect package that accompanies this book; James Bishop and the rest of the Production team; and Gill Colver, the proofreader. Finally, I would also like to thank the army of McGraw-Hill sales reps (Jamie, Eoin, Alexis, Bruce, Lauren, Phil, Bernie, Joris, Susan, Martin, Kenneth, Duncan and Nick) who enthusiastically trundle the halls of academe and engage with Finance academics trying to sell my three books. Truth be told, I think of you guys many times a year (but especially in August!).

This is now my third year of writing Finance textbooks and I'm sure my colleagues, friends and family are becoming heartily sick of me thanking them. However, I can't ignore the fact that their goodwill has given me the space and support that allows me to undertake this work.

Consequently, in no particular order, I would like to thank the following colleagues who have influenced my professional life over the course of writing *Fundamentals*: Emanuele Bajo, Marco Bigelli, Kostas Bozos, Pornanong Budsaratragoon, Charlie Cai, Iain Clacher, Dick Davies, Michelle Dickson, Paul Draper, Manapol Ekkayokkaya, Robert Faff, Allan Hodgson, Phil Holmes, Gration Kamugisha, Kevin Keasey, Joyce Khine Kyaw, Suntharee Lhaopadchan, Helix Li, Andy Marshall, Patrick McColgan, Krishna Paudyal, Julio Pindado, Paul Rugangira Kato, Pili Valcarcel, and Gianluca Veronesi.

I would also like to thank my friends: Ronnie and Anne Convery, Philip and Pauline Church, David and Morena Devine, Martin Kemmitt, Paul and Clare Lombardi, Anne and Nicky McLuskey, Pete and Katherine McCudden, Monsignor Tom Monaghan, and Garry and Stella Stern.

I would like to thank my mum, Marion, my siblings, Joe, Margaret, and Chris; my second family, Mary, Liam, John, Patrick and Quentin. Other family members I would like to mention are Bonnie, Cathy, Ian, Julie, Jennifer, Amy, Finn, Con and Nan.

Finally, and most importantly, I would like to thank my beautiful wife, Mary-Jo, and my children, Benjy, Danny, Con, Maria, Patrick and Saoirse, for putting up with me and my mad ways.

David Hillier
January 2011

The authors and publishers would like to pay special thanks to all those who participated in the text's development:

| | |
|---|---|
| Peter Anker | Rotterdam Business School |
| Edel Barnes | University College Cork |
| Jan Bartholdy | Aarhus School of Business |

| | |
|---|---|
| Tariq Bashir | University of East London |
| Uwe-Wilhelm Bloos | Johann Wolfgang Goethe-University |
| Tommy Bood | Karlstad University |
| Mike Buckle | Swansea University |
| Rachel Campbell | Maastricht University |
| Jean Chen | University of Surrey |
| Peter de Goeij | University of Tilburg |
| Everton Dockery | University of Portsmouth |
| Michael Dowling | University of Central Lancashire |
| Ken Dyson | University of Ulster |
| Roy Edwards | University of Southampton |
| Peter-Jan Engelen | Utrecht University |
| Bjarne Florentsen | Copenhagen University |
| Eleimon Gonis | University of the West of England |
| Jens Hagendorff | University of Leeds |
| Llang Han | University of Hull |
| Thomas Hartmann-Wendels | University of Cologne |
| Malcolm Hosking | Bournemouth University |
| Stavroula Iliopoulou | Royal Holloway, University of London |
| Antti Ilmari Rautiainen | University of Jyväskylä |
| Gregory Jabome | Liverpool University |
| Robert Kastner | ESSEC Business School |
| Robert Kelly | National University of Maynooth |
| Edward Kerr | University of Hertfordshire |
| Paul Klumpes | EDHEC Business School |
| Marc Kramer | University of Groningen |
| Jason Laws | Liverpool John Moores University |
| Edward Lee | University of Manchester |
| Joao Madeira | Exeter University |
| Shishir Malde | Nottingham Trent University |
| Marina Martynova | University of Sheffield |
| Omar Masood | University of East London |
| Conor McKeating | Dublin City University |
| Peder Nielsen | Aarhus University |
| Peter Oliver | University of Nottingham |
| Kean Ow-Yong | Birmingham University |
| Keith Parker | Cranfield University |
| Christian Riis Flor | University of Southern Denmark |
| James Ryan | University of Limerick |
| Gert Sandahl | University of Gothenburg |
| Frank Schuhmacher | University of Leipzig |
| Karl Shutes | Coventry University |
| Stefan Sjögren | University of Gothenburg |
| Eleni Sophocleous | University of Durham |
| Stefan Straetmans | Maastricht University |
| Sami Vähämaa | University of Vaasa |
| Katrien Van de Poel | Universiteit Antwerpen |
| Frank W. van den Berg | University of Amsterdam |
| Peter van der Meer | Utrecht University |
| Chaoyan Wang | University of York |
| Pengguo Wang | Imperial College London |
| Norman Williams | University of Greenwich |

# About the Authors

**David Hillier** is a professor of finance at the University of Strathclyde. Professor Hillier has published a wide range of peer-reviewed academic articles on corporate governance, corporate finance, insider trading, asset pricing, precious metals, auditing, and market microstructure. His research has attracted an ANBAR citation and a best paper prize from one of the top finance and management journals in South East Asia. He is on the editorial board and reviews for many of the world's top finance journals. Professor Hillier is an established teacher of executive programmes and has conducted courses for a variety of professional clients, including The World Bank and the UK National Health Service. Finally, he is a co-author of the European editions of *Financial Markets and Corporate Strategy* (McGraw-Hill, 2008) and *Corporate Finance* (McGraw-Hill, 2010).

**Iain Clacher** is a lecturer in Accounting and Finance at Leeds University Business School.

**Stephen A. Ross** is the Franco Modigliani Professor of Finance and Economics at the Sloan School of Management, Massachusetts Institute of Technology.

**Randolph W. Westerfield** is Dean Emeritus of the University of Southern California's Marshall School of Business and is the Charles B. Thornton Professor of Finance.

**Bradford D. Jordan** is Professor of Finance and holder of the Richard W. and Janis H. Furst Endowed Chair in Finance at the University of Kentucky.

# Introduction to Corporate Finance

## LEARNING OBJECTIVES

After studying this chapter, you should understand:

**LO1** The basic types of financial management decision, and the role of the financial manager.
**LO2** The goal of financial management.
**LO3** How financial markets work and the reason they exist.

RECENT YEARS HAVE SEEN corporate finance and financial events displace other newsworthy events from the front pages of newspapers. In 2007 financial markets and the world economy nearly imploded after banks were unable or unwilling to lend money to other companies. This led to a worldwide recession in 2008 and 2009, which saw job losses on an unprecedented scale, massive corporate bankruptcies, and governments spending billions to shore up their own economies.

While the corporate world was experiencing major difficulties, the financial markets performed exceptionally well, with some stock exchanges reporting their best performance on record. For example, while the United Kingdom underwent its longest and deepest recession on record, the London Stock Exchange FTSE 100 index (representing the combined value of its largest companies) grew by just under 50 per cent!

Does this make sense? Understanding the decisions facing corporations, the impact of these decisions, how they affect firm value, and the role of investors is the goal of this text. This takes us into issues involving corporate goals and firm valuation, all of which we introduce in this chapter.

To begin our study of modern corporate finance we need to address two central issues. First, what is corporate finance, and what is the role of the financial manager in the corporation? Second, what is the goal of financial management? For many companies, share price valuation is an exceptionally important issue, and so we also take a brief look at the financial markets and their impact on corporate decision-making.

## 1.1 Corporate Finance and the Financial Manager

In this section we discuss where the financial manager fits in the corporation. We start by defining *corporate finance* and the financial manager's job.

## What Is Corporate Finance?

Imagine that you were to start your own business. No matter what type you started, you would have to answer the following three questions in some form or another:

1   What long-term investments should you make? That is, what lines of business will you be in, and what sorts of buildings, machinery and equipment will you need?

2   Where will you get the long-term financing to pay for your investment? Will you bring in other owners, or will you borrow the money?

3   How will you manage your everyday financial activities, such as collecting from customers and paying suppliers?

These are not the only questions by any means, but they are among the most important. Corporate finance, broadly speaking, is the study of ways to answer these three questions. Accordingly, we'll be looking at each of them in the chapters ahead.

## The Financial Manager

A striking feature of large corporations is that the owners (the shareholders) are not usually directly involved in making business decisions, particularly on a day-to-day basis. Instead, the corporation employs managers to represent the owners' interests and make decisions on their behalf. In a large corporation the financial manager would be in charge of answering the three questions we raised in the preceding section.

The financial management function is usually associated with a top officer of the firm, such as a finance director (FD) or chief financial officer (CFO). Figure 1.1 is a simplified organizational chart that highlights the finance activity in a large firm. As shown, the finance director co-ordinates the activities of the treasurer and the controller. The controller's office handles cost and financial accounting, tax payments, and management information systems. The treasurer's office is responsible for managing the firm's cash and credit, its financial planning, and its capital expenditures.

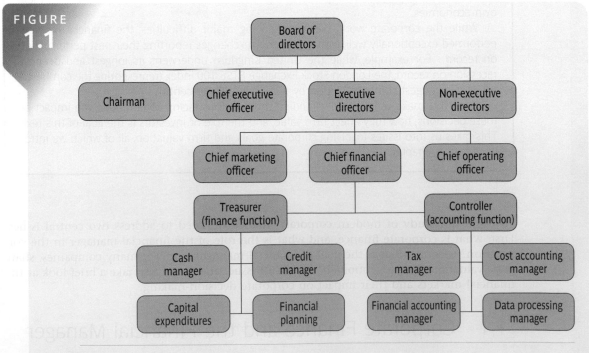

**FIGURE 1.1**

**Figure 1.1** A sample simplified organizational chart

You may be wondering what the difference is between the finance and accounting functions in a firm. The accounting function takes all the financial information and data that arises as a result of ongoing business activities, and presents this in ways that allow management to assess the performance and risk of their firm (financial accounting) and make informed decisions on future corporate activity (management accounting). To ensure that all firms provide comparable information, there are generally accepted accounting standards. In the European Union all firms that are listed on a stock exchange must follow International Accounting Standards (IAS), as set by the International Accounting Standards Board (IASB).

The finance function of the firm is related to the three general questions raised earlier, and the chapters ahead deal primarily with these issues. However, although our study bears mostly on activities associated with the finance function, we also discuss the accounting function whenever it is required to better understand the decisions made by corporations.

## Financial Management Decisions

As the preceding discussion suggests, the financial manager must be concerned with three basic types of question. We consider these in greater detail next.

**Capital Budgeting**   The first question concerns the firm's long-term investments. The process of planning and managing a firm's long-term investments is called **capital budgeting**. In capital budgeting the financial manager tries to identify investment opportunities that are worth more to the firm than they cost to acquire. Loosely speaking, this means that the value of the cash flow generated by an asset exceeds the cost of that asset.

> **capital budgeting**
> The process of planning and managing a firm's long-term investments.

The types of investment opportunity that would typically be considered depend in part on the nature of the firm's business. For example, for a large retailer such as Tesco, deciding whether to open another store would be an important capital budgeting decision. Similarly, for a software company such as Microsoft, the decision to develop and market a new spreadsheet program would be a major capital budgeting decision. Some decisions, such as what type of computer system to purchase, might not depend so much on a particular line of business.

Regardless of the specific nature of an opportunity under consideration, financial managers must be concerned not only with how much cash they expect to receive, but also with when they expect to receive it, and how likely they are to receive it. Evaluating the *size*, *timing* and *risk* of future cash flows is the essence of capital budgeting. In fact, as we shall see in the chapters ahead, whenever we evaluate a business decision, the size, timing and risk of the cash flows will be by far the most important things we shall consider.

**Capital Structure**   The second question for the financial manager concerns ways in which the firm obtains and manages the long-term financing it needs to support its long-term investments. A firm's **capital structure** (or financial structure) is the specific mixture of **long-term debt** and **equity** the firm uses to finance its operations. The financial manager has two concerns in this area. First, how much should the firm borrow? That is, what mixture of debt and equity is best? The mixture chosen will affect both the risk and the value of the firm. Second, what are the least expensive sources of funds for the firm?

> **capital structure**
> The mixture of long-term debt and equity maintained by a firm.
>
> **long-term debt**
> Long-term borrowing by the firm (longer than one year) to finance its long-term investments.
>
> **equity**
> The amount of money raised by the firm that comes from the owners' (shareholders') investment.

If we picture the firm as a pie, then the firm's capital structure determines how that pie is sliced – in other words, what percentage of the firm's cash flow goes to creditors and what percentage goes to shareholders. Firms have a great deal of flexibility in choosing a financial structure. The question of whether one structure is better than any other for a particular firm is the heart of the capital structure issue.

In addition to deciding on the financing mix, the financial manager has to decide exactly how and where to raise the money. The expenses associated with raising long-term financing can be considerable, so different possibilities must be carefully evaluated. Also, corporations borrow money from a variety of lenders in a number of different, and sometimes exotic, ways. Choosing among lenders and among loan types is another job handled by the financial manager.

**working capital**
A firm's short-term assets and liabilities.

**Working Capital Management**   The third question concerns **working capital** management. The term *working capital* refers to a firm's short-term assets, such as inventory, and its short-term liabilities, such as money owed to suppliers. Managing the firm's working capital is a day-to-day activity which ensures that the firm has sufficient resources to continue its operations and avoid costly interruptions. This involves a number of activities related to the firm's receipt and disbursement of cash.

Some questions about working capital that must be answered are the following:

1   How much cash and inventory should we keep on hand?

2   Should we sell on credit? If so, what terms will we offer, and to whom will we extend them?

3   How will we obtain any needed short-term financing? Will we purchase on credit, or will we borrow in the short term and pay cash? If we borrow in the short term, how and where should we do it?

These are just a small sample of the issues that arise in managing a firm's working capital.

**Conclusion**   The three areas of corporate financial management we have described – capital budgeting, capital structure, and working capital management – are very broad categories. Each includes a rich variety of topics, and we have indicated only a few questions that arise in the different areas. The chapters ahead contain greater detail.

**CONCEPT QUESTIONS**

1.1a   What is the capital budgeting decision?
1.1b   What do you call the specific mixture of long-term debt and equity that a firm chooses to use?
1.1c   Into what category of financial management does cash management fall?

## 1.2   The Goal of Financial Management

Assuming that we restrict ourselves to for-profit businesses, the main goal of financial management is to make money or add value for the owners. This goal is a little vague, of course, so we examine some different ways of formulating it to come up with a more precise definition. Such a definition is important, because it leads to an objective basis for making and evaluating financial decisions.

## Possible Goals

If we were to consider possible financial goals, we might come up with some ideas like the following:

- Survive.
- Avoid financial distress and bankruptcy.
- Beat the competition.
- Maximize sales or market share.
- Minimize costs.
- Maximize profits.
- Maintain steady earnings growth.

These are only a few of the goals we could list. Furthermore, each of these possibilities presents problems as a goal for the financial manager.

For example, it's easy to increase market share or unit sales: all we have to do is lower our prices or relax our credit terms. Similarly, we can always cut costs simply by doing away with things such as research and development. We can avoid bankruptcy by never borrowing any money or never taking any risks, and so on. However, it is not clear that any of these actions are in the shareholders' best interests.

Profit maximization would probably be the most commonly cited goal, but even this is not a precise objective. Do we mean profits this year? If so, we should note that actions such as deferring maintenance, letting inventories run down, and taking other short-run cost-cutting measures will tend to increase profits now, but these activities aren't necessarily desirable.

The goal of maximizing profits may refer to some sort of 'long-run' or 'average' profits, but it's still unclear exactly what this means. First, do we mean something like accounting net income or earnings per share? As we shall see in more detail in the next chapter, these accounting numbers may have little to do with what is good or bad for the firm. Second, what do we mean by the long run? As John Maynard Keynes, a famous economist, once remarked, in the long run we're all dead! More to the point, this goal doesn't tell us what the appropriate trade-off is between current and future profits.

The goals we've listed here are all different, but they tend to fall into two classes. The first of these relates to profitability. The goals involving sales, market share and cost control all relate, at least potentially, to different ways of earning or increasing profits. The goals in the second group, involving bankruptcy avoidance, stability and safety, relate in some way to controlling risk. Unfortunately, these two types of goal are somewhat contradictory. The pursuit of profit normally involves some element of risk, so it isn't really possible to maximize both safety and profit. What we need, therefore, is a goal that encompasses both factors.

## The Goal of Financial Management

The financial manager in a corporation makes decisions for the shareholders of the firm. Given this, instead of listing possible goals for the financial manager, we really need to answer a more fundamental question: from the shareholders' point of view, what is a good financial management decision?

If we assume that shareholders buy shares of a company's equity because they seek to gain financially, then the answer is obvious: good decisions increase the value of the equity, and poor decisions decrease the value of the equity.

Given our observations, it follows that the financial manager acts in the shareholders' best interests by making decisions that increase the value of the equity. The appropriate goal for the financial manager can thus be stated quite easily:

> *The goal of financial management is to maximize the current value per share of the existing equity.*

The goal of maximizing the value of the equity avoids the problems associated with the different goals we listed earlier. There is no ambiguity in the criterion, and there is no short-run versus long-run issue. We explicitly mean that our goal is to maximize the *current* share value.

If this goal seems a little strong or one-dimensional to you, keep in mind that the shareholders in a firm are residual owners. By this we mean that they are entitled only to what is left after employees, suppliers and creditors (and anyone else with a legitimate claim) are paid their due. If any of these groups go unpaid, the shareholders get nothing. So, if the shareholders are winning in the sense that the leftover, residual portion is growing, it must be true that everyone else is winning also.

Because the goal of financial management is to maximize the value of the equity, we need to learn how to identify investments and financing arrangements that impact favourably on the value of the equity. This is precisely what we shall be studying. In fact, we could have defined *corporate finance* as the study of the relationship between business decisions and the value of the equity in the business.

## A More General Goal

Given our goal as stated in the preceding section (to maximize the value of the equity), an obvious question comes up: what is the appropriate goal when the firm has no traded equity? Corporations are certainly not the only type of business, and the equity in many corporations rarely changes hands, so it's difficult to say what the value per share is at any given time.

As long as we are dealing with for-profit businesses, only a slight modification is needed. The total value of the equity in a corporation is simply equal to the value of the owners' equity. Therefore a more general way of stating our goal is as follows: maximize the market value of the existing owners' equity.

With this in mind, it doesn't matter what form the business takes. Good financial decisions increase the market value of the owners' equity, and poor financial decisions decrease it. In fact, although we focus on public corporations in the chapters ahead, the principles we develop apply to all forms of business. Many of them even apply to the not-for-profit sector.

Finally, our goal does not imply that the financial manager should take illegal or unethical actions in the hope of increasing the value of the equity in the firm. What we mean is that the financial manager best serves the owners of the business by identifying goods and services that add value to the firm because they are desired and valued in the free marketplace.

**EXAMPLE 1.1**

# Core Values

Every corporation will have a number of goals and objectives that contribute to the main financial management goal of increasing shareholder wealth. Consider the core values of Scottish and Southern Energy plc, the UK electrical utility firm. These are taken directly from their website (www.scottish-southern.co.uk).

**SAFETY**
We believe all accidents are preventable, so we do everything safely and responsibly or not at all.

**SERVICE**
We give our customers service we are proud of and make commitments that we deliver.

**EFFICIENCY**
We keep things simple, do the work that adds value and avoid wasting money, materials, energy or time.

**SUSTAINABILITY**
We operate ethically, taking the long-term view to achieve growth while safeguarding the environment.

**EXCELLENCE**
We strive to get better, smarter and more innovative and be the best in everything we do.

**TEAMWORK**
We support and value our colleagues and enjoy working together as a team in an open and honest way.

Consider each core value. Is it consistent with the goal to maximize shareholder wealth? If not, why not, and does this mean that there are other objectives that are not related to shareholder value?

| CONCEPT QUESTIONS | | |
|---|---|---|
| | 1.2a | What is the goal of financial management? |
| | 1.2b | What are some shortcomings of the goal of profit maximization? |
| | 1.2c | Can you give a definition of *corporate finance*? |

## 1.3 Financial Markets and the Corporation

In most countries the financial markets play a fundamental role in the operations of large corporations. Even if a firm is not traded on a stock exchange, the stock market is important, because it can inform management of the performance of their competitors, suppliers, customers and the economy as a whole. The primary advantage of financial markets is that they facilitate the flow of money from those that have surplus cash to those that need financing.

### Cash Flows To and From the Firm

The interplay between the corporation and the financial markets is illustrated in Fig. 1.2. The arrows in the figure trace the passage of cash from the financial markets to the firm, and from the firm back to the financial markets. Suppose we start with the firm selling shares of equity and borrowing money to raise cash. Cash flows to the firm from the financial markets (A). The firm invests the cash in assets (B). These can be short-term (current) or long-term (non-current), and they generate cash (C), some of which goes to pay corporate taxes (D). After taxes are paid, some of this cash flow is reinvested in the firm (E). The rest goes back to the financial markets as cash paid to creditors and shareholders (F).

The financial markets are not funded just by corporations paying cash to creditors or shareholders. The savings of households (G) also find their way into the financial markets. For example, whenever your salary goes into your bank account, whenever you pay insurance on your car, house or computers, and every time you pay your pension premium, this money will end up in the financial markets. This happens because the financial institutions (H) you pay your money to use it to invest in the financial markets. The difference between what financial institutions earn in the financial markets and what they have to pay you (in terms of monthly interest, random insurance payouts, and pensions) is their profit.

A financial market, like any market, is just a way of bringing buyers and sellers together. In financial markets it is debt and equity securities that are bought and sold. Financial markets differ in detail, however. The most important differences concern the types of security that are traded, how trading is conducted, and who the buyers and sellers are. Some of these differences are discussed next.

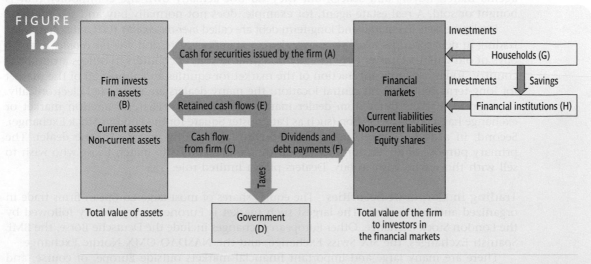

**Figure 1.2** Cash flows between the firm, the financial markets, and the economy

## Primary versus Secondary Markets

Financial markets function as both primary and secondary markets for debt and equity securities. The term *primary market* refers to the original sale of securities by governments and corporations. The *secondary markets* are those in which these securities are bought and sold after the original sale. Equities are, of course, issued solely by corporations. Debt securities are issued by both governments and corporations. In the discussion that follows, we focus on corporate securities only.

**Primary Markets**   In a primary market transaction the corporation is the seller, and the transaction raises money for the corporation. Corporations engage in two types of primary market transaction: public offerings and private placements. A public offering, as the name suggests, involves selling securities to the general public, whereas a private placement is a negotiated sale involving a specific buyer.

By law, public offerings of debt and equity must be registered with the securities regulator in the country where the offerings are made. For example, in the UK this is the Financial Services Authority, and in the Netherlands it is the Authority for Financial Markets (Autoriteit Financiële Markten). Registration requires the firm to disclose a great deal of information before selling any securities. The accounting, legal and selling costs of public offerings can be considerable.

Partly to avoid the various regulatory requirements and the expense of public offerings, debt and equity are often sold privately to large financial institutions such as life insurance companies or mutual funds. Such private placements do not normally have to be registered with securities regulators, and do not require the involvement of underwriters (investment banks that specialize in selling securities to the public).

**Secondary Markets**   A secondary market transaction involves one owner or creditor selling to another. Therefore the secondary markets provide the means for transferring ownership of corporate securities. Although a corporation is directly involved only in a primary market transaction (when it sells securities to raise cash), the secondary markets are still critical to large corporations. The reason is that investors are much more willing to purchase securities in a primary market transaction when they know that those securities can later be resold if desired.

**Dealer versus Auction Markets**   There are two kinds of secondary market: *auction* markets and *dealer* markets. Generally speaking, dealers buy and sell for themselves, at their own risk. A car dealer, for example, buys and sells automobiles. In contrast, brokers and agents match buyers and sellers, but they do not actually own the commodity that is bought or sold. A real estate agent, for example, does not normally buy and sell houses.

Dealer markets in equities and long-term debt are called *over-the-counter* (OTC) markets. Most trading in debt securities takes place over the counter. The expression *over the counter* refers to days of old when securities were literally bought and sold at counters in offices around the country. Today, a significant fraction of the market for equities and almost all of the market for long-term debt have no central location; the many dealers are connected electronically.

Auction markets differ from dealer markets in two ways. First, an auction market or exchange has a physical location (such as Paternoster Square for the London Stock Exchange). Second, in a dealer market, most of the buying and selling is done by the dealer. The primary purpose of an auction market, on the other hand, is to match those who wish to sell with those who wish to buy. Dealers play a limited role.

**Trading in Corporate Securities**   The equity shares of most large European firms trade in organized auction markets. The largest such market is Euronext, very closely followed by the London Stock Exchange. Other European exchanges include the Deutsche Börse, the BME Spanish Exchanges, the SIX Swiss Exchange, and the NASDAQ OMX Nordic Exchange.

There are many large and important financial markets outside Europe, of course, and European corporations often look to these markets to raise cash. The New York Stock Exchange, NASDAQ (US) and the Tokyo Stock Exchange are three well-known examples.

Because of globalization, financial markets have reached the point where trading in many investments never stops; it just travels around the world.

**Listing**   Securities that trade on an organized exchange are said to be *listed* on that exchange. To be listed, firms must meet certain minimum criteria concerning, for example, asset size and number of shareholders. These criteria differ from one exchange to another.

   Considering the London Stock Exchange as an illustrative case, the listing requirements are extensive. To be listed on the LSE a company must satisfy past track record requirements, have a minimum market value and number of publicly held shares, excellent future prospects, audited accounting information for three full years, appropriate corporate governance, and follow international accounting standards.

| CONCEPT QUESTIONS | |
|---|---|
| 1.3a | What is a dealer market? How do dealer and auction markets differ? |
| 1.3b | What does *OTC* stand for? The London Stock Exchange has a large OTC market for smaller equities and an auction market for its biggest equities. Why do you think this is the case? |
| 1.3c | What are the 10 largest stock exchanges in Europe? |

# Work the Web

The Web is a great place to learn more about individual companies, and there are a slew of sites available to help you. Search for 'Yahoo Finance' in your web browser and go to the site that is relevant for your country. Once you get there, you should see something like this on the page:

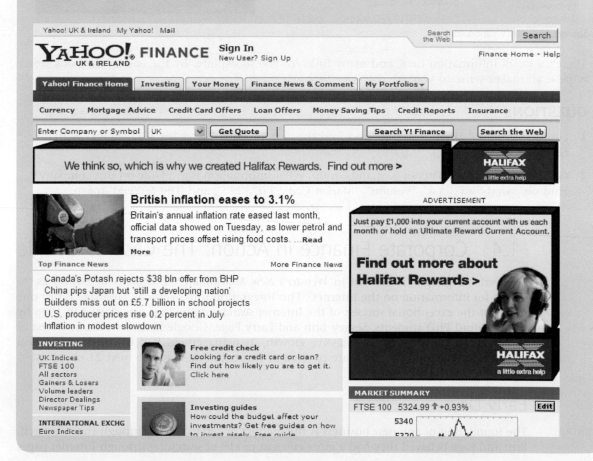

To look up a company, you must know its name or 'ticker symbol' (or just 'ticker' for short), which is a unique identifier. You can click on the 'Symbol Lookup' link and type in the company's name to find the ticker. For example, if we wished to investigate the international telephone directories firm Yell plc, we would type in 'YELL' in the box at the top of the page and click on 'Get Quote'. Here is a portion of what we got:

*Source*: uk.finance.yahoo.com.

There's a lot of information here, and many links for you to explore. By the end of the book we hope it all makes sense to you!

## QUESTIONS

1  Go to the Yahoo! Finance website and find the current share prices for WPP, Lloyds Banking Group, and Man Group.

2  Get a quote for Royal Bank of Scotland Group. What information is available on this company? Find out what 'Bid', 'Ask', 'Volume', 'Market Cap', 'P/E', 'EPS', and 'Div & Yield' mean.

## 1.4 Corporate Finance in Action: The Case of Google

The verb 'to google' is defined in *Webster's New Millennium™ Dictionary of English* as 'to search for information on the Internet'. This integration into everyday language is just one signal of the exceptional success of the Internet search engine that was started in 1996 by two Stanford PhD students, Sergey Brin and Larry Page. Google is now worth in excess of $130 billion. During Google's massive growth, its management had to consider and deal with many issues, all of which are covered in this textbook over the next 21 chapters.

### Early Days

The foundation of any new business is the product or service idea. Through their research, Brin and Page believed they had a more efficient model of searching through Internet pages than the search engines that existed in 1996. Armed only with this idea and a few working algorithms, they approached several potential investors and successfully attracted $100,000 from one of the founders of Sun Microsystems to develop their business concept. Within a year they had received a further $25 million from venture capitalists. To receive this financing, Brin and Page would have used accounting and finance information to create a business plan and cash flow forecast, from which potential investors were able to arrive at a valuation of the future company. Valuation of companies and projects is covered in Part Two of this text.

## The Google Share Issue

By 2004 Google had been so successful with its business model that it needed significant injections of cash to capture the emerging business opportunities that were becoming available. The company had two basic options. It could borrow the money (through a bank loan or public debt markets) or issue equity (through the equity markets). In the end, it chose to raise all the money in the form of equity financing. Google actually has no long-term debt. There are a number of reasons for this, and there are many factors to take into consideration when a firm chooses its own debt-to-equity mix, which is also known as its capital structure. Capital structure is covered in Part Three of the textbook.

The Google share issue was highly unusual in that it was organized wholly over the Internet. However, several fundamental issues had to be decided. First, what should the value of the new shares be? How risky are the shares? These questions are of huge importance to investors who are planning to invest their cash in any new investment. Assessing the risk of investments is covered in Part Four, and the process of issuing new securities is reviewed in Part Five.

## Google as a Business

Although Google is known as an Internet search firm, its success and size make it quite similar to other large firms in more capital-intensive industries. At the beginning of 2010 Google had approximately $5 billion invested in property, and 20,000 employees. Like all other firms, Google needs to ensure it has enough liquidity and cash available to pay off its creditors. Short-term financial planning is therefore crucial to its continued existence. This is covered in Part Six of the text.

Finally, Google has undertaken over 60 acquisitions since 2001. Most notably, it bought YouTube ($1.65 billion) in 2006, DoubleClick ($3.1 billion) in 2007, and AdMob ($750 million) in 2009. Its operations span many countries, making its global reach enormous. It is one of the biggest companies in the world, and will continue to evolve and develop in the future. The final part of this textbook deals with international corporate finance, and the salient decisions that are involved in this area. These are extremely important to all companies, and not just Google.

## So What Is Corporate Finance?

Many people who think of corporate finance tend to consider valuation as being most important. Others think of risk assessment, while many think that capital structure should be emphasized. Hopefully, this section shows that, for a business to be truly successful, the management of a firm and its shareholders must have a solid understanding of all corporate finance areas, and not just one or two topics. Google was a success, not just because it had a fantastic business idea, but also because it understands the fundamental basis of good business and corporate finance.

# Summary and Conclusions

This chapter introduced you to some of the basic ideas in corporate finance:

1 Corporate finance has three main areas of concern:

   (a) Capital budgeting: what long-term investments should the firm take?

   (b) Capital structure: where will the firm get the long-term financing to pay for its investments? In other words, what mixture of debt and equity should the firm use to fund operations?

   (c) Working capital management: how should the firm manage its everyday financial activities?

2 The goal of financial management in a for-profit business is to make decisions that increase the market value of the equity.

3 The advantages of the corporate form are enhanced by the existence of financial markets. Financial markets function as both primary and secondary markets for corporate securities, and can be organized as either dealer or auction markets.

Of the topics we've discussed thus far, the most important is the goal of financial management: maximizing the value of the equity. Throughout the text we shall be analysing many different financial decisions, but we shall always ask the same question: how does the decision under consideration affect the value of the company's equity?

# Concepts Review and Critical Thinking Questions

1 **The Financial Management Decision Process [LO1]** What are the three types of financial management decision? For each type of decision, give an example of a business transaction that would be relevant.

2 **Goal of Financial Management [LO2]** What goal should always motivate the actions of a firm's financial manager?

3 **Primary versus Secondary Markets [LO3]** You've probably noticed coverage in the financial press of an initial public offering (IPO) of a company's securities. Is an IPO a primary market transaction or a secondary market transaction?

4 **Auction versus Dealer Markets [LO3]** What does it mean when we say that Euronext is an auction market? How are auction markets different from dealer markets? What kind of market is the London Stock Exchange?

5 **Not-for-Profit Firm Goals [LO2]** Suppose you were the financial manager of a not-for-profit business (a not-for-profit hospital, perhaps). What kinds of goal do you think would be appropriate?

6 **Goal of the Firm [LO2]** Evaluate the following statement: Managers should not focus on the current equity value because doing so will lead to an overemphasis on short-term profits at the expense of long-term profits.

7 **Ethics and Firm Goals [LO2]** Can our goal of maximizing equity value conflict with other goals, such as avoiding unethical or illegal behaviour? In particular, do you think issues such as customer and employee safety, the environment, and the general good of society fit in this framework, or are they essentially ignored? Think of some specific examples to illustrate your answer.

8 **International Firm Goal [LO2]** Would our goal of maximizing equity value be different if we were thinking about financial management in a foreign country? Why or why not?

9  **Corporate Finance [LO1]**  Your grandmother sees you reading a fantastic book called *Fundamentals of Corporate Finance*. She asks you, 'What does corporate finance mean?' Explain to her in a way that doesn't put her to sleep.

10 **Financing Goals [LO2]**  Small firms tend to raise funds from private investors and venture capitalists. As these firms grow larger, they focus more on raising capital from the organized capital markets. Explain why this occurs.

11 **Financial Management Goals [LO2]**  You have read the first chapter of this textbook and have taken over a company that you now discover is losing £100,000 a week. At the rate things are going, the company won't have any cash left in 6 months to pay its creditors. What are your goals as a financial manager? Is this consistent with what you have read in this chapter? Explain.

12 **Financial Management Goals [LO2]**  If you are in charge of a private firm and it doesn't have a share price, what should be your goal as a financial manager? Explain.

13 **Financial Management Goals [LO2]**  You have been manager of a small company for 20 years and have become great friends with your employees. In the last month, new Norwegian owners have bought out the company's founding owner and have told you that they need to cut costs in order to maximize the value of the company. One of the things they suggest is to lay off 40 per cent of the workforce. However, you believe that the workforce is the company's greatest asset. On what basis do you argue against the new owners' opinions?

14 **Dealer versus Auction Markets [LO3]**  Explain the difference between dealer and auction markets. Why do you think both types of market exist? Is there one type of market that is the best? Explain.

15 **Financial Market Regulators [LO3]**  The UK's Financial Services Authority states that its objectives are to promote efficient, orderly and fair markets, help retail consumers achieve a fair deal, and improve the country's business capacity and effectiveness. The German financial markets regulator, BaFin, states that 'The objective of securities supervision is to ensure the transparency and integrity of the financial market and the protection of investors.' Are the British and German objectives consistent with each other? Explain.

## MINI CASE  Corporate Finance Information on the Web

A skill any financial manager must have is to be able to find and understand financial information. Visit the websites of the German firms Adidas, BASF and Commerzbank. Download their financial accounts for the most recent year. At first you may find it difficult to locate these, but persevere, because the information *is* there.

### QUESTIONS

1  For each firm, find the value of each company's total assets. Which firm is the biggest?

2  Visit the Yahoo! Finance website and find the share price of each firm. What does the share price history tell you about each company?

3  Find the market capitalization of each company. Which firm is the biggest?

4  On Yahoo! Finance read the news for each company. What does the news tell you about the fortunes of each company?

5  Combining all the information, which company do you think is the best investment? Explain.

# CHAPTER 2

# Corporate Governance

CORPORATE GOVERNANCE is concerned with how firms manage themselves, and the way in which this performance is monitored. When shareholders hire professional managers to run their company, it is important to ensure that business decisions are made that maximize the wealth of shareholders, and not the personal wealth of managers. Some ways in which this can be encouraged are by reducing the power of board members, appointing experienced independent non-executive directors to the company's board, and creating independent subcommittees to deal with executive remuneration, auditing and senior appointments.

Prior to 2007 the banking sector in Europe and the US led the world in providing financial services and products to companies and individuals. Commensurate with their importance to the global economy, all large Western banks followed their country's codes of corporate governance and also the principles of good governance as laid out by the Organization for Economic Co-operation and Development (OECD).

Even with excellent governance structures, banks were able to adopt exceptionally risky business strategies to maximize their growth rates and profits. Recent history has shown that this was a recipe for catastrophe, which led to a near-global financial meltdown, and pushed Western economies into deep recession.

Why, when banks were so well governed, did this come to pass? Does it mean that corporate governance is irrelevant? Does it mean that the corporate governance principles that Western companies follow are wrong? Over just a brief period, corporate governance has become one of the most important issues in corporate finance, and this chapter will explore some of the issues relating to the area.

To begin our study of corporate governance, it is important to understand the different ways in which companies are structured, and the pressures that management face in making business decisions.

## 2.1   Forms of Business Organization

Large European firms, such as BP, Renault and Vodafone, are almost all organized as corporations. We examine the three different legal forms of business organization – sole proprietorship, partnership and corporation – to see why this is so. Each form has distinct advantages and disadvantages for the life of the business, the ability of the business to raise cash, and how it is taxed. A key observation is that, as a firm grows, the advantages of the corporate form may come to outweigh the disadvantages.

## Sole Proprietorship

A **sole proprietorship** is a business owned by one person. This is the simplest type of business to start, and is the least regulated form of organization. Depending on where you live, you might be able to start a proprietorship by doing little more than getting a business licence and opening your doors. For this reason, there are substantially more sole proprietorships than any other type of business, and many businesses that later become large corporations start out as small proprietorships.

> **sole proprietorship**
> A business owned by a single individual.

The owner of a sole proprietorship keeps all the profits. That's the good news. The bad news is that the owner has *unlimited liability* for business debts. This means that creditors can look beyond business assets to the proprietor's personal assets for payment. Similarly, there is no distinction between personal and business income, so all business income is taxed as personal income.

The life of a sole proprietorship is limited to the owner's lifespan, and the amount of equity that can be raised is limited to the amount of the proprietor's personal wealth. This limitation often means that the business is unable to exploit new opportunities, because of insufficient capital. Ownership of a sole proprietorship may be difficult to transfer, because this transfer requires the sale of the entire business to a new owner.

Sole proprietorships tend to be exceptionally small, and these firms are normally called *micro companies* (between one and nine employees). Although tiny, they are by far the dominant business form in Europe, with over 18 million micro businesses, constituting nearly 92 per cent of all firms in the region (source: Eurostat).

## Partnership

A **partnership** is similar to a proprietorship except that there are two or more owners (partners). In a *general partnership*, all the partners share in gains or losses, and all have unlimited liability for *all* partnership debts, not just some particular share. The way partnership gains (and losses) are divided is described in the *partnership agreement*. This agreement can be an informal oral agreement, such as 'Let's start a lawnmowing business', or a lengthy, formal written document.

> **partnership**
> A business formed by two or more individuals or entities.

In a *limited partnership* one or more *general partners* will run the business and have unlimited liability, but there will be one or more *limited partners* who will not actively participate in the business. A limited partner's liability for business debts is limited to the amount that partner contributes to the partnership. This form of organization is common in law and accounting firms.

The advantages and disadvantages of a partnership are basically the same as those of a sole proprietorship. Partnerships based on a relatively informal agreement are easy and inexpensive to form. General partners have unlimited liability for partnership debts, and the partnership terminates when a general partner wishes to sell out or dies. All income is taxed as personal income to the partners, and the amount of equity that can be raised is limited to the partners' combined wealth. Ownership of a general partnership is not easily transferred, because a transfer requires that a new partnership be formed. A limited partner's interest can be sold without dissolving the partnership, but it may be difficult to find a buyer.

Because a partner in a general partnership can be held responsible for all partnership debts, it is very important to have a written agreement. Failure to spell out the rights and duties of the partners frequently leads to misunderstandings later on. Also, if you are a limited partner, you must not become deeply involved in business decisions unless you are willing to assume the obligations of a general partner. The reason is that, if things go badly, you may be deemed to be a general partner even though you say you are a limited partner.

There are notable differences in the definition of partnerships across Europe. The UK has a limited liability partnership (LLP), whereby the partnership is deemed to be an independent corporate body that can continue to exist if one or more partners leave the firm. Partners can also sign a partnership agreement that collectively takes on the responsibility for the overall firm, but bear no liability for any other partners' actions. The German Partnerschaftsgesellschaft (PartG) is similar to a limited liability partnership except that it is not a corporate entity. However, it owns property under its own name, and can sue or be sued.

Based on our discussion, the primary disadvantages of sole proprietorships and partnerships as forms of business organization are:

1  Unlimited liability for business debts on the part of the owners

2  Limited life of the business

3  Difficulty of transferring ownership

These three disadvantages add up to a single, central problem: the ability of such businesses to grow can be seriously limited by an inability to raise cash for investment.

## Corporation

**corporation**
A business created as a distinct legal entity composed of one or more individuals or entities.

The **corporation** is the most important form (in terms of size) of business organization in the world. A corporation is a legal 'person' separate and distinct from its owners, and it has many of the rights, duties and privileges of an actual person. Corporations can borrow money and own property, can sue and be sued, and can enter into contracts. A corporation can even be a general partner or a limited partner in a partnership, and a corporation can own equity in another corporation.

Not surprisingly, starting a corporation is somewhat more complicated than starting the other forms of business organization. Forming a corporation involves preparing *articles of incorporation* (or a charter) and a *memorandum of association*. The articles of incorporation must contain a number of things, including the corporation's name, its intended life (which can be for ever), its business purpose, and the number of shares that can be issued. This information must normally be supplied to the country in which the firm will be incorporated. For most legal purposes the corporation is a 'resident' of that country.

The memorandum of association consists of rules describing how the corporation regulates its existence. For example, the memorandum describes how directors are elected. This may be a simple statement of a few rules and procedures, or it may be quite extensive for a large corporation. The memorandum may be amended or extended from time to time by the shareholders.

In a large corporation the shareholders and managers are usually separate groups. In Europe there are two main ways in which directors of a company are elected. In single-tier board countries, such as the United Kingdom, Ireland and Sweden (and also the US), the shareholders elect the board of directors, who then select the managers. In two-tier board countries, such as Denmark, Germany and the Netherlands, there are two boards. The executive board manages the day-to-day operations of the company, and they report to the supervisory board who monitors their performance. The supervisory board will normally consist of representatives of major shareholders, creditors and employee groups. In both systems managers are charged with running the corporation's affairs in the shareholders' interests. In principle, shareholders control the corporation, because they elect the directors either directly or through a supervisory board.

As a result of the separation of ownership and management, the corporate form has several advantages. Ownership (represented by shares of equity) can be readily transferred, and the life of the corporation is therefore not limited. The corporation borrows money in its own name. As a result, the shareholders in a corporation have limited liability for corporate debts. The most they can lose is what they have invested.

The relative ease of transferring ownership, the limited liability for business debts, and the unlimited life of the business are why the corporate form is superior for raising cash. If a corporation needs new equity, for example, it can sell new shares and attract new investors. Apple is an example. Apple was a pioneer in the personal computer business. As demand for its products exploded, Apple had to convert to a corporation to raise the capital needed to fund growth and new product development. The number of owners can be huge: larger corporations have many thousands or even millions of shareholders. For example, in 2011 Royal Dutch Shell plc had several million shareholders and about 6 billion shares outstanding. In such cases ownership can change continuously without affecting the continuity of the business.

The corporate form has a significant disadvantage. Because a corporation is a legal person, it must pay taxes. Moreover, money paid out to shareholders in the form of dividends is taxed again as income to those shareholders. This is *double taxation*, meaning that corporate profits are taxed twice: at the corporate level when they are earned, and again at the personal level when they are paid out. Fortunately, in many countries, including the UK, shareholders are given a partial or full tax credit, which they can offset against the double tax that is levied on their dividends.

As the discussion in this section illustrates, the need of large businesses for outside investors and creditors is such that the corporate form will generally be the best for such firms. We focus on corporations in the chapters ahead because of the importance of the corporate form in the European and world economies. Also, a few important financial management issues, such as dividend policy, are unique to corporations. However, businesses of all types and sizes need financial management, so the majority of the subjects we discuss bear on any form of business.

## A Corporation by Any Other Name . . .

The corporate form of organization has many variations around the world. The exact laws and regulations differ from country to country, of course, but the essential features of public ownership and limited liability remain. These firms are often called *joint stock companies*, *public limited companies*, or *limited liability companies*, depending on the specific nature of the firm and the country of origin.

Table 2.1 gives the names of a number of corporate abbreviations, the countries in which they are used, a translation of the abbreviation, and a description of its meaning

| CONCEPT QUESTIONS | 2.1a | What are the three forms of business organization? |
| | 2.1b | What are the primary advantages and disadvantages of sole proprietorships and partnerships? |
| | 2.1c | What is the difference between a general and a limited partnership? |
| | 2.1d | Why is the corporate form superior when it comes to raising cash? |

## 2.2  The Agency Problem and Control of the Corporation

We've seen that the financial manager acts in the best interests of the shareholders by taking actions that increase the value of the company's equity. However, in many large corporations, particularly in the UK, Ireland and the US, ownership can be spread over a huge number of shareholders. This dispersion of ownership arguably means that management effectively controls the firm. In this case, will management necessarily act in the best interests of the shareholders? Put another way, might not management pursue its own goals at the shareholders' expense?

**TABLE 2.1**

| Type of corporation | Country of origin | In original language | Description |
|---|---|---|---|
| Pty Ltd | Australia | Proprietary Limited | Private limited |
| Limited | Australia | Limited | Publicly listed |
| AG | Austria, Germany | Aktiengesellschaft | Publicly listed |
| GmbH | Austria, Germany | Gesellschaft mit Beschränkter Haftung | Private limited |
| NV | Belgium, Netherlands | Naamloze Venootschap | Private/public |
| SA | Belgium, France, Luxembourg, Portugal, Spain | Société Anonyme/ Sociedade Anónima | Publicly listed |
| 股份有限公司 | China Mainland | 股份有限公司 | Publicly listed |
| 有限公司 | China Mainland | 有限公司 | Private limited |
| ApS | Denmark | Anpartsselkab | Private limited |
| A/S | Denmark | Aktieselskab | Publicly listed |
| SE | European Union | Societas Europaea | Publicly listed |
| Oy, AB | Finland, Sweden | Osakeyhtiö (Fin), Aktiebolag (Swe) | Private limited |
| Oyj, Abp | Finland, Sweden | Julkinen Osakeyhtiö (Fin), Publikt Aktiebolag (Swe) | Publicly listed |
| SARL | France, Luxembourg | Société à Responsibilité Limitée | Private limited |
| Pvt. Ltd | India | Private Limited Company | Private limited |
| Plc | India, Ireland, Thailand, UK | Public Limited Company | Publicly listed |
| Srl | Italy | Società a Responsabilità Limitata | Private limited |
| SpA | Italy | Società per Azioni | Publicly listed |
| AS | Norway | Aksjeselskap | Private limited |
| ASA | Norway | Allmennaksjeselskap | Publicly listed |
| (Pty) Ltd | South Africa | Privaat Maatskappy | Private limited |
| LTD | South Africa | Publieke Maatskappy | Publicly listed |
| SL | Spain | Sociedad Limitada | Private limited |
| Ltd | Ireland, UK, US | Limited | Private limited |
| Inc., Corp. | US | Incorporated, Corporation | Publicly listed |

**Table 2.1** International corporations

A different type of problem exists in many European firms. Whereas large British and American firms have a dispersed ownership structure, many businesses in Europe have a dominant shareholder with a very large ownership stake. Primarily, these shareholders are family groups, banks, or governments. In firms with a dominant shareholder it is possible that corporate objectives will be directed by only one individual or group at the expense of other, smaller, shareholders. In this case, managers are acting in the interests of only a subset of the company's owners.

The issues we have discussed above are caused by what we call *agency relationships*. In the following pages we briefly consider some of the arguments relating to this issue.

## Type I Agency Relationships

The relationship between shareholders and management is called a *type I agency relationship*. Such a relationship exists whenever someone (the principal) hires another (the agent) to represent his or her interests. For example, you might hire someone (an agent) to sell a car you own while you are away at university. In all such relationships, there is a possibility there may be a conflict of interest between the principal and the agent. Such a conflict is called a **type I agency problem**.

> **type I agency problem**
> The possibility of conflict of interest between the shareholders and management of a firm.

Suppose you hire someone to sell your car, and agree to pay that person a flat fee when he or she sells the car. The agent's incentive in this case is to make the sale, not necessarily to get you the best price. If you offer a commission of, say, 10 per cent of the sales price instead of a flat fee, then this problem might not exist. This example illustrates that the way in which an agent is compensated is one factor that affects agency problems.

## Management Goals

To see how management and shareholder interests might differ, imagine that the firm is considering a new investment. The new investment is expected to impact favourably on the share value, but it is also a relatively risky venture. The owners of the firm will wish to make the investment (because the share value will rise), but management may not, because there is the possibility that things will turn out badly, and management jobs will be lost. If management do not make the investment, then the shareholders may lose a valuable opportunity. This is one example of a type I agency cost.

In general, the term *agency cost* refers to the cost of the conflict of interest between shareholders and management (we shall consider later another agency relationship between controlling and minority shareholders). These costs can be indirect or direct. An indirect agency cost is a lost opportunity, such as the one we have just described.

Direct agency costs come in two forms. The first type is a corporate expenditure that benefits management but costs the shareholders. Perhaps the purchase of a luxurious and unneeded corporate jet would fall under this heading. The second type of direct agency cost is an expense that comes from the need to monitor management actions. Paying outside auditors to assess the accuracy of financial statement information could be one example.

It is sometimes argued that, left to themselves, managers would tend to maximize the amount of resources over which they have control or, more generally, corporate power or wealth. This goal could lead to an overemphasis on corporate size or growth. For example, cases in which management are accused of overpaying to buy up another company just to increase the business size or to demonstrate corporate power are not uncommon. Obviously, if overpayment does take place, such a purchase does not benefit the shareholders of the purchasing company.

Our discussion indicates that management may tend to overemphasize organizational survival to protect job security. Also, management may dislike outside interference, so independence and corporate self-sufficiency may be important goals.

## Do Managers Act in the Shareholders' Interests?

Whether managers will, in fact, act in the best interests of shareholders depends on two factors. First, how closely are management goals aligned with shareholder goals? This question relates, at least in part, to the way managers are compensated. Second, can managers be replaced if they do not pursue shareholder goals? This issue relates to control of the firm. As we shall discuss, there are a number of reasons to think that, even in the largest firms, management has a significant incentive to act in the interests of shareholders.

**Managerial Compensation**    Management will frequently have a significant economic incentive to increase share value, for two reasons. First, managerial compensation, particularly at the top, is usually tied to financial performance in general, and often to share value in particular. For example, managers are frequently given the option to buy equity at a bargain price. The more the equity is worth, the more valuable this option is. In fact, options are often used to motivate employees of all types, not just top managers. For example, in 2007 Google announced that it was issuing new share options to all of its 16,000 employees, thereby giving its workforce a significant stake in its share price, and achieving a better alignment of employee and shareholder interests. Many other corporations, large and small, have similar policies.

The second incentive managers have relates to job prospects. Better performers within the firm will tend to get promoted. More generally, managers who are successful in pursuing shareholder goals will be in greater demand in the labour market, and thus command higher salaries.

In fact, managers who are successful in pursuing shareholder goals can reap enormous rewards. For example, the best-paid executive in 2008 was Stephen Schwarzman, the CEO of Blackstone Group: according to *CNN* he made about £456 million (€523 million). By way of comparison, Schwarzman made quite a bit more than Larry Ellison of Oracle (£362 million/€415 million), Oprah Winfrey (£178 million/€205 million), and Lionel Messi (£30 million/€34 million). Information about executive compensation, along with lots of other information, can be easily found on the Web for almost any public company or even celebrity. Our nearby *Work the Web* box shows you how to get started.

# Work the Web

A great skill to develop is to be able to find company information easily on the Internet. In Chapter 1 you gained some experience with using a financial data provider, Yahoo! Finance, to find out information on share prices and other financial characteristics. In this chapter we shall look at a company's annual report.

Go to the Vodafone website (www.vodafone.com) and download the company's annual report for the most recent year. Click on the 'Investor Relations' tab and then 'Annual Report'. In this chapter we shall focus on the corporate governance of Vodafone. Take your time and read through the section on Governance. There's a lot of information here, and many links for you to explore.

## QUESTIONS

1   How many people are on the board of Vodafone? Who is the chairman, and who is the chief executive officer? How many non-executive directors and executive directors are there on the board of Vodafone?

2   How does the board of Vodafone evaluate its own performance?

3   How much did the chief executive of Vodafone earn in the most recent year?

**Control of the Firm**    Control of the firm ultimately rests with shareholders. They elect the board of directors, who in turn hire and fire managers. The fact that shareholders control the corporation was made abundantly clear by Steve Jobs's experience at Apple. Even though he was a founder of the corporation, and was largely responsible for its most successful products, there came a time when shareholders, through their elected directors, decided that Apple would be better off without him, so out he went. Of course, he was later rehired and helped turn Apple around with great new products such as the iPod, iPhone and iPad.

**Shareholder Rights** The conceptual structure of the corporation assumes that shareholders elect directors, who in turn hire managers to carry out their directives. Shareholders therefore control the corporation through the right to elect the directors. In countries with single-tier boards only shareholders have this right, and in two-tier board countries the supervisory board undertakes this task.

In two-tier board systems the supervisory board (which consists of the main shareholder representatives, major creditors, and employee representatives) chooses the executive board of directors. In companies with single-tier boards directors are elected each year at an annual meeting. Although there are exceptions (discussed next), the general idea is 'one share, one vote' (*not* one *shareholder*, one vote). Directors are elected at an annual shareholders' meeting by a vote of the holders of a majority of shares who are present and entitled to vote. However, the exact mechanism for electing directors differs across companies. The most important difference is whether shares must be voted cumulatively or voted straight.

To illustrate the two different voting procedures, imagine that a corporation has two shareholders: Smith with 20 shares and Jones with 80 shares. Both want to be a director. Jones does not want Smith, however. We assume there are a total of four directors to be elected.

The effect of **cumulative voting** is to permit minority participation. If cumulative voting is permitted, the total number of votes that each shareholder may cast is determined first. This is usually calculated as the number of shares (owned or controlled) multiplied by the number of directors to be elected.

> **cumulative voting**
> A procedure in which a shareholder may cast all votes for one member of the board of directors.

With cumulative voting the directors are elected all at once. In our example this means that the top four vote-getters will be the new directors. A shareholder can distribute votes however he or she wishes.

Will Smith get a seat on the board? If we ignore the possibility of a five-way tie, then the answer is yes. Smith will cast $20 \times 4 = 80$ votes, and Jones will cast $80 \times 4 = 320$ votes. If Smith gives all his votes to himself, he is assured of a directorship. The reason is that Jones can't divide 320 votes among four candidates in such a way as to give all of them more than 80 votes, so Smith will finish fourth at worst.

In general, if there are $N$ directors up for election, then $1/(N + 1)$ per cent of the shares plus one share will guarantee you a seat. In our current example this is $1/(4 + 1) = 20\%$. So the more seats that are up for election at one time, the easier (and cheaper) it is to win one.

> **straight voting**
> A procedure in which a shareholder may cast all votes for each member of the board of directors.

With **straight voting** the directors are elected one at a time. Each time, Smith can cast 20 votes and Jones can cast 80. As a consequence, Jones will elect all of the candidates. The only way to guarantee a seat is to own 50 per cent plus one share. This also guarantees that you will win every seat, so it's really all or nothing.

---

**EXAMPLE 2.1**

## Buying the Election

Shares in Sole SpA sell for €20 each, and feature cumulative voting. There are 10,000 shares outstanding. If three directors are up for election, how much does it cost to ensure yourself a seat on the board?

The question here is how many shares of equity it will take to get a seat. The answer is 2,501, so the cost is $2,501 \times €20 = €50,020$. Why 2,501? Because there is no way the remaining 7,499 votes can be divided among three people to give all of them more than 2,501 votes. For example, suppose two people receive 2,502 votes and the first two seats. A third person can receive at most $10,000 - 2,502 - 2,502 - 2,501 = 2,495$, so the third seat is yours.

---

As we've illustrated, straight voting can 'freeze out' minority shareholders: that is why many companies have mandatory cumulative voting. In companies where cumulative voting is mandatory, devices have been worked out to minimize its impact.

One such device is to stagger the voting for the board of directors. With staggered elections, only a fraction of the directorships are up for election at a particular time. Thus if only two directors are up for election at any one time, it will take $1/(2 + 1) = 33.33$ per cent of the equity plus one share to guarantee a seat.

Overall, staggering has two basic effects:

1   Staggering makes it more difficult for a minority to elect a director when there is cumulative voting, because there are fewer directors to be elected at one time.

2   Staggering makes takeover attempts less likely to be successful, because it makes it more difficult to vote in a majority of new directors.

We should note that staggering may serve a beneficial purpose. It provides 'institutional memory' – that is, continuity on the board of directors. This may be important for corporations with significant long-range plans and projects.

**proxy**
A grant of authority by a shareholder allowing another individual to vote his or her shares.

**Proxy Voting**   A **proxy** is the grant of authority by a shareholder to someone else to vote his or her shares. For convenience, much of the voting in large public corporations is actually done by proxy.

As we have seen, with straight voting each share of equity has one vote. The owner of 10,000 shares has 10,000 votes. Large companies have hundreds of thousands or even millions of shareholders. In single-tier board environments shareholders can come to the annual meeting and vote in person, or they can transfer their right to vote to another party.

Obviously, management always tries to get as many proxies as possible transferred to it. However, if shareholders are not satisfied with management, an 'outside' group of shareholders can try to obtain votes via proxy. They can vote by proxy in an attempt to replace management by electing enough directors. The resulting battle is called a *proxy fight*.

**Classes of Shares**   Some firms have more than one class of ordinary equity. Often the classes are created with unequal voting rights. Google, for example, has two classes of shares. The co-founders, Larry Page and Sergey Brin, own Class B shares, which have 10 votes for each share. Other shareholders have Class A shares, which are entitled to one vote per share. So, although the founders only own 5.7 per cent of Google, they have 57 per cent of the voting power.

A primary reason for creating dual or multiple classes of equity has to do with control of the firm. If such shares exist, management of a firm can raise equity capital by issuing non-voting or limited-voting shares while maintaining control.

The subject of unequal voting rights is controversial, and the idea of one share, one vote has a strong following and a long history. Interestingly, however, shares with unequal voting rights are quite common in the United Kingdom and elsewhere around the world.

**Other Rights**   The value of a share of equity in a corporation is directly related to the general rights of shareholders. In addition to the right to vote for directors, shareholders usually have the following rights:

1   The right to share proportionally in dividends paid.

2   The right to share proportionally in assets remaining after liabilities have been paid in a liquidation.

3   The right to vote on shareholder matters of great importance, such as a merger. Voting is usually done at the annual meeting or a special meeting.

In addition, shareholders sometimes have the right to share proportionally in any new equity sold. This is called the *pre-emptive right*.

Essentially, a pre-emptive right means that a company that wishes to sell equity must first offer it to the existing shareholders before offering it to the general public. The purpose is to give shareholders the opportunity to protect their proportionate ownership in the corporation.

**Dividends**    A distinctive feature of corporations is that they have shares of equity on which they are authorized by law to pay dividends to their shareholders. **Dividends** paid to shareholders represent a return on the capital directly or indirectly contributed to the corporation by the shareholders. The payment of dividends is at the discretion of the board of directors.

> **dividends**
> Payments by a corporation to shareholders, made in either cash or shares.

Some important characteristics of dividends include the following:

- Unless a dividend is declared by the board of directors of a corporation, it is not a liability of the corporation. A corporation cannot default on an undeclared dividend. As a consequence, corporations cannot become bankrupt because of non-payment of dividends. The amount of the dividend and even whether it is paid are decisions based on the business judgement of the board of directors.

- The payment of dividends by the corporation is not a business expense. Dividends are not deductible for corporate tax purposes. In short, dividends are paid out of the corporation's after-tax profits.

- Dividends received by individual shareholders are taxable.

There is a common belief that shareholders prefer companies to issue dividends, because it imposes a form of discipline on incumbent managers. If a company has high levels of cash, managers may invest in projects that will not normally be chosen simply because they can. By transferring the company's cash to shareholders through dividends, managers have less scope to squander resources.

The discussion so far has concerned the agency relationship between professional managers and outside shareholders. We shall now discuss a different type of agency relationship, which is more subtle and complex, and is known as a Type II agency relationship. A Type II agency relationship exists between shareholders who own a significant amount of a company's shares (controlling shareholders) and other shareholders who own only a small proportional amount (minority shareholders).

## Type II Agency Relationships

The relationship between a dominant or controlling shareholder and other shareholders who have a small proportional ownership stake is known as a *Type II agency relationship*. Such a relationship exists whenever a company has a concentrated ownership structure, which is common in many countries. When an investor owns a large percentage of a company's shares, they have the ability to remove or install a board of directors through their voting power. This means that, indirectly, they can make the firm's objectives aligned to their own personal objectives, which may not be the same as that of other shareholders with a smaller proportionate stake. This is the **Type II agency problem**.

> **Type II agency problem**
> The possibility of conflict of interest between controlling and minority shareholders.

It may seem strange that one set of shareholders can have a different objective from that of a different set of shareholders in the same company. Surely, all shareholders want to maximize the value of their firm? Agency theory recognizes that everyone has personal objectives, and these may not be congruent with other groups in an organization. Thus, for example, a dominant shareholder may benefit more from having one of her firms trading at advantageous prices with another firm she owns. This is known as a *related party transaction*.

Alternatively, a controlling shareholder may need cash for an investment in, for example, company A, and wish to take the cash from company B through an extraordinary dividend. This will obviously not be in the interests of company B's other shareholders, but in aggregate the action may be more profitable for the controlling shareholder of company B if it stands to make more money from an investment in company A.

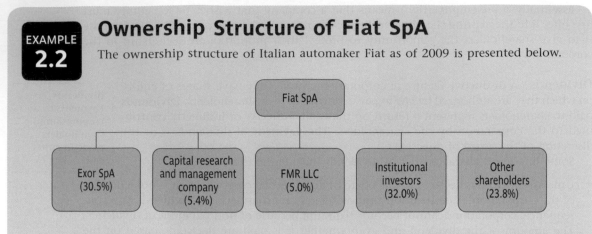

# Ownership Structure of Fiat SpA

The ownership structure of Italian automaker Fiat as of 2009 is presented below.

The dominant or controlling shareholder of Fiat SpA is Exor SpA, which owns 30.5 per cent of the company's outstanding shares. The next question is who owns Exor SpA? Exor is 100 per cent owned by *Giovanni Agnelli e C. S.a.p.az*, which is the investment company of the Agnelli family in Italy. Thus, indirectly, the Agnelli family is the dominant shareholder of Fiat.

## Conclusion

The available theory and evidence are consistent with the view that shareholders control the firm, and that shareholder wealth maximization is the relevant goal of the corporation. Even so, there will undoubtedly be times when management goals are pursued at the expense of some or all shareholders, at least temporarily.

## Stakeholders

**stakeholder**
Someone, other than a shareholder or creditor, who potentially has a claim on the cash flows of the firm.

Our discussion thus far implies that management and shareholders are the only parties with an interest in the firm's decisions. This is an oversimplification, of course. Employees, customers, suppliers, and even the government all have a financial interest in the firm.

Taken together, these various groups are called **stakeholders**. In general, a stakeholder is someone, other than a shareholder or creditor, who potentially has a claim on the cash flows of the firm. Such groups will also attempt to exert control over the firm, perhaps to the detriment of the owners.

**CONCEPT QUESTIONS**

2.2a  What is an agency relationship?

2.2b  What are agency problems, and how do they come about? What are agency costs?

2.2c  What incentives do managers in large corporations have to maximize share value?

## 2.3  International Corporate Governance

Variations in economic, social and religious culture can lead to differences in the way that companies are run. While corporate differences are to be expected across geographical regions, you may be surprised to learn that the corporate environment within Europe is very varied. Although monetary union has been enacted across much of the continent, the legal, institutional and governance structures in member countries are markedly different. In this section we shall discuss some differences in international corporate governance, and how they may impact upon the business decisions of corporations.

## Investor Protection: The Legal Environment

The legal environment in which a corporation does business can have a big impact on its decisions. In a common law system the law evolves as a result of the judgment decisions of courts, whereas in a civil law system judges interpret the law; they cannot change it. With respect to commercial decisions, the UK and Ireland follow a common law system, whereas the rest of Europe follows civil law.

The third form of legal system is based on religious principles: Canon Law for Christianity, Halakha for Judaism, and Sharia for Islam. Under religious law, specific religious principles form the basis of legal decisions. This can have a considerable impact on business activity, especially when religion forbids specific activities. For example, Islam forbids the use of interest in any economic transaction, and so financial loans are not allowed.

Figure 2.1 presents a snapshot of countries that follow different legal systems. Many countries do not follow one system alone, and the exact legal environment can be a hybrid of two systems. For example, India's legal system is based on common law, but personal laws are driven by religious law depending on an individual's religion. Scotland has a different legal system from the rest of the UK, with most laws based on continental or Roman civil law. Commercial law is an exception, and it is similar to the rest of the United Kingdom in this regard.

Because the corporate environment must respond quickly to different economic events, common law systems are able to adapt faster to these changes. For example, if a company can identify a loophole in the law that allows it to legally expropriate wealth from

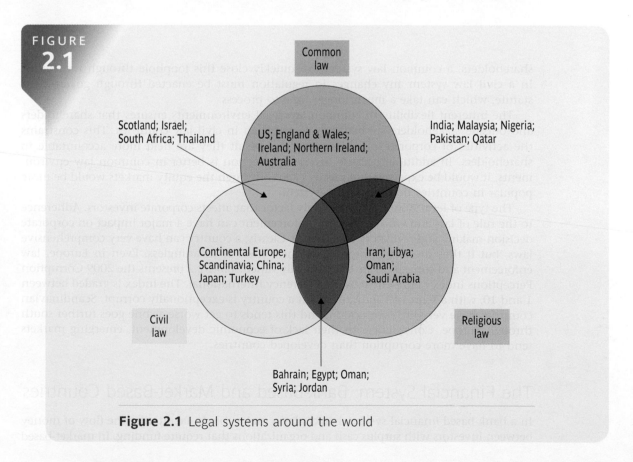

**Figure 2.1** Legal systems around the world

TABLE

2.2

| Country | Corruption perceptions index | Country | Corruption perceptions index |
|---|---|---|---|
| Denmark | 9.3 | Portugal | 5.8 |
| Singapore, Sweden | 9.2 | Taiwan | 5.6 |
| Switzerland | 9.0 | Oman, South Korea | 5.5 |
| Finland, Netherlands | 8.9 | Bahrain | 5.1 |
| Australia, Canada, Iceland | 8.7 | South Africa | 4.7 |
| Norway | 8.6 | Malaysia | 4.5 |
| Hong Kong, Luxembourg | 8.2 | Turkey | 4.4 |
| Germany, Ireland | 8.0 | Italy | 4.3 |
| Austria | 7.9 | Greece | 3.8 |
| UK, Japan | 7.7 | China | 3.6 |
| US | 7.5 | India, Thailand | 3.4 |
| Belgium | 7.1 | Tanzania | 2.6 |
| Qatar | 7.0 | Nigeria | 2.5 |
| France | 6.9 | Pakistan | 2.4 |
| UAE | 6.5 | Kenya, Russia | 2.2 |
| Spain, Israel | 6.1 | Iran | 1.8 |

*Source*: **Transparency International.**

**Table 2.2** Transparency International Corruption Perceptions Index 2009

shareholders, a common law system can quickly close this loophole through the courts. In a civil law system any changes in regulation must be enacted through government statute, which can take a much longer time to process.

The inherent flexibility of common law legal environments ensures that shareholders and outside stakeholders are better protected than in civil law countries. This constrains the activities of corporate managers, and as a result they are held more accountable to shareholders. In addition, because investor protection is better in common law environments, it would be expected that raising capital through the equity markets would be more popular in countries that follow this system.

The type of legal system is not the only factor that affects corporate investors. Adherence to the rule of law and efficiency of law enforcement can have a major impact on corporate decision-making and regulatory compliance. Clearly, a country can have very comprehensive laws, but if they are not enforced then their effect is meaningless. Even in Europe, law enforcement and corruption are exceptionally varied. Table 2.2 presents the 2009 Corruption Perceptions Index as presented by Transparency International. The index is graded between 1 and 10, with a score of 1 indicating that a country is exceptionally corrupt. Scandinavian countries have very little corruption, and this tends to get worse as one goes further south through Europe. Consistent with their lack of economic development, emerging markets tend to have more corruption than developed countries.

## The Financial System: Bank-Based and Market-Based Countries

In a bank-based financial system, banks play a major role in facilitating the flow of money between investors with surplus cash and organizations that require funding. In market-based

**TABLE 2.3**

| Country | Domestic bank deposits/ Stock market capitalization | Country | Domestic bank deposits/ Stock market capitalization | Country | Domestic bank deposits/ Stock market capitalization |
|---|---|---|---|---|---|
| South Africa | 0.40 | Denmark | 1.40 | Finland | 2.71 |
| Malaysia | 0.41 | Thailand | 1.44 | Israel | 2.76 |
| Singapore | 0.70 | Netherlands | 1.63 | Greece | 2.78 |
| Hong Kong | 0.76 | Japan | 1.66 | France | 3.11 |
| Sweden | 0.86 | New Zealand | 1.73 | Belgium | 3.31 |
| United States | 0.91 | Kenya | 1.80 | Cyprus | 3.73 |
| United Kingdom | 1.03 | Switzerland | 1.80 | Italy | 4.45 |
| Australia | 1.08 | Nigeria | 1.88 | Iceland | 4.50 |
| Canada | 1.12 | Pakistan | 2.17 | Germany | 5.01 |
| India | 1.24 | Indonesia | 2.67 | Portugal | 5.84 |
| Turkey | 1.35 | Norway | 2.69 | Egypt | 6.10 |
| Ireland | 1.36 | Spain | 3.20 | Austria | 10.24 |

*Source*: A. Demirguc-Kunt and R. Levine, 'Bank-based and market-based financial systems: cross-country comparisons', World Bank Working Paper.

**Table 2.3** Bank-based versus market-based financial systems

systems, financial markets take on the role of the main financial intermediary. Corporations in countries with very well-developed financial markets find it easier to raise money by issuing debt and equity to the public than through bank borrowing. Countries with bank-based systems have very strong banks that actively monitor corporations and are often involved in long-term strategic decisions.

It has been argued that corporations in market-based countries have a shorter-term focus than in bank-based countries, because of the emphasis on share price and market performance. When banks are the major source of funding to a company, managers may have longer investment horizons and be less willing to take risks. On the other hand, market-based systems have been argued to be more efficient at funding companies than bank systems. There are many ways in which a country's financial system can be classified as bank or market-based. Table 2.3 shows, for a number of countries, the level of domestic deposits in banks divided by stock market size. A country with a high ratio would be regarded as a bank-based financial system.

## Ownership Structure

Another factor that can affect business decision-making and corporate objectives is the ownership structure of companies. This is the make-up and constitution of shareholdings in a firm. In the UK and US most large companies are widely held, which means that no single investor has a large ownership stake in a firm. In such environments, Type I agency relationships dominate. The rest of the world is characterized by closely held firms, where governments, families and banks are the main shareholders in firms. Type II agency relationships are more important in closely held firms, and their corporate governance structure should reflect this.

Table 2.4 presents a breakdown of the ownership structure of the 20 largest corporations in a number of selected companies across the world. It is very clear from the table that no two countries are the exact same. For example, the UK is characterized by a widely held ownership structure, whereas most of the large firms in Greece are run by families.

TABLE
**2.4**

| Country | Widely held (%) | Family (%) | State (%) | Other (%) | Country | Widely held (%) | Family (%) | State (%) | Other (%) |
|---|---|---|---|---|---|---|---|---|---|
| Austria | 5 | 15 | 70 | 10 | Japan | 90 | 5 | 5 | 0 |
| Belgium | 5 | 50 | 5 | 40 | Netherlands | 30 | 20 | 5 | 45 |
| Denmark | 40 | 35 | 15 | 10 | Norway | 25 | 25 | 35 | 15 |
| Finland | 35 | 10 | 35 | 20 | Portugal | 10 | 45 | 25 | 20 |
| France | 60 | 20 | 15 | 5 | Spain | 35 | 15 | 30 | 20 |
| Germany | 50 | 10 | 25 | 15 | Sweden | 25 | 45 | 10 | 20 |
| Greece | 10 | 50 | 30 | 10 | Switzerland | 60 | 30 | 0 | 10 |
| Italy | 20 | 15 | 40 | 25 | UK | 100 | 0 | 0 | 0 |
| Ireland | 65 | 10 | 0 | 25 | US | 80 | 20 | 0 | 0 |

*Source*: R. La Porta, F. Lopez-de-Silanes, A. Shleifer and R.W. Vishny, 'Law and finance', *Journal of Political Economy* (1998), vol. 106, pp. 1113–1155.
The table presents the percentage of firms in a country that have a controlling shareholder with a greater than 20 per cent stake in the company. If no controlling shareholder exists, the firm is deemed to be widely held.

**Table 2.4** Ownership structure of 20 largest companies in each country

Governments have a major role to play in many European countries, with the Austrian government being the most involved in firms.

Ownership structure has a massive impact on corporate objectives. Whereas all shareholders wish to maximize the value of their investment, how value is assessed differs according to the individual. For example, if a firm is widely held in a market-based economy, such as the UK, corporate objectives are likely to be focused on maximizing share price performance. Family firms have slightly different objectives, because managers have to consider not only current shareholders but also the descendants of those shareholders. This would suggest that managers of family firms would have a longer-term perspective than other firms, which would influence the types of investment and funding they choose. Firms with a government as a major shareholder would have to consider political objectives, in addition to maximizing share value. A good example is the banking sector, which was bailed out by governments in 2008 and 2009. Although banks did not feel it appropriate to increase lending significantly under the economic conditions at the time, state shareholders insisted that lending be focused on first-time house buyers and small businesses.

## 2.4 Bringing It All Together

The basis of all good corporate finance decisions is a sound framework of corporate governance. This point can't be emphasized too much, because most of the problems that companies experience can usually be identified by failings in the way in which they are governed. When covering subjects in later chapters, the underlying assumption is that corporate executives are acting in the interests of shareholders, and that the firm is well governed.

When a company does not have strong corporate governance, it may make decisions that do not maximize share value. For example, a firm may choose to invest in projects that maximize managers' own wealth and not that of shareholders. They may also make financing decisions that minimize the risk of the firm for the management but not necessarily for shareholders. This would lead them to make investment and financing decisions different from those that would be recommended in later chapters.

| TABLE 2.5 | Country | Code |
|---|---|---|
| | Australia | Revised Corporate Governance Principles and Recommendations (2007) |
| | Austria | Austrian Code of Corporate Governance (2009) |
| | Belgium | The 2009 Belgian Code on Corporate Governance (2009) |
| | China | The Code of Corporate Governance for Listed Companies in China (2001) |
| | Denmark | Revised Recommendations for Corporate Governance in Denmark (2008) |
| | EU | Euroshareholders Corporate Governance Guidelines 2000 (2002) |
| | Finland | Finnish Corporate Governance Code (2008) |
| | France | Recommendations on Corporate Governance (2010) |
| | Germany | German Corporate Governance Code (2002, Amended 2009) |
| | Greece | Principles of Corporate Governance (2001) |
| | India | Corporate Governance Voluntary Guidelines (2009) |
| | Ireland | Corporate Governance, Share Option and Other Incentive Schemes (1999) |
| | Italy | Codice di Autodisciplina (2006) |
| | Netherlands | Dutch Corporate Governance Code (2008) |
| | Norway | The Norwegian Code of Practice for Corporate Governance (2009) |
| | OECD | OECD Principles of Corporate Governance (2004) |
| | Pakistan | Code of Corporate Governance (2002) |
| | Poland | Code of Best Practice for WSE Companies (2007) |
| | Portugal | CMVM Corporate Governance Code (2010) |
| | South Africa | King Code of Corporate Governance for South Africa (2009) |
| | Spain | Unified Good Governance Code (2006) |
| | Sweden | Swedish Code of Corporate Governance (2009) |
| | Switzerland | Swiss Code of Best Practice for Corporate Governance (2008) |
| | Thailand | The Principles of Good Corporate Governance for Listed Companies (2006) |
| | UK | The Stewardship Code for Institutional Investors (2010)<br>The Audit Firm Governance Code (2009)<br>Review of the Combined Code: Final Report (2009)<br>A Review of Corporate Governance in UK Banks and Other Financial Industry Entities (The Walker Review) (2009)<br>The Combined Code of Corporate Governance (2008) |
| | US | Key Agreed Principles to Strengthen Corporate Governance for US Publicly Traded Corporations (2008)<br>Final NYSE Corporate Governance Rules (2003)<br>The Sarbanes-Oxley Act (2002) |

**Table 2.5** Country codes of corporate governance

Transparency and timely information disclosure are major aspects of good governance. Without these, investors would find it extremely difficult to value a firm or assess the risk of its operations. Part Three of the textbook assumes that share prices efficiently incorporate information about a company. However, if the management of a firm do not see transparency and disclosure as important parts of their responsibilities, then share prices will be uninformative, and risk assessment would be meaningless.

Most countries have their own code of corporate governance that guides companies on how they should be governed. Largely, they are very similar, with only slight country-level differences. Table 2.5 lists the main corporate governance codes and their date of publication for different countries.

## Summary and Conclusions

All the material in this textbook makes the assumption that firms are run properly, efficiently, and ethically. Unfortunately, in practice this may not be the case. Corporate governance is concerned with the way in which a firm is managed. There are a number of basic principles that should be followed to minimize the danger of firms getting into difficulty because of the way they are managed. The budding financial manager must be aware of, and familiar with, the basic principles underlying the way in which his or her company should be run. Without this knowledge, he or she will not be in a position to make the best financial decisions for the company's shareholders.

## Concepts Review and Critical Thinking Questions

1  **Sole Proprietorships and Partnerships [LO1]**  What are the four primary disadvantages of the sole proprietorship and partnership forms of business organization? What benefits are there to these types of business organization as opposed to the corporate form?

2  **Corporations [LO1]**  What is the primary disadvantage of the corporate form of organization? Name at least two advantages of corporate organization.

3  **Agency Problems [LO2]**  Who owns a corporation? Describe the process whereby the owners control the firm's management. What is the main reason why an agency relationship exists in the corporate form of organization? In this context, what kinds of problem can arise?

4  **Agency Problems [LO2]**  Suppose you own equity in a company. The current share price is £25. Another company has just announced that it wants to buy your company, and will pay £35 per share to acquire all the outstanding shares. Your company's management immediately begins fighting off this hostile bid. Is management acting in the shareholders' best interests? Why or why not?

5  **Agency Problems and Corporate Ownership [LO3]**  Corporate ownership varies around the world. Historically, individuals have owned the majority of shares in public corporations in the United States. In Germany and Japan, however, banks and other large financial institutions own most of the equity in public corporations. Do you think agency problems are likely to be more or less severe in Germany and Japan than in the United States? Why? In recent years, large financial institutions such as mutual funds and pension funds have been becoming the dominant owners of shares in the United Kingdom, and these institutions are becoming more active in corporate affairs. What are the implications of this trend for agency problems and corporate control?

6  **Executive Compensation [LO2]**  Critics have charged that compensation to top managers in the banking sector is simply too high and should be cut back. Look at the financial accounts of some banks in your region and determine the total pay of their chief executive officers. Are such amounts excessive? In answering, it might be helpful to recognize that superstar athletes such as Cristiano Ronaldo and Lionel Messi, top entertainers such as Robert de Niro and Will Smith, and many others at the top of their respective fields earn at least as much, if not a great deal more.

7  **Private Limited and Publicly Listed Corporations [LO1]**  What are the main similarities and differences between private and public limited companies? Why are all firms not publicly listed?

8  **Macro Governance [LO3]**  Why do you think corporate behaviour in bank-based financial systems would be different from that in market-based financial systems? How do you think other differences in the macro environment can affect corporate objectives?

9   **Corporate Governance [LO3]**  Why is corporate governance important to the shareholders of a firm? Should the same corporate governance rules be applied to all companies? Why or why not?

10  **Corporate Governance [LO1]**  Explain why the corporate governance of a sole proprietorship should be different from that of a partnership, which in turn should be different from that of a limited corporation.

11  **Corporate Governance across the World [LO3]**  Why is there no single code of corporate governance applied to all the countries of the world? Would emerging-market firms have different issues to consider?

12  **Sole Proprietorship [LO1]**  Sole proprietorship is the most common type of corporation throughout the world. Why do you think this is the case? What are the benefits of sole proprietorships over other corporate forms?

13  **Partnerships [LO1]**  What are the differences between a general partnership and a limited partnership? Why do firms choose to be partnerships instead of limited liability corporations?

14  **Organizations [LO1]**  Review the differences between various corporate forms. Why would an owner move from being a sole owner to a partner to a controlling shareholder in a limited corporation?

15  **Government Ownership [LO3]**  In recent years, governments have taken control of banks through buying their shares. What impact does this have on the lending culture of these banks? Is this consistent with shareholder maximization? Use an example to illustrate your answer.

16  **Stakeholders [LO2]**  Discuss what is meant by a stakeholder. In what ways are stakeholders represented in two-tier board structures? How does this differ from companies with a unitary board structure? Use real examples to illustrate your answer.

17  **Institutional Shareholders [LO2]**  Regulators have developed a number of new policies with respect to institutional shareholder involvement in the running of firms. Review the reasons why regulators would prefer more or less involvement of institutions in the running of corporations. In addition, discuss the proposals that have been put forward by regulators in your own country, and whether these are likely to be effective.

18  **Managerial Objectives [LO2]**  Why would we expect managers of a corporation to pursue the objectives of shareholders? What about bondholders?

MINI CASE **Tadcaster Wines Limited**

In early 2007 Kevin and Michelle Tadcaster formed Tadcaster Wines Limited. The company produced a full line of English wines, and its specialities included tonic wine, crazy dog wine, Temeke Wine and Tyson Wine. The two formed the company as an outside interest, and both continued to work at their existing jobs. Kevin did all the wine growing, and Michelle handled the marketing and distribution. With good product quality and a sound marketing plan, the company grew rapidly. In early 2010 the company was featured in a widely distributed entrepreneurial magazine. Later that year the company was featured in *Gourmet Wines*, a leading speciality wine magazine. After the article appeared in *Gourmet Wines* sales exploded, and the company began receiving orders from all over the world.

Because of the increased sales, Kevin left his other job, followed shortly by Michelle. The company hired additional workers to meet demand. Unfortunately, the fast growth experienced by the company led to cash flow and capacity problems. The company is currently producing as many wines as possible with the assets it owns, but demand for its wines is still growing. Further, the company has been approached by a national supermarket chain with a proposal to put four of its wines in all of the chain's stores, and a national restaurant chain has contacted the company about selling Tadcaster Wines in its restaurants. The restaurant would sell the wines without a brand name.

Kevin and Michelle have operated the company as a sole proprietorship. They have approached you to help manage and direct the company's growth. Specifically, they have asked you to answer the following questions.

### QUESTIONS

1  What are the advantages and disadvantages of changing the company organization from a sole proprietorship to a partnership?

2  What are the advantages and disadvantages of changing the company organization from a sole proprietorship to a corporation?

3  Ultimately, what action would you recommend the company undertake? Why?

---

Online **Learning**Centre

To help you grasp the key concepts of this chapter check out the extra resources posted on the Online Learning Centre at **www.mcgraw-hill.co.uk/textbooks/hillier**

Among other helpful resources there are mini-cases tailored to each chapter.

# CHAPTER 3

# Financial Analysis and Planning

## KEY NOTATIONS

| | |
|---|---|
| *b* | retention ratio |
| NWC | net working capital |
| P/E ratio | price–earnings ratio |
| PPE | property, plant and equipment |
| ROA | return on assets |
| ROE | return on equity |

## LEARNING OBJECTIVES

After studying this chapter, you should understand:

LO1 The three main financial statements that are produced by corporations: the statement of financial position, the income statement, and the statement of cash flows.

LO2 How to compute and, more importantly, interpret some common ratios.

LO3 How to undertake long-term financial planning using financial statements.

A WRITE-OFF BY A COMPANY frequently means that the value of the company's assets has declined. In 2008 and 2009 almost all banks wrote off billions of euros of loans they did not expect to receive in the future. Royal Bank of Scotland, for example, took a write-off of £16.2 billion in 2008, meaning that it was reducing income for the year by that amount.

So did Royal Bank of Scotland shareholders actually lose £16.2 billion? The answer is no. Understanding why ultimately leads us to the main subject of this chapter: that all-important substance known as *cash flow*.

In this chapter we examine financial statements, taxes and cash flow. Our emphasis is not on preparing financial statements. Instead, we recognize that financial statements are frequently a key source of information for financial decisions, so our goal is to briefly examine such statements and point out some of their more relevant features. We also pay special attention to some of the practical details of cash flow.

As you read, pay particular attention to two important differences: (1) the difference between accounting value and market value; and (2) the difference between accounting income and cash flow. These distinctions will be important throughout the book.

## 3.1 The Annual Report

Every year, a company will release its annual report. In addition to information relating to the performance and activities of the firm over the previous year, the annual report presents three financial statements:

1  The statement of financial position, or balance sheet

2  The income statement

3  The statement of cash flows

We shall now discuss each statement in turn.

> **statement of financial position (balance sheet)** Financial statement showing a firm's accounting value on a particular date.

## The Statement of Financial Position

The **statement of financial position** or **balance sheet** is a snapshot of the firm. It is a convenient means of organizing and summarizing what a firm owns (its assets), what the firm owes (its liabilities), and the difference between the two (the firm's equity) at a given point in time. Figure 3.1 illustrates how the statement of financial position is constructed. As shown, the left side lists the assets of the firm, and the right side lists the liabilities and equity.

**Assets: The Left Side**    Assets are classified as either *current* or *non-current*. A non-current asset is one that has a relatively long life (greater than 12 months). Non-current assets can be either *tangible*, such as a truck or a computer, or *intangible*, such as a trademark or patent. A current asset has a life of less than one year. This means that the asset will convert to cash within 12 months. For example, inventory would normally be purchased and sold within a year, and is thus classified as a current asset. Obviously, cash itself is a current asset. Trade receivables (money owed to the firm by its customers) are also current assets.

**Liabilities and Owners' Equity: The Right Side**    The firm's liabilities are the first thing listed on the right side of the statement of financial position. These are classified as either *current* or *non-current*. Current liabilities, like current assets, have a life of less than one year (meaning they must be paid within the year), and are usually listed before non-current liabilities. Trade payables (money the firm owes to its suppliers) are one example of a current liability.

A debt that is not due in the coming year is classified as a non-current liability. A loan that the firm will pay off in five years is one such non-current liability. Firms borrow in the long term from a variety of sources. We shall tend to use the terms *bond* and *bondholders* generically to refer to long-term debt and long-term creditors, respectively.

**FIGURE 3.1**

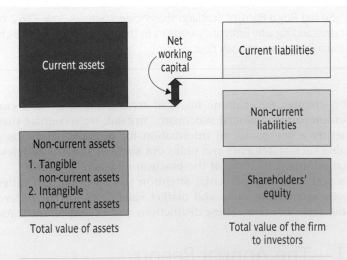

**Figure 3.1** The statement of financial position. Left side: total value of assets. Right side: total value of liabilities and shareholders' equity.

Finally, by definition, the difference between the total value of the assets (current and non-current) and the total value of the liabilities (current and non-current) is the *shareholders' equity*, also called *ordinary equity* or *owners' equity*. This feature of the statement of financial position is intended to reflect the fact that, if the firm were to sell all its assets and use the money to pay off its debts, then whatever residual value remained would belong to the shareholders. So the statement of financial position or balance sheet 'balances' because the value of the left side always equals the value of the right side. That is, the value of the firm's assets is equal to the sum of its liabilities and shareholders' equity:

$$\text{Assets} = \text{Liabilities} + \text{Shareholders' equity} \tag{3.1}$$

This is the *balance sheet identity*, or equation, and it always holds, because shareholders' equity is defined as the difference between assets and liabilities.

**Net Working Capital** As shown in Fig. 3.1, the difference between a firm's current assets and its current liabilities is called **net working capital**. Net working capital is positive when current assets exceed current liabilities. Based on the definitions of current assets and current liabilities, this means the cash that will become available over the next 12 months exceeds the cash that must be paid over the same period. For this reason, net working capital is usually positive in a healthy firm.

> **net working capital**
> Current assets less current liabilities.

## Building the Statement of Financial Position

**EXAMPLE 3.1**

From British Airways' 2009 annual report, it had current assets of £2.346 billion, non-current assets of £8.142 billion, current liabilities of £4.142 billion, and non-current liabilities of £4.5 billion. What does British Airways' statement of financial position or balance sheet look like? What is shareholders' equity? What is net working capital?

In this case, total assets are £2.346 + £8.142 = £10.488 billion and total liabilities are £4.142 + £4.5 = £8.642 billion, so shareholders' equity is the difference: £10.488 − £8.642 = £1.846 billion. The statement of financial position for British Airways would look like this:

| Assets (£ billions) | | Liabilities and shareholders' equity (£ billions) | |
|---|---|---|---|
| Current assets | 2.346 | Current liabilities | 4.142 |
| Non-current assets | 8.142 | Non-current liabilities | 4.5 |
| | | Shareholders' equity | 1.846 |
| Total assets | 10.488 | Total liabilities and shareholders' equity | 10.488 |

Net working capital is the difference between current assets and current liabilities, or £2.346 − £4.142 = −£1.796 billion. Given that British Airways' net working capital is negative, its managers would have had to consider ways in which to raise cash to meet the company's commitments in 2009/2010. History tells us that they merged with the Spanish airline Iberia to capture economies of scale and compete on a level playing field with other European operators, such as Air France-KLM.

Table 3.1 shows a real-life statement of financial position for the global plumbing and heating firm Wolseley plc. The assets on the statement of financial position can be listed in order of the length of time it takes for them to convert to cash in the normal course of business. Similarly, the liabilities are listed in the order in which they would normally be paid. There are other ways in which the statements can be presented. For example, in the UK, non-current assets are sometimes called *fixed assets*, non-current liabilities are known as *long-term debt,* and the statement of financial position is presented as fixed assets + current assets − current liabilities = long-term debt + shareholders' equity.

**Market Value versus Book Value** The values shown in the statement of financial position for the firm's assets are *book values*, and generally are not normally what the assets are

TABLE
3.1

| | Notes | 2009 £m | 2008 £m |
|---|---|---|---|
| **Group balance sheet** **As at 31 July 2009** | | | |
| **Assets** | | | |
| **Non-current assets** | | | |
| Intangible assets: goodwill | 12 | 1,514 | 1,995 |
| Intangible assets: other | 12 | 709 | 841 |
| Property, plant and equipment | 12 | 1,593 | 1,842 |
| Investment in associate | | 53 | – |
| Financial assets: available-for-sale investments | | 3 | 4 |
| Deferred tax assets | | 244 | 52 |
| Trade and other receivables | | 116 | 96 |
| Derivative financial assets | | 34 | – |
| | | 4,266 | 4,830 |
| **Current assets** | | | |
| Inventories | | 1,624 | 2,025 |
| Trade and other receivables | | 1,983 | 2,804 |
| Current tax receivable | | 124 | 18 |
| Financial assets: trading investments | | 155 | 5 |
| Derivative financial assets | | 23 | 16 |
| Financial receivables: construction loans (secured) | | 163 | 237 |
| Cash and cash equivalents | | 635 | 231 |
| | | 4,707 | 5,426 |
| Assets held for sale | | 88 | 43 |
| **Total assets** | | 9,061 | 10,299 |
| **Liabilities** | | | |
| **Current liabilities** | | | |
| Trade and other payables | | 2,586 | 2,956 |
| Current tax payable | | 173 | 219 |
| Borrowings: construction loans (unsecured) | | 163 | 237 |
| Bank loans and overdrafts | | 42 | 276 |
| Obligations under finance leases | | 12 | 19 |
| Derivative financial liabilities | | 25 | 8 |
| Provisions | 13 | 122 | 60 |
| Retirement benefit obligations | 14 | 33 | 22 |
| | | 3,156 | 3,797 |
| **Non-current liabilities** | | | |
| Trade and other payables | | 59 | 68 |
| Bank loans | | 1,657 | 2,440 |
| Obligations under finance leases | | 59 | 68 |

**Table 3.1** Statements of financial position

| TABLE 3.1 | | | |
|---|---|---:|---:|
| Derivative financial liabilities | | 11 | – |
| Deferred tax liabilities | | 176 | 235 |
| Provisions | 13 | 244 | 118 |
| Retirement benefit obligations | 14 | 308 | 214 |
| | | 2,514 | 3,143 |
| Liabilities of disposal groups held for sale | | 15 | – |
| **Total liabilities** | | 5,685 | 6,940 |
| **Net assets** | | 3,376 | 3,359 |
| **Shareholders' equity** | | | |
| Called up share capital | | 241 | 165 |
| Share premium account | | 1,152 | 949 |
| Foreign currency translation reserve | | 228 | (52) |
| Retained earnings | | 1,755 | 2,290 |
| **Equity shareholders' funds** | 15 | 3,376 | 3,359 |

Source: Wolseley plc 2009 annual report, www.wolseley.com

**Table 3.1** Continued

actually worth. Under **International Accounting Standards (IAS)** financial statements in Europe and many other countries can show assets in two ways. The most common presentation uses the *historical cost model*, in which assets are valued at what the firm paid for them, no matter how long ago they were purchased or how much they are worth today. Another approach uses the *revaluation model*, which present an asset's value as what it is worth in the market today. This is known as the *fair value amount*.

> **International Accounting Standards (IAS)**
> The common set of standards and procedures by which audited financial statements are prepared in Europe and many other countries.

For current assets market value and book value might be somewhat similar, because current assets are bought and converted into cash over a relatively short span of time. In other circumstances the two values might differ quite a bit. Moreover, for non-current assets under the cost model it would be purely a coincidence if the actual market value of an asset (what the asset could be sold for) were equal to its book value. For example, a railroad might own enormous tracts of land purchased a century or more ago. What the railroad paid for that land could be hundreds or thousands of times less than what the land is worth today. The statement of financial position would nonetheless show the historical cost if the cost model were used.

The difference between market value and book value is important for understanding the impact of reported gains and losses. For example, to open the chapter we discussed the huge charges against earnings taken by the Royal Bank of Scotland. What actually happened is that these charges came from recognizing a reduction in the book value of certain types of asset. However, this recognition had no effect on the amount the assets in question could actually sell for in the market. Instead, the market value of an asset depends on things such as its riskiness and cash flows, neither of which has anything to do with accounting.

The statement of financial position is potentially useful to many different parties. A supplier might look at the size of trade payables to see how promptly the firm pays its bills. A potential creditor would examine the liquidity and degree of financial leverage. Managers within the firm can track things such as the amount of cash and the amount of inventory the firm keeps on hand. Uses such as these are discussed in more detail later in the chapter.

Managers and investors will frequently be interested in knowing the value of the firm. This information is not in the statement of financial position. The fact that assets may be listed at cost means that there is no necessary connection between the total assets shown and the value of the firm. Indeed, many of the most valuable assets a firm might have – good management, a good reputation, talented employees – don't appear in the statement of financial position at all.

Similarly, the shareholders' equity figure in the statement of financial position and the true value of the equity need not be related. For example, in early 2010 the book value of BP's equity was about £55 billion, whereas the market value was £110 billion. Similarly, Wolseley's book value of equity was approximately £3.4 billion, and its market value was £3.9 billion.

For financial managers, then, the accounting value of the equity is not an especially important concern; it is the market value that matters. Henceforth, whenever we speak of the value of an asset or the value of the firm, we shall normally mean its *market value*. So, for example, when we say the goal of the financial manager is to increase the value of the equity, we mean the market value of the equity.

**EXAMPLE 3.2**

# Market Value versus Book Value

Siouxsie plc has non-current assets with a book value of £700 and an appraised market value of about £1,000. Net working capital is £400 on the books, but approximately £600 would be realized if all the current accounts were liquidated. Siouxsie has £500 in long-term debt, both book value and market value. What is the book value of the equity? What is the market value?

We can construct two simplified statements of financial position, one in accounting (book value) terms and one in economic (market value) terms:

| SIOUXSIE PLC Statements of financial position Market value versus book value | | | | | |
|---|---|---|---|---|---|
| **Assets** | | | **Liabilities and shareholders' equity** | | |
| | **Book £** | **Market £** | | **Book £** | **Market £** |
| Net working capital | 400 | 600 | Non-current liabilities | 500 | 500 |
| Non-current assets | 700 | 1,000 | Shareholders' equity | 600 | 1,100 |
| | 1,100 | 1,600 | | 1,100 | 1,600 |

In this example shareholders' equity is actually worth almost twice as much as what is shown on the books. The distinction between book and market values is important precisely because book values can be so different from true economic value.

## The Income Statement

**income statement**
Financial statement summarizing a firm's performance over a period of time.

The **income statement** measures performance over some period of time, usually a quarter, six months or a year. The income statement equation is

$$\text{Revenues} - \text{Expenses} = \text{Income} \tag{3.2}$$

If you think of the statement of financial position as a snapshot, then you can think of the income statement as a video recording covering the period between before and after pictures. Table 3.2 shows a real-life income statement for Wolseley plc.

TABLE
3.2

| | | 2009 Before exceptional items | 2009 Exceptional items | 2009 Total |
|---|---|---|---|---|
| **Group income statement** Year ended 31 July 2009 | | | | |
| | Notes | £m | £m | £m |
| *Continuing operations* | | | | |
| **Revenue** | 2 | 14,441 | – | 14,441 |
| Cost of sales | | (10,436) | (28) | (10,464) |
| **Gross profit** | | 4,005 | (28) | 3,977 |
| Distribution costs | | (2,831) | (266) | (3,097) |
| Administrative expenses: | | | | |
| amortization of acquired intangibles | | (105) | – | (105) |
| impairment of acquired intangibles | | (490) | – | (490) |
| other | | (743) | (164) | (907) |
| Administrative expenses: total | | (1,338) | (164) | (1,502) |
| Other income | | 16 | – | 16 |
| **Operating (loss)/profit** | 2 | (148) | (458) | (606) |
| Finance revenue | 4 | 72 | – | 72 |
| Finance costs | 5 | (217) | – | (217) |
| Share of after-tax loss of associate | 6 | (9) | (6) | (15) |
| **(Loss)/profit before tax** | | (302) | (464) | (766) |
| Tax income/(expense) | 7 | (72) | 106 | 34 |
| **(Loss)/profit from continuing operations** | | (374) | (358) | (732) |
| Loss from discontinued operations | 8 | (265) | (176) | (441) |
| **(Loss)/profit for the year attributable to equity shareholders** | | (639) | (534) | (1,173) |
| **(Loss)/earnings per share** | 10 | | | |
| *Continuing operations and discontinued operations* | | | | |
| Basic (loss)/earnings per share | | | | (558.0)p |
| Diluted (loss)/earnings per share | | | | (558.0)p |
| *Continuing operations only* | | | | |
| Basic (loss)/earnings per share | | | | (348.2)p |
| Diluted (loss)/earnings per share | | | | (348.2)p |

*Source*: Wolseley plc 2009 annual report, www.wolseley.com

**Table 3.2** Income statement

TABLE
3.3

| 15. Reconciliation of movements in shareholders' funds | 2009 £m | 2008 £m |
|---|---|---|
| (Loss)/profit for the year attributable to equity shareholders | (1,173) | 74 |
| Other recognized income and expense | 187 | 40 |
| Dividends paid | – | (215) |
| Credit to equity for share-based payments | 9 | 5 |
| New share capital subscribed | 999 | 4 |
| Purchase of own shares by employee benefit trusts | (5) | – |
| Net addition to/(reduction in) shareholders' funds | 17 | (92) |
| Opening shareholders' funds | 3,359 | 3,451 |
| Closing shareholders' funds | 3,376 | 3,359 |

*Source*: Wolseley plc 2009 annual report, www.wolseley.com

**Table 3.3** Note 15 to Wolseley 2009 annual report

The first thing reported in an income statement would usually be revenue and expenses from the firm's principal operations. Subsequent parts include, among other things, financing expenses such as interest paid. Taxes paid are reported separately. The last item is *(loss)/ profit from continuing operations*, also known as *net income* (the so-called bottom line). Net income is often expressed on a per-share basis and called *earnings per share (EPS)*.

Wolseley did not pay any dividends to its shareholders in 2009, probably because it had made such a large loss. You may also be wondering why shareholders' equity increased from £3.359 billion in 2008 to £3.376 billion in 2009 (see Table 3.1), when the firm lost £1.173 billion. This information can be found in the notes to the accounts, and is presented in Table 3.3. The main factor was that Wolseley raised £999 million in cash from shareholders, and this was used to shore up the company's finances during an exceptionally tough year.

**EXAMPLE 3.3**

## Calculating Earnings and Dividends per Share

Wolseley plc had 210 million shares after its 2009 share issue. Based on the income statement in Table 3.2, what was EPS? What were dividends per share?

From the income statement we see that Wolseley had a net loss of £732 million for the year from continuing operations. No dividends were paid. We can calculate earnings per share, or EPS, and dividends per share as follows:

Earnings per share  = profit/loss from continuing operations/Total shares outstanding
= −£732/210 = −£3.48 per share

Dividends per share = Total dividends/Total shares outstanding
= £0/210 = £0 per share

This is confirmed from looking at the bottom of Table 3.2. We could, of course, have used the profit/loss from continuing and discounted operations (£1,173 million) and arrived at an earnings per share of −£5.58 per share. Clearly, the two values are very different, and so it is exceptionally important to know what EPS is actually measuring.

When looking at an income statement, the financial manager needs to keep two main things in mind: International Accounting Standards (IAS) and cash versus non-cash items.

**IAS and the Income Statement**   An income statement prepared using International Accounting Standards will show revenue when it accrues. This is not necessarily when the cash comes in. The general rule (the *recognition* or *realization principle*) is to recognize revenue when the earnings process is virtually complete, and the value of an exchange of goods or services is known or can be reliably determined. In practice this principle usually means that revenue is recognized at the time of sale, which need not be the same as the time of collection.

Expenses shown on the income statement are based on the *matching principle*. The basic idea here is to first determine revenues as described previously and then match those revenues with the costs associated with producing them. So, if we manufacture a product and then sell it on credit, the revenue is realized at the time of sale. The production and other costs associated with the sale of that product will likewise be recognized at that time. Once again, the actual cash outflows may have occurred at some different time.

As a result of the way revenues and expenses are realized, the figures shown on the income statement may not be at all representative of the actual cash inflows and outflows that occurred during a particular period.

**Non-Cash Items**   A primary reason why accounting income differs from cash flow is that an income statement contains **non-cash items**. The most important of these is *depreciation*. Suppose a firm purchases an asset for €5,000 and pays in cash. Obviously, the firm has a €5,000 cash outflow at the time of purchase. However, instead of deducting the €5,000 as an expense, an accountant might depreciate the asset over its lifetime.

> **non-cash items**
> Expenses charged against revenues that do not directly affect cash flow, such as depreciation.

If the depreciation is straight-line and the asset is written down to zero over that period, then €5,000/5 = €1,000 will be deducted each year as an expense. The important thing to recognize is that this €1,000 deduction isn't cash – it's an accounting number. The actual cash outflow occurred when the asset was purchased.

The depreciation deduction is simply another application of the matching principle in accounting. The revenues associated with an asset would generally occur over some length of time. So the accountant seeks to match the expense of purchasing the asset with the benefits produced from owning it.

As we shall see, for the financial manager the actual timing of cash inflows and outflows is critical in coming up with a reasonable estimate of market value, so we need to learn how to separate the cash flows from the non-cash accounting entries. In reality, the difference between cash flow and accounting income can be pretty dramatic. For example, consider again Wolseley plc. For its 2009 fiscal year Wolseley reported a net loss of £1.173 billion. Sounds bad; but Wolseley also reported a *positive* cash flow of £395 million, a difference of about £1.5 billion! The main reason, as we have said, is that the company undertook a £999 million share issue in 2009 (see Table 3.3), and sold a considerable amount of property during the year.

Our nearby *Work the Web* box shows how to find this information online for almost any company.

# Work the Web

By far the simplest way to find companies' accounting information is to read their financial reports. Depending on where a company is listed, it will be required to produce quarterly, interim (six-monthly) and annual reports. Quarterly and interim statements are normally very brief, with only an income statement provided. The annual report will be much larger, and can run to over 100 pages. Although there are a number of websites that provide this information, it is often easier to check a company's website and look for a tab that says 'financial information', 'investor relations', or something similar. For example, consider the French luxury goods firm Compagnie Financière Richemont SA. Do an Internet search for 'Compagnie Financière Richemont SA annual report', and you should be directed to the company's homepage.

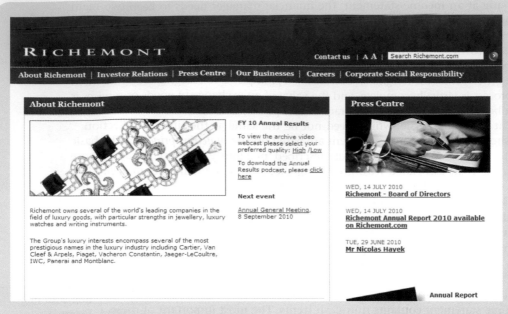

Click on the 'investor relations' tab and choose the 'reports' option. You will now be presented with a page with the company's most recent financial reports.

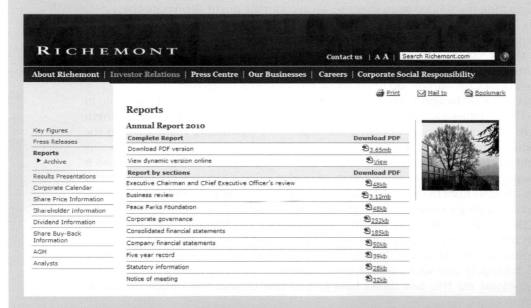

*Source*: www.richemont.com

Download these and read them at your leisure!

## QUESTIONS

1 Now it's over to you. Find the annual reports of Johnson Matthey plc, Intercontinental Hotels Group plc and Hammerson plc. Read these in detail and find out whether each company made a profit or loss in the most recent year, the book value of shareholders' equity, and the cash flow for the year.

2 Go to Yahoo! Finance and find the share price information and market capitalization for the three firms. Is the market value information significantly different from or similar to the accounting information for each firm? Why do you think this is the case?

# A Digression: Taxes

Taxes can be one of the largest cash outflows a firm experiences. For example, for the fiscal year 2008 the global energy firm Total SA's earnings before taxes were about €180 billion. Its tax bill, including all taxes paid worldwide, was a whopping €14 billion. Also for fiscal year 2008, Telefonica had a taxable income of €10.9 billion, and the company paid €3 billion in taxes, an average tax rate of 27.5 per cent.

The size of a company's tax bill is determined by the tax code, an often amended set of rules. In this section we examine corporate tax rates and how taxes are calculated. If the various rules of taxation seem a little bizarre or convoluted to you, keep in mind that the tax code is the result of political, not economic, forces. As a result, there is no reason why it has to make economic sense.

**Corporate Tax Rates**   An overview of corporate tax rates for a sample of countries that were in effect for 2010 is shown in Table 3.4. Corporate taxes are not normally a simple arithmetic deduction from profit before taxes. Almost all countries in the world allow firms to carry forward losses they've made in previous years to offset their tax bill in the future. In addition, there are a number of adjustments and modifications to the tax figure that affect what is actually paid. This is what happened in 2009 to British Airways, which made a loss of £401 million before taxes. Although the corporate tax rate in the UK was 28 per cent, British Airways received a tax credit (to offset the loss) of only £43 million. This is only 10.7 per cent of £401 million.

The tax rates presented in Table 3.4 are average tax rates for the largest companies. Many countries apply differential taxation, depending on how much a company earns in any given year. In the UK, for example, there are two corporation tax bands. Firms that earn between £0 and £300,000 per annum have a tax rate of 22 per cent. Firms that earn above £1,500,000 must pay 28 per cent (as presented in Table 3.4). Firms that report annual turnover between

| TABLE 3.4 | Country | Corporation tax (%) | Country | Corporation tax (%) |
|---|---|---|---|---|
| | Australia | 30 | New Zealand | 30 |
| | Austria | 25 | Nigeria | 30 |
| | Belgium | 33.99 | Norway | 28 |
| | Brazil | 34 | Pakistan | 35 |
| | Canada | 19.5 | Poland | 19 |
| | China | 25 | Portugal | 25 |
| | Denmark | 25 | Russia | 20 |
| | Finland | 26 | South Africa | 28 |
| | France | 33.33 | Spain | 32.50 |
| | Germany | 29.8 | Sweden | 28 |
| | Greece | 25 | Switzerland | 21.30 |
| | India | 30 | Taiwan | 25 |
| | Ireland | 12.50 | Tanzania | 30 |
| | Italy | 31.4 | Thailand | 30 |
| | Japan | 30 | Turkey | 20 |
| | Malaysia | 26 | United Kingdom | 28 |
| | Netherlands | 20/25.5 | United States | 40 |

*Source*: Federation of International Trade Associations, KPMG.

**Table 3.4** Corporate tax rates for large firms around the world

£300,000 and £1,500,000 receive a rebate called marginal tax relief that allows them to transition their tax rates gradually between the small companies tax rate and the standard rate.

**Average versus Marginal Tax Rates** In making financial decisions, it is frequently important to distinguish between average and marginal tax rates. Your average tax rate is your tax bill divided by your taxable income – in other words, the percentage of your income that goes to pay taxes. Your marginal tax rate is the tax you would pay (in per cent) if you earned one more unit of currency. The percentage tax rates shown in Table 3.4 for the Netherlands are marginal rates. On the first €200,000 of earnings, Dutch firms must pay 20 per cent tax. Any extra earnings are charged 25.5 per cent tax. Put another way, marginal tax rates apply to the part of income in the indicated range only, not all income.

The difference between average and marginal tax rates can best be illustrated with a simple example. Suppose our Dutch corporation has a taxable income of €400,000. What is the tax bill? Using Table 3.4, we can figure our tax bill like this:

$$
\begin{aligned}
0.20 \times €200,000 &= €40,000 \\
0.255 \times (€400,000 - 200,000) &= €51,000 \\
&= \underline{€91,000}
\end{aligned}
$$

Our total tax is thus €91,000.

In our example, what is the average tax rate? We had a taxable income of €400,000 and a tax bill of €91,000, so the average tax rate is €91,000/400,000 = 22.75%. What is the marginal tax rate? If we made one more euro, the tax on that euro would be 25.5 cents, so our marginal rate is 25.5 per cent.

With a flat-rate tax there is only one tax rate, so the rate is the same for all income levels. With such a tax the marginal tax rate is always the same as the average tax rate. As it stands now, corporate taxation in the United Kingdom is based on a modified flat-rate tax, which becomes a true flat rate for the highest incomes.

Normally, the marginal tax rate will be relevant for financial decision-making. The reason is that any new cash flows will be taxed at that marginal rate. Because financial decisions usually involve new cash flows or changes in existing ones, this rate will tell us the marginal effect of a decision on our tax bill.

## Statement of Cash Flows

At this point we are ready to discuss perhaps one of the most important pieces of financial information that can be gleaned from financial statements: cash flow. By *cash flow* we simply mean the difference between the cash that came in and the cash that went out. For example, if you were the owner of a business, you might be very interested in how much cash you actually took out of your business in a given year. How to determine this amount is one of the things we discuss next.

No standard financial statement always presents this information in the way that we wish. We shall therefore discuss how to calculate cash flow for Wolseley plc, and point out how the result may differ from that of standard financial statement calculations. It is also important to note that the accounting standards used in Europe are different from those in the US, and this leads to differences in the way the cash flow statement is presented. Our focus is on International Accounting Standards, because these are followed by large European firms.

**total cash flow**
The total of cash flow from operating activities, investing activities and financing activities.

From the balance sheet identity, we know that the value of a firm's assets is equal to the value of its liabilities plus the value of its equity. Similarly, the cash flow from the firm's assets must equal the sum of the cash flow to creditors and the cash flow to shareholders (or owners):

Cash flow from assets = Cash flow to creditors + Cash flow to shareholders    (3.3)

This is the *cash flow identity*. It says that the cash flow from the firm's assets is equal to the cash flow paid to suppliers of capital to the firm. What it reflects is the fact that a firm generates cash through its various activities, and that cash is either used to pay creditors or paid out to the owners of the firm.

Another way of presenting cash flow is to separate it according to the corporate activity to which it relates. Cash flows that arise because of the firm's core operations are known as **operating cash flow**. When a company buys or sells a warehouse, this is a long-term investment that will span many years, and a cash flow of this type relates to the firm's long-term investing activities. Finally, if a firm raises cash in the form of equity or debt, the cash flow would be part of its financing activities. Any cash flow that occurs can be identified as one of these three components:

> **operating cash flow**
> Cash generated from a firm's normal business activities.

$$\text{Total cash flow} = \frac{\text{Cash flow from}}{\text{operating activities}} + \frac{\text{Cash flow from}}{\text{investing activities}} + \frac{\text{Cash flow from}}{\text{financing activities}} \quad (3.4)$$

We discuss the various components that make up these cash flows next.

**Cash Flow from Operating Activities**    Operating cash flow refers to the cash flow that results from the firm's day-to-day activities of producing and selling. Expenses associated with the firm's financing of its assets or the purchase of buildings are not included, because they are not operating expenses.

To calculate operating cash flow (OCF), we want to calculate revenues minus costs plus changes in non-cash net working capital. We don't want to include depreciation, because it's not a cash outflow. We also don't want to include interest, because it's a financing expense. The only exception is when we are considering the accounts of a financial institution, such as a bank, where interest payments and receipts relate directly to operating income. Finally, we do want to include taxes, because they are (unfortunately) paid in cash.

International Accounting Standards require companies to present operating cash flows in one of two ways: the direct method, where actual cash outflows and inflows are presented; or the indirect method, which starts off with the company's profit or loss for the year and then extracts any non-cash items incurred (e.g. depreciation), cash flows arising from financing activities, and cash flows from investing activities. Both approaches will arrive at the same operating cash flow.

If we look at Wolseley plc's statement of cash generated from core operations (Table 3.5), we see that they used the indirect method to present cash flow from operating activities.

Wolseley plc had a 2009 net cash flow of £1.008 billion generated from its core operations. Notice the number of non-cash adjustments that were made to Wolseley's income statement to arrive at the £1.173 billion loss. In addition, cash flows from the sale of buildings have also been taken out because they are not operating cash flows.

Operating cash flow is an important number because it tells us, on a very basic level, whether a firm's cash inflows from its business operations are sufficient to cover its everyday cash outflows. For this reason, a negative operating cash flow is often a sign of trouble.

To complete our calculation of cash flow for Wolseley plc, we need to consider how much was reinvested in the firm and how much was raised from outside financing. We consider spending on non-current assets first.

**Cash Flow from Investing Activities**    Cash flow from investing activities (net capital spending) is just money spent on non-current assets less money received from the sale of non-current assets. Table 3.6 presents Wolseley plc's net capital spending for financial year 2008/2009.

> **cash flow from investing activities**
> Cash generated or expended from a firm's long-term investments.

During the year, Wolseley paid £18 million in buying other businesses, £91 million in property, plant and equipment, and £155 million in new financial investments. At the same time, it received £172 million from selling property, plant and equipment. In total, its spending on investing activities was £168 million.

Could cash flow from investing activities be positive? The answer is yes. This would happen if the firm sold off more assets than it purchased. You will often see cash flow from investing activities called CAPEX, which is an acronym for capital expenditure. It usually means the same thing.

TABLE
**3.5**

| Reconciliation of (loss)/profit to cash generated from operations Year ended 31 July 2009 | | |
|---|---|---|
| | 2009 £m | 2008 £m |
| (Loss)/profit for the year | (1,173) | 74 |
| Net finance costs | 145 | 156 |
| Share of after-tax loss of associate | 15 | – |
| Tax (income)/expense | (246) | 71 |
| Loss on disposal of businesses and revaluation of disposal groups | 121 | |
| Depreciation and impairment of property, plant and equipment | 286 | 212 |
| Amortization and impairment of non-acquired intangibles | 62 | 30 |
| Loss/(profit) on disposal of property, plant and equipment | 3 | (16) |
| Amortization and impairment of acquired intangibles | 894 | 306 |
| Decrease in inventories | 483 | 220 |
| Decrease in trade and other receivables | 928 | 247 |
| Decrease in trade and other payables | (565) | (61) |
| Increase in provisions and other liabilities | 238 | 18 |
| Share-based payments and other non-cash items | 9 | 5 |
| Cash generated from operations | 1,200 | 1,262 |
| **Cash flows from operating activities** | | |
| Cash generated from operations | 1,200 | 1,262 |
| Interest received | 66 | 70 |
| Interest paid | (231) | (205) |
| Tax paid | (27) | (99) |
| Net cash generated from operating activities | 1,008 | 1,028 |

*Source*: Wolseley plc 2009 annual report, www.wolseley.com

**Table 3.5** Moving from profit and loss to cash flow

**Cash Flow from Financing Activities** The last major component of a firm's cash flow comes from any actions it has taken during the year to raise cash from investors. The company may also have paid back outstanding borrowings, or repurchased its own shares. These cash flows can be substantial, and they constitute the third part of the cash flow statement.

**cash flow from financing activities**
Cash generated or expended as a result of its debt and equity choices.

During 2008/2009 Wolseley plc experienced a very tough time. The construction industry had its toughest period in more than 20 years, and most firms in the sector, not just Wolseley, incurred significant losses and very few cash inflows. Wolseley raised nearly £1 billion in a new share issue, so it could have enough cash to see it through the difficult economic conditions and pay off its creditors. This is reflected in the firm's *statement of cash flow from financing activities* (Table 3.7).

**Net Cash Flow** Given the figures we've come up with, we're ready to calculate cash flow for the firm. The total cash flow is found by adding the cash flow from operating activities to the cash flows from investing and financing activities. So, for Wolseley plc we have the figures shown in Table 3.8.

Wolseley generated net cash flow of £395 million, once the effect of converting some foreign cash flows into British pounds had been factored into the analysis. Clearly, if it had not raised £999 million in cash during the year, it is likely that the firm would have

TABLE
3.6

| Group cash flow statement Year ended 31 July 2009 | | | |
|---|---|---|---|
| | Notes | 2009 £m | 2008 £m |
| **Cash flows from investing activities** | | | |
| Acquisition of businesses (net of cash acquired) | | (18) | (199) |
| Disposals of businesses (net of cash disposed of) | | (15) | 16 |
| Purchases of property, plant and equipment | | (91) | (219) |
| Proceeds from sale of property, plant and equipment | | 172 | 84 |
| Purchases of intangible assets | | (66) | (98) |
| Purchases of investments | | (155) | – |
| Disposals of investments | | 5 | – |
| Net cash used in investing activities | | (168) | (416) |

*Source*: Wolseley plc 2009 annual report, www.wolseley.com

**Table 3.6** Wolseley plc cash flow from investing activities

TABLE
3.7

| Group cash flow statement Year ended 31 July 2009 | | | |
|---|---|---|---|
| | Notes | 2009 £m | 2008 £m |
| **Cash flows from financing activities** | | | |
| Proceeds from the issue of shares to shareholders | 15 | 999 | 4 |
| Purchased of shares by employee benefit trusts | 15 | (5) | – |
| Proceeds from new borrowings | | – | 283 |
| Repayments of borrowings and derivatives | | (1,437) | (529) |
| Finance lease capital payments | | (26) | (19) |
| Dividends paid to shareholders | | – | (215) |
| Net cash used in financing activities | | (469) | (476) |

*Source*: Wolseley plc 2009 annual report, www.wolseley.com

**Table 3.7** Wolseley plc cash flow from financing activities

been in exceptional difficulty. As the preceding discussion indicates, 'cash flow is king'. Without cash, a firm cannot exist.

CONCEPT
QUESTIONS

3.1a    What is the balance sheet identity?
3.1b    Explain the difference between accounting value and market value. Which is more important to the financial manager? Why?
3.1c    What is the income statement equation?
3.1d    Why is accounting income not the same as cash flow? Give two reasons.
3.1e    What is the difference between a marginal and an average tax rate?
3.1f    What is the cash flow identity? Explain what it says.
3.1g    What are the components of operating cash flow?

TABLE
**3.8**

| Group cash flow statement<br>Year ended 31 July 2009 | | | |
| --- | --- | --- | --- |
| | Notes | 2009<br>£m | 2008<br>£m |
| Net cash generated from operating activities | | 1,008 | 1,028 |
| Net cash used in investing activities | | (168) | (416) |
| Net cash used in financing activities | | (469) | (476) |
| Net cash generated | 16 | 371 | 136 |
| Effects of exchange rate changes | | 24 | 7 |
| Net increase in cash, cash equivalents and bank overdrafts | | 395 | 143 |
| Cash, cash equivalents and bank overdrafts at the beginning of the year | | 203 | 60 |
| Cash, cash equivalents and bank overdrafts at the end of the year | | 598 | 203 |

*Source*: Wolseley plc 2009 annual report, www.wolseley.com

**Table 3.8** Wolseley plc 2009 statement of cash flows

## 3.2 Ratio Analysis

**financial ratios**
Relationships determined from a firm's financial information and used for comparison purposes.

One of the main ways to understand how healthy a company is and how well it has performed is to carry out a ratio analysis and compare the **financial ratios** of the firm with its competitors. Such ratios are ways of comparing and investigating the relationships between different pieces of financial information.

Unfortunately, there is a problem in discussing financial ratios. Because a ratio is simply one number divided by another, and because there are so many accounting numbers out there, we could examine a huge number of possible ratios. Everybody has a favourite. We shall restrict ourselves to a representative sampling.

In this section we want only to introduce you to some commonly used financial ratios. These are not necessarily the ones we think are the best. In fact, some of them may strike you as illogical, or not as useful as some alternatives. If they do, don't be concerned. As a financial analyst, you can always decide how to compute your own ratios.

What you do need to worry about is the fact that different people and different sources seldom compute these ratios in exactly the same way, and this leads to much confusion. The specific definitions we use here may or may not be the same as ones you have seen or will see elsewhere. If you are ever using ratios as a tool for analysis, you should be careful to document how you calculate each one; and if you are comparing your numbers with numbers from another source, be sure you know how those numbers are computed.

We shall defer much of our discussion of how ratios are used, and some problems that come up with using them, until later in the chapter. For now, for each of the ratios we discuss, we consider several questions:

1  How is it computed?

2  What is it intended to measure, and why might we be interested?

3  What is the unit of measurement?

4 What might a high or low value tell us? How might such values be misleading?

5 How could this measure be improved?

Financial ratios are traditionally grouped into the following categories:

1 Short-term solvency, or liquidity, ratios

2 Long-term solvency, or financial leverage, ratios

3 Asset management, or turnover, ratios

4 Profitability ratios

5 Market value ratios

We shall consider each of these in turn.

## Short-Term Solvency, or Liquidity, Measures

As the name suggests, short-term solvency ratios as a group are intended to provide information about a firm's liquidity, and these ratios are sometimes called *liquidity measures*. The primary concern is the firm's ability to pay its bills over the short run without undue stress. Consequently, these ratios focus on current assets and current liabilities.

For obvious reasons, liquidity ratios are particularly interesting to short-term creditors. Because financial managers work constantly with banks and other short-term lenders, an understanding of these ratios is essential.

One advantage of looking at current assets and liabilities is that their book values and market values are likely to be similar. Often (though not always), these assets and liabilities just don't live long enough for the two to get seriously out of step. On the other hand, like any type of near-cash, current assets and liabilities can and do change fairly rapidly, so today's amounts may not be a reliable guide to the future. The most common liquidity ratios are as follows.

**Current Ratio**  One of the best known and most widely used ratios is the *current ratio*. As you might guess, the current ratio is defined as follows:

$$\text{Current ratio} = \frac{\text{Current assets}}{\text{Current liabilities}} \tag{3.5}$$

**The Quick (or Acid-Test) Ratio**  Inventory is often the least liquid current asset. It's also the one for which the book values are least reliable as measures of market value, because the quality of the inventory isn't considered. Some of the inventory may later turn out to be damaged, obsolete, or lost.

More to the point, relatively large inventories are often a sign of short-term trouble. The firm may have overestimated sales, and overbought or overproduced as a result. In this case, the firm may have a substantial portion of its liquidity tied up in slow-moving inventory.

To further evaluate liquidity, the *quick*, or *acid-test, ratio* is computed just like the current ratio, except that inventory is omitted:

$$\text{Quick ratio} = \frac{\text{Current assets} - \text{Inventory}}{\text{Current liabilities}} \tag{3.6}$$

Notice that using cash to buy inventory does not affect the current ratio, but it reduces the quick ratio. Again, the idea is that inventory is relatively illiquid compared with cash.

## Long-Term Solvency Measures

Long-term solvency ratios are intended to address the firm's long-term ability to meet its obligations, or, more generally, its financial leverage. These are sometimes called *financial leverage ratios* or just *leverage ratios*. We consider three commonly used measures and some variations.

**Total Debt Ratio**    The *total debt ratio* takes into account all debts of all maturities to all creditors. It can be defined in several ways, the easiest of which is this:

$$\text{Total debt ratio} = \frac{\text{Total assets} - \text{Total equity}}{\text{Total assets}} \tag{3.7}$$

We can define two useful variations on the total debt ratio – the *debt–equity ratio* and the *equity multiplier*:

$$\text{Debt–equity ratio} = \frac{\text{Total debt}}{\text{Total equity}} \tag{3.8}$$

$$\text{Equity multiplier} = \frac{\text{Total assets}}{\text{Total equity}} \tag{3.9}$$

The fact that the equity multiplier is 1 plus the debt–equity ratio is not a coincidence:

$$\text{Equity multiplier} = \frac{\text{Total assets}}{\text{Total equity}}$$

$$= \frac{\text{Total equity} + \text{Total debt}}{\text{Total equity}}$$

$$= 1 + \text{Debt–equity ratio}$$

The thing to notice here is that, given any one of these three ratios, you can immediately calculate the other two; so they all say exactly the same thing.

**Times Interest Earned**    Another common measure of long-term solvency is the *times interest earned (TIE) ratio*. Once again, there are several possible (and common) definitions, but we'll stick with the most traditional:

$$\text{Times interest earned ratio} = \frac{\text{Operating profit}}{\text{Interest}} \tag{3.10}$$

Operating profit is also known as *earnings before interest and taxes (EBIT)*, and you will see this term used in many books. As the name *times interest earned ratio* suggests, this ratio measures how well a company has its interest obligations covered, and it is often called the *interest coverage ratio*.

**Cash Coverage**    A problem with the TIE ratio is that it is based on operating profit, which is not really a measure of cash available to pay interest. The reason is that depreciation and other non-cash expenses have been deducted out. Because interest is definitely a cash outflow (to creditors), one way to define the *cash coverage ratio* is this:

$$\text{Cash coverage ratio} = \frac{\text{Operating profit} + \text{Non-cash deductions}}{\text{Interest}} \tag{3.11}$$

The numerator here, operating profit plus non-cash deductions, is often abbreviated to EBITDA (earnings before interest, taxes, depreciation and amortization – say 'ebbit-dah'). It is a basic measure of the firm's ability to generate cash from operations, and it is frequently used as a measure of cash flow available to meet financial obligations.

A common variation on EBITDA is earnings before interest, taxes, and depreciation (EBITD – say 'ebbit-dee'). In this variation, only depreciation is considered.

## Asset Management, or Turnover, Measures

We next turn our attention to the efficiency with which a company uses its assets. The measures in this section are sometimes called *asset utilization ratios*. The specific ratios we discuss can all be interpreted as measures of turnover. What they are intended to describe is how efficiently or intensively a firm uses its assets to generate sales. We first look at two important current assets: inventory and receivables.

**Inventory Turnover and Days' Sales in Inventory**    *Inventory turnover* can be calculated as follows:

$$\text{Inventory turnover} = \frac{\text{Cost of goods sold}}{\text{Inventory}} \tag{3.12}$$

As long as we are not running out of stock and thereby forgoing sales, the higher this ratio is, the more efficiently we are managing inventory.

If we know the inventory turnover, we can immediately figure out how long it took us to turn it over on average. The result is the average *days' sales in inventory*:

$$\text{Days' sales in inventory} = \frac{365 \text{ days}}{\text{Inventory turnover}} \tag{3.13}$$

In many of the ratios we discuss in this chapter, average figures could just as well be used. Again, it depends on whether we are worried about the past, in which case averages are appropriate, or the future, in which case ending figures might be better. Also, using ending figures is common in reporting industry averages; so, for comparison purposes, ending figures should be used in such cases.

**Receivables Turnover and Days' Sales in Receivables**    Our inventory measures give some indication of how fast we can sell our product. We now look at how fast we collect on those sales. The *receivables turnover* is defined much like inventory turnover:

$$\text{Receivable turnover} = \frac{\text{Sales}}{\text{Trade receivables}} \tag{3.14}$$

This ratio makes more sense if we convert it to days, so here is the *days' sales in receivables*:

$$\text{Days' sales in receivables} = \frac{365 \text{ days}}{\text{Receivables turnover}} \tag{3.15}$$

For obvious reasons, this ratio is frequently called the *average collection period (ACP)*.

**Asset Turnover Ratios**    Moving away from specific accounts such as inventory or receivables, we can consider several 'big picture' ratios. For example, *NWC turnover* is

$$\text{NWC turnover} = \frac{\text{Sales}}{\text{NWC}} \tag{3.16}$$

This ratio measures how much 'work' we get out of our working capital. Once again, assuming we aren't missing out on sales, a high value is preferred. (Why?)

Similarly, *PPE turnover* is

$$\text{PPE turnover} = \frac{\text{Sales}}{\text{Property, plant and equipment}} \tag{3.17}$$

Our final asset management ratio, the *total asset turnover*, comes up quite a bit. We shall see it later in this chapter. As the name suggests, the total asset turnover is

$$\text{Total asset turnover} = \frac{\text{Sales}}{\text{Total assets}} \qquad (3.18)$$

## Profitability Measures

The three measures we discuss in this section are probably the best known and most widely used of all financial ratios. In one form or another, they are intended to measure how efficiently a firm uses its assets and manages its operations. The focus in this group is on the bottom line, net income.

**Profit Margin**  Companies pay a great deal of attention to their *profit margins*:

$$\text{Profit margin} = \frac{\text{Net income}}{\text{Sales}} \qquad (3.19)$$

All other things being equal, a relatively high profit margin is obviously desirable. This situation corresponds to low expense ratios relative to sales. However, we hasten to add that other things are often not equal.

For example, lowering our sales price will usually increase unit volume, but will normally cause profit margins to shrink. Total profit (or, more important, operating cash flow) may go up or down; so the fact that margins are smaller isn't necessarily bad.

**Return on Assets**  *Return on assets (ROA)* is a measure of profit per unit cash of assets. It can be defined in several ways, but the most common is this:

$$\text{Return on assets} = \frac{\text{Net income}}{\text{Total assets}} \qquad (3.20)$$

**Return on Equity**  *Return on equity (ROE)* is a measure of how the shareholders fared during the year. Because benefiting shareholders is our goal, ROE is, in an accounting sense, the true bottom-line measure of performance. ROE is usually measured as follows:

$$\text{Return on equity} = \frac{\text{Net income}}{\text{Total equity}} \qquad (3.21)$$

Because ROA and ROE are such commonly cited numbers, we stress that it is important to remember they are accounting rates of return. For this reason, these measures should properly be called *return on book assets* and *return on book equity*. In fact, ROE is sometimes called *return on net worth*. Whatever it's called, it would be inappropriate to compare the result with, for example, an interest rate observed in the financial markets. We shall have more to say about accounting rates of return in later chapters.

## Market Value Measures

Our final group of measures is based, in part, on information not necessarily contained in financial statements – the market price per share of equity. Obviously, these measures can be calculated directly only for publicly traded companies.

**Price–Earnings Ratio**  The first of our market value measures, the *price–earnings (P/E) ratio* (or multiple), is defined here:

$$\text{P/E ratio} = \frac{\text{Price per share}}{\text{Earnings per share}} \qquad (3.22)$$

Earnings per share is simply net income divided by the number of shares.

Because the P/E ratio measures how much investors are willing to pay per unit of current earnings, higher P/Es are often taken to mean the firm has significant prospects for future growth. Of course, if a firm had no or almost no earnings, its P/E would probably be quite large: so, as always, care is needed in interpreting this ratio.

Sometimes analysts divide P/E ratios by expected future earnings growth rates (after multiplying the growth rate by 100). The result is the PEG ratio. The idea behind the PEG ratio is that whether a P/E ratio is high or low depends on expected future growth. High PEG ratios suggest that the P/E is too high relative to growth, and vice versa.

**Price–Sales Ratio**   In some cases, companies will have negative earnings for extended periods, so their P/E ratios are not very meaningful. A good example is a recent start-up. Such companies usually do have some revenues, so analysts will often look at the *price–sales ratio:*

$$\text{Price–sales ratio} = \frac{\text{Price per share}}{\text{Sales per share}} \tag{3.23}$$

As with P/E ratios, whether a particular price–sales ratio is high or low depends on the industry involved.

**Market-to-Book Ratio**   A second commonly quoted market value measure is the *market-to-book ratio*:

$$\text{Market-to-book ratio} = \frac{\text{Market value per share}}{\text{Book value per share}} \tag{3.24}$$

Notice that book value per share is total equity (not just ordinary shares) divided by the number of shares outstanding.

Because book value per share is an accounting number, it reflects historical costs. In a loose sense, the market-to-book ratio therefore compares the market value of the firm's investments with their cost. A value less than 1 could mean that the firm has not been successful overall in creating value for its shareholders.

Another ratio, called *Tobin's Q ratio*, is much like the market-to-book ratio. Tobin's Q is the market value of the firm's assets divided by their replacement cost:

$$\begin{aligned}
\text{Tobin's Q} &= \frac{\text{Market value of firm's assets}}{\text{Replacement cost of firm's assets}} \\
&= \frac{\text{Market value of firm's debt and equity}}{\text{Replacement cost of firm's assets}}
\end{aligned} \tag{3.25}$$

Notice that we used two equivalent numerators here: the market value of the firm's assets, and the market value of its debt and equity.

Conceptually, the Q ratio is superior to the market-to-book ratio, because it focuses on what the firm is worth today relative to what it would cost to replace it today. Firms with high Q ratios tend to be those with attractive investment opportunities or significant competitive advantages (or both). In contrast, the market-to-book ratio focuses on historical costs, which are less relevant.

As a practical matter, however, Q ratios are difficult to calculate with accuracy, because estimating the replacement cost of a firm's assets is not an easy task. Also, market values for a firm's debt are often unobservable. Book values can be used instead in such cases, but accuracy may suffer.

## Conclusion

This completes our definitions of some common ratios. We could tell you about more of them, but these are enough for now. We'll go on to discuss some ways of using these ratios instead of just how to calculate them. Table 3.9 summarizes the ratios we've discussed.

**TABLE 3.9**

### Short-term solvency, or liquidity, ratios

$$\text{Current ratio} = \frac{\text{Current assets}}{\text{Current liabilities}}$$

$$\text{Quick ratio} = \frac{\text{Current assets} - \text{Inventory}}{\text{Current liabilities}}$$

$$\text{Cash ratio} = \frac{\text{Cash}}{\text{Current liabilities}}$$

$$\frac{\text{Net working capital}}{\text{to total assets}} = \frac{\text{Net working capital}}{\text{Total assets}}$$

$$\frac{\text{Interval}}{\text{measure}} = \frac{\text{Current assets}}{\text{Average daily operating costs}}$$

### Asset management, or turnover, ratios

$$\text{Inventory turnover} = \frac{\text{Cost of goods sold}}{\text{Inventory}}$$

$$\frac{\text{Days' sales}}{\text{in inventory}} = \frac{365 \text{ days}}{\text{Inventory turnover}}$$

$$\frac{\text{Receivables}}{\text{turnover}} = \frac{\text{Sales}}{\text{Accounts receivable}}$$

$$\frac{\text{Days' sales in}}{\text{receivables}} = \frac{365 \text{ days}}{\text{Receivables turnover}}$$

$$\text{NWC turnover} = \frac{\text{Sales}}{\text{NWC}}$$

$$\frac{\text{PPE}}{\text{turnover}} = \frac{\text{Sales}}{\text{Property, plant and equipment}}$$

$$\text{Total asset turnover} = \frac{\text{Sales}}{\text{Total assets}}$$

### Long-term solvency, or financial leverage, ratios

$$\text{Total debt ratio} = \frac{\text{Total assets} - \text{Total equity}}{\text{Total assets}}$$

$$\text{Debt-equity ratio} = \frac{\text{Total debt}}{\text{Total equity}}$$

$$\text{Equity multiplier} = \frac{\text{Total assets}}{\text{Total equity}}$$

$$\frac{\text{Long-term}}{\text{debt ratio}} = \frac{\text{Long-term debt}}{\text{Long-term debt} + \text{Total equity}}$$

$$\frac{\text{Times interest}}{\text{earned ratio}} = \frac{\text{Operating profit}}{\text{Interest}}$$

$$\frac{\text{Cash}}{\text{coverage}} = \frac{\text{Operating profit} + \text{Non-cash adjustments}}{\text{Interest}}$$

### Profitability ratios

$$\text{Profit margin} = \frac{\text{Net income}}{\text{Sales}}$$

$$\text{Return on assets (ROA)} = \frac{\text{Net income}}{\text{Total assets}}$$

$$\text{Return on equity (ROE)} = \frac{\text{Net income}}{\text{Total equity}}$$

$$\text{ROE} = \frac{\text{Net income}}{\text{Sales}} \times \frac{\text{Sales}}{\text{Assets}} \times \frac{\text{Assets}}{\text{Equity}}$$

### Market value ratios

$$\text{Price-earnings ratio} = \frac{\text{Price per share}}{\text{Earnings per share}}$$

$$\text{PEG ratio} = \frac{\text{Price-earnings ratio}}{\text{Earnings growth rate (\%)}}$$

$$\text{Price-sales ratio} = \frac{\text{Price per share}}{\text{Sales per share}}$$

$$\frac{\text{Market-to-}}{\text{book ratio}} = \frac{\text{Market value per share}}{\text{Book value per share}}$$

$$\text{Tobin's } Q \text{ ratio} = \frac{\text{Market value of assets}}{\text{Replacement cost of assets}}$$

**Table 3.9** Common financial ratios

**CONCEPT QUESTIONS**

3.2a What are the five groups of ratios? Give two or three examples of each kind.

3.2b Given the total debt ratio, what other two ratios can be computed? Explain how.

3.2c Turnover ratios all have one of two figures as the numerator. What are these two figures? What do these ratios measure? How do you interpret the results?

3.2d Profitability ratios all have the same figure in the numerator. What is it? What do these ratios measure? How do you interpret the results?

## 3.3    The Du Pont Identity

As we mentioned in discussing ROA and ROE, the difference between these two profitability measures is a reflection of the use of debt financing, or financial leverage. We illustrate the relationship between these measures in this section by investigating a famous way of decomposing ROE into its component parts.

### A Closer Look at ROE

To begin, let's recall the definition of ROE:

$$\text{Return on equity} = \frac{\text{Net income}}{\text{Total equity}}$$

If we were so inclined, we could multiply this ratio by Assets/Assets without changing anything:

$$\text{Return on equity} = \frac{\text{Net income}}{\text{Total equity}} = \frac{\text{Net income}}{\text{Total equity}} \times \frac{\text{Assets}}{\text{Assets}}$$

$$= \frac{\text{Net income}}{\text{Assets}} \times \frac{\text{Assets}}{\text{Total equity}}$$

Notice that we have expressed the ROE as the product of two other ratios – ROA and the equity multiplier:

$$\text{ROE} = \text{ROA} \times \text{Equity multiplier}$$
$$= \text{ROA} \times (1 + \text{Debt–equity ratio})$$

The difference between ROE and ROA can be substantial, particularly for certain businesses that have borrowed a lot of money. We can further decompose ROE by multiplying the top and bottom by total sales:

$$\text{ROE} = \frac{\text{Sales}}{\text{Sales}} \times \frac{\text{Net income}}{\text{Assets}} \times \frac{\text{Assets}}{\text{Total equity}}$$

If we rearrange things a bit, ROE looks like this:

$$\text{ROE} = \underbrace{\frac{\text{Net income}}{\text{Sales}} \times \frac{\text{Sales}}{\text{Assets}}}_{\text{Return on assets}} \times \frac{\text{Assets}}{\text{Total equity}} \qquad \textbf{(3.26)}$$

$$= \text{Profit margin} \times \text{Total asset turnover} \times \text{Equity multiplier}$$

What we have now done is to partition ROA into its two component parts: profit margin and total asset turnover. The last expression of the preceding equation is called the **Du Pont identity**, after the Du Pont Corporation, which popularized its use.

The Du Pont identity tells us that ROE is affected by three things:

1   Operating efficiency (as measured by profit margin)

2   Asset use efficiency (as measured by total asset turnover)

3   Financial leverage (as measured by the equity multiplier)

Weakness in either operating or asset use efficiency (or both) will show up in a diminished return on assets, which will translate into a lower ROE.

Considering the Du Pont identity, it appears that the ROE could be leveraged up by increasing the amount of debt in the firm. However, notice that increasing debt also increases interest expense, which reduces profit margins, which acts to reduce

**Du Pont identity**
Popular expression breaking ROE into three parts: operating efficiency, asset use efficiency, and financial leverage.

ROE. So ROE could go up or down. More important, the use of debt financing has a number of other effects, and as we discuss at some length in Part Six, the amount of leverage a firm uses is governed by its capital structure policy.

The decomposition of ROE we've discussed in this section is a convenient way of systematically approaching financial statement analysis. If ROE is unsatisfactory by some measure, then the Du Pont identity tells you where to start looking for the reasons.

| CONCEPT QUESTIONS | | |
|---|---|---|
| | 3.3a | Return on assets, or ROA, can be expressed as the product of two ratios. Which two? |
| | 3.3b | Return on equity, or ROE, can be expressed as the product of three ratios. Which three? |

## 3.4 Using Financial Statement Information

We now discuss in more detail some practical aspects of financial statement analysis. In particular, we shall look at reasons for analysing financial statements, how to get benchmark information, and some problems that come up in the process.

### Why Evaluate Financial Statements?

As we have discussed, the primary reason for looking at accounting information is that we don't have, and can't reasonably expect to get, market value information. We stress that whenever we have market information, we shall use it instead of accounting data. Also, if there is a conflict between accounting and market data, market data should be given precedence.

Financial statement analysis is essentially an application of 'management by exception'. In many cases such analysis will boil down to comparing ratios for one business with average or representative ratios. Those ratios that seem to differ the most from the averages are tagged for further study.

**Internal Uses**    Financial statement information has a variety of uses within a firm. Among the most important of these is performance evaluation. For example, managers are frequently evaluated and compensated on the basis of accounting measures of performance such as profit margin and return on equity. Also, firms with multiple divisions frequently use financial statement information to compare the performance of those divisions.

Another important internal use we shall explore is planning for the future. As we shall see, historical financial statement information is useful for generating projections about the future, and for checking the realism of assumptions made in those projections.

**External Uses**    Financial statements are useful to parties outside the firm, including short-term and long-term creditors and potential investors. For example, we would find such information quite useful in deciding whether to grant credit to a new customer.

We would also use this information to evaluate suppliers, and suppliers would review our statements before deciding to extend credit to us. Large customers use this information to decide whether we are likely to be around in the future. Credit-rating agencies rely on financial statements in assessing a firm's overall creditworthiness. The common theme here is that financial statements are a prime source of information about a firm's financial health.

We would also find such information useful in evaluating our main competitors. We might be thinking of launching a new product. A prime concern would be whether the competition would jump in shortly thereafter. In this case we would be interested in learning about our competitors' financial strength to see whether they could afford the necessary development.

Finally, we might be thinking of acquiring another firm. Financial statement information would be essential in identifying potential targets and deciding what to offer.

## Choosing a Benchmark

Given that we want to evaluate a division or a firm based on its financial statements, a basic problem immediately comes up. How do we choose a benchmark, or a standard of comparison? In this section we describe some ways of getting started.

**Time Trend Analysis**   One standard we could use is history. Suppose we find that the current ratio for a particular firm is 2.4, based on the most recent financial statement information. Looking back over the last 10 years, we might find that this ratio has declined fairly steadily over that period.

Based on this, we might wonder whether the liquidity position of the firm has deteriorated. It could be, of course, that the firm has made changes that allow it to use its current assets more efficiently, that the nature of the firm's business has changed, or that business practices have changed. If we investigate, we might find any of these possible explanations behind the decline. This is an example of what we mean by management by exception – a deteriorating time trend may not be bad, but it does merit investigation.

**Peer Group Analysis**   The second means of establishing a benchmark is to identify firms similar in the sense that they compete in the same markets, have similar assets, and operate in similar ways. In other words, we need to identify a *peer group*. There are obvious problems with doing this, because no two companies are identical. Ultimately, the choice of which companies to use as a basis for comparison is subjective.

Also, we may be more concerned with a group of the top firms in an industry, not with the average firm. Such a group is called an *aspirant group*, because we aspire to be like its members. In this case, a financial statement analysis reveals how far we have to go.

There are many sources of ratio information in addition to the one we examine here. Our nearby *Work the Web* box shows how to get this information for just about any company, along with some useful benchmarking information. Be sure to look it over, and then benchmark your favourite company.

# Work the Web

As we have discussed in this chapter, ratios are an important tool for examining a company's performance. Gathering the necessary financial statements to calculate ratios can be tedious and time-consuming. Fortunately, many sites on the Web provide this information for free. One of the best is the Reuters website. We went there, entered a search for 'Volkswagen AG', and scrolled to the bottom of the page to see the key ratios statistics table. Here is a look at the results:

## Key Ratios and Statistics

| Share Related Items | | Dividend Information | |
|---|---|---|---|
| Market Cap (Mil.) | €32,419.28 | Yield % | -- |
| Shares Outstanding (Mil.) | 400.24 | Annual Dividend (€ EUR) | 1.93 |
| Float (Mil.) | 180.47 | Payout Ratio(TTM) % | 46.09 |

| Financial Strength | | Valuation Ratios | |
|---|---|---|---|
| Quick Ratio | 0.90 | Price/Earnings(TTM) | 19.21 |
| Current Ratio | 1.22 | Price/Sales(TTM) | 0.31 |
| LT Debt/Equity | 109.10 | Price/Book(TTM) | 0.92 |
| Total Debt/Equity | 216.52 | Price/Cash Flow(TTM) | 3.03 |

| Per Share Data | | Management Effectiveness | |
|---|---|---|---|
| Earnings(TTM) | €4.22 | Return on Equity(TTM) | 4.75 |
| Sales(TTM) | €263.52 | Return on Assets(TTM) | 0.93 |
| Book Value(MRQ) | €88.25 | Return on Investment(TTM) | 1.56 |
| Cash Flow(TTM) | €26.75 | | |
| Cash(MRQ) | €66.59 | Margins | |
| | | Gross Margin(TTM) % | 13.77 |
| | | Operating Margin(TTM) % | 2.78 |
| | | Profit Margin(TTM) % | 1.52 |

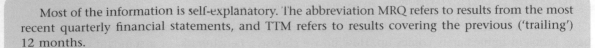

Most of the information is self-explanatory. The abbreviation MRQ refers to results from the most recent quarterly financial statements, and TTM refers to results covering the previous ('trailing') 12 months.

**QUESTIONS**

1 Go to the Reuters website and find the major ratio categories listed there. How do the categories differ from the categories listed in this textbook?

2 On the Reuters website, click on the 'Sectors & Industries' link, and choose 'Auto and Truck Manufacturers'. Compare the main ratios with those calculated for Volkswagen. How does Volkswagen compare to the industry average?

## Problems with Financial Statement Analysis

We close this section by discussing some additional problems that can arise from using financial statements. In one way or another, the basic problem with financial statement analysis is that there is no underlying theory to help us identify which quantities to look at or guide us in establishing benchmarks.

As we discuss in other chapters, there are many cases in which financial theory and economic logic provide guidance in making judgements about value and risk. Little such help exists with financial statements. This is why we can't say which ratios matter the most, or what a high or low value might be.

More generally, the kind of peer group analysis we have been describing works best when the firms are strictly in the same line of business, the industry is competitive, and there is only one way of operating. Another problem that is becoming increasingly common is that major competitors and natural peer group members in an industry may be scattered around the globe. The automobile industry is an obvious example. The problem here is that financial statements from outside Europe do not necessarily conform at all to International Accounting Standards. The existence of different standards and procedures makes it difficult to compare financial statements across national borders.

Several other general problems frequently crop up. First, different firms use different accounting procedures – for property, plant and equipment, for example. This makes it difficult to compare statements. Second, different firms end their fiscal years at different times. For firms in seasonal businesses (such as Tesco, with a large Christmas season), this can lead to difficulties in comparing statements of financial position, because of fluctuations in accounts during the year. Finally, for any particular firm, unusual or transient events – such as a one-time profit from an asset sale – may affect financial performance. In comparing firms, such events can give misleading signals.

| CONCEPT QUESTIONS | 3.4a | What are some uses for financial statement analysis? |
| | 3.4b | Why do we say that financial statement analysis is management by exception? |
| | 3.4c | What are some problems that can come up with financial statement analysis? |

## 3.5 Financial Planning

A lack of effective long-range planning is a commonly cited reason for financial distress and failure. As we discuss in this section, long-range planning is a means of systematically thinking about the future and anticipating possible problems before they arrive. There are no magic mirrors, of course, so the best we can hope for is a logical and organized procedure for exploring the unknown. Financial planning establishes guidelines for change and growth in a firm. It normally focuses on the big picture. This means it is concerned with the major elements of a firm's financial and investment policies, without examining the individual components of those policies in detail.

Financial planning formulates the way in which financial goals are to be achieved. A financial plan is thus a statement of what is to be done in the future. Many decisions have long lead times, which means they take a long time to implement. In an uncertain world, this requires that decisions be made far in advance of their implementation. If a firm wants to build a factory in 2014, for example, it might have to begin lining up contractors and financing in 2012 or even earlier.

## Growth as a Financial Management Goal

Because the subject of growth will be discussed in various places in this chapter, we need to start out with an important warning: growth, by itself, is not an appropriate goal for the financial manager. As we discussed in Chapter 1, the appropriate goal is increasing the market value of the owners' equity. Of course, if a firm is successful in doing this, then growth will usually result. Growth may thus be a desirable consequence of good decision-making, but it is not an end unto itself. We discuss growth simply because growth rates are so commonly used in the planning process. As we shall see, growth is a convenient means of summarizing various aspects of a firm's financial and investment policies. Also, if we think of growth as growth in the market value of the equity in the firm, then goals of growth and increasing the market value of the equity in the firm are not all that different.

## What Can Planning Accomplish?

Because a company is likely to spend a lot of time examining the different scenarios that will become the basis for its financial plan, it seems reasonable to ask what the planning process will accomplish.

**Examining Interactions** As we discuss in greater detail in the following pages, the financial plan must make explicit the linkages between investment proposals for the different operating activities of the firm and its available financing choices. In other words, if the firm is planning on expanding and undertaking new investments and projects, where will the financing be obtained to pay for this activity?

**Exploring Options** The financial plan allows the firm to develop, analyse, and compare many different scenarios in a consistent way. Various investment and financing options can be explored, and their impact on the firm's shareholders can be evaluated. Questions concerning the firm's future lines of business and optimal financing arrangements are addressed. Options such as marketing new products or closing plants might be evaluated.

**Avoiding Surprises** Financial planning should identify what may happen to the firm if different events take place. In particular, it should address what actions the firm will take if things go seriously wrong or, more generally, if assumptions made today about the future are seriously in error. As physicist Niels Bohr once observed, 'Prediction is very difficult, particularly when it concerns the future.' Thus one purpose of financial planning is to avoid surprises and develop contingency plans.

**Ensuring Feasibility and Internal Consistency** Beyond a general goal of creating value, a firm will normally have many specific goals. Such goals might be couched in terms of market share, return on equity, financial leverage, and so on. At times, the linkages between different goals and different aspects of a firm's business are difficult to see. Not only does a financial plan make these linkages explicit, it also imposes a unified structure for reconciling goals and objectives. In other words, financial planning is a way of verifying that the goals and plans made for specific areas of a firm's operations are feasible and internally consistent. Conflicting goals will often exist. To generate a coherent plan, goals and objectives will therefore have to be modified, and priorities will have to be established.

For example, one goal a firm might have would be 12 per cent growth in unit sales per year. Another goal might be to reduce the firm's total debt ratio from 40 to 20 per cent. Are these two goals compatible? Can they be accomplished simultaneously? Maybe yes, maybe no. As we shall discuss, financial planning is a way of finding out just what is possible – and, by implication, what is not possible.

**Conclusion**  Probably the most important result of the planning process is that it forces managers to think about goals and establish priorities. In fact, conventional business wisdom holds that financial plans don't work, but financial planning does. The future is inherently unknown. What we can do is establish the direction in which we want to travel, and make some educated guesses about what we shall find along the way. If we do a good job, we won't be caught off guard when the future rolls around.

---

**CONCEPT QUESTIONS**

3.5a  What are the two dimensions of the financial planning process?
3.5b  Why should firms draw up financial plans?

## 3.6 Financial Planning Models: A First Look

Just as companies differ in size and products, the financial planning process will differ from firm to firm. In this section we discuss some common elements in financial plans, and develop a basic model to illustrate these elements. What follows is just a quick overview; later sections will take up the various topics in more detail.

We can begin our discussion of long-term planning models with a relatively simple example. Chute SA's financial statements from the most recent year are as follows:

| Chute SA Financial statements | | | | | |
|---|---|---|---|---|---|
| **Income statement** | | | **Statement of financial position** | | |
| | € | | | € | | € |
| Sales | 1,000 | | Assets | 500 | | Debt | 250 |
| Costs | 800 | | | — | | Equity | 250 |
| Net profit | 200 | | Total | 500 | | Total | 500 |

Unless otherwise stated, the financial planners at Chute assume that all variables are tied directly to sales, and current relationships are optimal. This means that all items will grow at exactly the same rate as sales. This is obviously oversimplified; we use this assumption only to make a point.

Suppose sales increase by 20 per cent, rising from €1,000 to €1,200. Planners would then also forecast a 20 per cent increase in costs, from £800 to £800 × 1.2 = £960. The pro forma income statement would thus be:

| Pro forma income statement | |
|---|---|
| | **€** |
| Sales | 1,200 |
| Costs | 960 |
| Net profit | 240 |

The assumption that all variables will grow by 20 per cent lets us easily construct the pro forma statement of financial position as well:

| Pro forma balance sheet | | | |
|---|---|---|---|
| | **€** | | **€** |
| Assets | 600 (+100) | Debt | 300 (+50) |
| | | Equity | 300 (+50) |
| Total | 600 (+100) | Total | 600 (+100) |

Notice that we have simply increased every item by 20 per cent. The numbers in parentheses are the euro changes for the different items.

Now we have to reconcile these two pro formas. How, for example, can net profit be equal to €240 and equity increase by only €50? The answer is that Chute must have paid out the difference of €240 – 50 = €190, possibly as a cash dividend. In this case, dividends are the plug variable.

Suppose Chute does not pay out the €190. In this case, the addition to retained earnings is the full €240. Chute's equity will thus grow to €250 (the starting amount) plus €240 (net income), or €490, and debt must be retired to keep total assets equal to €600.

With €600 in total assets and €490 in equity, debt will have to be €600 – 490 = €110. Because we started with €250 in debt, Chute will have to retire €250 – 110 = €140 in debt. The resulting pro forma statement of financial position would look like this:

| Pro forma statement of financial position | | | |
|---|---|---|---|
| Assets | €600 (+100) | Debt | €110 (−140) |
| | | Equity | 490 (+240) |
| Total | €600 (+100) | Total | €600 (+100) |

In this case, debt is the plug variable used to balance projected total assets and liabilities.

This example shows the interaction between sales growth and financial policy. As sales increase, so do total assets. This occurs because the firm must invest in net working capital and non-current assets (such as property, plant and equipment) to support higher sales levels. Because assets are growing, total liabilities and equity (the right side of the balance sheet) will grow as well.

The thing to notice from our simple example is that the way the liabilities and owners' equity change depends on the firm's financing policy and its dividend policy. The growth in assets requires that the firm decides on how to finance that growth. This is strictly a managerial decision. Note that, in our example, the firm needed no outside funds.

In the Chute SA example we described a simple planning model in which every item increased at the same rate as sales. This may be a reasonable assumption for some elements. For others, such as long-term borrowing, it probably is not: the amount of long-term borrowing is something set by management, and it does not necessarily relate directly to the level of sales.

We now describe an extended version of our simple model. The basic idea is to separate the income statement and balance sheet accounts into two groups – those that vary directly with sales, and those that do not. Given a sales forecast, we shall then be able to calculate how much financing the firm will need to support the predicted sales level.

The financial planning model we describe next is based on the **percentage of sales approach**. Our goal here is to develop a quick and practical way of generating pro forma statements. We defer discussion of some 'bells and whistles' to a later section.

## The Income Statement

We start out with the most recent income statement for Bogle plc, as shown in Table 3.10. Notice that we have still simplified things by including costs, depreciation, and interest in a single cost figure.

Bogle has projected a 25 per cent increase in sales for the coming year, so we are anticipating sales of £1,000 × 1.25 = £1,250. To generate a pro forma income statement, we assume that total costs will continue to run at £800/1,000 = 80 per cent of sales. With this assumption, Bogle's pro forma income statement is shown in Table 3.11. The effect here of assuming that costs are a constant percentage of sales is to assume that the profit margin is constant. To check this, notice that the profit margin was £144/1,000 = 14.4 per cent. In our pro forma the profit margin is £180/1,250 = 14.4 per cent: so it is unchanged.

**TABLE 3.10**

| Bogle plc Income statement | | |
|---|---|---|
| | £ | £ |
| Sales | | 1,000 |
| Costs | | 800 |
| Profit before taxes | | 200 |
| Taxes (28%) | | 56 |
| Profit attributable to shareholders | | 144 |
| Dividends | 48 | |
| Addition to retained earnings | 96 | |

**Table 3.10** Bogle plc: income statement

**TABLE 3.11**

| Bogle plc Income statement | | |
|---|---|---|
| | £ | £ |
| Sales | | 1,250 |
| Costs | | 1,000 |
| Profit before taxes | | 250 |
| Taxes (28%) | | 70 |
| Profit attributable to shareholders | | 180 |
| Dividends | 60 | |
| Addition to retained earnings | 120 | |

**Table 3.11** Bogle plc: income statement

Next, we need to project the dividend payment. This amount is up to Bogle's management. We shall assume Bogle has a policy of paying out a constant fraction of net income in the form of a cash dividend. For the most recent year, the **dividend payout ratio** was this:

$$\text{Dividend payout ratio} = \text{Cash dividends/Net income} \quad (3.27)$$
$$= \pounds48/144 = 1/3$$

> **dividend payout ratio**
> The amount of cash paid out to shareholders divided by net income.

We can also calculate the ratio of the addition to retained earnings to net income:

$$\text{Addition to retained earnings/Net income} = \pounds96/144 = 2/3$$

This ratio is called the **retention ratio** or **ploughback ratio**, and it is equal to 1 minus the dividend payout ratio, because everything not paid out is retained. Assuming that the payout ratio is constant, here are the projected dividends and addition to retained earnings:

> **retention ratio**
> The addition to retained earnings divided by net income. Also called the **ploughback ratio**.

$$\text{Projected dividends paid to shareholders} = \pounds188 \times 1/3 = \pounds60$$
$$\text{Projected addition to retained earnings} = \pounds188 \times 2/3 = \underline{\pounds120}$$
$$\underline{\pounds180}$$

## The Statement of Financial Position

To generate a pro forma statement of financial position, we start with the most recent statement, as shown in Table 3.12.

On our statement of financial position, we assume that some items vary directly with sales and others do not. For items that vary with sales, we express each as a percentage of

**TABLE 3.12**

| | | | | | |
|---|---|---|---|---|---|
| Bogle plc<br>Statement of financial position | | | | | |
| **Assets** | | | **Liabilities and owners' equity** | | |
| | **£** | **Percentage of sales** | | **£** | **Percentage of sales** |
| **Current assets** | | | **Current liabilities** | | |
| Cash | 160 | 16 | Trade payables | 300 | 30 |
| Trade receivables | 440 | 44 | Notes payable | 100 | n/a |
| Inventory | 600 | 60 | | | |
| Total | 1,200 | 120 | Total | 400 | n/a |
| **Non-current assets** | | | **Long-term debt** | 800 | n/a |
| Property, plant and equipment | 1,800 | 180 | **Owners' equity** | | |
| | | | Ordinary shares and paid-in surplus | 800 | n/a |
| | | | Retained earnings | 1,000 | n/a |
| | | | Total | 1,800 | n/a |
| **Total assets** | 3,000 | 300 | **Total liabilities and owners' equity** | 3,000 | n/a |

**Table 3.12** Bogle plc: statement of financial position

sales for the year just completed. When an item does not vary directly with sales, we write 'n/a' for 'not applicable'.

For example, on the asset side, inventory is equal to 60 per cent of sales (= £600/1,000) for the year just ended. We assume this percentage applies to the coming year, so for each £1 increase in sales, inventory will rise by £0.60. More generally, the ratio of total assets to sales for the year just ended is £3,000/1,000 = 3, or 300 per cent.

> **capital intensity ratio**
> A firm's total assets divided by its sales, or the amount of assets needed to generate £1 in sales.

This ratio of total assets to sales is sometimes called the **capital intensity ratio**. It tells us the amount of assets needed to generate £1 in sales; so the higher the ratio, the more capital-intensive the firm. Notice also that this ratio is just the reciprocal of the total asset turnover ratio we defined in the last chapter.

For Bogle, assuming that this ratio is constant, it takes £3 in total assets to generate £1 in sales (apparently Bogle is in a relatively capital-intensive business). Therefore, if sales are to increase by £100, Bogle will have to increase total assets by three times this amount, or £300.

On the liability side of the statement of financial position, we show trade payables varying with sales. The reason is that we expect to place more orders with our suppliers as sales volume increases, so payables will change 'spontaneously' with sales. Notes payable, on the other hand, represent short-term debt such as bank borrowing. This item will not vary unless we take specific actions to change the amount, so we mark it as 'n/a'.

Similarly, we use 'n/a' for long-term debt because it won't automatically change with sales. The same is true for ordinary shares and paid-in surplus. The last item on the right side, retained earnings, will vary with sales, but it won't be a simple percentage of sales. Instead, we shall explicitly calculate the change in retained earnings based on our projected net income and dividends.

We can now construct a partial pro forma statement of financial position for Bogle. We do this by using the percentages we have just calculated wherever possible to calculate the projected amounts. For example, property, plant and equipment are 180 per cent of sales: so, with a new sales level of £1,250, the property, plant and equipment amount will be 1.80 × £1,250 = £2,250, representing an increase of £2,250 − 1,800 = £450. It is important to note that for items that don't vary directly with sales, we initially assume no change and simply write in the original amounts. The result is shown in Table 3.13. Notice that the change in retained earnings is equal to the £110 addition to retained earnings we calculated earlier.

Inspecting our pro forma statement of financial position, we notice that assets are projected to increase by £750. However, without additional financing, liabilities and equity will increase by only £195, leaving a shortfall of £750 − 185 = £555. We label this amount *external financing needed (EFN)*.

## A Particular Scenario

Our financial planning model now reminds us of one of those good news–bad news jokes. The good news is we're projecting a 25 per cent increase in sales. The bad news is that this isn't going to happen unless Bogle can somehow raise £555 in new financing.

This is a good example of how the planning process can point out problems and potential conflicts. If, for example, Bogle has a goal of not borrowing any additional funds and not selling any new equity, then a 25 per cent increase in sales is probably not feasible.

If we take the need for £555 in new financing as given, we know that Bogle has three possible sources: short-term borrowing, long-term borrowing, and new equity. The choice of some combination among these three is up to management; we shall illustrate only one of the many possibilities.

Suppose Bogle decides to borrow the needed funds. In this case, the firm might choose to borrow some over the short term and some over the long term. For example, current assets increased by £300 whereas current liabilities rose by only £75. Bogle could borrow £300 − 75 = £225 in short-term notes payable and leave total net working capital unchanged. With £555 needed, the remaining £555 − 225 = £330 would have to come from long-term debt. Table 3.14 shows the completed pro forma statement of financial position for Bogle.

TABLE
3.13

| Bogle plc Partial pro forma statement of financial position | | | | | |
|---|---|---|---|---|---|
| **Assets** | | | **Liabilities and owners' equity** | | |
| | Projected (£) | Change from previous year (£) | | Projected (£) | Change from previous year (£) |
| **Current assets** | | | **Current liabilities** | | |
| Cash | 200 | 40 | Trade payables | 375 | 75 |
| Trade receivables | 550 | 110 | Notes payable | 100 | 0 |
| Inventory | 750 | 150 | | | |
| Total | 1,500 | 300 | Total | 475 | 75 |
| **Non-current assets** | | | **Long-term debt** | 800 | 0 |
| Property, plant and equipment | 2,250 | 450 | **Owners' equity** | | |
| | | | Ordinary shares and paid-in surplus | 800 | 0 |
| | | | Retained earnings | 1,120 | 120 |
| | | | Total | 1,920 | 120 |
| **Total assets** | 3,750 | 750 | **Total liabilities and owners' equity** | 3,195 | 195 |
| | | | External financing needed | 555 | 555 |

**Table 3.13** Bogle plc: partial pro forma statement of financial position

TABLE
3.14

| Bogle plc Pro forma statement of financial position | | | | | |
|---|---|---|---|---|---|
| **Assets** | | | **Liabilities and owners' equity** | | |
| | Projected (£) | Change from previous year (£) | | Projected (£) | Change from previous year (£) |
| **Current assets** | | | **Current liabilities** | | |
| Cash | 200 | 40 | Trade payables | 375 | 75 |
| Trade receivables | 550 | 110 | Notes payable | 325 | 225 |
| Inventory | 750 | 150 | | | |
| Total | 1,500 | 300 | Total | 700 | 300 |
| **Non-current assets** | | | **Long-term debt** | 1,130 | 330 |
| Property, plant and equipment | 2,250 | 450 | **Owners' equity** | | |
| | | | Ordinary shares and paid-in surplus | 800 | 0 |
| | | | Retained earnings | 1,120 | 120 |
| | | | Total | 1,920 | 120 |
| **Total assets** | 3,750 | 750 | **Total liability and owners' equity** | 3,750 | 750 |

**Table 3.14** Bogle plc: pro forma statement of financial position

We have used a combination of short-term and long-term debt as the plug here, but we emphasize that this is just one possible strategy; it is not necessarily the best one by any means. There are many other scenarios we could (and should) investigate. The various ratios we discussed earlier in the chapter come in handy here. For example, with the scenario we have just examined, we would surely want to examine the current ratio and the total debt ratio to see whether we were comfortable with the new projected debt levels.

Now that we have finished our statement of financial position, we have all of the projected sources and uses of cash. We could finish off our pro formas by drawing up the projected statement of cash flows along the lines discussed earlier. We shall leave this as an exercise, and instead investigate an important alternative scenario.

## An Alternative Scenario

The assumption that assets are a fixed percentage of sales is convenient, but it may not be suitable in many cases. In particular, note that we effectively assumed that Bogle was using its non-current assets (property, plant and equipment) at 100 per cent of capacity, because any increase in sales led to an increase in fixed assets. For most businesses there would be some slack or excess capacity, and production could be increased by perhaps running an extra shift. For example, according to the European Commission, the overall capacity utilization for European manufacturing companies in the fourth quarter of 2009 was 71.4 per cent, down from 81.0 per cent a year earlier.

If we assume that Bogle is operating at only 71.4 per cent of capacity, then the need for external funds will be quite different. When we say '71.4 per cent of capacity', we mean that the current sales level is 71.4 per cent of the full-capacity sales level:

$$\text{Current sales} = £1,000 = 0.714 \times \text{Full-capacity sales}$$
$$\text{Full-capacity sales} = £1,000/0.714 = £1,401$$

This tells us that sales could increase by more than 40 per cent – from £1,000 to £1,401 – before any new fixed assets would be needed.

In our previous scenario we assumed it would be necessary to add £450 in property, plant and equipment. In the current scenario no spending on net fixed assets is needed, because sales are projected to rise only to £1,250, which is substantially less than the £1,401 full-capacity level.

As a result, our original estimate of £555 in external funds needed is too high. We estimated that £450 in new property, plant and equipment would be needed. Instead, no spending on new net fixed assets is necessary. Thus, if we are currently operating at 71.4 per cent capacity, we need only £555 – 450 = £105 in external funds. The excess capacity thus makes a considerable difference in our projections.

These alternative scenarios show that it is inappropriate to blindly manipulate financial statement information in the planning process. The results depend critically on the assumptions made about the relationships between sales and asset needs. We return to this point a little later.

One thing should be clear by now. Projected growth rates play an important role in the planning process. They are also important to outside analysts and potential investors. Our nearby *Work the Web* box shows you how to obtain growth rate estimates for real companies.

| CONCEPT QUESTIONS | 3.6a | What is the basic idea behind the percentage of sales approach? |
| | 3.6b | Unless it is modified, what does the percentage of sales approach assume about fixed asset capacity usage? |

# 3.7  External Financing and Growth

External financing needed (EFN) and growth are obviously related. All other things staying the same, the higher the rate of growth in sales or assets, the greater will be the need for external financing. In the previous section we took a growth rate as given, and then we determined the amount of external financing needed to support that growth. In this section we turn things around a bit. We shall take the firm's financial policy as given, and then examine the relationship between that financial policy and the firm's ability to finance new investments and thereby grow.

Once again, we emphasize that we are focusing on growth not because growth is an appropriate goal; instead, for our purposes, growth is simply a convenient means of examining the interactions between investment and financing decisions.

## EFN and Growth

The first thing we need to do is establish the relationship between EFN and growth. To do this, we introduce the simplified income statement and balance sheet (statement of financial position) for Hoffman AG in Table 3.15. Notice that we have simplified the statement of financial position by combining short-term and long-term debt into a single total debt figure. Effectively, we are assuming that none of the current liabilities varies spontaneously with sales. This assumption isn't as restrictive as it sounds. If any current liabilities (such as trade payables) vary with sales, we can assume that any such accounts have been netted out in current assets. Also, we continue to combine depreciation, interest, and costs on the income statement.

**TABLE 3.15**

| Hoffman AG Income statement | | |
|---|---|---|
| | € | € |
| Sales | | 500 |
| Costs | | 400 |
| Profit before taxes | | 100 |
| Taxes (34%) | | 34 |
| Profit attributable to shareholders | | 66 |
| Dividends | 22 | |
| Addition to retained earnings | 44 | |

| Statement of financial position | | | | | |
|---|---|---|---|---|---|
| **Assets** | | | **Liabilities and owners' equity** | | |
| | € | Percentage of sales | | € | Percentage of sales |
| Current assets | 200 | 40 | Total liabilities | 250 | n/a |
| Non-current assets | 300 | 60 | Owners' equity | 250 | n/a |
| Total assets | 500 | 100 | Total liabilities and owners' equity | 500 | n/a |

**Table 3.15** Hoffman AG: income statement and statement of financial position

TABLE
3.16

| Hoffman AG Income statement | | |
|---|---|---|
| | € | € |
| Sales (projected) | | 600.0 |
| Costs (80% of sales) | | 480.0 |
| Profit before taxes | | 120.0 |
| Taxes (34%) | | 40.8 |
| Profit attributable to shareholders | | 79.2 |
| Dividends | 26.4 | |
| Addition to retained earnings | 52.8 | |

| Statement of financial position | | | | | |
|---|---|---|---|---|---|
| **Assets** | | | **Liabilities and owners' equity** | | |
| | € | Percentage of sales | | € | Percentage of sales |
| Current assets | 240.0 | 40 | Total Liabilities | 50.0 | n/a |
| Non-current assets | 360.0 | 60 | Owners' equity | 302.8 | n/a |
| Total assets | 600.0 | 100 | Total liabilities and owners' equity | 552.8 | n/a |
| | | | External financing needed | 47.2 | n/a |

**Table 3.16** Hoffman AG: income statement and statement of financial position

Suppose Hoffman is forecasting next year's sales level at €600, a €100 increase. Notice that the percentage increase in sales is €100/500 = 20%. Using the percentage of sales approach and the figures in Table 3.15, we can prepare a pro forma income statement and balance sheet as in Table 3.16. As Table 3.16 illustrates, at a 20 per cent growth rate Hoffman needs €100 in new assets (assuming full capacity). The projected addition to retained earnings is €52.8, so the external financing needed is €100 − 52.8 = €47.2.

Notice that the debt–equity ratio for Hoffman was originally (from Table 3.15) equal to €250/250 = 1.0. We shall assume Hoffman does not wish to sell new equity. In this case, the €47.2 in EFN will have to be borrowed. What will the new debt–equity ratio be? From Table 3.16, we know that total owners' equity is projected at €302.8. The new total debt will be the original €250 plus €47.2 in new borrowing, or €297.2 total. The debt–equity ratio thus falls slightly from 1.0 to €297.2/302.8 = 0.98.

# Work the Web

Calculating company growth rates can involve detailed research, and a major part of an equity analyst's job is to estimate them. Places to find earnings and sales growth rates on the Web are Yahoo! Finance and Reuters. We visited Reuters, pulled up a quote for British Airways plc, and followed the 'Estimates' link. Here is an abbreviated look at the results:

**CONSENSUS ESTIMATES ANALYSIS**

Sales and Profit Figures in British Pound (GBP)
Earnings and Dividend Figures in British Pound (GBP)

| | # of Estimates | Mean | High | Low | 1 Year Ago |
|---|---|---|---|---|---|
| **SALES (in millions)** | | | | | |
| Quarter Ending Dec-09 | 1 | 1,964.00 | 1,964.00 | 1,964.00 | -- |
| Quarter Ending Mar-10 | 1 | 1,848.00 | 1,848.00 | 1,848.00 | -- |
| Year Ending Mar-09 | 20 | 9,086.05 | 9,317.90 | 8,942.10 | -- |
| Year Ending Mar-10 | 20 | 8,020.65 | 8,403.00 | 7,816.00 | 8,942.11 |
| Year Ending Mar-11 | 20 | 8,446.74 | 8,700.00 | 8,185.60 | 9,210.23 |
| **Earnings (per share)** | | | | | |
| Year Ending Mar-09 | 19 | -21.69 | -11.87 | -29.11 | -- |
| Year Ending Mar-10 | 19 | -38.29 | -23.80 | -58.20 | -2.67 |
| Year Ending Mar-11 | 15 | -6.51 | 3.78 | -18.40 | 14.51 |
| LT Growth Rate (%) | 1 | 10.00 | 10.00 | 10.00 | -20.47 |

As shown, we only have one estimate of long-term growth, 10 per cent. Interestingly, the mean year-on-year predictions, based on 20 analyst estimates, do not give the same picture. The consensus suggests that sales will fall from £9.086 billion in 2009 to £8.021 billion in 2010, and then increase to £8.447 billion in 2011. There is also a wide range in estimates, which makes things even more difficult to assess.

## QUESTIONS

1  One of the things shown here is the projected sales growth for British Airways during 2009 at the time this was captured from Reuters. How does the current sales projection or the actual sales number differ from this projection? Can you think of any reasons for the difference?

2  On the same Web page, you can find the earnings history for British Airways. How close have analysts been to estimating British Airways' earnings? In other words, what has the 'surprise' been in British Airways' earnings?

**TABLE 3.17**

| Projected sales growth (%) | Increase in assets required (€) | Addition to retained earnings (€) | External financing needed, EFN (€) | Projected debt–equity ratio |
|---|---|---|---|---|
| 0 | 0 | 44.0 | −44.0 | 0.70 |
| 5 | 25 | 46.2 | −21.2 | 0.77 |
| 10 | 50 | 48.4 | 1.6 | 0.84 |
| 15 | 75 | 50.6 | 24.4 | 0.91 |
| 20 | 100 | 52.8 | 47.2 | 0.98 |
| 25 | 125 | 55.0 | 70.0 | 1.05 |

**Table 3.17** Growth and projected EFN for Hoffman AG

Table 3.17 shows EFN for several different growth rates. The projected addition to retained earnings and the projected debt–equity ratio for each scenario are also given (you should probably calculate a few of these for practice). In determining the debt–equity ratios, we assumed that any needed funds were borrowed, and we also assumed that any surplus

FIGURE

**3.2**

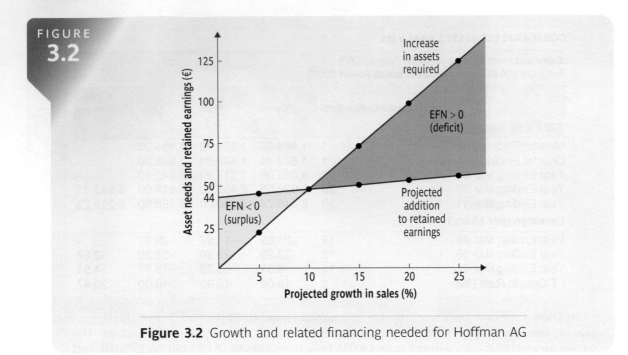

**Figure 3.2** Growth and related financing needed for Hoffman AG

funds were used to pay off debt. Thus, for the zero growth case, debt falls by €44, from €250 to €206. In Table 3.17 notice that the increase in assets required is simply equal to the original assets of €500 multiplied by the growth rate. Similarly, the addition to retained earnings is equal to the original €44 plus €44 times the growth rate.

Table 3.17 shows that for relatively low growth rates Hoffman will run a surplus, and its debt–equity ratio will decline. Once the growth rate increases to about 10 per cent, however, the surplus becomes a deficit. Furthermore, as the growth rate exceeds approximately 20 per cent, the debt–equity ratio passes its original value of 1.0.

Figure 3.2 illustrates the connection between growth in sales and external financing needed in more detail by plotting asset needs and additions to retained earnings from Table 3.17 against the growth rates. As shown, the need for new assets grows at a much faster rate than the addition to retained earnings, so the internal financing provided by the addition to retained earnings rapidly disappears.

## Financial Policy and Growth

Based on our preceding discussion, we see that there is a direct link between growth and external financing. In this section we discuss two growth rates that are particularly useful in long-range planning.

**internal growth rate**
The maximum growth rate a firm can achieve without external financing of any kind.

**The Internal Growth Rate** The first growth rate of interest is the maximum growth rate that can be achieved with no external financing of any kind. We shall call this the **internal growth rate**, because this is the rate the firm can maintain with internal financing only. In Fig. 3.2 this internal growth rate is represented by the point where the two lines cross. At this point the required increase in assets is exactly equal to the addition to retained earnings, and EFN is therefore zero. We have seen that this happens when the growth rate is slightly less than 10 per cent. With a little algebra we can define this growth rate more precisely:

$$\text{Internal growth rate} = \frac{\text{ROA} \times b}{1 - \text{ROA} \times b} \qquad (3.28)$$

Here ROA is the return on assets, and $b$ is the ploughback, or retention, ratio defined earlier in this chapter.

For Hoffman AG, net income was €66 and total assets were €500. ROA is thus €66/500 = 13.2 per cent. Of the €66 net income, €44 was retained, so the ploughback ratio, $b$, is €44/66 = 2/3. With these numbers, we can calculate the internal growth rate:

$$\text{Internal growth rate} = \frac{\text{ROA} \times b}{1 - \text{ROA} \times b}$$

$$= \frac{0.132 \times (2/3)}{1 - 0.132 \times (2/3)}$$

$$= 9.65\%$$

Thus Hoffman AG can expand at a maximum rate of 9.65 per cent per year without external financing.

**The Sustainable Growth Rate** We have seen that if Hoffman AG wishes to grow more rapidly than at a rate of 9.65 per cent per year, external financing must be arranged. The second growth rate of interest is the maximum growth rate a firm can achieve with no external *equity* financing while it maintains a constant debt–equity ratio. This rate is commonly called the **sustainable growth rate**, because it is the maximum rate of growth a firm can maintain without increasing its financial leverage.

> **sustainable growth rate** The maximum growth rate a firm can achieve without external equity financing while maintaining a constant debt–equity ratio.

There are various reasons why a firm might wish to avoid equity sales. For example, as we discuss in Chapter 14, new equity sales can be expensive. Alternatively, the current owners may not wish to bring in new owners or contribute additional equity. Why a firm might view a particular debt–equity ratio as optimal is discussed in Chapters 13 and 15; for now, we shall take it as given.

Based on Table 3.17, the sustainable growth rate for Hoffman is approximately 20 per cent, because the debt–equity ratio is near 1.0 at that growth rate. The precise value can be calculated:

$$\text{Sustainable growth rate} = \frac{\text{ROE} \times b}{1 - \text{ROE} \times b} \tag{3.29}$$

This is identical to the internal growth rate except that ROE, return on equity, is used instead of ROA.

For Hoffman AG, net income was €66 and total equity was €250; ROE is thus €66/250 = 26.4 per cent. The ploughback ratio, $b$, is still 2/3, so we can calculate the sustainable growth rate as follows:

$$\text{Sustainable growth rate} = \frac{\text{ROE} \times b}{1 - \text{ROE} \times b}$$

$$= \frac{0.264 \times (2/3)}{1 - 0.264 \times (2/3)}$$

$$= 21.36\%$$

Thus Hoffman AG can expand at a maximum rate of 21.36 per cent per year without external equity financing.

**Determinants of Growth** We have seen that the return on equity, ROE, could be decomposed into its various components using the Du Pont identity. Because ROE appears so prominently in the determination of the sustainable growth rate, it is obvious that the factors important in determining ROE are also important determinants of growth. We know that ROE can be written as the product of three factors:

$$\text{ROE} = \text{Profit margin} \times \text{Total asset turnover} \times \text{Equity multiplier}$$

If we examine our expression for the sustainable growth rate, we see that anything that increases ROE will increase the sustainable growth rate by making the top bigger and the bottom smaller. Increasing the ploughback ratio will have the same effect.

Putting it all together, what we have is that a firm's ability to sustain growth depends explicitly on the following four factors:

1  *Profit margin*: An increase in profit margin will increase the firm's ability to generate funds internally and thereby increase its sustainable growth.

2  *Dividend policy*: A decrease in the percentage of profit attributable to shareholders (net income) paid out as dividends will increase the retention ratio. This increases internally generated equity and thus increases sustainable growth.

3  *Financial policy*: An increase in the debt–equity ratio increases the firm's financial leverage. Because this makes additional debt financing available, it increases the sustainable growth rate.

4  *Total asset turnover*: An increase in the firm's total asset turnover increases the sales generated for each pound or euro in assets. This decreases the firm's need for new assets as sales grow and thereby increases the sustainable growth rate. Notice that increasing total asset turnover is the same thing as decreasing capital intensity.

The sustainable growth rate is a very useful planning number. What it illustrates is the explicit relationship between the firm's four major areas of concern: its operating efficiency as measured by profit margin, its asset use efficiency as measured by total asset turnover, its dividend policy as measured by the retention ratio, and its financial policy as measured by the debt–equity ratio.

Given values for all four of these, there is only one growth rate that can be achieved. This is an important point, so it bears restating:

*If a firm does not wish to sell new equity and its profit margin, dividend policy, financial policy and total asset turnover (or capital intensity) are all fixed, then there is only one possible growth rate.*

As we described early in this chapter, one of the primary benefits of financial planning is that it ensures internal consistency among the firm's various goals. The concept of the sustainable growth rate captures this element nicely. Also, we now see how a financial planning model can be used to test the feasibility of a planned growth rate. If sales are to grow at a rate higher than the sustainable growth rate, the firm must increase profit margins, increase total asset turnover, increase financial leverage, increase earnings retention, or sell new shares.

3.7a  How is a firm's sustainable growth related to its accounting return on equity (ROE)?

3.7b  What are the determinants of growth?

## 3.8 Some Caveats Regarding Financial Planning Models

Financial planning models do not always ask the right questions. A primary reason is that they tend to rely on accounting relationships and not financial relationships. In particular, the three basic elements of firm value tend to get left out – namely cash flow size, risk, and timing.

Because of this, financial planning models sometimes do not produce meaningful clues about what strategies will lead to increases in value. Instead, they divert the user's attention to questions concerning the association of, say, the debt–equity ratio and firm growth.

The financial model we used for Hoffman AG was simple – in fact, too simple. Our model, like many in use today, is really an accounting statement generator at heart. Such models are useful for pointing out inconsistencies and reminding us of financial needs, but they offer little guidance concerning what to do about these problems.

In closing our discussion, we should add that financial planning is an iterative process. Plans are created, examined, and modified over and over. The final plan will be a result negotiated between all the different parties to the process. Upper-level managers have a goal in mind, and it is up to the planning staff to rework and ultimately deliver a feasible plan that meets that goal.

The final plan will therefore implicitly contain different goals in different areas, and also satisfy many constraints. For this reason, such a plan need not be a dispassionate assessment of what we think the future will bring; it may instead be a means of reconciling the planned activities of different groups and a way of setting common goals for the future.

| CONCEPT QUESTIONS | 3.8a | What are some important elements that are often missing in financial planning models? |
| | 3.8b | Why do we say planning is an iterative process? |

## Summary and Conclusions

This chapter has introduced some of the basics of financial statements and planning. Financial statements are often the only basis on which to begin a financial analysis, and so it is important to understand them, how they are generated, and the weaknesses in using accounting information as compared with real cash flows.

Evaluating ratios of accounting numbers is a good way of comparing financial statement information. We therefore defined and discussed a number of the most commonly reported and used financial ratios. We also discussed the famous Du Pont identity as a way of analysing financial performance.

Finally, financial planning forces the firm to think about the future. We have examined a number of features of the planning process. We described what financial planning can accomplish, and the components of a financial model. We went on to develop the relationship between growth and financing needs, and we discussed how a financial planning model is useful in exploring that relationship.

Corporate financial planning should not become a purely mechanical activity. If it does, it will probably focus on the wrong things. In particular, plans all too often are formulated in terms of a growth target, with no explicit linkage to value creation, and they frequently are overly concerned with accounting statements. Nevertheless, the alternative to financial planning is stumbling into the future.

# Chapter Review and Self-Test Problems

**3.1    Financial Ratios**   Consider the 2008 statement of financial position for Thomas Cook Group.

| | December 2008 | | December 2008 |
|---|---:|---|---:|
| | **£m** | | **£m** |
| **Current assets** | | **Current liabilities** | |
| Cash | 761.3 | Accounts payable | 855.5 |
| Short-term investments | 390.8 | Accrued expenses | 809.6 |
| Trade receivables | 347.1 | Notes payable/short-term debt | 188.1 |
| Notes receivable: short term | 19.9 | Current port. of LT debt/ capital leases | 524.8 |
| Receivables: other | 131.6 | Other current liabilities | 1,370.4 |
| Total inventory | 24.2 | **Total current liabilities** | **3,748.4** |
| Other current assets | 404.8 | | |
| **Total current assets** | **2,079.7** | **Non-current liabilities** | |
| | | Long-term debt | 711.3 |
| **Non-current assets** | | Deferred income tax | 97.8 |
| Property/plant/equipment | 897.6 | Minority interest | 12.7 |
| Intangible assets | 3,432.4 | Other liabilities, total | 451.7 |
| Long-term investments | 143.4 | **Total non-current liabilities** | **1,273.5** |
| Note receivable: long term | 126.4 | | |
| Other long-term assets | 338.9 | **Total liabilities** | **5,021.9** |
| **Total non-current assets** | **4,938.7** | Ordinary share capital | 59.8 |
| | | Additional paid-in capital | 8.9 |
| | | Retained earnings (accumulated deficit) | 1,726.0 |
| | | Other equity, total | 201.8 |
| | | **Total equity** | **1,996.5** |
| **Total assets** | **7,018.4** | **Total liabilities and shareholders' equity** | **7,018.4** |

Based on the statement of financial position and income statement, calculate the following ratios for 2008:

Current ratio                   _____
Quick ratio                     _____
Cash ratio                      _____
Inventory turnover              _____
Receivables turnover            _____
Days' sales in inventory        _____
Days' sales in receivables      _____
Total debt ratio                _____
Long-term debt ratio            _____
Times interest earned ratio     _____
Cash coverage ratio             _____

**3.2 ROE and the Du Pont Identity** Calculate the 2008 ROE for Thomas Cook Group, and then break down your answer into its component parts using the Du Pont identity.

**3.3 Calculating EFN** Based on the following information for the pharmaceutical firm AstraZeneca plc, what is EFN if sales are predicted to grow by 15 per cent? Use the percentage of sales approach, and assume the company is operating at full capacity. The payout ratio is constant.

| AstraZeneca plc | | | | |
|---|---|---|---|---|
| **Financial statements for Y/E 2008** | | | | |
| **Income statement** | | **Statement of financial position** | | |
| | **$m** | **Assets** | **$m** | **Liabilities and owners' equity** |
| Sales | 31,601 | Current assets | 16,152 | Current liabilities | 13,320 |
| Costs | 22,920 | Non-current assets | 30,632 | Non-current liabilities | 17,552 |
| Profit before taxes | 8,861 | | | Owners' equity | 15,912 |
| Taxes (29.39%) | 2,551 | | | | |
| | | | | Total liabilities and owners' | |
| Net income | 6,130 | Total assets | 46,784 | equity | 46,784 |
| Dividends | 2,971 | | | | |
| Addition to retained earnings | 3,159 | | | | |

**3.4 EFN and Capacity Use** Based on the information in Problem 3.3, what is EFN, assuming 60 per cent capacity usage for non-current assets? What is it, assuming 95 per cent capacity?

**3.5 Sustainable Growth** Based on the information in Problem 3.3, what growth rate can AstraZeneca maintain if no external financing is used? What is the sustainable growth rate?

# Answers to Chapter Review and Self-Test Problems

**3.1** We've calculated the following ratios based on the ending figures.

| | | |
|---|---|---|
| Current ratio | £2,079.70/£3,748.40 | = 0.55 times |
| Quick ratio | £2,055.50/£3,748.40 | = 0.55 times |
| Cash ratio | £761.30/£3,748.40 | = 0.20 times |
| Inventory turnover | £6,282.50/£24.2 | = 259.61 times |
| Receivables turnover | £8,167.10/£347.1 | = 23.52 times |
| Days' sales in inventory | 365/259.61 | = 1.41 days |
| Days' sales in receivables | 365/23.52 | = 15.51 days |
| Total debt ratio | £5,021.90/£7,018.40 | = 71.55% |
| Long-term debt ratio | £711.30/£2,707.80 | = 26.27% |
| Times interest earned ratio | £109/£114 | = 0.96 times |
| Cash coverage ratio | £236.60/£114 | = 2.08 times |

3.2   The return on equity is the ratio of net income to total equity. For Thomas Cook Group, this is £44.7/£1,996.6 = 2.2 per cent, which is not outstanding.

Given the Du Pont identity, ROE can be written as follows:

$$
\begin{aligned}
\text{ROE} &= \text{Profit margin} \times \text{Total asset turnover} \times \text{Equity multiplier} \\
&= £44.7/£8,167.1 \times £8,167.1/£7,018.4 \times £7,018.4/£1,996.5 \\
&= 0.55\% \times 1.16 \times 3.52 \\
&= 2.2\%
\end{aligned}
$$

Notice that return on assets, ROA, is £44.7/£7,018.4 = 0.64 per cent.

3.3   We can calculate EFN by preparing the pro forma statements using the percentage of sales approach. Note that sales are forecast to be $31,601 × 1.10 = $34,761.

**AstraZeneca plc**
**Pro forma financial statements**

**Income statement ($m)**

| | | |
|---|---|---|
| Sales | 36,341 | Forecast |
| Costs | 26,358 | 72.53% of sales |
| Profit before taxes | 9,983 | |
| Taxes (29.39%) | 2,934 | |
| Net income | 7,050 | |
| Dividends | 3,417 | 48.47% of net income |
| Addition to retained earnings | 3,633 | |

**Statement of financial position**

| Assets | $m | % | Liabilities and owners' equity | $m | % |
|---|---|---|---|---|---|
| Current assets | 18,575 | 51.11 | Current liabilities | 15,318 | 42.15 |
| Non-current assets | 35,227 | 96.93 | Non-current liabilities | 17,552 | n/a |
| | | | Owners' equity | 19,545 | n/a |
| Total assets | 53,802 | 148.05 | Total liabilities and owners' equity | 52,415 | n/a |
| | | | EFN | 1,387 | n/a |

3.4   Full-capacity sales are equal to current sales divided by the capacity utilization. At 60 per cent of capacity:

$$
\begin{aligned}
\$31,601 &= 0.60 \times \text{Full-capacity sales} \\
\$52,668 &= \text{Full-capacity sales}
\end{aligned}
$$

With a sales level of $36,341, no new non-current assets will be needed, so our earlier estimate is too high. We estimated an increase in non-current assets of $35,227 − 30,632 = $4,595. The new EFN will thus be $1,387 − 4,595 = −$3,208, a surplus. No external financing is needed in this case.

At 95 per cent capacity, full-capacity sales are $33,264. The ratio of non-current assets to full-capacity sales is thus $30,632/33,264 = 92.08 per cent. At a sales level of $36,341, we shall thus need $36,341 × 0.9208 = $33,465 in non-current assets, an increase of $2,833. This is $4,595 − 2,833 = $1,762 less than we originally predicted, so the EFN is now $1,387 − 1,762 = −$375, a surplus. No additional financing is needed.

3.5   AstraZeneca retains b = 1 − 0.4847 = 51.53 per cent of net income. Return on assets is $6,130/46,784 = 13.10 per cent. The internal growth rate is thus

$$\frac{ROA \times b}{1 - (ROA \times b)} = \frac{0.1310 \times 0.5153}{1 - (0.1310 \times 0.5153)}$$
$$= 7.24\%$$

Return on equity for AstraZeneca is $6,130/15,912 = 38.52\%$, so we can calculate the sustainable growth rate as follows:

$$\frac{ROE \times b}{1 - (ROE \times b)} = \frac{0.3852 \times 0.5153}{1 - (0.3852 \times 0.5153)}$$
$$= 24.77\%$$

# Concepts Review and Critical Thinking Questions

1  **Accounting and Cash Flows [LO1]**  Why might the revenue and cost figures shown on a standard income statement not be representative of the actual cash inflows and outflows that occurred during a period?

2  **Book Values versus Market Values [LO1]**  In preparing a balance sheet, why do you think International Accounting Standards allow both historical cost and fair value approaches?

3  **Operating Cash Flow [LO1]**  In comparing accounting net income and operating cash flow, name two items you typically find in net income that are not in operating cash flow. Explain what each is, and why it is excluded in operating cash flow.

4  **Book Values versus Market Values [LO1]**  Under standard accounting rules, it is possible for a company's liabilities to exceed its assets. When this occurs, the owners' equity is negative. Can this happen with market values? Why or why not?

5  **Earnings Management [LO1]**  Companies often try to keep accounting earnings growing at a relatively steady pace, thereby avoiding large swings in earnings from period to period. They also try to meet earnings targets. To do so, they use a variety of tactics. The simplest way is to control the timing of accounting revenues and costs, which all firms can do to at least some extent. For example, if earnings are looking too low this year, then some accounting costs can be deferred until next year. This practice is called earnings management. It is common, and it raises a lot of questions. Why do firms do it? Why are firms even allowed to do it under International Accounting Standards? Is it ethical? What are the implications for cash flow and shareholder wealth?

6  **Current Ratio [LO2]**  What effect would the following actions have on a firm's current ratio? Assume that net working capital is positive.

(a)  Inventory is purchased.

(b)  A supplier is paid.

(c)  A short-term bank loan is repaid.

(d)  A long-term debt is paid off early.

(e)  A customer pays off a credit account.

(f)  Inventory is sold at cost.

(g)  Inventory is sold for a profit.

7  **Current Ratio [LO2]**  Explain what it means for a firm to have a current ratio equal to 0.50. Would the firm be better off if the current ratio were 1.50? What if it were 15.0? Explain your answers.

8  **Financial Ratios [LO2]**  Fully explain the kind of information the following financial ratios provide about a firm:

(a)  Quick ratio.

(b)  Cash ratio.

(c)  Total asset turnover.

(d)  Equity multiplier.

(e)  Long-term debt ratio.

(f)  Times interest earned ratio.

(g)  Profit margin.

(h)  Return on assets.

(i)  Return on equity.

(j)  Price–earnings ratio.

9  **Du Pont Identity [LO2]**  Why is the Du Pont identity a valuable tool for analysing the performance of a firm? Discuss the types of information it reveals, compared with ROE considered by itself.

10  **Industry-Specific Ratios [LO2]**  Specialized ratios are sometimes used in specific industries. For example, the so-called book-to-bill ratio is closely watched for semiconductor manu-facturers. A ratio of 0.93 indicates that for every €100 worth of chips shipped over some period, only €93 worth of new orders were received. In October 2009 the semiconductor equipment industry's book-to-bill ratio was 1.10, compared with 1.17 during the month of September 2009. The book-to-bill ratio reached a recent low of 0.47 during January 2009. The three-month average of worldwide bookings in October 2009 was $756.2 million, a decrease of $2.7 million from September 2009, while the three-month average of billings was $689.8 million, an increase of $41.1 million from September 2009. What is this ratio intended to measure? Why do you think it is so closely followed?

11  **Sustainable Growth [LO3]**  In the chapter we used Bogle plc to demonstrate how to calculate EFN. The ROE for Bogle is about 8 per cent, and the ploughback ratio is about 67 per cent. If you calculate the sustainable growth rate for Bogle, you will find it is only 5.63 per cent. In our calculation for EFN we used a growth rate of 25 per cent. Is this possible? (*Hint*: Yes. How?)

12  **External Financing Needed [LO3]**  GNR NV uses no external financing and maintains a positive retention ratio. When sales grow by 15 per cent, the firm has a negative projected EFN. What does this tell you about the firm's internal growth rate? How about the sustainable growth rate? At this same level of sales growth, what will happen to the projected EFN if the retention ratio is increased? What if the retention ratio is decreased? What happens to the projected EFN if the firm pays out all of its earnings in the form of dividends?

Use the following information to answer the next six questions. A small business called The Grandmother Calendar Company began selling personalized photo calendar kits. The kits were a hit, and sales soon sharply exceeded forecasts. The rush of orders created a huge backlog, so the company leased more space and expanded capacity, but it still could not keep up with demand. Equipment failed from overuse, and quality suffered. Working capital was drained to expand production, and at the same time payments from customers were often delayed until the product was shipped. Unable to deliver on orders, the company became so strapped for cash that employee pay cheques began to bounce. Finally, out of cash, the company ceased operations entirely, three years later.

13  **Product Sales [LO3]**  Do you think the company would have suffered the same fate if its product had been less popular? Why or why not?

14  **Cash Flow [LO3]**   The Grandmother Calendar Company clearly had a cash flow problem. What was the impact of customers not paying until orders were shipped?

15  **Product Pricing [LO3]**   The firm actually priced its product to be about 20 per cent less than that of competitors, even though the Grandmother calendar was more detailed. In retrospect, was this a wise choice?

16  **Corporate Borrowing [LO3]**   If the firm was so successful at selling, why wouldn't a bank or some other lender step in and provide it with the cash it needed to continue?

17  **Cash Flow [LO3]**   Which was the biggest culprit here: too many orders, too little cash, or too little production capacity?

18  **Cash Flow [LO3]**   What are some of the actions that a small company like The Grandmother Calendar Company can take if it finds itself in a situation in which growth in sales outstrips production capacity and available financial resources? What other options (besides expansion of capacity) are available to a company when orders exceed capacity?

## connect Questions and Problems

**BASIC**

**1–15**

1  **Building a Statement of Financial Position [LO1]**   On 31 March 2009 Cable & Wireless plc had current assets of £1.541 billion, non-current assets of £3.650 billion, current liabilities of £1.856 billion, and non-current liabilities of £1.291 billion. What is the value of the shareholders' equity account for this firm? How much is net working capital?

2  **Building an Income Statement [LO1]**   For the year ending 31 March 2009, Johnson Matthey plc had revenues of £7.848 billion, costs of £7.324 billion, depreciation expense of £108.9 million, interest expense of £42.7 million, and a tax rate of 28 per cent. What is the net income for this firm?

3  **Cost and Revaluation Methods of Accounting [LO1]**   Klingon Widgets plc purchased new cloaking machinery three years ago for £7 million. The machinery can be sold to the Romulans today for £4.9 million. Klingon's current statement of financial position shows non-current assets of £3.7 million, current liabilities of £1.1 million, and net working capital of £380,000. If all the current assets were liquidated today, the company would receive £1.6 million cash. What is the book value of Klingon's assets today if the historical cost method of accounting is used? What is the value of its assets if the revaluation method is used?

4  **Calculating Liquidity Ratios [LO2]**   For the year ending December 2008, Xstrata plc had current assets of $6,987, current liabilities of $5,060, and inventory of $3,573. What is the current ratio? What is the quick ratio?

5  **Calculating Profitability Ratios [LO2]**   For the year ending December 2008, Volkswagen AG had sales of €113,808 million, total assets of €167,919 million, and total debt of €69,380 million. If the profit margin is 4.173 per cent, what was net income? What was ROA? What was ROE?

6  **Calculating Leverage Ratios [LO2]**   GNR plc has a total debt ratio of 0.63. What is its debt–equity ratio? What is its equity multiplier?

7  **Calculating Market Value Ratios [LO2]**   Axel plc had additions to retained earnings for the year just ended of £430,000. The firm paid out £175,000 in cash dividends, and it has ending total equity of £5.3 million. If the company currently has 210,000 shares of equity outstanding, what are earnings per share? Dividends per share? Book value per share? If the equity currently sells for £63 per share, what is the market-to-book ratio? The price–earnings ratio? If the company had sales of £4.5 million, what is the price–sales ratio?

8 **Du Pont Identity [LO2]** If Roten Rooters NV has an equity multiplier of 2.80, total asset turnover of 1.15, and a profit margin of 5.5 per cent, what is its ROE?

9 **Pro Forma Statements [LO3]** Consider the following simplified 2008 financial statements for Nokia Oyj (ignoring taxes):

| Income statement | | Statement of financial position | | | |
|---|---|---|---|---|---|
| | €m | | €m | | €m |
| Sales | 50,710 | Assets | 39,582 | Debt | 23,072 |
| Costs | 45,740 | | | Equity | 16,510 |
| Net profit | 4,970 | Total | 39,582 | Total | 39,582 |

Nokia has predicted a sales increase of 15 per cent. It has predicted that every item on the statement of financial position will increase by 15 per cent as well. Create the pro forma statements, and reconcile them. What is the plug variable here?

10 **Pro Forma Statements and EFN [LO3]** In the previous question, assume Nokia pays out half of net profit in the form of a cash dividend. Costs and assets vary with sales, but debt and equity do not. Prepare the pro forma statements and determine the external financing needed.

11 **EFN [LO3]** The 2008 financial statements for WPP plc are shown here:

| Income statement | | Statement of financial position | | | |
|---|---|---|---|---|---|
| | £m | | £m | | £m |
| Sales | 7,477 | Current assets | 11,108 | Current liabilities | 12,136 |
| Costs | 6,730 | Non-current assets | 13,355 | Non-current liabilities | 6,565 |
| Profit before taxes | 747 | | | Total liabilities | 18,701 |
| Tax | 233 31.19% | | | Equity | 5,762 |
| Net profit | 514 | Total assets | 24,463 | Total | 24,463 |

Assets, costs, and current liabilities are proportional to sales. Non-current liabilities and equity are not. The company maintains a constant 40 per cent dividend payout ratio. As with every other firm in its industry, next year's sales are projected to increase by exactly 15 per cent. What is the external financing needed?

12 **Calculating Internal Growth [LO3]** The 2009 financial statements for Siemens AG are shown here:

| Income statement | | Statement of financial position | | | |
|---|---|---|---|---|---|
| | €m | | €m | | €m |
| Sales | 76,651 | Current assets | 44,129 | Current liabilities | 37,005 |
| Costs | 72,760 | Non-current assets | 50,797 | Non-current liabilities | 31,275 |
| Profit before taxes | 3,891 | | | Total liabilities | 68,280 |
| Tax | 1,434 36.85% | | | Equity | 26,646 |
| Net profit | 2,457 | Total assets | 94,926 | Total | 94,926 |

Assets and costs are proportional to sales. Debt and equity are not. The company maintains a constant 30 per cent dividend payout ratio. No external equity financing is possible. What is the internal growth rate?

13  **Calculating Sustainable Growth [LO3]**   For the company in the previous problem, what is the sustainable growth rate?

14  **Internal Growth [LO3]**  If the Football Shoppe has an 8 per cent ROA and a 20 per cent payout ratio, what is its internal growth rate?

15  **Sustainable Growth [LO3]**   If Garnett Ltd has a 15 per cent ROE and a 25 per cent payout ratio, what is its sustainable growth rate?

**INTERMEDIATE**

**16 – 31**

16  **Residual Claims [LO1]**   Moneyback Limited is obligated to pay its creditors £7,300 during the year.

(a)  What is the market value of the shareholders' equity if assets have a market value of £8,400?

(b)  What if assets equal £6,700?

17  **Net Income and OCF [LO1]**   During 2010, Cumbria Raines Umbrella Ltd had sales of £730,000. Cost of goods sold, administrative and selling expenses, and depreciation expenses were £580,000, £105,000 and £135,000 respectively. In addition, the company had an interest expense of £75,000 and a tax rate of 28 per cent. (Ignore any tax loss carry-back or carry-forward provisions.)

(a)  What is Cumbria Raines's net income for 2010?

(b)  What is its operating cash flow?

(c)  Explain your results in (a) and (b).

18  **Accounting Values versus Cash Flows [LO1]**   In Problem 17, suppose Cumbria Raines Umbrella Ltd paid out £25,000 in cash dividends. Is this possible? If spending on non-current assets and net working capital was zero, and if no new shares were issued during the year, what do you know about the firm's long-term debt?

19  **Calculating Cash Flows [LO1]**   Consider the following abbreviated financial statements for Parrothead Enterprises:

| Parrothead Enterprises 2009 and 2010 Partial balance sheets | | | | | | |
|---|---|---|---|---|---|---|
| **Assets** | | | | **Liabilities and owners' equity** | | |
| | **2009** £ | **2010** £ | | | **2009** £ | **2010** £ |
| Current assets | 653 | 707 | | Current liabilities | 261 | 293 |
| Non-current assets | 2,691 | 3,240 | | Non-current liabilities | 1,422 | 1,512 |

| Parrothead Enterprises 2010 Income statement | |
|---|---|
| | £ |
| Sales | 8,280 |
| Costs | 3,861 |
| Depreciation | 738 |
| Interest paid | 211 |

(a)  What is owners' equity for 2009 and 2010?

(b)  What is the change in net working capital for 2010?

(c)  In 2010, Parrothead Enterprises had capital expenditure of £1,350. How much in non-current assets did Parrothead Enterprises sell? What is the cash flow from investing activities for the year? (The tax rate is 28 per cent.)

**(d)** During 2010, Parrothead Enterprises raised £270 in new long-term debt. How much long-term debt must Parrothead Enterprises have paid off during the year? What is the cash flow from financing activities?

20    **Using the Du Pont Identity [LO2]**   Y3K plc has sales of £5,276, total assets of £3,105, and a debt–equity ratio of 1.40. If its return on equity is 15 per cent, what is its net income?

21    **Profit Margin [LO2]**   In response to complaints about high prices, a grocery chain runs the following advertising campaign: 'If you pay your child £3 to go and buy £50 worth of groceries, then your child makes twice as much on the trip as we do.' You've collected the following information from the grocery chain's financial statements:

| (millions) | |
|---|---|
| Sales | £750 |
| Net income | 22.5 |
| Total assets | 420 |
| Total debt | 280 |

Evaluate the grocery chain's claim. What is the basis for the statement? Is this claim misleading? Why or why not?

22    **Cost of Goods Sold [LO2]**   Holliman NV has current liabilities of €365,000, a quick ratio of 0.85, inventory turnover of 5.8, and a current ratio of 1.4. What is the cost of goods sold for the company?

Some recent financial statements for the luxury goods company LVMH Moet Hennessy Louis Vuitton SA follow. Use this information to work Problems 23–27.

| Income statements for LVMH Moet Hennessy Louis Vuitton | | |
|---|---|---|
| | Y/E Dec 08 | Y/E Dec 07 |
| | €m | €m |
| Revenue | 17,193 | 16,481 |
| Cost of revenue | 6,012 | 5,786 |
| **Gross profit** | **11,181** | **10,695** |
| Selling/general/admin. expenses | 7,553 | 7,140 |
| Amortization | 0 | 6 |
| Unusual expense (income) | 126 | 116 |
| Other operating expenses, total | 17 | 4 |
| **Operating profit** | **3,485** | **3,429** |
| Interest expense | −255 | −241 |
| Interest/invest income | 15 | 30 |
| Other, net | −41 | −41 |
| **Profit before taxes** | **3,204** | **3,177** |
| Provision for income taxes | 893 | 853 |
| **Profit after taxes** | **2,311** | **2,324** |
| Minority interest | −292 | −306 |
| Equity in affiliates | 7 | 7 |
| **Profit attributable to shareholders** | **2,026** | **2,025** |

| Statements of financial position LVMH Moet Hennessy Louis Vuitton | | | | | |
|---|---|---|---|---|---|
| | Dec 08 | Dec 07 | | Dec 08 | Dec 07 |
| | €m | €m | | €m | €m |
| **Current assets** | | | **Current liabilities** | | |
| Cash and short-term investments | 1,013 | 1,559 | Trade payables | 2,292 | 2,095 |
| Trade receivables | 1,650 | 1,595 | Accrued expenses | 1,866 | 1,552 |
| Receivables – other | 229 | 151 | Notes payable/ short-term debt | 1,571 | 2,212 |
| Total inventory | 5,767 | 4,812 | Current port. of LT debt/capital leases | 276 | 926 |
| Other current assets | 1,695 | 2,001 | Other current liabilities | 610 | 628 |
| **Total current assets** | **10,354** | **10,118** | **Total current liabilities** | **6,615** | **7,413** |
| **Non-current assets** | | | **Non-current liabilities** | | |
| Property/plant/ equipment | 6,081 | 5,419 | Total long-term debt | 3,738 | 2,477 |
| Goodwill, net | 4,423 | 4,818 | Deferred income tax | 3,113 | 2,843 |
| Intangibles, net | 8,523 | 7,999 | Minority interest | 989 | 938 |
| Long-term investments | 591 | 952 | Other liabilities | 4,224 | 5,123 |
| Other long-term assets | 1,511 | 1,078 | **Total non-current liabilities** | **12,064** | **11,381** |
| **Total non-current assets** | **21,129** | **20,266** | **Total liabilities** | **18,679** | **18,794** |
| | | | **Shareholders' equity** | | |
| | | | Ordinary shares | 147 | 147 |
| | | | Additional paid-in capital | 1,737 | 1,736 |
| | | | Retained earnings (accumulated deficit) | 12,274 | 11,192 |
| | | | Treasury stock – common | −983 | −877 |
| | | | Other equity, total | −371 | −608 |
| | | | **Total equity** | **12,804** | **11,590** |
| **Total assets** | **31,483** | **30,384** | **Total liabilities and shareholders' equity** | **31,483** | **30,384** |

23  **Calculating Financial Ratios [LO2]**  Find the following financial ratios for LVMH Moet Hennessy Louis Vuitton SA (use year-end figures rather than average values where appropriate):

**Short-term solvency ratios:**

(a)  Current ratio _____

(b)  Quick ratio _____

(c)  Cash ratio _____

**Asset utilization ratios:**

(d)  Total asset turnover _____

(e)  Inventory turnover _____

(f)  Receivables turnover _____

**Long-term solvency ratios:**

(g)  Total debt ratio _____

(h)  Debt–equity ratio _____

(i)  Equity multiplier _____

(j)  Times interest earned ratio _____

**Profitability ratios:**

(k)  Profit margin _____

(l)  Return on assets _____

(m)  Return on equity _____

24  **Du Pont Identity [LO2]**  Construct the Du Pont identity for LVMH Moet Hennessy Louis Vuitton SA.

25  **Market Value Ratios [LO2]**  LVMH Moet Hennessy Louis Vuitton SA has 473.06 million ordinary shares outstanding, and the market price for a share of equity at the end of 2008 was €46.79. What is the price–earnings ratio? What is the market-to-book ratio at the end of 2008? If the company's growth rate is 9 per cent, what is the PEG ratio?

26  **Tobin's Q [LO2]**  What is Tobin's Q for LVMH Moet Hennessy Louis Vuitton SA? What assumptions are you making about the book value of debt and the market value of debt? What about the book value of assets and the market value of assets? Are these assumptions realistic? Why or why not?

27  **Full-Capacity Sales [LO3]**  Seaweed Manufacturing is currently operating at only 95 per cent of non-current asset capacity. Current sales are £600,000. How fast can sales grow before any new non-current assets are needed?

28  **Non-Current Assets and Capacity Usage [LO3]**  For the company in the previous problem, suppose non-current assets are £440,000 and sales are projected to grow to £830,000. How much in new non-current assets is required to support this growth in sales? Assume the company maintains its current operating capacity.

29  **Growth and Assets [LO3]**  A firm wishes to maintain an internal growth rate of 8 per cent and a dividend payout ratio of 25 per cent. The current profit margin is 5 per cent, and the firm uses no external financing sources. What must total asset turnover be?

30  **Sustainable Growth Rate [LO3]**  Coheed plc had equity of £135,000 at the beginning of the year. At the end of the year the company had total assets of £250,000. During the year the company sold no new equity. Net income for the year was £19,000, and dividends were £3,500. What is the sustainable growth rate for the company? What is the sustainable growth rate if you use the formula $\text{ROE} \times b$ and beginning of period equity? What is the sustainable growth rate if you use end of period equity in this formula? Is this number too high or too low? Why?

31  **Internal Growth Rates [LO3]**  Calculate the internal growth rate for the company in the previous problem. Now calculate the internal growth rate using $\text{ROA} \times b$ for both beginning of period and end of period total assets. What do you observe?

**CHALLENGE**
**32–36**

32  **Non-Current Assets and Depreciation [LO1]**  On the simplified statement of financial position, the non-current assets (NCA) account is equal to the gross property, plant and equipment (PPE) account (which records the acquisition cost of property, plant and equipment) minus the accumulated depreciation (AD) account (which records the total depreciation taken by the firm against its property, plant and equipment). Using the fact that $\text{NCA} = \text{PPE} - \text{AD}$, show that the expression for net capital spending, $\text{NCA}_{\text{end}} - \text{NCA}_{\text{beg}} + D$ (where $D$ is the depreciation expense during the year), is equivalent to $\text{PPE}_{\text{end}} - \text{PPE}_{\text{beg}}$.

33  **Constraints on Growth [LO3]**  Nearside NV wishes to maintain a growth rate of 10 per cent per year and a debt–equity ratio of 0.50. Profit margin is 6.70 per cent, and the ratio of total assets to sales is constant at 1.35. Is this growth rate possible? To answer, determine what the dividend payout ratio must be. How do you interpret the result?

34  **EFN [LO3]**  Define the following:

$$S \quad = \text{Previous year's sales}$$
$$A \quad = \text{Total assets}$$
$$D \quad = \text{Total debt}$$
$$E \quad = \text{Total equity}$$
$$g \quad = \text{Projected growth in sales}$$
$$PM = \text{Profit margin}$$
$$b \quad = \text{Retention (ploughback) ratio}$$

Show that EFN can be written as follows:

$$EFN = -PM(S)b + [A - PM(S)b] \times g$$

*Hint*: Asset needs will equal $A \times g$. The addition to retained earnings will equal $PM(S)b \times (1 + g)$.

35  **Growth Rates [LO3]**  Based on the result in Problem 34, show that the internal and sustainable growth rates are as given in the chapter. *Hint:* For the internal growth rate, set EFN equal to zero and solve for $g$.

36  **Sustainable Growth Rate [LO3]**  In the chapter, we discussed the two versions of the sustainable growth rate formula. Derive the formula $ROE \times b$ from the formula given in the chapter, where ROE is based on beginning of period equity. Also, derive the formula $ROA \times b$ from the internal growth rate formula.

## MINI CASE  Ratios and Financial Planning at West Coast Yachts

Dan Ervin was recently hired by West Coast Yachts Ltd to assist the company with its short-term financial planning, and also to evaluate the company's financial performance. Dan graduated from university five years ago with a finance degree, and he has been employed in the treasury department of a FTSE 100 company since then.

West Coast Yachts was founded 10 years ago by Larissa Warren. The company's operations are located in a well-known marina, Inverkip, on the west coast of Scotland. The firm is structured as a private limited company. The company has manufactured custom, midsize, high-performance yachts for clients over this period, and its products have received high reviews for safety and reliability. The company's yachts have also recently received the highest award for customer satisfaction. The yachts are purchased primarily by wealthy individuals for pleasure use. Occasionally, a yacht is manufactured for purchase by a company for business purposes.

The custom yacht industry is fragmented, with a number of manufacturers. As with any industry, there are market leaders, but the diverse nature of the industry ensures that no manufacturer dominates the market. The competition in the market, as well as the product cost, ensures that attention to detail is a necessity. For instance, West Coast Yachts will spend 80 to 100 hours on hand-buffing the stainless steel stem-iron, which is the metal cap on the yacht's bow that conceivably could collide with a dock or another boat.

To get Dan started with his analyses, Larissa has provided the following financial statements. Larissa has gathered the industry ratios for the yacht manufacturing industry.

| West Coast Yachts 2010 Income statement | | |
|---|---|---|
| | £ | £ |
| Operating revenues | | 128,700,000 |
| Operating expenses | | 90,700,000 |
| Operating profit | | 38,000,000 |
| Depreciation | | 4,200,000 |
| Other non-operating expenses | | 15,380,000 |
| Interest | | 2,315,000 |
| Profit before taxes | | 16,105,000 |
| Taxes (28%) | | 4,509,400 |
| Profit for period attributable to equity holders | | 11,595,600 |
| Dividends | 6,957,360 | |
| Addition to retained earnings | 4,638,240 | |

| West Coast Yachts Statement of financial position as of 31 December 2010 | | | | |
|---|---|---|---|---|
| **Assets** | | | **Liabilities and equity** | |
| | £ | | | £ |
| Current assets | | | Current liabilities | |
| Cash | 2,340,000 | | Trade payables | 4,970,000 |
| Trade receivables | 4,210,000 | | Notes payable | 10,060,000 |
| Inventory | 4,720,000 | | | |
| Total | 11,270,000 | | Total | 15,030,000 |
| | | | | |
| Non-current assets | | | Non-current liabilities | 25,950,000 |
| Net plant and equipment | 72,280,000 | | | |
| | | | Shareholders' equity | |
| | | | Ordinary shares | 4,000,000 |
| | | | Retained earnings | 38,570,000 |
| | | | Total equity | 42,570,000 |
| Total assets | 83,550,000 | | Total liabilities and equity | 83,550,000 |

| Yacht industry ratios | | | |
|---|---|---|---|
| | **Lower quartile** | **Median** | **Upper quartile** |
| Current ratio | 0.50 | 1.43 | 1.89 |
| Quick ratio | 0.21 | 0.38 | 0.62 |
| Total asset turnover | 0.68 | 0.85 | 1.38 |
| Inventory turnover | 4.89 | 6.15 | 10.89 |
| Receivables turnover | 6.27 | 9.82 | 14.11 |
| Debt ratio | 0.44 | 0.52 | 0.61 |
| Debt–equity ratio | 0.79 | 1.08 | 1.56 |
| Equity multiplier | 1.79 | 2.08 | 2.56 |
| Interest coverage | 5.18 | 8.06 | 9.83 |
| Profit margin (%) | 4.05 | 6.98 | 9.87 |
| Return on assets (%) | 6.05 | 10.53 | 13.21 |
| Return on equity (%) | 9.93 | 16.54 | 26.15 |

1   Calculate all the ratios listed in the industry table for West Coast Yachts.

2   Compare the performance of West Coast Yachts with that of the industry as a whole.
    For each ratio, comment on why it might be viewed as positive or negative relative
    to the industry. Suppose you create an inventory ratio calculated as inventory divided
    by current liabilities. How do you interpret this ratio? How does West Coast Yachts
    compare with the industry average?

3   Calculate the sustainable growth rate of West Coast Yachts. Calculate external funds
    needed (EFN), and prepare a pro forma income statement and statement of financial
    position, assuming growth at precisely this rate. Recalculate the ratios in the previous
    question. What do you observe?

4   As a practical matter, West Coast Yachts is unlikely to be willing to raise external
    equity capital, in part because the owners don't want to dilute their existing owner-
    ship and control positions. However, West Coast Yachts is planning for a growth rate
    of 20 per cent next year. What are your conclusions and recommendations about the
    feasibility of West Coast's expansion plans?

5   Most assets can be increased as a percentage of sales. For instance, cash can be increased
    by any amount. However, non-current assets often must be increased in specific
    amounts, because it is impossible, as a practical matter, to buy part of a new plant
    or machine. In this case a company has a 'staircase' or 'lumpy' fixed cost structure.
    Assume that West Coast Yachts is currently producing at 100 per cent of capacity. As
    a result, to expand production, the company must set up an entirely new line at a
    cost of £25,000,000. Calculate the new EFN with this assumption. What does this
    imply about capacity utilization for West Coast Yachts next year?

Online LearningCentre

To help you grasp the key concepts of this chapter check out
the extra resources posted on the Online Learning Centre at
**www.mcgraw-hill.co.uk/textbooks/hillier**

Among other helpful resources there are mini-cases tailored
to individual chapters.

# CHAPTER 4

# Introduction to Valuation: The Time Value of Money

## LEARNING OBJECTIVES

After studying this chapter, you should understand:

**LO1** How to determine the future value of an investment made today.

**LO2** How to determine the present value of cash to be received at a future date.

**LO3** How to find the return on an investment.

**LO4** How long it takes for an investment to reach a desired value.

---

INTERCONTINFNTAL HOTELS offered some securities for sale to the public on 9 December 2009. Under the terms of the deal InterContinental promised to repay the owner of one of these securities £50,000 on 9 December 2016, and £3,000 every year in between. Investors paid InterContinental £49,732.50 for each of these securities; so they gave up £49,732.50 on 9 December 2009 for the promise of £71,000 (£21,000 in interest and £50,000 original amount) over the subsequent seven years. Is giving up £49,732.50 in exchange for £71,000 over seven years a good deal? On the plus side, you get back about £1.42 for every £1 you put up. That probably sounds good; but on the down side, you have to wait seven years to get it. What you need to know is how to analyse this trade-off; this chapter gives you the tools you need.

---

One of the basic problems faced by the financial manager is how to determine the value today of cash flows expected in the future. For example, the InterContinental security paid £71,000 in total. Does this mean that the security was worth £71,000? The answer is no, because the security was actually going to pay out over a seven-year period at a rate of £3,000 per year, with a final payment of £50,000 after seven years. How much was the security worth then? The answer depends on the time value of money, the subject of this chapter.

In the most general sense, the phrase *time value of money* refers to the fact that a euro (or pound) in the hand today is worth more than a euro promised at some time in the future. On a practical level, one reason for this is that you could earn interest while you waited; so a euro today would grow to more than a euro later. The trade-off between money now and money later thus depends on, among other things, the rate you can earn by investing. Our goal in this chapter is to evaluate explicitly this trade-off between euros (or any other currency) today and at some future time.

A thorough understanding of the material in this chapter is critical to understanding material in subsequent chapters, so you should study it with particular care. We shall present a number of examples in this chapter. In many problems your answer may differ from ours slightly. This can happen because of rounding, and is not a cause for concern.

## 4.1 Future Value and Compounding

The first thing we shall study is future value. **Future value (FV)** refers to the amount of money an investment will grow to over some period of time at some given interest rate. Put another way, future value is the cash value of an investment at some time in the future. We start out by considering the simplest case: a single-period investment.

> **future value (FV)**
> The amount an investment is worth after one or more periods.

### Investing for a Single Period

Suppose you invest £100 in a savings account that pays 10 per cent interest per year. How much will you have in one year? You will have £110. This £110 is equal to your original *principal* of £100 plus £10 in interest that you earn. We say that £110 is the future value of £100 invested for one year at 10 per cent, and we simply mean that £100 today is worth £110 in one year, given that 10 per cent is the interest rate.

In general, if you invest for one period at an interest rate of $r$, your investment will grow to $(1 + r)$ per pound invested. In our example, $r$ is 10 per cent, so your investment grows to $1 + 0.10 = 1.1$ pounds per pound invested. You invested £100 in this case, so you ended up with $£100 \times 1.10 = £110$.

> **compounding**
> The process of accumulating interest on an investment over time to earn more interest.

### Investing for More than One Period

Going back to our £100 investment, what will you have after two years, assuming the interest rate doesn't change? If you leave the entire £110 in the bank, you will earn $£110 \times 0.10 = £11$ in interest during the second year, so you will have a total of $£110 + 11 = £121$. This £121 is the future value of £100 in two years at 10 per cent. Another way of looking at it is that one year from now you are effectively investing £110 at 10 per cent for a year. This is a single-period problem, so you'll end up with £1.10 for every pound invested, or $£110 \times 1.1 = £121$ total.

This £121 has four parts. The first part is the £100 original principal. The second part is the £10 in interest you earned in the first year, and the third part is another £10 you earn in the second year, for a total of £120. The last £1 you end up with (the fourth part) is interest you earn in the second year on the interest paid in the first year: $£10 \times 0.10 = £1$.

This process of leaving your money and any accumulated interest in an investment for more than one period, and thereby *reinvesting* the interest, is called **compounding**. Compounding the interest means earning **interest on interest**, so we call the result **compound interest**. With **simple interest** the interest is not reinvested, so interest is earned each period only on the original principal.

> **interest on interest**
> Interest earned on the reinvestment of previous interest payments.

> **compound interest**
> Interest earned on both the initial principal and the interest reinvested from prior periods.

> **simple interest**
> Interest earned only on the original principal amount invested.

**EXAMPLE 4.1**

## Interest on Interest

Suppose you locate a two-year investment that pays 14 per cent per year. If you invest €325, how much will you have at the end of the two years? How much of this is simple interest? How much is compound interest?

At the end of the first year you will have €325 × (1 + 0.14) = €370.50. If you reinvest this entire amount and thereby compound the interest, you will have €370.50 × 1.14 = €422.37 at the end of the second year. The total interest you earn is thus €422.37 − 325 = €97.37. Your €325 original principal earns €325 × 0.14 = €45.50 in interest each year, for a two-year total of €91 in simple interest. The remaining €97.37 − 91 = €6.37 results from compounding. You can check this by noting that the interest earned in the first year is €45.50. The interest on interest earned in the second year thus amounts to €45.50 × 0.14 = €6.37, as we calculated.

We now take a closer look at how we calculated the £121 future value. We multiplied £110 by 1.1 to get £121. The £110, however, was £100 also multiplied by 1.1. In other words:

$$
\begin{aligned}
£121 &= £110 \times 1.1 \\
&= (£100 \times 1.1) \times 1.1 \\
&= £100 \times (1.1 \times 1.1) \\
&= £100 \times 1.1^2 \\
&= £100 \times 1.21
\end{aligned}
$$

At the risk of belabouring the obvious, let's ask: how much would our £100 grow to after three years? Once again, in two years we'll be investing £121 for one period at 10 per cent. We'll end up with £1.10 for every pound we invest, or £121 × 1.1 = £133.10 total. This £133.10 is thus

$$
\begin{aligned}
£133.10 &= £121 \times 1.1 \\
&= (£110 \times 1.1) \times 1.1 \\
&= (£100 \times 1.1) \times 1.1 \times 1.1 \\
&= £100 \times (1.1 \times 1.1 \times 1.1) \\
&= £100 \times 1.1^3 \\
&= £100 \times 1.331
\end{aligned}
$$

You're probably noticing a pattern to these calculations, so we can now go ahead and state the general result. As our examples suggest, the future value of £1 invested for $t$ periods at a rate of $r$ per period is this:

$$\text{Future value} = £1 \times (1 + r)^t \tag{4.1}$$

The expression $(1 + r)^t$ is sometimes called the *future value interest factor* (or just *future value factor*) for £1 invested at $r$ per cent for $t$ periods, and can be abbreviated as FVIF($r$, $t$).

In our example, what would your £100 be worth after five years? We can first compute the relevant future value factor as follows:

$$(1 + r)^t = (1 + 0.10)^5 = 1.1^5 = 1.6105$$

Your £100 will thus grow to

$$£100 \times 1.6105 = £161.05$$

The growth of your £100 each year is illustrated in Table 4.1. As shown, the interest earned in each year is equal to the beginning amount multiplied by the interest rate of 10 per cent.

In Table 4.1, notice that the total interest you earn is £61.05. Over the five-year span of this investment the simple interest is £100 × 0.10 = £10 per year, so you accumulate £50 this way. The other £11.05 is from compounding.

TABLE
4.1

| Year | Beginning amount (£) | Simple interest (£) | Compound interest (£) | Total interest earned (£) | Ending amount (£) |
|------|----------------------|---------------------|-----------------------|---------------------------|-------------------|
| 1 | 100.00 | 10 | 0.00 | 10.00 | 110.00 |
| 2 | 110.00 | 10 | 1.00 | 11.00 | 121.00 |
| 3 | 121.00 | 10 | 2.10 | 12.10 | 133.10 |
| 4 | 133.10 | 10 | 3.31 | 13.31 | 146.41 |
| 5 | 146.41 | 10 | 4.64 | 14.64 | 161.05 |
| | | Total £50 simple interest | Total £11.05 compound interest | Total £61.05 interest | |

**Table 4.1** Future value of £100 at 10 per cent

FIGURE
4.1

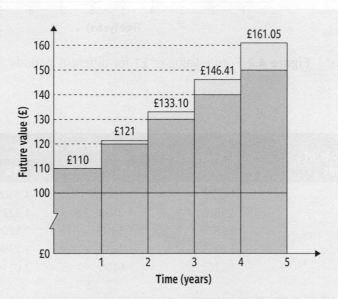

Growth of £100 original amount at 10% per year. The pink shaded area shows the simple interest. The green shaded area represents the portion of the total that results from compounding of interest.

**Figure 4.1** Future value, simple interest and compound interest

Figure 4.1 illustrates the growth of the compound interest in Table 4.1. Notice how the simple interest is constant each year, but the amount of compound interest you earn gets bigger every year. The amount of the compound interest keeps increasing because more and more interest builds up and there is thus more to compound.

Future values depend critically on the assumed interest rate, particularly for long-lived investments. Figure 4.2 illustrates this relationship by plotting the growth of £1 for different rates and lengths of time. Notice that the future value of £1 after 10 years is about £6.20 at a 20 per cent rate, but it is only about £2.60 at 10 per cent. In this case, doubling the interest rate more than doubles the future value.

To solve future value problems, we need to come up with the relevant future value factors. There are several different ways of doing this. In our example, we could have multiplied 1.1 by itself five times. This would work just fine, but it would get to be very tedious for, say, a 30-year investment.

FIGURE
**4.2**

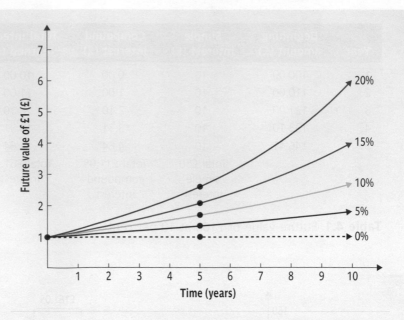

**Figure 4.2** Future value of £1 for different periods and rates

TABLE
**4.2**

| Number of periods | Interest rate (%) | | | |
|---|---|---|---|---|
| | 5 | 10 | 15 | 20 |
| 1 | 1.0500 | 1.1000 | 1.1500 | 1.2000 |
| 2 | 1.1025 | 1.2100 | 1.3225 | 1.4400 |
| 3 | 1.1576 | 1.3310 | 1.5209 | 1.7280 |
| 4 | 1.2155 | 1.4641 | 1.7490 | 2.0736 |
| 5 | 1.2763 | 1.6105 | 2.0114 | 2.4883 |

**Table 4.2** Future value interest factors

Fortunately, there are several easier ways to get future value factors. Most calculators have a key labelled '$y^x$.' You can usually just enter 1.1, press this key, enter 5, and press the '=' key to get the answer. This is an easy way to calculate future value factors, because it's quick and accurate.

Alternatively, you can use a table that contains future value factors for some common interest rates and time periods. Table 4.2 contains some of these factors. Table A.1 in the appendix at the end of the book contains a much larger set. To use the table, find the column that corresponds to 10 per cent. Then look down the rows until you come to five periods. You should find the factor that we calculated, 1.6105.

Tables such these are not as common as they once were, because they pre-date inexpensive calculators or spreadsheets, and are available only for a relatively small number of rates. Interest rates are often quoted to three or four decimal places, so the tables needed to deal with these accurately would be quite large. As a result, the real world has moved away from using them. We shall emphasize the use of a calculator or spreadsheet in this chapter.

These tables still serve a useful purpose, though. To make sure you are doing the calculations correctly, pick a factor from the table and then calculate it yourself to see that you get the same answer. There are plenty of numbers to choose from.

# Compound Interest

**EXAMPLE 4.2**

You've located an investment that pays 12 per cent per year. That rate sounds good to you, so you invest €400. How much will you have in three years? How much will you have in seven years? At the end of seven years, how much interest will you have earned? How much of that interest results from compounding?

Based on our discussion, we can calculate the future value factor for 12 per cent and three years as follows:

$$(1 + r)^t = 1.12^3 = 1.4049$$

Your €400 thus grows to

$$€400 \times 1.4049 = €561.97$$

After seven years you will have

$$€400 \times 1.12^7 = €400 \times 2.2107 = €884.27$$

Thus you will more than double your money over seven years.

Because you invested €400, the interest in the €884.27 future value is €884.27 − 400 = €484.27. At 12 per cent your €400 investment earns €400 × 0.12 = €48 in simple interest every year. Over seven years the simple interest thus totals 7 × €48 = €336. The other €484.27 − 336 = €148.27 is from compounding.

The effect of compounding is not great over short time periods, but it really starts to add up as the horizon grows. To take an extreme case, suppose one of your more frugal ancestors had invested £5 for you at a 6 per cent interest rate 200 years ago. How much would you have today? The future value factor is a substantial $1.06^{200} = 115,125.90$ (you won't find this one in a table), so you would have £5 × 115,125.90 = £575,629.52 today. Notice that the simple interest is just £5 × 0.06 = £0.30 per year. After 200 years, this amounts to £60. The rest is from reinvesting. Such is the power of compound interest!

# How Much for That Island?

**EXAMPLE 4.3**

To further illustrate the effect of compounding for long horizons, consider the case of Peter Minuit and the American Indians. In 1626 Minuit bought all of Manhattan Island for about $24 in goods and trinkets. This sounds cheap, but the Indians may have received the better end of the deal. To see why, suppose the Indians had sold the goods and invested the $24 at 10 per cent. How much would it be worth today?

About 385 years have passed since the transaction. At 10 per cent, $24 will grow by quite a bit over that time. How much? The future value factor is roughly

$$(1 + r)^t = 1.1^{385} \approx 8,600,000,000,000,000$$

That is, 8.6 followed by 14 zeros. The future value is thus of the order of $24 × 8.6 = $206 *quadrillion* (give or take a few hundreds of trillions).

Well, $206 quadrillion is a lot of money. How much? If you had it, you could buy the United States. All of it. Cash. With money left over to buy Canada, Mexico and the rest of the world, for that matter.

This example is something of an exaggeration, of course. In 1626 it would not have been easy to locate an investment that would pay 10 per cent every year without fail for the next 385 years.

## A Note About Compound Growth

If you are considering depositing money in an interest-bearing account, then the interest rate on that account is just the rate at which your money grows, assuming you don't remove any of it. If that rate is 10 per cent, then each year you simply have 10 per cent more money than you had the year before. In this case the interest rate is just an example of a compound growth rate.

The way we calculated future values is actually quite general, and lets you answer some other types of question related to growth. For example, your company currently has 10,000 employees. You've estimated that the number of employees grows by 3 per cent per year. How many employees will there be in five years? Here, we start with 10,000 people instead of pounds or euros, and we don't think of the growth rate as an interest rate, but the calculation is exactly the same:

$$10{,}000 \times 1.03^5 = 10{,}000 \times 1.1593 = 11{,}593 \text{ employees}$$

There will be about 1,593 net new hires over the coming five years.

To give another example, according to Reuters (a leading supplier of business information for investors), Arcelormittal SA's 2008 sales were about $124 billion. Suppose sales are projected to increase at a rate of 15 per cent per year. What will Arcelormittal's sales be in the year 2013 if this is correct? Verify for yourself that the answer is about $249 billion – just over twice as large.

## EXAMPLE 4.4 — Dividend Growth

In 2008 British Sky Broadcasting paid a cash dividend of £0.176 per share. You believe the dividend will be increased by 4 per cent each year indefinitely. How big will the dividend be in eight years?

Here we have a cash dividend growing because it is being increased by management; but once again the calculation is the same:

$$\text{Future value} = £0.176 \times 1.04^8 = £0.176 \times 1.3686 = £0.2409$$

The dividend will grow by £0.0649 over that period. Dividend growth is a subject we shall return to in a later chapter.

### CONCEPT QUESTIONS

4.1a   What do we mean by the future value of an investment?

4.1b   What does it mean to compound interest? How does compound interest differ from simple interest?

4.1c   In general, what is the future value of €1 invested at $r$ per period for $t$ periods?

## 4.2 Present Value and Discounting

When we discuss future value, we are thinking of questions such as: What will my €2,000 investment grow to if it earns a 6.5 per cent return every year for the next six years? The answer to this question is what we call the future value of €2,000 invested at 6.5 per cent for six years (verify that the answer is about €2,918).

Another type of question that comes up even more often is obviously related to future value. Suppose you need to have €10,000 in 10 years, and you can earn 6.5 per cent on your money. How much do you have to invest today to reach your goal? You can verify that the answer is €5,327.26. How do we know this? Read on.

## The Single-Period Case

We've seen that the future value of £1 invested for one year at 10 per cent is £1.10. We now ask a slightly different question: how much do we have to invest today at 10 per cent to get £1 in one year? In other words, we know the future value here is £1, but what is the **present value (PV)**? The answer isn't too hard to figure out. Whatever we invest today will be 1.1 times bigger at the end of the year. Because we need £1 at the end of the year:

**present value (PV)**
The current value of future cash flows discounted at the appropriate discount rate.

$$\text{Present value} \times 1.1 = \text{£1}$$

Or solving for the present value:

$$\text{Present value} = \text{£}1/1.1 = \text{£}0.909$$

In this case the present value is the answer to the following question: what amount, invested today, will grow to £1 in one year if the interest rate is 10 per cent? Present value is thus just the reverse of future value. Instead of compounding the money forward into the future, we **discount** it back to the present.

**discount**
Calculate the present value of some future amount.

---

**EXAMPLE 4.5**

## Single-Period PV

Suppose you need €400 to buy textbooks next year. You can earn 7 per cent on your money. How much do you have to put up today?

We need to know the PV of €400 in one year at 7 per cent. Proceeding as in the previous example:

$$\text{Present value} \times 1.07 = \text{€}400$$

We can now solve for the present value:

$$\text{Present value} = \text{€}400 \times (1/1.07) = \text{€}373.83$$

Thus €373.83 is the present value. Again, this just means that investing this amount for one year at 7 per cent will give you a future value of €400.

---

From our examples, the present value of £1 to be received in one period is generally given as follows:

$$PV = \text{£}1 \times \left(\frac{1}{1+r}\right)$$
$$= \frac{\text{£}1}{1+r}$$

We next examine how to get the present value of an amount to be paid in two or more periods into the future.

## Present Values for Multiple Periods

Suppose you need to have €1,000 in two years. If you can earn 7 per cent, how much do you have to invest to make sure you have the €1,000 when you need it? In other words, what is the present value of €1,000 in two years if the relevant rate is 7 per cent?

Based on your knowledge of future values, you know the amount invested must grow to €1,000 over the two years. In other words, it must be the case that:

$$€1,000 = PV \times 1.07 \times 1.07$$
$$= PV \times 1.07^2$$
$$= PV \times 1.1449$$

Given this, we can solve for the present value:

$$\text{Present value} = €1,000/1.1449 = €873.44$$

Therefore €873.44 is the amount you must invest to achieve your goal.

---

**EXAMPLE 4.6**

## Saving Up

You would like to buy a new car. You have £50,000 or so, but the car costs £68,500. If you can earn 9 per cent, how much do you have to invest today to buy the car in two years? Do you have enough? Assume the price will stay the same.

What we need to know is the present value of £68,500 to be paid in two years, assuming a 9 per cent rate. Based on our discussion, this is

$$PV = £68,500/1.09^2 = £68,500/1.1881 = £57,655.08$$

You're still about £7,655 short, even if you're willing to wait two years.

---

As you have probably recognized by now, calculating present values is quite similar to calculating future values, and the general result looks much the same. The present value of £1 to be received $t$ periods into the future at a discount rate of $r$ is

$$PV = £1 \times \left[ \frac{1}{(1 + r)^t} \right]$$

$$= \frac{£1}{(1 + r)^t}$$

(4.2)

**discount rate**
The rate used to calculate the present value of future cash flows.

**discounted cash flow (DCF) valuation**
Calculating the present value of a future cash flow to determine its value today.

The quantity in brackets, $1/(1 + r)^t$, goes by several different names. Because it's used to discount a future cash flow, it is often called a *discount factor*. With this name, it is not surprising that the rate used in the calculation is often called the **discount rate**. We shall tend to call it this in talking about present values. The quantity in brackets is also called the *present value interest factor* (or just *present value factor*) for £1 at $r$ per cent for $t$ periods, and is sometimes abbreviated as PVIF($r$, $t$). Finally, calculating the present value of a future cash flow to determine its worth today is commonly called **discounted cash flow (DCF) valuation**.

To illustrate, suppose you need €1,000 in three years. You can earn 15 per cent on your money. How much do you have to invest today? To find out, we have to determine the present value of €1,000 in three years at 15 per cent. We do this by discounting €1,000 back three periods at 15 per cent. With these numbers, the discount factor is

$$1/(1 + 0.15)^3 = 1/1.5209 = 0.6575$$

The amount you must invest is thus

$$€1,000 \times 0.6575 = €657.50$$

| TABLE 4.3 | Number of periods | Interest rate (%) | | | |
|---|---|---|---|---|---|
| | | 5 | 10 | 15 | 20 |
| | 1 | 0.9524 | 0.9091 | 0.8696 | 0.8333 |
| | 2 | 0.9070 | 0.8264 | 0.7561 | 0.6944 |
| | 3 | 0.8638 | 0.7513 | 0.6575 | 0.5787 |
| | 4 | 0.8227 | 0.6830 | 0.5718 | 0.4823 |
| | 5 | 0.7835 | 0.6209 | 0.4972 | 0.4019 |

**Table 4.3** Present value interest factors

We say that €657.50 is the present or discounted value of €1,000 to be received in three years at 15 per cent.

There are tables for present value factors just as there are tables for future value factors, and you use them in the same way (if you use them at all). Table 4.3 contains a small set. A much larger set can be found in Table A.2 in the book's appendix.

In Table 4.3 the discount factor we just calculated (0.6575) can be found by looking down the column labelled '15%' until you come to the third row.

**EXAMPLE 4.7**

# Deceptive Advertising?

Businesses sometimes advertise that you should 'Come try our product. If you do, we'll give you €100 just for coming by!' If you read the fine print, what you find out is that they will give you a savings certificate that will pay you €100 in 25 years or so. If the going interest rate on such certificates is 10 per cent per year, how much are they really giving you today?

What you're actually getting is the present value of €100 to be paid in 25 years. If the discount rate is 10 per cent per year, then the discount factor is

$$1/1.1^{25} = 1/10.8347 = 0.0923$$

This tells you that a euro in 25 years is worth a little more than nine cents today, assuming a 10 per cent discount rate. Given this, the promotion is actually paying you about $0.0923 \times €100 = €9.23$. Maybe this is enough to draw customers, but it's not €100.

As the length of time until payment grows, present values decline. As Example 4.7 illustrates, present values tend to become small as the time horizon grows. If you look out far enough, they will always approach zero. Also, for a given length of time, the higher the discount rate is, the lower is the present value. Put another way, present values and discount rates are inversely related. Increasing the discount rate decreases the PV and vice versa.

The relationship between time, discount rates, and present values is illustrated in Fig. 4.3. Notice that by the time we get to 10 years, the present values are all substantially smaller than the future amounts.

**CONCEPT QUESTIONS**

4.2a  What do we mean by the present value of an investment?
4.2b  The process of discounting a future amount back to the present is the opposite of doing what?
4.2c  What do we mean by discounted cash flow, or DCF, valuation?
4.2d  In general, what is the present value of £1 to be received in $t$ periods, assuming a discount rate of $r$ per period?

FIGURE
**4.3**

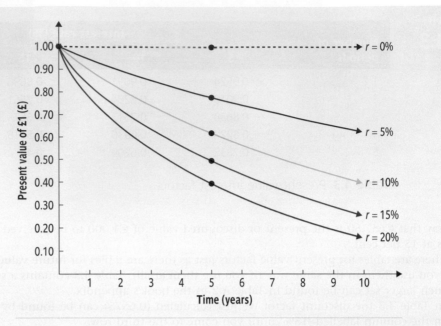

**Figure 4.3** Present value of £1 for different periods and rates

## 4.3 More about Present and Future Values

If you look back at the expressions we came up with for present and future values, you will see a simple relationship between the two. We explore this relationship and some related issues in this section.

### Present versus Future Value

What we called the present value factor is just the reciprocal of (that is, 1 divided by) the future value factor:

$$\text{Future value factor} = (1 + r)^t$$
$$\text{Present value factor} = 1/(1 + r)^t$$

In fact, the easy way to calculate a present value factor on many calculators is to first calculate the future value factor and then press the '1/ x' key to flip it over.

If we let $FV_t$ stand for the future value after $t$ periods, then the relationship between future value and present value can be written simply as one of the following:

$$PV \times (1 + r)^t = FV_t$$
$$PV = \frac{FV_t}{(1 + r)^t}$$
$$= FV_t \times \left[\frac{1}{(1 + r)^t}\right]$$
$$= FV_t \times (1 + r)^{-t}$$

(4.3)

This last result we shall call the *basic present value equation*. We shall use it throughout the text. A number of variations come up, but this simple equation underlies many of the most important ideas in corporate finance.

## Evaluating Investments

**EXAMPLE 4.8**

To give you an idea of how we shall be using present and future values, consider the following simple investment. Your company proposes to buy an asset for £335. This investment is very safe. You would sell off the asset in three years for £400. You know you could invest the £335 elsewhere at 10 per cent with very little risk. What do you think of the proposed investment?

This is not a good investment. Why not? Because you can invest the £335 elsewhere at 10 per cent. If you do, after three years it will grow to

$$£335 \times (1 + r)^t = £335 \times 1.1^3$$
$$= £335 \times 1.331$$
$$= £445.89$$

Because the proposed investment pays out only £400, it is not as good as other alternatives we have. Another way of seeing the same thing is to notice that the present value of £400 in three years at 10 per cent is

$$£400 \times \left[ \frac{1}{(1+r)^t} \right] = £400/1.1^3$$
$$= £400/1.331$$
$$= £300.53$$

This tells us that we have to invest only about £300 to get £400 in three years, not £335. We shall return to this type of analysis later on.

## Determining the Discount Rate

We frequently need to determine what discount rate is implicit in an investment. We can do this by looking at the basic present value equation:

$$PV = \frac{FV_t}{(1+r)^t}$$

There are only four parts to this equation: the present value (PV), the future value (FV$_t$), the discount rate ($r$), and the life of the investment ($t$). Given any three of these, we can always find the fourth.

## Finding *r* for a Single-Period Investment

**EXAMPLE 4.9**

You are considering a one-year investment. If you put up €1,250, you will get back €1,350. What rate is this investment paying?

First, in this single-period case, the answer is fairly obvious. You are getting a total of €100 in addition to your €1,250. The implicit rate on this investment is thus €100/1,250 = 8 per cent.

More formally, from the basic present value equation, the present value (the amount you must put up today) is €1,250. The future value (what the present value grows to) is €1,350. The time involved is one period, so we have

$$€1,250 = €1,350/(1 + r)^1$$
$$1 + r = €1,350/1,250 = 1.08$$
$$r = 8\%$$

In this simple case, of course, there was no need to go through this calculation. But as we describe next, it gets a little harder with more than one period.

To illustrate what happens with multiple periods, let's say we are offered an investment that costs us £100 and will double our money in eight years. To compare this with other investments, we should like to know what discount rate is implicit in these numbers. This discount rate is called the *rate of return*, or sometimes just the *return*, on the investment. In this case we have a present value of £100, a future value of £200 (double our money), and an eight-year life. To calculate the return, we can write the basic present value equation as

$$PV = \frac{FV_t}{(1+r)^t}$$

$$£100 = \frac{£200}{(1+r)^8}$$

It could also be written as

$$(1+r)^8 = £200/100 = 2$$

We now need to solve for *r*. There are three ways we could do it:

1 Use a financial calculator or a spreadsheet.

2 Solve the equation for 1 + *r* by taking the eighth root of both sides. Because this is the same thing as raising both sides to the power of 1/8 or 0.125, this is actually easy to do with the '$y^x$' key on a calculator. Just enter 2, then press '$y^x$', enter 0.125, and press the '=' key. The eighth root should be about 1.09, which implies that *r* is 9 per cent.

3 Use a future value table. The future value factor after eight years is equal to 2. If you look across the row corresponding to eight periods in Table A.1, you will see that a future value factor of 2 corresponds to the 9 per cent column, again implying that the return here is 9 per cent.

Actually, in this particular example there is a useful 'back of the envelope' means of solving for *r*: the Rule of 72. For reasonable rates of return, the time it takes to double your money is given approximately by 72/*r*%. In our example this means that 72/*r*% = 8 years, implying that *r* is 9 per cent, as we calculated. This rule is fairly accurate for discount rates in the range 5 to 20 per cent.

---

**EXAMPLE 4.10**

## Comic Collectibles as Investments

In January 2010 *Amazing Fantasy* No. 15, the first Marvel comic in which Spiderman appeared, was valued at $50,000 in mint condition. 'Experts' on such collectibles often argue that a mint condition *Amazing Fantasy* No. 15 would double in value to $100,000 by the end of 2019.

So would the comic have been a good investment? By the Rule of 72, you already know the experts were predicting that the comic would double in value in 10 years; so the return predicted would be about 72/10 = 7.2 per cent per year, which is only so-so.

---

At one time at least, a rule of thumb in the rarefied world of fine art collecting was 'Your money back in 5 years, double your money in 10 years.' Given this, let's see how an investment stacked up. In 1998 the Alberto Giacometti bronze statue *Homme Qui Marche III* sold for €2,016,000. Five years later the statue was sold again, walking out of the door at a price of €2,740,000. How did the seller do?

The rule of thumb has us doubling our money in 10 years; so, from the Rule of 72, we have that 7.2 per cent per year was the norm. The statue was resold in almost exactly five years. The present value is €2,016,000, and the future value is €2,740,000. We need to solve for the unknown rate, r, as follows:

$$€2,016,000 = \frac{€2,740,000}{(1+r)^5}$$
$$(1+r)^5 = 1.3591$$

Solving for r, we find that the seller earned about 6.33 per cent per year – less than the 7.2 per cent rule of thumb. At least the seller made his money back.

## Saving for University

**EXAMPLE 4.11**

You estimate that you will need about £80,000 to send your child to university in eight years. You have about £35,000 now. If you can earn 20 per cent per year, will you make it? At what rate will you just reach your goal?

If you can earn 20 per cent, the future value of your £35,000 in eight years will be

$$FV = £35,000 \times 1.20^8 = £35,000 \times 4.2998 = £150,493.59$$

So you will make it easily. The minimum rate is the unknown r in the following:

$$FV = £35,000 \times (1+r)^8 = £80,000$$
$$(1+r)^8 = £80,000/35,000 = 2.2857$$

Therefore the future value factor is 2.2857. Looking at the row in Table A.1 that corresponds to eight periods, we see that our future value factor is roughly halfway between the ones shown for 10 per cent (2.1436) and 12 per cent (2.4760), so you will just reach your goal if you earn approximately 11 per cent. To get the exact answer, we would solve for r:

$$(1+r)^8 = £80,000/35,000 = 2.2857$$
$$1 + r = 2.2857^{(1/8)} = 2.2857^{0.125} = 1.1089$$
$$r = 10.89\%$$

## Only 18,262.5 Days to Retirement

**EXAMPLE 4.12**

You would like to retire in 50 years as a millionaire. If you have €10,000 today, what rate of return do you need to earn to achieve your goal?

The future value is €1,000,000. The present value is €10,000, and there are 50 years until payment. We need to calculate the unknown discount rate in the following:

$$€10,000 = €1,000,000/(1 + r)^{50}$$
$$(1 + r)^{50} = 100$$

The future value factor is thus 100. You can verify that the implicit rate is about 9.65 per cent.

## Finding the Number of Periods

Suppose we are interested in purchasing an asset that costs £50,000. We currently have £25,000. If we can earn 12 per cent on this £25,000, how long until we have the £50,000? Finding the answer involves solving for the last variable in the basic present value equation, the number of periods. You already know how to get an approximate answer to this particular problem. Notice that we need to double our money. From the Rule of 72, this will take about $72/12 = 6$ years at 12 per cent.

To come up with the exact answer, we can again manipulate the basic present value equation. The present value is £25,000, and the future value is £50,000. With a 12 per cent discount rate, the basic equation takes one of the following forms:

$$£25,000 = £50,000/1.12^t$$
$$£50,000/25,000 = 1.12^t = 2$$

We thus have a future value factor of 2 for a 12 per cent rate. We now need to solve for $t$. If you look down the column in Table A.1 that corresponds to 12 per cent, you will see that a future value factor of 1.9738 occurs at six periods. It will thus take about six years, as we calculated. To get the exact answer, we have to explicitly solve for $t$. If you do this, you will see that the answer is 6.1163 years, so our approximation was quite close in this case.

---

**EXAMPLE 4.13**

# Waiting for Godot

You've been saving up to buy Godot Ltd. The total cost will be £10 million. You currently have about £2.3 million. If you can earn 5 per cent on your money, how long will you have to wait? At 16 per cent, how long must you wait?

At 5 per cent, you'll have to wait a long time. From the basic present value equation:

$$£2.3 \text{ million} = £10 \text{ million}/1.05^t$$
$$1.05^t = 4.35$$
$$t = 30 \text{ years}$$

At 16 per cent, things are a little better. Verify for yourself that it will take about 10 years.

---

# Spreadsheet Strategies

### Using a Spreadsheet for Time Value of Money Calculations

More and more, businesspeople from many different areas (not just finance and accounting) rely on spreadsheets to do all the different types of calculation that come up in the real world. As a result, in this section we shall show you how to use a spreadsheet to handle the various time value of money problems we presented in this chapter. We shall use Microsoft Excel™, but the commands are similar for other types of software. We assume you are already familiar with basic spreadsheet operations.

As we have seen, you can solve for any one of the following four potential unknowns: future value, present value, the discount rate, or the number of periods. With a spreadsheet, there is a separate formula for each. In Excel, these are as follows:

| To find | Enter this formula |
|---|---|
| Future value | = FV (rate,nper,pmt,pv) |
| Present value | = PV (rate,nper,pmt,fv) |
| Discount rate | = RATE (nper,pmt,pv,fv) |
| Number of periods | = NPER (rate,pmt,pv,fv) |

In these formulae, pv and fv are present and future value, nper is the number of periods, and rate is the discount, or interest, rate.

Two things are a little tricky here. First, the spreadsheet requires that the rate be entered as a decimal. Second, you have to put a negative sign on either the present value or the future value to solve for the rate or the number of periods. For the same reason, if you solve for a present value, the answer will have a negative sign unless you input a negative future value. The same is true when you compute a future value.

To illustrate how you might use these formulae, we shall go back to an example in the chapter. If you invest £25,000 at 12 per cent per year, how long until you have £50,000? You might set up a spreadsheet like this:

| | A | B | C | D | E | F | G | H |
|---|---|---|---|---|---|---|---|---|
| 1 | Present Value (pv) | £25,000 | | Periods | 6.116255 | | | |
| 2 | Future Value (fv) | £50,000 | | | | | | |
| 3 | Rate (rate) | 12% | | Formula in cell E1 is =NPER (B3,0,-B1,B2) | | | | |
| 4 | | | | | | | | |
| 5 | | | | | | | | |

This example finishes our introduction to basic time value concepts. Table 4.4 summarizes present and future value calculations for future reference.

**TABLE 4.4**

**Symbols**

PV = Present value; what future cash flows are worth today

$FV_t$ = Future value; what cash flows are worth in the future

R   = Interest rate, rate of return, or discount rate per period – typically, but not always, one year

T   = Number of periods – typically, but not always, the number of years

C   = Cash amount

**Future value of C invested at r per cent for t periods**

$FV_t = C \times (1 + r)^t$
The term $(1 + r)^t$ is called the *future value factor*.

**Present value of C to be received in t periods at r per cent per period**

$PV = C/(1 + r)^t$
The term $1/(1 + r)^t$ is called the *present value factor*.

**The basic present value equation giving the relationship between present and future value**

$PV = FV_t/(1 + r)^t$

**Table 4.4** Summary of time value calculations

**CONCEPT QUESTIONS**

4.3a   What is the basic present value equation?

4.3b   What is the Rule of 72?

## Summary and Conclusions

This chapter has introduced you to the basic principles of present value and discounted cash flow valuation. In it, we explained a number of things about the time value of money, including these:

1. For a given rate of return, we can determine the value at some point in the future of an investment made today by calculating the future value of that investment.

2. We can determine the current worth of a future cash flow or series of cash flows for a given rate of return by calculating the present value of the cash flow(s) involved.

3. The relationship between present value (PV) and future value (FV) for a given rate $r$ and time $t$ is given by the basic present value equation:

$$PV = \frac{FV_t}{(1 + r)^t}$$

As we have shown, it is possible to find any one of the four components (PV, $FV_t$, $r$ or $t$) given the other three.

The principles developed in this chapter will figure prominently in the chapters to come. The reason for this is that most investments, whether they involve real assets or financial assets, can be analysed using the discounted cash flow (DCF) approach. As a result, the DCF approach is broadly applicable and widely used in practice. Before going on, therefore, you might want to do some of the problems that follow.

## Chapter Review and Self-Test Problems

4.1 **Calculating Future Values** Assume you deposit 10,000 Swedish kroner today in an account that pays 6 per cent interest. How much will you have in five years?

4.2 **Calculating Present Values** Suppose you have just celebrated your 19th birthday. A rich uncle has set up a trust fund for you that will pay you £150,000 when you turn 30. If the relevant discount rate is 9 per cent, how much is this fund worth today?

4.3 **Calculating Rates of Return** You've been offered an investment that will double your money in 10 years. What rate of return are you being offered? Check your answer using the Rule of 72.

4.4 **Calculating the Number of Periods** You've been offered an investment that will pay you 9 per cent per year. If you invest £15,000, how long until you have £30,000? How long until you have £45,000?

## Answers to Chapter Review and Self-Test Problems

4.1 We need to calculate the future value of SKr10,000 at 6 per cent for five years. The future value factor is

$$1.06^5 = 1.3382$$

The future value is thus SKr10,000 × 1.3382 = SKr13,382.26.

4.2   We need the present value of £150,000 to be paid in 11 years at 9 per cent. The discount factor is

$$1/1.09^{11} = 1/2.5804 = 0.3875$$

The present value is thus about £58,130.

4.3   Suppose you invest €1,000. You will have €2,000 in 10 years with this investment. So €1,000 is the amount you have today, or the present value, and €2,000 is the amount you will have in 10 years, or the future value. From the basic present value equation we have

$$€2,000 = €1,000 \times (1 + r)^{10}$$
$$2 = (1 + r)^{10}$$

From here, we need to solve for $r$, the unknown rate. As shown in the chapter, there are several different ways to do this. We shall take the 10th root of 2 (by raising 2 to the power of 1/10):

$$2^{(1/10)} = 1 + r$$
$$1.0718 = 1 + r$$
$$r = 7.18\%$$

Using the Rule of 72, we have $72/t = r\%$, or $72/10 = 7.2\%$, so our answer looks good (remember that the Rule of 72 is only an approximation).

4.4   The basic equation is this:

$$£30,000 = £15,000 \times (1 + 0.09)^{t}$$
$$2 = (1 + 0.09)^{t}$$

If we solve for $t$, we find that $t = 8.04$ years. Using the Rule of 72, we get $72/9 = 8$ years, so once again our answer looks good. To get £45,000, verify for yourself that you will have to wait 12.75 years.

## Concepts Review and Critical Thinking Questions

1   **Present Value [LO2]**   The basic present value equation has four parts. What are they?

2   **Compounding [LO1, LO2]**   What is compounding? What is discounting?

3   **Compounding and Period [LO1]**   As you increase the length of time involved, what happens to future values? What happens to present values?

4   **Compounding and Interest Rates [LO1]**   What happens to a future value if you increase the rate $r$? What happens to a present value?

5   **Ethical Considerations [LO2]**   Take a look back at Example 4.7. Is it deceptive advertising? Is it unethical to advertise a future value like this without a disclaimer?

To answer the next five questions, consider a security issue by Spanish Word Ltd that provides that, in return for receiving £24,099 today from investors, they will pay back £100,000 in 30 years.

6   **Time Value of Money [LO2]**   Why would Spanish Word be willing to accept such a small amount today (£24,099) in exchange for a promise to repay about four times that amount (£100,000) in the future?

7   **Call Provisions [LO2]**   Spanish Word has the right to buy back the securities on the anniversary date at a price established when the securities were issued (this feature is a term of this particular deal). What impact does this feature have on the desirability of this security as an investment?

▶

> 8   **Time Value of Money [LO2]**   Would you be willing to pay £24,099 today in exchange for £100,000 in 30 years? What would be the key considerations in answering yes or no? Would your answer depend on who is making the promise to repay?
>
> 9   **Investment Comparison [LO2]**   Suppose that when Spanish Word offered the security for £24,099 the British government had offered an essentially identical security. Do you think it would have had a higher or lower price? Why?
>
> 10  **Length of Investment [LO2]**   The Spanish Word security is bought and sold on the London Stock Exchange. If you looked at the price today, do you think the price would exceed the £24,099 original price? Why? If you looked in the year 2021, do you think the price would be higher or lower than today's price? Why?

## connect Questions and Problems

BASIC
1–15

1   **Simple Interest versus Compound Interest [LO1]**   First City Bank pays 9 per cent simple interest on its savings account balances, whereas Second City Bank pays 9 per cent interest compounded annually. If you made a £5,000 deposit in each bank, how much more money would you earn from your Second City Bank account at the end of 10 years?

2   **Calculating Future Values [LO1]**   For each of the following, compute the future value:

| Present value (£) | Years | Interest rate (%) | Future value (£) |
|---|---|---|---|
| 2,250 | 10 | 10 | |
| 8,752 | 8 | 8 | |
| 76,355 | 16 | 17 | |
| 183,796 | 3 | 7 | |

3   **Calculating Present Values [LO2]**   For each of the following, compute the present value:

| Present value (£) | Years | Interest rate (%) | Future value (£) |
|---|---|---|---|
| | 6 | 8 | 15,451 |
| | 7 | 12 | 51,557 |
| | 23 | 11 | 886,073 |
| | 18 | 10 | 550,164 |

4   **Calculating Interest Rates [LO3]**   Solve for the unknown interest rate in each of the following:

| Present value (£) | Years | Interest rate (%) | Future value (£) |
|---|---|---|---|
| 240 | 3 | | 297 |
| 360 | 11 | | 1,080 |
| 39,000 | 12 | | 185,382 |
| 38,261 | 50 | | 531,618 |

5  **Calculating the Number of Periods [LO4]**  Solve for the unknown number of years in each of the following:

| Present value (NKr) | Years | Interest rate (%) | Future value (NKr) |
|---|---|---|---|
| 560 | | 10 | 1,284 |
| 810 | | 7 | 4,341 |
| 18,400 | | 15 | 364,518 |
| 21,500 | | 12 | 173,439 |

6  **Calculating Interest Rates [LO3]**  Assume the total cost of a university education will be €290,000 when your child enters college in 18 years. You currently have €40,000 to invest. What annual rate of interest must you earn on your investment to cover the cost of your child's university education?

7  **Calculating the Number of Periods [LO4]**  At 6 per cent interest, how long does it take to double your money? To quadruple it?

8  **Calculating Interest Rates [LO3]**  In 2010 the average price per metre for owner-occupied flats in Copenhagen was about 23,000 Danish kroner. In 1995 the average price was around 6,000 Danish kroner. What was the annual increase in selling price?

9  **Calculating the Number of Periods [LO4]**  You're trying to save to buy a new €170,000 Ferrari. You have €40,000 today that can be invested at your bank. The bank pays 5 per cent annual interest on its accounts. How long will it be before you have enough to buy the car?

10  **Calculating Present Values [LO2]**  Imprudential plc has an unfunded pension liability of £800 million that must be paid in 20 years. To assess the value of the firm's equity, financial analysts want to discount this liability back to the present. If the relevant discount rate is 7 per cent, what is the present value of this liability?

11  **Calculating Present Values [LO2]**  You have just received notification that you have won the €1 million first prize in the Euro Lottery. However, the prize will be awarded on your 100th birthday (assuming you're around to collect), 80 years from now. What is the present value of your windfall if the appropriate discount rate is 12 per cent?

12  **Calculating Future Values [LO1]**  Your coin collection contains fifty 1952 silver dollars. If your grandparents purchased them for their face value when they were new, how much will your collection be worth when you retire in 2057, assuming they appreciate at a 4.5 per cent annual rate?

13  **Calculating Interest Rates and Future Values [LO1, LO3]**  In 1968 prize money for the Wimbledon Tennis Championships was first awarded. The winner of the men's singles was £2,000 and for the ladies' singles it was £750. In 2009 both winners received £850,000. What was the percentage increase per year in the winner's cheque for men and women over this period? If the winner's prize increases at the same rate, what will the men's and ladies' singles tournament winners receive in 2040? Do you think this will actually happen? Explain.

14  **Calculating Interest Rates [LO3]**  In 2008 a gold Morgan dollar minted in 1895 sold for $43,125. For this to have been true, what rate of return did this coin return for the lucky numismatist?

15  **Calculating Rates of Return [LO3]**  On 8 February 2009 John Madejski, chairman of Reading Football Club, sold the Edgar Degas bronze sculpture *Petite Danseuse de Quatorze Ans* at auction for a world record price of £13.3 million. He bought the statue in 2004 for £5 million. What was his annual rate of return on this sculpture?

INTERMEDIATE

16–20

16 **Calculating Rates of Return [LO3]** Consider again the security issue by Spanish Word Ltd that in return for receiving £24,099 today from investors, they will pay back £100,000 in 30 years.

(a) Based on the £24,099 price, what rate was Spanish Word paying to borrow money?

(b) Suppose that in 2020 this security's price is £38,260. If an investor had purchased it for £24,099 in 2010 and sold it in 2020, what annual rate of return would she have earned?

(c) If an investor had purchased the security at market in 2020, and held it until it matured, what annual rate of return would she have earned?

17 **Calculating Present Values [LO2]** Suppose you are still committed to owning a €170,000 Ferrari (see Problem 9). If you believe your mutual fund can achieve a 12 per cent annual rate of return and you want to buy the car in 9 years on the day you turn 30, how much must you invest today?

18 **Calculating Future Values [LO1]** You have just made your first £4,000 contribution to your retirement account. Assuming you earn a 10 per cent rate of return and make no additional contributions, what will your account be worth when you retire in 45 years? What if you wait 10 years before contributing? (Does this suggest an investment strategy?)

19 **Calculating Future Values [LO1]** You are scheduled to receive £30,000 in two years. When you receive it, you will invest it for six more years at 8.4 per cent per year. How much will you have in eight years?

20 **Calculating the Number of Periods [LO4]** You expect to receive €10,000 at graduation in two years. You plan on investing it at 10 per cent until you have €75,000. How long will you have to wait from now?

To help you grasp the key concepts of this chapter check out the extra resources posted on the Online Learning Centre at **www.mcgraw-hill.co.uk/textbooks/hillier**

Among other helpful resources there are mini-cases tailored to individual chapters.

# CHAPTER 5

# Discounted Cash Flow Valuation

## KEY NOTATIONS

| | |
|---|---|
| APR | Annual percentage rate |
| C | Cash flow |
| EAR | Effective annual rate of return |
| g | Growth rate |
| m | Number of times interest is compounded a year |
| PVIFA | Present value interest factor for annuities |
| q | Quoted rate |
| r | Interest rate or discount rate |
| t | Number of periods |

## LEARNING OBJECTIVES

After studying this chapter, you should understand:

**LO1** How to determine the future and present value of investments with multiple cash flows.

**LO2** How loan payments are calculated, and how to find the interest rate on a loan.

**LO3** How loans are amortized or paid off.

**LO4** How interest rates are quoted (and misquoted).

THE SIGNING OF BIG-NAME ATHLETES is often accompanied by great fanfare, but the numbers are often misleading. For example, in 2009 footballer Cristiano Ronaldo reached a deal with Real Madrid, signing a contract with a reported value of £107 million. This amount was actually payable over six years, and consisted of £9.5 million in his first year, with a 25 per cent increase in salary each year for the remainder of his contract. Because his salary was paid over six years, we must consider the time value of money when considering the real value of Ronaldo's contract. How much did Cristiano Ronaldo really get? This chapter gives you the 'tools of knowledge' to answer this question.

In our previous chapter we covered the basics of discounted cash flow valuation. However, so far we have dealt only with single cash flows. In reality, most investments have multiple cash flows. For example, if Tesco is thinking of opening a new department store, there will be a large cash outlay in the beginning, and then cash inflows for many years. In this chapter, we begin to explore how to value such investments.

When you finish this chapter, you should have some very practical skills. For example, you will know how to calculate your own car payments or student loan payments. You will also be able to determine how long it will take to pay off a credit card if you make the minimum payment each month (a practice we do not recommend). We shall show you how to compare interest rates to determine which are the highest and which are the lowest, and we shall also show you how interest rates can be quoted in different – and at times deceptive – ways. Even financial securities, such as equities and bonds, can be valued using the techniques in this chapter.

## 5.1 Future and Present Values of Multiple Cash Flows

Thus far we have restricted our attention to either the future value of a lump sum present amount or the present value of some single future cash flow. In this section we begin to study ways to value multiple cash flows. We start with future value.

### Future Value with Multiple Cash Flows

Suppose you deposit €100 today in an account paying 8 per cent. In one year you will deposit another €100. How much will you have in two years? This particular problem is relatively easy. At the end of the first year you will have €108 plus the second €100 you deposit, for a total of €208. You leave this €208 on deposit at 8 per cent for another year. At the end of this second year, it is worth

$$€208 \times 1.08 = €224.64$$

Figure 5.1 is a *time line* that illustrates the process of calculating the future value of these two €100 deposits. Diagrams such as this are useful for solving complicated problems. Almost any time you are having trouble with a present or future value problem, drawing a time line will help you see what is happening.

In the first part of Fig. 5.1 we show the cash flows on the time line. The most important thing is that we write them down where they actually occur. Here, the first cash flow occurs today, which we label as time 0. We therefore put €100 at time 0 on the time line. The second €100 cash flow occurs one year from today, so we write it down at the point labelled as time 1. In the second part of Fig. 5.1 we calculate the future values, one period at a time, to come up with the final €224.64.

When we calculated the future value of the two €100 deposits, we simply calculated the balance as of the beginning of each year, and then rolled that amount forward to the next year. We could have done it another, quicker way. The first €100 is on deposit for two years at 8 per cent, so its future value is

$$€100 \times 1.08^2 = €100 \times 1.1664 = €116.64$$

The second €100 is on deposit for one year at 8 per cent, and its future value is thus

$$€100 \times 1.08 = €108$$

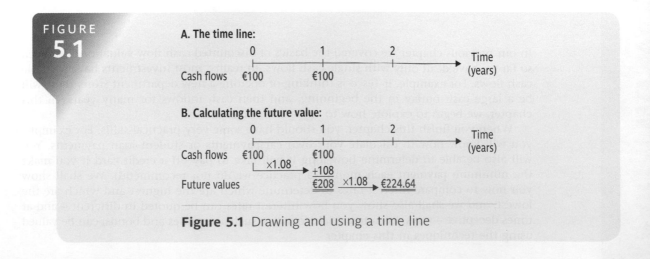

**Figure 5.1** Drawing and using a time line

FIGURE
5.2

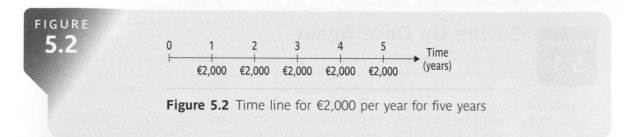

**Figure 5.2** Time line for €2,000 per year for five years

FIGURE
5.3

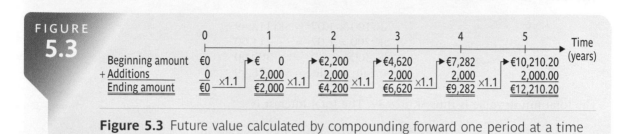

**Figure 5.3** Future value calculated by compounding forward one period at a time

FIGURE
5.4

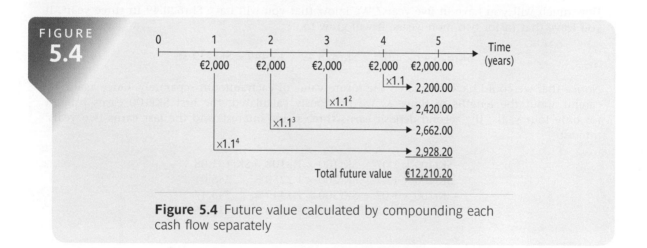

**Figure 5.4** Future value calculated by compounding each cash flow separately

The total future value, as we previously calculated, is equal to the sum of these two future values:

$$€116.64 + 108 = €224.64$$

Based on this example, there are two ways to calculate future values for multiple cash flows: (1) compound the accumulated balance forward one year at a time; or (2) calculate the future value of each cash flow first and then add them up. Both give the same answer, so you can do it either way.

To illustrate the two different ways of calculating future values, consider the future value of €2,000 invested at the end of each of the next five years. The current balance is zero, and the rate is 10 per cent. We first draw a time line, as shown in Fig. 5.2.

On the time line, notice that nothing happens until the end of the first year, when we make the first €2,000 investment. This first €2,000 earns interest for the next four (not five) years. Also notice that the last €2,000 is invested at the end of the fifth year, so it earns no interest at all.

Figure 5.3 illustrates the calculations involved if we compound the investment one period at a time. As illustrated, the future value is €12,210.20.

Figure 5.4 goes through the same calculations, but the second technique is used. Naturally, the answer is the same.

# Saving Up Once Again

**EXAMPLE 5.1**

If you deposit 100 Swedish kroner (SKr) in one year, SKr200 in two years, and SKr300 in three years, how much will you have in three years? How much of this is interest? How much will you have in five years if you don't add additional amounts? Assume a 7 per cent interest rate throughout.

We shall calculate the future value of each amount in three years. Notice that the SKr100 earns interest for two years, and the SKr200 earns interest for one year. The final SKr300 earns no interest. The future values are thus

$$SKr100 \times 1.07^2 = SKr114.49$$
$$SKr200 \times 1.07 = 214.00$$
$$+ SKr300 = \underline{300.00}$$
$$\text{Total future value} = \underline{SKr628.49}$$

The total future value is thus SKr628.49. The total interest is

$$SKr628.49 - (100 + 200 + 300) = SKr28.49$$

How much will you have in five years? We know that you will have SKr628.49 in three years. If you leave that in for two more years, it will grow to

$$SKr628.49 \times 1.07^2 = SKr628.49 \times 1.1449 = SKr719.56$$

Notice that we could have calculated the future value of each amount separately. Once again, be careful about the lengths of time. As we previously calculated, the first SKr100 earns interest for only four years, the second deposit earns three years' interest, and the last earns two years' interest:

$$SKr100 \times 1.07^4 = SKr100 \times 1.3108 = SKr131.08$$
$$SKr200 \times 1.07^3 = SKr200 \times 1.2250 = 245.01$$
$$+SKr300 \times 1.07^2 = SKr300 \times 1.1449 = \underline{343.47}$$
$$\text{Total future value} = \underline{SKr719.56}$$

## Present Value with Multiple Cash Flows

We often need to determine the present value of a series of future cash flows. As with future values, there are two ways we can do it. We can either discount back one period at a time, or we can just calculate the present values individually and add them up.

Suppose you need €1,000 in one year and €2,000 more in two years. If you can earn 9 per cent on your money, how much do you have to put up today to exactly cover these amounts in the future? In other words, what is the present value of the two cash flows at 9 per cent?

The present value of €2,000 in two years at 9 per cent is

$$€2,000/1.09^2 = €1,683.36$$

The present value of €1,000 in one year is

$$€1,000/1.09 = €917.43$$

Therefore the total present value is

$$€1,683.36 + 917.43 = €2,600.79$$

FIGURE
5.5

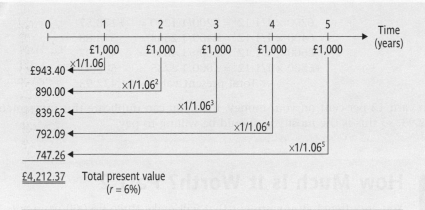

**Figure 5.5** Present value calculated by discounting each cash flow separately

FIGURE
5.6

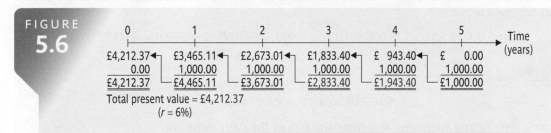

**Figure 5.6** Present value calculated by discounting back one period at a time

An alternative way of calculating present values for multiple future cash flows is to discount back to the present, one period at a time. To illustrate, suppose we had an investment that was going to pay £1,000 at the end of every year for the next five years. To find the present value, we could discount each £1,000 back to the present separately and then add them up. Figure 5.5 illustrates this approach for a 6 per cent discount rate; as shown, the answer is £4,212.37 (ignoring a small rounding error).

Alternatively, we could discount the last cash flow back one period and add it to the next-to-last cash flow:

$$(£1,000/1.06) + 1,000 = £943.40 + 1,000 = £1,943.40$$

We could then discount this amount back one period and add it to the year 3 cash flow:

$$(£1,943.40/1.06) + 1,000 = £1,833.40 + 1,000 = £2,833.40$$

This process could be repeated as necessary. Figure 5.6 illustrates this approach, and the remaining calculations.

## How Much Is It Worth?

EXAMPLE
5.2

You are offered an investment that will pay you £200 in one year, £400 the next year, £600 the next year, and £800 at the end of the fourth year. You can earn 12 per cent on similar investments. What is the most you should pay for this one?

We need to calculate the present value of these cash flows at 12 per cent. Taking them one at a time gives

$$£200 \times 1/1.12^1 = £200/1.1200 = \quad £178.57$$
$$£400 \times 1/1.12^2 = £400/1.2544 = \quad 318.88$$
$$£600 \times 1/1.12^3 = £600/1.4049 = \quad 427.07$$
$$+£800 \times 1/1.12^4 = £800/1.5735 = \quad \underline{508.41}$$
$$\text{Total present value} = \underline{\underline{£1,432.93}}$$

If you can earn 12 per cent on your money, then you can duplicate this investment's cash flows for £1,432.93, so this is the most you should be willing to pay.

---

**EXAMPLE 5.3**

## How Much Is It Worth? Part 2

You are offered an investment that will make three €5,000 payments. The first payment will occur four years from today. The second will occur in five years, and the third will follow in six years. If you can earn 11 per cent, what is the most this investment is worth today? What is the future value of the cash flows?

We shall answer the questions in reverse order to illustrate a point. The future value of the cash flows in six years is

$$(€5,000 \times 1.11^2) + (5,000 \times 1.11) + 5,000 = €6,160.50 + 5,550 + 5,000$$
$$= €16,710.50$$

The present value must be

$$€16,710.50/1.11^6 = €8,934.12$$

Let's check this. Taking them one at a time, the PVs of the cash flows are

$$€5,000 \times 1/1.11^6 = €5,000/1.8704 = €2,673.20$$
$$€5,000 \times 1/1.11^5 = €5,000/1.6851 = \quad 2,967.26$$
$$+€5,000 \times 1/1.11^4 = €5,000/1.5181 = \quad \underline{3,293.65}$$
$$\text{Total present value} = \underline{\underline{€8,934.12}}$$

This is as we previously calculated. The point we want to make is that we can calculate present and future values in any order, and convert between them using whatever way seems most convenient. The answers will always be the same as long as we stick with the same discount rate, and are careful to keep track of the right number of periods.

---

## Spreadsheet Strategies

### How to Calculate Present Values with Multiple Future Cash Flows Using a Spreadsheet

Just as we did in our previous chapter, we can set up a basic spreadsheet to calculate the present values of the individual cash flows as follows. Notice that we have simply calculated the present values one at a time and added them up:

| | A | B | C | D | E |
|---|---|---|---|---|---|
| 1 | Rate | 0.12 | | | |
| 2 | Year | 1 | 2 | 3 | 4 |
| 3 | Cash Flow | £200.00 | £400.00 | £600.00 | £800.00 |
| 4 | Present Value | £178.57 | £318.88 | £427.07 | £508.41 |
| 5 | Formula Used | =PV($B$1,B2,0,-B3) | =PV($B$1,C2,0,-C3) | =PV($B$1,D2,0,-D3) | =PV($B$1,E2,0,-E3) |
| 6 | | | | | |
| 7 | Total PV | £1,432.93 | | | |
| 8 | Formula Used | =SUM(B5:E5) | | | |
| 9 | | | | | |

## A Note about Cash Flow Timing

In present and future value problems, cash flow timing is critically important. In almost all such calculations, it is implicitly assumed that the cash flows occur at the *end* of each period. In fact, all the formulae we have discussed, all the numbers in a standard present value or future value table, and (very important) all the preset (or default) settings in a spreadsheet assume that cash flows occur at the end of each period. Unless you are explicitly told otherwise, you should always assume that this is what is meant.

As a quick illustration of this point, suppose you are told that a three-year investment has a first-year cash flow of £100, a second-year cash flow of £200, and a third-year cash flow of £300. You are asked to draw a time line. Without further information, you should always assume that the time line looks like this:

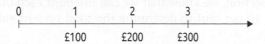

On our time line, notice how the first cash flow occurs at the end of the first period, the second at the end of the second period, and the third at the end of the third period.

We shall close this section by answering the question we posed at the beginning of the chapter concerning footballer Cristiano Ronaldo's contract. Recall that the contract called for £9.5 million in the first year, increasing by 25 per cent over the next five years. If 12 per cent is the appropriate interest rate, what kind of deal did the Real Madrid player have?

To answer, we can calculate the present value by discounting each year's salary back to the present as follows (notice we assume that all the payments are made at year-end):

$$
\begin{aligned}
&\text{Year 0 (2009):} && £9,500,000 && = £9,500,000.00 \\
&\text{Year 1 (2010):} && £9,500,000 \times 1.25 \times 1/1.12^1 && = £10,602,678.57 \\
&\text{Year 2 (2011):} && £9,500,000 \times 1.25^2 \times 1/1.12^2 && = £11,833,346.62 \\
&\text{Year 3 (2012):} && £9,500,000 \times 1.25^3 \times 1/1.12^3 && = £13,206,860.07 \\
&\text{Year 4 (2013):} && £9,500,000 \times 1.25^4 \times 1/1.12^4 && = £14,739,799.18 \\
&\text{Year 5 (2014):} && £9,500,000 \times 1.25^5 \times 1/1.12^5 && = £16,450,668.73
\end{aligned}
$$

Adding the individual cash flows together, you will see that Ronaldo's contract had a present value of about £76 million, or about 71 per cent of the stated £107 million value.

**CONCEPT QUESTIONS**

5.1a  Describe how to calculate the future value of a series of cash flows.

5.1b  Describe how to calculate the present value of a series of cash flows.

5.1c  Unless we are explicitly told otherwise, what do we always assume about the timing of cash flows in present and future value problems?

## 5.2  Valuing Level Cash Flows: Annuities and Perpetuities

We shall frequently encounter situations in which we have multiple cash flows that are all the same amount. For example, a common type of loan repayment plan calls for the borrower to repay the loan by making a series of equal payments over some length of time. Almost all consumer loans (such as car loans) and home mortgages feature equal payments, usually made each month.

| **annuity** |
| A level stream |
| of cash flows for |
| a fixed period |
| of time. |

More generally, a series of constant or level cash flows that occur at the end of each period for some fixed number of periods is called an ordinary **annuity**; more correctly, the cash flows are said to be in *ordinary annuity form*. Annuities appear frequently in financial arrangements, and there are some useful shortcuts for determining their values. We consider these next.

## Present Value for Annuity Cash Flows

Suppose we are examining an asset that promises to pay £500 at the end of each of the next three years. The cash flows from this asset are in the form of a three-year, £500 annuity. If we wanted to earn 10 per cent on our money, how much would we offer for this annuity?

From the previous section, we know that we can discount each of these £500 payments back to the present at 10 per cent to determine the total present value:

$$
\begin{aligned}
\text{Present value} &= (£500/1.1^1) + (500/1.1^2) + (500/1.1^3) \\
&= (£500/1.1) + (500/1.21) + (500/1.331) \\
&= £454.55 + 413.22 + 375.66 \\
&= £1{,}243.43
\end{aligned}
$$

This approach works just fine. However, we shall often encounter situations in which the number of cash flows is quite large. For example, a typical home mortgage calls for monthly payments over 25 years, for a total of 300 payments. If we were trying to determine the present value of those payments, it would be useful to have a shortcut.

Because the cash flows of an annuity are all the same, we can come up with a handy variation on the basic present value equation. The present value of an annuity of £$C$ (or any other currency) per period for $t$ periods when the rate of return or interest rate is $r$ is given by

$$
\begin{aligned}
\text{Annuity present value} &= C \bigg/ \left[ \frac{1 - \text{Present value factor}}{r} \right] \\
&= C \times \left\{ \frac{1 - [1/(1 + r)^t]}{r} \right\} \\
&= C \times \left\{ \frac{1}{r} - \frac{1}{r(1 + r)^t} \right\}
\end{aligned}
$$

(5.1)

The term in parentheses on the first line is sometimes called the *present value interest factor for annuities* and abbreviated PVIFA($r$, $t$).

The expression for the annuity present value may look a little complicated, but it isn't difficult to use. Notice that the term in square brackets on the second line, $1/(1 + r)^t$, is the same present value factor we've been calculating. In our example from the beginning of this section the interest rate is 10 per cent, and there are three years involved. The usual present value factor is thus

$$
\text{Present value factor} = 1/1.1^3 = 1/1.331 = 0.751315
$$

To calculate the annuity present value factor, we just plug this in:

$$
\begin{aligned}
\text{Annuity present value factor} &= (1 - \text{Present value factor})/r \\
&= (1 - 0.751315)/0.10 \\
&= 0.248685/0.10 = 2.48685
\end{aligned}
$$

Just as we calculated before, the present value of our £500 annuity is then

$$
\text{Annuity present value} = £500 \times 2.48685 = £1{,}243.43
$$

## EXAMPLE 5.4

## How Much Can You Afford?

After carefully going over your budget, you have determined that you can afford to pay €632 per month towards a new sports car. You call up your local bank, and find out that the going rate is 1 per cent per month for 48 months. How much can you borrow?

To determine how much you can borrow, we need to calculate the present value of €632 per month for 48 months at 1 per cent per month. The loan payments are in ordinary annuity form, so the annuity present value factor is

$$\text{Annuity PV factor} = (1 - \text{Present value factor})/r$$
$$= [1 - (1/1.01^{48})]/0.01$$
$$= (1 - 0.6203)/0.01$$
$$= 37.9740$$

With this factor we can calculate the present value of the 48 payments of €632 each as

$$\text{Present value} = €632 \times 37.9740 = €24{,}000$$

Therefore €24,000 is what you can afford to borrow and repay.

**Annuity Tables**   Just as there are tables for ordinary present value factors, there are tables for annuity factors as well. Table 5.1 contains a few such factors; Table A.3 in the appendix to the book contains a larger set. To find the annuity present value factor we calculated just before Example 5.4, look for the row corresponding to three periods and then find the column for 10 per cent. The number you see at that intersection should be 2.4869 (rounded to four decimal places), as we calculated. Once again, try calculating a few of these factors yourself and compare your answers with the ones in the table to make sure you know how to do it. If you are using a financial calculator, just enter £1 as the payment and calculate the present value; the result should be the annuity present value factor.

# Spreadsheet Strategies

## Annuity Present Values

Using a spreadsheet to find annuity present values goes like this:

|   | A | B | C |
|---|---|---|---|
| 1 | Payment Amount per Period | £500 | |
| 2 | Number of Payments | 3 | |
| 3 | Discount Rate | 10% | |
| 4 | | | |
| 5 | Annuity Present Value | £1,243.43 | |
| 6 | | | |
| 7 | | | |

Formula used: =PV(B3,B2,-B1)

**Finding the Payment**   Suppose you wish to start up a new business that specializes in the latest of health food trends, frozen yak milk. To produce and market your product, the Yakkee Doodle Dandy, you need to borrow €100,000. Because it strikes you as unlikely that this particular fad will be long-lived, you propose to pay off the loan quickly by making five equal annual payments. If the interest rate is 18 per cent, what will the payment be?

TABLE

5.1

| Number of periods | Interest rate (%) | | | |
|---|---|---|---|---|
| | 5 | 10 | 15 | 20 |
| 1 | 0.9524 | 0.9091 | 0.8696 | 0.8333 |
| 2 | 1.8594 | 1.7355 | 1.6257 | 1.5278 |
| 3 | 2.7232 | 2.4869 | 2.2832 | 2.1065 |
| 4 | 3.5460 | 3.1699 | 2.8550 | 2.5887 |
| 5 | 4.3295 | 3.7908 | 3.3522 | 2.9906 |

**Table 5.1** Annuity present value interest factors

In this case, we know the present value is €100,000. The interest rate is 18 per cent, and there are five years. The payments are all equal, so we need to find the relevant annuity factor and solve for the unknown cash flow:

$$\text{Annuity present value} = €100{,}000$$
$$= C \times [(1 - \text{Present value factor})/r]$$
$$= C \times \{[1 - (1/1.18^5)]/0.18\}$$
$$= C \times [(1 - 0.4371)/0.18]$$
$$= C \times 3.1272$$
$$C = €100{,}000/3.1272 = €31{,}978$$

Therefore you'll make five payments of just under €32,000 each.

# Spreadsheet Strategies

## Annuity Payments

Using a spreadsheet to work the same problem goes like this:

| | A | B | C |
|---|---|---|---|
| 1 | Annuity Present Value | 100000 | |
| 2 | Number of Payments | 5 | |
| 3 | Discount Rate | 18% | |
| 4 | | | |
| 5 | Annuity Present Value | 31977.78 | |
| 6 | | | |
| 7 | | | |

Formula used: =PV(B4,B3,-B2)

EXAMPLE

5.5

# Finding the Number of Payments

You ran a little short on your spring break holiday, so you put €1,000 on your credit card. You can afford only the minimum payment of €20 per month. The interest rate on the credit card is 1.5 per cent per month. How long will you need to pay off the €1,000?

What we have here is an annuity of €20 per month at 1.5 per cent per month for some unknown length of time. The present value is €1,000 (the amount you owe today). We need to do a little algebra (or use a calculator):

$$€1,000 = €20 \times [(1 - \text{Present value factor})/0.015]$$
$$(€1,000/20) \times 0.015 = 1 - \text{Present value factor}$$
$$\text{Present value factor} = 0.25 = 1/(1 + r)^t$$
$$1.015^t = 1/0.25 = 4$$

At this point the problem boils down to asking: how long does it take for your money to quadruple at 1.5 per cent per month? Based on our previous chapter, the answer is about 93 months:

$$1.015^{93} = 3.99 \approx 4$$

It will take you about 93/12 = 7.75 years to pay off the €1,000 at this rate.

**Finding the Rate**   The last question we might want to ask concerns the interest rate implicit in an annuity. For example, an insurance company offers to pay you £1,000 per year for 10 years if you will pay £6,710 up front. What rate is implicit in this 10-year annuity?

In this case we know the present value (£6,710), we know the cash flows (£1,000 per year), and we know the life of the investment (10 years). What we don't know is the discount rate:

$$£6,710 = £1,000 \times [(1 - \text{Present value factor})/r]$$
$$£6,710/1,000 = 6.71$$
$$= \{1 - [1/(1 + r)^{10}]\}/r$$

So the annuity factor for 10 periods is equal to 6.71, and we need to solve this equation for the unknown value of $r$. Unfortunately, this is mathematically impossible to do directly. The only way to do it is to use a table, or trial and error, to find a value for $r$.

If you look across the row corresponding to 10 periods in Table A.3 you will see a factor of 6.7101 for 8 per cent, so we see right away that the insurance company is offering just about 8 per cent. Alternatively, we could just start trying different values until we got very close to the answer. Using this trial-and-error approach can be a little tedious, but fortunately computers are good at that sort of thing.

To illustrate a situation in which finding the unknown rate can be useful, let us consider that a lottery offers you a choice of how to take your winnings. In a recent drawing participants were offered the option of receiving a lump sum payment of €250,000 or an annuity of €500,000 to be received in equal instalments over a 25-year period. Which option was better?

To answer, suppose you were to compare €250,000 today with an annuity of €500,000/ 25 = €20,000 per year for 25 years. At what rate do these have the same value? This is the same type of problem we've been looking at; we need to find the unknown rate $r$ for a present value of €250,000, a €20,000 payment, and a 25-year period. If you grind through the calculations (or get a little computer assistance), you should find that the unknown rate is about 6.24 per cent. You should take the annuity option if that rate is attractive relative to other investments available to you. Notice that we have ignored taxes in this example, and taxes can significantly affect our conclusion. Be sure to consult your tax adviser any time you win the lottery.

## Future Value for Annuities

Sometimes it's also handy to know a shortcut for calculating the future value of an annuity. As you might guess, there are future value factors for annuities as well as present value factors. In general, here is the future value factor for an annuity:

$$\text{Annuity FV factor} = \frac{\text{Future value factor} - 1}{r}$$

$$= \frac{(1 + r)^t - 1}{r} \tag{5.2}$$

$$= \frac{(1 + r)^t}{r} - \frac{1}{r}$$

To see how we use annuity future value factors, suppose you plan to contribute £2,000 every year to a retirement account paying 8 per cent. If you retire in 30 years, how much will you have?

The number of years here, $t$, is 30, and the interest rate, $r$, is 8 per cent; so we can calculate the annuity future value factor as:

$$\begin{aligned} \text{Annuity FV factor} &= (\text{Future value factor} - 1)/r \\ &= (1.08^{30} - 1)/0.08 \\ &= (10.0627 - 1)/0.08 \\ &= 113.2832 \end{aligned}$$

The future value of this 30-year, £2,000 annuity is thus

$$\begin{aligned} \text{Annuity future value} &= £2,000 \times 113.28 \\ &= £226,566 \end{aligned}$$

## A Note about Annuities Due

So far we have only discussed ordinary annuities. These are the most important, but there is a fairly common variation. Remember that with an ordinary annuity the cash flows occur at the end of each period. When you take out a loan with monthly payments, for example, the first loan payment normally occurs one month after you get the loan. However, when you lease an apartment, the first lease payment is usually due immediately. The second payment is due at the beginning of the second month, and so on. A lease is an example of an **annuity due**. An annuity due is an annuity for which the cash flows occur at the beginning of each period. Almost any type of arrangement in which we have to prepay the same amount each period is an annuity due.

> **annuity due**
> An annuity for which the cash flows occur at the beginning of the period.

Suppose an annuity due has five payments of £400 each, and the relevant discount rate is 10 per cent. The time line looks like this:

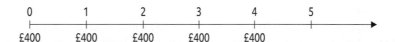

Notice how the cash flows here are the same as those for a *four*-year ordinary annuity, except that there is an extra £400 at time 0. For practice, check to see that the value of a four-year ordinary annuity at 10 per cent is £1,267.95. If we add on the extra £400, we get £1,667.95, which is the present value of this annuity due.

> **perpetuity**
> An annuity in which the cash flows continue for ever.
>
> **consol**
> A type of perpetuity.

## Perpetuities

We've seen that a series of level cash flows can be valued by treating those cash flows as an annuity. An important special case of an annuity arises when the level stream of cash flows continues for ever. Such an asset is called a **perpetuity**, because the cash flows are perpetual. Perpetuities are also called **consols**, particularly in the United Kingdom. See Example 5.6 for an important example of a perpetuity.

**TABLE 5.2**

| Symbols |
| --- |
| PV = Present value, what future cash flows are worth today |

PV = Present value, what future cash flows are worth today
$FV_t$ = Future value, what cash flows are worth in the future
r = Interest rate, rate of return, or discount rate per period – typically, but not always, one year
t = Number of periods – typically, but not always, the number of years
C = Cash amount

**Future value of C per period for t periods at r per cent per period**

$FV_t = C \times \{[(1 + r)^t - 1]/r\}$
A series of identical cash flows is called an *annuity*, and the term $[(1 + r)^t - 1]/r$ is called the *annuity future value factor*.

**Present value of C per period for t periods at r per cent per period**

$PV = C \times \{1 - [1/(1 + r)^t]\}/r$
The term $\{1 - [1/(1 + r)^t]\}/r$ is called the *annuity present value factor*.

**Present value of a perpetuity of C per period**

$PV = C/r$
A *perpetuity* has the same cash flow every year for ever.

**Table 5.2** Summary of annuity and perpetuity calculations

Because a perpetuity has an infinite number of cash flows, we obviously can't compute its value by discounting each one. Fortunately, valuing a perpetuity turns out to be the easiest possible case. The present value of a perpetuity is simply

$$\text{PV for a perpetuity} = C/r \qquad (5.3)$$

For example, an investment offers a perpetual cash flow of €500 every year. The return you require on such an investment is 8 per cent. What is the value of this investment? The value of this perpetuity is

$$\text{Perpetuity PV} = C/r = €500/0.08 = €6,250$$

For future reference, Table 5.2 contains a summary of the annuity and perpetuity basic calculations we have described.

**EXAMPLE 5.6**

## Preference Shares

*Preference shares* (or preferred stock) are an important example of a perpetuity. When a corporation sells preference shares, the buyer is promised a fixed cash dividend every period (usually every quarter or six months) for ever. This dividend must be paid before any dividend can be paid to regular shareholders – hence the term *preference*.

Suppose Wolfton plc wants to sell preference shares at £100 per share. A similar issue of preference shares already outstanding has a price of £40 per share and offers a dividend of £2 every six months. What dividend will Wolfton have to offer if the preference shares are going to sell?

The issue that is already out has a present value of £40 and a cash flow of £2 every six months for ever. Because this is a perpetuity:

$$\text{Present value} = £40 = £2 \times (1/r)$$
$$r = 5\%$$

To be competitive the new Wolfton issue will also have to offer 5 per cent *per six months*; so if the present value is to be £100, the dividend must be such that

$$\text{Present value} = £100 = C \times (1/0.05)$$
$$C = £5 \text{ (per six months)}$$

## Growing Annuities and Perpetuities

Annuities commonly have payments that grow over time. Suppose, for example, that we are looking at a lottery payout over a 20-year period. The first payment, made one year from now, will be €200,000. Every year thereafter the payment will grow by 5 per cent, so the payment in the second year will be €200,000 × 1.05 = €210,000. The payment in the third year will be €210,000 × 1.05 = €220,500, and so on. What's the present value if the appropriate discount rate is 11 per cent?

If we use the symbol $g$ to represent the growth rate, we can calculate the value of a growing annuity using a modified version of our regular annuity formula:

$$\text{Growing annuity present value} = C \times \left[ \frac{1 - \left( \dfrac{1+g}{1+r} \right)^t}{r - g} \right] \tag{5.4}$$

Plugging in the numbers from our lottery example (and letting $g = 0.05$), we get

$$PV = €200,000 \times \left[ \frac{1 - \left( \dfrac{1 + 0.05}{1 + 0.11} \right)^{20}}{0.11 - 0.05} \right]$$

$$= €200,000 \times 11.18169$$

$$= €2,236,337.06$$

There is also a formula for the present value of a growing perpetuity:

$$\text{Growing perpetuity present value} = C \times \left[ \frac{1}{r - g} \right] \tag{5.5}$$

$$= \frac{C}{r - g}$$

In our lottery example, now suppose the payments continue for ever. In this case, the present value is

$$PV = €200,000 \times \frac{1}{0.11 - 0.05}$$

$$= €200,000 \times 16.6667$$

$$= €3,333,333.33$$

The notion of a growing perpetuity may seem a little odd, because the payments get bigger every period for ever; but as we shall see in a later chapter, growing perpetuities play a key role in our analysis of share prices.

Before we go on, there is one important note about our formulae for growing annuities and perpetuities. In both cases, the cash flow in the formula, $C$, is the cash flow that is going to occur exactly one period from today.

## 5.3   Comparing Rates: The Effect of Compounding

The next issue we need to discuss has to do with the way interest rates are quoted. This subject causes a fair amount of confusion, because rates are quoted in many different ways. Sometimes the way a rate is quoted is the result of tradition, and sometimes it's the result of legislation. Unfortunately, at times, rates are quoted in deliberately deceptive ways to mislead borrowers and investors. We shall discuss these topics in this section.

### Effective Annual Percentage Rates and Compounding

If a rate is quoted as 10 per cent compounded semi-annually, this means the investment actually pays 5 per cent every six months. A natural question then arises: is 5 per cent every six months the same thing as 10 per cent per year? It's easy to see that it is not. If you invest €1 at 10 per cent per year, you will have €1.10 at the end of the year. If you invest at 5 per cent every six months, then you'll have the future value of €1 at 5 per cent for two periods:

$$€1 \times 1.05^2 = €1.1025$$

This is €0.0025 more. The reason is simple: your account was credited with €1 × 0.05 = 5 cents in interest after six months. In the following six months, you earned 5 per cent on that five cents, for an extra 5 × 0.05 = 0.25 cents.

As our example illustrates, 10 per cent compounded semi-annually is actually equivalent to 10.25 per cent per year. Put another way, we would be indifferent between 10 per cent compounded semi-annually and 10.25 per cent compounded annually. Any time we have compounding during the year, we need to be concerned about what the rate really is.

In our example, the 10 per cent is called a **nominal**, **stated** or **quoted interest rate**. Other names are used as well. The 10.25 per cent, which is actually the rate you will earn, is called the **effective annual percentage rate (EAR)**. To compare different investments or interest rates, we shall always need to convert to effective rates. Some general procedures for doing this are discussed next.

**nominal interest rate**
The interest rate expressed in terms of the interest payment made each period. Also known as the *stated or quoted interest rate*.

**effective annual percentage rate (EAR)**
The interest rate expressed as if it were compounded once per year.

### Calculating and Comparing Effective Annual Rates

To see why it is important to work only with effective rates, suppose you've shopped around and come up with the following three rates:

Bank A: 15 per cent compounded daily

Bank B: 15.5 per cent compounded quarterly

Bank C: 16 per cent compounded annually

Which of these is the best if you are thinking of opening a savings account? Which of these is best if they represent loan rates?

To begin, Bank C is offering 16 per cent per year. Because there is no compounding during the year, this is the effective rate. Bank B is actually paying $0.155/4 = 0.03875$ or 3.875 per cent per quarter. At this rate, an investment of £1 for four quarters would grow to

$$£1 \times 1.03875^4 = £1.1642$$

The effective annual rate (EAR), therefore, is 16.42 per cent. For a saver, this is much better than the 16 per cent rate Bank C is offering; for a borrower, it's worse.

Bank A is compounding every day. This may seem a little extreme, but it is common to calculate interest daily. In this case, the daily interest rate is actually

$$0.15/365 = 0.000411$$

This is 0.0411 per cent per day. At this rate, an investment of £1 for 365 periods would grow to

$$£1 \times 1.000411^{365} = £1.1618$$

The EAR is 16.18 per cent. This is not as good as Bank B's 16.42 per cent for a saver, and not as good as Bank C's 16 per cent for a borrower.

This example illustrates two things. First, the highest quoted rate is not necessarily the best. Second, compounding during the year can lead to a significant difference between the quoted rate and the effective rate. Remember that the effective rate is what you actually get or what you pay.

If you look at our examples, you see that we computed the EARs in three steps. We first divided the quoted rate by the number of times that the interest is compounded. We then added 1 to the result and raised it to the power of the number of times the interest is compounded. Finally, we subtracted the 1. If we let $m$ be the number of times the interest is compounded during the year, these steps can be summarized simply as

$$\text{EAR} = [1 + (\text{Quoted rate}/m)]^m - 1 \tag{5.6}$$

For example, suppose you are offered 12 per cent compounded monthly. In this case, the interest is compounded 12 times a year; so $m$ is 12. You can calculate the effective rate as

$$
\begin{aligned}
\text{EAR} &= [1 + (\text{Quoted rate}/m)]^m - 1 \\
&= [1 + (0.12/12)]^{12} - 1 \\
&= 1.01^{12} - 1 \\
&= 1.126825 - 1 \\
&= 12.6825\%
\end{aligned}
$$

**EXAMPLE 5.7**

## What's the EAR?

A bank is offering 12 per cent compounded quarterly. If you put £100 in an account, how much will you have at the end of one year? What's the EAR? How much will you have at the end of two years?

The bank is effectively offering $12\%/4 = 3\%$ every quarter. If you invest £100 for four periods at 3 per cent per period, the future value is

$$
\begin{aligned}
\text{Future value} &= £100 \times 1.03^4 \\
&= £100 \times 1.1255 \\
&= £112.55
\end{aligned}
$$

The EAR is 12.55 per cent: $£100 \times (1 + 0.1255) = £112.55$.

We can determine what you would have at the end of two years in two different ways. One way is to recognize that two years is the same as eight quarters. At 3 per cent per quarter, after eight quarters, you would have

$$£100 \times 1.03^8 = £100 \times 1.2668 = £126.68$$

Alternatively, we could determine the value after two years by using an EAR of 12.55 per cent; so after two years you would have

$$£100 \times 1.1255^2 = £100 \times 1.2688 = £126.68$$

Thus the two calculations produce the same answer. This illustrates an important point. Whenever we do a present or future value calculation, the rate we use must be an actual or effective rate. In this case the actual rate is 3 per cent per quarter. The effective annual percentage rate is 12.55 per cent. It doesn't matter which one we use once we know the EAR.

**EXAMPLE 5.8**

## Quoting a Rate

Now that you know how to convert a quoted rate to an EAR, consider going the other way. As a lender, you know you want to actually earn 18 per cent on a particular loan. You want to quote a rate that features monthly compounding. What rate do you quote?

In this case we know the EAR is 18 per cent, and we know this is the result of monthly compounding. Let $q$ stand for the quoted rate. We thus have

$$EAR = [1 + (\text{Quoted rate}/m)]^m - 1$$
$$0.18 = [1 + (q/12)]^{12} - 1$$
$$1.18 = [1 + (q/12)]^{12}$$

We need to solve this equation for the quoted rate. This calculation is the same as the ones we did to find an unknown interest rate in Chapter 4:

$$1.18^{(1/12)} = 1 + (q/12)$$
$$1.18^{0.08333} = 1 + (q/12)$$
$$1.0139 = 1 + (q/12)$$
$$q = 0.0139 \times 12$$
$$= 16.68\%$$

Therefore the rate you would quote is 16.68 per cent, compounded monthly.

## The Annual Percentage Rate

Given the many different ways in which interest rates can be presented to the public, the European Union introduced a directive in 2010 that harmonized the way in which interest rates in any credit agreement for under €75,000 are presented. The UK extended the directive to all regulated loans, and the Netherlands also uses it for mortgage loans. This harmonized interest rate is the **annual percentage rate (APR)**, and it expresses the *total* cost of borrowing or investing as a percentage interest rate.

The reason for an APR is that a credit agreement may include not only interest payments, but also management fees, arrangement fees, and other sundry costs that will affect the total charge for credit (TCC). In addition, knowledge of the interest rate is still not enough to guarantee full comparability of different loans or

**annual percentage rate (APR)**
The harmonized interest rate that expresses the total cost of borrowing or investing as a percentage interest rate.

investments. As shown above, the compounding frequency and the date when interest is charged will influence the effective annual rate of interest.

Under the EU directive, all providers of credit must show the APR prominently in any document or advertising material that promotes a particular type of loan or investment. To calculate APR, we use the standard present value formula. The main difference is in the cash flows that are included in the calculation.

$$PV = C_0 + \frac{C_1}{1 + APR} + \frac{C_2}{(1 + APR)^2} + \cdots + \frac{C_T}{(1 + APR)^T}$$

$$= C_0 + \sum_{i=1}^{T} \frac{C_i}{(1 + APR)^i}$$

(5.7)

---

**EXAMPLE 5.9**

## Annual Percentage Rate

After much deliberation, Mary Moan decides to buy a new Mercedes-Benz car for her family. The sale price of the car is £30,000. Mary arranges financing through the Mercedes dealer, who quotes a simple annual interest rate of 12 per cent on the original borrowed amount over three years, payable in 36 monthly instalments. This means that the lender will charge 12 per cent interest on the original loan of £30,000 every year for three years. Each year, the interest charge will be £3,600 (12% of £30,000), making a total interest payment of £10,800 over three years.

The regular monthly instalments that Mary must pay are

$$\text{Monthly instalment} = (£30{,}000 + £10{,}800)/36 = £1{,}133.33$$

In addition to the interest payments, the Mercedes dealer charges a £250 administration fee, which must be paid when the financing agreement is made. We now solve for APR in equation 5.7:

$$£30{,}000 = £250 + \frac{£1{,}133.33}{(1 + APR)^{1/12}} + \frac{£1{,}133.33}{(1 + APR)^{2/12}} + \cdots + \frac{£1{,}133.33}{(1 + APR)^{36/12}}$$

This gives an annual percentage rate (APR) of 24.13%! The lender must also state the total amount paid at the end of the loan, which in this case is £41,049.88, and the total charge for credit is £11,049.88 (£41,049.88 − £30,000).

---

The definition used by the European Union for APR is very different from the formula used in the United States, and this can cause considerable confusion when European students read finance textbooks aimed at an American market. In the US, the APR is simply the stated annual interest rate. Remember this if you ever plan to take out a loan overseas!

## Taking It to the Limit: A Note about Continuous Compounding

If you made a deposit in a savings account, how often could your money be compounded during the year? If you think about it, there isn't really any upper limit. We've seen that daily compounding, for example, isn't a problem. There is no reason to stop here, however. We could compound every hour or minute or second. How high would the EAR get in this case? Table 5.3 illustrates the EARs that result as 10 per cent is compounded at shorter and shorter intervals. Notice that the EARs do keep getting larger, but the differences get very small.

| TABLE 5.3 | Compounding period | Number of times compounded | Effective annual rate (%) |
|---|---|---|---|
| | Year | 1 | 10.00000 |
| | Quarter | 4 | 10.38129 |
| | Month | 12 | 10.47131 |
| | Week | 52 | 10.50648 |
| | Day | 365 | 10.51558 |
| | Hour | 8,760 | 10.51703 |
| | Minute | 525,600 | 10.51709 |

**Table 5.3** Compounding frequency and effective annual rates

As the numbers in Table 5.3 seem to suggest, there is an upper limit to the EAR. If we let $q$ stand for the quoted rate, then, as the number of times the interest is compounded gets extremely large, the EAR approaches

$$EAR = e^q - 1 \qquad\qquad (5.8)$$

where e is the number 2.71828 (look for a key labelled 'e$^x$' on your calculator). For example, with our 10 per cent rate, the highest possible EAR is

$$
\begin{aligned}
EAR &= e^q - 1 \\
&= 2.71828^{10} - 1 \\
&= 1.1051709 - 1 \\
&= 10.51709\%
\end{aligned}
$$

In this case we say that the money is continuously, or instantaneously, compounded. Interest is being credited the instant it is earned, so the amount of interest grows continuously.

| CONCEPT QUESTIONS | |
|---|---|
| 5.3a | If an interest rate is given as 12 per cent compounded daily, what do we call this rate? |
| 5.3b | What is an APR? What is an EAR? Are they the same thing? |
| 5.3c | In general, what is the relationship between a stated interest rate and an effective interest rate? Which is more relevant for financial decisions? |
| 5.3d | What does continuous compounding mean? |

## 5.4   Loan Types and Loan Amortization

Whenever a lender extends a loan, some provision will be made for repayment of the principal (the original loan amount). A loan might be repaid in equal instalments, for example, or it might be repaid in a single lump sum. Because the way that the principal and interest are paid is up to the parties involved, there are actually an unlimited number of possibilities.

In this section we describe a few forms of repayment that come up quite often, and more complicated forms can usually be built up from these. The three basic types of loan are pure discount loans, interest-only loans, and amortized loans. Working with these loans is a very straightforward application of the present value principles that we have already developed.

## Pure Discount Loans

The *pure discount loan* is the simplest form of loan. With such a loan the borrower receives money today, and repays a single lump sum at some time in the future. A one-year, 10 per cent pure discount loan, for example, would require the borrower to repay £1.10 in one year for every pound borrowed today.

Because a pure discount loan is so simple, we already know how to value one. Suppose a borrower was able to repay £25,000 in five years. If we, acting as the lender, wanted a 12 per cent interest rate on the loan, how much would we be willing to lend? Put another way, what value would we assign today to that £25,000 to be repaid in five years? Based on our work in Chapter 4, we know the answer is just the present value of £25,000 at 12 per cent for five years:

$$\text{Present value} = £25{,}000/1.12^5$$
$$= £25{,}000/1.7623$$
$$= £14{,}186$$

Pure discount loans are common when the loan term is short – say a year or less. In recent years they have become increasingly common for much longer periods.

## Treasury Bills

**EXAMPLE 5.10**

When a government borrows money on a short-term basis (a year or less), it does so by selling what are called *Treasury bills*, or *T-bills* for short. A T-bill is a promise by the government to repay a fixed amount at some time in the future – for example, 3 months or 12 months.

Treasury bills are pure discount loans. If a T-bill promises to repay £10,000 in 12 months, and the market interest rate is 7 per cent, how much will the bill sell for in the market?

Because the going rate is 7 per cent, the T-bill will sell for the present value of £10,000 to be repaid in one year at 7 per cent:

$$\text{Present value} = £10{,}000/1.07 = £9{,}345.79$$

## Interest-Only Loans

A second type of loan repayment plan calls for the borrower to pay interest each period, and to repay the entire principal (the original loan amount) at some point in the future. Loans with such a repayment plan are called *interest-only loans*. Notice that if there is just one period, a pure discount loan and an interest-only loan are the same thing.

For example, with a three-year, 10 per cent, interest-only loan of €1,000, the borrower would pay €1,000 × 0.10 = €100 in interest at the end of the first and second years. At the end of the third year the borrower would return the €1,000 along with another €100 in interest for that year. Similarly, a 50-year interest-only loan would call for the borrower to pay interest every year for the next 50 years, and then repay the principal. In the extreme, the borrower pays the interest every period for ever and never repays any principal. As we discussed earlier in the chapter, the result is a perpetuity.

Most corporate bonds have the general form of an interest-only loan. Because we shall be considering bonds in some detail in the next chapter, we shall defer further discussion of them for now.

## Amortized Loans

With a pure discount or interest-only loan the principal is repaid all at once. An alternative is an *amortized loan*, with which the lender may require the borrower to repay parts of the loan amount over time. The process of providing for a loan to be paid off by making regular principal reductions is called *amortizing* the loan.

A simple way of amortizing a loan is to have the borrower pay the interest each period, plus some fixed amount. This approach is common with medium-term business loans. For example, suppose a business takes out a £5,000, five-year loan at 9 per cent. The loan agreement calls for the borrower to pay the interest on the loan balance each year, and to reduce the loan balance each year by £1,000. Because the loan amount declines by £1,000 each year, it is fully paid in five years.

In the case we are considering, notice that the total payment will decline each year. The reason is that the loan balance goes down, resulting in a lower interest charge each year, whereas the £1,000 principal reduction is constant. For example, the interest in the first year will be £5,000 × 0.09 = £450. The total payment will be £1,000 + 450 = £1,450. In the second year the loan balance is £4,000, so the interest is £4,000 × 0.09 = £360, and the total payment is £1,360. We can calculate the total payment in each of the remaining years by preparing a simple *amortization schedule* as follows:

| Year | Beginning balance (£) | Total payment (£) | Interest paid (£) | Principal paid (£) | Ending balance (£) |
|------|----------------------|-------------------|-------------------|--------------------|--------------------|
| 1 | 5,000 | 1,450 | 450 | 1,000 | 4,000 |
| 2 | 4,000 | 1,360 | 360 | 1,000 | 3,000 |
| 3 | 3,000 | 1,270 | 270 | 1,000 | 2,000 |
| 4 | 2,000 | 1,180 | 180 | 1,000 | 1,000 |
| 5 | 1,000 | 1,090 | 90 | 1,000 | 0 |
| Totals | | 6,350 | 1,350 | 5,000 | |

Notice that in each year the interest paid is given by the beginning balance multiplied by the interest rate. Also notice that the beginning balance is given by the ending balance from the previous year.

Probably the most common way of amortizing a loan is to have the borrower make a single, fixed payment every period. Almost all consumer loans (such as car loans) and mortgages work this way. For example, suppose our five-year, 9 per cent, £5,000 loan was amortized this way. How would the amortization schedule look?

We first need to determine the payment. From our discussion earlier in the chapter we know that this loan's cash flows are in the form of an ordinary annuity. In this case, we can solve for the payment as follows:

$$£5,000 = C \times \{[1 - (1/1.09^5)]/0.09\}$$
$$= C \times [(1 - 0.6499)/0.09]$$

This gives us

$$C = £5,000/3.8897$$
$$= £1285.46$$

The borrower will therefore make five equal payments of £1,285.46. Will this pay off the loan? We shall check by filling in an amortization schedule.

In our previous example we knew the principal reduction each year. We then calculated the interest owed to get the total payment. In this example we know the total payment. We shall thus calculate the interest, and then subtract it from the total payment to calculate the principal portion in each payment.

In the first year the interest is £450, as we calculated before. Because the total payment is £1,285.46, the principal paid in the first year must be

$$\text{Principal paid} = £1,285.46 - 450 = £835.46$$

The ending loan balance is thus

$$\text{Ending balance} = £5,000 - 835.46 = £4,164.54$$

The interest in the second year is £4,164.54 × 0.09 = £374.81, and the loan balance declines by £1,285.46 − 374.81 = £910.65. We can summarize all of the relevant calculations in the following schedule:

| Year | Beginning balance (£) | Total payment (£) | Interest paid (£) | Principal paid (£) | Ending balance (£) |
|---|---|---|---|---|---|
| 1 | 5,000.00 | 1,285.46 | 450.00 | 835.46 | 4,164.54 |
| 2 | 4,164.54 | 1,285.46 | 374.81 | 910.65 | 3,253.88 |
| 3 | 3,253.88 | 1,285.46 | 292.85 | 992.61 | 2,261.27 |
| 4 | 2,261.27 | 1,285.46 | 203.51 | 1,081.95 | 1,179.32 |
| 5 | 1,179.32 | 1,285.46 | 106.14 | 1,179.32 | 0.00 |
| Totals | | 6,427.30 | 1,427.31 | 5,000.00 | |

Because the loan balance declines to zero, the five equal payments do pay off the loan. Notice that the interest paid declines each period. This isn't surprising, because the loan balance is going down. Given that the total payment is fixed, the principal paid must be rising each period.

If you compare the two loan amortizations in this section, you will see that the total interest is greater for the equal total payment case: £1,427.31 versus £1,350. The reason for this is that the loan is repaid more slowly early on, so the interest is somewhat higher. This doesn't mean that one loan is better than the other; it simply means that one is effectively paid off faster than the other. For example, the principal reduction in the first year is £835.46 in the equal total payment case as compared to £1,000 in the first case.

---

**EXAMPLE 5.11**

## Partial Amortization, or 'Bite the Bullet'

A common arrangement in property lending might call for a 5-year loan with, say, a 15-year amortization. What this means is that the borrower makes a payment every month of a fixed amount based on a 15-year amortization. However, after 60 months the borrower makes a single, much larger payment called a 'balloon' or 'bullet' to pay off the loan. Because the monthly payments don't fully pay off the loan, the loan is said to be partially amortized.

Suppose we have a €100,000 commercial mortgage with a 1 per cent monthly effective interest rate and a 20-year (240-month) amortization. Further suppose the mortgage has a five-year balloon. What will the monthly payment be? How big will the balloon payment be?

The monthly payment can be calculated based on an ordinary annuity with a present value of €100,000. There are 240 payments, and the interest rate is 1 per cent per month. The payment is

$$€100,000 = C \times \{[1 - (1/1.01^{240})]/0.01\}$$
$$= C \times 90.8194$$
$$C = €1,101.09$$

Now there is an easy way and a hard way to determine the balloon payment. The hard way is to actually amortize the loan for 60 months to see what the balance is at that time. The easy way is to recognize that, after 60 months, we have a 240 − 60 = 180-month loan. The payment is still €1,101.09 per month, and the interest rate is still 1 per cent per month. The loan balance is thus the present value of the remaining payments:

$$\text{Loan balance} = €1,101.09 \times \{[1 - (1/1.01^{180})]/0.01\}$$
$$= €1,101.09 \times 83.3217$$
$$= €91,744.69$$

The balloon payment is a substantial €91,744. Why is it so large? To get an idea, consider the first payment on the mortgage. The interest in the first month is €100,000 × 0.01 = €1,000. Your payment is €1,101.09, so the loan balance declines by only €101.09. Because the loan balance declines so slowly, the cumulative 'pay down' over five years is not great.

# Spreadsheet Strategies

## Loan Amortization Using a Spreadsheet

Loan amortization is a common spreadsheet application. To illustrate, we shall set up the problem that we examined earlier: a five-year, £5,000, 9 per cent loan with constant payments. Our spreadsheet looks like this:

| | A | B |
|---|---|---|
| 1 | Loan Amount | £5,000 |
| 2 | Interest rate | 9% |
| 3 | Loan Term | 5 |
| 4 | Loan Payment | £1,285.46 |
| 5 | | |
| 6 | | |

Loan payment formula: = PMT(B2,B3,-B1)

| | A | B | C | D | E | F | G |
|---|---|---|---|---|---|---|---|
| | | Beginning | Total | Interest | Principal | Ending | |
| 6 | Year | Balance | Payment | Paid | Paid | Balance | |
| 7 | 1 | £5,000 | £1,285.46 | 450 | £835.46 | £4,165 | |
| 8 | 2 | £4,165 | £1,285.46 | 374.809 | £910.65 | £3,254 | |
| 9 | 3 | £3,254 | £1,285.46 | 292.85 | £992.61 | £2,261 | |
| 10 | 4 | £2,261 | £1,285.46 | 203.515 | £1,081.94 | £1,179 | |
| 11 | 5 | £1,179 | £1,285.46 | 106.14 | £1,179.32 | £0 | |
| 12 | Totals | | £6,427.30 | 1427.31 | £4,999.99 | | |
| 13 | | | | | | | |
| 14 | | | | | | | |

Notice the slight rounding error in cell E12, which sometimes happens when one uses spreadsheets.

| Year | Beginning balance | Total payment | Interest paid | Principal paid | Ending balance |
|---|---|---|---|---|---|
| 1 | =B1 | =$B$4 | =B7*$B$2 | =C7-D7 | =B7-E7 |
| 2 | =F7 | =$B$4 | =B8*$B$2 | =C8-D8 | =B8-E8 |
| 3 | =F8 | =$B$4 | =B9*$B$2 | =C9-D9 | =B9-E9 |
| 4 | =F9 | =$B$4 | =B10*$B$2 | =C10-D10 | =B10-E10 |
| 5 | =F10 | =$B$4 | =B11*$B$2 | =C11-D11 | =B11-E11 |
| Totals | | =SUM(C7:C11) | =SUM(D7:D11) | =SUM(E7:E11) | |

| CONCEPT QUESTIONS | 5.4a | What is a pure discount loan? An interest-only loan? |
|---|---|---|
| | 5.4b | What does it mean to amortize a loan? |
| | 5.4c | What is a balloon payment? How do you determine its value? |

# Summary and Conclusions

This chapter rounded out your understanding of fundamental concepts related to the time value of money and discounted cash flow valuation. Several important topics were covered:

1   There are two ways of calculating present and future values when there are multiple cash flows. Both approaches are straightforward extensions of our earlier analysis of single cash flows.

2   A series of constant cash flows that arrive or are paid at the end of each period is called an ordinary annuity, and we described some useful shortcuts for determining the present and future values of annuities.

3   Interest rates can be quoted in a variety of ways. For financial decisions, it is important that any rates being compared be first converted to effective rates. The relationship between a quoted rate, and an effective annual rate (EAR) is given by

$$EAR = [1 + (Quoted\ rate/m)]^m - 1$$

where $m$ is the number of times during the year the money is compounded or, equivalently, the number of payments during the year.

4   Many loans are annuities. The process of providing for a loan to be paid off gradually is called amortizing the loan, and we discussed how amortization schedules are prepared and interpreted.

5   The annual percentage rate (APR) is used by countries in the European Union to provide a consistent way of presenting interest rates that have been applied to loans. The APR should include all fees and charges related to setting up a loan. The expression is

$$PV = C_0 + \frac{C_1}{1 + APR} + \frac{C_2}{(1 + APR)^2} + \ldots + \frac{C_T}{(1 + APR)^T}$$

$$= C_0 + \sum_{i=1}^{T} \frac{C_i}{(1 + APR)^i}$$

The principles developed in this chapter will figure prominently in the chapters to come. The reason for this is that most investments, whether they involve real assets or financial assets, can be analysed using the discounted cash flow (DCF) approach. As a result, the DCF approach is broadly applicable and widely used in practice. For example, the next two chapters show how to value bonds and shares using an extension of the techniques presented in this chapter. Before going on, therefore, you might want to do some of the problems that follow.

# Chapter Review and Self-Test Problems

5.1   **Present Values with Multiple Cash Flows**   A top footballer has been signed to a three-year, £10 million contract. The details provide for an immediate cash bonus of £2 million. The player is to receive £2 million in salary at the end of the first year, £3 million the next, and £3 million at the end of the last year. Assuming a 15 per cent discount rate, is this package worth £10 million? If not, how much is it worth?

5.2   **Future Value with Multiple Cash Flows**   You plan to make a series of deposits in an individual retirement account. You will deposit £1,000 today, £2,000 in two years, and £2,000 in five years. If you withdraw £1,500 in three years and £1,000 in seven years, assuming no withdrawal penalties, how much will you have after eight years if the interest rate is 7 per cent? What is the present value of these cash flows?

5.3 **Annuity Present Value**  You are looking into an investment that will pay you €12,000 per year for the next 10 years. If you require a 15 per cent return, what is the most you would pay for this investment?

5.4 **It's the Principal That Matters**  Suppose you borrow £10,000. You are going to repay the loan by making equal annual payments for five years. The interest rate on the loan is 14 per cent per year. Prepare an amortization schedule for the loan. How much interest will you pay over the life of the loan?

5.5 **Just a Little Bit Each Month**  You've recently finished your MBA. Naturally, you must purchase a new BMW immediately. The car costs about £21,000. The bank quotes a nominal annual interest rate of 15 per cent for a 72-month loan with a 10 per cent down payment. You plan on trading the car in for a new one in two years. What will your monthly payment be? What is the effective interest rate on the loan? What will the loan balance be when you trade the car in?

# Answers to Chapter Review and Self-Test Problems

5.1 Obviously, the package is not worth £10 million, because the payments are spread out over three years. The bonus is paid today, so it's worth £2 million. The present values for the three subsequent salary payments are

$$(£2/1.15) + (3/1.15^2) + (3/1.15^3) = (2/1.15) + (3/1.32) + (3/1.52)$$
$$= £5.99 \text{ million}$$

The package is worth a total of £5.99 million.

5.2 We shall calculate the future values for each of the cash flows separately, and then add them up. Notice that we treat the withdrawals as negative cash flows:

$$
\begin{array}{rcl}
£1,000 \times 1.07^8 = & £1,000 \times 1.7812 = & £1,718.19 \\
£2,000 \times 1.07^6 = & £2,000 \times 1.5007 = & £3,001.46 \\
-£1,500 \times 1.07^5 = & -£1,500 \times 1.4026 = & -£2,103.83 \\
£2,000 \times 1.07^3 = & £2,000 \times 1.2250 = & £2,450.09 \\
-£1,000 \times 1.07^1 = & -£1,000 \times 1.0700 = & \underline{-£1,070.00} \\
\text{Total future value} & = & \underline{£3,995.91}
\end{array}
$$

This value includes a small rounding error.

To calculate the present value, we could discount each cash flow back to the present, or we could discount back a single year at a time. However, because we already know that the future value in eight years is £3,995.91, the easy way to get the PV is just to discount this amount back eight years:

$$
\begin{aligned}
\text{Present value} &= £3,995.91/1.07^8 \\
&= £3,995.91/1.7182 \\
&= £2,325.64
\end{aligned}
$$

We again ignore a small rounding error. For practice, you can verify that this is what you get if you discount each cash flow back separately.

5.3 The most you would be willing to pay is the present value of €12,000 per year for 10 years at a 15 per cent discount rate. The cash flows here are in ordinary annuity form, so the relevant present value factor is

$$
\begin{aligned}
\text{Annuity present value factor} &= (1 - \text{Present value factor})/r \\
&= [1 - (1/1.15^{10})]/0.15 \\
&= (1 - 0.2472)/0.15 \\
&= 5.0188
\end{aligned}
$$

The present value of the 10 cash flows is thus

$$\text{Present value} = €12,000 \times 5.0188$$
$$= €60,225$$

This is the most you would pay.

5.4 We first need to calculate the annual payment. With a present value of £10,000, an interest rate of 14 per cent, and a term of five years, the payment can be determined from

$$£10,000 = \text{Payment} \times \{[1 - (1/1.14^5)]/0.14\}$$
$$= \text{Payment} \times 3.4331$$

Therefore the payment is £10,000/3.4331 = £2,912.84 (actually, it's £2,912.8355; this will create some small rounding errors in the following schedule). We can now prepare the amortization schedule as follows:

| Year | Beginning balance (£) | Total payment (£) | Interest paid (£) | Principal paid (£) | Ending balance (£) |
|---|---|---|---|---|---|
| 1 | 10,000.00 | 2,912.84 | 1,400.00 | 1,512.84 | 8,487.16 |
| 2 | 8,487.16 | 2,912.84 | 1,188.20 | 1,724.63 | 6,762.53 |
| 3 | 6,762.53 | 2,912.84 | 946.75 | 1,966.08 | 4,796.45 |
| 4 | 4,796.45 | 2,912.84 | 671.50 | 2,241.33 | 2,555.12 |
| 5 | 2,555.12 | 2,912.84 | 357.72 | 2,555.12 | 0.00 |
| Totals | | 14,564.17 | 4,564.17 | 10,000.00 | |

5.5 The cash flows on the car loan are in annuity form, so we need to find only the payment. The interest rate is 15%/12 = 1.25% per month, and there are 72 months. The first thing we need is the annuity factor for 72 periods at 1.25 per cent per period:

$$\text{Annuity present value factor} = (1 - \text{Present value factor})/r$$
$$= [1 - (1/1.0125^{72})]/0.0125$$
$$= [1 - (1/2.4459)]/0.0125$$
$$= (1 - 0.4088)/0.0125$$
$$= 47.2925$$

The present value is the amount we finance. With a 10 per cent down payment, we shall be borrowing 90 per cent of £21,000, or £18,900. To find the payment, we need to solve for C:

$$£18,900 = C \times \text{Annuity present value factor}$$
$$= C \times 47.2925$$

Rearranging things a bit, we have

$$C = £18,900 \times (1/47.2925)$$
$$= £18,900 \times 0.02115$$
$$= £399.64$$

Your payment is just under £400 per month.

The actual interest rate on this loan is 1.25 per cent per month. Based on our work in the chapter, we can calculate the effective annual rate as

$$\text{EAR} = (1.0125)^{12} - 1 = 16.08\%$$

The effective rate is about one point higher than the quoted rate.

To determine the loan balance in two years, we could amortize the loan to see what the balance is at that time. This would be fairly tedious to do by hand. Using the information already determined in this problem, we can instead simply calculate the present value of the remaining payments. After two years, we have made 24 payments, so there are 72 − 24 = 48 payments left. What is the present value of 48 monthly payments of £399.64 at 1.25 per cent per month? The relevant annuity factor is

$$
\begin{aligned}
\text{Annuity present value factor} &= (1 - \text{Present value factor})/r \\
&= [1 - (1/1.0125^{48})]/0.0125 \\
&= [1 - (1/1.8154)]/0.0125 \\
&= (1 - 0.5509)/0.0125 \\
&= 35.9315
\end{aligned}
$$

The present value is thus

$$
\text{Present value} = £399.64 \times 35.9315 = £14{,}359.66
$$

You will owe about £14,360 on the loan in two years.

# Concepts Review and Critical Thinking Questions

1  **Annuity Factors [LO1]**  There are four pieces to an annuity present value. What are they?

2  **Annuity Period [LO1]**  As you increase the length of time involved, what happens to the present value of an annuity? What happens to the future value?

3  **Interest Rates [LO1]**  What happens to the future value of an annuity if you increase the rate $r$? What happens to the present value?

4  **Present Value [LO1]**  What do you think about a lottery advertising a £1,000,000 prize when the payments are £250,000 per annum over four years? Is it deceptive advertising?

5  **Present Value [LO1]**  If you were an athlete negotiating a contract, would you want a big signing bonus payable immediately and smaller payments in the future, or vice versa? How about looking at it from the team's perspective?

6  **Quoted Rates and APR [LO4]**  Why did the European Union make it a requirement that most loans present their interest rate as an annual percentage rate?

7  **Time Value [LO1]**  On many government-subsidized student loans, interest does not begin to accrue until repayment begins. Who receives a bigger subsidy: a first-year student or a final-year student? Explain. In words, how would you go about valuing the subsidy on a student loan?

8  **Time Value [LO1]**  Eligibility for a student loan is based on current financial need, and is repaid out of future income (in the UK, you start paying back a student loan only when you earn more than £15,000). Does this payment schedule give a different subsidy to students studying different disciplines (e.g. medicine, social sciences, finance, engineering, education)? Is this fair? Explain.

9  **Time Value [LO1]**  A viatical settlement is a lump sum of money given to a terminally ill individual in exchange for his life insurance policy. When the insured person dies, the purchaser receives the payout from the life insurance policy. What factors determine the value of the viatical settlement? Do you think such settlements are ethical? Why or why not?

# connect Questions and Problems

**BASIC**

**1–28**

1 **Annual Percentage Rate [LO4]** You work for a jewellers and have sourced a good goldsmith who is able to sell you 100 ounces of gold for 1 million rand. You approach your two main customers. Mr Martyn says he will buy the gold from you in six months for R1,040,000, whereas Ms Kuchner tells you that she will be able to buy the gold from you in two years' time for R1,160,000. What are the annual percentage rates that Mr Martyn and Ms Kuchner are offering you? Which option should you go for?

2 **Present Value and Multiple Cash Flows [LO1]** Investment X offers to pay you £6,000 per year for nine years, whereas Investment Y offers to pay you £8,000 per year for six years. Which of these cash flow streams has the higher present value if the discount rate is 5 per cent? If the discount rate is 15 per cent?

3 **Future Value and Multiple Cash Flows [LO1]** Paradijs NV has identified an investment project with the following cash flows. If the discount rate is 12 per cent, what is the future value of these cash flows in year 5? What is the future value at a discount rate of 17 per cent? At 24 per cent?

| Year | Cash flow (€) |
|------|---------------|
| 1 | 950 |
| 2 | 1,190 |
| 3 | 1,540 |
| 4 | 1,905 |

4 **Calculating Annuity Present Value [LO1]** An investment offers £7,300 per year for 15 years, with the first payment occurring one year from now. If the required return is 7 per cent, what is the value of the investment? What would the value be if the payments occurred for 40 years? For 75 years? For ever?

5 **Calculating Annuity Cash Flows [LO1]** If you put up £44,000 today in exchange for an 8 per cent, 10-year annuity, what will the annual cash flow be?

6 **Calculating Annuity Values [LO1]** A 25-year fixed-rate mortgage has monthly payments of €717 per month and a mortgage interest rate of 6.14 per cent per year compounded monthly. If a buyer purchases a home with the cash proceeds of the mortgage loan plus an additional 20 per cent deposit, what is the purchase price of the home?

7 **Calculating Annuity Values [LO1]** If you deposit NKr4,000 at the end of each of the next 20 years into an account paying 11.2 per cent interest, how much money will you have in the account in 20 years? How much will you have if you make deposits for 40 years?

8 **Calculating Annuity Values [LO1]** You want to have DKr450,000 in your savings account 10 years from now, and you're prepared to make equal annual deposits into the account at the end of each year. If the account pays 7 per cent interest, what amount must you deposit each year?

9 **Calculating Annuity Values [LO2]** Dinero Bank offers you a £50,000, seven-year term loan at 7.5 per cent annual interest. What will your annual loan payment be?

10 **Calculating Perpetuity Values [LO1]** The Maybe Pay Life Insurance Co. is trying to sell you an investment policy that will pay you and your heirs £75,000 per year for ever. If the required return on this investment is 8 per cent, how much will you pay for the policy?

11 **Calculating Perpetuity Values [LO1]** In the previous problem, suppose a sales associate told you the policy costs £750,000. At what interest rate would this be a fair deal?

12  **Calculating EAR [LO4]**  Find the EAR in each of the following cases:

| Stated rate (APR) | Number of times compounded | Effective rate (EAR) |
|---|---|---|
| 4% | Quarterly | |
| 8% | Monthly | |
| 12% | Daily | |
| 16% | Infinite | |

13  **Calculating Quoted Rates [LO4]**  Find the quoted or stated rate in each of the following cases:

| Stated rate | Number of times compounded | Effective rate (EAR) |
|---|---|---|
| | Semi-annually | 8.6% |
| | Monthly | 19.8% |
| | Weekly | 9.4% |
| | Infinite | 16.5% |

14  **Calculating EAR [LO4]**  First National Bank charges 14.2 per cent compounded monthly on its business loans. First United Bank charges 14.5 per cent compounded semi-annually. As a potential borrower, which bank would you go to for a new loan?

15  **Calculating APR [LO4]**  Find the APR for the following five-year loan: a principal of £15,000 with a stated annual interest rate of 7 per cent on the original principal amount to be paid in 60 monthly instalments. The loan has a £250 arrangement fee to be paid as soon as the contract is signed.

16  **Calculating Future Values [LO1]**  What is the future value of €5,100 in 20 years assuming an interest rate of 10 per cent compounded semi-annually?

17  **Calculating Future Values [LO1]**  Gold Door Credit Bank is offering 9.3 per cent compounded daily on its savings accounts. If you deposit £4,500 today, how much will you have in the account in 5 years? In 10 years? In 20 years?

18  **Calculating Present Values [LO1]**  An investment will pay you £58,000 in seven years. If the appropriate discount rate is 10 per cent compounded daily, what is the present value?

19  **EAR, APR and Quoted Rates [LO4]**  Big Dom's Pawn Shop charges an interest rate of 30 per cent per month on loans to its customers. Like all lenders, Big Dom must report an APR to consumers. What rate should the shop report? What is the effective annual rate?

20  **Calculating Cash Flows [LO2, LO4]**  You are planning to save for retirement over the next 30 years. To do this, you will invest £500 a month in a share account and £500 a month in a bond account. The return of the share account is expected to be 7 per cent, and the bond account will pay 4 per cent. When you retire, you will combine your money into an account with a 6 per cent return. How much can you withdraw each month from your account, assuming a 25-year withdrawal period?

21  **Calculating Number of Periods [LO3]**  One of your customers is delinquent on his trade payables balance. You've mutually agreed to a repayment schedule of R5,000 per month. You will charge 1.3 per cent per month interest on the overdue balance. If the current balance is R180,000, how long will it take for the account to be paid off?

22  **Calculating EAR [LO4]**  Friendly's Quick Loans offers you 'two for four or I knock on your door.' This means you get £2 today and repay £4 when you get your wages in one week (or else). What's the effective annual return Friendly's earns on this lending business? If you were brave enough to ask, what quoted rate would Friendly's say you were paying?

23 **Valuing Perpetuities [LO1]** Live Forever Life Insurance Co. is selling a perpetuity contract that pays £1,800 monthly. The contract currently sells for £95,000. What is the monthly return on this investment vehicle? What is the APR?

24 **Calculating Annuity Future Values [LO1]** You are planning to make monthly deposits of £400 into a retirement account that pays 7 per cent interest compounded monthly. If your first deposit will be made one month from now, how large will your retirement account be in 40 years?

25 **Calculating Annuity Future Values [LO1]** In the previous problem, suppose you make £4,800 annual deposits into the same retirement account. How large will your account balance be in 40 years?

26 **Calculating Annuity Present Values [LO1]** Beginning three months from now, you want to be able to withdraw €2,300 each quarter from your bank account to cover university expenses over the next four years. If the account pays 0.65 per cent interest per quarter, how much do you need to have in your bank account today to meet your expense needs over the next four years?

27 **Discounted Cash Flow Analysis [LO1]** If the appropriate discount rate for the following cash flows is 11 per cent compounded quarterly, what is the present value of the cash flows?

| Year | Cash flow (£) |
|------|---------------|
| 1 | 725 |
| 2 | 980 |
| 3 | 0 |
| 4 | 1,360 |

28 **Discounted Cash Flow Analysis [LO1]** If the appropriate discount rate for the following cash flows is 9 per cent per year, what is the present value of the cash flows?

| Year | Cash flow (£) |
|------|---------------|
| 1 | 2,650 |
| 2 | 0 |
| 3 | 6,200 |
| 4 | 3,430 |

**INTERMEDIATE**

**29–55**

29 **Annual Percentage Rate [LO4]** You are serving on a jury. A plaintiff is suing the city for injuries sustained after a freak doggie pooh accident. In the trial, doctors testified that it will be five years before the plaintiff is able to return to work. The jury has already decided in favour of the plaintiff. You are the foreperson of the jury and propose that the jury give the plaintiff an award to cover the following. (1) The present value of two years' back pay. The plaintiff's annual salary for the last two years would have been €25,000 and €28,000, respectively. (2) The present value of five years' future salary. You assume the salary will be €28,000 per year. (3) €100,000 for pain, suffering and humiliation. (4) €20,000 for court costs. Assume that the salary payments are equal amounts paid at the end of each month. If the interest rate you choose is a 4 per cent APR, what is the size of the settlement? If you were the plaintiff, would you like to see a higher or lower interest rate?

30 **Calculating EAR [LO4]** You are looking at an investment that has an effective annual rate of 22 per cent. What is the effective semi-annual return? The effective quarterly return? The effective monthly return?

31 **Calculating Interest Expense [LO2]** You receive a credit card application from Shady Banks Savings and Loan offering an introductory rate of 1.5 per cent per

year, compounded monthly for the first six months, increasing thereafter to 18 per cent compounded monthly. Assuming you transfer the €5,000 balance from your existing credit card and make no subsequent payments, how much interest will you owe at the end of the first year?

32 **Calculating Future Values [LO1]** You have an investment that will pay you 1.17 per cent per month. How much will you have per euro invested in one year? In two years?

33 **Calculating Annuity Payments [LO1]** You want to be a millionaire when you retire in 40 years. How much do you have to save each month if you can earn a 10 per cent annual return? How much do you have to save if you wait 10 years before you begin your deposits? 20 years?

34 **Calculating Rates of Return [LO2]** Suppose an investment offers to triple your money in 12 months (don't believe it). What rate of return per quarter are you being offered?

35 **Comparing Cash Flow Streams [LO1]** You've just joined the investment banking firm of Dewey, Cheatum and Howe. They've offered you two different salary arrangements. You can have €120,000 per year for the next two years, or you can have €80,000 per year for the next two years, along with a €45,000 signing bonus today. The bonus is paid immediately, and the salary is paid at the end of each year. If the quoted interest rate is 12 per cent compounded monthly, which do you prefer?

36 **Growing Annuity [LO1]** You have just won the lottery and will receive €1,000,000 in one year. You will receive payments for 30 years, which will increase 5 per cent per year. If the appropriate discount rate is 8 per cent, what is the present value of your winnings?

37 **Growing Annuity [LO1]** Your job pays you only once a year for all the work you did over the previous 12 months. Today, 31 December, you have just received your salary of £50,000, and you plan to spend all of it. However, you want to start saving for retirement beginning next year. You have decided that one year from today you will begin depositing 5 per cent of your annual salary in an account that will earn 11 per cent per year. Your salary will increase at 4 per cent per year throughout your career. How much money will you have on the date of your retirement 40 years from today?

38 **Present Value and Interest Rates [LO1]** What is the relationship between the value of an annuity and the level of interest rates? Suppose you just bought a 20-year annuity of £19,000 per year at the current interest rate of 8 per cent per year. What happens to the value of your investment if interest rates suddenly drop to 3 per cent? What if interest rates suddenly rise to 13 per cent?

39 **Calculating the Number of Payments [LO2]** You're prepared to make monthly payments of €640, beginning at the end of this month, into an account that pays 9 per cent interest compounded monthly. How many payments will you have made when your account balance reaches €20,000?

40 **Calculating Annuity Present Values [LO2]** You want to borrow £100,000 from your local bank to buy a new yacht. You can afford to make monthly payments of £2,000, but no more. Assuming monthly compounding, what is the highest rate you can afford on a 60-month loan?

41 **Calculating Loan Payments [LO2]** You need a 25-year, fixed-rate mortgage to buy a new home for £450,000. Your mortgage bank will lend you the money at a 5.65 per cent APR for this 300-month loan. However, you can afford monthly payments of only £1,500, so you offer to pay off any remaining loan balance at the end of the loan in the form of a single balloon payment. How large will this balloon payment have to be for you to keep your monthly payments at £1,500?

42 **Present and Future Values [LO1]** The present value of the following cash flow stream is €9,000 when discounted at 8 per cent annually. What is the value of the missing cash flow?

| Year | Cash flow (€) |
|------|---------------|
| 1 | 1,700 |
| 2 | ? |
| 3 | 2,100 |
| 4 | 2,800 |

43 **Calculating Present Values [LO1]** You have just won the Lottery. You will receive £10 million today plus another 10 annual payments that increase by £1 million per year. Thus, in one year, you receive £11 million. In two years you get £12 million, and so on. If the appropriate interest rate is 9 per cent, what is the present value of your winnings?

44 **EAR versus Quoted Rate [LO4]** You have just purchased a new warehouse. To finance the purchase, you've arranged for a 30-year mortgage loan for 80 per cent of the £2,900,000 purchase price. The monthly payment on this loan will be £15,000. What is the APR on this loan? The quoted rate?

45 **Present Value and Break-Even Interest [LO1]** Consider a firm with a contract to sell an asset for £200,000 four years from now. The asset costs £95,000 to produce today. Given a relevant discount rate on this asset of 16 per cent per year, will the firm make a profit on this asset? At what rate does the firm just break even?

46 **Present Value and Multiple Cash Flows [LO1]** What is the present value of SKr4,000 per year, at a discount rate of 10 per cent, if the first payment is received 8 years from now and the last payment is received 25 years from now?

47 **Variable Interest Rates [LO1]** A 15-year annuity pays £1,500 per month, and payments are made at the end of each month. If the interest rate is 11 per cent compounded monthly for the first seven years, and 7 per cent compounded monthly thereafter, what is the present value of the annuity?

48 **Comparing Cash Flow Streams [LO1]** You have your choice of two investment accounts. Investment A is a 20-year annuity that features end-of-month NKr12,000 payments and has an interest rate of 6 per cent compounded monthly. Investment B is an 8 per cent continuously compounded lump sum investment, also good for 15 years. How much money would you need to invest in B today for it to be worth as much as investment A 20 years from now?

49 **Calculating Present Value of a Perpetuity [LO1]** Given an interest rate of 6.2 per cent per year, what is the value at date $t = 7$ of a perpetual stream of 3,500 payments that begins at date $t = 15$?

50 **Calculating APR [LO4]** A local finance company quotes a 16 per cent interest rate on one-year loans. So, if you borrow €25,000, the interest for the year will be €4,000. Because you must repay a total of €29,000 in one year, the finance company requires you to pay €29,000/12, or €2,416.67, per month over the next 12 months. Is this a 16 per cent loan? What rate would legally have to be quoted?

51 **Calculating Present Values [LO1]** A 10-year annuity of twenty £10,000 semi-annual payments will begin 8 years from now, with the first payment coming 8.5 years from now. If the discount rate is 10 per cent compounded monthly, what is the value of this annuity five years from now? What is the value three years from now? What is the current value of the annuity?

52 **Calculating Annuities Due [LO1]** Suppose you are going to receive £15,000 per year for four years. The appropriate interest rate is 10 per cent.

(a) What is the present value of the payments if they are in the form of an ordinary annuity? What is the present value if the payments are an annuity due?

(b) Suppose you plan to invest the payments for five years. What is the future value if the payments are an ordinary annuity? What if the payments are an annuity due?

(c) Which has the highest present value, the ordinary annuity or annuity due? Which has the highest future value? Will this always be true?

53 **Calculating Annuities Due [LO1]**   You want to buy a new Chrysler Grand Voyager car for £28,000. The contract is in the form of a 60-month annuity due at a 7.85 per cent APR. What will your monthly payment be?

54 **Amortization with Equal Payments [LO3]**   Prepare an amortization schedule for a five-year loan of R142,000. The interest rate is 10 per cent per year, and the loan calls for equal annual payments. How much interest is paid in the third year? How much total interest is paid over the life of the loan?

55 **Amortization with Equal Principal Payments [LO3]**   Rework Problem 54 assuming that the loan agreement calls for a principal reduction of R28,400 every year instead of equal annual payments.

56 **Calculating Annuity Values [LO1]**   Bilbo Baggins wants to save money to meet three objectives. First, he would like to be able to retire 30 years from now with retirement income of 40,000 gold coins per month for 25 years, with the first payment received 30 years and 1 month from now. Second, he would like to purchase a cabin in Rivendell in 10 years at an estimated cost of 380,000 gold coins. Third, after he passes on at the end of the 25 years of withdrawals, he would like to leave an inheritance of 900,000 gold coins to his nephew, Frodo. He can afford to save 2,500 gold coins per month for the next 10 years. If he can earn a 10 per cent EAR before he retires and a 7 per cent EAR after he retires, how much will he have to save each month in years 11–30?

**CHALLENGE**
**56–77**

57 **Calculating Annuity Values [LO1]**   After deciding to buy a new car, you can either lease the car or purchase it on a three-year loan. The car you wish to buy costs £32,000. The dealer has a special leasing arrangement where you pay £99 today and £450 per month for the next three years. If you purchase the car, you will pay it off in monthly payments over the next three years at a 12 per cent quoted rate of interest. You believe you will be able to sell the car for £23,000 in three years. Should you buy or lease the car? What break-even resale price in three years would make you indifferent between buying and leasing?

58 **Calculating Annuity Values [LO1]**   A golfer is in contract negotiations with his sponsors. The sponsors have offered the following salary structure:

| Time | Salary (£) |
|---|---|
| 0 | 7,000,000 |
| 1 | 4,500,000 |
| 2 | 5,000,000 |
| 3 | 6,000,000 |
| 4 | 6,800,000 |
| 5 | 7,900,000 |
| 6 | 8,800,000 |

All salaries are to be paid in lump sums. The player has asked you as his agent to renegotiate the terms. He wants a £19 million signing bonus payable today and a contract value increase of £1,000,000. He also wants an equal salary paid every three months, with the first payment three months from now. If the interest rate is 5 per cent compounded daily, what is the amount of his quarterly payment? Assume 365 days in a year.

59 **Discount Interest Loans [LO4]** This question illustrates what is known as *discount interest*. Imagine you are discussing a loan with a somewhat unscrupulous lender. You want to borrow £25,000 for one year. The interest rate is 15 per cent. You and the lender agree that the interest on the loan will be 0.15 × £25,000 = £3,750. So the lender deducts this interest amount from the loan up front and gives you £21,250. In this case, we say that the discount is £3,750. What's wrong here?

60 **Calculating Annuity Values [LO1]** You've just read a life-enhancing book that tells you that if you believe things will happen, they will! You decide that you want to become a millionaire by the time you are 65. You have just turned 22 and you decide to play the stock market. Your fantastic corporate finance textbook leads you to believe that you can earn 11.8 per cent per annum from investing in equities. How much must you invest each year in order to realize your dream? You've decided that investing each year will be boring, and so you just want to invest an amount today and leave it in an account for 43 years. How much should you invest today?

61 **Calculating EAR with Points [LO4]** You are looking at a one-year loan of €10,000. The interest rate is quoted as 8 per cent plus three points. A *point* on a loan is simply 1 per cent (one percentage point) of the loan amount. Quotes similar to this one are common with home mortgages. The interest rate quotation in this example requires the borrower to pay three points to the lender up front and repay the loan later with 8 per cent interest. What rate would you actually be paying here?

62 **Calculating EAR with Points [LO4]** The interest rate on a one-year loan is quoted as 11 per cent plus two points (see the previous problem). What is the EAR? Is your answer affected by the loan amount?

63 **EAR versus APR [LO4]** Two banks in the area offer 30-year, £240,000 mortgages at 6.8 per cent and charge a £2,300 loan application fee. However, the application fee charged by Insecurity Bank and Trust is refundable if the loan application is denied, whereas that charged by I.M. Greedy and Sons Mortgage Bank is not. The current disclosure law requires that any fees that will be refunded if the applicant is rejected be included in calculating the APR, but this is not required with non-refundable fees (presumably because refundable fees are part of the loan rather than a fee). What are the EARs on these two loans?

64 **Calculating EAR with Add-On Interest [LO4]** This problem illustrates a deceptive way of quoting interest rates called *add-on interest*. Imagine that you see an advertisement for Crazy Judy's Stereo City that reads something like this: '£1,000 Instant Credit! 14% Simple Interest! Three Years to Pay! Low, Low Monthly Payments!' You're not exactly sure what all this means, and somebody has spilled ink over the APR on the loan contract, so you ask the manager for clarification.

Judy explains that if you borrow £1,000 for three years at 14 per cent interest, in three years you will owe

$$£1,000 \times 1.14^3 = £1,000 \times 1.41854 = £1,481.54$$

Now, Judy recognizes that coming up with £1,481.54 all at once might be a strain, so she lets you make 'low, low monthly payments' of £1,481.54/36 = £41.15 per month, even though this is extra bookkeeping work for her.

Is this a 14 per cent loan? Why or why not? What is the APR on this loan? Why do you think this is called add-on interest?

65 **Calculating Annuity Payments [LO1]** This is a classic retirement problem. A time line will help in solving it. Your friend is celebrating her 35th birthday today, and wants to start saving for her anticipated retirement at age 65. She wants to be able to withdraw £105,000 from her savings account on each birthday for 20 years following her retirement; the first withdrawal will be on her 66th birthday. Your friend intends to invest her money in the local credit union, which offers 7 per cent

interest per year. She wants to make equal annual payments on each birthday into the account established at the credit union for her retirement fund.

(a) If she starts making these deposits on her 36th birthday and continues to make deposits until she is 65 (the last deposit will be on her 65th birthday), what amount must she deposit annually to be able to make the desired withdrawals at retirement?

(b) Suppose your friend has just inherited a large sum of money. Rather than make equal annual payments, she has decided to make one lump sum payment on her 35th birthday to cover her retirement needs. What amount does she have to deposit?

(c) Suppose your friend's employer will contribute £1,500 to the account every year as part of the company's profit-sharing plan. In addition, your friend expects a £150,000 distribution from a family trust fund on her 55th birthday, which she will also put into the retirement account. What amount must she deposit annually now to be able to make the desired withdrawals at retirement?

66 **Calculating the Number of Periods [LO2]**  Your Christmas skiing holiday was great, but it unfortunately ran a bit over budget. All is not lost: you just received an offer in the mail to transfer your €15,000 balance from your current credit card, which charges an annual rate of 21.4 per cent, to a new credit card charging a rate of 5 per cent. How much faster could you pay the loan off by making your planned monthly payments of €300 with the new card? What if there was a 2 per cent fee charged on any balances transferred?

67 **Future Value and Multiple Cash Flows [LO1]**  An insurance company is offering a new policy to its customers. Typically, the policy is bought by a parent or grandparent for a child at the child's birth. The details of the policy are as follows. The purchaser (say, the parent) makes the following six payments to the insurance company:

| | |
|---|---|
| First birthday: | £900 |
| Second birthday: | £900 |
| Third birthday: | £1,000 |
| Fourth birthday: | £1,000 |
| Fifth birthday: | £1,100 |
| Sixth birthday: | £1,100 |

After the child's sixth birthday, no more payments are made. When the child reaches age 65, he or she receives £500,000. If the relevant interest rate is 12 per cent for the first six years and 8 per cent for all subsequent years, is the policy worth buying?

68 **Calculating a Balloon Payment [LO2]**  You have just arranged for a €750,000 mortgage to finance the purchase of a large tract of land. The mortgage has an 8.1 per cent APR, and it calls for monthly payments over the next 30 years. However, the loan has an eight-year balloon payment, meaning that the loan must be paid off then. How big will the balloon payment be?

69 **Calculating Interest Rates [LO4]**  A financial planning service offers a university savings programme. The plan calls for you to make six annual payments of £9,000 each, with the first payment occurring today, your child's 12th birthday. Beginning on your child's 18th birthday, the plan will provide £20,000 per year for four years. What return is this investment offering?

70 **Break-Even Investment Returns [LO4]**  Your financial planner offers you two different investment plans. Plan X is a 100,000 dinari annual perpetuity. Plan Y is a 20-year, 150,000 dinari annual annuity. Both plans will make their first payment

one year from today. At what discount rate would you be indifferent between these two plans?

71 **Perpetual Cash Flows [LO1]** What is the value of an investment that pays £15,000 every *other* year for ever, if the first payment occurs one year from today and the discount rate is 10 per cent compounded daily? What is the value today if the first payment occurs four years from today?

72 **Ordinary Annuities and Annuities Due [LO1]** As discussed in the text, an annuity due is identical to an ordinary annuity except that the periodic payments occur at the beginning of each period and not at the end of the period. Show that the relationship between the value of an ordinary annuity and the value of an otherwise equivalent annuity due is

$$\text{Annuity due value} = \text{Ordinary annuity value} \times (1 + r)$$

Show this for both present and future values.

73 **Calculating Growing Annuities [LO1]** You have 40 years left until retirement and want to retire with £2 million. Your salary is paid annually, and you will receive £40,000 at the end of the current year. Your salary will increase at 3 per cent per year, and you can earn an 11 per cent return on the money you invest. If you save a constant percentage of your salary, what percentage of your salary must you save each year?

74 **Calculating EAR [LO4]** A pawnbroker's shop is in the business of making personal loans to walk-in customers. The shop makes only one-week loans at 7 per cent interest per week.

(a) What APR must the shop report to its customers?

(b) Now suppose the shop makes one-week loans at 7 per cent discount interest per week (see Problem 59). What's the APR now?

(c) The pawnbroker also makes one-month add-on interest loans at 7 per cent discount interest per week. Thus if you borrow €100 for one month (four weeks), the interest will be $(€100 \times 1.07^4) - 100 = €31.08$. Because this is discount interest, your net loan proceeds today will be €68.92. You must then repay the shop €100 at the end of the month. To help you out, though, the shop lets you pay off this €100 in instalments of €25 per week. What is the APR of this loan?

75 **Present Value of a Growing Perpetuity [LO1]** What is the equation for the present value of a growing perpetuity with a payment of $C$ one period from today if the payments grow by $C$ each period?

76 **Rule of 72 [LO4]** Earlier, we discussed the Rule of 72, a useful approximation for many interest rates and periods for the time it takes a lump sum to double in value. For a 10 per cent interest rate, show that the 'Rule of 73' is slightly better. For what rate is the Rule of 72 exact? (*Hint:* Use the Solver function in Microsoft Excel.)

77 **Rule of 69.3 [LO4]** A corollary to the Rule of 72 is the Rule of 69.3. The Rule of 69.3 is exactly correct except for rounding when interest rates are compounded continuously. Prove the Rule of 69.3 for continuously compounded interest.

# The MBA Decision

Ben Bates graduated from university six years ago with a finance undergraduate degree. Although he is satisfied with his current job, his goal is to become an investment banker. He feels that an MBA degree would allow him to achieve this goal. After examining schools, he has narrowed his choice to either Wilton University or Mount Perry University. Although internships are encouraged by both schools, to get class credit for the internship no salary can be paid. Other than internships, neither school will allow its students to work while enrolled in its MBA programme.

Ben currently works at the money management firm of Dewey and Louis. His annual salary at the firm is £75,000 per year, and his salary is expected to increase at 3 per cent per year until retirement. He is currently 28 years old and expects to work for 38 more years. His current job includes a fully paid health insurance plan, and his current average tax rate is 35 per cent. Ben has a savings account with enough money to cover the entire cost of his MBA programme.

The Ritter College of Business at Wilton University is one of the top MBA programmes in the country. The MBA degree requires two years of full-time enrolment at the university. The annual tuition fee is £30,000, payable at the beginning of each school year. Books and other supplies are estimated to cost £2,500 per year. Ben expects that after graduation from Wilton he will receive a job offer for about £98,000 per year, with a £15,000 signing bonus. The salary at this job will increase at 4 per cent per year. Because of the higher salary, his average income tax rate will increase to 40 per cent.

The Bradley School of Business at Mount Perry University began its MBA programme 16 years ago. The Bradley School is smaller and less well known than the Ritter College. Bradley offers an accelerated one-year programme, with a tuition cost of £20,000 to be paid upon matriculation. Books and other supplies for the programme are expected to cost £3,500. Ben thinks that he will receive an offer of £90,000 per year upon graduation, with a £10,000 signing bonus. The salary at this job will increase at 3.5 per cent per year. His average tax rate at this level of income will be 35 per cent.

Both schools offer a health insurance plan that will cost £3,000 per year, payable at the beginning of the year. Ben also estimates that room and board expenses will cost £20,000 per year at both schools. The appropriate discount rate is 6.5 per cent.

## QUESTIONS

1   How does Ben's age affect his decision to get an MBA?

2   What other, perhaps non-quantifiable, factors affect Ben's decision to get an MBA?

3   Assuming all salaries are paid at the end of each year, what is the best option for Ben from a strictly financial standpoint?

4   Ben believes that the appropriate analysis is to calculate the future value of each option. How would you evaluate this statement?

5   What initial salary would Ben need to receive to make him indifferent between attending Wilton University and staying in his current position?

6   Suppose, instead of being able to pay cash for his MBA, Ben must borrow the money. The current borrowing rate is 5.4 per cent. How would this affect his decision?

# CHAPTER
# 6

# Bond Valuation

KEY NOTATIONS

| | |
|---|---|
| C | Coupon |
| FV | Face value of bond |
| h | Inflation rate |
| PV | Present value |
| r | Interest rate or discount rate |
| t | Number of periods |
| YTM | Yield to maturity |

## LEARNING OBJECTIVES

After studying this chapter, you should understand:

**LO1** Important bond features and types of bond.

**LO2** Bond values and yields, and why they fluctuate.

**LO3** Bond ratings, and what they mean.

**LO4** The impact of inflation on interest rates.

**LO5** The term structure of interest rates, and the determinants of bond yields.

IN ITS MOST BASIC FORM, a bond is a fairly simple thing. You lend a company some money, say €1,000. The company pays you interest regularly, and it repays the original loan amount of €1,000 at some point in the future. Bonds can also have complex features, and in 2008 a type of bond known as *a mortgage-backed security*, or *MBS*, caused havoc in the global financial system.

An MBS, as the name suggests, is a bond that is backed by a pool of home mortgages. The bondholders receive payments derived from payments on the underlying mortgages, and these payments can be divided up in various ways to create different classes of bond. Defaults on the underlying mortgages lead to losses for MBS bondholders. Since most mortgage-backed securities were held and issued by banks, the collapse in the housing market (particularly in the US) led to a global credit crunch in 2008 that nearly halted the global business economy. Because some of the world's largest banks had to be rescued through state bail-outs, many governments had to implement stringent public sector spending cuts and tax increases to bring budgets back into balance. This was still affecting European countries in 2011, and the repercussions are likely to be felt for a number of years yet.

Our goal in this chapter is to introduce you to bonds. We begin by showing how the techniques we developed in Chapters 4 and 5 can be applied to bond valuation. From there, we go on to discuss bond features, and how bonds are bought and sold. One important thing we learn is that bond values depend, in large part, on interest rates. We therefore close the chapter with an examination of interest rates and their behaviour.

## 6.1 Bonds and Bond Valuation

When a corporation or government wishes to borrow money from the public on a long-term basis, it usually does so by issuing or selling debt securities that are generically called *bonds.* In this section we describe the various features of corporate bonds, and some of the terminology associated with bonds. We then discuss the cash flows associated with a bond, and how bonds can be valued using our discounted cash flow procedure.

## Bond Features and Prices

As we mentioned in our previous chapter, a bond is normally an interest-only loan, meaning that the borrower will pay the interest every period, but none of the principal will be repaid until the end of the loan. For example, suppose Pixie plc wants to borrow £1,000 for 30 years. The interest rate on similar debt issued by similar corporations is 12 per cent. Pixie will thus pay 0.12 × £1,000 = £120 in interest every year for 30 years. At the end of 30 years Pixie will repay the £1,000. As this example suggests, a bond is a fairly simple financing arrangement. There is, however, a rich jargon associated with bonds, so we shall use this example to define some of the more important terms.

In our example, the £120 regular interest payments that Pixie promises to make are called the bond's **coupons**. Because the coupon is constant and paid every year, the type of bond we are describing is sometimes called a *level coupon bond*. The amount that will be repaid at the end of the loan is called the bond's **face value**, or **par value**. As in our example, this par value is usually £1,000 for corporate bonds, and a bond that sells for its par value is called a *par value bond*. Government bonds frequently have much larger face, or par, values. Finally, the annual coupon divided by the face value is called the **coupon rate** on the bond: in this case, because £120/1,000 = 12%, the bond has a 12 per cent coupon rate.

The number of years until the face value is paid is called the bond's time to **maturity**. A corporate bond will frequently have a maturity of 30 years when it is originally issued, but this varies. Once the bond has been issued, the number of years to maturity declines as time goes by.

> **coupon**
> The stated interest payment made on a bond.
>
> **face value**
> The principal amount of a bond that is repaid at the end of the term. Also called *par value*.
>
> **coupon rate**
> The annual coupon divided by the face value of a bond.
>
> **maturity**
> The specified date on which the principal amount of a bond is paid.

## Bond Values and Yields

As time passes, interest rates change in the marketplace. The cash flows from a bond, however, stay the same. As a result, the value of the bond will fluctuate. When interest rates rise, the present value of the bond's remaining cash flows declines, and the bond is worth less. When interest rates fall, the bond is worth more.

To determine the value of a bond at a particular point in time, we need to know the number of periods remaining until maturity, the face value, the coupon, and the market interest rate for bonds with similar features. The interest rate required in the market on a bond is called the bond's **yield to maturity (YTM)**. This rate is sometimes called the bond's *yield* for short. Given all this information, we can calculate the present value of the cash flows as an estimate of the bond's current market value.

> **yield to maturity (YTM)**
> The rate required in the market on a bond.

For example, suppose Pixie plc were to issue a bond with 10 years to maturity. The Pixie bond has an annual coupon of £80. Similar bonds have a yield to maturity of 8 per cent. Based on our preceding discussion, the Pixie bond will pay £80 per year for the next 10 years in coupon interest. In 10 years, Pixie will pay £1,000 to the owner of the bond. The cash flows from the bond are shown in Fig. 6.1. What would this bond sell for?

As illustrated in Fig. 6.1, the Pixie bond's cash flows have an annuity component (the coupons) and a lump sum (the face value paid at maturity). We thus estimate the market value of the bond by calculating the present value of these two components separately and adding the results together. First, at the going rate of 8 per cent, the present value of the £1,000 paid in 10 years is

$$\text{Present value} = £1,000/1.08^{10} = £1,000/2.1589 = £463.19$$

FIGURE
6.1

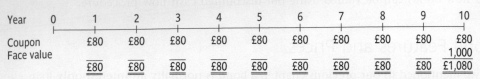

*Cash flows*

| Year | 0 | 1 | 2 | 3 | 4 | 5 | 6 | 7 | 8 | 9 | 10 |
|------|---|---|---|---|---|---|---|---|---|---|----|
| Coupon | | £80 | £80 | £80 | £80 | £80 | £80 | £80 | £80 | £80 | £80 |
| Face value | | | | | | | | | | | 1,000 |
| | | £80 | £80 | £80 | £80 | £80 | £80 | £80 | £80 | £80 | £1,080 |

As shown, the Pixie bond has an annual coupon of £80 and a face, or per, value of £1,000 paid at maturity in 10 years.

**Figure 6.1** Cash flows for Pixie plc bond

Second, the bond offers £80 per year for 10 years; the present value of this annuity stream is

$$\text{Annuity present value} = £80 \times (1 - 1/1.08^{10})/0.08$$
$$= £80 \times (1 - 1/2.1589)/0.08$$
$$= £80 \times 6.7101$$
$$= £536.81$$

We can now add the values for the two parts together to get the bond's value:

$$\text{Total bond value} = £463.19 + 536.81 = £1,000$$

This bond sells for exactly its face value. This is not a coincidence. The going interest rate in the market is 8 per cent. Considered as an interest-only loan, what interest rate does this bond have? With an £80 coupon, this bond pays exactly 8 per cent interest only when it sells for £1,000.

To illustrate what happens as interest rates change, suppose a year has gone by. The Pixie bond now has nine years to maturity. If the interest rate in the market has risen to 10 per cent, what will the bond be worth? To find out, we repeat the present value calculations with 9 years instead of 10, and a 10 per cent yield instead of an 8 per cent yield. First, the present value of the £1,000 paid in nine years at 10 per cent is

$$\text{Present value} = £1,000/1.10^9 = £1,000/2.3579 = £424.10$$

Second, the bond now offers £80 per year for nine years; the present value of this annuity stream at 10 per cent is

$$\text{Annuity present value} = £80 \times (1 - 1/1.10^9)/0.10$$
$$= £80 \times (1 - 1/2.3579)/0.10$$
$$= £80 \times 5.7590$$
$$= £460.72$$

We can now add the values for the two parts together to get the bond's value:

$$\text{Total bond value} = £424.10 + 460.72 = £884.82$$

Therefore the bond should sell for about £885. In the vernacular, we say that this bond, with its 8 per cent coupon, is priced to yield 10 per cent at £885.

The Pixie plc bond now sells for less than its £1,000 face value. Why? The market interest rate is 10 per cent. Considered as an interest-only loan of £1,000, this bond pays only 8 per cent, its coupon rate. Because this bond pays less than the going rate, investors are willing to lend only something less than the £1,000 promised repayment. Because the bond sells for less than face value, it is said to be a *discount bond*.

The only way to get the interest rate up to 10 per cent is to lower the price to less than £1,000 so that the purchaser, in effect, has a built-in gain. For the Pixie plc bond the price of £885 is £115 less than the face value, so an investor who purchased and kept the bond would get £80 per year and would have a £115 gain at maturity as well. This gain compensates the lender for the below-market coupon rate.

Another way to see why the bond is discounted by £115 is to note that the £80 coupon is £20 below the coupon on a newly issued par value bond, based on current market conditions. The bond would be worth £1,000 only if it had a coupon of £100 per year. In a sense, an investor who buys and keeps the bond gives up £20 per year for nine years. At 10 per cent, this annuity stream is worth

$$\text{Annuity present value} = £20 \times (1 - 1/1.10^9)/0.10$$
$$= £20 \times 5.7590$$
$$= £115.18$$

This is just the amount of the discount.

What would the Pixie bond sell for if interest rates had dropped by 2 per cent instead of rising by 2 per cent? As you might guess, the bond would sell for more than £1,000. Such a bond is said to sell at a *premium*, and is called a *premium bond*.

This case is just the opposite of that of a discount bond. The Pixie bond now has a coupon rate of 8 per cent when the market rate is only 6 per cent. Investors are willing to pay a premium to get this extra coupon amount. In this case, the relevant discount rate is 6 per cent, and there are nine years remaining. The present value of the £1,000 face amount is

$$\text{Present value} = £1,000/1.06^9 = £1,000/1.6895 = £591.89$$

The present value of the coupon stream is

$$\text{Annuity present value} = £80 \times (1 - 1/1.06^9)/0.06$$
$$= £80 \times (1 - 1/1.6895)/0.06$$
$$= £80 \times 6.8017$$
$$= £544.14$$

We can now add the values for the two parts together to get the bond's value:

$$\text{Total bond value} = £591.89 + 544.14 = £1,136.03$$

Total bond value is therefore about £136 in excess of par value. Once again, we can verify this amount by noting that the coupon is now £20 too high, based on current market conditions. The present value of £20 per year for nine years at 6 per cent is

$$\text{Annuity present value} = £20 \times (1 - 1/1.06^9)/0.06$$
$$= £20 \times 6.8017$$
$$= £136.03$$

This is just as we calculated.

Based on our examples, we can now write the general expression for the value of a bond. If a bond has (1) a face value of $F$ paid at maturity, (2) a coupon of $C$ paid per period, (3) $t$ periods to maturity, and (4) a yield of $r$ per period, its value is

$$\text{Bond value} = \underbrace{C \times \left[ \frac{1 - 1/(1+r)^t}{r} \right]}_{\substack{\text{Present value} \\ \text{of the coupons}}} + \underbrace{\frac{F}{(1+r)^t}}_{\substack{\text{Present value of} \\ \text{the face amount}}} \qquad (6.1)$$

<table><tr><td>EXAMPLE<br>**6.1**</td><td></td></tr></table>

# Semi-annual Coupons

Many bonds make coupon payments twice a year. So, if an ordinary bond has a coupon rate of 14 per cent and a face value of £100,000, then the owner will get a total of £14,000 per year, but this £14,000 will come in two payments of £7,000 each. Suppose we are examining such a bond. The yield to maturity is quoted at 16 per cent.

Bond yields are presented in the same way as quoted rates, which is equal to the actual rate per period multiplied by the number of periods. In this case, with a 16 per cent quoted yield and semi-annual payments, the true yield is 8 per cent per six months. The bond matures in seven years. What is the bond's price? What is the effective annual yield on this bond?

Based on our discussion, we know the bond will sell at a discount, because it has a coupon rate of 7 per cent every six months when the market requires 8 per cent every six months. So, if our answer exceeds £100,000, we know we have made a mistake.

To get the exact price, we first calculate the present value of the bond's face value of £100,000 paid in seven years. This seven-year period has 14 periods of six months each. At 8 per cent per period, the value is

$$\text{Present value} = £100,000/1.08^{14} = £100,000/2.9372 = £34,046$$

The coupons can be viewed as a 14-period annuity of £7,000 per period. At an 8 per cent discount rate, the present value of such an annuity is

$$\begin{aligned}\text{Annuity present value} &= £7,000 \times (1 - 1/1.08^{14})/0.08 \\ &= £7,000 \times (1 - 0.3405)/0.08 \\ &= £7,000 \times 8.2442 \\ &= £57,710\end{aligned}$$

The total present value gives us what the bond should sell for:

$$\text{Total present value} = £34,046 + 57,710 = £91,756$$

To calculate the effective yield on this bond, note that 8 per cent every six months is equivalent to

$$\text{Effective annual rate} = (1 + 0.08)^2 - 1 = 16.64\%$$

The effective yield, therefore, is 16.64 per cent.

As we have illustrated in this section, bond prices and interest rates always move in opposite directions. When interest rates rise, a bond's value, like any other present value, will decline. Similarly, when interest rates fall, bond values rise. Even if we are considering a bond that is riskless, in the sense that the borrower is certain to make all the payments, there is still risk in owning a bond. We discuss this next.

## Interest Rate Risk

The risk that arises for bond owners from fluctuating interest rates is called *interest rate risk*. How much interest rate risk a bond has depends on how sensitive its price is to interest rate changes. This sensitivity depends directly on two things: the time to maturity, and the coupon rate. As we shall see shortly, you should keep the following in mind when looking at a bond:

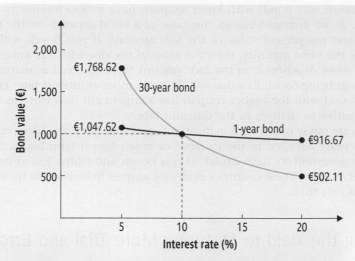

FIGURE
6.2

Value of a bond with a 10 per cent coupon rate for different interest rates and maturities

|  | Time to maturity | |
| Interest rate (%) | 1 year | 30 years |
| 5 | €1,047.62 | €1,768.62 |
| 10 | 1,000.00 | 1,000.00 |
| 15 | 966.52 | 671.70 |
| 20 | 916.67 | 502.11 |

**Figure 6.2** Interest rate risk and time to maturity

1 All other things being equal, the longer the time to maturity, the greater the interest rate risk.

2 All other things being equal, the lower the coupon rate, the greater the interest rate risk.

We illustrate the first of these two points in Fig. 6.2. As shown, we compute and plot prices under different interest rate scenarios for 10 per cent coupon bonds with maturities of one year and 30 years. Notice how the slope of the line connecting the prices is much steeper for the 30-year maturity than it is for the one-year maturity. This steepness tells us that a relatively small change in interest rates will lead to a substantial change in the bond's value. In comparison, the one-year bond's price is relatively insensitive to interest rate changes.

Intuitively, we can see that longer-term bonds have greater interest rate sensitivity, because a large portion of a bond's value comes from the €1,000 face amount. The present value of this amount isn't greatly affected by a small change in interest rates if the amount is to be received in one year. Even a small change in the interest rate, however, once it is compounded for 30 years, can have a significant effect on the present value. As a result, the present value of the face amount will be much more volatile with a longer-term bond.

The other thing to know about interest rate risk is that, like most things in finance and economics, it increases at a decreasing rate. In other words, if we compared a 10-year bond with a one-year bond, we would see that the 10-year bond has much greater interest rate risk. However, if you were to compare a 20-year bond with a 30-year bond, you would find that the 30-year bond had somewhat greater interest rate risk because it has a longer maturity, but the difference in the risk would be fairly small.

The reason why bonds with lower coupons have greater interest rate risk is essentially the same. As we discussed earlier, the value of a bond depends on the present value of its coupons and the present value of the face amount. If two bonds with different coupon rates have the same maturity, then the value of the one with the lower coupon is proportionately more dependent on the face amount to be received at maturity. As a result, all other things being equal, its value will fluctuate more as interest rates change. Put another way, the bond with the higher coupon has a larger cash flow early in its life, so its value is less sensitive to changes in the discount rate.

Bonds are rarely issued with maturities longer than 30 years. However, low interest rates in recent years have led to the issuance of much longer-term issues. Since 2005, several European governments have issued 50-year bonds and China issued its first 50-year bond at the end of 2009. These countries evidently wanted to lock in the historically low interest rates for a *long* time.

## Finding the Yield to Maturity: More Trial and Error

Frequently, we will know a bond's price, coupon rate and maturity date, but not its yield to maturity. For example, suppose we are interested in a six-year, 8 per cent coupon bond. A broker quotes a price of £955.14 for a bond with face value of £1,000. What is the yield on this bond?

We've seen that the price of a bond can be written as the sum of its annuity and lump sum components. Knowing that there is an £80 coupon for six years and a £1,000 face value, we can say that the price is

$$£955.14 = £80 \times \left[ \frac{1 - 1/(1 + r)^6}{r} \right] + \frac{1,000}{(1 + r)^6}$$

where $r$ is the unknown discount rate, or yield to maturity. We have one equation here and one unknown, but we cannot solve it for $r$ explicitly. The only way to find the answer is to use trial and error.

This problem is essentially identical to the one we examined in the last chapter when we tried to find the unknown interest rate on an annuity. However, finding the rate (or yield) on a bond is even more complicated, because of the £1,000 face amount.

We can speed up the trial-and-error process by using what we know about bond prices and yields. In this case, the bond has an £80 coupon and is selling at a discount. We thus know that the yield is greater than 8 per cent. If we compute the price at 10 per cent:

$$\text{Bond value} = £80 \times (1 - 1/1.10^6)/0.10 + 1,000/1.10^6$$
$$= £80 \times 4.3553 + 1,000/1.7716$$
$$= £912.89$$

At 10 per cent, the value we calculate is lower than the actual price, so 10 per cent is too high. The true yield must be somewhere between 8 and 10 per cent. At this point, it's 'plug and chug' to find the answer. You would probably want to try 9 per cent next. If you did, you would see that this is in fact the bond's yield to maturity.

**current yield**
A bond's annual coupon divided by its price.

A bond's yield to maturity should not be confused with its **current yield**, which is simply a bond's annual coupon divided by its price. In the previous example the bond's annual coupon was £80, and its price was £955.14. Given these numbers, we see that the current yield is £80/955.14 = 8.38 per cent, which is less than the yield to maturity of 9 per cent. The reason why the current yield is too low is that it considers only the coupon portion of your return; it doesn't consider the built-in gain from the price discount. For a premium bond the reverse is true, meaning that current yield would be higher because it ignores the built-in loss.

Our discussion of bond valuation is summarized in Table 6.1.

TABLE
6.1

**Finding the value of a bond**

Bond value = $C \times [1 - 1/(1 + r)^t]/r + F/(1 + r)^t$
where
$C$ = coupon paid each period
$r$ = rate per period
$t$ = number of periods
$F$ = bond's face value

**Finding the yield on a bond**

Given a bond value, coupon, time to maturity and face value, it is possible to find the implicit discount rate, or yield to maturity, by trial and error only. To do this, try different discount rates until the calculated bond value equals the given value (or let a financial calculator do it for you). Remember that increasing the rate decreases the bond value.

**Table 6.1** Summary of bond valuation

EXAMPLE
6.2

# Current Events

A bond has a quoted price of £108,042. It has a face value of £100,000, a semi-annual coupon of £3,000, and a maturity of five years. What is its current yield? What is its yield to maturity? Which is bigger? Why?

Notice that this bond makes semi-annual payments of £3,000, so the annual payment is £6,000. The current yield is thus £6,000/108,042 = 5.55 per cent. To calculate the yield to maturity, refer back to Example 6.1. In this case the bond pays £3,000 every six months, and has 10 six-month periods until maturity. So we need to find $r$ as follows:

$$£108,042 = £3,000 \times [1 - 1/(1 + r)^{10}]/r + 100,000/(1 + r)^{10}$$

After some trial and error we find that $r$ is equal to 2.1 per cent. But the tricky part is that this 2.1 per cent is the yield *per six months*. We have to double it to get the yield to maturity, so the yield to maturity is 4.2 per cent, which is less than the current yield. The reason is that the current yield ignores the built-in loss of the premium between now and maturity.

EXAMPLE
6.3

# Bond Yields

You're looking at two bonds identical in every way except for their coupons and, of course, their prices. Both have 12 years to maturity. The first bond has a 10 per cent annual coupon rate and sells for £93,508. The second has a 12 per cent annual coupon rate. What do you think it would sell for?

Because the two bonds are similar, they will be priced to yield about the same rate. We first need to calculate the yield on the 10 per cent coupon bond. Proceeding as before, we know that the yield must be greater than 10 per cent, because the bond is selling at a discount. The bond has a fairly long maturity of 12 years. We've seen that long-term bond prices are relatively sensitive to interest rate changes, so the yield is probably close to 10 per cent. A little trial and error reveals that the yield is actually 11 per cent:

$$\begin{aligned}
\text{Bond value} &= £10,000 \times (1 - 1/1.11^{12})/0.11 + 100,000/1.11^{12} \\
&= £10,000 \times 6.4924 + 100,000/3.4985 \\
&= £64,924 + 28,584 \\
&= £93,508
\end{aligned}$$

> With an 11 per cent yield, the second bond will sell at a premium because of its £12,000 coupon. Its value is
>
> $$\text{Bond value} = £12,000 \times (1 - 1/1.11^{12})/0.11 + 100,000/1.11^{12}$$
> $$= £12,000 \times 6.4924 + 100,000/3.4985$$
> $$= £77,908 + 28,584$$
> $$= £106,492$$

# Spreadsheet Strategies

## How to Calculate Bond Prices and Yields Using a Spreadsheet

Most spreadsheets have fairly elaborate routines available for calculating bond values and yields; many of these routines involve details we have not discussed. However, setting up a simple spreadsheet to calculate prices or yields is straightforward, as our next two spreadsheets show.

Suppose we have a bond with 22 years to maturity, a coupon rate of 8 per cent, and a yield to maturity of 9 per cent. If the bond makes semi-annual payments, what is its price today?

| | B8 | | $f_x$ | =PRICE(B1,B2,B3,B4,B5,B6) | |
|---|---|---|---|---|---|
| | A | B | C | D | |
| 1 | Settlement Date | 01/01/2010 | | | |
| 2 | Maturity Date | 01/01/2032 | | | |
| 3 | Annual Coupon Rate | 8% | | | |
| 4 | Yield to Maturity | 9% | | | |
| 5 | Face Value (% of par) | 100 | | | |
| 6 | Coupons per Year | 2 | | | |
| 7 | | | | | |
| 8 | Bond Price (% of par) | 90.49 | | | |

The formula for the bond price is given in the formula bar, and is '=PRICE(B1,B2,B3,B4,B5,B6)'. In our spreadsheet, notice that we had to enter two dates: a settlement date and a maturity date. The settlement date is just the date when you actually pay for the bond, and the maturity date is the day the bond actually matures. In most of our problems we don't explicitly have these dates, so we have to make them up. For example, because our bond has 22 years to maturity, we just picked 1/1/2010 (1 January 2010) as the settlement date and 1/1/2032 (1 January 2032) as the maturity date. Any two dates would do as long as they are exactly 22 years apart, but these are particularly easy to work with. Finally, notice that we had to enter the coupon rate and yield to maturity in annual terms and then explicitly provide the number of coupon payments per year.

Now suppose we have a bond with 22 years to maturity, a coupon rate of 8 per cent, and a price of €960.17. If the bond makes semi-annual payments, what is its yield to maturity?

| | A | B |
|---|---|---|
| 1 | Settlement Date | 01/01/2010 |
| 2 | Maturity Date | 01/01/2032 |
| 3 | Annual Coupon Rate | 8% |
| 4 | Bond Price (% of par) | 96.017 |
| 5 | Face Value (% of par) | 100 |
| 6 | Coupons per Year | 2 |
| 7 | | |
| 8 | Yield to Maturity | 8.40% |

The formula for yield to maturity is '=YIELD(B1,B2,B3,B4,B5,B6)'.

## 6.2   More about Bond Features

In this section we continue our discussion of corporate debt by describing in some detail the basic terms and features that make up a typical long-term corporate bond. We discuss additional issues associated with long-term debt in subsequent sections.

Securities issued by corporations may be classified roughly as *equity securities* or *debt securities*. At the crudest level, a debt represents something that must be repaid; it is the result of borrowing money. When corporations borrow, they generally promise to make regularly scheduled interest payments, and to repay the original amount borrowed (that is, the principal). The person or firm making the loan is called the *creditor* or *lender*. The corporation borrowing the money is called the *debtor* or *borrower*.

From a financial point of view, the main differences between debt and equity are the following.

1   Debt is not an ownership interest in the firm. Creditors generally do not have voting power.

2   The corporation's payment of interest on debt is considered a cost of doing business, and is fully tax deductible. Dividends paid to shareholders are *not* tax deductible.

3   Unpaid debt is a liability of the firm. If it is not paid, the creditors can legally claim the assets of the firm. This action can result in liquidation or reorganization, two of the possible consequences of bankruptcy. Thus one of the costs of issuing debt is the possibility of financial failure. This possibility does not arise when equity is issued.

### Is It Debt or Equity?

Sometimes it is not clear whether a particular security is debt or equity. For example, suppose a corporation issues a perpetual bond with interest payable solely from corporate income if and only if earned. Whether this is really a debt is hard to say, and is primarily a legal and semantic issue. Courts and tax authorities would have the final say.

Corporations are adept at creating exotic, hybrid securities that have many features of equity but are treated as debt. Obviously, the distinction between debt and equity is important for tax purposes. So one reason why corporations try to create a debt security that is really equity is to obtain the tax benefits of debt and the bankruptcy benefits of equity.

As a general rule, equity represents an ownership interest, and it is a residual claim. This means that equity holders are paid after debt holders. As a result, the risks and benefits associated with owning debt and equity are different. To give just one example, note that the maximum reward for owning a debt security is ultimately fixed by the amount of the loan, whereas there is no upper limit to the potential reward from owning an equity interest.

### Long-Term Debt: The Basics

Ultimately, all long-term debt securities are promises made by the issuing firm to pay principal when due, and to make timely interest payments on the unpaid balance. Beyond this, a number of features distinguish these securities from one another. We discuss some of these features next.

TABLE
**6.2**

| Term | | Explanation |
| --- | --- | --- |
| Amount of issue | €1 billion | The company issued €1 billion worth of bonds. |
| Date of issue | 3/02/2010 | The bonds were sold on 3 February 2010. |
| Maturity | 03/02/2015 | The bonds mature on 3 February 2015. |
| Face value | €1,000 | The denomination of the bonds is €1,000. |
| Annual coupon | 3.25 | Each bondholder will receive €32.50 per bond per year (3.25% of face value). |
| Offer price | 99.864 | The offer price was 99.864% of the €1,000 face value, or €998.64, per bond. |
| Coupon payment dates | 1 August, 1 February | Coupons of €32.50/2 = €16.25 will be paid on these dates. |
| Security | None | The bonds are guaranteed by the Kingdom of Spain. |
| Sinking fund | None | The bonds have no sinking fund. |
| Call provision | None | The bonds do not have a call provision. |
| Rating | Moody's Aaa; S&P AA+; Fitch AAA | The bonds have a very high credit rating. |

**Table 6.2** Features of an ICO bond

The maturity of a long-term debt instrument is the length of time the debt remains outstanding with some unpaid balance. Debt securities can be *short-term* (with maturities of one year or less) or *long-term* (with maturities of more than one year).[1] Short-term debt is sometimes referred to as *unfunded debt*.[2]

Debt securities are typically called *notes*, *debentures* or *bonds*. Strictly speaking, a bond is a secured debt. However, in common usage the word 'bond' refers to all kinds of secured and unsecured debt. We shall therefore continue to use the term generically to refer to long-term debt. Also, usually the only difference between a note and a bond is the original maturity. Issues with an original maturity of 10 years or less are often called notes. Longer-term issues are called bonds.

The two major forms of long-term debt are public issue and privately placed. We concentrate on public-issue bonds. Most of what we say about them holds true for private-issue, long-term debt as well. The main difference between public-issue and privately placed debt is that the latter is placed directly with a lender and not offered to the public. Because this is a private transaction, the specific terms are up to the parties involved.

There are many other aspects of long-term debt, including such things as security, call features, sinking funds, ratings and protective covenants. Table 6.2 illustrates these features for a bond issued by the Instituto de Crédito Oficial (ICO), the Spanish state financing organization. If some of these terms are unfamiliar, have no fear. We shall discuss them all presently.

Many of these features will be detailed in the bond indenture, so we discuss this first.

**indenture**
The written agreement between the corporation and the lender detailing the terms of the debt issue.

## The Indenture

The **indenture** is the written agreement between the corporation (the borrower) and its creditors. It is sometimes referred to as the *deed of trust*.[3] Usually, a trustee (a bank, perhaps) is appointed by the corporation to represent the bondholders. The trust company must: (1) make sure the terms of the indenture are obeyed; (2) manage the sinking fund (described in the following pages); and (3) represent the bondholders in default – that is, if the company defaults on its payments to them.

The bond indenture is a legal document. It can run to several hundred pages, and generally makes for tedious reading. It is an important document, however, because it generally includes the following provisions:

1  The basic terms of the bonds

2  The total quantity of bonds issued

3  A description of property used as security

4  The repayment arrangements

5  The call provisions

6  Details of the protective covenants

We discuss these features next.

**Terms of a Bond**    Corporate bonds usually have a face value (that is, a denomination) in multiples of 1,000 (for example, €1,000, €10,000 or €50,000). This *principal value* is stated on the bond certificate. So, if a corporation wanted to borrow €1 million, 1,000 bonds with a face value of €1,000 would have to be sold. The par value (that is, the initial accounting value) of a bond is almost always the same as the face value, and the terms are used interchangeably in practice.

Corporate bonds are usually in **registered form**. For example, the indenture might read as follows:

> *Interest is payable semi-annually on 1 July and 1 January of each year to the person in whose name the bond is registered at the close of business on 15 June or 15 December respectively.*

This means that the company has a registrar who will record the ownership of each bond, and record any changes in ownership. The company will pay the interest and principal by cheque, mailed directly to the address of the owner of record. A corporate bond may be registered and have attached 'coupons'. To obtain an interest payment the owner must separate a coupon from the bond certificate and send it to the company registrar (the paying agent).

Alternatively, the bond could be in **bearer form**. This means that the certificate is the basic evidence of ownership, and the corporation will 'pay the bearer'. Ownership is not otherwise recorded, and as with a registered bond with attached coupons, the holder of the bond certificate detaches the coupons and sends them to the company to receive payment.

There are two drawbacks to bearer bonds. First, they are difficult to recover if they are lost or stolen. Second, because the company does not know who owns its bonds, it cannot notify bondholders of important events. Bearer bonds are very common in Europe, and London is the financial centre of trading in these securities.

> **registered form**
> The form of bond issue in which the registrar of the company records ownership of each bond; payment is made directly to the owner of record.

> **bearer form**
> The form of bond issue in which the bond is issued without record of the owner's name; payment is made to whomever holds the bond.

**Security**    Debt securities are classified according to the collateral and mortgages used to protect the bondholder.

*Collateral* is a general term that frequently means securities (for example, bonds and equities) that are pledged as security for payment of debt. For example, collateral trust bonds often involve a pledge of equity shares held by the corporation. However, the term 'collateral' is commonly used to refer to any asset pledged on a debt.

*Mortgage securities* are secured by a mortgage on the real property of the borrower. The property involved is usually real estate – for example, land or buildings. The legal document that describes the mortgage is called a *mortgage trust indenture* or *trust deed*.

Sometimes mortgages are on specific property. More often, blanket mortgages are used. A *blanket mortgage* pledges all the real property owned by the company.[4]

Bonds frequently represent unsecured obligations of the company. An **unsecured bond** is a bond in which no specific pledge of property is made. The term **note** is

> **unsecured bond**
> An unsecured debt security, usually with a maturity of 10 years or more.

> **note**
> An unsecured debt security, usually with a maturity under 10 years.

generally used for such instruments if the maturity of the unsecured bond is less than 10 or so years when the bond is originally issued. Unsecured bondholders have a claim only on property not otherwise pledged – in other words, the property that remains after mortgages and collateral trusts are taken into account.

The terminology that we use here and elsewhere in this chapter is standard. However, across countries, these terms can have different meanings. For example, bonds ('gilts') issued by the British government are called treasury 'stock'. Also, in the United Kingdom, a debenture is a *secured* obligation, whereas in the US it is an *unsecured* obligation!

At present, public bonds issued in Europe by industrial and financial companies are typically unsecured.

**Seniority** In general terms, *seniority* indicates preference in position over other lenders, and debts are sometimes labelled as *senior* or *junior* to indicate seniority. Some debt is *subordinated*, as in, for example, a subordinated unsecured bond.

In the event of default, holders of subordinated debt must give preference to other specified creditors. Usually, this means that the subordinated lenders will be paid off only after the specified creditors have been compensated. However, debt cannot be subordinated to equity.

**Repayment** Bonds can be repaid at maturity, at which time the bondholder will receive the stated, or face, value of the bond; or they may be repaid in part or in entirety before maturity. Early repayment in some form is more typical, and is often handled through a sinking fund.

A **sinking fund** is an account managed by the bond trustee for the purpose of repaying the bonds. The company makes annual payments to the trustee, who then uses the funds to retire a portion of the debt. The trustee does this either by buying up some of the bonds in the market, or by calling in a fraction of the outstanding bonds. This second option is discussed in the next section.

There are many different kinds of sinking fund arrangement, and the details would be spelled out in the indenture. For example:

1 Some sinking funds start about 10 years after the initial issuance.

2 Some sinking funds establish equal payments over the life of the bond.

3 Some high-quality bond issues establish payments to the sinking fund that are not sufficient to redeem the entire issue. As a consequence, there is the possibility of a large 'balloon payment' at maturity.

**The Call Provision** A **call provision** allows the company to repurchase or 'call' part or all of the bond issue at stated prices over a specific period. Corporate bonds are usually callable.

Generally, the call price is above the bond's stated value (that is, the par value). The difference between the call price and the stated value is the **call premium**. The amount of the call premium may become smaller over time. One arrangement is initially to set the call premium equal to the annual coupon payment, and then make it decline to zero as the call date moves closer to the time of maturity.

Call provisions are often not operative during the first part of a bond's life. This makes the call provision less of a worry for bondholders in the bond's early years. For example, a company might be prohibited from calling its bonds for the first 10 years. This is a **deferred call provision**. During this period of prohibition the bond is said to be **call protected**.

In recent years a new type of call provision, a 'make-whole' call, has become widespread in the corporate bond market. With such a feature, bondholders receive approximately what the bonds are worth if they are called. Because bondholders don't suffer a loss in the event of a call, they are 'made whole'.

**sinking fund**
An account managed by the bond trustee for early bond redemption.

**call provision**
An agreement giving the corporation the option to repurchase a bond at a specified price prior to maturity.

**call premium**
The amount by which the call price exceeds the par value of a bond.

**deferred call provision**
A call provision prohibiting the company from redeeming a bond prior to a certain date.

**call-protected bond**
A bond that, during a certain period, cannot be redeemed by the issuer.

**protective covenant**
A part of the indenture limiting certain actions that might be taken during the term of the loan, usually to protect the lender's interest.

**Protective Covenants**  A **protective covenant** is that part of the indenture or loan agreement that limits certain actions a company might otherwise wish to take during the term of the loan. Protective covenants can be classified into two types: negative covenants and positive (or affirmative) covenants.

A *negative covenant* is a 'thou shalt not' type of covenant. It limits or prohibits actions the company might take. Here are some typical examples:

- The firm must limit the amount of dividends it pays according to some formula.
- The firm cannot pledge any assets to other lenders.
- The firm cannot merge with another firm.
- The firm cannot sell or lease any major assets without approval by the lender.
- The firm cannot issue additional long-term debt.

A *positive covenant* is a 'thou shalt' type of covenant. It specifies an action the company agrees to take, or a condition the company must abide by. Here are some examples:

- The company must maintain its working capital at or above some specified minimum level.
- The company must periodically furnish audited financial statements to the lender.
- The firm must maintain any collateral or security in good condition.

This is only a partial list of covenants; a particular indenture may feature many different ones.

<table>
<tr><td>**CONCEPT QUESTIONS**</td><td>6.2a</td><td>What are the distinguishing features of debt compared with equity?</td></tr>
<tr><td></td><td>6.2b</td><td>What is the indenture? What are protective covenants? Give some examples.</td></tr>
<tr><td></td><td>6.2c</td><td>What is a sinking fund?</td></tr>
</table>

## 6.3  Bond Ratings

Firms frequently pay to have their debt rated. The three leading bond-rating firms are Moody's, Standard & Poor's (S&P) and Fitch. The debt ratings are an assessment of the creditworthiness of the corporate issuer. The definitions of creditworthiness used by Moody's, S&P and Fitch are based on how likely the firm is to default, and on the protection that creditors have in the event of a default.

It is important to recognize that bond ratings are concerned *only* with the possibility of default. Earlier we discussed interest rate risk, which we defined as the risk of a change in the value of a bond resulting from a change in interest rates. Bond ratings do not address this issue. As a result, the price of a highly rated bond can still be quite volatile.

Bond ratings are constructed from information supplied by the corporation. The rating classes, and some information concerning them, are shown in Table 6.3.

The highest rating a firm's debt can have is AAA or Aaa, and such debt is judged to be the best quality and to have the lowest degree of risk. A large part of corporate borrowing takes the form of low-grade, or 'junk', bonds. If these low-grade corporate bonds are rated at all, they are rated below investment grade by the major rating agencies. Investment-grade bonds are bonds rated at least BBB by S&P and Fitch, or Baa by Moody's.

Rating agencies don't always agree. To illustrate, some bonds are known as 'crossover' or '5B' bonds. For example, in April 2008 CenterPoint Energy sold an issue of 10-year notes rated BBB by S&P and Ba1 by Moody's.

A bond's credit rating can change as the issuer's financial strength improves or deteriorates. For example, in January 2010 S&P downgraded Japan Airlines' long-term debt to junk bond status. Bonds that drop into junk territory like this are called *fallen angels*. After

**TABLE 6.3**

| | | Investment-quality bond ratings | | | | Low-quality, speculative and/or 'junk' bond ratings | | | | |
| --- | --- | --- | --- | --- | --- | --- | --- | --- | --- | --- |
| | | High grade | | Medium grade | | Low grade | | Very low grade | | |
| | Moody's | Aaa | Aa | A | Baa | Ba | B | Caa | Ca | C |
| | Standard & Poor's | AAA | AA | A | BBB | BB | B | CCC | CC | C | D |
| | Fitch | AAA | AA+ | A | BBB | BB | B | CCC | | | D |

| Moody's | S&P | Fitch | |
| --- | --- | --- | --- |
| Aaa | AAA | AAA | Debt rated Aaa and AAA has the highest rating. Capacity to pay interest and principal is extremely strong. |
| Aa | AA | AA+ | Debt rated Aa, AA and AA+ has a very strong capacity to pay interest and repay principal. Together with the highest rating, this group constitutes the high-grade bond class. |
| A | A | A | Debt rated A has a strong capacity to pay interest and repay principal, although it is somewhat more susceptible to the adverse effects of changes in circumstances and economic conditions than debt in high-rated categories. |
| Baa | BBB | BBB | Debt rated Baa and BBB is regarded as having an adequate capacity to pay interest and repay principal. Whereas it normally exhibits adequate protection parameters, adverse economic conditions or changing circumstances are more likely to lead to a weakened capacity to pay interest and repay principal for debt in this category than in higher-rated categories. These bonds are medium-grade obligations. |
| Ba; B Caa Ca C | BB; B CCC CC C | BB; B CCC | Debt rated in these categories is regarded, on balance, as predominantly speculative with respect to capacity to pay interest and repay principal in accordance with the terms of the obligation. BB and Ba indicate the lowest degree of speculation, and Ca, CC, and C the highest degree of speculation. Although such debt is likely to have some quality and protective characteristics, these are outweighed by large uncertainties or major risk exposures to adverse conditions. Issues rated C by Moody's are typically in default. |
| | D | D | Debt rated D is in default, and payment of interest and/or repayment of principal is in arrears. |

*Note*: At times, Moody's, S&P and Fitch use adjustments (called notches) to these ratings. S&P uses plus and minus signs: A+ is the strongest A rating and A– the weakest. Moody's uses a 1, 2, or 3 designation, with 1 being the highest.

**Table 6.3** Bond ratings

the downgrade, Japan Airlines declared bankruptcy on the basis that it could not pay its outstanding debts, rumoured to be in the region of £16 billion (€18 billion).

## Determinants of Credit Ratings

Many factors can influence the credit rating that is awarded to a bond. Considering sovereign bonds (bonds issued by governments in local or foreign currency) first, the primary determinants are political risk, economic strength and growth prospects, government debt, and monetary and fiscal flexibility. Political risk relates to the stability of a country's government, transparency in government decisions, public security and corruption. Economic strength is fairly self-explanatory, but it also includes financial sector development, the efficiency of the public sector in a country, the income gap between rich and poor, and flexibility in workforce patterns. Monetary and fiscal flexibility means that the country's economy is less subject to economic cycles, plus central bank independence, timely, transparent and accountable government reporting, and a sustainable level of pension obligations.

Corporate bond ratings are driven by a number of other factors, but most notably the most important determinant is financial risk, and whether the company is able to meet its debt payments. Other firm-level factors relate to the company's debt burden, and whether it is growing or getting smaller. Planned and committed capital expenditures and forecast earnings performance can also impact upon a corporation's credit rating.

Macroeconomic factors can cause corporate credit ratings to change. For example, if inflation is expected to increase, the cost of borrowing will also increase, and this could affect a company's investment plans. More recently, global oil price demand has pushed the cost of manufacturing up, which has affected most firms. The strength of a country's currency is also important.

As you can see, many factors can influence the credit rating of a company's bond issue. Some factors are quantitative and easily measured, whereas others are very subjective and difficult to quantify. Credit ratings can be influenced by the economy, by an industry's prospects, by the issuing company's performance, and by the bond itself. With such complexity, it is understandable that companies and investors pay a lot of money to subscribe to credit rating agencies to access all of their services.

| CONCEPT QUESTIONS | 6.3a | What does a bond rating say about the risk of fluctuations in a bond's value resulting from interest rate changes? |
| | 6.3b | What is a junk bond? |

## 6.4    Some Different Types of Bond

Thus far we have considered only 'plain vanilla' corporate bonds. In this section we briefly look at the characteristics of bonds issued by governments, and also at bonds with unusual features.

## Government Bonds

The biggest borrowers in the world – by a wide margin – are governments. According to Fitch, the credit ratings agency, European government borrowing in 2009 was €2.12 trillion, or about 17 per cent of GDP. France was the largest borrower (€454 billion), followed by Italy (€393 billion), Germany (€386 billion) and the UK (€279 billion) (source: www.

fitchratings.com). When a government wishes to borrow money for more than one year, it sells what are known as Treasury notes and bonds to the public (in fact, most governments do so every month). Treasury notes and bonds can have original maturities ranging from 2 to 100 years.

Most Treasury issues are just ordinary coupon bonds. Some older issues are callable, and a few have some unusual features. There are two important things to keep in mind, however. First, most government Treasury issues, unlike essentially all other bonds, have no default risk, because governments can always come up with the money to make the payments (i.e. print more money!). Countries in the European Monetary Union are an exception, because the European Central Bank decides on money supply, which means that individual countries in the EMU can have default risk. Second, many Treasury issues are exempt from income taxes.

In some countries, state and local governments also borrow money by selling notes and bonds. Such issues are called *municipal* notes and bonds, or just 'munis'. Unlike Treasury issues, munis have varying degrees of default risk, and in fact they are rated much like corporate issues. Also, they are almost always callable.

## Zero Coupon Bonds

> **zero coupon bond**
> A bond that makes no coupon payments and is thus initially priced at a deep discount. Also called *pure discount bonds*.

A bond that pays no coupons at all must be offered at a price that is much lower than its stated value. Such bonds are called **zero coupon bonds**, *pure discount bonds*, or just *zeros*.[5]

Suppose Bocelli SpA issues a €1,000 face value, five-year zero coupon bond. The initial price is set at €508.35. Even though no interest payments are made on the bond, zero coupon bond calculations use semi-annual periods to be consistent with coupon bond calculations. Using semi-annual periods, it is straightforward to verify that, at this price, the bond yields 14 per cent to maturity. The total interest paid over the life of the bond is €1,000 − 508.35 = €491.65.

For tax purposes, the issuer of a zero coupon bond deducts interest every year, even though no interest is actually paid. Similarly, the owner must pay taxes on interest accrued every year, even though no interest is actually received. The way in which the yearly interest on a zero coupon bond is calculated is governed by the tax law existing in each country.

Some bonds are zero coupon bonds for only part of their lives. For example, General Motors has a debenture outstanding that matures on 15 March 2036. For the first 20 years of its life no coupon payments will be made, but, after 20 years it will begin paying coupons semi-annually at a rate of 7.75 per cent per year.

## Floating-Rate Bonds

The conventional bonds we have talked about in this chapter have fixed obligations, because the coupon rates are set as fixed percentages of the par values. Similarly, the principal amounts are set equal to the par values. Under these circumstances, the coupon payments and principal are completely fixed.

With *floating-rate bonds (floaters)*, the coupon payments are adjustable. The adjustments are tied to an interest rate index such as the Treasury bill interest rate or the 30-year Treasury bond rate. The value of a floating-rate bond depends on exactly how the coupon payment adjustments are defined. In most cases the coupon adjusts with a lag to some base rate. For example, suppose a coupon rate adjustment is made on 1 June. The adjustment might be based on the simple average of Treasury bond yields during the previous three months. In addition, the majority of floaters have the following features:

1   The holder has the right to redeem the note at par on the coupon payment date after some specified amount of time. This is called a *put* provision, and it is discussed in the following section.

2 The coupon rate has a floor and a ceiling, meaning that the coupon is subject to a minimum and a maximum. In this case the coupon rate is said to be 'capped', and the upper and lower rates are sometimes called the *collar*.

A particularly interesting type of floating-rate bond is an *inflation-linked* bond. Such bonds have coupons that are adjusted according to the rate of inflation (the principal amount may be adjusted as well). The UK and French governments are the biggest European issuers of inflation-linked bonds, and they are called inflation-linked gilts (ILGs) in the UK and OATi and OAT€i in France. Other countries, including the US, Germany, Greece, Italy and Iceland, have issued similar securities.

## Other Types of Bond

Many bonds have unusual or exotic features. So-called *catastrophe*, or *cat*, *bonds* provide an interesting example. In December 2009 Swiss Reinsurance Company Ltd issued $150 million in cat bonds (reinsurance companies sell insurance to insurance companies). These cat bonds, which matured in late 2010, were issued at a large discount to par value. Investors in the cat bond would have received a high return if no trigger events (such as hurricanes, flooding or earthquakes) occurred. However, in the event of a major natural disaster, investors would lose their full investment.

The largest single cat bond issue to date is a series of six bonds sold by Merna Reinsurance in 2007. The six bond issues were to cover various catastrophes the company faced owing to its reinsurance of State Farm. The six bonds totalled about $1.2 billion in par value, a large portion of the record $7 billion in cat bonds issued during 2007.

At this point, cat bonds probably seem pretty risky. It might therefore be surprising to learn that, since cat bonds were first issued in 1997, only one has not been paid in full. Because of Hurricane Katrina, bondholders in that one issue lost $190 million.

Another possible bond feature is a *warrant*. A warrant gives the buyer of a bond the right to purchase shares of equity in the company at a fixed price. Such a right would be very valuable if the share price climbed substantially (a later chapter discusses this subject in greater depth). Because of the value of this feature, bonds with warrants are often issued at a very low coupon rate.

As these examples illustrate, bond features are really limited only by the imaginations of the parties involved. Unfortunately, there are far too many variations for us to cover in detail here. We therefore close this discussion by mentioning a few of the more common types.

*Income bonds* are similar to conventional bonds, except that coupon payments depend on company income. Specifically, coupons are paid to bondholders only if the firm's income is sufficient. This would appear to be an attractive feature, but income bonds are not very common.

A *convertible bond* can be swapped for a fixed number of shares of equity any time before maturity at the holder's option. Convertibles are relatively common, but the number has been decreasing in recent years.

A *put bond* allows the *holder* to force the issuer to buy back the bond at a stated price. For example, 3i Group plc, the private equity firm, has bonds outstanding that allow the holder to force 3i Group to buy the bonds back at 100 per cent of face value if certain relevant 'risk' events happen. One such event is a change in credit rating by Moody's or S&P from investment grade to lower than investment grade. The put feature is therefore just the reverse of the call provision.

A given bond may have many unusual features. Two of the most recent exotic bonds are *CoCo bonds*, which have a coupon payment, and *NoNo bonds*, which are zero coupon bonds. CoCo and NoNo bonds are contingent convertible, puttable, callable, subordinated bonds. The contingent convertible clause is similar to the normal conversion feature, except that the contingent feature must be met. For example, a contingent feature may require that the company equity trade at 110 per cent of the conversion price for 20 out of the most recent 30 days. Because they are so complex, valuation of NoNo and CoCo bonds is exceptionally difficult.

## 6.5 Bond Markets

Bonds are bought and sold in enormous quantities every day. You may be surprised to learn that the trading volume in bonds on a typical day is many, many times larger than the trading volume in equities (by *trading volume* we simply mean the amount of money that changes hands). Here is a finance trivia question: where does most trading of financial securities take place? Most people would guess the stock exchanges. In fact, the largest securities market in the world in terms of trading volume is the government treasury market.

### How Bonds Are Bought and Sold

Most trading in bonds takes place over the counter, or OTC, which means there is no particular place where buying and selling occur. Instead, dealers around the world stand ready to buy and sell. The various dealers are connected electronically. In 2010 the London Stock Exchange introduced a new electronic trading system for bonds that allowed private investors to buy bonds in denominations of £1,000. This retail market for individuals was a new innovation for UK bonds, since most British bonds have a face value of at least £50,000. In the Eurozone the main bond markets are Deutsche Böerse and Euronext, where many corporate bonds are traded through an electronic trading system.

One reason why the bond markets are so big is that the number of bond issues far exceeds the number of equity issues. There are two reasons for this. First, a corporation would typically have only one ordinary equity issue outstanding (there are exceptions to this, which we discuss in our next chapter). However, a single large corporation could easily have a dozen or more note and bond issues outstanding. Beyond this, government and local borrowing is simply enormous. For example, many large cities will have a wide variety of notes and bonds outstanding, representing money borrowed to pay for things such as roads, sewers and schools. When you think about how many large cities there are in the world, you begin to get the picture!

Although the total volume of trading in bonds far exceeds that in equities, only a small fraction of the total bond issues that exist actually trade on a given day. This fact, combined with the lack of transparency in the bond market, means that it can be difficult or impossible to get up-to-date prices on individual bonds, particularly for smaller corporate or municipal issues. Instead, a variety of sources of estimated prices exist and are commonly used.

### Bond Price Reporting

In recent years, transparency in the corporate bond market has improved dramatically. The advent of high-speed Internet connections has allowed real-time updates on bond prices and trading volumes directly from the stock exchange. Our nearby *Work the Web* box shows you how to get this information.

# Work the Web

Bond quotes have become more available with the rise of the Internet. The best place to find current bond prices is the stock exchange itself. We went to the Euronext website and searched for bonds issued by Air France-KLM. Here is a look at part of what we found:

The bond has a coupon rate of 4.97 per cent and matures on 1 April 2015. The last sale on this bond was at a price of €14.54. Not only does the site provide the most recent price and yield information, it also provides more important information about the bond, such as the credit rating, coupon date, call date and call price. We'll leave it up to you to have a look at the page and the rest of the information available there.

## QUESTIONS

1 Go to this website and find the bond shown above. When was this bond issued? What was the size of the bond issue? What were the yield to maturity and price when the bond was issued?

2 Search for Barclays bonds. Why do you think Barclays has issued so many different types of bond?

As shown in Fig. 6.3 for Euronext bonds, stock exchanges provide a daily snapshot of trading in the most active issues. The information shown is largely self-explanatory. Notice that the price of the AAB 4.7 per cent coupon bond to mature in 2019 was trading at 101.1 per cent of its face value, and 35,000 bonds were traded.

FIGURE
6.3

**Bonds**

Download >>>> Prices  Prices & features

| Name | ISIN | Market | Last | Currency | Accrued coupon % | Volume | Date - time (CET) | Maturity date |
|------|------|--------|------|----------|------------------|--------|-------------------|---------------|
| 11 CITIESB 5,75%62 | XS0151887584 | AMS | 0.00 | % | 3.229 | 0 | - | 26/07/62 |
| 11CITI 2A 0,937%71 | XS0178720107 | AMS | 0.00 | % | - | 0 | - | 20/10/71 |
| 11CITI2B 5,20%71 | XS0178720362 | AMS | 0.00 | % | 1.695 | 0 | - | 20/10/71 |
| 11CITI2C 5,7%71 | XS0178720446 | AMS | 0.00 | % | 1.858 | 0 | - | 20/10/71 |
| 11CITIES C 6,3%62 | XS0151890372 | AMS | 0.00 | % | 3.538 | 0 | - | 26/07/62 |
| 11CITIESA 0,973%62 | XS0151880142 | AMS | 0.00 | % | - | 0 | - | 26/07/62 |
| A BERG HY 0%13 | XS0224658483 | AMS | 0.00 | % | 0.00 | 0 | - | 29/07/13 |
| AAB 0%13 | XS0225867422 | AMS | 0.00 | % | 0.00 | 0 | | 01/08/13 |
| AAB 4,7%19 | NL0000122505 | AMS | 101.10 | % | - | 35,000 | 19/01/10 12:30 | 10/06/19 |
| AAB 3.75%12 | XS0267452927 | AMS | 103.19 | % | 0.359 | 50,000 | 15/01/10 16:41 | 12/01/12 |
| AAB 4,31%PL | XS0246487457 | AMS | 63.56 | % | 4.05 | 249,000 | 12/02/10 12:33 | - |
| AAB 1,034%11 | XS0211831135 | AMS | 0.00 | % | - | 0 | - | 07/02/11 |
| AAB 3 1/4%13 | XS0241183804 | AMS | 102.05 | % | 0.258 | 50,000 | 15/01/10 17:13 | 18/01/13 |
| AAB 3 1/4%15 | XS0230182338 | AMS | 99.49 | % | 1.317 | 50,000 | 15/01/10 16:42 | 21/09/15 |
| AAB 4 1/4%16 | XS0254035768 | AMS | 102.30 | % | 3.271 | 7,000 | 11/02/10 13:01 | 11/05/16 |
| AAB 4 3/4%14 | XS0180772484 | AMS | 105.20 | % | 0.559 | 20,000 | 10/02/10 11:56 | 04/01/14 |
| AAB 4 5/8%13 | XS0179253934 | AMS | 106.58 | % | 1.406 | 20,000 | 09/02/10 16:48 | 28/10/13 |
| AAB 5 3/8%12 | XS0150140597 | AMS | 105.81 | % | 3.445 | 15,000 | 11/01/10 15:26 | 27/06/12 |
| AAB 5 5/8%11 | XS0128758785 | AMS | 104.16 | % | 4.253 | 114,000 | 09/02/10 12:12 | 16/05/11 |
| AAB 6 1/4%10 | NL0000118024 | AMS | 101.37 | % | 3.989 | 32,000 | 11/02/10 14:18 | 28/06/10 |

**Figure 6.3** Sample Euronext bond quotations

FIGURE 6.4

### UK GILTS - cash market
www.ft.com/gilts

| Jan 8 | Price £ | Day's chng | W'ks chng | Int yield | Red yield | Day's chng | W'ks chng | Mth's chng | Year chng | 52 Week High | 52 Week Low | Amnt £m | Last xd date | Interest due |
|---|---|---|---|---|---|---|---|---|---|---|---|---|---|---|
| **Shorts (Lives up to Five Years)** | | | | | | | | | | | | | | |
| Tr 4.75pc '10 | 101.75 | -0.04 | -0.12 | 4.67 | 0.41 | +0.01 | +0.02 | +0.01 | -0.62 | 105.39 | 101.60 | 21,285 | 28/11 | 7 Jun/Dec |
| Tr 6.25pc '10 | 104.96 | -0.04 | -0.10 | 5.95 | 0.53 | -0.01 | -0.02 | -0.05 | -0.47 | 109.97 | 104.74 | 6,719 | 16/11 | 25 May/Nov |
| Tr 3.25pc '11 | 103.74 | -0.01 | +0.12 | 3.13 | 1.26 | 0.00 | -0.04 | +0.12 | -0.88 | 115.22 | 102.24 | 15,747 | 28/11 | 7 Jun/Dec |
| Tr 4.25pc '11 | 104.02 | -0.01 | +0.02 | 4.09 | 0.74 | -0.02 | -0.05 | +0.09 | -0.93 | 106.45 | 103.78 | 23,651 | 29/08 | 7 Mar/Sep |
| Cn 9pc Ln '11 | 111.98 | -0.05 | -0.08 | 8.03 | 0.95 | -0.01 | -0.04 | +0.08 | -0.77 | 118.61 | 99.40 | 7,312 | 01/07 | 12 Jan/Jul |
| Tr 5pc '12 | 107.30 | -0.01 | +0.04 | 4.66 | 1.54 | -0.01 | -0.01 | +0.20 | -0.68 | 109.96 | 106.56 | 26,867 | 29/08 | 7 Mar/Sep |
| Tr 5.25pc '12 | 108.08 | -0.02 | +0.02 | 4.86 | 1.80 | 0.00 | +0.01 | +0.24 | -0.51 | 111.11 | 107.21 | 21,583 | 28/11 | 7 Jun/Dec |
| Tr 9pc '12 ✠ | 117.81 | -0.03 | -0.07 | 7.64 | 1.87 | -0.01 | +0.01 | +0.22 | -0.56 | 124.11 | 116.18 | 204 | 28/07 | 6 Feb/Aug |
| Tr 8pc '13 | 119.98 | -0.04 | -0.15 | 6.67 | 2.34 | 0.00 | +0.05 | +0.26 | -0.23 | 125.99 | 119.27 | 8,377 | 16/09 | 27 Mar/Sep |
| Tr 4.5pc '13 | 106.80 | -0.01 | -0.01 | 4.21 | 2.25 | 0.00 | +0.04 | +0.24 | -0.23 | 109.94 | 105.08 | 29,287 | 29/08 | 7 Mar/Sep |
| Tr 2.25pc '14 | 98.15 | -0.03 | -0.09 | 2.29 | 2.72 | +0.01 | +0.08 | +0.30 | - | 120.73 | 95.03 | 29,123 | 29/08 | 7 Mar/Sep |
| Tr 5pc '14 | 109.28 | -0.04 | -0.13 | 4.57 | 2.86 | +0.01 | +0.07 | +0.28 | +0.14 | 115.60 | 108.74 | 28,057 | 29/08 | 7 Mar/Sep |
| **Five to Ten Years** | | | | | | | | | | | | | | |
| Tr 7.75pc '12-15 ✠ | 112.26 | -0.03 | -0.03 | 6.90 | 1.62 | -0.01 | -0.01 | +0.18 | -0.69 | 116.94 | 112.09 | 407 | 15/07 | 26 Jan/Jul |
| Tr 2.75pc '15 | 98.40 | -0.02 | +0.11 | 2.79 | 3.10 | +0.01 | +0.03 | +0.30 | - | 100.12 | 98.00 | 15,060 | 13/07 | 22 Jan/Jul |
| Tr 4.75pc '15 | 108.16 | -0.05 | -0.07 | 4.39 | 3.16 | +0.01 | +0.06 | +0.31 | +0.17 | 115.18 | 107.64 | 24,968 | 29/08 | 7 Mar/Sep |
| Tr 8pc '15 | 125.48 | -0.08 | -0.15 | 6.37 | 3.23 | +0.01 | +0.06 | +0.32 | -0.01 | 135.52 | 125.11 | 9,997 | 28/11 | 7 Jun/Dec |

*(Columns 'Day's chng', 'W'ks chng', 'Mth's chng', 'Year chng' after 'Red yield' fall under the heading Red yield)*

*Source*: REUTERS Ltd, via www.ft.com/gilts

**Figure 6.4** Sample *Financial Times* UK gilts cash market prices

If you go to the website and click on a particular bond, you will get a lot of information about the bond, including the credit rating, the call schedule, original issue information, and trade information.

As we mentioned before, the government Treasury market is the largest securities market in the world. As with bond markets in general, it is an OTC market, so there is limited transparency. However, unlike the situation with bond markets in general, trading in Treasury issues, particularly recently issued ones, is very heavy. Each day, representative prices for outstanding Treasury issues are reported.

Figure 6.4 shows a portion of the daily Treasury note and bond listings from the *Financial Times* website, ft.com. The entry that begins 'Tr 8pc '15' is highlighted. This information tells us that the bond will mature in 2015 and has an 8 per cent coupon. The next column is the price, which is £125.48. 'Day's chng' tells you that the price has fallen by £0.08 since the day before, and by £0.15 over the previous week. 'Int yield' is the interest yield or current yield (%), and you can calculate this by dividing the coupon (£8) by the bond price (£125.48). The redemption yield, 'Red yield', is the internal rate of return or yield to maturity of the bond, assuming that the bond is held to maturity and all the coupon payments are paid on time. For the 'Tr 8pc '15' bond this is 3.23 per cent. UK Treasury bonds (gilts) all make semi-annual payments and have a face value of £100, so this bond will pay £40 per six months until it matures.

The next four columns deal with changes in the bond's redemption yield (yield to maturity). Finally, the amount of bonds traded is presented (Amnt £m), the final date at which an individual is eligible to receive the bond's coupon (Last xd date), and the dates on which coupon payments are due.

If you examine the yields on the various issues in Fig. 6.4, you will clearly see that they vary by maturity. Why this occurs, and what it might mean, are things that we discuss in our next section.

## A Note about Bond Price Quotes

If you buy a bond between coupon payment dates, the price you pay is usually more than the price you are quoted. The reason is that standard convention in the bond market is to quote prices net of 'accrued interest', meaning that accrued interest is deducted to arrive at the quoted price. This quoted price is called the **clean price**. The price you actually pay, however, includes the accrued interest. This price is the **dirty price**,

---

**clean price**
The price of a bond net of accrued interest; this is the price that is typically quoted.

**dirty price**
The price of a bond including accrued interest, also known as the *full* or *invoice price*. This is the price the buyer actually pays.

also known as the 'full' or 'invoice' price. If you look back to Fig. 6.3, you will see the accrued interest presented for a number of corporate bonds.

An example is the easiest way to understand these issues. Suppose you buy a bond with a 12 per cent annual coupon, payable semi-annually. You actually pay €1,080 for this bond, so €1,080 is the dirty, or invoice, price. Further, on the day you buy it, the next coupon is due in four months, so you are between coupon dates. Notice that the next coupon will be €60.

The accrued interest on a bond is calculated by taking the fraction of the coupon period that has passed, in this case two months out of six, and multiplying this fraction by the next coupon, €60. So, the accrued interest in this example is $2/6 \times €60 = €20$. The bond's quoted price (that is, its clean price) would be €1,080 − €20 = €1,060.

---

**CONCEPT QUESTIONS**

6.5a  What is meant by a bond's redemption yield and interest yield?
6.5b  What is the difference between a bond's clean price and dirty price?

---

## 6.6  Inflation and Interest Rates

So far, we haven't considered the role of inflation in our various discussions of interest rates, yields and returns. Because this is an important consideration, we consider the impact of inflation next.

### Real versus Nominal Rates

**real rates**
Interest rates or rates of return that have been adjusted for inflation.

**nominal rates**
Interest rates or rates of return that have not been adjusted for inflation.

In examining interest rates, or any other financial market rates such as discount rates, bond yields, rates of return or required returns, it is often necessary to distinguish between **real rates** and **nominal rates**. Nominal rates are called 'nominal' because they have not been adjusted for inflation. Real rates are rates that have been adjusted for inflation.

To see the effect of inflation, suppose prices are currently rising by 5 per cent per year. In other words, the rate of inflation is 5 per cent. An investment is available that will be worth £115.50 in one year. It costs £100 today. Notice that with a present value of £100 and a future value in one year of £115.50, the investment has a 15.5 per cent rate of return. In calculating this 15.5 per cent return, we did not consider the effect of inflation, however, so this is the nominal return.

What is the impact of inflation here? To answer, suppose pizzas cost £5 apiece at the beginning of the year. With £100, we can buy 20 pizzas. Because the inflation rate is 5 per cent, pizzas will cost 5 per cent more, or £5.25, at the end of the year. If we take the investment, how many pizzas can we buy at the end of the year? Measured in pizzas, what is the rate of return on this investment?

Our £115.50 from the investment will buy us £115.50/5.25 = 22 pizzas. This is up from 20 pizzas, so our pizza rate of return is 10 per cent. What this illustrates is that even though the nominal return on our investment is 15.5 per cent, our buying power goes up by only 10 per cent, because of inflation. Put another way, we are really only 10 per cent richer. In this case we say that the real return is 10 per cent.

Alternatively, we can say that with 5 per cent inflation each of the £115.50 nominal pounds we get is worth 5 per cent less in real terms, so the real cash value of our investment in a year is

$$£115.50/1.05 = £110$$

What we have done is to *deflate* the £115.50 by 5 per cent. Because we give up £100 in current buying power to get the equivalent of £110, our real return is again 10 per cent.

Because we have removed the effect of future inflation here, this £110 is said to be measured in current pounds.

The difference between nominal and real rates is important, and bears repeating:

*The nominal rate on an investment is the percentage change in the amount of cash you have.*

*The real rate on an investment is the percentage change in how much you can buy with your cash – in other words, the percentage change in your buying power.*

## The Fisher Effect

Our discussion of real and nominal returns illustrates a relationship often called the **Fisher effect** (after the great economist Irving Fisher). Because investors are ultimately concerned with what they can buy with their money, they require compensation for inflation. Let $R$ stand for the nominal rate and $r$ stand for the real rate. The Fisher effect tells us that the relationship between nominal rates, real rates and inflation can be written as

> **Fisher effect**
> The relationship between nominal returns, real returns and inflation.

$$1 + R = (1 + r) \times (1 + h) \tag{6.2}$$

where $h$ is the inflation rate.

In the preceding example, the nominal rate was 15.50 per cent and the inflation rate was 5 per cent. What was the real rate? We can determine it by plugging in these numbers:

$$1 + 0.1550 = (1 + r) \times (1 + 0.05)$$
$$1 + r = 1.1550/1.05 = 1.10$$
$$r = 10\%$$

This real rate is the same as we found before. If we take another look at the Fisher effect, we can rearrange things a little as follows:

$$1 + R = (1 + r) \times (1 + h)$$
$$R = r + h + r \times h \tag{6.3}$$

What this tells us is that the nominal rate has three components. First, there is the real rate on the investment, $r$. Next, there is the compensation for the decrease in the value of the money originally invested because of inflation, $h$. The third component represents compensation for the fact that the money earned on the investment is also worth less because of the inflation.

This third component is usually small, so it is often dropped. The nominal rate is then approximately equal to the real rate plus the inflation rate:

$$R \approx r + h \tag{6.4}$$

---

**EXAMPLE 6.4**

## The Fisher Effect

If investors require a 10 per cent real rate of return, and the inflation rate is 8 per cent, what must be the approximate nominal rate? The exact nominal rate?

The nominal rate is approximately equal to the sum of the real rate and the inflation rate: 10% + 8% = 18%. From the Fisher effect, we have

$$1 + R = (1 + r) \times (1 + h)$$
$$= 1.10 \times 1.08$$
$$= 1.1880$$

Therefore the nominal rate will actually be closer to 19 per cent.

It is important to note that financial rates, such as interest rates, discount rates and rates of return, are almost always quoted in nominal terms. To remind you of this, we shall henceforth use the symbol $R$ instead of $r$ in most of our discussions about such rates.

## Inflation and Present Values

One question that often comes up is the effect of inflation on present value calculations. The basic principle is simple: either discount nominal cash flows at a nominal rate, or discount real cash flows at a real rate. As long as you are consistent, you will get the same answer.

To illustrate, suppose you want to withdraw money each year for the next three years, and you want each withdrawal to have £25,000 worth of purchasing power as measured in current pounds. If the inflation rate is 4 per cent per year, then the withdrawals will simply have to increase by 4 per cent each year to compensate. The withdrawals each year will thus be

$$C_1 = £25,000(1.04) = £26,000$$
$$C_2 = £25,000(1.04)^2 = £27,040$$
$$C_3 = £25,000(1.04)^3 = £28,121.60$$

What is the present value of these cash flows if the appropriate nominal discount rate is 10 per cent? This is a standard calculation, and the answer is

$$PV = \frac{£26,000}{1.10} + \frac{£27,040}{1.10^2} + \frac{£28,121.60}{1.10^3}$$
$$= £67,111.65$$

Notice that we discounted the nominal cash flows at a nominal rate.

To calculate the present value using real cash flows, we need the real discount rate. Using the Fisher equation, the real discount rate is obtained from

$$1 + R = (1 + r)(1 + h)$$
$$1 + 0.10 = (1 + r)(1 + 0.04)$$
$$r = 0.0577$$

By design, the real cash flows are an annuity of £25,000 per year. So the present value in real terms is

$$PV = £25,000[1 - (1/1.0577^3)]/0.0577 = £67,111.65$$

Thus we get exactly the same answer (after allowing for a small rounding error in the real rate). Of course, you could also use the growing annuity equation we discussed in the previous chapter. The withdrawals are increasing at 4 per cent per year: so, using the growing annuity formula, the present value is

$$PV = £26,000 \left[ \frac{1 - \left(\frac{1 + 0.04}{1 + 0.10}\right)^3}{0.10 - 0.04} \right]$$
$$= £26,000(2.58122)$$
$$= £67,111.65$$

This is exactly the same present value we calculated before.

**6.6a** What is the difference between a nominal and a real return? Which is more important to a typical investor?

**6.6b** What is the Fisher effect?

## 6.7 Determinants of Bond Yields

We are now in a position to discuss the determinants of a bond's yield. As we shall see, the yield on any particular bond reflects a variety of factors, some common to all bonds and some specific to the issue under consideration.

### The Term Structure of Interest Rates

At any one time, short-term and long-term interest rates will generally be different. Sometimes short-term rates are higher, sometimes lower. Figure 6.5 gives us a long-range perspective on this by showing over two centuries of short- and long-term interest rates for the US (this is the only country that has such a long time period of data). As shown, through time, the difference between short- and long-term rates has ranged from essentially zero to up to several percentage points, both positive and negative.

The relationship between short- and long-term interest rates is known as the **term structure of interest rates**. To be a little more precise, the term structure of interest rates tells us what *nominal* interest rates are on *default-free, pure discount* bonds of all maturities. These rates are, in essence, 'pure' interest rates, because they involve no risk of default and a single, lump sum future payment. In other words, the term structure tells us the pure time value of money for different lengths of time.

When long-term rates are higher than short-term rates, we say that the term structure is upward sloping; when short-term rates are higher, we say it is downward sloping. The

> **term structure of interest rates** The relationship between nominal interest rates on default-free, pure discount securities and time to maturity: that is, the pure time value of money.

FIGURE **6.5**

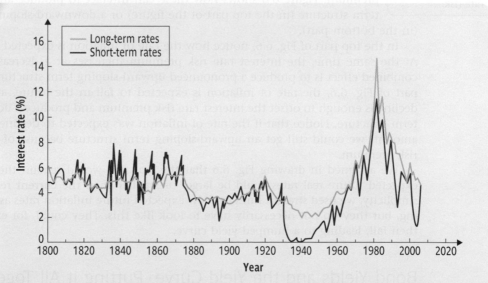

*Source*: J.J. Siegel, *Stocks for the Long Run*, 3rd edn (McGraw-Hill, 2004), updated by the authors.

**Figure 6.5** US interest rates: 1800–2007

term structure can also be 'humped'. When this occurs, it is usually because rates increase at first, but then begin to decline as we look at longer- and longer-term rates. The most common shape of the term structure, particularly in modern times, is upward sloping, but the degree of steepness has varied quite a bit.

What determines the shape of the term structure? There are three basic components. The first two are the ones we discussed in our previous section: the real rate of interest and the rate of inflation. The real rate of interest is the compensation that investors demand for forgoing the use of their money. You can think of it as the pure time value of money after adjusting for the effects of inflation.

The real rate of interest is the basic component underlying every interest rate, regardless of the time to maturity. When the real rate is high, all interest rates will tend to be higher, and vice versa. Thus the real rate doesn't really determine the shape of the term structure; instead, it mostly influences the overall level of interest rates.

In contrast, the prospect of future inflation strongly influences the shape of the term structure. Investors thinking about lending money for various lengths of time recognize that future inflation erodes the value of the cash that will be returned. As a result, investors demand compensation for this loss in the form of higher nominal rates. This extra compensation is called the **inflation premium**.

> **inflation premium**
> The portion of a nominal interest rate that represents compensation for expected future inflation.

If investors believe the rate of inflation will be higher in the future, then long-term nominal interest rates will tend to be higher than short-term rates. Thus an upward-sloping term structure may reflect anticipated increases in inflation. Similarly, a downward-sloping term structure probably reflects the belief that inflation will be falling in the future.

> **interest rate risk premium**
> The compensation investors demand for bearing interest rate risk.

The third, and last, component of the term structure has to do with interest rate risk. As we discussed earlier in the chapter, longer-term bonds have much greater risk of loss resulting from changes in interest rates than do shorter-term bonds. Investors recognize this risk, and they demand extra compensation in the form of higher rates for bearing it. This extra compensation is called the **interest rate risk premium**. The longer is the term to maturity, the greater is the interest rate risk, so the interest rate risk premium increases with maturity. However, as we discussed earlier, interest rate risk increases at a decreasing rate, so the interest rate risk premium does as well.[6]

Putting the pieces together, we see that the term structure reflects the combined effect of the real rate of interest, the inflation premium, and the interest rate risk premium. Figure 6.6 shows how these can interact to produce an upward-sloping term structure (in the top part of the figure) or a downward-sloping term structure (in the bottom part).

In the top part of Fig. 6.6, notice how the rate of inflation is expected to rise gradually. At the same time, the interest rate risk premium increases at a decreasing rate, so the combined effect is to produce a pronounced upward-sloping term structure. In the bottom part of Fig. 6.6, the rate of inflation is expected to fall in the future, and the expected decline is enough to offset the interest rate risk premium and produce a downward-sloping term structure. Notice that if the rate of inflation was expected to decline by only a small amount, we could still get an upward-sloping term structure because of the interest rate risk premium.

We assumed in drawing Fig. 6.6 that the real rate would remain the same. Actually, expected future real rates could be larger or smaller than the current real rate. Also, for simplicity, we used straight lines to show expected future inflation rates as rising or declining, but they do not necessarily have to look like this. They could, for example, rise and then fall, leading to a humped yield curve.

## Bond Yields and the Yield Curve: Putting It All Together

Going back to Fig. 6.4, recall that we saw that the yields on Treasury notes and bonds of different maturities are not the same. Each day, in addition to the Treasury prices and yields shown in Fig. 6.4, the *Financial Times* provides a plot of Treasury yields relative to maturity.

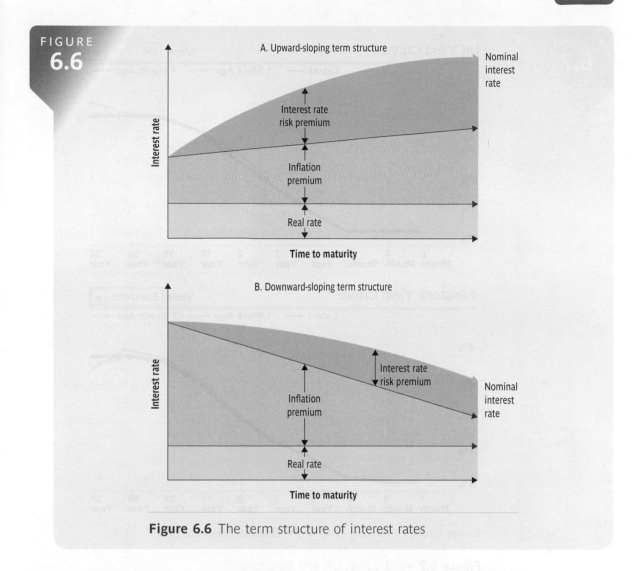

**Figure 6.6** The term structure of interest rates

This plot is called the **Treasury yield curve** (or just the *yield curve*). Figure 6.7 shows the yield curve for the UK and Eurozone in early 2010. As can be seen both are upward sloping.

As you probably now suspect, the shape of the yield curve reflects the term structure of interest rates. In fact, the Treasury yield curve and the term structure of interest rates are almost the same thing. The only difference is that the term structure is based on pure discount bonds, whereas the yield curve is based on coupon bond yields. As a result, Treasury yields depend on the three components that underlie the term structure – the real rate, expected future inflation, and the interest rate risk premium.

Treasury notes and bonds have three important features that we need to remind you of: they are default-free (except for Eurozone countries), they are taxable, and they are highly liquid. This is not true of bonds in general, so we need to examine what additional factors come into play when we look at bonds issued by corporations or municipalities.

The first thing to consider is credit risk – that is, the possibility of default. Investors recognize that in most countries (except the Eurozone) issuers other than the Treasury may or may not make all the promised payments on a bond, so they demand a higher yield as compensation for this risk. This extra compensation is called the **default risk premium**. Earlier in the chapter we saw how bonds were rated based on their credit risk. What you will find if you start looking at bonds of different ratings is that lower-rated bonds have higher yields.

**Treasury yield curve**
A plot of the yields on Treasury notes and bonds relative to maturity.

**default risk premium**
The portion of a nominal interest rate or bond yield that represents compensation for the possibility of default.

FIGURE
**6.7**

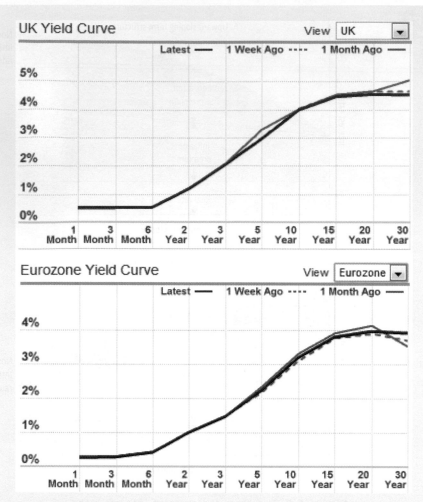

**Figure 6.7** Yield curve: UK and Eurozone

**taxability premium**
The portion of a nominal interest rate or bond yield that represents compensation for unfavourable tax status.

**liquidity premium**
The portion of a nominal interest rate or bond yield that represents compensation for lack of liquidity.

An important thing to recognize about a bond's yield is that it is calculated assuming that all the promised payments will be made. As a result, it is really a promised yield, and it may or may not be what you will earn. In particular, if the issuer defaults, your actual yield will be lower – probably much lower. This fact is particularly important when it comes to junk bonds. Thanks to a clever bit of marketing, such bonds are now commonly called high-yield bonds, which has a much nicer ring to it; but now you recognize that these are really high *promised* yield bonds.

Next, recall that we discussed earlier how government bonds are free from most taxes and, as a result, have much lower yields than taxable bonds. Investors demand the extra yield on a taxable bond as compensation for the unfavourable tax treatment. This extra compensation is the **taxability premium**.

Finally, bonds have varying degrees of liquidity. As we discussed earlier, there are an enormous number of bond issues, most of which do not trade regularly. As a result, if you wanted to sell quickly, you would probably not get as good a price as you could otherwise. Investors prefer liquid assets to illiquid ones, so they demand a **liquidity premium** on top of all the other premiums we have discussed. As a result, all else being the same, less liquid bonds will have higher yields than more liquid bonds.

## Conclusion

If we combine all of the things we have discussed regarding bond yields, we find that bond yields represent the combined effect of no fewer than six things. The first is the real rate of interest. On top of the real rate are five premiums representing compensation for:

1 Expected future inflation
2 Interest rate risk
3 Default risk
4 Taxability
5 Lack of liquidity

As a result, determining the appropriate yield on a bond requires careful analysis of each of these effects.

---

| CONCEPT QUESTIONS | 6.7a What is the term structure of interest rates? What determines its shape? |
| --- | --- |
| | 6.7b What is the Treasury yield curve? |
| | 6.7c What six components make up a bond's yield? |

---

# Summary and Conclusions

This chapter has explored bonds, bond yields, and interest rates:

1 Determining bond prices and yields is an application of basic discounted cash flow principles.

2 Bond values move in the direction opposite to that of interest rates, leading to potential gains or losses for bond investors.

3 Bonds have a variety of features, spelled out in a document called the indenture.

4 Bonds are rated based on their default risk. Some bonds, such as Treasury bonds, have no risk of default, whereas so-called junk bonds have substantial default risk.

5 A wide variety of bonds exist, many of which contain exotic or unusual features.

6 Much bond trading is OTC, with little or no market transparency in many cases. As a result, bond price and volume information can be difficult to find for some types of bond.

7 Bond yields and interest rates reflect the effect of six different things: the real interest rate, and five premiums that investors demand as compensation for inflation, interest rate risk, default risk, taxability and lack of liquidity.

In closing, we note that bonds are a vital source of financing for governments and corporations of all types. Bond prices and yields are a rich subject, and our one chapter necessarily touches on only the most important concepts and ideas. There is a great deal more we could say, but instead we shall move on to equities in our next chapter.

## Chapter Review and Self-Test Problems

**6.1 Bond Values** A Svenska AB bond has a 10 per cent coupon rate and a SKr1,000 face value. Interest is paid semi-annually, and the bond has 20 years to maturity. If investors require a 12 per cent yield, what is the bond's value? What is the effective annual yield on the bond?

**6.2 Bond Yields** An Ekornes ASA bond carries an 8 per cent coupon, paid semi-annually. The par value is NKr1,000, and the bond matures in six years. If the bond currently sells for NKr911.37, what is its yield to maturity? What is the effective annual yield?

## Answers to Chapter Review and Self-Test Problems

6.1 Because the bond has a 10 per cent coupon yield and investors require a 12 per cent return, we know that the bond must sell at a discount. Notice that, because the bond pays interest semi-annually, the coupons amount to SKr100/2 = SKr50 every six months. The required yield is 12%/2 = 6% every six months. Finally, the bond matures in 20 years, so there are a total of 40 six-month periods.

The bond's value is thus equal to the present value of SKr50 every six months for the next 40 six-month periods plus the present value of the SKr1,000 face amount:

$$\text{Bond value} = \text{SKr50} \times \left[\frac{1 - 1/1.06^{40}}{0.06}\right] + \frac{1,000}{1.06^{40}}$$
$$= \text{SKr50} \times 15.04630 + 1,000/10.2857$$
$$= \text{SKr849.54}$$

Notice that we discounted the SKr1,000 back 40 periods at 6 per cent per period, rather than 20 years at 12 per cent. The reason is that the effective annual yield on the bond is $1.06^2 - 1 = 12.36\%$, not 12 per cent. We thus could have used 12.36 per cent per year for 20 years when we calculated the present value of the SKr1,000 face amount, and the answer would have been the same.

6.2 The present value of the bond's cash flows is its current price, NKr911.37. The coupon is NKr40 every six months for 12 periods. The face value is NKr1,000. So the bond's yield is the unknown discount rate in the following:

$$\text{NKr911.37} = \text{NKr40} \times \left[\frac{1 - 1/(1 + r)^{12}}{r}\right] + \frac{1,000}{(1 + r)^{12}}$$

The bond sells at a discount. Because the coupon rate is 8 per cent, the yield must be something in excess of that.

If we were to solve this by trial and error, we might try 12 per cent (or 6 per cent per six months):

$$\text{Bond value} = \text{NKr40} \times \left[\frac{1 - 1/1.06^{12}}{0.06}\right] + \frac{1,000}{1.06^{12}}$$
$$= \text{NKr832.32}$$

This is less than the actual value, so our discount rate is too high. We now know that the yield is somewhere between 8 and 12 per cent. With further trial and error (or a little computer assistance), the yield works out to be 10 per cent, or 5 per cent every six months.

By convention, the bond's yield to maturity would be quoted as 2 × 5% = 10%. The effective yield is thus $1.05^2 - 1 = 10.25\%$.

# Concepts Review and Critical Thinking Questions

1   **Treasury Bonds [LO1]**   Is it true that a British Treasury security is risk-free? What about an Italian Treasury security?

2   **Interest Rate Risk [LO2]**   Which has greater interest rate risk, a 30-year Treasury bond or a 30-year BB corporate bond?

3   **Treasury Pricing [LO1]**   With regard to clean and dirty prices on a Treasury bond, is it possible for the clean price to be higher? Why or why not?

4   **Yield to Maturity [LO2]**   Treasury clean and dirty prices can be given in terms of yields, so there would be a clean yield and a dirty yield. Which do you think would be larger? Explain.

5   **Call Provisions [LO1]**   A company is contemplating a long-term bond issue. It is debating whether to include a call provision. What are the benefits to the company from including a call provision? What are the costs? How do these answers change for a put provision?

6   **Coupon Rate [LO1]**   How does a bond issuer decide on the appropriate coupon rate to set on its bonds? Explain the difference between the coupon rate and the required return on a bond.

7   **Real and Nominal Returns [LO4]**   Are there any circumstances under which an investor might be more concerned about the nominal return on an investment than the real return?

8   **Bond Ratings [LO3]**   Companies pay rating agencies such as Moody's, S&P and Fitch to rate their bonds, and the costs can be substantial. However, companies are not required to have their bonds rated; doing so is strictly voluntary. Why do you think they do it?

9   **Bond Ratings [LO3]**   US Treasury bonds are not rated. Why? Often, junk bonds are not rated. Why?

10   **Term Structure [LO5]**   What is the difference between the term structure of interest rates and the yield curve?

11   **Crossover Bonds [LO3]**   Looking back at the crossover bonds we discussed in the chapter, why do you think split ratings such as these occur?

12   **Bond Market [LO1]**   What are the implications for bond investors of the lack of transparency in the bond market?

13   **Rating Agencies [LO3]**   A controversy erupted regarding bond-rating agencies when some agencies began to provide unsolicited bond ratings. Why do you think this is controversial?

14   **Bonds as Equity [LO1]**   The 50-year bonds we discussed in the chapter have something in common with junk bonds. Critics charge that, in both cases, the issuers are really selling equity in disguise. What are the issues here? Why would a company want to sell 'equity in disguise'?

# connect Questions and Problems

BASIC

1–14

1 **Interpreting Bond Yields [LO1]** Is the yield to maturity on a bond the same thing as the required return? Is YTM the same thing as the coupon rate? Suppose today a 10 per cent coupon bond sells at par. Two years from now, the required return on the same bond is 8 per cent. What is the coupon rate on the bond then? The YTM?

2 **Interpreting Bond Yields [LO2]** Suppose you buy a 7 per cent coupon, 20-year bond today when it's first issued. If interest rates suddenly rise to 15 per cent, what happens to the value of your bond? Why?

3 **Bond Prices [LO2]** Staind plc has 8.5 per cent coupon bonds on the market that have 10 years left to maturity. The bonds make annual payments. If the YTM on these bonds is 9.75 per cent, what is the current bond price?

4 **Bond Yields [LO2]** Ackerman plc has 10 per cent coupon bonds on the market, with nine years left to maturity. The bonds make annual payments. If the bond currently sells for £9,340 and the face value of the bonds is £10,000, what is its YTM?

5 **Coupon Rates [LO2]** Steen Familie NV has bonds on the market making annual payments, with 13 years to maturity, and selling for €1,045. At this price, the bonds yield 7.5 per cent. What must the coupon rate be on the bonds?

6 **Bond Yields [LO2]** In March 2009 the auto firm Daimler AG issued a 15-month bond with a face value of €1,000, and an annual coupon rate of 6.875 per cent, paid every quarter. The issue price was €9,997. What was its YTM?

7 **Bond Yields [LO2]** Ngata SA issued 10-year bonds two years ago at a coupon rate of 7.5 per cent. The bonds make semi-annual payments. If these bonds currently sell for 105 per cent of par value, what is the YTM?

8 **Coupon Rates [LO2]** Stand AG has bonds on the market with 17.5 years to maturity, a YTM of 8 per cent, and a current price of €924. The bonds make semi-annual payments. What must the coupon rate be on these bonds?

9 **Calculating Real Rates of Return [LO4]** If Treasury bills are currently paying 7 per cent and the inflation rate is 3.8 per cent, what is the approximate real rate of interest? The exact real rate?

10 **Inflation and Nominal Returns [LO4]** Suppose the real rate is 4 per cent and the inflation rate is 4.7 per cent. What rate would you expect to see on a Treasury bill?

11 **Nominal and Real Returns [LO4]** An investment offers a 15 per cent total return over the coming year. You think the total real return on this investment will be only 9 per cent. What do you believe the inflation rate will be over the next year?

12 **Nominal versus Real Returns [LO4]** A six-year government bond makes annual coupon payments of 5 per cent and offers a yield of 3 per cent annually compounded. Suppose that one year later the bond still yields 3 per cent. What return has the bondholder earned over the 12-month period? Now suppose that the bond yields 2 per cent at the end of the year. What return would the bondholder earn in this case?

13 **Using Treasury Quotes [LO2]** Locate the 5 per cent coupon Treasury issue in Fig. 6.4 maturing in 2012. Is this a note or a bond? What is its interest yield? What is its redemption yield? What was the *previous* day's price?

14 **Using Treasury Quotes [LO2]** Locate the 2.75 per cent coupon Treasury bond in Fig. 6.4 maturing in 2015. Is this a premium or a discount bond? What is its current yield? What is its yield to maturity?

15 **Bond Price Movements [LO2]** Bond X is a premium bond making annual payments. The bond pays an 8 per cent coupon, has a YTM of 6 per cent, and has 13 years to maturity. Bond Y is a discount bond making annual payments. This bond pays a 6 per cent coupon, has a YTM of 8 per cent, and also has 13 years to maturity. If interest rates remain unchanged, what do you expect the price of these bonds to be one year from now? In three years? In eight years? In 12 years? In 13 years? What's going on here? Illustrate your answers by plotting bond prices against time to maturity.

16 **Interest Rate Risk [LO2]** Both Bond Tony and Bond Peter have 10 per cent coupons, make semi-annual payments, and are priced at par value. Bond Tony has 3 years to maturity, whereas Bond Peter has 20 years to maturity. If interest rates suddenly rise by 2 per cent, what is the percentage change in the price of Bond Tony? Of Bond Peter? If rates were to suddenly fall by 2 per cent instead, what would the percentage change in the price of Bond Tony be then? Of Bond Peter? Illustrate your answers by plotting bond prices against YTM. What does this problem tell you about the interest rate risk of longer-term bonds?

17 **Interest Rate Risk [LO2]** Bond J is a 4 per cent coupon bond. Bond K is a 12 per cent coupon bond. Both bonds have nine years to maturity, make semi-annual payments, and have a YTM of 8 per cent. If interest rates suddenly rise by 2 per cent, what is the percentage price change of these bonds? What if rates suddenly fall by 2 per cent instead? What does this problem tell you about the interest rate risk of lower-coupon bonds?

18 **Bond Yields [LO2]** One More Time Software has 10.2 per cent coupon bonds on the market with nine years to maturity. The bonds make semi-annual payments and currently sell for 105.8 per cent of par. What is the current yield on the bonds? The YTM? The effective annual yield?

19 **Bond Yields [LO2]** Seether plc wants to issue new 20-year bonds for some much-needed expansion projects. The company currently has 8 per cent coupon bonds on the market that sell for £93,000 with a par value of £100,000, make semi-annual payments, and mature in 20 years. What coupon rate should the company set on its new bonds if it wants them to sell at par?

20 **Accrued Interest [LO2]** You purchase a bond with an invoice price of £9,680. The bond has a coupon rate of 7.4 per cent, and there are four months to the next semi-annual coupon date. What is the clean price of the bond?

21 **Accrued Interest [LO2]** You purchase a bond with a coupon rate of 6.8 per cent and a clean price of £10,730. If the next semi-annual coupon payment is due in two months, what is the invoice price?

22 **Finding the Bond Maturity [LO2]** Fluss AB has 8 per cent coupon bonds making annual payments with a YTM of 7.2 per cent. The current yield on these bonds is 7.55 per cent. How many years do these bonds have left until they mature?

23 **Using Bond Quotes [LO2]** Suppose the following bond quotes for Giorni di Estate SpA appear in the financial page of today's newspaper. Assume the bond has a face value of €1,000 and the current date is 15 February 2010. What is the yield to maturity of the bond? What is the current yield?

| Company (ticker) | Coupon | Maturity | Last price | Last yield | Est vol (000s) |
|---|---|---|---|---|---|
| Giorni di Estate | 9.2 | 15 Feb 2023 | 108.96 | ?? | 1,827 |

24 **Bond Prices versus Yields [LO2]**

(a) What is the relationship between the price of a bond and its YTM?

(b) Explain why some bonds sell at a premium over par value while other bonds sell at a discount. What do you know about the relationship between the coupon rate and the YTM for premium bonds? What about for discount bonds? For bonds selling at par value?

(c) What is the relationship between the current yield and YTM for premium bonds? For discount bonds? For bonds selling at par value?

25 **Interest on Zeros [LO2]** Tesla plc needs to raise funds to finance a plant expansion, and it has decided to issue 20-year zero coupon bonds to raise the money. The required return on the bonds will be 12 per cent. What will these bonds sell for at issuance?

26 **Zero Coupon Bonds [LO2]** Suppose your company needs to raise €30 million and you want to issue 30-year bonds for this purpose. Assume the required return on your bond issue will be 8 per cent, and you're evaluating two issue alternatives: an 8 per cent semi-annual coupon bond and a zero coupon bond. Your company's tax rate is 35 per cent.

(a) How many of the coupon bonds would you need to issue to raise the €30 million? How many of the zeros would you need to issue?

(b) In 30 years, what will your company's repayment be if you issue the coupon bonds? What if you issue the zeros?

(c) Based on your answers in (a) and (b), why would you ever want to issue the zeros? To answer, calculate the firm's after-tax cash outflows for the first year under the two different scenarios.

27 **Finding the Maturity [LO2]** You've just found a 12 per cent coupon bond on the market that sells for par value. What is the maturity on this bond?

28 **Real Cash Flows [LO4]** You want to have €1.5 million in real euros in an account when you retire in 40 years. The nominal return on your investment is 11 per cent and the inflation rate is 3.8 per cent. What real amount must you deposit each year to achieve your goal?

29 **Components of Bond Returns [LO2]** Bond P is a premium bond with a 12 per cent coupon. Bond D is a 6 per cent coupon bond currently selling at a discount. Both bonds make annual payments, have a YTM of 9 per cent, and have five years to maturity. What is the current yield for bond P? For bond D? If interest rates remain unchanged, what is the expected capital gains yield over the next year for bond P? For bond D? Explain your answers and the interrelationships among the various types of yield.

CHALLENGE 29–35

30 **Holding Period Yield [LO2]** The YTM on a bond is the interest rate you earn on your investment if interest rates don't change. If you actually sell the bond before it matures, your realized return is known as the *holding period yield* (HPY).

(a) Suppose that today you buy a 7 per cent annual coupon bond for £106, when its face value is £100. The bond has 10 years to maturity. What rate of return do you expect to earn on your investment?

(b) Two years from now, the YTM on your bond has declined by 1 per cent, and you decide to sell. What price will your bond sell for? What is the HPY on your investment? Compare this yield with the YTM when you first bought the bond. Why are they different?

31 **Valuing Bonds [LO2]** Keegan plc has two different bonds currently outstanding. Bond M has a face value of £20,000 and matures in 20 years. The bond makes no payments for the first six years, then pays £1,100 every six months over the subsequent eight years, and finally pays £1,400 every six months over the last six years. Bond N also has a face value of £20,000 and a maturity of 20 years; it makes no coupon payments over the life of the bond. If the required return on both these bonds is 7 per cent compounded semi-annually, what is the current price of bond M? Of bond N?

32 **Valuing the Call Feature [LO2]**   Consider the prices in the following three Treasury issues as of 15 May 2010:

| Coupon | Maturity | Price | Change | YTM |
|--------|----------|-------|--------|-----|
| 6.500 | 16 May | 106:10 | –13 | 5.28 |
| 8.250 | 16 May | 103:14 | –3 | 5.24 |
| 12.000 | 16 May | 134:25 | –15 | 5.32 |

The bond in the middle is callable in February 2008. What is the implied value of the call feature? (*Hint*: Is there a way to combine the two non-callable issues to create an issue that has the same coupon as the callable bond?)

33 **Treasury Bonds [LO2]**   Consider the following Treasury bond on 11 May 2010:

| 9.125 | 15 May | 100:03 | . . . | –2.15 |
|-------|--------|--------|-------|-------|

Why would anyone buy this Treasury bond with a negative yield to maturity? How is this possible?

34 **Real Cash Flows [LO4]**   When Marilyn Monroe died, ex-husband Joe DiMaggio vowed to place fresh flowers on her grave every Sunday as long as he lived. The week after she died in 1962, a bunch of fresh flowers that the former baseball player thought appropriate for the star cost about $5. Based on actuarial tables, 'Joltin' Joe' could expect to live for 30 years after the actress died. Assume that the EAR is 8.4 per cent. Also, assume that the price of the flowers will increase at 3.7 per cent per year, when expressed as an EAR. Assuming that each year has exactly 52 weeks, what is the present value of this commitment? Joe began purchasing flowers the week after Marilyn died.

35 **Real Cash Flows [LO4]**   You are planning to save for retirement over the next 30 years. To save for retirement, you will invest £900 a month in an equity account in real pounds and £450 a month in a bond account in real pounds. The effective annual return of the equity account is expected to be 11 per cent, and the bond account will earn 7 per cent. When you retire, you will combine your money into an account with a 9 per cent effective return. The inflation rate over this period is expected to be 4 per cent. How much can you withdraw each month from your account in real terms, assuming a 25-year withdrawal period? What is the nominal pound amount of your last withdrawal?

---

**MINI CASE**

# Financing West Coast Yachts' Expansion Plans with a Bond Issue

Larissa Warren, the owner of West Coast Yachts, has decided to expand her operations. She asked her newly hired financial analyst, Dan Ervin, to enlist an underwriter to help sell £30 million in new 20-year bonds to finance new construction. Dan has entered into discussions with Robin Perry, an underwriter from the firm of Crowe & Mallard, about which bond features West Coast Yachts should consider, and also what coupon rate the issue is likely to have. Although Dan is aware of bond features, he is uncertain of the costs and benefits of some features, so he isn't sure how each feature would affect the coupon rate of the bond issue.

1 You are Robin's assistant, and she has asked you to prepare a memo to Dan describing the effect of each of the following bond features on the coupon rate of the bond. She would also like you to list any advantages or disadvantages of each feature.

(a) The security of the bond – that is, whether the bond has collateral.

(b) The seniority of the bond.

(c) The presence of a sinking fund.

(d) A call provision with specified call dates and call prices.

(e) A deferred call accompanying the call provision in (d).

(f) A make-whole call provision.

(g) Any positive covenants. Also, discuss several possible positive covenants West Coast Yachts might consider.

(h) Any negative covenants. Also, discuss several possible negative covenants West Coast Yachts might consider.

(i) A conversion feature (note that West Coast Yachts is not a publicly traded company).

(j) A floating-rate coupon.

Dan is also considering whether to issue coupon-bearing bonds or zero coupon bonds. The YTM on either bond issue will be 8 per cent. The coupon bond would have an 8 per cent coupon rate. The company's tax rate is 28 per cent.

2 How many of the coupon bonds must West Coast Yachts issue to raise the £30 million? How many of the zeros must it issue?

3 In 20 years, what will be the principal repayment due if West Coast Yachts issues the coupon bonds? What if it issues the zeros?

4 What are the company's considerations in issuing a coupon bond compared with a zero coupon bond?

5 Suppose West Coast Yachts issues the coupon bonds with a make-whole call provision. The make-whole call rate is the Treasury rate plus 0.40 per cent. If West Coast calls the bonds in 7 years when the Treasury rate is 5.6 per cent, what is the call price of the bond? What if it is 9.1 per cent?

6 Are investors really made whole with a make-whole call provision?

7 After considering all the relevant factors, would you recommend a zero coupon issue or a regular coupon issue? Why? Would you recommend an ordinary call feature or a make-whole call feature? Why?

# Endnotes

1 There is no universally agreed-upon distinction between short-term and long-term debt. In addition, people often refer to *intermediate-term debt*, which has a maturity of more than 1 year and less than 3 to 5, or even 10, years.

2 The word *funding* is part of the jargon of finance. It generally refers to the long term. Thus a firm planning to 'fund' its debt requirements may be replacing short-term debt with long-term debt.

3 The words *loan agreement* or *loan contract* are usually used for privately placed debt and term loans.

4 Real property includes land and things 'affixed thereto'. It does not include cash or inventories.

5 A bond issued with a very low coupon rate (as opposed to a zero coupon rate) is an *original-issue discount (OID) bond*.

6 In days of old, the interest rate risk premium was called a 'liquidity' premium. Today, the term *liquidity premium* has an altogether different meaning, which we explore in our next section. Also, the interest rate risk premium is sometimes called a *maturity risk premium*. Our terminology is consistent with the modern view of the term structure.

# CHAPTER 7

# Equity Valuation

## KEY NOTATIONS

| | |
|---|---|
| $D$ | Dividend |
| $g$ | Growth rate |
| $P$ | Share price |
| $r$ | Interest rate or discount rate |
| $t$ | Number of periods |

## LEARNING OBJECTIVES

After studying this chapter, you should understand:

**LO1** How share prices depend on future dividends and dividend growth.

**LO2** The different ways corporate directors are elected to office.

**LO3** How the equity markets work.

WHEN THE STOCK MARKET CLOSED on 19 February 2010, the equity of Daimler AG, manufacturer of automobiles, was selling for €32.36 per share. On that same day, shares in SAP AG, the software firm, closed at €32.90, while shares in Saint Gobain, the glass manufacturer, closed at €33.92. Because the share prices of these three companies were so similar, you might expect that they would be offering similar dividends to their shareholders, but you would be wrong. In fact, Daimler's annual dividend was €0.60 per share, Saint Gobain's was €1.98 per share, and SAP was paying no dividends at all!

As we shall see in this chapter, the dividends currently being paid are one of the primary factors we look at when attempting to value equities. However, it is obvious from looking at SAP that current dividends are not the end of the story. This chapter explores dividends, share prices, and the connection between the two.

In our previous chapter we introduced you to bonds and bond valuation. In this chapter, we turn to the other major source of financing for corporations: ordinary and preference shares. We first describe the cash flows associated with a share of equity, and then go on to develop a famous result, the dividend growth model. From there we move on to examine various important features of ordinary and preference shares, focusing on shareholder rights. We close the chapter with a discussion of how shares of equity are traded, and how share prices and other important information are reported in the financial press.

## 7.1 Share Valuation

Share prices are more difficult to value in practice than a bond, for at least three reasons. First, with equity, not even the promised cash flows are known in advance. Second, the life of the investment is essentially for ever, because equity has no maturity. Third, there is no way to easily observe the rate of return that the market requires. Nonetheless, as we shall see, there are cases in which we can come up with the present value of the future cash flows for a share of equity, and thus determine its value.

## Cash Flows

Imagine that you are considering buying a share of equity today. You plan to sell the equity in one year. You somehow know that it will be worth £70 at that time. You predict that the equity will also pay a £10 per share dividend at the end of the year. If you require a 25 per cent return on your investment, what is the most you would pay for the equity? In other words, what is the present value of the £10 dividend along with the £70 ending value at 25 per cent?

If you buy the equity today and sell it at the end of the year, you will have a total of £80 in cash. At 25 per cent:

$$\text{Present value} = \frac{£10 + 70}{1.25} = £64$$

Therefore £64 is the value you would assign to the equity today.

More generally, let $P_0$ be the current share price, and assign $P_1$ to be the price in one period. If $D_1$ is the cash dividend paid at the end of the period, then

$$P_0 = \frac{D_1 + P_1}{1 + R} \tag{7.1}$$

where $R$ is the required return in the market on this investment.

Notice that we really haven't said much so far. If we wanted to determine the share price today ($P_0$), we would first have to come up with the value in one year ($P_1$). This is even harder to do, so we've only made the problem more complicated.

What is the price in one period, $P_1$? We don't know in general. Instead, suppose we somehow knew the price in two periods, $P_2$. Given a predicted dividend in two periods, $D_2$, the share price in one period would be

$$P_1 = \frac{D_2 + P_2}{1 + R}$$

If we were to substitute this expression for $P_1$ into our expression for $P_0$, we would have

$$P_0 = \frac{D_1 + P_1}{1 + R} = \frac{D_1 + (D_2 + P_2)/(1 + R)}{1 + R}$$

$$= \frac{D_1}{(1 + R)^1} + \frac{D_2}{(1 + R)^2} + \frac{P_2}{(1 + R)^2}$$

Now we need to get a price in two periods. We don't know this either, so we can procrastinate again and write

$$P_2 = \frac{D_3 + P_3}{1 + R}$$

If we substitute this back in for $P_2$, we have

$$P_0 = \frac{D_1}{(1 + R)^1} + \frac{D_2}{(1 + R)^2} + \frac{P_2}{(1 + R)^2}$$

$$= \frac{D_1}{(1 + R)^1} + \frac{D_2}{(1 + R)^2} + \frac{(D_3 + P_3)/(1 + R)}{(1 + R)^2}$$

$$= \frac{D_1}{(1 + R)^1} + \frac{D_2}{(1 + R)^2} + \frac{D_3}{(1 + R)^3} + \frac{P_3}{(1 + R)^3}$$

You should start to notice that we can push the problem of coming up with the share price off into the future for ever. Note that no matter what the share price is, the present value is essentially zero if we push the sale of the equity far enough away.[1] What we are eventually left with is the result that the current price of the equity can be written as the present value of the dividends beginning in one period and extending out for ever:

$$P_0 = \frac{D_1}{(1+R)^1} + \frac{D_2}{(1+R)^2} + \frac{D_3}{(1+R)^3} + \frac{D_4}{(1+R)^4} + \frac{D_5}{(1+R)^5} + \ldots \qquad (7.2)$$

We have illustrated here that the share price today is equal to the present value of all of the future dividends. How many future dividends are there? In principle, there can be an infinite number. This means that we still can't compute a value for the equity, because we would have to forecast an infinite number of dividends and then discount them all. In the next section we consider some special cases in which we can get around this problem.

---

**EXAMPLE 7.1**

## Growth Stocks

You might be wondering about shares of equity in companies such as SAP AG that currently pay no dividends. In addition, small, growing companies frequently plough back everything and thus pay no dividends. Are such shares worth nothing? It depends. When we say that the value of the equity is equal to the present value of the future dividends, we don't rule out the possibility that some of those dividends are zero. They just can't *all* be zero.

Imagine a company that has a provision in its articles and memorandum of association that prohibits the paying of dividends now or ever. The corporation never borrows any money, never pays out any money to shareholders in any form whatsoever, and never sells any assets. Such a corporation couldn't really exist, because the tax authorities wouldn't like it, and the shareholders could always vote to amend the articles and memorandum if they wanted to. If it did exist, however, what would the equity be worth?

The shares are worth absolutely nothing. Such a company is a financial 'black hole'. Money goes in, but nothing valuable ever comes out. Because nobody would ever get any return on this investment, the investment has no value. This example is a little absurd, but it illustrates that when we speak of companies that don't pay dividends, what we really mean is that they are not *currently* paying dividends.

---

## Some Special Cases

In a few useful special circumstances we can come up with a value for the equity. What we have to do is make some simplifying assumptions about the pattern of future dividends. The three cases we consider are the following:

1   The dividend has a zero growth rate.

2   The dividend grows at a constant rate.

3   The dividend grows at a constant rate after some length of time.

We consider each of these separately.

**Zero Growth**   The case of zero growth is one we've already seen. A share of equity in a company with a constant dividend is much like a preference share. For a zero-growth share of equity, this implies that

$$D_1 = D_2 = D_3 = D = \text{constant}$$

So the value of the equity is

$$P_0 = \frac{D}{(1+R)^1} + \frac{D}{(1+R)^2} + \frac{D}{(1+R)^3} + \frac{D}{(1+R)^4} + \frac{D}{(1+R)^5} + \ldots$$

Because the dividend is always the same, the share price can be viewed as an ordinary perpetuity with a cash flow equal to $D$ every period. The per-share value is thus given by

$$P_0 = D/R \qquad (7.2)$$

where $R$ is the required return.

For example, suppose Paradise Prototyping has a policy of paying a €10 per share dividend every year. If this policy is to be continued indefinitely, what is the value of a share of equity if the required return is 20 per cent? The equity in this case amounts to an ordinary perpetuity, so it is worth €10/0.20 = €50 per share.

**Constant Growth**   Suppose we know that the dividend for some company always grows at a steady rate. Call this growth rate $g$. If we let $D_0$ be the dividend just paid, then the next dividend, $D_1$, is

$$D_1 = D_0 \times (1 + g)$$

The dividend in two periods is

$$
\begin{aligned}
D_2 &= D_1 \times (1 + g) \\
&= [D_0 \times (1 + g)] \times (1 + g) \\
&= D_0 \times (1 + g)^2
\end{aligned}
$$

We could repeat this process to come up with the dividend at any point in the future. In general, from our discussion of compound growth in Chapter 4, we know that the dividend $t$ periods into the future, $D_t$, is given by

$$D_t = D_0 \times (1 + g)^t$$

As we have previously seen, an asset with cash flows that grow at a constant rate for ever is called a *growing perpetuity*.

The assumption of steady dividend growth might strike you as peculiar. Why would the dividend grow at a constant rate? The reason is that, for many companies, steady growth in dividends is an explicit goal. For example, in 2009, Procter & Gamble, the US-based maker of personal care and household products, increased its dividend by 13.1 per cent to $1.64 per share: this increase was notable because it was the 53rd in a row. The subject of dividend growth falls under the general heading of dividend policy, so we shall defer further discussion of it to a later chapter.

## Dividend Growth

EXAMPLE
7.2

Oasis plc has just paid a dividend of £3 per share. The dividend of this company grows at a steady rate of 8 per cent per year. Based on this information, what will the dividend be in five years?

Here we have a £3 current amount that grows at 8 per cent per year for five years. The future amount is thus

$$£3 \times 1.08^5 = £3 \times 1.4693 = £4.41$$

The dividend will therefore increase by £1.41 over the coming five years.

If the dividend grows at a steady rate, then we have replaced the problem of forecasting an infinite number of future dividends with the problem of coming up with a single growth rate – a considerable simplification. In this case, if we take $D_0$ to be the dividend just paid, and $g$ to be the constant growth rate, the value of a share of equity can be written as

$$P_0 = \frac{D_1}{(1+R)^1} + \frac{D_2}{(1+R)^2} + \frac{D_3}{(1+R)^3} + \cdots$$

$$= \frac{D_0 \times (1+g)^1}{(1+R)^1} + \frac{D_0 \times (1+g)^2}{(1+R)^2} + \frac{D_0 \times (1+g)^3}{(1+R)^3} + \cdots$$

As long as the growth rate, $g$, is less than the discount rate, $r$, the present value of this series of cash flows can be written simply as

$$P_0 = \frac{D_0 \times (1+g)}{R-g}$$

$$= \frac{D_1}{R-g}$$

(7.3)

This elegant result goes by a lot of different names. We shall call it the **dividend growth model**. By any name, it is easy to use. To illustrate, suppose $D_0$ is £2.30, $R$ is 13 per cent, and $g$ is 5 per cent. The share price in this case is

$$P_0 = D_0 \times (1+g)/(R-g)$$
$$= £2.30 \times 1.05/(0.13 - 0.05)$$
$$= £2.415/0.08$$
$$= £30.19$$

> **dividend growth model**
> A model that determines the current share price as its dividend next period divided by the discount rate less the dividend growth rate.

We can actually use the dividend growth model to get the share price at any point in time, not just today. In general, the share price as of time $t$ is

$$P_t = \frac{D_t \times (1+g)}{R-g} = \frac{D_{t+1}}{R-g}$$

(7.4)

In our example, suppose we are interested in the share price in five years, $P_5$. We first need the dividend at time 5, $D_5$. Because the dividend just paid is £2.30 and the growth rate is 5 per cent per year, $D_5$ is

$$D_5 = £2.30 \times 1.05^5 = £2.30 \times 1.2763 = £2.935$$

From the dividend growth model, we get the share price in five years:

$$P_5 = \frac{D_5 \times (1+g)}{R-g}$$

$$= \frac{£2.935 \times 1.05}{0.13 - 0.05}$$

$$= \frac{£3.0822}{0.08}$$

$$= £38.53$$

---

**EXAMPLE 7.3**

## Gordon Growth Limited

The next dividend for Gordon Growth Limited will be £4 per share. Investors require a 16 per cent return on companies such as Gordon. Gordon's dividend increases by 6 per cent every year. Based on the dividend growth model, what is the value of Gordon's equity today? What is the value in four years?

The only tricky thing here is that the next dividend, $D_1$, is given as £4, so we won't multiply this by $(1+g)$. With this in mind, the share price is given by

$$P_0 = D_1/(R - g)$$
$$- £4/(0.16 - 0.06)$$
$$= £4/0.10$$
$$= £40$$

Because we already have the dividend in one year, we know that the dividend in four years is equal to $D_1 \times (1 + g)^3 = £4 \times 1.06^3 = £4.764$. The price in four years is therefore

$$P_4 = D_4 \times (1 + g)/(R - g)$$
$$= £4.764 \times 1.06/(0.16 - 0.06)$$
$$= £5.05/0.10$$
$$= £50.50$$

Notice in this example that $P_4$ is equal to $P_0 \times (1 + g)^4$:

$$P_4 = £50.50$$
$$= £40 \times 1.06^4$$
$$= P_0 \times (1 + g)^4$$

To see why this is so, notice first that

$$P_4 = D_5/(R - g)$$

However, $D_5$ is just equal to $D_1 \times (1 + g)^4$, so we can write $P_4$ as

$$P_4 = D_1 \times (1 + g)^4/(R - g)$$
$$= [D_1/(R - g)] \times (1 + g)^4$$
$$= P_0 \times (1 + g)^4$$

This last example illustrates that the dividend growth model makes the implicit assumption that the share price will grow at the same constant rate as the dividend. This really isn't too surprising. What it tells us is that if the cash flows on an investment grow at a constant rate through time, so does the value of that investment.

You might wonder what would happen with the dividend growth model if the growth rate, $g$, were greater than the discount rate, $R$. It looks like we would get a negative share price, because $R - g$ would be less than zero. This is not what would happen.

Instead, if the constant growth rate exceeds the discount rate, then the share price is infinitely large. Why? If the growth rate is bigger than the discount rate, the present value of the dividends keeps getting bigger. Essentially the same is true if the growth rate and the discount rate are equal. In both cases, the simplification that allows us to replace the infinite stream of dividends with the dividend growth model is 'illegal', so the answers we get from the dividend growth model are nonsense unless the growth rate is less than the discount rate.

Finally, the expression we came up with for the constant growth case will work for any growing perpetuity, not just dividends on ordinary equity. As we saw in Chapter 4, if $C$ is the next cash flow on a growing perpetuity, then the present value of the cash flows is given by

$$\text{Present value} = \frac{C_1}{(R - g)}$$
$$= \frac{C_0(1 + g)}{R - g}$$

Notice that this expression looks like the result for an ordinary perpetuity, except that we have $R - g$ on the bottom instead of just $R$.

**Non-constant Growth**  The next case we consider is non-constant growth. The main reason for considering this case is to allow for 'supernormal' growth rates over some finite length of time. As we discussed earlier, the growth rate cannot exceed the required return indefinitely, but it certainly could do so for some number of years. To avoid the problem of having to forecast and discount an infinite number of dividends, we shall require that the dividends start growing at a constant rate at some time in the future.

For a simple example of non-constant growth, consider the case of a company that is currently not paying dividends. You predict that, in five years, the company will pay a dividend for the first time. The dividend will be €0.50 per share. You expect that this dividend will then grow at a rate of 10 per cent per year indefinitely. The required return on companies such as this one is 20 per cent. What is the share price today?

To see what the equity is worth today, we first find out what it will be worth once dividends are paid. We can then calculate the present value of that future price to get today's price. The first dividend will be paid in five years, and the dividend will grow steadily from then on. Using the dividend growth model, we can say that the price in four years will be

$$
\begin{aligned}
P_4 &= D_4 \times (1 + g)/(R - g) \\
&= D_5/(R - g) \\
&= €0.50/(0.20 - 0.10) \\
&= €5
\end{aligned}
$$

If the equity will be worth €5 in four years, then we can get the current value by discounting this price back four years at 20 per cent:

$$
\begin{aligned}
P_0 &= €5/1.20^4 \\
&= €5/2.0736 \\
&= €2.41
\end{aligned}
$$

The equity is therefore worth €2.41 today.

The problem of non-constant growth is only slightly more complicated if the dividends are not zero for the first several years. For example, suppose you have come up with the following dividend forecasts for the next three years:

| Year | Expected dividend (€) |
|------|-----------------------|
| 1 | 1.00 |
| 2 | 2.00 |
| 3 | 2.50 |

After the third year, the dividend will grow at a constant rate of 5 per cent per year. The required return is 10 per cent. What is the share price today?

In dealing with non-constant growth, a time line can be helpful. Figure 7.1 illustrates one for this problem. The important thing to notice is when constant growth starts. As we've shown, for this problem, constant growth starts at time 3. This means we can use

**FIGURE 7.1**

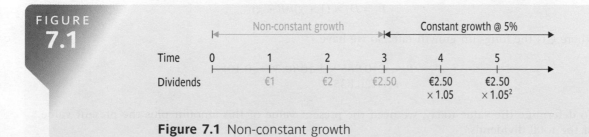

**Figure 7.1** Non-constant growth

our constant growth model to determine the share price at time 3, $P_3$. By far the most common mistake in this situation is to incorrectly identify the start of the constant growth phase and, as a result, calculate the future share price at the wrong time.

As always, the share price is the present value of all the future dividends. To calculate this present value we first have to compute the present value of the share price three years down the road, just as we did before. We then have to add in the present value of the dividends that will be paid between now and then. So the price in three years is

$$P_3 = D_3 \times (1 + g)/(R - g)$$
$$= €2.50 \times 1.05/(0.10 - 0.05)$$
$$= €52.50$$

We can now calculate the total value of the equity as the present value of the first three dividends plus the present value of the price at time 3, $P_3$:

$$P_0 = \frac{D_1}{(1 + R)^1} + \frac{D_2}{(1 + R)^2} + \frac{D_3}{(1 + R)^3} + \frac{P_3}{(1 + R)^3}$$
$$= \frac{€1}{1.10} + \frac{2}{1.10^2} + \frac{2.50}{1.10^3} + \frac{52.50}{1.10^3}$$
$$= €0.91 + 1.65 + 1.88 + 39.44$$
$$= €43.88$$

The share price today is thus €43.88.

**EXAMPLE 7.4**

# Supernormal Growth

Kettenreaktion AG has been growing at a phenomenal rate of 30 per cent per year because of its rapid expansion and explosive sales. You believe this growth rate will last for three more years, and will then drop to 10 per cent per year. If the growth rate then remains at 10 per cent indefinitely, what is the total value of the equity? Total dividends just paid were €5 million, and the required return is 20 per cent.

Kettenreaktion's situation is an example of supernormal growth. It is unlikely that a 30 per cent growth rate can be sustained for any extended time. To value the equity in this company, we first need to calculate the total dividends over the supernormal growth period:

| Year | Total dividends (in millions) |
|---|---|
| 1 | €5.00 × 1.3 = €6.500 |
| 2 | 6.50 × 1.3 =   8.450 |
| 3 | 8.45 × 1.3 = 10.985 |

The price at time 3 can be calculated as

$$P_3 = D_3 \times (1 + g)/(R - g)$$

where $g$ is the long-run growth rate. So we have

$$P_3 = €10.985 \times 1.10/(0.20 - 0.10)$$
$$= €120.835$$

To determine the value today, we need the present value of this amount plus the present value of the total dividends:

$$P_0 = \frac{D_1}{(1+R)^1} + \frac{D_2}{(1+R)^2} + \frac{D_3}{(1+R)^3} + \frac{P_3}{(1+R)^3}$$

$$= \frac{€6.50}{1.20} + \frac{8.45}{1.20^2} + \frac{10.985}{1.20^3} + \frac{120.835}{1.20^3}$$

$$= €5.42 + 5.87 + 6.36 + 69.93$$

$$= €87.58$$

The total value of the equity today is thus €87.58 million. If there were, for example, 20 million shares, then the equity would be worth €87.58/20 = €4.38 per share.

**Two-Stage Growth**   The last case we consider is a special case of non-constant growth: two-stage growth. Here, the idea is that the dividend will grow at a rate of $g_1$ for $t$ years and then grow at a rate of $g_2$ thereafter for ever. In this case the value of the equity can be written as

$$P_0 = \frac{D_1}{R - g_1} \times \left[1 - \left(\frac{1+g_1}{1+R}\right)^t\right] + \frac{P_t}{(1+R)^t} \tag{7.5}$$

Notice that the first term in our expression is the present value of a growing annuity, which we discussed in Chapter 4. In this first stage, $g_1$ can be greater than $R$. The second part is the present value of the share price once the second stage begins at time $t$.

We can calculate $P_t$ as follows:

$$P_t = \frac{D_{t+1}}{R - g_2} = \frac{D_0 \times (1+g_1)^t \times (1+g_2)}{R - g_2} \tag{7.6}$$

In this calculation we need the dividend at time $t + 1$, $D_{t+1}$, to get the share price at time $t$, $P_t$. Notice that, to get it, we grew the current dividend, $D_0$, at rate $g_1$ for $t$ periods and then grew it one period at rate $g_2$. Also, in this second stage, $g_2$ must be less than $R$.

**EXAMPLE 7.5**

## Two-Stage Growth

Alto Campo's dividend is expected to grow at 20 per cent for the next five years. After that, the growth is expected to be 4 per cent for ever. If the required return is 10 per cent, what's the value of the equity? The dividend just paid was €2.

There is a fair amount of computation here, but it is mostly just 'plug and chug' with a calculator. We can start by calculating the share price five years from now, $P_5$:

$$P_5 = \frac{D_6}{R - g_2} = \frac{D_0 \times (1+g_1)^5 \times (1+g_2)}{R - g_2}$$

$$= \frac{€2 \times (1+0.20)^5 \times (1+0.04)}{0.10 - 0.04}$$

$$= \frac{€5.18}{0.06}$$

$$= €86.26$$

We then plug into our two-stage growth formula to get the price today:

$$P_0 = \frac{D_1}{R - g_1} \times \left[ 1 - \left( \frac{1 + g_1}{1 + R} \right)^t \right] + \frac{P_t}{(1 + R)^t}$$

$$= \frac{€2 \times (1 + 0.20)}{0.10 - 0.20} \times \left[ 1 - \left( \frac{1 + 0.20}{1 + 0.10} \right)^5 \right] + \frac{€86.26}{(1 + 0.10)^5}$$

$$= €66.64$$

Notice that we were given $D_0 = €2$ here, so we had to grow it by 20 per cent for one period to get $D_1$. Notice also that $g_1$ is bigger than $R$ in this problem, but that fact does not cause a problem.

There are many reasons why dividend growth rates may change in the future. By far the most common reason is competition from other companies. Consider Apple, which has been incredibly successful over the past few years with its iPod, iPhone and iPad. Each product provided the company with exceptionally strong growth. However, within 12 months of launch, competitors released similar products. As competition grows, sales growth will naturally decrease, having a direct effect on dividend growth rates.

Dividend payout policy may also change, and this will also have an impact on growth rates. In Chapter 3 we discussed sustainable growth rates. If a company increases its total dividend as a proportion of its total earnings, growth will have to fall, because less money is retained to invest in value-maximizing projects. Holding everything else constant, if a company does increase its payout ratio, there will be a one-off increase in dividend (to reflect the bigger payout), followed by a lower growth rate in the future.

## Components of the Required Return

Thus far we have taken the required return, or discount rate, $R$, as given. We shall have quite a bit to say about this subject in Chapters 11 and 13. For now, we want to examine the implications of the dividend growth model for this required return. Earlier, we calculated $P_0$ as

$$P_0 = D_1/(R - g)$$

If we rearrange this to solve for $R$, we get

$$R - g = D_1/P_0$$
$$R = D_1/P_0 + g \qquad (7.7)$$

**dividend yield**
An equity's expected cash dividend divided by its current price.

**capital gains yield**
The dividend growth rate, or the rate at which the value of an investment grows.

This tells us that the total return, $R$, has two components. The first of these, $D_1/P_0$, is called the **dividend yield**. Because this is calculated as the expected cash dividend divided by the current price, it is conceptually similar to the current yield on a bond.

The second part of the total return is the growth rate, $g$. We know that the dividend growth rate is also the rate at which the share price grows (see Example 7.3). Thus this growth rate can be interpreted as the **capital gains yield** – that is, the rate at which the value of the investment grows.[2]

To illustrate the components of the required return, suppose we observe an equity selling for €20 per share. The next dividend will be €1 per share. You think that the dividend will grow by 10 per cent per year more or less indefinitely. What return does this equity offer if this is correct?

The dividend growth model calculates total return as

$$R = \text{Dividend yield} + \text{Capital gains yield}$$
$$= D_1/P_0 + g$$

In this case, total return works out to be

$$R = €1/20 + 10\%$$
$$= 5\% + 10\%$$
$$= 15\%$$

This equity therefore has an expected return of 15 per cent.

We can verify this answer by calculating the price in one year, $P_1$, using 15 per cent as the required return. Based on the dividend growth model, this price is

$$P_1 = D_1 \times (1 + g)/(R - g)$$
$$= €1 \times 1.10/(0.15 - 0.10)$$
$$= €1.10/0.05$$
$$= €22$$

Notice that this €22 is €20 × 1.1, so the share price has grown by 10 per cent as it should. If you pay €20 for the equity today, you will get a €1 dividend at the end of the year, and you will have a €22 − 20 = €2 gain. Your dividend yield is thus €1/20 = 5%. Your capital gains yield is €2/20 = 10%, so your total return would be 5% + 10% = 15%.

To get a feel for actual numbers in this context, consider that, according to Yahoo! Finance, Procter & Gamble's dividends were expected to grow by 8.5 per cent over the next five or so years, compared with a historical growth rate of 10.5 per cent over the preceding five years and 11 per cent over the preceding 10 years. In 2010 the projected dividend for the coming year was given as $1.77. The share price at that time was about $63 per share. What is the return investors require on P&G? Here, the dividend yield is 2.8 per cent and the capital gains yield is 8.5 per cent, giving a total required return of 11.3 per cent on P&G shares.

Our discussion of equity valuation is summarized in Table 7.1.

## The Price–Earnings Ratio

In Chapter 3, via our discussion on financial ratios, we introduced the price–earnings ratio. Recall that the price–earnings ratio is the share price divided by earnings per share. P/E ratios are used by analysts to compare equity values across an industry, and they are used to complement other methods of equity valuation. The dividend growth model tells us that share value increases with growth rates, and so it implies that companies with high growth opportunities will have higher price–earnings ratios.

This explanation seems to hold fairly well in the real world. Electronic and other high-tech shares generally sell at very high P/E ratios (or multiples, as they are often called), because they are perceived to have high growth rates. In fact, some technology shares sell at high prices even though the companies have never earned a profit. Conversely, railroads, utilities and steel companies sell at lower multiples because of the prospects of lower growth. Figure 7.2 contains summary data for different UK industries in April 2010.

Notice the variation across industries, and how the P/E ratios are related to growth opportunities. TTM means 'trailing twelve months', and it says that the data (earnings and sales) are taken from the most recent financial report from the past year. Care should be taken with blindly using data such as P/E ratios, because sometimes strange figures appear. From looking at Fig. 7.2 you may be surprised to learn that the average P/E ratio for a UK company over the past 30 years has been between 12 and 18. The reason why the values are so large in Fig. 7.2 is that 2009 (the period for the earnings and sales figures) was a terrible year for companies, and average earnings were very low. With the recovery in the stock markets and share valuations in 2010, this resulted in very high P/E and P/Sale ratios.

**TABLE 7.1**

### The general case

In general, the price today of a share of equity, $P_0$, is the present value of all of its future dividends, $D_1, D_2, D_3, \ldots$:

$$P_0 = \frac{D_1}{(1+R)^1} + \frac{D_2}{(1+R)^2} + \frac{D_3}{(1+R)^3} + \cdots$$

where $R$ is the required return.

### Constant growth case

If the dividend grows at a steady rate, $g$, then the price can be written as

$$P_0 = \frac{D_1}{R - g}$$

This result is called the *dividend growth model*.

### Non-constant growth

If the dividend grows steadily after $t$ periods, then the price can be written as

$$P_0 = \frac{D_1}{(1+R)^1} + \frac{D_2}{(1+R)^2} + \cdots + \frac{D_t}{(1+R)^t} + \frac{P_t}{(1+R)^t}$$

where

$$P_t = \frac{D_t \times (1+g)}{(R - g)}$$

### Two-stage growth

If the dividend grows at rate $g_1$ for $t$ periods and then grows at rate $g_2$ thereafter, then the price can be written as

$$P_0 = \frac{D_1}{R - g_1} \times \left[ 1 - \left( \frac{1 + g_1}{1 + R} \right)^t \right] + \frac{P_t}{(1+R)^t}$$

where

$$P_t = \frac{D_{t+1}}{R - g_2} = \frac{D_0 \times (1 + g_1)^t \times (1 + g_2)}{R - g_2}$$

### The required return

The required return, $R$, can be written as the sum of two things:

$$R = D_1/P_0 + g$$

where $D_1/P_0$ is the *dividend yield* and $g$ is the *capital gains yield* (which is the same thing as the growth rate in dividends for the steady growth case).

**Table 7.1** Summary of equity valuation

FIGURE
7.2

| Sectors | | | | | |
| --- | --- | --- | --- | --- | --- |
| **Performance  |  Summary** | | | | | |
| ▾ Sectors | Average Market Cap | P/E TTM | Div Yield | Price-To-Sales Ratio TTM | EPS Growth (5 years) |
| Basic Materials | 4.83t | 61.9 | 1.40% | 39.4 | +8.33% |
| Consumer Goods | 5.17t | 48.5 | 2.00% | 3.4 | +6.87% |
| Consumer Services | 4.24t | 69.6 | 1.82% | 7.1 | +7.40% |
| Financials | 11.41t | 52.9 | 2.28% | 67.7 | +7.10% |
| Health Care | 3.03t | 22.9 | 2.08% | 111.0 | +14.29% |
| Industrials | 79.98t | 4.1 | 0.14% | 177,553.2 | +0.64% |
| Oil & Gas | 4.74t | 25.0 | 2.54% | 28.5 | +7.19% |
| Technology | 3.87t | 35.8 | 1.06% | 6.6 | +17.11% |
| Telecommunications | 2.35t | 76.3 | 4.25% | 10.1 | +7.01% |
| Utilities | 2.18t | 20.0 | 3.71% | 2.6 | +11.99% |

As of Apr 15 2010 09:48 BST. Quotes are delayed by a least 20 minutes.

*Source*: *Financial Times*. © The Financial Times Ltd 2010.

**Figure 7.2** Summary equity data for selected UK industries, 15 April 2010

7.1a   What are the relevant cash flows for valuing a share of equity?
7.1b   Does the value of a share of equity depend on how long you expect to keep it?
7.1c   What is the value of a share of equity when the dividend grows at a constant rate?

## 7.2   Some Features of Ordinary and Preference Shares

In discussing ordinary equity features we focus on shareholder rights and dividend payments. For preference shares we explain what *preference* means, and we also debate whether preference shares are really debt or equity.

### Ordinary Equity Features

The term **ordinary equity** means different things to different people, but it is usually applied to equity that has no special preference either in receiving dividends or in bankruptcy.

### Preference Share Features

**Preference shares** differ from ordinary equity because they have preference over ordinary equity in the payment of dividends, and in the distribution of corporation

**ordinary equity**
Equity without priority for dividends or in bankruptcy.

**preference shares**
Equity with dividend priority over ordinary shares, normally with a fixed dividend rate, sometimes without voting rights.

assets in the event of liquidation. *Preference* means only that the holders of the preference shares must receive a dividend (in the case of an ongoing firm) before holders of ordinary shares are entitled to anything.

A preference share is a form of equity, from a legal and tax standpoint. It is important to note, however, that holders of preference shares sometimes have no voting privileges.

**Stated Value** Preference shares have a stated liquidating value, such as £100 or €100 per share. The cash dividend is described as a percentage of stated value. For example, Unilever plc '4% preference shares' easily translates into a dividend yield of 4 per cent of stated value, or £4 per share.

**Cumulative and Non-cumulative Dividends** A preference share dividend is *not* like interest on a bond. The board of directors may decide not to pay the dividends on preference shares, and their decision may have nothing to do with the current net income of the corporation.

Dividends payable on preference shares are either *cumulative* or *non-cumulative*; most are cumulative. If preferred dividends are cumulative and are not paid in a particular year, they will be carried forward as an *arrearage*. Usually, both the accumulated (past) preferred dividends and the current preferred dividends must be paid before the ordinary shareholders can receive anything.

Unpaid preferred dividends are *not* debts of the firm. Directors elected by the ordinary shareholders can defer preferred dividends indefinitely. However, in such cases ordinary shareholders must also forgo dividends. In addition, holders of preference shares are often granted voting and other rights if preferred dividends have not been paid for some time. Because preference shareholders receive no interest on the accumulated dividends, some have argued that firms have an incentive to delay paying preferred dividends, but, as we have seen, this may mean sharing control with preference shareholders.

**Are Preference Shares Really Debt?** A good case can be made that preference shares are really debt in disguise, a kind of equity bond. Preference shareholders receive a stated dividend only; and if the corporation is liquidated, preference shareholders get a stated value. Often, preference shares carry credit ratings much like those of bonds. Furthermore, preference shares are sometimes convertible into ordinary shares, and preference shares are often callable.

In addition, many preference share issues have obligatory sinking funds. The existence of such a sinking fund effectively creates a final maturity, because it means that the entire issue will ultimately be retired. For these reasons, preference shares seem to be a lot like debt. However, for tax purposes, preferred dividends are treated like ordinary share dividends.

International Accounting Standards (IAS 32: *Financial Instruments: Presentation*) recommend that the equity-like features of preference shares should be treated as equity in the company's financial accounts. Similarly, the bond-like features of a preference share should be treated as debt. So, if a preference share has a fixed dividend that has a mandatory redemption property at some future date, then it should be treated as a liability. If there is no redemption date, and the dividends are not mandatory, it should be treated as equity.

| CONCEPT QUESTIONS | 7.2a | Why is a preference share called *preference*? |
| | 7.2b | How can a preference share sometimes be treated as debt and at other times be treated as equity? |
| | 7.2c | What is the difference between cumulative and non-cumulative dividends? |

## 7.3 The Stock Markets

Back in Chapter 1 we briefly mentioned that shares of equity are bought and sold on various stock exchanges, the most important European exchanges being the London Stock Exchange, Euronext and Deutsche Börse. From our earlier discussion, recall that the stock market consists of a **primary market** and a **secondary market**. In the primary, or new issue, market, shares of equity are first brought to the market and sold to investors. In the secondary market, existing shares are traded among investors.

In the primary market, companies sell securities to raise money. We shall discuss this process in detail in a later chapter. We therefore focus mainly on secondary market activity in this section. We conclude with a discussion of how share prices are quoted in the financial press.

### Dealers and Brokers

Because most securities transactions involve dealers and brokers, it is important to understand exactly what is meant by the terms *dealer* and *broker*. A **dealer** maintains an inventory, and stands ready to buy and sell at any time. In contrast, a **broker** brings buyers and sellers together, but does not maintain an inventory. Thus, when we speak of used car dealers and real estate brokers, we recognize that the used car dealer maintains an inventory, whereas the real estate broker does not.

In the securities markets, a dealer stands ready to buy securities from investors wishing to sell them, and to sell securities to investors wishing to buy them. The price the dealer is willing to pay is called the *bid price*. The price at which the dealer will sell is called the *ask price* (sometimes called the asked, offered, or offering price). The difference between the bid and ask prices is called the *spread*, and it is the basic source of dealer profits.

Dealers exist in all areas of the economy, not just the stock markets. For example, your local university bookshop is probably both a primary and a secondary market textbook dealer. If you buy a new book, this is a primary market transaction. If you buy a used book, this is a secondary market transaction, and you pay the shop's ask price. If you sell the book back, you receive the shop's bid price (often half of the ask price). The bookshop's spread is the difference between the two prices.

In contrast, a securities broker arranges transactions between investors, matching investors wishing to buy securities with investors wishing to sell securities. The distinctive characteristic of security brokers is that they do not buy or sell securities for their own accounts. Facilitating trades by others is their business.

### Stock Market Reporting

In recent years the reporting of share prices and related information has increasingly moved from traditional print media, such as the *Financial Times*, to various websites. Yahoo! Finance (finance.yahoo.com) and FT.com are good examples. We went to Yahoo! Finance and requested a share price quote on Shire plc, which is listed on the London Stock Exchange. Here is a portion of what we found:

| **primary market** |
| --- |
| The market in which new securities are originally sold to investors. |

| **secondary market** |
| --- |
| The market in which previously issued securities are traded among investors. |

| **dealer** |
| --- |
| An agent who buys and sells securities from inventory. |

| **broker** |
| --- |
| An agent who arranges security transactions among investors. |

**SHIRE** ( LSE: SHP.L / ISIN JE00B2QKY057 )

| | | | |
| --- | --- | --- | --- |
| Last Trade: | 1,370.00 p | Day's Range: | 1,292.00 - 1,414.00 |
| Trade Time: | 19 Feb | 52wk Range: | 991.50 - 1,414.00 |
| Change: | ↑60.00 (4.58%) | | |
| Prev Close: | 1,310.00 | Volume: | 7,071,616 |
| Open: | 1,301.00 | Avg Vol (3m): | 1,387,010 |
| Bid: | 1,369.00 | Market Cap: | N/A |
| Ask: | 1,371.00 | P/E (ttm): | N/A |
| 1y Target Est: | 1,346.36 p | EPS (ttm): | N/A |
| | | Div & Yield: | 9.91 (0.76%) |

**TRADE** Buy/Sell for £9.95

- Add SHP.L to Your Portfolio
- Download Data
- Finance updates on your mobile

Most of this information is self-explanatory. The last trade price is £13.70. The reported change is from the previous day's closing price. The opening price is the first trade of the day. We see the bid and ask prices of £13.69 and £13.71. The '1y Target Est' is the average estimated share price one year ahead, based on estimates from security analysts who follow the company.

Moving to the second column, we have the range of prices for this day, followed by the range over the previous 52 weeks. Volume is the number of shares traded today, followed by average daily volume over the last three months. Market cap is number of shares outstanding (from the most recent financial statements) multiplied by the current price per share. P/E is the P/E ratio we discussed in Chapter 3. The earnings per share (EPS) used in the calculation is 'ttm', meaning 'trailing twelve months'. In Shire's case, this information is not available. Finally, we have the annual dividend on the share and the dividend yield. Notice that the yield is just the reported dividend divided by the previous day's closing share price: $9.91/1,370 = 0.009 = 0.76\%$.

| CONCEPT QUESTIONS | 7.3a | What is the difference between a securities broker and a securities dealer? |
|---|---|---|
| | 7.3b | Which is bigger, the bid price or the ask price? Why? |

## Summary and Conclusions

This chapter has covered the basics of equities and share valuation:

1  The cash flows from owning a share of equity come in the form of future dividends. We saw that in certain special cases it is possible to calculate the present value of all the future dividends and thus come up with a value for the equity.

2  In addition to ordinary shares, some corporations have issued preference shares. The name stems from the fact that preference shareholders must be paid first, before ordinary shareholders can receive anything. Preference shares have a fixed dividend.

3  The three biggest stock markets in Europe are the London Stock Exchange, Euronext, and Deutsche Börse. We discussed the organization and operation of these three markets, and we saw how share price information is reported in the financial press.

This chapter completes Part Two of our book. By now you should have a good grasp of what we mean by *present value*. You should also be familiar with how to calculate present values, loan payments, and so on. In Part Three we cover capital budgeting decisions. As you will see, the techniques you learned in Chapters 4–7 form the basis for our approach to evaluating business investment decisions.

## Chapter Review and Self-Test Problems

7.1  **Dividend Growth and Share Valuation**  Big Yellow Taxi plc has just paid a cash dividend of £2 per share. Investors require a 16 per cent return from investments such as this. If the dividend is expected to grow at a steady 8 per cent per year, what is the current value of the equity? What will the equity be worth in five years?

7.2  **More Dividend Growth and Share Valuation**  In Self-Test Problem 7.1, what would the share sell for today if the dividend was expected to grow at 20 per cent per year for the next three years and then settle down to 8 per cent per year, indefinitely?

# Answers to Chapter Review and Self-Test Problems

7.1 The last dividend, $D_0$, was £2. The dividend is expected to grow steadily at 8 per cent. The required return is 16 per cent. Based on the dividend growth model, we can say that the current price is

$$P_0 = D_1/(R - g) = D_0 \times (1 + g)/(R - g)$$
$$= £2 \times 1.08/(0.16 - 0.08)$$
$$= £2.16/0.08$$
$$= £27$$

We could calculate the price in five years by calculating the dividend in five years and then using the growth model again. Alternatively, we could recognize that the share price will increase by 8 per cent per year and calculate the future price directly. We'll do both. First, the dividend in five years will be

$$D_5 = D_0 \times (1 + g)^5$$
$$= £2 \times 1.08^5$$
$$= £2.9387$$

The price in five years would therefore be

$$P_5 = D_5 \times (1 + g)/(R - g)$$
$$= £2.9387 \times 1.08/0.08$$
$$= £3.1738/0.08$$
$$= £39.67$$

Once we understand the dividend model, however, it's easier to notice that

$$P_5 = P_0 \times (1 + g)^5$$
$$= £27 \times 1.08^5$$
$$= £27 \times 1.4693$$
$$= £39.67$$

Notice that both approaches yield the same price in five years.

7.2 In this scenario we have supernormal growth for the next three years. We'll need to calculate the dividends during the rapid growth period, and the share price in three years. The dividends are

$$D_1 = £2.00 \times 1.20 = £2.400$$
$$D_2 = £2.40 \times 1.20 = £2.880$$
$$D_3 = £2.88 \times 1.20 = £3.456$$

After three years the growth rate falls to 8 per cent indefinitely. The price at that time, $P_3$, is thus

$$P_3 = D_3 \times (1 + g)/(R - g)$$
$$= £3.456 \times 1.08/(0.16 - 0.08)$$
$$= £3.7325/0.08$$
$$= £46.656$$

To complete the calculation of the share's present value, we have to determine the present value of the three dividends and the future price:

$$P_0 = \frac{D_1}{(1 + R)^1} + \frac{D_2}{(1 + R)^2} + \frac{D_3}{(1 + R)^3} + \frac{P_3}{(1 + R)^3}$$
$$= \frac{£2.40}{1.16} + \frac{2.88}{1.16^2} + \frac{3.456}{1.16^3} + \frac{46.656}{1.16^3}$$
$$= £2.07 + 2.14 + 2.21 + 29.89$$
$$= £36.31$$

# Concepts Review and Critical Thinking Questions

1 **Share Valuation [LO1]** Why does the value of a share of equity depend on dividends?

2 **Share Valuation [LO1]** A substantial percentage of the companies listed on European stock exchanges don't pay dividends, but investors are nonetheless willing to buy shares in them. How is this possible, given your answer to the previous question?

3 **Dividend Policy [LO1]** Referring to the previous questions, under what circumstances might a company choose not to pay dividends?

4 **Dividend Growth Model [LO1]** Under what two assumptions can we use the dividend growth model presented in the chapter to determine the share price? Comment on the reasonableness of these assumptions.

5 **Ordinary versus Preference Shares [LO1]** Suppose a company has a preference share issue and an ordinary share issue. Both have just paid a £2 dividend. Which do you think will have a higher price, the preference share or the ordinary share?

6 **Dividend Growth Model [LO1]** Based on the dividend growth model, what are the two components of the total return on a share of equity? Which do you think is typically larger?

7 **Growth Rate [LO1]** In the context of the dividend growth model, is it true that the growth rate in dividends and the growth rate in the share price are identical?

8 **Share Valuation [LO1]** Evaluate the following statement: managers should not focus on the current share price, because doing so will lead to an overemphasis on short-term profits at the expense of long-term profits.

9 **Two-Stage Dividend Growth Model [LO1]** One of the assumptions of the two-stage growth model is that the dividends drop immediately from the high growth rate to the perpetual growth rate. What do you think about this assumption? What happens if this assumption is violated?

# connect Questions and Problems

**BASIC 1–9**

1 **Share Values [LO1]** In 2010, Daimler AG announced that it would not pay a dividend because of the atrocious trading conditions in the previous year. However, analysts expect the company to pay a dividend of €0.60 in 2011. If dividends are expected to grow at a constant rate of 8 per cent per year indefinitely, and investors require a 10 per cent return on the company, what is the current price? What will the price be in three years? In 15 years?

2 **Share Values [LO1]** The next dividend payment by Modern Times Group AB will be SKr5 per share. The dividends are anticipated to maintain a 5 per cent growth rate for ever. If the equity currently sells for SKr397.3 per share, what is the required return?

3 **Share Values [LO1]** For the company in the previous problem, what is the dividend yield? What is the expected capital gains yield?

4 **Share Values [LO1]** British American Tobacco plc will pay an £8.82 per share dividend next year. The company pledges to increase its dividend by 3.8 per cent per year indefinitely. If you require a 30 per cent return on your investment, how much will you pay for the company's equity today? Look up Yahoo! Finance and find the current price of British American Tobacco plc. How does the existing share price compare with the theoretical share price?

5 **Share Valuation [LO1]** Credit Agricole SA is expected to maintain a constant 5.2 per cent growth rate in its dividends indefinitely. If the company has a dividend yield of 4.27 per cent, what is the required return on the company's shares?

6 **Share Valuation [LO1]** Suppose you know that a company's equity currently sells for £47 per share, and the required return on the equity is 11 per cent. You also know that the total return on the equity is evenly divided between a capital gains yield and a dividend yield. If it's the company's policy to always maintain a constant growth rate in its dividends, what is the current dividend per share?

7 **Share Valuation [LO1]** Vivendi SA pays a constant €1.40 dividend on its equity. The company will maintain this dividend for the next 11 years, and will then cease paying dividends for ever. If the required return on this equity is 10 per cent, what is the current share price?

8 **Valuing Preference Shares [LO1]** Resnor plc has an issue of preference shares outstanding that pays a £3.40 dividend every year in perpetuity. If this issue currently sells for £69 per share, what is the required return?

9 **Share Valuation and Required Return [LO1]** Red plc, Yellow plc and Blue plc each will pay a dividend of £2.35 next year. The growth rate in dividends for all three companies is 5 per cent. The required return for each company's shares is 8 per cent, 11 per cent and 14 per cent, respectively. What is the share price for each company? What do you conclude about the relationship between the required return and the share price?

10 **Share Valuation [LO1]** Unilever NV just paid a dividend of €0.51 on its equity. The growth rate in dividends is expected to be a constant 5 per cent per year indefinitely. Investors require a 14 per cent return on the equity for the first three years, a 12 per cent return for the next three years, and a 10 per cent return thereafter. What is the current share price?

11 **Non-Constant Growth [LO1]** Metallica Bearings plc is a young start-up company. No dividends will be paid on the equity over the next nine years, because the firm needs to plough back its earnings to fuel growth. The company will pay a £1 per share dividend in 10 years, and will increase the dividend by 5 per cent per year thereafter. If the required return on this equity is 16 per cent, what is the current share price?

12 **Non-Constant Dividends [LO1]** Bread plc has an odd dividend policy. The company has just paid a dividend of £5 per share, and has announced that it will increase the dividend by £2 per share for each of the next five years, and then never pay another dividend. If you require an 18 per cent return on the company's equity, how much will you pay for a share today?

13 **Non-Constant Dividends [LO1]** Far Side SpA is expected to pay the following dividends over the next four years: €12, €10, €6 and €3. Subsequently, the company pledges to maintain a constant 5 per cent growth rate in dividends for ever. If the required return on the equity is 12 per cent, what is the current share price?

14 **Supernormal Growth [LO1]** Marcel AG is growing quickly. Dividends are expected to grow at a 30 per cent rate for the next three years, with the growth rate falling off to a constant 6 per cent thereafter. If the required return is 13 per cent and the company just paid a €1.80 dividend, what is the current share price?

15 **Supernormal Growth [LO1]** Eva AB is experiencing rapid growth. Dividends are expected to grow at 20 per cent per year during the next three years, 15 per cent over the following year, and then 10 per cent per year indefinitely. The required return on this equity is 13 per cent, and it currently sells for €56 per share. What is the projected dividend for the coming year?

**INTERMEDIATE**

**10–21**

16  **Negative Growth [LO1]**   Antiques R Us is a mature manufacturing firm. The company just paid a €12 dividend, but management expects to reduce the payout by 4 per cent per year indefinitely. If you require an 11 per cent return on this equity, what will you pay for a share today?

17  **Finding the Dividend [LO1]**   Teder plc shares currently sell for £64 per share. The market requires a 10 per cent return on the firm's equity. If the company maintains a constant 4.5 per cent growth rate in dividends, what was the most recent dividend per share paid on the equity?

18  **Valuing Preference Shares [LO1]**   E-Eyes.com Bank just issued some new preference shares. The issue will pay a £20 annual dividend in perpetuity, beginning 20 years from now. If the market requires a 6.4 per cent return on this investment, how much does a preference share cost today?

19  **Using Share Price Quotes [LO3]**   You have found the following share price quote for HBooks plc, in the financial pages of today's newspaper. What was the closing price for this equity that appeared in *yesterday's* paper? If the company currently has 25 million shares of equity outstanding, what was net income for the most recent year?

| 52-WEEK | | | | | | NET | |
| --- | --- | --- | --- | --- | --- | --- | --- |
| **HI** | **LO** | **EQUITY (DIV)** | **YLD %** | **P/E** | **VOL 100s** | **CLOSE** | **CHG** |
| 72.18 | 53.17 | HBOOKS 1.48 | 2.1 | 19 | 17652 | ?? | −.23 |

20  **Two-Stage Dividend Growth Model [LO1]**   Thirsty Cactus SA just paid a dividend of €2.50 per share. The dividends are expected to grow at 25 per cent for the next eight years, and then level off to an 8 per cent growth rate indefinitely. If the required return is 13 per cent, what is the share price today?

21  **Two-Stage Dividend Growth Model [LO1]**   Chartreuse County Choppers plc is experiencing rapid growth. The company expects dividends to grow at 20 per cent per year for the next 11 years before levelling off at 5 per cent into perpetuity. The required return on the company's equity is 14 per cent. If the dividend per share just paid was $1.74, what is the share price?

22  **Capital Gains versus Income [LO1]**   Consider four different equities, all of which have a required return of 16 per cent and a most recent dividend of £2.50 per share. Equities W, X and Y are expected to maintain constant growth rates in dividends for the foreseeable future of 10 per cent, 0 per cent and −5 per cent per year, respectively. Equity Z is a growth stock that will increase its dividend by 20 per cent for the next two years, and then maintain a constant 12 per cent growth rate thereafter. What is the dividend yield for each of these four equities? What is the expected capital gains yield? Discuss the relationship among the various returns that you find for each of these equities.

23  **Share Valuation [LO1]**   Most corporations pay semi-annual dividends on their ordinary equity rather than annual dividends. Barring any unusual circumstances during the year, the board raises, lowers or maintains the current dividend once a year and then pays this dividend out in equal six-monthly instalments to its shareholders.

(a)  Suppose a company currently pays a £3.20 annual dividend on its ordinary equity in a single annual instalment, and management plans to raise this dividend by 6 per cent per year indefinitely. If the required return on this equity is 14 per cent, what is the current share price?

(b)  Now suppose the company in (a) actually pays its annual dividend in equal six-monthly instalments: thus the company has just paid a £1.60 dividend per share, as it has for the previous six-month period. What is your value for the current share price now? (*Hint:* Find the equivalent annual end-of-year dividend for each year.) Comment on whether you think this model of share valuation is appropriate.

**CHALLENGE
22–28**

24  **Non-constant Growth [LO1]**  Storico plc has just paid a dividend of £2.45 per share. The company will increase its dividend by 20 per cent next year, and will then reduce its dividend growth rate by 5 percentage points per year until it reaches the industry average of 5 per cent dividend growth, after which the company will keep a constant growth rate for ever. If the required return on Storico shares is 11 per cent, what will a share of equity sell for today?

25  **Non-Constant Growth [LO1]**  This one's a little harder. Suppose the current share price for the firm in the previous problem is £63.82, and all the dividend information remains the same. What required return must investors be demanding on Storico equity? (*Hint:* Set up the valuation formula with all the relevant cash flows, and use trial and error to find the unknown rate of return.)

26  **Constant Dividend Growth Model [LO1]**  Assume an equity has dividends that grow at a constant rate for ever. If you value the shares using the constant dividend growth model, how many years worth of dividends constitute one-half of the share's current price?

27  **Two-Stage Dividend Growth [LO1]**  Regarding the two-stage dividend growth model in the chapter, show that the price of a share of equity today can be written as follows:

$$P_0 = \frac{D_0 \times (1 + g_1)}{R - g_1} \times \left[1 - \left(\frac{1 + g_1}{1 + R}\right)^t\right] + \left(\frac{1 + g_1}{1 + R}\right)^t \times \frac{D_0 \times (1 + g_2)}{R - g_2}$$

Can you provide an intuitive interpretation of this expression?

28  **Two-Stage Dividend Growth [LO1]**  The chapter shows that in the two-stage dividend growth model, the growth rate in the first stage, $g_1$, can be greater than or less than the discount rate, $R$. Can they be exactly equal? (*Hint:* Yes, but what does the expression for the share value look like?)

## MINI CASE  Share Valuation at Ragan plc.

Ragan plc was founded nine years ago by brother and sister Carrington and Genevieve Ragan. The company manufactures and installs commercial heating, ventilation and cooling (HVAC) units. Ragan plc has experienced rapid growth because of a proprietary technology that increases the energy efficiency of its units. The company is equally owned by Carrington and Genevieve. The original partnership agreement between the siblings gave each 50,000 shares of equity. In the event either wished to sell stock, the shares first had to be offered to the other at a discounted price.

Although neither sibling wants to sell, they have decided they should value their holdings in the company. To get started, they have gathered the following information about their main competitors:

| | EPS (£) | DPS (£) | Share price (£) | ROE (%) | R (%) |
|---|---|---|---|---|---|
| **Ragan plc competitors** | | | | | |
| Arctic Cooling plc | 0.79 | 0.20 | 14.18 | 10.00 | 10.00 |
| National Heating & Cooling | 1.38 | 0.62 | 11.87 | 13.00 | 13.00 |
| Expert HVAC plc | −0.48 | 0.38 | 13.21 | 14.00 | 12.00 |
| Industry Average | 0.56 | 0.40 | 13.09 | 12.33 | 11.67 |

Expert HVAC plc's negative earnings per share were the result of an accounting write-off last year. Without the write-off, earnings per share for the company would have been £1.06.

Last year, Ragan plc had an EPS of £4.54 and paid a dividend to Carrington and Genevieve of £63,000 each. The company also had a return on equity of 25 per cent. The siblings believe that 20 per cent is an appropriate required return for the company.

## QUESTIONS

1 Assuming the company continues its current growth rate, what is the share price of the company's equity?

2 To verify their calculations, Carrington and Genevieve have hired Josh Schlessman as a consultant. Josh was previously an equity analyst, and covered the HVAC industry. Josh has examined the company's financial statements, as well as examining its competitors. Although Ragan plc currently has a technological advantage, his research indicates that other companies are investigating methods to improve efficiency. Given this, Josh believes that the company's technological advantage will last only for the next five years. After that period, the company's growth is likely to slow to the industry growth average. Additionally, Josh believes that the required return used by the company is too high. He believes the industry average required return is more appropriate. Under this growth rate assumption, what is your estimate of the share price?

3 What is the industry average price–earnings ratio? What is the price–earnings ratio for Ragan plc? Is this the relationship you would expect between the two ratios? Why?

4 Carrington and Genevieve are unsure how to interpret the price–earnings ratio. After some head scratching, they've come up with the following expression for the price–earnings ratio:

$$\frac{P_0}{E_1} = \frac{1-b}{R - (\text{ROE} \times b)}$$

Beginning with the constant dividend growth model, verify this result. What does this expression imply about the relationship between the dividend payout ratio, the required return on the equity, and the company's ROE?

5 Assume the company's growth rate slows to the industry average in five years. What future return on equity does this imply, assuming a constant payout ratio?

6 After discussing the share value with Josh, Carrington and Genevieve agree that they would like to increase the value of the company equity. Like many small business owners, they want to retain control of the company, but they do not want to sell equity to outside investors. They also feel that the company's debt is at a manageable level, and do not want to borrow more money. How can they increase the share price? Are there any conditions under which this strategy would not increase the share price?

## Endnotes

1 The only assumption we make about the share price is that it is a finite number, no matter how far away we push it. It can be extremely large, just not infinitely so. Because no one has ever observed an infinite share price, this assumption is plausible.

2 Here and elsewhere, we use the term *capital gains* a little loosely. For the record, a capital gain (or loss) is, strictly speaking, something defined by a country's tax authority. For our purposes, it would be more accurate (but less common) to use the term *price appreciation* instead of *capital gain*.

# CHAPTER 8

# Net Present Value and Other Investment Criteria

## KEY NOTATIONS

| | |
|---|---|
| AAR | Average accounting return |
| IRR | Internal rate of return |
| NPV | Net present value |
| PI | Profitability index |
| R | Discount rate |

## LEARNING OBJECTIVES

After studying this chapter, you should understand:

**LO1** The reasons why the net present value criterion is the best way to evaluate proposed investments.

**LO2** The payback rule, and some of its shortcomings.

**LO3** The discounted payback rule, and some of its shortcomings.

**LO4** Accounting rates of return, and some of the problems with them.

**LO5** The internal rate of return criterion, and its strengths and weaknesses.

**LO6** The modified internal rate of return.

**LO7** The profitability index, and its relation to net present value.

IN 2010 THE EUROPEAN TELECOMMUNICATIONS INDUSTRY was facing its next big challenge. Its challenge was whether to invest heavily in new fibre optic technology that would significantly improve broadband Internet speed and potentially allow new premium streaming services to customers.

After a couple of years, in which it slashed capital expenditure, France Telecom announced that between 2010 and 2015 it would roll out an extensive fibre optic network in Paris and 15 other French cities, at a cost of €2 billion. Although the French government encouraged the company to undertake its plans, many of France Telecom's shareholders were worried about the return that could be earned on such an investment. Furthermore, France Telecom's fixed-line competitors, SFR and Free, had no plans to compete in the fibre optic market, because of difficulties they had in previous years to sell premium on-demand products. The directors of France Telecom, on the other hand, believed that high-speed lines would return customers that had previously been lost to SFR and Free, as well as introducing new income streams from video on demand and HD games streaming over the Internet.

France Telecom's fibre optic network roll-out is an example of a capital budgeting decision. Decisions such as this one, with a price tag of €2 billion, are obviously major undertakings, and the risks and rewards must be carefully weighed. In this chapter we discuss the basic tools used in making such decisions.

In Chapter 1 we saw that increasing the value of the equity in a company is the goal of financial management. Thus what we need to know is how to tell whether a particular investment will achieve that or not. This chapter considers a variety of techniques that are used in practice for this purpose. More important, it shows how many of these techniques can be misleading, and it explains why the net present value approach is the right one.

In Chapter 1 we identified the three key areas of concern to the financial manager. The first of these involved the question: what non-current assets should we buy? We called this the *capital budgeting decision.* In this chapter we begin to deal with the issues that arise in answering this question.

The process of allocating or budgeting capital is usually more involved than just deciding whether to buy a particular non-current asset. We frequently face broader issues, such as whether we should launch a new product or enter a new market. Decisions such as these determine the nature of a firm's operations and products for years to come, primarily because non-current asset investments are generally long-lived and not easily reversed once they are made.

The most fundamental decision a business must make concerns its product line. What services shall we offer or what shall we sell? In what markets will we compete? What new products shall we introduce? The answer to any of these questions will require that the firm commit its scarce and valuable capital to certain types of asset. As a result, all these strategic issues fall under the general heading of capital budgeting. The process of capital budgeting could thus be given a more descriptive (not to mention impressive) name: *strategic asset allocation.*

For the reasons we have discussed, the capital budgeting question is probably the most important issue in corporate finance. How a firm chooses to finance its operations (the capital structure question) and how a firm manages its short-term operating activities (the working capital question) are certainly issues of concern, but the non-current assets define the business of the firm. Airlines, for example, are airlines because they operate airplanes, regardless of how they finance them.

Any firm possesses a huge number of possible investments. Each possible investment is an option available to the firm. Some options are valuable and some are not. The essence of successful financial management, of course, is learning to identify which are which. With this in mind, our goal in this chapter is to introduce you to the techniques used to analyse potential business ventures to decide which are worth undertaking.

We present and compare a number of different procedures used in practice. Our primary goal is to acquaint you with the advantages and disadvantages of the various approaches. As we shall see, the most important concept in this area is the idea of net present value. We consider this next.

## 8.1    Net Present Value

In Chapter 1 we argued that the goal of financial management is to create value for the shareholders. The financial manager must thus examine a potential investment in the light of its likely effect on the value of the firm's shares. In this section we describe a widely used procedure for doing this: the net present value approach.

### The Basic Idea

An investment is worth undertaking if it creates value for its owners. In the most general sense, we create value by identifying an investment worth more in the marketplace than it costs us to acquire. How can something be worth more than it costs? It's a case of the whole being worth more than the cost of the parts.

For example, suppose you buy a run-down house for £25,000 and spend another £25,000 on painters, plumbers and so on to get it renovated. Your total investment is £50,000. When the work is completed, you place the house back on the market and find that it's worth £60,000. The market value (£60,000) exceeds the cost (£50,000) by £10,000. What you have done here is act as a manager and bring together some non-current assets (a house), some labour (plumbers, carpenters, and others) and some materials (carpeting, paint, and so on). The net result is that you have created £10,000 in value. Put another way, this £10,000 is the *value added* by management.

With our house example, it turned out *after the fact* that £10,000 in value had been created. Things thus worked out nicely. The real challenge, of course, would have been somehow to identify *ahead of time* whether investing the necessary £50,000 was a good idea in the first place. This is what capital budgeting is all about – namely, trying to determine whether a proposed investment or project will be worth more, once it is in place, than it costs.

For reasons that will be obvious in a moment, the difference between an investment's market value and its cost is called the **net present value** of the investment, abbreviated to **NPV**. In other words, net present value is a measure of how much value is created or added today by undertaking an investment. Given our goal of creating value for the shareholders, the capital budgeting process can be viewed as a search for investments with positive net present values.

With our run-down house, you can probably imagine how we would go about making the capital budgeting decision. We would first look at what comparable, renovated properties were selling for in the market. We would then get estimates of the cost of buying a particular property and bringing it to market. At this point, we would have an estimated total cost and an estimated market value. If the difference was positive, then this investment would be worth undertaking, because it would have a positive estimated net present value. There is risk, of course, because there is no guarantee that our estimates will turn out to be correct.

As our example illustrates, investment decisions are greatly simplified when there is a market for assets similar to the investment we are considering. Capital budgeting becomes much more difficult when we cannot observe the market price for at least roughly comparable investments. The reason is that we then face the problem of estimating the value of an investment using only indirect market information. Unfortunately, this is precisely the situation the financial manager usually encounters. We examine this issue next.

> **net present value (NPV)**
> The difference between an investment's market value and its cost.

## Estimating Net Present Value

Imagine we are thinking of starting a business to produce and sell a new product – organic fertilizer, say. We can estimate the start-up costs with reasonable accuracy, because we know what we shall need to buy to begin production. Would this be a good investment? Based on our discussion, you know that the answer depends on whether the value of the new business exceeds the cost of starting it. In other words, does this investment have a positive NPV?

This problem is much more difficult than our renovated house example, because entire fertilizer companies are not routinely bought and sold in the marketplace, so it is essentially impossible to observe the market value of a similar investment. As a result, we must somehow estimate this value by other means.

Based on our work in Chapters 4 and 5, you may be able to guess how we shall go about estimating the value of our fertilizer business. We shall first try to estimate the future cash flows we expect the new business to produce. We shall then apply our basic discounted cash flow procedure to estimate the present value of those cash flows. Once we have this estimate, we shall then estimate NPV as the difference between the present value of the future cash flows and the cost of the investment. As we mentioned in Chapter 5, this procedure is often called **discounted cash flow (DCF) valuation**.

> **discounted cash flow (DCF) valuation**
> The process of valuing an investment by discounting its future cash flows.

FIGURE
**8.1**

| Time (years) | 0 | 1 | 2 | 3 | 4 | 5 | 6 | 7 | 8 |
|---|---|---|---|---|---|---|---|---|---|
| Initial cost | −£30 | | | | | | | | |
| Inflows | | £20 | £20 | £20 | £20 | £20 | £20 | £20 | £20 |
| Outflows | | −14 | −14 | −14 | −14 | −14 | −14 | −14 | −14 |
| Net inflow | | £ 6 | £ 6 | £ 6 | £ 6 | £ 6 | £ 6 | £ 6 | £ 6 |
| Salvage | | | | | | | | | 2 |
| Net cash flow | −£30 | £ 6 | £ 6 | £ 6 | £ 6 | £ 6 | £ 6 | £ 6 | £ 8 |

**Figure 8.1** Project cash flows (£000)

To see how we might go about estimating NPV, suppose we believe the cash revenues from our fertilizer business will be £20,000 per year, assuming everything goes as expected. Cash costs (including taxes) will be £14,000 per year. We shall wind down the business in eight years. Plant, property and equipment will be worth £2,000 as salvage at that time. The project costs £30,000 to launch. We use a 15 per cent discount rate on new projects such as this one. Is this a good investment? If there are 1,000 shares of equity outstanding, what will be the effect on the share price of taking this investment?

From a purely mechanical perspective, we need to calculate the present value of the future cash flows at 15 per cent. The net cash inflow will be £20,000 cash income less £14,000 in costs per year for eight years. These cash flows are illustrated in Fig. 8.1. As Fig. 8.1 suggests, we effectively have an eight-year annuity of £20,000 − 14,000 = £6,000 per year, along with a single lump-sum inflow of £2,000 in eight years. Calculating the present value of the future cash flows thus comes down to the same type of problem we considered in Chapter 5. The total present value is

$$\text{Present value} = £6,000 \times [1 - (1/1.15^8)]/0.15 + (2,000/1.15^8)$$
$$= (£6,000 \times 4.4873) + (2,000/3.0590)$$
$$= £26,924 + 654$$
$$= £27,578$$

When we compare this with the £30,000 estimated cost, we see that the NPV is

$$\text{NPV} = -£30,000 + 27,578 = -£2,422$$

Therefore this is *not* a good investment. Based on our estimates, taking it would *decrease* the total value of the equity by £2,422. With 1,000 shares outstanding, our best estimate of the impact of taking this project is a loss of value of £2,422/1,000 = £2.42 per share.

Our fertilizer example illustrates how NPV estimates can be used to determine whether an investment is desirable. From our example, notice that if the NPV is negative, the effect on share value will be unfavourable. If the NPV were positive, the effect would be favourable. As a consequence, all we need to know about a particular proposal for the purpose of making an accept–reject decision is whether the NPV is positive or negative.

Given that the goal of financial management is to increase share value, our discussion in this section leads us to the *net present value rule*:

*An investment should be accepted if the net present value is positive, and rejected if it is negative.*

In the unlikely event that the net present value turned out to be exactly zero, we would be indifferent between taking the investment and not taking it.

Two comments about our example are in order. First, and foremost, it is not the rather mechanical process of discounting the cash flows that is important. Once we have the cash flows and the appropriate discount rate, the required calculations are fairly straightforward. The task of coming up with the cash flows and the discount rate is much more challenging. We shall have much more to say about this in the next few chapters. For the remainder of this chapter we take it as a given that we have estimates of the cash revenues and costs and, where needed, an appropriate discount rate.

The second thing to keep in mind about our example is that the –£2,422 NPV is an estimate. Like any estimate, it can be high or low. The only way to find out the true NPV would be to place the investment up for sale and see what we could get for it. We generally won't be doing this, so it is important that our estimates are reliable. Once again, we shall say more about this later. For the rest of this chapter we shall assume that the estimates are accurate.

---

## EXAMPLE 8.1

## Using the NPV Rule

Suppose we are asked to decide whether a new consumer product should be launched. Based on projected sales and costs, we expect that the cash flows over the five-year life of the project will be £2,000 in the first two years, £4,000 in the next two, and £5,000 in the last year. It will cost about £10,000 to begin production. We use a 10 per cent discount rate to evaluate new products. What should we do here?

Given the cash flows and discount rate, we can calculate the total value of the product by discounting the cash flows back to the present:

$$Present\ value = (£2,000/1.1) + (2,000/1.1^2) + (4,000/1.1^3)$$
$$+ (4,000/1.1^4) + (5,000/1.1^5)$$
$$= £1,818 + 1,653 + 3,005 + 2,732 + 3,105$$
$$= £12,313$$

The present value of the expected cash flows is £12,313, but the cost of getting those cash flows is only £10,000, so the NPV is £12,313 – 10,000 = £2,313. This is positive; so, based on the net present value rule, we should take on the project.

---

As we have seen in this section, estimating NPV is one way of assessing the value of a proposed investment. It is certainly not the only way value is assessed, and we now turn to some alternatives. As we shall see, when compared with NPV, each of the alternative ways we shall examine is flawed in some key way; so NPV is the preferred approach in principle, if not always in practice.

# Spreadsheet Strategies

## Calculating NPVs with a Spreadsheet

Spreadsheets are commonly used to calculate NPVs. Examining the use of spreadsheets in this context also allows us to issue an important warning. Let's redo Example 8.1:

|   | A | B | C | D | E | F | G | H |
|---|---|---|---|---|---|---|---|---|
| 1 | Year | 0 | 1 | 2 | 3 | 4 | 5 | |
| 2 | Cash Flow | -£10,000 | £2,000 | £2,000 | £4,000 | £4,000 | £5,000 | |
| 3 | | | | | | | | |
| 4 | Discount Rate | 10% | | | | | | |
| 5 | | | | | | | | |
| 6 | NPV = | £2,102.72 | WRONG!!! Incorrect formula is =NPV(B4,B2:G2) | | | | | |
| 7 | NPV = | £2,312.99 | CORRECT!!! Formula is =NPV(B4,C2:G2)+B2 | | | | | |
| 8 | | | | | | | | |
| 9 | | | | | | | | |

In our spreadsheet example, notice that we have provided two answers. By comparing the answers with that found in Example 8.1, we see that the first answer is wrong, even though we used the spreadsheet's NPV formula. What happened is that the 'NPV' function in our spreadsheet is actually a PV function; unfortunately, one of the original spreadsheet programs many years ago got the definition wrong, and subsequent spreadsheets have copied it! Our second answer shows how to use the formula properly.

The example here illustrates the danger of blindly using calculators or computers without understanding what is going on; we shudder to think of how many capital budgeting decisions in the real world are based on incorrect use of this particular function. We shall see another example of something that can go wrong with a spreadsheet later in the chapter.

**CONCEPT QUESTIONS**

8.1a  What is the net present value rule?

8.1b  If we say an investment has an NPV of €1,000, what exactly do we mean?

## 8.2  The Payback Rule

It is common in practice to talk of the payback on a proposed investment. Loosely, the *payback* is the length of time it takes to recover our initial investment. Because this idea is widely understood and used, we shall examine it in some detail.

### Defining the Rule

**payback period**
The amount of time required for an investment to generate cash flows sufficient to recover its initial cost.

We can illustrate how to calculate a payback with an example. Figure 8.2 shows the cash flows from a proposed investment. How many years do we have to wait until the accumulated cash flows from this investment equal or exceed the cost of the investment? As Fig. 8.2 indicates, the initial investment is £50,000. After the first year, the firm has recovered £30,000, leaving £20,000. The cash flow in the second year is exactly £20,000, so this investment 'pays for itself' in exactly two years. Put another way, the **payback period** is two years. If we require a payback of, say, three years or less, then this investment is acceptable. This illustrates the *payback period rule*:

*Based on the payback rule, an investment is acceptable if its calculated payback period is less than some pre-specified number of years.*

In our example, the payback works out to be exactly two years. This won't usually happen, of course. When the numbers don't work out exactly, it is customary to work with fractional years. For example, suppose the initial investment is £60,000, and the cash flows are £20,000 in the first year and £90,000 in the second. The cash flows over the first two years are £110,000, so the project obviously pays back some time in the second year. After the first year, the project has paid back £20,000, leaving £40,000 to be recovered. To figure

**FIGURE 8.2**

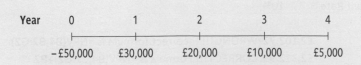

| Year | 0 | 1 | 2 | 3 | 4 |
|------|-----|-----|-----|-----|-----|
| | −£50,000 | £30,000 | £20,000 | £10,000 | £5,000 |

**Figure 8.2** Net project cash flows

out the fractional year, note that this £40,000 is £40,000/90,000 = 4/9 of the second year's cash flow. Assuming that the £90,000 cash flow is received uniformly throughout the year, the payback would be $1\frac{4}{9}$ years.

| EXAMPLE 8.2 | Calculating Payback |
|---|---|

Here are the projected cash flows from a proposed investment:

| Year | Cash flow (€) |
|---|---|
| 1 | 100 |
| 2 | 200 |
| 3 | 500 |

This project costs €500. What is the payback period for this investment?

The initial cost is €500. After the first two years, the cash flows total €300. After the third year, the total cash flow is €800, so the project pays back some time between the end of year 2 and the end of year 3. Because the accumulated cash flows for the first two years are €300, we need to recover €200 in the third year. The third-year cash flow is €500, so we shall have to wait €200/500 = 0.4 year to do this. The payback period is thus 2.4 years, or about two years and five months.

| TABLE 8.1 | | | | | |
|---|---|---|---|---|---|
| **Year** | **A (€)** | **B (€)** | **C (€)** | **D (€)** | **E (€)** |
| 0 | −100 | −200 | −200 | −200 | −50 |
| 1 | 30 | 40 | 40 | 100 | 100 |
| 2 | 40 | 20 | 20 | 100 | −50,000,000 |
| 3 | 50 | 10 | 10 | −200 | |
| 4 | 60 | | 130 | 200 | |

**Table 8.1** Expected cash flows for projects A–E

Now that we know how to calculate the payback period on an investment, using the payback period rule for making decisions is straightforward. A particular cut-off time is selected – say, two years – and all investment projects that have payback periods of two years or less are accepted, whereas any that pay off in more than two years are rejected.

Table 8.1 illustrates cash flows for five different projects. The figures shown as the year 0 cash flows are the costs of the investments. We examine these to indicate some peculiarities that can, in principle, arise with payback periods.

The payback for the first project, A, is easily calculated. The sum of the cash flows for the first two years is €70, leaving us with €100 – 70 = €30 to go. Because the cash flow in the third year is €50, the payback occurs some time in that year. When we compare the €30 we need with the €50 that will be coming in, we get €30/50 = 0.6: so payback will occur 60 per cent of the way into the year. The payback period is thus 2.6 years.

Project B's payback is also easy to calculate: it *never* pays back, because the cash flows never total up to the original investment. Project C has a payback of exactly four years, because it supplies the €130 that B is missing in year 4. Project D is a little strange. Because of the negative cash flow in year 3, you can easily verify that it has two different payback periods, two years and four years. Which of these is correct? Both of them; the way the payback period is calculated doesn't guarantee a single answer. Finally, project E is obviously unrealistic, but it does pay back in six months, thereby illustrating the point that a rapid payback does not guarantee a good investment.

| TABLE 8.2 | Year | Long (€) | Short (€) |
|---|---|---|---|
| | 0 | −250 | −250 |
| | 1 | 100 | 100 |
| | 2 | 100 | 200 |
| | 3 | 100 | 0 |
| | 4 | 100 | 0 |

**Table 8.2** Investment projected cash flows

## Analysing the Rule

When compared with the NPV rule, the payback period rule has some rather severe short-comings. First, we calculate the payback period by simply adding up the future cash flows. There is no discounting involved, so the time value of money is completely ignored. The payback rule also fails to consider any risk differences. The payback would be calculated the same way for both very risky and very safe projects.

Perhaps the biggest problem with the payback period rule is coming up with the right cut-off period: we don't really have an objective basis for choosing a particular number. Put another way, there is no economic rationale for looking at payback in the first place, so we have no guide for how to pick the cut-off. As a result, we end up using a number that is arbitrarily chosen.

Suppose we have somehow decided on an appropriate payback period of two years or less. As we have seen, the payback period rule ignores the time value of money for the first two years. More seriously, cash flows after the second year are ignored entirely. To see this, consider the two investments, Long and Short, in Table 8.2. Both projects cost €250. Based on our discussion, the payback on Long is 2 + (€50/100) = 2.5 years, and the payback on Short is 1 + (€150/200) = 1.75 years. With a cut-off of two years, Short is acceptable and Long is not.

Is the payback period rule guiding us to the right decisions? Maybe not. Suppose we require a 15 per cent return on this type of investment. We can calculate the NPV for these two investments as

$$\text{NPV(Short)} = -€250 + (100/1.15) + (200/1.15^2) = -€11.81$$
$$\text{NPV(Long)} = -€250 + (100 \times \{[1 - (1/1.15^4)]/0.15\}) = €35.50$$

Now we have a problem. The NPV of the shorter-term investment is actually negative, meaning that taking it diminishes the value of the shareholders' equity. The opposite is true for the longer-term investment – it increases share value.

Our example illustrates two primary shortcomings of the payback period rule. First, by ignoring time value, we may be led to take investments (like Short) that are actually worth less than they cost. Second, by ignoring cash flows beyond the cut-off, we may be led to reject profitable long-term investments (like Long). More generally, using a payback period rule will tend to bias us towards shorter-term investments.

## Redeeming Qualities of the Rule

Despite its shortcomings, the payback period rule is often used by large and sophisticated companies when they are making relatively minor decisions. There are several reasons for this. The primary reason is that many decisions simply do not warrant detailed analysis, because the cost of the analysis would exceed the possible loss from a mistake. As a practical matter, it can be said that an investment that pays back rapidly and has benefits extending beyond the cut-off period probably has a positive NPV.

Small investment decisions are made by the hundreds every day in large organizations. Moreover, they are made at all levels. As a result, it would not be uncommon for a corporation to require, for example, a two-year payback on all investments of a very small amount (say, less than £10,000). Larger investments would be subjected to greater scrutiny. The requirement of a two-year payback is not perfect, for reasons we have seen, but it does exercise some control over expenditures, and thus limits possible losses.

In addition to its simplicity, the payback rule has two other positive features. First, because it is biased towards short-term projects, it is biased towards liquidity. In other words, a payback rule tends to favour investments that free up cash for other uses quickly. This could be important for a small business; it would be less so for a large corporation. Second, the cash flows that are expected to occur later in a project's life are probably more uncertain. Arguably, a payback period rule adjusts for the extra riskiness of later cash flows, but it does so in a rather draconian fashion – by ignoring them altogether.

We should note here that some of the apparent simplicity of the payback rule is an illusion. The reason is that we must still come up with the cash flows first, and, as we discussed earlier, this is not at all easy to do. Thus it would probably be more accurate to say that the *concept* of a payback period is both intuitive and easy to understand.

## Summary of the Rule

To summarize, the payback period is a kind of 'break-even' measure. Because time value is ignored, you can think of the payback period as the length of time it takes to break even in an accounting sense, but not in an economic sense. The biggest drawback to the payback period rule is that it doesn't ask the right question. The relevant issue is the impact an investment will have on the value of the equity, not how long it takes to recover the initial investment.

Nevertheless, because it is so simple, companies often use it as a screen for dealing with the myriad minor investment decisions they have to make. There is certainly nothing wrong with this practice. As with any simple rule of thumb, there will be some errors in using it; but it wouldn't have survived all this time if it weren't useful. Now that you understand the rule, you can be on the alert for circumstances under which it might lead to problems. To help you remember, Table 8.3 lists the pros and cons of the payback period rule.

| TABLE 8.3 | Advantages | Disadvantages |
|---|---|---|
| | 1 Easy to understand. | 1 Ignores the time value of money. |
| | 2 Adjusts for uncertainty of later cash flows. | 2 Requires an arbitrary cut-off point. |
| | 3 Biased towards liquidity. | 3 Ignores cash flows beyond the cut-off date. |
| | | 4 Biased against long-term projects, such as research and development, and new projects. |

**Table 8.3** Advantages and disadvantages of the payback period rule

**CONCEPT QUESTIONS**

8.2a  In words, what is the payback period? The payback period rule?
8.2b  Why do we say that the payback period is, in a sense, an accounting break-even measure?

## 8.3 The Discounted Payback

> **discounted payback period**
> The length of time required for an investment's discounted cash flows to equal its initial cost.

We saw that one shortcoming of the payback period rule was that it ignored time value. A variation of the payback period, the discounted payback period, fixes this particular problem. The **discounted payback period** is the length of time until the sum of the discounted cash flows is equal to the initial investment. The *discounted payback rule* would be:

*Based on the discounted payback rule, an investment is acceptable if its discounted payback is less than some pre-specified number of years.*

To see how we might calculate the discounted payback period, suppose we require a 12.5 per cent return on new investments. We have an investment that costs €300 and has cash flows of €100 per year for five years. To get the discounted payback, we have to discount each cash flow at 12.5 per cent and then start adding them. We do this in Table 8.4. In Table 8.4 we have both the discounted and the undiscounted cash flows. Looking at the accumulated cash flows, we see that the regular payback is exactly three years. The discounted cash flows total €300 only after four years, however, so the discounted payback is four years, as shown.[1]

How do we interpret the discounted payback? Recall that the ordinary payback is the time it takes to break even in an accounting sense. Because it includes the time value of money, the discounted payback is the time it takes to break even in an economic or financial sense. Loosely speaking, in our example, we get our money back, along with the interest we could have earned elsewhere, in four years.

Figure 8.3 illustrates this idea by comparing the *future* value at 12.5 per cent of the €300 investment with the *future* value of the €100 annual cash flows at 12.5 per cent. Notice that the two lines cross at exactly four years. This tells us that the value of the project's cash flows catches up and then passes the original investment in four years.

Table 8.4 and Fig. 8.3 illustrate another interesting feature of the discounted payback period. If a project ever pays back on a discounted basis, then it must have a positive NPV.[2] This is true because, by definition, the NPV is zero when the sum of the discounted cash flows equals the initial investment. For example, the present value of all the cash flows in Table 8.4 is €355. The cost of the project was €300, so the NPV is obviously €55. This €55 is the value of the cash flow that occurs *after* the discounted payback (see the last line in Table 8.4). In general, if we use a discounted payback rule, we won't accidentally take any projects with a negative estimated NPV.

Based on our example, the discounted payback would seem to have much to recommend it. You may be surprised to find that it is rarely used in practice. Why? Probably because it really isn't any simpler to use than NPV. To calculate a discounted payback, you have to discount cash flows, add them up, and compare them with the cost, just as you do with NPV. So, unlike an ordinary payback, the discounted payback is not especially simple to calculate.

**TABLE 8.4**

| Year | Cash flow (€) | | Accumulated cash flow (€) | |
| | Undiscounted | Discounted | Undiscounted | Discounted |
| --- | --- | --- | --- | --- |
| 1 | 100 | 89 | 100 | 89 |
| 2 | 100 | 79 | 200 | 168 |
| 3 | 100 | 70 | 300 | 238 |
| 4 | 100 | 62 | 400 | 300 |
| 5 | 100 | 55 | 500 | 355 |

**Table 8.4** Ordinary and discounted payback

FIGURE
8.3

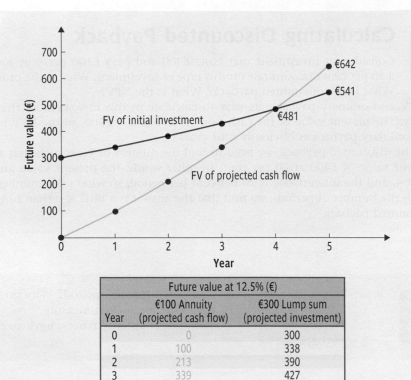

| | Future value at 12.5% (€) | |
|---|---|---|
| Year | €100 Annuity (projected cash flow) | €300 Lump sum (projected investment) |
| 0 | 0 | 300 |
| 1 | 100 | 338 |
| 2 | 213 | 390 |
| 3 | 339 | 427 |
| 4 | 481 | 481 |
| 5 | 642 | 541 |

**Figure 8.3** Future value of project cash flows

A discounted payback period rule has a couple of other significant drawbacks. The biggest one is that the cut-off still has to be arbitrarily set, and cash flows beyond that point are ignored.[3] As a result, a project with a positive NPV may be found unacceptable because the cut-off is too short. Also, just because one project has a shorter discounted payback than another does not mean it has a larger NPV.

All things considered, the discounted payback is a compromise between a regular payback and NPV that lacks the simplicity of the first and the conceptual rigour of the second. Nonetheless, if we need to assess the time it will take to recover the investment required by a project, then the discounted payback is better than the ordinary payback, because it considers time value. In other words, the discounted payback recognizes that we could have invested the money elsewhere and earned a return on it. The ordinary payback does not take this into account. The advantages and disadvantages of the discounted payback rule are summarized in Table 8.5.

TABLE
8.5

| Advantages | Disadvantages |
|---|---|
| 1 Includes time value of money. | 1 May reject positive-NPV investments. |
| 2 Easy to understand. | 2 Requires an arbitrary cut-off point. |
| 3 Does not accept negative estimated NPV investments. | 3 Ignores cash flows beyond the cut-off date. |
| 4 Biased towards liquidity. | 4 Biased against long-term projects, such as research and development, and new projects. |

**Table 8.5** Advantages and disadvantages of the discounted payback period rule

EXAMPLE 8.3

# Calculating Discounted Payback

Consider an investment that costs £400 and pays £100 per year for ever. We use a 20 per cent discount rate on this type of investment. What is the ordinary payback? What is the discounted payback? What is the NPV?

The NPV and ordinary payback are easy to calculate in this case, because the investment is a perpetuity. The present value of the cash flows is £100/0.2 = £500, so the NPV is £500 − 400 = £100. The ordinary payback is obviously four years.

To get the discounted payback, we need to find the number of years such that a £100 annuity has a present value of £400 at 20 per cent. In other words, the present value annuity factor is £400/100 = 4, and the interest rate is 20 per cent per period; so what's the number of periods? If we solve for the number of periods, we find that the answer is a little less than nine years, so this is the discounted payback.

CONCEPT QUESTIONS

8.3a In words, what is the discounted payback period? Why do we say it is, in a sense, a financial or economic break-even measure?

8.3b What advantage(s) does the discounted payback have over the ordinary payback?

## 8.4 The Average Accounting Return

**average accounting return (AAR)**
An investment's average net income divided by its average book value.

Another attractive, but flawed, approach to making capital budgeting decisions involves the **average accounting return (AAR)**. There are many different definitions of the AAR. However, in one form or another, the AAR is always defined as

$$\frac{\text{Some measure of average accounting profit}}{\text{Some measure of average accounting value}}$$

The specific definition we shall use is

$$\frac{\text{Average net income}}{\text{Average book value}}$$

To see how we might calculate this number, suppose we are deciding whether to open a store in a new shopping centre. The required investment in improvements is £500,000. The store would have a five-year life, because everything reverts to the centre owners after that time. We shall assume that the required investment would be 100 per cent depreciated (straight-line) over five years,[4] so the depreciation would be £500,000/5 = £100,000 per year. The tax rate is 25 per cent. Table 8.6 contains the projected revenues and expenses. Net income in each year, based on these figures, is also shown.

To calculate the average book value for this investment, we note that we started out with a book value of £500,000 (the initial cost) and ended up at £0. The average book value during the life of the investment is thus (£500,000 + 0)/2 = £250,000. As long as we use straight-line depreciation, the average investment will always be one-half of the initial investment.[5]

Looking at Table 8.6, we see that net income is £100,000 in the first year, £150,000 in the second year, £50,000 in the third year, £0 in Year 4, and −£50,000 in Year 5. The average net income, then, is

$$[£100,000 + 150,000 + 50,000 + 0 + (-50,000)]/5 = £50,000$$

| TABLE 8.6 | | Year 1 | Year 2 | Year 3 | Year 4 | Year 5 |
|---|---|---|---|---|---|---|
| | Revenue (£) | 433,333 | 450,000 | 266,667 | 200,000 | 133,333 |
| | Expenses (£) | 200,000 | 150,000 | 100,000 | 100,000 | 100,000 |
| | Earnings before depreciation (£) | 233,333 | 300,000 | 166,667 | 100,000 | 33,333 |
| | Depreciation (£) | 100,000 | 100,000 | 100,000 | 100,000 | 100,000 |
| | Earnings before taxes (£) | 133,333 | 200,000 | 66,667 | 0 | −66,667 |
| | Taxes (25%) (£) | 33,333 | 50,000 | 16,667 | 0 | −16,667 |
| | Net income (£) | 100,000 | 150,000 | 50,000 | 0 | −50,000 |

$$\text{Average net income} = \frac{£100,000 + 150,000 + 50,000 + 0 - 50,000}{5} = £50,000$$

$$\text{Average book value} = \frac{£500,000 + 0}{2} = £250,000$$

**Table 8.6** Projected yearly revenue and costs for average accounting return

The average accounting return is

$$\text{AAR} = \frac{\text{Average net income}}{\text{Average book value}} = \frac{£50,000}{£250,000} = 20\%$$

If the firm has a target AAR of less than 20 per cent, then this investment is acceptable; otherwise it is not. The *average accounting return rule* is thus

> Based on the average accounting return rule, a project is acceptable if its average accounting return exceeds a target average accounting return.

As we shall now see, the use of this rule has a number of problems.

You should recognize the chief drawback of the AAR immediately. Above all else, the AAR is not a rate of return in any meaningful economic sense. Instead, it is the ratio of two accounting numbers, and it is not comparable to the returns offered, for example, in financial markets.[6]

One of the reasons why the AAR is not a true rate of return is that it ignores time value. When we average figures that occur at different times, we are treating the near future and the more distant future in the same way. There was no discounting involved when we computed the average net income, for example.

The second problem with the AAR is similar to the problem we had with the payback period rule concerning the lack of an objective cut-off period. Because a calculated AAR is really not comparable to a market return, the target AAR must somehow be specified. There is no generally agreed-upon way to do this. One way of doing it is to calculate the AAR for the firm as a whole and use this as a benchmark, but there are lots of other ways as well.

The third, and perhaps worst, flaw in the AAR is that it doesn't even look at the right things. Instead of cash flow and market value, it uses net income and book value. These are both poor substitutes. As a result, an AAR doesn't tell us what the effect on share price will be of taking an investment, so it doesn't tell us what we really want to know.

Does the AAR have any redeeming features? About the only one is that it almost always can be computed. The reason is that accounting information will almost always be available, both for the project under consideration and for the firm as a whole. We hasten to add that once the accounting information is available, we can always convert it to cash flows, so even this is not a particularly important fact. The AAR is summarized in Table 8.7.

TABLE
8.7

| Advantages | Disadvantages |
|---|---|
| 1 Easy to calculate. | 1 Not a true rate of return; time value of money is ignored. |
| 2 Needed information will usually be available. | 2 Uses an arbitrary benchmark cut-off rate. |
| | 3 Based on accounting (book) values, not cash flows and market values. |

**Table 8.7** Advantages and disadvantages of the average accounting return

8.4a  What is an average accounting rate of return (AAR)?
8.4b  What are the weaknesses of the AAR rule?

## 8.5 The Internal Rate of Return

**internal rate of return (IRR)**
The discount rate that makes the NPV of an investment zero.

We now come to the most important alternative to NPV, the **internal rate of return**, universally known as the **IRR**. As we shall see, the IRR is closely related to NPV. With the IRR, we try to find a single rate of return that summarizes the merits of a project. Furthermore, we want this rate to be an 'internal' rate in the sense that it depends only on the cash flows of a particular investment, not on rates offered elsewhere.

To illustrate the idea behind the IRR, consider a project that costs €100 today and pays €110 in one year. Suppose you were asked, 'What is the return on this investment?' What would you say? It seems both natural and obvious to say that the return is 10 per cent, because for every euro we put in, we get €1.10 back. In fact, as we shall see in a moment, 10 per cent is the internal rate of return, or IRR, on this investment.

Is this project with its 10 per cent IRR a good investment? Once again, it would seem apparent that this is a good investment only if our required return is less than 10 per cent. This intuition is also correct, and illustrates the *IRR rule*:

*Based on the IRR rule, an investment is acceptable if the IRR exceeds the required return. It should be rejected otherwise.*

Imagine that we want to calculate the NPV for our simple investment. At a discount rate of $R$, the NPV is

$$\text{NPV} = -€100 + [110/(1 + R)]$$

Now, suppose we don't know the discount rate. This presents a problem, but we can still ask how high the discount rate would have to be before this project was deemed unacceptable. We know that we are indifferent between taking and not taking this investment when its NPV is just equal to zero. In other words, this investment is *economically* a break-even proposition when the NPV is zero, because value is neither created nor destroyed. To find the break-even discount rate we set NPV equal to zero and solve for $R$:

$$\text{NPV} = 0 = -€100 + [110/(1 + R)]$$
$$€100 = €110/(1 + R)$$
$$1 + R = €110/100 = 1.1$$
$$R = 10\%$$

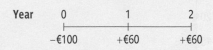

Figure 8.4 Project cash flows

This 10 per cent is what we have already called the return on this investment. What we have now illustrated is that the internal rate of return on an investment (or just 'return' for short) is the discount rate that makes the NPV equal to zero. This is an important observation, so it bears repeating:

*The IRR on an investment is the required return that results in a zero NPV when it is used as the discount rate.*

The fact that the IRR is simply the discount rate that makes the NPV equal to zero is important, because it tells us how to calculate the returns on more complicated investments. As we have seen, finding the IRR turns out to be relatively easy for a single-period investment. However, suppose you were now looking at an investment with the cash flows shown in Fig. 8.4. As illustrated, this investment costs €100 and has a cash flow of €60 per year for two years, so it's only slightly more complicated than our single-period example. However, if you were asked for the return on this investment, what would you say? There doesn't seem to be any obvious answer (at least not to us). However, based on what we now know, we can set the NPV equal to zero and solve for the discount rate:

$$NPV = 0 = -€100 + [60/(1 + IRR)] + [60/(1 + IRR)^2]$$

Unfortunately, the only way to find the IRR in general is by trial and error, either by hand or by calculator. This is precisely the same problem that came up in Chapter 4 when we found the unknown rate for an annuity and in Chapter 6 when we found the yield to maturity on a bond. In fact, we now see that in both of those cases we were finding an IRR.

In this particular case the cash flows form a two-period, €60 annuity. To find the unknown rate, we can try some different rates until we get the answer. If we were to start with a 0 per cent rate, the NPV would obviously be €120 − 100 = €20. At a 10 per cent discount rate, we would have

$$NPV = -€100 + (60/1.1) + (60/1.1^2) = €4.13$$

Now, we're getting close. We can summarize these and some other possibilities as shown in Table 8.8. From our calculations the NPV appears to be zero with a discount rate between 10 per cent and 15 per cent, so the IRR is somewhere in that range. With a little more effort we can find that the IRR is about 13.1 per cent.[7] So, if our required return were less than 13.1 per cent, we would take this investment. If our required return exceeded 13.1 per cent, we would reject it.

| Discount rate (%) | NPV (€) |
| --- | --- |
| 0 | 20.00 |
| 5 | 11.56 |
| 10 | 4.13 |
| 15 | −2.46 |
| 20 | −8.33 |

Table 8.8 NPV at different discount rates

FIGURE
**8.5**

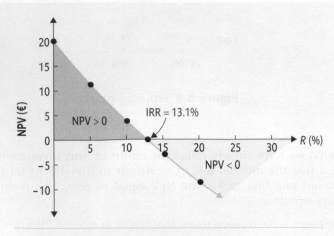

**Figure 8.5** An NPV profile

By now you have probably noticed that the IRR rule and the NPV rule appear to be quite similar. In fact, the IRR is sometimes simply called the *discounted cash flow return*, or *DCF return*. The easiest way to illustrate the relationship between NPV and IRR is to plot the numbers we calculated for Table 8.8. We put the different NPVs on the vertical axis, or *y*-axis, and the discount rates on the horizontal axis, or *x*-axis. If we had a very large number of points the resulting picture would be a smooth curve called a **net present value profile**. Figure 8.5 illustrates the NPV profile for this project. Beginning with a 0 per cent discount rate, we have €20 plotted directly on the *y*-axis. As the discount rate increases, the NPV declines smoothly. Where will the curve cut through the *x*-axis? This will occur where the NPV is just equal to zero, so it will happen right at the IRR of 13.1 per cent.

> **net present value profile**
> A graphical representation of the relationship between an investment's NPVs and various discount rates.

In our example the NPV rule and the IRR rule lead to identical accept–reject decisions. We shall accept an investment using the IRR rule if the required return is less than 13.1 per cent. As Fig. 8.5 illustrates, however, the NPV is positive at any discount rate less than 13.1 per cent, so we would accept the investment using the NPV rule as well. The two rules give equivalent results in this case.

---

| EXAMPLE **8.4** | ## Calculating the IRR |
|---|---|

A project has a total up-front cost of €435.44. The cash flows are €100 in the first year, €200 in the second year, and €300 in the third year. What's the IRR? If we require an 18 per cent return, should we take this investment?

We'll describe the NPV profile and find the IRR by calculating some NPVs at different discount rates. You should check our answers for practice. Beginning with 0 per cent, we have:

| Discount rate (%) | NPV (€) |
|---|---|
| 0 | 164.56 |
| 5 | 100.36 |
| 10 | 46.15 |
| 15 | 0.00 |
| 20 | −39.61 |

The NPV is zero at 15 per cent, so 15 per cent is the IRR. If we require an 18 per cent return, then we should not take the investment. The reason is that the NPV is negative at 18 per cent (verify that it is −€24.47). The IRR rule tells us the same thing in this case. We shouldn't take this investment, because its 15 per cent return is below our required 18 per cent return.

At this point you may be wondering whether the IRR and NPV rules always lead to identical decisions. The answer is yes, as long as two very important conditions are met. First, the project's cash flows must be *conventional*, meaning that the first cash flow (the initial investment) is negative and all the rest are positive. Second, the project must be *independent*, meaning that the decision to accept or reject this project does not affect the decision to accept or reject any other. The first of these conditions is typically met, but the second often is not. In any case, when one or both of these conditions are not met, problems can arise. We discuss some of these next.

## Spreadsheet Strategies

### Calculating IRRs with a Spreadsheet

Because IRRs are so tedious to calculate by hand, spreadsheets are generally used and, as the following example illustrates, using a spreadsheet is easy.

Suppose we have a four-year project that costs £500. The cash flows over the four-year life will be £100, £200, £300 and £400, respectively. What is the IRR?

The spreadsheet could be laid out as follows:

|   | A | B | C | D | E | F |
|---|---|---|---|---|---|---|
| 1 | Year | 0 | 1 | 2 | 3 | 4 |
| 2 | Cash Flow | -500 | 100 | 200 | 300 | 400 |
| 3 |   |   |   |   |   |   |
| 4 | IRR = | =IRR(B2:F2) |   |   |   |   |

The formula in cell B4 gives an IRR of 27.27 per cent.

## Problems with the IRR

The problems with the IRR come about when the cash flows are not conventional, or when we are trying to compare two or more investments to see which is best. In the first case, surprisingly, the simple question 'What's the return?' can become difficult to answer. In the second case, the IRR can be a misleading guide.

**Non-Conventional Cash Flows**  Suppose we have a strip-mining project that requires a €60 investment. Our cash flow in the first year will be €155. In the second year the mine will be depleted, but we shall have to spend €100 to restore the terrain. As Fig. 8.6 illustrates, both the first and third cash flows are negative.

**FIGURE 8.6**

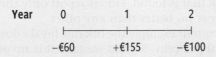

| Year | 0 | 1 | 2 |
|------|---|---|---|
|  | −€60 | +€155 | −€100 |

**Figure 8.6** Project cash flows

FIGURE

**8.7**

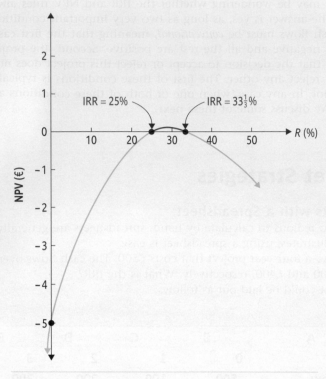

**Figure 8.7** NPV profile

To find the IRR on this project, we can calculate the NPV at various rates:

| Discount rate (%) | NPV (€) |
|---|---|
| 0 | −5.00 |
| 10 | −1.74 |
| 20 | −0.28 |
| 30 | 0.06 |
| 40 | −0.31 |

The NPV appears to be behaving in a peculiar fashion here. First, as the discount rate increases from 0 per cent to 30 per cent, the NPV starts out negative and becomes positive. This seems backward, because the NPV is rising as the discount rate rises. It then starts getting smaller, and becomes negative again. What's the IRR? To find out, we draw the NPV profile as shown in Fig. 8.7.

In Fig. 8.7, notice that the NPV is zero when the discount rate is 25 per cent, so this is the IRR. Or is it? The NPV is also zero at $33^{1}/_{3}$ per cent. Which of these is correct? The answer is both or neither; more precisely, there is no unambiguously correct answer. This is the **multiple rates of return** problem. Many financial computer packages (including a best-seller for personal computers) aren't aware of this problem and just report the first IRR that is found. Others report only the smallest positive IRR, even though this answer is no better than any other.

**multiple rates of return**
The possibility that more than one discount rate will make the NPV of an investment zero.

In our current example the IRR rule breaks down completely. Suppose our required return is 10 per cent. Should we take this investment? Both IRRs are greater than 10 per cent, so, by the IRR rule, perhaps we should. However, as Fig. 8.7 shows, the NPV is negative at any discount rate less than 25 per cent, so this is not a good investment. When should we take it? Looking at Fig. 8.7 one last time, we see that the NPV is positive only if our required return is between 25 per cent and $33^{1}/_{3}$ per cent.

Non-conventional cash flows can occur in a variety of ways. For example, ore mining firms open and close operations depending on the price of the ore that is being extracted. This results in negative cash flows during the periods in which the mine is closed, and positive cash flows when it is open. Sometimes the cost of maintaining a disused mine is significantly better than running a loss-making mining operation.

The moral of the story is that when the cash flows aren't conventional, strange things can start to happen to the IRR. This is not anything to get upset about, however, because the NPV rule, as always, works just fine. This illustrates the fact that, oddly enough, the obvious question – What's the rate of return? – may not always have a good answer.

---

**EXAMPLE 8.5**

## What's the IRR?

You are looking at an investment that requires you to invest €51 today. You'll get €100 in one year, but you must pay out €50 in two years. What is the IRR on this investment?

You're on the alert now for the non-conventional cash flow problem, so you probably wouldn't be surprised to see more than one IRR. However, if you start looking for an IRR by trial and error, it will take you a long time. The reason is that there is no IRR. The NPV is negative at every discount rate, so we shouldn't take this investment under any circumstances. What's the return on this investment? Your guess is as good as ours.

---

**EXAMPLE 8.6**

## 'I Think, Therefore I Know How Many IRRs There Can Be.'

We've seen that it's possible to get more than one IRR. If you wanted to make sure that you had found all the possible IRRs, how could you do it? The answer comes from the great mathematician, philosopher and financial analyst Descartes (of 'I think, therefore I am' fame). Descartes' Rule of Sign says that the maximum number of IRRs that there can be is equal to the number of times that the cash flows change sign from positive to negative and/or negative to positive.[8]

In our example with the 25 per cent and $33^1/_3$ per cent IRRs, could there be yet another IRR? The cash flows flip from negative to positive, then back to negative, for a total of two sign changes. Therefore, according to Descartes' rule, the maximum number of IRRs is two and we don't need to look for any more. Note that the actual number of IRRs can be less than the maximum (see Example 8.5).

---

**Mutually Exclusive Investments**  Even if there is a single IRR, another problem can arise concerning **mutually exclusive investment decisions**. If two investments, X and Y, are mutually exclusive, then taking one of them means that we cannot take the other. Two projects that are not mutually exclusive are said to be independent. For example, if we own one corner lot, then we can build a petrol station or an apartment building, but not both. These are mutually exclusive alternatives.

Thus far we have asked whether a given investment is worth undertaking. However, a related question comes up often: given two or more mutually exclusive investments, which one is the best? The answer is simple enough: the best one is the one with the largest NPV. Can we also say that the best one has the highest return? As we show, the answer is no.

To illustrate the problem with the IRR rule and mutually exclusive investments, consider the following cash flows from two mutually exclusive investments:

> **mutually exclusive investment decisions** A situation in which taking one investment prevents the taking of another.

| Year | Investment A (€) | Investment B (€) |
|------|------------------|------------------|
| 0 | −100 | −100 |
| 1 | 50 | 20 |
| 2 | 40 | 40 |
| 3 | 40 | 50 |
| 4 | 30 | 60 |

The IRR for A is 24 per cent, and the IRR for B is 21 per cent. Because these investments are mutually exclusive, we can take only one of them. Simple intuition suggests that investment A is better because of its higher return. Unfortunately, simple intuition is not always correct.

To see why investment A is not necessarily the better of the two investments, we've calculated the NPV of these investments for different required returns:

| Discount rate (%) | NPV(A) (€) | NPV(B) (€) |
|-------------------|-----------|-----------|
| 0 | 60.00 | 70.00 |
| 5 | 43.13 | 47.88 |
| 10 | 29.06 | 29.79 |
| 15 | 17.18 | 14.82 |
| 20 | 7.06 | 2.31 |
| 25 | −1.63 | −8.22 |

The IRR for A (24 per cent) is larger than the IRR for B (21 per cent). However, if you compare the NPVs, you'll see that which investment has the higher NPV depends on our required return. B has greater total cash flow, but it pays back more slowly than A. As a result, it has a higher NPV at lower discount rates.

In our example, the NPV and IRR rankings conflict for some discount rates. If our required return is 10 per cent, for instance, then B has the higher NPV and is thus the better of the two, even though A has the higher return. If our required return is 15 per cent, then there is no ranking conflict: A is better.

The conflict between the IRR and NPV for mutually exclusive investments can be illustrated by plotting the investments' NPV profiles as we have done in Fig. 8.8. In Fig. 8.8

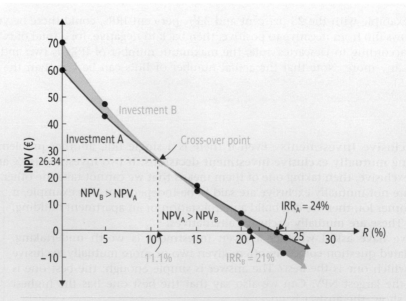

**Figure 8.8** NPV profiles for mutually exclusive investments

notice that the NPV profiles cross at about 11 per cent. Notice also that at any discount rate less than 11 per cent the NPV for B is higher. In this range, taking B benefits us more than taking A, even though A's IRR is higher. At any rate greater than 11 per cent, investment A has the greater NPV.

This example illustrates that when we have mutually exclusive projects, we shouldn't rank them based on their returns. More generally, whenever we are comparing investments to determine which is best, looking at IRRs can be misleading. Instead, we need to look at the relative NPVs to avoid the possibility of choosing incorrectly. Remember, we're ultimately interested in creating value for the shareholders, so the option with the higher NPV is preferred, regardless of the relative returns.

If this seems counterintuitive, think of it this way. Suppose you have two investments. One has a 10 per cent return and makes you €100 richer immediately. The other has a 20 per cent return and makes you €50 richer immediately. Which one do you like better? We would rather have €100 than €50, regardless of the returns, so we like the first one better.

---

**EXAMPLE 8.7**

## Calculating the Crossover Rate

In Fig. 8.8 the NPV profiles cross at about 11 per cent. How can we determine just what this crossover point is? The *crossover rate*, by definition, is the discount rate that makes the NPVs of two projects equal. To illustrate, suppose we have the following two mutually exclusive investments:

| Year | Investment A (€) | Investment B (€) |
|---|---|---|
| 0 | −400 | −500 |
| 1 | 250 | 320 |
| 2 | 280 | 340 |

What's the crossover rate?

To find the crossover, first consider moving out of investment A and into investment B. If you make the move, you'll have to invest an extra €100 (= $500 − 400). For this €100 investment, you'll get an extra €70 (= €320 − 250) in the first year and an extra €60 (= €340 − 280) in the second year. Is this a good move? In other words, is it worth investing the extra €100?

Based on our discussion, the NPV of the switch, NPV(B − A), is

$$NPV(B − A) = −€100 + [70/(1 + R)] + [60/(1 + R)^2]$$

We can calculate the return on this investment by setting the NPV equal to zero and solving for the IRR:

$$NPV(B − A) = 0$$
$$= −€100 + [70/(1 + R)] + [60/(1 + R)^2]$$

If you go through this calculation you will find the IRR is exactly 20 per cent. What this tells us is that, at a 20 per cent discount rate, we are indifferent between the two investments, because the NPV of the difference in their cash flows is zero. As a consequence, the two investments have the same value, so this 20 per cent is the crossover rate. Check to see that the NPV at 20 per cent is €2.78 for both investments.

In general, you can find the crossover rate by taking the difference in the cash flows and calculating the IRR using the difference. It doesn't make any difference which one you subtract from which. To see this, find the IRR for (A − B); you'll see it's the same number. Also, for practice, you might want to find the exact crossover in Fig. 8.8. (*Hint*: It's 11.0704 per cent.)

**Investing or Financing?**   Consider the following two independent investments:

| Year | Investment A (€) | Investment B (€) |
|------|-----------------|------------------|
| 0    | −100            | −100             |
| 1    | 130             | −130             |

The company initially pays out cash with investment A and initially receives cash for investment B. Most projects are more like investment A, but projects like investment B also occur. For example, consider a corporation conducting a seminar where the participants pay in advance. Because large expenses are frequently incurred at the seminar date, cash inflows precede cash outflows.

For these two projects, suppose the required return for each investment project is 12 per cent. According to the IRR decision rule, which, if either, project should we accept? If you calculate the IRRs, you will find that they are 30 per cent for both projects.

According to the IRR decision rule, we should accept both projects. However, if we calculate the NPV of B at 12 per cent, we get

$$ €100 - \frac{€130}{1.12} = -€16.07 $$

In this case the NPV and IRR decision rules disagree. To see what's going on, Fig. 8.9 shows the NPV profile for each project. As you can see, the NPV profile for B is upward sloping. Thus the project should be accepted if the required return is *greater* than 30 per cent.

When a project has cash flows like investment B's, the IRR is really a rate that you are paying, not receiving. For this reason we say that the project has *financing-type* cash flows, whereas investment A has *investing-type* cash flows. You should take a project with financing-type cash flows only if it is an inexpensive source of financing, meaning that its IRR is *lower* than your required return.

## Redeeming Qualities of the IRR

Despite its flaws, the IRR is very popular in practice – more so even than the NPV. It probably survives because it fills a need that the NPV does not. In analysing investments, people in general, and financial analysts in particular, seem to prefer talking about rates of return rather than cash values.

In a similar vein, the IRR also appears to provide a simple way of communicating information about a proposal. One manager might say to another, 'Remodelling the clerical wing has a 20 per cent return.' This may somehow seem simpler than saying, 'At a 10 per cent discount rate, the net present value is £4,000.'

**FIGURE 8.9**

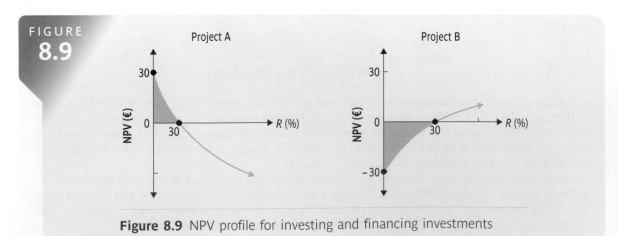

**Figure 8.9** NPV profile for investing and financing investments

| TABLE 8.9 | Advantages | Disadvantages |
|---|---|---|
| | **1** Closely related to NPV, often leading to identical decisions. | **1** May result in multiple answers, or not deal with non-conventional cash flows. |
| | **2** Easy to understand and communicate. | **2** May lead to incorrect decisions in comparisons of mutually exclusive investments. |

**Table 8.9** Advantages and disadvantages of the internal rate of return

Finally, under certain circumstances, the IRR may have a practical advantage over the NPV. We can't estimate the NPV unless we know the appropriate discount rate, but we can still estimate the IRR. Suppose we didn't know the required return on an investment, but we found, for example, that it had a 40 per cent return. We would probably be inclined to take it, because it would be unlikely that the required return would be that high. The advantages and disadvantages of the IRR are summarized in Table 8.9.

## The Modified Internal Rate of Return (MIRR)

To address some of the problems that can crop up with the standard IRR, it is often proposed that a modified version be used. As we shall see, there are several different ways of calculating a modified IRR, or MIRR, but the basic idea is to modify the cash flows first and then calculate an IRR using the modified cash flows.

To illustrate, let's go back to the cash flows in Fig. 8.6: −€60, +€155 and −€100. As we saw, there are two IRRs, 25 per cent and $33^1/_3$ per cent. We next illustrate three different MIRRs, all of which have the property that only one answer will result, thereby eliminating the multiple IRR problem.

**Method 1: The Discounting Approach**   With the discounting approach, the idea is to discount all negative cash flows back to the present at the required return and add them to the initial cost, and then calculate the IRR. Because only the first modified cash flow is negative, there will be only one IRR. The discount rate used might be the required return, or it might be some other externally supplied rate. We shall use the project's required return.

If the required return on the project is 20 per cent, then the modified cash flows look like this:

$$\text{Time 0: } -€60 + \frac{-€100}{1.20^2} = -€129.44$$

Time 1: +€155
Time 2: +€0

If you calculate the MIRR now, you should get 19.74 per cent.

**Method 2: The Reinvestment Approach**   With the reinvestment approach, we compound *all* cash flows (positive and negative) except the first out to the end of the project's life, and then calculate the IRR. In a sense, we are 'reinvesting' the cash flows, and not taking them out of the project until the very end. The rate we use could be the required return on the project, or it could be a separately specified 'reinvestment rate'. We shall use the project's required return. When we do, here are the modified cash flows:

Time 0: −€60
Time 1: +0
Time 2: −€100 + (€155 × 1.2) = €86

The MIRR on this set of cash flows is 19.72 per cent, or a little lower than we got using the discounting approach.

**Method 3: The Combination Approach**    As the name suggests, the combination approach blends our first two methods. Negative cash flows are discounted back to the present, and positive cash flows are compounded to the end of the project. In practice, different discount or compounding rates might be used, but we shall again stick with the project's required return.

With the combination approach, the modified cash flows are as follows:

$$\text{Time 0: } -€60 + \frac{-€100}{1.20^2} = -€129.44$$

$$\text{Time 1: } +0$$

$$\text{Time 2: } €155 \times 1.2 = €186$$

See if you don't agree that the MIRR is 19.87 per cent, the highest of the three.

**MIRR or IRR: Which Is Better?**    MIRRs are controversial. At one extreme are those who claim that MIRRs are always superior to IRRs. For example, by design, they clearly don't suffer from the multiple rate of return problem.

At the other end, detractors say that MIRR should stand for 'meaningless internal rate of return'. As our example makes clear, one problem with MIRRs is that there are different ways of calculating them, and there is no clear reason to say that one of our three methods is better than any other. The differences are small with our simple cash flows, but they could be much larger for a more complex project. Moreover, it's not clear how to interpret an MIRR. It may look like a rate of return, but it's a rate of return on a modified set of cash flows, not the project's actual cash flows.

We're not going to take sides. However, notice that calculating an MIRR requires discounting, compounding, or both, which leads to two obvious observations. First, if we have the relevant discount rate, why not calculate the NPV and be done with it? Second, because an MIRR depends on an externally supplied discount (or compounding) rate, the answer you get is not truly an 'internal' rate of return, which by definition depends only on the project's cash flows.

We shall take a stand on one issue that frequently comes up in this context. The value of a project does not depend on what the firm does with the cash flows generated by that project. A firm might use a project's cash flows to fund other projects, to pay dividends, or to buy an executive jet. It doesn't matter: how the cash flows are spent in the future does not affect their value today. As a result, there is generally no need to consider reinvestment of interim cash flows.

| | | |
|---|---|---|
| **CONCEPT QUESTIONS** | 8.5a | Under what circumstances will the IRR and NPV rules lead to the same accept–reject decisions? When might they conflict? |
| | 8.5b | Is it generally true that an advantage of the IRR rule over the NPV rule is that we don't need to know the required return to use the IRR rule? |

## 8.6    The Profitability Index

**profitability index (PI)**
The present value of an investment's future cash flows divided by its initial cost.
Also called the *benefit–cost ratio*.

Another tool used to evaluate projects is called the **profitability index (PI)** or benefit–cost ratio. This index is defined as the present value of the future cash flows divided by the initial investment. So, if a project costs €200 and the present value of its future cash flows is €220, the profitability index value would be €220/200 = 1.1. Notice that the NPV for this investment is €20, so it is a desirable investment.

More generally, if a project has a positive NPV, then the present value of the future cash flows must be bigger than the initial investment. The profitability index

| TABLE 8.10 | Advantages | Disadvantages |
|---|---|---|
| | **1** Closely related to NPV, generally leading to identical decisions. | **1** May lead to incorrect decisions in comparisons of mutually exclusive investments. |
| | **2** Easy to understand and communicate. | |
| | **3** May be useful when available investment funds are limited. | |

**Table 8.10** Advantages and disadvantages of the profitability index

would thus be bigger than 1 for a positive-NPV investment and less than 1 for a negative-NPV investment.

How do we interpret the profitability index? In our example, the PI was 1.1. This tells us that, per euro invested, €1.10 in value or €0.10 in NPV results. The profitability index thus measures the value created per cash unit invested. For this reason, it is often proposed as a measure of performance for government or other not-for-profit investments. Also, when capital is scarce, it may make sense to allocate it to projects with the highest PIs. We shall return to this issue in a later chapter.

The PI is obviously similar to the NPV. However, consider an investment that costs €5 and has a €10 present value, and an investment that costs €100 with a €150 present value. The first of these investments has an NPV of €5 and a PI of 2. The second has an NPV of €50 and a PI of 1.5. If these are mutually exclusive investments, then the second one is preferred even though it has a lower PI. This ranking problem is similar to the IRR ranking problem we saw in the previous section. In all, there seems to be little reason to rely on the PI instead of the NPV. Our discussion of the PI is summarized in Table 8.10.

| CONCEPT QUESTIONS | 8.6a | What does the profitability index measure? |
|---|---|---|
| | 8.6b | How would you state the profitability index rule? |

# 8.7 The Practice of Capital Budgeting

Given that NPV seems to be telling us directly what we want to know, you might be wondering why there are so many other procedures, and why alternative procedures are commonly used. Recall that we are trying to make an investment decision, and that we are frequently operating under considerable uncertainty about the future. We can only *estimate* the NPV of an investment in this case. The resulting estimate can be very 'soft', meaning that the true NPV might be quite different.

Because the true NPV is unknown, the astute financial manager seeks clues to help in assessing whether the estimated NPV is reliable. For this reason, firms would typically use multiple criteria for evaluating a proposal. For example, suppose we have an investment with a positive estimated NPV. Based on our experience with other projects, this one appears to have a short payback and a very high AAR. In this case, the different indicators seem to agree that it's 'all systems go'. Put another way, the payback and the AAR are consistent with the conclusion that the NPV is positive.

On the other hand, suppose we had a positive estimated NPV, a long payback, and a low AAR. This could still be a good investment, but it looks as though we need to be much more careful in making the decision, because we are getting conflicting signals. If the estimated NPV is based on projections in which we have little confidence, then further analysis is probably in order. We shall consider how to evaluate NPV estimates in more detail in the next two chapters.

EXAMPLE
8.8

# Bringing It All Together: Evaluating a Project Using Several Capital Budgeting Appraisal Techniques

Sandy Grey Ltd is in the process of deciding whether or not to revise its line of mobile phones that it manufactures and sells. Its sole market is large corporations, and it has not as yet focused on the retail sector. The company has estimated that the revision will cost £220,000. Cash flows from increased sales will be £80,000 in the first year. These cash flows will increase by 5% per year. The company estimates that the new line will be obsolete five years from now. Assume the initial cost is paid now, and all revenues are received at the end of each year. If the company requires a 10 per cent return for such an investment, should it undertake the revision? Use three investment evaluation techniques to arrive at your answer.

We shall look at NPV, IRR and the profitability index. However, it is easy to consider the payback period or discounted payback period.

If the cash flows increase by 5 per cent per year, they will be as follows:

| Year | 0 | 1 | 2 | 3 | 4 | 5 |
|---|---|---|---|---|---|---|
| Cash flow (£) | −220,000 | 80,000 | 84,000 | 88,200 | 92,610 | 97,240.5 |

The NPV of the investment is

$$NPV = -£220,000 + \frac{£80,000}{(1+0.10)} + \frac{£84,000}{(1+0.10)^2} + \frac{£88,200}{(1+0.10)^3} + \frac{£92,610}{(1+0.10)^4} + \frac{£97,240.5}{(1+0.10)^5}$$

$$= £112,047$$

The IRR of the investment is

$$NPV = 0$$

$$= -£220,000 + \frac{£80,000}{(1+IRR)} + \frac{£84,000}{(1+IRR)^2} + \frac{£88,200}{(1+IRR)^3} + \frac{£92,610}{(1+IRR)^4} + \frac{£97,240.5}{(1+IRR)^5}$$

Using trial and error, the IRR is

$$IRR = 27.69\%$$

The profitability index of the investment is

$$PI = \left[ \frac{£80,000}{(1+IRR)} + \frac{£84,000}{(1+IRR)^2} + \frac{£88,200}{(1+IRR)^3} + \frac{£92,610}{(1+IRR)^4} + \frac{£97,240.5}{(1+IRR)^5} \right] \Big/ £220,000$$

$$= 1.509$$

With all methods the project looks viable, and should be undertaken.

So far this chapter has asked 'Which capital budgeting methods should companies be using?' An equally important question is this: which methods *are* companies using? Table 8.11 helps to answer this question. As can be seen from the table, there is quite a strong variation in the frequency with which different techniques are utilized. Other more advanced techniques, such as real options, break-even and sensitivity analysis, are covered in later chapters.

Most companies use the IRR and NPV methods. This is not surprising, given the theoretical advantages of these approaches. The most interesting point is that for the UK, Germany and France, payback period is the most popular technique to appraise new projects, which is surprising, given the conceptual problems with this approach. However, as we have discussed, the flaws of payback period may be relatively easy to correct. For example,

TABLE
8.11

| | US | UK | The Netherlands | Germany | France |
|---|---|---|---|---|---|
| Net present value | 74.93 | 46.97 | 70.00 | 47.58 | 35.09 |
| Internal rate of return | 75.61 | 53.13 | 56.00 | 42.15 | 44.07 |
| Accounting rate of return | 20.29 | 38.10 | 25.00 | 32.17 | 16.07 |
| Profitability index | 11.87 | 15.87 | 8.16 | 16.07 | 37.74 |
| Payback period | 56.74 | 69.23 | 64.71 | 50.00 | 50.88 |
| Discounted payback | 29.45 | 25.40 | 25.00 | 30.51 | 11.32 |
| Hurdle rate | 56.94 | 26.98 | 41.67 | 28.81 | 3.85 |
| Sensitivity analysis | 51.54 | 42.86 | 36.73 | 28.07 | 10.42 |
| Real options | 26.56 | 29.03 | 34.69 | 44.04 | 53.06 |

*Source*: Table 2 from D. Brounen, A. de Jong and K. Koedijk, 'Corporate finance in Europe: confronting theory and practice', *Journal of Banking and Finance* (2006), vol. 30, no. 5, pp. 1409–1442.

**Table 8.11** Capital budgeting techniques in practice

although the payback method ignores all cash flows after the payback period, an alert manager can make ad hoc adjustments for a project with back-loaded cash flows.

For future reference, the various criteria we have discussed are summarized in Table 8.12.

TABLE
8.12

**Discounted cash flow criteria**

**A**  *Net present value (NPV)*: The NPV of an investment is the difference between its market value and its cost. The NPV rule is to take a project if its NPV is positive. NPV is frequently estimated by calculating the present value of the future cash flows (to estimate market value) and then subtracting the cost. NPV has no serious flaws; it is the preferred decision criterion.

**B**  *Internal rate of return (IRR)*: The IRR is the discount rate that makes the estimated NPV of an investment equal to zero; it is sometimes called the *discounted cash flow (DCF) return*. The IRR rule is to take a project when its IRR exceeds the required return. IRR is closely related to NPV, and it leads to exactly the same decisions as NPV for conventional, independent projects. When project cash flows are not conventional there may be no IRR, or there may be more than one. More seriously, the IRR cannot be used to rank mutually exclusive projects; the project with the highest IRR is not necessarily the preferred investment.

**C**  *Modified internal rate of return (MIRR)*: The MIRR is a modification to the IRR. A project's cash flows are modified by: (1) discounting the negative cash flows back to the present; (2) compounding cash flows to the end of the project's life; or (3) combining (1) and (2). An IRR is then computed on the modified cash flows. MIRRs are guaranteed to avoid the multiple rate of return problem, but it is unclear how to interpret them; and they are not truly 'internal', because they depend on externally supplied discounting or compounding rates.

**D**  *Profitability index (PI)*: The PI, also called the *benefit–cost ratio*, is the ratio of present value to cost. The PI rule is to take an investment if the index exceeds 1. The PI measures the present value of an investment per unit of currency invested. It is quite similar to NPV, but, like IRR, it cannot be used to rank mutually exclusive projects. However, it is sometimes used to rank projects when a firm has more positive NPV investments than it can currently finance.

**Table 8.12** Summary of investment criteria

TABLE
8.12

**Payback criteria**

A  *Payback period*: The payback period is the length of time until the sum of an investment's cash flows equals its cost. The payback period rule is to take a project if its payback is less than some cut-off. The payback period is a flawed criterion, primarily because it ignores risk, the time value of money, and cash flows beyond the cut-off point.

B  *Discounted payback period*: The discounted payback period is the length of time until the sum of an investment's discounted cash flows equals its cost. The discounted payback period rule is to take an investment if the discounted payback is less than some cut-off. The discounted payback rule is flawed, primarily because it ignores cash flows after the cut-off.

**Accounting criterion**

A  *Average accounting return (AAR)*: The AAR is a measure of accounting profit relative to book value. It is *not* related to the IRR, but it is similar to the accounting return on assets (ROA) measure in Chapter 3. The AAR rule is to take an investment if its AAR exceeds a benchmark AAR. The AAR is seriously flawed for a variety of reasons, and it has little to recommend it.

**Table 8.12** *Continued*

CONCEPT
QUESTIONS

8.7a   What are the most commonly used capital budgeting procedures?
8.7b   If NPV is conceptually the best procedure for capital budgeting, why do you think multiple measures are used in practice?

# Summary and Conclusions

This chapter has covered the different criteria used to evaluate proposed investments. The seven criteria, in the order we discussed them, are these:

1  Net present value (NPV)

2  Payback period

3  Discounted payback period

4  Average accounting return (AAR)

5  Internal rate of return (IRR)

6  Modified internal rate of return (MIRR)

7  Profitability index (PI)

We illustrated how to calculate each of these, and discussed the interpretation of the results. We also described the advantages and disadvantages of each of them. Ultimately a good capital budgeting criterion must tell us two things. First, is a particular project a good investment? Second, if we have more than one good project, but we can take only one of them, which one should we take? The main point of this chapter is that only the NPV criterion can always provide the correct answer to both questions.

For this reason, NPV is one of the two or three most important concepts in finance, and we shall refer to it many times in the chapters ahead. When we do, keep two things in mind: (1) NPV is always just the difference between the market value of an asset or project and its cost; and (2) the financial manager acts in the shareholders' best interests by identifying and taking positive-NPV projects.

Finally, we noted that NPVs can't normally be observed in the market; instead, they must be estimated. Because there is always the possibility of a poor estimate, financial managers use multiple criteria for examining projects. The other criteria provide additional information about whether a project truly has a positive NPV.

# Chapter Review and Self-Test Problems

**8.1 Investment Criteria**  This problem will give you some practice calculating NPVs and paybacks. A proposed overseas expansion has the following cash flows:

| Year | Cash flow (£) |
| --- | --- |
| 0 | −200 |
| 1 | 50 |
| 2 | 60 |
| 3 | 70 |
| 4 | 200 |

Calculate the payback, the discounted payback, and the NPV at a required return of 10 per cent.

**8.2 Mutually Exclusive Investments**  Consider the following two mutually exclusive investments. Calculate the IRR for each, and the crossover rate. Under what circumstances will the IRR and NPV criteria rank the two projects differently?

| Year | Investment A (€) | Investment B (€) |
| --- | --- | --- |
| 0 | −75 | −75 |
| 1 | 20 | 60 |
| 2 | 40 | 50 |
| 3 | 70 | 15 |

**8.3 Average Accounting Return**  You are looking at a three-year project with a projected net income of €2,000 in year 1, €4,000 in year 2, and €6,000 in year 3. The cost is €12,000, which will be depreciated straight-line to zero over the three-year life of the project. What is the average accounting return (AAR)?

# Answers to Chapter Review and Self-Test Problems

8.1 In the following table we have listed the cash flow, cumulative cash flow, discounted cash flow (at 10 per cent), and cumulative discounted cash flow for the proposed project.

| | Cash flow (£) | | Accumulated cash flow (£) | |
|---|---|---|---|---|
| Year | Undiscounted | Discounted | Undiscounted | Discounted |
| 1 | 50 | 45.45 | 50 | 45.45 |
| 2 | 60 | 49.59 | 110 | 95.04 |
| 3 | 70 | 52.59 | 180 | 147.63 |
| 4 | 200 | 136.60 | 380 | 284.23 |

Recall that the initial investment was £200. When we compare this with accumulated undiscounted cash flows, we see that payback occurs between years 3 and 4. The cash flows for the first three years are £180 total, so, going into the fourth year, we are short by £20. The total cash flow in year 4 is £200, so the payback is 3 + (£20/200) = 3.10 years.

Looking at the accumulated discounted cash flows, we see that the discounted payback occurs between years 3 and 4. The sum of the discounted cash flows is £284.23, so the NPV is £84.23. Notice that this is the present value of the cash flows that occur after the discounted payback.

8.2 To calculate the IRR, we might try some guesses, as in the following table:

| Discount rate (%) | NPV(A) (€) | NPV(B) (€) |
|---|---|---|
| 0 | 55.00 | 50.00 |
| 10 | 28.83 | 32.14 |
| 20 | 9.95 | 18.40 |
| 30 | −4.09 | 7.57 |
| 40 | −14.80 | −1.17 |

Several things are immediately apparent from our guesses. First, the IRR on A must be between 20 per cent and 30 per cent (why?). With some more effort, we find that it's 26.79 per cent. For B, the IRR must be a little less than 40 per cent (again, why?); it works out to be 38.54 per cent. Also, notice that at rates between 0 per cent and 10 per cent, the NPVs are very close, indicating that the crossover is in that vicinity.

To find the crossover exactly, we can compute the IRR on the difference in the cash flows. If we take the cash flows from A minus the cash flows from B, the resulting cash flows are:

| Year | A − B (€) |
|---|---|
| 0 | 0 |
| 1 | −40 |
| 2 | −10 |
| 3 | 55 |

These cash flows look a little odd, but the sign changes only once, so we can find an IRR. With some trial and error you'll see that the NPV is zero at a discount rate of 5.42 per cent, so this is the crossover rate.

The IRR for B is higher. However, as we've seen, A has the larger NPV for any discount rate less than 5.42 per cent, so the NPV and IRR rankings will conflict in that range. Remember, if there's a conflict, we shall go with the higher NPV. Our decision rule is thus simple: take A if the required return is less than 5.42 per cent, take B if the required return is between 5.42 per cent and 38.54 per cent (the IRR on B), and take neither if the required return is more than 38.54 per cent.

8.3 Here we need to calculate the ratio of average net income to average book value to get the AAR. Average net income is

$$\text{Average net income} = (€2,000 + 4,000 + 6,000)/3 = €4,000$$

Average book value is

$$\text{Average book value} = €12{,}000/2 = €6{,}000$$

So the average accounting return is

$$\text{AAR} = €4{,}000/6{,}000 = 66.67\%$$

This is an impressive return. Remember, however, that it isn't really a rate of return like an interest rate or an IRR, so the size doesn't tell us a lot. In particular, our money is probably not going to grow at a rate of 66.67 per cent per year, we're sorry to say.

# Concepts Review and Critical Thinking Questions

1 **Payback Period and Net Present Value [LO1, LO2]**   If a project with conventional cash flows has a payback period less than the project's life, can you definitively state the algebraic sign of the NPV? Why or why not? If you know that the discounted payback period is less than the project's life, what can you say about the NPV? Explain.

2 **Net Present Value [LO1]**   Suppose a project has conventional cash flows and a positive NPV. What do you know about its payback? Its discounted payback? Its profitability index? Its IRR? Explain.

3 **Payback Period [LO2]**   Concerning payback:

(a) Describe how the payback period is calculated, and describe the information this measure provides about a sequence of cash flows. What is the payback criterion decision rule?

(b) What are the problems associated with using the payback period to evaluate cash flows?

(c) What are the advantages of using the payback period to evaluate cash flows? Are there any circumstances under which using payback might be appropriate? Explain.

4 **Discounted Payback [LO3]**   Concerning discounted payback:

(a) Describe how the discounted payback period is calculated, and describe the information this measure provides about a sequence of cash flows. What is the discounted payback criterion decision rule?

(b) What are the problems associated with using the discounted payback period to evaluate cash flows?

(c) What conceptual advantage does the discounted payback method have over the regular payback method? Can the discounted payback ever be longer than the regular payback? Explain.

5 **Average Accounting Return [LO4]**   Concerning AAR:

(a) Describe how the average accounting return is usually calculated, and describe the information this measure provides about a sequence of cash flows. What is the AAR criterion decision rule?

(b) What are the problems associated with using the AAR to evaluate a project's cash flows? What underlying feature of AAR is most troubling to you from a financial perspective? Does the AAR have any redeeming qualities?

6   **Net Present Value [LO1]**   Concerning NPV:

(a)   Describe how NPV is calculated, and describe the information this measure provides about a sequence of cash flows. What is the NPV criterion decision rule?

(b)   Why is NPV considered a superior method of evaluating the cash flows from a project? Suppose the NPV for a project's cash flows is computed to be £2,500. What does this number represent with respect to the firm's shareholders?

7   **Internal Rate of Return [LO5]**   Concerning IRR:

(a)   Describe how the IRR is calculated, and describe the information this measure provides about a sequence of cash flows. What is the IRR criterion decision rule?

(b)   What is the relationship between IRR and NPV? Are there any situations in which you might prefer one method over the other? Explain.

(c)   Despite its shortcomings in some situations, why do most financial managers use IRR along with NPV when evaluating projects? Can you think of a situation in which IRR might be a more appropriate measure to use than NPV? Explain.

8   **Profitability Index [LO7]**   Concerning the profitability index:

(a)   Describe how the profitability index is calculated, and describe the information this measure provides about a sequence of cash flows. What is the profitability index decision rule?

(b)   What is the relationship between the profitability index and NPV? Are there any situations in which you might prefer one method over the other? Explain.

9   **Payback and Internal Rate of Return [LO2, LO5]**   A project has perpetual cash flows of $C$ per period, a cost of $I$, and a required return of $R$. What is the relationship between the project's payback and its IRR? What implications does your answer have for long-lived projects with relatively constant cash flows?

10   **International Investment Projects [LO1]**   In January 2008 automobile manufacturer Volkswagen announced plans to build an automatic transmission and engine plant in the US. Volkswagen apparently felt that it would be better able to compete and create value in the US with US-based facilities rather than export its automobiles from Europe. Other companies, such as BMW, Fiat and Mercedes, have reached similar conclusions and taken similar actions. What are some of the reasons why manufacturers might arrive at the same conclusion to set up facilities abroad rather than simply export their products?

11   **Capital Budgeting Problems [LO1]**   What difficulties might come up in actual applications of the various criteria we have discussed in this chapter? Which one would be the easiest to implement in actual applications? The most difficult?

12   **Capital Budgeting in Not-for-Profit Entities [LO1]**   Are the capital budgeting criteria we have discussed applicable to not-for-profit corporations? How should such entities make capital budgeting decisions? What about governments? Should they evaluate spending proposals using these techniques?

13   **Modified Internal Rate of Return [LO6]**   One of the less flattering interpretations of the acronym MIRR is 'meaningless internal rate of return'. Why do you think this term is applied to MIRR?

14   **Net Present Value [LO1]**   It is sometimes stated that 'the net present value approach assumes reinvestment of the intermediate cash flows at the required return'. Is this claim correct? To answer, suppose you calculate the NPV of a project in the usual way. Next, suppose you do the following:

(a) Calculate the future value (as of the end of the project) of all the cash flows other than the initial outlay, assuming they are reinvested at the required return, and producing a single future value figure for the project.

(b) Calculate the NPV of the project using the single future value calculated in the previous step, and the initial outlay. It is easy to verify that you will get the same NPV as in your original calculation only if you use the required return as the reinvestment rate in the previous step.

15 **Internal Rate of Return [LO5]**   It is sometimes stated that 'the internal rate of return approach assumes reinvestment of the intermediate cash flows at the internal rate of return'. Is this claim correct? To answer, suppose you calculate the IRR of a project in the usual way. Next, suppose you do the following:

(a) Calculate the future value (as of the end of the project) of all the cash flows other than the initial outlay, assuming they are reinvested at the IRR, and producing a single future value figure for the project.

(b) Calculate the IRR of the project using the single future value calculated in the previous step and the initial outlay. It is easy to verify that you will get the same IRR as in your original calculation only if you use the IRR as the reinvestment rate in the previous step.

# connect Questions and Problems

BASIC

1 – 19

1 **Calculating Payback [LO2]**   What is the payback period for the following set of cash flows?

| Year | Cash flow (R) |
|------|---------------|
| 0 | −6,400 |
| 1 | 1,600 |
| 2 | 1,900 |
| 3 | 2,300 |
| 4 | 1,400 |

2 **Calculating Payback [LO2]**   An investment project provides cash inflows of £765 per year for eight years. What is the project payback period if the initial cost is £2,400? What if the initial cost is £3,600? What if it is £6,500?

3 **Calculating Payback [LO2]**   Koop Kust NV imposes a payback cut-off of three years for its international investment projects. If the company has the following two projects available, should it accept either of them?

| Year | Cash flow (A) (€) | Cash flow (B) (€) |
|------|-------------------|-------------------|
| 0 | −50,000 | −60,000 |
| 1 | 9,000 | 24,000 |
| 2 | 35,000 | 7,000 |
| 3 | 18,000 | 24,000 |
| 4 | 6,000 | 270,000 |

4 **Calculating Discounted Payback [LO3]**   An investment project has annual cash inflows of €4,200, €5,300, €6,100 and €7,400, and a discount rate of 14 per cent. What is the discounted payback period for these cash flows if the initial cost is €7,000? What if the initial cost is €10,000? What if it is €13,000?

5 **Calculating Discounted Payback [LO3]** An investment project costs €30,000, and has annual cash flows of €8,300 for six years. What is the discounted payback period if the discount rate is zero per cent? What if the discount rate is 7 per cent? If it is 20 per cent?

6 **Calculating AAR [LO4]** You're trying to determine whether to expand your business by building a new manufacturing plant. The plant has an installation cost of £15 million, which will be depreciated straight-line to zero over its four-year life. If the plant has projected net income of £1,938,200, £2,201,600, £1,876,000 and £1,329,500 over these four years, what is the project's average accounting return (AAR)?

7 **Calculating IRR [LO5]** A firm evaluates all of its projects by applying the IRR rule. If the required return is 20 per cent, should the firm accept the following project?

| Year | Cash flow (€) |
|---|---|
| 0 | −30,000 |
| 1 | 15,000 |
| 2 | 17,000 |
| 3 | 14,000 |

8 **Calculating NPV [LO1]** For the cash flows in the previous problem, suppose the firm uses the NPV decision rule. At a required return of 12 per cent, should the firm accept this project? What if the required return was 40 per cent?

9 **Calculating NPV and IRR [LO1, 5]** A project that provides annual cash flows of €28,500 for nine years costs €138,000 today. Is this a good project if the required return is 8 per cent? What if it's 20 per cent? At what discount rate would you be indifferent between accepting the project and rejecting it?

10 **Calculating IRR [LO5]** What is the IRR of the following set of cash flows?

| Year | Cash flow (£) |
|---|---|
| 1 | 9,800 |
| 2 | 10,300 |
| 3 | 8,600 |

11 **Calculating NPV [LO1]** For the cash flows in the previous problem, what is the NPV at a discount rate of zero per cent? What if the discount rate is 5 per cent? If it is 15 per cent? If it is 25 per cent?

12 **NPV versus IRR [LO1, LO5]** Mahjong SA has identified the following two mutually exclusive projects:

| Year | Cash flow (A) (€) | Cash flow (B) (€) |
|---|---|---|
| 0 | −43,000 | −43,000 |
| 1 | 23,000 | 7,000 |
| 2 | 17,900 | 13,800 |
| 3 | 12,400 | 24,000 |
| 4 | 9,400 | 26,000 |

(a) What is the IRR for each of these projects? Using the IRR decision rule, which project should the company accept? Is this decision necessarily correct?

(b) If the required return is 11 per cent, what is the NPV for each of these projects? Which project will the company choose if it applies the NPV decision rule?

(c)    Over what range of discount rates would the company choose project A? Project B? At what discount rate would the company be indifferent between these two projects? Explain.

13   **NPV versus IRR [LO1, LO5]**   Consider the following two mutually exclusive projects:

| Year | Cash flow (X) (DKr) | Cash flow (Y) (DKr) |
|---|---|---|
| 0 | −15,000 | −15,000 |
| 1 | 8,150 | 7,700 |
| 2 | 5,050 | 5,150 |
| 3 | 6,800 | 7,250 |

Sketch the NPV profiles for X and Y over a range of discount rates from zero to 25 per cent. What is the crossover rate for these two projects?

14   **Problems with IRR [LO5]**   Light Sweet Petroleum AG is trying to evaluate a generation project with the following cash flows:

| Year | Cash flow (SKr) |
|---|---|
| 0 | −45,000,000 |
| 1 | 78,000,000 |
| 2 | −14,000,000 |

(a)    If the company requires a 12 per cent return on its investments, should it accept this project? Why?

(b)    Compute the IRR for this project. How many IRRs are there? Using the IRR decision rule, should the company accept the project? What's going on here?

15   **Calculating Profitability Index [LO7]**   What is the profitability index for the following set of cash flows if the relevant discount rate is 10 per cent? What if the discount rate is 15 per cent? If it is 22 per cent?

| Year | Cash flow (€) |
|---|---|
| 0 | −14,000 |
| 1 | 7,300 |
| 2 | 6,900 |
| 3 | 5,700 |

16   **Problems with Profitability Index [LO1, LO7]**   Weiland Computers GmbH is trying to choose between the following two mutually exclusive design projects:

| Year | Cash flow (I) (€) | Cash flow (II) (€) |
|---|---|---|
| 0 | −53,000 | −16,000 |
| 1 | 27,000 | 9,100 |
| 2 | 27,000 | 9,100 |
| 3 | 27,000 | 9,100 |

(a)    If the required return is 10 per cent and the company applies the profitability index decision rule, which project should the firm accept?

(b)    If the company applies the NPV decision rule, which project should it take?

(c)    Explain why your answers in (a) and (b) are different.

17 **Comparing Investment Criteria [LO1, LO2, LO3, LO5, LO7]** Consider the following two mutually exclusive projects:

| Year | Cash flow (A) (NKr) | Cash flow (B) (NKr) |
|------|---------------------|---------------------|
| 0 | −300,000 | −40,000 |
| 1 | 20,000 | 19,000 |
| 2 | 50,000 | 12,000 |
| 3 | 50,000 | 18,000 |
| 4 | 390,000 | 10,500 |

Whichever project you choose, if any, you require a 15 per cent return on your investment.

(a) If you apply the payback criterion, which investment will you choose? Why?

(b) If you apply the discounted payback criterion, which investment will you choose? Why?

(c) If you apply the NPV criterion, which investment will you choose? Why?

(d) If you apply the IRR criterion, which investment will you choose? Why?

(e) If you apply the profitability index criterion, which investment will you choose? Why?

(f) Based on your answers in (a)–(e), which project will you finally choose? Why?

18 **NPV and Discount Rates [LO1]** An investment has an installed cost of €700,000. The cash flows over the four-year life of the investment are projected to be €250,000, €300,000, €225,000 and €175,000. If the discount rate is zero, what is the NPV? If the discount rate is infinite, what is the NPV? At what discount rate is the NPV just equal to zero? Sketch the NPV profile for this investment, based on these three points.

19 **MIRR [LO6]** Slow Ride plc is evaluating a project with the following cash flows:

| Year | Cash flow (£) |
|------|---------------|
| 0 | −19,000 |
| 1 | 7,100 |
| 2 | 8,800 |
| 3 | 9,400 |
| 4 | 4,500 |
| 5 | −7,100 |

The company uses a 12 per cent interest rate on all of its projects. Calculate the MIRR of the project using all three methods.

20 **MIRR [LO6]** Suppose the company in the previous problem uses an 11 per cent discount rate and an 8 per cent reinvestment rate on all of its projects. Calculate the MIRR of the project using all three methods using these interest rates.

21 **NPV and the Profitability Index [LO1, LO7]** If we define the NPV index as the ratio of NPV to cost, what is the relationship between this index and the profitability index?

22 **Cash Flow Intuition [LO1, LO2]** A project has an initial cost of $I$, has a required return of $R$, and pays $C$ annually for $N$ years.

INTERMEDIATE

20–22

(a) Find $C$ in terms of $I$ and $N$ such that the project has a payback period just equal to its life.

(b) Find $C$ in terms of $I$, $N$ and $R$ such that this is a profitable project according to the NPV decision rule.

(c) Find $C$ in terms of $I$, $N$ and $R$ such that the project has a benefit–cost ratio of 2.

**CHALLENGE**

**23 – 28**

23 **Payback and NPV [LO1, LO2]** An investment under consideration has a payback of seven years and a cost of €724,000. If the required return is 12 per cent, what is the worst-case NPV? The best-case NPV? Explain. Assume the cash flows are conventional.

24 **Multiple IRRs [LO5]** This problem is useful for testing the ability of financial calculators and computer software. Consider the following cash flows. How many different IRRs are there? (*Hint*: Search between 20 per cent and 70 per cent.) When should we take this project?

| Year | Cash flow (£) |
|------|---------------|
| 0    | −1,512        |
| 1    | 8,586         |
| 2    | −18,210       |
| 3    | 17,100        |
| 4    | −6,000        |

25 **NPV Valuation [LO1]** Yuvhadit Ltd wants to set up a private cemetery business. According to the CFO, Barry M. Deep, business is 'looking up'. As a result, the cemetery project will provide a net cash inflow of €80,000 for the firm during the first year, and the cash flows are projected to grow at a rate of 6 per cent per year for ever. The project requires an initial investment of €800,000.

(a) If Yuvhadit requires a 12 per cent return on such undertakings, should the cemetery business be started?

(b) The company is somewhat unsure about the assumption of a 6 per cent growth rate in its cash flows. At what constant growth rate would the company just break even if it still required a 12 per cent return on investment?

26 **Problems with IRR [LO5]** A project has the following cash flows:

| Year | Cash flow (£) |
|------|---------------|
| 0    | 58,000        |
| 1    | −34,000       |
| 2    | −45,000       |

What is the IRR for this project? If the required return is 12 per cent, should the firm accept the project? What is the NPV of this project? What is the NPV of the project if the required return is 0 per cent? 24 per cent? What is going on here? Sketch the NPV profile to help you with your answer.

27 **Problems with IRR [LO5]** McKeekin plc has a project with the following cash flows:

| Year | Cash flow (£) |
|------|---------------|
| 0    | 20,000        |
| 1    | −26,000       |
| 2    | 13,000        |

What is the IRR of the project? What is happening here?

28  **NPV and IRR [LO1, LO5]**  Gulliver International Limited is evaluating a project in Lilliput. The project will create the following cash flows:

| Year | Cash flow (LP) |
|---|---|
| 0 | −750,000 |
| 1 | 205,000 |
| 2 | 265,000 |
| 3 | 346,000 |
| 4 | 220,000 |

All cash flows will occur in Lilliput and are expressed in Lilliputian pounds (LP). In an attempt to improve its economy, the Lilliputian government has declared that all cash flows created by a foreign company are 'blocked', and must be reinvested with the government for one year. The reinvestment rate for these funds is 4 per cent. If Gulliver uses an 11 per cent required return on this project, what are the NPV and IRR of the project? Is the IRR you calculated the MIRR of the project? Why or why not?

MINI
CASE # Davis Gold Mining

Dick Davies, the owner of Davies Gold Mining, is evaluating a new gold mine in Tanzania. Barry Koch, the company's geologist, has just finished his analysis of the mine site. He has estimated that the mine would be productive for eight years, after which the gold would be completely mined. Barry has taken an estimate of the gold deposits to Andy Marshall, the company's financial officer. Andy has been asked by Dick to perform an analysis of the new mine and present his recommendation on whether the company should open the new mine.

Andy has used the estimates provided by Barry to determine the revenues that could be expected from the mine. He has also projected the expense of opening the mine, and the annual operating expenses. If the company opens the mine, it will cost £500 million today, and it will have a cash outflow of £80 million nine years from today in costs associated with closing the mine and reclaiming the area surrounding it. The expected cash flows each year from the mine are shown in the following table. Davies Gold Mining has a 12 per cent required return on all of its gold mines.

| Year | Cash flow (£) |
|---|---|
| 0 | −500,000,000 |
| 1 | 60,000,000 |
| 2 | 90,000,000 |
| 3 | 170,000,000 |
| 4 | 230,000,000 |
| 5 | 205,000,000 |
| 6 | 140,000,000 |
| 7 | 110,000,000 |
| 8 | 70,000,000 |
| 9 | −80,000,000 |

1  Construct a spreadsheet to calculate the payback period, internal rate of return, modified internal rate of return, and net present value of the proposed mine.

2  Based on your analysis, should the company open the mine?

3  Bonus question: Most spreadsheets do not have a built-in formula to calculate the payback period. Write a VBA script that calculates the payback period for a project.

# Endnotes

1 In this case the discounted payback is an even number of years. This won't ordinarily happen, of course. However, calculating a fractional year for the discounted payback period is more involved than it is for the ordinary payback, and it is not commonly done.

2 This argument assumes that the cash flows, other than the first, are all positive. If they are not, then these statements are not necessarily correct. Also, there may be more than one discounted payback.

3 If the cut-off were for ever, then the discounted payback rule would be the same as the NPV rule. It would also be the same as the profitability index rule considered in a later section.

4 Straight-line depreciation is not the normal way to depreciate assets in Europe, where the reducing-balance method is more common. To estimate reducing-balance depreciation you would subtract a certain percentage from the residual value of the asset. For example, assume that the asset is worth £500,000 and you are applying 20 per cent reducing-balance depreciation. The depreciation for this year would be 20% of £500,000, which is equal to £100,000. Next year, the residual value is £500,000 − £100,000 = £400,000, and depreciation next year would be 20% of this amount, £400,000, which is £80,000, and so on.

5 We could, of course, calculate the average of the six book values directly. In thousands, we would have (£500 + 400 + 300 + 200 + 100 + 0)/6 = £250.

6 The AAR is closely related to the return on assets (ROA) discussed in Chapter 3. In practice, the AAR is sometimes computed by first calculating the ROA for each year and then averaging the results. This produces a number that is similar, but not identical, to the one we computed.

7 With a lot more effort (or a personal computer), we can find that the IRR is approximately (to nine decimal places) 13.066238629 per cent – not that anybody would ever want this many decimal places!

8 To be more precise, the number of IRRs that are larger than −100 per cent is equal to the number of sign changes, or it differs from the number of sign changes by an even number. Thus, for example, if there are five sign changes, there are five IRRs, three IRRs, or one IRR. If there are two sign changes, there are either two IRRs or no IRRs.

---

 **Online LearningCentre**

To help you grasp the key concepts of this chapter check out the extra resources posted on the Online Learning Centre at **www.mcgraw-hill.co.uk/textbooks/hillier**

Among other helpful resources there are mini-cases tailored to individual chapters.

# CHAPTER

# 9

# Making Capital Investment Decisions

MAKING CAPITAL INVESTMENT DECISIONS is not just about investing in one specific project. In an environment where cash is scarce, an investment decision in one area may lead to spending cuts in another area. This is what happened with Anglo American, the global mining firm, in 2010. With a number of potentially lucrative projects in the pipeline, the company had to reserve cash from its operations to fund the new investment. It refused to pay a dividend for 18 months, redesigned its global supply chain, and made 20,000 employees redundant in 2009, leading to cost savings of £1 billion (€1.14 billion). However, in return it invested £2.5 billion (€2.8 billion) in a large Brazilian iron ore project and invested new capital in its two affiliate companies, Anglo Platinum and De Beers. Management of Anglo American argued that the combined investment and cost savings would increase firm value by £1.3 billion (€1.5 billion).

As you no doubt recognize from your study of the previous chapter, Anglo American's decision to invest in new mining operations represents a capital budgeting decision. However, other decisions made by the firm are inextricably linked to the investments. In this chapter we further investigate such decisions, how they are made, and how to look at them objectively.

This chapter follows up on the previous one by delving more deeply into capital budgeting. We have two main goals. First, recall that in the last chapter we saw that cash flow estimates are the critical input into a net present value analysis, but we didn't say much about where these cash flows come from, so we shall now examine this question in some detail. Our second goal is to learn how to critically examine NPV estimates and, in particular, how to evaluate the sensitivity of NPV estimates to assumptions made about the uncertain future.

So far we've covered various parts of the capital budgeting decision. Our task in this chapter is to start bringing these pieces together. In particular, we'll show you how to 'spread the numbers' for a proposed investment or project and, based on those numbers, make an initial assessment about whether the project should be undertaken.

In the discussion that follows, we focus on the process of setting up a discounted cash flow analysis. From the previous chapter we know that the projected future cash flows are the key element in such an evaluation. Accordingly, we emphasize working with financial and accounting information to come up with these figures.

In evaluating a proposed investment we pay special attention to deciding what information is relevant to the decision at hand, and what information is not. As we shall see, it is easy to overlook important pieces of the capital budgeting puzzle.

We shall wait until the next chapter to describe in detail how to go about evaluating the results of our discounted cash flow analysis. Also, where needed, we shall assume that we know the relevant required return, or discount rate. We continue to defer in-depth discussion of this subject to Part Five.

# 9.1    Project Cash Flows: A First Look

The effect of taking a project is to change the firm's overall cash flows today, and in the future. To evaluate a proposed investment we must consider these changes in the firm's cash flows, and then decide whether they add value to the firm. The first (and most important) step, therefore, is to decide which cash flows are relevant.

## Relevant Cash Flows

What is a relevant cash flow for a project? The general principle is simple enough: a relevant cash flow for a project is a change in the firm's overall future cash flow that comes about as a *direct* consequence of the decision to take that project. Because the relevant cash flows are defined in terms of changes in, or increments to, the firm's existing cash flow, they are called the **incremental cash flows** associated with the project.

The concept of incremental cash flow is central to our analysis, so we shall state a general definition, and refer back to it as needed:

> *The incremental cash flows for project evaluation consist of* any and all *changes in the firm's future cash flows that are a direct consequence of taking the project.*

This definition of incremental cash flows has an obvious and important corollary: any cash flow that exists regardless of *whether or not* a project is undertaken is *not* relevant.

> **incremental cash flows**
> The difference between a firm's future cash flows with a project and those without the project.

## The Stand-Alone Principle

In practice, it would be cumbersome to actually calculate the future total cash flows to the firm with and without a project, especially for a large firm. Fortunately, it is not really necessary to do so. Once we have identified the effect of undertaking the proposed project on the firm's cash flows, we need focus only on the project's resulting incremental cash flows. This is called the **stand-alone principle**.

What the stand-alone principle says is that, once we have determined the incremental cash flows from undertaking a project, we can view that project as a kind of 'mini-firm' with its own future revenues and costs, its own assets and, of course, its own cash flows. We shall then be interested primarily in comparing the cash flows from this mini-firm with the cost of acquiring it. An important consequence of this approach is that we shall be evaluating the proposed project purely on its own merits, in isolation from any other activities or projects.

> **stand-alone principle**
> The assumption that evaluation of a project may be based on the project's incremental cash flows.

## 9.2 Incremental Cash Flows

We are concerned here only with cash flows that are incremental, and which result from a project. Looking back at our general definition, we might think it would be easy enough to decide whether a cash flow is incremental. Even so, in a few situations it is easy to make mistakes. In this section we describe some common pitfalls, and how to avoid them.

### Sunk Costs

**sunk cost**
A cost that has already been incurred and cannot be removed, and which therefore should not be considered in an investment decision.

A **sunk cost**, by definition, is a cost we have already paid, or have already incurred the liability to pay. Such a cost cannot be changed by the decision today to accept or reject a project. Put another way, the firm will have to pay this cost no matter what. Based on our general definition of incremental cash flow, such a cost is clearly not relevant to the decision at hand. So we shall always be careful to exclude sunk costs from our analysis.

That a sunk cost is not relevant seems obvious given our discussion. Nonetheless, it's easy to fall prey to the fallacy that a sunk cost should be associated with a project. For example, suppose General Milk plc hires a financial consultant to help evaluate whether a line of chocolate milk should be launched. When the consultant turns in the report, General Milk objects to the analysis, because the consultant did not include the hefty consulting fee as a cost of the chocolate milk project.

Who is correct? By now, we know that the consulting fee is a sunk cost: it must be paid whether or not the chocolate milk line is actually launched (this is an attractive feature of the consulting business).

### Opportunity Costs

**opportunity cost**
The most valuable alternative that is given up if a particular investment is undertaken.

When we think of costs, we normally think of out-of-pocket costs – namely those that require us to actually spend some amount of cash. An **opportunity cost** is slightly different; it requires us to give up a benefit. A common situation arises in which a firm already owns some of the assets a proposed project will be using. For example, we might be thinking of converting an old rustic cotton mill we bought years ago for €100,000 into up-market apartments.

If we undertake this project, there will be no direct cash outflow associated with buying the old mill, because we already own it. For purposes of evaluating the apartment project, should we then treat the mill as 'free'? The answer is no. The mill is a valuable resource used by the project. If we didn't use it here, we could do something else with it. Like what? The obvious answer is that, at a minimum, we could sell it. Using the mill for the apartment complex thus has an opportunity cost: we give up the valuable opportunity to do something else with the mill.

There is another issue here. Once we agree that the use of the mill has an opportunity cost, how much should we charge the apartment project for this use? Given that we paid €100,000, it might seem that we should charge this amount to the apartment project. Is this correct? The answer is no, and the reason is based on our discussion concerning sunk costs.

The fact that we paid €100,000 some years ago is irrelevant. That cost is sunk. At a minimum, the opportunity cost that we charge the project is what the mill would sell for today (net of any selling costs), because this is the amount we give up by using the mill instead of selling it.[1]

## Side Effects

Remember that the incremental cash flows for a project include all the resulting changes in the *firm's* future cash flows. It would not be unusual for a project to have side, or spillover, effects, both good and bad. For example, in 2010 the time between the theatrical release of a feature film and the release of the DVD had shrunk to 98 days, compared with 200 days ten years earlier. This shortened release time was blamed for at least part of the decline in average movie theatre box office receipts. Of course, retailers cheered the move, because it was credited with increasing DVD sales. A negative impact on the cash flows of an existing product from the introduction of a new product is called **erosion**.[2] In this case the cash flows from the new line should be adjusted downwards to reflect lost profits on other lines.

| erosion |
| :--- |
| The cash flows of a new project that come at the expense of a firm's existing projects. |

In accounting for erosion, it is important to recognize that any sales lost as a result of launching a new product might be lost anyway because of future competition. Erosion is relevant only when the sales would not otherwise be lost.

Side effects show up in a lot of different ways. For example, one of Walt Disney Company's concerns when it built Euro Disney was that the new park would drain visitors from the Florida park, a popular vacation destination for Europeans.

There are beneficial spillover effects, of course. For example, you might think that Hewlett-Packard would have been concerned when the price of a printer that sold for £500–£600 in 1994 declined to below £100 by 2010, but such was not the case. HP realized that the big money is in the consumables that printer owners buy to keep their printers going, such as inkjet cartridges, laser toner cartridges and special paper. The profit margins for these products are substantial.

## Net Working Capital

Normally a project will require that the firm invest in net working capital in addition to long-term assets. For example, a project will generally need some amount of cash on hand to pay any expenses that arise. In addition, a project will need an initial investment in inventories and trade receivables (to cover credit sales). Some of the financing for this will be in the form of amounts owed to suppliers (trade payables), but the firm will have to supply the balance. This balance represents the investment in net working capital.

It's easy to overlook an important feature of net working capital in capital budgeting. As a project winds down, inventories are sold, receivables are collected, bills are paid, and cash balances can be drawn down. These activities free up the net working capital originally invested. So the firm's investment in project net working capital closely resembles a loan. The firm supplies working capital at the beginning, and recovers it towards the end.

## Financing Costs

In analysing a proposed investment, we shall *not* include interest paid or any other financing costs such as dividends or principal repaid, because we are interested in the cash flow generated by the assets of the project. As we mentioned in Chapter 3, interest paid, for example, is a component of cash flow to creditors, not cash flow from assets.

More generally, our goal in project evaluation is to compare the cash flow from a project with the cost of acquiring that project in order to estimate NPV. The particular mixture of debt and equity a firm actually chooses to use in financing a project is a managerial variable, and determines primarily how project cash flow is divided between owners and creditors. This is not to say that financing arrangements are unimportant; they are just something to be analysed separately. We shall cover this in later chapters.

## Other Issues

There are some other things to watch out for. First, we are interested only in measuring cash flow. Moreover, we are interested in measuring it when it actually occurs, not when it accrues in an accounting sense. Second, we are always interested in *after-tax* cash flow, because taxes are definitely a cash outflow. In fact, whenever we write *incremental cash flows*, we mean after-tax incremental cash flows. Remember, however, that after-tax cash flow and accounting profit, or net income, are entirely different things.

---

**CONCEPT QUESTIONS**

9.2a   What is a sunk cost? An opportunity cost?
9.2b   Explain what erosion is, and why it is relevant.
9.2c   Explain why interest paid is not a relevant cash flow for project evaluation.

---

## 9.3   Pro Forma Financial Statements and Project Cash Flows

The first thing we need when we begin evaluating a proposed investment is a set of pro forma, or projected, financial statements. Given these, we can develop the projected cash flows from the project. Once we have the cash flows, we can estimate the value of the project using the techniques we described in the previous chapter.

### Getting Started: Pro Forma Financial Statements

**pro forma financial statements**
Financial statements projecting future years' operations.

**Pro forma financial statements** are a convenient and easily understood means of summarizing much of the relevant information for a project. To prepare these statements, we shall need estimates of quantities such as unit sales, the selling price per unit, the variable cost per unit, and total fixed costs. We shall also need to know the total investment required, including any investment in net working capital.

To illustrate, suppose we think we can sell 50,000 cans of shark attractant per year at a price of £4 per can. It costs us about £2.50 per can to make the attractant, and a new product such as this one typically has only a three-year life (perhaps because the customer base dwindles rapidly). We require a 20 per cent return on new products.

Fixed costs for the project, including such things as rent on the production facility, will run to £12,000 per year.[3] Further, we shall need to invest a total of £90,000 in manufacturing equipment. For simplicity, we shall assume that this £90,000 will be 100 per cent depreciated straight-line over the three-year life of the project.[4] Furthermore, the cost of removing the equipment will roughly equal its actual value in three years, so it will be essentially worthless on a market value basis as well. Finally, the project will require an initial £20,000 investment in net working capital, and the tax rate is 34 per cent.

In Table 9.1 we organize these initial projections by first preparing the pro forma income statement. Once again, notice that we have *not* deducted any interest expense. This will always be so. As we described earlier, interest paid is a financing expense, not a component of operating cash flow.

We can also prepare a series of abbreviated statements of financial position that show the capital requirements for the project, as we've done in Table 9.2. Here we have net working capital of £20,000 in each year. Non-current assets are £90,000 at the start of the project's life (year 0), and they decline by the £30,000 in depreciation each year, ending up at zero. Notice that the total investment given here for future years is the total book, or accounting, value, not market value.

At this point, we need to start converting this accounting information into cash flows. We consider how to do this next.

| TABLE 9.1 | | |
|---|---|---|
| Sales (50,000 units at £4/unit) | | 200,000 |
| Variable costs (£2.50/unit) | | 125,000 |
| Gross profit (£) | | 75,000 |
| Fixed costs (£) | | 12,000 |
| Depreciation (£90,000/3) | | 30,000 |
| Profit before taxes (£) | | 33,000 |
| Taxes (34%) (£) | | 11,220 |
| Net income (£) | | 21,780 |

**Table 9.1** Projected income statement, shark attractant project

| TABLE 9.2 | Year | | | |
|---|---|---|---|---|
| | 0 | 1 | 2 | 3 |
| Net working capital (£) | 20,000 | 20,000 | 20,000 | 20,000 |
| Net non-current assets (£) | 90,000 | 60,000 | 30,000 | 0 |
| Total investment (£) | 110,000 | 80,000 | 50,000 | 20,000 |

**Table 9.2** Projected capital requirements, shark attractant project

## Project Cash Flows

To develop the cash flows from a project, we should recall (from Chapter 3) that net cash flow comes from three components: operating activities, financing activities, and investing activities. When considering the cash flows attributable to a project, we must consider only those cash flows that arise directly as a result of making the investment. As explained earlier in the chapter, financing activities should be ignored, because we are interested only in the cash flows from the project. To evaluate a project, or mini-firm, we need to estimate the cash flows from operating activities and investing activities that are a result of the new investment.

Once we have estimates of the components of cash flow, we shall calculate cash flow for our mini-firm just as we did in Chapter 3 for an entire firm:

Project cash flow = Project operating cash flow − Project capital spending

We consider these components next.

**Project Operating Cash Flow**    To determine the operating cash flow associated with a project, we first need to recall the definition of operating cash flow:

Operating cash flow = Net income
+ Depreciation
− Increase (+ Decrease) in net working capital

To illustrate the calculation of operating cash flow, we shall use the projected information from the shark attractant project.

Given the income statement in Table 9.2, calculating the operating cash flow is straightforward. As we see in Table 9.3, projected operating cash flow (ignoring changes in net working capital) for the shark attractant project is £51,780.

TABLE
9.3

| | |
|---|---|
| Net income (£) | 21,780 |
| Depreciation (£) | +30,000 |
| Operating cash flow (£) | 51,780 |

**Table 9.3** Projected operating cash flow (ignoring changes in net working capital), shark attractant project

TABLE
9.4

| | | Year | | |
|---|---|---|---|---|
| | 0 | 1 | 2 | 3 |
| Opening cash flow (£) | | 51,780 | 51,780 | 51,780 |
| Changes in NWC (£) | −20,000 | | | +20,000 |
| Capital spending (£) | −90,000 | | | |
| Total project cash flow (£) | −110,000 | 51,780 | 51,780 | 71,780 |

**Table 9.4** Projected total cash flows, shark attractant project

**Project Net Working Capital and Capital Spending**  We next need to take care of the non-current asset and net working capital requirements. Based on our statements of financial position, we know that the firm must spend £90,000 up front for non-current assets and invest an additional £20,000 in net working capital. The immediate outflow is thus £110,000. At the end of the project's life, the non-current assets will be worthless, but the firm will recover the £20,000 that was tied up in working capital.[5] This will lead to a £20,000 *inflow* in the last year.

On a purely mechanical level, notice that whenever we have an investment in net working capital, that same investment has to be recovered: in other words, the same number needs to appear at some time in the future with the opposite sign.

## Projected Total Cash Flow and Value

Given the information we've accumulated, we can finish the preliminary cash flow analysis, as illustrated in Table 9.4.

Now that we have cash flow projections, we are ready to apply the various criteria we discussed in the last chapter. First, the NPV at the 20 per cent required return is

$$\text{NPV} = -£110,000 + 51,780/1.2 + 51,780/1.2^2 + 71,780/1.2^3$$
$$= £10,648$$

Based on these projections, the project creates over £10,000 in value and should be accepted. Also, the return on this investment obviously exceeds 20 per cent (because the NPV is positive at 20 per cent). After some trial and error, we find that the IRR works out to be about 25.8 per cent.

In addition, if required, we could calculate the payback and the average accounting return, or AAR. Inspection of the cash flows shows that the payback on this project is just a little over two years (verify that it's about 2.1 years).[6]

From the previous chapter we know that the AAR is average net income divided by average book value. The net income each year is £21,780. The average (in thousands) of the four book values (from Table 9.2) for total investment is (£110 + 80 + 50 + 20)/4 = £65. So the AAR is £21,780/65,000 = 33.51 per cent.[7] We've already seen that the return on this investment (the IRR) is about 26 per cent. The fact that the AAR is larger illustrates again why the AAR cannot be meaningfully interpreted as the return on a project.

## 9.4  More about Project Cash Flow

In this section we take a closer look at some aspects of project cash flow. In particular, we discuss project net working capital in more detail. We then examine current tax laws regarding depreciation. Finally, we work through a more involved example of the capital investment decision.

### A Closer Look at Net Working Capital

In calculating operating cash flow, we did not explicitly consider the fact that some of our sales might be on credit. Also, we may not have actually paid some of the costs shown. In either case, the cash flow in question would not yet have occurred. We show here that these possibilities are not a problem as long as we don't forget to include changes in net working capital in our analysis. This discussion thus emphasizes the importance and the effect of doing so.

Suppose that during a particular year of a project we have the following simplified income statement:

| | |
|---|---|
| Sales (€) | 500 |
| Costs (€) | 310 |
| Net income (€) | 190 |

Depreciation and taxes are zero. No non-current assets are purchased during the year. Also, to illustrate a point, we assume that the only components of net working capital are trade receivables and payables. The beginning and ending amounts for these accounts are as follows:

| | Beginning of year | End of year | Change |
|---|---|---|---|
| Trade receivables (€) | 880 | 910 | +30 |
| Trade payables (€) | 550 | 605 | +55 |
| Net working capital (€) | 330 | 305 | −25 |

Based on this information, what is total cash flow for the year? We can first just mechanically apply what we have been discussing to come up with the answer. Operating cash flow in this particular case is the same as net income, because there are no taxes or depreciation: thus it equals €190. Also, notice that net working capital actually *declined* by €25. This just means that €25 was freed up during the year. There was no capital spending, so the total cash flow for the year is

$$\begin{aligned} \text{Total cash flow} &= \text{Operating cash flow} - \text{Change in NWC} - \text{Capital spending} \\ &= €190 - (-25) - 0 \\ &= €215 \end{aligned}$$

Now, we know that this €215 total cash flow has to be 'euros in' less 'euros out' for the year. We could therefore ask a different question: what were cash revenues for the year? Also, what were cash costs?

To determine cash revenues, we need to look more closely at net working capital. During the year, we had sales of €500. However, trade receivables rose by €30 over the same time period. What does this mean? The €30 increase tells us that sales exceeded collections by €30. In other words, we haven't yet received the cash from €30 of the €500 in sales. As a result, our cash inflow is €500 − 30 = €470. In general, cash income is sales minus the increase in trade receivables.

Cash outflows can be similarly determined. We show costs of €310 on the income statement, but trade payables increased by €55 during the year. This means that we have not yet paid €55 of the €310, so cash costs for the period are just €310 − 55 = €255. In other words, in this case, cash costs equal costs less the increase in accounts payable.[8]

Putting this information together, we calculate that cash inflows less cash outflows are €470 − 255 = €215, just as we had before. Notice that

$$
\begin{aligned}
\text{Cash flow} &= \text{Cash inflow} - \text{Cash outflow} \\
&= (€500 - 30) - (310 - 55) \\
&= (€500 - 310) - (30 - 55) \\
&= \text{Operating cash flow} - \text{Change in NWC} \\
&= €190 - (-25) \\
&= €215
\end{aligned}
$$

More generally, this example illustrates that including net working capital changes in our calculations has the effect of adjusting for the discrepancy between accounting sales and costs and actual cash receipts and payments.

## Cash Collections and Costs

**EXAMPLE 9.1**

For the year just completed, Combat Womble Telestat plc (CWT) reports sales of £998 and costs of £734. You have collected the following beginning and ending statement of financial position information:

|  | Beginning | Ending |
|---|---|---|
| Trade receivables (£) | 100 | 110 |
| Inventory (£) | 100 | 80 |
| Trade payables (£) | 100 | 70 |
| Net working capital (£) | 100 | 120 |

Based on these figures, what are cash inflows? Cash outflows? What happened to each account? What is net cash flow?

Sales were £998, but receivables rose by £10. So cash collections were £10 less than sales, or £988. Costs were £734, but inventories fell by £20. This means that we didn't replace £20 worth of inventory, so costs are actually overstated by this amount. Also, payables fell by £30. This means that, on a net basis, we actually paid our suppliers £30 more than we received from them, resulting in a £30 understatement of costs. Adjusting for these events, we calculate that cash costs are £734 − 20 + 30 = £744. Net cash flow is £988 − 744 = £244.

Finally, notice that net working capital increased by £20 overall. We can check our answer by noting that the original accounting sales less costs (= £998 − 734) are £264. In addition, CWT spent £20 on net working capital, so the net result is a cash flow of £264 − 20 = £244, as we calculated.

## Depreciation

As we note elsewhere, accounting depreciation is a non-cash deduction. As a result, depreciation has cash flow consequences only because it influences the tax bill. The way that depreciation is computed for tax purposes is thus the relevant method for capital investment decisions. Not surprisingly, the procedures are governed by tax law. We now discuss some specifics of the depreciation system that is enacted within the European Union. This system is known as the **reducing-balance method** (compared with the straight-line method presented in earlier examples).

**Reducing-Balance Depreciation**    The calculation of depreciation is normally mechanical, and assets are depreciated according to the tax rules that apply in each country. The UK system is very simple, with only two asset categories for depreciation: plant and machinery, and buildings. However, other countries may have more complex systems for estimating depreciation expenses, and these should be considered before carrying out a capital budgeting analysis.

> **reducing-balance method** A depreciation method allowing for the accelerated write-off of assets under various classifications.

Depreciation rates change regularly, and a financial manager must be up to date with the current applicable rates. For example, from 2010 the UK applied 20 per cent reducing-balance depreciation on plant and machinery. Buildings are depreciated using the straight-line method.

To understand how reducing-balance depreciation is calculated, it is useful to compare the methodology with the much simpler straight-line depreciation. Assume that you purchase an asset for €500,000, which has a five-year life, and at the end of its life the asset will be worthless.

With straight-line depreciation, since the asset's life is five years and its residual value is zero, the annual depreciation will be

$$\text{Annual depreciation} = €500,000/5 = €100,000$$

**Reducing-balance Depreciation:**

Assume that we apply 20 per cent reducing-balance method. This means that we shall depreciate the written-down (or residual) value of the asset by 20 per cent per annum.

| | Year | | | | |
| --- | --- | --- | --- | --- | --- |
| | 1 | 2 | 3 | 4 | 5 |
| Initial value (€) | 500,000 | 400,000 | 320,000 | 256,000 | 204,800 |
| Depreciation (20%) (€) | 100,000 | 80,000 | 64,000 | 51,200 | 204,800 |
| Written-down value (€) | 400,000 | 320,000 | 256,000 | 204,800 | 0 |

Note how the depreciation amounts fall over time. This is because the amount that is being depreciated is less each year. In addition, given that the asset is worthless at the end of five years, the final-year depreciation is simply the starting year 5 value.

Currently, each country in the European Union has its own tax system, and this is seen as one of the major obstacles for full integration of the different European economies. However, a working group has been set up to develop a Common Consolidated Corporate Tax Base (CCCTB) for all countries. Although it will take several years for it to be enacted, the CCCTB is definitely a step in the right direction. The main recommendations of the working group are that all countries apply 20 per cent reducing-balance depreciation on plant and machinery, 2.5 per cent straight-line depreciation for buildings, and 4 per cent straight-line depreciation for long-term tangible assets (i.e. assets that will last for more than 25 years).

**Book Value versus Market Value**    In calculating depreciation under current tax law, the economic life and future market value of the asset are not an issue. As a result, the book value of an asset can differ substantially from its actual market value. Take, for example, a top of the range Chrysler Grand Voyager that is worth £35,000 new. With 20 per cent reducing-balance depreciation, the book value after the first year is £35,000 less the first year's depreciation of £7,000, or £28,000. The remaining book values are summarized in Table 9.5. After five years, the book value of the car is £11,469.

TABLE
9.5

| | Year | | | | |
|---|---|---|---|---|---|
| | **1** | **2** | **3** | **4** | **5** |
| Initial value (£) | 35,000 | 28,000 | 22,400 | 17,920 | 14,336 |
| Depreciation (20%) (£) | 7,000 | 5,600 | 4,480 | 3,584 | 2,867 |
| Written-down value (£) | 28,000 | 22,400 | 17,920 | 14,336 | 11,469 |

**Table 9.5** Chrysler Grand Voyager book values

Suppose we wanted to sell the car after five years. Based on historical averages, it would be worth, say, 50 per cent of the purchase price, or $0.50 \times £35,000 = £17,500$. If we actually sold it for this, then we would have to pay taxes at the ordinary income tax rate on the difference between the sale price of £17,500 and the book value of £11,469. For a corporation in the 28 per cent bracket, the tax liability would be $0.28 \times £6,031 = £1,688.74$.

The reason why taxes must be paid in this case is that the difference between market value and book value is 'excess' depreciation, and it must be 'recaptured' when the asset is sold. What this means is that, as it turns out, we over-depreciated the asset by $£17,500 - £11,469 = £6,031$. Because we deducted £6,031 too much in depreciation, we paid £1,688.74 too little in taxes, and we simply have to make up the difference.

Notice that this is *not* a tax on a capital gain. As a general (albeit rough) rule, a capital gain occurs only if the market price exceeds the original cost. However, what is and what is not a capital gain is ultimately up to the taxation authorities, and the specific rules can be complex. We shall ignore capital gains taxes for the most part.

Finally, if the book value exceeds the market value, then the difference is treated as a loss for tax purposes. For example, if we sell the car after two years for £10,000, then the book value exceeds the market value by £1,469. In this case, a tax saving of $0.28 \times £1,469 = £411.32$ occurs.

**EXAMPLE
9.2**

# Reducing-Balance Depreciation

Staple Supply Ltd has just purchased a new computerized information system with an installed cost of €160,000. What are the yearly depreciation allowances if 20 per cent reducing-balance depreciation is used? Based on historical experience, we think that the system will be worth only €10,000 when Staple gets rid of it in four years. What are the tax consequences of the sale if the tax rate is 34 per cent? What is the total after-tax cash flow from the sale?

The yearly depreciation allowances are presented below:

| | Year | | | |
|---|---|---|---|---|
| | **1** | **2** | **3** | **4** |
| Initial value (€) | 160,000 | 128,000 | 102,400 | 81,920 |
| Depreciation (20%) (€) | 32,000 | 25,600 | 20,480 | 16,384 |
| Written-down value (€) | 128,000 | 102,400 | 81,920 | 65,536 |

Notice that we have also computed the book value of the system as at the end of each year. The book value at the end of year 4 is €65,536. If Staple sells the system for €10,000 at that time, it will have a loss of €55,536 (the difference) for tax purposes. This loss, of course, is like depreciation because it isn't a cash expense.

What really happens? Two things. First, Staple gets €10,000 from the buyer. Second, it saves $0.34 \times €55,536 = €18,882$ in taxes. So the total after-tax cash flow from the sale is a €28,882 cash inflow.

## An Example: Majestic Mulch and Compost Ltd (MMC)

At this point we want to go through a somewhat more involved capital budgeting analysis. Keep in mind as you read that the basic approach here is exactly the same as that in the shark attractant example used earlier. We have just added some real-world detail (and a lot more numbers).

MMC is investigating the feasibility of a new line of power mulching tools aimed at the growing number of home composters. Based on exploratory conversations with buyers for large garden shops, MMC projects unit sales as follows:

| Year | Unit sales |
|---|---|
| 1 | 3,000 |
| 2 | 5,000 |
| 3 | 6,000 |
| 4 | 6,500 |
| 5 | 6,000 |
| 6 | 5,000 |
| 7 | 4,000 |
| 8 | 3,000 |

The new power mulcher will sell for £120 per unit to start. When the competition catches up after three years, however, MMC anticipates that the price will drop to £110.

The power mulcher project will require £20,000 in net working capital at the start. Subsequently, total net working capital at the end of each year will be about 15 per cent of sales for that year. The variable cost per unit is £60, and total fixed costs are £25,000 per year.

It will cost about £800,000 to buy the equipment necessary to begin production. This investment is primarily in industrial equipment, which should be depreciated using the 20 per cent reducing-balance method. The equipment will actually be worth about 20 per cent of its cost in eight years, or $0.20 \times £800,000 = £160,000$. The relevant tax rate is 28 per cent, and the required return is 15 per cent. Based on this information, should MMC proceed?

**Operating Cash Flows** There is a lot of information here that we need to organize. The first thing we can do is calculate projected sales. Sales in the first year are projected at 3,000 units at £120 apiece, or £360,000 total. The remaining figures are shown in Table 9.6.

| TABLE 9.6 | Year | Unit price (£) | Unit sales | Revenues (£) |
|---|---|---|---|---|
| | 1 | 120 | 3,000 | 360,000 |
| | 2 | 120 | 5,000 | 600,000 |
| | 3 | 120 | 6,000 | 720,000 |
| | 4 | 110 | 6,500 | 715,000 |
| | 5 | 110 | 6,000 | 660,000 |
| | 6 | 110 | 5,000 | 550,000 |
| | 7 | 110 | 4,000 | 440,000 |
| | 8 | 110 | 3,000 | 330,000 |

Table 9.6 Projected revenues, power mulcher project

TABLE
9.7

| Year | Initial value (£) | Depreciation (£) | Residual value (£) |
|---|---|---|---|
| 1 | 800,000 | 160,000 | 640,000 |
| 2 | 640,000 | 128,000 | 512,000 |
| 3 | 512,000 | 102,400 | 409,600 |
| 4 | 409,600 | 81,920 | 327,680 |
| 5 | 327,680 | 65,536 | 262,144 |
| 6 | 262,144 | 52,429 | 209,715 |
| 7 | 209,715 | 41,943 | 167,772 |
| 8 | 167,772 | 7,772 | 160,000 |

**Table 9.7** Annual depreciation, power mulcher project

TABLE
9.8

| | Year | | | | | | | |
|---|---|---|---|---|---|---|---|---|
| | 1 | 2 | 3 | 4 | 5 | 6 | 7 | 8 |
| Unit price (£) | 120 | 120 | 120 | 110 | 110 | 110 | 110 | 110 |
| Unit sales | 3,000 | 5,000 | 6,000 | 6,500 | 6,000 | 5,000 | 4,000 | 3,000 |
| Revenues (£) | 360,000 | 600,000 | 720,000 | 715,000 | 660,000 | 550,000 | 440,000 | 330,000 |
| Variable cost (£) | 180,000 | 300,000 | 360,000 | 390,000 | 360,000 | 300,000 | 240,000 | 180,000 |
| Fixed costs (£) | 25,000 | 25,000 | 25,000 | 25,000 | 25,000 | 25,000 | 25,000 | 25,000 |
| Depreciation (£) | 160,000 | 128,000 | 102,400 | 81,920 | 65,536 | 52,429 | 41,943 | 7,772 |
| Profit before taxes (£) | −5,000 | 147,000 | 232,600 | 218,080 | 209,464 | 172,571 | 133,057 | 117,228 |
| Taxes (28%) (£) | −1,400 | 41,160 | 65,128 | 61,062 | 58,650 | 48,320 | 37,256 | 32,824 |
| Net income (£) | −3,600 | 105,840 | 167,472 | 157,018 | 150,814 | 124,251 | 95,801 | 84,404 |

**Table 9.8** Projected income statements, power mulcher project

Next, we compute the depreciation on the £800,000 investment in Table 9.7. With this information, we can prepare the pro forma income statements, as shown in Table 9.8. From here, computing the operating cash flows is straightforward. The results are illustrated in the first part of Table 9.10.

**Change in NWC** Now that we have the operating cash flows, we need to determine the changes in NWC. By assumption, net working capital requirements change as sales change. In each year, MMC will generally either add to or recover some of its project net working capital. Recalling that NWC starts out at £20,000 and then rises to 15 per cent of sales, we can calculate the amount of NWC for each year, as shown in Table 9.9.

As illustrated, during the first year net working capital grows from £20,000 to $0.15 \times £360,000 = £54,000$. The increase in net working capital for the year is thus £54,000 − 20,000 = £34,000. The remaining figures are calculated in the same way.

Remember that an increase in net working capital is a cash outflow, so we use a negative sign in this table to indicate an additional investment that the firm makes in net working capital. A positive sign represents net working capital returning to the firm. Thus, for example, £16,500 in NWC flows back to the firm in year 6. Over the project's life, net working capital builds to a peak of £108,000, and declines from there as sales begin to drop off.

| TABLE 9.9 | Year | Revenues (£) | Net working capital (£) | Cash flow (£) |
|---|---|---|---|---|
| | 0 | | 20,000 | −20,000 |
| | 1 | 360,000 | 54,000 | −34,000 |
| | 2 | 600,000 | 90,000 | −36,000 |
| | 3 | 720,000 | 108,000 | −18,000 |
| | 4 | 715,000 | 107,250 | 750 |
| | 5 | 660,000 | 99,000 | 8,250 |
| | 6 | 550,000 | 82,500 | 16,500 |
| | 7 | 440,000 | 66,000 | 16,500 |
| | 8 | 330,000 | 49,500 | 16,500 |

**Table 9.9** Changes in net working capital, power mulcher project

We show the result for changes in net working capital in the second part of Table 9.10. Notice that at the end of the project's life there is £49,500 in net working capital still to be recovered. Therefore, in the last year, the project returns £16,500 of NWC during the year and then returns the remaining £49,500 at the end of the year for a total of £66,000.

Capital Spending   Finally, we have to account for the long-term capital invested in the project. In this case MMC invests £800,000 at year 0. By assumption, this equipment will be worth £160,000 at the end of the project. In Table 9.7, this figure is given as the ending value, and the depreciation has been calculated accordingly. This means that the book and market values of the equipment are the same, resulting in no tax effects from disposal. These figures are shown in the third part of Table 9.10.

Total Cash Flow and Value   We now have all the cash flow pieces, and we put them together in Table 9.11. In addition to the total project cash flows, we have calculated the cumulative cash flows and the discounted cash flows. At this point, it's essentially plug-and-chug to calculate the net present value, internal rate of return, and payback.

If we sum the discounted cash flows and the initial investment, the net present value (at 15 per cent) works out to be £95,864. This is positive, so, based on these preliminary projections, the power mulcher project is acceptable. The internal, or DCF, rate of return is greater than 15 per cent, because the NPV is positive. It works out to be 18.20 per cent, again indicating that the project is acceptable.

Looking at the cumulative cash flows, we can see that the project has almost paid back after four years, because the table shows that the cumulative cash flow is almost zero at that time. As indicated, the fractional year works out to be £8,200/£224,600 = 0.03, so the payback is 4.03 years. We can't say whether or not this is good because we don't have a benchmark for MMC. This is the usual problem with payback periods.

Conclusion   This completes our preliminary DCF analysis. Where do we go from here? If we have a great deal of confidence in our projections, there is no further analysis to be done. MMC should begin production and marketing immediately. It is unlikely that this will be the case. It is important to remember that the result of our analysis is an estimate of NPV, and we shall usually have less than complete confidence in our projections. This means we have more work to do. In particular, we shall almost surely want to spend some time evaluating the quality of our estimates. We shall take up this subject in the next chapter. For now, we look at some alternative definitions of operating cash flow, and we illustrate some different cases that arise in capital budgeting.

| | | | | | Year | | | | |
|---|---|---|---|---|---|---|---|---|---|
| | **0** | **1** | **2** | **3** | **4** | **5** | **6** | **7** | **8** |
| **I. Operating cash flow** | | | | | | | | | |
| Net income (£) | | −3,600 | 105,840 | 167,472 | 157,018 | 150,814 | 124,251 | 95,801 | 84,404 |
| Depreciation (£) | | 160,000 | 128,000 | 102,400 | 81,920 | 65,536 | 52,429 | 41,943 | 7,772 |
| Operating cash flow (£) | | 156,400 | 233,840 | 269,872 | 238,938 | 216,350 | 176,680 | 137,744 | 92,176 |
| **II. Net working capital** | | | | | | | | | |
| Initial NWC (£) | −20,000 | | | | | | | | |
| Change in NWC (£) | | −34,000 | −36,000 | −18,000 | 750 | 8,250 | 16,500 | 16,500 | 16,500 |
| NWC recovery (£) | | | | | | | | | 49,500 |
| Total change in NWC (£) | −20,000 | −34,000 | −36,000 | −18,000 | 750 | 8,250 | 16,500 | 16,500 | 66,000 |
| **III. Capital spending** | | | | | | | | | |
| Initial outlay (£) | −800,000 | | | | | | | | |
| After-tax salvage (£) | | | | | | | | | 160,000 |

**Table 9.10** Projected cash flows, power mulcher project

| | | | | | Year | | | | |
|---|---|---|---|---|---|---|---|---|---|
| | **0** | **1** | **2** | **3** | **4** | **5** | **6** | **7** | **8** |
| Operating cash flow (£) | | 156,400 | 233,840 | 269,872 | 238,938 | 216,350 | 176,680 | 137,744 | 92,176 |
| Change in NWC (£) | −20,000 | −34,000 | −36,000 | −18,000 | 750 | 8,250 | 16,500 | 16,500 | 66,000 |
| Capital spending (£) | −800,000 | | | | | | | | 160,000 |
| **Net cash flow (£)** | **−820,000** | **122,400** | **197,840** | **251,872** | **239,688** | **224,600** | **193,180** | **154,244** | **318,176** |
| Cumulative cash flow (£) | −820,000 | −697,600 | −499,760 | −247,888 | −8,200 | 216,400 | 409,580 | 563,824 | 882,000 |
| **DCF @ 15% (£)** | **−820,000** | **106,435** | **149,595** | **165,610** | **137,042** | **111,666** | **83,517** | **57,986** | **104,012** |
| NPV @ 15% (£) | 95,864 | | | | | | | | |
| Internal rate of return (%) | 18.20 | | | | | | | | |
| Payback (years) | 4.04 | | | | | | | | |

**Table 9.11** Projected total cash flows, power mulcher project

## 9.5   Alternative Definitions of Operating Cash Flow

The analysis we went through in the previous section is quite general, and can be adapted to just about any capital investment problem. In the next section we illustrate some particularly useful variations. Before we do so, we need to discuss the fact that there are different definitions of project operating cash flow that are commonly used, both in practice and in finance texts.

As we shall see, the different approaches to operating cash flow that exist all measure the same thing. If they are used correctly, they all produce the same answer, and one is not necessarily any better or more useful than another. Unfortunately, the fact that alternative definitions are used does sometimes lead to confusion. For this reason, we examine several of these variations next, to see how they are related.

In the discussion that follows, keep in mind that when we speak of cash flow, we literally mean cash in less cash out. This is all we are concerned with. Different definitions of operating cash flow simply amount to different ways of manipulating basic information about sales, costs, depreciation and taxes to get at cash flow.

For a particular project and year under consideration, suppose we have the following estimates:

Sales = €1,500
Costs = €700
Depreciation = €600

With these estimates, notice that earnings before interest and taxes (EBIT) is

$$EBIT = Sales - Costs - Depreciation$$
$$= €1,500 - 700 - 600$$
$$= €200$$

Once again, we assume that no interest is paid, so the tax bill is

$$Taxes = EBIT \times T$$
$$= €200 \times 0.34 = €68$$

where $T$, the corporate tax rate, is 34 per cent.

When we put all of this together, we see that project operating cash flow, OCF, is

$$OCF = EBIT + Depreciation - Taxes$$
$$= €200 + 600 - 68 = €732$$

There are some other ways to determine OCF that could be (and are) used. We consider these next.

### The Bottom-Up Approach

Because we are ignoring any financing expenses, such as interest, in our calculations of project OCF, we can write project net income as

$$\text{Project net income} = \text{EBIT} - \text{Taxes}$$
$$= \text{€}200 - 68$$
$$= \text{€}132$$

If we simply add the depreciation to both sides, we arrive at a slightly different and very common expression for OCF:

$$\text{OCF} = \text{Net income} + \text{Depreciation}$$
$$= \text{€}132 + 600 \qquad\qquad (9.1)$$
$$= \text{€}732$$

This is the *bottom-up* approach. Here, we start with the accountant's bottom line (net income) and add back any non-cash deductions such as depreciation. It is crucial to remember that this definition of operating cash flow as net income plus depreciation is correct only if there is no interest expense subtracted in the calculation of net income.

For the shark attractant project, net income was £21,780 and depreciation was £30,000, so the bottom-up calculation is

$$\text{OCF} = £21,780 + 30,000 = £51,780$$

## The Top-Down Approach

Perhaps the most obvious way to calculate OCF is

$$\text{OCF} = \text{Sales} - \text{Costs} - \text{Taxes}$$
$$= \text{€}1,500 - 700 - 68 = \text{€}732 \qquad\qquad (9.2)$$

This is the *top-down* approach, the second variation on the basic OCF definition. Here, we start at the top of the income statement with sales, and work our way down to net cash flow by subtracting costs, taxes and other expenses. Along the way, we simply leave out any strictly non-cash items such as depreciation.

For the shark attractant project the operating cash flow can be readily calculated using the top-down approach. With sales of £200,000, total costs (fixed plus variable) of £137,000, and a tax bill of £11,220, the OCF is

$$\text{OCF} = £200,000 - 137,000 - 11,220 = £51,780$$

This is just as we had before.

## The Tax Shield Approach

The third variation on our basic definition of OCF is the *tax shield* approach. This approach will be useful for some problems we consider in the next section. The tax shield definition of OCF is

$$\text{OCF} = (\text{Sales} - \text{Costs}) \times (1 - T) + \text{Depreciation} \times T \qquad\qquad (9.3)$$

where $T$ is again the corporate tax rate. Assuming that $T = 34\%$, the OCF works out to be

$$\text{OCF} = (\text{€}1,500 - 700) \times 0.66 + 600 \times 0.34$$
$$= \text{€}528 + 204$$
$$= \text{€}732$$

This is just as we had before.

This approach views OCF as having two components. The first part is what the project's cash flow would be if there were no depreciation expense. In this case, this would-have-been cash flow is €528.

The second part of OCF in this approach is the depreciation deduction multiplied by the tax rate. This is called the **depreciation tax shield**. We know that depreciation is a non-cash expense. The only cash flow effect of deducting depreciation is to reduce our taxes, a benefit to us. At a 34 per cent corporate tax rate, every euro in depreciation expense saves us 34 cents in taxes. So, in our example, the €600 depreciation deduction saves us €600 × 0.34 = €204 in taxes.

For the shark attractant project we considered earlier in the chapter, the depreciation tax-shield would be £30,000 × 0.34 = £10,200. The after-tax value for sales less costs would be (£200,000 − 137,000) × (1 − 0.34) = £41,580. Adding these together yields the value of OCF:

$$OCF = £41,580 + 10,200 = £51,780$$

This calculation verifies that the tax shield approach is completely equivalent to the approach we used before.

## Conclusion

Now that we've seen that all of these approaches are the same, you're probably wondering why everybody doesn't just agree on one of them. One reason, as we shall see in the next section, is that different approaches are useful in different circumstances. The best one to use is whichever happens to be the most convenient for the problem at hand.

| CONCEPT QUESTIONS | |
|---|---|
| 9.5a | What are the top-down and bottom-up definitions of operating cash flow? |
| 9.5b | What is meant by the term *depreciation tax shield*? |

## 9.6  Some Special Cases of Discounted Cash Flow Analysis

To finish our chapter, we look at three common cases involving discounted cash flow analysis. The first case involves investments that are aimed primarily at improving efficiency and thereby cutting costs. The second case we consider comes up when a firm is involved in submitting competitive bids. The third and final case arises in choosing between equipment options with different economic lives.

We could consider many other special cases, but these three are particularly important, because problems similar to these are so common. Also, they illustrate some diverse applications of cash flow analysis and DCF valuation.

### Evaluating Cost-Cutting Proposals

One decision we frequently face is whether to upgrade existing facilities to make them more cost-effective. The issue is whether the cost savings are large enough to justify the necessary capital expenditure.

For example, suppose we are considering automating some part of an existing production process. The necessary equipment costs €80,000 to buy and install. The automation will save €22,000 per year (before taxes) by reducing labour and material costs. For simplicity, assume that the equipment has a five-year life and is depreciated to zero on a straight-line basis over that period. It will actually be worth €20,000 in five years. Should we automate? The tax rate is 34 per cent, and the discount rate is 10 per cent.

As always, the first step in making such a decision is to identify the relevant incremental cash flows. First, determining the relevant capital spending is easy enough. The initial cost is €80,000. The after-tax salvage value is €20,000 × (1 − 0.34) = €13,200, because the book value will be zero in five years. Second, there are no working capital consequences here, so we don't need to worry about changes in net working capital.

Operating cash flows are the third component to consider. Buying the new equipment affects our operating cash flows in two ways. First, we save €22,000 before taxes every year. In other words, the firm's operating income increases by €22,000, so this is the relevant incremental project operating income.

Second (and it's easy to overlook this), we have an additional depreciation deduction. In this case, the depreciation is €80,000/5 = €16,000 per year.

Because the project has an operating income of €22,000 (the annual pre-tax cost saving) and a depreciation deduction of €16,000, taking the project will increase the firm's EBIT by €22,000 − 16,000 = €6,000, so this is the project's EBIT.

Finally, because EBIT is rising for the firm, taxes will increase. This increase in taxes will be €6,000 × 0.34 = €2,040. With this information, we can compute operating cash flow in the usual way:

|  | € |
|---|---|
| EBIT | 6,000 |
| + Depreciation | 16,000 |
| − Taxes | 2,040 |
| Operating cash flow | 19,960 |

So our after-tax operating cash flow is €19,960.

It might be somewhat more enlightening to calculate operating cash flow using a different approach. What is actually going on here is very simple. First, the cost savings increase our pre-tax income by €22,000. We have to pay taxes on this amount, so our tax bill increases by 0.34 × €22,000 = €7,480. In other words, the €22,000 pre-tax saving amounts to €22,000 × (1 − 0.34) = €14,520 after taxes.

Second, the extra €16,000 in depreciation isn't really a cash outflow, but it does reduce our taxes by €16,000 × 0.34 = €5,440. The sum of these two components is €14,520 + 5,440 = €19,960, just as we had before. Notice that the €5,440 is the depreciation tax shield we discussed earlier, and we have effectively used the tax shield approach here.

We can now finish our analysis. Based on our discussion, here are the relevant cash flows:

|  | Year | | | | | |
|---|---|---|---|---|---|---|
|  | 0 | 1 | 2 | 3 | 4 | 5 |
| Operating cash flow (€) |  | 19,960 | 19,960 | 19,960 | 19,960 | 19,960 |
| Capital spending (€) | −80,000 |  |  |  |  | 13,200 |
| Total cash flow (€) | −80,000 | 19,960 | 19,960 | 19,960 | 19,960 | 33,160 |

At 10 per cent, it's straightforward to verify that the NPV here is €3,860, so we should go ahead and automate.

**EXAMPLE 9.3**

# To Buy or Not to Buy

We are considering the purchase of a €200,000 computer-based inventory management system. It will be depreciated 20 per cent reducing-balance over its four-year life. It will be worth €30,000 at the end of that time. The system will save us €60,000 before taxes in inventory-related costs. The relevant tax rate is 39 per cent. Because the new set-up is more efficient than our existing one, we shall be able to carry less total inventory and thus free up €45,000 in net working capital. What is the NPV at 16 per cent? What is the DCF return (the IRR) on this investment?

We can first calculate the operating cash flow. The depreciation schedule is given below:

| Year | Initial value (€) | Depreciation (€) | Residual value (€) |
|---|---|---|---|
| 1 | 200,000 | 40,000 | 160,000 |
| 2 | 160,000 | 32,000 | 128,000 |
| 3 | 128,000 | 25,600 | 102,400 |
| 4 | 102,400 | 72,400 | 30,000 |

Operating cash flow now follows:

| | Year | | | |
|---|---|---|---|---|
| | 1 | 2 | 3 | 4 |
| Cash savings (€) | 60,000 | 60,000 | 60,000 | 60,000 |
| Depreciation (€) | 40,000 | 32,000 | 25,600 | 72,400 |
| Profit before taxes (€) | 20,000 | 28,000 | 34,400 | −12,400 |
| Taxes (39%) (€) | 7,800 | 10,920 | 13,416 | −4,836 |
| Net income (€) | 12,200 | 17,080 | 20,984 | −7,564 |
| Plus depreciation (€) | 40,000 | 32,000 | 25,600 | 72,400 |
| Operating cash flow (€) | 52,200 | 49,080 | 46,584 | 64,836 |

Finally, and this is the somewhat tricky part, the initial investment in net working capital is a €45,000 *inflow*, because the system frees up working capital. Furthermore, we shall have to put this back in at the end of the project's life. What this really means is simple: while the system is in operation, we have €45,000 to use elsewhere.

To finish our analysis, we can compute the total cash flows:

| | Year | | | | |
|---|---|---|---|---|---|
| | 0 | 1 | 2 | 3 | 4 |
| Operating cash flow (€) | | 52,200 | 49,080 | 46,584 | 64,836 |
| Change in NWC (€) | 45,000 | | | | −45,000 |
| Capital spending (€) | −200,000 | | | | 30,000 |
| Net cash flow (€) | −155,000 | 52,200 | 49,080 | 46,584 | 49,836 |

At 16 per cent the NPV is −€16,157, so the investment is not attractive. After some trial and error, we find that the NPV is zero when the discount rate is 10.62 per cent, so the IRR on this investment is about 10.6 per cent.

## Setting the Bid Price

Early on, we used discounted cash flow analysis to evaluate a proposed new product. A somewhat different (and common) scenario arises when we must submit a competitive bid to win a job. Under such circumstances, the winner is whoever submits the lowest bid.

There is an old joke concerning this process: the low bidder is whoever makes the biggest mistake. This is called the *winner's curse*. In other words, if you win, there is a good chance you underbid. In this section we look at how to go about setting the bid price to avoid the winner's curse. The procedure we describe is useful whenever we have to set a price on a product or service.

As with any other capital budgeting project, we must be careful to account for all relevant cash flows. For example, industry analysts estimated that the materials in Microsoft's Xbox 360 cost £313 before assembly. Other items such as the power supply, cables and controllers increased the materials cost by another £37. At a retail price of £160, Microsoft obviously loses a significant amount on each Xbox 360 it sells in the UK. Why would a manufacturer sell at a price well below break-even? A Microsoft spokesperson stated that the company believed that sales of its game software would make the Xbox 360 a profitable project.

To illustrate how to go about setting a bid price, imagine we are in the business of buying stripped-down truck platforms and then modifying them to customer specifications for resale. A local distributor has requested bids for five specially modified trucks each year for the next four years, for a total of 20 trucks in all.

We need to decide what price per truck to bid. The goal of our analysis is to determine the lowest price we can profitably charge. This maximizes our chances of being awarded the contract, while guarding against the winner's curse.

Suppose we can buy the truck platforms for €10,000 each. The facilities we need can be leased for €24,000 per year. The labour and material cost to do the modification works out to be about €4,000 per truck. Total cost per year will thus be €24,000 + 5 × (10,000 + 4,000) = €94,000.

We shall need to invest €60,000 in new equipment. For simplicity, this equipment will be depreciated straight-line to a zero salvage value over the four years. It will be worth about €5,000 at the end of that time. We shall also need to invest €40,000 in raw materials inventory and other working capital items. The relevant tax rate is 39 per cent. What price per truck should we bid if we require a 20 per cent return on our investment?

We start by looking at the capital spending and net working capital investment. We have to spend €60,000 today for new equipment. The after-tax salvage value is €5,000 × (1 − 0.39) = €3,050. Furthermore, we have to invest €40,000 today in working capital. We shall get this back in four years.

We can't determine the operating cash flow just yet, because we don't know the sales price. Thus, if we draw a time line, here is what we have so far:

| | Year | | | | |
| --- | --- | --- | --- | --- | --- |
| | **0** | **1** | **2** | **3** | **4** |
| Operating cash flow | | +OCF | +OCF | +OCF | +OCF |
| Change in NWC (€) | −40,000 | | | | 40,000 |
| Capital spending (€) | −60,000 | | | | 3,050 |
| Total cash flow (€) | −100,000 | +OCF | +OCF | +OCF | +OCF + 43,050 |

With this in mind, note that the key observation is the following: the lowest possible price we can profitably charge will result in a zero NPV at 20 per cent. At that price, we earn exactly 20 per cent on our investment.

Given this observation, we first need to determine what the operating cash flow must be for the NPV to equal zero. To do this, we calculate the present value of the €43,050 non-operating cash flow from the last year, and subtract it from the €100,000 initial investment:

$$€100,000 - 43,050/1.20^4 = €100.000 - 20,761$$
$$= €79,239$$

Once we have done this, our time line is as follows:

| | Year | | | |
|---|---|---|---|---|
| | **0** | **1** | **2** | **3** | **4** |
| Total cash flow (€) | −79,239 | +OCF | +OCF | +OCF | +OCF |

As the time line suggests, the operating cash flow is now an unknown ordinary annuity amount. The four-year annuity factor for 20 per cent is 2.58873, so we have

$$NPV = 0 = -€79,239 + OCF \times 2.58873$$

This implies that

$$OCF = €79,239/2.58873 = €30,609$$

So the operating cash flow needs to be €30,609 each year.

We're not quite finished. The final problem is to find out what sales price results in an operating cash flow of €30,609. The easiest way to do this is to recall that operating cash flow can be written as net income plus depreciation (the bottom-up definition). The depreciation here is €60,000/4 = €15,000. Given this, we can determine what net income must be:

$$Operating\ cash\ flow = Net\ income + Depreciation$$
$$€30,609 = Net\ income + €15,000$$
$$Net\ income = €15,609$$

From here, we work our way backward up the income statement. If net income is €15,609, then our income statement is as follows:

| Sales | ? |
|---|---|
| Costs (€) | 94,000 |
| Depreciation (€) | 15,000 |
| Taxes (39%) (€) | ? |
| Net income (€) | 15,609 |

We can solve for sales by noting that

$$Net\ income = (Sales - Costs - Depreciation) \times (1 - T)$$
$$€15,609 = (Sales - €94,000 - €15,000) \times (1 - 0.39)$$
$$Sales = €15,609/0.61 + 94,000 + 15,000$$
$$= €134,589$$

Sales per year must be €134,589. Because the contract calls for five trucks per year, the sales price has to be €134,589/5 = €26,918. If we round this up a bit, it looks as though we need to bid about €27,000 per truck. At this price, were we to get the contract, our return would be just over 20 per cent.

## Evaluating Equipment Options with Different Lives

The final problem we consider involves choosing among different possible systems, equipment set-ups, or procedures. Our goal is to choose the most cost-effective. The approach we consider here is necessary only when two special circumstances exist. First, the possibilities under evaluation have different economic lives. Second, and just as important, we shall need whatever we buy more or less indefinitely. As a result, when it wears out, we shall buy another one.

We can illustrate this problem with a simple example. Imagine we are in the business of manufacturing stamped metal subassemblies. Whenever a stamping mechanism wears out, we have to replace it with a new one to stay in business. We are considering which of two stamping mechanisms to buy.

Machine A costs €100 to buy and €10 per year to operate. It wears out, and must be replaced every two years. Machine B costs €140 to buy and €8 per year to operate. It lasts for three years, and must then be replaced. Ignoring taxes, which one should we choose if we use a 10 per cent discount rate?

In comparing the two machines, we notice that the first is cheaper to buy, but it costs more to operate, and it wears out more quickly. How can we evaluate these trade-offs? We can start by computing the present value of the costs for each:

$$\text{Machine A: PV} = -€100 + -10/1.1 + -10/1.1^2 = -€117.36$$
$$\text{Machine B: PV} = -€140 + -8/1.1 + -8/1.1^2 + -8/1.1^3 = -€159.89$$

Notice that *all* the numbers here are costs, so they all have negative signs. If we stopped here, it might appear that A is more attractive, because the PV of the costs is less. However, all we have really discovered so far is that A effectively provides two years' worth of stamping service for €117.36, whereas B effectively provides three years' worth for €159.89. These costs are not directly comparable, because of the difference in service periods.

| |
|---|
| **equivalent annual cost (EAC)** The present value of a project's costs, calculated on an annual basis. |

We need to somehow work out a cost per year for these two alternatives. To do this, we ask: what amount, paid each year over the life of the machine, has the same PV of costs? This amount is called the **equivalent annual cost (EAC)**.

Calculating the EAC involves finding an unknown payment amount. For example, for machine A we need to find a two-year ordinary annuity with a PV of −€117.36 at 10 per cent. Going back to Chapter 5, we know that the two-year annuity factor is

$$\text{Annuity factor} = (1 − 1/1.10^2)/0.10 = 1.7355$$

For machine A, then, we have

$$\text{PV of costs} = -€117.36 = \text{EAC} \times 1.7355$$
$$\text{EAC} = -€117.36/1.7355$$
$$= €67.62$$

For machine B the life is three years, so we first need the three-year annuity factor:

$$\text{Annuity factor} = (1 − 1/1.10^3)/0.10 = 2.4869$$

We calculate the EAC for B just as we did for A:

$$\text{PV of costs} = -€159.89 = \text{EAC} \times 2.4869$$
$$\text{EAC} = -€159.89/2.4869$$
$$= -€64.29$$

Based on this analysis, we should purchase B, because it effectively costs €64.29 per year compared with €67.62 for A. In other words, all things considered, B is cheaper. In this case, the longer life and lower operating cost are more than enough to offset the higher initial purchase price.

## Evaluating Equipment Options with Different Lives

# Equivalent Annual Costs

**EXAMPLE 9.4**

This extended example illustrates what happens to the EAC when we consider taxes. You are evaluating two different pollution control options. A filtration system will cost €1.1 million to install and €60,000 annually, before taxes, to operate. It will have to be completely replaced every five years. A precipitation system will cost €1.9 million to install but only €10,000 per year to operate. The precipitation equipment has an effective operating life of eight years. To simplify matters, straight-line depreciation is used throughout, and neither system has any salvage value. Which option should we select if we use a 12 per cent discount rate? The tax rate is 34 per cent.

We need to consider the EACs for the two systems, because they have different service lives and will be replaced as they wear out. The relevant information can be summarized as follows:

| | Filtration system | Precipitation system |
|---|---|---|
| After-tax operating cost (€) | −39,600 | −6,600 |
| Depreciation tax shield (€) | 74,800 | 80,750 |
| Operating cash flow (€) | 35,200 | 74,150 |
| Economic life (years) | 5 | 8 |
| Annuity factor (12%) (€) | 3.6048 | 4.9676 |
| Present value of operating cash flow (€) | 126,888 | 368,350 |
| Capital spending (€) | −1,100,000 | −1,900,000 |
| Total PV of costs (€) | −973,112 | −1,531,650 |

Notice that the operating cash flow is actually positive in both cases because of the large depreciation tax shields. This can occur whenever the operating cost is small relative to the purchase price.

To decide which system to purchase, we compute the EACs for both using the appropriate annuity factors:

$$\text{Filtration system:}$$
$$-€973,112 = \text{EAC} \times 3.6048$$
$$\text{EAC} = -€269,951$$

$$\text{Precipitation system:}$$
$$-€1,531,650 = \text{EAC} \times 4.9676$$
$$\text{EAC} = -€308,328$$

The filtration system is the cheaper of the two, so we select it. In this case the longer life and smaller operating cost of the precipitation system are not sufficient to offset its higher initial cost.

**CONCEPT QUESTIONS**

9.6a In setting a bid price, we used a zero NPV as our benchmark. Explain why this is appropriate.

9.6b Under what circumstances do we have to worry about unequal economic lives? How do you interpret the EAC?

# Summary and Conclusions

This chapter has described how to put together a discounted cash flow analysis. In it, we covered:

1 The identification of relevant project cash flows. We discussed project cash flows, and described how to handle some issues that often come up, including sunk costs, opportunity costs, financing costs, net working capital, and erosion.

2   Preparing and using pro forma, or projected, financial statements. We showed how information from such financial statements is useful in coming up with projected cash flows, and we also looked at some alternative definitions of operating cash flow.

3   The role of net working capital and depreciation in determining project cash flows. We saw that including the change in net working capital was important in cash flow analysis, because it adjusted for the discrepancy between accounting revenues and costs and cash revenues and costs. We also went over the calculation of depreciation expense under current tax law.

4   Some special cases encountered in using discounted cash flow analysis. Here we looked at three special issues: evaluating cost-cutting investments, how to go about setting a bid price, and the unequal lives problem.

The discounted cash flow analysis we've covered here is a standard tool in the business world. It is a very powerful tool, so care should be taken in its use. The most important thing is to identify the cash flows in a way that makes economic sense. This chapter gives you a good start in learning to do this.

# Chapter Review and Self-Test Problems

**9.1**   **Capital Budgeting for Project X**   Based on the following information for project X, should we undertake the venture? To answer, first prepare a pro forma income statement for each year. Next calculate operating cash flow. Finish the problem by determining total cash flow and then calculating NPV assuming a 28 per cent required return. Use a 34 per cent tax rate throughout. For help, look back at our shark attractant and power mulcher examples.

     Project X involves a new type of graphite composite in-line skate wheel. We think we can sell 6,000 units per year at a price of €1,000 each. Variable costs will be about €400 per unit, and the product should have a four-year life.

     Fixed costs for the project will be €450,000 per year. Further, we shall need to invest a total of €1,250,000 in manufacturing equipment. This equipment is depreciated using 20 per cent reducing-balance for tax purposes. In four years the equipment will be worth about half of what we paid for it. We shall have to invest €1,150,000 in net working capital at the start. After that, net working capital requirements will be 25 per cent of sales.

**9.2**   **Calculating Operating Cash Flow**   Kilimanjaro Tents Ltd have projected a sales volume of R1,650 for the second year of a proposed expansion project. Costs normally run at 60 per cent of sales, or about R990 in this case. The depreciation expense will be R100, and the tax rate is 35 per cent. What is the operating cash flow? Calculate your answer using all the approaches (including the top-down, bottom-up and tax shield approaches) described in the chapter.

**9.3**   **Spending Money to Save Money?**   For help on this one, refer back to the computerized inventory management system in Example 9.3. Here, we're contemplating a new automatic surveillance system to replace our current contract security system. It will cost SKr450,000 to get the new system. The cost will be depreciated straight-line to zero over the system's four-year expected life. The system is expected to be worth SKr250,000 at the end of four years after removal costs.

     We think the new system will save us SKr125,000, before taxes, per year in contract security costs. The tax rate is 34 per cent. What are the NPV and IRR for buying the new system? The required return is 17 per cent.

# Answers to Chapter Review and Self-Test Problems

9.1 To develop the pro forma income statements, we need to calculate the depreciation for each of the four years. The asset is worth €625,000 in the fourth year, so the depreciation schedule is as follows:

| Year | Initial value (€) | Depreciation (€) | Residual value (€) |
|---|---|---|---|
| 1 | 1,250,000 | 250,000 | 1,000,000 |
| 2 | 1,000,000 | 200,000 | 800,000 |
| 3 | 800,000 | 160,000 | 640,000 |
| 4 | 640,000 | 15,000 | 625,000 |

The projected income statements, therefore, are as follows:

| | Year | | | |
|---|---|---|---|---|
| | 1 | 2 | 3 | 4 |
| Sales (€) | 6,000,000 | 6,000,000 | 6,000,000 | 6,000,000 |
| Variable costs (€) | 2,400,000 | 2,400,000 | 2,400,000 | 2,400,000 |
| Fixed costs (€) | 450,000 | 450,000 | 450,000 | 450,000 |
| Depreciation (€) | 250,000 | 200,000 | 160,000 | 15,000 |
| Profit before taxes (€) | 2,900,000 | 2,950,000 | 2,990,000 | 3,135,000 |
| Taxes (34%) (€) | 986,000 | 1,003,000 | 1,016,600 | 1,065,900 |
| Net income (€) | 1,914,000 | 1,947,000 | 1,973,400 | 2,069,100 |

Based on this information, here are the operating cash flows:

| | Year | | | |
|---|---|---|---|---|
| | 1 | 2 | 3 | 4 |
| Net income (€) | 1,914,000 | 1,947,000 | 1,973,400 | 2,069,100 |
| Plus depreciation (€) | 250,000 | 200,000 | 160,000 | 15,000 |
| Operating cash flow (€) | 2,164,000 | 2,147,000 | 2,133,400 | 2,084,100 |

We now have to worry about the non-operating cash flows. Net working capital starts out at €1,150,000 and then rises to 25 per cent of sales, or €1,500,000. This is a €350,000 change in net working capital.

Finally, we have to invest €1,250,000 to get started, and in four years the estimated market value is €625,000 (half of the cost). When we combine all this information, the projected cash flows for project X are as follows:

| | Year | | | | |
|---|---|---|---|---|---|
| | 0 | 1 | 2 | 3 | 4 |
| Operating cash flow (€) | | 2,164,000 | 2,147,000 | 2,133,400 | 2,084,100 |
| Change in NWC (€) | −1,150,000 | −350,000 | | | 1,500,000 |
| Capital spending (€) | −1,250,000 | | | | 625,000 |
| Net cash flow (€) | −2,400,000 | 1,814,000 | 2,147,000 | 2,133,400 | 4,209,100 |

With these cash flows, the NPV at 28 per cent is

$$NPV = -€2,400,000 + 1,814,000/1.28 + 2,147,000/1.28^2$$
$$+ 2,133,400/1.28^3 + 4,209,100/1.28^4$$
$$= €2,912,909$$

So this project appears quite profitable.

9.2 First, we can calculate the project's EBIT, its tax bill, and its net income:

$$EBIT = Sales - Costs - Depreciation$$
$$= R1,650 - 990 - 100 = R560$$
$$Taxes = R560 × 0.35 = R196$$
$$Net\ income = R560 - 196 = R364$$

With these numbers, operating cash flow is

$$OCF = EBIT + Depreciation - Taxes$$
$$= R560 + 100 - 196$$
$$= R464$$

Using the other OCF definitions, we have

$$Bottom\text{-}up\ OCF = Net\ income + Depreciation$$
$$= R364 + 100$$
$$= R464$$
$$Top\text{-}down\ OCF = Sales - Costs - Taxes$$
$$= R1,650 - 990 - 196$$
$$= R464$$
$$Tax\ shield\ OCF = (Sales - Costs) × (1 - 0.35) + Depreciation × 0.35$$
$$= (R1,650 - 990) × 0.65 + 100 × 0.35$$
$$= R464$$

As expected, all these definitions produce exactly the same answer.

9.3 The SKr125,000 pre-tax saving amounts to $(1 - 0.34) × SKr125,000 = SKr82,500$ after taxes. The annual depreciation of $SKr450,000/4 = SKr112,500$ generates a tax shield of $0.34 × SKr112,500 = SKr38,250$ each year. Putting these together, we calculate that the operating cash flow is $SKr82,500 + 38,250 = SKr120,750$. Because the book value is zero in four years, the after-tax salvage value is $(1 - 0.34) × SKr250,000 = SKr165,000$. There are no working capital consequences, so here are the cash flows:

| | | Year | | | |
|---|---|---|---|---|---|
| | **0** | **1** | **2** | **3** | **4** |
| Operating cash flow (SKr) | | 120,750 | 120,750 | 120,750 | 120,750 |
| Capital spending (SKr) | −450,000 | | | | 165,000 |
| Total cash flow (SKr) | −450,000 | 120,750 | 120,750 | 120,750 | 285,750 |

You can verify that the NPV at 17 per cent is −SKr30,702, and the return on the new surveillance system is only about 13.96 per cent. The project does not appear to be profitable.

# Concepts Review and Critical Thinking Questions

1   **Opportunity Cost [LO1]**   In the context of capital budgeting, what is an opportunity cost?

2   **Depreciation [LO1]**   Given the choice, would a firm prefer to use reducing-balance depreciation or straight-line depreciation? Why?

3   **Net Working Capital [LO1]**   In our capital budgeting examples, we assumed that a firm would recover all of the working capital it invested in a project. Is this a reasonable assumption? When might it not be valid?

4   **Stand-Alone Principle [LO1]**   Suppose a financial manager is quoted as saying, 'Our firm uses the stand-alone principle. Because we treat projects like mini-firms in our evaluation process, we include financing costs because they are relevant at the firm level.' Critically evaluate this statement.

5   **Equivalent Annual Cost [LO4]**   When is EAC analysis appropriate for comparing two or more projects? Why is this method used? Are there any implicit assumptions required by this method that you find troubling? Explain.

6   **Cash Flow and Depreciation [LO1]**   'When evaluating projects, we're concerned with only the relevant incremental after-tax cash flows. Therefore, because depreciation is a non-cash expense, we should ignore its effects when evaluating projects.' Critically evaluate this statement.

7   **Capital Budgeting Considerations [LO1]**   A major university textbook publisher has an existing finance textbook. The publisher is debating whether to produce an 'essentialized' version, meaning a shorter (and lower-priced) book. What are some of the considerations that should come into play?

To answer the next three questions, refer to the following example. In 2003 Porsche unveiled its new sports utility vehicle (SUV), the Cayenne. With a price tag of over £40,000 (€43,000), the Cayenne went from zero to 62 mph in 9.7 seconds. Porsche's decision to enter the SUV market was a response to the runaway success of other high-priced SUVs such as the Mercedes-Benz M-class. Vehicles in this class had generated years of high profits. The Cayenne certainly spiced up the market, and Porsche subsequently introduced the Cayenne Turbo, which goes from zero to 60 mph in 4.9 seconds and has a top speed of 171 mph. The price tag for the Cayenne Turbo in 2008? About £76,000 (€84,000)!

   Some analysts questioned Porsche's entry into the luxury SUV market. The analysts were concerned not only that Porsche was a late entry into the market, but also that the introduction of the Cayenne would damage Porsche's reputation as a maker of high-performance automobiles.

8   **Erosion [LO1]**   In evaluating the Cayenne, would you consider the possible damage to Porsche's reputation to be erosion?

9   **Capital Budgeting [LO1]**   Porsche was one of the last manufacturers to enter the sports utility vehicle market. Why would one company decide to proceed with a product when other companies, at least initially, decide not to enter the market?

10   **Capital Budgeting [LO1]**   In evaluating the Cayenne, what do you think Porsche needs to assume regarding the substantial profit margins that exist in this market? Is it likely that they will be maintained as the market becomes more competitive, or will Porsche be able to maintain the profit margin because of its image and the performance of the Cayenne?

# connect Questions and Problems

BASIC

1 – 17

1 **Relevant Cash Flows [LO1]** Parker & Stone NV is looking at setting up a new manufacturing plant in Rotterdam to produce garden tools. The company bought some land six years ago for €6 million in anticipation of using it as a warehouse and distribution site, but the company has since decided to rent these facilities from a competitor instead. If the land were sold today, the company would net €6.4 million. The company wants to build its new manufacturing plant on this land; the plant will cost €14.2 million to build, and the site requires €890,000 worth of grading before it is suitable for construction. What is the proper cash flow amount to use as the initial investment in non-current assets when evaluating this project? Why?

2 **Relevant Cash Flows [LO1]** Winnebagel plc currently sells 30,000 mobile caravans per year at £53,000 each, and 12,000 luxury stationary caravans per year at £91,000 each. The company wants to introduce a new caravanette to fill out its product line; it hopes to sell 19,000 of these caravanettes per year at £13,000 each. An independent consultant has determined that if Winnebagel introduces the new caravanettes, it should boost the sales of its existing luxury stationary caravans by 4,500 units per year, and reduce the sales of its mobile caravans by 900 units per year. What is the amount to use as the annual sales figure when evaluating this project? Why?

3 **Calculating Projected Net Income [LO1]** A proposed new investment has projected sales of £830,000. Variable costs are 60 per cent of sales, and fixed costs are £181,000; depreciation is £77,000. Prepare a pro forma income statement assuming a tax rate of 28 per cent. What is the projected net income?

4 **Calculating OCF [LO1]** Consider the following income statement:

| | |
|---|---|
| Sales (£) | 1,824,500 |
| Costs (£) | 838,900 |
| Depreciation (£) | 226,500 |
| Profit before taxes (£) | ? |
| Taxes (28%) (£) | ? |
| Net income (£) | ? |

Fill in the missing numbers and then calculate the OCF. What is the depreciation tax shield?

5 **OCF from Several Approaches [LO1]** A proposed new project has projected sales of NKr108,000, costs of NKr51,000, and depreciation of NKr6,800. The tax rate is 35 per cent. Calculate operating cash flow using the four different approaches described in the chapter, and verify that the answer is the same in each case.

6 **Calculating Depreciation [LO1]** A piece of newly purchased industrial equipment costs €1,080,000, and is depreciated using 20 per cent reducing-balance. Calculate the annual depreciation allowances and end-of-the-year book values for this equipment.

7 **Calculating Salvage Value [LO1]** Consider an asset that costs €548,000 and is depreciated using 20 per cent reducing-balance. The asset is to be used in a five-year project; at the end of the project, the asset can be sold for €105,000. If the relevant tax rate is 35 per cent, what is the after-tax cash flow from the sale of this asset?

8 **Calculating Salvage Value [LO1]** An asset used in a four-year project is to be depreciated using the 20 per cent reducing-balance method. The asset has an acquisition cost of DKr7,900,000 and will be sold for DKr1,400,000 at the end of the project. If the tax rate is 25 per cent, what is the after-tax salvage value of the asset?

**9   Calculating Project OCF [LO1]**   Summer Tyme plc is considering a new three-year expansion project that requires an initial non-current asset investment of £3.9 million. The non-current asset will be depreciated using the 20 per cent reducing-balance method. At the end of three years it will be worthless. The project is estimated to generate £2,650,000 in annual sales, with costs of £840,000. If the tax rate is 28 per cent, what is the OCF for each year of this project?

**10   Calculating Project NPV [LO1]**   In the previous problem, suppose the required return on the project is 12 per cent. What is the project's NPV?

**11   Calculating Project Cash Flow from Assets [LO1]**   In the previous problem, suppose the project requires an initial investment in net working capital of £300,000, and the non-current asset will have a market value of £210,000 at the end of the project. What is the project's year 0 net cash flow? Year 1? Year 2? Year 3? What is the new NPV?

**12   NPV and Straight-Line Depreciation [LO1]**   In the previous problem, suppose the non-current asset actually is depreciated straight-line to zero over the three years of the project. All the other facts are the same. What is the project's year 1 net cash flow now? Year 2? Year 3? What is the new NPV?

**13   Project Evaluation [LO1]**   Dog Up! Franks is looking at a new sausage system with an installed cost of €390,000. This cost will be depreciated straight-line to zero over the project's five-year life, at the end of which the sausage system can be scrapped for €60,000. The sausage system will save the firm €120,000 per year in pre-tax operating costs, and the system requires an initial investment in net working capital of €28,000. If the tax rate is 34 per cent and the discount rate is 10 per cent, what is the NPV of this project?

**14   Project Evaluation [LO1]**   Your firm is contemplating the purchase of a new £925,000 computer-based order entry system. The system will be depreciated using the 20 per cent reducing-balance method over its five-year life. It will be worth £90,000 at the end of that time. You will save £360,000 before taxes per year in order-processing costs, and you will be able to reduce working capital by £125,000 (this is a one-time reduction). If the tax rate is 28 per cent, what is the IRR for this project?

**15   Calculating EAC [LO4]**   A five-year project has an initial fixed non-current asset investment of £270,000, an initial NWC investment of £25,000, and an annual OCF of –£42,000. The non-current asset is depreciated 20 per cent reducing-balance over the life of the project, and has no salvage value. If the required return is 11 per cent, what is this project's equivalent annual cost, or EAC?

**16   Calculating EAC [LO4]**   You are evaluating two different silicon wafer milling machines. The Techron I costs €210,000, has a three-year life, and has pre-tax operating costs of €34,000 per year. The Techron II costs €320,000, has a five-year life, and has pre-tax operating costs of €23,000 per year. For both milling machines, use 20 per cent reducing-balance depreciation over the project's life and assume a salvage value of €20,000. If your tax rate is 35 per cent and your discount rate is 14 per cent, compute the EAC for both machines. Which do you prefer? Why?

**17   Calculating a Bid Price [LO3]**   Alson Enterprises needs someone to supply it with 185,000 cartons of machine screws per year to support its manufacturing needs over the next five years, and you've decided to bid for the contract. It will cost you £940,000 to install the equipment necessary to start production; you'll depreciate this cost straight-line to zero over the project's life. You estimate that, in five years, this equipment can be salvaged for £70,000. Your fixed production costs will be £305,000 per year, and your variable production costs should be £9.25 per carton. You also need an initial investment in net working capital of £75,000. If your tax rate is 35 per cent and you require a 12 per cent return on your investment, what bid price should you submit?

INTERMEDIATE

18 – 29

18 **Cost-Cutting Proposals [LO2]** Geary Machine Shop is considering a four-year project to improve its production efficiency. Buying a new machine press for £560,000 is estimated to result in £210,000 in annual pre-tax cost savings. The press is depreciated using the 20 per cent reducing-balance method, and it will have a salvage value at the end of the project of £80,000. The press also requires an initial investment in spare parts inventory of £20,000, along with an additional £3,000 in inventory for each succeeding year of the project. If the shop's tax rate is 28 per cent and its discount rate is 9 per cent, should the company buy and install the machine press?

19 **Comparing Mutually Exclusive Projects [LO1]** Hagar Industrial Systems Company (HISC) is trying to decide between two different conveyor belt systems. System A costs 430,000 Norwegian kroner (NKr), has a four-year life, and requires NKr120,000 in pre-tax annual operating costs. System B costs NKr540,000, has a six-year life, and requires NKr80,000 in pre-tax annual operating costs. Both systems are to be depreciated using the reducing-balance method of 50 per cent per annum, and will have zero salvage value at the end of their life. Whichever system is chosen, it will not be replaced when it wears out. If the tax rate is 28 per cent and the discount rate is 20 per cent, which system should the firm choose?

20 **Comparing Mutually Exclusive Projects [LO4]** Suppose in the previous problem that HISC always needs a conveyor belt system; when one wears out, it must be replaced. Which project should the firm choose now?

21 **Calculating a Bid Price [LO3]** Consider a project to supply 100 million postage stamps per year to the Royal Mail for the next five years. You have an idle parcel of land available that cost £2,400,000 five years ago; if the land were sold today, it would net you £2,700,000 after tax. In five years the land can be sold for £3,200,000 after tax. You will need to install £4.1 million in new manufacturing plant and equipment to actually produce the stamps: this plant and equipment will be depreciated straight-line to zero over the project's five-year life. The equipment can be sold for £540,000 at the end of the project. You will also need £600,000 in initial net working capital for the project, and an additional investment of £50,000 in every year thereafter. Your production costs are 0.5 pence per stamp, and you have fixed costs of £950,000 per year. If your tax rate is 34 per cent and your required return on this project is 12 per cent, what bid price should you submit on the contract?

22 **Interpreting a Bid Price [LO3]** In the previous problem, suppose you could keep working capital investments down to only £25,000 per year. How would this new information affect your calculated bid price?

23 **Comparing Mutually Exclusive Projects [LO4]** Vandalay Industries is considering the purchase of a new machine for the production of latex. Machine A costs £2,900,000 and will last for six years. Variable costs are 35 per cent of sales, and fixed costs are £170,000 per year. Machine B costs £5,100,000 and will last for nine years. Variable costs for this machine are 30 per cent of sales, and fixed costs are £130,000 per year. The sales for each machine will be £10 million per year. The required return is 10 per cent, and the tax rate is 35 per cent. Both machines will be depreciated on a straight-line basis. If the company plans to replace the machine when it wears out on a perpetual basis, which machine should you choose?

24 **Equivalent Annual Cost [LO4]** Compact fluorescent lamps (CFLs) have become more popular in recent years, but do they make financial sense? Suppose a typical 60 watt incandescent light bulb costs £0.50 and lasts 1,000 hours. A 15 watt CFL, which provides the same light, costs £3.50 and lasts for 12,000 hours. A kilowatt-hour of electricity costs £0.101, which is about the national average. A kilowatt-hour is 1,000 watts for 1 hour. If you require a 10 per cent return and use a light fixture for 500 hours per year, what is the equivalent annual cost of each light bulb?

**25  Break-Even Cost [LO2]**   The previous problem suggests that using CFLs instead of incandescent bulbs is a no-brainer. However, electricity costs actually vary quite a bit, depending on location and user type (you can get information on your rates from your local power company). An industrial user in the Scottish Highlands might pay £0.04 per kilowatt-hour, whereas a residential user in Essex might pay £0.25. What's the break-even cost per kilowatt-hour in Problem 24?

**26  Break-Even Replacement [LO2]**   The previous two problems suggest that using CFLs is a good idea from a purely financial perspective unless you live in an area where power is relatively inexpensive, but there is another wrinkle. Suppose you have a residence with a lot of incandescent bulbs that are used on average for 500 hours a year. The average bulb will be about halfway through its life, so it will have 500 hours remaining (and you can't tell which bulbs are older or newer). At what cost per kilowatt-hour does it make sense to replace your incandescent bulbs today?

**27  Issues in Capital Budgeting [LO1]**   The debate regarding CFLs versus incandescent bulbs (see Problems 24–26) has even more wrinkles. In no particular order:

- Incandescent bulbs generate a lot more heat than CFLs.

- CFL prices will probably decline relative to incandescent bulbs.

- CFLs unavoidably contain small amounts of mercury, a significant environmental hazard, and special precautions must be taken in disposing of burned-out units (and also in cleaning up a broken lamp). Currently, there is no agreed-upon way to recycle a CFL. Incandescent bulbs pose no disposal/breakage hazards.

- Depending on a light's location (or the number of lights), there can be a non-trivial cost to change bulbs (i.e., labour cost in a business).

- Coal-fired power generation accounts for a substantial portion of the mercury emissions in Europe, though the emissions will drop sharply in the relatively near future.

- Power generation accounts for a substantial portion of $CO_2$ emissions in Europe.

- CFLs are more energy and material intensive to manufacture. On-site mercury contamination and worker safety are issues.

- If you install a CFL in a permanent lighting fixture in a building, you will probably move long before the CFL burns out.

- Another lighting technology based on light-emitting diodes (LEDs) exists, and is improving. LEDs are currently much more expensive than CFLs, but costs are coming down. LEDs last much longer than CFLs, and use even less power. Also, LEDs don't contain mercury.

Qualitatively, how do these issues affect your position in the CFL versus incandescent light bulb debate? Australia recently proposed banning the sale of incandescent bulbs altogether, as have several European countries. Does your analysis suggest such a move is wise? Are there other regulations, short of an outright ban, that make sense to you?

**28  Replacement Decisions [LO2]**   Your small remodelling business has two hydrogen-battery/petrol hybrid eco-vehicles. One is a small passenger car used for job-site visits and for other general business purposes. The other is a heavy truck used to haul equipment. The car gets 50 miles per litre. The truck gets 20 miles per litre. You want to improve petrol mileage to save money, and you have enough money to upgrade one vehicle. The upgrade cost will be the same for both vehicles. An upgraded car will get 80 miles per litre; an upgraded truck will get 25 miles per litre. The cost of petrol is £1.09 per litre. Assuming an upgrade is a good idea in the first place, which one should you upgrade? Both vehicles are driven 12,000 miles per year.

29  **Replacement Decisions [LO2]**   In the previous problem, suppose you drive the truck *x* miles per year. How many miles would you have to drive the car before upgrading the car would be the better choice? (*Hint:* Look at the relative petrol savings.)

**CHALLENGE**
**30 – 34**

30  **Calculating Project NPV [LO1]**   You have been hired as a consultant for Pristine Urban-Tech Zither plc (PUTZ), manufacturers of fine zithers. The market for zithers is growing quickly. The company bought some land three years ago for £1.4 million in anticipation of using it as a toxic waste dump site, but has recently hired another company to handle all toxic materials. Based on a recent appraisal, the company believes it could sell the land for £1.5 million on an after-tax basis. In four years the land could be sold for £1.6 million after taxes. The company also hired a marketing firm to analyse the zither market, at a cost of £125,000. An excerpt of the marketing report is as follows:

> The zither industry will have a rapid expansion in the next four years. With the brand name recognition that PUTZ brings to bear, we feel that the company will be able to sell 3,200, 4,300, 3,900 and 2,800 units each year for the next four years, respectively. Again, capitalizing on the name recognition of PUTZ, we feel that a premium price of £780 can be charged for each zither. Because zithers appear to be a fad, we feel that, at the end of the four-year period, sales should be discontinued.

PUTZ believes that fixed costs for the project will be £425,000 per year, and variable costs are 15 per cent of sales. The equipment necessary for production will cost £4.2 million, and will be depreciated according to the 20 per cent reducing-balance method. At the end of the project the equipment can be scrapped for £400,000. Net working capital of £125,000 will be required immediately. PUTZ has a 28 per cent tax rate, and the required return on the project is 13 per cent. What is the NPV of the project? Assume the company has other profitable projects.

31  **Project Evaluation [LO1]**   Aguilera Acoustics (AA) projects unit sales for a new seven-octave voice emulation implant as follows:

| Year | Unit sales |
|------|------------|
| 1 | 85,000 |
| 2 | 98,000 |
| 3 | 106,000 |
| 4 | 114,000 |
| 5 | 93,000 |

Production of the implants will require €1,500,000 in net working capital to start, and additional net working capital investments each year equal to 15 per cent of the projected sales increase for the following year. Total fixed costs are €900,000 per year, variable production costs are €240 per unit, and the units are priced at €325 each. The equipment needed to begin production has an installed cost of €21,000,000. Because the implants are intended for professional singers, this equipment is considered industrial machinery, and is thus depreciated by the reducing-balance method at 20 per cent per annum. In five years this equipment can be sold for about 20 per cent of its acquisition cost. AA is in the 35 per cent marginal tax bracket, and has a required return on all its projects of 18 per cent. Based on these preliminary project estimates, what is the NPV of the project? What is the IRR?

32  **Calculating Required Savings [LO2]**   A proposed cost-saving device has an installed cost of £480,000. The device will be used in a five-year project, and will be depreciated using the reducing-balance method at 20 per cent per annum. The required initial net working capital investment is £40,000, the marginal tax rate is 28 per cent, and the project discount rate is 12 per cent. The device has an estimated year 5 salvage value of £45,000. What level of pre-tax cost savings do we require for this project to be profitable?

33  **Calculating a Bid Price [LO3]**  Your company has been approached to bid on a contract to sell 10,000 voice recognition (VR) computer keyboards a year for four years. Because of technological improvements, beyond that time they will be outdated, and no sales will be possible. The equipment necessary for the production will cost £2.4 million and will be depreciated on a reducing-balance (20 per cent) method. Production will require an investment in net working capital of £75,000 to be returned at the end of the project, and the equipment can be sold for £200,000 at the end of production. Fixed costs are £500,000 per year, and variable costs are £165 per unit. In addition to the contract, you feel your company can sell 3,000, 6,000, 8,000 and 5,000 additional units to companies in other countries over the next four years, respectively, at a price of £275. This price is fixed. The tax rate is 28 per cent, and the required return is 13 per cent. Additionally, the managing director of the company will undertake the project only if it has an NPV of £100,000. What bid price should you set for the contract?

34  **Replacement Decisions [LO2]**  Suppose we are thinking about replacing an old computer with a new one. The old one cost us €650,000; the new one will cost €780,000. The new machine will be depreciated straight-line to zero over its five-year life. It will probably be worth about €150,000 after five years.

The old computer is being depreciated straight-line at a rate of €130,000 per year. It will be completely written off in three years. If we don't replace it now, we shall have to replace it in two years. We can sell it now for €210,000; in two years, it will probably be worth €60,000. The new machine will save us €145,000 per year in operating costs. The tax rate is 38 per cent, and the discount rate is 12 per cent.

(a)  Suppose we recognize that, if we don't replace the computer now, we shall be replacing it in two years. Should we replace now or should we wait? (*Hint*: What we effectively have here is a decision either to 'invest' in the old computer (by not selling it) or to invest in the new one. Notice that the two investments have unequal lives.)

(b)  Suppose we consider only whether we should replace the old computer now without worrying about what's going to happen in two years. What are the relevant cash flows? Should we replace it or not? (*Hint*: Consider the net change in the firm's after-tax cash flows if we do the replacement.)

## MINI CASE  Conch Republic Electronics, Part 1

Conch Republic Electronics is a mid-sized electronics manufacturer located in Emilia-Romagna, Italy. The company president is Morena Moscardini, who inherited the company. When it was founded, over 70 years ago, the company originally repaired radios and other household appliances. Over the years the company expanded into manufacturing, and is now a reputable manufacturer of various electronic items. Jay McCanless, a recent MBA graduate, has been hired by the company's finance department.

One of the major revenue-producing items manufactured by Conch Republic is a personal digital assistant (PDA). Conch Republic currently has one PDA model on the market, and sales have been excellent. The PDA is a unique item in that it comes in a variety of tropical colours and is pre-programmed to play Billy Bragg music. However, as with any electronic item, technology changes rapidly, and the current PDA has limited features in comparison with newer models. Conch Republic spent €750,000 to develop a prototype for a new PDA that has all the features of the existing PDA but adds new features such as cell-phone capability. The company has spent a further €200,000 for a marketing study to determine the expected sales figures for the new PDA.

Conch Republic can manufacture the new PDA for €155 each in variable costs. Fixed costs for the operation are estimated to be €4.7 million per year. The estimated sales volumes are 74,000, 95,000, 125,000, 105,000 and 80,000 per year for the next five years, respectively. The unit price of the new PDA will be €360. The necessary equipment can be purchased for €21.5 million, and will be depreciated using the 20 per cent reducing-balance method. It is believed the value of the equipment in five years will be €4.1 million.

As previously stated, Conch Republic currently manufactures a PDA. Production of the existing model is expected to be terminated in two years. If Conch Republic does not introduce the new PDA, sales will be 80,000 units and 60,000 units for the next two years, respectively. The price of the existing PDA is €290 per unit, with variable costs of €120 each and fixed costs of €1,800,000 per year. If Conch Republic does introduce the new PDA, sales of the existing PDA will fall by 15,000 units per year, and the price of the existing units will have to be lowered to €255 each. Net working capital for the PDAs will be 20 per cent of sales, and will occur with the timing of the cash flows for the year: for example, there is no initial outlay for NWC, but changes in NWC will first occur in year 1 with the first year's sales. Conch Republic has a 35 per cent corporate tax rate and a 12 per cent required return.

Morena has asked Jay to prepare a report that answers the following questions.

## QUESTIONS

1 What is the payback period of the project?

2 What is the profitability index of the project?

3 What is the IRR of the project?

4 What is the NPV of the project?

# Endnotes

1 If the asset in question is unique, then the opportunity cost might be higher, because there might be other valuable projects we could undertake that would use it. However, if the asset in question is of a type that is routinely bought and sold (a used car, perhaps), then the opportunity cost is always the going price in the market, because that is the cost of buying another similar asset.

2 More colourfully, erosion is sometimes called *piracy* or *cannibalism*.

3 By *fixed cost* we mean a cash outflow that will occur regardless of the level of sales. This should not be confused with some sort of accounting period charge.

4 We shall also assume that a full year's depreciation can be taken in the first year.

5 In reality, the firm would probably recover something less than 100 per cent of this amount because of bad debts, inventory loss, and so on. If we wanted to, we could just assume that, for example, only 90 per cent was recovered, and proceed from there.

6 We're guilty of a minor inconsistency here. When we calculated the NPV and the IRR, we assumed that all the cash flows occurred at end of year. When we calculated the payback, we assumed that the cash flows occurred uniformly throughout the year.

7 Notice that the average total book value is not the initial total of £110,000 divided by 2. The reason is that the £20,000 in working capital doesn't 'depreciate'.

8 If there were other accounts, we might have to make some further adjustments. For example, a net increase in inventory would be a cash outflow.

# Project Analysis and Evaluation

## KEY NOTATIONS

| | |
|---|---|
| D | Depreciation |
| DCF | Discounted cash flow |
| DOL | Degree of operating leverage |
| FC | Total fixed cost |
| NPV | Net present value |
| P | Price per unit |
| Q | Total quantity of output |
| S | Total sales = $P \times Q$ |
| T | Tax rate |
| TC | Total cost |
| v | Variable cost per unit |
| VC | Total variable cost |

## LEARNING OBJECTIVES

After studying this chapter, you should understand:

**LO1** How to perform and interpret a sensitivity analysis for a proposed investment.

**LO2** How to perform and interpret a scenario analysis for a proposed investment.

**LO3** How to determine and interpret cash, accounting and financial break-even points.

**LO4** How the degree of operating leverage can affect the cash flows of a project.

**LO5** How capital rationing affects the ability of a company to accept projects.

IN THE SUMMER OF 2008 the movie *Speed Racer*, starring Emile Hirsch and Christina Ricci, spun its wheels at the box office. The *Speed Racer* slogan is 'Go Speed Racer, Go!', but critics said, 'Don't go (see) *Speed Racer*, don't go!' One critic said 'the races felt like a drag'. Others were even more harsh, saying the movie was 'like spending two hours caroming through a pinball machine' and a 'long, dreary, migraine-inducing slog'.

Looking at the numbers, Warner Brothers spent close to $150 million making the movie, plus millions more for marketing and distribution. Unfortunately for Warner Brothers, *Speed Racer* crashed and burned, pulling in only $90 million worldwide. In fact, about 4 of 10 movies lose money at the box office, though DVD sales often help the final tally. Of course, there are movies that do quite well. In 2009 the independent offering *Paranormal Activity* raked in over $100 million worldwide at a production cost of just $15,000!

Obviously, Warner Brothers didn't *plan* to lose $60 million on *Speed Racer*, but it happened. As the box office results for *Speed Racer* show, projects don't always go as companies think they will. This chapter explores how this can happen, and what companies can do to analyse and possibly avoid these situations.

In our previous chapter we discussed how to identify and organize the relevant cash flows for capital investment decisions. Our primary interest there was in coming up with a preliminary estimate of the net present value for a proposed project. In this chapter we focus on assessing the reliability of such an estimate, and on some additional considerations in project analysis.

We begin by discussing the need for an evaluation of cash flow and NPV estimates. We go on to develop some useful tools for such an evaluation. We also examine additional complications and concerns that can arise in project evaluation.

## 10.1    Evaluating NPV Estimates

As we discussed in Chapter 9, an investment has a positive net present value if its market value exceeds its cost. Such an investment is desirable, because it creates value for its owner. The primary problem in identifying such opportunities is that usually we can't actually observe the relevant market value; instead, we estimate it. Having done so, it is only natural to wonder whether our estimates are at least close to the true values. We consider this question next.

### The Basic Problem

Suppose we are working on a preliminary discounted cash flow analysis along the lines we described in the previous chapter. We carefully identify the relevant cash flows, avoiding such things as sunk costs, and we remember to consider working capital requirements. We add back any depreciation; we account for possible erosion; and we pay attention to opportunity costs. Finally, we double-check our calculations; when all is said and done, the bottom line is that the estimated NPV is positive.

Now what? Do we stop here and move on to the next proposal? Probably not. The fact that the estimated NPV is positive is definitely a good sign; but, more than anything, this tells us that we need to take a closer look.

If you think about it, there are two circumstances under which a DCF analysis could lead us to conclude that a project has a positive NPV. The first possibility is that the project really does have a positive NPV. That's the good news. The bad news is the second possibility: a project may appear to have a positive NPV because our estimate is inaccurate.

Notice that we could also err in the opposite way. If we conclude that a project has a negative NPV when the true NPV is positive, we lose a valuable opportunity.

### Projected versus Actual Cash Flows

There is a somewhat subtle point we need to make here. When we say something like 'The projected cash flow in year 4 is €700', what exactly do we mean? Does this mean that we think the cash flow will actually be €700? Not really. It could happen, of course, but we would be surprised to see it turn out exactly that way. The reason is that the €700 projection is based only on what we know today. Almost anything could happen between now and then to change that cash flow.

Loosely speaking, we really mean that if we took all the possible cash flows that could occur in four years and averaged them, the result would be €700. So we don't really expect a projected cash flow to be exactly right in any one case. What we *do* expect is that, if we evaluate a large number of projects, our projections will be right – on average.

### Forecasting Risk

The key inputs into a DCF analysis are projected future cash flows. If the projections are seriously in error, then we have a classic GIGO (garbage in, garbage out) system. In such a case, no matter how carefully we arrange the numbers and manipulate them, the resulting answer can still be grossly misleading. This is the danger in using a relatively sophisticated technique like DCF. It is sometimes easy to get caught up in number crunching and forget the underlying nuts-and-bolts economic reality.

**forecasting risk**
The possibility that errors in projected cash flows will lead to incorrect decisions. Also, *estimation risk*.

The possibility that we shall make a bad decision because of errors in the projected cash flows is called **forecasting risk** (or *estimation risk*). Because of forecasting risk, there is the danger that we shall think a project has a positive NPV when really it does not. How is this possible? It happens if we are overly optimistic about the future, and, as a result, our projected cash flows don't realistically reflect the possible future cash flows.

Forecasting risk can take many forms. For example, Microsoft spent several billion dollars developing and bringing the Xbox game console to market. Technologically more sophisticated than existing products on the market, the Xbox was the best way to play against competitors over the Internet. Unfortunately, Microsoft sold only 9 million Xboxes in the first 14 months of sales, at the low end of Microsoft's expected range. The Xbox was arguably the best available game console at the time, so why didn't it sell better? The reason given by analysts was that there were far fewer games made for the Xbox. For example, the PlayStation enjoyed a two-to-one advantage in the number of games made for it.

So far, we have not explicitly considered what to do about the possibility of errors in our forecasts, so one of our goals in this chapter is to develop some tools that are useful in identifying areas where potential errors exist, and where they might be especially damaging. In one form or another, we shall be trying to assess the economic 'reasonableness' of our estimates. We shall also be wondering how much damage will be done by errors in those estimates.

## Sources of Value

The first line of defence against forecasting risk is simply to ask, 'What is it about this investment that leads to a positive NPV?' We should be able to point to something specific as the source of value. For example, if the proposal under consideration involved a new product, then we might ask questions such as the following. Are we certain that our new product is significantly better than that of the competition? Can we truly manufacture at lower cost, or distribute more effectively, or identify undeveloped market niches, or gain control of a market?

These are just a few of the potential sources of value. There are many others. For example, in 2004 Google announced a new, free email service: Gmail. Why? Free email services were already widely available from big hitters like Microsoft and Yahoo! The answer is that Google's mail service is integrated with its acclaimed search engine, thereby giving it an edge. Also, offering email lets Google expand its lucrative keyword-based advertising delivery. So Google's source of value is leveraging its proprietary web search and advertisement delivery technologies.

A key factor to keep in mind is the degree of competition in the market. A basic principle of economics is that positive-NPV investments will be rare in a highly competitive environment. Therefore proposals that appear to show significant value in the face of stiff competition are particularly troublesome, and the likely reaction of the competition to any innovations must be closely examined.

To give an example, in 2010 demand for touch screen smartphones was high, prices were high, and profit margins were fat for retailers. But also in 2010 manufacturers of smartphones, such as Apple, Nokia and HTC, were projected to pour several billion euros into new production facilities as the market matured. Thus anyone thinking of entering this highly profitable market would do well to reflect on what the supply (and profit margin) situation will look like in just a few years.

It is also necessary to think about *potential* competition. For example, suppose home improvement retailer B&Q identifies an area that is underserved, and is thinking about opening a store. If the store is successful, what will happen? The answer is that Focus or Homebase (other competitors) would probably also build a store, thereby driving down volume and profits. So we always need to keep in mind that success attracts imitators and competitors.

The point to remember is that positive-NPV investments are probably not all that common, and the number of positive-NPV projects is almost certainly limited for any given firm. If we can't articulate some sound economic basis for thinking – ahead of time – that we have found something special, then the conclusion that our project has a positive NPV should be viewed with some suspicion.

10.1a    What is forecasting risk? Why is it a concern for the financial manager?
10.1b    What are some potential sources of value in a new project?

## 10.2  Scenario and Other What-If Analyses

Our basic approach to evaluating cash flow and NPV estimates involves asking what-if questions. Accordingly, we discuss some organized ways of going about a what-if analysis. Our goal in performing such an analysis is to assess the degree of forecasting risk, and to identify the most critical components of the success or failure of an investment.

### Getting Started

We are investigating a new project. Naturally, the first thing we do is estimate NPV, based on our projected cash flows. We shall call this initial set of projections the *base case*. Now, however, we recognize the possibility of error in these cash flow projections. After completing the base case, we thus wish to investigate the impact on our estimates of different assumptions about the future.

One way to organize this investigation is to put upper and lower bounds on the various components of the project. For example, suppose we forecast sales at 100 units per year. We know this estimate may be high or low, but we are relatively certain it is not off by more than 10 units in either direction. We thus pick a lower bound of 90 and an upper bound of 110. We go on to assign such bounds to any other cash flow components we are unsure about.

When we pick these upper and lower bounds, we are not ruling out the possibility that the actual values could be outside this range. What we are saying, again loosely speaking, is that it is unlikely that the true average (as opposed to our estimated average) of the possible values is outside this range.

An example is useful to illustrate the idea here. The project under consideration costs €200,000, has a five-year life, and has no salvage value. For simplicity, depreciation is straight-line to zero. The required return is 12 per cent, and the tax rate is 34 per cent. In addition, we have compiled the following information:

|                          | Base case | Lower bound | Upper bound |
|--------------------------|-----------|-------------|-------------|
| Unit sales               | 6,000     | 5,500       | 6,500       |
| Price per unit (€)       | 80        | 75          | 85          |
| Variable costs per unit (€) | 60     | 58          | 62          |
| Fixed costs per year (€) | 50,000    | 45,000      | 55,000      |

With this information we can calculate the base-case NPV by first calculating net income:

| Sales (€)              | 480,000 |
|------------------------|---------|
| Variable costs (€)     | 360,000 |
| Fixed costs (€)        | 50,000  |
| Depreciation (€)       | 40,000  |
| Profit before taxes (€)| 30,000  |
| Taxes (34%) (€)        | 10,200  |
| Net income             | 19,800  |

Operating cash flow is thus €19,800 + 40,000 = €59,800 per year. At 12 per cent, the five-year annuity factor is 3.6048, so the base-case NPV is

$$\text{Base-case NPV} = -€200,000 + 59,800 \times 3.6048$$
$$= €15,567$$

Thus the project looks good so far.

## Scenario Analysis

The basic form of what-if analysis is called **scenario analysis**. What we do is investigate the changes in our NPV estimates that result from asking questions such as: what if unit sales realistically should be projected at 5,500 units instead of 6,000?

Once we start looking at alternative scenarios, we might find that most of the plausible ones result in positive NPVs. In this case we have some confidence in proceeding with the project. If a substantial percentage of the scenarios look bad, the degree of forecasting risk is high, and further investigation is in order.

We can consider a number of possible scenarios. A good place to start is with the worst-case scenario. This will tell us the minimum NPV of the project. If this turns out to be positive, we shall be in good shape. While we are at it, we shall go ahead and determine the other extreme, the best case. This puts an upper bound on our NPV.

To get the worst case, we assign the least favourable value to each item. This means *low* values for items such as units sold and price per unit, and *high* values for costs. We do the reverse for the best case. For our project, these values would be the following:

> **scenario analysis**
> The determination of what happens to NPV estimates when we ask what-if questions.

| | Worst case | Best case |
|---|---|---|
| Unit sales | 5,500 | 6,500 |
| Price per unit (€) | 75 | 85 |
| Variable costs per unit (€) | 62 | 58 |
| Fixed costs per year (€) | 55,000 | 45,000 |

With this information we can calculate the net income and cash flows under each scenario (check these for yourself):

| Scenario | Net income (€) | Cash flow (€) | Net present value (€) | IRR (%) |
|---|---|---|---|---|
| Base case | 19,800 | 59,800 | 15,567 | 15.1 |
| Worst case* | –15,510 | 24,490 | –111,719 | –14.4 |
| Best case | 59,730 | 99,730 | 159,504 | 40.9 |

*We assume a tax credit is created in our worst-case scenario.

What we learn is that, under the worst scenario, the cash flow is still positive at €24,490. That's good news. The bad news is that the return is –14.4 per cent in this case, and the NPV is –€111,719. Because the project costs €200,000, we stand to lose a little more than half of the original investment under the worst possible scenario. The best case offers an attractive 41 per cent return.

The terms *best case* and *worst case* are commonly used, and we shall stick with them; but they are somewhat misleading. The absolutely best thing that could happen would be something absurdly unlikely, such as launching a new diet soft drink and subsequently learning that our (patented) formulation also just happens to cure the common cold. Similarly, the true worst case would involve some incredibly remote possibility of total disaster. We're not claiming that these things don't happen; once in a while they do. Some products, such as iPhones, succeed beyond the wildest expectations; and some, such as asbestos, turn out to be absolute catastrophes. Our point is that, in assessing the reasonableness of an NPV estimate, we need to stick to cases that are reasonably likely to occur.

Instead of *best* and *worst*, then, it is probably more accurate to use the words *optimistic* and *pessimistic*. In broad terms, if we were thinking about a reasonable range for, say, unit sales, then what we call the best case would correspond to something near the upper end of that range. The worst case would simply correspond to the lower end.

Depending on the project, the best- and worst-case estimates can vary greatly. For example, in 2008 Roche Carolina, a subsidiary of the Roche Group, a Swiss global health care company, announced plans for converting its site to a solar heating and cooling system. The initial cost was estimated at €350,000, including a government grant. The range used for this initial cost was ±15 per cent. The annual savings were estimated at €29,000, with a range of ±30 per cent. In the end, the NPV was estimated at €125,000, with a range of €42,000 to €208,000, and the IRR was 18 per cent, with a range of 11 per cent to 25 per cent.

As we have mentioned, there are an unlimited number of different scenarios that we could examine. At a minimum, we might want to investigate two intermediate cases by going halfway between the base amounts and the extreme amounts. This would give us five scenarios in all, including the base case.

Beyond this point, it is hard to know when to stop. As we generate more and more possibilities, we run the risk of experiencing 'paralysis of analysis'. The difficulty is that, no matter how many scenarios we run, all we can learn are possibilities – some good and some bad. Beyond that, we don't get any guidance as to what to do. Scenario analysis is thus useful in telling us what could happen, and in helping us gauge the potential for disaster, but it does not tell us whether to take a project.

Unfortunately, in practice, even the worst-case scenarios may not be low enough. Two recent examples show what we mean. The Eurotunnel, or Chunnel, may be one of the new wonders of the world. The tunnel under the English Channel connects Britain to France and covers 38 km. It took 8,000 workers eight years to remove 7.5 million cubic metres of rock. When the tunnel was finally built, it cost £11.9 billion (€13.1 billion), or slightly more than twice the original estimate of £5.9 billion (€6.5 billion). And things got worse. Forecasts called for 16.8 million passengers in the first year, but only 4 million actually used it. Revenue estimates for 2003 were £1.92 billion (€2.12 billion), but actual revenue was only about one-third of that. The major problems faced by the Eurotunnel were increased competition from ferry services, which dropped their prices, and the rise of low-cost airlines. In 2006 things got so bad that the company operating the Eurotunnel was forced into negotiations with creditors to chop its £7.4 billion (€8.2 billion) debt in half to avoid bankruptcy. The debt reduction appeared to help. In 2007 the Eurotunnel reported its first profit, of £0.9 million (€1 million). Of course, this profit paled in comparison with the £185 million (€204 million) in losses accumulated since the Chunnel first opened in 1994.

Another example is Toyota, which had long been regarded as a very reliable carmaker. In 2010 complaints started to trickle out that the accelerator pedal in some of its cars would stick, leading to uncontrolled increases in speed. By April 2010 Toyota had recalled over 8 million cars, which resulted in a catastrophic decline in its reputation, and a collapse in Toyota car sales throughout the world.

Moving forward to 2010, analysts would have had even more difficulty in forecasting the eruption of the Icelandic volcano, Eyjafjallajökull, which grounded European flights for weeks and forced many people into using other sources of transport, such as the Eurotunnel. The last time that Eyjafjallajökull erupted (in the nineteenth century), its eruptions lasted for nearly two years. Furthermore, the volcano's larger neighbour, Katla, could also erupt, and if this happens, European flights will be the least of our worries . . .

**sensitivity analysis**
Investigation of what happens to NPV when only one variable is changed.

## Sensitivity Analysis

**Sensitivity analysis** is a variation on scenario analysis that is useful in pinpointing the areas where forecasting risk is especially severe. The basic idea with a sensitivity analysis is to freeze all of the variables except one, and then see how sensitive our estimate of NPV is to changes in that one variable. If our NPV estimate turns out to be very sensitive to relatively small changes in the projected value of some component of project cash flow, then the forecasting risk associated with that variable is high.

To illustrate how sensitivity analysis works, we go back to our base case for every item except unit sales. We can then calculate cash flow and NPV using the largest and smallest unit sales figures:

| Scenario | Unit sales | Cash flow (€) | Net present value (€) | IRR (%) |
|----------|-----------|---------------|----------------------|---------|
| Base case | 6,000 | 59,800 | 15,567 | 15.1 |
| Worst case | 5,500 | 53,200 | −8,226 | 10.3 |
| Best case | 6,500 | 66,400 | 39,357 | 19.7 |

For comparison, we now freeze everything except fixed costs and repeat the analysis:

| Scenario | Fixed costs (€) | Cash flow (€) | Net present value (€) | IRR (%) |
|----------|-----------------|---------------|----------------------|---------|
| Base case | 50,000 | 59,800 | 15,567 | 15.1 |
| Worst case | 55,000 | 56,500 | 3,670 | 12.7 |
| Best case | 45,000 | 63,100 | 27,461 | 17.4 |

What we see here is that, given our ranges, the estimated NPV of this project is more sensitive to changes in projected unit sales than it is to changes in projected fixed costs. In fact, under the worst case for fixed costs, the NPV is still positive.

The results of our sensitivity analysis for unit sales can be illustrated graphically as in Fig. 10.1. Here we place NPV on the vertical axis and unit sales on the horizontal axis. When we plot the combinations of unit sales versus NPV, we see that all possible combinations fall on a straight line. The steeper the resulting line, the greater the sensitivity of the estimated NPV to changes in the projected value of the variable being investigated.

As we have illustrated, sensitivity analysis is useful in pinpointing which variables deserve the most attention. If we find that our estimated NPV is especially sensitive to changes in a variable that is difficult to forecast (such as unit sales), then the degree of

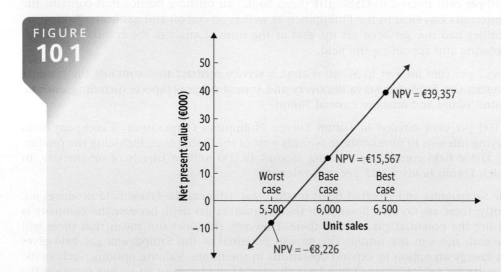

**Figure 10.1** Sensitivity analysis for unit sales

forecasting risk is high. We might decide that further market research would be a good idea in this case.

Because sensitivity analysis is a form of scenario analysis, it suffers from the same drawbacks. Sensitivity analysis is useful for pointing out where forecasting errors will do the most damage, but it does not tell us what to do about possible errors.

## Case Study: Forum Energy plc

In this section we shall consider the problems you may face in valuing a full company instead of a single project. Recall the balance sheet equation (3.1) from Chapter 3, where the value of a firm's assets equals the value of its debt plus equity. We've already shown how to value debt and equity, and this is good enough when a company is large, and its securities are frequently traded on a stock exchange. However, in many cases you may prefer to work with the other side of the balance sheet equation and value a company's assets directly.

Valuing a firm's assets is similar to valuing a project. You estimate the future cash flows coming from all the operations of the company, and discount those cash flows at the appropriate discount rate. If the firm has several distinct operations in different industries or geographical locations, you may wish to use separate discount rates for each stream of cash flows.

In this case study we shall arrive at a valuation for Forum Energy plc, which is a gas firm with all of its operations in the Philippines. You can visit its website, www.forumenergyplc.com, for more information on the company's history and operations. Our approach will be necessarily simplistic, so as to focus on the fundamentals of valuation. However, although we may seem to be making lots of assumptions, the detail of the analysis is actually at the same level as provided by many commercial providers of valuation services!

As of April 2010, Forum Energy was listed on the UK small companies exchange, AIM, and its share price was £0.715. It had 33,092,533 shares outstanding, making its market capitalization of equity equal to £0.715 × 33,092,533 = £23.7 million. The company had no debt, and so, according to the share price, the value of the company was £23.7 million.

Let us now focus on the firm's assets and operations. According to its audited annual accounts of 31 December 2009 and its website, Forum Energy plc had three main areas of operations:

1  A 70 per cent interest in GSEC 101 (Reed Bank), an offshore licence that contains the Sampaguita Gas Field in the Philippines, as well as several oil and gas leads. Production facilities had not yet been set up, and at the time of analysis the company was still exploring and appraising the field.

2  A 66.7 per cent interest in SC 40 (Cebu), a service contract that contains the onshore Libertad Gas Field and Maya discovery and several other prospects including onshore Jibitnil Island and offshore Central Tañon.

3  A 100 per cent interest in Forum Energy Philippines Corporation, a company with varying interests in nine offshore oilfields west of the Philippines, including the producing Galoc field currently producing around 10,000 million barrels of oil per day, in which Forum holds a 2.27 per cent interest.

The Sampaguita and Libertad fields produce gas, whereas the Galoc field produces oil. Currently, there are no cash flows from the Sampaguita gas field, because the company is appraising the potential gas reserves there. However, this does not mean that there will not be cash flows in the future. The growth potential of the Sampaguita gas field gives Forum Energy an option to expand operations in the future. Valuing options, such as the Sampaguita gas field, is covered in a later chapter. At the moment let us just focus on the two existing production facilities, Libertad and Galoc.

Given that Libertad produces gas and Galoc produces oil, we can concentrate on three main uncertainties: the future gas price, the future oil price, and the future extraction capabilities of the hydrocarbon fields owned by Forum Energy.

The wholesale gas price in April 2010 was around £2.63 per barrel and the oil price was around £54.61 per barrel. Assume that one barrel of gas is equal to 6 cubic feet. The expected extraction rates and other information for each hydrocarbon field are as follows:

| Field | Interest | Expected reserves | Reserves × Interest | Barrels equivalent | Annual output |
|---|---|---|---|---|---|
| Libertad Gas | 66.7% | 1.14 billion cubic feet | 760 million cubic feet | 127 million barrels | 423,333 barrels/year (assuming 300 years' life) |
| Galoc Oil | 2.27% | 2.3 million barrels/year | 52,210 barrels/year | 52,210 barrels/year | 52,210 barrels/year |

This is all the information we have to work with, and so we have to make a number of assumptions. Assume that the relevant discount rate for the oil field is 12 per cent, and the discount rate for the gas field is 15 per cent. Assume also that the oil field lasts for 10 years, and the gas field has enough gas to last for 300 years. Also assume that energy prices may be 20 per cent higher or lower than anticipated, and extraction capabilities may be 10 per cent higher or lower than expected. The assumptions are provided in tabular form below:

| Input | Worst case | Expected | Best case |
|---|---|---|---|
| Oil price (£) | 43.68 | 54.61 | 65.53 |
| Gas price (£) | 2.11 | 2.63 | 3.16 |
| Oil extraction capacity (barrels) | 46,989 | 52,210 | 57,431 |
| Gas extraction capacity (barrels) | 381,000 | 423,333 | 465,667 |

Now that we have our different assumptions, we are in a position to value Forum Energy plc. Taking the expected scenario first, we value the oil and gas fields separately:

- **Galoc oil field** The oil in the Galoc field will last for 10 years. If the oil price is £54.61 per barrel, and 52,210 barrels are extracted annually, then the annual revenues from Galoc will be £54.61 × 52,210 = £2,850,941. The present value of a 10-year annuity of £2,850,941 discounted at a rate of 12 per cent is approximately equal to £16,108,451.

- **Libertad gas field** The gas in the Libertad field will last for 300 years. The gas price is £2.63 per barrel, and 423,333 barrels are extracted annually, giving annual cash flows of £2.63 × 423,333 = £1,114,034. The present value of a 300-year annuity of £1,114,034 discounted at a rate of 15 per cent is approximately equal to £7,426,895.

The total market value of Forum Energy's assets (ignoring the Sampaguita gas field) is equal to the sum of the two main operations, which is £16,108,451 + £7,426,895 = £23,535,346. With 33,092,533 shares, the expected share price should be £0.711, which is almost exactly the same as the actual share price of £0.715. This gives us confidence that our analysis is in roughly the same area as that of the market. If our valuation was significantly different from the existing share price, it would be important to reassess the various inputs into the analysis.

For information, the spreadsheet that was used in the analysis is presented overleaf. Clearly any layout could be used.

| | A | B | C | D | E |
|---|---|---|---|---|---|
| 1 | Forum Energy plc | | | | |
| 2 | | | | | |
| 3 | Share Price | £0.715 | | | |
| 4 | Number of Shares | 33092533 | | | |
| 5 | Market Cap | £23,661,161 | | | |
| 6 | | | | | |
| 7 | $/£ | 1.52 | | | |
| 8 | Oil Price ($83) | £54.61 | | | |
| 9 | Gas Price ($4) | £2.63 | | | |
| 10 | | | | | |
| 11 | Oil Barrels | 52,210 | | Gas Barrels | 423,333 |
| 12 | Annual Oil Revenu | £2,850,940.79 | | Annual Gas Revenues | £1,114,034.21 |
| 13 | years | 10 | | years | 300 |
| 14 | r | 12% | | r | 15% |
| 15 | | | | | |
| 16 | PV Oil | £16,108,451.30 | | PV Gas | £7,426,894.74 |
| 17 | | | | | |
| 18 | Total Value | £23,535,346.04 | | | |
| 19 | Share Price | £0.711 | | | |
| 20 | | | | | |

The next stage in our valuation should be the sensitivity analysis. In the table below we present the expected share prices in each situation by varying only one input at a time. From the table it can be seen that the Forum Energy share price is most sensitive to changes in the oil price. Thus analysts should focus more heavily on predicting changes in future oil prices when considering Forum Energy's value.

| Worst case Oil = £43.68 | Best case Oil = £65.53 | Worst case Gas = £2.11 | Best case Gas = £3.16 |
|---|---|---|---|
| Share price = £0.614 | Share price = £0.809 | Share price = £0.667 | Share price = £0.756 |
| | | | |
| Worst case Oil = 46,989 barrels | Best case Oil = 57,431 barrels | Worst case Gas = 381,000 barrels | Best case Gas = 465,667 barrels |
| Share price = £0.662 | Share price = £0.760 | Share price = £0.689 | Share price = £0.734 |

We can also carry out a scenario analysis for Forum Energy by looking at the best- and worst-case scenarios. These are the times when the worst (or best) case estimates for all the inputs occur simultaneously. When the worst-case scenario occurs, the gas price will be £2.11, the oil price will be £43.68, the oil production will be 46,989 barrels, and the gas production will be 381,000 barrels. The share price of Forum Energy plc when this happens will only be £0.512, significantly less than the current share price. Similarly, under the best-case scenario, Forum Energy's share price will be £0.939.

So what should the share price be? It all depends on the likelihood of each scenario or outcome in the future. Further analysis is definitely required at this point. For example, we have not considered the valuation effects of the Sampaguita gas field and the possible revenue streams that are likely to arise from extraction operations there. In addition, we could have considered our assumptions in more detail and, for example, considered gas and oil price changes for every year in the future.

## Simulation Analysis

Scenario analysis and sensitivity analysis are widely used. With scenario analysis, we let all the different variables change, but we let them take on only a few values. With sensitivity analysis, we let only one variable change, but we let it take on many values. If we combine the two approaches, the result is a crude form of **simulation analysis**.

> **simulation analysis**
> A combination of scenario and sensitivity analysis.

If we want to let all the items vary at the same time, we have to consider a very large number of scenarios, and computer assistance is almost certainly needed. In the simplest case we start with unit sales, and assume that any value in our 5,500 to 6,500 range is equally likely. We start by randomly picking one value (or by instructing a computer to do so). We then randomly pick a price, a variable cost, and so on.

Once we have values for all the relevant components, we calculate an NPV. We repeat this sequence as much as we desire, probably several thousand times. The result is many NPV estimates that we summarize by calculating the average value and some measure of how spread out the different possibilities are. For example, it would be of some interest to know what percentage of the possible scenarios result in negative estimated NPVs.

Because simulation analysis (or simulation) is an extended form of scenario analysis, it has the same problems. Once we have the results, no simple decision rule tells us what to do. Also, we have described a relatively simple form of simulation. To really do it right, we would have to consider the interrelationships between the different cash flow components. Furthermore, we assumed that the possible values were equally likely to occur. It is probably more realistic to assume that values near the base case are more likely than extreme values, but coming up with the probabilities is difficult, to say the least.

For these reasons, the use of simulation is somewhat limited in practice. However, recent advances in computer software and hardware (and user sophistication) lead us to believe it may become more common in the future, particularly for large-scale projects.

---

**CONCEPT QUESTIONS**

10.2a   What are scenario, sensitivity and simulation analysis?
10.2b   What are the drawbacks to the various types of what-if analysis?

---

## 10.3  Break-Even Analysis

It will frequently turn out that the crucial variable for a project is sales volume. If we are thinking of creating a new product or entering a new market, for example, the hardest thing to forecast accurately is how much we can sell. For this reason, sales volume is usually analysed more closely than other variables.

Break-even analysis is a popular and commonly used tool for analysing the relationship between sales volume and profitability. There are a variety of different break-even measures, and we have already seen several types. For example, we discussed (in Chapter 8) how the payback period can be interpreted as the length of time until a project breaks even, ignoring time value.

All break-even measures have a similar goal. Loosely speaking, we shall always be asking, 'How bad do sales have to get before we actually begin to lose money?' Implicitly, we shall also be asking, 'Is it likely that things will get that bad?' To get started on this subject, we first discuss fixed and variable costs.

## Fixed and Variable Costs

In discussing break-even, the difference between fixed and variable costs becomes very important. As a result, we need to be a little more explicit about the difference than we have been so far.

> **variable costs**
> Costs that change when the quantity of output changes.

**Variable Costs**   By definition, **variable costs** change as the quantity of output changes, and they are zero when production is zero. For example, direct labour costs and raw material costs are usually considered variable. This makes sense, because if we shut down operations tomorrow, there will be no future costs for labour or raw materials.

We shall assume that variable costs are a constant amount per unit of output. This simply means that total variable cost is equal to the cost per unit multiplied by the number of units. In other words, the relationship between total variable cost (VC), cost per unit of output ($v$) and total quantity of output ($Q$) can be written simply as

$$\text{Total variable cost} = \text{Total quantity of output} \times \text{Cost per unit of output}$$
$$VC = Q \times v$$

For example, suppose variable costs ($v$) are €2 per unit. If total output ($Q$) is 1,000 units, what will total variable costs (VC) be?

$$VC = Q \times v$$
$$= 1,000 \times \text{€}2$$
$$= \text{€}2,000$$

Similarly, if $Q$ is 5,000 units, then VC will be $5,000 \times \text{€}2 = \text{€}10,000$. Figure 10.2 illustrates the relationship between output level and variable costs in this case. In Fig. 10.2, notice that increasing output by one unit results in variable costs rising by €2, so 'the rise over the run' (the slope of the line) is given by €2/1 = €2.

FIGURE
**10.2**

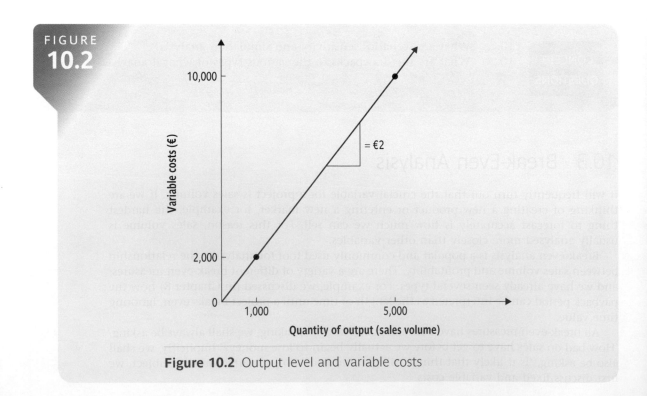

**Figure 10.2** Output level and variable costs

**EXAMPLE 10.1**

# Variable Costs

Blume plc is a manufacturer of pencils. It has received an order for 5,000 pencils, and the company has to decide whether to accept the order. From recent experience, the company knows that each pencil requires £0.05 in raw materials and £0.50 in direct labour costs. These variable costs are expected to continue to apply in the future. What will Blume's total variable costs be if it accepts the order?

In this case the cost per unit is £0.50 in labour plus £0.05 in materials, for a total of £0.55 per unit. At 5,000 units of output, we have

$$\begin{aligned} VC &= Q \times v \\ &= 5,000 \times £0.55 \\ &= £2,750 \end{aligned}$$

Therefore total variable costs will be £2,750.

**Fixed Costs** **Fixed costs**, by definition, do not change during a specified time period. So, unlike variable costs, they do not depend on the amount of goods or services produced during a period (at least within some range of production). For example, the lease payment on a production facility and the company chairman's salary are fixed costs, at least over some period.

Naturally, fixed costs are not fixed for ever. They are fixed only during some particular time, say a quarter or a year. Beyond that time, leases can be terminated and executives 'retired'. More to the point, any fixed cost can be modified or eliminated given enough time; so, in the long run, all costs are variable.

Notice that when a cost is fixed, that cost is effectively a sunk cost, because we are going to have to pay it no matter what.

> **fixed costs**
> Costs that do not change when the quantity of output changes during a particular time period.

**Total Costs** Total costs (TC) for a given level of output are the sum of variable costs (VC) and fixed costs (FC):

$$\begin{aligned} TC &= VC + FC \\ &= v \times Q + FC \end{aligned}$$

So, for example, if we have variable costs of €3 per unit and fixed costs of €8,000 per year, our total cost is

$$TC = €3 \times Q + €8,000$$

If we produce 6,000 units, our total production cost will be €3 × 6,000 + €8,000 = €26,000. At other production levels, we have the following:

| Quantity produced | Total variable costs (€) | Fixed costs (€) | Total costs (€) |
|---|---|---|---|
| 0 | 0 | 8,000 | 8,000 |
| 1,000 | 3,000 | 8,000 | 11,000 |
| 5,000 | 15,000 | 8,000 | 23,000 |
| 10,000 | 30,000 | 8,000 | 38,000 |

By plotting these points in Fig. 10.3 we see that the relationship between quantity produced and total costs is given by a straight line. In Fig. 10.3, notice that total costs equal fixed costs when sales are zero. Beyond that point, every one-unit increase in production leads to a €3 increase in total costs, so the slope of the line is 3. In other words, the **marginal**, or **incremental**, **cost** of producing one more unit is €3.

> **marginal, or incremental, cost**
> The change in costs that occurs when there is a small change in output.

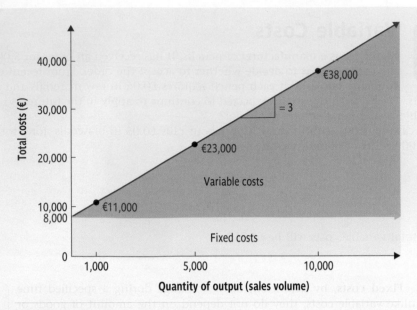

**Figure 10.3** Output level and total costs

---

<table>
<tr><td>EXAMPLE<br>**10.2**</td><td></td></tr>
</table>

## Average Cost versus Marginal Cost

Suppose Blume plc has a variable cost per pencil of £0.55. The lease payment on the production facility is £5,000 per month. If Blume produces 100,000 pencils per year, what are the total costs of production? What is the average cost per pencil?

The fixed costs are £5,000 per month, or £60,000 per year. The variable cost is £0.55 per pencil. So the total cost for the year, assuming that Blume produces 100,000 pencils, is

$$
\begin{aligned}
\text{Total cost} &= v \times Q + \text{FC} \\
&= £0.55 \times 100,000 + £60,000 \\
&= £115,000
\end{aligned}
$$

The average cost per pencil is £115,000/100,000 = £1.15.

Now suppose that Blume has received a special, one-off order for 5,000 pencils. Blume has sufficient capacity to manufacture the 5,000 pencils on top of the 100,000 already produced, so no additional fixed costs will be incurred. Also, there will be no effect on existing orders. If Blume can get £0.75 per pencil for this order, should the order be accepted?

What this boils down to is a simple proposition. It costs £0.55 to make another pencil. Anything Blume can get for this pencil in excess of the £0.55 incremental cost contributes in a positive way towards covering fixed costs. The £0.75 **marginal**, or **incremental**, **revenue** exceeds the £0.55 marginal cost, so Blume should take the order.

The fixed cost of £60,000 is not relevant to this decision, because it is effectively sunk, at least for the current period. In the same way, the fact that the average cost is £1.15 is irrelevant, because this average reflects the fixed cost. As long as producing the extra 5,000 pencils truly does not cost anything beyond the £0.55 per pencil, then Blume should accept anything over £0.55.

> **marginal, or incremental, revenue**
> The change in revenue that occurs when there is a small change in output.

## Accounting Break-Even

The most widely used measure of break-even is **accounting break-even**. The accounting break-even point is simply the sales level that results in a zero project net income.

To determine a project's accounting break-even, we start off with some common sense. Suppose we retail USB flash drives for £5 apiece. We can buy drives from a wholesale supplier for £3 apiece. We have accounting expenses of £600 in fixed costs and £300 in depreciation. How many drives do we have to sell to break even – that is, for net income to be zero?

For every drive we sell, we pick up £5 − 3 = £2 towards covering our other expenses (this £2 difference between the selling price and the variable cost is often called the *contribution margin per unit*). We have to cover a total of £600 + 300 = £900 in accounting expenses, so we obviously need to sell £900/2 = 450 drives. We can check this by noting that at a sales level of 450 units our revenues are £5 × 450 = £2,250 and our variable costs are £3 × 450 = £1,350. Thus here is the income statement:

| | |
|---|---|
| Sales (£) | 2,250 |
| Variable costs (£) | 1,350 |
| Fixed costs (£) | 600 |
| Depreciation (£) | 300 |
| Profit before taxes (£) | 0 |
| Taxes (28%) (£) | 0 |
| Net income (£) | 0 |

Remember, because we are discussing a proposed new project, we do not consider any interest expense in calculating net income or cash flow from the project. Also, notice that we include depreciation in calculating expenses here, even though depreciation is not a cash outflow. That is why we call it an *accounting* break-even. Finally, notice that when net income is zero, so are pre-tax income and, of course, taxes. In accounting terms, our revenues are equal to our costs, so there is no profit to tax.

Figure 10.4 presents another way to see what is happening. This figure looks a lot like Fig. 10.3 except that we add a line for revenues. As indicated, total revenues are zero when output is zero. Beyond that, each unit sold brings in another £5, so the slope of the revenue line is 5.

From our preceding discussion we know that we break even when revenues are equal to total costs. The line for revenues and the line for total costs cross exactly where output is at 450 units. As illustrated, at any level of output below 450 our accounting profit is negative, and at any level above 450 we have a positive net income.

## Accounting Break-Even: A Closer Look

In our numerical example, notice that the break-even level is equal to the sum of fixed costs and depreciation, divided by price per unit less variable costs per unit. This is always true. To see why, we recall all of the following variables:

$P$ = Selling price per unit

$v$ = Variable cost per unit

$Q$ = Total units sold

$S$ = Total sales = $P \times Q$

VC = Total variable costs = $v \times Q$

FC = Fixed costs

$D$ = Depreciation

$T$ = Tax rate

FIGURE
**10.4**

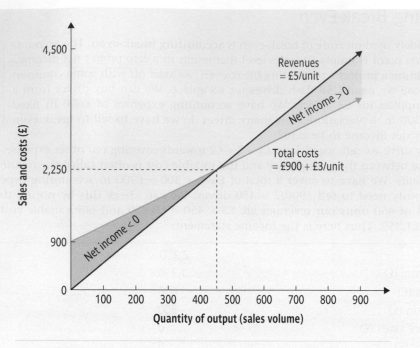

**Figure 10.4** Accounting break-even

Project net income is given by

Net income = (Sales − Variable costs − Fixed costs − Depreciation) × (1 − $T$)
= ($S$ − VC − FC − $D$) × (1 − $T$)

From here, it is not difficult to calculate the break-even point. If we set this net income equal to zero, we get

Net income $\overset{\text{SET}}{=}$ 0 = ($S$ − VC − FC − $D$) × (1 − $T$)

Divide both sides by (1 − $T$) to get

$$S - \text{VC} - \text{FC} - D = 0$$

As we have seen, this says that when net income is zero, so is pre-tax income. If we recall that $S = P \times Q$ and VC = $v \times Q$, then we can rearrange the equation to solve for the break-even level:

$$
\begin{aligned}
S - \text{VC} &= \text{FC} + D \\
P \times Q - v \times Q &= \text{FC} + D \\
(P - v) \times Q &= \text{FC} + D \\
Q &= (\text{FC} + D)/(P - v)
\end{aligned}
$$

(10.1)

This is the same result we described earlier.

## Uses for the Accounting Break-Even

Why would anyone be interested in knowing the accounting break-even point? To illustrate how it can be useful, suppose we are a small ice cream manufacturer with a strictly local distribution. We are thinking about expanding into new markets. Based on the estimated cash flows, we find that the expansion has a positive NPV.

Going back to our discussion of forecasting risk, we know that it is likely that what will make or break our expansion is sales volume. The reason is that, in this case at least, we probably have a fairly good idea of what we can charge for the ice cream. Further, we know relevant production and distribution costs reasonably well, because we are already in the business. What we do not know with any real precision is how much ice cream we can sell.

Given the costs and selling price, however, we can immediately calculate the break-even point. Once we have done so, we might find that we need to get 30 per cent of the market just to break even. If we think that this is unlikely to occur, because, for example, we have only 10 per cent of our current market, then we know our forecast is questionable, and there is a real possibility that the true NPV is negative. On the other hand, we might find that we already have firm commitments from buyers for about the break-even amount, so we are almost certain we can sell more. In this case the forecasting risk is much lower, and we have greater confidence in our estimates.

There are several other reasons why knowing the accounting break-even can be useful. First, as we shall discuss in more detail later, accounting break-even and payback period are similar measures. Like payback period, accounting break-even is relatively easy to calculate and explain.

Second, managers are often concerned with the contribution a project will make to the firm's total accounting earnings. A project that does not break even in an accounting sense actually reduces total earnings.

Third, a project that just breaks even on an accounting basis loses money in a financial or opportunity cost sense. This is true because we could have earned more by investing elsewhere. Such a project does not lose money in an out-of-pocket sense. As described in the following pages, we get back exactly what we put in. For non-economic reasons, opportunity losses may be easier to live with than out-of-pocket losses.

| CONCEPT QUESTIONS | 10.3a | How are fixed costs similar to sunk costs? |
| --- | --- | --- |
| | 10.3b | What is net income at the accounting break-even point? What about taxes? |
| | 10.3c | Why might a financial manager be interested in the accounting break-even point? |

# 10.4 Operating Cash Flow, Sales Volume and Break-Even

Accounting break-even is one tool that is useful for project analysis. Ultimately, however, we are more interested in cash flow than in accounting income. So, for example, if sales volume is the critical variable, then we need to know more about the relationship between sales volume and cash flow than just the accounting break-even.

Our goal in this section is to illustrate the relationship between operating cash flow and sales volume. We also discuss some other break-even measures. To simplify matters somewhat, we shall ignore the effect of taxes. We start off by looking at the relationship between accounting break-even and cash flow.

## Accounting Break-Even and Cash Flow

Now that we know how to find the accounting break-even, it is natural to wonder what happens with cash flow. To illustrate, suppose Wettway Yachts Ltd is considering whether to launch its new Margo-class yacht. The selling price will be £40,000 per boat. The variable costs will be about half that, or £20,000 per boat, and fixed costs will be £500,000 per year.

**The Base Case**  The total investment needed to undertake the project is £3,500,000. For simplicity, this amount will be depreciated straight-line to zero over the five-year life of the equipment.[1] The salvage value is zero, and there are no working capital consequences. Wettway has a 20 per cent required return on new projects.

Based on market surveys and historical experience, Wettway projects total sales for the five years at 425 boats, or about 85 boats per year. Ignoring taxes, should this project be launched?

To begin, ignoring taxes, the operating cash flow at 85 boats per year is

$$
\begin{aligned}
\text{Operating cash flow} &= \text{EBIT} + \text{Depreciation} - \text{Taxes} \\
&= (S - VC - FC - D) + D - 0 \\
&= 85 \times (£40,000 - 20,000) - 500,000 \\
&= £1,200,000 \text{ per year}
\end{aligned}
$$

At 20 per cent, the five-year annuity factor is 2.9906, so the NPV is

$$
\begin{aligned}
\text{NPV} &= -£3,500,000 + 1,200,000 \times 2.9906 \\
&= -£3,500,000 + 3,588,720 \\
&= £88,720
\end{aligned}
$$

In the absence of additional information, the project should be launched.

**Calculating the Break-Even Level**  To begin looking a little closer at this project, you might ask a series of questions. For example, how many new boats does Wettway need to sell for the project to break even on an accounting basis? If Wettway does break even, what will be the annual cash flow from the project? What will be the return on the investment in this case?

Before fixed costs and depreciation are considered, Wettway generates £40,000 – 20,000 = £20,000 per boat (this is revenue less variable cost). Depreciation is £3,500,000/5 = £700,000 per year. Fixed costs and depreciation together total £1.2 million, so Wettway needs to sell $(FC + D)/(P - v) = £1.2$ million/20,000 = 60 boats per year to break even on an accounting basis. This is 25 boats fewer than projected sales: so, assuming that Wettway is confident its projection is accurate to within, say, 15 boats, it appears unlikely that the new investment will fail to at least break even on an accounting basis.

To calculate Wettway's cash flow in this case, we note that if 60 boats are sold, net income will be exactly zero. Recalling from the previous chapter that operating cash flow for a project can be written as net income plus depreciation (the bottom-up definition), we can see that the operating cash flow is equal to the depreciation, or £700,000 in this case. The internal rate of return is exactly zero (why?).

**Payback and Break-Even**  As our example illustrates, whenever a project breaks even on an accounting basis, the cash flow for that period will equal the depreciation. This result makes perfect accounting sense. For example, suppose we invest £100,000 in a five-year project. The depreciation is straight-line to a zero salvage, or £20,000 per year. If the project exactly breaks even in every period, then the cash flow will be £20,000 per period.

The sum of the cash flows for the life of this project is 5 × £20,000 = £100,000, the original investment. What this shows is that a project's payback period is exactly equal to its life if the project breaks even in every period. Similarly, a project that does better than break even has a payback that is shorter than the life of the project, and has a positive rate of return.

The bad news is that a project that just breaks even on an accounting basis has a negative NPV and a zero return. For our yacht project, the fact that Wettway will almost surely break even on an accounting basis is partially comforting, because it means that the firm's 'downside' risk (its potential loss) is limited, but we still don't know whether the project is truly profitable. More work is needed.

## Sales Volume and Operating Cash Flow

At this point we can generalize our example and introduce some other break-even measures. From our discussion in the previous section, we know that, ignoring taxes, a project's operating cash flow, OCF, can be written simply as EBIT plus depreciation:

$$OCF = [(P - v) \times Q - FC - D] + D$$
$$= (P - v) \times Q - FC$$

(10.2)

For the Wettway yacht project the general relationship (in thousands of pounds) between operating cash flow and sales volume is thus

$$OCF = (P - v) \times Q - FC$$
$$= (£40 - 20) \times Q - 500$$
$$= -£500 + 20 \times Q$$

What this tells us is that the relationship between operating cash flow and sales volume is given by a straight line with a slope of £20 and a $y$-intercept of –£500. If we calculate some different values, we get

| Quantity sold | Operating cash flow (£) |
|---|---|
| 0 | –500 |
| 15 | –200 |
| 30 | 100 |
| 50 | 500 |
| 75 | 1,000 |

These points are plotted in Fig. 10.5, where we have indicated three different break-even points. We discuss these next.

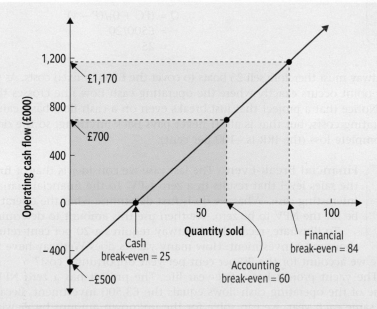

FIGURE

10.5

**Figure 10.5** Operating cash flow and sales volume

## Cash Flow, Accounting and Financial Break-Even Points

We know from the preceding discussion that the relationship between operating cash flow and sales volume (ignoring taxes) is:

$$OCF = (P - v) \times Q - FC$$

If we rearrange this and solve for $Q$, we get

$$Q = \frac{FC + OCF}{P - v} \qquad\qquad (10.3)$$

This tells us what sales volume ($Q$) is necessary to achieve any given OCF, so this result is more general than the accounting break-even. We use it to find the various break-even points in Fig. 10.5.

**Accounting Break-Even Revisited**   Looking at Fig. 10.5, suppose operating cash flow is equal to depreciation ($D$). Recall that this situation corresponds to our break-even point on an accounting basis. To find the sales volume, we substitute the £700 depreciation amount for OCF in our general expression:

$$
\begin{aligned}
Q &= (FC + OCF)/(P - v) \\
&= (£500 + 700)/20 \\
&= 60
\end{aligned}
$$

This is the same quantity we had before.

**Cash Break-Even**   We have seen that a project that breaks even on an accounting basis has a net income of zero, but it still has a positive cash flow. At some sales level below the accounting break-even, the operating cash flow actually goes negative. This is a particularly unpleasant occurrence. If it happens, we actually have to supply additional cash to the project just to keep it afloat.

> **cash break-even**
> The sales level that results in a zero operating cash flow.

To calculate the **cash break-even** (the point where operating cash flow is equal to zero), we put in a zero for OCF:

$$
\begin{aligned}
Q &= (FC + 0)/(P - v) \\
&= £500/20 \\
&= 25
\end{aligned}
$$

Wettway must therefore sell 25 boats to cover the £500 in fixed costs. As we show in Fig. 10.5, this point occurs exactly where the operating cash flow line crosses the horizontal axis.

Notice that a project that just breaks even on a cash flow basis can cover its own fixed operating costs, but that is all. It never pays back anything, so the original investment is a complete loss (the IRR is −100 per cent).

> **financial break-even**
> The sales level that results in a zero NPV.

**Financial Break-Even**   The last case we consider is that of **financial break-even**, the sales level that results in a zero NPV. To the financial manager this is the most interesting case. What we do is first determine what the operating cash flow has to be for the NPV to be zero. We then use this amount to determine the sales volume.

To illustrate, recall that Wettway requires a 20 per cent return on its £3,500 (in thousands) investment. How many yachts does Wettway have to sell to break even once we account for the 20 per cent per year opportunity cost?

The yacht project has a five-year life. The project has a zero NPV when the present value of the operating cash flows equals the £3,500 investment. Because the cash flow is the same each year, we can solve for the unknown amount by viewing it as an ordinary annuity. The five-year annuity factor at 20 per cent is 2.9906, and the OCF can be determined as follows:

$$£3,500 = OCF \times 2.9906$$
$$OCF = £3,500/2.9906$$
$$= £1,170$$

Wettway thus needs an operating cash flow of £1,170 each year to break even. We can now plug this OCF into the equation for sales volume:

$$Q = (£500 + 1,170)/20$$
$$= 83.5$$

So, Wettway needs to sell about 84 boats per year. This is not good news.

As indicated in Fig. 10.5, the financial break-even is substantially higher than the accounting break-even. This will often be the case. Moreover, what we have discovered is that the yacht project has a substantial degree of forecasting risk. We project sales of 85 boats per year, but it takes 84 just to earn the required return.

**Conclusion**   Overall, it seems unlikely that the Wettway yacht project would fail to break even on an accounting basis. However, there appears to be a very good chance that the true NPV is negative. This illustrates the danger in looking at just the accounting break-even.

What should Wettway do? Is the new project all wet? The decision at this point is essentially a managerial issue – a judgement call. The crucial questions are these:

1 How much confidence do we have in our projections?

2 How important is the project to the future of the company?

3 How badly will the company be hurt if sales turn out to be low? What options are available to the company in this case?

We shall consider questions such as these in a later section. For future reference, our discussion of the different break-even measures is summarized in Table 10.1.

| CONCEPT QUESTIONS | |
|---|---|
| 10.4a | If a project breaks even on an accounting basis, what is its operating cash flow? |
| 10.4b | If a project breaks even on a cash basis, what is its operating cash flow? |
| 10.4c | If a project breaks even on a financial basis, what do you know about its *discounted* payback? |

## 10.5  Operating Leverage

We have discussed how to calculate and interpret various measures of break-even for a proposed project. What we have not explicitly discussed is what determines these points, and how they might be changed. We now turn to this subject.

### The Basic Idea

**Operating leverage** is the degree to which a project or firm is committed to fixed production costs. A firm with low operating leverage will have low fixed costs compared with a firm with high operating leverage. Generally speaking, projects with a relatively heavy investment in plant and equipment will have a relatively high degree of operating leverage. Such projects are said to be *capital intensive*.

Whenever we are thinking about a new venture, there will normally be alternative ways of producing and delivering the product. For example, Wettway can purchase the necessary equipment and build all the components for its yachts in-house. Alternatively, some of the work could be farmed out to other firms. The

**operating leverage**
The degree to which a firm or project relies on fixed costs.

TABLE
**10.1**

### The general break-even expression

Ignoring taxes, the relation between operating cash flow (OCF) and quantity of output or sales volume ($Q$) is

$$Q = \frac{FC + OCF}{P - v}$$

where
  FC = Total fixed costs
  P = Price per unit
  v = Variable cost per unit

As shown next, this relation can be used to determine the accounting, cash, and financial break-even points.

### The accounting break-even point

Accounting break-even occurs when net income is zero. Operating cash flow is equal to depreciation when net income is zero, so the accounting break-even point is

$$Q = \frac{FC + D}{P - v}$$

A project that always just breaks even on an accounting basis has a payback exactly equal to its life, a negative NPV, and an IRR of zero.

### The cash break-even point

Cash break-even occurs when operating cash flow is zero. The cash break-even point is thus

$$Q = \frac{FC}{P - v}$$

A project that always just breaks even on a cash basis never pays back, has an NPV that is negative and equal to the initial outlay, and has an IRR of −100 per cent.

### The financial break-even point

Financial break-even occurs when the NPV of the project is zero. The financial break-even point is thus

$$Q = \frac{FC + OCF^*}{P - v}$$

where OCF* is the level of OCF that results in a zero NPV. A project that breaks even on a financial basis has a discounted payback equal to its life, a zero NPV, and an IRR just equal to the required return.

**Table 10.1** Summary of break-even measures

first option involves a greater investment in plant and equipment, greater fixed costs and depreciation, and, as a result, a higher degree of operating leverage.

## Implications of Operating Leverage

Regardless of how it is measured, operating leverage has important implications for project evaluation. Fixed costs act like a lever in the sense that a small percentage change in operating revenue can be magnified into a large percentage change in operating cash flow and NPV. This explains why we call it operating 'leverage'.

The higher the degree of operating leverage, the greater is the potential danger from forecasting risk. The reason is that relatively small errors in forecasting sales volume can get magnified, or 'levered up', into large errors in cash flow projections.

From a managerial perspective, one way of coping with highly uncertain projects is to keep the degree of operating leverage as low as possible. This will generally have the effect of keeping the break-even point (however measured) at its minimum level. We shall illustrate this point shortly, but first we need to discuss how to measure operating leverage.

## Measuring Operating Leverage

One way of measuring operating leverage is to ask: if quantity sold rises by 5 per cent, what will be the percentage change in operating cash flow? In other words, the **degree of operating leverage (DOL)** is defined such that

> **degree of operating leverage (DOL)** The percentage change in operating cash flow relative to the percentage change in quantity sold.

$$\text{Percentage change in OCF} = \text{DOL} \times \text{Percentage change in } Q$$

Based on the relationship between OCF and Q, DOL can be written as[2]

$$\text{DOL} = 1 + \text{FC/OCF} \tag{10.4}$$

The ratio FC/OCF simply measures fixed costs as a percentage of total operating cash flow. Notice that zero fixed costs would result in a DOL of 1, implying that percentage changes in quantity sold would show up one for one in operating cash flow. In other words, no magnification, or leverage, effect would exist.

To illustrate this measure of operating leverage, we go back to the Wettway yacht project. Fixed costs were £500 and $(P - v)$ was £20, so OCF was

$$\text{OCF} = -£500 + 20 \times Q$$

Suppose Q is currently 50 boats. At this level of output, OCF is $-£500 + 1,000 = £500$.

If Q rises by 1 unit to 51, then the percentage change in Q is $(51 - 50)/50 = 0.02$, or 2 per cent. OCF rises to £520, a change of $P - v = £20$. The percentage change in OCF is $(£520 - 500)/500 = 0.04$, or 4 per cent. So a 2 per cent increase in the number of boats sold leads to a 4 per cent increase in operating cash flow. The degree of operating leverage must be exactly 2.00. We can check this by noting that

$$\begin{aligned} \text{DOL} &= 1 + \text{FC/OCF} \\ &= 1 + £500/500 \\ &= 2 \end{aligned}$$

This verifies our previous calculations.

Our formulation of DOL depends on the current output level, Q. However, it can handle changes from the current level of any size, not just one unit. For example, suppose Q rises from 50 to 75, a 50 per cent increase. With DOL equal to 2, operating cash flow should increase by 100 per cent, or exactly double. Does it? The answer is yes, because, at a Q of 75, OCF is

$$\text{OCF} = -£500 + 20 \times 75 = £1,000$$

Notice that operating leverage declines as output (Q) rises. For example, at an output level of 75, we have

$$\begin{aligned} \text{DOL} &= 1 + £500/1,000 \\ &= 1.50 \end{aligned}$$

The reason why DOL declines is that fixed costs, considered as a percentage of operating cash flow, get smaller and smaller, so the leverage effect diminishes.

| EXAMPLE 10.3 | **Operating Leverage** |

Peigi Ltd currently sells gourmet dog food for £1.20 per can. The variable cost is £0.80 per can, and the packaging and marketing operations have fixed costs of £360,000 per year. Depreciation is £60,000 per year. What is the accounting break-even? Ignoring taxes, what will be the increase in operating cash flow if the quantity sold rises to 10 per cent above the break-even point?

The accounting break-even is £420,000/0.40 = 1,050,000 cans. As we know, the operating cash flow is equal to the £60,000 depreciation at this level of production, so the degree of operating leverage is

$$DOL = 1 + FC/OCF$$
$$= 1 + £360,000/60,000$$
$$= 7$$

Given this, a 10 per cent increase in the number of cans of dog food sold will increase operating cash flow by a substantial 70 per cent.

To check this answer, we note that if sales rise by 10 per cent, then the quantity sold will rise to 1,050,000 × 1.1 = 1,155,000. Ignoring taxes, the operating cash flow will be 1,155,000 × £0.40 − 360,000 = £102,000. Compared with the £60,000 cash flow we had, this is exactly 70 per cent more: £102,000/60,000 = 1.70.

## Operating Leverage and Break-Even

We illustrate why operating leverage is an important consideration by examining the Wettway yacht project under an alternative scenario. At a Q of 85 boats, the degree of operating leverage for the yacht project under the original scenario is

$$DOL = 1 + FC/OCF$$
$$= 1 + £500/1,200$$
$$= 1.42$$

Also, recall that the NPV at a sales level of 85 boats was £88,720, and that the accounting break-even was 60 boats.

An option available to Wettway is to subcontract production of the boat hull assemblies. If the company does this, the necessary investment falls to £3,200,000 and the fixed operating costs fall to £180,000. However, variable costs will rise to £25,000 per boat, because subcontracting is more expensive than producing in-house. Ignoring taxes, evaluate this option.

For practice, see if you don't agree with the following:

> NPV at 20% (85 units) = £74,720
> Accounting break-even = 55 boats
> Degree of operating leverage = 1.16

What has happened? This option results in a slightly lower estimated net present value, and the accounting break-even point falls to 55 boats from 60 boats.

Given that this alternative has the lower NPV, is there any reason to consider it further? Perhaps there is. The degree of operating leverage is substantially lower in the second case. If Wettway is worried about the possibility of an overly optimistic projection, then it might prefer to subcontract.

There is another reason why Wettway might consider the second arrangement. If sales turned out to be better than expected, the company would always have the option of starting to produce in-house at a later date. As a practical matter, it is much easier to increase operating leverage (by purchasing equipment) than to decrease it (by selling off equipment). As we discuss in a later chapter, one of the drawbacks of discounted cash flow analysis is that it is difficult to explicitly include options of this sort in the analysis, even though they may be quite important.

## 10.6  Capital Rationing

**Capital rationing** is said to exist when we have profitable (positive NPV) investments available, but we can't get the funds needed to undertake them. For example, as division managers for a large corporation, we might identify €5 million in excellent projects, but find that, for whatever reason, we can spend only €2 million. Now what? Unfortunately, for reasons we shall discuss, there may be no truly satisfactory answer.

**capital rationing**
The situation that exists if a firm has positive-NPV projects but cannot find the necessary financing.

### Soft Rationing

The situation we have just described is called **soft rationing**. This occurs when, for example, different units in a business are allocated some fixed amount of money each year for capital spending. Such an allocation is primarily a means of controlling and keeping track of overall spending. The important thing to note about soft rationing is that the corporation as a whole isn't short of capital; more can be raised on ordinary terms if management so desires.

**soft rationing**
The situation that occurs when units in a business are allocated a certain amount of financing for capital budgeting.

If we face soft rationing, the first thing to do is to try to get a larger allocation. Failing that, one common suggestion is to generate as large a net present value as possible within the existing budget. This amounts to choosing projects with the largest benefit–cost ratio (profitability index).

Strictly speaking, this is the correct thing to do only if the soft rationing is a one-time event – that is, if it won't exist next year. If the soft rationing is a chronic problem, then something is amiss. The reason goes all the way back to Chapter 1. Ongoing soft rationing means we are constantly bypassing positive-NPV investments. This contradicts our goal of the firm. If we are not trying to maximize value, then the question of which projects to take becomes ambiguous, because we no longer have an objective goal in the first place.

### Hard Rationing

With **hard rationing**, a business cannot raise capital for a project under any circumstances. For large, healthy corporations this situation probably does not occur very often. This is fortunate, because with hard rationing our DCF analysis breaks down, and the best course of action is ambiguous.

**hard rationing**
The situation that occurs when a business cannot raise financing for a project under any circumstances.

The reason why DCF analysis breaks down has to do with the required return. Suppose we say our required return is 20 per cent. Implicitly, we are saying we shall take a project with a return that exceeds this. However, if we face hard rationing, then we are not going to take a new project, no matter what the return on that project is, so the whole concept of a required return is ambiguous. About the only interpretation we can give this situation is that the required return is so large that no project has a positive NPV in the first place.

Hard rationing can occur when a company experiences financial distress, meaning that bankruptcy is a possibility. Also, a firm may not be able to raise capital without violating a pre-existing contractual agreement. We discuss these situations in greater detail in a later chapter.

| | |
|---|---|
| **CONCEPT QUESTIONS** | 10.6a What is capital rationing? What types are there? |
| | 10.6b What problems does capital rationing create for discounted cash flow analysis? |

# Summary and Conclusions

In this chapter we looked at some ways of evaluating the results of a discounted cash flow analysis; we also touched on some of the problems that can come up in practice:

1  Net present value estimates depend on projected future cash flows. If there are errors in those projections, then our estimated NPVs can be misleading. We called this possibility *forecasting risk*.

2  Scenario and sensitivity analysis are useful tools for identifying which variables are critical to the success of a project, and where forecasting problems can do the most damage.

3  Break-even analysis in its various forms is a particularly common type of scenario analysis that is useful for identifying critical levels of sales.

4  Operating leverage is a key determinant of break-even levels. It reflects the degree to which a project or a firm is committed to fixed costs. The degree of operating leverage tells us the sensitivity of operating cash flow to changes in sales volume.

5  Projects usually have future managerial options associated with them. These options may be important, but standard discounted cash flow analysis tends to ignore them.

6  Capital rationing occurs when apparently profitable projects cannot be funded. Standard discounted cash flow analysis is troublesome in this case, because NPV is not necessarily the appropriate criterion.

The most important thing to carry away from reading this chapter is that estimated NPVs or returns should not be taken at face value. They depend critically on projected cash flows. If there is room for significant disagreement about those projected cash flows, the results from the analysis have to be taken with a pinch of salt.

Despite the problems we have discussed, discounted cash flow analysis is still *the* way of attacking problems, because it forces us to ask the right questions. What we have learned in this chapter is that knowing the questions to ask does not guarantee we shall get all the answers.

## Chapter Review and Self-Test Problems

Use the following base-case information to work the self-test problems:

A project under consideration costs €750,000, has a five-year life, and has no salvage value. Depreciation is straight-line to zero. The required return is 17 per cent, and the tax rate is 34 per cent. Sales are projected at 500 units per year. Price per unit is €2,500, variable cost per unit is €1,500, and fixed costs are €200,000 per year.

**10.1 Scenario Analysis**   Suppose you think that the unit sales, price, variable cost and fixed cost projections given here are accurate to within 5 per cent. What are the upper and lower bounds for these projections? What is the base-case NPV? What are the best- and worst-case scenario NPVs?

**10.2 Break-Even Analysis**   Given the base-case projections in the previous problem, what are the cash, accounting and financial break-even sales levels for this project? Ignore taxes in answering.

## Answers to Chapter Review and Self-Test Problems

10.1   We can summarize the relevant information as follows:

|  | Base case | Lower bound | Upper bound |
|---|---|---|---|
| Unit sales | 500 | 475 | 525 |
| Price per unit (€) | 2,500 | 2,375 | 2,625 |
| Variable cost per unit (€) | 1,500 | 1,425 | 1,575 |
| Fixed cost per year (€) | 200,000 | 190,000 | 210,000 |

Depreciation is €150,000 per year; knowing this, we can calculate the cash flows under each scenario. Remember that we assign high costs and low prices and volume for the worst case, and just the opposite for the best case:

| Scenario | Unit sales | Unit price (€) | Unit variable cost (€) | Fixed costs (€) | Cash flow (€) |
|---|---|---|---|---|---|
| Base case | 500 | 2,500 | 1,500 | 200,000 | 249,000 |
| Best case | 525 | 2,625 | 1,425 | 190,000 | 341,400 |
| Worst case | 475 | 2,375 | 1,575 | 210,000 | 163,200 |

At 17 per cent the five-year annuity factor is 3.19935, so the NPVs are

$$\text{Base-case NPV} = -€750,000 + 3.19935 \times €249,000$$
$$= €46,638$$
$$\text{Best-case NPV} = -€750,000 + 3.19935 \times €341,400$$
$$= €342,258$$
$$\text{Worst-case NPV} = -€750,000 + 3.19935 \times €163,200$$
$$= -€227,866$$

10.2   In this case we have €200,000 in cash fixed costs to cover. Each unit contributes €2,500 − 1,500 = €1,000 towards covering fixed costs. The cash break-even is thus €200,000/€1,000 = 200 units. We have another €150,000 in depreciation, so the accounting break-even is (€200,000 + 150,000)/€1,000 = 350 units.

To get the financial break-even, we need to find the OCF such that the project has a zero NPV. As we have seen, the five-year annuity factor is 3.19935 and the project costs €750,000, so the OCF must be such that

$$€750,000 = OCF \times 3.19935$$

So, for the project to break even on a financial basis, the project's cash flow must be €750,000/3.19935, or €234,423 per year. If we add this to the €200,000 in cash fixed costs, we get a total of €434,423 that we have to cover. At €1,000 per unit, we need to sell €434,423/€1,000 = 435 units.

## Concepts Review and Critical Thinking Questions

1 **Forecasting Risk [LO1]** What is forecasting risk? In general, would the degree of forecasting risk be greater for a new product or a cost-cutting proposal? Why?

2 **Sensitivity Analysis and Scenario Analysis [LO1, LO2]** What is the essential difference between sensitivity analysis and scenario analysis?

3 **Marginal Cash Flows [LO3]** A co-worker claims that looking at all this marginal this and incremental that is just a bunch of nonsense, saying, 'Listen, if our average revenue doesn't exceed our average cost, then we shall have a negative cash flow, and we shall go broke!' How do you respond?

4 **Operating Leverage [LO4]** Because of the strength of trade unions in many European countries, it is very difficult to make employees redundant. What are the implications of this for the degree of operating leverage a company faces?

5 **Operating Leverage [LO4]** Airlines offer an example of an industry in which the degree of operating leverage is fairly high. Why?

6 **Break-Even [LO3]** As a shareholder of a firm that is contemplating a new project, would you be more concerned with the accounting break-even point, the cash break-even point, or the financial break-even point? Why?

7 **Break-Even [LO3]** Assume a firm is considering a new project that requires an initial investment, and has equal sales and costs over its life. Will the project reach the accounting, cash, or financial break-even point first? Which will it reach next? Last? Will this ordering always apply?

8 **Capital Rationing [LO5]** How are soft rationing and hard rationing different? What are the implications if a firm is experiencing soft rationing? Hard rationing?

9 **Capital Rationing [LO5]** Going all the way back to the beginning of the book, recall that we saw that partnerships and proprietorships can face difficulties when it comes to raising capital. In the context of this chapter, the implication is that small businesses will generally face what problem?

## connect Questions and Problems

BASIC
1 – 15

1 **Calculating Costs and Break-Even [LO3]** Night Shades NV (NS) manufactures biotech sunglasses. The variable materials cost is €5.43 per unit, and the variable labour cost is €3.13 per unit.

(a) What is the variable cost per unit?

(b) Suppose NS incurs fixed costs of €720,000 during a year in which total production is 280,000 units. What are the total costs for the year?

(c)   If the selling price is €19.99 per unit, does NS break even on a cash basis? If depreciation is €220,000 per year, what is the accounting break-even point?

2   **Computing Average Cost [LO3]** Makaveli SpA can manufacture mountain climbing shoes for €24.86 per pair in variable raw material costs and €14.08 per pair in variable labour expense. The shoes sell for €135 per pair. Last year, production was 120,000 pairs. Fixed costs were €1,550,000. What were total production costs? What is the marginal cost per pair? What is the average cost? If the company is considering a one-time order for an extra 5,000 pairs, what is the minimum acceptable total revenue from the order? Explain.

3   **Scenario Analysis [LO2]** Olin Transmissions plc has the following estimates for its new gear assembly project: price = £1,900 per unit; variable costs = £240 per unit; fixed costs = £4.8 million; quantity = 95,000 units. Suppose the company believes all of its estimates are accurate only to within ±15 per cent. What values should the company use for the four variables given here when it performs its best-case scenario analysis? What about the worst-case scenario?

4   **Sensitivity Analysis [LO1]** For the company in the previous problem, suppose management is most concerned about the impact of its price estimate on the project's profitability. How could you address this concern? Describe how you would calculate your answer. What values would you use for the other forecast variables?

5   **Sensitivity Analysis and Break-Even [LO1, LO3]** We are evaluating a project that costs £724,000, has an eight-year life, and has no salvage value. Assume that depreciation is straight-line to zero over the life of the project. Sales are projected at 90,000 units per year. Price per unit is £43, variable cost per unit is £29, and fixed costs are £780,000 per year. The tax rate is 28 per cent, and we require a 15 per cent return on this project.

(a)   Calculate the accounting break-even point. What is the degree of operating leverage at the accounting break-even point?

(b)   Calculate the base-case cash flow and NPV. What is the sensitivity of NPV to changes in the sales figure? Explain what your answer tells you about a 500-unit decrease in projected sales.

(c)   What is the sensitivity of OCF to changes in the variable cost figure? Explain what your answer tells you about a £1 decrease in estimated variable costs.

6   **Scenario Analysis [LO2]** In the previous problem, suppose the projections given for price, quantity, variable costs and fixed costs are all accurate to within ±10 per cent. Calculate the best-case and worst-case NPV figures.

7   **Calculating Break-Even [LO3]** In each of the following cases, calculate the accounting break-even and the cash break-even points. Ignore any tax effects in calculating the cash break-even.

| Unit price (NKr) | Unit variable cost (NKr) | Fixed costs (NKr) | Depreciation (NKr) |
|---|---|---|---|
| 3,020 | 2,275 | 14,000,000 | 6,500,000 |
| 2,938 | 27 | 73,000 | 150,000 |
| 2,811 | 4 | 1,200 | 840 |

8 **Calculating Break-Even [LO3]** In each of the following cases, find the unknown variable.

| Accounting break-even | Unit price (£) | Unit variable cost (£) | Fixed costs (£) | Depreciation (£) |
|---|---|---|---|---|
| 212,800 | 41 | 30 | 820,000 | ? |
| 165,000 | ? | 33 | 3,200,000 | 1,150,000 |
| 4,385 | 98 | ? | 90,000 | 105,000 |

9 **Calculating Break-Even [LO3]** A project has the following estimated data: price = £60 per unit; variable costs = £32 per unit; fixed costs = £9,000; required return = 12 per cent; initial investment = £18,000; life = four years. Ignoring the effect of taxes, what is the accounting break-even quantity? The cash break-even quantity? The financial break-even quantity? What is the degree of operating leverage at the financial break-even level of output?

10 **Using Break-Even Analysis [LO3]** Consider a project with the following data: accounting break-even quantity = 17,500 units; cash break-even quantity = 13,200 units; life = five years; fixed costs = £140,000; variable costs = £24 per unit; required return = 16 per cent. Ignoring the effect of taxes, find the financial break-even quantity.

11 **Calculating Operating Leverage [LO4]** At an output level of 80,000 units, you calculate that the degree of operating leverage is 3.40. If output falls to 70,000 units, what will the percentage change in operating cash flow be? Will the new level of operating leverage be higher or lower? Explain.

12 **Leverage [LO4]** In the previous problem, suppose fixed costs are £130,000. What is the operating cash flow at 58,000 units? The degree of operating leverage?

13 **Operating Cash Flow and Leverage [LO4]** A proposed project has fixed costs of £83,000 per year. The operating cash flow at 8,000 units is £97,500. Ignoring the effect of taxes, what is the degree of operating leverage? If units sold rise from 8,000 to 8,500, what will be the increase in operating cash flow? What is the new degree of operating leverage?

14 **Cash Flow and Leverage [LO4]** At an output level of 10,000 units, you have calculated that the degree of operating leverage is 2.1. The operating cash flow is £43,000 in this case. Ignoring the effect of taxes, what are fixed costs? What will the operating cash flow be if output rises to 11,000 units? If output falls to 9,000 units?

15 **Leverage [LO4]** In the previous problem, what will be the new degree of operating leverage in each case?

16 **Break-Even Intuition [LO3]** Consider a project with a required return of $R$ per cent that costs $€I$ and will last for $N$ years. The project uses straight-line depreciation to zero over the $N$-year life; there is no salvage value or net working capital requirements.

INTERMEDIATE

16–24

(a) At the accounting break-even level of output, what is the IRR of this project? The payback period? The NPV?

(b) At the cash break-even level of output, what is the IRR of this project? The payback period? The NPV?

(c) At the financial break-even level of output, what is the IRR of this project? The payback period? The NPV?

17 **Sensitivity Analysis [LO1]** Consider a four-year project with the following information: initial fixed asset investment = €490,000; 20 per cent reducing-balance

depreciation over the four-year life; zero salvage value; price = €32; variable costs = €19; fixed costs = €210,000; quantity sold = 110,000 units; tax rate = 34 per cent. How sensitive is OCF to changes in quantity sold?

18 **Operating Leverage [LO4]** In the previous problem, what is the degree of operating leverage at the given level of output? What is the degree of operating leverage at the accounting break-even level of output?

19 **Project Analysis [LO1, LO2, LO3, LO4]** You are considering a new product launch. The project will cost £1,700,000, have a four-year life, and have no salvage value; depreciation is 20 per cent reducing-balance. Sales are projected at 190 units per year; price per unit will be £18,000, variable cost per unit will be £11,200, and fixed costs will be £410,000 per year. The required return on the project is 12 per cent, and the relevant tax rate is 28 per cent.

   (a) Based on your experience, you think the unit sales, variable cost and fixed cost projections given here are probably accurate to within ±10 per cent. What are the upper and lower bounds for these projections? What is the base-case NPV? What are the best-case and worst-case scenarios?

   (b) Evaluate the sensitivity of your base-case NPV to changes in fixed costs.

   (c) What is the cash break-even level of output for this project (ignoring taxes)?

   (d) What is the accounting break-even level of output for this project? What is the degree of operating leverage at the accounting break-even point? How do you interpret this number?

20 **Project Analysis [LO1, LO2]** McGilla Golf has decided to sell a new line of golf clubs. The clubs will sell for €750 per set and have a variable cost of €330 per set. The company has spent €150,000 for a marketing study which determined that the company will sell 51,000 sets per year for seven years. The marketing study also determined that the company will lose sales of 11,000 sets of its high-priced clubs. The high-priced clubs sell at €1,200 and have variable costs of €650. The company will also increase sales of its cheap clubs by 9,500 sets. The cheap clubs sell for €420 and have variable costs of €190 per set. The fixed costs each year will be €8,100,000. The company has also spent €1,000,000 on research and development for the new clubs. The plant and equipment required will cost €22,400,000 and will be depreciated on a straight-line basis. The new clubs will also require an increase in net working capital of €1,250,000 that will be returned at the end of the project. The tax rate is 40 per cent, and the cost of capital is 10 per cent. Calculate the payback period, the NPV, and the IRR.

21 **Scenario Analysis [LO2]** In the previous problem, you feel that the values are accurate to within only ±10 per cent. What are the best-case and worst-case NPVs? (*Hint*: The price and variable costs for the two existing sets of clubs are known with certainty; only the sales gained or lost are uncertain.)

22 **Sensitivity Analysis [LO1]** McGilla Golf would like to know the sensitivity of NPV to changes in the price of the new clubs and the quantity of new clubs sold. What is the sensitivity of the NPV to each of these variables?

23 **Break-Even Analysis [LO3]** Hybrid cars are touted as a 'green' alternative; however, the financial aspects of hybrid ownership are not as clear. Consider the 2010 Toyota Prius Hatchback, which had a list price of £18,390 (including tax consequences) compared with an equivalent Toyota Corolla with a list price of £15,855. Additionally, the annual ownership costs (other than fuel) for the Prius are expected to be £300 more than the Corolla. The EPA mileage estimate was 40 km/l for the Prius and 32 km/l for the Corolla.

   (a) Assume that petrol costs £1.03 per litre, and you plan to keep either car for six years. How many kilometres per year would you need to drive to make the decision to buy the Prius worthwhile, ignoring the time value of money?

(b) If you drive 15,000 miles per year and keep either car for six years, what price per litre would make the decision to buy the Prius worthwhile, ignoring the time value of money?

(c) Rework parts (a) and (b) assuming the appropriate interest rate is 10 per cent and all cash flows occur at the end of the year.

(d) What assumption did the analysis in the previous parts make about the resale value of each car?

24 **Break-Even Analysis [LO3]** In an effort to capture the large jet market, Airbus invested €10.2 billion developing its A380, which is capable of carrying 800 passengers. The plane has a list price of €206 million. In discussing the plane, Airbus stated that the company would break even when 249 A380s were sold.

(a) Assuming the break-even sales figure given is the cash flow break-even, what is the cash flow per plane?

(b) Airbus promised its shareholders a 20 per cent rate of return on the investment. If sales of the plane continue in perpetuity, how many planes must the company sell per year to deliver on this promise?

(c) Suppose instead that the sales of the A380 last for only 10 years. How many planes must Airbus sell per year to deliver the same rate of return?

25 **Break-Even and Taxes [LO3]** This problem concerns the effect of taxes on the various break-even measures.

(a) Show that, assuming straight-line depreciation, when we consider taxes, the general relationship between operating cash flow, OCF, and sales volume, $Q$, can be written as

$$Q = \frac{FC + (OCF - T \times D)/(1 - T)}{P - v}$$

(b) Use the expression in part (a) to find the cash, accounting, and financial break-even points for the Wettway yacht example in the chapter. Assume a 38 per cent tax rate.

(c) In part (b), the accounting break-even should be the same as before. Why? Verify this algebraically.

26 **Operating Leverage and Taxes [LO4]** Show that if we consider the effect of taxes, the degree of operating leverage can be written as

$$DOL = 1 + \frac{FC \times (1 - T) - T \times D}{OCF}$$

Assume straight-line depreciation. Notice that this reduces to our previous result if $T = 0$. Can you interpret this in words?

27 **Scenario Analysis [LO2]** Consider a project to supply Detroit with 35,000 tons of machine screws annually for automobile production. You will need an initial $3,200,000 investment in threading equipment to get the project started; the project will last for five years. The accounting department estimates that annual fixed costs will be $450,000 and that variable costs should be $185 per ton; accounting will depreciate the initial fixed asset investment straight-line to zero over the five-year project life. It also estimates a salvage value of $500,000 after dismantling costs. The marketing department estimates that the automakers will let the contract at a selling price of $230 per ton. The engineering department estimates you will need an initial net working capital investment of $360,000. You require a 13 per cent return, and face a marginal tax rate of 38 per cent on this project.

(a)  What is the estimated OCF for this project? The NPV? Should you pursue this project?

(b)  Suppose you believe that the accounting department's initial cost and salvage value projections are accurate only to within ±15 per cent; the marketing department's price estimate is accurate only to within ±10 per cent; and the engineering department's net working capital estimate is accurate only to within ±5 per cent. What is your worst-case scenario for this project? Your best-case scenario? Do you still want to pursue the project?

28  **Sensitivity Analysis [LO1]**  In Problem 27, suppose you're confident about your own projections, but you're a little unsure about Detroit's actual machine screw requirement. What is the sensitivity of the project OCF to changes in the quantity supplied? What about the sensitivity of NPV to changes in quantity supplied? Given the sensitivity number you calculated, is there some minimum level of output below which you wouldn't want to operate? Why?

29  **Break-Even Analysis [LO3]**  Use the results of Problem 25 to find the accounting, cash, and financial break-even quantities for the company in Problem 27.

30  **Operating Leverage [LO4]**  Use the results of Problem 26 to find the degree of operating leverage for the company in Problem 27 at the base-case output level of 35,000 units. How does this number compare with the sensitivity figure you found in Problem 28? Verify that either approach will give you the same OCF figure at any new quantity level.

**MINI CASE**

# Conch Republic Electronics, Part 2

Morena Moscardini, the owner of Conch Republic Electronics, had received the capital budgeting analysis from Jay McCanless for the new PDA the company is considering. Morena was pleased with the results, but she still had concerns about the new PDA. Conch Republic had used a small market research firm for the past 20 years, but recently the founder of that firm retired. Because of this, she was not convinced the sales projections presented by the market research firm were entirely accurate. Additionally, because of rapid changes in technology, she was concerned that a competitor could enter the market. This would probably force Conch Republic to lower the sales price of its new PDA. For these reasons, she has asked Jay to analyse how changes in the price of the new PDA and changes in the quantity sold will affect the NPV of the project.

Morena has asked Jay to prepare a memo answering the following questions.

## QUESTIONS

1  How sensitive is the NPV to changes in the price of the new PDA?

2  How sensitive is the NPV to changes in the quantity sold of the new PDA?

# Endnotes

1  We use straight-line depreciation to provide the intuition underlying break-even analysis. In practice, one would use the reducing-balance method. Given that the depreciation amount would be different each year, one would need to use a spreadsheet to find the break-even level. However, the intuition underlying the discussion remains the same.

2  To see this, note that if $Q$ goes up by one unit, OCF will go up by $(P - v)$. In this case, the percentage change in $Q$ is $1/Q$, and the percentage change in OCF is $(P - v)/\text{OCF}$. Given this, we have

$$\text{Percentage change in OCF} = \text{DOL} \times \text{Percentage change in } Q$$
$$(P - v)/\text{OCF} = \text{DOL} \times 1/Q$$
$$\text{DOL} = (P - v) \times Q/\text{OCF}$$

Also, based on our definitions of OCF:

$$\text{OCF} + \text{FC} = (P - v) \times Q$$

Thus DOL can be written as

$$\text{DOL} = (\text{OCF} + \text{FC})/\text{OCF}$$
$$= 1 + \text{FC}/\text{OCF}$$

To help you grasp the key concepts of this chapter check out the extra resources posted on the Online Learning Centre at **www.mcgraw-hill.co.uk/textbooks/hillier**

Among other helpful resources there are mini-cases tailored to individual chapters.

# Some Lessons from Recent Capital Market History

## KEY NOTATIONS

| | |
|---|---|
| $D$ | Dividend |
| $P$ | Share price |
| $R$ | Return |
| $\bar{R}$ | Average return |
| $SD(R)$ or $\sigma$ | Standard deviation of returns |
| $T$ | Number of historical returns |
| $Var(R)$ or $\sigma^2$ | Variance of returns |

## LEARNING OBJECTIVES

After studying this chapter, you should understand:

**LO1** How to calculate the return on an investment.

**LO2** The historical returns on various important types of investment.

**LO3** The historical risks on various important types of investment.

**LO4** The implications of market efficiency.

RECENT YEARS have seen significant movements in financial markets, both up and down. Take the FTSE 100 as an example. Representing the fortunes of the 100 largest companies in the UK, it had an index value of 6,457 at the end of 2007. In the aftermath of the global credit crisis and the resulting collapse in equity valuations, it fell by 31 per cent to 4,434 – its worst calendar year performance since the index started in 1984. Although it slipped further in the early months of 2009 (its lowest point was in March, when it had a value of 3,512), it made an incredibly sharp recovery, and within one year (March 2010) it hit 5,600. As can be seen, between 2007 and 2010 there were tremendous potential profits to be made, but there was also the risk of losing money – lots of it. So what should you, as a stock market investor, expect when you invest your own money? In this chapter, we study market history to find out.

Thus far we haven't had much to say about what determines the required return on an investment. In one sense, the answer is simple: the required return depends on the risk of the investment. The greater the risk, the greater is the required return.

Having said this, we are left with a somewhat more difficult problem. How can we measure the amount of risk present in an investment? Put another way, what does it mean to say that one investment is riskier than another? Obviously, we need to define what we mean by *risk* if we are going to answer these questions. This is our task in the next two chapters.

From the last several chapters, we know that one of the responsibilities of the financial manager is to assess the value of proposed real asset investments. In doing this, it is important that we first look at what financial investments have to offer. At a minimum, the return we require from a proposed non-financial investment must be greater than what we can get by buying financial assets of similar risk.

Our goal in this chapter is to provide a perspective on what capital market history can tell us about risk and return. The most important thing to get out of this chapter is a feel for the numbers. What is a high return? What is a low one? More generally, what returns should we expect from financial assets, and what are the risks of such investments? This perspective is essential for understanding how to analyse and value risky investment projects.

We start our discussion of risk and return by describing the experience of investors in the world's financial markets. The introduction to this chapter showed the extent of volatility in the UK equity markets since 2007, which experienced the greatest year-on-year movements since the index started in 1984. The US has an even longer period to consider. In 1931, for example, the US stock market lost 43 per cent of its value, gaining 54 per cent just two years later. In more recent memory, the US market lost about 25 per cent of its value on one day alone (19 October 1987). What lessons, if any, can financial managers learn from such shifts in the stock market? We shall explore market history to find out.

Two central lessons emerge from our study of market history. First, there is a reward for bearing risk. Second, the greater the potential reward is, the greater is the risk. To illustrate these facts about market returns, we devote much of this chapter to reporting the statistics and numbers that make up the modern capital market history of Europe. In the next chapter these facts provide the foundation for our study of how financial markets put a price on risk.

## 11.1 Returns

We wish to discuss historical returns on different types of financial asset. The first thing we need to do, then, is to briefly discuss how to calculate the return from investing.

### Cash Returns

If you buy an asset of any sort, your gain (or loss) from that investment is called the *return on your investment*. This return will usually have two components. First, you may receive some cash directly while you own the investment. This is called the *income component* of your return. Second, the value of the asset you purchase will often change. In this case, you have a capital gain or capital loss on your investment.[1]

To illustrate, suppose Video Concept has several thousand shares of equity outstanding. You purchased some of these shares at the beginning of the year. It is now year-end, and you want to determine how well you have done on your investment.

First, over the year, a company may pay cash dividends to its shareholders. As a shareholder in Video Concept, you are a part owner of the company. If the company is profitable, it may choose to distribute some of its profits to shareholders (we discuss the details of dividend policy in a later chapter). So, as the owner of some equity, you will receive some cash. This cash is the income component from owning the shares.

In addition to the dividend, the other part of your return is the capital gain or capital loss on the equity. This part arises from changes in the value of your investment. For example, consider the cash flows illustrated in Fig. 11.1. At the beginning of the year the equity was selling for £37 per share. If you had bought 100 shares, you would have had a total outlay of £3,700. Suppose that, over the year, the equity paid a dividend of £1.85 per share. By the end of the year, then, you would have received income of

$$\text{Dividend} = £1.85 \times 100 = £185$$

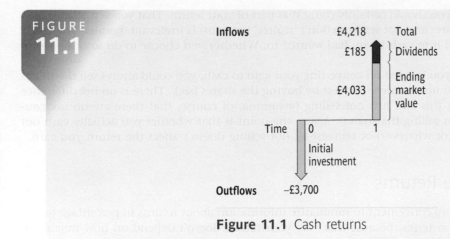

**Figure 11.1** Cash returns

Also, the value of the equity has risen to £40.33 per share by the end of the year. Your 100 shares are now worth £4,033, so you have a capital gain of

$$\text{Capital gain} = (£40.33 - 37) \times 100 = £333$$

On the other hand, if the price had dropped to, say, £34.78, you would have a capital loss of

$$\text{Capital loss} = (£34.78 - 37) \times 100 = -£222$$

Notice that a capital loss is the same thing as a negative capital gain.

The total cash return on your investment is the sum of the dividend and the capital gain:

$$\text{Total cash return} = \text{Dividend income} + \text{Capital gain (or loss)} \quad \textbf{(11.1)}$$

In our first example, the total cash return is thus given by

$$\text{Total cash return} = £185 + 333 = £518$$

Notice that if you sold the equity at the end of the year, the total amount of cash you would have would equal your initial investment plus the total return. In the preceding example, then:

$$\begin{aligned} \text{Total cash if equity is sold} &= \text{Initial investment} + \text{Total return} \quad \textbf{(11.2)} \\ &= £3,700 + 518 \\ &= £4,218 \end{aligned}$$

As a check, notice that this is the same as the proceeds from the sale of the equity plus the dividends:

$$\begin{aligned} \text{Proceeds from equity sale} + \text{Dividends} &= £40.33 \times 100 + 185 \\ &= £4,033 + 185 \\ &= £4,218 \end{aligned}$$

Suppose you hold on to your Video Concept shares and don't sell them at the end of the year. Should you still consider the capital gain as part of your return? Isn't this only a 'paper' gain and not really a cash flow if you don't sell the equity?

The answer to the first question is a strong yes, and the answer to the second is an equally strong no. The capital gain is every bit as much a part of your return as the dividend, and you should certainly count it as part of your return. That you actually decided to keep the shares and not sell (you don't 'realize' the gain) is irrelevant, because you could have converted it to cash if you had wanted to. Whether you choose to do so or not is up to you.

After all, if you insisted on converting your gain to cash, you could always sell the shares at year-end and immediately reinvest by buying the shares back. There is no net difference between doing this and just not selling (assuming, of course, that there are no tax consequences from selling the shares). Again, the point is that whether you actually cash out and buy beer (or whatever) or reinvest by not selling doesn't affect the return you earn.

## Percentage Returns

It is usually more convenient to summarize information about returns in percentage terms, rather than cash terms, because that way your return doesn't depend on how much you actually invest. The question we want to answer is this: how much do we get for each unit of cash we invest?

To answer this question, let $P_t$ be the share price at the beginning of the year and let $D_{t+1}$ be the dividend paid during the year. Consider the cash flows in Fig. 11.2. These are the same as those in Fig. 11.1, except that we have now expressed everything on a per-share basis.

In our example, the price at the beginning of the year was £37 per share and the dividend paid during the year on each share was £1.85. As we discussed in Chapter 7, expressing the dividend as a percentage of the beginning share price results in the dividend yield:

$$\text{Dividend yield} = D_{t+1}/P_t$$
$$= £1.85/37 = 0.05 = 5\%$$

This says that for each pound we invest, we get five pence in dividends.

The second component of our percentage return is the capital gains yield. Recall (from Chapter 7) that this is calculated as the change in the price during the year (the capital gain) divided by the beginning price:

$$\text{Capital gains yield} = (P_{t+1} - P_t)/P_t$$
$$= (£40.33 - 37)/37$$
$$= £3.33/37$$
$$= 9\%$$

So, per pound invested, we get nine pence in capital gains.

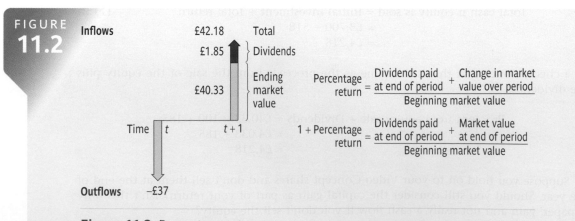

**Figure 11.2** Percentage returns

Putting it together, per pound invested, we get 5 pence in dividends and 9 pence in capital gains; so we get a total of 14 pence. Our percentage return is 14 pence on the pound, or 14 per cent.

To check this, notice that we invested £3,700 and ended up with £4,218. By what percentage did our £3,700 increase? As we saw, we picked up £4,218 − 3,700 = £518. This is a £518/3,700 = 14% increase.

---

**EXAMPLE 11.1**

## Calculating Returns

Suppose you bought some equity at the beginning of the year for €25 per share. At the end of the year, the share price is €35. During the year, you got a €2 dividend per share. This is the situation illustrated in Fig. 11.3. What is the dividend yield? The capital gains yield? The percentage return? If your total investment was €1,000, how much do you have at the end of the year?

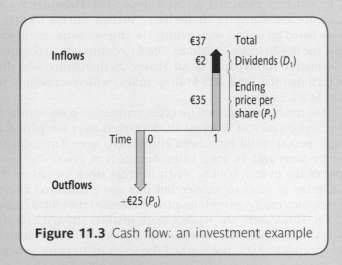

**Figure 11.3** Cash flow: an investment example

Your €2 dividend per share works out to a dividend yield of

$$\text{Dividend yield} = D_{t+1}/P_t$$
$$= €2/25 = 0.08 = 8\%$$

The per-share capital gain is €10, so the capital gains yield is

$$\text{Capital gains yield} = (P_{t-1} - P_t)/P_t$$
$$= (€35 - 25)/25$$
$$= €10/25$$
$$= 40\%$$

The total percentage return is thus 48 per cent.

If you had invested €1,000, you would have €1,480 at the end of the year, representing a 48 per cent increase. To check this, note that your €1,000 would have bought you €1,000/25 = 40 shares. Your 40 shares would then have paid you a total of 40 × €2 = €80 in cash dividends. Your €10 per share gain would give you a total capital gain of €10 × 40 = €400. Add these together, and you get the €480 increase.

---

To give another example, equity in the mining firm Fresnillo began 2009 at £2.30 per share. Fresnillo paid dividends of £0.077 during 2009, and the share price at the end of the year was £7.819. What was the return on Fresnillo for the year? For practice, see if you agree that the answer is 243.3 per cent. Of course, negative returns occur as well. For example, again in 2009, Royal Bank of Scotland's share price at the beginning of the year was £0.494, and no dividends were paid. The equity ended the year at £0.292 per share. Verify that the loss was 40.8 per cent for the year.

| CONCEPT QUESTIONS | 11.1a | What are the two parts of total return? |
| --- | --- | --- |
| | 11.1b | Why are unrealized capital gains or losses included in the calculation of returns? |
| | 11.1c | What is the difference between a cash return and a percentage return? Why are percentage returns more convenient? |

## 11.2 The Historical Record

In this section we shall discuss the historical rates of return on a number of different securities in different countries across Europe. The countries we look at are Belgium, Denmark, France, Germany, the Netherlands, Sweden and the UK. The large company share portfolios are based on indices representing the largest companies in each country. These are, respectively, the Bel-20 Index (Belgium), OMX Copenhagen 20 (Denmark), CAC 40 (France), DAX30 (Germany), Amsterdam SE All Shares (Netherlands), and the FTSE 100 (UK). We have also included the FTSE 250 Midcap Index, which represents smaller companies on the London Stock Exchange.

None of the returns are adjusted for taxes, transaction costs or inflation. Figure 11.4 shows the relative performance of different stock markets over the period 2001–2010. Clearly, a much longer period could have been considered, since European stock exchanges have been open for years and, in some cases, hundreds of years. The period (2001) starts with the collapse of the hi-tech bubble, when Internet stock valuations dropped precipitously. It took a number of years to recover, but this was a sustained growth period until 2007, when the subprime mortgage crisis erupted and caused the global credit crunch that markets faced in 2008. Fortunately, the world's stock markets showed exceptional performance in 2009, giving much needed returns to Europe's investors. Unfortunately, valuations in most European countries had still not reached the levels of 10 years earlier, and an investor who

**FIGURE 11.4**

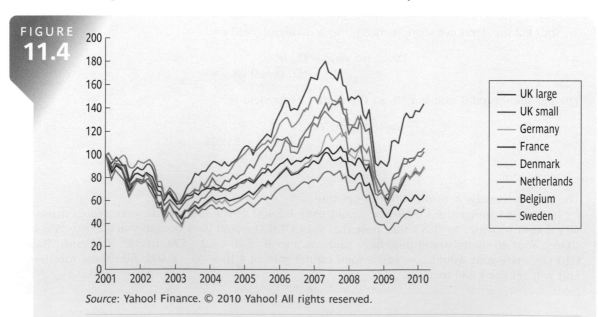

*Source*: Yahoo! Finance. © 2010 Yahoo! All rights reserved.

**Figure 11.4** Stock market index levels for a number of European countries, 2001–2010

| Date | UK large | UK small | Germany | France | Denmark | Netherlands | Belgium | Sweden |
|---|---|---|---|---|---|---|---|---|
| Jan 2000 | 6,268 | 6,181 | 6,835 | 5,659 | 250 | 612 | 2,806 | N/A |
| Jan 2001 | 6,297 | 6,735 | 6,795 | 5,998 | 347 | 639 | 2,968 | 303 |
| Jan 2002 | 5,164 | 5,849 | 5,107 | 4,461 | 263 | 500 | 2,764 | 225 |
| Jan 2003 | 3,567 | 4,016 | 2,747 | 2,937 | 186 | 294 | 1,882 | 144 |
| Jan 2004 | 4,390 | 6,023 | 4,058 | 3,638 | 261 | 353 | 2,383 | 205 |
| Jan 2005 | 4,852 | 7,166 | 4,254 | 3,913 | 291 | 360 | 2,997 | 229 |
| Jan 2006 | 5,760 | 9,172 | 5,674 | 4,947 | 389 | 450 | 3,744 | 307 |
| Jan 2007 | 6,203 | 11,100 | 6,789 | 5,608 | 462 | 499 | 4,433 | 386 |
| Jan 2008 | 5,879 | 9,881 | 6,851 | 4,869 | 407 | 441 | 3,722 | 309 |
| Jan 2009 | 4,149 | 6,250 | 4,338 | 2,973 | 261 | 248 | 1,900 | 192 |
| Jan 2010 | 5,188 | 9,237 | 5,608 | 3,739 | 354 | 327 | 2,505 | 301 |

*Source*: Yahoo! Finance. © 2010 Yahoo!

**Table 11.1** Year-by-year stock market index levels for different countries, 2000–2010

bought shares in 2001 would have not recouped her investment in 2010 had she invested in large UK, French, German, Dutch or Belgian firms.

Table 11.1 presents the index values for each stock market for every year between 2001 and 2010. The numbers in Table 11.1 also show that an investor must be careful when reading information on company or stock market performance. For example, if one were to look at the return for the United Kingdom between 2000 and 2010, and compare this with the return for the same country in 2009, conflicting messages would be given. The average annual return (calculate the annual return for each year, and average over the full sample period) for the years 2000–2010 is 0.19 per cent, compared with the annual return for 2009 of 25.04 per cent! Which is the correct performance measure? Unfortunately, both are correct from different perspectives.

Figure 11.4 gives the growth of an investment in various stock markets between 2000 and 2010. In other words, it shows what the worth of the investment would have been if the money that was initially invested had been left in the stock market, and if each year the dividends from the previous year had been reinvested in more shares. If $R_t$ is the return in year $t$ (expressed in decimals), the value you would have at the end of year $T$ is the product of 1 plus the return in each of the years:

$$(1 + R_1) \times (1 + R_2) \times \cdots \times (1 + R_t) \times \cdots \times (1 + R_T)$$

For example, in Table 11.2 the index values in Table 11.1 are presented as annual percentage returns.

The next thing to consider is the difference in performance between large and small companies (shown here for the UK). Notice how, in almost every year, small companies had larger returns (whether positive or negative) than large companies. We shall discuss why later in the chapter.

| CONCEPT QUESTIONS | |
|---|---|
| 11.2a | With 20/20 hindsight, what would you say was the best investment for the period from 2000 through 2010? |
| 11.2b | Why doesn't everyone just buy small equities as investments? |
| 11.2c | About how many times did large-company equities return more than 30 per cent? How many times did they return less than −20 per cent? |
| 11.2d | What was the longest 'winning streak' (years without a negative return) for large-company equities? |

TABLE
**11.2**

| Year | UK large | UK small | Germany | France | Denmark | Netherlands | Belgium | Sweden |
|------|----------|----------|---------|--------|---------|-------------|---------|--------|
| 2000 | 0.46 | 8.96 | −0.59 | 5.99 | 38.80 | 4.41 | 5.77 | – |
| 2001 | −17.99 | −13.16 | −24.84 | −25.63 | −24.21 | −21.75 | −6.87 | −25.74 |
| 2002 | −30.93 | −31.34 | −46.21 | −34.16 | −29.28 | −41.20 | −31.91 | −36.00 |
| 2003 | 23.07 | 49.98 | 47.72 | 23.87 | 40.32 | 20.07 | 26.62 | 42.36 |
| 2004 | 10.52 | 18.98 | 4.83 | 7.56 | 11.49 | 1.98 | 25.77 | 11.71 |
| 2005 | 18.71 | 27.99 | 33.38 | 26.42 | 33.68 | 25.00 | 24.92 | 34.06 |
| 2006 | 7.69 | 21.02 | 19.65 | 13.36 | 18.77 | 10.89 | 18.40 | 25.73 |
| 2007 | −5.22 | −10.98 | 0.91 | −13.18 | −11.90 | −11.62 | −16.04 | −19.95 |
| 2008 | −29.43 | −36.75 | −36.68 | −38.94 | −35.87 | −43.76 | −48.95 | −37.86 |
| 2009 | 25.04 | 47.79 | 29.28 | 25.77 | 35.63 | 31.85 | 31.84 | 56.77 |

**Table 11.2** Year-by-year stock market returns (percentages) for different countries, 2000–2009

# 11.3  Average Returns: The First Lesson

As you've probably begun to notice, the history of capital market returns is too complicated to be of much use in its undigested form. We need to begin summarizing all these numbers. Accordingly, we discuss how to go about condensing the detailed data. We start out by calculating average returns.

## Calculating Average Returns

The obvious way to calculate the average returns on the different indices in Table 11.2 is simply to add up the yearly returns and divide by 10. The result is the historical average of the individual values.

For example, if you add up the returns for the UK large company equities for the 10 years, you will get about 1.94. The average annual return is thus 1.94/10 = 0.194%. You interpret this 0.194 per cent, just like any other average. If you were to pick a year at random from the 10-year history, and you had to guess what the return in that year was, the best guess would be 0.194 per cent.

## Average Returns: The Historical Record

Table 11.3 shows the average returns for the indices we have discussed. As shown, in a typical year, UK small company equities increased in value by 8.25 per cent. Notice also how much larger the small company returns are than the large company returns.

Clearly, the 10-year period between 2001 and 2010 has been exceptional in the history of stock markets. A much longer period to assess average returns would be better, because then short-term volatility would be likely to even out. Fortunately, the US has data starting in 1927, and the average returns for a variety of instruments are presented in Table 11.4.

These averages are of course nominal, because we haven't worried about inflation. Notice that the average inflation rate in the US was 3.1 per cent per year over this 82-year span. The nominal return on US Treasury bills was 3.8 per cent per year. The average real return on US Treasury bills was thus approximately 0.7 per cent per year: so the real return on US T-bills has been quite low historically.

| TABLE 11.3 | Investment | Average return (%) |
|---|---|---|
| | UK large companies | 0.19 |
| | UK small companies | 8.25 |
| | Belgian companies | 2.96 |
| | Danish companies | 7.74 |
| | French companies | −0.89 |
| | German companies | 2.75 |
| | Dutch companies | −2.41 |
| | Swedish companies (from 2002) | 5.68 |

**Table 11.3** Average annual returns: 2001–2010

| TABLE 11.4 | Investment | Average return (%) |
|---|---|---|
| | US large companies | 12.3 |
| | US small companies | 17.1 |
| | Long-term corporate bonds | 6.2 |
| | Long-term government bonds | 5.8 |
| | US Treasury bills | 3.8 |
| | Inflation | 3.1 |

**Table 11.4** Average annual returns for US securities: 1926–2007

At the other extreme, small company equities had an average real return of about 17.1% – 3.1% = 14%, which is relatively large. If you remember the Rule of 72 (Chapter 5), then you know that a quick back-of-the-envelope calculation tells us that 14 per cent real growth doubles your buying power about every five years. Notice also that the real value of the large-company stock portfolio increased by over 9 per cent in a typical year.

## Risk Premiums

Now that we have computed some average returns, it seems logical to see how they compare with each other. One such comparison involves government-issued securities. These are free of much of the variability we see in the stock market, for example.

The government borrows money by issuing bonds in different forms. The ones we shall focus on are the Treasury bills. These have the shortest time to maturity of the different government bonds. Because the government can always raise taxes to pay its bills, the debt represented by T-bills is virtually free of any default risk over its short life. Thus we shall call the rate of return on such debt the *risk-free return*, and we shall use it as a kind of benchmark.

A particularly interesting comparison involves the virtually risk-free return on T-bills and the very risky return on ordinary equities. The difference between these two returns

| Investment | Average return (%) | Risk premium (%) |
|---|---|---|
| Large companies | 12.3 | 8.5 |
| Small companies | 17.1 | 13.3 |
| Long-term corporate bonds | 6.2 | 2.4 |
| Long-term government bonds | 5.8 | 2.0 |
| US Treasury bills | 3.8 | 0.0 |

*Source: Ibbotson® Stocks, Bonds, Bills and Inflation 2008 Yearbook;* annually updates work by Roger G. Ibbotson and Rex A. Sinquefield (Chicago: Morningstar). All rights reserved.

**Table 11.5** Average US annual returns and risk premiums: 1926–2007

can be interpreted as a measure of the *excess return* on the average risky asset (assuming that the equity of a large corporation has about average risk compared with all risky assets).

**risk premium**
The excess return required from an investment in a risky asset over that required from a risk-free investment.

We call this the 'excess' return, because it is the additional return we earn by moving from a relatively risk-free investment to a risky one. Because it can be interpreted as a reward for bearing risk, we shall call it a **risk premium**.

Using Table 11.4, we can calculate the risk premiums for the different investments: these are shown in Table 11.5. We report only the nominal risk premiums, because there is only a slight difference between the historical nominal and real risk premiums.

The risk premium on T-bills is shown as zero in the table because we have assumed that they are riskless.

## The First Lesson

Looking at Table 11.3, one would be worried about investing in European equities. However, over the longer term there is much less volatility in returns. For US securities over a significantly longer period (Table 11.3), we see that the average risk premium earned by a typical US large-company equity is 12.3% – 3.8% = 8.5%. This is a significant reward. The fact that it exists historically is an important observation, and it is the basis for our first lesson: over the long term, risky assets, on average, earn a risk premium. Put another way, there is a reward for bearing risk.

Why is this so? Why, for example, is the risk premium for small-company equities so much larger than the risk premium for large-company equities? More generally, what determines the relative sizes of the risk premiums for the different assets? The answers to these questions are at the heart of modern finance, and the next chapter is devoted to them. For now, we can find part of the answer by looking at the historical variability of the returns on these different investments. So, to get started, we now turn our attention to measuring variability in returns.

---

**CONCEPT QUESTIONS**

11.3a   What do we mean by *excess return* and *risk premium*?

11.3b   What was the real (as opposed to nominal) risk premium on the US large company portfolio?

11.3c   What was the nominal risk premium on US corporate bonds? The real risk premium?

11.3d   What is the first lesson from capital market history?

## 11.4  The Variability of Returns: The Second Lesson

We have already seen that the year-to-year returns on equities tend to be more volatile than the returns on, say, long-term government bonds. We now discuss measuring this variability of equity returns so that we can begin examining the subject of risk.

### Return Variability

What we need to do is to measure the spread in returns. We know, for example, that the return on UK small company equities in a typical year was 8.25 per cent. We now want to know how much the actual return deviates from this average in a typical year. In other words, we need a measure of how volatile the return is. The **variance** and its square root, the **standard deviation**, are the most commonly used measures of volatility. We describe how to calculate them next.

> **variance**
> The average squared difference between the actual return and the average return.
>
> **standard deviation**
> The positive square root of the variance.

### The Historical Variance and Standard Deviation

The variance essentially measures the average squared difference between the actual returns and the average return. The bigger this number is, the more the actual returns tend to differ from the average return. Also, the larger the variance or standard deviation is, the more spread out the returns will be.

The way we calculate the variance and standard deviation will depend on the specific situation. In this chapter we are looking at historical returns, so the procedure we describe here is the correct one for calculating the *historical* variance and standard deviation. If we were examining projected future returns, then the procedure would be different. We describe this procedure in the next chapter.

To illustrate how we calculate the historical variance, suppose a particular investment has had returns of 10 per cent, 12 per cent, 3 per cent and –9 per cent over the last four years. The average return is $(0.10 + 0.12 + 0.03 - 0.09)/4 = 4\%$. Notice that the return is never actually equal to 4 per cent. Instead, the first return deviates from the average by $0.10 - 0.04 = 0.06$, the second return deviates from the average by $0.12 - 0.04 = 0.08$, and so on. To compute the variance, we square each of these deviations, add them up, and divide the result by the number of returns less 1, or 3 in this case. Most of this information is summarized in the following table:

| | (1)<br>Actual return | (2)<br>Average return | (3)<br>Deviation (1)–(2) | (4)<br>Squared deviation |
|---|---|---|---|---|
| | 0.10 | 0.04 | 0.06 | 0.0036 |
| | 0.12 | 0.04 | 0.08 | 0.0064 |
| | 0.03 | 0.04 | −0.01 | 0.0001 |
| | −0.09 | 0.04 | −0.13 | 0.0169 |
| Totals | 0.16 | | 0.00 | 0.0270 |

In the first column we write the four actual returns. In the third column we calculate the difference between the actual returns and the average by subtracting 4 per cent. Finally, in the fourth column we square the numbers in the third column to get the squared deviations from the average.

The variance can now be calculated by dividing 0.0270, the sum of the squared deviations, by the number of returns less 1. Let Var($R$), or $\sigma^2$ (read this as 'sigma squared'), stand for the variance of the return:

$$\text{Var}(R) = \sigma^2 = 0.027/(4 - 1) = 0.009$$

The standard deviation is the square root of the variance. So if SD($R$), or $\sigma$, stands for the standard deviation of return:

$$\text{SD}(R) = \sigma = \sqrt{0.009} = 0.09487$$

The square root of the variance is used because the variance is measured in 'squared' percentages and thus is hard to interpret. The standard deviation is an ordinary percentage, so the answer here could be written as 9.487 per cent.

In the preceding table, notice that the sum of the deviations is equal to zero. This will always be the case, and it provides a good way to check your work. In general, if we have $T$ historical returns, where $T$ is some number, we can write the historical variance as

$$\text{Var}(R) = \frac{1}{T-1}[(R_1 - \bar{R})^2 + \cdots + (R_T - \bar{R})^2] \tag{11.3}$$

This formula tells us to do what we just did: take each of the $T$ individual returns ($R_1$, $R_2$, ...) and subtract the average return, $\bar{R}$; square the results, and add them all up; and finally, divide this total by the number of returns less 1, $(T - 1)$. The standard deviation is always the square root of Var(R). Standard deviations are a widely used measure of volatility. Our nearby Work the Web box gives a real-world example.

---

**EXAMPLE 11.2**

# Calculating the Variance and Standard Deviation

Suppose Supertech and Hyperdrive have experienced the following returns in the last four years:

| Year | Supertech return | Hyperdrive return |
|------|------------------|-------------------|
| 2007 | −0.20 | 0.05 |
| 2008 | 0.50 | 0.09 |
| 2009 | 0.30 | −0.12 |
| 2010 | 0.10 | 0.20 |

What are the average returns? The variances? The standard deviations? Which investment was more volatile?

To calculate the average returns, we add up the returns and divide by 4. The results are:

$$\text{Supertech average return } \bar{R} = 0.70/4 = 0.175$$
$$\text{Hyperdrive average return } \bar{R} = 0.22/4 = 0.055$$

To calculate the variance for Supertech, we can summarize the relevant calculations as follows:

| Year | (1) Actual return | (2) Average return | (3) Deviation (1)−(2) | (4) Squared deviation |
|------|------|------|------|------|
| 2007 | −0.20 | 0.175 | −0.375 | 0.140625 |
| 2008 | 0.50 | 0.175 | 0.325 | 0.105625 |
| 2009 | 0.30 | 0.175 | 0.125 | 0.015625 |
| 2010 | 0.10 | 0.175 | −0.075 | 0.005625 |
| Totals | 0.70 | | 0.000 | 0.267500 |

Because there are four years of returns, we calculate the variance by dividing 0.2675 by $(4 - 1) = 3$:

|  | Supertech | Hyperdrive |
|------|------|------|
| Variance ($\sigma^2$) | 0.2675/3 = 0.0892 | 0.0529/3 = 0.0176 |
| Standard deviation ($\sigma$) | $\sqrt{0.0892} = 0.2987$ | $\sqrt{0.0176} = 0.1327$ |

For practice, verify that you get the same answer as we do for Hyperdrive. Notice that the standard deviation for Supertech, 29.87 per cent, is a little more than twice Hyperdrive's 13.27 per cent: Supertech is thus the more volatile investment.

FIGURE
11.5

| Series | Average return (%) | Standard deviation (%) | Distribution |
|---|---|---|---|
| US large-company equities | 12.3 | 20.0 |  |
| US small-company equities | 17.1 | 32.6 | 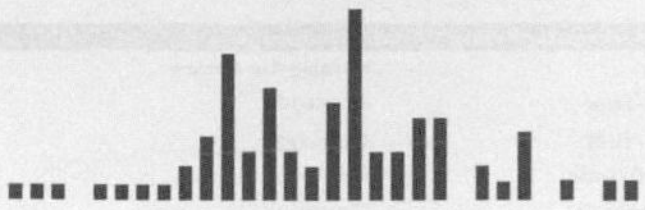 |
| Long-term corporate bonds | 6.2 | 8.4 |  |
| Long-term government bonds | 5.8 | 9.2 |  |
| Intermediate-term government bonds | 5.5 | 5.7 | 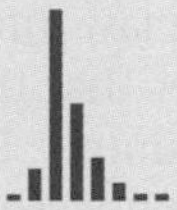 |
| US Treasury bills | 3.8 | 3.1 | |
| Inflation | 3.1 | 4.2 | 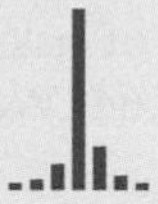 |

The 1933 small company equity total return was 142.9 per cent.

*Source*: Modified from *Ibbotson® Stocks, Bonds, Bills and Inflation 2008 Yearbook*; annually updates work by Roger G. Ibbotson and Rex A. Sinquefield (Chicago: Morningstar). All rights reserved.

**Figure 11.5** US historical returns, standard deviations, and frequency distributions: 1926–2007

## The Historical Record

Figure 11.5 summarizes US capital market history in more detail. It displays average returns, standard deviations and frequency distributions of annual returns on a common scale. In Fig. 11.5, for example, notice that the standard deviation for the small company portfolio (32.6 per cent per year) is more than 10 times larger than the T-bill portfolio's standard deviation (3.1 per cent per year). We shall return to these figures shortly.

## Normal Distribution

For many different random events in nature, a particular frequency distribution, the **normal distribution** (or *bell curve*), is useful for describing the probability of ending up in a given range.

**normal distribution**
A symmetric, bell-shaped frequency distribution that is completely defined by its mean and standard deviation.

# Work the Web

Standard deviations are widely reported for mutual funds. For example, consider the Henderson All Stocks Credit A Investment Trust. How volatile is it? To find out, we went to www.morningstar.co.uk, searched on the fund's name, and hit the 'Risk/Measures' link. Here is what we found:

**Henderson All Stocks Credit A Inc**

| Morningstar Rating™ (Relative to Category) | | | 28/02/2010 |
|---|---|---|---|
| | Morningstar Return | Morningstar Risk | Morningstar Rating™ |
| 3-Year | Average | Below Average | ★★★★ |
| 5-Year | Average | Below Average | ★★★★ |
| 10-Year | - | - | Not Rated |
| Overall | Average | Below Average | ★★★★ |

Category : Sterling Corporate Bond          Click here to see our Methodology

| Volatility Measurements | | | 28/02/2010 |
|---|---|---|---|
| 3-Yr Std Dev | 6.19 % | 3-Yr Sharpe Ratio | -0.13 |
| 3-Yr Mean Return | 3.00 % | | |

| Modern Portfolio Statistics | | | 28/02/2010 |
|---|---|---|---|
| | | Standard Index | Best Fit Index |
| | | IBOXX GBP Corp TR | IBOXX GBP Corp TR |
| 3-Yr R-Squared | | 85.11 | 85.11 |
| 3-Yr Beta | | 0.64 | 0.64 |
| 3-Yr Alpha | | 0.21 | 0.21 |

Over the last three years the standard deviation of the return on the fund was 6.19 per cent. When you consider that the average share price has a standard deviation of about 50 per cent, this seems like a low number. But the All Stocks Credit A fund is a relatively well-diversified portfolio of low-risk corporate bonds, so this is an illustration of the power of diversification and asset risk, a subject we shall discuss in detail later. The mean is the average return: so over the last three years investors in the Henderson fund experienced fairly poor performance, with a return of 3 per cent per year. Also under the Volatility Measurements section you will see the Sharpe ratio. The Sharpe ratio is defined as the risk premium of the asset divided by the standard deviation. It is a measure of return to the level of risk taken (as measured by standard deviation). The 'beta' for the All Stocks Credit A Fund is 0.64. We shall have more to say about this number – lots more – in the next chapter.

## QUESTIONS

1  Go to the Morningstar website at www.morningstar.com. Get a quote for the Aberdeen Asian Income fund. How does this compare with the Henderson All Stocks Investment Trust?

2  What style is this fund? What are the five sectors that have the highest percentage investment for this fund? What are the five equities with the highest percentage investment?

Figure 11.6 illustrates a normal distribution, and its distinctive bell shape. As you can see, this distribution has a much cleaner appearance than the actual return distributions illustrated in Fig. 11.5. Even so, like the normal distribution, the actual distributions do appear to be at least roughly mound-shaped and symmetric. When this is true, the normal distribution is often a very good approximation.

Also, keep in mind that the distributions in Fig. 11.5 are based on only 82 yearly observations, whereas Fig. 11.6 is, in principle, based on an infinite number. So if we had been able to observe returns for, say, 1,000 years, we might have filled in a lot of the irregularities and ended up with a much smoother picture in Fig. 11.5. For our purposes it is enough to observe that the returns are at least roughly normally distributed.

The usefulness of the normal distribution stems from the fact that it is completely described by the average and the standard deviation. If you have these two numbers, then there is nothing else to know. For example, with a normal distribution, the probability that we shall end up within one standard deviation of the average is about 2/3. The probability that we shall end up within two standard deviations is about 95 per cent. Finally, the probability of being more than three standard deviations away from the average is less than 1 per cent. These ranges, and the probabilities, are illustrated in Fig. 11.6.

To see why this is useful, recall from Fig. 11.5 that the standard deviation of returns on the US large company equities is 20 per cent. The average return is 12.3 per cent. So,

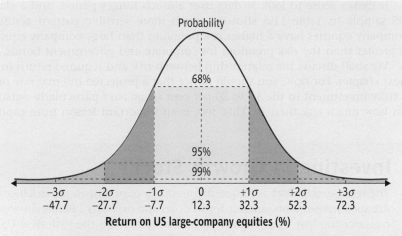

**Figure 11.6** The normal distribution

Note: Illustrated returns are based on the historical return and standard deviation for a portfolio of US large firm equities.

assuming that the frequency distribution is at least approximately normal, the probability that the return in a given year is in the range –7.7 to 32.3 per cent (12.3 per cent plus or minus one standard deviation, 20 per cent) is about 2/3. This range is illustrated in Fig. 11.6. In other words, there is about one chance in three that the return will be *outside* this range. This literally tells you that, if you buy equities in large US companies, you should expect to be outside this range in one year out of every three. This reinforces our earlier observations about stock market volatility. However, there is only a 5 per cent chance (approximately) that we would end up outside the range –27.7 to 52.3 per cent (12.3 per cent plus or minus 2 × 20%). These points are also illustrated in Fig. 11.6.

## The Second Lesson

Our observations concerning the year-to-year variability in returns are the basis for our second lesson from capital market history. On average, bearing risk is handsomely rewarded; but in a given year there is a significant chance of a dramatic change in value. Thus our second lesson is this: the greater the potential reward, the greater is the risk.

## Using Capital Market History

Based on the discussion in this section, you should begin to have an idea of the risks and rewards from investing. For example, in early 2010 one-year UK Treasury bills were paying about 0.75 per cent. Suppose we had an investment that we thought had about the same risk as a portfolio of small UK company equities. At a minimum, what return would this investment have to offer for us to be interested?

From Table 11.3 we see that the average return earned by small UK company equities was 8.25 per cent per annum, and so a reasonable estimate of the risk premium was 7.5 per cent (= 8.25 – 0.75) over the 10-year period 2001 to 2010. This may strike you as being high, but if we were thinking of starting a new business, then the risks of doing so might resemble those of investing in small-company equities.

Clearly, there are major problems with this analysis when such a short period is used to estimate risk premiums. Take, for example, large UK company equities, which had an average annual return of 0.19 per cent over the period 2001–2010. In this case the estimated risk premium is negative, which is nonsense.

It makes sense to look at data over a much longer period, and a glance at the 82-year US sample in Table 11.5 shows a much more sensible pattern across securities. Small-company equities have a higher risk premium than large-company equities, which in turn is greater than the risk premium for corporate and government bonds.

We shall discuss the relationship between risk and required return in more detail in the next chapter. For now, you should notice that a projected internal rate of return, or IRR, on a risky investment in the 10 to 20 per cent range isn't particularly outstanding. It depends on how much risk there is. This, too, is an important lesson from capital market history.

---

**EXAMPLE 11.3**

## Investing in Growth Stocks

The term *growth stock* is frequently used as a euphemism for small-company equities. Are such investments suitable for 'widows and orphans'? Before answering, you should consider the historical volatility. For example, from the historical US record, what is the approximate probability that you will actually lose more than 16 per cent of your money in a single year if you buy a portfolio of shares of such companies?

Looking back at Fig. 11.5, we see that the average return on small US company equities is 17.1 per cent, and the standard deviation is 32.6 per cent. Assuming the returns are approximately normal, there is about a 1/3 probability that you will experience a return outside the range −15.5 to 49.7 per cent (17.1% ± 32.6%).

Because the normal distribution is symmetric, the odds of being above or below this range are equal. There is thus a 1/6 chance (half of 1/3) that you will lose more than 15.5 per cent. So you should expect this to happen once in every six years, on average. Such investments can thus be *very* volatile, and they are not well suited for those who cannot afford the risk.

---

## More on the Stock Market Risk Premium

As we have discussed, the historical stock market risk premium has been substantial. In fact, based on standard economic models, it has been argued that the historical risk premium is *too* big, and is thus an overestimate of what is likely to happen in the future.

Of course, whenever we use the past to predict the future, there is the danger that the past period we observe isn't representative of what the future will hold. For example, in this chapter we have studied the period 2001–2010. Investors were obviously highly unlucky over this period, and earned abysmally low returns. With that in mind, the average annual return (March to February) on the FTSE 100 since it started in 1984 is 7.9 per cent, significantly greater than 0.19 per cent (2001–2010), but still low compared with other major countries, such as the US.

Data from earlier years are available, but are not of such high quality. Figure 11.7 shows the historical average stock market risk premium for 17 countries over the 106-year period 1900–2005. Looking at the numbers, we can see that Italy had the highest risk premium, at 10.5 per cent, and Denmark was lowest, at 4.5 per cent. The overall average risk premium is 7.1 per cent. These numbers make it clear most investors did well, but not exceptionally well.

So, are market risk premiums estimated too high? The evidence seems to suggest that the answer is 'maybe a little' for some countries and 'definitely not' for others.

---

**CONCEPT QUESTIONS**

11.4a  In words, how do we calculate a variance? A standard deviation?
11.4b  With a normal distribution, what is the probability of ending up more than one standard deviation below the average?
11.4c  Assuming that long-term corporate bonds have an approximately normal distribution, what is the approximate probability of earning 14.6 per cent or more in a given year? With T-bills, roughly what is this probability?
11.4d  What is the second lesson from capital market history?

FIGURE
**11.7**

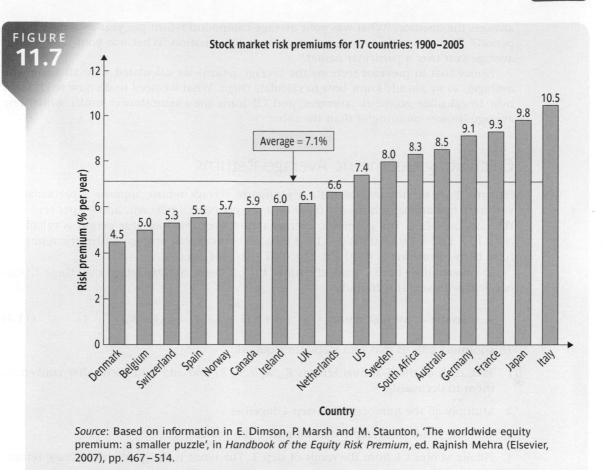

Source: Based on information in E. Dimson, P. Marsh and M. Staunton, 'The worldwide equity premium: a smaller puzzle', in *Handbook of the Equity Risk Premium*, ed. Rajnish Mehra (Elsevier, 2007), pp. 467–514.

**Figure 11.7** Stock market risk premiums for 17 countries: 1900–2005

## 11.5  More about Average Returns

Thus far in this chapter we have looked closely at simple average returns. But there is another way of computing an average return. The fact that average returns are calculated in two different ways leads to some confusion, so our goal in this section is to explain the two approaches, and also the circumstances under which each is appropriate.

## Arithmetic versus Geometric Averages

Let's start with a simple example. Suppose you buy a particular equity for £100. Unfortunately, the first year you own it, it falls to £50. The second year you own it, it rises back to £100, leaving you where you started (no dividends were paid).

What was your average return on this investment? Common sense seems to say that your average return must be exactly zero, because you started with £100 and ended with £100. But if we calculate the returns year by year, we see that you lost 50 per cent the first year (you lost half of your money). The second year, you made 100 per cent (you doubled your money). Your average return over the two years was thus (−50% + 100%)/2 = 25%!

So which is correct, 0 per cent or 25 per cent? Both are correct: they just answer different questions. The 0 per cent is called the **geometric average return**. The 25 per cent is called the **arithmetic average return**. The geometric average return

> **geometric average return**
> The average compound return earned per year over a multi-year period.
>
> **arithmetic average return**
> The return earned in an average year over a multi-year period.

answers the question 'What was your average compound return per year over a particular period?' The arithmetic average return answers the question 'What was your return in an average year over a particular period?'

Notice that in previous sections the average returns we calculated were all arithmetic averages, so we already know how to calculate them. What we need to do now is: (1) learn how to calculate geometric averages; and (2) learn the circumstances under which one average is more meaningful than the other.

## Calculating Geometric Average Returns

First, to illustrate how we calculate a geometric average return, suppose a particular investment had annual returns of 10 per cent, 12 per cent, 3 per cent, and –9 per cent over the last four years. The geometric average return over this four-year period is calculated as $(1.10 \times 1.12 \times 1.03 \times 0.91)^{1/4} - 1 = 3.66\%$. In contrast, the average arithmetic return we have been calculating is $(0.10 + 0.12 + 0.03 - 0.09)/4 = 4.0\%$.

In general, if we have $T$ years of returns, the geometric average return over these $T$ years is calculated using this formula:

$$\text{Geometric average return} = [(1 + R_1) \times (1 + R_2) \times \cdots \times (1 + R_T)]^{1/T} - 1 \qquad (11.4)$$

This formula tells us that four steps are required:

1. Take each of the $T$ annual returns $R_1, R_2, \ldots, R_T$ and add 1 to each (after converting them to decimals!).

2. Multiply all the numbers from step 1 together.

3. Take the result from step 2 and raise it to the power $1/T$.

4. Finally, subtract 1 from the result of step 3. The result is the geometric average return.

## Calculating the Geometric Average Return

EXAMPLE 11.4

Calculate the geometric average return for Danish equities for the first five years in Table 11.1, 2001–2005.

First, convert percentages to decimal returns, add 1, and then calculate their product:

| Danish returns (%) | Product |
|---|---|
| 38.80 | 1.3880 |
| −24.21 | × 0.7579 |
| −29.28 | × 0.7072 |
| 40.32 | × 1.4032 |
| 11.49 | × 1.1149 |
| | 1.1640 |

Notice that the number 1.1640 is what our investment is worth after five years if we started with a 1 kroner investment. The geometric average return is then calculated as follows:

$$\text{Geometric average return} = 1.1640^{1/5} - 1 = 0.0308, \text{ or } 3.08\%$$

Thus the geometric average return is about 3.08 per cent in this example. Here is a tip: if you are using a financial calculator, you can put '1' in as the present value, '1.5291' as the future value, and '5' as the number of periods. Then solve for the unknown rate. You should get the same answer that we did.

| TABLE 11.6 | | Average return (%) | | Standard deviation (%) |
| --- | --- | --- | --- | --- |
| Series | | Geometric | Arithmetic | |
| Large US company equities | | 10.4 | 12.3 | 20.0 |
| Small US company equities | | 12.5 | 17.1 | 32.6 |
| Long-term US corporate bonds | | 5.9 | 6.2 | 8.4 |
| Long-term US government bonds | | 5.5 | 5.8 | 9.2 |
| Intermediate-term US government bonds | | 5.3 | 5.5 | 5.7 |
| US Treasury bills | | 3.7 | 3.8 | 3.1 |
| Inflation | | 3.0 | 3.1 | 4.2 |

**Table 11.6** Geometric versus arithmetic average US returns: 1926–2007

One thing you may have noticed in our examples thus far is that the geometric average returns seem to be smaller. This will always be true (as long as the returns are not all identical, in which case the two 'averages' would be the same). To illustrate, Table 11.6 shows the arithmetic averages and standard deviations from Fig. 11.5, along with the geometric average returns.

As shown in Table 11.6, the geometric averages are all smaller, but the magnitude of the difference varies quite a bit. The reason is that the difference is greater for more volatile investments. In fact, there is a useful approximation. Assuming all the numbers are expressed in decimals (as opposed to percentages), the geometric average return is approximately equal to the arithmetic average return minus half the variance. For example, looking at the large company equities, the arithmetic average is 0.123 and the standard deviation is 0.20, implying that the variance is 0.04. The approximate geometric average is thus 0.123 − 0.04/2 = 0.103, which is quite close to the actual value.

## More Geometric Averages

EXAMPLE 11.5

Take a look back at Table 11.1. There we showed that the small UK company index grew from 6,181 to 9,237 over 10 years. The 10-year return is given below:

$$\text{Ten-year return} = (9{,}237/6{,}181) - 1 = 49.44\%$$

The geometric average annual return is thus

$$\text{Geometric average return} = 1.4944^{1/10} - 1 = 0.0409, \text{ or } 4.09\%$$

For practice, check some of the other countries in Table 11.1 the same way.

## Arithmetic Average Return or Geometric Average Return?

When we look at historical returns, the difference between the geometric and arithmetic average returns isn't too hard to understand. To put it slightly differently, the geometric average tells you what you actually earned per year on average, compounded annually. The arithmetic average tells you what you earned in a typical year. You should use whichever one answers the question you want answered.

A somewhat trickier question concerns which average return to use when forecasting future wealth levels, and there's a lot of confusion on this point among analysts and financial planners. First, let's get one thing straight: if you *know* the true arithmetic average return, then this is what you should use in your forecast. For example, if you know the arithmetic return is 10 per cent, then your best guess of the value of a €1,000 investment in 10 years is the future value of €1,000 at 10 per cent for 10 years, or €2,593.74.

The problem we face, however, is that we usually have only *estimates* of the arithmetic and geometric returns, and estimates have errors. In this case the arithmetic average return is probably too high for longer periods, and the geometric average is probably too low for shorter periods. So you should regard long-run projected wealth levels calculated using arithmetic averages as optimistic. Short-run projected wealth levels calculated using geometric averages are probably pessimistic.

The good news is that there is a simple way of combining the two averages, which we shall call *Blume's formula*.[2] Suppose we have calculated geometric and arithmetic return averages from $N$ years of data, and we wish to use these averages to form a $T$-year average return forecast, $R(T)$, where $T$ is less than $N$. Here's how we do it:

$$R(T) = \frac{T-1}{N-1} \times \text{Geometric average} + \frac{N-T}{N-1} \times \text{Arithmetic average} \qquad \textbf{(11.5)}$$

For example, suppose that from 25 years of annual returns data we calculate an arithmetic average return of 12 per cent and a geometric average return of 9 per cent. From these averages we wish to make one-year, five-year and ten-year average return forecasts. These three average return forecasts are calculated as follows:

$$R(1) = \frac{1-1}{24} \times 9\% + \frac{25-1}{24} \times 12\% = 12\%$$

$$R(5) = \frac{5-1}{24} \times 9\% + \frac{25-5}{24} \times 12\% = 11.5\%$$

$$R(10) = \frac{10-1}{24} \times 9\% + \frac{25-10}{24} \times 12\% = 10.875\%$$

Thus we see that one-year, five-year and ten-year forecasts are 12 per cent, 11.5 per cent and 10.875 per cent, respectively.

As a practical matter, Blume's formula says that if you are using averages calculated over a long period to forecast up to a decade or so into the future, then you should use the arithmetic average. If you are forecasting a few decades into the future (as you might do for retirement planning), then you should just split the difference between the arithmetic and geometric average returns. Finally, if for some reason you are doing very long forecasts covering many decades, use the geometric average.

This concludes our discussion of geometric versus arithmetic averages. One last note: in the future, when we say 'average return', we mean arithmetic unless we explicitly say otherwise.

**CONCEPT QUESTIONS**

11.5a  If you want to forecast what the stock market is going to do over the next year, should you use an arithmetic or geometric average?

11.5b  If you want to forecast what the stock market is going to do over the next century, should you use an arithmetic or geometric average?

## 11.6 Capital Market Efficiency

Capital market history suggests that the market values of equities and bonds can fluctuate widely from year to year. Why does this occur? At least part of the answer is that prices change because new information arrives, and investors reassess asset values based on that information.

The behaviour of market prices has been extensively studied. A question that has received particular attention is whether prices adjust quickly and correctly when new information arrives. A market is said to be 'efficient' if this is the case. To be more precise, in an **efficient capital market** current market prices fully reflect available information. By this we simply mean that, based on available information, there is no reason to believe that the current price is too low or too high.

The concept of market efficiency is a rich one, and much has been written about it. A full discussion of the subject goes beyond the scope of our study of corporate finance. However, because the concept figures so prominently in studies of market history, we briefly describe the key points here.

> **efficient capital market**
> A market in which security prices reflect available information.

## Price Behaviour in an Efficient Market

To illustrate how prices behave in an efficient market, suppose F-Stop Camera Corporation (FCC) has, through years of secret research and development, developed a camera with an autofocusing system whose speed will double that of the autofocusing systems now available. FCC's capital budgeting analysis suggests that launching the new camera will be a highly profitable move; in other words, the NPV appears to be positive and substantial. The key assumption thus far is that FCC has not released any information about the new system, so the fact of its existence is 'inside' information only.

Now consider a share of equity in FCC. In an efficient market, its price reflects what is known about FCC's current operations and profitability, and it reflects market opinion about FCC's potential for future growth and profits. The value of the new autofocusing system is not reflected, however, because the market is unaware of the system's existence.

If the market agrees with FCC's assessment of the value of the new project, FCC's share price will rise when the decision to launch is made public. For example, assume the announcement is made in a press release on Wednesday morning. In an efficient market, the price of shares in FCC will adjust quickly to this new information. Investors should not be able to buy the equity on Wednesday afternoon and make a profit on Thursday. This would imply that it took the stock market a full day to realize the implication of the FCC press release. If the market is efficient, the FCC share price on Wednesday afternoon will already reflect the information contained in the Wednesday morning press release.

Figure 11.8 presents three possible share price adjustments for FCC. In Fig. 11.8 day 0 represents the announcement day. As illustrated, before the announcement FCC sells for £140 per share. The NPV per share of the new system is, say, £40, so the new price will be £180 once the value of the new project is fully reflected.

The solid line in Fig. 11.8 represents the path taken by the share price in an efficient market. In this case the price adjusts immediately to the new information, and no further changes in the share price take place. The broken line in Fig. 11.8 depicts a delayed reaction. Here it takes the market eight days or so to fully absorb the information. Finally, the dotted line illustrates an overreaction and subsequent adjustment to the correct price.

The broken line and the dotted line in Fig. 11.8 illustrate paths that the share price might take in an inefficient market. If, for example, share prices don't adjust immediately to new information (the broken line), then buying shares immediately following the release of new information and then selling it several days later would be a positive-NPV activity because the price is too low for several days after the announcement.

## The Efficient Markets Hypothesis

The **efficient markets hypothesis (EMH)** asserts that well-organized capital markets, such as the London Stock Exchange or Euronext, are efficient markets, at least as a practical matter. In other words, an advocate of the EMH might argue that although inefficiencies may exist, they are relatively small and not common.

If a market is efficient, then there is a very important implication for market participants: all investments in that market are zero-NPV investments. The reason is not complicated. If prices are neither too low nor too high, then the difference between the market value of an investment and its cost is zero: hence the NPV is zero. As a

> **efficient markets hypothesis (EMH)**
> The hypothesis that actual capital markets are efficient.

FIGURE
**11.8**

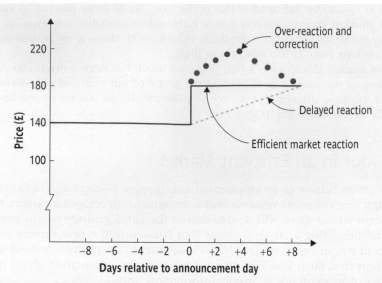

*Efficient market reaction*: The price instantaneously adjusts to and fully reflects new information; there is no tendency for subsequent increases and decreases to occur.
*Delayed reaction*: The price partially adjusts to the new information; eight days elapse before the price completely reflects the new information.
*Over-reaction*: The price over-adjusts to the new information; it overshoots the new price and subsequently corrects.

**Figure 11.8** Share price reaction to new information in efficient and inefficient markets

result, in an efficient market investors get exactly what they pay for when they buy securities, and firms receive exactly what their equities and bonds are worth when they sell them.

What makes a market efficient is competition among investors. Many individuals spend their entire lives trying to find mispriced equities. For any given equity, they study what has happened in the past to the share price and the equity's dividends. They learn, to the extent possible, what a company's earnings have been, how much the company owes to creditors, what taxes it pays, what businesses it is in, what new investments are planned, how sensitive it is to changes in the economy, and so on.

Not only is there a great deal to know about any particular company, but there is also a powerful incentive for knowing it – namely, the profit motive. If you know more about some company than other investors in the marketplace, you can profit from that knowledge by investing in the company's shares if you have good news and by selling them if you have bad news.

The logical consequence of all this information-gathering and analysis is that mispriced equities will become fewer and fewer. In other words, because of competition among investors, the market will become increasingly efficient. A kind of equilibrium comes into being, with which there is just enough mispricing around for those who are best at identifying it to make a living at it. For most other investors the activity of information-gathering and analysis will not pay.[3]

## Some Common Misconceptions about the EMH

No other idea in finance has attracted as much attention as that of efficient markets, and not all of the attention has been flattering. Rather than rehash the arguments here, we shall be content to observe that some markets are more efficient than others. For example, financial markets on the whole are probably much more efficient than real asset markets.

Having said this, however, we can also say that much of the criticism of the EMH is misguided, because it is based on a misunderstanding of what the hypothesis says and what it doesn't say. For example, when the notion of market efficiency was first publicized and debated in the popular financial press, it was often characterized by words to the effect that 'throwing darts at the financial page will produce a portfolio that can be expected to do as well as any managed by professional security analysts'.[4]

Confusion over statements of this sort has often led to a failure to understand the implications of market efficiency. For example, sometimes it is wrongly argued that market efficiency means that it doesn't matter how you invest your money, because the efficiency of the market will protect you from making a mistake. However, a random dart thrower might wind up with all of the darts sticking into one or two high-risk equities that deal in genetic engineering. Would you really want all of your money in two such companies?

A contest run by the *Wall Street Journal* provides a good example of the controversy surrounding market efficiency. Each month the *Journal* asked four professional money managers to pick one equity each. At the same time it threw four darts at the equities page to select a comparison group. In the 147 five- and one-half month contests from July 1990 to September 2002 the pros won 90 times.

The fact that the pros are ahead of the darts by 90 to 57 suggests that markets are not efficient. Or does it? One problem is that the darts naturally tend to select equities of average risk. The pros, however, are playing to win, and naturally select riskier equities, or so it is argued. If this is true, then on average we *expect* the pros to win. Furthermore, the pros' picks are announced to the public at the start. This publicity may boost the prices of the shares involved somewhat, leading to a partially self-fulfilling prophecy. Unfortunately, the *Journal* discontinued the contest in 2002, so this test of market efficiency is no longer continuing.

More than anything else, what efficiency implies is that the price a firm will obtain when it sells a share of its equity is a 'fair' price in the sense that it reflects the value of that equity, given the information available about the firm. Shareholders do not have to worry that they are paying too much for an equity with a low dividend or some other sort of characteristic, because the market has already incorporated that characteristic into the price. We sometimes say that the information has been 'priced out'.

The concept of efficient markets can be explained further by replying to a frequent objection. It is sometimes argued that the market cannot be efficient, because share prices fluctuate from day to day. If the prices are right, the argument goes, then why do they change so much and so often? From our discussion of the market we can see that these price movements are in no way inconsistent with efficiency. Investors are bombarded with information every day. The fact that prices fluctuate is, at least in part, a reflection of that information flow. In fact, the absence of price movements in a world that changes as rapidly as ours would suggest inefficiency.

## The Forms of Market Efficiency

It is common to distinguish between three forms of market efficiency. Depending on the degree of efficiency, we say that markets are either *weak-form efficient*, *semi-strong-form efficient*, or *strong-form efficient*. The difference between these forms relates to what information is reflected in prices.

We start with the extreme case. If the market is strong-form efficient, then *all* information of *every* kind is reflected in share prices. In such a market there is no such thing as inside information. Therefore, in our FCC example, we apparently were assuming that the market was not strong-form efficient.

Casual observation, particularly in recent years, suggests that inside information does exist, and it can be valuable to possess. Whether it is lawful or ethical to use that information is another issue. In any event, we conclude that private information about a particular equity may exist that is not currently reflected in the share price. For example, prior knowledge of a takeover attempt could be very valuable.

The second form of efficiency, semi-strong-form efficiency, is the most controversial. If a market is semi-strong-form efficient, then all *public* information is reflected in the share price. The reason why this form is controversial is that it implies that a security analyst who tries to identify mispriced equities using, for example, financial statement information is wasting time, because that information is already reflected in the current price.

The third form of efficiency, weak-form efficiency, suggests that, at a minimum, the current share price reflects the equity's own past prices. In other words, studying past prices in an attempt to identify mispriced securities is futile if the market is weak-form efficient. Although this form of efficiency might seem rather mild, it implies that searching for patterns in historical prices that will be useful in identifying mispriced equities will not work (this practice is quite common).

What does capital market history say about market efficiency? Here again there is great controversy. At the risk of going out on a limb, we can say that the evidence seems to tell us three things. First, prices appear to respond rapidly to new information, and the response is at least not grossly different from what we would expect in an efficient market. Second, the future of market prices, particularly in the short run, is difficult to predict based on publicly available information. Third, if mispriced equities exist, then there is no obvious means of identifying them. Put another way, simple-minded schemes based on public information will probably not be successful.

Many people do not believe that markets are efficient at all. The recent stock market bubbles at the beginning of the century and, more recently, in the mid-2000s have led to a new interest in what is known as *behavioural finance*. This is covered in more detail in Chapter 19.

| CONCEPT QUESTIONS | 11.6a What is an efficient market? |
| | 11.6b What are the forms of market efficiency? |

## Summary and Conclusions

This chapter has explored the subject of capital market history. Such history is useful, because it tells us what to expect in the way of returns from risky assets. We summed up our study of market history with two key lessons:

1 Risky assets, on average, earn a risk premium. There is a reward for bearing risk.

2 The greater the potential reward from a risky investment, the greater is the risk.

These lessons have significant implications for the financial manager. We shall consider these implications in the chapters ahead.

We also discussed the concept of market efficiency. In an efficient market, prices adjust quickly and correctly to new information. Consequently, asset prices in efficient markets are rarely too high or too low. How efficient capital markets (such as the London Stock Exchange or Euronext) are is a matter of debate; but, at a minimum, they are probably much more efficient than most real asset markets.

# Chapter Review and Self-Test Problems

**11.1   Recent Return History**   Use Table 11.1 to calculate the average return over the years 2001–2010 for all the indices presented in the table.

**11.2   More Recent Return History**   Calculate the standard deviation for each index using information from Problem 11.1. Which of the investments was the most volatile over this period?

# Answers to Chapter Review and Self-Test Problems

**11.1**   We calculate the averages as follows:

| Date | UK large (%) | UK small (%) | Germany (%) | France (%) | Denmark (%) | Netherlands (%) | Belgium (%) | Sweden (%) |
|---|---|---|---|---|---|---|---|---|
| 2000 | 0.46 | 8.96 | −0.59 | 5.99 | 38.80 | 4.41 | 5.77 | – |
| 2001 | −17.99 | −13.16 | −24.84 | −25.63 | −24.21 | −21.75 | −6.87 | −25.74 |
| 2002 | −30.93 | −31.34 | −46.21 | −34.16 | −29.28 | −41.20 | −31.91 | −36.00 |
| 2003 | 23.07 | 49.98 | 47.72 | 23.87 | 40.32 | 20.07 | 26.62 | 42.36 |
| 2004 | 10.52 | 18.98 | 4.83 | 7.56 | 11.49 | 1.98 | 25.77 | 11.71 |
| 2005 | 18.71 | 27.99 | 33.38 | 26.42 | 33.68 | 25.00 | 24.92 | 34.06 |
| 2006 | 7.69 | 21.02 | 19.65 | 13.36 | 18.77 | 10.89 | 18.40 | 25.73 |
| 2007 | −5.22 | −10.98 | 0.91 | −13.18 | −11.90 | −11.62 | −16.04 | −19.95 |
| 2008 | −29.43 | −36.75 | −36.68 | −38.94 | −35.87 | −43.76 | −48.95 | −37.86 |
| 2009 | 25.04 | 47.79 | 29.28 | 25.77 | 35.63 | 31.85 | 31.84 | 56.77 |
| Average | 0.19 | 8.25 | 2.75 | −0.89 | 7.74 | −2.41 | 2.96 | 5.68 |

**11.2**   We first need to calculate the deviations from the average returns. Using the averages from Problem 11.1, we get the following values:

| Date | UK large (%) | UK small (%) | Germany (%) | France (%) | Denmark (%) | Netherlands (%) | Belgium (%) | Sweden (%) |
|---|---|---|---|---|---|---|---|---|
| 2000 | 0.27 | 0.71 | −3.33 | 6.88 | 31.06 | 6.83 | 2.82 | – |
| 2001 | −18.19 | −21.40 | −27.59 | −24.73 | −31.95 | −19.34 | −9.83 | −31.42 |
| 2002 | −31.12 | −39.59 | −48.96 | −33.27 | −37.02 | −38.79 | −34.87 | −41.68 |
| 2003 | 22.88 | 41.73 | 44.98 | 24.76 | 32.58 | 22.48 | 23.67 | 36.69 |
| 2004 | 10.33 | 10.73 | 2.08 | 8.45 | 3.75 | 4.40 | 22.81 | 6.03 |
| 2005 | 18.52 | 19.74 | 30.63 | 27.32 | 25.93 | 27.41 | 21.97 | 28.39 |
| 2006 | 7.50 | 12.77 | 16.91 | 14.26 | 11.02 | 13.30 | 15.45 | 20.06 |
| 2007 | −5.42 | −19.23 | −1.83 | −12.28 | −19.65 | −9.21 | −18.99 | −25.62 |
| 2008 | −29.62 | −45.00 | −39.43 | −38.05 | −43.62 | −41.35 | −51.91 | −43.54 |
| 2009 | 24.85 | 39.54 | 26.53 | 26.66 | 27.89 | 34.27 | 28.89 | 51.10 |

We square these deviations and calculate the variances and standard deviations:

| Date | UK large (%) | UK small (%) | Germany (%) | France (%) | Denmark (%) | Netherlands (%) | Belgium (%) | Sweden (%) |
|---|---|---|---|---|---|---|---|---|
| 2000 | 0.00 | 0.01 | 0.11 | 0.47 | 9.65 | 0.47 | 0.08 | – |
| 2001 | 3.31 | 4.58 | 7.61 | 6.12 | 10.21 | 3.74 | 0.97 | 9.87 |
| 2002 | 9.68 | 15.67 | 23.97 | 11.07 | 13.71 | 15.04 | 12.16 | 17.37 |
| 2003 | 5.23 | 17.41 | 20.23 | 6.13 | 10.61 | 5.05 | 5.60 | 13.46 |
| 2004 | 1.07 | 1.15 | 0.04 | 0.71 | 0.14 | 0.19 | 5.20 | 0.36 |
| 2005 | 3.43 | 3.90 | 9.38 | 7.46 | 6.73 | 7.51 | 4.83 | 8.06 |
| 2006 | 0.56 | 1.63 | 2.86 | 2.03 | 1.22 | 1.77 | 2.39 | 4.02 |
| 2007 | 0.29 | 3.70 | 0.03 | 1.51 | 3.86 | 0.85 | 3.61 | 6.57 |
| 2008 | 8.77 | 20.25 | 15.54 | 14.48 | 19.02 | 17.10 | 26.94 | 18.96 |
| 2009 | 6.17 | 15.64 | 7.04 | 7.11 | 7.78 | 11.74 | 8.34 | 26.11 |
| Variance | 4.28 | 9.33 | 9.65 | 6.34 | 9.21 | 7.05 | 7.79 | 13.10 |
| Standard deviation | 20.69 | 30.54 | 31.06 | 25.19 | 30.35 | 26.56 | 27.91 | 36.19 |

To calculate the variances we added up the squared deviations and divided by 9, the number of returns less 1. Notice that most of the equity indices had roughly the same level of volatility.

# Concepts Review and Critical Thinking Questions

1 **Investment Selection [LO4]** Given that the Zimbabwe Industrials Index was up by over 12,000 per cent in 2007, why didn't all investors take a position in Zimbabwe during in 2007?

2 **Investment Selection [LO4]** Given that the Chinese stock markets were down by 46 per cent in the first six months of 2008, why did investors continue to hold shares in China? Why didn't they sell out before the market declined so sharply?

3 **Risk and Return [LO2, LO3]** We have seen that, over long periods, equity investments have tended to substantially outperform bond investments. However, it is common to observe investors with long horizons holding entirely bonds. Are such investors irrational?

4 **Market Efficiency Implications [LO4]** Explain why a characteristic of an efficient market is that investments in that market have zero NPVs.

5 **Efficient Markets Hypothesis [LO4]** A stock market analyst is able to identify mispriced equities by comparing the average price for the last 10 days with average price for the last 60 days. If this is true, what do you know about the market?

6 **Semi-Strong Efficiency [LO4]** If a market is semi-strong-form efficient, is it also weak-form efficient? Explain.

7 **Efficient Markets Hypothesis [LO4]** What are the implications of the efficient markets hypothesis for investors who buy and sell equities in an attempt to 'beat the market'?

8 **Stocks versus Gambling [LO4]** Critically evaluate the following statement: 'Playing the stock market is like gambling. Such speculative investing has no social value other than the pleasure people get from this form of gambling.'

9 **Efficient Markets Hypothesis [LO4]** Several celebrated investors and stock pickers frequently mentioned in the financial press have recorded huge returns on their investments over the past two decades. Is the success of these particular investors an invalidation of the EMH? Explain.

10 **Efficient Markets Hypothesis [LO4]** For each of the following scenarios, discuss whether profit opportunities exist from trading in the equity of the firm under the conditions that: (1) the market is not weak-form efficient; (2) the market is weak-form but not semi-strong-form efficient; (3) the market is semi-strong-form but not strong-form efficient; and (4) the market is strong-form efficient.

(a) The share price has risen steadily each day for the past 30 days.

(b) The financial statements for a company were released three days ago, and you believe you've uncovered some anomalies in the company's inventory and cost control reporting techniques that are causing the firm's true liquidity strength to be understated.

(c) You observe that the senior managers of a company have been buying a lot of the company's equities on the open market over the past week.

## connect Questions and Problems

**BASIC**
**1 – 11**

1 **Calculating Returns [LO1]** At the beginning of 2009 the price of Anheuser-Busch was €19.67, it paid a dividend of €0.28 per share during the year, and had an ending share price of €36.40. Compute the percentage total return.

2 **Calculating Yields [LO1]** In Problem 1, what was the dividend yield? The capital gains yield?

3 **Return Calculations [LO1]** Rework Problems 1 and 2 assuming the ending share price is €30.

4 **Calculating Returns [LO1]** Suppose you bought a 7 per cent coupon bond one year ago for £104. The bond sells for £107 today.

(a) Assuming a £100 face value, what was your total cash return on this investment over the past year?

(b) What was your total nominal rate of return on this investment over the past year?

(c) If the inflation rate last year was 4 per cent, what was your total real rate of return on this investment?

5 **Nominal versus Real Returns [LO2]** What was the average annual return on UK large company shares from 2001 through to 2010:

(a) In nominal terms?

(b) In real terms if the average rate of inflation was 1 per cent?

6 **Bond Returns [LO2]** What is the historical real return on long-term US government bonds? On long-term US corporate bonds?

7 **Calculating Returns and Variability [LO1]** Using the following returns, calculate the arithmetic average returns, the variances, and the standard deviations for X and Y.

| | Returns (%) | |
|---|---|---|
| Year | X | Y |
| 1 | 8 | 16 |
| 2 | 21 | 38 |
| 3 | 17 | 14 |
| 4 | −16 | −21 |
| 5 | 9 | 26 |

8 **Risk Premiums [LO2, LO3]** Refer to Table 11.1 in the text and look at the period from 2003 through to 2007.

(a) Calculate the arithmetic average returns for all the indices in the table over this period.

(b) Calculate the standard deviation of the returns for all the indices over this period.

9 **Calculating Returns and Variability [LO1]** You've observed the following returns on Crash-n-Burn Computers' equity over the past five years: 7 per cent, −12 per cent, 11 per cent, 38 per cent and 14 per cent.

(a) What was the arithmetic average return on Crash-n-Burn's shares over this five-year period?

(b) What was the variance of Crash-n-Burn's returns over this period? The standard deviation?

10 **Calculating Real Returns and Risk Premiums [LO1]** For Problem 9, suppose the average inflation rate over this period was 3.5 per cent and the average T-bill rate over the period was 4.2 per cent.

(a) What was the average real return on Crash-n-Burn's shares?

(b) What was the average nominal risk premium on Crash-n-Burn's shares?

11 **Calculating Real Rates [LO1]** Given the information in Problem 10, what was the average real risk-free rate over this time period? What was the average real risk premium?

12 **Calculating Investment Returns [LO1]** You bought one of Blueboy plc's 8 per cent coupon bonds one year ago for £103,000. These bonds make annual payments, and mature six years from now. Suppose you decide to sell your bonds today, when the required return on the bonds is 8 per cent. If the inflation rate was 3.2 per cent over the past year, what was your total real return on investment?

13 **Calculating Returns and Variability [LO1]** You find a certain equity that had returns of 7 per cent, −12 per cent, 18 per cent and 19 per cent for four of the last five years. If the average return of the equity over this period was 10.5 per cent, what was the equity's return for the missing year? What is the standard deviation of the equity's return?

14 **Arithmetic and Geometric Returns [LO1]** An equity has had returns of 6 per cent, 14 per cent, 21 per cent, −15 per cent, 29 per cent and −13 per cent over the last six years. What are the arithmetic and geometric returns for the equity?

**INTERMEDIATE**

**12–20**

15   **Arithmetic and Geometric Returns [LO1]**   An equity has had the following year-end prices and dividends:

| Year | Price (£) | Dividend (£) |
|------|-----------|--------------|
| 1 | 60.18 | – |
| 2 | 73.66 | 0.60 |
| 3 | 94.18 | 0.64 |
| 4 | 89.35 | 0.72 |
| 5 | 78.49 | 0.80 |
| 6 | 95.05 | 1.20 |

What are the arithmetic and geometric returns for the equity?

16   **Using Return Distributions [LO3]**   Suppose the returns on long-term corporate bonds are normally distributed. Based on the historical record, what is the approximate probability that your return on these bonds will be less than −2.2 per cent in a given year? What range of returns would you expect to see 95 per cent of the time? What range would you expect to see 99 per cent of the time?

17   **Using Return Distributions [LO3]**   Assuming that the returns from holding Dutch equities are normally distributed, what is the approximate probability that your money will double in value in a single year? What about triple in value?

18   **Distributions [LO3]**   In Problem 17, what is the probability that the return is less than −100 per cent (think)? What are the implications for the distribution of returns?

19   **Blume's Formula [LO1]**   Over a 40-year period an asset had an arithmetic return of 15.3 per cent and a geometric return of 11.9 per cent. Using Blume's formula, what is your best estimate of the future annual returns over 5 years? 10 years? 20 years?

20   **Blume's Formula [LO1, LO2]**   Assume that the historical return on German equities is a predictor of the future returns. What return would you estimate for German equities over the next year? The next 5 years?

21   **Using Probability Distributions [LO3]**   Suppose the returns on large company UK equities are normally distributed. Based on the historical record, use the cumulative normal probability table (rounded to the nearest table value) in the appendix of the text to determine the probability that in any given year you will lose money by investing in small company UK equities.

22   **Using Probability Distributions [LO3]**   Suppose the returns on German and Danish equities are normally distributed. Based on the historical record, use the cumulative normal probability table (rounded to the nearest table value) in the appendix of the text to answer the following questions:

(a)   What is the probability that, in any given year, the return on German equities will be greater than 10 per cent? Less than 0 per cent?

(b)   What is the probability that in any given year, the return on Danish equities will be greater than 10 per cent? Less than 0 per cent?

(c)   In 2008 the return on German equities was −36.68 per cent. How likely is it that such a low return will recur at some point in the future? In 2009 German equities had a return of 29.28 per cent. How likely is it that such a high return on German equities will recur at some point in the future?

**CHALLENGE**
**21 – 22**

# A Job at West Coast Yachts

You recently graduated from university, and your job search led you to West Coast Yachts at Kip Marina. Because you felt the company's business was seaworthy, you accepted a job offer. The first day on the job, while you are finishing your employment paperwork, Dan Ervin, who works in Finance, stops by to inform you about the company's retirement plan.

Retirement plans are offered by many companies, and are tax-deferred savings vehicles, meaning that any deposits you make into the plan are deducted from your current pre-tax income, so no current taxes are paid on the money. For example, assume your salary will be £50,000 per year. If you contribute £3,000 to the plan, you will pay taxes on only £47,000 in income. There are also no taxes paid on any capital gains or income while you are invested in the plan, but you do pay taxes when you withdraw money at retirement. As is fairly common, the company also has a 5 per cent matched funding. This means that the company will match your contribution up to 5 per cent of your salary, but you must contribute to get the match.

The retirement plan has several options for investments, most of which are mutual funds. A mutual fund is a portfolio of assets. When you purchase shares in a mutual fund, you are actually purchasing partial ownership of the fund's assets. The return of the fund is the weighted average of the return of the assets owned by the fund, minus any expenses. The largest expense is typically the management fee paid to the fund manager. The management fee is compensation for the manager, who makes all the investment decisions for the fund.

West Coast Yachts uses Skandla Life Assurance Company Ltd as its retirement plan administrator. Here are the investment options offered for employees:

- **Company Shares** One option in the retirement plan is equity ownership of West Coast Yachts. The company is currently privately held. However, when you were interviewed by the owner, Larissa Warren, she informed you that the company shares were expected to go public in the next three to four years. Until then, a company share price is simply set each year by the board of directors.

- **Skandla Market Index Fund** This mutual fund tracks the FTSE 100 index. Equities in the fund are weighted exactly the same as the FTSE 100. This means that the fund return is approximately the return on the FTSE 100, minus expenses. Because an index fund purchases assets based on the compensation of the index it is following, the fund manager is not required to research stocks or make investment decisions. The result is that the fund expenses are usually low. The Skandla Index Fund charges expenses of 0.15 per cent of assets per year.

- **Skandla Small-Cap Fund** This fund invests primarily in small-capitalization companies. The returns of the fund are therefore more volatile. The fund can also invest 10 per cent of its assets in companies based outside the United Kingdom. This fund charges 1.70 per cent in expenses.

- **Skandla Large-Company Equity Fund** This fund invests primarily in large-capitalization companies based in the United Kingdom. The fund is managed by Evan Skandla, and has outperformed the market in six of the last eight years. The fund charges 1.50 per cent in expenses.

- **Skandla Bond Fund** This fund invests in long-term corporate bonds issued by UK-domiciled companies. The fund is restricted to investments in bonds with an investment-grade credit rating. This fund charges 1.40 per cent in expenses.

- **Skandla Money Market Fund** This fund invests in short-term, high–credit quality debt instruments, which include Treasury bills. The return on the money market fund is therefore only slightly higher than the return on Treasury bills. Because of the credit quality and short-term nature of the investments, there is only a very slight risk of negative return. The fund charges 0.60 per cent in expenses.

## QUESTIONS

1   What advantages do the mutual funds offer compared with the company equity?

2   Assume that you invest 5 per cent of your salary and receive the full 5 per cent match from West Coast Yachts. What APR do you earn from the match? What conclusions do you draw about matching plans?

3   Assume you decide you should invest at least part of your money in large-capitalization companies based in the United Kingdom. What are the advantages and disadvantages of choosing the Skandla Large-Company Equity Fund compared with the Skandla Market Index Fund?

4   The returns on the Skandla Small-Cap Fund are the most volatile of all the mutual funds offered in the retirement plan. Why would you ever want to invest in this fund? When you examine the expenses of the mutual funds, you will notice that this fund also has the highest expenses. Does this affect your decision to invest in this fund?

5   A measure of risk-adjusted performance that is often used is the Sharpe ratio. The Sharpe ratio is calculated as the risk premium of an asset divided by its standard deviation. The standard deviation and return of the funds over the past 10 years are listed here. Calculate the Sharpe ratio for each of these funds. Assume that the expected return and standard deviation of the company equity will be 18 per cent and 70 per cent, respectively. Calculate the Sharpe ratio for the company shares. How appropriate is the Sharpe ratio for these assets? When would you use the Sharpe ratio?

| | 10-Year annual return (%) | Standard deviation (%) |
|---|---|---|
| Skandla Market Index Fund | 11.48 | 15.82 |
| Skandla Small-Cap Fund | 16.68 | 19.64 |
| Skandla Large-Company Equity Fund | 11.85 | 15.41 |
| Skandla Bond Fund | 9.67 | 10.83 |

6   What portfolio allocation would you choose? Why? Explain your thinking carefully.

## Endnotes

1   As we mentioned in an earlier chapter, strictly speaking, what is and what is not a capital gain (or loss) is determined by a country's tax authority. We thus use the terms loosely.

2   This elegant result is due to Marshal Blume ('Unbiased estimates of long-run expected rates of return', *Journal of the American Statistical Association*, September 1974, pp. 634–638).

3   The idea behind the EMH can be illustrated by the following short story. A student was walking down the hall with her finance professor when they both saw a €500 note on the ground. As the student bent down to pick it up, the professor shook his head slowly and, with a look of disappointment on his face, said patiently to the student, 'Don't bother. If it were really there, someone else would have picked it up already.' The moral of the story reflects the logic of the efficient markets hypothesis: if you think you have found a pattern in share prices or a simple device for picking winners, you probably have not.

4   B.G. Malkiel, *A Random Walk Down Wall Street* (revised and updated ed.) (New York: Norton, 2003).

# Return, Risk and the Security Market Line

## KEY NOTATIONS

| | |
|---|---|
| CAPM | Capital asset pricing model |
| E(R) | Expected return |
| $R_f$ | Risk-free rate of return |
| $R_P$ | Portfolio return |
| $\beta$ | Beta or systematic risk |
| $\beta_P$ | Portfolio beta |
| $\sigma$ | Standard deviation of returns |
| $\sigma^2$ | Variance of returns |

## LEARNING OBJECTIVES

After studying this chapter, you should understand:

LO1 How to calculate expected returns.

LO2 The impact of diversification.

LO3 The systematic risk principle.

LO4 The security market line and the risk-return trade-off.

EVERY DAY, companies release news about their operations, and share prices respond as a result. In March 2010, WPP, ITV and Standard Chartered joined a host of other companies in announcing earnings. WPP announced a 'brutal year', with pre-tax profits down by 16.1 per cent. ITV stated that, while group revenues were down 7 per cent, it was able to make a pre-tax profit of £25 million. Finally, Standard Chartered announced a 13 per cent increase in pre-tax profits and a 7.2 per cent increase in dividends to shareholders. You would expect earnings increases to be good news and decreases to be bad news – they usually are. Even so, WPP's share price increased by 4.2 per cent, ITV fell by 3.5 per cent, and Standard Chartered grew by 6.4 per cent.

Although WPP's news seemed negative, its share price went up. Similarly, ITV's news seemed positive, but its share price fell. So when is good news really good news? The answer is fundamental to understanding risk and return, and the good news is this chapter explores it in some detail.

In our last chapter we learned some important lessons from capital market history. Most importantly, we learned that there is a reward, on average, for bearing risk. We called this reward a *risk premium*. The second lesson is that this risk premium is larger for riskier investments. This chapter explores the economic and managerial implications of this basic idea.

Thus far we have concentrated mainly on the return behaviour of a few large portfolios. We need to expand our consideration to include individual assets. Specifically, we have two tasks to accomplish. First, we have to define risk, and discuss how to measure it. We then must quantify the relationship between an asset's risk and its required return.

When we examine the risks associated with individual assets, we find there are two types of risk: systematic and unsystematic. This distinction is crucial, because, as we shall see, systematic risk affects almost all assets in the economy, at least to some degree, whereas unsystematic risk affects at most a small number of assets. We then develop the principle of diversification, which shows that highly diversified portfolios will tend to have almost no unsystematic risk.

The principle of diversification has an important implication: to a diversified investor, only systematic risk matters. It follows that in deciding whether to buy a particular individual asset, a diversified investor will be concerned only with that asset's systematic risk. This is a key observation, and it allows us to say a great deal about the risks and returns on individual assets. In particular, it is the basis for a famous relationship between risk and return called the *security market line*, or SML. To develop the SML we introduce the equally famous *beta* coefficient, one of the centrepieces of modern finance. Beta and the SML are key concepts, because they supply us with at least part of the answer to the question of how to determine the required return on an investment.

# 12.1  Expected Returns and Variances

In our previous chapter we discussed how to calculate average returns and variances using historical data. We now begin to discuss how to analyse returns and variances when the information we have concerns future possible returns and their probabilities.

## Expected Return

We start with a straightforward case. Consider a single period of time – say a year. We have two equities, L and U, which have the following characteristics. Equity L is expected to have a return of 25 per cent in the coming year. Equity U is expected to have a return of 20 per cent for the same period.

In a situation like this, if all investors agreed on the expected returns, why would anyone want to hold Equity U? After all, why invest in one equity when the expectation is that another will do better? Clearly, the answer must depend on the risk of the two investments. The return on Equity L, although it is *expected* to be 25 per cent, could actually turn out to be higher or lower.

For example, suppose the economy booms. In this case we think Equity L will have a 70 per cent return. If the economy enters a recession, we think the return will be −20 per cent. In this case we say that there are two *states of the economy*, which means that these are the only two possible situations. This set-up is oversimplified, of course, but it allows us to illustrate some key ideas without a lot of computation.

Suppose we think a boom and a recession are equally likely to happen, for a 50–50 chance of each. Table 12.1 illustrates the basic information we have described, and some

| State of economy | Probability of state of economy | Rate of return if state occurs (%) | |
|---|---|---|---|
| | | Equity L | Equity U |
| Recession | 0.50 | −20 | 30 |
| Boom | 0.50 | 70 | 10 |
| | 1.00 | | |

**Table 12.1** States of the economy and equity returns

TABLE
12.2

| (1)<br>State of<br>economy | (2)<br>Probability<br>of state of<br>economy | Equity L | | Equity U | |
|---|---|---|---|---|---|
| | | (3)<br>Rate of return<br>if state occurs | (4)<br>Product<br>(2) × (3) | (5)<br>Rate of return<br>if state occurs | (6)<br>Product<br>(2) × (5) |
| Recession | 0.50 | −0.20 | −0.10 | 0.30 | 0.15 |
| Boom | 0.50 | 0.70 | 0.35 | 0.10 | 0.05 |
| | 1.00 | | $E(R_L) = 0.25 = 25\%$ | | $E(R_U) = 0.20 = 20\%$ |

**Table 12.2** Calculation of expected return

additional information about Equity U. Notice that Equity U earns 30 per cent if there is a recession, and 10 per cent if there is a boom.

Obviously, if you buy one of these equities, say Equity U, what you earn in any particular year depends on what the economy does during that year. However, suppose the probabilities stay the same through time. If you hold Equity U for a number of years, you'll earn 30 per cent about half the time and 10 per cent the other half. In this case we say that your **expected return** on Equity U, $E(R_U)$, is 20 per cent:

> **expected return**
> The return on a risky asset expected in the future.

$$E(R_U) = 0.50 \times 30\% + 0.50 \times 10\% = 20\%$$

In other words, you should expect to earn 20 per cent from this equity, on average.

For Equity L the probabilities are the same, but the possible returns are different. Here, we lose 20 per cent half the time, and we gain 70 per cent the other half. The expected return on L, $E(R_L)$, is thus 25 per cent:

$$E(R_L) = 0.50 \times -20\% + 0.50 \times 70\% = 25\%$$

Table 12.2 illustrates these calculations.

In our previous chapter we defined the risk premium as the difference between the return on a risky investment and that on a risk-free investment, and we calculated the historical risk premiums on some different investments. Using our projected returns, we can calculate the *projected*, or *expected*, *risk premium* as the difference between the expected return on a risky investment and the certain return on a risk-free investment.

For example, suppose risk-free investments are currently offering 8 per cent. We shall say that the risk-free rate, which we label as $R_f$, is 8 per cent. Given this, what is the projected risk premium on Equity U? On Equity L? Because the expected return on Equity U, $E(R_U)$, is 20 per cent, the projected risk premium is

$$\begin{align} \text{Risk premium} &= \text{Expected return} - \text{Risk-free rate} \qquad \text{(12.1)}\\ &= E(R_U) - R_f \\ &= 20\% - 8\% \\ &= 12\% \end{align}$$

Similarly, the risk premium on Equity L is 25% − 8% = 17%.

In general, the expected return on a security or other asset is simply equal to the sum of the possible returns multiplied by their probabilities. So, if we had 100 possible returns, we would multiply each one by its probability and add up the results. The result would be the expected return. The risk premium would then be the difference between this expected return and the risk-free rate.

EXAMPLE
12.1

# Unequal Probabilities

Look again at Tables 12.1 and 12.2. Suppose you think a boom will occur only 20 per cent of the time instead of 50 per cent. What are the expected returns on Equities U and L in this case? If the risk-free rate is 10 per cent, what are the risk premiums?

The first thing to notice is that a recession must occur 80 per cent of the time (1 − 0.20 = 0.80), because there are only two possibilities. With this in mind, we see that Equity U has a 30 per cent return in 80 per cent of the years and a 10 per cent return in 20 per cent of the years. To calculate the expected return, we again just multiply the possibilities by the probabilities and add up the results:

$$E(R_U) = 0.80 \times 30\% + 0.20 \times 10\% = 26\%$$

Table 12.3 summarizes the calculations for both equities. Notice that the expected return on L is −2 per cent.

The risk premium for Equity U is 26% − 10% = 16% in this case. The risk premium for Equity L is negative: −2% − 10% = −12%. This is a little odd; but, for reasons we discuss later, it is not impossible.

| (1) State of economy | (2) Probability of state of economy | Equity L | | Equity U | |
|---|---|---|---|---|---|
| | | (3) Rate of return if state occurs | (4) Product (2) × (3) | (5) Rate of return if state occurs | (6) Product (2) × (5) |
| Recession | 0.80 | −0.20 | −0.16 | 0.30 | 0.24 |
| Boom | 0.20 | 0.70 | 0.14 | 0.10 | 0.02 |
| | | | $E(R_L) = -0.2\%$ | | $E(R_U) = 0.26\%$ |

**Table 12.3** Calculation of expected return

## Calculating the Variance

To calculate the variances of the returns on our two equities, we first determine the squared deviations from the expected return. We then multiply each possible squared deviation by its probability. We add these up, and the result is the variance. The standard deviation, as always, is the square root of the variance.

To illustrate, let us return to the Equity U we originally discussed, which has an expected return of $E(R_U) = 20\%$. In a given year it will actually return either 30 per cent or 10 per cent. The possible deviations are thus 30% − 20% = 10% and 10% − 20% = −10%. In this case, the variance is

$$\text{Variance} = \sigma^2 = 0.50 \times (10\%)^2 + 0.50 \times (-10\%)^2 = 0.01$$

The standard deviation is the square root of this:

$$\text{Standard deviation} = \sigma = \sqrt{0.01} = 0.10 = 10\%$$

TABLE
**12.4**

| (1) State of economy | (2) Probability of state of economy | (3) Return deviation from expected return | (4) Squared return deviation from expected return | (5) Product (2) × (4) |
|---|---|---|---|---|
| *Equity L* | | | | |
| Recession | 0.50 | $-0.20 - 0.25 = -0.45$ | $-0.45^2 = 0.2025$ | 0.10125 |
| Boom | 0.50 | $0.70 - 0.25 = 0.45$ | $0.45^2 = 0.2025$ | 0.10125 |
| | | | | $\sigma_L^2 = 0.20250$ |
| *Equity U* | | | | |
| Recession | 0.50 | $0.30 - 0.20 = 0.10$ | $0.10^2 = 0.01$ | 0.005 |
| Boom | 0.50 | $0.10 - 0.20 = -0.45$ | $-0.10^2 = 0.01$ | 0.005 |
| | | | | $\sigma_U^2 = 0.010$ |

**Table 12.4** Calculation of variance

Table 12.4 summarizes these calculations for both equities. Notice that Equity L has a much larger variance.

When we put the expected return and variability information for our two equities together, we have the following:

| | Equity L | Equity U |
|---|---|---|
| Expected return, $E(R)$ (%) | 25 | 20 |
| Variance, $\sigma^2$ | 0.2025 | 0.0100 |
| Standard deviation, $\sigma$ (%) | 45 | 10 |

Equity L has a higher expected return, but U has less risk. You could get a 70 per cent return on your investment in L, but you could also lose 20 per cent. Notice that an investment in U will always pay at least 10 per cent.

Which of these two equities should you buy? We can't really say; it depends on your personal preferences. We can be reasonably sure that some investors would prefer L to U, and some would prefer U to L.

You've probably noticed that the way we have calculated expected returns and variances here is somewhat different from the way we did it in the last chapter. The reason is that in Chapter 11 we were examining actual historical returns, so we estimated the average return and the variance based on some actual events. Here, we have projected *future* returns and their associated probabilities, so this is the information with which we must work.

**EXAMPLE 12.2**

# More Unequal Probabilities

Going back to Example 12.1, what are the variances on the two equities once we have unequal probabilities? The standard deviations?

We can summarize the needed calculations as follows:

| (1) State of economy | (2) Probability of state of economy | (3) Return deviation from expected return | (4) Squared return deviation from expected return | (5) Product (2) × (4) |
|---|---|---|---|---|
| *Equity L* | | | | |
| Recession | 0.80 | $-0.20 - (-0.02) = -0.18$ | 0.0324 | 0.02592 |
| Boom | 0.20 | $0.70 - (-0.02) = 0.72$ | 0.5184 | 0.10368 |
| | | | | $\sigma_L^2 = 0.12960$ |
| *Equity U* | | | | |
| Recession | 0.80 | $0.30 - 0.26 = 0.04$ | 0.0016 | 0.00128 |
| Boom | 0.20 | $0.10 - 0.26 = -0.16$ | 0.0256 | 0.00512 |
| | | | | $\sigma_U^2 = 0.00640$ |

Based on these calculations, the standard deviation for L is $\sigma_L = \sqrt{0.1296} = 0.36 = 36\%$. The standard deviation for U is much smaller: $\sigma_U = \sqrt{0.0064} = 0.08 = 8\%$.

**CONCEPT QUESTIONS**

**12.1a** How do we calculate the expected return on a security?

**12.1b** In words, how do we calculate the variance of the expected return?

## 12.2 Portfolios

Thus far in this chapter we have concentrated on individual assets considered separately. However, most investors actually hold a **portfolio** of assets. All we mean by this is that investors tend to own more than just a single equity, bond, or other asset. Given that this is so, portfolio return and portfolio risk are of obvious relevance. Accordingly, we now discuss portfolio expected returns and variances.

> **portfolio**
> A group of assets such as equities and bonds held by an investor.

### Portfolio Weights

There are many equivalent ways of describing a portfolio. The most convenient approach is to list the percentage of the total portfolio's value that is invested in each portfolio asset. We call these percentages the **portfolio weights**.

For example, if we have €50 in one asset and €150 in another, our total portfolio is worth €200. The percentage of our portfolio in the first asset is €50/€200 = 0.25. The percentage of our portfolio in the second asset is €150/€200, or 0.75. Our portfolio weights are thus 0.25 and 0.75. Notice that the weights have to add up to 1.00, because all of our money is invested somewhere.[1]

> **portfolio weight**
> The percentage of a portfolio's total value that is in a particular asset.

### Portfolio Expected Returns

Let's go back to Equities L and U. You put half your money in each. The portfolio weights are obviously 0.50 and 0.50. What is the pattern of returns on this portfolio? The expected return?

TABLE
**12.5**

| (1)<br>State of<br>economy | (2)<br>Probability of<br>state of economy | (3)<br>Portfolio return<br>if state occurs | (4)<br>Product<br>(2) × (3) |
|---|---|---|---|
| Recession | 0.50 | $0.50 \times -20\% + 0.50 \times 30\% = 5\%$ | 0.025 |
| Boom | 0.50 | $0.50 \times 70\% + 0.50 \times 10\% = 40\%$ | 0.200 |
| | | | $E(R_\text{p}) = 22.5\%$ |

**Table 12.5** Expected return on an equally weighted portfolio of Equity L and Equity U

To answer these questions, suppose the economy actually enters a recession. In this case, half your money (the half in L) loses 20 per cent. The other half (the half in U) gains 30 per cent. Your portfolio return, $R_\text{p}$, in a recession is thus

$$R_\text{p} = 0.50 \times -20\% + 0.50 \times 30\% = 5\%$$

Table 12.5 summarizes the remaining calculations. Notice that when a boom occurs, your portfolio will return 40 per cent:

$$R_\text{p} = 0.50 \times 70\% + 0.50 \times 10\% = 40\%$$

As indicated in Table 12.5, the expected return on your portfolio, $E(R_\text{p})$, is 22.5 per cent.

We can save ourselves some work by calculating the expected return more directly. Given these portfolio weights, we could have reasoned that we expect half of our money to earn 25 per cent (the half in L) and half of our money to earn 20 per cent (the half in U). Our portfolio expected return is thus

$$\begin{aligned} E(R_\text{p}) &= 0.50 \times E(R_\text{L}) + 0.50 \times E(R_\text{U}) \\ &= 0.50 \times 25\% + 0.50 \times 20\% \\ &= 22.5\% \end{aligned}$$

This is the same portfolio expected return we calculated previously.

This method of calculating the expected return on a portfolio works no matter how many assets there are in the portfolio. Suppose we had $n$ assets in our portfolio, where $n$ is any number. If we let $x_i$ stand for the percentage of our money in Asset $i$, then the expected return would be

$$E(R_\text{p}) = x_1 \times E(R_1) + x_2 \times E(R_2) + \ldots + x_n \times E(R_n) \qquad \text{(12.2)}$$

This says that the expected return on a portfolio is a straightforward combination of the expected returns on the assets in that portfolio. This seems somewhat obvious; but, as we shall examine next, the obvious approach is not always the right one.

EXAMPLE
**12.3**

## Portfolio Expected Return

Suppose we have the following projections for three equities:

| State of<br>economy | Probability<br>of state of<br>economy | Returns if state occurs (%) | | |
|---|---|---|---|---|
| | | **Equity A** | **Equity B** | **Equity C** |
| Boom | 0.40 | 10 | 15 | 20 |
| Bust | 0.60 | 8 | 4 | 0 |

We want to calculate portfolio expected returns in two cases. First, what would be the expected return on a portfolio with equal amounts invested in each of the three equities? Second, what would be the expected return if half of the portfolio were in A, with the remainder equally divided between B and C?

Based on what we've learned from our earlier discussions, we can determine that the expected returns on the individual equities are (check these for practice):

$E(R_A) = 8.8\%$

$E(R_B) = 8.4\%$

$E(R_C) = 8.0\%$

If a portfolio has equal investments in each asset, the portfolio weights are all the same. Such a portfolio is said to be *equally weighted*. Because there are three equities in this case, the weights are all equal to $1/3$. The portfolio expected return is thus

$$E(R_P) = (1/3) \times 8.8\% + (1/3) \times 8.4\% + (1/3) \times 8\% = 8.4\%$$

In the second case, verify that the portfolio expected return is 8.5 per cent.

## Portfolio Variance

From our earlier discussion, the expected return on a portfolio that contains equal investments in Equities U and L is 22.5 per cent. What is the standard deviation of return on this portfolio? Simple intuition might suggest that because half of the money has a standard deviation of 45 per cent and the other half has a standard deviation of 10 per cent, the portfolio's standard deviation might be calculated as

$$\sigma_P = 0.50 \times 45\% + 0.50 \times 10\% = 27.5\%$$

Unfortunately, this approach is completely incorrect!

Let's see what the standard deviation really is. Table 12.6 summarizes the relevant calculations. As we see, the portfolio's variance is about 0.031, and its standard deviation is less than we thought – it's only 17.5 per cent. What is illustrated here is that the variance on a portfolio is not generally a simple combination of the variances of the assets in the portfolio.

We can illustrate this point a little more dramatically by considering a slightly different set of portfolio weights. Suppose we put 2/11 (about 18 per cent) in L and the other 9/11 (about 82 per cent) in U. If a recession occurs, this portfolio will have a return of:

$$R_P = (2/11) \times -20\% + (9/11) \times 30\% = 20.91\%$$

| TABLE 12.6 | (1) State of economy | (2) Probability of state of economy | (3) Portfolio return if state occurs (%) | (4) Squared deviation from expected return | (5) Product (2) × (4) |
|---|---|---|---|---|---|
| | Recession | 0.50 | 5 | $(0.05 - 0.225)^2 = 0.030625$ | 0.0153125 |
| | Boom | 0.50 | 40 | $(0.40 - 0.225)^2 = 0.030625$ | 0.0153125 |
| | | | | $\sigma_P^2 = 0.030625$ | |
| | | | | $\sigma_P = \sqrt{0.030625} = 17.5\%$ | |

**Table 12.6** Variance on an equally weighted portfolio of Equity L and Equity U

If a boom occurs, this portfolio will have a return of

$$R_P = (2/11) \times 70\% + (9/11) \times 10\% = 20.91\%$$

Notice that the return is the same, no matter what happens. No further calculations are needed: this portfolio has a zero variance. Apparently, combining assets into portfolios can substantially alter the risks faced by the investor. This is a crucial observation, and we shall begin to explore its implications in the next section.

---

**EXAMPLE 12.4**

## Portfolio Variance and Standard Deviation

In Example 12.3, what are the standard deviations on the two portfolios? To answer, we first have to calculate the portfolio returns in the two states. We shall work with the second portfolio, which has 50 per cent in Equity A and 25 per cent in each of Equities B and C. The relevant calculations can be summarized as follows:

| State of economy | Probability of state of economy | Rate of return if state occurs (%) | | | |
| --- | --- | --- | --- | --- | --- |
| | | Equity A | Equity B | Equity C | Portfolio |
| Boom | 0.40 | 10 | 15 | 20 | 13.75 |
| Bust | 0.60 | 8 | 4 | 0 | 5.00 |

The portfolio return when the economy booms is calculated as

$$E(R_P) = 0.50 \times 10\% + 0.25 \times 15\% + 0.25 \times 20\% = 13.75\%$$

The return when the economy goes bust is calculated the same way. The expected return on the portfolio is 8.5 per cent. The variance is thus

$$\sigma_P^2 = 0.40 \times (0.1375 - 0.085)^2 + 0.60 \times (0.05 - 0.085)^2$$
$$= 0.0018375$$

The standard deviation is thus about 4.3 per cent. For our equally weighted portfolio, check to see that the standard deviation is about 5.4 per cent.

---

**CONCEPT QUESTIONS**

12.2a   What is a portfolio weight?
12.2b   How do we calculate the expected return on a portfolio?
12.2c   Is there a simple relationship between the standard deviation on a portfolio and the standard deviations of the assets in the portfolio?

## 12.3 Announcements, Surprises and Expected Returns

Now that we know how to construct portfolios and evaluate their returns, we begin to describe more carefully the risks and returns associated with individual securities. Thus far, we have measured volatility by looking at the difference between the actual return on an asset or portfolio, $R$, and the expected return, $E(R)$. We now look at why those deviations exist.

## Expected and Unexpected Returns

To begin, for concreteness, we consider the return on the equity of a company called Flyers. What will determine this equity's return in, say, the coming year?

The return on any equity traded in a financial market is composed of two parts. First, the normal, or expected, return from the equity is the part of the return that shareholders in the market predict or expect. This return depends on the information shareholders have that bears on the equity, and it is based on the market's understanding today of the important factors that will influence the share price in the coming year.

The second part of the return on the equity is the uncertain, or risky, part. This is the portion that comes from unexpected information revealed within the year. A list of all possible sources of such information would be endless, but here are a few examples:

- News about Flyers research
- Government figures released on gross domestic product (GDP)
- The results from the latest arms control talks
- The news that Flyers' sales figures are higher than expected
- A sudden, unexpected drop in interest rates

Based on this discussion, one way to express the return on Flyers' equity in the coming year would be

$$\text{Total return} = \text{Expected return} + \text{Unexpected return}$$
$$R = E(R) + U \tag{12.3}$$

where $R$ stands for the actual total return in the year, $E(R)$ stands for the expected part of the return, and $U$ stands for the unexpected part of the return. What this says is that the actual return, $R$, differs from the expected return, $E(R)$, because of surprises that occur during the year. In any given year, the unexpected return will be positive or negative; but, through time, the average value of $U$ will be zero. This simply means that, on average, the actual return equals the expected return.

## Announcements and News

We need to be careful when we talk about the effect of news items on the return. For example, suppose Flyers' business is such that the company prospers when GDP grows at a relatively high rate, and suffers when GDP is stagnant. In this case, in deciding what return to expect this year from owning equity in Flyers, shareholders either implicitly or explicitly must think about what GDP is likely to be for the year.

When the government actually announces GDP figures for the year, what will happen to the value of Flyers' equity? Obviously, the answer depends on what figure is released. More to the point, however, the impact depends on how much of that figure is *new* information.

At the beginning of the year, market participants will have some idea or forecast of what the yearly GDP will be. To the extent that shareholders have predicted GDP, that prediction will already be factored into the expected part of the return on the equity, $E(R)$. On the other hand, if the announced GDP is a surprise, the effect will be part of $U$, the unanticipated portion of the return. As an example, suppose shareholders in the market had forecast that the GDP increase this year would be 0.5 per cent. If the actual announcement this year is exactly 0.5 per cent, the same as the forecast, then the shareholders don't really learn anything, and the announcement isn't news. There will be no impact on the share price as a result. This is like receiving confirmation of something you suspected all along; it doesn't reveal anything new.

A common way of saying that an announcement isn't news is to say that the market has already 'discounted' the announcement. The use of the word *discount* here is different from the use of the term in computing present values, but the spirit is the same. When we discount cash in the future, we say it is worth less to us because of the time value of money. When we discount an announcement or a news item, we say that it has less of an impact on the price, because the market already knew much of it.

Going back to Flyers, suppose the government announces that the actual GDP increase during the year has been 1.5 per cent. Now shareholders have learned something – namely, that the increase is one percentage point higher than they had forecast. This difference between the actual result and the forecast, one percentage point in this example, is sometimes called the *innovation* or the *surprise*.

This distinction explains why what seems to be good news can actually be bad news (and vice versa). Going back to the companies we discussed in our chapter opener, even though ITV's earnings were up £25 million, the company experienced a drop in revenues, and the share price fell. Clearly, shareholders were concerned more by the fall in revenues than by the increase in earnings.

A key idea to keep in mind about news and price changes is that news about the future is what matters. For WPP, analysts accepted the bad news about earnings, but also noted that those numbers were, in a very real sense, yesterday's news. Looking to the future, the company's CEO announced that 2009 was a brutal year but 2010 'should be less worse!' and the market would stabilize.

To summarize, an announcement can be broken into two parts: the anticipated, or expected, part and the surprise, or innovation:

$$\text{Announcement} = \text{Expected part} + \text{Surprise} \tag{12.4}$$

The expected part of any announcement is the part of the information that the market uses to form the expectation, $E(R)$, of the return on the equity. The surprise is the news that influences the unanticipated return on the equity, $U$.

Our discussion of market efficiency in the previous chapter bears on this discussion. We are assuming that relevant information known today is already reflected in the expected return. This is identical to saying that the current price reflects relevant publicly available information. We are thus implicitly assuming that markets are at least reasonably efficient in the semi-strong form.

Henceforth, when we speak of news, we shall mean the surprise part of an announcement, and not the portion that the market has expected and therefore already discounted.

| | |
|---|---|
| **CONCEPT QUESTIONS** | 12.3a  What are the two basic parts of a return? |
| | 12.3b  Under what conditions will a company's announcement have no effect on common share prices? |

## 12.4  Risk: Systematic and Unsystematic

The unanticipated part of the return, that portion resulting from surprises, is the true risk of any investment. After all, if we always receive exactly what we expect, then the investment is perfectly predictable and, by definition, risk-free. In other words, the risk of owning an asset comes from surprises – unanticipated events.

There are important differences, though, among various sources of risk. Look back at our previous list of news stories. Some of these stories are directed specifically at Flyers, and some are more general. Which of the news items are of specific importance to Flyers?

Announcements about interest rates or GDP are clearly important for nearly all companies, whereas news about Flyers' chairman, its research, or its sales is of specific interest to Flyers. We shall distinguish between these two types of event because, as we shall see, they have different implications.

## Systematic and Unsystematic Risk

The first type of surprise – the one that affects many assets – we shall label **systematic risk**. A systematic risk is one that influences a large number of assets, each to a greater or lesser extent. Because systematic risks have market-wide effects, they are sometimes called *market risks*.

The second type of surprise we shall call **unsystematic risk**. An unsystematic risk is one that affects a single asset or a small group of assets. Because these risks are unique to individual companies or assets, they are sometimes called *unique* or *asset-specific risks*. We shall use these terms interchangeably.

As we have seen, uncertainties about general economic conditions (such as GDP, interest rates, or inflation) are examples of systematic risks. These conditions affect nearly all companies to some degree. An unanticipated increase, or surprise, in inflation, for example, affects wages and the costs of the supplies that companies buy; it affects the value of the assets that companies own; and it affects the prices at which companies sell their products. Forces such as these, to which all companies are susceptible, are the essence of systematic risk.

In contrast, the announcement of an oil strike by a company will primarily affect that company and, perhaps, a few others (such as main competitors and suppliers). It is unlikely to have much of an effect on the world oil market, however, or on the affairs of companies not in the oil business, so this is an unsystematic event.

> **systematic risk**
> A risk that influences a large number of assets. Also, *market risk*.
>
> **unsystematic risk**
> A risk that affects at most a small number of assets. Also, *unique* or *asset-specific risk*.

## Systematic and Unsystematic Components of Return

The distinction between a systematic risk and an unsystematic risk is never really as exact as we make it out to be. Even the most narrow and peculiar bit of news about a company ripples through the economy. This is true because every enterprise, no matter how tiny, is a part of the economy. It's like the tale of a kingdom that was lost because one horse lost a shoe. This is mostly hairsplitting, however. Some risks are clearly much more general than others. We'll see some evidence on this point in just a moment.

The distinction between the types of risk allows us to break down the surprise portion, $U$, of the return on Flyers' equity into two parts. Earlier, we had the actual return broken down into its expected and surprise components:

$$R = E(R) + U$$

We now recognize that the total surprise component for Flyers, $U$, has a systematic and an unsystematic component, so:

$$R = E(R) + \text{Systematic portion} + \text{Unsystematic portion} \quad (12.5)$$

Because it is traditional, we shall use the Greek letter epsilon, $\varepsilon$, to stand for the unsystematic portion. Because systematic risks are often called market risks, we shall use the letter $m$ to stand for the systematic part of the surprise. With these symbols, we can rewrite the formula for the total return:

$$R = E(R) + U$$
$$= E(R) + m + \varepsilon$$

The important thing about the way we have broken down the total surprise, $U$, is that the unsystematic portion, $\varepsilon$, is more or less unique to Flyers. For this reason, it is unrelated to the unsystematic portion of return on most other assets. To see why this is important, we need to return to the subject of portfolio risk.

**CONCEPT QUESTIONS**

12.4a  What are the two basic types of risk?
12.4b  What is the distinction between the two types of risk?

## 12.5 Diversification and Portfolio Risk

We've seen earlier that portfolio risks can, in principle, be quite different from the risks of the assets that make up the portfolio. We now look more closely at the riskiness of an individual asset versus the risk of a portfolio of many different assets. We shall once again examine some market history to get an idea of what happens with actual investments in European capital markets.

### The Effect of Diversification: Another Lesson from Market History

In our previous chapter we saw that the standard deviation of the annual return on a portfolio of large European equities has historically been between 20 and 30 per cent per year. Does this mean that the standard deviation of the annual return on a typical equity in Europe is between 20 and 30 per cent? As you might suspect by now, the answer is *no*. This is an extremely important observation.

To illustrate the relationship between portfolio size and portfolio risk, Table 12.7 illustrates typical average annual standard deviations for equally weighted portfolios that contain different numbers of randomly selected securities.

In column 2 of Table 12.7 we see that the standard deviation for a 'portfolio' of one security is about 49 per cent. What this means is that if you randomly selected a single equity and put all your money into it, your standard deviation of return would typically be a substantial 49 per cent per year. If you were to randomly select two equities and invest half your money in each, your standard deviation would be about 37 per cent on average, and so on.

| TABLE 12.7 | | |
|---|---|---|
| (1) Number of equities in portfolio | (2) Average standard deviation of annual portfolio returns (%) | (3) Ratio of portfolio standard deviation to standard deviation of a single equity |
| 1 | 49.24 | 1.00 |
| 2 | 37.36 | 0.76 |
| 4 | 29.69 | 0.60 |
| 6 | 26.64 | 0.54 |
| 8 | 24.98 | 0.51 |
| 10 | 23.93 | 0.49 |
| 20 | 21.68 | 0.44 |
| 30 | 20.87 | 0.42 |
| 40 | 20.46 | 0.42 |
| 50 | 20.20 | 0.41 |
| 100 | 19.69 | 0.40 |
| 200 | 19.42 | 0.39 |
| 300 | 19.34 | 0.39 |
| 400 | 19.29 | 0.39 |
| 500 | 19.27 | 0.39 |
| 1,000 | 19.21 | 0.39 |

*Source*: Table 1 in M. Statman, 'How many stocks make a diversified portfolio?' *Journal of Financial and Quantitative Analysis* (1987), vol. 22, no. 3, pp. 353–364. Derived from E.J. Elton and M.J. Gruber, 'Risk reduction and portfolio size: an analytic solution', *Journal of Business* (1977), vol. 50, October, pp. 415–437.

**Table 12.7** Standard deviations of annual portfolio returns

The important thing to notice in Table 12.7 is that the standard deviation declines as the number of securities is increased. By the time we have 100 randomly chosen equities, the portfolio's standard deviation has declined by about 60 per cent, from 49 per cent to about 20 per cent. With 500 securities the standard deviation is 19.27 per cent, similar to the 20 per cent we saw in our previous chapter for the large UK company portfolio.

## The Principle of Diversification

Figure 12.1 illustrates the point we've been discussing. What we have plotted is the standard deviation of return versus the number of equities in the portfolio. Notice in Fig. 12.1 that the benefit in terms of risk reduction from adding securities drops off as we add more and more. By the time we have 10 securities, most of the effect is already realized; and by the time we get to 30 or so, there is little remaining benefit.

Figure 12.1 illustrates two key points. First, some of the riskiness associated with individual assets can be eliminated by forming portfolios. The process of spreading an investment across assets (and thereby forming a portfolio) is called *diversification*. The **principle of diversification** tells us that spreading an investment across many assets will eliminate some of the risk. The blue shaded area in Fig. 12.1, labelled 'Diversifiable risk', is the part that can be eliminated by diversification.

> **principle of diversification**
> Spreading an investment across a number of assets will eliminate some, but not all, of the risk.

The second point is equally important. There is a minimum level of risk that cannot be eliminated simply by diversifying. This minimum level is labelled 'Non-diversifiable risk' in Fig. 12.1. Taken together, these two points are another important lesson from capital market history: diversification reduces risk, but only up to a point. Put another way, some risk is diversifiable and some is not.

To give a recent example of the impact of diversification, the FTSE 100, which is a widely followed stock market index of 100 large, well-known British companies, stayed level on 9 March 2010. The biggest individual gainers for the day were Antofagasta (up 1.1 per cent), GlaxoSmithKline (up 1.6 per cent), and SAB Miller (up 1.1 per cent). The losers included Liberty International (down 4.1 per cent) and various banks (e.g. Lloyds Banking Group, Royal Bank of Scotland, and HSBC), who were down between 0.7 and 2.8 per cent. Again, the lesson is clear: diversification reduces exposure to extreme outcomes, both good and bad.

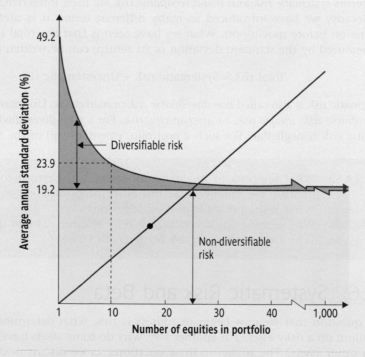

**FIGURE 12.1**

**Figure 12.1** Portfolio diversification

## Diversification and Unsystematic Risk

From our discussion of portfolio risk, we know that some of the risk associated with individual assets can be diversified away and some cannot. We are left with an obvious question: why is this so? It turns out that the answer hinges on the distinction we made earlier between systematic and unsystematic risk.

By definition, an unsystematic risk is one that is particular to a single asset or, at most, a small group. For example, if the asset under consideration is equity in a single company, the discovery of positive-NPV projects such as successful new products and innovative cost savings will tend to increase the value of the equity. Unanticipated lawsuits, industrial accidents, strikes and similar events will tend to decrease future cash flows and thereby reduce share values.

Here is the important observation: if we held only a single equity, the value of our investment would fluctuate because of company-specific events. If we hold a large portfolio, on the other hand, some of the equities in the portfolio will go up in value because of positive company-specific events and some will go down in value because of negative events. The net effect on the overall value of the portfolio will be relatively small, however, because these effects will tend to cancel each other out.

Now we see why some of the variability associated with individual assets is eliminated by diversification. When we combine assets into portfolios, the unique, or unsystematic, events – both positive and negative – tend to 'wash out' once we have more than just a few assets.

This is an important point that bears repeating:

*Unsystematic risk is eliminated by diversification, so a portfolio with many assets has almost no unsystematic risk.*

In fact, the terms *diversifiable risk* and *unsystematic risk* are often used interchangeably.

## Diversification and Systematic Risk

We've seen that unsystematic risk can be eliminated by diversifying. What about systematic risk? Can it also be eliminated by diversification? The answer is no, because, by definition, a systematic risk affects almost all assets to some degree. As a result, no matter how many assets we put into a portfolio, the systematic risk doesn't go away. Thus, for obvious reasons, the terms *systematic risk* and *non-diversifiable risk* are used interchangeably.

Because we have introduced so many different terms, it is useful to summarize our discussion before moving on. What we have seen is that the total risk of an investment, as measured by the standard deviation of its return, can be written as

$$\text{Total risk} = \text{Systematic risk} + \text{Unsystematic risk} \qquad (12.6)$$

Systematic risk is also called *non-diversifiable risk* or *market risk*. Unsystematic risk is also called *diversifiable risk*, *unique risk*, or *asset-specific risk*. For a well-diversified portfolio, the unsystematic risk is negligible. For such a portfolio, essentially all of the risk is systematic.

| CONCEPT QUESTIONS | | |
|---|---|---|
| | 12.5a | What happens to the standard deviation of return for a portfolio if we increase the number of securities in the portfolio? |
| | 12.5b | What is the principle of diversification? |
| | 12.5c | Why is some risk diversifiable? Why is some risk not diversifiable? |
| | 12.5d | Why can't systematic risk be diversified away? |

## 12.6  Systematic Risk and Beta

The question that we now begin to address is this: what determines the size of the risk premium on a risky asset? Put another way, why do some assets have a larger risk premium than other assets? The answer to these questions, as we discuss next, is also based on the distinction between systematic and unsystematic risk.

## The Systematic Risk Principle

Thus far, we've seen that the total risk associated with an asset can be decomposed into two components: systematic and unsystematic risk. We have also seen that unsystematic risk can essentially be eliminated by diversification. The systematic risk present in an asset, on the other hand, cannot be eliminated by diversification.

Based on our study of capital market history, we know that there is a reward, on average, for bearing risk. However, we now need to be more precise about what we mean by risk. The **systematic risk principle** states that the reward for bearing risk depends only on the systematic risk of an investment. The underlying rationale for this principle is straightforward: because unsystematic risk can be eliminated at virtually no cost (by diversifying), there is no reward for bearing it. Put another way, the market does not reward risks that are borne unnecessarily.

The systematic risk principle has a remarkable and very important implication:

*The expected return on an asset depends only on that asset's systematic risk.*

There is an obvious corollary to this principle: no matter how much total risk an asset has, only the systematic portion is relevant in determining the expected return (and the risk premium) on that asset.

> **systematic risk principle**
> The expected return on a risky asset depends only on that asset's systematic risk.

## Measuring Systematic Risk

Because systematic risk is the crucial determinant of an asset's expected return, we need some way of measuring the level of systematic risk for different investments. The specific measure we shall use is called the **beta coefficient**, for which we shall use the Greek letter $\beta$. A beta coefficient, or beta for short, tells us how much systematic risk a particular asset has relative to an average asset. By definition, an average asset has a beta of 1.0 relative to itself. An asset with a beta of 0.50, therefore, has half as much systematic risk as an average asset; an asset with a beta of 2.0 has twice as much.

Table 12.8 contains the estimated beta coefficients for the equities of some well-known companies. The range of betas in Table 12.8 is typical for equities of large European corporations. Betas outside this range occur, but they are less common.

The important thing to remember is that the expected return, and thus the risk premium, of an asset depends only on its systematic risk. Because assets with larger betas have greater systematic risks, they will have greater expected returns. Thus, from Table 12.8, an investor who buys equity in Volkswagen, with a beta of 0.40, should expect to earn less, on average, than an investor who buys equity in Renault, with a beta of about 1.64.

One cautionary note is in order: not all betas are created equal. Different providers use somewhat different methods for estimating betas, and significant differences sometimes

> **beta coefficient**
> The amount of systematic risk present in a particular risky asset relative to that in an average risky asset.

**TABLE 12.8**

| Equity | Beta |
|---|---|
| Alcatel-Lucent | 1.44 |
| L'Oreal | 0.45 |
| SAP | 0.56 |
| Siemens | 1.51 |
| Daimler | 1.25 |
| Philips Electron | 0.92 |
| Renault | 1.64 |
| Volkswagen | 0.40 |

*Source*: Yahoo! Finance. © 2010 Yahoo! All rights reserved.

**Table 12.8** Beta coefficients for selected companies

occur. As a result, it is a good idea to look at several sources. See our nearby Work the Web box for more about beta.

**EXAMPLE 12.5**

# Total Risk versus Beta

Consider the following information about two securities. Which has greater total risk? Which has greater systematic risk? Greater unsystematic risk? Which asset will have a higher risk premium?

| | Standard deviation (%) | Beta |
|---|---|---|
| Security A | 40 | 0.50 |
| Security B | 20 | 1.50 |

From our discussion in this section, Security A has greater total risk, but it has substantially less systematic risk. Because total risk is the sum of systematic and unsystematic risk, Security A must have greater unsystematic risk. Finally, from the systematic risk principle, Security B will have a higher risk premium and a greater expected return, despite the fact that it has less total risk.

## Portfolio Betas

Earlier, we saw that the riskiness of a portfolio has no simple relationship to the risks of the assets in the portfolio. A portfolio beta, however, can be calculated, just like a portfolio expected return. For example, looking again at Table 12.8, suppose you put half of your money in L'Oréal and half in Siemens. What would the beta of this combination be? Because L'Oréal has a beta of 0.45 and Siemens has a beta of 1.51, the portfolio's beta, $\beta_P$, would be

$$\beta_P = 0.50 \times \beta_{L'Oréal} + 0.50 \times \beta_{Siemens}$$
$$= 0.50 \times 0.45 + 0.50 \times 1.51$$
$$= 0.98$$

# Work the Web

You can find beta estimates at many sites on the Web. One of the best is Yahoo! Finance. Here is a snapshot of the 'Key Statistics' screen for the brokerage firm ICAP plc:

| RISK ANALYSIS | |
|---|---|
| Alpha: | -0.004 |
| Beta: | 1.5436 |
| R2: | 0.329 |
| Relative Performance: | -23.9528% |
| Relative Strength: | -2.8183 |
| Retractment from maximum: | -22.2198% |
| Quarterly Volatility: | 57.6177% |
| Distance to 20 days moving average: | 9.797% |
| Distance to 200 days moving average: | -13.886% |

The reported beta for ICAP is 1.54, which means that ICAP has about one and a half times the systematic risk of a typical equity. You would expect that the company is quite risky; and, looking at the other numbers, we agree.

## QUESTIONS

1   Explore the other pages on Yahoo! Finance relating to ICAP plc. From your own assessment, explain why you think ICAP has greater risk than the average equity.

2   What growth rate are analysts projecting for ICAP plc? How does this growth rate compare with the industry?

In general, if we had many assets in a portfolio, we would multiply each asset's beta by its portfolio weight and then add the results to get the portfolio's beta.

---

**EXAMPLE 12.6**

## Portfolio Betas

Suppose we had the following investments:

| Security | Amount invested (€) | Expected return (%) | Beta |
|----------|---------------------|---------------------|------|
| Equity A | 1,000 | 8 | 0.80 |
| Equity B | 2,000 | 12 | 0.95 |
| Equity C | 3,000 | 15 | 1.10 |
| Equity D | 4,000 | 18 | 1.40 |

What is the expected return on this portfolio? What is the beta of this portfolio? Does this portfolio have more or less systematic risk than an average asset?

To answer, we first have to calculate the portfolio weights. Notice that the total amount invested is €10,000. Of this, €1,000/10,000 = 10% is invested in Equity A. Similarly, 20 per cent is invested in Equity B, 30 per cent is invested in Equity C, and 40 per cent is invested in Equity D. The expected return, $E(R_P)$, is thus

$$E(R_P) = 0.10 \times E(R_A) + 0.20 \times E(R_B) + 0.30 \times E(R_C) + 0.40 \times E(R_D)$$
$$= 0.10 \times 8\% + 0.20 \times 12\% + 0.30 \times 15\% + 0.40 \times 18\%$$
$$= 14.9\%$$

Similarly, the portfolio beta, $\beta_P$, is

$$\beta_P = 0.10 \times \beta_A + 0.20 \times \beta_B + 0.30 \times \beta_C + 0.40 \times \beta_D$$
$$= 0.10 \times 0.80 + 0.20 \times 0.95 + 0.30 \times 1.10 + 0.40 \times 1.40$$
$$= 1.16$$

This portfolio thus has an expected return of 14.9 per cent and a beta of 1.16. Because the beta is larger than 1, this portfolio has greater systematic risk than an average asset.

---

**CONCEPT QUESTIONS**

12.6a   What is the systematic risk principle?

12.6b   What does a beta coefficient measure?

12.6c   True or false: the expected return on a risky asset depends on that asset's total risk. Explain.

12.6d   How do you calculate a portfolio beta?

# 12.7 The Security Market Line

We're now in a position to see how risk is rewarded in the marketplace. To begin, suppose that Asset A has an expected return of $E(R_A) = 20\%$ and a beta of $\beta_A = 1.6$. Furthermore, suppose that the risk-free rate is $R_f = 8\%$. Notice that a risk-free asset, by definition, has no systematic risk (or unsystematic risk), so a risk-free asset has a beta of zero.

## Beta and the Risk Premium

Consider a portfolio made up of Asset A and a risk-free asset. We can calculate some different possible portfolio expected returns and betas by varying the percentages invested in these two assets. For example, if 25 per cent of the portfolio is invested in Asset A, then the expected return is

$$E(R_P) = 0.25 \times E(R_A) + (1 - 0.25) \times R_f$$
$$= 0.25 \times 20\% + 0.75 \times 8\%$$
$$= 11\%$$

Similarly, the beta on the portfolio, $\beta_P$, would be

$$\beta_P = 0.25 \times \beta_A + (1 - 0.25) \times 0$$
$$= 0.25 \times 1.6$$
$$= 0.40$$

Notice that because the weights have to add up to 1, the percentage invested in the risk-free asset is equal to 1 minus the percentage invested in Asset A.

One thing that you might wonder about is whether it is possible for the percentage invested in Asset A to exceed 100 per cent. The answer is yes. This can happen if the investor borrows at the risk-free rate. For example, suppose an investor has €100 and borrows an additional €50 at 8 per cent, the risk-free rate. The total investment in Asset A would be €150, or 150 per cent of the investor's wealth. The expected return in this case would be

$$E(R_P) = 1.50 \times E(R_A) + (1 - 1.50) \times R_f$$
$$= 1.50 \times 20\% - 0.50 \times 8\%$$
$$= 26\%$$

The beta on the portfolio would be

$$\beta_P = 1.50 \times \beta_A + (1 - 1.50) \times 0$$
$$= 1.50 \times 1.6$$
$$= 2.4$$

We can calculate some other possibilities, as follows:

| Percentage of portfolio in Asset A (%) | Portfolio expected return (%) | Portfolio beta |
|---|---|---|
| 0 | 8 | 0.0 |
| 25 | 11 | 0.4 |
| 50 | 14 | 0.8 |
| 75 | 17 | 1.2 |
| 100 | 20 | 1.6 |
| 125 | 23 | 2.0 |
| 150 | 26 | 2.4 |

In Fig. 12.2 these portfolio expected returns are plotted against the portfolio betas. Notice that all the combinations fall on a straight line.

**The Reward-to-Risk Ratio**    What is the slope of the straight line in Fig. 12.2(a)? As always, the slope of a straight line is equal to 'the rise over the run'. In this case, as we move out of the risk-free asset into Asset A, the beta increases from zero to 1.6 (a 'run' of 1.6). At the same time, the expected return goes from 8 per cent to 20 per cent, a 'rise' of 12 per cent. The slope of the line is thus 12%/1.6 = 7.5%.

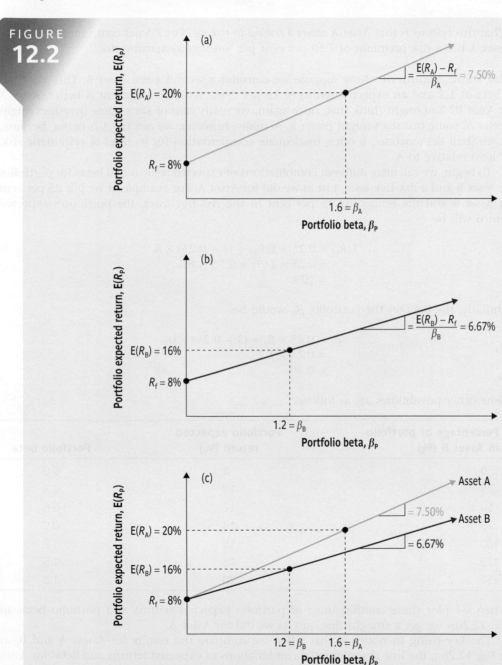

**Figure 12.2** (a) Portfolio expected returns and betas for Asset A; (b) Portfolio expected returns and betas for Asset B; (c) Portfolio expected returns and betas for both assets

Notice that the slope of our line is just the risk premium on Asset A, $E(R_A) - R_f$, divided by Asset A's beta, $\beta_A$:

$$\text{Slope} = \frac{E(R_A) - R_f}{\beta_A}$$

$$= \frac{20\% - 8\%}{1.6}$$

$$= 7.5\%$$

What this tells us is that Asset A offers a *reward-to-risk* ratio of 7.5 per cent.[2] In other words, Asset A has a risk premium of 7.50 per cent per 'unit' of systematic risk.

**The Basic Argument** Now suppose we consider a second asset, Asset B. This asset has a beta of 1.2 and an expected return of 16 per cent. Which investment is better, Asset A or Asset B? You might think that, once again, we really cannot say – some investors might prefer A; some investors might prefer B. Actually, however, we *can* say A is better, because, as we shall demonstrate, B offers inadequate compensation for its level of systematic risk, at least relative to A.

To begin, we calculate different combinations of expected returns and betas for portfolios of Asset B and a risk-free asset, just as we did for Asset A. For example, if we put 25 per cent in Asset B and the remaining 75 per cent in the risk-free asset, the portfolio's expected return will be

$$E(R_P) = 0.25 \times E(R_B) + (1 - 0.25) \times R_f$$

$$= 0.25 \times 16\% + 0.75 \times 8\%$$

$$= 10\%$$

Similarly, the beta on the portfolio, $\beta_P$, would be

$$\beta_P = 0.25 \times \beta_B + (1 - 0.25) \times 0$$

$$= 0.25 \times 1.2$$

$$= 0.30$$

Some other possibilities are as follows:

| Percentage of portfolio in Asset B (%) | Portfolio expected return (%) | Portfolio beta |
|---|---|---|
| 0 | 8 | 0.0 |
| 25 | 10 | 0.3 |
| 50 | 12 | 0.6 |
| 75 | 14 | 0.9 |
| 100 | 16 | 1.2 |
| 125 | 18 | 1.5 |
| 150 | 20 | 1.8 |

When we plot these combinations of portfolio expected returns and portfolio betas in Fig. 12.2(b) we get a straight line, just as we did for Asset A.

The key thing to notice is that when we compare the results for Assets A and B, as in Fig. 12.2(c), the line describing the combinations of expected returns and betas for Asset A is higher than the one for Asset B. This tells us that for any given level of systematic risk (as measured by $\beta$), some combination of Asset A and the risk-free asset always offers a larger return. This is why we were able to state that Asset A is a better investment than Asset B.

Another way of seeing that A offers a superior return for its level of risk is to note that the slope of our line for Asset B is

$$\text{Slope} = \frac{E(R_B) - R_f}{\beta_B}$$

$$= \frac{16\% - 8\%}{1.2}$$

$$= 6.67\%$$

Thus Asset B has a reward-to-risk ratio of 6.67 per cent, which is less than the 7.5 per cent offered by Asset A.

**The Fundamental Result**  The situation we have described for Assets A and B could not persist in a well-organized, active market, because investors would be attracted to Asset A and away from Asset B. As a result, Asset A's price would rise and Asset B's price would fall. Because prices and returns move in opposite directions, A's expected return would decline and B's would rise.

This buying and selling would continue until the two assets plotted on exactly the same line, which means they would offer the same reward for bearing risk. In other words, in an active, competitive market, we must have the situation that

$$\frac{E(R_A) - R_f}{\beta_A} = \frac{E(R_B) - R_f}{\beta_B}$$

This is the fundamental relationship between risk and return.

Our basic argument can be extended to more than just two assets. In fact, no matter how many assets we had, we would always reach the same conclusion:

*The reward-to-risk ratio must be the same for all the assets in the market.*

This result is really not so surprising. What it says is that, for example, if one asset has twice as much systematic risk as another asset, its risk premium will simply be twice as large.

Because all of the assets in the market must have the same reward-to-risk ratio, they all must plot on the same line. This argument is illustrated in Fig. 12.3. As shown, Assets A and B plot directly on the line and thus have the same reward-to-risk ratio. If an asset plotted above the line, such as C in Fig. 12.3, its price would rise and its expected

**FIGURE 12.3**

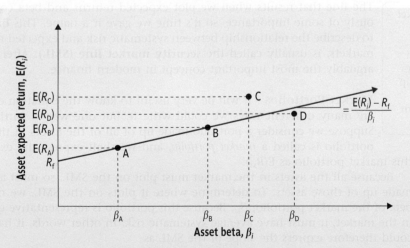

The fundamental relationship between beta and expected return is that all assets must have the same reward-to-risk ratio, $[E(R_i) - R_f]/\beta_i$. This means that they would all plot on the same straight line. Assets A and B are examples of this behaviour. Asset C's expected return is too high; asset D's is too low.

**Figure 12.3** Expected returns and systematic risk

return would fall until it plotted exactly on the line. Similarly, if an asset plotted below the line, such as D in Fig. 12.3, its expected return would rise until it too plotted directly on the line.

The arguments we have presented apply to active, competitive, well-functioning markets. The financial markets, including the LSE, Euronext and Deutsche Börse, best meet these criteria. Other markets, such as real asset markets, may or may not. For this reason these concepts are most useful in examining financial markets. We shall thus focus on such markets here. However, as discussed in a later section, the information about risk and return gleaned from financial markets is crucial in evaluating the investments that a corporation makes in real assets.

---

**EXAMPLE 12.7**

# Buy Low, Sell High

An asset is said to be *overvalued* if its price is too high, given its expected return and risk. Suppose you observe the following situation:

| Security | Beta | Expected return (%) |
|---|---|---|
| SWMS plc | 1.3 | 14 |
| Insec plc | 0.8 | 10 |

The risk-free rate is currently 6 per cent. Is one of the two securities overvalued relative to the other?

To answer, we compute the reward-to-risk ratio for both. For SWMS, this ratio is $(14\% - 6\%)/1.3 = 6.15\%$. For Insec, this ratio is 5 per cent. What we conclude is that Insec offers an insufficient expected return for its level of risk, at least relative to SWMS. Because its expected return is too low, its price is too high. In other words, Insec is overvalued relative to SWMS, and we would expect to see its price fall relative to SWMS's. Notice that we could also say SWMS is undervalued relative to Insec.

---

## The Security Market Line

**security market line (SML)**
A positively sloped straight line displaying the relationship between expected return and beta.

The line that results when we plot expected returns and beta coefficients is obviously of some importance, so it's time we gave it a name. This line, which we use to describe the relationship between systematic risk and expected return in financial markets, is usually called the **security market line (SML)**. After NPV, the SML is arguably the most important concept in modern finance.

**Market Portfolios**   It will be very useful to know the equation of the SML. There are many different ways we could write it, but one way is particularly common. Suppose we consider a portfolio made up of all of the assets in the market. Such a portfolio is called a *market portfolio*, and we shall express the expected return on this market portfolio as $E(R_M)$.

Because all the assets in the market must plot on the SML, so must a market portfolio made up of those assets. To determine where it plots on the SML, we need to know the beta of the market portfolio, $\beta_M$. Because this portfolio is representative of all of the assets in the market, it must have average systematic risk. In other words, it has a beta of 1. We could therefore express the slope of the SML as

$$\text{SML slope} = \frac{E(R_M) - R_f}{\beta_M}$$
$$= \frac{E(R_M) - R_f}{1}$$
$$= E(R_M) - R_f$$

The term $E(R_M) - R_f$ is often called the **market risk premium**, because it is the risk premium on a market portfolio.

**The Capital Asset Pricing Model**   To finish up, if we let $E(R_i)$ and $\beta_i$ stand for the expected return and beta, respectively, on any asset in the market, then we know that asset must plot on the SML. As a result, we know that its reward-to-risk ratio is the same as the overall market's:

$$\frac{E(R_i) - R_f}{\beta_i} = E(R_M) - R_f$$

If we rearrange this, then we can write the equation for the SML as

$$E(R_i) = R_f + [E(R_M) - R_f] \times \beta_i \qquad (12.7)$$

This result is the famous **capital asset pricing model (CAPM)**.

The CAPM shows that the expected return for a particular asset depends on three things:

1  *The pure time value of money*: As measured by the risk-free rate, $R_f$, this is the reward for merely waiting for your money, without taking any risk.

2  *The reward for bearing systematic risk*: As measured by the market risk premium, $E(R_M) - R_f$, this component is the reward the market offers for bearing an average amount of systematic risk in addition to waiting.

3  *The amount of systematic risk*: As measured by $\beta_i$, this is the amount of systematic risk present in a particular asset or portfolio, relative to that in an average asset.

By the way, the CAPM works for portfolios of assets just as it does for individual assets. In an earlier section we saw how to calculate a portfolio's $\beta$. To find the expected return on a portfolio, we simply use this $\beta$ in the CAPM equation.

Figure 12.4 summarizes our discussion of the SML and the CAPM. As before, we plot expected return against beta. Now we recognize that, based on the CAPM, the slope of the SML is equal to the market risk premium, $E(R_M) - R_f$.

> **market risk premium**
> The slope of the SML – the difference between the expected return on a market portfolio and the risk-free rate.
>
> **capital asset pricing model (CAPM)**
> The equation of the SML showing the relationship between expected return and beta.

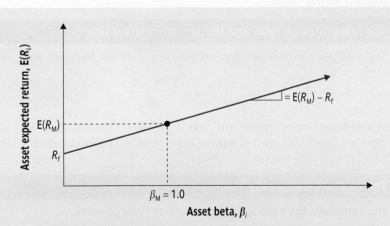

**FIGURE 12.4**

The slope of the security market line is equal to the market risk premium – that is, the reward for bearing an average amount of systematic risk. The equation describing the SML can be written:

$$E(R_i) = R_f + [E(R_M) - R_f] \times \beta_i$$

which is the capital asset pricing model (CAPM).

**Figure 12.4** The security market line (SML)

This concludes our presentation of concepts related to the risk–return trade-off. For future reference, Table 12.9 summarizes the various concepts in the order in which we discussed them.

TABLE
**12.9**

**Total risk**

The *total risk* of an investment is measured by the variance or, more commonly, the standard deviation of its return.

**Total return**

The *total return* on an investment has two components: the expected return and the unexpected return. The unexpected return comes about because of unanticipated events. The risk from investing stems from the possibility of an unanticipated event.

**Systematic and unsystematic risks**

*Systematic risks* (also called *market risks*) are unanticipated events that affect almost all assets to some degree because the effects are economy-wide. *Unsystematic risks* are unanticipated events that affect single assets or small groups of assets. Unsystematic risks are also called *unique* or *asset-specific risks*.

**The effect of diversification**

Some, but not all, of the risk associated with a risky investment can be eliminated by diversification. The reason is that unsystematic risks, which are unique to individual assets, tend to wash out in a large portfolio, but systematic risks, which affect all of the assets in a portfolio to some extent, do not.

**The systematic risk principle and beta**

Because unsystematic risk can be freely eliminated by diversification, the *systematic risk principle* states that the reward for bearing risk depends only on the level of systematic risk. The level of systematic risk in a particular asset, relative to the average, is given by the beta of that asset.

**The reward-to-risk ratio and the security market line**

The *reward-to-risk ratio* for Asset $i$ is the ratio of its risk premium, $E(R_i) - R_f$, to its beta, $\beta_i$:

$$\frac{E(R_i) - R_f}{\beta_i}$$

In a well-functioning market this ratio is the same for every asset. As a result, when asset expected returns are plotted against asset betas, all assets plot on the same straight line, called the *security market line* (SML).

**The capital asset pricing model**

From the SML, the expected return on Asset $i$ can be written:

$$E(R_i) = R_f + [E(R_M) - R_f] \times \beta_i$$

This is the *capital asset pricing model* (CAPM). The expected return on a risky asset thus has three components. The first is the pure time value of money $(R_f)$, the second is the market risk premium $[E(R_M) - R_f]$, and the third is the beta for that asset, $(\beta_i)$.

**Table 12.9** Summary of risk and return

## EXAMPLE 12.8   Risk and Return

Suppose the risk-free rate is 4 per cent, the market risk premium is 8.6 per cent, and a particular equity has a beta of 1.3. Based on the CAPM, what is the expected return on this equity? What would the expected return be if the beta were to double?

With a beta of 1.3, the risk premium for the equity is 1.3 × 8.6%, or 11.18 per cent. The risk-free rate is 4 per cent, so the expected return is 15.18 per cent. If the beta were to double to 2.6, the risk premium would double to 22.36 per cent, so the expected return would be 26.36 per cent.

---

**CONCEPT QUESTIONS**

12.7a   What is the fundamental relationship between risk and return in well-functioning markets?

12.7b   What is the security market line? Why must all assets plot directly on it in a well-functioning market?

12.7c   What is the capital asset pricing model (CAPM)? What does it tell us about the required return on a risky investment?

## 12.8   The SML and the Cost of Capital: A Preview

Our goal in studying risk and return is twofold. First, risk is an extremely important consideration in almost all business decisions, so we want to discuss just what risk is and how it is rewarded in the market. Our second purpose is to learn what determines the appropriate discount rate for future cash flows. We briefly discuss this second subject now; we shall discuss it in more detail in a subsequent chapter.

### The Basic Idea

The security market line tells us the reward for bearing risk in financial markets. At an absolute minimum, any new investment our firm undertakes must offer an expected return that is no worse than what the financial markets offer for the same risk. The reason for this is simply that our shareholders can always invest for themselves in the financial markets.

The only way we benefit our shareholders is by finding investments with expected returns that are superior to what the financial markets offer for the same risk. Such an investment will have a positive NPV. So, if we ask 'What is the appropriate discount rate?', the answer is that we should use the expected return offered in financial markets on investments with the same systematic risk.

In other words, to determine whether an investment has a positive NPV, we essentially compare the expected return on that new investment with what the financial market offers on an investment with the same beta. This is why the SML is so important: it tells us the 'going rate' for bearing risk in the economy.

### The Cost of Capital

The appropriate discount rate on a new project is the minimum expected rate of return an investment must offer to be attractive. This minimum required return is often called the **cost of capital** associated with the investment. It is called this because the required return is what the firm must earn on its capital investment in

**cost of capital**
The minimum required return on a new investment.

a project just to break even. It can thus be interpreted as the opportunity cost associated with the firm's capital investment.

Notice that when we say an investment is attractive if its expected return exceeds what is offered in financial markets for investments of the same risk, we are effectively using the internal rate of return (IRR) criterion that we developed and discussed in Chapter 8. The only difference is that we now have a much better idea of what determines the required return on an investment. This understanding will be critical when we discuss cost of capital and capital structure in Part Five of our book.

| | |
|---|---|
| **CONCEPT QUESTIONS** | 12.8a If an investment has a positive NPV, would it plot above or below the SML? Why? |
| | 12.8b What is meant by the term *cost of capital*? |

# Summary and Conclusions

This chapter has covered the essentials of risk. Along the way we have introduced a number of definitions and concepts. The most important of these is the security market line, or SML. The SML is important because it tells us the reward offered in financial markets for bearing risk. Once we know this, we have a benchmark against which we can compare the returns expected from real asset investments to determine whether they are desirable.

Because we have covered quite a bit of ground, it's useful to summarize the basic economic logic underlying the SML as follows:

1 Based on capital market history, there is a reward for bearing risk. This reward is the risk premium on an asset.

2 The total risk associated with an asset has two parts: systematic risk and unsystematic risk. Unsystematic risk can be freely eliminated by diversification (this is the principle of diversification), so only systematic risk is rewarded. As a result, the risk premium on an asset is determined by its systematic risk. This is the systematic risk principle.

3 An asset's systematic risk, relative to the average, can be measured by its beta coefficient, $\beta_i$. The risk premium on an asset is then given by its beta coefficient multiplied by the market risk premium, $[E(R_M) - R_f] \times \beta_i$.

4 The expected return on an asset, $E(R_i)$, is equal to the risk-free rate, $R_f$, plus the risk premium:

$$E(R_i) = R_f + [E(R_M) - R_f] \times \beta_i$$

This is the equation of the SML, and it is often called the capital asset pricing model (CAPM).

This chapter completes our discussion of risk and return. Now that we have a better understanding of what determines a firm's cost of capital for an investment, the next several chapters will examine more closely how firms raise the long-term capital needed for investment.

## Chapter Review and Self-Test Problems

12.1 **Expected Return and Standard Deviation** This problem will give you some practice calculating measures of prospective portfolio performance. There are two assets and three states of the economy:

| State of economy | Probability of state of economy | Rate of return if state occurs | |
|---|---|---|---|
| | | Equity A | Equity B |
| Recession | 0.20 | −0.15 | 0.20 |
| Normal | 0.50 | 0.20 | 0.30 |
| Boom | 0.30 | 0.60 | 0.40 |

What are the expected returns and standard deviations for these two equities?

12.2 **Portfolio Risk and Return** Using the information in the previous problem, suppose you have £20,000 total. If you put £15,000 in Equity A and the remainder in Equity B, what will be the expected return and standard deviation of your portfolio?

12.3 **Risk and Return** Suppose you observe the following situation:

| Security | Beta | Expected return (%) |
|---|---|---|
| Cooley NV | 1.8 | 22.00 |
| Moyer NV | 1.6 | 20.44 |

If the risk-free rate is 7 per cent, are these securities correctly priced? What would the risk-free rate have to be if they are correctly priced?

12.4 **CAPM** Suppose the risk-free rate is 8 per cent. The expected return on the market is 16 per cent. If a particular equity has a beta of 0.7, what is its expected return based on the CAPM? If another equity has an expected return of 24 per cent, what must its beta be?

# Answers to Chapter Review and Self-Test Problems

12.1 The expected returns are just the possible returns multiplied by the associated probabilities:

$$E(R_A) = (0.20 \times -0.15) + (0.50 \times 0.20) + (0.30 \times 0.60) = 25\%$$
$$E(R_B) = (0.20 \times 0.20) + (0.50 \times 0.30) + (0.30 \times 0.40) = 31\%$$

The variances are given by the sums of the squared deviations from the expected returns multiplied by their probabilities:

$$\sigma_A^2 = 0.20 \times (-0.15 - 0.25)^2 + 0.50 \times (0.20 - 0.25)^2 + 0.30 \times (0.60 - 0.25)^2$$
$$= (0.20 \times -0.40^2) + (0.50 \times -0.05^2) + (0.30 \times 0.35^2)$$
$$= (0.20 \times 0.16) + (0.50 \times 0.0025) + (0.30 \times 0.1225)$$
$$= 0.0700$$

$$\sigma_B^2 = 20 \times (0.20 - 0.31)^2 + 0.50 \times (0.30 - 0.31)^2 + 0.30 \times (0.40 - 0.31)^2$$
$$= (0.20 \times 0.11^2) + (0.50 \times 0.01^2) + (0.30 \times 0.09^2)$$
$$= (0.20 \times 0.0121) + (0.50 \times 0.0001) + (0.30 \times 0.0081)$$
$$= 0.0049$$

The standard deviations are thus

$$\sigma_A = \sqrt{0.0700} = 26.46\%$$
$$\sigma_B = \sqrt{0.0049} = 7\%$$

12.2 The portfolio weights are £15,000/20,000 = 0.75 and £5,000/20,000 = 0.25. The expected return is thus

$$E(R_P) = 0.75 \times E(R_A) + 0.25 \times E(R_B)$$
$$= (0.75 \times 25\%) + (0.25 \times 31\%)$$
$$= 26.5\%$$

Alternatively, we could calculate the portfolio's return in each of the states:

| State of economy | Probability of state of economy | Portfolio return if state occurs |
|---|---|---|
| Recession | .20 | (0.75 × −0.15) + (0.25 × 0.20) = −0.0625 |
| Normal | .50 | (0.75 × 0.20) + (0.25 × 0.30) = 0.2250 |
| Boom | .30 | (0.75 × 0.60) + (0.25 × 0.40) = 0.5500 |

The portfolio's expected return is

$$E(R_P) = (0.20 \times -0.0625) + (0.50 \times 0.2250) + (0.30 \times 0.5500) = 26.5\%$$

This is the same as we had before.
   The portfolio's variance is

$$\sigma_P^2 = 0.20 \times (-0.0625 - 0.265)^2 + 0.50 \times (0.225 - 0.265)^2$$
$$+ 0.30 \times (0.55 - 0.265)^2$$
$$= 0.0466$$

So the standard deviation is $\sqrt{0.0466} = 21.59\%$.

12.3 If we compute the reward-to-risk ratios, we get (22% − 7%)/1.8 = 8.33% for Cooley versus 8.4% for Moyer. Relative to that of Cooley, Moyer's expected return is too high, so its price is too low.

If they are correctly priced, then they must offer the same reward-to-risk ratio. The risk-free rate would have to be such that

$$(22\% - R_f)/1.8 = (20.44\% - R_f)/1.6$$

With a little algebra, we find that the risk-free rate must be 8 per cent:

$$22\% - R_f = (20.44\% - R_f)(1.8/1.6)$$
$$22\% - 20.44\% \times 1.125 = R_f - R_f \times 1.125$$
$$R_f = 8\%$$

12.4 Because the expected return on the market is 16 per cent, the market risk premium is 16% − 8% = 8%. The first equity has a beta of 0.7, so its expected return is 8% + 0.7 × 8% = 13.6%.

For the second equity, notice that the risk premium is 24% − 8% = 16%. Because this is twice as large as the market risk premium, the beta must be exactly equal to 2. We can verify this using the CAPM:

$$E(R_i) = R_f + [E(R_M) - R_f]\,\beta_i$$
$$24\% = 8\% + (16\% - 8\%) \times \beta_i$$
$$\beta_i = 16\%/8\%$$
$$= 2.0$$

# Concepts Review and Critical Thinking Questions

1  **Diversifiable and Non-Diversifiable Risks [LO3]**  In broad terms, why is some risk diversifiable? Why are some risks non-diversifiable? Does it follow that an investor can control the level of unsystematic risk in a portfolio, but not the level of systematic risk?

2  **Information and Market Returns [LO3]**  Suppose the government announces that, based on a just-completed survey, the growth rate in the economy is likely to be 2 per cent in the coming year, as compared with 5 per cent for the past year. Will security prices increase, decrease, or stay the same following this announcement? Does it make any difference whether the 2 per cent figure was anticipated by the market? Explain.

3  **Systematic versus Unsystematic Risk [LO3]**  Classify the following events as mostly systematic or mostly unsystematic. Is the distinction clear in every case?

   (a)  Short-term interest rates increase unexpectedly.

   (b)  The interest rate a company pays on its short-term debt borrowing is increased by its bank.

   (c)  Oil prices unexpectedly decline.

   (d)  An oil tanker ruptures, creating a large oil spill.

   (e)  A manufacturer loses a multimillion-dollar product liability suit.

   (f)  A European Court of Human Rights decision substantially broadens producer liability for injuries suffered by product users.

4  **Systematic versus Unsystematic Risk [LO3]**  Indicate whether the following events might cause equities in general to change price, and whether they might cause Big Widget's share price to change:

   (a)  The government announces that inflation unexpectedly jumped by 2 per cent last month.

   (b)  Big Widget's earnings report, just issued, generally fell in line with analysts' expectations.

   (c)  The government reports that economic growth last year was at 3 per cent, which generally agreed with most economists' forecasts.

   (d)  The directors of Big Widget die in a plane crash.

   (e)  Parliament approves changes to the tax code that will increase the top marginal corporate tax rate. The legislation had been debated for the previous six months.

5  **Expected Portfolio Returns [LO1]**  If a portfolio has a positive investment in every asset, can the expected return on the portfolio be greater than that on every asset in the portfolio? Can it be less than that on every asset in the portfolio? If you answer yes to one or both of these questions, give an example to support your answer.

6  **Diversification [LO2]**  True or false: the most important characteristic in determining the expected return of a well-diversified portfolio is the variance of the individual assets in the portfolio. Explain.

7  **Portfolio Risk [LO2]**  If a portfolio has a positive investment in every asset, can the standard deviation on the portfolio be less than that on every asset in the portfolio? What about the portfolio beta?

8 **Beta and CAPM [LO4]** Is it possible that a risky asset could have a beta of zero? Explain. Based on the CAPM, what is the expected return on such an asset? Is it possible that a risky asset could have a negative beta? What does the CAPM predict about the expected return on such an asset? Can you give an explanation for your answer?

9 **Corporate Downsizing [LO1]** In recent years it has been common for companies to experience significant share price increases in reaction to announcements of massive layoffs. Critics charge that such events encourage companies to fire long-time employees, and that investors are cheering them on. Do you agree or disagree?

10 **Earnings and Equity Returns [LO1]** As indicated by a number of examples in this chapter, earnings announcements by companies are closely followed by, and frequently result in, share price revisions. Two issues should come to mind. First, earnings announcements concern past periods. If the market values equities based on expectations of the future, why are numbers summarizing past performance relevant? Second, these announcements concern accounting earnings. Going back to Chapter 3, such earnings may have little to do with cash flow – so, again, why are they relevant?

## connect Questions and Problems

**BASIC**

**1 – 20**

1 **Determining Portfolio Weights [LO1]** What are the portfolio weights for a portfolio that has 200 shares of Equity A that sell for £4.50 per share and 100 shares of Equity B that sell for £2.70 per share?

2 **Portfolio Expected Return [LO1]** You own a portfolio that has €2,950 invested in Equity A and €3,700 invested in Equity B. If the expected returns on these equities are 11 per cent and 15 per cent, respectively, what is the expected return on the portfolio?

3 **Portfolio Expected Return [LO1]** You own a portfolio that is 60 per cent invested in Equity X, 25 per cent in Equity Y, and 15 per cent in Equity Z. The expected returns on these three equities are 9 per cent, 17 per cent and 13 per cent, respectively. What is the expected return on the portfolio?

4 **Portfolio Expected Return [LO1]** You have £10,000 to invest in an equity portfolio. Your choices are Equity X with an expected return of 14 per cent and Equity Y with an expected return of 10.5 per cent. If your goal is to create a portfolio with an expected return of 12.4 per cent, how much money will you invest in Equity X? In Equity Y?

5 **Calculating Expected Return [LO1]** Based on the following information, calculate the expected return:

| State of economy | Probability of state of economy | Portfolio return if state occurs |
|---|---|---|
| Recession | 0.25 | −0.08 |
| Boom | 0.75 | 0.21 |

6 **Calculating Expected Return [LO1]** Based on the following information, calculate the expected return:

| State of economy | Probability of state of economy | Portfolio return if state occurs |
|---|---|---|
| Recession | 0.20 | −0.05 |
| Normal | 0.50 | 0.12 |
| Boom | 0.30 | 0.21 |

7   **Calculating Returns and Standard Deviations [LO1]**   Based on the following information, calculate the expected return and standard deviation for the two equities:

| State of economy | Probability of state of economy | Rate of return if state occurs | |
|---|---|---|---|
| | | **Equity A** | **Equity B** |
| Recession | 0.25 | 0.05 | −0.17 |
| Normal | 0.55 | 0.08 | 0.12 |
| Boom | 0.20 | 0.13 | 0.29 |

8   **Calculating Expected Returns [LO1]**   A portfolio is invested 25 per cent in Equity G, 55 per cent in Equity J, and 20 per cent in Equity K. The expected returns on these equities are 8 per cent, 15 per cent and 24 per cent, respectively. What is the portfolio's expected return? How do you interpret your answer?

9   **Returns and Variances [LO1]**   Consider the following information:

| State of economy | Probability of state of economy | Rate of returns if state occurs | | |
|---|---|---|---|---|
| | | **Equity A** | **Equity B** | **Equity C** |
| Boom | 0.35 | 0.07 | 0.15 | 0.33 |
| Bust | 0.65 | 0.13 | 0.03 | −0.06 |

(a)   What is the expected return on an equally weighted portfolio of these three equities?

(b)   What is the variance of a portfolio invested 20 per cent each in A and B and 60 per cent in C?

10   **Returns and Standard Deviations [LO1]**   Consider the following information:

| State of economy | Probability of state of economy | Rate of returns if state occurs | | |
|---|---|---|---|---|
| | | **Equity A** | **Equity B** | **Equity C** |
| Boom | 0.05 | 0.30 | 0.45 | 0.33 |
| Good | 0.45 | 0.12 | 0.10 | 0.15 |
| Poor | 0.35 | 0.01 | −0.15 | −0.05 |
| Bust | 0.15 | −0.06 | −0.30 | −0.09 |

(a)   Your portfolio is invested 30 per cent each in A and C, and 40 per cent in B. What is the expected return of the portfolio?

(b)   What is the variance of this portfolio? The standard deviation?

11   **Calculating Portfolio Betas [LO4]**   You own an equity portfolio invested 25 per cent in Equity Q, 20 per cent in Equity R, 15 per cent in Equity S, and 40 per cent in Equity T. The betas for these four equities are 0.84, 1.17, 1.11, and 1.36, respectively. What is the portfolio beta?

12   **Calculating Portfolio Betas [LO4]**   You own a portfolio equally invested in a risk-free asset and two equities. If one of the equities has a beta of 1.38 and the total portfolio is equally as risky as the market, what must the beta be for the other equity in your portfolio?

13   **Using CAPM [LO4]**   An equity has a beta of 1.05, the expected return on the market is 11 per cent, and the risk-free rate is 5.2 per cent. What must the expected return on this equity be?

14    **Using CAPM [LO4]**   An equity has an expected return of 11.2 per cent, the risk-free rate is 1.5 per cent, and the market risk premium is 8.5 per cent. What must the beta of this equity be?

15    **Using CAPM [LO4]**   An equity has an expected return of 13.5 per cent, its beta is 1.17, and the risk-free rate is 5.5 per cent. What must the expected return on the market be?

16    **Using CAPM [LO4]**   An equity has an expected return of 14 per cent, its beta is 1.45, and the expected return on the market is 11.5 per cent. What must the risk-free rate be?

17    **Using CAPM [LO4]**   An equity has a beta of 1.35 and an expected return of 16 per cent. A risk-free asset currently earns 4.8 per cent.

(a)    What is the expected return on a portfolio that is equally invested in the two assets?

(b)    If a portfolio of the two assets has a beta of 0.95, what are the portfolio weights?

(c)    If a portfolio of the two assets has an expected return of 8 per cent, what is its beta?

(d)    If a portfolio of the two assets has a beta of 2.70, what are the portfolio weights? How do you interpret the weights for the two assets in this case? Explain.

18    **Using the SML [LO4]**   Asset W has an expected return of 15.2 per cent and a beta of 1.25. If the risk-free rate is 5.3 per cent, complete the following table for portfolios of Asset W and a risk-free asset. Illustrate the relationship between portfolio expected return and portfolio beta by plotting the expected returns against the betas. What is the slope of the line that results?

| Percentage of portfolio in Asset W | Portfolio expected return | Portfolio beta |
|---|---|---|
| 0 | | |
| 25 | | |
| 50 | | |
| 75 | | |
| 100 | | |
| 125 | | |
| 150 | | |

19    **Reward-to-Risk Ratios [LO4]**   Equity Y has a beta of 1.4 and an expected return of 18.5 per cent. Equity Z has a beta of 0.80 and an expected return of 12.1 per cent. If the risk-free rate is 2 per cent and the market risk premium is 7.5 per cent, are these equities correctly priced?

20    **Reward-to-Risk Ratios [LO4]**   In the previous problem, what would the risk-free rate have to be for the two equities to be correctly priced?

21    **Portfolio Returns [LO2]**   Using information from the previous chapter on capital market history, determine the return on a portfolio that is equally invested in large UK company equities and small UK company equities. What is the return on a portfolio that is equally invested in German and French equities?

22    **CAPM [LO4]**   Using the CAPM, show that the ratio of the risk premiums on two assets is equal to the ratio of their betas.

23    **Portfolio Returns and Deviations [LO2]**   Consider the following information about three equities:

| State of economy | Probability of state of economy | Rate of returns if state occurs | | |
|---|---|---|---|---|
| | | Equity A | Equity B | Equity C |
| Boom | 0.25 | 0.24 | 0.36 | 0.55 |
| Good | 0.50 | 0.17 | 0.13 | 0.09 |
| Bust | 0.25 | 0.00 | −0.28 | −0.45 |

(a) If your portfolio is invested 40 per cent each in A and B and 20 per cent in C, what is the portfolio expected return? The variance? The standard deviation?

(b) If the expected T-bill rate is 3.80 per cent, what is the expected risk premium on the portfolio?

(c) If the expected inflation rate is 3.50 per cent, what are the approximate and exact expected real returns on the portfolio? What are the approximate and exact expected real risk premiums on the portfolio?

24 **Analysing a Portfolio [LO2]**   You want to create a portfolio equally as risky as the market, and you have £1,000,000 to invest. Given this information, fill in the rest of the following table:

| Asset | Investment (£) | Beta |
|---|---|---|
| Equity A | 210,000 | 0.85 |
| Equity B | 320,000 | 1.20 |
| Equity C | | 1.35 |
| Risk-free asset | | |

25 **Analysing a Portfolio [LO2, LO4]**   You have £100,000 to invest in a portfolio containing Equity X and Equity Y. Your goal is to create a portfolio that has an expected return of 16.5 per cent. If Equity X has an expected return of 15.2 per cent and a beta of 1.4, and Equity Y has an expected return of 11.6 per cent and a beta of 0.95, how much money will you invest in equity Y? How do you interpret your answer? What is the beta of your portfolio?

26 **Systematic versus Unsystematic Risk [LO3]**   Consider the following information about Equities I and II:

| State of economy | Probability of state of economy | Rate of return if state occurs | |
|---|---|---|---|
| | | Equity I | Equity II |
| Recession | 0.25 | 0.11 | −0.40 |
| Normal | 0.50 | 0.29 | 0.10 |
| Irrational exuberance | 0.25 | 0.13 | 0.56 |

The market risk premium is 8 per cent, and the risk-free rate is 4 per cent. Which equity has the most systematic risk? Which one has the most unsystematic risk? Which equity is 'riskier'? Explain.

27 **SML [LO4]**   Suppose you observe the following situation:

| Security | Beta | Expected Return |
|---|---|---|
| Pete plc | 1.35 | 0.132 |
| Repete plc | 0.80 | 0.101 |

Assume these securities are correctly priced. Based on the CAPM, what is the expected return on the market? What is the risk-free rate?

**CHALLENGE**

**25 – 28**

28   **SML [LO4]**   Suppose you observe the following situation:

| State of economy | Probability of state | Return if state occurs Equity A | Return if state occurs Equity B |
|---|---|---|---|
| Bust | 0.25 | −0.08 | −0.05 |
| Normal | 0.70 | 0.13 | 0.14 |
| Boom | 0.05 | 0.48 | 0.29 |

(a)   Calculate the expected return on each equity.

(b)   Assuming the capital asset pricing model holds, and equity B's beta is greater than equity A's beta by 0.25, what is the expected market risk premium?

## MINI CASE   The Beta for Vodafone

Joey Moss, a recent finance graduate, has just begun his job with the investment firm of Covili and Wyatt. Paul Covili, one of the firm's founders, has been talking to Joey about the firm's investment portfolio.

As with any investment, Paul is concerned about the risk of the investment as well as the potential return. More specifically, because the company holds a diversified portfolio, Paul is concerned about the systematic risk of current and potential investments. One such position the company currently holds is equity in Vodafone. Vodafone is the well-known mobile telecommunications firm that has operations throughout the world.

Covili and Wyatt currently uses a commercial data vendor for information about its positions. Because of this, Paul is unsure exactly how the numbers provided are calculated. The data provider considers its methods proprietary, and it will not disclose how equity betas and other information are calculated. Paul is uncomfortable with not knowing exactly how these numbers are being computed, and also believes that it could be less expensive to calculate the necessary statistics in-house. To explore this question, Paul has asked Joey to do the following assignments.

### QUESTIONS

1   Go to Yahoo! Finance and download the ending monthly equity prices for Vodafone for the last 60 months. Use the adjusted closing price, which adjusts for dividend payments and stock splits. Next, download the ending value of the FTSE 100 index over the same period. For the historical risk-free rate, download the historical three-month Treasury bill secondary market rate. What are the monthly returns, average monthly returns and standard deviations for Vodafone equity, the three-month Treasury bill, and the FTSE 100 for this period?

2   Beta is often estimated by linear regression. A model often used is called the *market model*, which is

$$R_t - R_{ft} = \alpha_i + \beta_i \, [R_{Mt} - R_{ft}] + \varepsilon_t$$

In this regression $R_t$ is the return on the equity and $R_{ft}$ is the risk-free rate for the same period. $R_{Mt}$ is the return on a stock market index such as the FTSE 100 index. $\alpha_i$ is the regression intercept, and $\beta_i$ is the slope (and the equity's estimated beta). $\varepsilon_t$ represents the residuals for the regression. What do you think is the motivation for this particular regression? The intercept, $\alpha_i$, is often called *Jensen's alpha*. What does it measure? If an asset has a positive Jensen's alpha, where would it plot with respect to the SML? What is the financial interpretation of the residuals in the regression?

3   Use the market model to estimate the beta for Vodafone using the last 36 months of returns (the regression procedure in Microsoft Excel is one easy way to do this). Plot the monthly returns on Vodafone against the index, and also show the fitted line.

4   When the beta of an equity is calculated using monthly returns, there is a debate over the number of months that should be used in the calculation. Rework the previous questions using the last 60 months of returns. How does this answer compare with what you calculated previously? What are some arguments for and against using shorter versus longer periods? Also, you've used monthly data, which are a common choice. You could have used daily, weekly, quarterly, or even annual data. What do you think are the issues here?

5   Compare your beta for Vodafone with the beta you find on Yahoo! Finance. How similar are they? Why might they be different?

## Endnotes

1   Some of it could be in cash, of course, but we would then just consider the cash to be one of the portfolio assets.

2   This ratio is sometimes called the *Treynor index*, after one of its originators.

Online **Learning Centre**

To help you grasp the key concepts of this chapter check out the extra resources posted on the Online Learning Centre at **www.mcgraw-hill.co.uk/textbooks/hillier**

Among other helpful resources there are mini-cases tailored to individual chapters.

# CHAPTER 13

# Cost of Capital

## LEARNING OBJECTIVES

After studying this chapter, you should understand:

LO1 How to determine a firm's cost of equity capital.

LO2 How to determine a firm's cost of debt.

LO3 How to determine a firm's overall cost of capital.

LO4 How to correctly include flotation costs in capital budgeting projects.

LO5 Some of the pitfalls associated with a firm's overall cost of capital, and what to do about them.

WITH OVER 95,000 EMPLOYEES ON FIVE CONTINENTS, Germany-based BASF is a major international company. The company operates in a variety of industries, including agriculture, oil and gas, chemicals, and plastics. In an attempt to increase value, BASF launched BASF 2015, a comprehensive plan that included all functions within the company, and challenged and encouraged all employees to act in an entrepreneurial manner. The major financial component of the strategy was that the company expected to earn its weighted average cost of capital, or WACC, plus a premium. So, what exactly is the WACC?

The WACC is the minimum return a company needs to earn to satisfy all of its investors, including shareholders, bondholders and preference shareholders. In 2007, for example, BASF pegged its WACC at 9 per cent, and it increased this figure to 10 per cent in 2008. In this chapter we learn how to compute a firm's cost of capital, and find out what it means to the firm and its investors. We shall also learn when to use the firm's cost of capital and, perhaps more important, when not to use it.

Suppose you have just become the chief executive of a large company, and the first decision you face is whether to go ahead with a plan to renovate the company's warehouse distribution system. The plan will cost the company €50 million, and it is expected to save €12 million per year after taxes over the next six years.

This is a familiar problem in capital budgeting. To address it, you would determine the relevant cash flows, discount them, and, if the net present value was positive, take on the project; if the NPV was negative, you would scrap it. So far, so good; but what should you use as the discount rate?

From our discussion of risk and return, you know that the correct discount rate depends on the riskiness of the project to renovate the warehouse distribution system. In particular, the new project will have a positive NPV only if its return exceeds what the financial markets offer on investments of similar risk. We called this minimum required return the *cost of capital* associated with the project.

Thus, to make the right decision as chief executive, you must examine what the capital markets have to offer, and use this information to arrive at an estimate of the project's cost of capital. Our primary purpose in this chapter is to describe how to go about doing this. There are a variety of approaches to this task, and a number of conceptual and practical issues arise.

One of the most important concepts we develop is that of the *weighted average cost of capital* (WACC). This is the cost of capital for the firm as a whole, and it can be interpreted as the required return on the overall firm. In discussing the WACC we shall recognize the fact that a firm will normally raise capital in a variety of forms, and that these different forms of capital may have different costs associated with them.

We also recognize in this chapter that taxes are an important consideration in determining the required return on an investment: we are always interested in valuing the after-tax cash flows from a project. We shall therefore discuss how to incorporate taxes explicitly into our estimates of the cost of capital.

## 13.1 The Cost of Capital: Some Preliminaries

In Chapter 12 we developed the security market line, or SML, and used it to explore the relationship between the expected return on a security and its systematic risk. We concentrated on how the risky returns from buying securities looked from the viewpoint of, for example, a shareholder in the firm. This helped us understand more about the alternatives available to an investor in the capital markets.

In this chapter we turn things around a bit and look more closely at the other side of the problem, which is how these returns and securities look from the viewpoint of the companies that issue them. The important fact to note is that the return an investor in a security receives is the cost of that security to the company that issued it.

### Required Return versus Cost of Capital

When we say that the required return on an investment is, say, 10 per cent, we usually mean that the investment will have a positive NPV only if its return exceeds 10 per cent. Another way of interpreting the required return is to observe that the firm must earn 10 per cent on the investment just to compensate its investors for the use of the capital needed to finance the project. This is why we could also say that 10 per cent is the cost of capital associated with the investment.

To illustrate the point further, imagine that we are evaluating a risk-free project. In this case, how to determine the required return is obvious: we look at the capital markets and observe the current rate offered by risk-free investments, and we use this rate to discount the project's cash flows. Thus the cost of capital for a risk-free investment is the risk-free rate.

If a project is risky, then, assuming that all the other information is unchanged, the required return is obviously higher. In other words, the cost of capital for this project, if it is risky, is greater than the risk-free rate, and the appropriate discount rate would exceed the risk-free rate.

We shall henceforth use the terms *required return*, *appropriate discount rate* and *cost of capital* more or less interchangeably, because, as the discussion in this section suggests, they all mean essentially the same thing. The key fact to grasp is that the cost of capital associated with an investment depends on the risk of that investment. This is one of the most important lessons in corporate finance, so it bears repeating:

> *The cost of capital depends primarily on the use of the funds, not the source.*

It is a common error to forget this crucial point, and fall into the trap of thinking that the cost of capital for an investment depends primarily on how and where the capital is raised.

## Financial Policy and Cost of Capital

We know that the particular mixture of debt and equity a firm chooses to employ – its capital structure – is a managerial variable. In this chapter we shall take the firm's financial policy as given. In particular, we shall assume that the firm has a fixed debt–equity ratio that it maintains. This ratio reflects the firm's *target* capital structure. How a firm might choose that ratio is the subject of a later chapter.

From the preceding discussion we know that a firm's overall cost of capital will reflect the required return on the firm's assets as a whole. Given that a firm uses both debt and equity capital, this overall cost of capital will be a mixture of the returns needed to compensate its creditors and those needed to compensate its shareholders. In other words, a firm's cost of capital will reflect both its cost of debt capital and its cost of equity capital. We discuss these costs separately in the sections that follow.

**CONCEPT QUESTIONS**

**13.1a** What is the primary determinant of the cost of capital for an investment?
**13.1b** What is the relationship between the required return on an investment and the cost of capital associated with that investment?

## 13.2 The Cost of Equity

**cost of equity**
The return that equity investors require on their investment in the firm.

We begin with the most difficult question on the subject of cost of capital: what is the firm's overall **cost of equity**? The reason why this is a difficult question is that there is no way of directly observing the return that the firm's equity investors require on their investment. Instead, we must somehow estimate it. This section discusses two approaches to determining the cost of equity: the dividend growth model approach and the security market line (SML) approach.

### The Dividend Growth Model Approach

The easiest way to estimate the cost of equity capital is to use the dividend growth model we developed in Chapter 7. Recall that, under the assumption that the firm's dividend will grow at a constant rate $g$, the share price, $P_0$, can be written as

$$P_0 = \frac{D_0 \times (1 + g)}{R_E - g} = \frac{D_1}{R_E - g}$$

where $D_0$ is the dividend just paid and $D_1$ is the next period's projected dividend. Notice that we have used the symbol $R_E$ (the E stands for equity) for the required return on the equity.

As we discussed in Chapter 7, we can rearrange this to solve for $R_E$ as follows:

$$R_E = D_1/P_0 + g \qquad (13.1)$$

Because $R_E$ is the return that the shareholders require on the equity, it can be interpreted as the firm's cost of equity capital.

**Implementing the Approach**    To estimate $R_E$ using the dividend growth model approach, we obviously need three pieces of information: $P_0$, $D_0$ and $g$.[1] Of these, for a publicly traded, dividend-paying company, the first two can be observed directly, so they are easily obtained. Only the third component, the expected growth rate for dividends, must be estimated.

To illustrate how we estimate $R_E$, suppose Great Country Public Service, a large public utility, paid a dividend of €4 per share last year. The equity currently sells for €60 per share. You estimate that the dividend will grow steadily at a rate of 6 per cent per year into the indefinite future. What is the cost of equity capital for Great Country?

Using the dividend growth model, we can calculate that the expected dividend for the coming year, $D_1$, is

$$D_1 = D_0 \times (1 + g)$$
$$= €4 \times 1.06$$
$$= €4.24$$

Given this, the cost of equity, $R_E$, is

$$R_E = D_1/P_0 + g$$
$$= €4.24/60 + 0.06$$
$$= 13.07\%$$

The cost of equity is thus 13.07 per cent.

**Estimating $g$**    To use the dividend growth model, we must come up with an estimate for $g$, the growth rate. There are essentially two ways of doing this: (1) use historical growth rates; or (2) use analysts' forecasts of future growth rates. Analysts' forecasts are available from a variety of sources, such as Yahoo! Finance. Naturally, different sources will have different estimates, so one approach might be to obtain multiple estimates and then average them.

Alternatively, we might observe dividends for the previous, say, five years, calculate the year-to-year growth rates, and average them. For example, suppose we observe the following for some company:

| Year | Dividend (£) |
|------|--------------|
| 2006 | 1.10 |
| 2007 | 1.20 |
| 2008 | 1.35 |
| 2009 | 1.40 |
| 2010 | 1.55 |

We can calculate the percentage change in the dividend for each year as follows:

| Year | Dividend (£) | Absolute change (£) | Percentage change (%) |
|------|--------------|----------------------|------------------------|
| 2006 | 1.10 | – | – |
| 2007 | 1.20 | 0.10 | 9.09 |
| 2008 | 1.35 | 0.15 | 12.50 |
| 2009 | 1.40 | 0.05 | 3.70 |
| 2010 | 1.55 | 0.15 | 10.71 |

Notice that we calculated the change in the dividend on a year-to-year basis, and then expressed the change as a percentage. Thus in 2007, for example, the dividend rose from £1.10 to £1.20, an increase of £0.10. This represents a £0.10/1.10 = 9.09% increase.

If we average the four growth rates the result is (9.09 + 12.50 + 3.70 + 10.71)/4 = 9%, so we could use this as an estimate for the expected growth rate, $g$. Notice that this 9 per cent growth rate we have calculated is a simple, or arithmetic, average. Going back to Chapter 11, we also could calculate a geometric growth rate. Here, the dividend grows from £1.10 to £1.55 over a four-year period. What's the compound, or geometric, growth rate? See if you don't agree that it's 8.95 per cent; you can view this as a simple time value of money problem, where £1.10 is the present value and £1.55 is the future value.

As usual, the geometric average (8.95 per cent) is lower than the arithmetic average (9 per cent), but the difference here is not likely to be of any practical significance. In general, if the dividend has grown at a relatively steady rate, as we assume when we use this approach, then it can't make much difference which way we calculate the average dividend growth rate.

**Advantages and Disadvantages of the Approach**   The primary advantage of the dividend growth model approach is its simplicity. It is both easy to understand and easy to use. There are a number of associated practical problems and disadvantages.

First and foremost, the dividend growth model is obviously applicable only to companies that pay dividends. This means that the approach is useless in many cases. Furthermore, even for companies that do pay dividends, the key underlying assumption is that the dividend grows at a constant rate. As our previous example illustrates, this will never be *exactly* the case. More generally, the model is really applicable only to cases in which reasonably steady growth is likely to occur.

A second problem is that the estimated cost of equity is very sensitive to the estimated growth rate. For a given share price, an upward revision of $g$ by just one percentage point, for example, increases the estimated cost of equity by at least a full percentage point. Because $D_1$ will probably be revised upwards as well, the increase will actually be somewhat larger than that.

Finally, this approach really does not explicitly consider risk. Unlike the SML approach (which we consider next), there is no direct adjustment for the riskiness of the investment. For example, there is no allowance for the degree of certainty or uncertainty surrounding the estimated growth rate for dividends. As a result, it is difficult to say whether or not the estimated return is commensurate with the level of risk.[2]

## The SML Approach

In Chapter 12 we discussed the security market line, or SML. Our primary conclusion was that the required or expected return on a risky investment depends on three things:

1   The risk-free rate, $R_f$.

2   The market risk premium, $E(R_M) - R_f$.

3   The systematic risk of the asset relative to average, which we called its beta coefficient, $\beta$.

Using the SML, we can write the expected return on the company's equity, $E(R_E)$, as

$$E(R_E) = R_f + \beta_E \times [E(R_M) - R_f]$$

where $\beta_E$ is the estimated beta. To make the SML approach consistent with the dividend growth model, we shall drop the Es denoting expectations and henceforth write the required return from the SML, $R_E$, as

$$R_E = R_f + \beta_E \times (R_M - R_f) \tag{13.2}$$

**Implementing the Approach** To use the SML approach, we need a risk-free rate, $R_f$, an estimate of the market risk premium, $R_M - R_f$, and an estimate of the relevant beta, $\beta_E$. In Chapter 11 we saw that one estimate of the market risk premium (based on large UK equities) is about 6.1 per cent (see Figure 11.7). Assume that Treasury bills are paying about 0.5 per cent, so we shall use this as our risk-free rate for the UK. Beta coefficients for publicly traded companies are widely available.[3]

To illustrate, according to Yahoo! Finance, Associated British Foods plc (ABF) had an estimated beta of 0.37 in 2010. We could thus estimate ABF's cost of equity as

$$R_E = R_f + \beta_{ABF} \times (R_M - R_f)$$
$$= 0.5\% + 0.37 \times 6.1\%$$
$$= 7.26\%$$

Thus, using the SML approach, we calculate that ABF's cost of equity is about 7.26 per cent.

**Advantages and Disadvantages of the Approach** The SML approach has two primary advantages. First, it explicitly adjusts for risk. Second, it is applicable to companies other than just those with steady dividend growth. Thus it may be useful in a wider variety of circumstances.

There are drawbacks, of course. The SML approach requires that two things be estimated: the market risk premium and the beta coefficient. To the extent that our estimates are poor, the resulting cost of equity will be inaccurate. For example, our estimate of the UK market risk premium, 6.1 per cent, is based on a large number of years of returns on particular equity portfolios and markets. Using different time periods or different equities and markets could result in very different estimates.

Finally, as with the dividend growth model, we essentially rely on the past to predict the future when we use the SML approach. Economic conditions can change quickly: so, as always, the past may not be a good guide to the future. In the best of all worlds, both approaches (the dividend growth model and the SML) are applicable, and the two result in similar answers. If this happens, we might have some confidence in our estimates. We might also wish to compare the results with those for other similar companies as a reality check.

EXAMPLE
**13.1**

# The Cost of Equity

Suppose equity in Alpha Air Freight has a beta of 1.2. The market risk premium is 7 per cent, and the risk-free rate is 6 per cent. Alpha's last dividend was €2 per share, and the dividend is expected to grow at 8 per cent indefinitely. The equity currently sells for €30. What is Alpha's cost of equity capital?

We can start off by using the SML. Doing this, we find that the expected return on the equity of Alpha Air Freight is

$$R_E = R_f + \beta_E \times (R_M - R_f)$$
$$= 6\% + 1.2 \times 7\%$$
$$= 14.4\%$$

This suggests that 14.4 per cent is Alpha's cost of equity. We next use the dividend growth model. The projected dividend is $D_0 \times (1 + g) = €2 \times 1.08 = €2.16$, so the expected return using this approach is

$$R_E = D_1/P_0 + g$$
$$= €2.16/30 + 0.08$$
$$= 15.2\%$$

Our two estimates are reasonably close, so we might just average them to find that Alpha's cost of equity is approximately 14.8 per cent.

TABLE
**13.1**

| | US | UK | The Netherlands | Germany | France |
|---|---|---|---|---|---|
| Capital asset pricing model | 73.49 | 47.06 | 55.56 | 33.96 | 45.16 |
| Historical returns | 39.41 | 31.25 | 30.77 | 18.00 | 27.27 |
| Multifactor models[4] | 34.29 | 27.27 | 15.38 | 16.07 | 30.30 |
| Backed out from dividend growth model (i.e. $P = Div/r$) | 15.74 | 10.00 | 10.71 | 10.42 | 10.34 |
| Determined by investors | 13.93 | 18.75 | 44.83 | 39.22 | 34.38 |
| Determined by regulators | 7.04 | 16.13 | 3.70 | 0.00 | 16.13 |

*Source*: Table 3 from D. Brounen, A. de Jong and K. Koedijk, 'Corporate finance in Europe: confronting theory and practice', *Journal of Banking and Finance* (2006), vol. 30, no. 5, pp. 1409–1442.

**Table 13.1** Of firms that estimate cost of capital, the percentage that use specific methods

## How Do Corporations Estimate Cost of Capital in Practice?

The material in this chapter is quite complex, and the reader may be left wondering what firms actually do when they calculate the cost of capital in practice. Recently, a survey was undertaken of executives in France, Germany, the Netherlands and the UK on the methods they used to estimate the cost of capital for their firm. The responses are presented in Table 13.1.

There are notable differences across countries, but the most commonly used method is CAPM and beta. Historical returns on share prices are also commonly used, and in the Netherlands a surprisingly large number of companies use a cost of capital estimate that is set by investors. Regulators play an important role in the UK and France, whereas in Germany they are not considered at all.

| | |
|---|---|
| **CONCEPT QUESTIONS** | 13.2a   What do we mean when we say that a corporation's cost of equity capital is 16 per cent? |
| | 13.2b   What are two approaches to estimating the cost of equity capital? |

## 13.3   The Costs of Debt and Preference Shares

In addition to ordinary equity, firms use debt and, to a lesser extent, preference shares to finance their investments. As we discuss next, determining the costs of capital associated with these sources of financing is much easier than determining the cost of equity.

### The Cost of Debt

**cost of debt**
The return that lenders require on the firm's debt.

The **cost of debt** is the return the firm's creditors demand on new borrowing. In principle, we could determine the beta for the firm's debt and then use the SML to estimate the required return on debt, just as we estimated the required return on equity. This isn't really necessary, however.

Unlike a firm's cost of equity, its cost of debt can normally be observed either directly or indirectly: the cost of debt is simply the interest rate the firm must pay on new borrowing, and we can observe interest rates in the financial markets. For example, if the firm already has bonds outstanding, then the yield to maturity on those bonds is the market-required rate on the firm's debt.

Alternatively, if we know that the firm's bonds are rated, say, AA, then we can simply find the interest rate on newly issued AA-rated bonds. Either way, there is no need to estimate a beta for the debt, because we can directly observe the rate we want to know.

There is one thing to be careful about, though. The coupon rate on the firm's outstanding debt is irrelevant here. That rate just tells us roughly what the firm's cost of debt was back when the bonds were issued, not what the cost of debt is today.[5] This is why we have to look at the yield on the debt in today's marketplace. For consistency with our other notation, we shall use the symbol $R_D$ for the cost of debt.

---

## EXAMPLE 13.2 — The Cost of Debt

Suppose General Tools issued a 30-year, 7 per cent bond 8 years ago. The bond is currently selling for 96 per cent of its face value of £50,000, or £48,000. What is General Tool's cost of debt?

Going back to Chapter 6, we need to calculate the yield to maturity on this bond. Because the bond is selling at a discount, the yield is apparently greater than 7 per cent, but not much greater, because the discount is fairly small. You can check to see that the yield to maturity is about 7.37 per cent, assuming annual coupons. General Tool's cost of debt, $R_D$, is thus 7.37 per cent.

---

## The Cost of Preference Shares

Determining the *cost of preference shares* is quite straightforward. As we discussed in Chapters 5 and 7, preference shares have a fixed dividend paid every period for ever, so a single preference share is essentially a perpetuity. The cost of preference shares, $R_P$, is thus

$$R_P = D/P_0 \qquad (13.3)$$

where $D$ is the fixed dividend and $P_0$ is the current preference share price. Notice that the cost of preference shares is simply equal to the dividend yield on the preference share. Alternatively, because preference shares are rated in much the same way as bonds, the cost of preference shares can be estimated by observing the required returns on other, similarly rated preference shares.

---

## EXAMPLE 13.3 — Edinburgh Power's Cost of Preference Shares

On 30 May 2010 Edinburgh Power had two issues of ordinary preference shares with a £25 par value. One issue paid £1.30 annually per share and sold for £21.05 per share. The other paid £1.46 per share annually and sold for £24.35 per share. What is Edinburgh Power's cost of preference shares?

Using the first issue, we calculate that the cost of preference shares is

$$
\begin{aligned}
R_P &= D/P_0 \\
&= £1.30/21.05 \\
&= 6.2\%
\end{aligned}
$$

Using the second issue, we calculate that the cost is

$$
\begin{aligned}
R_P &= D/P_0 \\
&= £1.46/24.35 \\
&= 6\%
\end{aligned}
$$

So Edinburgh Power's cost of preference shares appears to be about 6.1 per cent.

# 13.4    The Weighted Average Cost of Capital

Now that we have the costs associated with the main sources of capital the firm employs, we need to worry about the specific mix. As we mentioned earlier, we shall take this mix, which is the firm's capital structure, as given for now. Also, we shall focus mostly on debt and ordinary equity in this discussion.

In Chapter 3 we mentioned that financial analysts frequently focus on a firm's total capitalization, which is the sum of its long-term debt and equity. This is particularly true in determining cost of capital; short-term liabilities are often ignored in the process. We shall not explicitly distinguish between total value and total capitalization in the following discussion; the general approach is applicable with either.

## The Capital Structure Weights

We shall use the symbol E (for equity) to stand for the *market* value of the firm's equity. We calculate this by taking the number of shares outstanding and multiplying it by the share price. Similarly, we shall use the symbol $D$ (for debt) to stand for the *market* value of the firm's debt. For long-term debt we calculate this by multiplying the market price of a single bond by the number of bonds outstanding.

If there are multiple bond issues (as there normally would be), we repeat this calculation of $D$ for each, and then add up the results. If there is debt that is not publicly traded (because it is held by a life insurance company, for example), we must observe the yield on similar publicly traded debt and then estimate the market value of the privately held debt, using this yield as the discount rate. For short-term debt the book (accounting) values and market values should be somewhat similar, so we might use the book values as estimates of the market values.

Finally, we shall use the symbol $V$ (for value) to stand for the combined market value of the debt and equity:

$$V = E + D \tag{13.4}$$

If we divide both sides by $V$, we can calculate the percentages of the total capital represented by the debt and equity:

$$100\% = E/V + D/V \tag{13.5}$$

These percentages can be interpreted just like portfolio weights, and they are often called the *capital structure weights*.

For example, if the total market value of a company's equity were calculated as £200 million and the total market value of the company's debt were calculated as £50 million, then the combined value would be £250 million. Of this total, E/V = £200 million/250 million = 80%, so 80 per cent of the firm's financing would be equity and the remaining 20 per cent would be debt.

We emphasize here that the correct way to proceed is to use the *market* values of the debt and equity. Under certain circumstances, such as when calculating figures for a privately owned company, it may not be possible to get reliable estimates of these quantities. In this case we might go ahead and use the accounting values for debt and equity. Although this would probably be better than nothing, we would have to take the answer with a pinch of salt.

## Taxes and the Weighted Average Cost of Capital

There is one final issue we need to discuss. Recall that we are always concerned with after-tax cash flows. If we are determining the discount rate appropriate to those cash flows, then the discount rate also needs to be expressed on an after-tax basis.

As we have discussed previously in various places in this book (and as we shall discuss later), the interest paid by a corporation is deductible for tax purposes. Payments to shareholders, such as dividends, are not. What this means, effectively, is that the government pays some of the interest. Thus, in determining an after-tax discount rate, we need to distinguish between the pre-tax and the after-tax cost of debt.

To illustrate, suppose a firm borrows €1 million at 9 per cent interest. The corporate tax rate is 34 per cent. What is the after-tax interest rate on this loan? The total interest bill will be €90,000 per year. This amount is tax deductible, however, so the €90,000 interest reduces the firm's tax bill by $0.34 \times €90,000 = €30,600$. The after-tax interest bill is thus €90,000 − 30,600 = €59,400. The after-tax interest rate is thus €59,400/1 million = 5.94%.

Notice that, in general, the after-tax interest rate is simply equal to the pre-tax rate multiplied by 1 minus the tax rate. If we use the symbol $T_C$ to stand for the corporate tax rate, then the after-tax rate can be written as $R_D \times (1 - T_C)$. For example, using the numbers from the preceding paragraph, we find that the after-tax interest rate is $9\% \times (1 - 0.34) = 5.94\%$.

> **weighted average cost of capital (WACC)**
> The weighted average of the cost of equity and the after-tax cost of debt.

Bringing together the various topics we have discussed in this chapter, we now have the capital structure weights along with the cost of equity and the after-tax cost of debt. To calculate the firm's overall cost of capital we multiply the capital structure weights by the associated costs, and add them up. The total is the **weighted average cost of capital (WACC)**:

$$\text{WACC} = (E/V) \times R_E + (D/V) \times R_D \times (1 - T_C) \tag{13.6}$$

This WACC has a straightforward interpretation. It is the overall return the firm must earn on its existing assets to maintain the value of its equity. It is also the required return on any investments by the firm that have essentially the same risks as existing operations. So, if we were evaluating the cash flows from a proposed expansion of our existing operations, this is the discount rate we would use.

If a firm uses preference shares in its capital structure, then our expression for the WACC needs a simple extension. If we define $P/V$ as the percentage of the firm's financing that comes from preference shares, then the WACC is simply

$$\text{WACC} = (E/V) \times R_E + (P/V) \times R_P + (D/V) \times R_D \times (1 - T_C) \tag{13.7}$$

where $R_P$ is the cost of preference shares.

## Calculating the WACC

**EXAMPLE 13.4**

Travis SpA has 1.4 million shares of equity outstanding. The equity currently sells for €20 per share. The firm's debt is publicly traded, and was recently quoted at 93 per cent of face value. It has a total face value of €5 million, and it is currently priced to yield 11 per cent. The risk-free rate is 8 per cent, and the market risk premium is 7 per cent. You've estimated that Travis has a beta of 0.74. If the corporate tax rate is 34 per cent, what is the WACC of Travis SpA?

We can first determine the cost of equity and the cost of debt. Using the SML, we find that the cost of equity is $8\% + 0.74 \times 7\% = 13.18\%$. The total value of the equity is 1.4 million × €20 = €28 million. The pre-tax cost of debt is the current yield to maturity on the outstanding debt, 11 per cent. The debt sells for 93 per cent of its face value, so its current market value is

0.93 × €5 million = €4.65 million. The total market value of the equity and debt together is €28 million + 4.65 million = €32.65 million.

From here, we can calculate the WACC easily enough. The percentage of equity used by Travis to finance its operations is €28 million/€32.65 million = 85.76%. Because the weights have to add up to 1, the percentage of debt is 1 − 0.8576 = 14.24%. The WACC is thus

$$\text{WACC} = (E/V) \times R_\text{E} + (D/V) \times R_\text{D} \times (1 - T_\text{C})$$
$$= 0.8576 \times 13.18\% + 0.1424 \times 11\% \times (1 - 0.34)$$
$$= 12.34\%$$

Travis thus has an overall weighted average cost of capital of 12.34 per cent.

## Calculating the WACC for Deutsche Börse Group

In this section we illustrate how to calculate the WACC for the European stock exchange operator Deutsche Börse Group, in the same way that a financial analyst would. Our goal is to take you through, on a step-by-step basis, the process of finding and using the information needed using online sources. As you will see, there is a fair amount of detail involved, but the necessary information is, for the most part, readily available.

**Deutsche Börse's Cost of Equity**    Our first stop is the main screen for Deutsche Börse available at Yahoo! Finance. As of mid-2010, here's what it looked like:

**DEUTSCHE BOERSE N** ( XETRA: DB1.DE / ISIN DE0005810055 )

| | | | |
|---|---|---|---|
| Last Trade: | **53.88 €** | Day's Range: | 53.46 - 53.94 |
| Trade Time: | 8:22am | 52wk Range: | 45.45 - 62.62 |
| Change: | ↑0.45 (0.84%) | Volume: | 80,023 |
| Prev Close: | 53.43 | Avg Vol (3m): | 1,369,000 |
| Open: | 53.70 | Market Cap: | 10.51B |
| Bid: | 53.88 | P/E (ttm): | 20.18 x |
| Ask: | 53.89 | EPS (ttm): | 2.67 € |
| 1y Target Est: | 60.46 € | Div & Yield: | 2.10 (3.93%) |

As you can see, the total value of equity is €10.51 billion. To estimate Deutsche Börse's cost of equity, we shall assume a market risk premium of 9.1 per cent (see Fig. 11.7 for Germany). Deutsche Börse's beta on Yahoo! is 1.51, which is much higher than the beta of the average equity. To check this number, we went to Reuters and FT.com. The beta estimates we found there were both 1.08. These estimates are more realistic, and some financial judgement is required here. Because the beta estimate from Yahoo! is so much higher, we shall ignore it and use the beta from the other two websites. Thus the beta estimate we shall use is 1.08. According to the bond section of FT.com, T-bills were paying about 0.36 per cent. Using the CAPM to estimate the cost of equity, we find:

$$R_\text{E} = 0.0036 + 1.08 \,(0.091) = 0.1018 \text{ or } 10.18\%$$

To calculate the growth rate in dividends for Deutsche Börse, we check the analysts' estimates link in the Deutsche Börse page at FT.com. We found the following:

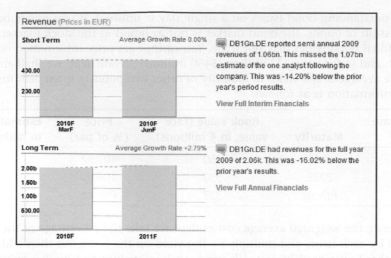

*Source: Financial Times.* © The Financial Times Ltd 2010.

Analysts estimate that the growth in earnings per share for the company will be 2.79 per cent over the next two years. For now we shall use this growth rate in the dividend discount model to estimate the cost of equity; the link between earnings growth and dividends is discussed in a later chapter. The estimated cost of equity using the dividend discount model is

$$R_E = \left[ \frac{€2.10(1 + 0.0279)}{€53.88} \right] + 0.0279$$
$$= 0.0680 \text{ or } 6.80\%$$

Notice that the estimates for the cost of equity are different. This is often the case. Remember that each method of estimating the cost of equity relies on different assumptions, so different estimates of the cost of equity should not surprise us. If the estimates are different, there are two simple solutions. First, we could ignore one of the estimates. We would look at each estimate to see whether one of them seemed too high or too low to be reasonable. Second, we could average the two estimates. Averaging the two estimates for Deutsche Börse's cost of equity gives us a cost of equity of 8.49 per cent. This seems like a reasonable number, so we shall use it in calculating the cost of capital in this example.

**Deutsche Börse's Cost of Debt**   We found out about Deutsche Börse's outstanding bonds by going to its website and looking at its financial information. It has two relatively long-term bond issues plus private loans that account for essentially all of its long-term debt (see below).

| Exchange listed debt instruments of Deutsche Börse AG | | | | | | | |
|---|---|---|---|---|---|---|---|
| Type | Issue volume | ISIN | Term | Maturity | Coupon p.a. | Listing | More information |
| Fixed-income bearer bond | €650 m | XS0353963225 | 5 years | April 2013 | 5,00 % | Luxembourg/ Frankfurt | more |
| Hybrid bond | €550 m | XS0369549570 | 30 years* | June 2038 | 7,50 %** | Luxembourg/ Frankfurt | more |

* Premature right of termination after 5 and 10 years and in each year thereafter

** Until June 2013: fixed-income 7.50 percent p.a.; from June 2013 to June2018: fixed-income mid swap + 285 basis points; from June 2018: variable interest rate

In additon, Deutsche Börse AG has until now issued private placements with a total value of approximately $460 million. Furthermore, Deutsche Börse AG issues Commercial Paper on a regular basis.

To calculate the cost of debt we shall have to combine these three debt issues. What we shall do is compute a weighted average. Since we know each security's International Security Identification Number (ISIN), we can easily get the most recent quote for each of the two publicly traded bonds. We should note here that finding the yield to maturity for all of a company's outstanding bond issues on a single day is unusual. If you remember our previous discussion of bonds, the bond market is not as liquid as the stock market; on many days, individual bond issues may not trade. You cannot get price information on privately placed debt, and so for the €337 million ($460 million) private debt, we shall approximate by using the average of the yields to maturity of other two publicly listed debt instruments. The basic information is as follows:

| Coupon rate (%) | Maturity | Book value (face value, in € millions) | Price (% of par) | Estimated yield to maturity (%) |
|---|---|---|---|---|
| 5.00 | 2013 | 650 | 107.32 | 2.440 |
| 7.50 | 2038 | 550 | 106.00 | 7.005 |
| Private | Private | 337 | Private | 4.723 |

To calculate the weighted average cost of debt we take the percentage of the total debt represented by each issue, and multiply by the yield on the issue. We then add to get the overall weighted average debt cost. We use both book values and market values here for comparison. The results of the calculations are as follows (totals for book values and market values are exact figures; the values in the individual cells are rounded):

| Coupon rate (%) | Book value (face value, in € millions) | Percentage of total (%) | Market value (in € millions) | Percentage of total (%) | Yield to maturity (%) | Book values (%) | Market values (%) |
|---|---|---|---|---|---|---|---|
| 5.00 | 650 | 0.42 | 697.58 | 0.43 | 2.440 | 1.03 | 1.05 |
| 7.00 | 550 | 0.36 | 583.00 | 0.36 | 7.005 | 2.51 | 2.52 |
| Private | 337 | 0.22 | 337.00 | 0.21 | 4.723 | 1.04 | 0.98 |
| | 1,537 | 1.00 | 1,617.58 | 1.00 | | 4.57 | 4.56 |

As these calculations show, Deutsche Börse's cost of debt is 4.57 per cent on a book value basis, and 4.56 per cent on a market value basis. Thus, for Deutsche Börse, whether market values or book values are used makes no real difference. The reason is simply that the market values and book values are very similar. This will often be the case, and it explains why companies frequently use book values for debt in WACC calculations. Also, Deutsche Börse has no preference shares, so we don't need to consider its cost.

**Deutsche Börse's WACC**    We now have the various pieces necessary to calculate Deutsche Börse's WACC. First, we need to calculate the capital structure weights. On a book value basis, Deutsche Börse's equity and debt are worth €2.789 billion and €1.537 billion (source: Reuters), respectively. The total value is €4.326 billion, so the equity and debt weights are €2.789 billion/4.326 billion = 0.64 and €1.537 billion/4.326 billion = 0.36, respectively. Assuming a tax rate of 33 per cent, Deutsche Börse's WACC is

$$\text{WACC} = 0.64 \times 8.49\% + 0.36 \times 4.57\% \times (1 - 0.33) = 6.54\%$$

Thus, using book value capital structure weights, we get about 6.54 per cent for Deutsche Börse's WACC.

If we use market value weights, however, the WACC will be higher. To see why, notice that on a market value basis Deutsche Börse's equity and debt are worth €10.51 billion and €1.618 billion, respectively. The capital structure weights are therefore €10.51 billion/12.128 billion = 0.87 and €1.618 billion/12.128 billion = 0.13, so the equity percentage is much higher. With these weights, Deutsche Börse's WACC is

$$\text{WACC} = 0.87 \times 8.49\% + 0.13 \times 4.57\% \times (1 - 0.33) = 7.78\%$$

Thus, using market value weights, we get about 7.78 per cent for Deutsche Börse's WACC, which is about 1.2 per cent higher than the 6.54 per cent WACC we got using book value weights.

As this example illustrates, using book values can lead to trouble, particularly if equity book values are used. Going back to Chapter 3, recall that we discussed the market-to-book ratio (the ratio of market value per share to book value per share). This ratio is usually substantially bigger than 1. For Deutsche Börse, for example, verify that it's about 3.77; so book values significantly overstate the percentage of Deutsche Börse's financing that comes from debt. In addition, if we were computing a WACC for a company that did not have publicly traded equity, we would try to come up with a suitable market-to-book ratio by looking at publicly traded companies, and we would then use this ratio to adjust the book value of the company under consideration. As we have seen, failure to do so can lead to significant underestimation of the WACC.

## Solving the Warehouse Problem and Similar Capital Budgeting Problems

Now we can use the WACC to solve the warehouse problem we posed at the beginning of the chapter. However, before we rush to discount the cash flows at the WACC to estimate NPV, we need to make sure we are doing the right thing.

Going back to first principles, we need to find an alternative in the financial markets that is comparable to the warehouse renovation. To be comparable, an alternative must be of the same level of risk as the warehouse project. Projects that have the same risk are said to be in the same risk class.

The WACC for a firm reflects the risk and the target capital structure of the firm's existing assets as a whole. As a result, strictly speaking, the firm's WACC is the appropriate discount rate only if the proposed investment is a replica of the firm's existing operating activities.

In broader terms, whether or not we can use the firm's WACC to value the warehouse project depends on whether the warehouse project is in the same risk class as the firm. We shall assume that this project is an integral part of the overall business of the firm. In such cases it is natural to think that the cost savings will be as risky as the general cash flows of the firm, and the project will thus be in the same risk class as the overall firm. More generally, projects like the warehouse renovation that are intimately related to the firm's existing operations are often viewed as being in the same risk class as the overall firm.

We can now see what the chief executive should do. Suppose the firm has a target debt–equity ratio of 1/3. From Chapter 3 we know that a debt–equity ratio of $D/E = 1/3$ implies that $E/V$ is 0.75 and $D/V$ is 0.25. The cost of debt is 10 per cent, and the cost of equity is 20 per cent. Assuming a 34 per cent tax rate, the WACC will be

$$
\begin{aligned}
\text{WACC} &= (E/V) \times R_\text{E} + (D/V) \times R_\text{D} \times (1 - T_\text{C}) \\
&= 0.75 \times 20\% + 0.25 \times 10\% \times (1 - 0.34) \\
&= 16.65\%
\end{aligned}
$$

Recall that the warehouse project had a cost of €50 million and expected after-tax cash flows (the cost savings) of €12 million per year for six years. The NPV (in millions) is thus

$$
\text{NPV} = -€50 + \frac{12}{(1 + \text{WACC})^1} + \cdots + \frac{12}{(1 + \text{WACC})^6}
$$

Because the cash flows are in the form of an ordinary annuity, we can calculate this NPV using 16.65 per cent (the WACC) as the discount rate as follows:

$$
\begin{aligned}
\text{NPV} &= -€50 + 12 \times \frac{1 - [1/(1 + 0.1665)^6]}{0.1665} \\
&= -€50 + 12 \times 3.6222 \\
&= -€6.53
\end{aligned}
$$

Should the firm take on the warehouse renovation? The project has a negative NPV using the firm's WACC. This means that the financial markets offer superior projects in the same risk class (namely, the firm itself). The answer is clear: the project should be rejected. For future reference, our discussion of the WACC is summarized in Table 13.2.

**The cost of equity, $R_E$**

A. Dividend growth model approach (from Chapter 7):

$$R_E = D_1/P_0 + g$$

where $D_1$ is the expected dividend in one period, $g$ is the dividend growth rate, and $P_0$ is the current share price.

B. SML approach (from Chapter 12):

$$R_E = R_f + \beta_E \times (R_M - R_f)$$

where $R_E$ is the risk-free rate, $R_M$ is the expected return on the overall market, and $\beta_E$ is the systematic risk of the equity.

**The cost of debt, $R_D$**

A. For a firm with publicly held debt, the cost of debt can be measured as the yield to maturity on the outstanding debt. The coupon rate is irrelevant. Yield to maturity is covered in Chapter 6.

B. If the firm has no publicly traded debt, then the cost of debt can be measured as the yield to maturity on similarly rated bonds (bond ratings are discussed in Chapter 6).

**The weighted average cost of capital, WACC**

A. The firm's WACC is the overall required return on the firm as a whole. It is the appropriate discount rate to use for cash flows similar in risk to those of the overall firm.

B. The WACC is calculated as

$$\text{WACC} = (E/V) \times R_E + (D/V) \times R_D \times (1 - T_C)$$

where $T_C$ is the corporate tax rate, $E$ is the *market* value of the firm's equity, $D$ is the *market* value of the firm's debt, and $V = E + D$. Note that E/V is the percentage of the firm's financing (in market value terms) that is equity, and D/V is the percentage that is debt.

**Table 13.2** Summary of capital cost calculations

## EXAMPLE 13.5    Using the WACC

A firm is considering a project that will result in initial after-tax cash savings of £5 million at the end of the first year. These savings will grow at the rate of 5 per cent per year. The firm has a debt–equity ratio of 0.5, a cost of equity of 29.2 per cent, and a cost of debt of 10 per cent. The cost-saving proposal is closely related to the firm's core business, so it is viewed as having the same risk as the overall firm. Should the firm take on the project?

Assuming a 28 per cent tax rate, the firm should take on this project if it costs less than £29.64 million. To see this, first note that the PV is

$$PV = \frac{£5 \text{ million}}{WACC - 0.05}$$

This is an example of a growing perpetuity, as discussed in Chapter 7. The WACC is

$$\begin{aligned} WACC &= (E/V) \times R_E + (D/V) \times R_D \times (1 - T_C) \\ &= 2/3 \times 29.2\% + 1/3 \times 10\% \times (1 - 0.28) \\ &= 21.87\% \end{aligned}$$

The PV is thus

$$PV = \frac{£5 \text{ million}}{0.2187 - 0.05} = £29.64 \text{ million}$$

The NPV will be positive only if the cost is less than £29.64 million.

## Performance Evaluation: Another Use of the WACC

Performance evaluation is another use of the WACC. Probably the best-known approach in this area is the economic value added (EVA) method developed by Stern Stewart and Co. Similar approaches include market value added (MVA) and shareholder value added (SVA).

Although the details differ, the basic idea behind EVA and similar strategies is straightforward. Suppose we have €100 million in capital (debt and equity) tied up in our firm, and our overall WACC is 12 per cent. If we multiply these together, we get €12 million. Referring back to Chapter 3, if our cash flow from assets is less than this, we are, on an overall basis, destroying value; if cash flow from assets exceeds €12 million, we are creating value.

In practice, evaluation strategies such as these suffer to a certain extent from problems with implementation. For example, it appears that many companies make extensive use of book values for debt and equity in computing cost of capital. Even so, by focusing on value creation, WACC-based evaluation procedures force employees and management to pay attention to the real bottom line: increasing share prices.

| | | |
|---|---|---|
| **CONCEPT QUESTIONS** | 13.4a | How is the WACC calculated? |
| | 13.4b | Why do we multiply the cost of debt by $(1 - T_C)$ when we compute the WACC? |
| | 13.4c | Under what conditions is it correct to use the WACC to determine NPV? |

## 13.5  Divisional and Project Costs of Capital

As we have seen, using the WACC as the discount rate for future cash flows is appropriate only when the proposed investment is similar to the firm's existing activities. This is not as restrictive as it sounds. If we are in the pizza business, for example, and we are thinking of opening a new location, then the WACC is the discount rate to use. The same is true of a retailer thinking of a new store, a manufacturer thinking of expanding production, or a consumer products company thinking of expanding its markets.

Nonetheless, despite the usefulness of the WACC as a benchmark, there will clearly be situations in which the cash flows under consideration have risks distinctly different from those of the overall firm. We consider how to cope with this problem next.

FIGURE
**13.1**

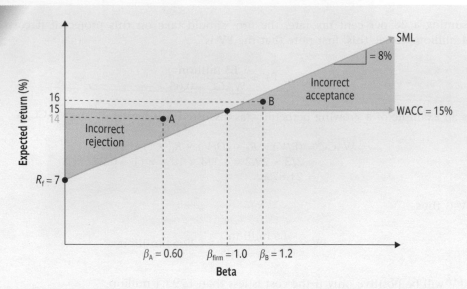

If a firm uses its **WACC** to make accept–reject decisions for all types of project, it will have a tendency towards incorrectly accepting risky projects and incorrectly rejecting less risky projects.

**Figure 13.1** The security market line (SML) and the weighted average cost of capital (WACC)

## The SML and the WACC

When we are evaluating investments with risks that are substantially different from those of the overall firm, use of the WACC will potentially lead to poor decisions. Figure 13.1 illustrates why.

In Fig. 13.1 we have plotted an SML corresponding to a risk-free rate of 7 per cent and a market risk premium of 8 per cent. To keep things simple, we consider an all-equity company with a beta of 1. As we have indicated, the WACC and the cost of equity are exactly equal to 15 per cent for this company, because there is no debt.

Suppose our firm uses its WACC to evaluate all investments. This means that any investment with a return of greater than 15 per cent will be accepted, and any investment with a return of less than 15 per cent will be rejected. We know from our study of risk and return, however, that a desirable investment is one that plots above the SML. As Fig. 13.1 illustrates, using the WACC for all types of project can result in the firm's incorrectly accepting relatively risky projects and incorrectly rejecting relatively safe ones.

For example, consider point A. This project has a beta of $\beta_A = 0.60$, as compared with the firm's beta of 1.0. It has an expected return of 14 per cent. Is this a desirable investment? The answer is yes, because its required return is only

$$\text{Required return} = R_f + \beta_A \times (R_M - R_f)$$
$$= 7\% + 0.60 \times 8\%$$
$$= 11.8\%$$

However, if we use the WACC as a cut-off, then this project will be rejected, because its return is less than 15 per cent. This example illustrates that a firm that uses its WACC as a cut-off will tend to reject profitable projects with risks less than those of the overall firm.

At the other extreme, consider point B. This project has a beta of $\beta_B = 1.2$. It offers a 16 per cent return, which exceeds the firm's cost of capital. This is not a good investment, however, because, given its level of systematic risk, its return is inadequate. Nonetheless, if we use the WACC to evaluate it, it will appear to be attractive. So the second error that will arise if we use the WACC as a cut-off is that we shall tend to make unprofitable investments with risks greater than those of the overall firm. As a consequence, through time, a firm that uses its WACC to evaluate all projects will have a tendency both to accept unprofitable investments and to become increasingly risky.

## Divisional Cost of Capital

The same type of problem with the WACC can arise in a corporation with more than one line of business. Imagine, for example, a corporation that has two divisions: a regulated telephone company and an electronics manufacturing operation. The first of these (the phone operation) has relatively low risk; the second has relatively high risk.

In this case, the firm's overall cost of capital is really a mixture of two different costs of capital, one for each division. If the two divisions were competing for resources, and the firm used a single WACC as a cut-off, which division would tend to be awarded greater funds for investment?

The answer is that the riskier division would tend to have greater returns (ignoring the greater risk), so it would tend to be the 'winner'. The less glamorous operation might have great profit potential that would end up being ignored. Large corporations in Europe are aware of this problem, and many work to develop separate divisional costs of capital.

## The Pure Play Approach

We've seen that using the firm's WACC inappropriately can lead to problems. How can we come up with the appropriate discount rates in such circumstances? Because we cannot observe the returns on these investments, there generally is no direct way of coming up with a beta, for example. Instead, what we must do is examine other investments outside the firm that are in the same risk class as the one we are considering, and use the market-required return on these investments as the discount rate. In other words, we shall try to determine what the cost of capital is for such investments by trying to locate some similar investments in the marketplace.

For example, going back to our telephone division, suppose we wanted to come up with a discount rate to use for that division. What we could do is identify several other phone companies that have publicly traded securities. We might find that a typical phone company has a beta of 0.80, AA-rated debt, and a capital structure that is about 50 per cent debt and 50 per cent equity. Using this information, we could develop a WACC for a typical phone company and use this as our discount rate.

Alternatively, if we were thinking of entering a new line of business, we would try to develop the appropriate cost of capital by looking at the market-required returns on companies already in that business. In the language of financial markets, a company that focuses on a single line of business is called a *pure play*. For example, if you wanted to bet on the price of crude oil by purchasing equities, you would try to identify companies that dealt exclusively with this product, because they would be the most affected by changes in the price of crude oil. Such companies would be called 'pure plays on the price of crude oil'.

What we try to do here is to find companies that focus as exclusively as possible on the type of project in which we are interested. Our approach, therefore, is called the **pure play approach** to estimating the required return on an investment. To illustrate, suppose McDonald's decides to enter the personal computer and network server business with a line of machines called McPuters. The risks involved are quite different from those in the fast-food business. As a result, McDonald's would need to look at companies already in the personal computer business to compute a cost of capital for the new division. An obvious pure play candidate would be Dell, which is predominantly in this line of business. HP, on the other hand, would not be as good a choice because its primary focus is elsewhere, and it has many different product lines.

**pure play approach** The use of a WACC that is unique to a particular project, based on companies in similar lines of business.

In Chapter 3 we discussed the subject of identifying similar companies for comparison purposes. The same problems we described there come up here. The most obvious one is that we may not be able to find any suitable companies. In this case, how to determine a discount rate objectively becomes a difficult question. Even so, the important thing is to be aware of the issue, so that we at least reduce the possibility of the kinds of mistake that can arise when the WACC is used as a cut-off on all investments.

## The Subjective Approach

Because of the difficulties that exist in establishing discount rates objectively for individual projects, firms often adopt an approach that involves making subjective adjustments to the overall WACC. To illustrate, suppose a firm has an overall WACC of 14 per cent. It places all proposed projects into four categories, as follows:

| Category | Examples | Adjustment factor (%) | Discount rate (%) |
|---|---|---|---|
| High risk | New products | +6 | 20 |
| Moderate risk | Cost savings, expansion of existing lines | +0 | 14 |
| Low risk | Replacement of existing equipment | −4 | 10 |
| Mandatory | Pollution control equipment | n/a | n/a |

n/a = Not applicable.

The effect of this crude partitioning is to assume that all projects either fall into one of three risk classes or else are mandatory. In the last case, the cost of capital is irrelevant, because the project must be taken. With the subjective approach, the firm's WACC may change through time as economic conditions change. As this happens, the discount rates for the different types of projects will also change.

Within each risk class, some projects will presumably have more risk than others, and the danger of making incorrect decisions still exists. Figure 13.2 illustrates this point.

FIGURE

**13.2**

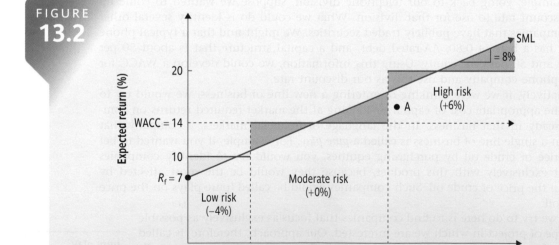

With the subjective approach, the firm places projects into one of several risk classes. The discount rate used to value the project is then determined by adding (for high risk) or subtracting (for low risk) an adjustment factor to or from the firm's WACC. This results in fewer incorrect decisions than if the firm simply used the WACC to make the decisions.

**Figure 13.2** The security market line (SML) and the subjective approach

Comparing Figs 13.1 and 13.2, we see that similar problems exist, but the magnitude of the potential error is less with the subjective approach. For example, the project labelled A would be accepted if the WACC were used, but it is rejected once it is classified as a high-risk investment. What this illustrates is that some risk adjustment, even if it is subjective, is probably better than no risk adjustment.

It would be better, in principle, to determine the required return objectively for each project separately. However, as a practical matter, it may not be possible to go much beyond subjective adjustments, because either the necessary information is unavailable or the cost and effort required are simply not worthwhile.

| CONCEPT QUESTIONS | 13.5a | What are the likely consequences if a firm uses its WACC to evaluate all proposed investments? |
| | 13.5b | What is the pure play approach to determining the appropriate discount rate? When might it be used? |

## 13.6 Flotation Costs and the Weighted Average Cost of Capital

So far we have not included issue, or flotation, costs in our discussion of the weighted average cost of capital. If a company accepts a new project, it may be required to issue, or float, new bonds and shares. This means that the firm will incur some costs, which we call *flotation costs*. The nature and magnitude of flotation costs are discussed in some detail in Chapter 14.

Sometimes it is suggested that the firm's WACC should be adjusted upwards to reflect flotation costs. This is really not the best approach, because, once again, the required return on an investment depends on the risk of the investment, not on the source of the funds. This is not to say that flotation costs should be ignored. Because these costs arise as a consequence of the decision to undertake a project, they are relevant cash flows. We therefore briefly discuss how to include them in project analysis.

### The Basic Approach

We start with a simple case. Spatt Ltd, an all-equity firm, has a cost of equity of 20 per cent. Because this firm is 100 per cent equity, its WACC and its cost of equity are the same. Spatt is contemplating a large-scale, €100 million expansion of its existing operations. The expansion would be funded by selling new equity.

Based on conversations with its investment banker, Spatt believes its flotation costs will run to 10 per cent of the amount issued. This means that Spatt's proceeds from the equity sale will be only 90 per cent of the amount sold. When flotation costs are considered, what is the cost of the expansion?

As we discuss in more detail in Chapter 14, Spatt needs to sell enough equity to raise €100 million *after* covering the flotation costs. In other words:

$$€100 \text{ million} = (1 - 0.10) \times \text{Amount raised}$$
$$\text{Amount raised} = €100 \text{ million}/0.90 = €111.11 \text{ million}$$

Spatt's flotation costs are thus €11.11 million, and the true cost of the expansion is €111.11 million once we include flotation costs.

Things are only slightly more complicated if the firm uses both debt and equity. For example, suppose Spatt's target capital structure is 60 per cent equity, 40 per cent debt. The flotation costs associated with equity are still 10 per cent, but the flotation costs for debt are less – say 5 per cent.

Earlier, when we had different capital costs for debt and equity, we calculated a weighted average cost of capital using the target capital structure weights. Here we shall do much the same thing. We can calculate a weighted average flotation cost, $f_A$, by multiplying the equity flotation cost, $f_E$, by the percentage of equity ($E/V$) and the debt flotation cost, $f_D$, by the percentage of debt ($D/V$), and then adding the two together:

$$
\begin{aligned}
f_A &= (E/V) \times f_E + (D/V) \times f_D \\
&= 60\% \times 0.10 + 40\% \times 0.05 \\
&= 8\%
\end{aligned}
\tag{13.8}
$$

The weighted average flotation cost is thus 8 per cent. What this tells us is that for every euro in outside financing needed for new projects, the firm must actually raise €1/(1 − 0.08) = €1.087. In our example the project cost is €100 million when we ignore flotation costs. If we include them, then the true cost is €100 million/(1 − $f_A$) = €100 million/0.92 = €108.7 million.

In taking issue costs into account, the firm must be careful not to use the wrong weights. The firm should use the target weights, even if it can finance the entire cost of the project with either debt or equity. The fact that a firm can finance a specific project with debt or equity is not directly relevant. If a firm has a target debt–equity ratio of 1, for example, but chooses to finance a particular project with all debt, it will have to raise additional equity later on to maintain its target debt–equity ratio. To take this into account, the firm should always use the target weights in calculating the flotation cost.

---

**EXAMPLE 13.6**

## Calculating the Weighted Average Flotation Cost

Wendy plc has a target capital structure that is 80 per cent equity, 20 per cent debt. The flotation costs for equity issues are 20 per cent of the amount raised; the flotation costs for debt issues are 6 per cent. If Wendy needs £65 million for a new manufacturing facility, what is the true cost once flotation costs are considered?

We first calculate the weighted average flotation cost, $f_A$:

$$
\begin{aligned}
f_A &= (E/V) \times f_E + (D/V) \times f_D \\
&= 80\% \times 0.20 + 20\% \times 0.06 \\
&= 17.2\%
\end{aligned}
$$

The weighted average flotation cost is thus 17.2 per cent. The project cost is £65 million when we ignore flotation costs. If we include them, then the true cost is £65 million/(1 − $f_A$) = £65 million/0.828 = £78.5 million, again illustrating that flotation costs can be a considerable expense.

---

## Flotation Costs and NPV

To illustrate how flotation costs can be included in an NPV analysis, suppose Tripleday Printing SA is currently at its target debt–equity ratio of 100 per cent. It is considering building a new €500,000 printing plant in Lyon. This new plant is expected to generate after-tax cash flows of €73,150 per year for ever. The tax rate is 34 per cent. There are two financing options:

1   A €500,000 new issue of equity. The issuance costs of the new equity would be about 10 per cent of the amount raised. The required return on the company's new equity is 20 per cent.

2   A €500,000 issue of 30-year bonds. The issuance costs of the new debt would be 2 per cent of the proceeds. The company can raise new debt at 10 per cent.

What is the NPV of the new printing plant?

To begin, because printing is the company's main line of business, we shall use the company's weighted average cost of capital to value the new printing plant:

$$\text{WACC} = (E/V) \times R_E + (D/V) \times R_D \times (1 - T_C)$$
$$= 0.50 \times 20\% + 0.50 \times 10\% \times (1 - 0.34)$$
$$= 13.3\%$$

Because the cash flows are €73,150 per year for ever, the PV of the cash flows at 13.3 per cent per year is

$$\text{PV} = \frac{€73,150}{0.133} = €550,000$$

If we ignore flotation costs, the NPV is

$$\text{NPV} = €550,000 - 500,000 = €50,000$$

With no flotation costs, the project generates an NPV that is greater than zero, so it should be accepted.

What about financing arrangements and issue costs? Because new financing must be raised, the flotation costs are relevant. From the information given, we know that the flotation costs are 2 per cent for debt and 10 per cent for equity. Because Tripleday uses equal amounts of debt and equity, the weighted average flotation cost, $f_A$, is

$$f_A = (E/V) \times f_E + (D/V) \times f_D$$
$$= 0.50 \times 10\% + 0.50 \times 2\%$$
$$= 6\%$$

Remember, the fact that Tripleday can finance the project with all debt or all equity is irrelevant. Because Tripleday needs €500,000 to fund the new plant, the true cost, once we include flotation costs, is €500,000/$(1 - f_A)$ = €500,000/0.94 = €531,915. Because the PV of the cash flows is €550,000, the plant has an NPV of €550,000 − 531,915 = €18,085, so it is still a good investment. However, its value is less than we initially might have thought.

## Internal Equity and Flotation Costs

Our discussion of flotation costs to this point implicitly assumes that firms always have to raise the capital needed for new investments. In reality, most firms rarely sell equity at all. Instead, their internally generated cash flow is sufficient to cover the equity portion of their capital spending. Only the debt portion must be raised externally.

The use of internal equity doesn't change our approach. However, we now assign a value of zero to the flotation cost of equity, because there is no such cost. In our Tripleday example, the weighted average flotation cost would therefore be

$$f_A = (E/V) \times f_E + (D/V) \times f_D$$
$$= 0.50 \times 0\% + 0.50 \times 2\%$$
$$= 1\%$$

Notice that whether equity is generated internally or externally makes a big difference, because external equity has a relatively high flotation cost.

| | |
|---|---|
| **CONCEPT QUESTIONS** | 13.6a  What are flotation costs? |
| | 13.6b  How are flotation costs included in an NPV analysis? |

## Summary and Conclusions

This chapter has discussed cost of capital. The most important concept is the weighted average cost of capital, or WACC, which we interpreted as the required rate of return on the overall firm. It is also the discount rate appropriate for cash flows that are similar in risk to those of the overall firm. We described how the WACC can be calculated, and we illustrated how it can be used in certain types of analysis.

We also pointed out situations in which it is inappropriate to use the WACC as the discount rate. To handle such cases we described some alternative approaches to developing discount rates, such as the pure play approach. We also discussed how the flotation costs associated with raising new capital can be included in an NPV analysis.

## Chapter Review and Self-Test Problems

13.1    **Calculating the Cost of Equity**    Suppose equity in Watta plc has a beta of 0.80. The market risk premium is 6 per cent, and the risk-free rate is 6 per cent. Watta's last dividend was £1.20 per share, and the dividend is expected to grow at 8 per cent indefinitely. The equity currently sells for £45 per share. What is Watta's cost of equity capital?

13.2    **Calculating the WACC**    In addition to the information given in the previous problem, suppose Watta has a target debt–equity ratio of 50 per cent. Its cost of debt is 9 per cent before taxes. If the tax rate is 28 per cent, what is the WACC?

13.3    **Flotation Costs**    Suppose in the previous problem Watta is seeking £30 million for a new project. The necessary funds will have to be raised externally. Watta's flotation costs for selling debt and equity are 2 per cent and 16 per cent, respectively. If flotation costs are considered, what is the true cost of the new project?

## Answers to Chapter Review and Self-Test Problems

13.1    We start off with the SML approach. Based on the information given, the expected return on Watta's equity is

$$R_E = R_f + \beta_E \times (R_M - R_f)$$
$$= 6\% + 0.80 \times 6\%$$
$$= 10.80\%$$

We now use the dividend growth model. The projected dividend is $D_0 \times (1 + g) = £1.20 \times 1.08 = £1.296$, so the expected return using this approach is

$$R_E = D_1/P_0 + g$$
$$= £1.296/45 + 0.08$$
$$= 10.88\%$$

Because these two estimates, 10.80 per cent and 10.88 per cent, are fairly close, we shall average them. Watta's cost of equity is approximately 10.84 per cent.

13.2    Because the target debt–equity ratio is 0.50, Watta uses £0.50 in debt for every £1 in equity. In other words, Watta's target capital structure is 1/3 debt and 2/3 equity. The WACC is thus

$$WACC = (E/V) \times R_E + (D/V) \times R_D \times (1 - T_C)$$
$$= 2/3 \times 10.84\% + 1/3 \times 9\% \times (1 - 0.28)$$
$$= 9.387\%$$

13.3 Because Watta uses both debt and equity to finance its operations, we first need the weighted average flotation cost. As in the previous problem, the percentage of equity financing is 2/3, so the weighted average cost is

$$f_A = (E/V) \times f_E + (D/V) \times f_D$$
$$= 2/3 \times 16\% + 1/3 \times 2\%$$
$$= 11.33\%$$

If Watta needs £30 million after flotation costs, then the true cost of the project is £30 million/ $(1 - f_A)$ = £30 million/0.8867 = £33.83 million.

# Concepts Review and Critical Thinking Questions

1 **WACC [LO3]**  On the most basic level, if a firm's WACC is 12 per cent, what does this mean?

2 **Book Values versus Market Values [LO3]**  In calculating the WACC, if you had to use book values for either debt or equity, which would you choose? Why?

3 **Project Risk [LO5]**  If you can borrow all the money you need for a project at 6 per cent, doesn't it follow that 6 per cent is your cost of capital for the project?

4 **WACC and Taxes [LO3]**  Why do we use an after-tax figure for cost of debt but not for cost of equity?

5 **DCF Cost of Equity Estimation [LO1]**  What are the advantages of using the DCF model for determining the cost of equity capital? What are the disadvantages? What specific piece of information do you need to find the cost of equity using this model? What are some of the ways in which you could get this estimate?

6 **SML Cost of Equity Estimation [LO1]**  What are the advantages of using the SML approach to finding the cost of equity capital? What are the disadvantages? What specific pieces of information are needed to use this method? Are all of these variables observable, or do they need to be estimated? What are some of the ways in which you could get these estimates?

7 **Cost of Debt Estimation [LO2]**  How do you determine the appropriate cost of debt for a company? Does it make a difference if the company's debt is privately placed as opposed to being publicly traded? How would you estimate the cost of debt for a firm whose only debt issues are privately held by institutional investors?

8 **Cost of Capital [LO5]**  Suppose Tom O'Bedlam, chief executive of Bedlam Products, has hired you to determine the firm's cost of debt and cost of equity capital.

   (a) The equity currently sells for €50 per share, and the dividend per share will probably be about €5. Tom argues, 'It will cost us €5 per share to use the shareholders' money this year, so the cost of equity is equal to 10 per cent (= €5/50).' What's wrong with this conclusion?

   (b) Based on the most recent financial statements, Bedlam Products' total liabilities are €8 million. Total interest expense for the coming year will be about €1 million. Tom therefore reasons, 'We owe €8 million, and we shall pay €1 million interest. Therefore our cost of debt is obviously €1 million/8 million = 12.5%.' What's wrong with this conclusion?

   (c) Based on his own analysis, Tom is recommending that the company increase its use of equity financing, because 'debt costs 12.5 per cent, but equity costs only 10 per cent; thus equity is cheaper.' Ignoring all the other issues, what do you think about the conclusion that the cost of equity is less than the cost of debt?

9  **Company Risk versus Project Risk [LO5]**  Both MacLean Chemicals, a large natural gas user, and Superior Oil, a major natural gas producer, are thinking of investing in natural gas wells near the Falkland Islands. Both companies are all equity-financed. MacLean and Superior are looking at identical projects. They've analysed their respective investments, which would involve a negative cash flow now and positive expected cash flows in the future. These cash flows would be the same for both firms. No debt would be used to finance the projects. Both companies estimate that their projects would have a net present value of £1 million at an 18 per cent discount rate and a –£1.1 million NPV at a 22 per cent discount rate. MacLean has a beta of 1.25, whereas Superior has a beta of 0.75. The expected risk premium on the market is 8 per cent, and risk-free bonds are yielding 12 per cent. Should either company proceed? Should both? Explain.

10  **Divisional Cost of Capital [LO5]**  Under what circumstances would it be appropriate for a firm to use different costs of capital for its different operating divisions? If the overall firm WACC were used as the hurdle rate for all divisions, would the riskier divisions or the more conservative divisions tend to get most of the investment projects? Why? If you were to try to estimate the appropriate cost of capital for different divisions, what problems might you encounter? What are two techniques you could use to develop a rough estimate for each division's cost of capital?

# connect Questions and Problems

**BASIC**

**1–19**

1  **Calculating Cost of Equity [LO1]**  Down and Out NV just issued a dividend of €2.40 per share on its equity. The company is expected to maintain a constant 5.5 per cent growth rate in its dividends indefinitely. If the equity sells for €52 a share, what is the company's cost of equity?

2  **Calculating Cost of Equity [LO1]**  Up and Coming NV's equity has a beta of 1.05. If the risk-free rate is 5.3 per cent and the expected return on the market is 12 per cent, what is the company's cost of equity capital?

3  **Calculating Cost of Equity [LO1]**  Equity in Landsväg AG has a beta of 0.85. The market risk premium is 8 per cent, and T-bills are currently yielding 5 per cent. The company's most recent dividend was SKr1.60 per share, and dividends are expected to grow at a 6 per cent annual rate indefinitely. If the equity sells for SKr37 per share, what is your best estimate of the company's cost of equity?

4  **Estimating the DCF Growth Rate [LO1]**  Suppose Found Ltd just issued a dividend of £1.43 per share on its equity. The company paid dividends of £1.05, £1.12, £1.19 and £1.30 per share in the last four years. If the equity currently sells for £45, what is your best estimate of the company's cost of equity capital using the arithmetic average growth rate in dividends? What if you use the geometric average growth rate?

5  **Calculating Cost of Preference Shares [LO1]**  Holdup Bank has an issue of preference shares with a €6 stated dividend that just sold for €96 per share. What is the bank's cost of preference shares?

6  **Calculating Cost of Debt [LO2]**  Hendrix plc is trying to determine its cost of debt. The firm has a debt issue outstanding with 15 years to maturity that is quoted at 107 per cent of face value. The issue makes semi-annual payments and has an embedded cost of 7 per cent annually. What is the company's pre-tax cost of debt? If the tax rate is 28 per cent, what is the after-tax cost of debt?

7  **Calculating Cost of Debt [LO2]**  Door De Storm NV issued a 30-year, 8 per cent semi-annual bond 7 years ago. The bond currently sells for 95 per cent of its face value. The company's tax rate is 35 per cent.

(a)   What is the pre-tax cost of debt?

(b)   What is the after-tax cost of debt?

(c)   Which is more relevant, the pre-tax or the after-tax cost of debt? Why?

8   **Calculating Cost of Debt [LO2]**   For the firm in Problem 7, suppose the book value of the debt issue is €80 million. In addition, the company has a second debt issue on the market, a zero coupon bond with seven years left to maturity; the book value of this issue is €35 million, and the bonds sell for 61 per cent of par. What is the company's total book value of debt? The total market value? What is your best estimate of the after-tax cost of debt now?

9   **Calculating WACC [LO3]**   Mullineaux has a target capital structure of 60 per cent equity, 5 per cent preference shares, and 35 per cent debt. Its cost of equity is 14 per cent, the cost of preference shares is 6 per cent, and the cost of debt is 8 per cent. The relevant tax rate is 28 per cent.

(a)   What is Mullineaux's WACC?

(b)   The company chief executive has approached you about Mullineaux's capital structure. He wants to know why the company doesn't use more preference share financing, because it costs less than debt. What would you tell the chief executive?

10   **Taxes and WACC [LO3]**   Sixx AM Manufacturing has a target debt–equity ratio of 0.65. Its cost of equity is 15 per cent, and its cost of debt is 9 per cent. If the tax rate is 35 per cent, what is the company's WACC?

11   **Finding the Target Capital Structure [LO3]**   Fama's Llamas has a weighted average cost of capital of 8.9 per cent. The company's cost of equity is 12 per cent, and its pre-tax cost of debt is 7.9 per cent. The tax rate is 30 per cent. What is the company's target debt–equity ratio?

12   **Book Value versus Market Value [LO3]**   Filer Manufacturing has 11 million shares of equity outstanding. The current share price is £68, and the book value per share is £6. Filer Manufacturing also has two bond issues outstanding. The first bond issue has a face value of £70 million, has a 7 per cent coupon, and sells for 93 per cent of par. The second issue has a face value of £55 million, has an 8 per cent coupon, and sells for 104 per cent of par. The first issue matures in 21 years, the second in 6 years.

(a)   What are Filer's capital structure weights on a book value basis?

(b)   What are Filer's capital structure weights on a market value basis?

(c)   Which are more relevant, the book or market value weights? Why?

13   **Calculating the WACC [LO3]**   In Problem 12, suppose the most recent dividend was £4.10 and the dividend growth rate is 6 per cent. Assume that the overall cost of debt is the weighted average of that implied by the two outstanding debt issues. Both bonds make semi-annual payments. The tax rate is 28 per cent. What is the company's WACC?

14   **WACC [LO3]**   Urskov has a target debt–equity ratio of 1.05. Its WACC is 9.4 per cent, and the tax rate is 35 per cent.

(a)   If Urskov's cost of equity is 14 per cent, what is its pre-tax cost of debt?

(b)   If instead you know that the after-tax cost of debt is 6.8 per cent, what is the cost of equity?

15   **Finding the WACC [LO3]**   Given the following information for Evenflow Power, find the WACC. Assume the company's tax rate is 28 per cent.

| | |
|---|---|
| *Debt*: | 400 6.5 per cent coupon bonds outstanding, £50,000 par value, 20 years to maturity, selling for 92 per cent of par; the bonds make semi-annual payments. |
| *Equity*: | 250,000 shares outstanding, selling for £57 per share; the beta is 1.05. |
| *Preference shares*: | 15,000 of 5 per cent preference shares outstanding, currently selling for £93 per share against a face value of £100. |
| *Market*: | 8 per cent market risk premium and 4.5 per cent risk-free rate. |

16  **Finding the WACC [LO3]**   Titan Mining has 9 million shares of equity outstanding, 250,000 of 6 per cent preference shares outstanding, and 105,000 7.5 per cent semi-annual bonds outstanding, par value €1,000 each. The equity currently sells for €34 per share and has a beta of 1.25, the preference shares currently sell for €91 per share, and the bonds have 15 years to maturity and sell for 93 per cent of par. The market risk premium is 8.5 per cent, T-bills are yielding 5 per cent, and Titan Mining's tax rate is 35 per cent.

(a)   What is the firm's market value capital structure?

(b)   If Titan Mining is evaluating a new investment project that has the same risk as the firm's typical project, what rate should the firm use to discount the project's cash flows?

17  **SML and WACC [LO1]**   An all-equity firm is considering the following projects:

| Project | Beta | Expected return (%) |
|---|---|---|
| W | 0.80 | 10 |
| X | 0.90 | 12 |
| Y | 1.45 | 13 |
| Z | 1.60 | 15 |

The T-bill rate is 5 per cent, and the expected return on the market is 11 per cent.

(a)   Which projects have a higher expected return than the firm's 11 per cent cost of capital?

(b)   Which projects should be accepted?

(c)   Which projects would be incorrectly accepted or rejected if the firm's overall cost of capital were used as a hurdle rate?

18  **Calculating Flotation Costs [LO4]**   Suppose your company needs £20 million to build a new assembly line. Your target debt–equity ratio is 0.75. The flotation cost for new equity is 8 per cent, but the flotation cost for debt is only 5 per cent. Your boss has decided to fund the project by borrowing money, because the flotation costs are lower and the required funds are relatively small.

(a)   What do you think about the rationale behind borrowing the entire amount?

(b)   What is your company's weighted average flotation cost, assuming all equity is raised externally?

(c)   What is the true cost of building the new assembly line after taking flotation costs into account? Does it matter in this case that the entire amount is being raised from debt?

19  **Calculating Flotation Costs [LO4]**   Southern Alliance needs to raise €45 million to start a new project, and will raise the money by selling new bonds. The company will generate no internal equity for the foreseeable future. The company has a target capital structure of 65 per cent equity, 5 per cent preference shares, and 30 per cent debt. Flotation costs for issuing new equity are 9 per cent, for new preference shares,

6 per cent, and for new debt, 3 per cent. What is the true initial cost figure Southern should use when evaluating its project?

INTERMEDIATE

20–23

20 **WACC and NPV [LO3, LO5]**   Scanlin is considering a project that will result in initial after-tax cash savings of £2.7 million at the end of the first year, and these savings will grow at a rate of 4 per cent per year indefinitely. The firm has a target debt–equity ratio of 0.90, a cost of equity of 13 per cent, and an after-tax cost of debt of 4.8 per cent. The cost-saving proposal is somewhat riskier than the usual project the firm undertakes; management uses the subjective approach and applies an adjustment factor of +2 per cent to the cost of capital for such risky projects. Under what circumstances should the company take on the project?

21 **Flotation Costs [LO4]**   Purple Haze recently issued new securities to finance a new TV show. The project cost €15 million, and the company paid €850,000 in flotation costs. In addition, the equity issued had a flotation cost of 7 per cent of the amount raised, whereas the debt issued had a flotation cost of 3 per cent of the amount raised. If Purple Haze issued new securities in the same proportion as its target capital structure, what is the company's target debt–equity ratio?

22 **Calculating the Cost of Debt [LO2]**   Ying Imports has several bond issues outstanding, each making semi-annual interest payments. The bonds are listed in the following table. If the corporate tax rate is 28 per cent, what is the after-tax cost of Ying's debt?

| Bond | Coupon rate (%) | Price quote | Maturity (years) | Face value (£) |
|---|---|---|---|---|
| 1 | 7.00 | 103.00 | 5 | 40,000,000 |
| 2 | 8.50 | 108.00 | 8 | 35,000,000 |
| 3 | 8.20 | 97.00 | 15½ | 55,000,000 |
| 4 | 9.80 | 111.00 | 25 | 50,000,000 |

23 **Calculating the Cost of Equity [LO1]**   Floyd Industries equity has a beta of 1.50. The company just paid a dividend of £0.80, and the dividends are expected to grow at 5 per cent. The expected return of the market is 12 per cent, and Treasury bills are yielding 5.5 per cent. The most recent share price for Floyd is £61.

(a) Calculate the cost of equity using the DCF method.

(b) Calculate the cost of equity using the SML method.

(c) Why do you think your estimates in (a) and (b) are so different?

CHALLENGE

24–26

24 **Flotation Costs and NPV [LO3, LO4]**   Photochronograph Creative (PC) manufactures time series photographic equipment. It is currently at its target debt–equity ratio of 0.70. It's considering building a new £45 million manufacturing facility. This new plant is expected to generate after-tax cash flows of £6.2 million in perpetuity. The company raises all equity from outside financing. There are three financing options:

1 *A new issue of equity.* The flotation costs of the new equity would be 8 per cent of the amount raised. The required return on the company's new equity is 14 per cent.

2 *A new issue of 20-year bonds.* The flotation costs of the new bonds would be 4 per cent of the proceeds. If the company issues these new bonds at an annual coupon rate of 8 per cent, they will sell at par.

3 *Increased use of accounts payable financing.* Because this financing is part of the company's ongoing daily business, it has no flotation costs, and the company assigns it a cost that is the same as the overall firm WACC. Management has a target ratio of accounts payable to long-term debt of 0.20. (Assume there is no difference between the pre-tax and after-tax accounts payable cost.)

What is the NPV of the new plant? Assume that PC has a 28 per cent tax rate.

25  **Flotation Costs [LO4]** Trower has a debt–equity ratio of 1.20. The company is considering a new plant that will cost €145 million to build. When the company issues new equity, it incurs a flotation cost of 8 per cent. The flotation cost on new debt is 3.5 per cent. What is the initial cost of the plant if the company raises all equity externally? What if it typically uses 60 per cent retained earnings? What if all equity investment is financed through retained earnings?

26  **Project Evaluation [LO3, LO4]** This is a comprehensive project evaluation problem bringing together much of what you have learned in this and previous chapters. Suppose you have been hired as a financial consultant to Defence Electronics International (DEI), a large, publicly traded firm that is the market share leader in radar detection systems (RDSs). The company is looking at setting up a manufacturing plant overseas to produce a new line of RDSs. This will be a five-year project. The company bought some land three years ago for £4 million in anticipation of using it as a toxic dump site for waste chemicals, but it built a piping system to discard the chemicals safely instead. The land was appraised last week at £5.1 million. In five years the after-tax value of the land will be £6 million, but the company expects to keep the land for a future project. The company wants to build its new manufacturing plant on this land; the plant and equipment will cost £35 million to build. The following market data on DEI's securities are current:

| | |
|---|---|
| *Debt*: | 2,400,000 7.5 per cent coupon bonds outstanding, 20 years to maturity, selling for 94 per cent of par; the bonds have a £100 par value each and make semi-annual payments. |
| *Equity*: | 9,000,000 shares outstanding, selling for £71 per share; the beta is 1.2. |
| *Preference shares*: | 400,000 of 5.5 per cent preference shares outstanding, selling for £81 per share. |
| *Market*: | 8 per cent expected market risk premium; 5 per cent risk-free rate. |

DEI uses G. M. Wharton as its lead underwriter. Wharton charges DEI spreads of 8 per cent on new equity issues, 6 per cent on new preference share issues, and 4 per cent on new debt issues. Wharton has included all direct and indirect issuance costs (along with its profit) in setting these spreads. Wharton has recommended to DEI that it raise the funds needed to build the plant by issuing new shares of equity. DEI's tax rate is 28 per cent. The project requires £1,300,000 in initial net working capital investment to get operational. Assume Wharton raises all equity for new projects externally.

(a)  Calculate the project's initial time 0 cash flow, taking into account all side effects.

(b)  The new RDS project is somewhat riskier than a typical project for DEI, primarily because the plant is being located overseas. Management has told you to use an adjustment factor of +2 per cent to account for this increased riskiness. Calculate the appropriate discount rate to use when evaluating DEI's project.

(c)  The manufacturing plant has an eight-year tax life, and DEI uses 20 per cent reducing-balance depreciation. At the end of the project (that is, the end of year 5), the plant and equipment can be scrapped for £6 million. What is the after-tax salvage value of this plant and equipment?

(d)  The company will incur £7,000,000 in annual fixed costs. The plan is to manufacture 18,000 RDSs per year and sell them at £10,900 per machine; the variable production costs are £9,400 per RDS. What is the annual operating cash flow (OCF) from this project?

(e) DEI's financial controller is interested primarily in the impact of DEI's investments on the bottom line of reported accounting statements. What will you tell her is the accounting break-even quantity of RDSs sold for this project?

(f) Finally, DEI's chief executive wants you to throw all your calculations, assumptions, and everything else into the report for the chief financial officer; all he wants to know is what the RDS project's internal rate of return (IRR) and net present value (NPV) are. What will you report?

## MINI CASE

# The Cost of Capital for Goff Technological Printing

You have recently been hired by Goff Technological Printing, in the finance area. GTP was founded eight years ago by Chris Goff, and currently operates 74 shops in the United Kingdom. GTP is privately owned by Chris and his family, and had sales of £97 million last year.

GTP sells primarily to in-store customers. Customers come to the shop and talk to a sales representative. The sales representative assists the customer in determining the type of printing and labelling solutions that are necessary for the individual customer's computing needs. After the order is taken, the customer pays for the order immediately, and the printing technology is assembled to fill the order. Delivery of the printing technology averages 15 days, but is guaranteed in 30 days.

GTP's growth to date has been financed from its profits. Whenever the company had sufficient capital, it would open a new shop. Relatively little formal analysis has been used in the capital budgeting process. Chris has just read about capital budgeting techniques, and has come to you for help. The company has never attempted to determine its cost of capital, and Chris would like you to perform the analysis. Because the company is privately owned, it is difficult to determine the cost of equity for the company. You have determined that to estimate the cost of capital for GTP, you will use Domino Printing Sciences plc as a representative company. The following steps will allow you to calculate this estimate:

1 All publicly traded UK corporations are required to submit financial reports to Companies House detailing their financial operations over the previous six months or year, respectively. These corporate filings are always available on the company's website. Go to the Domino Printing Sciences website, follow the 'Investor Relations' link, and download the most recent set of financial accounts for Domino Printing Sciences. Look in the balance sheet to find the book value of debt and the book value of equity. If you look further down the report, you should find a section titled 'Borrowings' in the Notes to the Accounts, which will list a breakdown of Domino Printing Sciences' long-term debt. For 2009, this was

| 30. Financial Instruments continued | | | | | |
|---|---|---|---|---|---|
| Company | Less than 1 year £000 | 1–2 years £000 | 2–5 years £000 | >5 years £000 | Total £000 |
| **2009** | | | | | |
| Non-interest bearing | 34,038 | – | – | – | 34,038 |
| Fixed interest rate instruments | 11,540 | 416 | 3,205 | – | 15,161 |
| Variable interest rate instruments | 3,919 | – | – | – | 3,919 |
| | 49,497 | 416 | 3,205 | – | 53,118 |
| **2008** | | | | | |
| Non-interest bearing | 43,067 | – | – | – | 43,067 |
| Fixed interest rate instruments | 212 | 273 | 3,153 | – | 3,638 |
| Variable interest rate instruments | 3,314 | – | – | – | 3,314 |
| | 46,593 | 273 | 3,153 | – | 50,019 |

2 To estimate the cost of equity for Domino Printing Sciences, go to www.reuters.com and enter the ticker symbol 'DOPR'. Follow the various links to find answers to the following questions. What is the most recent share price listed for Domino Printing Sciences? What is the market value of equity, or market capitalization? How many shares of equity does Domino Printing Sciences have outstanding? What is the beta

for Domino Printing Sciences? Now go to www.ft.com, follow the 'Markets Data' link and then the 'Bonds and Rates' link. What is the yield on 3-month UK Treasury bills?

3   We now need to estimate the historical market risk premium. Go to Yahoo! Finance, and download the monthly historical prices for the FTSE 100 index for the last five years. Calculate the monthly returns, take the average, and multiply this by 12 to get the annualized historical return on the FTSE 100. What is the historical market risk premium for UK? Using the historical market risk premium, what is the cost of equity for Domino Printing Sciences using the CAPM?

4   Go to www.reuters.com and find the list of competitors in the industry. Find the beta for each of these competitors, and then calculate the industry average beta. Using the industry average beta, what is the cost of equity? Does it matter if you use the beta for Domino Printing Sciences or the beta for the industry in this case?

5   You now need to calculate the cost of debt for Domino Printing Sciences. Use the information on Domino Printing Sciences bonds to find the weighted average cost of debt for Domino using the book value weights. Try and find bond prices for Domino Pricing Sciences' debt. What should you do if no information is available? Does it make a difference in this case if you use book value weights or market value weights? Explain.

6   You now have all the necessary information to calculate the weighted average cost of capital for Domino Printing Sciences. Calculate the weighted average cost of capital for Domino Printing Sciences using book value weights and market value weights, assuming Domino has a 30 per cent effective tax rate. Which cost of capital number is more relevant?

7   You used Domino Printing Sciences as a representative company to estimate the cost of capital for GTP. What are some of the potential problems with this approach in this situation? What improvements might you suggest?

*Source*: © Domino Printing Sciences plc.

# Endnotes

1   Notice that if we have $D_0$ and $g$, we can simply calculate $D_1$ by multiplying $D_0$ by $(1 + g)$.

2   There is an implicit adjustment for risk, because the current share price is used. All other things being equal, the higher the risk, the lower is the share price. Further, the lower the share price, the greater is the cost of equity, again assuming all the other information is the same.

3   We can also estimate beta coefficients directly by using historical data. For a discussion of how to do this, see Chapters 10, 11 and 13 in D. Hillier, S.A. Ross, R.W. Westerfield and J.J. Jaffe, *Corporate Finance: European Edition*, 1st edn (McGraw-Hill, 2009).

4   For a discussion of multifactor models, see D. Hillier, S.A. Ross, R.W. Westerfield and J.J. Jaffe, *Corporate Finance: European Edition*, 1st edn (McGraw-Hill, 2009).

5   The firm's cost of debt based on its historic borrowing is sometimes called the *embedded debt cost*.

# Raising Capital

## KEY NOTATIONS

**EPS** Earnings per share
**IPO** Initial public offering
**SEO** Seasoned equity offering

## LEARNING OBJECTIVES

After studying this chapter, you should understand:

**LO1** The venture capital market, and its role in the financing of new, high-risk ventures.
**LO2** How securities are sold to the public, and the role of investment banks in the process.
**LO3** Initial public offerings, and some of the costs of going public.
**LO4** How rights are issued to existing shareholders, and how to value those rights.

WHEN A FIRM WISHES TO RAISE CAPITAL for new investment, it has two basic choices. One option is to issue new equity. Another option is to borrow funds from financial institutions, or through the public issue of debt. Every day in the financial press you will read about companies that have gone to the markets to raise new equity.

Take the Royal Bank of Scotland Group (RBSG) as an example. In 2007 it had undertaken a very expensive takeover of the Dutch bank ABN AMRO. Then, in the wake of the financial crisis, the bank reported total bad debts amounting to £5.9 billion. With a sharply deteriorating economic outlook, the bank sought equity financing of £12 billion. Unfortunately, the capital injection was not enough to save the bank, and in October 2008 the British government effectively nationalized RBSG by investing £5 billion in preference shares and underwriting a further £15 billion equity issue.

In this chapter we examine the process by which companies such as Royal Bank of Scotland Group plc sell equity to the public, the costs of doing so, and the role of intermediaries in the process. We pay particular attention to what is probably the most important stage in a company's financial life cycle – the initial public offering. Such offerings are the process by which companies convert from being privately owned to being publicly owned. For many people, starting a company, growing it, and taking it public are the ultimate entrepreneurial dream.

All firms must, at different times, obtain capital. To do so, a firm must either borrow the money (debt financing), or sell a portion of the firm (equity financing), or both. How a firm raises capital depends a great deal on the size of the firm, its life-cycle stage, and its growth prospects.

In this chapter we examine some of the ways in which firms actually raise capital. We begin by looking at companies in the early stages of their lives, and the importance of venture capital for such firms. We then look at the process of going public, and the role of investment banks. Along the way we discuss many of the issues associated with selling securities to the public, and their implications for all types of firm. We close the chapter with a discussion of sources of debt capital.

## 14.1   The Financing Life Cycle of a Firm: Early-Stage Financing and Venture Capital

One day, you and a friend have a great idea for a new computer software product that helps users communicate using the next-generation meganet. Filled with entrepreneurial zeal, you christen the product Megacomm and set about bringing it to market.

Working at nights and weekends, you are able to create a prototype of your product. It doesn't actually work, but at least you can show it around to illustrate your idea. To develop the product you need to hire programmers, buy computers, rent office space, and so on. Unfortunately, because you are both university students, your combined assets are not sufficient to fund a pizza party, much less a start-up company. You need what is often referred to as OPM – other people's money.

> **venture capital (VC)**
> Financing for new, often high-risk ventures.

Your first thought might be to approach a bank for a loan. You would probably discover, however, that banks are generally not interested in making loans to start-up companies with no assets (other than an idea) run by fledgling entrepreneurs with no track record. Instead your search for capital would probably lead you to the private equity and **venture capital (VC)** market.

### The Private Equity Firm

A large amount of private equity investment is undertaken by professional private equity managers representing large institutional investors such as mutual funds and pension funds. Private equity has been important for both traditional start-up companies and established public firms. The private equity market can be divided into venture equity and non-venture equity markets. A large part of the non-venture market is made up of firms in financial distress. Firms in financial distress are not likely to be able to issue public equity, and typically cannot use traditional forms of debt such as bank loans or public debt. For these firms the best alternative is to find a private equity market firm.

Outside the United States, the UK and Sweden are the leading centres for private equity, and most private equity firms are based there. Figure 14.1 shows a breakdown of all European private equity investments in 2008 as a percentage of each country's GDP.

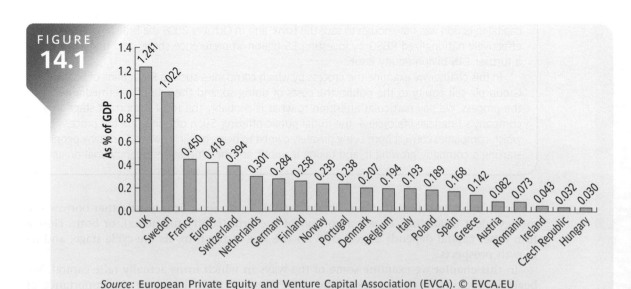

FIGURE **14.1**

*Source*: European Private Equity and Venture Capital Association (EVCA). © EVCA.EU

**Figure 14.1** All European private equity investments in 2008 as a percentage of each country's GDP

## Suppliers of Venture Capital

As we have pointed out, venture capital is an important part of the private equity market. There are at least four types of supplier of venture capital. First, a few old-line, wealthy families have traditionally provided start-up capital to promising businesses. For example, over the years, the Rockefeller family has made the initial capital contribution to a number of successful businesses. Such families have been involved in venture capital for at least a century.

Second, a number of private partnerships and corporations have been formed to provide investment funds. The organizer behind the partnership might raise capital from institutional investors, such as insurance companies and pension funds. Alternatively, a group of individuals might provide the funds to be ultimately invested with budding entrepreneurs.

Venture capital is a sub-activity of all private equity financing. The most common form of private equity financing in recent years is through buy-outs. Examples of private equity buy-out activity include EMI, Boots and Chrysler. Figure 14.2 provides a breakdown of European private equity funding in 2008 across industrial sectors. The majority of venture capital investments are in business and industrial products. Private equity buyout deals were substantially more common than venture capital investments because of the global financial crisis in 2008. This was due to a general lack of financing opportunities, an inability to exit from private equity investments, and falling valuations.

Stories used to abound about how easily an individual could obtain venture capital. Though that may have been the case in an earlier era, it is certainly not the case today. Venture capital firms employ various screening procedures to prevent inappropriate funding. For example, because of the large demand for funds, many venture capitalists have at least one employee whose full-time job consists of reading business plans. Only the very best plans can expect to attract funds.

Third, large industrial or financial corporations have established venture capital subsidiaries. Manufacturers Hanover Venture Capital Corp., Citicorp Venture Capital and Chemical Venture Capital Corporation of Chemical Bank are examples of this type. However, subsidiaries of this type appear to make up only a small portion of the venture capital market.

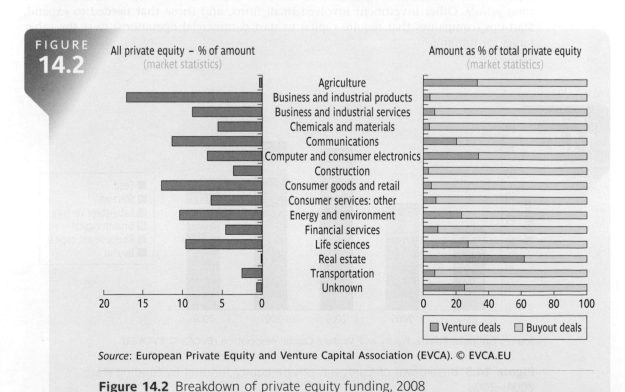

FIGURE 14.2

Source: European Private Equity and Venture Capital Association (EVCA). © EVCA.EU

**Figure 14.2** Breakdown of private equity funding, 2008

Fourth, there are also participants in an informal venture capital market. Rather than belonging to any venture capital firm, these investors (often referred to as *angels*) act as individuals when providing financing. They should not, by any means, be viewed as isolated, and there is a rich network of angels, continually relying on each other for advice.

## Stages of Financing

There are six stages in private equity financing:

1  *Seed money*: A small amount of financing needed to prove a concept or develop a product. Marketing is not included in this stage.

2  *Start-up*: Financing for firms that started within the past year. Funds are likely to pay for marketing and product development expenditures.

3  *Later stage capital*: Additional money to begin sales and manufacturing after a firm has spent its start-up funds.

4  *Growth capital*: Funds earmarked for a firm to enable it to reach its potential and achieve successful growth.

5  *Replacement capital*: Financing for a company to buy out other investors in the firm.

6  *Buyout financing*: Money provided for managers and outside investors to acquire a fully functioning firm.

Although these categories may seem vague to the reader, we have found that the terms are well accepted within the industry. For example, the European Private Equity and Venture Capital Association uses these stages to disaggregate the level of private equity and venture capital activity. Figure 14.3 presents a breakdown of where private equity funding was made in Europe in 2008. The majority of investment was in buyouts, where a publicly listed firm is bought out and taken off the stock exchange. This is known as *going private*. Other investment involved small firms, and those that needed to expand. Start-ups (companies that require capital to start commercial operations) were the other target for funding.

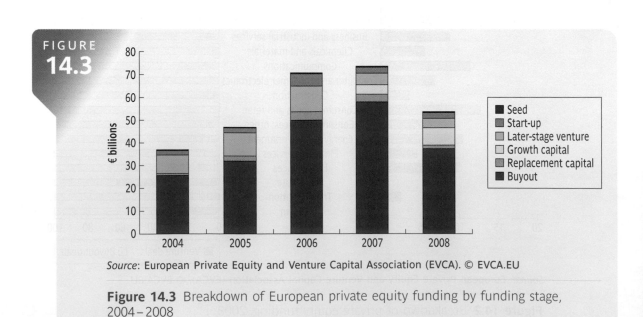

*Source*: European Private Equity and Venture Capital Association (EVCA). © EVCA.EU

**Figure 14.3** Breakdown of European private equity funding by funding stage, 2004–2008

The penultimate stage in venture capital finance is the initial public offering. Venture capitalists are very important participants in initial public offerings. Venture capitalists rarely sell all of the shares they own at the time of the initial public offering. Instead they usually sell out in subsequent public offerings. However, there is considerable evidence that venture capitalists can successfully time IPOs by taking firms public when the market values are at the highest.

## Some Venture Capital Realities

Although there is a large venture capital market, the truth is that access to venture capital is really very limited. Venture capital companies receive huge numbers of unsolicited proposals, the vast majority of which end up in the bin, unread. Venture capitalists rely heavily on informal networks of lawyers, accountants, bankers and other venture capitalists to help identify potential investments. As a result, personal contacts are important in gaining access to the venture capital market; it is very much an 'introduction' market.

Another simple fact about venture capital is that it is incredibly expensive. In a typical deal the venture capitalist will demand (and get) 40 per cent or more of the equity in the company. Venture capitalists frequently hold voting preference shares, giving them various priorities in the event that the company is sold or liquidated. The venture capitalist will typically demand (and get) several seats on the company's board of directors, and may even appoint one or more members of senior management.

## Conclusion

If a start-up succeeds, the big pay-off frequently comes when the company is sold to another company or goes public. Either way, investment bankers are often involved in the process. We discuss the process of selling securities to the public in the next several sections, paying particular attention to the process of going public.

| CONCEPT QUESTIONS | 14.1a What is venture capital? |
| | 14.1b Why is venture capital often provided in stages? |

# 14.2 Selling Securities to the Public: The Basic Procedure

When considering the steps involved in a public issue of securities, it is important to remember that each country has its own specific regulations and traditions, although the European Union has a comprehensive directive that covers all member countries. Table 14.1 illustrates the process for the UK, which is very similar to those of most other European countries.

| CONCEPT QUESTIONS | 14.2a What are the basic procedures in selling a new issue? |
| | 14.2b What is a prospectus? |

TABLE
**14.1**

| Steps in public offering | Time | Activities |
|---|---|---|
| **1** Pathfinder prospectus | Several months before issue | An initial indicative prospectus is released that presents the proposed offering. |
| **2** Pre-underwriting conferences | About 4 weeks before the full prospectus is issued | The amount of money to be raised and the type of security to be issued are discussed. Initial expressions of interest are collected, and an issue price is set. An underwriter and approved adviser will be appointed. |
| **3** Full prospectus | Several weeks before the offering takes place | The prospectus contains all relevant financial and business information. |
| **4** Public offering and sale | Shortly after the last day of the registration period | In a typical firm commitment contract the underwriter buys a stipulated amount of equity from the firm, and sells it at a higher price. The selling group assists in the sale. |
| **5** Market stabilization | Usually within 30 days of the offering | The underwriter stands ready to place orders to buy at a specified price on the market. |

**Table 14.1** The process of raising capital

**general cash offer**
An issue of securities offered for sale to the general public on a cash basis.
**rights issue**
A public issue of securities in which securities are first offered to existing shareholders. Also called a *rights offering*.
**initial public offering**
A company's first equity issue made available to the public. Also called an *unseasoned new issue* or an *IPO*.
**seasoned equity offering (SEO)**
A new equity issue of securities by a company that has previously issued securities to the public.

## 14.3 Alternative Issue Methods

When a company decides to issue a new security, it can sell it as a public issue or a private issue. In the case of a public issue, the firm is required to register the issue with the stock exchange it plans to list on. However, if the issue is to be sold to a small number of investors, the sale may be carried out privately.

For equity sales, there are two kinds of public issue: a **general cash offer** and a **rights issue** (or *rights offering*). With a cash offer, securities are offered to the general public. With a rights issue, securities are initially offered only to existing owners. Rights issues are very common in Europe.

The first public equity issue that is made by a company is referred to as an **initial public offering**, an *IPO*, or an *unseasoned new issue*. This issue occurs when a company decides to go public. Obviously, all initial public offerings are cash offers. If the firm's existing shareholders wanted to buy the shares, the firm wouldn't have to sell them publicly in the first place.

A **seasoned equity offering (SEO)** is a new issue for a company with securities that have been previously issued.[1] A seasoned equity offering can be made by using a cash offer or a rights offer.

These methods of issuing new securities are shown in Table 14.2. They are discussed in Sections 14.4–14.8.

| | |
|---|---|
| **CONCEPT QUESTIONS** | 14.3a What is the difference between a rights offer and a cash offer? |
| | 14.3b Why is an initial public offering necessarily a cash offer? |

| TABLE 14.2 | Method | Type | Definition |
|---|---|---|---|
| | Public traditional negotiated cash offer | Firm commitment cash offer | The company negotiates an agreement with an investment firm or bank to underwrite and distribute the new shares. A specified number of shares are bought by underwriters and sold at a higher price. |
| | | Best efforts cash offer | The company has an investment firm or bank sell as many of the new shares as possible at the agreed-upon price. There is no guarantee concerning how much cash will be raised. |
| | | Dutch auction cash offer | The company has an investment firm or bank auction shares to determine the highest offer price obtainable for a given number of shares to be sold. |
| | Privileged subscription | Direct rights issue | The company offers the new equity directly to its existing shareholders. |
| | | Standby rights issue | Like the direct rights issue, this contains a privileged subscription arrangement with existing shareholders. The net proceeds are guaranteed by the underwriters. |
| | Non-traditional cash offer | Shelf cash offer | Qualifying companies can authorize all shares they expect to sell over a two-year period and sell them when needed. |
| | | Competitive firm cash offer | The company can elect to award the underwriting contract through a public auction instead of negotiation. |
| | Private | Direct placement | Securities are sold directly to the purchaser, who, at least until recently, generally could not resell securities for at least two years. |

**Table 14.2** The methods of issuing new securities

## 14.4 Underwriters

If the public issue of securities is a cash offer, **underwriters** are usually involved. Underwriting is an important line of business for large investment firms (such as Merrill Lynch) and banks (such as HSBC). Underwriters perform services such as the following for corporate issuers:

* Formulating the method used to issue the securities
* Pricing the new securities
* Selling the new securities

Typically, the underwriter buys the securities for less than the offering price, and accepts the risk of not being able to sell them. Because underwriting involves risk, underwriters usually combine to form an underwriting group called a **syndicate** to share the risk and to help sell the issue.

In a syndicate, one or more managers arrange, or co-manage, the offering. The lead manager typically has the responsibility of dealing with the issuer and pricing the securities. The other underwriters in the syndicate serve primarily to distribute the issue and produce research reports later on. In recent years it has become fairly common for a syndicate to consist of only a small number of co-managers.

The difference between the underwriter's buying price and the offering price is called the **gross spread**, or underwriting discount. It is the basic compensation received by the underwriter. Sometimes, on smaller deals, the underwriter will get non-cash compensation in the form of warrants and shares in addition to the spread.[2]

**underwriters** Investment firms that act as intermediaries between a company selling securities and the investing public.

**syndicate** A group of underwriters formed to share the risk and to help sell an issue.

**gross spread** Compensation to the underwriter, determined by the difference between the underwriter's buying price and the offering price.

## Choosing an Underwriter

A firm can offer its securities to the highest bidding underwriter on a *competitive offer* basis, or it can negotiate directly with an underwriter. Except for a few large firms, companies usually do new issues of debt and equity on a *negotiated offer* basis.

There is evidence that competitive underwriting is cheaper to use than negotiated underwriting. The underlying reasons for the dominance of negotiated underwriting in Europe are the subject of ongoing debate.

## Types of Underwriting

**firm commitment underwriting**
The type of underwriting in which the underwriter buys the entire issue, assuming full financial responsibility for any unsold shares.

**best efforts underwriting**
The type of underwriting in which the underwriter sells as much of the issue as possible, but can return any unsold shares to the issuer without financial responsibility.

**Dutch auction underwriting**
The type of underwriting in which the offer price is set based on competitive bidding by investors. Also known as a *uniform price auction*.

Three basic types of underwriting are involved in a cash offer: firm commitment, best efforts, and Dutch auction.

**Firm Commitment Underwriting** In **firm commitment underwriting** the issuer sells the entire issue to the underwriters, who then attempt to resell it. This is the most prevalent type of underwriting in Europe. For a new issue of seasoned equity, the underwriters can look at the market price to determine what the issue should sell for, and more than 95 per cent of all such new issues are firm commitments.

If the underwriter cannot sell all of the issue at the agreed-upon offering price, it may have to lower the price on the unsold shares. Nonetheless, with firm commitment underwriting the issuer receives the agreed-upon amount, and all the risk associated with selling the issue is transferred to the underwriter.

Because the offering price usually isn't set until the underwriters have investigated how receptive the market is to the issue, this risk is usually minimal. Also, because the offering price usually is not set until just before selling commences, the issuer doesn't know precisely what its net proceeds will be until that time.

**Best Efforts Underwriting** In **best efforts underwriting** the underwriter is legally bound to use 'best efforts' to sell the securities at the agreed-upon offering price. Beyond this, the underwriter does not guarantee any particular amount of money to the issuer. This form of underwriting has become uncommon in recent years.

**Dutch Auction Underwriting** With **Dutch auction underwriting** the underwriter does not set a fixed price for the shares to be sold. Instead, the underwriter conducts an auction in which investors bid for shares. The offer price is determined based on the submitted bids. A Dutch auction is also known by the more descriptive name *uniform price auction*. This approach to selling securities to the public is relatively new in the IPO market, and has not been widely used there, but it is very common in the bond markets. For example, it is the sole procedure used by governments to sell enormous quantities of notes, bonds and bills to the public.

The best way to understand a Dutch or uniform price auction is to consider a simple example. Suppose Rial plc wants to sell 400 shares to the public. The company receives five bids as follows:

| Bidder | Quantity (shares) | Price (£) |
|---|---|---|
| A | 100 | 16 |
| B | 100 | 14 |
| C | 200 | 12 |
| D | 100 | 12 |
| E | 200 | 10 |

Thus bidder A is willing to buy 100 shares at £16 each, bidder B is willing to buy 100 shares at £14, and so on. Rial plc examines the bids to determine the highest price that will result in all 400 shares being sold. So, for example, at £14, A and B would buy only 200 shares, so that price is too high. Working our way down, all 400 shares won't be sold until we hit a price of £12, so £12 will be the offer price in the IPO. Bidders A–D will receive shares; bidder E will not.

There are two additional important points to observe in our example. First, all the winning bidders will pay £12 – even bidders A and B, who actually bid a higher price. The fact that all successful bidders pay the same price is the reason for the name 'uniform price auction'. The idea in such an auction is to encourage bidders to bid aggressively, by providing some protection against bidding a price that is too high.

Second, notice that at the £12 offer price there are actually bids for 500 shares, which exceeds the 400 shares Rial wants to sell. Thus there has to be some sort of allocation. How this is done varies, but in the IPO market the approach has been to simply compute the ratio of shares offered to shares bid at the offer price or better, which in our example is 400/500 = 0.8, and allocate bidders that percentage of their bids. In other words, bidders A–D would each receive 80 per cent of the shares they bid at a price of £12 per share.

## The Aftermarket

The period after a new issue is initially sold to the public is referred to as the *aftermarket*. During this time the members of the underwriting syndicate generally do not sell securities for less than the offering price.

In most countries the principal underwriter is permitted to buy shares if the market price falls below the offering price. The purpose of this would be to support the market and stabilize the price against temporary downward pressure. If the issue remains unsold after a time (for example, 30 days), members can leave the group and sell their shares at whatever price the market will allow.

## The Green Shoe Provision

Many underwriting contracts contain a **Green Shoe provision** (sometimes called the *overallotment option*), which gives the members of the underwriting group the option to purchase additional shares from the issuer at the offering price.[3] Essentially all IPOs and SEOs include this provision, but ordinary debt offerings generally do not. The stated reason for the Green Shoe option is to cover excess demand and oversubscriptions. Green Shoe options usually last for 30 days and involve 15 per cent of the newly issued shares.

In practice, usually underwriters initially go ahead and sell 115 per cent of the shares offered. If the demand for the issue is strong after the offering, the underwriters exercise the Green Shoe option to get the extra 15 per cent from the company. If demand for the issue is weak, the underwriters buy the needed shares in the open market, thereby helping to support the price of the issue in the aftermarket.

## Lock-Up Agreements

Although they are not required by law, almost all underwriting contracts contain so-called **lock-up agreements**. Such agreements specify how long insiders must wait after an IPO before they can sell some or all of their equity. Lock-up periods have become fairly standardized in recent years at 180 days. Thus, following an IPO, insiders can't cash out until six months have gone by, which ensures that they maintain a significant economic interest in the company going public.

---

**Green Shoe provision**
A contract provision giving the underwriter the option to purchase additional shares from the issuer at the offering price. Also called the *overallotment option*.

**lock-up agreement**
The part of the underwriting contract that specifies how long insiders must wait after an IPO before they can sell equity.

Lock-up periods are also important because it is not unusual for the number of locked-up shares to exceed the number of shares held by the public, sometimes by a substantial multiple. On the day the lock-up period expires, there is the possibility that a large number of shares will hit the market on the same day and thereby depress values. The evidence suggests that, on average, venture-capital-backed companies are particularly likely to experience a loss in value on the lock-up expiration day.

## The Quiet Period

Once a firm begins to seriously contemplate an IPO, stock exchange authorities normally require that a firm and its managing underwriters observe a 'quiet period'. This means that all communications with the public must be limited to ordinary announcements and other purely factual matters. The logic is that all relevant information should be contained in the prospectus, and an important result of this requirement is that the underwriter's analysts are prohibited from making recommendations to investors. As soon as the quiet period ends, however, the managing underwriters typically publish research reports, usually accompanied by a favourable 'buy' recommendation.

| **CONCEPT QUESTIONS** | 14.4a  What do underwriters do? |
| | 14.4b  What is the Green Shoe provision? |

## 14.5   IPOs and Underpricing

Determining the correct offering price is the most difficult thing an underwriter must do for an initial public offering. The issuing firm faces a potential cost if the offering price is set too high or too low. If the issue is priced too high, it may be unsuccessful and have to be withdrawn. If the issue is priced below the true market value, the issuer's existing shareholders will experience an opportunity loss when the issuer sells shares for less than they are worth.

Underpricing is fairly common. It obviously helps new shareholders earn a higher return on the shares they buy. However, the existing shareholders of the issuing firm are not helped by underpricing. To them it is an indirect cost of issuing new securities. For example, consider a hypothetical IPO. The new issue opens at €44 and rises to a first-day high of €69, before closing at €56.50, a gain of about 28 per cent. Based on these numbers, the IPO is underpriced by about €12.50 per share, which means the company missed out on significant capital that could be used in its operations.

### IPO Underpricing: The European Experience

In Europe, unseasoned new equity issues are generally offered below their true market price. Figure 14.4 shows the issue date average return on new IPOs for a variety of countries.

There were some incredibly high initial returns experienced by IPO firms in Europe during the period 1990–2003. In particular, Polish firms experienced underpricing of greater than 60 per cent, which dwarfs the nearest country, Greece, which experienced 40 per cent underpricing. Even with their highly developed capital markets, German and UK firms experienced IPO returns of around 30 per cent. If you're interested in finding out how IPOs have done recently, check out our nearby Work the Web box.

## Work the Web

So how many companies have had underpriced IPOs recently? We went to FT.com to see and here is what we found for early 2010:

### UK RECENT EQUITY ISSUES

| issue date | issue price p | Sector | Stock code | Stock | Close price p | +/- | High | Low | Volume 000's | Mkt cap (£m) |
|---|---|---|---|---|---|---|---|---|---|---|
| 9/3 | 100 | AIM | SIAG | Sherborne Inv A | 102.50 | - | 102.50 | 102.50 | - | 107.6 |
| 8/3 | - | IvCo | FASS | Fidelity Asian Val Sub | 29 | - | 29 | 29 | 403 | 3.5 |
| 4/3 | §100 | AIM | DGB | Digital Barriers | 140 | - | 140 | 114.50 | 95 | 28.0 |
| 4/3 | 100 | IvCo | FTVP | Foresight VCT Exit | 102.50 | - | 102.50 | 102.50 | - | 1.2 |
| 4/3 | 100 | IvCo | FTNP | Foresight VCT2 Exit | 102.50 | - | 102.50 | 102.50 | - | 1.2 |
| 26/2 | §17.5 | AIM | PAL | Equatorial Palm | 14.25 | -0.25 | 18.50 | 13.75 | 7,373 | 11.6 |
| 24/2 | §4.6 | AIM | SGZ | Scotgold Resources | 7.13 | -0.25 | 7.75 | 6 | 306 | 8.4 |
| 12/2 | 1.75 | AIM | ONG | Oxford Nutrascience | 3.38 | -0.38 | 3.75 | 1.88 | 79 | 15.7 |
| 5/2 | 100 | IvCo | DA2O | Downing Abs Inc VCT 2 | 100 | - | 100 | 100 | - | 1.7 |
| 5/2 | 0.15 | IvCo | DA2A | Downing Abs Inc VCT 2 A | 0.15 | - | 0.15 | 0.15 | - | 0.0 |
| 5/2 | 100 | IvCo | OTV4 | Octopus Titan VCT 4 | 100 | - | 100 | 100 | - | 1.0 |
| 15/1 | 100 | IvCo | DO1B | Downing Strct VCT1 B | 100 | - | 100 | 100 | - | 1.2 |
| 15/1 | 0.1 | IvCo | DO1C | Downing Strct VCT1 C | 0.10 | - | 0.10 | 0.10 | - | 0.0 |
| 14/1 | §5 | PLUS | USOP | US Oil & Gas | 11.50 | 1 | 11.50 | 7 | 130 | 3.1 |
| 12/1 | 100 | IvCo | DP2D | Downing Plan 2D | 100 | - | 100 | 100 | - | 1.2 |
| 12/1 | 100 | IvCo | DP3D | Downing Plan 3D | 100 | - | 100 | 100 | - | 1.2 |
| 12/1 | 0.1 | IvCo | DP2E | Downing Plan Do 2E | 0.10 | - | 2.53 | 0.10 | - | 0.0 |
| 12/1 | 0.1 | IvCo | DP3E | Downing Plan Do 3E | 0.10 | - | 2.53 | 0.10 | - | 0.0 |

§Placing price. * Introduction. ‡ When issued. Annual report/prospectus available, see London Shares Page. For a full explanation of all other symbols please refer to London Share Service notes.

*Source*: www.ft.com. © The Financial Times Ltd 2010.

Comparing the closing price with the issue price, almost all IPOs from February 2010 to March 2010 were underpriced. Notice also that one company, Equatorial Palm, dropped in value from 17.5p to 14.25p, even though it reached a high of 18.5p during the day.

### QUESTIONS

1 Go to FT.com and find the companies that have had public offerings recently. What company was underpriced the most as a percentage of the issue price?

2 Did any company go down in price on the issue day? Look up recent news items on the company. Was there a reason for the price falling?

## Why Does Underpricing Exist?

Based on the evidence we've examined, an obvious question is why underpricing continues to exist. As we discuss, there are various explanations; but, to date, there is a lack of complete agreement among researchers as to which is correct.

We present some pieces of the underpricing puzzle by stressing two important caveats to our preceding discussion. First, the average figures we have examined tend to obscure the fact that much of the apparent underpricing is attributable to the smaller, more highly speculative issues. This point is illustrated in Table 14.3, which shows the extent of underpricing for US IPOs over the period from 1980 through to 2007. Here, the firms are grouped based on their total sales in the 12 months prior to the IPO.

| | 1980–1989 | | 1990–1998 | | 1999–2000 | | 2001–2007 | |
|---|---|---|---|---|---|---|---|---|
| Annual sales of issuing firms | Number of firms | First-day average return (%) | Number of firms | First-day average return (%) | Number of firms | First-day average return (%) | Number of firms | First-day average return (%) |
| $0 ≤ sales < $10m | 392 | 10.2 | 676 | 17.3 | 332 | 69.2 | 131 | 6.4 |
| $10m ≤ sales < $20m | 250 | 8.6 | 385 | 18.5 | 139 | 80.1 | 40 | 8.9 |
| $20m ≤ sales < $50m | 469 | 7.7 | 775 | 18.8 | 150 | 75.5 | 124 | 12.9 |
| $50m ≤ sales < $100m | 350 | 6.5 | 579 | 13.0 | 89 | 60.4 | 133 | 16.6 |
| $100m ≤ sales < $200m | 238 | 4.7 | 446 | 11.8 | 57 | 34.9 | 115 | 15.1 |
| $200m ≤ sales | 287 | 3.4 | 629 | 8.7 | 86 | 26.3 | 312 | 11.3 |
| All | 2,013 | 7.2 | 3,490 | 14.8 | 853 | 64.4 | 855 | 12.0 |

Sales, measured in millions, are for the last 12 months prior to going public. All sales have been converted into dollars of 2003 purchasing power, using the Consumer Price Index. There are 6,854 IPOs, after excluding IPOs with an offer price of less than $5.00 per share, units, REITs, ADRs, closed-end funds, banks and S&Ls, firms not listed on CRSP within six months of the offer date, and 140 firms with missing sales. The average first-day return is 18.5 per cent.

*Source:* Professor Jay R. Ritter, University of Florida

**Table 14.3** Average first-day returns, categorized by sales, for IPOs, 1980–2007

TABLE
**14.3**

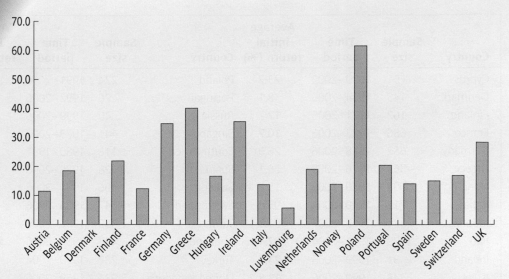

*Source*: A. Ljunqvist, 'IPO underpricing', In Chapter 7 of *Handbook of Corporate Finance: Empirical Corporate Finance*, Volume A, ed. B. Espen Eckbo (Handbooks in Finance Series, Elsevier/North Holland, 2006), Chapter 7

**Figure 14.4** Equal weighted average initial IPO returns in per cent for 19 European countries between 1990 and 2003

As illustrated in Table 14.3, the underpricing tends to be higher for firms with few to no sales in the previous year. These firms tend to be young firms, and such young firms can be very risky investments. Arguably, they must be significantly underpriced, on average, just to attract investors, and this is one explanation for the underpricing phenomenon.

# In Their Own Words . . .

## Jay Ritter on IPO Underpricing Around the World

In general, countries with developed capital markets have more moderate underpricing than in emerging markets. The following table gives a summary of the average first-day returns on IPOs in a number of countries around the world, with the figures collected from a number of studies by various authors.

| Country | Sample size | Time period | Average initial return (%) | Country | Sample size | Time period | Average initial return (%) |
|---|---|---|---|---|---|---|---|
| Argentina | 20 | 1991–1994 | 4.4 | Japan | 2,458 | 1970–2006 | 40.1 |
| Australia | 1,103 | 1976–2006 | 19.8 | Korea | 1,417 | 1980–2007 | 57.4 |
| Austria | 96 | 1971–2006 | 6.5 | Malaysia | 350 | 1980–2006 | 69.6 |
| Belgium | 114 | 1984–2006 | 13.5 | Mexico | 88 | 1987–1994 | 15.9 |
| Brazil | 180 | 1979–2006 | 48.7 | Netherlands | 181 | 1982–2006 | 10.2 |
| Bulgaria | 9 | 2004–2007 | 36.5 | New Zealand | 214 | 1979–2006 | 20.3 |
| Canada | 635 | 1971–2006 | 7.1 | Nigeria | 114 | 1989–2006 | 12.7 |
| Chile | 65 | 1982–2006 | 8.4 | Norway | 153 | 1984–2006 | 9.6 |
| China | 1,394 | 1990–2005 | 164.5 | Philippines | 123 | 1987–2006 | 21.2 |

| Country | Sample size | Time period | Average initial return (%) | Country | Sample size | Time period | Average initial return (%) |
|---|---|---|---|---|---|---|---|
| Cyprus | 51 | 1999–2002 | 23.7 | Poland | 224 | 1991–2006 | 22.9 |
| Denmark | 145 | 1984–2006 | 8.1 | Portugal | 28 | 1992–2006 | 11.6 |
| Finland | 162 | 1971–2006 | 17.2 | Russia | 40 | 1999–2006 | 4.2 |
| France | 686 | 1983–2006 | 10.7 | Singapore | 441 | 1973–2006 | 28.3 |
| Germany | 652 | 1978–2006 | 26.9 | South Africa | 118 | 1980–1991 | 32.7 |
| Greece | 363 | 1976–2005 | 25.1 | Spain | 128 | 1986–2006 | 10.9 |
| Hong Kong | 1,008 | 1980–2006 | 15.9 | Sweden | 406 | 1980–2006 | 27.3 |
| India | 2,713 | 1990–2004 | 95.4 | Switzerland | 147 | 1983–2006 | 29.3 |
| Indonesia | 321 | 1989–2007 | 21.1 | Taiwan | 1,312 | 1980–2006 | 37.2 |
| Iran | 279 | 1991–2004 | 22.4 | Thailand | 447 | 1987–2006 | 36.9 |
| Ireland | 31 | 1999–2006 | 23.7 | Turkey | 282 | 1990–2004 | 10.8 |
| Israel | 348 | 1990–2006 | 13.8 | United Kingdom | 3,986 | 1959–2006 | 16.8 |
| Italy | 233 | 1985–2006 | 18.2 | United States | 15,649 | 1960–2007 | 18.0 |

Jay R. Ritter is Cordell Professor of Finance at the University of Florida. An outstanding scholar, he is well known for his insightful analyses of new issues and going public.

The second caveat is that relatively few IPO buyers will actually get the initial high average returns observed in IPOs, and many will actually lose money. Although it is true that, on average, IPOs have positive initial returns, a significant fraction of them have price drops. Furthermore, when the price is too low, the issue is often 'oversubscribed'. This means investors will not be able to buy all the shares they want, and the underwriters will allocate the shares among investors.

The average investor will find it difficult to get shares in a 'successful' offering (one in which the price increases), because there will not be enough shares to go around. On the other hand, an investor blindly submitting orders for IPOs tends to get more shares in issues that go down in price.

To illustrate, consider this tale of two investors. Smith knows very accurately what Bonanza Ltd is worth when its shares are offered. She is confident that the shares are underpriced. Jones knows only that prices usually rise one month after an IPO. Armed with this information, Jones decides to buy 1,000 shares of every IPO. Does he actually earn an abnormally high return on the initial offering?

The answer is no, and at least one reason is Smith. Knowing about Bonanza Ltd, Smith invests all her money in its IPO. When the issue is oversubscribed, the underwriters have to somehow allocate the shares between Smith and Jones. The net result is that when an issue is underpriced, Jones doesn't get to buy as much of it as he wanted.

Smith also knows that the Blue Sky Ltd IPO is overpriced. In this case she avoids its IPO altogether, and Jones ends up with a full 1,000 shares. To summarize this tale, Jones gets fewer shares when more knowledgeable investors swarm to buy an underpriced issue, and gets all he wants when the smart money avoids the issue.

This is an example of a 'winner's curse', and it is thought to be another reason why IPOs have such a large average return. When the average investor 'wins' and gets the entire allocation, it may be because those who knew better avoided the issue. The only way underwriters can counteract the winner's curse and attract the average investor is to under-price new issues (on average) so that the average investor still makes a profit.

Another reason for underpricing is that it is a kind of insurance for the underwriters. Conceivably, an underwriter could be sued successfully by angry customers if it consistently overpriced securities. Underpricing guarantees that, at least on average, customers will come out ahead.

A final reason for underpricing is that, before the offer price is established, underwriters talk to big institutional investors to gauge the level of interest in the equity, and to gather opinions about a suitable price. Underpricing is a way that the bank can reward these investors for truthfully revealing what they think the equity is worth and the number of shares they would like to buy.

| CONCEPT QUESTIONS | 14.5a | Why is underpricing a cost to the issuing firm? |
|---|---|---|
| | 14.5b | Suppose a stockbroker calls you up out of the blue and offers to sell you 'all the shares you want' of a new issue. Do you think the issue will be more or less underpriced than average? |

## 14.6 New Equity Sales and the Value of the Firm

We now turn to a consideration of seasoned offerings, which, as we discussed earlier, are offerings by firms that already have outstanding securities. It seems reasonable to believe that new long-term financing is arranged by firms after positive net present value projects are put together. As a consequence, when the announcement of external financing is made, the firm's market value should go up. Interestingly, this is not what happens. Share prices tend to decline following the announcement of a new equity issue, although they tend to not change much following a debt announcement. A number of researchers have studied this issue. Plausible reasons for this strange result include the following:

1   *Managerial information*: If management has superior information about the market value of the firm, it may know when the firm is overvalued. If it does, it will attempt to issue new shares of equity when the market value exceeds the correct value. This will benefit existing shareholders. However, the potential new shareholders are not stupid, and they will anticipate this superior information and discount it in lower market prices at the new-issue date.

2   *Debt usage*: A company issuing new equity may reveal that the company has too much debt or too little liquidity. One version of this argument says that the equity issue is a bad signal to the market. After all, if the new projects are favourable ones, why should the firm let new shareholders in on them? It could just issue debt and let the existing shareholders have all the gain.

3   *Issue costs*: As we discuss next, there are substantial costs associated with selling securities.

The drop in value of existing shares following the announcement of a new issue is an example of an indirect cost of selling securities. This drop might typically be of the order of 3 per cent for an industrial corporation (and somewhat smaller for a public utility); so, for a large company, it can represent a substantial amount of money. We label this drop the *abnormal return* in our discussion of the costs of new issues that follows.

| CONCEPT QUESTIONS | 14.6a | What are some possible reasons why the share price drops on the announcement of a new equity issue? |
|---|---|---|
| | 14.6b | Explain why we might expect a firm with a positive-NPV investment to finance it with debt instead of equity. |

## 14.7 The Costs of Issuing Securities

Issuing securities to the public isn't free, and the costs of different methods are important determinants of which is used. These costs associated with *floating* a new issue are generically called *flotation costs*. In this section we take a closer look at the flotation costs associated with equity sales to the public.

## The Costs of Selling Stock to the Public

The costs of selling equity are classified in the following list, and fall into six categories:

1 *Gross spread*: The gross spread consists of direct fees paid by the issuer to the underwriting syndicate – the difference between the price the issuer receives and the offer price.

2 *Other direct expenses*: These are direct costs, incurred by the issuer, that are not part of the compensation to underwriters. These costs include filing fees, legal fees, and taxes – all reported on the prospectus.

3 *Indirect expenses*: These costs are not reported on the prospectus, and include the costs of management time spent working on the new issue.

4 *Abnormal returns*: In a seasoned issue of equity, the price of the existing shares drops on average by 3 per cent on the announcement of the issue. This drop is called the abnormal return.

5 *Underpricing*: For initial public offerings, losses arise from selling the equity below the true value.

6 *Green Shoe option*: The Green Shoe option gives the underwriters the right to buy additional shares at the offer price to cover overallotments.

Research on issues costs provide a number of insights. First, with the possible exception of straight debt offerings (about which we shall have more to say later), there are substantial economies of scale. The underwriter spreads are smaller on larger issues, and other direct costs fall sharply as a percentage of the amount raised – a reflection of the mostly fixed nature of such costs. Second, the costs associated with selling debt are substantially less than the costs of selling equity. Third, IPOs have higher expenses than SEOs, but the difference is not as great as might originally be guessed. Finally, straight bonds are cheaper to float than convertible bonds.

As we have discussed, the underpricing of IPOs is an additional cost to the issuer. To give a better idea of the total cost of going public, Table 14.4 provides a comparison of direct issue costs with underpricing experienced by firms in the US. Comparing the total

| TABLE 14.4 | Proceeds ($ millions) | Number of issues | Gross spread (%) | Other direct expense (%) | Total direct cost (%) | Underpricing (%) |
|---|---|---|---|---|---|---|
| | 2.00–9.99 | 1,007 | 9.40 | 15.82 | 25.22 | 20.42 |
| | 10.00–19.99 | 810 | 7.39 | 7.30 | 14.69 | 10.33 |
| | 20.00–39.99 | 1,422 | 6.96 | 7.06 | 14.03 | 17.03 |
| | 40.00–59.99 | 880 | 6.89 | 2.87 | 9.77 | 28.26 |
| | 60.00–79.99 | 522 | 6.79 | 2.16 | 8.94 | 28.36 |
| | 80.00–99.99 | 327 | 6.71 | 1.84 | 8.55 | 32.92 |
| | 100.00–199.99 | 702 | 6.39 | 1.57 | 7.96 | 21.55 |
| | 200.00–499.99 | 440 | 5.81 | 1.03 | 6.84 | 6.19 |
| | 500.00 and up | 155 | 5.01 | .49 | 5.50 | 6.64 |
| | Total/average | 6,265 | 7.19 | 3.18 | 10.37 | 19.34 |

*Source*: I. Lee, S. Lochhead, J. Ritter and Q. Zhao, 'The costs of raising capital', *Journal of Financial Research* (1996), vol. 19, Spring, pp. 59–74, updated by the authors.

**Table 14.4** Direct and indirect costs, in percentages, of equity IPOs, 1990–2008

direct costs (in the fifth column) with the underpricing (in the sixth column), we see that they are roughly the same size, so the direct costs are only about half of the total. Overall, across all size groups, the total direct costs amount to 10 per cent of the amount raised, and the underpricing amounts to 19 per cent.

Finally, with regard to debt offerings, there is a general pattern in issue costs. Recall from Chapter 6 that bonds carry different credit ratings. Higher-rated bonds are said to be investment grade, whereas lower-rated bonds are non-investment grade. Research has shown that there are substantial economies of scale with debt offerings as well, and that investment-grade issues have much lower direct costs, particularly for straight bonds.

For UK and US issues the underwriting discount and other non-underwriting direct expenses are presented in Table 14.5. The total issue costs decline as the gross proceeds of the offering increase, for both US and UK companies. Thus it appears that issue costs are subject to substantial economies of scale. In addition, issue costs in the US are higher than in the UK for most levels of gross proceeds. Last, and perhaps most important, the costs of issuing securities to the public are quite large. For example, total direct expenses are approximately 6 per cent in the UK, and this rises to nearly 15 per cent for small issues. This implies that issuing equity is a weighty decision, especially for smaller companies. Although there are many benefits, such as raising needed capital and spreading ownership, the costs cannot be ignored.

**TABLE 14.5**

| UK rights issues and open offers, purged sample | | | | | US SEOs | | |
|---|---|---|---|---|---|---|---|
| Gross proceeds (£m) | N | Non-underwriting costs (%) | Underwriting costs (%) | Total costs (%) | Gross proceeds ($m) | N | Total costs (%) |
| 312.5+ | 19 | 0.72 | 1.44 | 2.17 | 500+ | 9 | 3.15 |
| 125.0–312.4 | 32 | 0.88 | 1.77 | 2.65 | 200–499.9 | 55 | 3.47 |
| 62.5–124.9 | 48 | 1.07 | 1.71 | 2.79 | 100–199.9 | 152 | 4.22 |
| 50.0–62.4 | 21 | 1.60 | 1.94 | 3.54 | 80–99.9 | 71 | 4.73 |
| 37.5–49.9 | 31 | 1.35 | 1.71 | 3.07 | 60–79.9 | 143 | 5.18 |
| 25.0–37.4 | 44 | 1.87 | 1.83 | 3.70 | 40–59.9 | 261 | 5.87 |
| 12.5–24.9 | 85 | 2.03 | 1.67 | 3.68 | 20–39.9 | 425 | 6.93 |
| 6.25–12.4 | 86 | 3.72 | 1.41 | 5.16 | 10–19.9 | 310 | 8.72 |
| 1.25–6.24 | 180 | 6.90 | 1.39 | 8.27 | 2–9.9 | 167 | 13.28 |
| 0.1–1.24 | 37 | 13.48 | 0.99 | 14.36 | | | |
| Total | 583 | 4.18 | 1.53 | 5.78 | | 1,593 | 7.11 |
| Median | | 2.55 | 1.75 | 4.28 | | | |

*Source*: Table 1 from S. Armitage, 'The direct costs of UK rights issues and open offers', *European Financial Management* (2000), vol. 6, pp. 57–68.

**Table 14.5** Cost of issue by issue size

**CONCEPT QUESTIONS**

14.7a  What are the different costs associated with security offerings?

14.7b  What lessons do we learn from studying issue costs?

## 14.8 Rights

When new shares of equity are sold to the general public, the proportional ownership of existing shareholders is likely to be reduced. However, if a pre-emptive right is contained in the firm's articles of incorporation, the firm must first offer any new issue of equity to existing shareholders. If the articles of incorporation do not include a pre-emptive right, the firm has a choice of offering the issue of equity directly to existing shareholders or to the public.

An issue of equity offered to existing shareholders is called a *rights issue*, *rights offering*, or a *privileged subscription*. In a rights issue each shareholder is issued rights to buy a specified number of new shares from the firm at a specified price within a specified time, after which the rights are said to *expire*. The terms of the rights offering are evidenced by certificates known as *share warrants* or *rights*. Such rights are often traded on securities exchanges or over the counter.

Rights issues have some interesting advantages relative to cash offers. For example, they appear to be cheaper for the issuing firm than cash offers. In fact, a firm can undertake a rights issue without using an underwriter, whereas, as a practical matter, an underwriter is almost a necessity in a cash offer. In Europe, rights issues are more common than cash offers, but fairly rare in the United States. Why this is true is a bit of a mystery, and the source of much debate; but to our knowledge no definitive answer exists.

### The Mechanics of a Rights Issue

The various considerations confronting a financial manager in a rights issue are illustrated by the situation of the Royal Bank of Scotland, whose initial financial statements are given in Table 14.6.

The Royal Bank of Scotland earned £7.712 billion after taxes and had approximately 10 billion shares outstanding. Earnings per share was £0.764, and the equity sold at 4.68 times earnings (that is, its price–earnings ratio was 4.68). The market price of each share was therefore £3.58. The company planned to raise just over £12 billion of new equity funds by a rights offering.

The process of issuing rights differs from the process of issuing shares of equity for cash. Existing shareholders are notified that they have been given one right for each share of

| TABLE 14.6 | Royal Bank of Scotland Group plc<br>Statement of financial position and income statement for 2007 | | |
|---|---|---|---|
| **Statement of financial position (£ millions)** | | | |
| Assets | Shareholder equity | | |
| | Ordinary shares | | 53,038 |
| | Retained earnings | | 1,847,481 |
| Total 1,900,519 | Total | | 1,900,519 |
| **Income statement (£ millions)** | | | |
| Earnings before taxes | 9,908 | | |
| Taxes | 2,188 | | |
| Net income | 7,712 | | |
| Earnings per share (£) | 0.764 | | |
| Shares outstanding (millions) | 10,094.24 | | |
| Market price per share (£) | 3.58 | | |
| Total market value (£ millions) | 36,137 | | |

**Table 14.6** Financial statement before rights issues

equity they own. Exercise occurs when a shareholder sends payment to the firm's subscription agent (usually a bank) and turns in the required number of rights. Shareholders of Royal Bank of Scotland had several choices: (1) subscribe for the full number of entitled shares; (2) order all the rights sold; or (3) do nothing and let the rights expire.

The financial management of Royal Bank of Scotland had to answer the following questions:

1 What price should the existing shareholders be allowed to pay for a share of new equity?

2 How many rights will be required to purchase one share of equity?

3 What effect will the rights offering have on the existing share price of the company?

**Subscription Price** In a rights issue the subscription price is the price that existing shareholders are allowed to pay for a share of equity. A rational shareholder will subscribe to the rights offering only if the subscription price is below the market price of the equity on the offer's expiration date. For example, if the share price at expiration is £1.50 and the subscription price is £2.00, no rational shareholder will subscribe. Why pay £2.00 for something worth £1.50? The Royal Bank of Scotland chose a price of £2.00, which was well below the existing market price of £3.58. As long as the market price did not fall below the subscription price of £2.00 before expiration, the rights offering would succeed.

**Number of Rights Needed to Purchase a Share** Royal Bank of Scotland wanted to raise £12,246,020,924 in new equity. With a subscription price of £2.00, it needed to issue 6,123,010,462 new shares. This can be determined by dividing the total amount to be raised by the subscription price:

$$\text{Number of new shares} = \frac{\text{Funds to be raised}}{\text{Subscription price}}$$

$$= \frac{£12,246,020,924}{£2.00}$$

$$= 6,123,010,462 \text{ shares}$$

Because shareholders typically get one right for each share of equity they own, just over 6 billion rights were issued by Royal Bank of Scotland. To determine how many rights must be exercised to get one share of equity, we can divide the number of existing outstanding shares of equity by the number of new shares:

$$\frac{\text{Number of rights needed}}{\text{to buy a share of equity}} = \frac{\text{'Old' shares}}{\text{'New' shares}}$$

$$= \frac{10,094,241,000}{6,123,010,462}$$

$$= 1.648 \text{ rights}$$

Clearly, it is impossible to own exactly 1.648 shares, and so in a rights issue one must construct terms so that the number of rights and shares are integers. In the Royal Bank of Scotland's case the correct terms were 18 'old' shares for 11 'new' Shares (18/11 = 1.64). In markets parlance this would be called an '11 for 18 rights issue of 6,123,010,462 shares at £2.00 per share'. Thus each shareholder had to give up 18 rights plus £22.00 to receive 11 shares of new equity. If all the shareholders do this, the Royal Bank of Scotland will raise the required £12.246 billion.

It should be clear that the subscription price, the number of new shares, and the number of rights needed to buy a new share of equity are interrelated. If the Royal Bank of Scotland lowered the subscription price, it would have had to issue more new shares to raise £12.246 billion in new equity. Several alternatives appear here:

| Subscription price (£) | Number of new shares | Number of rights needed to buy a share of equity |
|---|---|---|
| 3.00 | 4,082,006,974 | 2.47 |
| 2.00 | 6,123,010,462 | 1.648 |
| 1.00 | 12,246,020,924 | 1 |

**The Effect of a Rights Offer on the Share Price**   Rights clearly have value. In the case of the Royal Bank of Scotland the right to be able to buy a share of equity worth £3.58 for £2.00 was valuable.

Suppose a shareholder of the Royal Bank of Scotland owns 18 shares of equity just before the rights offering. This situation is depicted in Table 14.7. Initially the price of the Royal Bank of Scotland was £3.58 per share, so the shareholder's total holding is worth $18 \times £3.58 = £64.44$. The shareholder who has 18 shares will receive 18 rights. The Royal Bank of Scotland rights issue gave shareholders with 18 rights the opportunity to purchase 11 additional shares for £2.00. The holding of the shareholder who exercises these rights and buys the new shares would increase to $18 + 11 = 29$ shares. The value of the new holding would be $£64.44 + £22 = £86.44$ (the £64.44 initial value plus the £22 paid to the company). Because the shareholder now holds 29 shares, the price per share would drop to $£86.44/29 = £2.98$ (rounded to two decimal places).

The difference between the old share price of £3.58 and the new share price of £2.98 reflects the fact that the old shares carried rights to subscribe to the new issue. The difference must be equal to the value of one right – that is, $£3.58 – £2.98 = £0.60$.

Table 14.8 shows what happens to the Royal Bank of Scotland. If all shareholders exercise their rights, the number of shares will increase to 16,217,251,462 and the value of the firm will increase to £48,327,409,357. After the rights offering the value of each share will drop to £2.98 (= £48,327,409,357/16,217,251,462).

An investor holding no shares of the Royal Bank of Scotland equity who wants to subscribe to the new issue can do so by buying rights. An outside investor buying 18 rights

| **TABLE 14.7** | The shareholder |
|---|---|
| Initial position | |
|    Number of shares | 18 |
|    Share price | £3.58 |
|    Value of holding | £64.44 |
| Terms of offer | |
|    Subscription price | £2.00 |
|    Number of rights issued | 18 |
|    Number of rights for a share | 11 |
| After offer | |
|    Number of shares | 29 |
|    Value of holding | £86.44 |
|    Share price | £2.98 |
| Value of a right | |
|    Old price – New price | £3.58 – £2.98 = £0.60 |
|    $\dfrac{\text{New price – Subscription price}}{\text{Number of rights for a share}}$ | (£2.98 – £2.00)/1.648 = £0.60 |

**Table 14.7** The value to the individual shareholder of the Royal Bank of Scotland's rights

| TABLE 14.8 | | |
|---|---|---|
| Initial position | | |
| Number of 'old' shares | | 10,094,241,000 |
| Share price (£) | | 3.58 |
| Value of firm (£) | | 36,137,382,780 |
| Terms of offer | | |
| Subscription price (£) | | 2.00 |
| Number of rights issued | | 10,094,241,000 |
| Number of 'new' shares | | 6,123,010,462 |
| After offer | | |
| Number of shares | | 16,217,251,462 |
| Share price (£) | | 2.98 |
| Value of firm (£) | | 48,327,409,357 |
| Value of one right (£) | | 3.58 − 2.98 = 0.60 |
| | | or (£2.98 − £2.00)/1.648 = 0.60 |

**Table 14.8** The Royal Bank of Scotland rights offering

will pay £0.60 × 18 = £10.78 (to account for previous rounding). If the investor exercises the rights at a subscription cost of £2.00 to purchase 11 new shares, the total cost will be £22 + £10.78 = £32.78. In return for this expenditure the investor will receive 11 shares of the new equity (worth £2.98 per share), totalling £32.78.

Of course, outside investors can also buy the Royal Bank of Scotland shares directly at £2.98 per share. In an efficient stock market it will make no difference whether new equity is obtained via rights or via direct purchase.

**Effects on Shareholders** Shareholders can exercise their rights or sell them. In either case the shareholder will neither win nor lose by the rights offering. The hypothetical holder of 18 shares of the Royal Bank of Scotland has a portfolio worth £64.44. On the one hand, if the shareholder exercises the rights, he or she ends up with 11 shares worth a total of £32.78. In other words, by spending £32.78 the investor increases the value of the holding by £32.78, which means that he or she is neither better nor worse off.

On the other hand, a shareholder who sells the 18 rights for £0.60 each obtains £0.60 × 18 = £10.78 in cash. Because the 18 shares are each worth £2.98, the holdings are valued at

$$\text{Shares} = 18 \times £2.98 = £53.64$$
$$\text{Sold rights} = 18 \times £0.60 = \underline{£10.80}$$
$$\text{Total} = £64.44$$

The new £53.64 market value plus £10.80 in cash is exactly the same as the original holding of £64.44. Thus shareholders can neither lose nor gain from exercising or selling rights.

It is obvious that the new market price of the firm's equity will be lower after the rights offering than it was before the rights issue. The lower the subscription price, the greater the price decline of a rights issue. However, our analysis shows that the shareholders have suffered no loss because of the rights issue.

## The Underwriting Arrangements

Rights issues are typically arranged using **standby underwriting**. In standby under-writing the issuer makes a rights issue, and the underwriter makes a firm commitment

**standby underwriting** The type of underwriting in which the underwriter agrees to purchase the unsubscribed portion of the issue.

**standby fee**
An amount paid to an underwriter participating in a standby underwriting agreement.

to 'take up' (that is, purchase) the unsubscribed portion of the issue. The underwriter usually gets a **standby fee** and additional amounts based on the securities taken up.

Standby underwriting protects the firm against undersubscription, which can occur if investors throw away rights, or if bad news causes the market price of the equity to fall below the subscription price.

In practice, only a small percentage (fewer than 10 per cent) of shareholders fail to exercise valuable rights. This failure can probably be attributed to ignorance or holidays. Furthermore, shareholders are usually given an **oversubscription privilege**, which enables them to purchase unsubscribed shares at the subscription price. The oversubscription privilege makes it unlikely that the corporate issuer would have to turn to its underwriter for help.

---

**CONCEPT QUESTIONS**

14.8a How does a rights issue work?

14.8b What questions must financial managers answer in a rights issue?

14.8c How is the value of a right determined?

14.8d When does a rights issue affect the value of a company's shares?

14.8e Does a rights issue cause share prices to decrease? How are existing shareholders affected by a rights offering?

---

## 14.9 Dilution

A subject that comes up quite a bit in discussions involving the selling of securities is **dilution**. Dilution refers to a loss in existing shareholders' value. There are several kinds:

1  Dilution of proportionate ownership

2  Dilution of market value

3  Dilution of book value and earnings per share

**oversubscription privilege**
A privilege that allows shareholders to purchase unsubscribed shares in a rights offering at the subscription price.

**dilution**
Loss in existing shareholders' value in terms of ownership, market value, book value, or EPS.

The differences between these three types can be a little confusing, and there are some common misconceptions about dilution, so we discuss it in this section.

### Dilution of Proportionate Ownership

The first type of dilution can arise whenever a firm sells shares to the general public. For example, Joe Smith owns 5,000 shares of Merit Shoes. Merit Shoes currently has 50,000 shares of equity outstanding; each share gets one vote. Joe thus controls 10 per cent (= 5,000/50,000) of the votes, and gets 10 per cent of the dividends.

If Merit Shoes issues 50,000 new shares of equity to the public via a general cash offer, Joe's ownership in Merit Shoes may be diluted. If Joe does not participate in the new issue, his ownership will drop to 5 per cent (= 5,000/100,000). Notice that the value of Joe's shares is unaffected; he just owns a smaller percentage of the firm.

Because a rights issue would ensure that Joe Smith has an opportunity to maintain his proportionate 10 per cent share, dilution of the ownership of existing shareholders can be avoided by using a rights issue.

### Dilution of Value: Book versus Market Values

We now examine dilution of value by looking at some accounting numbers. We do this to illustrate a fallacy concerning dilution; we do not mean to suggest that accounting value dilution is more important than market value dilution. As we illustrate, quite the reverse is true.

Suppose North Country Manufacturing (NCM) wants to build a new electricity-generating plant to meet future anticipated demands. As shown in Table 14.9, NCM currently has

| TABLE 14.9 | | After taking on new project | |
|---|---|---|---|
| | Initial | With dilution | With no dilution |
| Number of shares | 1,000,000 | 1,400,000 | 1,400,000 |
| Book value (€) | 10,000,000 | 12,000,000 | 12,000,000 |
| Book value per share, $B$ (€) | 10 | 8.57 | 8.57 |
| Market value (€) | 5,000,000 | 6,000,000 | 8,000,000 |
| Market price, $P$ (€) | 5 | 4.29 | 5.71 |
| Net income (€) | 1,000,000 | 1,200,000 | 1,600,000 |
| Return on equity, ROE | 0.10 | 0.10 | 0.13 |
| Earnings per share, EPS (€) | 1 | 0.86 | 1.14 |
| EPS/P | 0.20 | 0.20 | 0.20 |
| P/EPS | 5 | 5 | 5 |
| P/B | 0.5 | 0.5 | 0.67 |
| Project cost €2,000,000 | | NPV = −€1,000,000 | NPV = €1,000,000 |

**Table 14.9** New issues and dilution: the case of North Country Manufacturing

1 million shares outstanding and no debt. Each share is selling for €5, and the company has a €5 million market value. NCM's book value is €10 million total, or €10 per share.

NCM has experienced a variety of difficulties in the past, including cost overruns, regulatory delays in building a nuclear-powered electricity-generating plant, and below-normal profits. These difficulties are reflected in the fact that NCM's market-to-book ratio is €5/10 = 0.50 (successful firms rarely have market prices below book values).

Net income for NCM is currently €1 million. With 1 million shares, earnings per share are €1, and the return on equity is €1/10 = 10%.[4] NCM thus sells for five times earnings (the price–earnings ratio is 5). NCM has 200 shareholders, each of whom holds 5,000 shares. The new plant will cost €2 million, so NCM will have to issue 400,000 new shares (€5 × 400,000 = €2 million). There will thus be 1.4 million shares outstanding after the issue.

The ROE on the new plant is expected to be the same as for the company as a whole. In other words, net income is expected to go up by 0.10 × €2 million = €200,000. Total net income will thus be €1.2 million. The following will result if the plant is built:

1　With 1.4 million shares outstanding, EPS will be €1.2/1.4 = €.857, down from €1.

2　The proportionate ownership of each old shareholder will drop from 0.50 per cent to 5,000/1.4 million = 0.36 per cent.

3　If the equity continues to sell for five times earnings, then the value will drop to 5 × €0.857 = €4.29, representing a loss of €.71 per share.

4　The total book value will be the old €10 million plus the new €2 million, for a total of €12 million. Book value per share will fall to €12 million/1.4 million = €8.57.

If we take this example at face value, then dilution of proportionate ownership, accounting dilution and market value dilution all occur. NCM's shareholders appear to suffer significant losses.

**A Misconception**　Our example appears to show that selling equity when the market-to-book ratio is less than 1 is detrimental to shareholders. Some managers claim that the resulting dilution occurs because EPS will go down whenever shares are issued when the market value is less than the book value.

When the market-to-book ratio is less than 1, increasing the number of shares does cause EPS to go down. Such a decline in EPS is accounting dilution, and accounting dilution will always occur under these circumstances.

Is it also true that market value dilution will necessarily occur? The answer is *no*. There is nothing incorrect about our example, but why the market price has decreased is not obvious. We discuss this next.

**The Correct Arguments**  In this example the market price falls from €5 per share to €4.29. This is true dilution, but why does it occur? The answer has to do with the new project. NCM is going to spend €2 million on the new plant. However, as shown in Table 14.9, the total market value of the company is going to rise from €5 million to €6 million, an increase of only €1 million. This simply means that the NPV of the new project is −€1 million. With 1.4 million shares, the loss per share is €1/1.4 = €0.71, as we calculated before.

So true dilution takes place for the shareholders of NCM because the NPV of the project is negative, not because the market-to-book ratio is less than 1. This negative NPV causes the market price to drop, and the accounting dilution has nothing to do with it.

Suppose the new project has a positive NPV of €1 million. The total market value rises by €2 million + 1 million = €3 million. As shown in Table 14.9 (third column), the share price rises to €5.71. Notice that accounting dilution still takes place because the book value per share still falls, but there is no economic consequence of that fact. The market value of the equity rises.

The €0.71 increase in share value comes about because of the €1 million NPV, which amounts to an increase in value of about €0.71 per share. Also, as shown, if the ratio of price to EPS remains at 5, then EPS must rise to €5.71/5 = €1.14. Total earnings (net income) rises to €1.14 per share × 1.4 million shares = €1.6 million. Finally, ROE will rise to €1.6 million/12 million = 13.33%.

| CONCEPT QUESTIONS | 14.9a  What are the different kinds of dilution? |
| | 14.9b  Is dilution important? |

## 14.10  Issuing Long-Term Debt

The general procedures followed in a public issue of bonds are the same as those for equities: the issue must be registered with the stock exchange authorities, there must be a prospectus, and so on. The registration statement for a public issue of bonds, however, is different from the one for equities. For bonds the registration statement must indicate an indenture.

> **term loans**
> Direct business loans of typically one to five years.

> **private placements**
> Loans (usually long-term) provided directly by a limited number of investors.

Another important difference is that more than 50 per cent of all debt is issued privately. There are two basic forms of direct private long-term financing: term loans and private placement.

**Term loans** are direct business loans. These loans have maturities of between one year and five years. Most term loans are repayable during the life of the loan. The lenders include commercial banks, insurance companies, and other lenders that specialize in corporate finance. **Private placements** are similar to term loans except that the maturity is longer.

The important differences between direct private long-term financing and public issues of debt are these:

- A direct long-term loan avoids the cost of stock exchange registration.

- Direct placement is likely to have more restrictive covenants.

- It is easier to renegotiate a term loan or a private placement in the event of a default. It is harder to renegotiate a public issue, because hundreds of holders are usually involved.

- Life insurance companies and pension funds dominate the private placement segment of the bond market. Banks are significant participants in the term loan market.

- The costs of distributing bonds are lower in the private market.

The interest rates on term loans and private placements are usually higher than those on an equivalent public issue. This difference reflects the trade-off between a higher interest rate and more flexible arrangements in the event of financial distress, as well as the lower costs associated with private placements.

An additional, and very important, consideration is that the flotation costs associated with selling debt are much less than the comparable costs associated with selling equity.

> **CONCEPT QUESTIONS**
>
> 14.10a What is the difference between private and public bond issues?
> 14.10b A private placement is likely to have a higher interest rate than a public issue. Why?

## 14.11 Shelf Registration

To simplify the procedures for issuing securities, many stock exchanges allow **shelf registration**. This permits a corporation to register an offering that it reasonably expects to sell within a specified number of years. A master registration statement is filed at the time of registration. The company is permitted to sell the issue whenever it wants over the shelf registration period as long as it distributes a short-form statement.

Shelf registration allows firms to use a *dribble* method of new equity issuance. In dribbling, a company registers the issue and hires an underwriter as its selling agent. The company sells shares in 'dribs and drabs' from time to time directly via a stock exchange (for example, the LSE or Euronext).

Shelf registration has been controversial, and arguments against it are these:

> **shelf registration** Registration permitted by many stock exchanges that allows a company to register all issues it expects to sell within a certain period at one time, with subsequent sales at any time within that period.

1 The costs of new issues might go up, because underwriters might not be able to provide as much current information to potential investors as they would otherwise, so investors would pay less. The expense of selling the issue piece by piece might therefore be higher than that of selling it all at once.

2 Some investment bankers have argued that shelf registration will cause a 'market overhang' that will depress market prices. In other words, the possibility that the company may increase the supply of equity at any time will have a negative impact on the current share price.

> **CONCEPT QUESTIONS**
>
> 14.11a What is shelf registration?
> 14.11b What are the arguments against shelf registration?

## Summary and Conclusions

This chapter has looked at how corporate securities are issued. The following are the main points:

1 The costs of issuing securities can be quite large. They are much lower (as a percentage) for larger issues.

2 The direct and indirect costs of going public can be substantial. However, once a firm is public, it can raise additional capital with much greater ease.

3 Rights issues are cheaper than general cash offers.

4 The private equity market consists of taking public firms private, and the venture capital industry. In recent years the private equity market has been dominated by buy-outs.

## Chapter Review and Self-Test Problems

**14.1  Flotation Costs**  L5 plc is considering an equity issue to finance a new space station. A total of €15 million in new equity is needed. If the direct costs are estimated at 7 per cent of the amount raised, how large does the issue need to be? What is the euro amount of the flotation cost?

**14.2  Rights Issues**  Hadron SA currently has 3 million shares outstanding. The equity sells for €40 per share. To raise $20 million for a new particle accelerator, the firm is considering a rights offering at €25 per share. What is the value of a right in this case? The ex-rights price?

## Answers to Chapter Review and Self-Test Problems

**14.1**  The firm needs to net €15 million after paying the 7 per cent flotation costs. So the amount raised is given by

$$\text{Amount raised} \times (1 - 0.07) = €15 \text{ million}$$
$$\text{Amount raised} = €15 \text{ million}/0.93 = €16.129 \text{ million}$$

The total flotation cost is thus €1.129 million.

**14.2**  To raise €20 million at €25 per share, €20 million/25 = 800,000 shares will have to be sold. Before the offering, the firm is worth 3 million × €40 = €120 million. The issue will raise €20 million, and there will be 3.8 million shares outstanding. The value of an ex-rights share will therefore be €140 million/3.8 million = €36.84. The value of a right is thus €40 − 36.84 = €3.16.

## Concepts Review and Critical Thinking Questions

1  **Debt versus Equity Offering Size [LO2]**  In the aggregate, debt offerings are much more common than equity offerings and typically much larger as well. Why?

2  **Debt versus Equity Flotation Costs [LO2]**  Why are the costs of selling equity so much larger than the costs of selling debt?

3  **Bond Ratings and Flotation Costs [LO2]**  Why do non-investment-grade bonds have much higher direct costs than investment-grade issues?

4  **Underpricing in Debt Offerings [LO2]**  Why is underpricing not a great concern with bond offerings?

Use the following information to answer the next three questions. Eyetech Pharmaceuticals, Inc., a company that develops treatments for eye problems, went public in January 2004. Assisted by the investment bank Merrill Lynch, Eyetech sold 6.5 million shares at $21 each, thereby raising a total of $136.5 million. At the end of the first day of trading the equity sold for $32.40 per share, down slightly from a high of $33.00. Based on the end-of-day numbers, Eyetech shares were apparently underpriced by about $11 each, meaning that the company missed out on an additional $67 million.

5  **IPO Pricing [LO3]**  The Eyetech IPO was underpriced by about 54 per cent. Should Eyetech be upset at Merrill Lynch over the underpricing?

**6 IPO Pricing [LO3]** In the previous question, would it affect your thinking to know that the company was incorporated less than four years earlier, had only $30 million in revenues for the first nine months of 2003, and had never earned a profit? Additionally, the company had only one product, Macugen, which had won fast-track status from the FDA, but still did not have approval to be sold.

**7 IPO Pricing [LO3]** In the previous two questions, how would it affect your thinking to know that, in addition to the 6.5 million shares offered in the IPO, Eyetech had an additional 32 million shares outstanding? Of those 32 million shares, 10 million shares were owned by pharmaceutical giant Pfizer, and 12 million shares were owned by the 13 directors and executive officers.

**8 Cash Offer versus Rights Offer [LO4]** Ren-Stimpy International is planning to raise fresh equity capital by selling a large new issue of equity. Ren-Stimpy is currently a publicly traded corporation, and it is trying to choose between an underwritten cash offer and a rights offering (not underwritten) to current shareholders. Ren-Stimpy management is interested in minimizing the selling costs, and has asked you for advice on the choice of issue methods. What is your recommendation, and why?

**9 IPO Underpricing [LO3]** In 1980 a certain assistant professor of finance bought 12 initial public offerings of equity. He held each of these for approximately one month and then sold. The investment rule he followed was to submit a purchase order for every firm commitment initial public offering of oil and gas exploration companies. There were 22 of these offerings, and he submitted a purchase order for approximately $1,000 in equity for each of the companies. With 10 of these, no shares were allocated to this assistant professor. With 5 of the 12 offerings that were purchased, fewer than the requested number of shares were allocated.

The year 1980 was very good for oil and gas exploration company owners: on average, for the 22 companies that went public, the equities were selling for 80 per cent above the offering price a month after the initial offering date. The assistant professor looked at his performance record and found that the $8,400 invested in the 12 companies had grown to $10,000, representing a return of only about 20 per cent (commissions were negligible). Did he have bad luck, or should he have expected to do worse than the average initial public offering investor? Explain.

**10 IPO Pricing [LO3]** The following material represents the cover page and summary of the prospectus for the initial public offering of the Pest Investigation Control Corporation SA (PICC), which is going public tomorrow with a firm commitment initial public offering managed by the investment banking firm of Bigelli and Bajo.

Answer the following questions:

(a) Assume that you know nothing about PICC other than the information contained in the prospectus. Based on your knowledge of finance, what is your prediction for the price of PICC tomorrow? Provide a short explanation of why you think this will occur.

(b) Assume that you have several thousand euros to invest. When you get home from class tonight, you find that your stockbroker, to whom you have not talked for weeks, has called. She has left a message that PICC is going public tomorrow, and that she can get you several hundred shares at the offering price if you call her back first thing in the morning. Discuss the merits of this opportunity.

**PROSPECTUS**

**PICC**

## 200,000 shares
## PEST INVESTIGATION CONTROL CORPORATION

Of the shares being offered hereby, all 200,000 are being sold by the Pest Investigation Control Corporation SA ('the Company'). Before the offering there has been no public market for the shares of PICC, and no guarantee can be given that any such market will develop.

*These securities have not been approved or disapproved by the Autorité des Marchés Financiers, nor has the Authority passed judgement upon the accuracy or adequacy of this prospectus. Any representation to the contrary is a criminal offence.*

|  | **Price to public** | **Underwriting discount** | **Proceeds to company*** |
|---|---|---|---|
| Per share | €11.00 | €1.10 | €9.90 |
| Total | €2,200,000 | €220,000 | €1,980,000 |

*Before deducting expenses estimated at €27,000 and payable by the company.

*This is an initial public offering. The ordinary shares are being offered, subject to prior sale, when, as, and if delivered to and accepted by the Underwriters and subject to approval of certain legal matters by their Counsel and by Counsel for the Company. The Underwriters reserve the right to withdraw, cancel, or modify such offer and to reject offers in whole or in part.*

**Bigelli and Bajo, Bankers**
**12 July 2010**
**Prospectus Summary**

| | |
|---|---|
| The company | The Pest Investigation Control Corporation (PICC) breeds and markets toads and tree frogs as ecologically safe insect-control mechanisms. |
| The offering | 200,000 ordinary shares of equity, no par value. |
| Listing | The Company will seek listing on Euronext. |
| Shares outstanding | As of 30 June 2010, 400,000 ordinary shares of equity were outstanding. After the offering, 600,000 ordinary shares of equity will be outstanding. |
| Use of proceeds | To finance expansion of inventory and receivables and general working capital, and to pay for country club memberships for certain finance professors. |

**Selected financial information**
**(amounts in € thousands except per-share data)**

| | **Fiscal year ended 30 June** | | | | **As of 30 June 2010** | |
|---|---|---|---|---|---|---|
| | **2008** | **2009** | **2010** | | **Actual** | **As adjusted for this offering** |
| Revenues | 60.00 | 120.00 | 240.00 | Working capital | 0.8 | 1,961 |
| Net earnings | 3.80 | 15.90 | 36.10 | Total assets | 511 | 2,464 |
| Earnings per share | 0.01 | 0.04 | 0.09 | Shareholders' equity | 423 | 2,376 |

# connect Questions and Problems

1   **Rights Issues [LO4]**   Again plc is proposing a rights offering. Currently there are 350,000 shares outstanding at £85 each. There will be 70,000 new shares offered at £70 each.

   (a)   What is the new market value of the company?

   (b)   How many rights are associated with one of the new shares?

   (c)   What is the ex-rights price?

   (d)   What is the value of a right?

   (e)   Ignoring regulations, why might a company have a rights offering rather than a general cash offer?

2   **Rights Issues [LO4]**   Faff plc has announced a rights issue to raise £50 million for a new journal, the *Journal of Financial Excess*. This journal will review potential articles after the author pays a non-refundable reviewing fee of £5,000 per page. The equity currently sells for £40 per share, and there are 5.2 million shares outstanding.

   (a)   What is the maximum possible subscription price? What is the minimum?

   (b)   If the subscription price is set at £35 per share, how many shares must be sold? How many rights will it take to buy one share?

   (c)   What is the ex-rights price? What is the value of a right?

   (d)   Show how a shareholder with 1,000 shares before the offering and no desire (or money) to buy additional shares is not harmed by the rights offer.

3   **Rights [LO4]**   Stone Shoe plc has concluded that additional equity financing will be needed to expand operations, and that the needed funds will be best obtained through a rights issue. It has correctly determined that, as a result of the rights issue, the share price will fall from £80 to £74.50 (£80 is the 'rights-on' price; £74.50 is the ex-rights price, also known as the *when-issued* price). The company is seeking £15 million in additional funds with a per-share subscription price equal to £40. How many shares are there currently, before the offering? (Assume that the increment to the market value of the equity equals the gross proceeds from the offering.)

4   **IPO Underpricing [LO3]**   Carlyle plc and Mullan plc have both announced IPOs at £40 per share. One of these is undervalued by £11, and the other is overvalued by £6, but you have no way of knowing which is which. You plan on buying 1,000 shares of each issue. If an issue is underpriced, it will be rationed, and only half your order will be filled. If you *could* get 1,000 shares in Carlyle and 1,000 shares in Mullan, what would your profit be? What profit do you actually expect? What principle have you illustrated?

5   **Calculating Flotation Costs [LO3]**   Educated Horses plc needs to raise £60 million to finance its expansion into new markets. The company will sell new shares of equity via a general cash offering to raise the needed funds. If the offer price is £21 per share and the company's underwriters charge a 9 per cent spread, how many shares need to be sold?

6   **Calculating Flotation Costs [LO3]**   In the previous problem, if the stock exchange filing fee and associated administrative expenses of the offering are £900,000, how many shares need to be sold?

7   **Calculating Flotation Costs [LO3]**   Groene Heuvels NV has just gone public. Under a firm commitment agreement, Groene Heuvels received €19.75 for each of the 5 million shares sold. The initial offering price was €21 per share, and the equity rose to €26 per share in the first few minutes of trading. Groene Heuvels paid €800,000 in direct legal and other costs and €250,000 in indirect costs. What was the flotation cost as a percentage of funds raised?

8 **Price Dilution [LO3]** Raggio SpA has 100,000 shares of equity outstanding. Each share is worth €90, so the company's market value of equity is €9,000,000. Suppose the firm issues 20,000 new shares at the following prices: €90, €85 and €70. What will the effect be of each of these alternative offering prices on the existing price per share?

INTERMEDIATE

9–15

9 **Dilution [LO3]** Larme SA wishes to expand its facilities. The company currently has 10 million shares outstanding, and no debt. The equity sells for €50 per share, but the book value per share is €40. Net income for Larme is currently €15 million. The new facility will cost €35 million, and it will increase net income by €500,000.

(a) Assuming a constant price–earnings ratio, what will the effect be of issuing new equity to finance the investment? To answer, calculate the new book value per share, the new total earnings, the new EPS, the new share price, and the new market-to-book ratio. What is going on here?

(b) What would the new net income for Larme have to be for the share price to remain unchanged?

10 **Dilution [LO3]** Elvis Heavy Metal Mining (EHMM) plc wants to diversify its operations. Some recent financial information for the company is shown here:

| | |
|---|---|
| Share price (£) | 98 |
| Number of shares | 14,000 |
| Total assets (£) | 6,000,000 |
| Total liabilities (£) | 2,400,000 |
| Net income (£) | 630,000 |

EHMM is considering an investment that has the same P/E ratio as the firm. The cost of the investment is £1,100,000, and it will be financed with a new equity issue. The return on the investment will equal EHMM's current ROE. What will happen to the book value per share, the market value per share, and the EPS? What is the NPV of this investment? Does dilution take place?

11 **Dilution [LO3]** In the previous problem, what would the ROE on the investment have to be if we wanted the price after the offering to be £98 per share? (Assume the P/E ratio remains constant.) What is the NPV of this investment? Does any dilution take place?

12 **Rights [LO4]** Hoobastink Manufacturing is considering a rights offer. The company has determined that the ex-rights price would be €52. The current price is €55 per share, and there are 5 million shares outstanding. The rights issue would raise a total of €60 million. What is the subscription price?

13 **Value of a Right [LO4]** Show that the value of a right just prior to expiration can be written as

$$\text{Value of a right} = P_{RO} - P_X = (P_{RO} - P_S)/(N + 1)$$

where $P_{RO}$, $P_S$ and $P_X$ stand for the rights-on price, the subscription price and the ex-rights price, respectively, and $N$ is the number of rights needed to buy one new share at the subscription price.

14 **Selling Rights [LO4]** Wuttke plc wants to raise £3.65 million via a rights issue. The company currently has 490,000 ordinary shares outstanding that sell for £30 per share. Its underwriter has set a subscription price of £22 per share, and will charge Wuttke a 6 per cent spread. If you currently own 6,000 shares of equity in the company and decide not to participate in the rights issue, how much money can you get by selling your rights?

15 **Valuing a Right [LO4]** Mitsi Inventory Systems has announced a rights offer. The company has announced that it will take four rights to buy a new share in the offering at a subscription price of €40. At the close of business the day before the ex-rights day the company's shares sell for €80 per share. The next morning you notice that the equity sells for €72 per share and the rights sell for €6 each. Are the equity and/or the rights correctly priced on the ex-rights day? Describe a transaction in which you could use these prices to create an immediate profit.

## MINI CASE West Coast Yachts Goes Public

Larissa Warren and Dan Ervin have been discussing the future of West Coast Yachts. The company has been experiencing fast growth, and the future looks like clear sailing. However, the fast growth means that the company's growth can no longer be funded by internal sources, so Larissa and Dan have decided the time is right to take the company public. To this end, they have entered into discussions with the bank of Crowe & Mallard. The company has a working relationship with Robin Perry, the underwriter who assisted with the company's previous bond offering. Crowe & Mallard has helped numerous small companies in the IPO process, so Larissa and Dan feel confident with this choice.

Robin begins by telling Larissa and Dan about the process. Although Crowe & Mallard charged an underwriter fee of 4 per cent on the bond offering, the underwriter fee is 7 per cent on all initial equity offerings of the size of West Coast Yachts' initial offering. Robin tells Larissa and Dan that the company can expect to pay about £1,200,000 in legal fees and expenses, £12,000 in registration fees, and £15,000 in other filing fees. Additionally, to be listed on the London Stock Exchange, the company must pay £100,000. There are also transfer agent fees of £6,500 and engraving expenses of £450,000. The company should also expect to pay £75,000 for other expenses associated with the IPO.

Finally, Robin tells Larissa and Dan that to file with the London Stock Exchange the company must provide three years' worth of audited financial statements. She is unsure of the costs of the audit. Dan tells Robin that the company provides audited financial statements as part of its bond indenture, and the company pays £300,000 per year for the outside auditor.

### QUESTIONS

1 At the end of the discussion Dan asks Robin about the Dutch auction IPO process. What are the differences in the expenses to West Coast Yachts if it uses a Dutch auction IPO compared with a traditional IPO? Should the company go public with a Dutch auction or use a traditional underwritten offering?

2 During the discussion of the potential IPO and West Coast Yachts' future, Dan states that he feels the company should raise £50 million. However, Larissa points out that if the company needs more cash soon, a secondary offering close to the IPO would be potentially problematic. Instead she suggests that the company should raise £80 million in the IPO. How can we calculate the optimal size of the IPO? What are the advantages and disadvantage of increasing the size of the IPO to £80 million?

3 After deliberation, Larissa and Dan have decided that the company should use a firm commitment offering, with Crowe & Mallard as the lead underwriter. The IPO will be for £60 million. Ignoring underpricing, how much will the IPO cost the company as a percentage of the funds received?

4 Many of the employees of West Coast Yachts have shares of equity in the company because of an existing employee stock purchase plan. To sell the equity, the employees can tender their shares to be sold in the IPO at the offering price, or the employees can retain their equity and sell it in the secondary market after West Coast Yachts goes public (once the 180-day lock-up expires). Larissa asks you to advise the employees about which option is best. What would you suggest to the employees?

# Endnotes

1 The terms *follow-on offering* and *secondary offering* are also commonly used.

2 Warrants are options to buy shares at a fixed price for some fixed period.

3 The term *Green Shoe provision* sounds quite exotic, but the origin is relatively mundane. The term comes from the name of the Green Shoe Manufacturing Company, which in 1963 was the first issuer that granted such an option.

4 Return on equity, or ROE, is equal to earnings per share divided by book value per share, or, equivalently, net income divided by common equity. We discuss this and other financial ratios in some detail in Chapter 3.

To help you grasp the key concepts of this chapter check out the extra resources posted on the Online Learning Centre at **www.mcgraw-hill.co.uk/textbooks/hillier**

Among other helpful resources there are mini-cases tailored to individual chapters.

# CHAPTER

# 15

# Financial Leverage and Capital Structure Policy

## KEY NOTATIONS

| | |
|---|---|
| $D$ | Market value of debt |
| $E$ | Market value of equity |
| EBIT | Earnings before interest and taxes |
| EPS | Earnings per share |
| $R_A$ | Return on assets |
| $R_D$ | Return on debt |
| $R_E$ | Return on equity |
| ROE | Return on equity |
| $T_C$ | Corporate tax rate |
| $V_L$ | Market value of a levered firm |
| $V_U$ | Market value of a unlevered firm |
| WACC | Weighted average cost of capital |

## LEARNING OBJECTIVES

After studying this chapter, you should understand:

LO1 The effect of financial leverage.

LO2 The impact of taxes and bankruptcy on capital structure choice.

LO3 The essentials of the bankruptcy process.

IN RECENT YEARS analysts of British soccer clubs have become seriously concerned about the level of indebtedness in their largest institutions. Prior to 2007, British soccer had seen unparalleled injections of cash from worldwide television deals. This additional spending power led to massive transfer fees, which in turn required more funding. Several clubs, including Liverpool and Manchester United, were bought by wealthy individuals backed by significant debt. As for its banking counterparts, the debt that funded British soccer would expire and need to be renewed. Several questions arise. Is the level of debt in British soccer too high? Will we see a fallout in the soccer sector in the same way as the banking sector? How should a company choose a capital structure for itself, and what are the important factors driving this? To answer these questions, this chapter covers the basic ideas underlying optimal debt policies, and how firms establish them.

Thus far we have taken the firm's capital structure as given. Debt–equity ratios don't just drop on firms from the sky, of course, so now it's time to wonder where they come from. Going back to Chapter 1, recall that we refer to decisions about a firm's debt–equity ratio as *capital structure decisions*.[1]

For the most part, a firm can choose any capital structure it wants. If management so desired, a firm could issue some bonds and use the proceeds to buy back some equity, thereby increasing the debt–equity ratio. Alternatively, it could issue equity and use the money to pay off some debt, thereby reducing the debt–equity ratio. Activities such as these, which alter the firm's existing capital structure, are called capital *restructurings*. In general, such restructurings take place whenever the firm substitutes one capital structure for another while leaving the firm's assets unchanged.

Because the assets of a firm are not directly affected by a capital restructuring, we can examine the firm's capital structure decision separately from its other activities. This means that a firm can consider capital restructuring decisions in isolation from its investment decisions. In this chapter, then, we shall ignore investment decisions and focus on the long-term financing, or capital structure, question.

What we shall see in this chapter is that capital structure decisions can have important implications for the value of the firm and its cost of capital. We shall also find that important elements of the capital structure decision are easy to identify, but precise measures of these elements are generally not obtainable. As a result, we are able to give only an incomplete answer to the question of what the best capital structure might be for a particular firm at a particular time.

## 15.1 The Capital Structure Question

How should a firm go about choosing its debt–equity ratio? Here, as always, we assume that the guiding principle is to choose the course of action that maximizes the value of a share of equity. As we discuss next, however, when it comes to capital structure decisions, this is essentially the same thing as maximizing the value of the whole firm, and, for convenience, we shall tend to frame our discussion in terms of firm value.

### Firm Value and Equity Value: An Example

The following example illustrates that the capital structure that maximizes the value of the firm is the one that financial managers should choose for the shareholders, so there is no conflict in our goals. To begin, suppose the market value of J.J. Sprint plc is £1,000. The company currently has no debt, and J.J. Sprint's 100 shares sell for £10 each. Further suppose that J.J. Sprint restructures itself by borrowing £500 and then paying out the proceeds to shareholders as an extra dividend of £500/100 = £5 per share.

This restructuring will change the capital structure of the firm, with no direct effect on the firm's assets. The immediate effect will be to increase debt and decrease equity. However, what will be the final impact of the restructuring? Table 15.1 illustrates three possible

**TABLE 15.1**

|                | No debt | Debt plus dividend | | |
|----------------|---------|------|------|------|
|                |         | I    | II   | III  |
| Debt (£)       | 0       | 500  | 500  | 500  |
| Equity (£)     | 1,000   | 750  | 500  | 250  |
| Firm value (£) | 1,000   | 1,250 | 1,000 | 750  |

**Table 15.1** Possible firm values: no debt versus debt plus dividend

TABLE
15.2

| | Debt plus dividend | | |
|---|---|---|---|
| | **I** | **II** | **III** |
| Equity value reduction (£) | −250 | −500 | −750 |
| Dividends (£) | 500 | 500 | 500 |
| Net effect (£) | +250 | 0 | −250 |

**Table 15.2** Possible pay-offs to shareholders: debt plus dividend

outcomes in addition to the original no-debt case. Notice that in Scenario II the value of the firm is unchanged at £1,000. In Scenario I firm value rises to £1,250; it falls by £250, to £750, in Scenario III. We haven't yet said what might lead to these changes. For now, we just take them as possible outcomes to illustrate a point.

Because our goal is to benefit the shareholders, we next examine, in Table 15.2, the net pay-offs to the shareholders in these scenarios. We see that, if the value of the firm stays the same, shareholders will experience a capital loss exactly offsetting the extra dividend. This is Scenario II. In Scenario I the value of the firm increases to £1,250, and the shareholders come out ahead by £250. In other words, the restructuring has an NPV of £250 in this scenario. The NPV in Scenario III is −£250.

The key observation to make here is that the change in the value of the firm is the same as the net effect on the shareholders. Financial managers can therefore try to find the capital structure that maximizes the value of the firm. Put another way, the NPV rule applies to capital structure decisions, and the change in the value of the overall firm is the NPV of a restructuring. Thus J.J. Sprint should borrow £500 if it expects Scenario I. The crucial question in determining a firm's capital structure is, of course, which scenario is likely to occur.

## Capital Structure and the Cost of Capital

In Chapter 13 we discussed the concept of the firm's weighted average cost of capital, or WACC. You may recall that the WACC tells us that the firm's overall cost of capital is a weighted average of the costs of the various components of the firm's capital structure. When we described the WACC, we took the firm's capital structure as given. Thus one important issue that we shall want to explore in this chapter is what happens to the cost of capital when we vary the amount of debt financing, or the debt–equity ratio.

A primary reason for studying the WACC is that the value of the firm is maximized when the WACC is minimized. To see this, recall that the WACC is the appropriate discount rate for the firm's overall cash flows. Because values and discount rates move in opposite directions, minimizing the WACC will maximize the value of the firm's cash flows.

Thus we shall want to choose the firm's capital structure so that the WACC is minimized. For this reason, we shall say that one capital structure is better than another if it results in a lower weighted average cost of capital. Further, we say that a particular debt–equity ratio represents the *optimal capital structure* if it results in the lowest possible WACC. This optimal capital structure is sometimes called the firm's *target* capital structure as well.

| | |
|---|---|
| **CONCEPT QUESTIONS** | **15.1a** Why should financial managers choose the capital structure that maximizes the value of the firm? |
| | **15.1b** What is the relationship between the WACC and the value of the firm? |
| | **15.1c** What is an optimal capital structure? |

## 15.2 The Effect of Financial Leverage

The previous section described why the capital structure that produces the highest firm value (or the lowest cost of capital) is the one most beneficial to shareholders. In this section we examine the impact of financial leverage on the pay-offs to shareholders. As you may recall, *financial leverage* refers to the extent to which a firm relies on debt. The more debt financing a firm uses in its capital structure, the more financial leverage it employs.

As we describe, financial leverage can dramatically alter the pay-offs to shareholders in the firm. Remarkably, however, financial leverage may not affect the overall cost of capital. If this is true, then a firm's capital structure is irrelevant, because changes in capital structure won't affect the value of the firm. We shall return to this issue a little later.

### The Basics of Financial Leverage

We start by illustrating how financial leverage works. For now, we ignore the impact of taxes. Also, for ease of presentation, we describe the impact of leverage in terms of its effects on earnings per share, EPS, and return on equity, ROE. These are of course accounting numbers, and as such are not our primary concern. Using cash flows instead of these accounting numbers would lead to precisely the same conclusions, but a little more work would be needed. We discuss the impact on market values in a subsequent section.

**Financial Leverage, EPS and ROE: An Example**   Autoveloce SpA currently has no debt in its capital structure. The firm is considering a restructuring that would involve issuing debt and using the proceeds to buy back some of the outstanding equity. Table 15.3 presents both the current and proposed capital structures. As shown, the firm's assets have a market value of €8 million, and there are 400,000 shares outstanding. Because Autoveloce is an all-equity firm, the price per share is €20.

The proposed debt issue would raise €4 million; the interest rate would be 10 per cent. Because the equity sells for €20 per share, the €4 million in new debt would be used to purchase €4 million/20 = 200,000 shares, leaving 200,000. After the restructuring, Autoveloce would have a capital structure that was 50 per cent debt, so the debt–equity ratio would be 1. Notice that, for now, we assume that the equity price will remain at €20.

To investigate the impact of the proposed restructuring, Table 15.4 compares the firm's current capital structure with the proposed capital structure under three scenarios. The scenarios reflect different assumptions about the firm's EBIT. Under the expected scenario the EBIT is €1 million. In the recession scenario EBIT falls to €500,000. In the expansion scenario it rises to €1.5 million.

To illustrate some of the calculations behind the figures in Table 15.4, consider the expansion case. EBIT is €1.5 million. With no debt (the current capital structure) and no

| TABLE 15.3 | | Current | Proposed |
|---|---|---|---|
| Assets (€) | | 8,000,000 | 8,000,000 |
| Debt (€) | | 0 | 4,000,000 |
| Equity (€) | | 8,000,000 | 4,000,000 |
| Debt–equity ratio | | 0 | 1 |
| Share price (€) | | 20 | 20 |
| Shares outstanding | | 400,000 | 200,000 |
| Interest rate (%) | | 10 | 10 |

**Table 15.3** Current and proposed capital structures for Autoveloce SpA

TABLE
15.4

| Current capital structure: no debt | | | |
|---|---|---|---|
| | Recession | Expected | Expansion |
| EBIT (€) | 500,000 | 1,000,000 | 1,500,000 |
| Interest (€) | 0 | 0 | 0 |
| Net income (€) | 500,000 | 1,000,000 | 1,500,000 |
| ROE (%) | 6.25 | 12.50 | 18.75 |
| EPS (€) | 1.25 | 2.50 | 3.75 |
| Proposed capital structure: Debt = €4 million | | | |
| EBIT (€) | 500,000 | 1,000,000 | 1,500,000 |
| Interest (€) | 400,000 | 400,000 | 400,000 |
| Net income (€) | 100,000 | 600,000 | 1,100,000 |
| ROE (%) | 2.50 | 15.00 | 27.50 |
| EPS (€) | 0.50 | 3.00 | 5.50 |

**Table 15.4** Capital structure scenarios for Autoveloce SpA

taxes, net income is also €1.5 million. In this case there are 400,000 shares worth €8 million total. EPS is therefore €1.5 million/400,000 = €3.75. Also, because accounting return on equity, ROE, is net income divided by total equity, ROE is €1.5 million/8 million = 18.75%.[2]

With €4 million in debt (the proposed capital structure), things are somewhat different. Because the interest rate is 10 per cent, the interest bill is €400,000. With EBIT of €1.5 million, interest of €400,000, and no taxes, net income is €1.1 million. Now there are only 200,000 shares worth €4 million total. EPS is therefore €1.1 million/200,000 = €5.50, versus the €3.75 that we calculated in the previous scenario. Furthermore, ROE is €1.1 million/4 million = 27.5%. This is well above the 18.75 per cent we calculated for the current capital structure.

**EPS versus EBIT** The impact of leverage is evident when the effect of the restructuring on EPS and ROE is examined. In particular, the variability in both EPS and ROE is much larger under the proposed capital structure. This illustrates how financial leverage acts to magnify gains and losses to shareholders.

In Fig. 15.1 we take a closer look at the effect of the proposed restructuring. This figure plots earnings per share, EPS, against earnings before interest and taxes, EBIT, for the current and proposed capital structures. The first line, labelled 'No debt', represents the case of no leverage. This line begins at the origin, indicating that EPS would be zero if EBIT were zero. From there, every €400,000 increase in EBIT increases EPS by €1 (because there are 400,000 shares outstanding).

The second line represents the proposed capital structure. Here, EPS is negative if EBIT is zero. This follows because €400,000 of interest must be paid, regardless of the firm's profits. Because there are 200,000 shares in this case, the EPS is −€2 as shown. Similarly, if EBIT were €400,000, EPS would be exactly zero.

The important thing to notice in Fig. 15.1 is that the slope of the line in this second case is steeper. In fact, for every €400,000 increase in EBIT, EPS rises by €2, so the line is twice as steep. This tells us that EPS is twice as sensitive to changes in EBIT because of the financial leverage employed.

Another observation to make in Fig. 15.1 is that the lines intersect. At that point, EPS is exactly the same for both capital structures. To find this point, note that EPS is equal to EBIT/400,000 in the no-debt case. In the with-debt case, EPS is (EBIT − €400,000)/200,000. If we set these equal to each other, EBIT is given by

FIGURE
**15.1**

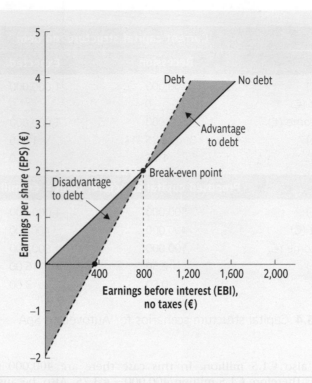

**Figure 15.1** Financial leverage: EPS and EBIT for Autoveloce SpA

$$EBIT/400,000 = (EBIT - €400,000)/200,000$$
$$EBIT = 2 \times (EBIT - €400,000)$$
$$= €800,000$$

When EBIT is €800,000, EPS is €2 under either capital structure. This is labelled as the break-even point in Fig. 15.1; we could also call it the indifference point. If EBIT is above this level, leverage is beneficial; if it is below this point, it is not.

There is another, more intuitive, way of seeing why the break-even point is €800,000. Notice that, if the firm has no debt and its EBIT is €800,000, its net income is also €800,000. In this case the ROE is 10 per cent. This is precisely the same as the interest rate on the debt, so the firm earns a return that is just sufficient to pay the interest.

In Fig. 15.1, we have plotted the firm's EPS against its EBIT for the two possible capital structures. These lines represent earnings per share, EPS, against earnings before interest and taxes, EBIT, for the cur-

EXAMPLE
**15.1**

# Break-Even EBIT

MPD plc has decided in favour of a capital restructuring. Currently, MPD uses no debt financing. Following the restructuring, however, debt will be £1 million. The interest rate on the debt will be 9 per cent. MPD currently has 200,000 shares outstanding, and the share price is £20. If the restructuring is expected to increase EPS, what is the minimum level for EBIT that MPD's management must be expecting? Ignore taxes in answering.

To answer, we calculate the break-even EBIT. At any EBIT above this the increased financial leverage will increase EPS, so this will tell us the minimum level for EBIT. Under the old capital structure EPS is simply EBIT/200,000. Under the new capital structure the interest expense will be £1 million × 0.09 = £90,000. Furthermore, with the £1 million proceeds, MPD will repurchase £1 million/20 = 50,000 shares of equity, leaving 150,000 outstanding. EPS will thus be (EBIT − £90,000)/150,000.

Now that we know how to calculate EPS under both scenarios, we set them equal to each other and solve for the break-even EBIT:

$$EBIT/200{,}000 = (EBIT - £90{,}000)/150{,}000$$
$$EBIT = 4/3 \times (EBIT - £90{,}000)$$
$$= £360{,}000$$

Verify that, in either case, EPS is £1.80 when EBIT is £360,000. Management at MPD is apparently of the opinion that EPS will exceed £1.80.

## Corporate Borrowing and Homemade Leverage

Based on Tables 15.3 and 15.4 and Fig. 15.1, Autoveloce draws the following conclusions:

1   The effect of financial leverage depends on the company's EBIT. When EBIT is relatively high, leverage is beneficial.

2   Under the expected scenario, leverage increases the returns to shareholders, as measured by both ROE and EPS.

3   Shareholders are exposed to more risk under the proposed capital structure, because the EPS and ROE are much more sensitive to changes in EBIT in this case.

4   Because of the impact that financial leverage has on both the expected return to shareholders and the riskiness of the equity, capital structure is an important consideration.

The first three of these conclusions are clearly correct. Does the last conclusion necessarily follow? Surprisingly, the answer is no. As we discuss next, the reason is that shareholders can adjust the amount of financial leverage by borrowing and lending on their own. This use of personal borrowing to alter the degree of financial leverage is called **homemade leverage**.

We shall now illustrate that it actually makes no difference whether or not Autoveloce adopts the proposed capital structure, because any shareholder who prefers the proposed capital structure can simply create it using homemade leverage. To begin, the first part of Table 15.5 shows what will happen to an investor who buys €2,000 worth of Autoveloce equity if the proposed capital structure is adopted. This investor purchases 100 shares of equity. From Table 15.4 we know that EPS will be €0.50, €3 or €5.50, so the total earnings for 100 shares will be either €50, €300 or €550 under the proposed capital structure.

> **homemade leverage**
> The use of personal borrowing to change the overall amount of financial leverage to which the individual is exposed.

Now, suppose that Autoveloce does not adopt the proposed capital structure. In this case EPS will be €1.25, €2.50 or €3.75. The second part of Table 15.5 demonstrates how a shareholder who prefers the pay-offs under the proposed structure can create them using personal borrowing. To do this, the shareholder borrows €2,000 at 10 per cent on her or his own. Our investor uses this amount, along with the original €2,000, to buy 200 shares of equity. As shown, the net pay-offs are exactly the same as those for the proposed capital structure.

How did we know to borrow €2,000 to create the right pay-offs? We are trying to replicate Autoveloce's proposed capital structure at the personal level. The proposed capital structure results in a debt–equity ratio of 1. To replicate this structure at the personal level, the shareholder must borrow enough to create this same debt–equity ratio. Because the shareholder has €2,000 in equity invested, the borrowing of another €2,000 will create a personal debt–equity ratio of 1.

This example demonstrates that investors can always increase financial leverage themselves to create a different pattern of pay-offs. It thus makes no difference whether Autoveloce chooses the proposed capital structure.

TABLE
15.5

| Proposed capital structure | | | |
|---|---|---|---|
| | Recession | Expected | Expansion |
| EPS (€) | 0.50 | 3.00 | 5.50 |
| Earnings for 100 shares (€) | 50.00 | 300.00 | 550.00 |
| Net cost = 100 shares × €20 = €2,000 | | | |

| Original capital structure and homemade leverage | | | |
|---|---|---|---|
| EPS (€) | 1.25 | 2.50 | 3.75 |
| Earnings for 200 shares (€) | 250.00 | 500.00 | 750.00 |
| Less: Interest on €2,000 at 10% (€) | 200.00 | 200.00 | 200.00 |
| Net earnings (€) | 50.00 | 300.00 | 550.00 |
| Net cost = 200 shares × €20 − Amount borrowed = €4,000 − 2,000 = €2,000 | | | |

**Table 15.5** Proposed capital structure versus original capital structure with homemade leverage

## Unlevering the Equity

EXAMPLE **15.2**

In our Autoveloce example, suppose management adopts the proposed capital structure. Further suppose that an investor who owned 100 shares preferred the original capital structure. Show how this investor could 'unlever' the equity to recreate the original pay-offs.

To create leverage, investors borrow on their own. To undo leverage, investors must lend money. In the case of Autoveloce, the corporation borrowed an amount equal to half its value. The investor can unlever the equity by simply lending money in the same proportion. In this case the investor sells 50 shares for €1,000 total, and then lends the €1,000 at 10 per cent. The pay-offs are calculated in the following table:

| | Recession | Expected | Expansion |
|---|---|---|---|
| EPS (proposed structure) (€) | 0.50 | 3.00 | 5.50 |
| Earnings for 50 shares (€) | 25.00 | 150.00 | 275.00 |
| Plus: Interest on €1,000 (€) | 100.00 | 100.00 | 100.00 |
| Total pay-off (€) | 125.00 | 250.00 | 375.00 |

These are precisely the pay-offs the investor would have experienced under the original capital structure.

CONCEPT
QUESTIONS

15.2a   What is the impact of financial leverage on shareholders?
15.2b   What is homemade leverage?
15.2c   Why is Autoveloce's capital structure irrelevant?

## 15.3 Capital Structure and the Cost of Equity Capital

We have seen that there is nothing special about corporate borrowing, because investors can borrow or lend on their own. As a result, whichever capital structure Autoveloce

FIGURE
**15.2**

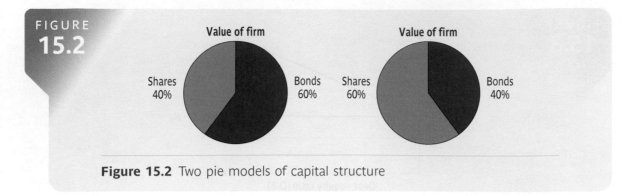

**Figure 15.2** Two pie models of capital structure

chooses, the equity price will be the same. Autoveloce's capital structure is thus irrelevant, at least in the simple world we have examined.

Our Autoveloce example is based on a famous argument advanced by two Nobel laureates, Franco Modigliani and Merton Miller, whom we shall henceforth call M&M. What we illustrated for the Autoveloce Corporation is a special case of **M&M Proposition I**. M&M Proposition I states that it is completely irrelevant how a firm chooses to arrange its finances.

> **M&M Proposition I**
> The proposition that the value of the firm is independent of the firm's capital structure.

## M&M Proposition I: The Pie Model

One way to illustrate M&M Proposition I is to imagine two firms that are identical on the left side of the balance sheet. Their assets and operations are exactly the same. The right sides are different, because the two firms finance their operations differently. In this case we can view the capital structure question in terms of a 'pie' model. Why we choose this name is apparent from Fig. 15.2. Figure 15.2 gives two possible ways of cutting up the pie between the equity slice, $E$, and the debt slice, $D$: 40%–60% and 60%–40%. However, the size of the pie in Fig. 15.2 is the same for both firms, because the value of the assets is the same. This is precisely what M&M Proposition I states: The size of the pie doesn't depend on how it is sliced.

## The Cost of Equity and Financial Leverage: M&M Proposition II

Although changing the capital structure of the firm does not change the firm's *total* value, it does cause important changes in the firm's debt and equity. We now examine what happens to a firm financed with debt and equity when the debt–equity ratio is changed. To simplify our analysis, we shall continue to ignore taxes.

Based on our discussion in Chapter 13, if we ignore taxes, the weighted average cost of capital, WACC, is

$$\text{WACC} = (E/V) \times R_E + (D/V) \times R_D$$

where $V = E + D$. We also saw that one way of interpreting the WACC is as the required return on the firm's overall assets. To remind us of this, we shall use the symbol $R_A$ to stand for the WACC, and write

$$R_A = (E/V) \times R_E + (D/V) \times R_D$$

If we rearrange this to solve for the cost of equity capital, we see that

$$R_E = R_A + (R_A - R_D) \times (D/E) \tag{15.1}$$

FIGURE

**15.3**

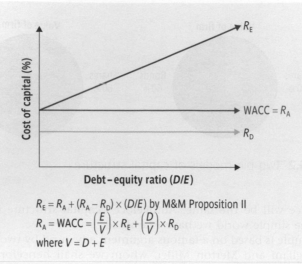

$$R_E = R_A + (R_A - R_D) \times (D/E) \text{ by M\&M Proposition II}$$
$$R_A = \text{WACC} = \left(\frac{E}{V}\right) \times R_E + \left(\frac{D}{V}\right) \times R_D$$
where $V = D + E$

**Figure 15.3** The cost of equity and the WACC: M&M Propositions I and II with no taxes

**M&M Proposition II**
The proposition that a firm's cost of equity capital is a positive linear function of the firm's capital structure.

This is the famous **M&M Proposition II**, which tells us that the cost of equity depends on three things: the required rate of return on the firm's assets, $R_A$; the firm's cost of debt, $R_D$; and the firm's debt–equity ratio, $D/E$.

Figure 15.3 summarizes our discussion thus far by plotting the cost of equity capital, $R_E$, against the debt–equity ratio. As shown, M&M Proposition II indicates that the cost of equity, $R_E$, is given by a straight line with a slope of $(R_A - R_D)$. The $y$-intercept corresponds to a firm with a debt–equity ratio of zero, so $R_A = R_E$ in that case. Figure 15.3 shows that as the firm raises its debt–equity ratio, the increase in leverage raises the risk of the equity and therefore the required return or cost of equity ($R_E$).

Notice in Fig. 15.3 that the WACC doesn't depend on the debt–equity ratio; it's the same no matter what the debt–equity ratio is. This is another way of stating M&M Proposition I: the firm's overall cost of capital is unaffected by its capital structure. As illustrated, the fact that the cost of debt is lower than the cost of equity is exactly offset by the increase in the cost of equity from borrowing. In other words, the change in the capital structure weights ($E/V$ and $D/V$) is exactly offset by the change in the cost of equity ($R_E$), so the WACC stays the same.

EXAMPLE

**15.3**

# The Cost of Equity Capital

Ricard NV has a weighted average cost of capital (ignoring taxes) of 12 per cent. It can borrow at 8 per cent. Assuming that Ricard has a target capital structure of 80 per cent equity and 20 per cent debt, what is its cost of equity? What is the cost of equity if the target capital structure is 50 per cent equity? Calculate the WACC using your answers to verify that it is the same.

According to M&M Proposition II, the cost of equity, $R_E$, is

$$R_E = R_A + (R_A - R_D) \times (D/E)$$

In the first case, the debt–equity ratio is $0.2/0.8 = 0.25$, so the cost of the equity is

$$R_E = 12\% + (12\% - 8\%) \times 0.25$$
$$= 13\%$$

In the second case, verify that the debt–equity ratio is 1.0, so the cost of equity is 16 per cent.

We can now calculate the WACC assuming that the percentage of equity financing is 80 per cent, the cost of equity is 13 per cent, and the tax rate is zero:

$$\text{WACC} = (E/V) \times R_\text{E} + (D/V) \times R_\text{D}$$
$$= 0.80 \times 13\% + 0.20 \times 8\%$$
$$= 12\%$$

In the second case, the percentage of equity financing is 50 per cent and the cost of equity is 16 per cent. The WACC is

$$\text{WACC} = (E/V) \times R_\text{E} + (D/V) \times R_\text{D}$$
$$= 0.50 \times 16\% + 0.50 \times 8\%$$
$$= 12\%$$

As we have calculated, the WACC is 12 per cent in both cases.

# In Their Own Words . . .

### Merton H. Miller on Capital Structure: M&M 30 Years Later

How difficult it is to summarize briefly the contribution of these papers was brought home to me very clearly after Franco Modigliani was awarded the Nobel Prize in Economics, in part – but, of course, only in part – for his work in finance. The television camera crews from our local stations in Chicago immediately descended upon me. 'We understand,' they said, 'that you worked with Modigliani some years back in developing these M&M theorems, and we wonder if you could explain them briefly to our television viewers.' 'How briefly?' I asked. 'Oh, take 10 seconds,' was the reply.

Ten seconds to explain the work of a lifetime! Ten seconds to describe two carefully reasoned articles, each running to more than 30 printed pages and each with 60 or so long footnotes! When they saw the look of dismay on my face, they said, 'You don't have to go into details. Just give us the main points in simple, common-sense terms.'

The main point of the cost-of-capital article was, in principle at least, simple enough to make. It said that in an economist's ideal world, the total market value of all the securities issued by a firm would be governed by the earning power and risk of its underlying real assets and would be independent of how the mix of securities issued to finance it was divided between debt instruments and equity capital. Some corporate treasurers might well think that they could enhance total value by increasing the proportion of debt instruments because yields on debt instruments, given their lower risk, are, by and large, substantially below those on equity capital. But, under the ideal conditions assumed, the added risk to the shareholders from issuing more debt will raise required yields on the equity by just enough to offset the seeming gain from use of low-cost debt.

Such a summary would not only have been too long, but it relied on shorthand terms and concepts that are rich in connotations to economists, but hardly so to the general public. I thought, instead, of an analogy that we ourselves had invoked in the original paper. 'Think of the firm,' I said, 'as a gigantic tub of whole milk. The farmer can sell the whole milk as is. Or he can separate out the cream and sell it at a considerably higher price than the whole milk would bring. (Selling cream is the analogue of a firm selling low-yield and hence high-priced debt securities.) But, of course, what the farmer would have left would be skim milk, with low butterfat content, and that would sell for much less than whole milk. Skim milk corresponds to the levered equity. The M&M proposition says that if there were no costs of separation (and, of course, no government dairy support programmes), the cream plus the skim milk would bring the same price as the whole milk.'

The television people conferred among themselves for a while. They informed me that it was still too long, too complicated, and too academic. 'Have you anything simpler?' they asked. I thought of another way in which the M&M proposition is presented that stresses the role of securities as devices for 'partitioning' a firm's pay-offs among the group of its capital suppliers. 'Think of the firm,' I said, 'as a gigantic pizza, divided into quarters. If, now, you cut each quarter in half into eighths, the M&M proposition says that you will have more pieces, but not more pizza.'

Once again whispered conversation. This time, they shut the lights off. They folded up their equipment. They thanked me for my co-operation. They said they would get back to me. But I knew that I had somehow lost my chance to start a new career as a packager of economic wisdom for TV viewers in convenient 10-second sound bites. Some have the talent for it; and some just don't.

*The late Merton H. Miller was famous for his groundbreaking work with Franco Modigliani on corporate capital structure, cost of capital, and dividend policy. He received the Nobel Prize in Economics for his contributions shortly after this essay was prepared.*

## Business and Financial Risk

**business risk**
The equity risk that comes from the nature of the firm's operating activities.

**financial risk**
The equity risk that comes from the financial policy (the capital structure) of the firm.

M&M Proposition II shows that the firm's cost of equity can be broken down into two components. The first component, $R_A$, is the required return on the firm's assets overall, and it depends on the nature of the firm's operating activities. The risk inherent in a firm's operations is called the **business risk** of the firm's equity. Referring back to Chapter 12, note that this business risk depends on the systematic risk of the firm's assets. The greater a firm's business risk, the greater $R_A$ will be, and, all other things being the same, the greater will be the firm's cost of equity.

The second component in the cost of equity, $(R_A - R_D) \times (D/E)$, is determined by the firm's financial structure. For an all-equity firm this component is zero. As the firm begins to rely on debt financing, the required return on equity rises. This occurs because the debt financing increases the risks borne by the shareholders. This extra risk that arises from the use of debt financing is called the **financial risk** of the firm's equity.

The total systematic risk of the firm's equity thus has two parts: business risk and financial risk. The first part (the business risk) depends on the firm's assets and operations, and is not affected by capital structure. Given the firm's business risk (and its cost of debt), the second part (the financial risk) is completely determined by financial policy. As we have illustrated, the firm's cost of equity rises when the firm increases its use of financial leverage, because the financial risk of the equity increases while the business risk remains the same.

**CONCEPT QUESTIONS**

15.3a   What does M&M Proposition I state?
15.3b   What are the three determinants of a firm's cost of equity?
15.3c   The total systematic risk of a firm's equity has two parts. What are they?

## 15.4 M&M Propositions I and II with Corporate Taxes

Debt has two distinguishing features that we have not taken into proper account. First, as we have mentioned in a number of places, interest paid on debt is tax deductible. This is good for the firm, and it may be an added benefit of debt financing. Second, failure to meet debt obligations can result in bankruptcy. This is not good for the firm, and it may be an added cost of debt financing. Because we haven't explicitly considered either of these two features of debt, we realize that we may get a different answer about capital structure once we do. Accordingly, we consider taxes in this section and bankruptcy in the next.

We can start by considering what happens to M&M Propositions I and II when we consider the effect of corporate taxes. To do this, we shall examine two firms: Firm U (unlevered) and Firm L (levered). These two firms are identical on the left side of the balance sheet, so their assets and operations are the same.

We assume that EBIT is expected to be €1,000 every year for ever for both firms. The difference between the firms is that Firm L has issued €1,000 worth of perpetual bonds on which it pays 8 per cent interest each year. The interest bill is thus $0.08 \times €1,000 = €80$ every year for ever. Also, we assume that the corporate tax rate is 30 per cent.

For our two firms, U and L, we can now calculate the following:

|  | Firm U | Firm L |
|---|---|---|
| EBIT (€) | 1,000 | 1,000 |
| Interest (€) | 0 | 80 |
| Taxable income (€) | 1,000 | 920 |
| Taxes (30%) (€) | 300 | 276 |
| Net income | 700 | 644 |

## The Interest Tax Shield

To simplify things, we shall assume that depreciation is zero. We shall also assume that capital spending is zero, and that there are no changes in NWC. In this case, cash flow from assets is simply equal to EBIT – Taxes. For Firms U and L we thus have

| Cash flow from assets | Firm U | Firm L |
|---|---|---|
| EBIT (€) | 1,000 | 1,000 |
| – Taxes (€) | 300 | 276 |
| Total (€) | 700 | 724 |

We immediately see that capital structure is now having some effect, because the cash flows from U and L are not the same, even though the two firms have identical assets.

To see what's going on, we can compute the cash flow to shareholders and bondholders:

| Cash flow (€) | Firm U | Firm L |
|---|---|---|
| To shareholders | 700 | 644 |
| To bondholders | 0 | 80 |
| Total | 700 | 724 |

What we are seeing is that the total cash flow to L is €24 more. This occurs because L's tax bill (which is a cash outflow) is €24 less. The fact that interest is deductible for tax purposes has generated a tax saving equal to the interest payment (€80) multiplied by the corporate tax rate (30 per cent): $€80 \times 0.30 = €24$. We call this tax saving the **interest tax shield**.

> **interest tax shield**
> The tax saving attained by a firm from interest expense.

## Taxes and M&M Proposition I

Because the debt is perpetual, the same €24 shield will be generated every year for ever. The after-tax cash flow to L will thus be the same €700 that U earns plus the €24 tax shield. Because L's cash flow is always €24 greater, Firm L is worth more than Firm U, the difference being the value of this €24 perpetuity.

Because the tax shield is generated by paying interest, it has the same risk as the debt, and 8 per cent (the cost of debt) is therefore the appropriate discount rate. The value of the tax shield is thus

$$PV = \frac{€24}{0.08}$$

$$= \frac{0.30 \times €1,000 \times 0.08}{0.08}$$

$$= 0.30 \times €1,000$$

$$= €300$$

As our example illustrates, the present value of the interest tax shield can be written as

$$\text{Present value of the interest tax shield} = \frac{T_C \times D \times R_D}{R_D} \qquad (15.2)$$

$$= T_C \times D$$

We have now come up with another famous result, M&M Proposition I with corporate taxes. We have seen that the value of Firm L, $V_L$, exceeds the value of Firm U, $V_U$, by the present value of the interest tax shield, $T_C \times D$. M&M Proposition I with taxes therefore states that

$$V_L = V_U + T_C \times D \qquad (15.3)$$

The effect of borrowing in this case is illustrated in Fig. 15.4. We have plotted the value of the levered firm, $V_L$, against the amount of debt, $D$. M&M Proposition I with corporate taxes implies that the relationship is given by a straight line with a slope of $T_C$ and a $y$-intercept of $V_U$.

In Fig. 15.4 we have also drawn a horizontal line representing $V_U$. As indicated, the distance between the two lines is $T_C \times D$, the present value of the tax shield.

> **unlevered cost of capital**
> The cost of capital for a firm that has no debt.

Suppose that the cost of capital for Firm U is 10 per cent. We shall call this the **unlevered cost of capital**, and we shall use the symbol $R_U$ to represent it. We can think of $R_U$ as the cost of capital a firm would have if it had no debt. Firm U's cash flow is €700 every year for ever, and, because U has no debt, the appropriate discount rate is $R_U = 10\%$. The value of the unlevered firm, $V_U$, is simply:

**FIGURE 15.4**

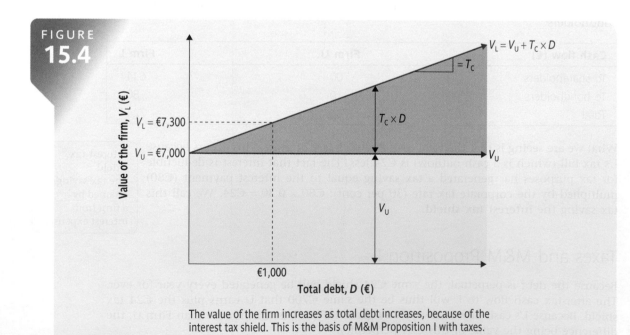

The value of the firm increases as total debt increases, because of the interest tax shield. This is the basis of M&M Proposition I with taxes.

**Figure 15.4** M&M Proposition I with taxes

$$V_U = \frac{\text{EBIT} \times (1 - T_C)}{R_U}$$

$$= \frac{\text{€}700}{0.10}$$

$$= \text{€}7{,}000$$

The value of the levered firm, $V_L$, is

$$V_L = V_U + T_C \times D$$
$$= \text{€}7{,}000 + 0.30 \times 1{,}000$$
$$= \text{€}7{,}300$$

As Fig. 15.4 indicates, the value of the firm goes up by €0.30 for every €1 in debt. In other words, the NPV *per euro* of debt is €0.30. It is difficult to imagine why any corporation would not borrow to the absolute maximum under these circumstances.

The result of our analysis in this section is the realization that, once we include taxes, capital structure definitely matters. However, we immediately reach the illogical conclusion that the optimal capital structure is 100 per cent debt.

## Taxes, the WACC and Proposition II

We can also conclude that the best capital structure is 100 per cent debt by examining the weighted average cost of capital. From Chapter 13 we know that once we consider the effect of taxes, the WACC is

$$\text{WACC} = (E/V) \times R_E + (D/V) \times R_D \times (1 - T_C)$$

To calculate this WACC we need to know the cost of equity. M&M Proposition II with corporate taxes states that the cost of equity is

$$R_E = R_U + (R_U - R_D) \times (D/E) \times (1 - T_C) \tag{15.4}$$

To illustrate, recall that we saw a moment ago that Firm L is worth €7,300 in total. Because the debt is worth €1,000, the equity must be worth €7,300 − 1,000 = €6,300. For Firm L, the cost of equity is thus

$$R_E = 0.10 + (0.10 - 0.08) \times (\text{€}1{,}000/6{,}300) \times (1 - 0.30)$$
$$= 10.22\%$$

The weighted average cost of capital is

$$\text{WACC} = (\text{€}6{,}300/7{,}300) \times 10.22\% + (1{,}000/7{,}300) \times 8\% \times (1 - 0.30)$$
$$= 9.6\%$$

Without debt, the WACC is over 10 per cent; with debt, it is 9.6 per cent. Therefore the firm is better off with debt.

## Conclusion

Figure 15.5 summarizes our discussion concerning the relationship between the cost of equity, the after-tax cost of debt, and the weighted average cost of capital. For reference, we have included $R_U$, the unlevered cost of capital. In Fig. 15.5 we have the debt–equity ratio on the horizontal axis. Notice how the WACC declines as the debt–equity ratio grows. This illustrates again that the more debt the firm uses, the lower is its WACC. Table 15.6 summarizes the key results of our analysis of the M&M propositions for future reference.

FIGURE
15.5

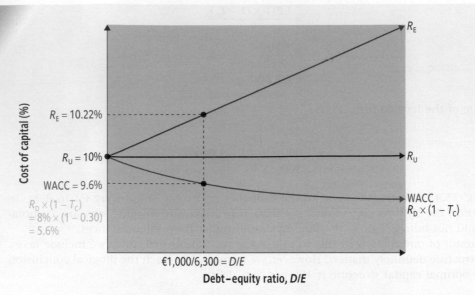

M&M Proposition I with taxes implies that a firm's WACC decreases as the firm relies more heavily on debt financing:

$$WACC = \left(\frac{E}{V}\right) \times R_E + \left(\frac{D}{V}\right) \times R_D \times (1 - T_c)$$

M&M Proposition II with taxes implies that a firm's cost of equity, $R_E$, rises as the firm relies more heavily on debt financing:

$$R_E = R_U + (R_U - R_D) \times (D/E) \times (1 - T_c)$$

**Figure 15.5** The cost of equity and the WACC: M&M Proposition II with taxes

TABLE
15.6

**The no-tax case**

**A** Proposition I: The value of the firm levered ($V_L$) is equal to the value of the firm unlevered ($V_U$):

$$V_L = V_U$$

Implications of Proposition I:

1 A firm's capital structure is irrelevant.

2 A firm's weighted average cost of capital (WACC) is the same, no matter what mixture of debt and equity is used to finance the firm.

**B** Proposition II: The cost of equity, $R_E$, is

$$R_E = R_A + (R_A - R_D) \times (D/E)$$

where $R_A$ is the WACC, $R_D$ is the cost of debt, and $D/E$ is the debt–equity ratio. Implications of Proposition II:

1 The cost of equity rises as the firm increases its use of debt financing.

2 The risk of the equity depends on two things: the riskiness of the firm's operations (*business risk*), and the degree of financial leverage (*financial risk*). Business risk determines $R_A$; financial risk is determined by $D/E$.

**Table 15.6** Modigliani and Miller summary

**TABLE 15.6**

**The tax case**

**A** Proposition I with taxes: The value of the firm levered ($V_L$) is equal to the value of the firm unlevered ($V_U$) plus the present value of the interest tax shield:

$$V_L = V_U + T_C \times D$$

where $T_C$ is the corporate tax rate and $D$ is the amount of debt.
Implications of Proposition I:

1 Debt financing is highly advantageous, and in the extreme a firm's optimal capital structure is 100 per cent debt.

2 A firm's weighted average cost of capital (WACC) decreases as the firm relies more heavily on debt financing.

**B** Proposition II with taxes: The cost of equity, $R_E$, is

$$R_E = R_U + (R_U - R_D) \times (D/E) \times (1 - T_C)$$

where $R_U$ is the *unlevered cost of capital* – that is, the cost of capital for the firm if it has no debt. Unlike the case with Proposition I, the general implications of Proposition II are the same whether there are taxes or not.

**Table 15.6** *Continued*

**EXAMPLE 15.4**

# The Cost of Equity and the Value of the Firm

This is a comprehensive example that illustrates most of the points we have discussed thus far. You are given the following information for Fermat SA:

$$\text{EBIT} = €151.52$$
$$T_C = 0.34$$
$$D = €500$$
$$R_U = 0.20$$

The cost of debt capital is 10 per cent. What is the value of Fermat's equity? What is the cost of equity capital for Fermat? What is the WACC?

This one's easier than it looks. Remember that all the cash flows are perpetuities. The value of the firm if it has no debt, $V_U$, is

$$
V_U = \frac{\text{EBIT} - \text{Taxes}}{R_U}
$$
$$
= \frac{\text{EBIT} \times (1 - T_C)}{R_U}
$$
$$
= \frac{€100}{0.20}
$$
$$
= €500
$$

From M&M Proposition I with taxes we know that the value of the firm with debt is

$$
V_L = V_U + T_C \times D
$$
$$
= €500 + 0.34 \times 500
$$
$$
= €670
$$

Because the firm is worth €670 total, and the debt is worth €500, the equity is worth €170:

$$E = V_L - D$$
$$= €670 - 500$$
$$= €170$$

Based on M&M Proposition II with taxes, the cost of equity is

$$R_E = R_U + (R_U - R_D) \times (D/E) \times (1 - T_C)$$
$$= 0.20 + (0.20 - 0.10) \times (€500/170) \times (1 - 0.34)$$
$$= 39.4\%$$

Finally, the WACC is

$$WACC = (€170/670) \times 39.4\% + (500/670) \times 10\% \times (1 - 0.34)$$
$$= 14.92\%$$

Notice that this is substantially lower than the cost of capital for the firm with no debt ($R_U = 20\%$), so debt financing is highly advantageous.

| | |
|---|---|
| **CONCEPT QUESTIONS** | **15.4a** What is the relationship between the value of an unlevered firm and the value of a levered firm once we consider the effect of corporate taxes? |
| | **15.4b** If we consider only the effect of taxes, what is the optimal capital structure? |

## 15.5 Bankruptcy Costs

One limiting factor affecting the amount of debt a firm might use comes in the form of *bankruptcy costs*. As the debt–equity ratio rises, so too does the probability that the firm will be unable to pay its bondholders what was promised to them. When this happens, ownership of the firm's assets is ultimately transferred from the shareholders to the bondholders.

In principle, a firm becomes bankrupt when the value of its assets equals the value of its debt. When this occurs, the value of equity is zero, and the shareholders turn over control of the firm to the bondholders. When this takes place, the bondholders hold assets whose value is exactly equal to what is owed on the debt. In a perfect world there are no costs associated with this transfer of ownership, and the bondholders don't lose anything.

This idealized view of bankruptcy is not, of course, what happens in the real world. Ironically, it is expensive to go bankrupt. As we discuss, the costs associated with bankruptcy may eventually offset the tax-related gains from leverage.

### Direct Bankruptcy Costs

When the value of a firm's assets equals the value of its debt, then the firm is economically bankrupt in the sense that the equity has no value. However, the formal turning over of the assets to the bondholders is a *legal* process, not an economic one. There are legal and administrative costs to bankruptcy, and it has been remarked that bankruptcies are to lawyers what blood is to sharks.

One of the most well-publicized bankruptcies in recent years concerned Lehman Brothers, at the time one of the biggest banks in the world. This bankruptcy followed large write-downs on subprime mortgage assets and a general collapse in interbank credit in September 2008. *Businessweek* stated:

*The Lehman Brothers bankruptcy is quickly becoming one giant mess.*

*Scores of hedge funds that had hundreds of millions in cash and other securities parked with Lehman's prime brokerage operation in London have had their accounts frozen. A number of these hedge funds have filed formal objections with the bankruptcy court and at least one fund, New York-based Bay Harbour Management, is mounting a legal challenge to the court's hastily approved sale of Lehman's brokerage arm to Barclays Capital.*

*Now a new and even more troubling scenario is arising: legal disputes stemming from the estimated $1 trillion in derivatives transactions that Lehman had entered into on behalf of itself and some of its customers. Already, at least three lawsuits have been filed, alleging that nearly $600 million in collateral posted by some of Lehman's trading partners in derivatives transactions hasn't been returned and is in jeopardy of disappearing as the bankruptcy process unfolds.*

*To date, the most aggrieved of Lehman's trading partners is Bank of America, which at one time was considering buying Lehman as the investment firm was lurching towards bankruptcy. The Charlotte, NC based lender is seeking to recover nearly $500 million the bank 'posted as collateral to "support derivative transactions between BofA and the respective Lehman Entities,"' according to a lawsuit filed in New York State Supreme Court.*[3]

Bankruptcy costs can be absolutely massive with large companies like Lehman Brothers. For example, as of 2009, the direct costs of Enron's bankruptcy (in 2001) included thousands of jobs, more than $60 billion in market value, $2 billion in pension plans, $7.3 billion in compensation, and at least $30 billion of claims still in courts.

Because of the expenses associated with bankruptcy, bondholders won't get all that they are owed. Some fraction of the firm's assets will 'disappear' in the legal process of going bankrupt. These are the legal and administrative expenses associated with the bankruptcy proceeding. We call these costs **direct bankruptcy costs**.

> **direct bankruptcy costs**
> The costs that are directly associated with bankruptcy, such as legal and administrative expenses.

These direct bankruptcy costs are a disincentive to debt financing. If a firm goes bankrupt, then, suddenly, a piece of the firm disappears. This amounts to a bankruptcy 'tax'. So a firm faces a trade-off: borrowing saves a firm money on its corporate taxes, but the more a firm borrows, the more likely it is that the firm will become bankrupt and have to pay the bankruptcy tax.

## Indirect Bankruptcy Costs

Because it is expensive to go bankrupt, a firm will spend resources to avoid doing so. When a firm is having significant problems in meeting its debt obligations, we say that it is experiencing financial distress. Some financially distressed firms ultimately file for bankruptcy, but most do not, because they are able to recover or otherwise survive.

> **indirect bankruptcy costs**
> The costs of avoiding a bankruptcy filing incurred by a financially distressed firm.

The costs of avoiding a bankruptcy filing incurred by a financially distressed firm are called **indirect bankruptcy costs**. We use the term **financial distress costs** to refer generically to the direct and indirect costs associated with going bankrupt or avoiding a bankruptcy filing.

> **financial distress costs**
> The direct and indirect costs associated with going bankrupt or experiencing financial distress.

The problems that come up in financial distress are particularly severe, and the financial distress costs are thus larger, when the shareholders and the bondholders are different groups. Until the firm is legally bankrupt, the shareholders control it. They, of course, will take actions in their own economic interests. Because the shareholders can be wiped out in a legal bankruptcy, they have a very strong incentive to avoid a bankruptcy filing.

The bondholders, on the other hand, are concerned primarily with protecting the value of the firm's assets, and will try to take control away from shareholders. They have a strong incentive to seek bankruptcy to protect their interests and keep shareholders from further dissipating the assets of the firm. The net effect of all this fighting is that a long, drawn-out, and potentially quite expensive legal battle gets started.

Meanwhile, as the wheels of justice turn in their ponderous way, the assets of the firm lose value, because management is busy trying to avoid bankruptcy instead of running the business. Normal operations are disrupted, and sales are lost. Valuable employees leave, potentially fruitful programmes are dropped to preserve cash, and otherwise profitable investments are not taken.

For example, in 2008 many loyal HBOS and Royal Bank of Scotland customers switched to other banks when rumours of the banks' funding situation spread. These buyers questioned whether they would be able to get access to their money were the banks to fail. Sometimes the taint of impending bankruptcy is enough to drive customers away.

These are all indirect bankruptcy costs, or costs of financial distress. Whether or not the firm ultimately goes bankrupt, the net effect is a loss of value because the firm chose to use debt in its capital structure. It is this possibility of loss that limits the amount of debt that a firm will choose to use.

## Agency Costs

When a firm has debt, conflicts of interest arise between shareholders and bondholders. Because of this, shareholders are tempted to pursue selfish strategies. These conflicts of interest, which are magnified when financial distress is incurred, impose agency costs on the firm. We describe three kinds of selfish strategy that shareholders use to hurt the bondholders and help themselves. These strategies are costly, because they will lower the market value of the whole firm.

**Selfish Investment Strategy 1: Incentive to Take Large Risks**   Firms near bankruptcy often take great chances, because they believe that they are playing with someone else's money. To see this, imagine a levered firm considering two mutually exclusive projects, a low-risk one and a high-risk one. There are two equally likely outcomes, recession and boom. The firm is in such dire straits that, should a recession hit, it will come near to bankruptcy with one project and actually fall into bankruptcy with the other. To save themselves and their jobs managers will take the high-risk project, because, irrespective of a recession or boom, the firm will become bankrupt with the low-risk investment. With the high-risk project there is a strong probability the firm will fail, and a very small chance that the firm will survive. Clearly, managers will choose the high-risk project, even though it may not actually have a positive NPV.

Thus financial economists argue that shareholders expropriate value from the bondholders by selecting high-risk projects.

**Selfish Investment Strategy 2: Incentive towards Underinvestment**   Shareholders of a firm with a significant probability of bankruptcy often find that new investment helps the bondholders at the shareholders' expense. The simplest case might be a property owner facing imminent bankruptcy. If he took €100,000 out of his own pocket to refurbish the building, he could increase the building's value by, say, €150,000. Although this investment has a positive net present value, he will turn it down if the increase in value cannot prevent bankruptcy. 'Why,' he asks, 'should I use my own funds to improve the value of a building that the bank will soon repossess?'

The discussion of selfish strategy 2 is quite similar to the discussion of selfish strategy 1. In both cases an investment strategy for the levered firm is different from the one for the unlevered firm. Thus leverage results in distorted investment policy. Whereas the unlevered corporation always chooses projects with positive net present value, the levered firm may deviate from this policy.

**Selfish Investment Strategy 3: Milking the Property**   Another strategy is to pay out extra dividends or other distributions in times of financial distress, leaving less in the firm for the bondholders. This is known as *milking the property*, a phrase taken from real estate. Strategies 2 and 3 are very similar. In Strategy 2 the firm chooses not to raise new equity. Strategy 3 goes one step further, because equity is actually withdrawn through the dividend.

**Summary of Selfish Strategies**   The distortions just discussed occur only when there is a probability of bankruptcy or financial distress. Thus these distortions should not affect, say, Vodafone, because bankruptcy is not a realistic possibility for a diversified, blue-chip firm such as this. In other words, Vodafone's debt will be virtually risk-free, regardless of the projects it accepts. The same argument could be made for nationalized banks, such as the Royal Bank of Scotland, that are protected by the government. By contrast, small firms in risky industries, such as computers, are more likely to experience financial distress and, in turn, to be affected by such distortions.

Who pays for the cost of selfish investment strategies? We argue that it is ultimately the shareholders. Rational bondholders know that when financial distress is imminent, they cannot expect help from shareholders. Rather, shareholders are likely to choose investment strategies that reduce the value of the bonds. Bondholders protect themselves accordingly by raising the interest rate that they require on the bonds. Because the shareholders must pay these high rates, they ultimately bear the costs of selfish strategies. For firms that face these distortions, debt will be difficult and costly to obtain. These firms will have low leverage ratios.

| | | |
|---|---|---|
| **CONCEPT QUESTIONS** | 15.5a | What are direct bankruptcy costs? |
| | 15.5b | What are indirect bankruptcy costs? |
| | 15.5c | Explain what is meant by agency costs. |

# 15.6  Optimal Capital Structure

Our previous two sections have established the basis for determining an optimal capital structure. A firm will borrow because the interest tax shield is valuable. At relatively low debt levels the probability of bankruptcy and financial distress is low, and the benefit from debt outweighs the cost. At very high debt levels the possibility of financial distress is a chronic, ongoing problem for the firm, so the benefit from debt financing may be more than offset by the financial distress costs. Based on our discussion, it would appear that an optimal capital structure exists somewhere in between these extremes.

## The Static Theory of Capital Structure

The theory of capital structure that we have outlined is called the **static theory of capital structure**. It says that firms borrow up to the point where the tax benefit from an extra pound or euro in debt is exactly equal to the cost that comes from the increased probability of financial distress. We call this the static theory because it assumes that the firm is fixed in terms of its assets and operations, and it considers only possible changes in the debt–equity ratio.

The static theory is illustrated in Fig. 15.6, which plots the value of the firm, $V_L$, against the amount of debt, $D$. In Fig. 15.6 we have drawn lines corresponding to three different stories. The first represents M&M Proposition I with no taxes. This is the horizontal line extending from $V_U$, and it indicates that the value of the firm is unaffected by its capital structure. The second case, M&M Proposition I with corporate taxes, is represented by the upward-sloping straight line. These two cases are exactly the same as the ones we previously illustrated in Fig. 15.4.

The third case in Fig. 15.6 illustrates our current discussion: the value of the firm rises to a maximum and then declines beyond that point. This is the picture that we get from our static theory. The maximum value of the firm, $V_L^*$, is reached at $D^*$, so this point represents the optimal amount of borrowing. Put another way, the firm's optimal capital structure is composed of $D^*/V_L^*$ in debt and $1 - D^*/V_L^*$ in equity.

> **static theory of capital structure** The theory that a firm borrows up to the point where the tax benefit from an extra pound or euro in debt is exactly equal to the cost that comes from the increased probability of financial distress.

FIGURE
15.6

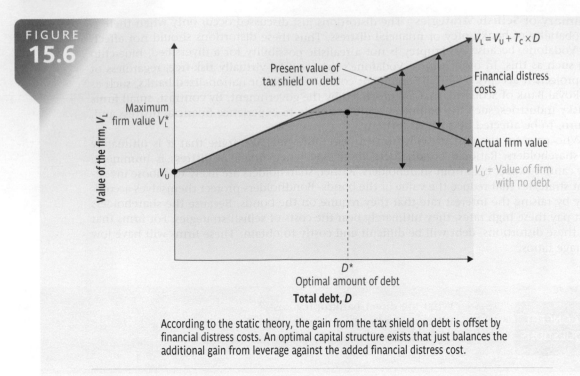

According to the static theory, the gain from the tax shield on debt is offset by financial distress costs. An optimal capital structure exists that just balances the additional gain from leverage against the added financial distress cost.

**Figure 15.6** The static theory of capital structure: the optimal capital structure and the value of the firm

The final thing to notice in Fig. 15.6 is that the difference between the value of the firm in our static theory and the M&M value of the firm with taxes is the loss in value from the possibility of financial distress. Also, the difference between the static theory value of the firm and the M&M value with no taxes is the gain from leverage, net of distress costs.

## Optimal Capital Structure and the Cost of Capital

As we discussed earlier, the capital structure that maximizes the value of the firm is also the one that minimizes the cost of capital. Figure 15.7 illustrates the static theory of capital structure in terms of the weighted average cost of capital and the costs of debt and equity. Notice in Fig. 15.7 that we have plotted the various capital costs against the debt–equity ratio, $D/E$.

Figure 15.7 is much the same as Fig. 15.5 except that we have added a new line for the WACC. This line, which corresponds to the static theory, declines at first. This occurs because the after-tax cost of debt is cheaper than equity, so, at least initially, the overall cost of capital declines.

At some point the cost of debt begins to rise, and the fact that debt is cheaper than equity is more than offset by the financial distress costs. From this point, further increases in debt actually increase the WACC. As illustrated, the minimum WACC* occurs at the point $D*/E*$, just as we described before.

## Optimal Capital Structure: A Recap

With the help of Fig. 15.8 we can review our discussion of capital structure and cost of capital. As we have noted, there are essentially three cases. We shall use the simplest of the three cases as a starting point, and then build up to the static theory of capital structure. Along the way we shall pay particular attention to the connection between capital structure, firm value, and cost of capital.

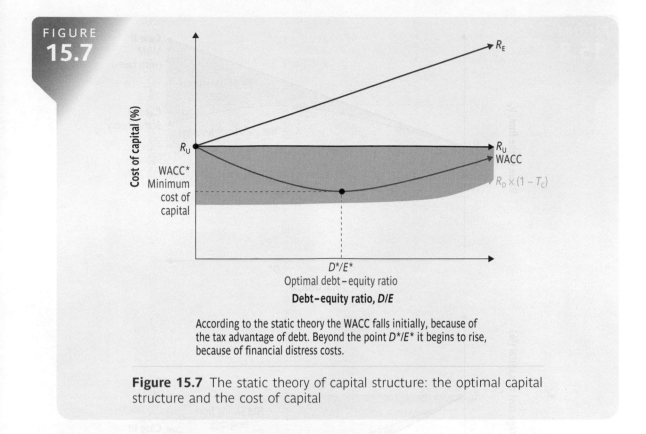

FIGURE
15.7

According to the static theory the WACC falls initially, because of
the tax advantage of debt. Beyond the point $D^*/E^*$ it begins to rise,
because of financial distress costs.

**Figure 15.7** The static theory of capital structure: the optimal capital
structure and the cost of capital

Figure 15.8 presents the original M&M no-tax, no-bankruptcy argument as Case I. This
is the most basic case. In the top part of the figure we have plotted the value of the firm,
$V_L$, against total debt, $D$. When there are no taxes, bankruptcy costs, or other real-world
imperfections, we know that the total value of the firm is not affected by its debt policy,
so $V_L$ is simply constant. The bottom part of Fig. 15.8 tells the same story in terms of the
cost of capital. Here the weighted average cost of capital, WACC, is plotted against the
debt–equity ratio, $D/E$. As with total firm value, the overall cost of capital is not affected
by debt policy in this basic case, so the WACC is constant.

Next we consider what happens to the original M&M argument once taxes are introduced. As Case II illustrates, we now see that the firm's value critically depends on its debt
policy. The more the firm borrows, the more it is worth. From our earlier discussion we
know this happens because interest payments are tax deductible, and the gain in firm value
is just equal to the present value of the interest tax shield.

In the bottom part of Fig. 15.8 notice how the WACC declines as the firm uses more
and more debt financing. As the firm increases its financial leverage, the cost of equity
does increase; but this increase is more than offset by the tax break associated with debt
financing. As a result, the firm's overall cost of capital declines.

To finish our story, we include the impact of bankruptcy or financial distress costs to get
Case III. As shown in the top part of Fig. 15.8, the value of the firm will not be as large as
we previously indicated. The reason is that the firm's value is reduced by the present value of
the potential future bankruptcy costs. These costs grow as the firm borrows more and more,
and they eventually overwhelm the tax advantage of debt financing. The optimal capital
structure occurs at $D^*$, the point at which the tax saving from an additional pound or
euro in debt financing is exactly balanced by the increased bankruptcy costs associated
with the additional borrowing. This is the essence of the static theory of capital structure.

The bottom part of Fig. 15.8 presents the optimal capital structure in terms of the cost
of capital. Corresponding to $D^*$, the optimal debt level, is the optimal debt–equity ratio,
$D^*/E^*$. At this level of debt financing the lowest possible weighted average cost of capital,
WACC*, occurs.

FIGURE
**15.8**

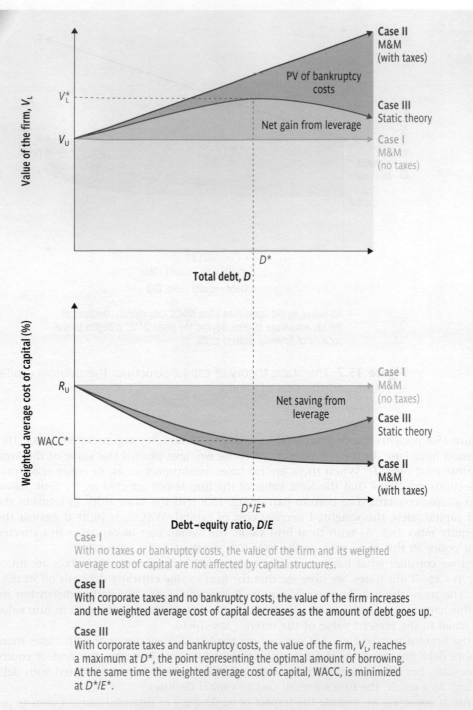

Case II
M&M
(with taxes)

PV of bankruptcy
costs

$V_L^*$

Case III
Static theory

Net gain from leverage

$V_U$

Case I
M&M
(no taxes)

$D^*$

**Total debt, $D$**

Case I
M&M
(no taxes)

Net saving from
leverage

$R_U$

Case III
Static theory

WACC*

$D^*/E^*$

Case II
M&M
(with taxes)

**Debt–equity ratio, $D/E$**

**Case I**
With no taxes or bankruptcy costs, the value of the firm and its weighted
average cost of capital are not affected by capital structures.

**Case II**
With corporate taxes and no bankruptcy costs, the value of the firm increases
and the weighted average cost of capital decreases as the amount of debt goes up.

**Case III**
With corporate taxes and bankruptcy costs, the value of the firm, $V_L$, reaches
a maximum at $D^*$, the point representing the optimal amount of borrowing.
At the same time the weighted average cost of capital, WACC, is minimized
at $D^*/E^*$.

**Figure 15.8** The capital structure question

## Capital Structure: Some Managerial Recommendations

The static model that we have described is not capable of identifying a precise optimal
capital structure, but it does point out two of the more relevant factors: taxes and financial
distress. We can draw some limited conclusions concerning these.

**Taxes**  First of all, the tax benefit from leverage is obviously important only to firms that
are in a tax-paying position. Firms with substantial accumulated losses will get little value

from the interest tax shield. Furthermore, firms that have substantial tax shields from other sources, such as depreciation, will get less benefit from leverage.

Also, not all firms have the same tax rate. The higher the tax rate, the greater the incentive to borrow.

**Financial Distress**  Firms with a greater risk of experiencing financial distress will borrow less than firms with a lower risk of financial distress. For example, all other things being equal, the greater the volatility in EBIT, the less a firm should borrow.

In addition, financial distress is more costly for some firms than for others. The costs of financial distress depend primarily on the firm's assets. In particular, financial distress costs will be determined by how easily ownership of those assets can be transferred.

For example, a firm with mostly tangible assets that can be sold without great loss in value will have an incentive to borrow more. For firms that rely heavily on intangibles, such as employee talent or growth opportunities, debt will be less attractive, because these assets effectively cannot be sold.

**CONCEPT QUESTIONS**

15.6a  Can you describe the trade-off that defines the static theory of capital structure?

15.6b  What are the important factors in making capital structure decisions?

## 15.7  The Pie Again

Although it is comforting to know that the firm might have an optimal capital structure when we take account of such real-world matters as taxes and financial distress costs, it is disquieting to see the elegant original M&M intuition (that is, the no-tax version) fall apart in the face of these matters.

Critics of the M&M theory often say that it fails to hold as soon as we add in real-world issues, and that the M&M theory is really just that: a theory that doesn't have much to say about the real world that we live in. In fact, they would argue that it is the M&M theory that is irrelevant, not capital structure. As we discuss next, however, taking that view blinds critics to the real value of the M&M theory.

### The Extended Pie Model

To illustrate the value of the original M&M intuition, we briefly consider an expanded version of the pie model that we introduced earlier. In the extended pie model taxes just represent another claim on the cash flows of the firm. Because taxes are reduced as leverage is increased, the value of the government's claim (G) on the firm's cash flows decreases with leverage.

Bankruptcy costs are also a claim on the cash flows. They come into play as the firm comes close to bankruptcy and has to alter its behaviour to attempt to stave off the event itself, and they become large when bankruptcy actually takes place. Thus the value of this claim (B) on the cash flows rises with the debt–equity ratio.

The extended pie theory simply holds that all these claims can be paid from only one source: the cash flows (CF) of the firm. Algebraically, we must have

CF = Payments to shareholders + Payments to creditors
+ Payments to the government
+ Payments to bankruptcy courts and lawyers
+ Payments to any and all other claimants to the cash flows of the firm

The extended pie model is illustrated in Fig. 15.9. Notice that we have added a few slices for the additional groups. Notice also the change in the relative sizes of the slices as the firm's use of debt financing is increased.

FIGURE
**15.9**

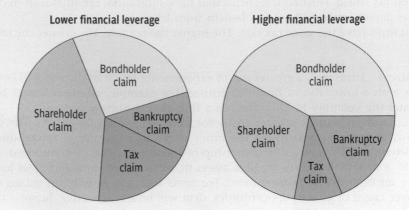

In the extended pie model the value of all the claims against the firm's cash flows is not affected by capital structure, but the *relative* values of claims change as the amount of debt financing is increased.

**Figure 15.9** The extended pie model

With the list we have developed, we have not even begun to exhaust the potential claims on the firm's cash flows. To give an unusual example, we might say that everyone reading this book has an economic claim on the cash flows of Mercedes-Benz. After all, if you are injured in an accident, you might sue Mercedes-Benz, and, win or lose, Mercedes-Benz will expend some of its cash flow in dealing with the matter. For Mercedes-Benz, or any other company, there should thus be a slice of the pie representing potential lawsuits. This is the essence of the M&M intuition and theory: the value of the firm depends on the total cash flow of the firm. The firm's capital structure just cuts that cash flow up into slices without altering the total. What we recognize now is that the shareholders and the bondholders may not be the only ones who can claim a slice.

## Marketed Claims versus Non-Marketed Claims

With our extended pie model there is an important distinction between claims such as those of shareholders and bondholders, on the one hand, and those of the government and potential litigants in lawsuits on the other. The first set of claims are *marketed claims*, and the second set are *non-marketed claims*. A key difference is that the marketed claims can be bought and sold in financial markets, but the non-marketed claims cannot.

When we speak of the value of the firm, we are generally referring to just the value of the marketed claims, $V_M$, and not the value of the non-marketed claims, $V_N$. If we write $V_T$ for the total value of *all* the claims against a corporation's cash flows, then

$$V_T = E + D + G + B + \cdots$$
$$= V_M + V_N$$

The essence of our extended pie model is that this total value, $V_T$, of all the claims to the firm's cash flows is unaltered by capital structure. However, the value of the marketed claims, $V_M$, may be affected by changes in the capital structure.

Based on the pie theory, any increase in $V_M$ must imply an identical decrease in $V_N$. The optimal capital structure is thus the one that maximizes the value of the marketed claims or, equivalently, minimizes the value of non-marketed claims such as taxes and bankruptcy costs.

| CONCEPT QUESTIONS | | |
|---|---|---|
| | 15.7a | What are some of the claims on a firm's cash flows? |
| | 15.7b | What is the difference between a marketed claim and a non-marketed claim? |
| | 15.7c | What does the extended pie model say about the value of all the claims on a firm's cash flows? |

# 15.8 Signalling

The previous section pointed out that the corporate leverage decision involves a trade-off between a tax subsidy and financial distress costs. This idea was graphed in Fig. 15.8, where the marginal tax subsidy of debt exceeds the distress costs of debt for low levels of debt. The reverse holds for high levels of debt. The firm's capital structure is optimized where the marginal subsidy to debt equals the marginal cost.

Let's explore this idea a little more. What is the relationship between a company's profitability and its debt level? A firm with low anticipated profits will probably take on a low level of debt. A small interest deduction is all that is needed to offset all of this firm's pre-tax profits. And too much debt would raise the firm's expected distress costs. A more successful firm would probably take on more debt. This firm could use the extra interest to reduce the taxes from its greater earnings. Being more financially secure, this firm would find its extra debt increasing the risk of bankruptcy only slightly. In other words, rational firms raise debt levels (and the concomitant interest payments) when profits are expected to increase.

How do investors react to an increase in debt? Rational investors are likely to infer a higher firm value from a higher debt level. Thus these investors are likely to bid up a firm's share price after the firm has, say, issued debt in order to buy back equity. We say that investors view debt as a signal of firm value.

Now we get to the incentives of managers to fool the public. Consider a firm whose level of debt is optimal. That is, the marginal tax benefit of debt exactly equals the marginal distress costs of debt. However, imagine that the firm's manager desires to increase the firm's current share price, perhaps because he knows that many of his shareholders want to sell their equity soon. This manager might want to increase the level of debt just to make investors think that the firm is more valuable than it really is. If the strategy works, investors will push up the price of the shares.

This implies that firms can fool investors by taking on some additional leverage. Now let's ask the big question. Are there benefits to extra debt but no costs, implying that all firms will take on as much debt as possible? The answer, fortunately, is that there are costs as well. Imagine that a firm has issued extra debt just to fool the public. At some point the market will learn that the company is not that valuable after all. At this time the share price should actually fall below what it would have been had the debt never been increased. Why? Because the firm's debt level is now above the optimal level. That is, the marginal tax benefit of debt is below the marginal cost of debt. Thus if the current shareholders plan to sell, say, half of their shares now and retain the other half, an increase in debt will help them on immediate sales but probably hurt them on later ones.

Now here is the important point: we said that in a world where managers do not attempt to fool investors, valuable firms issue more debt than less valuable ones. It turns out that even when managers attempt to fool investors, the more valuable firms will still want to issue more debt than the less valuable firms. That is, while all firms will increase debt levels somewhat to fool investors, the costs of extra debt prevent the less valuable firms from issuing more debt than the more valuable firms issue. Thus investors can still treat debt level as a signal of firm value. In other words, investors can still view an announcement of debt as a positive sign for the firm.

The foregoing is a simplified example of debt signalling, and you might argue that it is too simplified. For example, perhaps the shareholders of some firms want to sell most of their equity immediately, whereas the shareholders of other firms want to sell only a little of theirs now. It is impossible to tell here whether the firms with the most debt are the most valuable, or merely the ones with the most impatient shareholders. Because other objections can be brought up as well, signalling theory is best validated by empirical evidence. Fortunately, the empirical evidence tends to support the theory.

15.8a What is meant by signalling?
15.8b Why would managers wish to fool investors if, by doing so, they run the risk of getting discovered?

## 15.9 The Pecking-Order Theory

The static theory we have developed in this chapter has dominated thinking about capital structure for a long time, but it has some shortcomings. Perhaps the most obvious is that many large, financially sophisticated, and highly profitable firms use little debt. This is the opposite of what we would expect. Under the static theory these are the firms that should use the *most* debt, because there is little risk of bankruptcy and the value of the tax shield is substantial. Why do they use so little debt? The pecking-order theory, which we consider next, may be part of the answer.

### Internal Financing and the Pecking Order

The pecking-order theory is an alternative to the static theory. A key element in the pecking-order theory is that firms prefer to use internal financing whenever possible. A simple reason is that selling securities to raise cash can be expensive, so it makes sense to avoid doing so if possible. If a firm is very profitable, it might never need external financing: so it would end up with little or no debt. For example, in early 2010 Google's balance sheet showed assets of $40.5 billion, of which almost $24.5 billion was classified as either cash or marketable securities. In fact, Google held so much of its assets in the form of securities that, at one point, it was in danger of being regulated as a mutual fund!

There is a more subtle reason why companies may prefer internal financing. Suppose you are the manager of a firm, and you need to raise external capital to fund a new venture. As an insider, you are privy to a lot of information that isn't known to the public. Based on your knowledge, the firm's future prospects are considerably brighter than outside investors realize. As a result, you think your equity is currently undervalued. Should you issue debt or equity to finance the new venture?

If you think about it, you definitely don't want to issue equity in this case. The reason is that your equity is undervalued, and you don't want to sell it too cheaply. So you issue debt instead.

Would you ever want to issue equity? Suppose you thought your firm's equity was overvalued. It makes sense to raise money at inflated prices, but a problem crops up. If you try to sell equity, investors will realize that the shares are probably overvalued, and your equity price will take a hit. In other words, if you try to raise money by selling equity, you run the risk of signalling to investors that the price is too high. In fact, in the real world, companies rarely sell new equity, and the market reacts negatively to such sales when they occur.

So we have a pecking order. Companies will use internal financing first. Then they will issue debt if necessary. Equity will be sold pretty much as a last resort.

### Implications of the Pecking Order

The pecking-order theory has several significant implications, a couple of which are at odds with our static trade-off theory:

1   *No target capital structure*: Under the pecking-order theory there is no target or optimal debt–equity ratio. Instead, a firm's capital structure is determined by its need for external financing, which dictates the amount of debt the firm will have.

2   *Profitable firms use less debt*: Because profitable firms have greater internal cash flow, they will need less external financing, and will therefore have less debt. As we mentioned earlier, this is a pattern that we seem to observe, at least for some companies.

3   *Companies will want financial slack*: To avoid selling new equity, companies will want to stockpile internally generated cash. Such a cash reserve is known as *financial slack*. It gives management the ability to finance projects as they appear, and to move quickly if necessary.

Which theory, static trade-off or pecking order, is correct? Financial researchers have not reached a definitive conclusion on this issue, but we can make a few observations. The trade-off theory speaks more to long-run financial goals or strategies. The issues of tax shields and financial distress costs are plainly important in that context. The pecking-order theory is concerned more with the shorter-run, tactical issue of raising external funds to finance investments. So both theories are useful ways of understanding corporate use of debt. For example, it is probably the case that firms have long-run, target capital structures, but it is also probably true that they will deviate from those long-run targets as needed to avoid issuing new equity.

| | |
|---|---|
| **CONCEPT QUESTIONS** | **15.9a** Under the pecking-order theory, what is the order in which firms will obtain financing?<br>**15.9b** Why might firms prefer not to issue new equity?<br>**15.9c** What are some differences in implications of the static and pecking-order theories? |

## 15.10  Observed Capital Structures

No two firms have identical capital structures. Nonetheless, we see some regular elements when we start looking at actual capital structures. We discuss a few of these next.

The most striking thing we observe about European capital structures is that they are so varied across countries. Most corporations use much less debt financing than equity financing. To illustrate, Fig. 15.10 shows the debt-to-equity ratios of firms in different European countries in recent years.

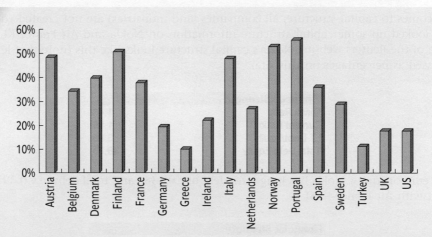

FIGURE **15.10**

*Source*: J.P.H. Fan, S. Titman and G. Twite, 'An international comparison of capital structure and debt maturity choices' (2006), working paper

**Figure 15.10** Estimated ratios of debt to equity, various European countries

TABLE
15.7

| Debt to asset ratios | Germany | The Netherlands | United Kingdom |
|---|---|---|---|
| Consumer goods | 22.10 | 25.18 | 20.52 |
| Consumer services | 22.34 | 22.98 | 26.83 |
| Financials | 43.30 | 31.80 | 25.13 |
| Healthcare | 20.94 | 20.20 | 13.00 |
| Industrial | 22.32 | 23.42 | 20.65 |
| Materials | 20.04 | 26.08 | 20.18 |
| Oil and gas | 13.19 | 24.74 | 15.90 |
| Technology | 11.88 | 18.55 | 10.74 |
| Telecommunication | 16.50 | 32.84 | 26.49 |
| Utility | 13.39 | 29.71 | 34.09 |

*Source*: Adapted from Thomson Reuters, www.thomsonreuters.com.

**Table 15.7** Average capital structure ratios for various industries in Germany, the Netherlands and the United Kingdom, 1998–2007

There are also significant inter-industry differences in debt ratios that persist over time. As can be seen in Table 15.7, debt–asset ratios tend to be quite low in high-growth industries, such as the healthcare and technology industries, with ample future investment opportunities. This is true even when the need for external financing is great. Industries with large investments in tangible assets, such as real estate, tend to have high leverage. Consistent with Fig. 15.10, there are also differences in average industry capital structures across countries.

Table 15.7 makes it clear that corporations have not, in general, issued debt up to the point where tax shelters have been completely used up, and we conclude that there must be limits to the amount of debt corporations can use. Take a look at our nearby Work the Web box for more about actual capital structures.

# Work the Web

When it comes to capital structure, all companies (and industries) are not created equal. To illustrate, we looked up some capital structure information on Nokia and Air France-KLM using the Ratio area of the Reuters website. Nokia's capital structure looks like this (note that leverage ratios are expressed as percentages on this site):

| Financial Strength | |
|---|---|
| Quick Ratio | 1.43 |
| Current Ratio | 1.55 |
| LT Debt/Equity | 33.86 |
| Total Debt/Equity | 39.75 |

For every euro of equity, Nokia has long-term debt of €0.3386 and total debt of €0.3975. Compare this result with Air France-KLM:

| Financial Strength | |
|---|---|
| Quick Ratio | 0.66 |
| Current Ratio | 0.79 |
| LT Debt/Equity | 156.83 |
| Total Debt/Equity | 189.61 |

For every euro of equity, Air France-KLM has €1.5683 of long-term debt and total debt of €1.8961. When we examine the industry and sector averages, the differences are again apparent. Although the choice of capital structure is a management decision, it is clearly influenced by industry characteristics.

## QUESTIONS

1 The ratios shown for these companies were based on March 2010 figures. Go to www.reuters. com and find the current long-term debt-to-equity and total debt-to-equity ratios for both Nokia and Air France-KLM. How have these ratios changed over this time?

2 Go to www.reuters.com and find the long-term debt-to-equity and total debt-to-equity ratios for Barclays, ICI and BSkyB. Why do you think these three companies use different amounts of debt?

Because different industries have different operating characteristics in terms of, for example, EBIT volatility and asset types, there does appear to be some connection between these characteristics and capital structure. Our story involving tax savings, financial distress costs and potential pecking orders undoubtedly supplies part of the reason, but to date there is no fully satisfactory theory that explains these regularities in capital structures.

As can be seen in Fig. 15.11, the great majority of European firms across countries have a target debt–equity ratio, though the strictness of the targets varies across companies. A notable exception to this is in France, where most firms do not pursue a target debt ratio. Even in the UK, nearly half of all firms do not consider a target debt ratio to be important.

**CONCEPT QUESTIONS**

15.10a  Do European corporations rely heavily on debt financing?
15.10b  What regularities do we observe in capital structures?

FIGURE 15.11

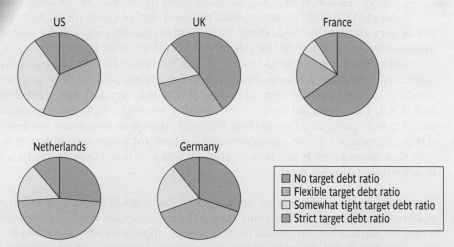

Legend:
- No target debt ratio
- Flexible target debt ratio
- Somewhat tight target debt ratio
- Strict target debt ratio

*Source*: Figure 1 of D. Brounen, A. de Jong and K. Koedijk, 'Capital structure policies in Europe: survey evidence', *Journal of Banking and Finance* (2006), vol. 30, no. 5, pp. 1409–1442

**Figure 15.11** Survey results on the use of target debt–equity ratios

## 15.11 A Quick Look at the Bankruptcy Process

As we have discussed, one consequence of using debt is the possibility of financial distress, which can be defined in several ways:

1  *Business failure*: This term is usually used to refer to a situation in which a business has terminated with a loss to creditors; but even an all-equity firm can fail.

2  *Legal bankruptcy*: Firms or creditors bring petitions to a court for bankruptcy. **Bankruptcy** is a legal proceeding for liquidating or reorganizing a business.

3  *Technical insolvency*: Technical insolvency occurs when a firm is unable to meet its financial obligations.

4  *Accounting insolvency*: Firms with negative net worth are insolvent on the books. This happens when the total book liabilities exceed the book value of the total assets.

We now very briefly discuss some of the terms and more relevant issues associated with bankruptcy and financial distress.

**bankruptcy**
A legal proceeding for liquidating or reorganizing a business.

**liquidation**
Termination of the firm as a going concern.

**reorganization**
Financial restructuring of a failing firm to attempt to continue operations as a going concern.

### Liquidation and Reorganization

Firms that cannot or choose not to make contractually required payments to creditors have two basic options: liquidation or reorganization. **Liquidation** means termination of the firm as a going concern, and it involves selling off the assets of the firm. The proceeds, net of selling costs, are distributed to creditors in order of established priority. **Reorganization** is the option of keeping the firm a going concern; it often involves issuing new securities to replace old securities. Liquidation or reorganization is the result of a bankruptcy proceeding. Which occurs depends on whether the firm is worth more 'dead or alive'.

### Bankruptcy Law

Bankruptcy law across the world is converging to a similar process. However, there are important country-level differences. The European Union introduced its bankruptcy regulation in 2002, 'Regulation on Insolvency Proceedings', which has been adopted by all EU countries, with the exception of Denmark. As European bankruptcy law is very similar, the regulations facing British bankruptcy will be discussed in detail, followed by an overview of the salient differences in other countries.

Financially distressed firms in the UK can be voluntarily or compulsorily dissolved or liquidated. Liquidation means that the firm's assets are sold to allow payment of the outstanding liabilities of the firm. However, this is the very last and least desirable option, and it will be considered only when all other strategies have been exhausted. An alternative is to appoint an administrator, who will attempt to restructure the firm's outstanding claims, introduce a viable business model, or look for a potential buyer. It is important to note that when a firm is in administration, it will continue business until a solution (which may be liquidation) is found.

**Liquidation**  For a firm to be liquidated or made insolvent, a creditor, the directors, or shareholders must petition a court for a winding-up order. If a judge decides that there is a case for liquidation, an official receiver will be appointed who liquidates the assets of the firm and distributes the proceeds to all creditors. Normally, creditors will not be paid all that they are due, because of direct bankruptcy costs from legal and administration fees.

**Priority of Claims**  Once a corporation is determined to be bankrupt, liquidation takes place. The distribution of the proceeds of the liquidation occurs according to the following general priority:

1 Administration expenses associated with liquidating the bankrupt's assets

2 Unsecured claims arising after the filing of an involuntary bankruptcy petition

3 Wages, salaries and commissions

4 Contributions to employee benefit plans arising within a set period before the filing date

5 Consumer claims

6 Tax claims

7 Secured and unsecured creditors' claims

8 Preference shareholder claims

9 Ordinary shareholder claims

The priority rule in liquidation is known as the **absolute priority rule (APR)**.

One qualification to this list concerns secured creditors. Liens on property are outside APR ordering. However, if the secured property is liquidated, and provides cash insufficient to cover the amount owed them, the secured creditors join with unsecured creditors in dividing the remaining liquidating value. In contrast, if the secured property is liquidated for proceeds greater than the secured claim, the net proceeds are used to pay unsecured creditors and others.

> **absolute priority rule** The order of creditor claims distribution in the event of a liquidation.

**Administration**   When a company enters administration, the administrator will attempt to restructure the company's liabilities, look for a buyer, or break up the company into viable parts. Possible strategies also include exchanging debt for equity, which allows the financially distressed firm to dispense with paying interest on debt and at the same time gives the creditor a stake in the company should it recover.

The legal agreement that details how the firm's liabilities are to be restructured is known as a *company voluntary agreement* (CVA). If creditors reject the CVA, or the company does not submit a CVA to the court, the judge can give the corporation an extension during which it must come up with an acceptable plan or ask the creditors to come up with their own reorganization plan. In most cases at least one extension is granted. Under UK bankruptcy law a CVA will be accepted if at least 75 per cent of the company's claimholders, including shareholders, vote in favour of it. Once accepted, the agreement is legally binding.

In Scotland, bankruptcy law is slightly more complex. In addition to administration and insolvency procedures, firms may also go into receivership. This is also a characteristic of bankruptcy law in England and Wales for firms that have outstanding securities issued before 2003. The differences between administration and receivership are important. When in administration, the financially distressed firm is legally protected from its creditors while a CVA is prepared. An insolvency practitioner, such as an accounting firm, is normally appointed to run the business while the agreement is being drawn up. A firm will go into receivership if its creditors do not believe that the company can recover and repay its liabilities. A receiver, again normally an accounting firm, will thus be appointed to sell the assets of the firm so that the creditors can be paid.

**Bankruptcy in Other Countries**   Bankruptcy procedures in most countries follow the same model as that in the United Kingdom. In the United States, financially distressed firms may file for Chapter 11 bankruptcy (equivalent to administration) or for Chapter 7 bankruptcy (equivalent to liquidation). All other aspects of the system are practically the same.

Countries in the European Union follow the 2002 'Regulation on Insolvency Proceedings'. Some country-level differences do exist, however. Under Spanish insolvency law a creditors' meeting is organized to form a CVA, and if it is not possible to come to an agreement, the firm will be liquidated. France has a three-stage process. The first stage involves pre-insolvency hearings, which can occur if the firm's auditor is concerned about the financial health of the firm. If the hearings cannot resolve the auditor's concerns, a petition will be made to a commercial court. The firm may at this point request a three-month window to draw up a CVA that will be acceptable to all parties. If this is unsuccessful, the firm will be wound up. Finally, although South Africa follows a similar system to other countries, there is no administration process. Thus creditors, shareholders or the company itself will go directly to the South African

High Court to request that the firm be placed in liquidation. The process is then worked through the system, and restructuring or winding-up may be an outcome of this process.

15.11a  What is the APR?
15.11b  What is the difference between liquidation and reorganization?

# Summary and Conclusions

The ideal mixture of debt and equity for a firm – its optimal capital structure – is the one that maximizes the value of the firm and minimizes the overall cost of capital. If we ignore taxes, financial distress costs, and any other imperfections, we find that there is no ideal mixture. Under these circumstances the firm's capital structure is simply irrelevant.

If we consider the effect of corporate taxes, we find that capital structure matters a great deal. This conclusion is based on the fact that interest is tax deductible, and thus generates a valuable tax shield. Unfortunately, we also find that the optimal capital structure is 100 per cent debt, which is not something we observe in healthy firms.

We next introduced costs associated with bankruptcy or, more generally, financial distress. These costs reduce the attractiveness of debt financing. We concluded that an optimal capital structure exists when the net tax saving from an additional pound or euro in interest just equals the increase in expected financial distress costs. This is the essence of the static theory of capital structure.

We also considered the pecking-order theory of capital structure as an alternative to the static trade-off theory. This theory suggests that firms will use internal financing as much as possible, followed by debt financing if needed. Equity will not be issued if possible. As a result, a firm's capital structure just reflects its historical needs for external financing, so there is no optimal capital structure.

When we examine actual capital structures, we find two regularities. First, firms in Europe typically do not use great amounts of debt, but they pay substantial taxes. This suggests that there is a limit to the use of debt financing to generate tax shields. Second, firms in similar industries tend to have similar capital structures, suggesting that the nature of their assets and operations is an important determinant of capital structure.

# Chapter Review and Self-Test Problems

15.1  **EBIT and EPS**  Suppose Blackhead plc has decided in favour of a capital restructuring that involves increasing its existing £80 million in debt to £125 million. The interest rate on the debt is 9 per cent, and is not expected to change. The firm currently has 10 million shares outstanding, and the share price is £45. If the restructuring is expected to increase the ROE, what is the minimum level for EBIT that BDJ's management must be expecting? Ignore taxes in your answer.

15.2  **M&M Proposition II (No Taxes)**  Habitat has a WACC of 16 per cent. Its cost of debt is 13 per cent. If Habitat's debt–equity ratio is 2, what is its cost of equity capital? Ignore taxes in your answer.

15.3  **M&M Proposition I (with Corporate Taxes)**  Gypco expects an EBIT of €10,000 every year for ever. Gypco can borrow at 7 per cent. Suppose Gypco currently has no debt, and its cost of equity is 17 per cent. If the corporate tax rate is 35 per cent, what is the value of the firm? What will the value be if Gypco borrows €15,000 and uses the proceeds to repurchase equity?

# Answers to Chapter Review and Self-Test Problems

15.1 To answer, we can calculate the break-even EBIT. At any EBIT above this the increased financial leverage will increase EPS. Under the old capital structure the interest bill is £80 million × 0.09 = £7,200,000. There are 10 million shares of equity: so, ignoring taxes, EPS is (EBIT − £7.2 million)/10 million.

Under the new capital structure the interest expense will be £125 million × 0.09 = £11.25 million. Furthermore, the debt rises by £45 million. This amount is sufficient to repurchase £45 million/£45 = 1 million shares of equity, leaving 9 million outstanding. EPS is thus (EBIT − £11.25 million)/9 million.

Now that we know how to calculate EPS under both scenarios, we set the two calculations equal to each other and solve for the break-even EBIT:

$$(\text{EBIT} − £7.2 \text{ million})/10 \text{ million} = (\text{EBIT} − £11.25 \text{ million})/9 \text{ million}$$
$$\text{EBIT} − £7.2 \text{ million} = 1.11 \times (\text{EBIT} − £11.25 \text{ million})$$
$$\text{EBIT} = £47,700,000$$

Verify that, in either case, EPS is £4.05 when EBIT is £47.7 million.

15.2 According to M&M Proposition II (no taxes), the cost of equity is

$$R_E = R_A + (R_A − R_D) \times (D/E)$$
$$= 16\% + (16\% − 13\%) \times 2$$
$$= 22\%$$

15.3 With no debt, Gypco's WACC is 17 per cent. This is also the unlevered cost of capital. The after-tax cash flow is €10,000 × (1 − 0.35) = €6,500, so the value is just $V_U$ = €6,500/0.17 = €38,235.

After the debt issue, Gypco will be worth the original €38,235 plus the present value of the tax shield. According to M&M Proposition I with taxes, the present value of the tax shield is $T_C \times D$, or 0.35 × €15,000 = €5,250: so the firm is worth €38,235 + 5,250 = €43,485.

# Concepts Review and Critical Thinking Questions

1 **Business Risk versus Financial Risk [LO1]** Explain what is meant by *business risk* and *financial risk*. Suppose Firm A has greater business risk than Firm B. Is it true that Firm A also has a higher cost of equity capital? Explain.

2 **M&M Propositions [LO1]** How would you answer in the following debate?

Q: Isn't it true that the riskiness of a firm's equity will rise if the firm increases its use of debt financing?

A: Yes, that's the essence of M&M Proposition II.

Q: And isn't it true that, as a firm increases its use of borrowing, the likelihood of default increases, thereby increasing the risk of the firm's debt?

A: Yes.

Q: In other words, increased borrowing increases the risk of the equity *and* the debt?

A: That's right.

Q: Well, given that the firm uses only debt and equity financing, and given that the risks of both are increased by increased borrowing, does it not follow that increasing debt increases the overall risk of the firm and therefore decreases the value of the firm?

A: ??

3 **Optimal Capital Structure [LO1]** Is there an easily identifiable debt–equity ratio that will maximize the value of a firm? Why or why not?

4 **Observed Capital Structures [LO1]** Refer to the observed capital structures given in Table 15.7 of the text. What do you notice about the types of industry with respect to their average debt–equity ratios? Are certain types of industry more likely to be highly leveraged than others? What are some possible reasons for this observed segmentation? Do the operating results and tax history of the firms play a role? How about their future earnings prospects? Explain.

5 **Financial Leverage [LO1]** Why is the use of debt financing referred to as financial 'leverage'?

6 **Homemade Leverage [LO1]** What is homemade leverage?

7 **Bankruptcy and Corporate Ethics [LO3]** Some firms have filed for bankruptcy because of actual or likely litigation-related losses. Is this a proper use of the bankruptcy process?

8 **Bankruptcy and Corporate Ethics [LO3]** Firms sometimes use the threat of a bankruptcy filing to force creditors to renegotiate terms. Critics argue that in such cases the firm is using bankruptcy laws 'as a sword rather than a shield'. Is this an ethical tactic?

9 **Bankruptcy and Corporate Ethics [LO3]** Consider a company that files for bankruptcy as a means of reducing labour costs. Is this ethical? Give both sides of the argument.

10 **Capital Structure Goal [LO1]** What is the basic goal of financial management with regard to capital structure?

## connect Questions and Problems

**BASIC**

**1–15**

1 **EBIT and Leverage [LO1]** Geld NV has no debt outstanding, and a total market value of €150,000. Earnings before interest and taxes, EBIT, are projected to be €14,000 if economic conditions are normal. If there is strong expansion in the economy, then EBIT will be 30 per cent higher. If there is a recession, then EBIT will be 60 per cent lower. Geld is considering a €60,000 debt issue with a 5 per cent interest rate. The proceeds will be used to repurchase shares of equity. There are currently 2,500 shares outstanding. Ignore taxes for this problem.

(a) Calculate earnings per share, EPS, under each of the three economic scenarios before any debt is issued. Also calculate the percentage changes in EPS when the economy expands or enters a recession.

(b) Repeat part (a) assuming that Geld goes through with recapitalization. What do you observe?

2 **EBIT, Taxes and Leverage [LO2]** Repeat parts (a) and (b) in Problem 1 assuming Geld has a tax rate of 20 per cent.

3 **ROE and Leverage [LO1, LO2]** Suppose the company in Problem 1 has a market-to-book ratio of 1.0.

(a) Calculate return on equity (ROE) under each of the three economic scenarios before any debt is issued. Also calculate the percentage changes in ROE for economic expansion and recession, assuming no taxes.

(b) Repeat part (a) assuming the firm goes through with the proposed recapitalization.

(c) Repeat parts (a) and (b) of this problem assuming the firm has a tax rate of 20 per cent.

4  **Break-Even EBIT [LO1]**   Rolston plc is comparing two different capital structures: an all-equity plan (Plan I) and a levered plan (Plan II). Under Plan I Rolston would have 150,000 shares of equity outstanding. Under Plan II there would be 60,000 shares of equity outstanding and £1.5 million in debt outstanding. The interest rate on the debt is 10 per cent, and there are no taxes.

   (a)  If EBIT is £200,000, which plan will result in the higher EPS?

   (b)  If EBIT is £700,000, which plan will result in the higher EPS?

   (c)  What are the break-even EBIT?

5  **M&M and Equity Value [LO1]**   In Problem 4 use M&M Proposition I to find the share price under each of the two proposed plans. What is the value of the firm?

6  **Break-Even EBIT and Leverage [LO1, LO2]**   Kolby SpA is comparing two different capital structures. Plan I would result in 1,100 shares of equity and €16,500 in debt. Plan II would result in 900 shares of equity and €27,500 in debt. The interest rate on the debt is 10 per cent.

   (a)  Ignoring taxes, compare both of these plans with an all-equity plan assuming that EBIT will be €10,000. The all-equity plan would result in 1,400 shares of equity outstanding. Which of the three plans has the highest EPS? The lowest?

   (b)  In part (a) what are the break-even levels of EBIT for each plan as compared with that for an all-equity plan? Is one higher than the other? Why?

   (c)  Ignoring taxes, when will EPS be identical for Plans I and II?

   (d)  Repeat parts (a), (b) and (c) assuming that the corporate tax rate is 31.4 per cent. Are the break-even levels of EBIT different from before? Why or why not?

7  **Leverage and Equity Value [LO1]**   Ignoring taxes in Problem 6, what is the share price under Plan I? Plan II? What principle is illustrated by your answers?

8  **Homemade Leverage [LO1]**   Star plc, a prominent consumer products firm, is debating whether or not to convert its all-equity capital structure to one that is 40 per cent debt. Currently there are 2,000 shares outstanding, and the share price is £70. EBIT is expected to remain at £16,000 per year for ever. The interest rate on new debt is 8 per cent, and there are no taxes.

   (a)  Ms Brown, a shareholder of the firm, owns 100 shares of equity. What is her cash flow under the current capital structure, assuming the firm has a dividend payout rate of 100 per cent?

   (b)  What will Ms Brown's cash flow be under the proposed capital structure of the firm? Assume that she keeps all 100 of her shares.

   (c)  Suppose Star does convert, but Ms Brown prefers the current all-equity capital structure. Show how she could unlever her shares to recreate the original capital structure.

   (d)  Using your answer to part (c), explain why Star's choice of capital structure is irrelevant.

9  **Homemade Leverage and WACC [LO1]**   ABC AG and XYZ AG are identical firms in all respects except for their capital structure. ABC is all equity financed, with NKr600,000 in equity shares. XYZ uses both shares and perpetual debt; its equity is worth NKr300,000, and the interest rate on its debt is 10 per cent. Both firms expect EBIT to be NKr73,000. Ignore taxes.

   (a)  Knut owns NKr30,000 worth of XYZ's shares. What rate of return is he expecting?

   (b)  Show how Knut could generate exactly the same cash flows and rate of return by investing in ABC and using homemade leverage.

(c) What is the cost of equity for ABC? What is it for XYZ?

(d) What is the WACC for ABC? For XYZ? What principle have you illustrated?

10 **M&M [LO1]** Nina plc uses no debt. The weighted average cost of capital is 13 per cent. If the current market value of the equity is £35 million, and there are no taxes, what is EBIT?

11 **M&M and Taxes [LO2]** In the previous problem, suppose the corporate tax rate is 28 per cent. What is EBIT in this case? What is the WACC? Explain.

12 **Calculating WACC [LO1]** Weston Industries has a debt–equity ratio of 1.5. Its WACC is 12 per cent, and its cost of debt is 12 per cent. The corporate tax rate is 35 per cent.

(a) What is Weston's cost of equity capital?

(b) What is Weston's unlevered cost of equity capital?

(c) What would the cost of equity be if the debt–equity ratio were 2? What if it were 1.0? What if it were zero?

13 **Calculating WACC [LO1]** Shadow plc has no debt, but can borrow at 8 per cent. The firm's WACC is currently 12 per cent, and the tax rate is 28 per cent.

(a) What is Shadow's cost of equity?

(b) If the firm converts to 25 per cent debt, what will its cost of equity be?

(c) If the firm converts to 50 per cent debt, what will its cost of equity be?

(d) What is Shadow's WACC in part (b)? In part (c)?

14 **M&M and Taxes [LO2]** Bruce & Co. expects its EBIT to be £95,000 every year for ever. The firm can borrow at 11 per cent. Bruce currently has no debt, and its cost of equity is 22 per cent. If the tax rate is 28 per cent, what is the value of the firm? What will the value be if Bruce borrows £60,000 and uses the proceeds to repurchase shares?

15 **M&M and Taxes [LO2]** In Problem 14, what is the cost of equity after recapitalization? What is the WACC? What are the implications for the firm's capital structure decision?

16 **M&M [LO2]** Tool Manufacturing has an expected EBIT of £35,000 in perpetuity and a tax rate of 28 per cent. The firm has £70,000 in outstanding debt at an interest rate of 9 per cent, and its unlevered cost of capital is 14 per cent. What is the value of the firm according to M&M Proposition I with taxes? Should Tool change its debt–equity ratio if the goal is to maximize the value of the firm? Explain.

17 **Firm Value [LO2]** Old School Corporation expects an EBIT of £9,000 every year for ever. Old School currently has no debt, and its cost of equity is 17 per cent. The firm can borrow at 10 per cent. If the corporate tax rate is 28 per cent, what is the value of the firm? What will the value be if Old School converts to 50 per cent debt? To 100 per cent debt?

18 **Homemade Leverage [LO1]** The Veblen Company and the Knight Company are identical in every respect except that Veblen is not levered. The market value of Knight Company's 6 per cent bonds is SKr1 million. Financial information for the two firms appears here. All earnings streams are perpetuities. Neither firm pays taxes. Both firms distribute all earnings available to ordinary shareholders immediately.

|  | Veblen | Knight |
|---|---|---|
| Projected operating income (SKr) | 300,000 | 300,000 |
| Year-end interest on debt (SKr) | – | 60,000 |
| Market value of stock (SKr) | 2,400,000 | 1,714,000 |
| Market value of debt (SKr) | – | 1,000,000 |

**INTERMEDIATE**

**16–18**

(a) An investor who can borrow at 6 per cent per year wishes to purchase 5 per cent of Knight's equity. Can he increase his kroner return by purchasing 5 per cent of Veblen's equity if he borrows so that the initial net costs of the two strategies are the same?

(b) Given the two investment strategies in (a), which will investors choose? When will this process cease?

**CHALLENGE**
**19–22**

19 **Weighted Average Cost of Capital [LO1]**   In a world of corporate taxes only, show that the WACC can be written as WACC = $R_U \times [1 - T_C(D/V)]$.

20 **Cost of Equity and Leverage [LO1]**   Assuming a world of corporate taxes only, show that the cost of equity, $R_E$, is as given in the chapter by M&M Proposition II with corporate taxes.

21 **Business and Financial Risk [LO1]**   Assume a firm's debt is risk-free, so that the cost of debt equals the risk-free rate, $R_f$. Define $\beta_A$ as the firm's *asset* beta – that is, the systematic risk of the firm's assets. Define $\beta_E$ to be the beta of the firm's equity. Use the capital asset pricing model (CAPM) along with M&M Proposition II to show that $\beta_E = \beta_A \times (1 + D/E)$, where $D/E$ is the debt–equity ratio. Assume the tax rate is zero.

22. **Shareholder Risk [LO1]**   Suppose a firm's business operations are such that they mirror movements in the economy as a whole very closely: that is, the firm's asset beta is 1.0. Use the result of Problem 21 to find the equity beta for this firm for debt–equity ratios of 0, 1, 5 and 20. What does this tell you about the relationship between capital structure and shareholder risk? How is the shareholders' required return on equity affected? Explain.

MINI
CASE

# Stephenson Real Estate Recapitalization

Stephenson Real Estate was founded 25 years ago by the current CEO, Robert Stephenson. The company purchases real estate, including land and buildings, and rents the property to tenants. The company has shown a profit every year for the past 18 years, and the shareholders are satisfied with the company's management. Prior to founding Stephenson Real Estate, Robert was the founder and CEO of a failed sheep farming operation. The resulting bankruptcy made him extremely averse to debt financing. As a result, the company is entirely equity-financed, with 15 million shares outstanding. The shares currently trade at £32.50 per share.

Stephenson is evaluating a plan to purchase a huge tract of land in south-eastern England for £100 million. The land will subsequently be leased to tenant farmers. This purchase is expected to increase Stephenson's annual pre-tax earnings by £25 million in perpetuity. Kim Weyand, the company's new CFO, has been put in charge of the project. Kim has determined that the company's current cost of capital is 12.5 per cent. She feels that the company would be more valuable if it included debt in its capital structure, so she is evaluating whether the company should issue debt to finance the project entirely. Based on some conversations with investment banks, she thinks that the company can issue bonds at par value with an 8 per cent coupon rate. Based on her analysis, she also believes that a capital structure in the range of 70 per cent equity/30 per cent debt would be optimal. If the company goes beyond 30 per cent debt, its bonds would carry a lower rating and a much higher coupon, because the possibility of financial distress and the associated costs would rise sharply. Stephenson has a 28 per cent corporate tax rate.

1 If Stephenson wishes to maximize its total market value, would you recommend that it issue debt or equity to finance the land purchase? Explain.

2 Construct Stephenson's market value balance sheet before it announces the purchase.

3 Suppose Stephenson decides to issue equity to finance the purchase.

(a)    What is the net present value of the project?

(b)    Construct Stephenson's market value balance sheet after it announces that the firm will finance the purchase using equity. What would be the new price per share of the firm's equity? How many shares will Stephenson need to issue to finance the purchase?

(c)    Construct Stephenson's market value balance sheet after the equity issue but before the purchase has been made. How many shares of equity does Stephenson have outstanding? What is the price per share of the firm's equity?

(d)    Construct Stephenson's market value balance sheet after the purchase has been made.

4    Suppose Stephenson decides to issue debt to finance the purchase.

(a)    What will the market value of the Stephenson company be if the purchase is financed with debt?

(b)    Construct Stephenson's market value balance sheet after both the debt issue and the land purchase. What is the price per share of the firm's equity?

5    Which method of financing maximizes the per-share price of Stephenson's equity?

# Endnotes

1    It is conventional to refer to decisions regarding debt and equity as *capital structure decisions*. However, the term *financial structure decisions* would be more accurate, and we use the terms interchangeably.

2    ROE is discussed in some detail in Chapter 3.

3    'Lehman bankruptcy gets ugly', *Businessweek*, 2 October 2008.

To help you grasp the key concepts of this chapter check out the extra resources posted on the Online Learning Centre at **www.mcgraw-hill.co.uk/textbooks/hillier**

Among other helpful resources there are mini-cases tailored to individual chapters.

# 16

# Dividends and Payout Policy

## KEY NOTATIONS

D  Dividend
P  Share price
r  Interest rate or discount rate

## LEARNING OBJECTIVES

After studying this chapter, you should understand:

LO1  Dividend types, and how dividends are paid.
LO2  The issues surrounding dividend policy decisions.
LO3  The difference between cash and stock dividends.
LO4  Why share repurchases are an alternative to dividends.

> ON 11 MARCH 2010 the UK cinema chain Cineworld announced an increase in its annual dividend following the release of the 3D movie *Avatar*. Cineworld, which was an early investor in 3D technology, showed an 11 per cent increase in revenues. As a result, the company increased its dividend from 9p (in 2009) to 10p. At the same time the share price fell by 1p from £1.71 to £1.70. Why do prices fall on the announcement of some dividends and rise on the announcement of others? To find out, this chapter explores several issues concerning dividends, and their implications for shareholders.

Dividend policy is an important subject in corporate finance, and dividends are a major cash outlay for many corporations. For example, British companies were expected to pay about £59.6 billion in dividends in 2010, a slight increase from £56.9 billion in 2009 (source: Reuters citing a Capita Registrars report). BP (before the Gulf of Mexico oil spill disaster), Royal Dutch Shell, HSBC, Vodafone and GlaxoSmithKline were the biggest payers. How much? The five companies paid out nearly 50 per cent of the total UK dividends in 2010. In contrast, more than a third paid no dividends at all.

At first glance it may seem obvious that a firm would always want to give as much as possible back to its shareholders by paying dividends. It might seem equally obvious, however, that a firm could always invest the money for its shareholders instead of paying it out. The heart of the dividend policy question is just this: should the firm pay out money to its shareholders, or should it take that money and invest it for its shareholders?

In this chapter we shall cover a variety of topics related to dividends and corporate payout policies. We first discuss the various types of cash dividend, and how they are paid. We ask whether dividend policy matters, and we consider arguments in favour of both high- and low-dividend payouts. Next we examine share repurchases, which have become an important alternative to cash dividends. We then bring together several decades of research on dividends and corporate payouts to describe the key trade-offs involved in establishing a payout policy. We conclude the chapter by discussing stock splits and stock dividends.

# 16.1 Cash Dividends and Dividend Payment

**dividend**
A payment made out of a firm's earnings to its owners, in the form of either cash or stock.

**distribution**
A payment made by a firm to its owners from sources other than current or accumulated retained earnings.

The term **dividend** usually refers to cash paid out of earnings. If a payment is made from sources other than current or accumulated retained earnings, the term **distribution**, rather than *dividend*, is used. However, it is acceptable to refer to a distribution from earnings as a dividend, and a distribution from capital as a liquidating dividend. More generally, any direct payment by the corporation to the shareholders may be considered a dividend or a part of dividend policy.

Dividends come in several different forms. The basic types of cash dividend are these:

1 Regular cash dividends

2 Extra dividends

3 Special dividends

4 Liquidating dividends

Later in the chapter we discuss dividends paid in equity instead of cash. We also consider another alternative to cash dividends: share repurchases.

## Cash Dividends

**regular cash dividend**
A cash payment made by a firm to its owners in the normal course of business, usually paid four times a year.

The most common type of dividend is a cash dividend. Commonly, public companies pay **regular cash dividends** two or four times a year. As the name suggests, these are cash payments made directly to shareholders, and they are made in the regular course of business. In other words, management sees nothing unusual about the dividend, and no reason why it won't be continued.

Sometimes firms will pay a regular cash dividend and an *extra cash dividend*. By calling part of the payment 'extra', management is indicating that the 'extra' part may or may not be repeated in the future. A *special dividend* is similar, but the name usually indicates that this dividend is viewed as a truly unusual or one-time event, and won't be repeated. For example, in December 2004 Microsoft paid a special dividend of $3 per share. The total payout of $32 billion was the largest one-time corporate dividend in history. Founder Bill Gates received about $3 billion, which he pledged to donate to charity. Finally, the payment of a *liquidating dividend* usually means that some or all of the business has been liquidated – that is, sold off.

However it is labelled, a cash dividend payment reduces corporate cash and retained earnings, except in the case of a liquidating dividend (which may reduce paid-in capital).

## Standard Method of Cash Dividend Payment

The decision to pay a dividend rests in the hands of the board of directors of the corporation. When a dividend has been declared, it becomes a debt of the firm, and cannot easily be rescinded. Some time after it has been declared, a dividend is distributed to all shareholders as of some specific date.

Commonly, the amount of the cash dividend is expressed in terms of cash per share (*dividends per share*). As we have seen in other chapters, it is also expressed as a percentage of the market price (the *dividend yield*), or as a percentage of net income or earnings per share (the *dividend payout*).

## Dividend Payment: A Chronology

The mechanics of a cash dividend payment can be illustrated by the example in Fig. 16.1 and the following description:

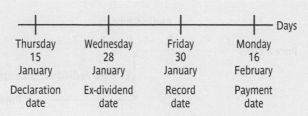

FIGURE
**16.1**

1 *Declaration date*: The board of directors declares a payment of dividends.
2 *Record date*: The declared dividends are distributable to shareholders of record on a specific date.
3 *Ex-dividend date*: A share of equity becomes ex dividend on the date the seller is entitled to keep the dividend; under stock exchange rules, shares are traded ex dividend on and after the second business day before the record date.
4 *Payment date*: The dividend cheques are mailed to shareholders of record.

**Figure 16.1** Example of procedure for dividend payment

1  **Declaration date**: On 15 January the board of directors passes a resolution to pay a dividend of £1 per share on 16 February to all holders of record as of 30 January.

2  **Ex-dividend date**: To make sure that dividend payments go to the right people, brokerage firms and stock exchanges establish an ex-dividend date. This date is normally two business days before the date of record (discussed next). If you buy the equity before this date, you are entitled to the dividend. If you buy on this date or after, the previous owner will get the dividend.

    In Fig. 16.1, Wednesday 28 January is the ex-dividend date. Before this date, the equity is said to trade 'with dividend' or 'cum dividend'. Afterward, the equity trades 'ex dividend'.

    The ex-dividend date convention removes any ambiguity about who is entitled to the dividend. Because the dividend is valuable, the share price will be affected when the equity goes 'ex'. We examine this effect in a moment.

3  **Date of record**: Based on its records, the corporation prepares a list on 30 January of all individuals believed to be shareholders. These are the *holders of record*, and 30 January is the *date of record* (or record date). The word *believed* is important here. If you buy the equity just before this date, the corporation's records may not reflect that fact, because of mailing or other delays. Without some modification, some of the dividend payments will go to the wrong people. This is the reason for the ex-dividend day convention.

4  **Date of payment**: The dividend is paid on 16 February.

> **declaration date**
> The date on which the board of directors passes a resolution to pay a dividend.
>
> **ex-dividend date**
> The date two business days before the date of record, establishing those individuals entitled to a dividend.
>
> **date of record**
> The date by which a holder must be on record to be designated to receive a dividend.
>
> **date of payment**
> The date on which the dividend is paid.

## More About the Ex-Dividend Date

The ex-dividend date is important, and is a common source of confusion. We examine what happens to the equity when it goes ex, meaning that the ex-dividend date arrives. To illustrate, suppose we have an equity that sells for £10 per share. The board of directors declares a dividend of £1 per share, and the record date is set to be Tuesday 12 June. Based on our previous discussion, we know that the ex date will be two business (not calendar) days earlier, on Friday 8 June.

    If you buy the equity on Thursday 7 June, just as the market closes, you'll get the £1 dividend, because the equity is trading cum dividend. If you wait, and buy it just as the market opens on Friday, you won't get the £1 dividend. What happens to the value of the equity overnight?

FIGURE
16.2

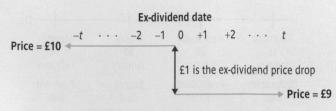

**Ex-dividend date**

$-t$ · · · $-2$ $-1$ $0$ $+1$ $+2$ · · · $t$

Price = £10

£1 is the ex-dividend price drop

Price = £9

The share price will fall by the amount of the dividend on the ex-dividend date (Time 0). If the dividend is £1 per share, the price will be £10 − 1 = £9 on the ex-dividend date:

Before ex-dividend date (Time −1), dividend = £0    Price = £10
On ex-dividend date (Time 0), dividend = £1    Price = £9

**Figure 16.2** Price behaviour around the ex-dividend date for a £1 cash dividend

If you think about it, you will see that the equity is worth about £1 less on Friday morning, so its price will drop by this amount between close of business on Thursday and the Friday opening. In general, we expect that the share price will go down by about the dividend amount when the equity goes ex dividend. The key word here is *about*. Because dividends are taxed, the actual price drop might be closer to some measure of the after-tax value of the dividend. Determining this value is complicated, because of the different tax rates and tax rules that apply for different buyers.

The series of events described here is illustrated in Fig. 16.2.

**EXAMPLE
16.1**

## 'Ex' Marks the Day

The board of directors of Divided Airlines has declared a dividend of €2.50 per share payable on Tuesday 30 May, to shareholders of record as of Tuesday 9 May. You buy 100 shares of Divided on Tuesday 2 May for €150 per share. What is the ex date? Describe the events that will occur with regard to the cash dividend and the share price.

The ex date is two business days before the date of record, Tuesday, 9 May: so the equity will go ex on Friday 5 May. You buy the shares on Tuesday 2 May, so you purchase the equity cum dividend. In other words, you will get €2.50 × 100 = €250 in dividends. You will be paid on Tuesday 30 May. Just before the equity does go ex on Friday, its value will drop overnight by about €2.50 per share.

As an example of the price drop on the ex-dividend date, we return to the enormous dividend Microsoft paid in December 2004. The total dividends paid by all the companies in the S&P 500 for the year amounted to $213.6 billion, so Microsoft's $32 billion special dividend represented about 15 per cent of all dividends paid by S&P 500 companies for the year. To give you another idea of the size of the special dividend, consider that, in December, when the dividend was sent to investors, personal income in the United States rose by 3.7 per cent. Without the dividend, personal income rose only 0.3 per cent; so the dividend payment accounted for about 3 per cent of all personal income in the United States for the month!

The equity went ex-dividend on 15 November 2004 with a total dividend of $3.08 per share, consisting of a $3 special dividend and a $0.08 regular dividend. The share price chart here shows the change in Microsoft equity four days prior to the ex-dividend date and on the ex-dividend date.

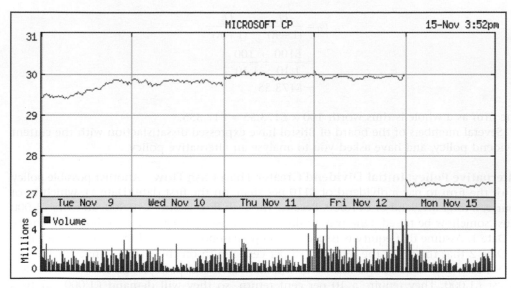

*Source*: http://finance.yahoo.com. © 2004 Yahoo! Inc.

The equity closed at $29.97 on 12 November (a Friday) and opened at $27.34 on 15 November – a drop of $2.63. With a 15 per cent tax rate on dividends, we would have expected a drop of $2.62, so the actual price drop was almost exactly what we expected (we discuss dividends and taxes in more detail in a subsequent section).

CONCEPT QUESTIONS

16.1a　What are the different types of cash dividend?
16.1b　What are the mechanics of the cash dividend payment?
16.1c　How should the share price change when it goes ex dividend?

## 16.2　Does Dividend Policy Matter?

To decide whether or not dividend policy matters, we first have to define what we mean by dividend *policy*. All other things being the same, of course dividends matter. Dividends are paid in cash, and cash is something that everybody likes. The question we shall be discussing here is whether the firm should pay out cash now, or invest the cash and pay it out later. Dividend policy, therefore, is the time pattern of dividend payout. In particular, should the firm pay out a large percentage of its earnings now, or a small (or even zero) percentage? This is the dividend policy question.

### An Illustration of the Irrelevance of Dividend Policy

A powerful argument can be made that dividend policy does not matter. We illustrate this by considering the simple case of Bristol plc. Bristol is an all-equity firm that has existed for 10 years. The current financial managers plan to dissolve the firm in two years. The total cash flows the firm will generate, including the proceeds from liquidation, will be £10,000 in each of the next two years.

**Current Policy: Dividends Set Equal to Cash Flow**　At present, dividends at each date are set equal to the cash flow of £10,000. There are 100 shares outstanding, so the dividend per share is £100. In Chapter 7 we showed that the value of the equity is equal to the present value of the future dividends. Assuming a 10 per cent required return, the share price today, $P_0$, is

$$P_0 = \frac{D_1}{(1+R)^1} + \frac{D_2}{(1+R)^2}$$

$$= \frac{£100}{1.10} + \frac{100}{1.10^2}$$

$$= £173.55$$

The firm as a whole is thus worth $100 \times £173.55 = £17,355$.

Several members of the board of Bristol have expressed dissatisfaction with the current dividend policy, and have asked you to analyse an alternative policy.

**Alternative Policy: Initial Dividend Greater Than Cash Flow**    Another possible policy is for the firm to pay a dividend of £110 per share on the first date (Date 1), which is, of course, a total dividend of £11,000. Because the cash flow is only £10,000, an extra £1,000 must somehow be raised. One way to do this is to issue £1,000 worth of bonds or equity at Date 1. Assume that equity is issued. The new shareholders will desire enough cash flow at Date 2 that they earn the required 10 per cent return on their Date 1 investment.[1]

What is the value of the firm with this new dividend policy? The new shareholders invest £1,000. They require a 10 per cent return, so they will demand $£1,000 \times 1.10 = £1,100$ of the Date 2 cash flow, leaving only £8,900 to the old shareholders. The dividends to the old shareholders will be as follows:

|  | Date 1 | Date 2 |
|---|---|---|
| Aggregate dividends to old shareholders (£) | 11,000 | 8,900 |
| Dividends per share (£) | 110 | 89 |

The present value of the dividends per share is therefore

$$P_0 = \frac{£110}{1.10} + \frac{89}{1.10^2} = £173.55$$

This is the same value we had before.

The value of the equity is not affected by this switch in dividend policy, even though we have to sell some new equity just to finance the new dividend. In fact, no matter what pattern of dividend payout the firm chooses, the value of the equity will always be the same in this example. In other words, for Bristol plc, dividend policy makes no difference. The reason is simple: any increase in a dividend at some point in time is exactly offset by a decrease somewhere else: so the net effect, once we account for time value, is zero.

## Homemade Dividends

There is an alternative and perhaps more intuitively appealing explanation of why dividend policy doesn't matter in our example. Suppose individual investor X prefers dividends per share of £100 at both Dates 1 and 2. Would she be disappointed if informed that the firm's management was adopting the alternative dividend policy (dividends of £110 and £89 on the two dates, respectively)? Not necessarily: she could easily reinvest the £10 of unneeded funds received on Date 1 by buying more Bristol plc shares. At 10 per cent, this investment would grow to £11 by Date 2. Thus X would receive her desired net cash flow of $£110 - 10 = £100$ at Date 1 and $£89 + 11 = £100$ at Date 2.

Conversely, imagine that investor Z, preferring £110 of cash flow at Date 1 and £89 of cash flow at Date 2, finds that management will pay dividends of £100 at both Dates 1 and 2. This investor can simply sell £10 worth of equity to boost his total cash at Date 1 to £110. Because this investment returns 10 per cent, Investor Z gives up £11 at Date 2 ($£10 \times 1.1$), leaving him with $£100 - 11 = £89$.

Our two investors are able to transform the corporation's dividend policy into a different policy by buying or selling on their own. The result is that investors

**homemade dividend policy** The tailored dividend policy created by individual investors who undo corporate dividend policy by reinvesting dividends or selling shares of equity.

are able to create a **homemade dividend policy**. This means that dissatisfied shareholders can alter the firm's dividend policy to suit themselves. As a result, there is no particular advantage to any one dividend policy the firm might choose.

Many corporations actually assist their shareholders in creating homemade dividend policies by offering *automatic dividend reinvestment plans* (ADRs or DRIPs). As the name suggests, with such a plan shareholders have the option of automatically reinvesting some or all of their cash dividend in shares of equity. In some cases they actually receive a discount on the shares, which makes such a plan very attractive.

## A Test

Our discussion to this point can be summarized by considering the following true–false test questions:

1   Dividends are irrelevant: true or false?

2   Dividend policy is irrelevant: true or false?

The first statement is surely false, and the reason follows from common sense. Clearly, investors prefer higher dividends to lower dividends at any single date if the dividend level is held constant at every other date. To be more precise regarding the first question, if the dividend per share at a given date is raised while the dividend per share at every other date is held constant, the share price will rise. The reason is that the present value of the future dividends must go up if this occurs. This action can be accomplished by management decisions that improve productivity, increase tax savings, strengthen product marketing, or otherwise improve cash flow.

The second statement is true, at least in the simple case we have been examining. Dividend policy by itself cannot raise the dividend at one date while keeping it the same at all other dates. Rather, dividend policy merely establishes the trade-off between dividends at one date and dividends at another date. Once we allow for time value, the present value of the dividend stream is unchanged. Thus, in this simple world, dividend policy does not matter, because managers choosing either to raise or to lower the current dividend do not affect the current value of their firm. However, we have ignored several real-world factors that might lead us to change our minds; we pursue some of these in subsequent sections.

| CONCEPT QUESTIONS | 16.2a   How can an investor create a homemade dividend? |
|---|---|
| | 16.2b   Are dividends irrelevant? |

## 16.3   Real-World Factors Favouring a Low-Dividend Payout

The example we used to illustrate the irrelevance of dividend policy ignored taxes and flotation costs. In this section we shall see that these factors might lead us to prefer a low-dividend payout.

## Taxes

Tax laws are complex, and they affect dividend policy in a number of ways. The key tax feature has to do with the taxation of dividend income and capital gains. For individual shareholders, *effective* tax rates on dividend income are normally higher than the tax rates on capital gains. However, this is not always the case, and in many countries the opposite is true. Historically, dividends received have been taxed as ordinary income. Capital gains have been taxed at somewhat lower rates, and the tax on a capital gain is deferred until the equity is sold. This second aspect of capital gains taxation makes the effective tax rate much lower, because the present value of the tax is less.[2]

## Flotation Costs

In our example showing that dividend policy doesn't matter, we saw that the firm could sell some new equity if necessary to pay a dividend. As we mentioned in Chapter 13, selling new equity can be very expensive. If we include flotation costs in our argument, then we shall find that the share price decreases if we sell new equity.

More generally, imagine two firms identical in every way except that one pays out a greater percentage of its cash flow in the form of dividends. Because the other firm ploughs back more, its equity grows faster. If these two firms are to remain identical, then the one with the higher payout will have to periodically sell some equity to catch up. Because this is expensive, a firm might be inclined to have a low payout.

## Dividend Restrictions

In some cases a corporation may face restrictions on its ability to pay dividends. For example, as we discussed in Chapter 6, a common feature of a bond indenture is a covenant prohibiting dividend payments above some level. Also, a corporation may be prohibited by law from paying dividends if the dividend amount exceeds the firm's retained earnings.

**CONCEPT QUESTIONS**

16.3a   What are the tax benefits of low dividends?
16.3b   Why do flotation costs favour a low payout?

## 16.4 Real-World Factors Favouring a High-Dividend Payout

In this section we consider reasons why a firm might pay its shareholders higher dividends, even if it means the firm must issue more shares of equity to finance the dividend payments.

In a classic textbook, Benjamin Graham, David Dodd and Sidney Cottle have argued that firms should generally have high-dividend payouts because:

1  'The discounted value of near dividends is higher than the present worth of distant dividends.'

2  Between 'two companies with the same general earning power and same general position in an industry, the one paying the larger dividend will almost always sell at a higher price'.[3]

Two additional factors favouring a high-dividend payout have also been mentioned frequently by proponents of this view: the desire for current income, and the resolution of uncertainty.

## Desire for Current Income

It has been argued that many individuals desire current income. The classic example is the group of retired people and others living on a fixed income (the proverbial widows and orphans).

It is argued that this group is willing to pay a premium to get a higher dividend yield. If this is true, then it lends support to the second claim made by Graham, Dodd and Cottle.

It is easy to see, however, that this argument is not relevant in our simple case. An individual preferring high current cash flow but holding low-dividend securities can easily sell off shares to provide the necessary funds. Similarly, an individual desiring a low current cash flow but holding high-dividend securities can just reinvest the dividend. This is just our homemade dividend argument again. Thus, in a world of no transaction costs, a policy of high current dividends would be of no value to the shareholder.

The current income argument may have relevance in the real world. Here the sale of low-dividend equities would involve brokerage fees and other transaction costs. These direct cash expenses could be avoided by an investment in high-dividend securities. In addition, the expenditure of the shareholder's own time in selling securities, and the natural (though not necessarily rational) fear of consuming out of principal, might further lead many investors to buy high-dividend securities.

Even so, to put this argument in perspective, remember that financial intermediaries such as mutual funds can (and do) perform these 'repackaging' transactions for individuals at very low cost. Such intermediaries could buy low-dividend equities and, through a controlled policy of realizing gains, they could pay their investors at a higher rate.

## Tax and Other Benefits from High Dividends

Earlier, we saw that dividends were regularly taxed unfavourably for individual investors. This fact is a powerful argument for a low payout. However, there are a number of other investors who do not receive unfavourable tax treatment from holding high-dividend yield, rather than low-dividend yield, securities.

**Tax-Exempt Investors**    We have pointed out both the tax advantages and the tax disadvantages of a low-dividend payout. Of course, this discussion is irrelevant to those in zero-tax brackets. This group includes (in most countries) some of the largest investors in the economy, such as pension funds, endowment funds and trust funds.

Institutions such as university endowment funds and trust funds are frequently prohibited from spending any of the principal. Such institutions might therefore prefer to hold high-dividend yield equities so they have some ability to spend. Like widows and orphans, this group thus prefers current income. However, unlike widows and orphans, this group is very large in terms of the amount of equity owned.

## Conclusion

Overall, individual investors (for whatever reason) may have a desire for current income, and may thus be willing to pay the dividend tax. In addition, some very large investors such as tax-free institutions may have a very strong preference for high-dividend payouts.

| CONCEPT QUESTIONS | 16.4a | Why might some individual investors favour a high-dividend payout? |
| | 16.4b | Why might some non-individual investors prefer a high-dividend payout? |

## 16.5  A Resolution of Real-World Factors?

In the previous sections we presented some factors that favour a low-dividend policy and others that favour a high-dividend policy. In this section we discuss two important concepts related to dividends and dividend policy: the information content of dividends, and the clientele effect. The first topic illustrates both the importance of dividends in general and the importance of distinguishing between dividends and dividend policy. The second topic suggests that, despite the many real-world considerations we have discussed, the dividend payout ratio may not be as important as we originally imagined.

## Information Content of Dividends

To begin, we quickly review some of our earlier discussion. Previously, we examined three different positions on dividends:

1   Based on the homemade dividend argument, dividend policy is irrelevant.

2   Because of tax effects for individual investors and new issue costs, a low-dividend policy is best.

3   Because of the desire for current income and related factors, a high-dividend policy is best.

If you wanted to decide which of these positions is the right one, an obvious way to get started would be to look at what happens to share prices when companies announce dividend changes. You would find with some consistency that share prices rise when the current dividend is unexpectedly increased (except for our opening example!), and they generally fall when the dividend is unexpectedly decreased. What does this imply about any of the three positions just stated?

At first glance, the behaviour we describe seems consistent with the third position and inconsistent with the other two. In fact, many writers have argued this. If share prices rise in response to dividend increases and fall in response to dividend decreases, then isn't the market saying that it approves of higher dividends?

Other authors have pointed out that this observation doesn't really tell us much about dividend policy. Everyone agrees that dividends are important, all other things being equal. Companies cut dividends only with great reluctance. Thus a dividend cut is often a signal that the firm is in trouble.

More to the point, a dividend cut is usually not a voluntary, planned change in dividend policy. Instead, it usually signals that management does not think that the current dividend policy can be maintained. As a result, expectations of future dividends should generally be revised downwards. The present value of expected future dividends falls, and so does the share price.

In this case, the share price declines following a dividend cut because future dividends are generally expected to be lower, not because the firm has changed the percentage of its earnings it will pay out in the form of dividends.

In a similar vein, an unexpected increase in the dividend signals good news. Management will raise the dividend only when future earnings, cash flow and general prospects are expected to rise to such an extent that the dividend will not have to be cut later. A dividend increase is management's signal to the market that the firm is expected to do well.

The share price reacts favourably because expectations of future dividends are revised upwards, not because the firm has increased its payout.

**information content effect**
The market's reaction to a change in corporate dividend payout.

In both of these cases the share price reacts to the dividend change. The reaction can be attributed to changes in the expected amount of future dividends, not necessarily a change in dividend payout policy. This reaction is called the **information content effect** of the dividend. The fact that dividend changes convey information about the firm to the market makes it difficult to interpret the effect of the dividend policy of the firm.

## The Clientele Effect

In our earlier discussion we saw that some groups (wealthy individuals, for example) have an incentive to pursue low-payout (or zero-payout) equities. Other groups (charities, for example) have an incentive to pursue high-payout equities. Companies with high payouts will thus attract one group, and low-payout companies will attract another.

These different groups are called *clienteles*, and what we have described is a **clientele effect**. The clientele effect argument states that different groups of investors desire different levels of dividend. When a firm chooses a particular dividend policy, the only effect is to attract a particular clientele. If a firm changes its dividend policy, then it just attracts a different clientele.

> **clientele effect**
> The observable fact that equities attract particular groups based on dividend yield and the resulting tax effects.

What we are left with is a simple supply and demand argument. Suppose 40 per cent of all investors prefer high dividends, but only 20 per cent of the firms pay high dividends. Here the high-dividend firms will be in short supply: thus their share prices will rise. Consequently, low-dividend firms will find it advantageous to switch policies until 40 per cent of all firms have high payouts. At this point the *dividend market* is in equilibrium. Further changes in dividend policy are pointless, because all the clienteles are satisfied. The dividend policy for any individual firm is now irrelevant.

To see if you understand the clientele effect, consider the following statement. In spite of the theoretical argument that dividend policy is irrelevant, or that firms should not pay dividends, many investors like high dividends: because of this fact, a firm can boost its share price by having a higher dividend payout ratio. True or false?

The answer is 'false' if clienteles exist. As long as enough high-dividend firms satisfy the dividend-loving investors, a firm won't be able to boost its share price by paying high dividends. An unsatisfied clientele must exist for this to happen, and there is no evidence that this is the case.

---

| CONCEPT QUESTIONS | | |
|---|---|---|
| | 16.5a | How does the market react to unexpected dividend changes? What does this tell us about dividends? About dividend policy? |
| | 16.5b | What is a dividend clientele? All things considered, would you expect a risky firm with significant but highly uncertain growth prospects to have a low- or high-dividend payout? |

---

## 16.6  Share Repurchases: An Alternative to Cash Dividends

Thus far in our chapter we have considered cash dividends. However, cash dividends are not the only way corporations distribute cash. Instead, a company can **repurchase** its own equity. Repurchases (or *buybacks*) have become an increasingly popular tool, and the amount spent on repurchases has become huge.

> **share repurchase**
> The purchase, by a corporation, of its own shares of equity; also known as a *buyback*.

Another way to see how important repurchases have become is to compare them with cash dividends. Consider Fig. 16.3, which shows the average ratios of dividends to earnings, repurchases to earnings, and total payout (both dividends and repurchases) to earnings for US industrial firms over the years from 1984 to 2004. As can be seen, the ratio of repurchases to earnings was far less than the ratio of dividends to earnings in the early years. However, the ratio of repurchases to earnings exceeded the ratio of dividends to earnings by 1998. This trend reversed after 1999, with the ratio of repurchases to earnings falling slightly below the ratio of dividends to earnings by 2004.

Across Europe the pattern is historically quite different, most notably because share repurchases were not common, and in several cases were illegal, on the continent and in the UK. For example, in 2002 less than 1 per cent of all British firms repurchased shares. Similarly, although the level of British repurchases was low, the activity was significantly more common in the UK than in the rest of Europe combined. However, in recent years the pattern has shifted significantly, and by 2005 share repurchases were over half the value of all cash dividends in the European Union. Table 16.1 shows the trend in share

FIGURE
**16.3**

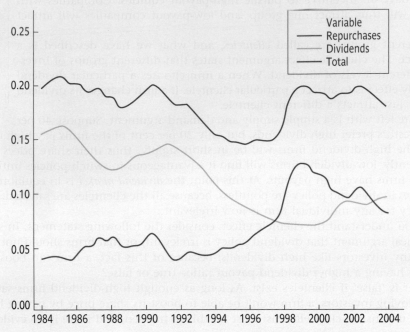

The graph shows the average ratios of repurchases, dividends and total payout (both repurchases and dividends) to earnings for US industrial companies over the years from 1984 to 2004. The graph indicates growth in repurchases over much of the sample period.

*Source*: Figure 3 of B. Julio and D. Ikenberry, 'Reappearing dividends', *Journal of Applied Corporate Finance* (2004), vol. 16, no. 4, 89–100.

**Figure 16.3** Ratios of various payouts to earnings

repurchases over the period 1989 to 2005. It is clear that, in all countries, share repurchases have become a much more important part of payout policy since 1999.

Share repurchases are typically accomplished in one of three ways. First, companies may simply purchase their own equity, just as anyone would buy shares of a particular equity. In these *open market purchases* the firm does not reveal itself as the buyer. Thus the seller does not know whether the shares were sold back to the firm, or to just another investor.

Second, the firm could institute a *tender offer*. Here the firm announces to all of its shareholders that it is willing to buy a fixed number of shares at a specific price. For example, suppose Kunst en Ambacht NV (K&A) has 1 million shares of equity outstanding, with a share price of €50 per share. The firm makes a tender offer to buy back 300,000 shares at €60 per share. K&A chooses a price above €50 to induce shareholders to sell – that is, tender – their shares. In fact, if the tender price is set high enough, shareholders may very well want to sell more than the 300,000 shares. In the extreme case where all outstanding shares are tendered, K&A will buy back 3 out of every 10 shares that a shareholder has.

Finally, firms may repurchase shares from specific individual shareholders. This procedure has been called a *targeted repurchase*. For example, suppose International Biotechnology AB purchased approximately 10 per cent of the outstanding equity of Prime Robotics Ltd (P-R Ltd) in April at around SKr38 per share. At that time, International Biotechnology announced to the Stockholm Stock Exchange that it might eventually try to take control of P-R Ltd. In May, P-R Ltd repurchased the International Biotechnology holdings in P-R Ltd at SKr48 per share, well above the market price at that time. This offer was not extended to other shareholders.

Source: H. von Eije and W.L. Megginson, 'Dividends and share repurchases in the European Union', Journal of Financial Economics (2008), vol. 89, no. 2, pp. 347–374.

**TABLE 16.1**

| Year | Austria | Belgium | Denmark | Finland | France | Germany | Greece | Ireland | Italy | Luxembourg | Netherlands | Portugal | Spain | Sweden | United Kingdom | All countries |
|---|---|---|---|---|---|---|---|---|---|---|---|---|---|---|---|---|
| 1989 | 0 | 0 | 8 | 129 | 577 | 0 | 0 | 0 | 260 | 0 | 114 | 6 | 46 | 40 | 4,965 | 6,146 |
| 1990 | 0 | 0 | 27 | 134 | 278 | 54 | 0 | 0 | 366 | 0 | 19 | 0 | 37 | 3 | 1,543 | 2,461 |
| 1991 | 0 | 0 | 0 | 22 | 99 | 0 | 0 | 0 | 99 | 0 | 19 | 0 | 2 | 17 | 316 | 575 |
| 1992 | 0 | 0 | 0 | 83 | −11 | 210 | 0 | 5 | 202 | 0 | 18 | 3 | 6 | 35 | 462 | 1,013 |
| 1993 | 0 | 5 | 1 | 9 | 91 | 45 | 0 | 58 | 1 | 0 | 1 | −14 | 33 | 14 | 1,049 | 1,293 |
| 1994 | 0 | 0 | 16 | 5 | 151 | 70 | 0 | 6 | 0 | 0 | 432 | 11 | 23 | 0 | 1,100 | 1,813 |
| 1995 | 0 | 0 | 2 | 40 | 252 | 2 | 0 | 71 | 0 | 5 | 5 | 7 | 59 | 2 | 898 | 1,344 |
| 1996 | 0 | 0 | 0 | 104 | 86 | 1 | 0 | 1 | 0 | 3 | 140 | 16 | 82 | 363 | 1,152 | 1,946 |
| 1997 | 1 | 0 | 16 | 20 | 472 | 71 | 0 | 13 | 27 | 2 | 540 | 17 | 67 | 1,743 | 6,726 | 9,717 |
| 1998 | 0 | 0 | 331 | 388 | 888 | 4 | 0 | 66 | 182 | 3 | 1,405 | 60 | 218 | 610 | 13,569 | 17,723 |
| 1999 | 24 | 0 | 463 | 247 | 5,019 | 1,601 | 0 | 29 | 153 | 1 | 1,464 | 36 | 177 | 408 | 6,706 | 16,329 |
| 2000 | 105 | 107 | 665 | 542 | 4,291 | 4,583 | 4 | 16 | 697 | 0 | 1,443 | 38 | 173 | 2,874 | 10,518 | 26,056 |
| 2001 | 160 | 190 | 176 | 689 | 11,875 | 2,289 | 162 | 43 | 1,797 | 6 | 1,639 | 39 | 168 | 1,685 | 9,695 | 30,611 |
| 2002 | 19 | 341 | 449 | 351 | 5,883 | 1,164 | 0 | 65 | 824 | 2 | 1,176 | 28 | 257 | 415 | 13,409 | 24,382 |
| 2003 | 4 | 57 | 492 | 1,595 | 5,917 | 1,424 | 4 | 13 | 658 | 35 | 837 | 54 | 189 | 477 | 10,123 | 21,880 |
| 2004 | 0 | 363 | 704 | 2,727 | 8,419 | 2,234 | 43 | 34 | 182 | 265 | 1,091 | 32 | 382 | 1,001 | 13,335 | 30,814 |
| 2005 | 35 | 1,076 | 984 | 4,428 | 6,184 | 3,508 | 256 | 349 | 1,355 | 48 | 7,383 | 31 | 1,126 | 2,733 | 29,344 | 58,841 |
| Total | 349 | 2,138 | 4,336 | 11,515 | 50,473 | 17,259 | 468 | 767 | 6,804 | 370 | 17,726 | 363 | 3,047 | 12,420 | 124,909 | 252,943 |

**Table 16.1** Share repurchases in Europe (€ millions) between 1989 and 2005

## Cash Dividends versus Repurchase

Imagine an all-equity company with excess cash of £300,000. The firm pays no dividends, and its net income for the year just ended is £49,000. The market value balance sheet at the end of the year is represented here:

| Market value balance sheet (before paying out excess cash) | | | |
|---|---|---|---|
| | £ | | £ |
| Excess cash | 300,000 | Debt | 0 |
| Other assets | 700,000 | Equity | 1,000,000 |
| Total | 1,000,000 | Total | 1,000,000 |

There are 100,000 shares outstanding. The total market value of the equity is £1 million, so the share price is £10. Earnings per share (EPS) are £49,000/100,000 = £0.49, and the price–earnings ratio (P/E) is £10/0.49 = 20.4.

One option the company is considering is a £300,000/100,000 = £3 per share extra cash dividend. Alternatively, the company is thinking of using the money to repurchase £300,000/10 = 30,000 shares of equity.

If commissions, taxes and other imperfections are ignored in our example, the shareholders shouldn't care which option is chosen. Does this seem surprising? It shouldn't, really. What is happening here is that the firm is paying out £300,000 in cash. The new balance sheet is represented here:

| Market value balance sheet (after paying out excess cash) | | | |
|---|---|---|---|
| | £ | | £ |
| Excess cash | 0 | Debt | 0 |
| Other assets | 700,000 | Equity | 700,000 |
| Total | 700,000 | Total | 700,000 |

If the cash is paid out as a dividend, there are still 100,000 shares outstanding, so each is worth £7.

The fact that the per-share value fell from £10 to £7 is not a cause for concern. Consider a shareholder who owns 100 shares. At £10 per share before the dividend, the total value is £1,000.

After the £3 dividend, this same shareholder has 100 shares worth £7 each, for a total of £700, plus 100 × £3 = £300 in cash, for a combined total of £1,000. This just illustrates what we saw early on: a cash dividend doesn't affect a shareholder's wealth if there are no imperfections. In this case, the share price simply fell by £3 when the equity went ex dividend.

Also, because total earnings and the number of shares outstanding haven't changed, EPS is still 49 pence. The price–earnings ratio, however, falls to £7/0.49 = 14.3. Why we are looking at accounting earnings and P/E ratios will be apparent in just a moment.

Alternatively, if the company repurchases 30,000 shares, there are 70,000 left outstanding. The balance sheet looks the same:

| Market value balance sheet (after share repurchase) | | | |
|---|---|---|---|
| | £ | | £ |
| Excess cash | 0 | Debt | 0 |
| Other assets | 700,000 | Equity | 700,000 |
| Total | 700,000 | Total | 700,000 |

The company is worth £700,000 again, so each remaining share is worth £700,000/70,000 = £10. Our shareholder with 100 shares is obviously unaffected. For example, if she was so inclined, she could sell 30 shares and end up with £300 in cash and £700 in equity, just as she has if the firm pays the cash dividend. This is another example of a homemade dividend.

In this second case, EPS goes up because total earnings remain the same while the number of shares goes down. The new EPS is £49,000/70,000 = £0.70. However, the important thing to notice is that the P/E ratio is £10/0.70 = 14.3, just as it was following the dividend.

This example illustrates the important point that, if there are no imperfections, a cash dividend and a share repurchase are essentially the same thing. This is just another illustration of dividend policy irrelevance when there are no taxes or other imperfections.

## Real-World Considerations in a Repurchase

The example we have just described shows that a repurchase and a cash dividend are the same thing in a world without taxes and transaction costs. In the real world there are some accounting differences between a share repurchase and a cash dividend, but the most important difference is in the tax treatment.

Under current tax laws a repurchase has a significant tax advantage over a cash dividend. A dividend is taxed, and a shareholder has no choice about whether or not to receive the dividend. In a repurchase, a shareholder pays taxes only if: (1) the shareholder actually chooses to sell; and (2) the shareholder has a capital gain on the sale.

For example, suppose a dividend of £1 per share is taxed at ordinary rates. Investors in the 28 per cent tax bracket who own 100 shares of the security pay £100 × 0.28 = £28 in taxes. Selling shareholders would pay far lower taxes if £100 worth of equity were repurchased. This is because taxes are paid only on the profit from a sale. Thus the gain on a sale would be only £40 if shares sold at £100 were originally purchased at £60. The capital gains tax would be 0.28 × £40 = £11.20.

## Share Repurchase and EPS

You may read in the popular financial press that a share repurchase is beneficial because it causes earnings per share to increase. As we have seen, this will happen. The reason is simply that a share repurchase reduces the number of outstanding shares, but it has no effect on total earnings. As a result, EPS rises.

However, the financial press may place undue emphasis on EPS figures in a repurchase agreement. In our preceding example we saw that the value of the equity wasn't affected by the EPS change. In fact, the P/E ratio was exactly the same when we compared a cash dividend with a repurchase.

| | | |
|---|---|---|
| **CONCEPT QUESTIONS** | 16.6a | Why might a share repurchase make more sense than an extra cash dividend? |
| | 16.6b | What is the effect of a share repurchase on a firm's EPS? On its P/E? |

## 16.7 What We Know and Do Not Know about Dividend and Payout Policies

### Dividends and Dividend Payers

As we have discussed, there are numerous good reasons favouring a dividend policy of low (or no) payout. Nonetheless, in Europe, aggregate dividends paid by companies are quite large. In Europe the total real dividends (share repurchases and cash dividends) have increased significantly since 2000. For example, consider Fig. 16.4, which shows the total real cash

FIGURE
16.4

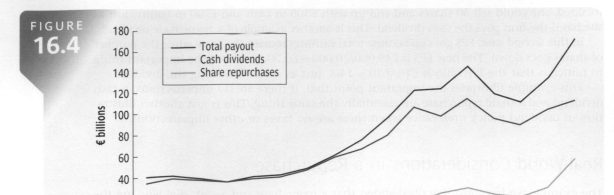

*Source*: Figure 4 of H. von Eije and W. Megginson, 'Dividends and share repurchases in the European Union', *Journal of Financial Economics* (2008), vol. 89, no. 2, pp. 347–374

**Figure 16.4** Dividends and share repurchases in the European Union

FIGURE
16.5

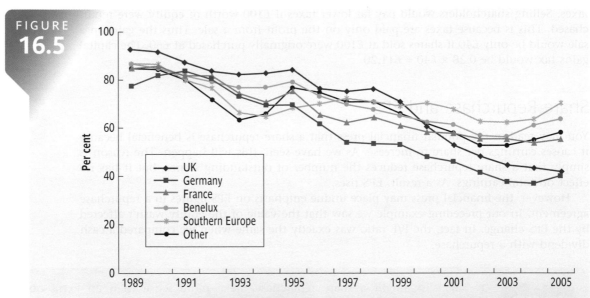

*Source*: Figure 3 of H. von Eije and W. Megginson, 'Dividends and share repurchases in the European Union', *Journal of Financial Economics* (2008), vol. 89, no. 2, pp. 347–374

**Figure 16.5** Proportion of cash dividend payers among European industrial firms

dividends and share repurchases by the EU15 companies between 1989 and 2005. Share repurchases increased from virtually zero in 1996 to €60 billion (2000 prices) in 2005. Similarly, cash dividends grew from approximately €40 billion in 1993 to over €170 billion in 2005.

While we know dividends are large in the aggregate, we also know that the number of companies that pay dividends has declined. Although dividends are substantial, von Eije and Megginson point out that the percentage of European companies paying cash dividends has fallen over the last few decades, and that these have largely been replaced by share repurchases. Figure 16.5 shows that the proportion of cash dividend payers among European industrial firms dropped substantially between 1989 and 2005. This figure also shows an increase in the proportion of dividend payers across the whole of Europe from 2002 to 2005.

The fact that aggregate dividends grew while the number of payers fell so sharply seems a bit paradoxical, but the explanation is straightforward: dividend payments are heavily concentrated in a relatively small set of large firms. In 2010, for example, about 50 per cent of aggregate dividends paid in the UK came from just five firms. Thus the reason why dividends grew while dividend payers shrank is that the decline in dividend payers is due almost entirely to smaller firms, which tend to pay smaller dividends in the first place.

One important reason why the percentage of dividend-paying firms has declined is that the population of firms has changed. There has been a huge increase in the number of newly listed firms over the last 25 or so years. Newly listed firms tend to be younger and less profitable. Such firms need their internally generated cash to fund growth, and typically do not pay dividends.

Another factor at work is that firms appear to be more likely to begin making payouts using share repurchases, which are flexible, rather than committing themselves to making cash distributions. Such a policy seems quite sensible, given our previous discussions. However, after controlling for the changing mix of firms and the increase in share repurchasing activity, there still appears to be a decreased propensity to pay dividends among certain types of older, better-established firms, although further research is needed on this question.

The fact that the number of dividend-paying firms has declined so sharply is an interesting phenomenon. Making matters even more interesting is evidence showing that the trend may have begun to reverse itself. Take another look at Fig. 16.5. As shown, there is a pronounced downward trend, but that trend appears to bottom out in 2002 and then reverse in 2003. The apparent reversal in the decline of dividend payers is a recent phenomenon, so its significance remains to be seen. It may prove to be just a transient event in the middle of a long decline. We shall have to wait and see.

## Corporations Smooth Dividends

As we previously observed, dividend cuts are frequently viewed as very bad news by market participants. As a result, companies cut dividends only when there is no other acceptable alternative. For the same reason, companies are also reluctant to increase dividends unless they are sure the new dividend level can be sustained.

In practice, what we observe is that dividend-paying companies tend to raise dividends only after earnings have risen, and they don't increase or cut dividends in response to temporary earnings fluctuations. In other words: (1) dividend growth lags earnings growth; and (2) dividend growth will tend to be much smoother than earnings growth.

To see how important dividend stability and steady growth are to financial managers, consider that in 2009, amid exceptionally unbelievably difficult trading conditions, more than a quarter of FTSE All Share companies increased their dividend.

## Putting It All Together

Much of what we have discussed in this chapter (and much of what we know about dividends from decades of research) can be pulled together and summarized in the following five observations:[4]

1   Aggregate dividend and share repurchases are massive, and they have increased steadily in both nominal and real terms over the years.

2   Dividends are heavily concentrated among a relatively small number of large, mature firms.

3   Managers are very reluctant to cut dividends, normally doing so only because of firm-specific problems.

4   Managers smooth dividends, raising them slowly and incrementally as earnings grow.

5   Share prices react to unanticipated changes in dividends.

The challenge now is to fit these five pieces into a reasonably coherent picture. With regard to payouts in general, meaning the combination of share repurchases and cash dividends, a simple life cycle theory fits points 1 and 2. The key ideas are straightforward. First, relatively young and less profitable firms generally should not make cash distributions. They need the cash to fund investments (and flotation costs discourage the raising of outside cash).

However, as a firm matures, it begins to generate free cash flow (which, you will recall, is internally generated cash flow beyond that needed to fund profitable investment activities). Significant free cash flow can lead to agency problems if it is not distributed. Managers may become tempted to pursue empire building or otherwise spend the excess cash in ways not in the shareholders' best interests. Thus firms come under pressure to make distributions rather than hoard cash. And, consistent with what we observe, we expect large firms with a history of profitability to make large distributions.

Thus the life cycle theory says that firms trade off the agency costs of excess cash retention against the potential future costs of external equity financing. A firm should begin making distributions when it generates sufficient internal cash flow to fund its investment needs now and into the foreseeable future.

The more complex issue concerns the type of distribution: cash dividends versus repurchase. The tax argument in favour of repurchases is a clear and strong one. Further, repurchases are a much more flexible option (and managers greatly value financial flexibility), so the question is: why would firms ever choose a cash dividend?

If we are to answer this question, we have to ask a different question. What can a cash dividend accomplish that a share repurchase cannot? One answer is that when a firm makes a commitment to pay a cash dividend now and into the future, it sends a two-part signal to the markets. As we have already discussed, one signal is that the firm anticipates being profitable, with the ability to make the payments on an ongoing basis. Note that a firm cannot benefit by trying to fool the market in this regard, because the firm would ultimately be punished when it couldn't make the dividend payment (or couldn't make it without relying on external financing). Thus a cash dividend may let a firm distinguish itself from less profitable rivals.

A second, and more subtle, signal takes us back to the agency problem of free cash flow. By committing itself to pay cash dividends now and in the future, the firm signals that it won't be hoarding cash (or at least not as much cash), thereby reducing agency costs and enhancing shareholder wealth.

This two-part signalling story is consistent with points 3–5 above, but an obvious objection remains. Why don't firms just commit themselves to a policy of setting aside whatever money would be used to pay dividends, and use it instead to buy back shares? After all, either way, a firm is committing itself to pay out cash to shareholders.

A fixed repurchase strategy suffers from two drawbacks. The first is verifiability. A firm could announce an open market repurchase and then simply not do it. By suitably fudging its books, it would be some time before the deception was discovered. Thus it would be necessary for shareholders to develop a monitoring mechanism, meaning some sort of way for shareholders to know for sure that the repurchase was in fact done. Such a mechanism wouldn't be difficult to build (it could be a simple trustee relationship, such as we observe in the bond markets), but it currently does not exist. Of course, a tender offer repurchase needs little or no verification, but such offers have expenses associated with them. The beauty of a cash dividend is that it needs no monitoring. A firm is forced to make dividend payments two or four times a year, year in and year out.

A second objection to a fixed repurchase strategy is more controversial. Suppose managers, as insiders, are better able than shareholders to judge whether their share price is too high or too low. (Note that this idea does not conflict with semi-strong market efficiency if inside information is the reason.) In this case, a fixed repurchase commitment forces management to buy back shares even in circumstances when the equity is overvalued. In other words, it forces management into making negative-NPV investments.

More research on the cash dividend versus share repurchase question is needed, but the historical trend seems to be favouring continued growth in repurchases relative to dividends.

**TABLE 16.2**

| Pros | Cons |
|---|---|
| 1 Cash dividends can underscore good results and provide support for the share price. | 1 Dividends are taxed to recipients. |
| 2 Dividends may attract institutional investors who prefer some return in the form of dividends. A mix of institutional and individual investors may allow a firm to raise capital at lower cost because of the ability of the firm to reach a wider market. | 2 Dividends can reduce internal sources of financing. Dividends may force the firm to forgo positive-NPV projects or rely on costly external equity financing. |
| 3 Share prices usually increase with the announcement of a new or increased dividend. | 3 Once dividends are established, dividend cuts are hard to make without adversely affecting a firm's share price. |
| 4 Dividends absorb excess cash flow, and may reduce the agency costs that arise from conflicts between management and shareholders. | |

**Table 16.2** The pros and cons of paying dividends

**TABLE 16.3**

| Policy statements | Proportion of respondents who agree or strongly agree (%) |
|---|---|
| 1 We try to avoid reducing dividends per share. | 93.8 |
| 2 We try to maintain a smooth dividend from year to year. | 89.6 |
| 3 We consider the level of dividends per share that we have paid in recent quarters. | 88.2 |
| 4 We are reluctant to make dividend changes that might have to be reversed in the future. | 77.9 |
| 5 We consider the change or growth in dividends per share. | 66.7 |
| 6 We consider the cost of raising external capital to be smaller than the cost of cutting dividends. | 42.8 |
| 7 We pay dividends to attract investors subject to 'prudent man' investment restrictions. | 41.7 |

Survey respondents were asked the question, 'Do these statements describe factors that affect your company's dividend decisions?'

*Source*: Adapted from Table 4 of A. Brav, J.R. Graham, C.R. Harvey and R. Michaely, 'Payout policy in the 21st century', *Journal of Financial Economics* (2005), vol. 77, no. 3, pp. 483–527.

**Table 16.3** Survey responses on dividend decisions

## Some Survey Evidence on Dividends

A recent study surveyed a large number of financial executives regarding dividend policy. One of the questions asked was, 'Do these statements describe factors that affect your company's dividend decisions?' Table 16.3 shows some of the results.

TABLE

16.4

| Policy statements | Proportion of respondents who think this is important or very important (%) |
|---|---|
| 1 Maintaining consistency with our historic dividend policy. | 84.1 |
| 2 Stability of future earnings. | 71.9 |
| 3 A sustainable change in earnings. | 67.1 |
| 4 Attracting institutional investors to purchase our stock. | 52.5 |
| 5 The availability of good investment opportunities for our firm to pursue. | 47.6 |
| 6 Attracting retail investors to purchase our stock. | 44.5 |
| 7 Personal taxes our shareholders pay when receiving dividends. | 21.1 |
| 8 Flotation costs of issuing new equity. | 9.3 |

Survey respondents were asked the question, 'How important are the following factors to your company's dividend decision?'

*Source*: Adapted from Table 5 of A. Brav, J.R. Graham, C.R. Harvey and R. Michaely, 'Payout policy in the 21st century', *Journal of Financial Economics* (2005), vol. 77, no. 3, pp. 483–527.

**Table 16.4** Survey responses on dividend decisions

As shown in Table 16.3, financial managers are very disinclined to cut dividends. Moreover, they are very conscious of their previous dividends, and desire to maintain a relatively steady dividend. In contrast, the cost of external capital and the desire to attract 'prudent man' investors (those with fiduciary duties) are less important.

Table 16.4 is drawn from the same survey, but here the responses are to the question, 'How important are the following factors to your company's dividend decision?' Not surprisingly, given the responses in Table 16.3 and our earlier discussion, the highest priority is maintaining a consistent dividend policy. The next several items are also consistent with our previous analysis. Financial managers are very concerned about earnings stability and future earnings levels in making dividend decisions, and they consider the availability of good investment opportunities. Survey respondents also believed that attracting both institutional and individual (retail) investors was relatively important.

In contrast to our discussion of taxes and flotation costs in the earlier part of this chapter, the financial managers in this survey did not think that personal taxes paid on dividends by shareholders were very important. And even fewer thought that equity flotation costs were relevant.

## 16.8 Stock Dividends and Stock Splits

Another type of dividend is paid out in shares of equity. This type of dividend is called a **share** or **stock dividend**. A stock dividend is not a true dividend, because it is not paid in cash. The effect of a stock dividend is to increase the number of shares that each owner holds. Because there are more shares outstanding, each is simply worth less.

**stock dividend** A payment made by a firm to its owners in the form of equity, diluting the value of each share outstanding.

A stock dividend is commonly expressed as a percentage: for example, a 20 per cent stock dividend means that a shareholder receives one new share for every five currently owned (a 20 per cent increase). Because every shareholder receives 20 per cent more shares, the total number of shares outstanding rises by 20 per cent. As we shall see in a moment, the result is that each share of equity is worth about 20 per cent less.

A **stock split** is essentially the same thing as a stock dividend, except that it is expressed as a ratio instead of a percentage. When a split is declared, each share is split up to create additional shares. For example, in a three-for-one stock split, each old share is split into three new shares.

> **stock split**
> An increase in a firm's shares outstanding without any change in owners' equity.

## Some Details about Stock Splits and Stock Dividends

Stock splits and stock dividends have essentially the same impacts on the corporation and the shareholder: they increase the number of shares outstanding and reduce the value per share. Unlike US accounting standards, IFRS makes no distinction between a cash dividend and a stock dividend. IFRS considers a stock dividend as being a cash dividend to shareholders with a simultaneous purchase of shares by the same shareholders.

By convention, stock dividends of less than 20 to 25 per cent are called *small stock dividends*. The accounting procedure for such a dividend is discussed next. A stock dividend greater than this value of 20 to 25 per cent is called a *large stock dividend*. Large stock dividends are not uncommon, and except for some relatively minor accounting differences, a stock dividend has the same effect as a stock split.

## Value of Stock Splits and Stock Dividends

The laws of logic tell us that stock splits and stock dividends can: (1) leave the value of the firm unaffected; (2) increase its value; or (3) decrease its value. Unfortunately, the issues are complex enough that we cannot easily determine which of the three relationships holds.

**The Benchmark Case**   A strong case can be made that stock dividends and splits do not change either the wealth of any shareholder or the wealth of the firm as a whole. Consider an all-equity firm with a total market value of €660,000 and 10,000 shares. With a 10 per cent stock dividend, the number of shares increases to 11,000, so it seems that each would be worth €660,000/11,000 = €60.

For example, a shareholder who had 100 shares worth €66 each before the dividend would have 110 shares worth €60 each afterwards. The total value of the equity is €6,600 either way; so the stock dividend doesn't really have any economic effect.

Now consider a two-for-one split. After the stock split there are 20,000 shares outstanding, so each should be worth €660,000/20,000 = €33. In other words, the number of shares double and the price halves. From these calculations it appears that stock dividends and splits are just paper transactions.

Although these results are relatively obvious, reasons are often given to suggest that there may be some benefits to these actions. The typical financial manager is aware of many real-world complexities: for that reason, the stock split or stock dividend decision is not treated lightly in practice.

**Popular Trading Range**   Proponents of stock dividends and stock splits frequently argue that a security has a proper **trading range**. When the security is priced above this level, many investors do not have the funds to buy the common trading unit of 100 shares, called a *round lot*. Although securities can be purchased in *odd-lot* form (fewer than 100 shares), the commissions are greater. Thus firms will split the equity to keep the price in this trading range.

> **trading range**
> The price range between the highest and lowest prices at which an equity is traded.

For example, Microsoft has split nine times since the company went public in 1986. The equity has split three-for-two on two occasions and two-for-one a total of seven times. So for every share of Microsoft you owned in 1986 when the company first went public, you would own 288 shares as of the most recent stock split. Similarly, since Wal-Mart went public in 1970, it has split its equity two-for-one 11 times, and Dell has split three-for-two once and two-for-one six times since going public in 1988.

Although this argument is a popular one, its validity is questionable, for a number of reasons. Mutual funds, pension funds and other institutions have steadily increased their trading activity since World War II, and now handle a sizable percentage of total trading volume (of the order of 80 per cent of stock exchange trading volume, for example). Because these institutions buy and sell in huge amounts, the individual share price is of little concern.

Furthermore, we sometimes observe share prices that are quite large that do not appear to cause problems. To take an extreme case, consider the Swiss chocolatier Lindt. In February 2006 Lindt shares were selling for around 24,595 Swiss francs each, or about £13,878 (€16,288). This is fairly expensive, but also consider Berkshire-Hathaway, the company run by legendary investor Warren Buffet. In March 2010 each share in the company sold for about €92,490!

Finally, there is evidence that stock splits may actually decrease the liquidity of the company's shares. Following a two-for-one split, the number of shares traded should more than double if liquidity is increased by the split. This doesn't appear to happen, and the reverse is sometimes observed.

## Reverse Splits

**reverse split**
A stock split in which a firm's number of shares outstanding is reduced.

A less frequently encountered financial manoeuvre is the **reverse split**. For example, in 2008 Ericsson, the multinational telecommunications firm, underwent a one-for-five reverse stock split. In a one-for-five reverse split each investor exchanges five old shares for one new share. The par value is quintupled in the process. As with stock splits and stock dividends, a case can be made that a reverse split has no real effect.

Given real-world imperfections, three related reasons are cited for reverse splits. First, transaction costs to shareholders may be less after the reverse split. Second, the liquidity and marketability of a company's equity might be improved when its price is raised to the popular trading range. Third, equities selling at prices below a certain level are not considered respectable, meaning that investors underestimate these firms' earnings, cash flow, growth and stability. Some financial analysts argue that a reverse split can achieve instant respectability. As was the case with stock splits, none of these reasons is particularly compelling, especially not the third one.

There are two other reasons for reverse splits. First, stock exchanges have minimum share price requirements. A reverse split may bring the share price up to such a minimum. Second, companies sometimes perform reverse splits and, at the same time, buy out any shareholders who end up with less than a certain number of shares.

**CONCEPT QUESTIONS**

16.8a   What is the effect of a stock split on shareholder wealth?
16.8b   How does the accounting treatment of a stock split differ from that used with a stock dividend?

## Summary and Conclusions

In this chapter we first discussed the types of dividend and how they are paid. We then defined dividend policy, and examined whether or not dividend policy matters. Next, we illustrated how a firm might establish a dividend policy, and described an important alternative to cash dividends, a share repurchase.

In covering these subjects, we saw these points:

1   Dividend policy is irrelevant when there are no taxes or other imperfections, because shareholders can effectively undo the firm's dividend strategy. Shareholders who receive dividends greater than desired can reinvest the excess. Conversely, shareholders who receive dividends smaller than desired can sell off extra shares of equity.

2 Individual shareholder income taxes and new issue flotation costs are real-world considerations that favour a low-dividend payout. With taxes and new issue costs, the firm should pay out dividends only after all positive-NPV projects have been fully financed.

3 There are groups in the economy that may favour a high payout. These include many large institutions, such as pension plans. Recognizing that some groups prefer a high payout and some prefer a low payout, the clientele-effect argument supports the idea that dividend policy responds to the needs of shareholders. For example, if 40 per cent of the shareholders prefer low dividends and 60 per cent of the shareholders prefer high dividends, approximately 40 per cent of companies will have a low-dividend payout and 60 per cent will have a high payout. This sharply reduces the impact of any individual firm's dividend policy on its market price.

4 A share repurchase acts much like a cash dividend, but has a significant tax advantage. Stock repurchases are therefore a very useful part of overall dividend policy.

5 We discussed recent research and thinking on dividend policy. We saw that dividends are heavily concentrated in a relatively small number of larger, older firms, and that the use of share repurchases continues to grow. We described a simple life cycle theory of distributions, in which firms trade off the agency costs of excess cash retention against the future costs of external equity financing. The implication is that younger firms with significant growth opportunities will not distribute cash, but older, profitable firms with significant free cash flow will do so.

To close our discussion of dividends, we emphasize one last time the difference between dividends and dividend policy. Dividends are important, because the value of a share of equity is ultimately determined by the dividends that will be paid. What is less clear is whether the time pattern of dividends (more now versus more later) matters. This is the dividend policy question, and it is not easy to give a definitive answer to it.

# Concepts Review and Critical Thinking Questions

1 **Dividend Policy Irrelevance [LO2]**   How is it possible that dividends are so important but, at the same time, dividend policy is irrelevant?

2 **Share Repurchases [LO4]**   What is the impact of a share repurchase on a company's debt ratio? Does this suggest another use for excess cash?

3 **Dividend Chronology [LO1]**   On Tuesday 8 December, Home Potere SpA's board of directors declares a dividend of 75 cents per share payable on Wednesday 17 January to shareholders of record as of Wednesday 3 January. When is the ex-dividend date? If a shareholder buys equity before that date, who gets the dividends on those shares – the buyer or the seller?

4 **Alternative Dividends [LO1]**   Some corporations, like one British company that offers its large shareholders free crematorium use, pay dividends in kind (that is, offer their services to shareholders at below-market cost). Should mutual funds invest in equities that pay these dividends in kind? (The fundholders do not receive these services.)

5 **Dividends and Share Price [LO1]**   If increases in dividends tend to be followed by (immediate) increases in share prices, how can it be said that dividend policy is irrelevant?

6 **Dividends and Share Price [LO1]**   Last month, Central Virginia Power Company, which had been having trouble with cost overruns on a nuclear power plant that it had been building, announced that it was 'temporarily suspending payments due to the cash flow crunch associated with its investment programme'. The company's share price dropped from $28.50 to $25 when this announcement was made. How would you interpret this change in the share price (that is, what would you say caused it)?

7  **Dividend Reinvestment Plans [LO1]**   DRK plc has recently developed a dividend reinvestment plan, or DRIP. The plan allows investors to reinvest cash dividends automatically in DRK in exchange for new shares of equity. Over time, investors in DRK will be able to build their holdings by reinvesting dividends to purchase additional shares of the company.

Many companies offer dividend reinvestment plans. Most companies with DRIPs charge no brokerage or service fees. In fact, the shares of DRK will be purchased at a 10 per cent discount from the market price. A consultant for DRK estimates that about 75 per cent of DRK's shareholders will take part in this plan. This is somewhat higher than the average.

Evaluate DRK's dividend reinvestment plan. Will it increase shareholder wealth? Discuss the advantages and disadvantages involved here.

8  **Dividend Policy [LO1]**   The fourth quarter of 2009 saw an upturn in initial public offerings in Europe, with about €5 billion raised and up 400 per cent from the previous quarter. Relatively few of the 61 firms involved paid cash dividends. Why do you think that most chose not to pay cash dividends?

Use the following information to answer the next two questions:

Historically, the US tax code treated dividend payments made to shareholders as ordinary income. Thus dividends were taxed at the investor's marginal tax rate, which was as high as 38.6 per cent in 2002. Capital gains were taxed at a capital gains tax rate, which was the same for most investors and fluctuated through the years. In 2002 the capital gains tax rate stood at 20 per cent. In an effort to stimulate the economy, President George W. Bush presided over a tax plan overhaul that included changes in dividend and capital gains tax rates. The new tax plan, which was implemented in 2003, called for a 15 per cent tax rate on both dividends and capital gains for investors in higher tax brackets. For lower-tax-bracket investors the tax rate on dividends and capital gains was set at 5 per cent through 2007, dropping to zero in 2008.

9  **Ex-Dividend Share Prices [LO1]**   How do you think this tax law change affects ex-dividend share prices?

10  **Share Repurchases [LO4]**   How do you think this tax law change affected the relative attractiveness of share repurchases compared with dividend payments?

## connect Questions and Problems

**BASIC**
**1–9**

1  **Dividends and Taxes [LO2]**   Lea SpA has declared a €6 per-share dividend. Italy has a gradual tax system, where higher tax rates are charged at higher salary bands. Capital gains are taxed, dependent on how long you hold the shares of the company, and the amount recorded for tax purposes is deflated by the inflation rate between the date of purchase and the date of sale. We're going to make things simple. Suppose the tax rate on capital gains and dividends is zero. Lea sells for €80 per share, and the equity is about to go ex dividend. What do you think the ex-dividend price will be?

2  **Stock Dividends [LO3]**   The owners' equity accounts for Hexagon International are shown here:

|  | £ |
| --- | --- |
| Ordinary shares (£1 par value) | 10,000 |
| Capital surplus | 180,000 |
| Retained earnings | 586,500 |
| Total owners' equity | 776,500 |

(a) If Hexagon shares currently sell for £25 per share, and a 10 per cent stock dividend is declared, how many new shares will be distributed? Show how the equity accounts would change.

(b) If Hexagon declared a 25 per cent stock dividend, how would the accounts change?

3 **Stock Splits [LO3]**   For the company in Problem 2, show how the equity accounts will change if:

(a) Hexagon declares a four-for-one stock split. How many shares are outstanding now? What is the new par value per share?

(b) Hexagon declares a one-for-five reverse stock split. How many shares are outstanding now? What is the new par value per share?

4 **Stock Splits and Stock Dividends [LO3]**   Roll AB currently has 150,000 shares outstanding that sell for SKr65 per share. Assuming no market imperfections or tax effects exist, what will the share price be after:

(a) a five-for-three stock split?

(b) a 15 per cent stock dividend?

(c) a 42.5 per cent stock dividend?

(d) a four-for-seven reverse stock split?

Determine the new number of shares outstanding in parts (a)–(d).

5 **Regular Dividends [LO1]**   The balance sheet for Levy AG is shown here in market value terms. There are 5,000 shares outstanding.

| Market value balance sheet | | | |
|---|---|---|---|
| | **€** | | **€** |
| Cash | 20,000 | Equity | 175,000 |
| Fixed assets | 155,000 | | |
| Total | 175,000 | Total | 175,000 |

The company has declared a dividend of €1.50 per share. The equity goes ex dividend tomorrow. Ignoring any tax effects, what are the shares selling for today? What will they sell for tomorrow? What will the market value balance sheet look like after the dividends are paid?

6 **Share Repurchase [LO4]**   In the previous problem, suppose Levy has announced it is going to repurchase €4,025 worth of equity. What effect will this transaction have on the equity of the firm? How many shares will be outstanding? What will the price per share be after the repurchase? Ignoring tax effects, show how the share repurchase is effectively the same as a cash dividend.

7 **Stock Dividends [LO3]**   The market value balance sheet for Outbox Manufacturing is shown here. Outbox has declared a 25 per cent stock dividend. The stock goes ex dividend tomorrow (the chronology for a stock dividend is similar to that for a cash dividend). There are 15,000 shares of equity outstanding. What will the ex-dividend price be?

| Market value balance sheet | | | |
|---|---|---|---|
| | **£** | | **£** |
| Cash | 190,000 | Debt | 160,000 |
| Fixed assets | 330,000 | Equity | 360,000 |
| Total | 520,000 | Total | 520,000 |

8 **Stock Dividends [LO3]** The company with the equity accounts shown here has declared a 12 per cent stock dividend when the market value of its equity is €20 per share. What effects on the equity accounts will the distribution of the stock dividend have?

| | € |
| --- | --- |
| Ordinary shares (€1 par value) | 350,000 |
| Capital surplus | 1,650,000 |
| Retained earnings | 3,000,000 |
| Total owners' equity | 5,000,000 |

9 **Stock Splits [LO3]** In the previous problem, suppose the company instead decides on a five-for-one stock split. The firm's 70 pence per share cash dividend on the new (post-split) shares represents an increase of 10 per cent over last year's dividend on the pre-split equity. What effect does this have on the equity accounts? What was last year's dividend per share?

INTERMEDIATE
10–12

10 **Homemade Dividends [LO2]** You own 1,000 shares of equity in Avondale Property ASA. You will receive a 0.70 krone (NKr) per share dividend in one year. In two years, Avondale will pay a liquidating dividend of NKr40 per share. The required return on Avondale shares is 15 per cent. What is the current share price of your equity (ignoring taxes)? If you would rather have equal dividends in each of the next two years, show how you can accomplish this by creating homemade dividends. (*Hint*: Dividends will be in the form of an annuity.)

11 **Homemade Dividends [LO2]** In the previous problem, suppose you want only NKr200 total in dividends the first year. What will your homemade dividend be in two years?

12 **Share Repurchase [LO4]** Flychucker SA is evaluating an extra dividend versus a share repurchase. In either case €5,000 would be spent. Current earnings are €0.95 per share, and the equity currently sells for €40 per share. There are 200 shares outstanding. Ignore taxes and other imperfections in answering parts (a) and (b).

(a) Evaluate the two alternatives in terms of the effect on the price per share of the equity and shareholder wealth.

(b) What will be the effect on Flychucker's EPS and P/E ratio under the two different scenarios?

(c) In the real world, which of these actions would you recommend? Why?

CHALLENGE
13–16

13 **Expected Return, Dividends and Taxes [LO2]** Gecko Company and Gordon Company are two firms whose business risk is the same but which have different dividend policies. Gecko pays no dividend, whereas Gordon has an expected dividend yield of 6 per cent. Suppose the capital gains tax rate is zero, whereas the dividend tax rate is 12.5 per cent. Gecko has an expected earnings growth rate of 15 per cent annually, and its share price is expected to grow at this same rate. If the after-tax expected returns on the two equities are equal (because they are in the same risk class), what is the pre-tax required return on Gordon's shares?

14 **Dividends and Taxes [LO2]** As discussed in the text, in the absence of market imperfections and tax effects, we would expect the share price to decline by the amount of the dividend payment when the stock goes ex dividend. Once we consider the role of taxes, however, this is not necessarily true. One model has been proposed that incorporates tax effects into determining the ex-dividend price:[8]

$$(P_0 - P_X)/D = (1 - T_P)/(1 - T_G)$$

where $P_0$ is the price just before the equity goes ex, $P_X$ is the ex-dividend share price, $D$ is the amount of the dividend per share, $T_P$ is the relevant marginal personal tax rate on dividends, and $T_G$ is the effective marginal tax rate on capital gains.

(a) If $T_P = T_G = 0$, how much will the share price fall when the equity goes ex?

(b) If $T_P = 15$ per cent and $T_G = 0$, how much will the share price fall?

(c) If $T_P = 15$ per cent and $T_G = 30$ per cent, how much will the share price fall?

(d) What does this problem tell you about real-world tax considerations and the dividend policy of the firm?

15 **Dividends versus Reinvestment [LO2]** National Business Machine plc (NBM) has £2 million of extra cash after taxes have been paid. NBM has two choices to make use of this cash. One alternative is to invest the cash in financial assets. The resulting investment income will be paid out as a special dividend at the end of three years. In this case, the firm can invest in either Treasury bills yielding 7 per cent or an 11 per cent preferred stock. Another alternative is to pay out the cash now as dividends. This would allow the shareholders to invest on their own in Treasury bills with the same yield, or in preferred stock. The corporate tax rate is 28 per cent. Assume the investor has a 40 per cent personal income tax rate, which is applied to interest income and preferred stock dividends. The personal dividend tax rate is 12.5 per cent on cash dividends. Should the cash be paid today or in three years? Which of the two options generates the highest after-tax income for the shareholders?

16 **Dividends versus Reinvestment [LO2]** After completing its capital spending for the year, Carlson Manufacturing has £1,000 extra cash. Carlson's managers must choose between investing the cash in Treasury bonds that yield 8 per cent or paying the cash out to investors, who would invest in the bonds themselves.

(a) If the corporate tax rate is 28 per cent, what personal tax rate would make the investors equally willing to receive the dividend or let Carlson invest the money?

(b) Is the answer to (a) reasonable? Why or why not?

(c) Suppose the only investment choice is a preference share that yields 12 per cent. What personal tax rate will make the shareholders indifferent to the outcome of Carlson's dividend decision?

Is this a compelling argument for a low-dividend payout ratio? Why or why not?

## MINI CASE    Electronic Calendrier SA

Electronic Calendrier (EC) is a small company founded 15 years ago by electronics engineers Georges Thiébald and Louis-Lucien Klotz. EC manufactures integrated circuits to capitalize on the complex mixed-signal design technology, and has recently entered the market for frequency timing generators, or silicon timing devices, which provide the timing signals or 'clocks' necessary to synchronize electronic systems. Its clock products originally were used in PC video graphics applications, but the market subsequently expanded to include motherboards, PC peripheral devices, and other digital consumer electronics such as digital television boxes and game consoles. EC also designs and markets custom application-specific integrated circuits (ASICs) for industrial customers. The ASICs' design combines analogue and digital, or mixed-signal, technology. In addition to Georges and Louis-Lucien, Katherine Pancol, who provided capital for the company, is the third primary owner. Each owns 25 per cent of the 1 million shares outstanding. Several other individuals, including current employees, own the remaining company shares.

Recently, the company has designed a new computer motherboard. The company's design is both more efficient and less expensive to manufacture, and the EC design is expected to become standard in many personal computers. After investigating the possibility of manufacturing the new motherboard, EC determined that the costs involved in building a new plant would be prohibitive. The owners also decided that they were unwilling to bring in another large outside owner. Instead, EC sold the design to an outside firm. The sale of the motherboard design was completed for an after-tax payment of €30 million.

1 Georges believes the company should use the extra cash to pay a special one-time dividend. How will this proposal affect the share price? How will it affect the value of the company?

2 Louis-Lucent believes that the company should use the extra cash to pay off debt, and upgrade and expand its existing manufacturing capability. How would Louis-Lucent's proposals affect the company?

3 Katherine is in favour of a share repurchase. She argues that a repurchase will increase the company's P/E ratio, return on assets, and return on equity. Are her arguments correct? How will a share repurchase affect the value of the company?

4 Another option discussed by Georges, Louis-Lucent and Katherine would be to begin a regular dividend payment to shareholders. How would you evaluate this proposal?

5 One way to value a share of equity is the dividend growth, or growing perpetuity, model. Consider the following. The dividend payout ratio is 1 minus $b$, where $b$ is the 'retention' or 'ploughback' ratio. So the dividend next year will be the earnings next year, $E_1$, times 1 minus the retention ratio. The most commonly used equation to calculate the sustainable growth rate is the return on equity times the retention ratio. Substituting these relationships into the dividend growth model, we get the following equation to calculate the price of a share of equity today:

$$P_0 = \frac{E_1(1-b)}{R_S - \text{ROE} \times b}$$

What are the implications of this result in terms of whether the company should pay a dividend or upgrade and expand its manufacturing capability? Explain.

6 Does the question of whether the company should pay a dividend depend on whether the company is organized as a corporation or as a partnership?

## Endnotes

1 The same results would occur after an issue of bonds, although the arguments would be less easily presented.

2 In fact, capital gains taxes can sometimes be avoided altogether. Although we do not recommend this particular tax avoidance strategy, the capital gains tax may be avoided by dying. Your heirs are not considered to have a capital gain, so the tax liability dies when you do. In this instance, you *can* take it with you.

3 B. Graham, D. Dodd and S. Cottle, *Security Analysis* (New York: McGraw-Hill, 1962).

4 This list is distilled in part from a longer list in H. DeAngelo and L. DeAngelo, 'Payout policy pedagogy: what matters and why', *European Financial Management* (2007), vol. 13, no. 1, pp. 11–27.

# HAPTER
# 17

# Short-Term Financial Planning and Management

## LEARNING OBJECTIVES

After studying this chapter, you should understand:

**LO1** The importance of float, and how it affects the cash balances.

**LO2** How firms manage their cash, and some of the collection, concentration and disbursement techniques used.

**LO3** The advantages and disadvantages of holding cash, and some of the ways to invest idle cash.

**LO4** How firms manage their receivables, and the basic components of a firm's credit policies.

**LO5** How to analyse the decision by a firm to grant credit.

**LO6** The types of inventory and inventory management system used by firms.

**LO7** How to determine the costs of carrying inventory, and the optimal inventory level.

AS MOST PEOPLE KNOW, many banks ran out of cash in 2008 and 2009 as bad debts, lack of short-term financing, and poor profitable opportunities combined to cause the most severe crisis in the financial sector for decades. Governments stepped into the breach and used taxpayers' money to shore up their institutions. The non-financial sector was also seriously affected. All across Europe, construction companies and other firms, such as estate agents, found that they had no cash, because the housing market was almost non-existent. The automobile industry suffered deeply, and many firms changed their manufacturing strategy, made workers redundant, and cut production to save cash. Cash is one of the most important issues a firm needs to consider. Even if a firm is growing and has excellent performance, if it runs out of cash it cannot survive.

This chapter is about how firms manage cash and other short-term financial assets. The basic objective in short-term financial management is to keep the investment in cash and other short-term assets as low as possible while still keeping the firm operating efficiently and effectively. This goal usually reduces to the dictum 'Collect early and pay late'. Accordingly, we discuss ways of accelerating collections and managing disbursements.

In addition, firms must invest temporarily idle cash in short-term marketable securities. As we discuss in various places, these securities can be bought and sold in the financial markets. As a group, they have very little default risk, and most are highly marketable. There are different types of these so-called money market securities, and we discuss a few of the most important ones.

## 17.1 Reasons for Holding Cash

John Maynard Keynes, in his classic work *The General Theory of Employment, Interest and Money*, identified three motives for liquidity: the speculative motive, the precautionary motive, and the transaction motive. We discuss these next.

**speculative motive**
The need to hold cash to take advantage of additional investment opportunities, such as bargain purchases.

**precautionary motive**
The need to hold cash as a safety margin to act as a financial reserve.

**transaction motive**
The need to hold cash to satisfy normal disbursement and collection activities associated with a firm's ongoing operations.

### The Speculative and Precautionary Motives

The **speculative motive** is the need to hold cash in order to be able to take advantage of, for example, bargain purchases that might arise, attractive interest rates, and (in the case of international firms) favourable exchange rate fluctuations.

For most firms, reserve borrowing ability and marketable securities can be used to satisfy speculative motives. Thus there might be a speculative motive for maintaining liquidity, but not necessarily for holding cash *per se*. Think of it this way: if you have a credit card with a very large credit limit, then you can probably take advantage of any unusual bargains that come along without carrying any cash.

This is also true, to a lesser extent, for precautionary motives. The **precautionary motive** is the need for a safety supply to act as a financial reserve. Once again, there probably is a precautionary motive for maintaining liquidity. However, given that the value of money market instruments is relatively certain, and that instruments such as T-bills are extremely liquid, there is no real need to hold substantial amounts of cash for precautionary purposes.

### The Transaction Motive

Cash is needed to satisfy the **transaction motive**: the need to have cash on hand to pay bills. Transaction-related needs come from the normal disbursement and collection activities of the firm. The disbursement of cash includes the payment of wages and salaries, trade debts, taxes and dividends.

Cash is collected from product sales, the selling of assets, and new financing. The cash inflows (collections) and outflows (disbursements) are not perfectly synchronized, and some level of cash holdings is necessary to serve as a buffer.

As electronic funds transfers and other high-speed 'paperless' payment mechanisms continue to develop, even the transaction demand for cash may all but disappear. Even if it does, however, there will still be a demand for liquidity and a need to manage it efficiently.

## Compensating Balances

Compensating balances are another reason to hold cash. Cash balances are kept at banks to compensate for banking services the firm receives. A minimum compensating balance requirement may impose a lower limit on the level of cash a firm holds.

## Costs of Holding Cash

When a firm holds cash in excess of some necessary minimum, it incurs an opportunity cost. The opportunity cost of excess cash (held in currency or bank deposits) is the interest income that could be earned in the next best use, such as investment in marketable securities.

Given the opportunity cost of holding cash, why would a firm hold cash in excess of its compensating balance requirements? The answer is that a cash balance must be maintained to provide the liquidity necessary for transaction needs – paying bills. If the firm maintains too small a cash balance, it may run out of cash. If this happens, the firm may have to raise cash on a short-term basis. This could involve, for example, selling marketable securities or borrowing.

Activities such as selling marketable securities and borrowing involve various costs. As we've discussed, holding cash has an opportunity cost. To determine the appropriate cash balance, the firm must weigh the benefits of holding cash against these costs. We discuss this subject in more detail in the sections that follow.

## Cash Management versus Liquidity Management

Before we move on, we should note that it is important to distinguish between true cash management and a more general subject, liquidity management. The distinction is a source of confusion, because the word *cash* is used in practice in two different ways. First of all, it has its literal meaning: actual cash on hand. However, financial managers frequently use the word to describe a firm's holdings of cash along with its marketable securities, and marketable securities are sometimes called *cash equivalents* or *near-cash*.

The distinction between liquidity management and cash management is straightforward. Liquidity management concerns the optimal quantity of liquid assets a firm should have on hand, and it is one particular aspect of the current asset management policies we discus in this chapter. Cash management is much more closely related to optimizing mechanisms for collecting and disbursing cash.

**CONCEPT QUESTIONS**

17.1a What is the transaction motive, and how does it lead firms to hold cash?

17.1b What is the cost to the firm of holding excess cash?

## 17.2 Understanding Float

> **float**
> The difference between book cash and bank cash, representing the net effect of cheques in the process of clearing.

A firm's cash balance as reported in its financial statements (book cash or ledger cash) is not the same thing as the balance shown in its bank account (bank cash or collected bank cash). The difference between bank cash and book cash is called **float**, and represents the net effect of cheques in the process of *clearing* (moving through the banking system).

### Disbursement Float

Cheques written by a firm generate *disbursement float*, causing a decrease in the firm's book balance but no change in its available balance. For example, suppose General Mechanics plc currently has £100,000 on deposit with its bank. On 8 June it buys some raw materials and pays with a cheque for £100,000. The company's book balance is immediately reduced by £100,000 as a result.

GM's bank, however, will not find out about this cheque until it is presented to GM's bank for payment on, say, 14 June. Until the cheque is presented, the firm's available balance is greater than its book balance by £100,000. In other words, before 8 June, GM has a zero float:

$$\text{Float} = \text{Firm's available balance} - \text{Firm's book balance}$$
$$= £100,000 - 100,000$$
$$= £0$$

GM's position from 8 June to 14 June is

$$\text{Disbursement float} = \text{Firm's available balance} - \text{Firm's book balance}$$
$$= £100,000 - 0$$
$$= £100,000$$

While the cheque is clearing, GM has a balance with the bank of £100,000. It can obtain the benefit of this cash during this period. For example, the available balance could be temporarily invested in marketable securities and thus earn some interest. We shall return to this subject a little later.

### Collection Float and Net Float

Cheques received by the firm create *collection float*. Collection float increases book balances but does not immediately change available balances. For example, suppose GM receives a cheque from a customer for £100,000 on 8 October. Assume, as before, that the company has £100,000 deposited at its bank, and a zero float. It deposits the cheque and increases its book balance by £100,000 to £200,000. However, the additional cash is not available to GM until its bank has presented the cheque to the customer's bank and received £100,000. This will occur on, say, 14 October. In the meantime, the cash position at GM will reflect a collection float of £100,000. We can summarize these events. Before 8 October, GM's position is

$$\text{Float} = \text{Firm's available balance} - \text{Firm's book balance}$$
$$= £100,000 - 100,000$$
$$= £0$$

GM's position from 8 October to 14 October is

$$\text{Collection float} = \text{Firm's available balance} - \text{Firm's book balance}$$
$$= £100,000 - 200,000$$
$$= -£100,000$$

In general, a firm's payment (disbursement) activities generate disbursement float, and its collection activities generate collection float. The net effect – that is, the sum of the total collection and disbursement floats – is the *net float*. The net float at a point in time is simply the overall difference between the firm's available balance and its book balance. If the net float is positive, then the firm's disbursement float exceeds its collection float, and its available balance exceeds its book balance. If the available balance is less than the book balance, then the firm has a net collection float.

A firm should be concerned with its net float and available balance more than with its book balance. If a financial manager knows that a cheque written by the company will not clear for several days, that manager will be able to keep a lower cash balance at the bank than might be possible otherwise. This can generate a great deal of money.

For example, take the case of Royal Dutch Shell plc. The average daily sales of Royal Dutch Shell are about £780 million. If Royal Dutch Shell's collections could be speeded up by a single day, then the company could release £780 million for investing. At a relatively modest 0.01 per cent daily rate, the interest earned would be in the order of £78,000 per day.

---

**EXAMPLE 17.1**

## Staying Afloat

Suppose you have €5,000 on deposit. One day, you write a cheque for €1,000 to pay for books, and you deposit €2,000. What are your disbursement, collection and net floats?

After you have written the €1,000 cheque, you show a balance of €4,000 on your books, but the bank shows €5,000 while the cheque is clearing. The difference is a disbursement float of €1,000.

After you have deposited the €2,000 cheque, you show a balance of €6,000. Your available balance doesn't rise until the cheque clears. This results in a collection float of −€2,000. Your net float is the sum of the collection and disbursement floats, or −€1,000.

Overall, you show €6,000 on your books. The bank shows a €7,000 balance, but only €5,000 is available, because your deposit has not been cleared. The discrepancy between your available balance and your book balance is the net float (−€1,000), and it is bad for you. If you write another cheque for €5,500 there may not be sufficient available funds to cover it, and it may bounce. This is why financial managers have to be concerned more with available balances than with book balances.

---

## Float Management

Float management involves controlling the collection and disbursement of cash. The objective in cash collection is to speed up collections and reduce the lag between the time customers pay their bills and the time the cash becomes available. The objective in cash disbursement is to control payments and minimize the firm's costs associated with making payments.

Total collection or disbursement times can be broken down into three parts: mailing time, processing delay, and availability delay:

1 *Mailing time* is the part of the collection and disbursement process during which cheques are trapped in the postal system.

2 *Processing delay* is the time it takes the receiver of a cheque to process the payment and deposit it in a bank for collection.

3 *Availability delay* refers to the time required to clear a cheque through the banking system.

Speeding up collections involves reducing one or more of these components. Slowing down disbursements involves increasing one of them. We shall describe some procedures for managing collection and disbursement times later. First, we need to discuss how float is measured.

**Measuring Float**    The size of the float depends on both the cash levels and the time delay involved. For example, suppose you mail a cheque for €500 to another Eurozone country each month. It takes five days in the mail for the cheque to reach its destination (the mailing time), and one day for the recipient to get over to the bank (the processing delay). The recipient's bank holds foreign country cheques for three days (availability delay). The total delay is $5 + 1 + 3 = 9$ days.

In this case, what is your average daily disbursement float? There are two equivalent ways of calculating the answer. First, you have a €500 float for nine days, so we say that the total float is $9 \times €500 = €4,500$. Assuming 30 days in the month, the average daily float is €4,500/30 = €150.

Alternatively, your disbursement float is €500 for 9 days out of the month and zero for the other 21 days (again assuming 30 days in a month). Your average daily float is thus

$$
\begin{aligned}
\text{Average daily float} &= (9 \times €500 + 21 \times 0)/30 \\
&= 9/30 \times €500 + 21/30 \times 0 \\
&= €4,500/30 \\
&= €150
\end{aligned}
$$

This means that, on an average day, your book balance is €150 less than your available balance, representing a €150 average disbursement float.

Things are only a little more complicated when there are multiple disbursements or receipts. To illustrate, suppose Concepts NV receives two items each month as follows:

| Amount | Processing and availability delay | Total float |
|---|:---:|---:|
| Item 1: €5,000,000 | × 9 | = €45,000,000 |
| Item 2: €3,000,000 | × 5 | = €15,000,000 |
| Total €8,000,000 | | €60,000,000 |

The average daily float is equal to

$$
\begin{aligned}
\text{Average daily float} &= \frac{\text{Total float}}{\text{Total days}} \\
&= \frac{€60 \text{ million}}{30} \\
&= €2 \text{ million}
\end{aligned}
\qquad \text{(17.1)}
$$

So, on an average day, there is €2 million that is uncollected and not available.

Another way to see this is to calculate the average daily receipts and multiply by the weighted average delay. Average daily receipts are

$$
\begin{aligned}
\text{Average daily receipts} &= \frac{\text{Total receipts}}{\text{Total days}} \\
&= \frac{€8 \text{ million}}{30} \\
&= €266,666.67
\end{aligned}
$$

Of the €8 million total receipts, €5 million, or $5/8$ of the total, is delayed for nine days. The other $3/8$ is delayed for five days. The weighted average delay is thus

$$
\begin{aligned}
\text{Weighted average delay} &= (5/8) \times 9 \text{ days} + (3/8) \times 5 \text{ days} \\
&= 5.625 + 1.875 \\
&= 7.50 \text{ days}
\end{aligned}
$$

The average daily float is thus

$$
\begin{aligned}
\text{Average daily float} &= \text{Average daily receipts} \times \text{Weighted average delay} \\
&= €266,666.67 \times 7.50 \text{ days} \\
&= €2 \text{ million}
\end{aligned}
\qquad \text{(17.2)}
$$

**Some Details** In measuring float there is an important difference to note between collection and disbursement float. We defined *float* as the difference between the firm's available cash balance and its book balance. With a disbursement, the firm's book balance goes down when the cheque is *mailed*, so the mailing time is an important component in disbursement float. However, with a collection, the firm's book balance isn't increased until the cheque is *received*, so mailing time is not a component of collection float.

This doesn't mean that mailing time is not important. The point is that when collection *float* is calculated, mailing time should not be considered. As we shall discuss, when total collection *time* is considered, the mailing time is a crucial component.

Also, when we talk about availability delay, how long it actually takes a cheque to clear isn't really crucial. What matters is how long we must wait before the bank grants availability – that is, use of the funds. Banks actually use availability schedules to determine how long a cheque is held, based on time of deposit and other factors. Beyond this, availability delay can be a matter of negotiation between the bank and a customer. In a similar vein, for outgoing cheques, what matters is the date our account is debited, not when the recipient is granted availability.

**Cost of the Float** The basic cost of collection float to the firm is simply the opportunity cost of not being able to use the cash. At a minimum, the firm could earn interest on the cash if it were available for investing.

**Ethical and Legal Questions** The cash manager must work with collected bank cash balances and not the firm's book balance (which reflects cheques that have been deposited but not collected). If this is not done, a cash manager could be drawing on uncollected cash as a source of funds for short-term investing. Most banks charge a penalty rate for the use of uncollected funds. However, banks may not have good enough accounting and control procedures to be fully aware of the use of uncollected funds. This raises some ethical and legal questions for the firm.

# The End of Float?

The use of cheques in Europe has fallen dramatically in recent years. For example, in 2009, 3.8 million cheques were written every day in the UK compared with 10.9 million in 1990. The main reason why cheques are becoming less common is that there are now significantly more efficient ways to transfer cash between companies.

*Electronic data interchange* (EDI) is a general term that refers to the growing practice of direct, electronic information exchange between all types of business. One important use of EDI, often called *financial EDI* or *FEDI*, is to transfer financial information and funds between parties electronically, thereby eliminating paper invoices, paper cheques, mailing and handling. For example, it is now possible to arrange to have your account debited directly each month to pay many types of bill. More generally, EDI allows a seller to send a bill electronically to a buyer, thereby avoiding the mail. The buyer can then authorize payment, which also occurs electronically. Its bank then transfers the funds to the seller's account at a different bank. The net effect is that the length of time required to initiate and complete a business transaction is shortened considerably, and much of what we normally think of as float is sharply reduced or eliminated.

The Single Euro Payments Area (SEPA) is an attempt to reduce payment times across most countries in Europe. The initiative aims to harmonize payments across Europe by treating the different countries within the region as a single area. As a result, the payment system in Europe will be akin to a domestic market, and clearing times will be improved accordingly. The process towards full SEPA adoption began in January 2007, when all banks in Europe agreed to use an IBAN (International Bank Account Number) to identify transactions. The forms of payment affected by SEPA are credit transfers, direct debits, and credit and debit card payments. Full adoption of SEPA is expected by the beginning of 2011. Finally, the UK has begun to phase out the use of cheques altogether, and from 2016 cheques will no longer be allowed to transfer cash from one account to another.

## 17.3  Investing Idle Cash

If a firm has a temporary cash surplus, it can invest in short-term securities. As we have mentioned at various times, the market for short-term financial assets is called the *money market*. The maturity of short-term financial assets that trade in the money market is one year or less.

Most large firms manage their own short-term financial assets, carrying out transactions through banks and dealers. Some large firms and many small firms use money market mutual funds. These are funds that invest in short-term financial assets for a management fee. The management fee is compensation for the professional expertise and diversification provided by the fund manager.

Among the many money market mutual funds, some specialize in corporate customers. In addition, banks offer arrangements in which the bank takes all excess available funds at the close of each business day and invests them for the firm.

### Temporary Cash Surpluses

Firms have temporary cash surpluses for various reasons. Two of the most important are the financing of seasonal or cyclical activities of the firm and the financing of planned or possible expenditures.

**Seasonal or Cyclical Activities**   Some firms have a predictable cash flow pattern. They have surplus cash flows during part of the year and deficit cash flows for the rest of the year. For example, Toys Я Us, a retail toy firm, has a seasonal cash flow pattern influenced by the holiday season.

A firm such as Toys Я Us may buy marketable securities when surplus cash flows occur, and sell marketable securities when deficits occur. Of course, bank loans are another short-term financing device. The use of bank loans and marketable securities to meet temporary financing needs is illustrated in Fig. 17.1. In this case, the firm is following a compromise working capital policy.

**Planned or Possible Expenditures**   Firms frequently accumulate temporary investments in marketable securities to provide the cash for a plant construction programme, dividend payment, or other large expenditure. Thus firms may issue bonds and shares before the cash is needed, investing the proceeds in short-term marketable securities and then selling the securities to finance the expenditures. Also, firms may face the possibility of having to make a large cash outlay. An obvious example would involve the possibility of losing a large lawsuit. Firms may build up cash surpluses against such a contingency.

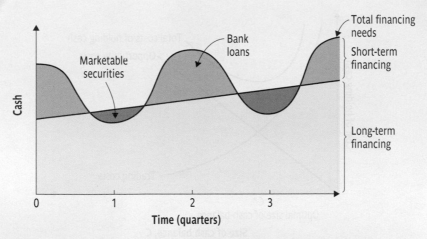

Time 1: A surplus cash flow exists. Seasonal demand for assets is low. The surplus cash flow is invested in short-term marketable securities.

Time 2: A deficit cash flow exists. Seasonal demand for assets is high. The financial deficit is financed by selling marketable securities and by bank borrowing.

**Figure 17.1** Seasonal cash demands

## 17.4 Determining the Target Cash Balance

The **target cash balance** involves a trade-off between the opportunity costs of holding too much cash (the carrying costs) and the costs of holding too little (the shortage costs, also called **adjustment costs**). The nature of these costs depends on the firm's working capital policy.

If the firm has a flexible working capital policy, it will probably maintain a marketable securities portfolio. In this case the adjustment, or shortage, costs will be the trading costs associated with buying and selling securities. If the firm has a restrictive working capital policy, it will probably borrow in the short term to meet cash shortages. The costs in this case will be the interest and other expenses associated with arranging a loan.

In our discussion that follows, we shall assume the firm has a flexible policy. Its cash management, then, consists of moving money in and out of marketable securities. This is a traditional approach to the subject, and it is a nice way of illustrating the costs and benefits of holding cash. Keep in mind, however, that the distinction between cash and money market investments is becoming increasingly blurred.

> **target cash balance**
> A firm's desired cash level as determined by the trade-off between carrying costs and shortage costs.
>
> **adjustment costs**
> The costs associated with holding too little cash. Also, *shortage costs*.

### The Basic Idea

Figure 17.2 presents the cash management problem for our flexible firm. If a firm tries to keep its cash holdings too low, it will find itself running out of cash more often than is desirable, and thus selling marketable securities (and perhaps later buying marketable securities to replace those sold) more frequently than would be the case if the cash balance were higher. Thus trading costs will be high when the cash balance is small. These costs will fall as the cash balance becomes larger.

In contrast, the opportunity costs of holding cash are low if the firm holds little cash. These costs increase as the cash holdings rise, because the firm is giving up more interest that could have been earned.

In Fig. 17.2 the sum of the costs is given by the total cost curve. As shown, the minimum total cost occurs where the two individual cost curves cross at point C*. At this point

FIGURE
**17.2**

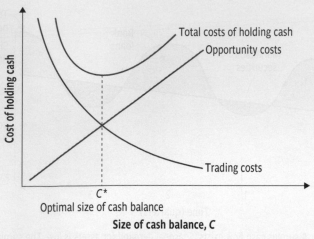

Trading costs are increased when the firm must sell securities to establish a cash balance. Opportunity costs are increased when there is a cash balance because there is no return on cash.

**Figure 17.2** Cost of holding cash

the opportunity costs and the trading costs are equal. This point represents the target cash balance, and it is the point the firm should try to find.

## The BAT Model

The Baumol–Allais–Tobin (BAT) model is a classic means of analysing our cash management problem. We shall show how this model can be used to actually establish the target cash balance. It is a straightforward model useful for illustrating the factors in cash management and, more generally, current asset management.

To develop the BAT model, suppose Golden Socks plc starts off at week 0 with a cash balance of $C = £1.2$ million. Each week, outflows exceed inflows by £600,000. As a result, the cash balance will drop to zero at the end of week 2. The average cash balance will be the beginning balance (£1.2 million) plus the ending balance (£0) divided by 2, or (£1.2 million + 0)/2 = £600,000, over the two-week period. At the end of week 2, Golden Socks replenishes its cash by depositing another £1.2 million.

As we have described, the simple cash management strategy for Golden Socks boils down to depositing £1.2 million every two weeks. This policy is shown in Fig. 17.3. Notice how the cash balance declines by £600,000 per week. Because the company brings the account up to £1.2 million, the balance hits zero every two weeks.

Implicitly, we assume that the net cash outflow is the same every day and is known with certainty. These two assumptions make the model easy to handle. We shall indicate in the next section what happens when they do not hold.

If $C$ were set higher, at £2.4 million, say, cash would last four weeks before the firm would have to sell marketable securities; but the firm's average cash balance would increase to £1.2 million (from £600,000). If $C$ were set at £600,000, cash would run out in one week, and the firm would have to replenish cash more frequently; but the average cash balance would fall from £600,000 to £300,000.

Because transaction costs (for example, the brokerage costs of selling marketable securities) must be incurred whenever cash is replenished, establishing large initial balances will lower the trading costs connected with cash management. However, the larger the average cash balance, the greater is the opportunity cost (the return that could have been earned on marketable securities).

**FIGURE 17.3**

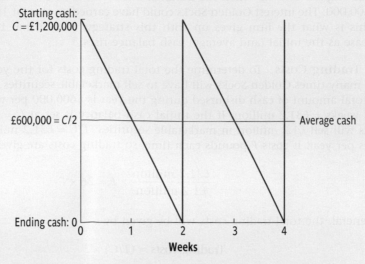

Golden Socks plc starts at week 0 with cash of £1,200,000. The balance drops to zero by the second week. The average cash balance is C/2 = £1,200,000/2 = £600,000 over the period.

**Figure 17.3** Cash balances for Golden Socks plc

To determine the optimal strategy, Golden Socks needs to know the following three things:

$F$ = The fixed cost of making a securities trade to replenish cash.
$T$ = The total amount of new cash needed for transaction purposes over the relevant planning period – say, one year.
$R$ = The opportunity cost of holding cash. This is the interest rate on marketable securities.

With this information, Golden Socks can determine the total costs of any particular cash balance policy. It can then determine the optimal cash balance policy.

**The Opportunity Costs**   To determine the opportunity costs of holding cash, we have to find out how much interest is forgone. Golden Socks has, on average, $C/2$ in cash. This amount could be earning interest at rate $R$. So the total opportunity costs of cash balances are equal to the average cash balance multiplied by the interest rate:

$$\text{Opportunity costs} = (C/2) \times R \qquad (17.3)$$

For example, the opportunity costs of various alternatives are given here, assuming that the interest rate is 10 per cent:

| Initial cash balance, C (£) | Average cash balance, C/2 (£) | Opportunity cost, (C/2) × R (£) (R = 0.10) |
|---|---|---|
| 4,800,000 | 2,400,000 | 240,000 |
| 2,400,000 | 1,200,000 | 120,000 |
| 1,200,000 | 600,000 | 60,000 |
| 600,000 | 300,000 | 30,000 |
| 300,000 | 150,000 | 15,000 |

In our original case, in which the initial cash balance is £1.2 million, the average balance is £600,000. The interest Golden Socks could have earned on this (at 10 per cent) is £60,000, so this is what the firm gives up with this strategy. Notice that the opportunity costs increase as the initial (and average) cash balance rises.

**The Trading Costs**   To determine the total trading costs for the year, we need to know how many times Golden Socks will have to sell marketable securities during the year. First, the total amount of cash disbursed during the year is £600,000 per week, so $T$ = £600,000 × 52 weeks = £31.2 million. If the initial cash balance is set at $C$ = £1.2 million, Golden Socks will sell £1.2 million in marketable securities: $T/C$ = £31.2 million/1.2 million = 26 times per year. It costs $F$ pounds each time, so trading costs are given by

$$\frac{£31.2 \text{ million}}{£1.2 \text{ million}} \times F = 26 \times F$$

In general, the total trading costs will be given by

$$\text{Trading costs} = (T/C) \times F \tag{17.4}$$

In this example, if $F$ were £1,000 (an unrealistically large amount), the trading costs would be £26,000.

We can calculate the trading costs associated with some different strategies as follows:

| Total amount of disbursements during relevant period, $T$ (£) | Initial cash balance, $C$ (£) | Trading costs, $(T/C) \times F$ (£) $(F = £1,000)$ |
|---|---|---|
| 31,200,000 | 4,800,000 | 6,500 |
| 31,200,000 | 2,400,000 | 13,000 |
| 31,200,000 | 1,200,000 | 26,000 |
| 31,200,000 | 600,000 | 52,000 |
| 31,200,000 | 300,000 | 104,000 |

**The Total Cost**   Now that we have the opportunity costs and the trading costs, we can calculate the total cost by adding them together:

$$\text{Total cost} = \text{Opportunity costs} + \text{Trading costs}$$
$$= (C/2) \times R + (T/C) \times F \tag{17.5}$$

Using the numbers generated earlier, we have the following:

| Cash balance (£) | Opportunity costs (£) | + | Trading costs (£) | = | Total cost (£) |
|---|---|---|---|---|---|
| 4,800,000 | 240,000 | | 6,500 | | 246,500 |
| 2,400,000 | 120,000 | | 13,000 | | 133,000 |
| 1,200,000 | 60,000 | | 26,000 | | 86,000 |
| 600,000 | 30,000 | | 52,000 | | 82,000 |
| 300,000 | 15,000 | | 104,000 | | 119,000 |

Notice how the total cost starts out at almost £250,000 and declines to about £82,000 before starting to rise again.

**The Solution**   We can see from the preceding schedule that a £600,000 cash balance results in the lowest total cost of the possibilities presented: £82,000. But what about £700,000 or £500,000, or other possibilities? It appears that the optimal balance is somewhere between £300,000 and £1.2 million. With this in mind, we could easily proceed by trial and error to find the optimal balance. It is not difficult to find it directly, however, so we do this next.

Take a look back at Fig. 17.2. As the figure is drawn, the optimal size of the cash balance, $C^*$, occurs right where the two lines cross. At this point the opportunity costs and the trading costs are exactly equal. So, at $C^*$, we must have that

$$\text{Opportunity costs} = \text{Trading costs}$$
$$(C^*/2) \times R = (T/C^*) \times F$$

With a little algebra, we can write

$$C^{*2} = (2T \times F)/R$$

To solve for $C^*$, we take the square root of both sides to get

$$C^* = \sqrt{(2T \times F)/R} \qquad (17.6)$$

This is the optimal initial cash balance.

For Golden Socks we have $T = £31.2$ million, $F = £1,000$, and $R = 10\%$. We can now find the optimal cash balance:

$$C^* = \sqrt{(2 \times £31,200,000 \times 1,000)/0.10}$$
$$= \sqrt{£624 \text{ billion}}$$
$$= £789,937$$

We can verify this answer by calculating the various costs at this balance, as well as a little above and a little below:

| Cash balance (£) | Opportunity costs (£) | + | Trading costs (£) | = | Total cost (£) |
|---|---|---|---|---|---|
| 850,000 | 42,500 | | 36,706 | | 79,206 |
| 800,000 | 40,000 | | 39,000 | | 79,000 |
| 789,937 | 39,497 | | 39,497 | | 78,994 |
| 750,000 | 37,500 | | 41,600 | | 79,100 |
| 700,000 | 35,000 | | 44,571 | | 79,571 |

The total cost at the optimal cash level is £78,994, and it does appear to increase as we move in either direction.

**EXAMPLE 17.2**

## The BAT Model

Vulcan SA has cash outflows of €100 per day, seven days a week. The interest rate is 5 per cent, and the fixed cost of replenishing cash balances is €10 per transaction. What is the optimal initial cash balance? What is the total cost?

The total cash needed for the year is 365 days × €100 = €36,500. From the BAT model, we have that the optimal initial balance is

$$C^* = \sqrt{(2T \times F)/R}$$
$$= \sqrt{2 \times €36,500 \times 10/0.05}$$
$$= \sqrt{€14.6 \text{ million}}$$
$$= €3,821$$

The average cash balance is €3,821/2 = €1,911, so the opportunity cost is €1,911 × 0.05 = €96. Because Vulcan needs €100 per day, the €3,821 balance will last €3,821/100 = 38.21 days. The firm needs to resupply the account 365/38.21 = 9.6 times per year, so the trading (order) cost is €96. The total cost is €192.

**Conclusion** The BAT model is possibly the simplest and most stripped-down sensible model for determining the optimal cash position. Its chief weakness is that it assumes steady, certain cash outflows. We next discuss a more involved model designed to deal with this limitation.

## The Miller–Orr Model: A More General Approach

We now describe a cash management system designed to deal with cash inflows and outflows that fluctuate randomly from day to day. With this model we again concentrate on the cash balance. But in contrast to the situation with the BAT model, we assume that this balance fluctuates up and down randomly, and that the average change is zero.

**The Basic Idea** Figure 17.4 shows how the system works. It operates in terms of an upper limit ($U^*$) and a lower limit ($L$) to the amount of cash, as well as a target cash balance ($C^*$). The firm allows its cash balance to wander around between the lower and upper limits. As long as the cash balance is somewhere between $U^*$ and $L$, nothing happens.

When the cash balance reaches the upper limit ($U^*$), as it does at point $X$, the firm moves $U^* - C^*$ cash out of the account and into marketable securities. This action moves the cash balance down to $C^*$. In the same way, if the cash balance falls to the lower limit ($L$), as it does at point $Y$, the firm will sell $C^* - L$ worth of securities and deposit the cash in the account. This action takes the cash balance up to $C^*$.

**Using the Model** To get started, management sets the lower limit ($L$). This limit essentially defines a safety stock, so where it is set depends on how much risk of a cash shortfall the firm is willing to tolerate. Alternatively, the minimum might just equal a required compensating balance.

As with the BAT model, the optimal cash balance depends on trading costs and opportunity costs. Once again, the cost per transaction of buying and selling marketable securities, $F$, is assumed to be fixed. Also, the opportunity cost of holding cash is $R$, the interest rate per period on marketable securities.

The only extra piece of information needed is $\sigma^2$, the variance of the net cash flow per period. For our purposes the period can be anything – a day or a week, for example – as long as the interest rate and the variance are based on the same length of time.

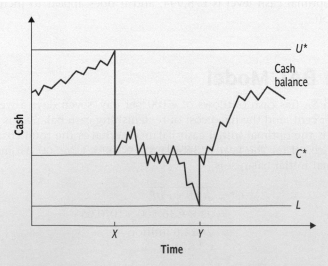

**FIGURE 17.4**

$U^*$ is the upper control limit. $L$ is the lower control limit. The target cash balance is $C^*$. As long as cash is between $L$ and $U^*$, no transaction is made.

**Figure 17.4** The Miller–Orr model

Given $L$, which is set by the firm, Miller and Orr show that the cash balance target, $C^*$, and the upper limit, $U^*$, that minimize the total costs of holding cash are

$$C^* = L + (3/4 \times F \times \sigma^2/R)^{1/3} \qquad (17.7)$$

$$U^* = 3 \times C^* - 2 \times L \qquad (17.8)$$

Also, the average cash balance in the Miller–Orr model is

$$\text{Average cash balance} = (4 \times C^* - L)/3 \qquad (17.9)$$

The derivation of these expressions is relatively complex, so we shall not present it here. Fortunately, as we illustrate next, the results are not difficult to use.

For example, suppose $F = €10$, the interest rate is 1 per cent per month, and the standard deviation of the monthly net cash flows is €200. The variance of the monthly net cash flows is

$$\sigma^2 = €200^2 = €40,000$$

We assume a minimum cash balance of $L = €100$. We can calculate the cash balance target, $C^*$, as follows:

$$
\begin{aligned}
C^* &= L + (3/4 \times F \times \sigma^2/R)^{1/3} \\
&= €100 + (3/4 \times 10 \times 40,000/0.01)^{1/3} \\
&= €100 + 30,000,000^{1/3} \\
&= €100 + 311 = €411
\end{aligned}
$$

The upper limit, $U^*$, is thus

$$
\begin{aligned}
U^* &= 3 \times C^* - 2 \times L \\
&= 3 \times €411 - 2 \times 100 \\
&= €1,033
\end{aligned}
$$

Finally, the average cash balance will be

$$
\begin{aligned}
\text{Average cash balance} &= (4 \times C^* - L)/3 \\
&= (4 \times €411 - 100)/3 \\
&= €515
\end{aligned}
$$

## Implications of the BAT and Miller–Orr Models

Our two cash management models differ in complexity, but they have some similar implications. In both cases, all other things being equal, we see that:

1  The greater the interest rate, the lower is the target cash balance.

2  The greater the order cost, the higher is the target balance.

These implications are both fairly obvious. The advantage of the Miller–Orr model is that it improves our understanding of the problem of cash management by considering the effect of uncertainty, as measured by the variation in net cash inflows.

The Miller–Orr model shows that the greater the uncertainty is (the higher $\sigma^2$ is), the greater is the difference between the target balance and the minimum balance. Similarly, the greater the uncertainty is, the higher is the upper limit and the higher is the average cash balance. These statements all make intuitive sense. For example, the greater the variability is, the greater is the chance that the balance will drop below the minimum. We thus keep a higher balance to guard against this happening.

## Other Factors Influencing the Target Cash Balance

Before moving on, we briefly discuss two additional considerations that affect the target cash balance.

First, in our discussion of cash management, we assume cash is invested in marketable securities such as Treasury bills. The firm obtains cash by selling these securities. Another alternative is to borrow cash. Borrowing introduces additional considerations to cash management:

1 Borrowing is likely to be more expensive than selling marketable securities, because the interest rate is likely to be higher.

2 The need to borrow will depend on management's desire to hold low cash balances. A firm is more likely to have to borrow to cover an unexpected cash outflow with greater cash flow variability and lower investment in marketable securities.

Second, for large firms, the trading costs of buying and selling securities are small when compared with the opportunity costs of holding cash. For example, suppose a firm has £1 million in cash that won't be needed for 24 hours. Should the firm invest the money or leave it sitting?

Suppose the firm can invest the money at an annualized rate of 7.57 per cent per year. The daily rate in this case is about two basis points (0.02 per cent or 0.0002). The daily return earned on £1 million is thus $0.0002 \times £1$ million = £200. In many cases, the order cost will be much less than this; so a large firm will buy and sell securities very often before it will leave substantial amounts of cash idle.

---

**CONCEPT QUESTIONS**

17.4a What is a target cash balance?
17.4b What is the basic trade-off in the BAT model?
17.4c Describe how the Miller–Orr model works.

---

# 17.5 Credit and Receivables

When a firm sells goods and services, it can demand cash on or before the delivery date, or it can extend credit to customers and allow some delay in payment. The next few sections provide an idea of what is involved in the firm's decision to grant credit to its customers. Granting credit is making an investment in a customer – an investment tied to the sale of a product or service.

Why do firms grant credit? Not all do, but the practice is extremely common. The obvious reason is that offering credit is a way of stimulating sales. The costs associated with granting credit are not trivial. First, there is the chance that the customer will not pay. Second, the firm has to bear the costs of carrying the receivables. The credit policy decision thus involves a trade-off between the benefits of increased sales and the costs of granting credit.

From an accounting perspective, when credit is granted, a trade receivable is created. Such receivables include credit to other firms, called *trade credit*, and credit granted to consumers, called *consumer credit*. About one-sixth of all the assets of industrial firms are in the form of trade receivables, so receivables obviously represent a major investment of financial resources by businesses.

## Components of Credit Policy

If a firm decides to grant credit to its customers, then it must establish procedures for extending credit and collecting. In particular, the firm will have to deal with the following components of credit policy:

1 **Terms of sale**: The terms of sale establish how the firm proposes to sell its goods and services. A basic decision is whether the firm will require cash or will extend credit. If the firm does grant credit to a customer, the terms of sale will specify (perhaps implicitly) the credit period, the cash discount and discount period, and the type of credit instrument.

2 **Credit analysis**: In granting credit, a firm determines how much effort to expend trying to distinguish between customers who will pay and customers who will not pay. Firms use a number of devices and procedures to determine the probability that customers will not pay: put together, these are called credit analysis.

3 **Collection policy**: After credit has been granted, the firm has the potential problem of collecting the cash, for which it must establish a collection policy.

In the next several sections, we shall discuss these components of credit policy, which collectively make up the decision to grant credit.

> **terms of sale**
> The conditions under which a firm sells its goods and services for cash or credit.
>
> **credit analysis**
> The process of determining the probability that customers will not pay.
>
> **collection policy**
> The procedures followed by a firm in collecting trade receivables.

## The Cash Flows from Granting Credit

In Chapter 3 we described the trade receivables period as the time it takes to collect on a sale. There are several events that occur during this period. These events are the cash flows associated with granting credit, and they can be illustrated with a cash flow diagram:

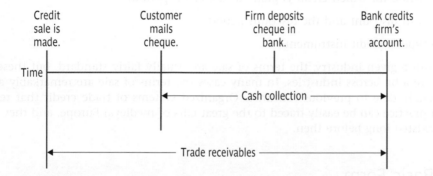

As our time line indicates, the typical sequence of events when a firm grants credit is as follows:

1 The credit sale is made.

2 The customer sends a cheque to the firm.

3 The firm deposits the cheque.

4 The firm's account is credited for the amount of the cheque.

Based on our discussion in a previous section, it is apparent that one of the factors influencing the receivables period is float. Thus one way to reduce the receivables period is to speed up the cheque mailing, processing and clearing. Because we cover this subject elsewhere, we shall ignore float in the subsequent discussion, and focus on what is likely to be the major determinant of the receivables period: credit policy.

## The Investment in Receivables

The investment in trade receivables for any firm depends on the amount of credit sales and the average collection period. For example, if a firm's average collection period, ACP, is 30 days, then at any given time there will be 30 days' worth of sales outstanding. If credit sales run £1,000 per day, the firm's trade receivables will then be equal to 30 days × £1,000 per day = £30,000, on average.

As our example illustrates, a firm's receivables generally will be equal to its average daily sales multiplied by its average collection period:

$$\text{Trade receivables} = \text{Average daily sales} \times \text{ACP} \qquad (17.10)$$

Thus a firm's investment in trade receivables depends on factors that influence credit sales and collections.

We have seen the average collection period in various places, including Chapter 3. Recall that we use the terms *days' sales in receivables*, *receivables period*, and *average collection period* interchangeably to refer to the length of time it takes for the firm to collect on a sale.

| CONCEPT QUESTIONS | 17.5a What are the basic components of credit policy? |
|---|---|
| | 17.5b What are the basic components of the terms of sale if a firm chooses to sell on credit? |

## 17.6 Terms of the Sale

As we described previously, the terms of a sale are made up of three distinct elements:

1 The period for which credit is granted (the credit period)

2 The cash discount and the discount period

3 The type of credit instrument

Within a given industry, the terms of sale are usually fairly standard, but these terms vary quite a bit across industries. In many cases the terms of sale are remarkably archaic, and literally date to previous centuries. Organized systems of trade credit that resemble current practice can be easily traced to the great fairs of medieval Europe, and they almost surely existed long before then.

### The Basic Form

The easiest way to understand the terms of sale is to consider an example. Terms such as '2/10, net 60' are common. This means that customers have 60 days from the invoice date (discussed a bit later) to pay the full amount; however, if payment is made within 10 days, a 2 per cent cash discount can be taken.

Consider a buyer who places an order for €1,000, and assume that the terms of the sale are 2/10, net 60. The buyer has the option of paying €1,000 × (1 − 0.02) = €980 in 10 days, or paying the full €1,000 in 60 days. If the terms are stated as just net 30, then the customer has 30 days from the invoice date to pay the entire €1,000, and no discount is offered for early payment.

In general, credit terms are interpreted in the following way:

<take this discount off the invoice price>/<if you pay in this many days>,
<else pay the full invoice amount in this many days>

Thus '5/10, net 45' means take a 5 per cent discount from the full price if you pay within 10 days, or else pay the full amount in 45 days.

**credit period**
The length of time for which credit is granted.

### The Credit Period

The **credit period** is the basic length of time for which credit is granted. The credit period varies widely from industry to industry, but it is almost always between 30 and 120 days. If a cash discount is offered, then the credit period has two components: the net credit period and the cash discount period.

The net credit period is the length of time the customer has to pay. The cash discount period is the time during which the discount is available. With 2/10, net 30, for example, the net credit period is 30 days and the cash discount period is 10 days.

**The Invoice Date**    The invoice date is the beginning of the credit period. An **invoice** is a written account of services provided or merchandise shipped to the buyer. For individual items, by convention, the invoice date is usually the shipping date or the billing date, *not* the date on which the buyer receives the goods or the bill.

> **invoice**
> A bill for goods or services provided by the seller to the purchaser.

Many other arrangements exist. For example, the terms of sale might be ROG, for *receipt of goods*. In this case the credit period starts when the customer receives the order. This might be used when the customer is in a remote location.

With EOM dating, all sales made during a particular month are assumed to be made at the end of that month. This is useful when a buyer makes purchases throughout the month, but the seller bills only once a month.

For example, terms of 2/10th, EOM tell the buyer to take a 2 per cent discount if payment is made by the 10th of the month; otherwise the full amount is due. Confusingly, the end of the month is sometimes taken to be the 25th day of the month. MOM, for middle of month, is another variation.

Seasonal dating is sometimes used to encourage sales of seasonal products during the off-season. A product sold primarily in the summer (suntan oil?) can be shipped in January with credit terms of 2/10, net 30. However, the invoice might be dated 1 May so that the credit period actually begins at that time. This practice encourages buyers to order early.

**Length of the Credit Period**    Several factors influence the length of the credit period. Two important ones are the *buyer's* inventory period and operating cycle. All else equal, the shorter these are, the shorter the credit period will be.

The operating cycle has two components: the inventory period and the receivables period. The buyer's inventory period is the time it takes the buyer to acquire inventory (from us), process it, and sell it. The buyer's receivables period is the time it then takes the buyer to collect on the sale. Note that the credit period we offer is effectively the buyer's payables period.

By extending credit, we finance a portion of our buyer's operating cycle and thereby shorten that buyer's cash cycle. If our credit period exceeds the buyer's inventory period, then we are financing not only the buyer's inventory purchases, but also part of the buyer's receivables.

Furthermore, if our credit period exceeds our buyer's operating cycle, then we are effectively providing financing for aspects of our customer's business beyond the immediate purchase and sale of our merchandise. The reason is that the buyer effectively has a loan from us even after the merchandise is resold, and the buyer can use that credit for other purposes. For this reason, the length of the buyer's operating cycle is often cited as an appropriate upper limit to the credit period.

There are a number of other factors that influence the credit period. Many of these also influence our customer's operating cycles; so, once again, these are related subjects. Among the most important are these:

1  *Perishability and collateral value*: Perishable items have relatively rapid turnover and relatively low collateral value. Credit periods are thus shorter for such goods. For example, a food wholesaler selling fresh fruit and produce might use net seven days. Alternatively, jewellery might be sold for 5/30, net four months.

2  *Consumer demand*: Products that are well established generally have more rapid turnover. Newer or slow-moving products will often have longer credit periods associated with them to entice buyers. Also, as we have seen, sellers may choose to extend much longer credit periods for off-season sales (when customer demand is low).

3  *Cost, profitability and standardization*: Relatively inexpensive goods tend to have shorter credit periods. The same is true for relatively standardized goods and raw materials. These all tend to have lower mark-ups and higher turnover rates, both of which lead to shorter credit periods. However, there are exceptions. Car dealers, for example, generally pay for the vehicles as they are received.

4  *Credit risk*: The greater the credit risk of the buyer, the shorter the credit period is likely to be (if credit is granted at all).

5  *Size of the account*: If an account is small, the credit period may be shorter because small accounts cost more to manage, and the customers are less important.

6  *Competition*: When the seller is in a highly competitive market, longer credit periods may be offered as a way of attracting customers.

7  *Customer type*: A single seller might offer different credit terms to different buyers. A food wholesaler, for example, might supply groceries, bakeries and restaurants. Each group would probably have different credit terms. More generally, sellers often have both wholesale and retail customers, and they frequently quote different terms to the two types.

## Cash Discounts

> **cash discount**
> A discount given to induce prompt payment. Also, *sales discount*.

As we have seen, **cash discounts** are often part of the terms of sale. One reason why discounts are offered is to speed up the collection of receivables. This will have the effect of reducing the amount of credit being offered, and the firm must trade this off against the cost of the discount.

Notice that when a cash discount is offered, the credit is essentially free during the discount period. The buyer pays for the credit only after the discount expires.

With 2/10, net 30, a rational buyer either pays in 10 days to make the greatest possible use of the free credit or pays in 30 days to get the longest possible use of the money in exchange for giving up the discount. By giving up the discount, the buyer effectively gets 30 − 10 = 20 days' credit.

Another reason for cash discounts is that they are a way of charging higher prices to customers that have had credit extended to them. In this sense, cash discounts are a convenient way of charging for the credit granted to customers.

**Cost of the Credit**   In our examples it might seem that the discounts are rather small. With 2/10, net 30, for example, early payment gets the buyer only a 2 per cent discount. Does this provide a significant incentive for early payment? The answer is yes, because the implicit interest rate is extremely high.

To see why the discount is important, we shall calculate the cost to the buyer of not paying early. To do this, we shall find the interest rate that the buyer is effectively paying for the trade credit. Suppose the order is for £1,000. The buyer can pay £980 in 10 days or wait another 20 days and pay £1,000. It's obvious that the buyer is effectively borrowing £980 for 20 days and that the buyer pays £20 in interest on the 'loan'. What's the interest rate?

This interest is ordinary discount interest, which we discussed in Chapter 5. With £20 in interest on £980 borrowed, the rate is £20/980 = 2.0408%. This is relatively low, but remember that this is the rate per 20-day period. There are 365/20 = 18.25 such periods in a year: so, by not taking the discount, the buyer is paying an effective annual rate (EAR) of

$$EAR = 1.020408^{18.25} - 1 = 44.6\%$$

From the buyer's point of view this is an expensive source of financing!

Given that the interest rate is so high here, it is unlikely that the seller benefits from early payment. Ignoring the possibility of default by the buyer, the decision of a customer to forgo the discount almost surely works to the seller's advantage.

**Trade Discounts**   In some circumstances the discount is not really an incentive for early payment but is instead a *trade discount*, a discount routinely given to some type of buyer. For example, with our 2/10th, EOM terms, the buyer takes a 2 per cent discount if the invoice is paid by the 10th, but the bill is considered due on the 10th, and overdue after that. Thus the credit period and the discount period are effectively the same, and there is no reward for paying before the due date.

**The Cash Discount and the ACP**   To the extent that a cash discount encourages customers to pay early, it will shorten the receivables period and, all other things being equal, reduce the firm's investment in receivables.

For example, suppose a firm currently has terms of net 30 and an average collection period (ACP) of 30 days. If it offers terms of 2/10, net 30, then perhaps 50 per cent of its customers (in terms of volume of purchases) will pay in 10 days. The remaining customers will still take an average of 30 days to pay. What will the new ACP be? If the firm's annual sales are £15 million (before discounts), what will happen to the investment in receivables?

If half of the customers take 10 days to pay and half take 30, then the new average collection period will be

$$\text{New ACP} = 0.50 \times 10 \text{ days} + 0.50 \times 30 \text{ days} = 20 \text{ days}$$

The ACP thus falls from 30 days to 20 days. Average daily sales are £15 million/365 = £41,096 per day. Receivables will thus fall by £41,096 × 10 = £410,960.

## Credit Instruments

The **credit instrument** is the basic evidence of indebtedness. Most trade credit is offered on *open account*. This means that the only formal instrument of credit is the invoice, which is sent with the shipment of goods and which the customer signs as evidence that the goods have been received. Afterwards, the firm and its customers record the exchange on their books of account.

> **credit instrument**
> The evidence of indebtedness.

At times, the firm may require that the customer sign a *promissory note*. This is a basic IOU, and might be used when the order is large, when there is no cash discount involved, or when the firm anticipates a problem in collections. Promissory notes are not common, but they can eliminate possible controversies later about the existence of debt.

One problem with promissory notes is that they are signed after delivery of the goods. One way to obtain a credit commitment from a customer before the goods are delivered is to arrange a *commercial draft*. Typically, the firm draws up a commercial draft calling for the customer to pay a specific amount by a specified date. The draft is then sent to the customer's bank with the shipping invoices.

If immediate payment is required on the draft, it is called a *sight draft*. If immediate payment is not required, then the draft is a *time draft*. When the draft is presented and the buyer 'accepts' it, meaning that the buyer promises to pay it in the future, then it is called a *trade acceptance* and is sent back to the selling firm. The seller can then keep the acceptance or sell it to someone else. If a bank accepts the draft, meaning that the bank is guaranteeing payment, then the draft becomes a *banker's acceptance*. This arrangement is common in international trade, and banker's acceptances are actively traded in the money market.

A firm can also use a conditional sales contract as a credit instrument. With such an arrangement the firm retains legal ownership of the goods until the customer has completed payment. Conditional sales contracts are usually paid in instalments, and have an interest cost built into them.

| | |
|---|---|
| **CONCEPT QUESTIONS** | 17.6a   What considerations enter the determination of the terms of sale? |
| | 17.6b   Explain what terms of '3/45, net 90' mean. What is the effective interest rate? |

# 17.7 Analysing Credit Policy

In this section we take a closer look at the factors that influence the decision to grant credit. Granting credit makes sense only if the NPV from doing so is positive. We thus need to look at the NPV of the decision to grant credit.

## Credit Policy Effects

In evaluating credit policy, there are five basic factors to consider:

1 *Revenue effects*: If the firm grants credit, then there will be a delay in revenue collections as some customers take advantage of the credit offered and pay later. However, the firm may be able to charge a higher price if it grants credit, and it may be able to increase the quantity sold. Total revenues may thus increase.

2 *Cost effects*: Although the firm may experience delayed revenues if it grants credit, it will still incur the costs of sales immediately. Whether the firm sells for cash or credit, it will still have to acquire or produce the merchandise (and pay for it).

3 *The cost of debt*: When the firm grants credit, it must arrange to finance the resulting receivables. As a result, the firm's cost of short-term borrowing is a factor in the decision to grant credit.

4 *The probability of non-payment*: If the firm grants credit, some percentage of the credit buyers will not pay. This can't happen, of course, if the firm sells for cash.

5 *The cash discount*: When the firm offers a cash discount as part of its credit terms, some customers will choose to pay early to take advantage of the discount.

## Evaluating a Proposed Credit Policy

To illustrate how credit policy can be analysed, we shall start with a relatively simple case. Locust Software has been in existence for two years, and it is one of several successful firms that develop computer programs. Currently, Locust sells for cash only.

Locust is evaluating a request from some major customers to change its current policy to net one month (30 days). To analyse this proposal, we define the following:

$$P = \text{Price per unit}$$
$$v = \text{Variable cost per unit}$$
$$Q = \text{Current quantity sold per month}$$
$$Q' = \text{Quantity sold under new policy}$$
$$R = \text{Monthly required return}$$

For now, we ignore discounts and the possibility of default. Also, we ignore taxes, because they don't affect our conclusions.

**NPV of Switching Policies**   To illustrate the NPV of switching credit policies, suppose we have the following for Locust:

$$P = €49$$
$$v = €20$$
$$Q = 100$$
$$Q' = 110$$

If the required return, $R$, is 2 per cent per month, should Locust make the switch?

Currently, Locust has monthly sales of $P \times Q = €4,900$. Variable costs each month are $v \times Q = €2,000$, so the monthly cash flow from this activity is

$$\text{Cash flow with old policy} = (P - v)Q \qquad \textbf{(17.11)}$$
$$= (€49 - 20) \times 100$$
$$= €2,900$$

This is not the total cash flow for Locust, of course, but it is all that we need to look at, because fixed costs and other components of cash flow are the same whether or not the switch is made.

If Locust does switch to net 30 days on sales, then the quantity sold will rise to $Q' = 110$. Monthly revenues will increase to $P \times Q'$, and costs will be $v \times Q'$. The monthly cash flow under the new policy will thus be

$$\text{Cash flow with new policy} = (P - v)Q' \qquad \textbf{(17.12)}$$
$$= (€49 - 20) \times 110$$
$$= €3,190$$

Going back to Chapter 9, we know that the relevant incremental cash flow is the difference between the new and old cash flows:

$$\text{Incremental cash inflow} = (P - v)(Q' - Q)$$
$$= (€49 - 20) \times (110 - 100)$$
$$= €290$$

This says that the benefit each month of changing policies is equal to the gross profit per unit sold, $P - v = €29$, multiplied by the increase in sales, $Q' - Q = 10$. The present value of the future incremental cash flows is thus

$$PV = [(P - v)(Q' - Q)]/R \qquad \textbf{(17.13)}$$

For Locust, this present value works out to be

$$PV = (€29 \times 10)/0.02 = €14,500$$

Notice that we have treated the monthly cash flow as a perpetuity, because the same benefit will be realized each month for ever.

Now that we know the benefit of switching, what's the cost? There are two components to consider. First, because the quantity sold will rise from $Q$ to $Q'$, Locust will have to produce $Q' - Q$ more units at a cost of $v(Q' - Q) = €20 \times (110 - 100) = €200$. Second, the sales that would have been collected this month under the current policy ($P \times Q = €4,900$) will not be collected. Under the new policy, the sales made this month won't be collected until 30 days later. The cost of the switch is the sum of these two components:

$$\text{Cost of switching} = PQ + v(Q' - Q) \qquad \textbf{(17.14)}$$

For Locust this cost would be €4,900 + 200 = €5,100.

Putting it all together, we see that the NPV of the switch is

$$\text{NPV of switching} = -[PQ + v(Q' - Q)] + [(P - v)(Q' - Q)]/R \qquad \textbf{(17.15)}$$

For Locust, the cost of switching is €5,100. As we saw earlier, the benefit is €290 per month, for ever. At 2 per cent per month, the NPV is

$$NPV = -€5,100 + 290/0.02$$
$$= -€5,100 + 14,500$$
$$= €9,400$$

Therefore the switch is very profitable.

**EXAMPLE 17.3**

# We'd Rather Fight Than Switch

Suppose a company is considering a switch from all cash to net 30, but the quantity sold is not expected to change. What is the NPV of the switch? Explain.

In this case, $Q' - Q$ is zero, so the NPV is just $-PQ$. What this says is that the effect of the switch is simply to postpone one month's collections for ever, with no benefit from doing so.

**A Break-Even Application**  Based on our discussion thus far, the key variable for Locust is $Q' - Q$, the increase in unit sales. The projected increase of 10 units is only an estimate, so there is some forecasting risk. Under the circumstances, it's natural to wonder what increase in unit sales is necessary to break even.

Earlier, the NPV of the switch was defined as

$$\text{NPV} = -[PQ + v(Q' - Q)] + [(P - v)(Q' - Q)]/R$$

We can calculate the break-even point explicitly by setting the NPV equal to zero and solving for $(Q' - Q)$:

$$\text{NPV} = 0 = -[PQ + v(Q' - Q)] + \frac{(P - v)(Q' - Q)}{R}$$

$$Q' - Q = \frac{PQ}{(P - v)/(R - v)}$$

(17.16)

For Locust, the break-even sales increase is thus:

$$Q' - Q = €4,900/(29/0.02 - 20)$$
$$= 3.43 \text{ units}$$

This tells us that the switch is a good idea as long as Locust is confident that it can sell at least 3.43 more units per month.

**CONCEPT QUESTIONS**

**17.7a**  What are the important effects to consider in a decision to offer credit?

**17.7b**  Explain how to estimate the NPV of a credit policy switch.

## 17.8 Optimal Credit Policy

So far, we've discussed how to compute net present values for a switch in credit policy. We have not discussed the optimal amount of credit, or the optimal credit policy. In principle, the optimal amount of credit is determined by the point at which the incremental cash flows from increased sales are exactly equal to the incremental costs of carrying the increase in investment in trade receivables.

### The Total Credit Cost Curve

The trade-off between granting credit and not granting credit isn't hard to identify, but it is difficult to quantify precisely. As a result, we can only describe an optimal credit policy.

FIGURE
17.5

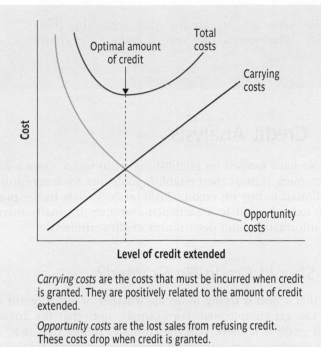

Carrying costs are the costs that must be incurred when credit
is granted. They are positively related to the amount of credit
extended.

Opportunity costs are the lost sales from refusing credit.
These costs drop when credit is granted.

**Figure 17.5** The costs of granting credit

To begin, the carrying costs associated with granting credit come in three forms:

1  The required return on receivables

2  The losses from bad debts

3  The costs of managing credit and credit collections

We have already discussed the first and second of these. The third cost, the cost of managing credit, consists of the expenses associated with running the credit department. Firms that don't grant credit have no such department, and no such expense. These three costs will all increase as credit policy is relaxed.

If a firm has a very restrictive credit policy, then all the associated costs will be low. In this case the firm will have a 'shortage' of credit, so there will be an opportunity cost. This opportunity cost is the extra potential profit from credit sales that are lost because credit is refused. This forgone benefit comes from two sources: the increase in quantity sold, $Q'$ minus $Q$, and (potentially) a higher price. The opportunity costs go down as credit policy is relaxed.

The sum of the carrying costs and the opportunity costs of a particular credit policy is called the total **credit cost curve**. We have drawn such a curve in Fig. 17.5. As Fig. 17.5 illustrates, there is a point where the total credit cost is minimized. This point corresponds to the optimal amount of credit or, equivalently, the optimal investment in receivables.

If the firm extends more credit than this minimum, the additional net cash flow from new customers will not cover the carrying costs of the investment in receivables. If the level of receivables is below this amount, then the firm is forgoing valuable profit opportunities.

In general, the costs and benefits from extending credit will depend on the characteristics of particular firms and industries. All other things being equal, for example, it is likely that firms with (1) excess capacity, (2) low variable operating costs, and (3) repeat customers will extend credit more liberally than other firms. See if you can explain why each of these characteristics contributes to a more liberal credit policy.

> **credit cost curve**
> A graphical representation of the sum of the carrying costs and the opportunity costs of a credit policy.

17.8a   What are the carrying costs of granting credit?
17.8b   What are the opportunity costs of not granting credit?

## 17.9  Credit Analysis

Thus far we have focused on establishing credit terms. Once a firm decides to grant credit to its customers, it must then establish guidelines for determining who will and who will not be allowed to buy on credit. *Credit analysis* refers to the process of deciding whether or not to extend credit to a particular customer. It usually involves two steps: gathering relevant information, and determining creditworthiness.

### When Should Credit Be Granted?

Imagine that a firm is trying to decide whether or not to grant credit to a customer. This decision can get complicated. For example, note that the answer depends on what will happen if credit is refused. Will the customer simply pay cash? Or will the customer not make the purchase at all? To avoid being bogged down by this and other difficulties, we shall use some special cases to illustrate the key points.

**A One-Time Sale**   We start by considering the simplest case. A new customer wishes to buy one unit on credit at a price of $P$ per unit. If credit is refused, the customer will not make the purchase.

Furthermore, we assume that, if credit is granted, then, in one month, the customer will either pay up or default. The probability of the second of these events is $\pi$. In this case the probability ($\pi$) can be interpreted as the percentage of *new* customers who will not pay. Our business does not have repeat customers, so this is strictly a one-time sale. Finally, the required return on receivables is $R$ per month, and the variable cost is $v$ per unit.

The analysis here is straightforward. If the firm refuses credit, then the incremental cash flow is zero. If it grants credit, then it spends $v$ (the variable cost) this month, and expects to collect $(1 - \pi)P$ next month. The NPV of granting credit is

$$\text{NPV} = -v + (1 - \pi)P/(1 + R) \tag{17.17}$$

For example, for Locust Software, this NPV is

$$\text{NPV} = -\text{€}20 + (1 - \pi) \times 49/1.02$$

With, say, a 20 per cent rate of default, this works out to be

$$\text{NPV} = -\text{€}20 + 0.80 \times 49/1.02 = \text{€}18.43$$

Therefore credit should be granted. Notice that we have divided by $(1 + R)$ here instead of by $R$, because we now assume that this is a one-time transaction.

Our example illustrates an important point. In granting credit to a new customer, a firm risks its variable cost ($v$) but it stands to gain the full price ($P$). For a new customer, then, credit may be granted even if the default probability is high. For example, the break-even probability in this case can be determined by setting the NPV equal to zero and solving for $\pi$:

$$\text{NPV} = 0 = -\text{€}20 + (1 - \pi) \times 49/1.02$$
$$1 - \pi = \text{€}20/49 \times 1.02$$
$$\pi = 58.4\%$$

Locust should extend credit as long as there is a $1 - 0.584 = 41.6\%$ chance or better of collecting. This explains why firms with higher mark-ups tend to have looser credit terms.

This percentage (58.4%) is the maximum acceptable default probability for a *new* customer. If a returning, cash-paying customer wanted to switch to a credit basis, the analysis would be different, and the maximum acceptable default probability would be much lower.

The important difference is that, if we extend credit to a returning customer, we risk the total sales price ($P$), because this is what we collect if we don't extend credit. If we extend credit to a new customer, we risk only our variable cost.

**Repeat Business**    A second, very important factor to keep in mind is the possibility of repeat business. We can illustrate this by extending our one-time sale example. We make one important assumption: a new customer who does not default the first time around will remain a customer for ever and never default.

If the firm grants credit, it spends $v$ this month. Next month, it gets nothing if the customer defaults, or it gets $P$ if the customer pays. If the customer pays, then the customer will buy another unit on credit and the firm will spend $v$ again. The net cash inflow for the month is thus $P - v$. In every subsequent month, this same $P - v$ will occur as the customer pays for the previous month's order and places a new one.

It follows from our discussion that, in one month, the firm will receive €0 with probability $\pi$. With probability $(1 - \pi)$, however, the firm will have a permanent new customer. The value of a new customer is equal to the present value of $(P - v)$ every month for ever:

$$PV = (P - v)/R$$

The NPV of extending credit is therefore

$$NPV = -v + (1 - \pi)(P - v)/R \qquad \textbf{(17.18)}$$

For Locust, this is

$$NPV = -€20 + (1 - \pi) \times (49 - 20)/0.02$$
$$= -€20 + (1 - \pi) \times 1{,}450$$

Even if the probability of default is 90 per cent, the NPV is

$$NPV = -€20 + 0.10 \times 1{,}450 = €125$$

Locust should extend credit unless default is a virtual certainty. The reason is that it costs only €20 to find out who is a good customer and who is not. A good customer is worth €1,450, however, so Locust can afford quite a few defaults.

Our repeat business example probably exaggerates the acceptable default probability, but it does illustrate that it will often turn out that the best way to do credit analysis is simply to extend credit to almost anyone. It also points out that the possibility of repeat business is a crucial consideration. In such cases the important thing is to control the amount of credit initially offered to any one customer, so that the possible loss is limited. The amount can be increased with time. Most often, the best predictor of whether or not someone will pay in the future is whether or not they have paid in the past.

**CONCEPT QUESTIONS**

17.9a  What is credit analysis?

17.9b  Should credit always be given?

## 17.10 Collection Policy

Collection policy is the final element in credit policy. Collection policy involves monitoring receivables to spot trouble, and obtaining payment on past-due accounts.

### Monitoring Receivables

To keep track of payments by customers, most firms will monitor outstanding accounts. First of all, a firm will normally keep track of its average collection period (ACP) through time. If a firm is in a seasonal business, the ACP will fluctuate during the year; but unexpected increases in the ACP are a cause for concern. Either customers in general are taking longer to pay, or some percentage of trade receivables are seriously overdue.

> **ageing schedule**
> A compilation of trade receivables by the age of each account.

The **ageing schedule** is a second basic tool for monitoring receivables. To prepare one, the credit department classifies accounts by age. Suppose a firm has £100,000 in receivables. Some of these accounts are only a few days old, but others have been outstanding for quite some time. The following is an example of an ageing schedule:

| Age of account (days) | Amount (£) | Percentage of total value of trade receivables (%) |
|---|---|---|
| 0–10 | 50,000 | 50 |
| 11–60 | 25,000 | 25 |
| 61–80 | 20,000 | 20 |
| Over 80 | 5,000 | 5 |
| | 100,000 | 100 |

If this firm has a credit period of 60 days, then 25 per cent of its accounts are late. Whether or not this is serious depends on the nature of the firm's collections and customers. It is often the case that accounts beyond a certain age are almost never collected. Monitoring the age of accounts is very important in such cases.

Firms with seasonal sales will find the percentages on the ageing schedule changing during the year. For example, if sales in the current month are very high, then total receivables will also increase sharply. This means that the older accounts, as a percentage of total receivables, become smaller and might appear less important. Some firms have refined the ageing schedule so that they have an idea of how it should change with peaks and valleys in their sales.

### Collection Effort

A firm usually goes through the following sequence of procedures for customers whose payments are overdue:

1 It sends out a delinquency letter informing the customer of the past-due status of the account.

2 It makes a telephone call to the customer.

3 It employs a collection agency.

4 It takes legal action against the customer.

At times, a firm may refuse to grant additional credit to customers until arrears are cleared up. This may antagonize a normally good customer, which points to a potential conflict between the collections department and the sales department.

In probably the worst case, the customer files for bankruptcy. When this happens, the credit-granting firm is just another unsecured creditor. The firm can simply wait, or it can sell its receivable.

## 17.11 Inventory Management

Like receivables, inventories represent a significant investment for many firms. For a typical manufacturing operation, inventories will often exceed 15 per cent of assets. For a retailer, inventories could represent more than 25 per cent of assets. From our discussion earlier, we know that a firm's operating cycle is made up of its inventory period and its receivables period. This is one reason for considering credit and inventory policy in the same chapter. Beyond this, both credit policy and inventory policy are used to drive sales, and the two must be co-ordinated to ensure that the process of acquiring inventory, selling it, and collecting on the sale proceeds smoothly. For example, changes in credit policy designed to stimulate sales must be accompanied by planning for adequate inventory.

### The Financial Manager and Inventory Policy

Despite the size of a typical firm's investment in inventories, the financial manager of a firm will not normally have primary control over inventory management. Instead, other functional areas such as purchasing, production and marketing will usually share decision-making authority regarding inventory. Inventory management has become an increasingly important speciality in its own right, and financial management will often only have input into the decision. For this reason we shall just survey some basics of inventory and inventory policy.

### Inventory Types

For a manufacturer, inventory is normally classified into one of three categories. The first category is *raw material*. This is whatever the firm uses as a starting point in its production process. Raw materials might be something as basic as iron ore for a steel manufacturer, or something as sophisticated as disk drives for a computer manufacturer.

The second type of inventory is *work in progress*, which is just what the name suggests – unfinished product. How big this portion of inventory is depends in large part on the length of the production process. For an airframe manufacturer, for example, work in progress can be substantial. The third and final type of inventory is *finished goods* – that is, products ready to ship or sell.

### Inventory Costs

Two basic types of costs are associated with current assets in general, and with inventory in particular. The first of these is *carrying costs*. Here, carrying costs represent all of the direct and opportunity costs of keeping inventory on hand. These include:

* Storage and tracking costs

* Insurance and taxes

* Losses due to obsolescence, deterioration, or theft

* The opportunity cost of capital on the invested amount

The sum of these costs can be substantial, ranging roughly from 20 to 40 per cent of inventory value per year.

The other type of costs associated with inventory is *shortage costs*. Shortage costs are costs associated with having inadequate inventory on hand. The two components of shortage costs are restocking costs and costs related to safety reserves. Depending on the firm's business, restocking or order costs are either the costs of placing an order with suppliers or the costs of setting up a production run. The costs related to safety reserves are opportunity losses such as lost sales and loss of customer goodwill that result from having inadequate inventory.

A basic trade-off exists in inventory management, because carrying costs increase with inventory levels, whereas shortage or restocking costs decline with inventory levels. The basic goal of inventory management is thus to minimize the sum of these two costs. We consider ways to reach this goal in the next section.

---

**CONCEPT QUESTIONS**

17.11a  What are the different types of inventory?

17.11b  What is the basic goal of inventory management?

---

## 17.12 Inventory Management Techniques

As we described earlier, the goal of inventory management is usually framed as cost minimization. Three techniques are discussed in this section, ranging from the relatively simple to the very complex.

### The ABC Approach

The ABC approach is a simple approach to inventory management, in which the basic idea is to divide inventory into three (or more) groups. The underlying rationale is that a small portion of inventory in terms of quantity might represent a large portion in terms of inventory value. For example, this situation would exist for a manufacturer that uses some relatively expensive, high-tech components and some relatively inexpensive basic materials in producing its products.

Figure 17.6 illustrates an ABC comparison of items in terms of the percentage of inventory value represented by each group versus the percentage of items represented. As Fig. 17.6

**FIGURE 17.6**

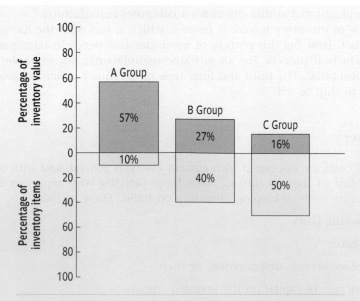

**Figure 17.6** ABC inventory analysis

shows, the A Group constitutes only 10 per cent of inventory by item count, but it represents over half of the value of inventory. The A Group items are thus monitored closely, and inventory levels are kept relatively low. At the other end, basic inventory items, such as nuts and bolts, also exist; but because these are crucial and inexpensive, large quantities are ordered and kept on hand. These would be C Group items. The B Group is made up of in-between items.

## The Economic Order Quantity Model

The economic order quantity (EOQ) model is the best-known approach for explicitly establishing an optimal inventory level. The basic idea is illustrated in Fig. 17.7, which plots the various costs associated with holding inventory (on the vertical axis) against inventory levels (on the horizontal axis). As shown, inventory-carrying costs rise and restocking costs decrease as inventory levels increase. From our general discussion earlier in this chapter, and our discussion of the total credit cost curve, the general shape of the total inventory cost curve is familiar. With the EOQ model, we shall attempt to specifically locate the minimum total cost point, $Q^*$.

In our discussion that follows, an important point to keep in mind is that the actual cost of the inventory itself is not included. The reason is that the *total* amount of inventory the firm needs in a given year is dictated by sales. What we are analysing here is how much the firm should have on hand at any particular time. More precisely, we are trying to determine what order size the firm should use when it restocks its inventory.

**Inventory Depletion**   To develop the EOQ, we shall assume that the firm's inventory is sold off at a steady rate until it hits zero. At that point, the firm restocks its inventory back to some optimal level. For example, suppose Eyssell plc starts out today with 3,600 units of a particular item in inventory. Annual sales of this item are 46,800 units, which is about 900 per week. If Eyssell sells off 900 units of inventory each week, all

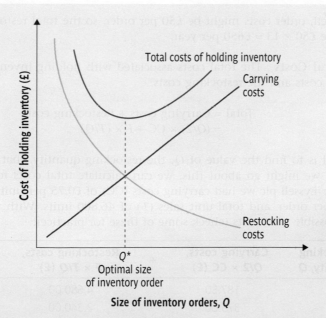

**Figure 17.7** Costs of holding inventory

the available inventory will be sold after four weeks, and Eyssell will restock by ordering (or manufacturing) another 3,600 and start again. This selling and restocking process produces a sawtooth pattern for inventory holdings. On average, then, inventory is half of 3,600, or 1,800 units.

**The Carrying Costs**   As Fig. 17.7 illustrates, carrying costs are normally assumed to be directly proportional to inventory levels. Suppose we let $Q$ be the quantity of inventory that Eyssell orders each time (3,600 units): we shall call this the *restocking quantity*. Average inventory would then just be $Q/2$, or 1,800 units. If we let CC be the carrying cost per unit per year, Eyssell's total carrying costs will be

$$\text{Total carrying costs} = \text{Average inventory} \times \text{Carrying costs per unit}$$
$$= (Q/2) \times \text{CC} \qquad (17.19)$$

In Eyssell's case, if carrying costs were £0.75 per unit per year, total carrying costs would be the average inventory of 1,800 multiplied by £0.75, or £1,350 per year.

**The Shortage Costs**   For now, we shall focus only on the restocking costs. In essence, we shall assume that the firm never actually runs short of inventory, so that costs relating to safety reserves are not important. We shall return to this issue later.

Restocking costs are normally assumed to be fixed. In other words, every time we place an order, fixed costs are associated with that order (remember that the cost of the inventory itself is not considered here). Suppose we let $T$ be the firm's total unit sales per year. If the firm orders $Q$ units each time, then it will need to place a total of $T/Q$ orders. For Eyssell, annual sales are 46,800, and the order size is 3,600. Eyssell thus places a total of $46,800/3,600 = 13$ orders per year. If the fixed cost per order is $F$, the total restocking cost for the year would be

$$\text{Total restocking cost} = \text{Fixed cost per order} \times \text{Number of orders}$$
$$= F \times (T/Q) \qquad (17.20)$$

For Eyssell, order costs might be £50 per order, so the total restocking cost for 13 orders would be £50 × 13 = £650 per year.

**The Total Costs**   The total costs associated with holding inventory are the sum of the carrying costs and the restocking costs:

$$\text{Total} = \text{Carrying costs} + \text{Restocking costs}$$
$$= (Q/2) \times \text{CC} + F \times (T/Q) \qquad (17.21)$$

Our goal is to find the value of $Q$, the restocking quantity, that minimizes this cost. To see how we might go about this, we can calculate total costs for some different values of $Q$. For Eyssell plc we had carrying costs (CC) of £0.75 per unit per year, fixed costs ($F$) of £50 per order, and total unit sales ($T$) of 46,800 units. With these numbers, here are some possible total costs (check some of these for practice):

| Restocking quantity, Q | Carrying costs, Q/2 × CC (£) | + | Restocking costs, F × T/Q (£) | = | Total costs (£) |
|---|---|---|---|---|---|
| 500 | 187.50 | | 4,680.00 | | 4,867.50 |
| 1,000 | 375.00 | | 2,340.00 | | 2,715.00 |
| 1,500 | 562.50 | | 1,560.00 | | 2,122.50 |
| 2,000 | 750.00 | | 1,170.00 | | 1,920.00 |
| **2,500** | **937.50** | | **936.00** | | **1,873.50** |
| 3,000 | 1,125.00 | | 780.00 | | 1,905.00 |
| 3,500 | 1,312.50 | | 668.60 | | 1,981.10 |

Inspecting the numbers, we see that total costs start out at almost £5,000 and decline to just under £1,900. The cost-minimizing quantity is about 2,500.

To find the cost-minimizing quantity, we can look back at Fig. 17.7. What we notice is that the minimum point occurs exactly where the two lines cross. At this point, carrying costs and restocking costs are the same. For the particular types of costs we have assumed here, this will always be true; so we can find the minimum point just by setting these costs equal to each other and solving for $Q^*$:

$$\text{Carrying costs} = \text{Restocking costs}$$
$$(Q^*/2) \times CC = F \times (T/Q^*) \qquad (17.22)$$

With a little algebra, we get

$$Q^{*2} = \frac{2T \times F}{CC} \qquad (17.23)$$

To solve for $Q^*$, we take the square root of both sides to find

$$Q^* = \sqrt{\frac{2T \times F}{CC}} \qquad (17.24)$$

This reorder quantity, which minimizes the total inventory cost, is called the **economic order quantity (EOQ)**. For Eyssell plc, the EOQ is

$$
\begin{aligned}
Q^* &= \sqrt{\frac{2T \times F}{CC}} \\
&= \sqrt{\frac{(2 \times 46{,}800) \times £50}{0.75}} \\
&= \sqrt{6{,}240{,}000} \\
&= 2{,}498 \text{ units}
\end{aligned}
$$

> **economic order quantity (EOQ)** The restocking quantity that minimizes the total inventory costs.

Thus, for Eyssell, the economic order quantity is 2,498 units. At this level, verify that the restocking costs and carrying costs are both £936.75.

## Carrying Costs

**EXAMPLE 17.4**

Thiewes Shoes begins each period with 100 pairs of hiking boots in stock. This stock is depleted each period and reordered. If the carrying cost per pair of boots per year is £3, what are the total carrying costs for the hiking boots?

Inventories always start at 100 items and end up at zero, so average inventory is 50 items. At an annual cost of £3 per item, total carrying costs are £150.

## Restocking Costs

**EXAMPLE 17.5**

In Example 17.4, suppose Thiewes sells a total of 600 pairs of boots in a year. How many times per year does Thiewes restock? Suppose the restocking cost is £20 per order. What are total restocking costs?

Thiewes orders 100 items each time. Total sales are 600 items per year, so Thiewes restocks six times per year, or about every two months. The restocking costs would be 6 orders × £20 per order = £120.

## The EOQ

**EXAMPLE 17.6**

Based on our previous two examples, what size orders should Thiewes place to minimize costs? How often will Thiewes restock? What are the total carrying and restocking costs? The total costs?

We know that the total number of pairs of boots ordered for the year ($T$) is 600. The restocking cost ($F$) is £20 per order, and the carrying cost (CC) is £3. We can calculate the EOQ for Thiewes as follows:

$$\text{EOQ} = \sqrt{\frac{2T \times F}{\text{CC}}}$$
$$= \sqrt{\frac{(2 \times 600) \times £20}{3}}$$
$$= \sqrt{8,000}$$
$$= 89.44 \text{ units}$$

Because Thiewes sells 600 pairs per year, it will restock $600/89.44 = 6.71$ times. The total restocking costs will be $£20 \times 6.71 = £134.16$. Average inventory will be $89.44/2 = 44.72$. The carrying costs will be $£3 \times 44.72 = £134.16$, the same as the restocking costs. The total costs are thus £268.33.

## Extensions to the EOQ Model

Thus far we have assumed that a company will let its inventory run down to zero and then reorder. In reality, a company will wish to reorder before its inventory goes to zero, for two reasons. First, by always having at least some inventory on hand, the firm minimizes the risk of a stock-out and the resulting losses of sales and customers. Second, when a firm does reorder, there will be some time lag before the inventory arrives. Thus, to finish our discussion of the EOQ, we consider two extensions: safety stocks and reordering points.

**Safety Stocks** A *safety stock* is the minimum level of inventory that a firm keeps on hand. Inventories are reordered whenever the level of inventory falls to the safety stock level. The top of Fig. 17.8 illustrates how a safety stock can be incorporated into an EOQ model. Notice that adding a safety stock simply means that the firm does not run its inventory all the way down to zero. Other than this, the situation here is identical to that described in our earlier discussion of the EOQ.

**Reorder Points** To allow for delivery time, a firm will place orders before inventories reach a critical level. The *reorder points* are the times at which the firm will actually place its inventory orders. These points are illustrated in the middle of Fig. 17.8. As shown, the reorder points simply occur some fixed number of days (or weeks or months) before inventories are projected to reach zero.

One of the reasons why a firm will keep a safety stock is to allow for uncertain delivery times. We can therefore combine our reorder point and safety stock discussions in the bottom part of Fig. 17.8. The result is a generalized EOQ model in which the firm orders in advance of anticipated needs, and also keeps a safety stock of inventory.

## Managing Derived-Demand Inventories

The third type of inventory management technique is used to manage derived-demand inventories. As we described earlier, demand for some inventory types is derived from or dependent on other inventory needs. A good example is given by the car manufacturing industry, in which the demand for finished products depends on consumer demand, marketing programmes, and other factors related to projected unit sales. The demand for inventory items such as tyres, batteries, headlights and other components is then completely determined

FIGURE
17.8

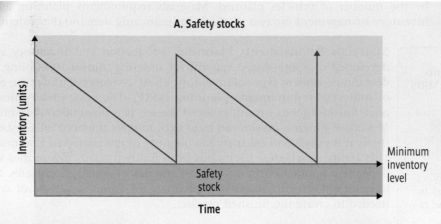

**A. Safety stocks**

With a safety stock, the firm reorders when inventory reaches a minimum level.

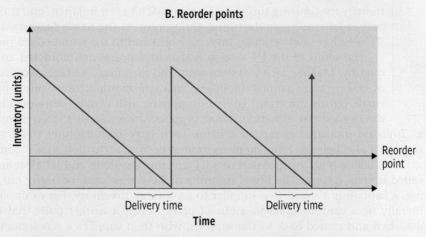

**B. Reorder points**

When there are lags in delivery or production times, the firm reorders when inventory reaches the reorder point.

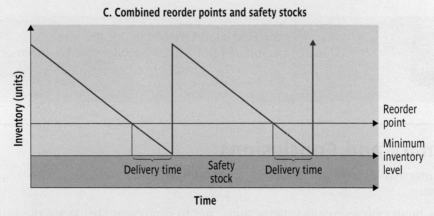

**C. Combined reorder points and safety stocks**

By combining safety stocks and reorder points, the firm maintains a buffer against unforeseen events.

**Figure 17.8** Safety stocks and reorder points

by the number of vehicles planned. Materials requirements planning and just-in-time inventory management are two methods for managing demand-dependent inventories.

**materials requirements planning (MRP)**
A set of procedures used to determine inventory levels for demand-dependent inventory types such as work in progress and raw materials.

**just-in-time (JIT) inventory**
A system for managing demand-dependent inventories that minimizes inventory holdings.

**Materials Requirements Planning**  Production and inventory specialists have developed computer-based systems for ordering and/or scheduling production of demand-dependent types of inventory. These systems fall under the general heading of **materials requirements planning (MRP)**. The basic idea behind MRP is that, once finished goods inventory levels are set, it is possible to determine what levels of work-in-progress inventories must exist to meet the need for finished goods. From there, it is possible to calculate the quantity of raw materials that must be on hand. This ability to schedule backwards from finished goods inventories stems from the dependent nature of work-in-progress and raw materials inventories. MRP is particularly important for complicated products for which a variety of components are needed to create the finished product.

**Just-in-Time Inventory**  **Just-in-time (JIT) inventory** is a modern approach to managing dependent inventories. The goal of JIT is to minimize such inventories, thereby maximizing turnover. The approach began in Japan, and it is a fundamental part of Japanese manufacturing philosophy. As the name suggests, the basic goal of JIT is to have only enough inventory on hand to meet immediate production needs.

The result of the JIT system is that inventories are reordered and restocked frequently. Making such a system work and avoiding shortages requires a high degree of co-operation among suppliers. Japanese manufacturers often have a relatively small, tightly integrated group of suppliers, with whom they work closely to achieve the needed co-ordination. These suppliers are a part of a large manufacturer's (such as Toyota's) industrial group, or *keiretsu*. Each large manufacturer tends to have its own *keiretsu*. It also helps to have suppliers located nearby, a situation that is common in Japan.

The *kanban* is an integral part of a JIT inventory system, and JIT systems are sometimes called *kanban systems*. The literal meaning of *kanban* is 'card' or 'sign'; but, broadly speaking, a kanban is a signal to a supplier to send more inventory. For example, a kanban can literally be a card attached to a bin of parts. When a worker pulls that bin, the card is detached and routed back to the supplier, who then supplies a replacement bin.

A JIT inventory system is an important part of a larger production planning process. A full discussion of it would necessarily shift our focus away from finance to production and operations management, so we shall leave it here.

**CONCEPT QUESTIONS**

17.12a  What does the EOQ model determine for the firm?
17.12b  Which cost component of the EOQ model does JIT inventory minimize?

## Summary and Conclusions

This chapter has covered the basics of short-term financial planning. With respect to cash management:

1  A firm holds cash to conduct transactions, and to compensate banks for the various services they render.

2  The difference between a firm's available balance and its book balance is the firm's net float. The float reflects the fact that some cheques have not cleared, and are thus uncollected. The financial manager must always work with collected cash balances, and not with the company's book balance. To do otherwise is to use the bank's cash without the bank's knowing it, which raises ethical and legal questions.

3 The firm can make use of a variety of procedures to manage the collection and disbursement of cash in such a way as to speed up the collection of cash and slow down the payments.

4 Because of seasonal and cyclical activities, to help finance planned expenditures, or as a contingency reserve, firms temporarily hold a cash surplus. The money market offers a variety of possible vehicles for 'parking' this idle cash.

With respect to credit and working capital:

1 We discussed the terms of sale, credit analysis, and collection policy. Under the general subject of terms of sale, the credit period, the cash discount and discount period, and the credit instrument were described.

2 We developed the cash flows from the decision to grant credit, and showed how the credit decision can be analysed in an NPV setting. The NPV of granting credit depends on five factors: revenue effects, cost effects, the cost of debt, the probability of non-payment, and the cash discount.

3 The optimal amount of credit the firm should offer depends on the competitive conditions under which the firm operates. These conditions will determine the carrying costs associated with granting credit, and the opportunity costs of the lost sales resulting from refusing to offer credit. The optimal credit policy minimizes the sum of these two costs.

4 We looked at the decision to grant credit to a particular customer. We saw that two considerations are very important: the cost relative to the selling price, and the possibility of repeat business.

5 Collection policy determines the method of monitoring the age of trade receivables and dealing with past-due accounts. We described how an ageing schedule can be prepared, and the procedures a firm might use to collect on past-due accounts.

6 We described the different inventory types, and how they differ in terms of liquidity and demand.

7 The two basic inventory costs are carrying costs and restocking costs; we discussed how inventory management involves a trade-off between these two costs.

8 We described the ABC approach and the EOQ model approach to inventory management. We also briefly touched on materials requirements planning (MRP) and just-in-time (JIT) inventory management.

## Chapter Review and Self-Test Problems

**17.1 The BAT Model** Given the following information, calculate the target cash balance using the BAT model:

| | |
|---|---|
| Annual interest rate | 12% |
| Fixed order cost | €100 |
| Total cash needed | €240,000 |

What are the opportunity cost of holding cash, the trading cost, and the total cost? What would these be if €15,000 were held instead? If €25,000 were held?

**17.2 Credit Policy** Cold Fusion plc (manufacturer of the Mr Fusion home power plant) is considering a new credit policy. The current policy is cash only. The new policy would involve extending credit for one period. Based on the following information, determine if a switch is advisable. The interest rate is 2.0 per cent per period:

|  | **Current policy** | **New policy** |
|---|---|---|
| Price per unit (£) | 175 | 175 |
| Cost per unit (£) | 130 | 130 |
| Sales per period (units) | 1,000 | 1,100 |

17.3 **Credit Where Credit Is Due**  You are trying to decide whether or not to extend credit to a particular customer. Your variable cost is €15 per unit; the selling price is €22. This customer wants to buy 1,000 units today and pay in 30 days. You think there is a 15 per cent chance of default. The required return is 3 per cent per 30 days. Should you extend credit? Assume that this is a one-time sale, and that the customer will not buy if credit is not extended.

17.4 **The EOQ**  Annondale Manufacturing starts each period with 10,000 'Long John' golf clubs in stock. This stock is depleted each month and reordered. If the carrying cost per golf club is £1, and the fixed order cost is £5, is Annondale following an economically advisable strategy?

# Answers to Chapter Review and Self-Test Problems

17.1 From the BAT model, we know that the target cash balance is

$$
\begin{aligned}
C^* &= \sqrt{(2T \times F)/R} \\
&= \sqrt{(2 \times €240,000 \times 100)/0.12} \\
&= \sqrt{€400,000,000} \\
&= €20,000
\end{aligned}
$$

The average cash balance will be $C^*/2 = €20,000/2 = €10,000$. The opportunity cost of holding €10,000 when the going rate is 12 per cent is €10,000 × 0.12 = €1,200. There will be €240,000/20,000 = 12 orders during the year, so the order cost, or trading cost, is also 12 × €100 = €1,200. The total cost is thus €2,400.

   If €15,000 is held, the average balance is €7,500. Verify that the opportunity, trading and total costs in this case are €900, €1,600 and €2,500, respectively. If €25,000 is held, these numbers are €1,500, €960 and €2,460, respectively.

17.2 If the switch is made, an extra 100 units per period will be sold at a gross profit of £175 − 130 = £45 each. The total benefit is thus £45 × 100 = £4,500 per period. At 2.0 per cent per period for ever, the PV is £4,500/0.02 = £225,000.

   The cost of the switch is equal to this period's revenue of £175 × 1,000 units = £175,000 plus the cost of producing the extra 100 units: 100 × £130 = £13,000. The total cost is thus £188,000, and the NPV is £225,000 − 188,000 = £37,000. The switch should be made.

17.3 If the customer pays in 30 days, then you will collect €22 × 1,000 = €22,000. There's only an 85 per cent chance of collecting this; so you expect to get €22,000 × 0.85 = €18,700 in 30 days. The present value of this is €18,700/1.03 = €18,155.34. Your cost is €15 × 1,000 = €15,000; so the NPV is €18,155.34 − 15,000 = €3,155.34. Credit should be extended.

17.4 We can answer by first calculating Annondale's carrying and restocking costs. The average inventory is 5,000 clubs, and, because the carrying costs are £1 per club, total carrying costs are £5,000. Annondale restocks every month at a fixed order cost of £5, so the total restocking costs are £60. What we see is that carrying costs are large relative to reorder costs, so Annondale is carrying too much inventory.

   To determine the optimal inventory policy, we can use the EOQ model. Because Annondale orders 10,000 golf clubs 12 times per year, total needs (T) are 120,000 golf clubs. The fixed order cost is £5, and the carrying cost per unit (CC) is £1. The EOQ is therefore

$$EOQ = \sqrt{\frac{2T \times F}{CC}}$$

$$= \sqrt{\frac{(2 \times 120,000) \times £5}{1}}$$

$$= \sqrt{1,200,000}$$

$$= 1,095.45 \text{ units}$$

We can check this by noting that the average inventory is about 550 clubs, so the carrying cost is £550. Annondale will have to reorder $120,000/1,095.45 = 109.54 \approx 110$ times. The fixed order cost is £5, so the total restocking cost is also £550.

## Concepts Review and Critical Thinking Questions

1  **Cash Management [LO3]**   Is it possible for a firm to have too much cash? Why would shareholders care if a firm accumulates large amounts of cash?

2  **Agency Issues [LO3]**   Are stockholders and creditors likely to agree on how much cash a firm should keep on hand?

3  **Cash Management versus Liquidity Management [LO3]**   What is the difference between cash management and liquidity management?

4  **Collection and Disbursement Floats [LO1]**   Which would a firm prefer: a net collection float or a net disbursement float? Why?

5  **Agency Issues [LO3]**   It is sometimes argued that excess cash held by a firm can aggravate agency problems (discussed in Chapter 2) and, more generally, reduce incentives for shareholder wealth maximization. How would you frame the issue here?

6  **Float [LO1]**   An unfortunately common practice goes like this (Warning: don't try this at home). Suppose you are out of money in your bank account; however, your local grocery store will, as a convenience to you as a customer, cash a cheque for you. So you cash a cheque for £200. Of course, this cheque will bounce unless you do something. To prevent this, you go to the grocery the next day and cash another cheque for £200. You take this £200 and deposit it. You repeat this process every day, and, in doing so, you make sure that no cheques bounce. Eventually, manna from heaven arrives (perhaps in the form of money from home), and you are able to cover your outstanding cheques.

To make it interesting, suppose you are absolutely certain that no cheques will bounce along the way. Assuming this is true, and ignoring any question of legality (what we have described is probably illegal cheque kiting), is there anything unethical about this? If you say yes, then why? In particular, who is harmed?

7  **Credit Instruments [LO4]**   Describe each of the following:

(a)  Sight draft.

(b)  Time draft.

(c)  Banker's acceptance.

(d)  Promissory note.

(e)  Trade acceptance.

8  **Receivables Costs [LO4]**   What costs are associated with carrying receivables? What costs are associated with not granting credit? What do we call the sum of the costs for different levels of receivables?

9 **Credit Period Length [LO4]** What are some of the factors that determine the length of the credit period? Why is the length of the buyer's operating cycle often considered an upper bound on the length of the credit period?

10 **Inventory Types [LO6]** What are the different inventory types? How do the types differ? Why are some types said to have dependent demand whereas other types are said to have independent demand?

11 **Inventory Costs [LO6]** If a company's inventory-carrying costs are £5 million per year and its fixed order costs are £8 million per year, do you think the firm keeps too much inventory on hand or too little? Why?

## connect Questions and Problems

**BASIC**

**1–10**

1 **Calculating Float [LO1]** In a typical month, Jeremy Ltd receives 80 cheques totalling £156,000. These are delayed four days on average. What is the average daily float?

2 **Costs of Float [LO1]** Purple Feet Wine receives an average of €19,000 in cheques per day. The delay in clearing is typically three days. The current interest rate is 0.019 per cent per day.

(a) What is the company's float?

(b) What is the most Purple Feet should be willing to pay today to eliminate its float entirely?

(c) What is the highest daily fee the company should be willing to pay to eliminate its float entirely?

3 **Using Weighted Average Delay [LO1]** A mail-order firm processes 5,300 cheques per month. Of these, 60 per cent are for £55 and 40 per cent are for £80. The £55 cheques are delayed two days on average; the £80 cheques are delayed three days on average.

(a) What is the average daily collection float? How do you interpret your answer?

(b) What is the weighted average delay? Use the result to calculate the average daily float.

(c) How much should the firm be willing to pay to eliminate the float?

(d) If the interest rate is 7 per cent per year, calculate the daily cost of the float.

(e) How much should the firm be willing to pay to reduce the weighted average float by 1.5 days?

4 **Value of Delay [LO2]** No More Pencils disburses cheques every two weeks that average £93,000 and take seven days to clear. How much interest can the company earn annually if it delays transfer of funds from an interest-bearing account that pays 0.015 per cent per day for these seven days? Ignore the effects of compounding interest.

5 **Cash Discounts [LO4]** You place an order for 400 units of inventory at a unit price of €125. The supplier offers terms of 1/10, net 30.

(a) How long do you have to pay before the account is overdue? If you take the full period, how much should you remit?

(b) What is the discount being offered? How quickly must you pay to get the discount? If you do take the discount, how much should you remit?

(c) If you don't take the discount, how much interest are you paying implicitly? How many days' credit are you receiving?

6 **ACP and Trade Receivables [LO4]** Kyoto Joe sells earnings forecasts for Japanese securities. Its credit terms are 2/10, net 30. Based on experience, 65 per cent of all customers will take the discount.

(a) What is the average collection period for Kyoto Joe?

(b) If Kyoto Joe sells 1,300 forecasts every month at a price of €1,700 each, what is its average balance sheet amount in trade receivables?

7 **Terms of Sale [LO4]** A firm offers terms of 1/10, net 35. What effective annual interest rate does the firm earn when a customer does not take the discount? Without doing any calculations, explain what will happen to this effective rate if:

(a) The discount is changed to 2 per cent.

(b) The credit period is increased to 60 days.

(c) The discount period is increased to 15 days.

8 **Size of Trade Receivables [LO4]** Essence of Skunk Fragrances Ltd sells 5,600 units of its perfume collection each year at a price per unit of €425. All sales are on credit, with terms of 1/10, net 40. The discount is taken by 60 per cent of the customers. What is the amount of the company's trade receivables? In reaction to sales by its main competitor, Sewage Spray, Essence of Skunk is considering a change in its credit policy to terms of 2/10, net 30 to preserve its market share. How will this change in policy affect trade receivables?

9 **Evaluating Credit Policy [LO5]** Air Spares is a wholesaler that stocks engine components and test equipment for the commercial aircraft industry. A new customer has placed an order for eight high-bypass turbine engines, which increase fuel economy. The variable cost is £1.6 million per unit, and the credit price is £1.87 million each. Credit is extended for one period and, based on historical experience, payment for about 1 out of every 200 such orders is never collected. The required return is 2.9 per cent per period.

(a) Assuming that this is a one-time order, should it be filled? The customer will not buy if credit is not extended.

(b) What is the break-even probability of default in part (a)?

(c) Suppose that customers who don't default become repeat customers and place the same order every period for ever. Further assume that repeat customers never default. Should the order be filled? What is the break-even probability of default?

(d) Describe in general terms why credit terms will be more liberal when repeat orders are a possibility.

10 **EOQ [LO7]** Redan Manufacturing uses 2,500 switch assemblies per week and then reorders another 2,500. If the relevant carrying cost per switch assembly is €9, and the fixed order cost is €1,700, is Redan's inventory policy optimal? Why or why not?

11 **EOQ Derivation [LO7]** Prove that when carrying costs and restocking costs are as described in the chapter, the EOQ must occur at the point where the carrying costs and restocking costs are equal.

12 **Credit Policy Evaluation [LO5]** Harrington plc is considering a change in its cash-only policy. The new terms would be net one period. Based on the following information, determine whether Harrington should proceed or not. The required return is 2.5 per cent per period.

| | Current policy | New policy |
|---|---|---|
| Price per unit (£) | 91 | 94 |
| Cost per unit (£) | 47 | 47 |
| Unit sales per month | 3,850 | 3,940 |

13  **Credit Policy Evaluation [LO5]**  Happy Times currently has an all-cash credit policy. It is considering making a change in the credit policy by going to terms of net 30 days. Based on the following information, what do you recommend? The required return is 0.95 per cent per month.

| | Current policy | New policy |
|---|---|---|
| Price per unit (€) | 290 | 295 |
| Cost per unit (€) | 230 | 234 |
| Unit sales per month | 1,105 | 1,125 |

**CHALLENGE 14**

14  **Safety Stocks and Order Points [LO4]**  Saché SA expects to sell 700 of its designer suits every week. The store is open seven days a week, and expects to sell the same number of suits every day. The company has an EOQ of 500 suits and a safety stock of 100 suits. Once an order is placed, it takes three days for Saché to get the suits in. How many orders does the company place per year? Assume that it is Monday morning before the store opens, and a shipment of suits has just arrived. When will Saché place its next order?

**MINI CASE**

# Credit Policy at Schwarzwald AG

Dagmar Bamberger, the president of Schwarzwald AG, has been exploring ways of improving the company's financial performance. Schwarzwald manufactures and sells office equipment to retailers. The company's growth has been relatively slow in recent years, but with an expansion in the economy it appears that sales may increase more quickly in the future. Dagmar has asked Johann Rüstow, the company's treasurer, to examine Schwarzwald's credit policy to see whether a different credit policy could help increase profitability.

The company currently has a policy of net 30. As with any credit sales, default rates are always of concern. Because of Schwarzwald's screening and collection process, the default rate on credit is currently only 1.5 per cent. Johann has examined the company's credit policy in relation to other vendors, and he has determined that three options are available.

The first option is to relax the company's decision on when to grant credit. The second option is to increase the credit period to net 45, and the third option is a combination of the relaxed credit policy and the extension of the credit period to net 45. On the positive side, each of the three policies under consideration would increase sales. The three policies have the drawbacks that default rates would increase, the administrative costs of managing the firm's receivables would increase, and the receivables period would increase. The credit policy change would affect all four of these variables to different degrees. Johann has prepared the following table outlining the effect on each of these variables:

| | Annual sales (€ millions) | Default rate (% of sales) | Administrative costs (% of sales) | Receivables period (days) |
|---|---|---|---|---|
| Current policy | 120 | 1.5 | 2.1 | 38 |
| Option 1 | 140 | 2.4 | 3.1 | 41 |
| Option 2 | 137 | 1.7 | 2.3 | 51 |
| Option 3 | 150 | 2.1 | 2.9 | 49 |

Schwarzwald's variable costs of production are 45 per cent of sales, and the relevant interest rate is a 6 per cent effective annual rate. Which credit policy should the company use? Also, notice that in option 3 the default rate and administrative costs are below those in option 2. Is this plausible? Why or why not?

# International Corporate Finance

## KEY NOTATIONS

| | |
|---|---|
| $F$ | Forward exchange rate |
| FC | Foreign country |
| $h$ | Inflation rate |
| HC | Home country |
| IFE | International Fisher effect |
| IRP | Interest rate parity |
| NPV | Net present value |
| $P$ | Price |
| PPP | Purchasing power parity |
| $R$ | Risk-free rate |
| $S$ | Exchange rate |
| UFR | Unbiased forward rate |
| UIP | Uncovered interest parity |

## LEARNING OBJECTIVES

After studying this chapter, you should understand:

LO1 How exchange rates are quoted, what they mean, and the difference between spot and forward exchange rates.

LO2 Purchasing power parity, interest rate parity, unbiased forward rates, uncovered interest rate parity and the international Fisher effect, and their implications for exchange rate changes.

LO3 The different types of exchange rate risk, and ways in which firms manage exchange rate risk.

LO4 The impact of political risk on international business investing.

RELATIVELY FEW LARGE COMPANIES operate in a single country. As a financial manager in a corporation, even if your sales are not overseas, it is highly likely that you have competitors or suppliers with operations overseas. In most industries, raw materials and components are sourced and imported from abroad, and many services and products are sold to other countries.

For example, an analysis of 2009 import and export revenue for the United Kingdom shows that most of Britain's export revenue comes from the US (13.8%), Germany (11.5%), the Netherlands (7.8%) France (7.6%), Ireland (7.5%), Belgium (5.3%) and Spain (4.1%). Similarly, the United Kingdom's main import partners are Germany (13%), the US (8.7%), China (7.5%), the Netherlands (7.4%), France (6.8%), Belgium (4.7%) and Italy (4.1%).

Currency fluctuations will clearly have an impact on firms. For example, if the euro strengthens against the British pound, British exports become more competitive in Europe. Similarly, raw materials sourced from Europe will become more expensive, and British corporations will look elsewhere for cheaper inputs. One of the reasons why European Monetary Union was adopted in 2000 was precisely that many countries in the Eurozone traded heavily with each other. With a single currency, the risk of fluctuations is eradicated. For companies outside the Eurozone who have Eurozone customers or suppliers, currency fluctuations (and hence currency risk) may even become worse. For example, when Greek sovereign debt was reduced to junk status in 2010, the euro was exceptionally volatile. In this chapter we explore the roles played by currencies and exchange rates, along with a number of other key topics in international corporate finance.

Corporations with significant foreign operations are often called *international corporations* or *multinationals*. Such corporations must consider many financial factors that do not directly affect purely domestic firms. These include foreign exchange rates, differing interest rates from country to country, complex accounting methods for foreign operations, foreign tax rates, and foreign government intervention.

The basic principles of corporate finance still apply to international corporations: like domestic companies, these firms seek to invest in projects that create more value for the shareholders than they cost, and to arrange financing that raises cash at the lowest possible cost. In other words, the net present value principle holds for both foreign and domestic operations, although it is usually more complicated to apply the NPV rule to foreign investments.

One of the most significant complications of international finance is foreign exchange. The foreign exchange markets provide important information and opportunities for an international corporation when it undertakes capital budgeting and financing decisions. As we shall discuss, international exchange rates, interest rates and inflation rates are closely related. We shall spend much of this chapter exploring the connection between these financial variables.

We shan't have much to say here about the role of cultural and social differences in international business. Nor shall we be discussing the implications of differing political and economic systems. These factors are of great importance to international businesses, but it would take another book to do them justice. Consequently, we shall focus only on some purely financial considerations in international finance, and on some key aspects of foreign exchange markets.

## 18.1 Terminology

A common buzzword for the student of business finance is *globalization*. The first step in learning about the globalization of financial markets is to conquer the new vocabulary. As with any speciality, international finance is rich in jargon. Accordingly, we get started on the subject with a highly eclectic vocabulary exercise.

The terms that follow are presented alphabetically, and they are not all of equal importance. We choose these particular ones either because they appear frequently in the financial press, or because they illustrate the colourful nature of the language of international finance.

**American depositary receipt (ADR)** A security issued in the United States representing shares of a foreign equity, and allowing that equity to be traded in the United States.

**cross-rate** The implicit exchange rate between two currencies quoted in some third currency.

**Eurobonds** International bonds issued in multiple countries but denominated in a single currency (usually the issuer's currency).

1  An **American depositary receipt (ADR)** is a security issued in the United States that represents shares of a foreign equity, allowing that equity to be traded in the United States. Foreign companies use ADRs, which are issued in US dollars, to expand the pool of potential US investors. ADRs are available in two forms for a large and growing number of foreign companies: company-sponsored, which are listed on an exchange; and unsponsored, which usually are held by the bank that makes a market in the ADR. Both forms are available to individual investors, but only company-sponsored issues are quoted daily in newspapers. A *global depositary receipt* (GDR) is an equivalent security denominated in sterling or euros, and issued and traded in financial centres such as London or Frankfurt.

2  The **cross-rate** is the implicit exchange rate between two currencies when both are quoted in some third currency.

3  A **Eurobond** is a bond issued in multiple countries, but denominated in a single currency, usually the issuer's home currency. Such bonds have become an important way to raise capital for many international companies and governments. Eurobonds are issued outside the restrictions that apply to domestic offerings, and are syndicated and traded mostly from London. Trading takes place anywhere there is a buyer and a seller.

4   **Eurocurrency** is money deposited in a financial centre outside the country whose currency is involved. For instance, Eurodollars – the most widely used Eurocurrency – are US dollars deposited in banks outside the US. Eurosterling and euroyen are British and Japanese equivalents.

5   **Foreign bonds**, unlike Eurobonds, are issued in a single country and are usually denominated in that country's currency. Often, the country in which these bonds are issued will draw distinctions between them and bonds issued by domestic issuers, including different tax laws, restrictions on the amount issued, and tougher disclosure rules.

Foreign bonds often are nicknamed for the country where they are issued: Yankee bonds (United States), Samurai bonds (Japan), Rembrandt bonds (the Netherlands), and Bulldog bonds (Britain). Partly because of tougher regulations and disclosure requirements, the foreign bond market hasn't grown in past years with the vigour of the Eurobond market.

6   **Gilts**, technically, are British and Irish government securities, although the term also includes issues of local British authorities and some overseas public sector offerings.

7   The **London Interbank Offered Rate (LIBOR)** is the rate that most international banks charge one another for loans overnight in the London market. LIBOR is a cornerstone in the pricing of money market issues and other short-term debt issues by both government and corporate borrowers. Interest rates are frequently quoted as some spread over LIBOR, and they then float with the LIBOR rate. EURIBOR is the Eurozone equivalent.

8   There are two basic kinds of **swap**: interest rate swaps and currency swaps. An interest rate swap occurs when two parties exchange a floating-rate payment for a fixed-rate payment or vice versa. Currency swaps are agreements to deliver one currency in exchange for another. Often, both types of swap are used in the same transaction when debt denominated in different currencies is swapped.

**Eurocurrency**
Money deposited in a financial centre outside the country whose currency is involved.

**foreign bonds**
International bonds issued in a single country, usually denominated in that country's currency.

**gilts**
British and Irish government securities.

**London Interbank Offered Rate (LIBOR)**
The rate most international banks charge one another for overnight loans.

**swaps**
Agreements to exchange two securities or currencies.

---

**CONCEPT QUESTIONS**

18.1a   What are the differences between a Eurobond and a foreign bond?
18.1b   What are Eurodollars?

---

## 18.2   Foreign Exchange Markets and Exchange Rates

The **foreign exchange market** is undoubtedly the world's largest financial market. It is the market where one country's currency is traded for another's. Most of the trading takes place in a few currencies: the US dollar ($), the British pound sterling (£), the Japanese yen (¥) and the euro (€). Table 18.1 lists some of the more common currencies and their symbols.

The foreign exchange market is an over-the-counter market, so there is no single location where traders get together. Instead, market participants are located in the major banks around the world. They communicate using computer terminals, telephones, and other telecommunications devices. For example, one communications network for foreign transactions is maintained by the Society for Worldwide Interbank Financial Telecommunication (SWIFT), a Belgian not-for-profit co-operative. Using data transmission lines, a bank in New York can send messages to a bank in London via SWIFT regional processing centres.

**foreign exchange market**
The market in which one country's currency is traded for another's.

TABLE
18.1

| Country | Currency | Symbol |
|---|---|---|
| Australia | Dollar | A$ |
| Canada | Dollar | C$ |
| China | Yuan (renminbi) | ¥ |
| Denmark | Krone | DKr |
| EMU (Eurozone) | Euro | € |
| India | Rupee | Rs |
| Iran | Rial | IR |
| Japan | Yen | ¥ |
| Kuwait | Dinar | KD |
| Mexico | Peso | Ps |
| Norway | Krone | NKr |
| Saudi Arabia | Riyal | SR |
| Singapore | Dollar | S$ |
| South Africa | Rand | R |
| Sweden | Krona | SKr |
| Switzerland | Franc | SFr |
| United Kingdom | Pound | £ |
| United States | Dollar | $ |

**Table 18.1** International currency symbols

# Work the Web

You have just returned from your dream backpacking trip to Vietnam, and you feel rich because you have 10,000 Vietnamese dong left over. You now need to convert this to euros. How much will you have? You can look up the current exchange rate and do the conversion yourself, or simply work the Web. We went to www.xe.com and used the currency converter on the site to find out. This is what we found:

It looks as though you left Vietnam just before you ran out of money!

## QUESTIONS

1   Using this currency converter, what is the current EUR/VND exchange rate?

2   The website www.xe.com also lists cross-rates. What is the current ¥/€ cross-rate?

The many different types of participant in the foreign exchange market include the following:

1 Importers who pay for goods using foreign currencies

2 Exporters who receive foreign currency and may want to convert to the domestic currency

3 Portfolio managers who buy or sell foreign equities and bonds

4 Foreign exchange brokers who match buy and sell orders

5 Traders who 'make a market' in foreign currencies

6 Speculators who try to profit from changes in exchange rates

## Exchange Rates

> **exchange rate**
> The price of one country's currency expressed in terms of another country's currency.

An **exchange rate** is simply the price of one country's currency expressed in terms of another country's currency. In practice, almost all trading of currencies takes place in terms of the US dollar, the yen and the euro. For example, both the Swiss franc and the Japanese yen are traded with their prices quoted in US dollars. Exchange rates are constantly changing. Our nearby Work the Web box shows you how to get up-to-the-minute rates.

**Exchange Rate Quotations**    Figure 18.1 reproduces exchange rate quotations as they appeared in the *Financial Times* in 2010. The three main columns give the number of units of foreign currency it takes to buy one dollar, euro or pound, respectively. Because this is the price in foreign currency with respect to dollars, euros or pounds, it is called an indirect quote. For example, the Thai baht is quoted at 49.2861 against the pound, which means that you can buy one British pound with 49.2861 Thai baht.

**Cross-Rates and Triangle Arbitrage**    The *Financial Times* quotes exchange rates in terms of the US dollar, euro and British pound. Using any of these currencies as the common denominator in quoting exchange rates greatly reduces the number of possible cross-currency quotes. For example, with five major currencies there would potentially be ten exchange rates instead of just four.[1] Also, the fact that one currency (the dollar, euro or pound) is used throughout decreases inconsistencies in the exchange rate quotations.

---

**EXAMPLE 18.1**

## A Yen for Euros

Suppose you have £1,000. Based on the rates in Fig. 18.1, how many South African rand can you get? Alternatively, if a Porsche costs €100,000, how many pounds will you need to buy it?

The exchange rate in terms of rand per pound is 11.1965. Your £1,000 will thus get you

$$£1,000 \times 11.1965 \text{ rand per } £1 = 11,197 \text{ rand}$$

Because the exchange rate in terms of pounds per euro is 0.9056, you will need

$$€100,000 \times £0.9056 \text{ per } € = £90,560$$

---

Earlier, we defined the cross-rate as the exchange rate for a foreign currency expressed in terms of another foreign currency. For example, suppose we observe the following for the Russian rouble and the Bahraini dinar:

$$\text{Russian rouble per } €1 = 45.8022$$
$$\text{Bahraini dinar per } €1 = 0.4831$$

**Figure 18.1** Exchange rate quotations

*Source:* ft.com, 17 March 2010. © The Financial Times Ltd 2010.

| Mar 16 | Currency | DOLLAR Closing Mid | DOLLAR Day's Change | EURO Closing Mid | EURO Day's Change | POUND Closing Mid | POUND Day's Change |
|---|---|---|---|---|---|---|---|
| Argentina | (Peso) | 3.8613 | -0.0018 | 5.3124 | 0.0388 | 5.8664 | 0.0557 |
| Australia | (A$) | 1.0933 | -0.0037 | 1.5042 | 0.0066 | 1.6611 | 0.0109 |
| Bahrain | (Dinar) | 0.3770 | 0.0000 | 0.5187 | 0.0040 | 0.5728 | 0.0057 |
| Bolivia | (Boliviano) | 7.0200 | | 9.6581 | 0.0747 | 10.6655 | 0.1060 |
| Brazil | (R$) | 1.7622 | -0.0048 | 2.4244 | 0.0122 | 2.6773 | 0.0193 |
| Canada | (C$) | 1.0149 | -0.0068 | 1.3963 | 0.0015 | 1.5419 | 0.0050 |
| Chile | (Peso) | 523.950 | 7.7000 | 720.850 | 16.0917 | 796.037 | 19.4940 |
| China | (Yuan) | 6.8259 | -0.0001 | 9.3911 | 0.0725 | 10.3706 | 0.1030 |
| Colombia | (Peso) | 1896.45 | -6.0500 | 2609.14 | 11.9381 | 2881.28 | 19.5361 |
| Costa Rica | (Colon) | 527.820 | -13.7850 | 726.176 | -13.1971 | 801.918 | -12.7654 |
| Czech Rep. | (Koruna) | 18.5347 | -0.1446 | 25.5000 | | 28.1598 | 0.0624 |
| Denmark | (DKr) | 5.4081 | -0.0426 | 7.4405 | -0.0006 | 8.2166 | 0.0176 |
| Egypt | (Egypt £) | 5.4815 | -0.0005 | 7.5415 | 0.0577 | 8.3281 | 0.0820 |
| Estonia | (Kroon) | 11.3727 | -0.0887 | 15.6465 | | 17.2785 | 0.0383 |
| Hong Kong | (HK$) | 7.7608 | 0.0017 | 10.6772 | 0.0850 | 11.7909 | 0.1199 |
| Hungary | (Forint) | 191.838 | -2.1705 | 263.930 | -0.9200 | 291.459 | -0.3681 |
| India | (Rs) | 45.5350 | -0.0500 | 62.6471 | 0.4167 | 69.1813 | 0.6123 |
| Indonesia | (Rupiah) | 9165.00 | | 12609.2 | 97.6075 | 13924.4 | 138.391 |
| Iran | (Rial) | 9887.50 | | 13603.2 | 105.302 | 15022.1 | 149.301 |
| Israel | (Shk) | 3.7263 | -0.0023 | 5.1266 | 0.0366 | 5.6613 | 0.0529 |
| Japan | (Y) | 90.4300 | -0.0350 | 124.414 | 0.9153 | 137.390 | 1.3129 |
| One Month | | 90.4102 | 0.0001 | 124.390 | 0.0018 | 137.335 | 0.0024 |
| Three Month | | 90.3755 | 0.0010 | 124.344 | 0.0021 | 137.235 | 0.0022 |
| One Year | | 89.9980 | 0.0015 | 123.746 | 0.0012 | 136.495 | -0.0109 |
| Kenya | (Shilling) | 76.9000 | 0.0500 | 105.799 | 0.8872 | 116.834 | 1.2364 |
| Kuwait | (Dinar) | 0.2879 | -0.0003 | 0.3961 | 0.0026 | 0.4374 | 0.0039 |
| Malaysia | (M$) | 3.3200 | -0.0010 | 4.5677 | 0.0339 | 5.0441 | 0.0486 |
| Mexico | (New Peso) | 12.5208 | -0.0448 | 17.2261 | 0.0722 | 19.0228 | 0.1218 |
| New Zealand | (NZ$) | 1.4139 | -0.0150 | 1.9453 | -0.0053 | 2.1482 | -0.0012 |
| Nigeria | (Naira) | 150.000 | -0.4300 | 206.370 | 1.0105 | 227.895 | 1.6182 |
| Norway | (NKr) | 5.8260 | -0.0494 | 8.0154 | -0.0053 | 8.8515 | 0.0138 |
| Pakistan | (Rupee) | 84.4000 | -0.1000 | 116.118 | 0.7624 | 128.229 | 1.1241 |
| Peru | (New Sol) | 2.8368 | -0.0027 | 3.9029 | 0.0265 | 4.3100 | 0.0387 |
| Philippines | (Peso) | 45.7200 | 0.0075 | 62.9016 | 0.4972 | 69.4624 | 0.7017 |

| Currency | | DOLLAR Closing Mid | DOLLAR Day's Change | EURO Closing Mid | EURO Day's Change | POUND Closing Mid | POUND Day's Change |
|---|---|---|---|---|---|---|---|
| Poland | (Zloty) | 2.8203 | -0.0334 | 3.8802 | -0.0156 | 4.2849 | -0.0078 |
| Romania | (New Leu) | 2.9738 | -0.0219 | 4.0913 | 0.0018 | 4.5180 | 0.0120 |
| Russia | (Rouble) | 29.3013 | -0.1480 | 40.3127 | 0.1099 | 44.5174 | 0.2198 |
| Saudi Arabia | (SR) | 3.7503 | 0.0001 | 5.1596 | 0.0401 | 5.6978 | 0.0567 |
| Singapore | (S$) | 1.3950 | -0.0031 | 1.9192 | 0.0107 | 2.1194 | 0.0165 |
| South Africa | (R) | 7.3695 | -0.0505 | 10.1390 | 0.0095 | 11.1965 | 0.0353 |
| South Korea | (Won) | 1132.65 | -2.0500 | 1558.30 | 9.2642 | 1720.84 | 14.0194 |
| Sweden | (SKr) | 7.0648 | -0.0691 | 9.7198 | -0.0190 | 10.7336 | 0.0029 |
| Switzerland | (SFr) | 1.0557 | -0.0077 | 1.4524 | 0.0006 | 1.6039 | 0.0042 |
| Taiwan | (T$) | 31.8155 | 0.0005 | 43.7718 | 0.3395 | 48.3373 | 0.4812 |
| Thailand | (Bt) | 32.4400 | -0.1300 | 44.6310 | 0.1680 | 49.2861 | 0.2943 |
| Tunisia | (Dinar) | 1.3769 | -0.0097 | 1.8944 | 0.0015 | 2.0920 | 0.0062 |
| Turkey | (Lira) | 1.5227 | -0.0076 | 2.0949 | 0.0058 | 2.3134 | 0.0116 |
| U A E | (Dirham) | 3.6730 | | 5.0533 | 0.0391 | 5.5804 | 0.0555 |
| UK (0.6582)* | (£) | 1.5193 | 0.0151 | 0.9056 | -0.0020 | | |
| One Month | | 1.5190 | 0.0000 | 0.9058 | | | |
| Three Month | | 1.5185 | 0.0000 | 0.9061 | | | |
| One Year | | 1.5167 | -0.0001 | 0.9066 | 0.0001 | | |
| Ukraine | (Hrywnja) | 7.9875 | 0.0140 | 10.9892 | 10.9892 | 12.1355 | 0.1417 |
| Uruguay | (Peso) | 19.5500 | 0.0500 | 26.8969 | 26.8969 | 29.7024 | 0.3704 |
| USA | ($) | | | 1.3758 | | 1.5193 | 0.0151 |
| One Month | | | | 1.3759 | 0.0000 | 1.5190 | 0.0000 |
| Three Month | | | | 1.3759 | 0.0000 | 1.5185 | 0.0000 |
| One Year | | | | 1.3750 | 0.0001 | 1.5167 | -0.0001 |
| Venezuela †(Bolivar Fuerte) | | 4.2947 | | 5.9086 | 0.0458 | 6.5249 | 0.0649 |
| Vietnam | (Dong) | 19090.0 | | 26264.0 | 203.309 | 29003.4 | 288.259 |

| | | DOLLAR Closing Mid | DOLLAR Day's Change | EURO Closing Mid | EURO Day's Change | POUND Closing Mid | POUND Day's Change |
|---|---|---|---|---|---|---|---|
| Euro (0.7268)* | (Euro) | 1.3758 | 0.0106 | | | 1.1043 | 0.0025 |
| One Month | | 1.3759 | 0.0000 | | | 1.1041 | |
| Three Month | | 1.3759 | 0.0000 | | | 1.1037 | |
| One Year | | 1.3750 | 0.0001 | | | 1.1030 | -0.0001 |
| SDR | | 0.6508 | -0.0024 | 0.8953 | 0.0036 | 0.9887 | 0.0062 |

Suppose the cross-rate is quoted as

$$\text{Dinar per rouble} = 0.01$$

**What do you think?**

The cross-rate here is inconsistent with the exchange rates. To see this, suppose you have €100. If you convert this to Russian roubles, you will receive

$$€100 \times 45.8022 \text{ roubles per } €1 = 4,580.22 \text{ roubles}$$

If you convert this to dinar at the cross-rate, you will have

$$4,580.22 \text{ roubles} \times 0.01 \text{ per rouble} = 45.8022 \text{ dinar}$$

However, if you just convert your euros to dinar without going through Russian roubles, you will have

$$€100 \times 0.4831 \text{ dinar per } €1 = 48.31 \text{ dinar}$$

What we see is that the dinar has two prices, 0.4831 dinar per €1 and 0.4580 dinar per €1, with the price we pay depending on how we get the dinar.

To make money, we want to buy low and sell high. The important thing to note is that dinar are cheaper if you buy them with euros, because you get 0.4831 dinar instead of just 0.4580 dinar. You should proceed as follows:

1   Buy 48.31 dinar for €100.

2   Use the 48.31 dinar to buy Russian roubles at the cross-rate. Because it takes 0.01 dinar to buy a Russian rouble, you will receive 48.31 dinar/0.01 roubles = 4,831 roubles.

3   Use the 4,831 roubles to buy euros. Because the exchange rate is 45.8022 roubles per euro, you receive 4,831 roubles/45.8022 = €105.48, for a round-trip profit of €5.48.

4   Repeat steps 1–3.

This particular activity is called *triangle arbitrage*, because the arbitrage involves moving through three different exchange rates:

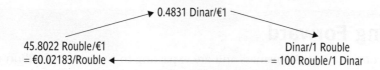

To prevent such opportunities, it is not difficult to see that because a euro will buy you either 45.8022 Russian roubles or 0.4831 Bahraini dinar, the cross-rate must be

$$(0.4831 \text{ dinar/}€1)/(45.8022 \text{ rouble/}€1) = 0.010548 \text{ dinar/rouble}$$

That is, the cross-rate must be 0.010548 Bahraini dinar per 1 Russian rouble. If it were anything else, there would be a triangle arbitrage opportunity.

---

**EXAMPLE 18.2**

## Shedding Some Pounds

According to Fig. 18.1, the exchange rates for the British pound against the euro and dollar are

$$€/£ = 1.1043$$
$$\$/£ = 1.5193$$

The US dollar/euro exchange rate is quoted as $1.3758/€. Show that the exchange rates are consistent.

Taking the two British pound exchange rates, we find that the cross-rate is

$$\$/€ = (\$/£)/(€/£) = 1.5193/1.1043 = 1.3758$$

The exchange rates are consistent.

**spot trade**
An agreement to trade currencies based on the exchange rate today for settlement within two business days.

**spot exchange rate**
The exchange rate on a spot trade.

**forward trade**
An agreement to exchange currency at some time in the future.

**forward exchange rate**
The agreed-upon exchange rate to be used in a forward trade.

**Types of Transaction**   There are two basic types of trade in the foreign exchange market: spot trades and forward trades. A **spot trade** is an agreement to exchange currency 'on the spot', which actually means that the transaction will be completed or settled within two business days. The exchange rate on a spot trade is called the **spot exchange rate**. Implicitly, all the exchange rates and transactions we have discussed so far have referred to the spot market.

A **forward trade** is an agreement to exchange currency at some time in the future. The exchange rate that will be used is agreed upon today and is called the **forward exchange rate**. A forward trade will normally be settled some time in the next 12 months.

If you look back at Fig. 18.1 you will see forward exchange rates quoted for the dollar, the euro and the pound. For example, the spot €/£ exchange rate is €1.1043/£. The one-year forward exchange rate is €1.1030/£. This means that you can buy a pound today for €1.1043, or you can agree to take delivery of a pound in one year and pay €1.1030 at that time.

Notice that the British pound is less expensive in the forward market (€1.1030 versus €1.1043). Because the British pound is less expensive in the future than it is today, it is said to be selling at a *discount* relative to the euro. For the same reason, the euro is said to be selling at a *premium* relative to the British pound.

Why does the forward market exist? One answer is that it allows businesses and individuals to lock in a future exchange rate today, thereby eliminating any risk from unfavourable shifts in the exchange rate.

## EXAMPLE 18.3    Looking Forward

Suppose you are a British business and are expecting to receive one million euros in three months, and you agree to a forward trade to exchange your euros for pounds. Based on Fig. 18.1, how many pounds will you get in three months? Is the euro selling at a discount or a premium relative to the pound?

In Fig. 18.1 the spot exchange rate and the three-month forward rate in terms of pounds per euros are £0.9056 = €1 and £0.9061 = €1, respectively. If you expect €1 million in three months, then you will get €1 million × 0.9061 per pound = £906,100. Because it is less expensive to buy a pound in the forward market than in the spot market (£0.9061 versus £0.9056), the pound is said to be selling at a discount relative to the euro.

As we mentioned earlier, it is standard practice around the world (with a few exceptions) to quote exchange rates in terms of the dollar, euro or pound. This means that rates are quoted as the amount of currency per dollar, euro or pound. For the remainder of this chapter we shall stick with this form. Things can get extremely confusing if you forget this. Thus when we say things like 'the exchange rate is expected to rise', it is important to remember that we are talking about the exchange rate quoted as units of foreign currency per dollar, euro or pound.

| CONCEPT QUESTIONS | 18.2a | What is triangle arbitrage? |
|---|---|---|
| | 18.2b | What do we mean by the 90-day forward exchange rate? |
| | 18.2c | If we say that the exchange rate is €1.1/£, what do we mean? |

## 18.3 Purchasing Power Parity

Now that we have discussed what exchange rate quotations mean, we can address an obvious question: what determines the level of the spot exchange rate? In addition, because we know that exchange rates change through time, we can ask the related question: what determines the rate of change in exchange rates? At least part of the answer in both cases goes by the name of **purchasing power parity** (PPP): the idea that the exchange rate adjusts to keep purchasing power constant among currencies. As we discuss next, there are two forms of PPP, *absolute* and *relative*.

> **purchasing power parity (PPP)**
> The idea that the exchange rate adjusts to keep purchasing power constant among currencies.

### Absolute Purchasing Power Parity

The basic idea behind **absolute purchasing power parity** is that a commodity costs the same, regardless of what currency is used to purchase it or where it is selling. This is a straightforward concept. If a beer costs 50 kroner in Oslo, and the exchange rate is NKr10 per pound, then a beer costs NKr50/10 = £5 in London. In other words, absolute PPP says that £1 or €1 will buy you the same number of, say, beers anywhere in the world.

More formally, let $S_0$ be the spot exchange rate between the euro and the dollar today (time 0), and we are quoting exchange rates as the amount of foreign currency per euro. Let $P_{US}$ and $P_{euro}$ be the current US and euro prices, respectively, on a particular commodity, say, apples. Absolute PPP simply says that

$$P_{US} = S_0 \times P_{euro}$$

This tells us that the US price for something is equal to the euro price for that same something multiplied by the exchange rate.

The rationale behind PPP is similar to that behind triangle arbitrage. If PPP did not hold, arbitrage would be possible (in principle) if apples were moved from one country to another. For example, suppose apples are selling in Milan for €2 per bushel, whereas in New York the price is $3 per bushel. Absolute PPP implies that

$$P_{US} = S_0 \times P_{euro}$$
$$\$3 = S_0 \times €2$$
$$S_0 = \$3/€2 = \$1.50/€$$

That is, the implied spot exchange rate is $1.50 per euro. Equivalently, a dollar is worth €1/$1.5 = €0.667/$.

Suppose instead that the actual exchange rate is $1.2815/€. Starting with €2, a trader could buy a bushel of apples in Madrid, ship it to New York, and sell it there for $3. Our trader could then convert the $3 into euros at the prevailing exchange rate, $S_0 = \$1.2815/€$, yielding a total of $3/€1.2815 = €2.34. The round-trip gain would be 34 cents.

Because of this profit potential, forces are set in motion to change the exchange rate and/or the price of apples. In our example, apples would begin moving from Madrid to New York. The reduced supply of apples in Madrid would raise the price of apples there, and the increased supply in the US would lower the price of apples in New York.

In addition to moving apples around, apple traders would be busily converting dollars back into euros to buy more apples. This activity would increase the supply of dollars, and simultaneously increase the demand for euros. We would expect the value of a dollar to fall. This means that the euro would be getting more valuable, so it would take more dollars to buy one euro. Because the exchange rate is quoted as dollars per euro, we would expect the exchange rate to rise from $1.2815/£.

For absolute PPP to hold absolutely, several things must be true:

1 The transactions costs of trading apples – shipping, insurance, spoilage, and so on – must be zero.

2 There must be no barriers to trading apples – no tariffs, taxes, or other political barriers.

3 Finally, an apple in New York must be identical to an apple in Madrid. It won't do for you to send red apples to Madrid if the Spanish eat only green apples.

Given the fact that the transactions costs are not zero, and that the other conditions are rarely exactly met, it is not surprising that absolute PPP is really applicable only to traded goods, and then only to very uniform ones.

For this reason, absolute PPP does not imply that a Mercedes costs the same as a Ford, or that a nuclear power plant in France costs the same as one in New York. In the case of the cars, they are not identical. In the case of the power plants, even if they were identical, they are expensive and would be very difficult to ship. On the other hand, we would be surprised to see a significant violation of absolute PPP for gold.

Examples of violations of absolute purchasing power parity are not too hard to find. One of the more famous violations of absolute PPP is the Big Mac Index constructed by *The Economist*. To construct the index, prices for a Big Mac in different countries are gathered from McDonald's. Below you will find the January 2010 Big Mac index from www.economist.com. (We shall leave it to you to find the most recent index.)

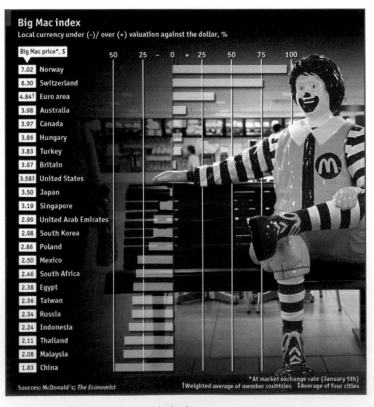

As you can see from the index, absolute PPP does not seem to hold, at least for the Big Mac. In fact, in only 11 of the 23 currencies surveyed by *The Economist* is the exchange rate within 25 per cent of that predicted by absolute PPP. The largest disparity is in Norway, where the currency is apparently overvalued by just under 100 per cent!

# Relative Purchasing Power Parity

As a practical matter, a relative version of purchasing power parity has evolved. *Relative purchasing power parity* does not tell us what determines the absolute level of the exchange rate. Instead, it tells what determines the *change* in the exchange rate over time.

**The Basic Idea**   Suppose the British pound–US dollar exchange rate is currently $S_0 = \$1.30$. Further suppose that the inflation rate in the US is predicted to be 10 per cent over the coming year, and (for the moment) the inflation rate in the United Kingdom is predicted to be zero. What do you think the exchange rate will be in a year?

If you think about it, you see that a pound currently costs $1.30 in the US. With 10 per cent inflation, we expect prices in the US to generally rise by 10 per cent. So we expect that the price of a pound will go up by 10 per cent, and the exchange rate should rise to $\$1.30 \times 1.1 = \$1.43$.

If the inflation rate in the United Kingdom is not zero, then we need to worry about the relative inflation rates in the two countries. For example, suppose the UK inflation rate is predicted to be 4 per cent. Relative to prices in the United Kingdom, prices in the US are rising at a rate of 10 per cent − 4 per cent = 6 per cent per year. So we expect the price of the pound to rise by 6 per cent, and the predicted exchange rate is $\$1.30 \times 1.06 = \$1.378$.

**The Result**   In general, relative PPP says that the change in the exchange rate is determined by the difference in the inflation rates of the two countries. To be more specific, we shall use the following notation:

$S_0$  = Current (time 0) spot exchange rate (foreign currency per dollar)
$E(S_t)$ = Expected exchange rate in $t$ periods
$h_{HC}$ = Inflation rate in the home currency
$h_{FC}$ = Foreign country inflation rate

Based on our preceding discussion, relative PPP says that the expected percentage change in the exchange rate over the next year, $[E(S_1) - S_0]/S_0$, is

$$\frac{E(S_1) - S_0}{S_0} = h_{FC} - h_{HC} \qquad (18.1)$$

In words, relative PPP simply says that the expected percentage change in the exchange rate is equal to the difference in inflation rates. If we rearrange this slightly, we get

$$E(S_1) = S_0 \times [1 + (h_{FC} - h_{HC})] \qquad (18.2)$$

This result makes a certain amount of sense, but care must be used in quoting the exchange rate.

In our example involving Britain and the United States, relative PPP tells us that the exchange rate will rise by $h_{FC} - h_{HC} = 10\% - 4\% = 6\%$ per year. Assuming the difference in inflation rates doesn't change, the expected exchange rate in two years, $E(S_2)$, will therefore be

$$\begin{aligned}
E(S_2) &= E(S_1) \times (1 + 0.06) \\
&= 1.378 \times 1.06 \\
&= 1.461
\end{aligned}$$

Notice that we could have written this as

$$\begin{aligned}
E(S_2) &= 1.378 \times 1.06 \\
&= 1.30 \times (1.06 \times 1.06) \\
&= 1.30 \times 1.06^2
\end{aligned}$$

In general, relative PPP says that the expected exchange rate at some time in the future, $E(S_t)$, is

$$E(S_t) = S_0 \times [1 + (h_{FC} - h_{HC})]^t$$

As we shall see, this is a very useful relationship.

Because we don't really expect absolute PPP to hold for most goods, we shall focus on relative PPP in our following discussion. Henceforth, when we refer to PPP without further qualification, we mean relative PPP.

---

**EXAMPLE 18.4**

## It's All Relative

From Fig. 18.1, the Turkish lira–euro exchange rate is 2.0949 lira per euro. The inflation rate in Turkey over the next three years will be, say, 10 per cent per year, whereas the Eurozone inflation rate will be 2 per cent. Based on relative PPP, what will the exchange rate be in three years?

Because the Eurozone inflation rate is lower, we expect that a euro will become more valuable. The exchange rate change will be 10 per cent – 2 per cent = 8 per cent per year. Over three years the exchange rate will rise to

$$
\begin{aligned}
E(S_3) &= S_0 \times [1 + (h_{FC} - h_{HC})]^3 \\
&= 2.0949 \times [1 + (0.08)]^3 \\
&= 2.6390
\end{aligned}
$$

---

**Currency Appreciation and Depreciation**  We frequently hear things like 'the euro strengthened (or weakened) in financial markets today' or 'the euro is expected to appreciate (or depreciate) relative to the pound.' When we say that the euro strengthens or appreciates, we mean that the value of a euro rises, so it takes more foreign currency to buy a euro.

What happens to the exchange rates as currencies fluctuate in value depends on how exchange rates are quoted. Because we are quoting them as units of foreign currency per home currency, the exchange rate moves in the same direction as the value of the home currency: it rises as the home currency strengthens, and it falls as the home currency weakens.

Relative PPP tells us that the exchange rate will rise if the home currency inflation rate is lower than the foreign country's. This happens because the foreign currency depreciates in value and therefore weakens relative to the home currency.

---

**CONCEPT QUESTIONS**

18.3a  What does absolute PPP say? Why might it not hold for many types of goods?

18.3b  According to relative PPP, what determines the change in exchange rates?

---

## 18.4 Interest Rate Parity, Unbiased Forward Rates and the International Fisher Effect

The next issue we need to address is the relationship between spot exchange rates, forward exchange rates, and interest rates. To get started, we need some additional notation:

$$
\begin{aligned}
F_t &= \text{Forward exchange rate for settlement at time } t \\
R_{HC} &= \text{Home country nominal risk-free interest rate} \\
R_{FC} &= \text{Foreign country nominal risk-free interest rate}
\end{aligned}
$$

As before, we shall use $S_0$ to stand for the spot exchange rate. You can take the home country's nominal risk-free rate, $R_{HC}$, to be the home country's T-bill rate.

## Covered Interest Arbitrage

We observe the following information about the British pound and the US dollar:

$$S_0 = \$1.5193$$
$$F_1 = \$1.5167$$
$$R_{HC} = 2.13\%$$
$$R_{FC} = 0.27\%$$

where $R_{FC}$ is the nominal risk-free rate in the United States. The period is one year, so $F_1$ is the 360-day forward rate.

Do you see an arbitrage opportunity here? Suppose you have £10,000 to invest, and you want a riskless investment. One option you have is to invest the £10,000 in a riskless UK investment such as a 360-day T-bill. If you do this, then in one period your £1 will be worth

$$£ \text{ value in 1 period} = £1 \times (1 + R_{HC})$$
$$= £10,213$$

Alternatively, you can invest in the US risk-free investment. To do this, you need to convert your £10,000 to US dollars and simultaneously execute a forward trade to convert dollars back to pounds in one year. The necessary steps would be as follows:

1   Convert your £10,000 to £10,000 × $S_0$ = \$15,193.

2   At the same time, enter into a forward agreement to convert US dollars back to pounds in one year. Because the forward rate is \$1.5167, you will get £1 for every \$1.5167 that you have in one year.

3   Invest your \$15,193 in the United States at $R_{FC}$. In one year, you will have

$$\$ \text{ value in 1 year} = \$15,193 \times (1 + R_{FC})$$
$$= \$15,193 \times 1.0027$$
$$= \$15,234$$

4   Convert your \$15,234 back to pounds at the agreed-upon rate of \$1.5167 = £1. You end up with

$$£ \text{ value in 1 year} = \$15,234/1.5167$$
$$= £10,044$$

Notice that the value in one year resulting from this strategy can be written as

$$£ \text{ value in 1 year} = £10,000 \times S_0 \times (1 + R_{FC})/F_1$$
$$= £10,000 \times 1.5193 \times 1.0027/1.5167$$
$$= £10,044$$

The return on this investment is apparently 0.44 per cent. This is lower than the 2.13 per cent we get from investing in the United Kingdom. Because both investments are risk-free, there is an arbitrage opportunity.

To exploit the difference in interest rates, you need to borrow, say, \$10 million at the lower US rate and invest it at the higher British rate. What is the round-trip profit from doing this? To find out, we can work through the steps outlined previously:

1   Convert the \$10 million at \$1.5193/£ to get £6,581,979.

2   Agree to exchange dollars for pounds in one year at \$1.5167 to the pound.

3   Invest the £6,581,979 for one year at $R_{UK}$ = 2.13 per cent. You end up with £6,722,175.

4   Convert the £6,722,175 back to dollars to fulfil the forward contract. You receive £6,722,175 × \$1.5167/£ = \$10,195,522.

5   Repay the loan with interest. You owe \$10 million plus 0.27 per cent interest, for a total of \$10,027,000. You have \$10,195,522, so your round-trip profit is a risk-free \$168,522.

The activity that we have illustrated here goes by the name of *covered interest arbitrage*. The term *covered* refers to the fact that we are covered in the event of a change in the exchange rate because we lock in the forward exchange rate today.

## Interest Rate Parity

If we assume that significant covered interest arbitrage opportunities do not exist, then there must be some relationship between spot exchange rates, forward exchange rates, and relative interest rates. To see what this relationship is, note that, in general, Strategy 1, from the preceding discussion, investing in a riskless home country investment, gives us $1 + R_{HC}$ for every unit of cash in home currency we invest. Strategy 2, investing in a foreign risk-free investment, gives us $S_0 \times (1 + R_{FC})/F_1$ for every unit of cash in home currency we invest. Because these have to be equal to prevent arbitrage, it must be the case that

$$1 + R_{HC} = S_0 \times \frac{1 + R_{FC}}{F_1}$$

> **interest rate parity (IRP)**
> The condition stating that the interest rate differential between two countries is equal to the percentage difference between the forward exchange rate and the spot exchange rate.

Rearranging this a bit gets us the famous **interest rate parity (IRP)** condition:

$$\frac{F_1}{S_0} = \frac{1 + R_{FC}}{1 + R_{HC}} \qquad (18.3)$$

There is a very useful approximation for IRP that illustrates very clearly what is going on, and is not difficult to remember. If we define the percentage forward premium or discount as $(F_1 - S_0)/S_0$, then IRP says that this percentage premium or discount is *approximately* equal to the difference in interest rates:

$$(F_1 - S_0)/S_0 = R_{FC} - R_{HC} \qquad (18.4)$$

Very loosely, what IRP says is that any difference in interest rates between two countries for some period is just offset by the change in the relative value of the currencies, thereby eliminating any arbitrage possibilities. Notice that we could also write

$$F_1 = S_0 \times [1 + (R_{FC} - R_{HC})] \qquad (18.5)$$

In general, if we have $t$ periods instead of just one, the IRP approximation is written as

$$F_t = S_0 \times [1 + (R_{FC} - R_{HC})]^t \qquad (18.6)$$

---

### EXAMPLE 18.5

## Parity Check

Suppose the exchange rate for the South African rand, $S_0$, is currently R13.0745 = €1. If the interest rate in the Eurozone is $R_{Euro}$ = 2.12 per cent and the interest rate in South Africa is $R_{SA}$ = 10.95 per cent, then what must the forward rate be to prevent covered interest arbitrage?

From IRP, we have

$$
\begin{aligned}
F_1 &= S_0 \times [1 + (R_{SA} - R_{Euro})] \\
&= \text{R}13.0745 \times [1 + (0.1095 - 0.0212)] \\
&= \text{R}13.0745 \times 1.0883 \\
&= \text{R}14.2290
\end{aligned}
$$

Notice that the rand will sell at a discount relative to the euro. (Why?)

# Forward Rates and Future Spot Rates

**unbiased forward rates (UFR)**
The condition stating that the current forward rate is an unbiased predictor of the future spot exchange rate.

In addition to PPP and IRP, we need to discuss one more basic relationship. What is the connection between the forward rate and the expected future spot rate? The **unbiased forward rates (UFR)** condition says that the forward rate, $F_1$, is equal to the *expected* future spot rate, $E(S_1)$:

$$F_1 = E(S_1)$$

With $t$ periods, UFR would be written as

$$F_t = E(S_t)$$

Loosely, the UFR condition says that, on average, the forward exchange rate is equal to the future spot exchange rate.

If we ignore risk, then the UFR condition should hold. Suppose the forward rate for the South African rand is consistently lower than the future spot rate by, say, 10 rand. This means that anyone who wanted to convert euros to rand in the future would consistently get more rand by not agreeing to a forward exchange. The forward rate would have to rise to get anyone interested in a forward exchange.

Similarly, if the forward rate were consistently higher than the future spot rate, then anyone who wanted to convert rand to euros would get more euros per rand by not agreeing to a forward trade. The forward exchange rate would have to fall to attract such traders.

For these reasons, the forward and actual future spot rates should be equal to each other on average. What the future spot rate will actually be is uncertain, of course. The UFR condition may not hold if traders are willing to pay a premium to avoid this uncertainty. If the condition does hold, then the 180-day forward rate that we see today should be an unbiased predictor of what the exchange rate will actually be in 180 days.

# Putting It All Together

We have developed three relationships, PPP, IRP and UFR, that describe the interaction between key financial variables such as interest rates, exchange rates and inflation rates. We now explore the implications of these relationships as a group.

**Uncovered Interest Parity**    To start, it is useful to collect our international financial market relationships in one place:

$$\text{PPP: } E(S_1) = S_0 \times [1 + (h_{FC} - h_{HC})]$$
$$\text{IRP: } F_1 = S_0 \times [1 + (R_{FC} - R_{HC})]$$
$$\text{UFR: } F_1 = E(S_1)$$

We begin by combining UFR and IRP. Because we know that $F_1 = E(S_1)$ from the UFR condition, we can substitute $E(S_1)$ for $F_1$ in IRP. The result is

$$\text{UIP: } E(S_1) = S_0 \times [1 + (R_{FC} - R_{HC})] \qquad (18.7)$$

**uncovered interest parity (UIP)**
The condition stating that the expected percentage change in the exchange rate is equal to the difference in interest rates.

This important relationship is called **uncovered interest parity (UIP)**, and it will play a key role in our international capital budgeting discussion that follows. With $t$ periods, UIP becomes

$$E(S_t) = S_0 \times [1 + (R_{FC} - R_{HC})]^t \qquad (18.8)$$

**The International Fisher Effect**    Next, we compare PPP and UIP. Both of them have $E(S_1)$ on the left-hand side, so their right-hand sides must be equal. We thus have that

**international Fisher effect (IFE)**
The theory that real interest rates are equal across countries.

$$S_0 \times [1 + (h_{FC} - h_{HC})] = S_0 \times [1 + (R_{FC} - R_{HC})]$$
$$h_{FC} - h_{HC} = R_{FC} - R_{HC}$$

This tells us that the difference in returns between the home country and a foreign country is just equal to the difference in inflation rates. Rearranging this slightly gives us the **international Fisher effect (IFE)**:

$$\text{IFE: } R_{HC} - h_{HC} = R_{FC} - h_{FC} \tag{18.9}$$

The IFE says that *real* rates are equal across countries.[2]

The conclusion that real returns are equal across countries is really basic economics. If real returns were higher in, say, Britain than in the Eurozone, money would flow out of Eurozone financial markets and into British markets. Asset prices in Britain would rise and their returns would fall. At the same time, asset prices in Europe would fall and their returns would rise. This process acts to equalize real returns.

Having said all this, we need to note a couple of things. First of all, we really haven't explicitly dealt with risk in our discussion. We might reach a different conclusion about real returns once we do, particularly if people in different countries have different tastes and attitudes towards risk. Second, there are many barriers to the movement of money and capital around the world. Real returns might be different in two different countries for long periods of time if money can't move freely between them.

Despite these problems, we expect that capital markets will become increasingly internationalized. As this occurs, any differences in real rates that do exist will probably diminish. The laws of economics have very little respect for national boundaries.

---

**CONCEPT QUESTIONS**

18.4a   What is covered interest arbitrage?
18.4b   What is the international Fisher effect?

---

## 18.5  International Capital Budgeting

Kihlstrom Equipment, a US-based international company, is evaluating an overseas investment. Kihlstrom's exports of drill bits have increased to such a degree that it is considering building a distribution centre in France. The project will cost €2 million to launch. The cash flows are expected to be €0.9 million a year for the next three years.

The current spot exchange rate for euros is €0.5. Recall that this is euros per dollar, so a euro is worth $1/0.5 = $2. The risk-free rate in the United States is 5 per cent, and the risk-free rate in the Eurozone is 7 per cent. Note that the exchange rate and the two interest rates are observed in financial markets, not estimated.[3] Kihlstrom's required return on dollar investments of this sort is 10 per cent.

Should Kihlstrom take this investment? As always, the answer depends on the NPV; but how do we calculate the net present value of this project in US dollars? There are two basic methods:

1   *The home currency approach*: Convert all the euro cash flows into dollars, and then discount at 10 per cent to find the NPV in dollars. Notice that for this approach we have to come up with the future exchange rates to convert the future projected euro cash flows into dollars.

2   *The foreign currency approach*: Determine the required return on euro investments, and then discount the euro cash flows to find the NPV in euros. Then convert this euro NPV to a dollar NPV. This approach requires us to somehow convert the 10 per cent dollar required return to the equivalent euro required return.

The difference between these two approaches is primarily a matter of when we convert from euros to dollars. In the first case we convert before estimating the NPV. In the second case we convert after estimating the NPV.

It might appear that the second approach is superior, because we have to come up with only one number, the euro discount rate. Furthermore, because the first approach requires us to forecast future exchange rates, it probably seems that there is greater room for error with this approach. As we illustrate next, however, based on our previous results, the two approaches are really the same.

## Method 1: The Home Currency Approach

To convert the projected future cash flows into dollars, we shall invoke the uncovered interest parity, or UIP, relation to come up with the projected exchange rates. Based on our earlier discussion, the expected exchange rate at time $t$, $E(S_t)$, is

$$E(S_t) = S_0 \times [1 + (R_\epsilon - R_{US})]^t$$

where $R_\epsilon$ stands for the nominal risk-free rate in the Eurozone. Because $R_\epsilon$ is 7 per cent, $R_{US}$ is 5 per cent, and the current exchange rate ($S_0$) is €0.5:

$$E(S_t) = 0.5 \times [1 + (0.07 - 0.05)]^t$$
$$= 0.5 \times 1.02^t$$

The projected exchange rates for the drill bit project are thus

| Year | Expected exchange rate |
|------|------------------------|
| 1 | €0.5 × 1.02$^1$ = €0.5100 |
| 2 | €0.5 × 1.02$^2$ = €0.5202 |
| 3 | €0.5 × 1.02$^3$ = €0.5306 |

Using these exchange rates, along with the current exchange rate, we can convert all of the euro cash flows to dollars (note that all of the cash flows in this example are in millions):

| Year | (1)<br>Cash flow<br>in € millions | (2)<br>Expected exchange<br>rate (€/$) | (3)<br>Cash flow in<br>$ millions (1)/(2) |
|------|-----------------------------------|----------------------------------------|-------------------------------------------|
| 0 | −2.0 | 0.5000 | −4.00 |
| 1 | 0.9 | 0.5100 | 1.76 |
| 2 | 0.9 | 0.5202 | 1.73 |
| 3 | 0.9 | 0.5306 | 1.70 |

To finish off, we calculate the NPV in the ordinary way:

$$NPV_\$ = -\$4 + \$1.76/1.10 + \$1.73/1.10^2 + \$1.70/1.10^3$$
$$= \$0.3 \text{ million}$$

So the project appears to be profitable.

## Method 2: The Foreign Currency Approach

Kihlstrom requires a nominal return of 10 per cent on the dollar-denominated cash flows. We need to convert this to a rate suitable for euro-denominated cash flows. Based on the international Fisher effect, we know that the difference in the nominal rates is

$$R_\epsilon - R_{US} = h_\epsilon - h_{US}$$
$$= 7\% - 5\%$$
$$= 2\%$$

The appropriate discount rate for estimating the euro cash flows from the drill bit project is approximately equal to 10 per cent plus an extra 2 per cent to compensate for the greater euro inflation rate.

If we calculate the NPV of the euro cash flows at this rate, we get

$$NPV_\epsilon = -\text{€}2 + \text{€}0.9/1.12 + \text{€}0.9/1.12^2 + \text{€}0.9/1.12^3$$
$$= \text{€}0.16 \text{ million}$$

The NPV of this project is €0.16 million. Taking this project makes us €0.16 million richer today. What is this in dollars? Because the exchange rate today is €0.5, the dollar NPV of the project is

$$NPV_\$ = NPV_\epsilon/S_0$$
$$= \text{€}0.16/0.5$$
$$= \$0.3 \text{ million}$$

This is the same dollar NPV that we previously calculated.

The important thing to recognize from our example is that the two capital budgeting procedures are actually the same, and will always give the same answer.[4] In this second approach, the fact that we are implicitly forecasting exchange rates is simply hidden. Even so, the foreign currency approach is computationally a little easier.

## Unremitted Cash Flows

The previous example assumed that all after-tax cash flows from the foreign investment could be remitted to (paid out to) the parent firm. Actually, substantial differences can exist between the cash flows generated by a foreign project and the amount that can actually be remitted, or 'repatriated', to the parent firm.

A foreign subsidiary can remit funds to a parent in many forms, including the following:

- Dividends

- Management fees for central services

- Royalties on the use of trade names and patents

However cash flows are repatriated, international firms must pay special attention to remittances, because there may be current and future controls on remittances. Many governments are sensitive to the charge of being exploited by foreign national firms. In such cases, governments are tempted to limit the ability of international firms to remit cash flows. Funds that cannot currently be remitted are sometimes said to be *blocked*.

**CONCEPT QUESTIONS**

18.5a  What financial complications arise in international capital budgeting? Describe two procedures for estimating NPV in the case of an international project.

18.5b  What are blocked funds?

**exchange rate risk**
The risk related to having international operations in a world where relative currency values vary.

## 18.6  Exchange Rate Risk

**Exchange rate risk** is the natural consequence of international operations in a world where relative currency values move up and down. Managing exchange rate risk is an important part of international finance. As we discuss next, there are three different types of exchange rate risk, or exposure: short-run exposure, long-run exposure, and translation exposure.

## Short-Run Exposure

The day-to-day fluctuations in exchange rates create short-run risks for international firms. Most such firms have contractual agreements to buy and sell goods in the near future at set prices. When different currencies are involved, such transactions have an extra element of risk.

For example, imagine that you are importing imitation pasta from Italy and reselling it in the United Kingdom under the Impasta brand name. Your largest customer has ordered 10,000 cases of Impasta. You place the order with your supplier today, but you won't pay until the goods arrive in 60 days. Your selling price is £6 per case. Your cost is €8.4 per case, and the exchange rate is currently €1.50, so it takes €1.50 to buy £1.

At the current exchange rate, your cost in pounds of filling the order is €8.4/0.5 = £5.60 per case, so your pre-tax profit on the order is 10,000 × (£6 – 5.60) = £4,000. However, the exchange rate in 60 days will probably be different, so your profit will depend on what the future exchange rate turns out to be.

For example, if the rate goes to €1.6, your cost is €8.4/1.6 = £5.25 per case. Your profit goes to £7,500. If the exchange rate goes to, say, €1.4, then your cost is €8.4/1.4 = £6, and your profit is zero.

The short-run exposure in our example can be reduced or eliminated in several ways. The most obvious way is by entering into a forward exchange agreement to lock in an exchange rate. For example, suppose the 60-day forward rate is €1.58. What will be your profit if you hedge? What profit should you expect if you don't?

If you hedge, you lock in an exchange rate of €1.58. Your cost in pounds will thus be €8.4/1.58 = £5.32 per case, so your profit will be 10,000 × (£6 – 5.32) = £6,800. If you don't hedge, then, assuming that the forward rate is an unbiased predictor (in other words, assuming the UFR condition holds), you should expect that the exchange rate will actually be €1.58 in 60 days. You should expect to make £6,800.

Alternatively, if this strategy is not feasible, you could simply borrow the pounds today, convert them into euros, and invest the euros for 60 days to earn some interest. Based on IRP, this amounts to entering into a forward contract.

## Long-Run Exposure

In the long run, the value of a foreign operation can fluctuate because of unanticipated changes in relative economic conditions. For example, imagine that we own a labour-intensive assembly operation located in another country to take advantage of lower wages. Through time, unexpected changes in economic conditions can raise the foreign wage levels to the point where the cost advantage is eliminated, or even becomes negative.

The impact of changes in exchange rate levels can be substantial. For example, during early 2010 the euro varied between €1.15/£ and €1.10/£, with it strengthening over the period and then weakening because of the Greek debt crisis. This meant that Eurozone manufacturers took home less for each pound's worth of sales they made, depending on when they traded. Currency gains and losses can be enormous. For example, during 2009 Barclays lost £853 million as a result of exchange rate changes. This compares with a gain of £2,233 million in 2008.

Hedging long-run exposure is more difficult than hedging short-term risks. For one thing, organized forward markets don't exist for such long-term needs. Instead, the primary option that firms have is to try to match up foreign currency inflows and outflows. The same thing goes for matching foreign-currency-denominated assets and liabilities. For example, a firm that sells in a foreign country might try to concentrate its raw material purchases and labour expense in that country. In that way, the home currency values of its revenues and costs will move up and down together. Probably the best examples of this type of hedging are the so-called *transplant auto manufacturers* such as BMW, Honda, Mercedes and Toyota, which now build in the United States a substantial portion of the cars they sell there, thereby obtaining some degree of immunization against exchange rate movements.

For example, BMW produces 160,000 cars in the US and exports about 100,000 of them. The costs of manufacturing the cars are paid mostly in dollars; when BMW exports the cars to Europe, it receives euros. When the dollar weakens, these vehicles become more profitable for BMW. At the same time, BMW exports about 217,000 cars to the United States each year. The costs of manufacturing these imported cars are mostly in euros, so they become less profitable when the dollar weakens. Taken together, these gains and losses tend to offset each other and provide BMW with a natural hedge.

Similarly, a firm can reduce its long-run exchange rate risk by borrowing in the foreign country. Fluctuations in the value of the foreign subsidiary's assets will then be at least partially offset by changes in the value of the liabilities.

## Translation Exposure

When a British company calculates its accounting net income and EPS for some period, it must 'translate' everything into pounds. This can create some problems for the accountants when there are significant foreign operations. In particular, two issues arise:

1   What is the appropriate exchange rate to use for translating each balance sheet account?

2   How should balance sheet accounting gains and losses from foreign currency translation be handled?

To illustrate the accounting problem, suppose we started a small foreign subsidiary in Lilliputia a year ago. The local currency is the gulliver, abbreviated GL. At the beginning of the year, the exchange rate was GL2 = €1, and the balance sheet in gullivers looked like this:

| **GL** | | | **GL** |
|---|---|---|---|
| Assets | 1,000 | Liabilities | 500 |
| | | Equity | 500 |

At two gullivers to the euro, the beginning balance sheet in euros was as follows:

| **€** | | | **€** |
|---|---|---|---|
| Assets | 500 | Liabilities | 250 |
| | | Equity | 250 |

Lilliputia is a quiet place, and nothing at all actually happened during the year. As a result, net income was zero (before consideration of exchange rate changes). However, the exchange rate did change to 4 gullivers = €1, purely because the Lilliputian inflation rate is much higher than the Eurozone inflation rate.

Because nothing happened, the accounting ending balance sheet in gullivers is the same as the beginning one. However, if we convert it to euros at the new exchange rate, we get

| **€** | | | **€** |
|---|---|---|---|
| Assets | 250 | Liabilities | 125 |
| | | Equity | 125 |

Notice that the value of the equity has gone down by €125, even though net income was exactly zero. Despite the fact that absolutely nothing really happened, there is a €125 accounting loss. How to handle this €125 loss has been a controversial accounting question.

One obvious and consistent way to handle this loss is simply to report the loss on the parent's income statement. During periods of volatile exchange rates this kind of treatment can dramatically impact on an international company's reported EPS. This is a purely accounting phenomenon; but, even so, such fluctuations are disliked by some financial managers.

The current approach to handling translation gains and losses is based on rules set out in the International Accounting Standards Board (IASB) International Accounting Standard No. 21 (IAS 21). For the most part, IAS 21 requires that all assets and liabilities be translated from the subsidiary's currency into the parent's currency using the exchange rate that currently prevails. Income and expenses are treated differently, and these are translated at the exchange rate that prevails at the time of the transaction, or at the average rate for the period when this is a reasonable approximation. In contrast to US accounting rules, the impact of translation gains and losses is explicitly recognized in net income. In the US, the translation gain or loss is not recognized until the underlying assets and liabilities are sold or otherwise liquidated.

## Managing Exchange Rate Risk

For a large multinational firm the management of exchange rate risk is complicated by the fact that there can be many different currencies involved in many different subsidiaries. A change in some exchange rate will probably benefit some subsidiaries and hurt others. The net effect on the overall firm depends on its net exposure.

For example, suppose a firm has two divisions. Division A buys goods in Italy for euros and sells them in Britain for pounds. Division B buys goods in Britain for pounds and sells them in Italy for euros. If these two divisions are of roughly equal size in terms of their inflows and outflows, then the overall firm obviously has little exchange rate risk.

In our example the firm's net position in pounds (the amount coming in less the amount going out) is small, so the exchange rate risk is small. However, if one division, acting on its own, were to start hedging its exchange rate risk, then the overall firm's exchange rate risk would go up. The moral of the story is that multinational firms have to be conscious of their overall positions in a foreign currency. For this reason, management of exchange rate risk is probably best handled on a centralized basis.

| CONCEPT QUESTIONS | 18.6a | What are the different types of exchange rate risk? |
| | 18.6b | How can a firm hedge short-run exchange rate risk? Long-run exchange rate risk? |

## 18.7  Political Risk

One final element of risk in international investing is **political risk**. Political risk refers to changes in value that arise as a consequence of political actions. This is not a problem faced exclusively by international firms. For example, changes in British tax laws and regulations may benefit some British firms and hurt others, so political risk exists nationally as well as internationally.

> **political risk**
> Risk related to changes in value that arise because of political actions.

Some countries do have more political risk than others, however. When firms operate in these riskier countries, the extra political risk may lead the firms to require higher returns on overseas investments to compensate for the possibility that funds may be blocked, critical operations interrupted, or contracts abrogated. In the most extreme case the possibility of outright confiscation may be a concern in countries with relatively unstable political environments.

Political risk also depends on the nature of the business: some businesses are less likely to be confiscated, because they are not particularly valuable in the hands of a different owner. An assembly operation supplying subcomponents that only the parent company uses would not be an attractive 'takeover' target, for example. Similarly, a manufacturing operation that requires the use of specialized components from the parent is of little value without the parent company's co-operation.

Natural resource developments, such as copper mining or oil drilling, are just the opposite. Once the operation is in place, much of the value is in the commodity. The political risk for such investments is much higher for this reason. Also, the issue of exploitation is more pronounced with such investments, again increasing the political risk.

Corruption is a very big issue in many countries, and the payment of kickbacks or 'business facilitation fees' is the norm in many areas. Government officials, petty bureaucrats and cumbersome administrative regulations can significantly restrict the efficiency of international operations.

Many organizations present rankings of political risk in countries, and it is important that these are considered before any foreign direct investment takes place. Transparency International's 'perceptions of corruption' ranking is an example of such an assessment, and is presented in Table 18.2.

Political risk can be hedged in several ways, particularly when confiscation or nationalization is a concern. The use of local financing, perhaps from the government of the foreign country in question, reduces the possible loss, because the company can refuse to pay the debt in the event of unfavourable political activities. Based on our discussion in this section, structuring the operation in such a way that it requires significant parent company involvement to function is another way to reduce political risk.

**TABLE 18.2**

| Country/territory | CPI 2009 score | Country/territory | CPI 2009 score |
|---|---|---|---|
| New Zealand | 9.4 | United States | 7.5 |
| Denmark | 9.3 | Belgium | 7.1 |
| Sweden | 9.2 | France | 6.9 |
| Switzerland | 9.0 | Cyprus | 6.6 |
| Finland | 8.9 | Spain | 6.1 |
| Netherlands | 8.9 | Portugal | 5.8 |
| Australia | 8.7 | South Africa | 4.7 |
| Iceland | 8.7 | Italy | 4.3 |
| Norway | 8.6 | Greece | 3.8 |
| Germany | 8.0 | China | 3.6 |
| Ireland | 8.0 | India | 3.4 |
| Austria | 7.9 | Thailand | 3.4 |
| Japan | 7.7 | Tanzania | 2.6 |
| United Kingdom | 7.7 | Somalia | 1.1 |

Countries with lower numbers are more corrupt. *Source*: Transparency International.

**Table 18.2** Perceptions of Corruption Index 2009

**CONCEPT QUESTIONS**

18.7a  What is political risk?

18.7b  What are some ways of hedging political risk?

# Summary and Conclusions

The international firm has a more complicated life than the purely domestic firm. Management must understand the connection between interest rates, foreign currency exchange rates and inflation, and it must become aware of many different financial market regulations and tax systems. This chapter is intended to be a concise introduction to some of the financial issues that come up in international investing.

Our coverage has been necessarily brief. The main topics we discussed are the following:

1　*Some basic vocabulary*: We briefly defined some exotic terms such as LIBOR and Eurocurrency.

2　*The basic mechanics of exchange rate quotations*: We discussed the spot and forward markets, and how exchange rates are interpreted.

3　*The fundamental relationships between international financial variables*:

(a)　Absolute and relative purchasing power parity, PPP.

(b)　Interest rate parity, IRP.

(c)　Unbiased forward rates, UFR.

Absolute purchasing power parity states that £1 or €1 should have the same purchasing power in each country. This means that an orange costs the same whether you buy it in London or in Madrid.

Relative purchasing power parity means that the expected percentage change in exchange rates between the currencies of two countries is equal to the difference in their inflation rates.

Interest rate parity implies that the percentage difference between the forward exchange rate and the spot exchange rate is equal to the interest rate differential. We showed how covered interest arbitrage forces this relationship to hold.

The unbiased forward rates condition indicates that the current forward rate is a good predictor of the future spot exchange rate.

4　*International capital budgeting*: We showed that the basic foreign exchange relationships imply two other conditions:

(a)　Uncovered interest parity.

(b)　The international Fisher effect.

By invoking these two conditions, we learned how to estimate NPVs in foreign currencies and how to convert foreign currencies into home currencies to estimate NPV in the usual way.

5　*Exchange rate and political risk*: We described the various types of exchange rate risk, and discussed some commonly used approaches to managing the effect of fluctuating exchange rates on the cash flows and value of the international firm. We also discussed political risk, and some ways of managing exposure to it.

# Chapter Review and Self-Test Problems

18.1　**Relative Purchasing Power Parity**　The inflation rate in the United Kingdom is projected at 3 per cent per year for the next several years. The Swiss inflation rate is projected to be 5 per cent during that time. The exchange rate is currently SFr 1.66. Based on relative PPP, what is the expected exchange rate in two years?

18.2　**Covered Interest Arbitrage**　The spot and 360-day forward rates on the Turkish lira to the euro are L2.1/€ and L1.9/€, respectively. Assume that the risk-free interest rate in Europe is 6 per cent, and the risk-free rate in Turkey is 4 per cent. Is there an arbitrage opportunity here? How would you exploit it?

# Answers to Chapter Review and Self-Test Problems

18.1 Based on relative PPP, the expected exchange rate in two years, $E(S_2)$, is

$$E(S_2) = S_0 \times [1 + (h_{FC} - h_{HC})]^2$$

where $h_{FC}$ is the Swiss inflation rate. The current exchange rate is SFr 1.66, so the expected exchange rate is

$$
\begin{aligned}
E(S_2) &= \text{SFr}1.66 \times [1 + (0.05 - 0.03)]^2 \\
&= \text{SFr}1.66 \times 1.02^2 \\
&= \text{SFr}1.73
\end{aligned}
$$

18.2 Based on interest rate parity, the forward rate should be (approximately)

$$
\begin{aligned}
F_1 &= S_0 \times [1 + (R_{FC} - R_{HC})] \\
&= 2.1 \times [1 + (0.04 - 0.06)] \\
&= 2.06
\end{aligned}
$$

Because the forward rate is actually L1.9/€, there is an arbitrage opportunity.

To exploit the arbitrage opportunity, you first note that euros are selling for L1.9 each in the forward market. Based on IRP, this is too cheap, because they should be selling for L2.06. So you want to arrange to buy euros with Turkish lira in the forward market. To do this, you can:

1 *Today*: Borrow, say, €1 million for 360 days. Convert it to L2.1 million in the spot market, and buy a forward contract at L1.9 to convert it back to euros in 360 days. Invest the L2.1 million at 4 per cent.

2 *In one year*: Your investment has grown to L2.1 million × 1.04 = L2.184 million. Convert this to euros at the rate of L1.9/€. You will have L2.184 million/1.9 = €1,149,474. Pay off your loan with 6 per cent interest at a cost of €1 million × 1.06 = €1,060,000 and pocket the difference of €89,474.

# Concepts Review and Critical Thinking Questions

1 **Spot and Forward Rates [LO1]** Suppose the exchange rate for the Norwegian krone is quoted as NKr9.96/£ in the spot market and NKr10/£ in the 90-day forward market.

(a) Is the British pound selling at a premium or a discount relative to the krone?

(b) Does the financial market expect the krone to weaken relative to the pound? Explain.

(c) What do you suspect is true about relative economic conditions in the United Kingdom and Norway?

2 **Exchange Rates [LO1]** Suppose the rate of inflation in the Eurozone will be about 3 per cent higher than the UK inflation rate over the next several years. All other things being the same, what will happen to the euro versus pound exchange rate? What relationship are you relying on in answering?

3 **Bulldog Bonds [LO3]** Which of the following most accurately describes a Bulldog bond?

(a) A bond issued by Vodafone in Frankfurt with the interest payable in British pounds.

(b) A bond issued by Vodafone in Frankfurt with the interest payable in euros.

(c) A bond issued by BMW in Germany with the interest payable in British pounds.

(d) A bond issued by BMW in London with the interest payable in British pounds.

(e) A bond issued by BMW worldwide with the interest payable in British pounds.

4 **Exchange Rates [LO1]** Are exchange rate changes necessarily good or bad for a particular company?

5 **International Risks [LO4]** At one point, Duracell International confirmed that it was planning to open battery-manufacturing plants in China and India. Manufacturing in these countries allows Duracell to avoid import duties of between 30 and 35 per cent that have made alkaline batteries prohibitively expensive for some consumers. What additional advantages might Duracell see in this proposal? What are some of the risks to Duracell?

6 **Multinational Corporations [LO3]** Given that many multinationals based in many countries have much greater sales outside their domestic markets than within them, what is the particular relevance of their domestic currency?

7 **Exchange Rate Movements [LO3]** Are the following statements true or false? Explain why.

(a) If the general price index in Great Britain rises faster than that in the United States, we would expect the pound to appreciate relative to the dollar.

(b) Suppose you are a German machine tool exporter, and you invoice all of your sales in foreign currency. Further suppose that the European Central Bank begins to undertake an expansionary monetary policy. If it is certain that the easy money policy will result in higher inflation rates in Germany relative to those in other countries, then you should use the forward markets to protect yourself against future losses resulting from the deterioration in the value of the euro.

(c) If you could accurately estimate differences in the relative inflation rates of two countries over a long period while other market participants were unable to do so, you could successfully speculate in spot currency markets.

8 **Exchange Rate Movements [LO3]** Some countries encourage movements in their exchange rate relative to those of some other country as a short-term means of addressing foreign trade imbalances. For each of the following scenarios, evaluate the impact the announcement would have on a Danish importer and a Danish exporter doing business with the foreign country:

(a) Officials in the Danish government announce that they are comfortable with a rising krone relative to the euro.

(b) The Bank of England announces that it feels the krone has been driven too low by currency speculators relative to the British pound.

(c) The European Central Bank announces that it will print billions of new euros and inject them into the economy in an effort to reduce the country's unemployment rate.

9 **International Capital Market Relationships [LO2]** We discussed five international capital market relationships: relative PPP, IRP, UFR, UIP and the international Fisher effect. Which of these would you expect to hold most closely? Which do you think would be most likely to be violated?

# connect Questions and Problems

BASIC

1 – 14

1 **Using Exchange Rates [LO1]** Take a look back at Fig. 18.1 to answer the following questions:

(a) If you have €100, how many British pounds can you get?

(b) How much is one pound worth?

(c) If you have 5 million pounds, how many euros do you have?

(d) Which is worth more, a New Zealand dollar or a Singapore dollar?

(e) Which is worth more, a Mexican peso or a Chilean peso?

(f) How many Mexican pesos can you get for an Israeli sheqel? What do you call this rate?

(g) Per unit, what is the most valuable currency of those listed? The least valuable?

2 **Using the Cross-Rate [LO1]** Use the information in Fig. 18.1 to answer the following questions:

(a) Which would you rather have, €100 or £100? Why?

(b) Which would you rather have, 100 Swiss francs (SFr) or 100 Norwegian kroner (NKr)? Why?

(c) What is the cross-rate for Swiss francs in terms of Norwegian kroner? For Norwegian kroner in terms of Swiss francs?

3 **Forward Exchange Rates [LO1]** Use the information in Fig. 18.1 to answer the following questions:

(a) What is the three-month forward rate for the US dollar per euro? Is the dollar selling at a premium or a discount? Explain.

(b) What is the three-month forward rate for British pounds in euros per pound? Is the euro selling at a premium or a discount? Explain.

(c) What do you think will happen to the value of the euro relative to the dollar and the pound, based on the information in the figure? Explain.

4 **Using Spot and Forward Exchange Rates [LO1]** Suppose the spot exchange rate for the South African rand is R15/£ and the six-month forward rate is R16/£.

(a) Which is worth more, the British pound or the South African rand?

(b) Assuming absolute PPP holds, what is the cost in the United Kingdom of a Castle beer if the price in South Africa is R20? Why might the beer actually sell at a different price in the United Kingdom?

(c) Is the British pound selling at a premium or a discount relative to the South African rand?

(d) Which currency is expected to appreciate in value?

(e) Which country do you think has higher interest rates – the United Kingdom or South Africa? Explain.

5 **Cross-Rates and Arbitrage [LO1]** Use Fig. 18.1 to answer the following questions

(a) What is the cross-rate in terms of Iranian rial per Thai baht?

(b) Suppose the cross-rate is 279 rial = 1 Thai baht. Is there an arbitrage opportunity here? If there is, explain how to take advantage of the mispricing.

6 **Interest Rate Parity [LO2]** Use Fig. 18.1 to answer the following questions: Suppose interest rate parity holds, and the current one-year risk-free rate in the Eurozone is

3.8 per cent. What must the one-year risk-free rate be in Great Britain? In Japan? In the US?

7  **Interest Rates and Arbitrage [LO2]**   The treasurer of a major British firm has £30 million to invest for three months. The annual interest rate in the United Kingdom is 0.45 per cent per month. The interest rate in the Eurozone is 0.6 per cent per month. The spot exchange rate is €1.12/£, and the three-month forward rate is €1.15/€. Ignoring transaction costs, in which country would the treasurer want to invest the company's funds? Why?

8  **Inflation and Exchange Rates [LO2]**   Suppose the current exchange rate for the Polish zloty is Z5/£. The expected exchange rate in three years is Z5.2/£. What is the difference in the annual inflation rates for the United Kingdom and Poland over this period? Assume that the anticipated rate is constant for both countries. What relationship are you relying on in answering?

9  **Exchange Rate Risk [LO3]**   Suppose your company, which is based in Nantes, imports computer motherboards from Singapore. The exchange rate is S$1.9361/€1. You have just placed an order for 30,000 motherboards at a cost to you of 168.5 Singapore dollars each. You will pay for the shipment when it arrives in 90 days. You can sell the motherboards for €100 each. Calculate your profit if the exchange rate goes up or down by 10 per cent over the next 90 days. What is the break-even exchange rate? What percentage rise or fall does this represent in terms of the Singapore dollar versus the euro?

10  **Exchange Rates and Arbitrage [LO2]**   Suppose the spot and six-month forward rates on the Swedish krona are SKr11.95/£ and SKr12.00/£, respectively. The annual risk-free rate in the United Kingdom is 2.5 per cent, and the annual risk-free rate in Sweden is 1.13 per cent.

(a)  Is there an arbitrage opportunity here? If so, how would you exploit it?

(b)  What must the six-month forward rate be to prevent arbitrage?

11  **The International Fisher Effect [LO2]**   You observe that the inflation rate in the United Kingdom is 3.5 per cent per year, and that T-bills currently yield 3.9 per cent annually. What do you estimate the inflation rate to be in

(a)  Australia if short-term Australian government securities yield 5 per cent per year?

(b)  Canada if short-term Canadian government securities yield 7 per cent per year?

(c)  Taiwan if short-term Taiwanese government securities yield 10 per cent per year?

12  **Spot versus Forward Rates [LO1]**   Suppose the spot and three-month forward rates for the Indian rupee are R62.5/€ and R61.8/€, respectively.

(a)  Is the rupee expected to get stronger or weaker?

(b)  What would you estimate is the difference between the inflation rates of the Eurozone and India?

13.  **Expected Spot Rates [LO2]**   Suppose the spot exchange rate for the Tanzanian shilling is TSh2000/£. The inflation rate in the United Kingdom is 3.5 per cent and it is 8.6 per cent in Tanzania. What do you predict the exchange rate will be in one year? In two years? In five years? What relationship are you using?

14  **Capital Budgeting [LO2]**   The Dutch firm ABS Equipment has an investment opportunity in the United Kingdom. The project costs £12 million, and is expected to produce cash flows of £2.7 million in year 1, £3.5 million in year 2, and £3.3 million in year 3. The current spot exchange rate is €1.12/£ and the current

risk-free rate in the Eurozone is 2.12 per cent, compared with that in the United Kingdom of 2.13 per cent. The appropriate discount rate for the project is estimated to be 13 per cent, the Eurozone cost of capital for the company. In addition, the subsidiary can be sold at the end of three years for an estimated £7.4 million. What is the NPV of the project?

INTERMEDIATE

15–17

15 **Capital Budgeting [LO2]** As a German company, you are evaluating a proposed expansion of an existing subsidiary located in Switzerland. The cost of the expansion would be SFr27.0 million. The cash flows from the project would be SFr7.5 million per year for the next five years. The euro required return is 13 per cent per year, and the current exchange rate is SFr1.48/€. The going rate on EURIBOR is 8 per cent per year. It is 7 per cent per year on Swiss francs.

(a) What do you project will happen to exchange rates over the next four years?

(b) Based on your answer in (a), convert the projected franc flows into euro cash flows and calculate the NPV.

(c) What is the required return on franc cash flows? Based on your answer, calculate the NPV in francs and then convert to euros.

16 **Translation Exposure [LO3]** Atreides International has operations in Arrakis. The balance sheet for this division in Arrakeen solaris shows assets of 23,000 solaris, debt in the amount of 9,000 solaris, and equity of 14,000 solaris.

(a) If the current exchange ratio is 1.20 solaris per euro, what does the balance sheet look like in euros?

(b) Assume that one year from now the balance sheet in solaris is exactly the same as at the beginning of the year. If the exchange rate is 1.40 solaris per euro, what does the balance sheet look like in euros now?

(c) Rework part (b) assuming the exchange rate is 1.12 solaris per euro.

17 **Translation Exposure [LO3]** In the previous problem, assume the equity increases by 1,250 solaris as a result of retained earnings. If the exchange rate at the end of the year is 1.24 solaris per euro, what does the balance sheet look like?

CHALLENGE

18

18 **Using the Exact International Fisher Effect [LO2]** From our discussion of the Fisher effect in Chapter 6, we know that the actual relationship between a nominal rate $R$, a real rate $r$ and an inflation rate $h$ can be written as

$$1 + r = (1 + R)/(1 + h)$$

This is the *domestic* Fisher effect.

(a) What is the non-approximate form of the international Fisher effect?

(b) Based on your answer in (a), what is the exact form for UIP? (*Hint*: Recall the exact form of IRP, and use UFR.)

(c) What is the exact form for relative PPP? (*Hint*: Combine your previous two answers.)

(d) Recalculate the NPV for the Kihlstrom drill bit project (discussed in Sec. 18.5) using the exact forms for UIP and the international Fisher effect. Verify that you get precisely the same answer either way.

# MINI CASE

## West Coast Yachts Goes International

Larissa Warren, the owner of West Coast Yachts, has been in discussions with a yacht dealer in Monaco about selling the company's yachts in Europe. Jarek Jachowicz, the dealer, wants to add West Coast Yachts to his current retail line. Jarek has told Larissa that he feels the retail sales will be approximately €5 million per month. All sales will be made in euros, and Jarek will retain 5 per cent of the retail sales as commission, which will be paid in euros. Because the yachts will be customized to order, the first sales will take place in one month. Jarek will pay West Coast Yachts for the order 90 days after it is filled. This payment schedule will continue for the length of the contract between the two companies.

Larissa is confident the company can handle the extra volume with its existing facilities, but she is unsure about any potential financial risks of selling yachts in Europe. In her discussion with Jarek she found that the current exchange rate is €1.12/£. At this exchange rate the company would spend 70 per cent of the sales income on production costs. This number does not reflect the sales commission to be paid to Jarek.

Larissa has decided to ask Dan Ervin, the company's financial analyst, to prepare an analysis of the proposed international sales. Specifically she asks Dan to answer the following questions:

1  What are the pros and cons of the international sales plan? What additional risks will the company face?

2  What will happen to the company's profits if the British pound strengthens? What if the British pound weakens?

3  Ignoring taxes, what are West Coast Yacht's projected gains or losses from this proposed arrangement at the current exchange rate of €1.12/£? What will happen to profits if the exchange rate changes to €1.20/£? At what exchange rate will the company break even?

4  How can the company hedge its exchange rate risk? What are the implications for this approach?

5  Taking all factors into account, should the company pursue international sales further? Why or why not?

## Endnotes

1  There are four exchange rates instead of five because one exchange rate would involve the exchange of a currency for itself. More generally, it might seem that there should be 25 exchange rates with five currencies. There are 25 different combinations, but, of these, five involve the exchange of a currency for itself. Of the remaining 20, half are redundant because they are just the reciprocals of another exchange rate. Of the remaining 10, six can be eliminated by using a common denominator.

2  Notice that our result here is in terms of the approximate real rate, $R - h$ (see Chapter 6), because we used approximations for PPP and IRP. For the exact result see Problem 18 at the end of the chapter.

3  For example, the interest rates might be the short-term Eurodollar and euro deposit rates offered by large money centre banks.

4  Actually, there will be a slight difference because we are using the approximate relationships. If we calculate the required return as $1.10 \times (1 + 0.02) - 1 = 12.2\%$, then we get exactly the same NPV. See Problem 18 for more detail.

# CHAPTER 19

# Behavioural Finance

EUROPEAN STOCK MARKETS WERE RAGING in the mid-2000s, and most stock indices nearly doubled in value between 2003 and 2007. Of course, that spectacular run came to a jarring halt when the global credit crunch imploded market valuations in October 2007. Take, for example, the UK, where the FTSE 100 Index fell by 50 per cent between its highest point in October 2007 and its lowest point in March 2009. The FTSE 350 Construction and Materials Index, an index of construction-related UK companies, rose from 1,561 in March 2003 to 6,386 in October 2007, a gain of about 300 per cent. It then fell like a rock to 2,472 by October 2008. The performance of the FTSE 100 over this period, and particularly the rise and fall of construction companies, has been described by many as a major bubble. The argument is that prices were inflated to economically ridiculous levels by market participants (banks in particular) before investors came to their senses, which then caused the bubble to pop and prices to plunge. Debate over whether the stock market movements of recent years have been bubbles has generated much controversy. In this chapter we introduce the subject of behavioural finance, which deals with questions such as how bubbles can come to exist. Some of the issues we discuss are quite controversial and unsettled. We shall describe competing ideas, present some evidence on both sides, and examine the implications for financial managers.

Be honest: do you think of yourself as a better than average driver? If you do, you are not alone. About 80 per cent of the people who are asked this question will say yes. Evidently, we tend to overestimate our abilities behind the wheel. Is the same true when it comes to making financial management decisions?

It will probably not surprise you when we say that human beings sometimes make errors in judgement. How these errors, and other aspects of human behaviour, affect financial managers falls under the general heading of *behavioural finance*. In this chapter our goal is to acquaint you with some common types of mistake, and their financial implications. As you will see, researchers have identified a wide variety of potentially damaging behaviours. By learning to recognize situations in which mistakes are common, you will become a better decision-maker, both in the context of financial management and elsewhere.

## 19.1 Introduction to Behavioural Finance

Sooner or later, you are going to make a financial decision that winds up costing you (and possibly your employer and/or shareholders) a lot of money. Why is this going to happen? You already know the answer. Sometimes you make sound decisions, but you get unlucky in the sense that something happens that you could not have reasonably anticipated. At other times (however painful it is to admit) you just make a bad decision, one that could (and should) have been avoided. The beginning of business wisdom is to recognize the circumstances that lead to poor decisions, and thereby cut down on the damage done by financial blunders.

> **behavioural finance**
> The area of finance dealing with the implications of reasoning errors on financial decisions.

As we have previously noted, the area of research known as **behavioural finance** attempts to understand and explain how reasoning errors influence financial decisions. Much of the research done in the behavioural finance area stems from work in cognitive psychology, which is the study of how people, including financial managers, think, reason, and make decisions. Errors in reasoning are often called *cognitive errors*. In the next several subsections we shall review three main categories of such errors: (1) biases; (2) framing effects; and (3) heuristics.

## 19.2 Biases

If your decisions exhibit systematic biases, then you will make systematic errors in judgement. The type of error depends on the type of bias. In this section, we discuss three particularly relevant biases: (1) overconfidence; (2) over-optimism; and (3) confirmation bias.

### Overconfidence

Serious errors in judgement occur in the business world as a result of **overconfidence**. We are all overconfident about our abilities in at least some areas (recall our question about driving ability at the beginning of the chapter). Here is another example that we see a lot: ask yourself what grade you will receive in this course (in spite of the arbitrary and capricious nature of the professor). In our experience, almost everyone will either say 'A' or, at worst 'B'. Sadly, when this happens, we are always confident (but not overconfident) that at least some of our students are going to be disappointed.

> **overconfidence**
> The belief that your abilities are better than they really are.

In general, you are overconfident when you overestimate your ability to make the correct choice or decision. For example, most business decisions require judgements about the unknown future. The belief that you can forecast the future with precision is a common form of overconfidence.

Another good example of overconfidence comes from studies of equity investors. Researchers have examined large numbers of actual brokerage accounts to see how investors fare when they choose equities. Overconfidence by investors would cause them to overestimate their ability to pick the best equities, leading to excessive trading. The evidence supports this view. First, investors hurt themselves by trading. The accounts that have the most trading significantly underperform the accounts with the least trading, primarily because of the costs associated with trades.

A second finding is equally interesting. Accounts registered to men underperform those registered to women. The reason is that men trade more on average. This extra trading is consistent with evidence from psychology that men have greater degrees of overconfidence than women.

## Over-Optimism

> **over-optimism**
> Taking an overly optimistic view of potential outcomes.
>
> **confirmation bias**
> Searching for (and giving more weight to) information and opinion that confirms what you believe, rather than information and opinion to the contrary.

**Over-optimism** leads to overestimating the likelihood of a good outcome and underestimating the likelihood of a bad outcome. Over-optimism and overconfidence are related, but they are not the same thing. An overconfident individual could (overconfidently) forecast a bad outcome, for example.

Optimism is usually thought of as a good thing. Optimistic people have 'upbeat personalities' and 'sunny dispositions'. However, excessive optimism leads to bad decisions. In a capital budgeting context, overly optimistic analysts will consistently overestimate cash flows and underestimate the probability of failure. Doing so leads to upward-biased estimates of project NPVs, a common occurrence in the business world.

## Confirmation Bias

When you are evaluating a decision, you collect information and opinions. A common bias in this regard is to focus more on information that agrees with your opinion, and to downplay or ignore information that doesn't agree with or support your position. This phenomenon is known as **confirmation bias**, and people who suffer from it tend to spend too much time trying to prove themselves right rather than searching for information that might prove them wrong.

Here is a classic example from psychology. Below are four cards. Notice that the cards are labelled *a*, *b*, 2 and 3. You are asked to evaluate the following statement: 'Any card with a vowel on one side has an even number on the other.' You are asked which of the four cards has to be turned over to decide whether the statement is true or false. It costs €100 to turn over a card, so you want to be economical as possible. What do you do?

You would probably begin by turning over the card with an *a* on it, which is correct. If we find an odd number, then we are done, because the statement is not correct.

Suppose we find an even number. What next? Most people will turn over the card with a 2. Is that the right choice? If we find a vowel, then we confirm the statement, but if we find a consonant, we don't learn anything. In other words, this card can't prove that the statement is wrong; it can only confirm it, so selecting this card is an example of confirmation bias.

Continuing, there is no point in turning over the card labelled '*b*', because the statement doesn't say anything about consonants, which leaves us with the last card. Do we have to turn it over? The answer is yes, because it might have a vowel on the other side, which would disprove the statement, but most people will choose the 2 card over the 3 card.

Confirmation bias can lead managers to ignore negative information about potential investments and focus only on that information which proves they are correct in their opinions. This can lead to a number of poor decisions that reduce firm value. For example, in 2007 most investors believed that the banking system was stable, and that the incredibly high levels of lending were sustainable in the long term. Even though the signs were there to see that people and companies were becoming over-indebted, most individuals didn't see the signals until it was too late.

---

**CONCEPT QUESTIONS**

19.2a  What is overconfidence? How is it likely to be costly?
19.2b  What is over-optimism? How is it likely to be costly?
19.2c  What is confirmation bias? How is it likely to be costly?

## 19.3   Framing Effects

You are susceptible to framing effects if your decisions depend on how a problem or question is framed. Consider the following example. A disaster has occurred, 600 people are at risk, and you are in charge. You must choose between the two following rescue operations:

**Scenario 1**

Option A: Exactly 200 people will be saved.

Option B: There is a 1/3 chance that all 600 people will be saved and a 2/3 chance that no people will be saved.

Which would you choose? There is no necessarily right answer, but most people will choose Option A. Now suppose your choices are as follows:

**Scenario 2**

Option C: Exactly 400 people will die.

Option D: There is a 1/3 chance that nobody will die and a 2/3 chance that all 600 will die.

Now which do you pick? Again, there is no right answer, but most people will choose option D. Although most people will choose options A and D in our hypothetical scenarios, you probably see that doing so is inconsistent, because options A and C are identical, as are options B and D. Why do people make inconsistent choices? It's because the options are framed differently. The first scenario is positive, because it emphasizes the number that will be saved. The second is negative, because it focuses on losses, and people react differently to positive and negative framing, which is a form of **frame dependence**.

> **frame dependence**
> The tendency of individuals to make different (and potentially inconsistent) decisions, depending on how a question or problem is framed.

## Loss Aversion

Here is another example that illustrates a particular type of frame dependence:

**Scenario 1**

Suppose we give you £1,000. You have the following choices:

Option A: You can receive another £500 for sure.

Option B: You can flip a fair coin. If the coin flip comes up heads, you get another £1,000, but if it comes up tails, you get nothing.

**Scenario 2**

Suppose we give you £2,000. You have the following choices:

Option C: You can lose £500 for sure.

Option D: You can flip a fair coin. If the coin flip comes up heads, you lose £1,000, but if it comes up tails, you lose nothing.

What were your answers? Did you choose option A in the first scenario and option D in the second? If that's what you did, you are guilty of focusing just on gains and losses, and not paying attention to what really matters, namely the impact on your wealth. However, you are not alone. About 85 per cent of the people who are presented with the first scenario choose option A, and about 70 per cent of the people who are presented with the second scenario choose option D.

If you look closely at the two scenarios, you will see that they are actually identical. You end up with £1,500 for sure if you pick option A or C, or else you end up with a

50–50 chance of either £1,000 or £2,000 if you pick option B or D. So you should pick the same option in both scenarios. Which option you prefer is up to you, but the point is that you should never pick option A in our first scenario and option D in our second one.

This example illustrates an important aspect of financial decision-making. Focusing on gains and losses instead of overall wealth is an example of narrow framing, and it leads to a phenomenon known as *loss aversion*. In fact, the reason why most people avoid option C in scenario 2 in our example is that it is expressed as a sure loss of £500. In general, researchers have found that individuals are reluctant to realize losses and will, for example, gamble at unfavourable odds to avoid doing so.

Loss aversion is also known as the *break-even effect*, because it frequently shows up as individuals and companies hang on to bad investments and projects (and perhaps even invest more), hoping that something will happen that will allow them to break even and thereby escape without a loss. For example, we discussed the irrelevance of sunk costs in the context of capital budgeting, and the idea of a sunk cost seems clear. Nonetheless, we constantly see companies (and individuals) throw good money after bad rather than just recognize a loss in the face of sunk costs.

How destructive is the break-even effect? Perhaps the most famous case occurred in 1995, when 28-year-old Nicholas Leeson caused the collapse of his employer, the 233-year-old Barings Bank. At the end of 1992 Mr Leeson had lost about £2 million, which he hid in a secret account. By the end of 1993 his losses were about £23 million, and they mushroomed to £208 million at the end of 1994.

Instead of admitting to these losses, Mr Leeson gambled more of the bank's money in an attempt to 'double up and catch up'. On 23 February 1995 Mr Leeson's losses were about £827 million, and his trading irregularities were uncovered. Although he attempted to flee from prosecution, he was caught, arrested, tried, convicted and imprisoned. Also, his wife divorced him.

Do you suffer from the break-even effect? Perhaps so. Consider the following scenario. You have just lost €78 somehow. You can just live with the loss, or you can make a bet. If you make the bet, there is an 80 per cent chance that your loss will grow to €100 (from €78) and a 20 per cent chance that your loss will be nothing. Do you take the loss or take the bet? We bet you choose the bet. If you do, you suffer from the break-even effect, because the bet is a bad one. Instead of a sure loss of €78, your expected loss from the bet is $0.80 \times €100 + 0.20 \times €0 = €80$.

In corporate finance, loss aversion can be quite damaging. We have already mentioned the pursuit of sunk costs. We also might see managers bypassing positive-NPV projects because they have the possibility of large losses (perhaps with low probability). Another phenomenon that we see is *debt avoidance*. As we discuss in our coverage of capital structure, debt financing generates valuable tax shields for profitable companies. Even so, there are hundreds of profitable companies listed on major stock exchanges that completely (or almost completely) avoid debt financing. Because debt financing increases the likelihood of losses, and even bankruptcy, this potentially costly behaviour could be due to loss aversion.

## House Money

Casinos know all about a concept called *playing with house money*. They have found that gamblers are far more likely to take big risks with money that they have won from the casino (i.e., house money). Also, casinos have found that gamblers are not as upset about losing house money as they are about losing the money they brought with them to gamble.

It may seem natural for you to feel that some money is precious, because you earned it through hard work, sweat and sacrifice, whereas other money is less precious, because it came to you as a windfall. But these feelings are plainly irrational, because any cash you have buys the same amount of goods and services, no matter how you obtained that cash.

Let's consider another common situation to illustrate several of the ideas we have explored thus far. Consider the following two investments:

**Investment 1:** You bought 100 shares in Jayz plc for £35 per share. The shares immediately fell to £20 each.

**Investment 2:** At the same time you bought 100 shares in Streets plc for £5 per share. The shares immediately jumped to £20 each.

How would you feel about your investments? You would probably feel pretty good about your Streets investment and be unhappy with your Jayz investment. Here are some other things that might occur:

1   You might tell yourself that your Streets investment was a great idea on your part; you're a stock-picking genius. The drop in value on the Jayz shares wasn't your fault – it was just bad luck. This is a form of confirmation bias, and it also illustrates self-attribution bias, which is taking credit for good outcomes that occur for reasons beyond your control, while attributing bad outcomes to bad luck or misfortune.

2   You might be unhappy that your big winner was essentially nullified by your loser, but notice in our example that your overall wealth did not change. Suppose instead that shares in both companies didn't change in price at all, so that your overall wealth was unchanged. Would you feel the same way?

3   You might be inclined to sell your Streets shares to 'realize' the gain, but hold on to your Jayz shares in hopes of avoiding the loss (which is, of course, loss aversion). The tendency to sell winners and hold losers is known as the *disposition effect*. Plainly, the rational thing to do is to decide whether the equities are attractive investments at their new prices, and react accordingly.

Suppose you decide to keep both equities a little longer. Once you do, both decline to £15. You might now feel very differently about the decline, depending on which equity you looked at. With Jayz, the decline makes a bad situation even worse. Now you are down £20 per share on your investment. On the other hand, with Streets you only 'give back' some of your 'paper profit'. You are still way ahead. This kind of thinking is playing with house money; whether you lose from your original investment or from your investment gains is irrelevant.

Our Jayz and Streets example illustrates what can happen when you become emotionally invested in decisions such as equity purchases. When you add a new equity to your portfolio, it is human nature for you to associate the equity with its purchase price. As the share price changes through time, you will have unrealized gains or losses when you compare the current price with the purchase price. Through time, you will mentally account for these gains and losses, and how you feel about the investment depends on whether you are ahead or behind. This behaviour is known as *mental accounting*.

When you engage in mental accounting, you unknowingly have a personal relationship with each of your investments. As a result, it becomes harder to sell one of them. It is as if you have to 'break up' with this investment, or 'fire' it from your portfolio. As with personal relationships, these investment relationships can be complicated and, believe it or not, make selling shares or dropping projects difficult at times. What can you do about mental accounting? Legendary investor Warren Buffet offers the following advice: 'The investment doesn't know you own it. You have feelings about it, but it has no feelings about you. The investment doesn't know what you paid. People shouldn't get emotionally involved with their investments.'

Loss aversion, mental accounting and the house money effect are important examples of how narrow framing leads to poor decisions. Other, related types of judgement error have been documented. Here are a few examples:

1   *Myopic loss aversion*: This behaviour is the tendency to focus on avoiding short-term losses, even at the expense of long-term gains. For example, you might fail to invest in equities for long-term retirement purposes because you have a fear of loss in the near term. Another example is that managers may avoid investing in long-term projects with little positive cash flow for a number of years because they fear the impact the investment has on the firm's short-term earnings. Projects with shorter payback periods may be preferred in this case.

2 *Regret aversion*: This aversion is the tendency to avoid making a decision because you fear that, in hindsight, the decision would have been less than optimal. Regret aversion relates to myopic loss aversion.

3 *Endowment effect*: This effect is the tendency to consider something that you own to be worth more than it would be if you did not own it. Because of the endowment effect, people sometimes demand more money to give up something than they would be willing to pay to acquire it. The endowment effect can sometimes explain why acquiring firms find it so difficult to persuade shareholders of a target firm that the value of the target is less than the shareholders believe.

4 *Money illusion*: If you suffer from a money illusion, you are confused between real buying power and nominal buying power (i.e., you do not account for the effects of inflation).

---

**CONCEPT QUESTIONS**

19.3a  What is frame dependence? How is it likely to be costly?
19.3b  What is loss aversion? How is it likely to be costly?
19.3c  What is the house money effect? Why is it irrational?

---

# 19.4 Heuristics

Financial managers (and managers in general) often rely on rules of thumb, or **heuristics**, in making decisions. For example, a manager might decide that any project with a payback period of less than two years is acceptable, and therefore not bother with additional analysis. As a practical matter, this mental shortcut might be fine for most circumstances, but we know that sooner or later it will lead to the acceptance of a negative-NPV project.

> **heuristics**
> Shortcuts or rules of thumb used to make decisions.

> **affect heuristic**
> The reliance on instinct instead of analysis in making decisions.

## The Affect Heuristic

We frequently hear business and political leaders talk about following their gut instinct. In essence, such people are making decisions based on whether the chosen outcome or path feels 'right' emotionally. Psychologists use the term *affect* (as in *affection*) to refer to emotional feelings, and the reliance on gut instinct is called the **affect heuristic**.

Reliance on instinct is closely related to reliance on intuition and/or experience. Both intuition and experience are important, and, used properly, help decision-makers to identify potential risks and rewards. However, instinct, intuition and experience should be viewed as complements to formal analysis, not substitutes. Overreliance on emotions in making decisions will almost surely lead (at least on occasion) to costly outcomes that could have been avoided with careful, structured thinking. An obvious example would be making capital budgeting decisions based on instinct rather than on market research and discounted cash flow analysis.

## The Representativeness Heuristic

People often assume that a particular person, object or outcome is broadly representative of a larger class. For example, suppose an employer hired a graduate of your high-quality educational institution and, in fact, is quite pleased with that person. The employer might be inclined to look to your institution again for future employees, because the students are so good. Of course, in doing so, the employer is assuming that the recent hire is representative of all the students, which is an example of the **representativeness heuristic**. A little more generally, the representativeness heuristic is the reliance on stereotypes, analogies or limited samples to form opinions about an entire class.

> **representativeness heuristic**
> The reliance on instinct instead of analysis in making decisions.

## Representativeness and Randomness

Another implication of the representativeness heuristic has to do with perceiving patterns or causes where none exist. For example, soccer fans generally believe that success breeds success. Suppose we look at the recent performance of two football players named Wayne and Cristiano. Both of these players have a 50 per cent goal to shoot ratio. But Wayne has just scored two goals in a row, whereas Cristiano has just missed two in a row. Researchers have found that if they ask 100 football fans which player has the better chance of scoring the next goal, 91 of them will say Wayne. Further, 84 of these fans believe that it is important for teammates to pass the ball to Wayne after he has scored two or three goals in a row.

But, and the sports fans among you will have a hard time with this, researchers have found that this (known as the *hot hands effect* from basketball) is an illusion. That is, players really do not deviate much from their long-run scoring averages – although fans, players, commentators and coaches think they do. Cognitive psychologists actually studied the shooting percentage of one professional basketball team for a season. Here is what they found:

| Shooting percentages and the history of previous attempts | |
| --- | --- |
| **Shooting percentage on next shot (%)** | **History of previous attempts** |
| 46 | Has made 3 in a row |
| 50 | Has made 2 in a row |
| 51 | Has made 1 in a row |
| 52 | First shot of the game |
| 54 | Has missed 1 in a row |
| 53 | Has missed 2 in a row |
| 56 | Has missed 3 in a row |

Detailed analysis of scoring data failed to show that players score or miss shots more or less frequently than what would be expected by chance. That is, statistically speaking, all the scoring percentages listed here are the same.

It is true that footballers score in streaks. But these streaks are within the bounds of long-run goal scoring percentages. So it is an illusion that players are either 'hot' or 'cold'. If you are a believer in the hot hand (or hot foot), however, you are likely to reject these facts, because you 'know better' from watching your favourite teams over the years. If you do, you are being fooled by randomness.

The *clustering illusion* is our human belief that random events that occur in clusters are not really random. For example, it strikes most people as very unusual if heads comes up four times in a row during a series of coin flips. However, if a fair coin is flipped 20 times, there is about a 50 per cent chance of getting four heads in a row. Ask yourself, if you flip four heads in a row, do you think you have a 'hot hand' at coin flipping?

## The Gambler's Fallacy

People commit the *gambler's fallacy* when they assume that a departure from what occurs on average, or in the long run, will be corrected in the short run. Interestingly, some people suffer from both the hot-hand illusion (which predicts continuation in the short run) and the gambler's fallacy (which predicts reversal in the short run)! The idea is that because an event has not happened recently, it has become overdue and is more likely to occur. People sometimes refer (wrongly) to the law of averages in such cases.

Roulette is a random gambling game where gamblers can make various bets on the spin of the wheel. There are 37 numbers on a roulette table: 1 green one, 18 red ones, and 18 black ones. One possible bet is whether the spin will result in a red number or in a black number. Suppose a red number has appeared five times in a row. Gamblers will often become (over) confident that the next spin will be black, when the true chance remains at about 50 per cent (of course, it is exactly 18 in 37).

The misconception arises from the human intuition that the overall odds of the wheel must be reflected in a small number of spins. That is, gamblers often become convinced that the wheel is 'due' to hit a black number after a series of red numbers. Gamblers do know that the odds of a black number appearing are always unchanged: 18 in 37. But gamblers cannot help but feel that after a long series of red numbers, a black one must appear to restore the balance between red and black numbers over time.

Of course, there are many other related errors and biases due to heuristics. Here is a partial list:

1   *Law of small numbers*: If you believe in the law of small numbers, you believe that a small sample of outcomes always resembles the long-run distribution of outcomes. If your investment guru has been right five out of seven times recently, you might believe that his long-run average of being correct is also five out of seven. The law of small numbers is related to recency bias (see our next item), and to the gambler's fallacy.

2   *Recency bias*: Humans tend to give recent events more importance than less recent events. For example, during the great bull market that occurred from 2003 to 2007, many investors thought the market would continue its big gains for a long time – forgetting that bear markets also occur (which happened from 2007 to 2008). Recency bias is related to the law of small numbers.

3   *Anchoring and adjustment*: People have an anchoring bias when they are unable to account for new information in a correct way. That is, they become 'anchored' to a previous price or other value. If you have an anchoring bias, you will tend to be overly conservative in the face of fresh news.

4   *Aversion to ambiguity*: This bias results when people shy away from the unknown. For example, consider the following choice. You get £1,000 for sure, or you can draw a ball out of a big bin containing 100 balls. If the ball is blue, you win £2,000. If it is red, you win nothing. When people are told that there are 50 blue balls and 50 red balls in the bin, about 40 per cent choose to draw a ball. When they are told nothing about how many balls in the bin are blue, most choose to take the £1,000 – ignoring the possibility that the odds might really be in their favour. That is, there could be more than 50 blue balls in the bin.

5   *False consensus*: This is the tendency to think that other people are thinking the same thing you are thinking (with no real evidence). False consensus relates to overconfidence and confirmation bias.

6   *Availability bias*: You suffer from availability bias when you put too much weight on information that is easily available, and place too little weight on information that is hard to obtain. Your financial decisions will suffer if you consider only information that is easy to obtain.

| | | |
|---|---|---|
| **CONCEPT QUESTIONS** | 19.4a | What is the affect heuristic? How is it likely to be costly? |
| | 19.4b | What is the representativeness heuristic? How is it likely to be costly? |
| | 19.4c | What is the gambler's fallacy? |

## 19.5 Behavioural Finance and Market Efficiency

Our discussion thus far has focused on how cognitive errors by individuals can lead to poor business decisions. It seems both clear and non-controversial that such errors are both real and financially important. We now venture into a much less clear area – the implications of behavioural finance for share prices.

In Chapter 11 we introduced the notion of market efficiency. The key idea is that, in an efficient market, prices fully reflect available information. Put differently, prices are correct in the sense that an equity purchase or sale is a zero-NPV investment. In a well-organized, liquid market such as the LSE or Euronext, the argument is that competition among profit-motivated, economically rational traders ensures that prices can never drift far from their zero-NPV level.

In this chapter we have already seen a few examples of how cognitive errors, such as overconfidence, can lead to damaging decisions in the context of share ownership. If many traders behave in ways that are economically irrational, then is there still reason to think that markets are efficient?

First off, it is important to realize that the efficient markets hypothesis does not require every investor to be rational. Instead, all that is required for a market to be efficient is at least some smart and well-financed investors. These investors are prepared to buy and sell to take advantage of any mispricing in the marketplace. This activity is what keeps markets efficient. It is sometimes said that market efficiency doesn't require that *everyone* be rational, just that *some* be.

## Limits to Arbitrage

Investors who buy and sell to exploit mispricings are engaging in a form of *arbitrage* and are known as *arbitrageurs* (or just *arbs* for short). Sometimes, however, a problem arises in this context. The term **limits to arbitrage** refers to the notion that, under certain circumstances, it may not be possible for rational, well-capitalized traders to correct a mispricing, at least not quickly. The reason is that strategies designed to eliminate mispricings are often risky, costly, or somehow restricted.

Three important such problems are:

1   *Firm-specific risk*: This issue is the most obvious risk facing a would-be arbitrageur. Suppose that you believe that the observed price of BMW equity is too low, so you purchase many, many shares. Then there is some unanticipated negative news that drives the share price of BMW even lower. Of course, you could try to hedge some of the firm-specific risk, but any hedge you create is likely to be either imperfect and/or costly.

2   *Noise trader risk*: A **noise trader** is someone whose trades are not based on information or financially meaningful analysis. Noise traders could, in principle, act together to worsen a mispricing in the short run. Noise trader risk is important, because the worsening of a mispricing could force the arbitrageur to liquidate early and sustain steep losses. As Keynes once famously observed, 'Markets can remain irrational longer than you can remain solvent'.

    Noise trader risk is also called **sentiment-based risk**, meaning the risk that an asset's price is being influenced by sentiment (or irrational belief) rather than fact-based financial analysis. If sentiment-based risk exists, then it is another source of risk beyond the systematic and unsystematic risks we discussed in an earlier chapter.

3   *Implementation costs*: All trades cost money. In some cases, the cost of correcting a mispricing may exceed the potential gains. For example, suppose you believe a small, thinly traded equity is significantly undervalued. You want to buy a large quantity. The problem is that as soon as you try to place a huge order, the price would jump because the equity isn't heavily traded.

When these or other risks and costs are present, a mispricing may persist because arbitrage is too risky or too costly. Collectively, these risks and costs create barriers or limits to arbitrage. How important these limits are is difficult to say, but we do know that mispricings occur, at least on occasion. To illustrate, we next consider two well-known examples.

> **limits to arbitrage** The notion that the price of an asset may not equal its correct value because of barriers to arbitrage.
>
> **noise trader** A trader whose trades are not based on information or meaningful financial analysis.
>
> **sentiment-based risk** A source of risk to investors above and beyond firm-specific risk and overall market risk.

**The 3Com/Palm Mispricing**  On 2 March 2000 3Com, a profitable provider of computer networking products and services, sold 5 per cent of its Palm subsidiary to the public via an initial public offering (IPO). 3Com planned to distribute the remaining Palm shares to 3Com shareholders at a later date. Under the plan, if you owned one share of 3Com, you would receive 1.5 shares of Palm. So, after 3Com sold part of Palm via the IPO, investors could buy Palm shares directly, or they could buy them indirectly by purchasing shares of 3Com.

What makes this case interesting is what happened in the days that followed the Palm IPO. If you owned one 3Com share, you would be entitled, eventually, to 1.5 shares of Palm. Therefore each 3Com share should be worth *at least* 1.5 times the value of each Palm share. We say *at least*, because the other parts of 3Com were profitable. As a result, each 3Com share should have been worth much more than 1.5 times the value of one Palm share. But, as you might guess, things did not work out this way.

The day before the Palm IPO, shares in 3Com sold for $104.13. After the first day of trading, Palm closed at $95.06 per share. Multiplying $95.06 by 1.5 results in $142.59, which is the minimum value one would expect to pay for 3Com. But the day Palm closed at $95.06, 3Com shares closed at $81.81, more than $60 lower than the price implied by Palm. It gets stranger.

A 3Com price of $81.81 when Palm is selling for $95.06 implies that the market values the rest of 3Com's businesses (per share) at: $81.81 − 142.59 = −$60.78. Given the number of 3Com shares outstanding at the time, this means the market placed a *negative value* of about −$22 billion on the rest of 3Com's businesses. Of course, a share price cannot be negative. This means, then, that the price of Palm relative to 3Com was much too high, and investors should have bought and sold such that the negative value was instantly eliminated.

What happened? As you can see in Fig. 19.1, the market valued 3Com and Palm shares in such a way that the non-Palm part of 3Com had a negative value for about two months, from 2 March 2000 until 8 May 2000. Even then, it took approval by the US tax authorities for 3Com to proceed with the planned distribution of Palm shares before the non-Palm part of 3Com once again had a positive value.

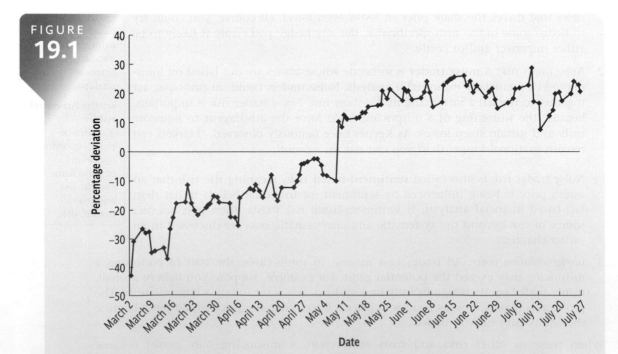

FIGURE 19.1

**Figure 19.1** The percentage difference between 1 share of 3Com and 1.5 shares of Palm, 2 March 2000 to 27 July 2000

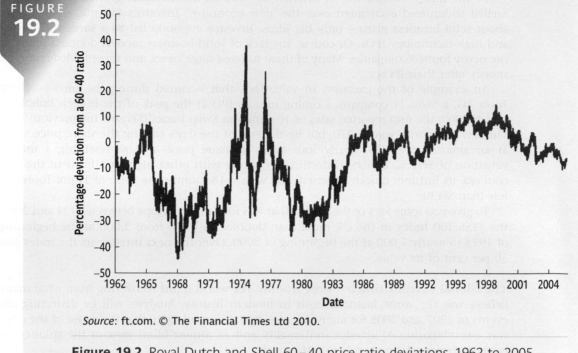

**Figure 19.2** Royal Dutch and Shell 60–40 price ratio deviations, 1962 to 2005

*Source*: ft.com. © The Financial Times Ltd 2010.

**The Royal Dutch/Shell Price Ratio**    Another fairly well-known example of an apparent mispricing involves two large oil companies. In 1907 Royal Dutch of the Netherlands and Shell of the UK agreed to merge their business enterprises and split operating profits on a 60–40 basis. So, whenever the share prices of Royal Dutch and Shell are not in a 60–40 ratio, there is a potential opportunity to make an arbitrage profit.

Figure 19.2 contains a plot of the daily deviations from the 60–40 ratio of the Royal Dutch price to the Shell price. If the prices of Royal Dutch and Shell are in a 60–40 ratio, there is a zero percentage deviation. If the price of Royal Dutch is too high compared with the Shell price, there is a positive deviation. If the price of Royal Dutch is too low compared with the price of Shell, there is a negative deviation. As you can see in Fig. 19.2, there have been large and persistent deviations from the 60–40 ratio. In fact, the ratio is seldom at 60–40 for most of the time from 1962 until mid-2005 (when the companies merged).

## Bubbles and Crashes

A **bubble** occurs when market prices soar far in excess of what normal and rational analysis would suggest. Investment bubbles eventually pop, because they are not based on fundamental values. When a bubble does pop, investors find themselves holding assets with plummeting values.

A **crash** is a significant and sudden drop in market-wide values. Crashes are generally associated with a bubble. Typically, a bubble lasts much longer than a crash. A bubble can form over weeks, months, or even years. Crashes, on the other hand, are sudden, generally lasting less than a week. However, the disastrous financial aftermath of a crash can last for years.

**The High-Technology Bubble and Crash**    How many websites do you think existed at the end of 1994? Would you believe only about 10,000? By the end of 1999 the number of active websites stood at about 9,500,000, and at the beginning of 2010 there were about 108,000,000 active websites.

**bubble**
A situation where observed prices soar far higher than fundamentals and rational analysis would suggest.

**crash**
A situation where market prices collapse significantly and suddenly.

By the mid-1990s the rise in Internet use and its international growth potential had fuelled widespread excitement over the 'new economy'. Investors did not seem to care about solid business plans – only big ideas. Investor euphoria led to a surge in Internet and high-technology IPOs. Of course, the lack of solid business models doomed many of the newly formed companies. Many of them suffered huge losses, and some folded relatively shortly after their IPOs.

An example of the craziness in valuations that occurred during the time is Think Tools AG, a Swiss IT company. Coming into its IPO at the peak of the hi-tech bubble in March 2000, the firm reported sales of 10.6 million Swiss francs (SFr) for the previous year. The IPO issue price was SFr270, but by the end of the day's trading the share price stood at an amazing SFr1,050, nearly four times its issue price, and representing a market valuation of SFr2.52 billion. Unfortunately, along with other high-tech firms of the dot-com era, its fortunes quickly reversed, and within 18 months the price of Think Tools was less than SFr30.

To give you some idea of the bubble that was forming in Europe between 1994 and 2000, the FTSE 100 Index in the UK more than doubled in value from 3,000 at the beginning of 1994 to nearly 7,000 at the beginning of 2000. Over the next three years the index lost 50 per cent of its value.

**The Global Credit Crunch**  More recently, the world is just recovering from what many believe was the worst financial crisis in modern history. Analysts will be dissecting the events of 2007 and 2008 for many decades, but almost all agree that the cause of the crisis was a combination of investor irrationality and an almost blind view of the riskiness of bank strategies in the years before the crash.

Although the crisis originated in the US through the mass provision of risky subprime mortgages to people ill placed to afford them over the longer term, Europe gleefully took full advantage of the cheap credit that was available at the time. Faced with increasing competition from other countries, many banks maximized the size of their loan portfolios through significantly increased levels of lending to risky borrowers. What made this strategy particularly risky was that the long-term loans were funded by short-term borrowing in the money markets. Since 2001, short-term borrowing had been exceptionally cheap, and bankers believed this was going to continue for the foreseeable future. To further cement their view, the increase in loan portfolios led to very high earnings growth, which was supported by shareholders, who were delighted with the returns they were receiving. Governments, too, were happy to allow the risky funding strategy to continue, because they were receiving significant tax revenues on the back of the banks' performance.

It is clear that several behavioural biases were at work here. First, everyone was overly optimistic about the cheap credit continuing. Even with inflation growing fast, and bad debt levels increasing, market participants ignored the warning signs. Confirmation bias was also exhibited by bankers and shareholders, who argued that the bank funding and lending strategy was obviously a good one, because it had provided such strong performance in the recent past.

As markets descended into chaos in 2008, share price valuations exhibited massive degrees of volatility, as can be seen for the VDAX index of German market volatility in Fig. 19.3. Moreover, the heightened levels of market volatility did not return to pre-crisis levels until late 2009.

The global financial crisis of 2008 is the most recent and dramatic example of a bubble and crash. However, there are many more examples of bubbles, and some of these are presented in Table 19.1.

As a result of the events of recent years, many people now believe that markets are not efficient, but instead are driven by behavioural biases of the type discussed in this chapter. However, many others believe that the markets are efficient in general, but that there are times when a fundamental shock leads to a period of transition.

Behavioural finance supporters may have the final say in this debate by stating that the global credit crunch and the resulting financial crisis were actually caused by traders who blindly believed in efficient markets. Because they think that share prices will always

**TABLE 19.1**

| Period | Name | Description |
|---|---|---|
| 1633–1637 | Tulpenmanie | The price of one tulip bulb in The Netherlands rose to 10 times the annual income of a skilled worker, and cost the equivalent of 12 acres (5 hectares) of land. When the bubble burst, the bulb price fell to 0.001 per cent of its previous high. |
| 1720 | The South Sea Bubble | Share valuations in European companies that traded in South America grew 1,000 per cent and collapsed to pre-bubble levels within one year. A very famous example of the silliness was the successful public equity issue of a company whose business model was to 'carry out an undertaking of great advantage'. We still don't know today what that undertaking was. |
| 1920–1929 | The Roaring Twenties | Very similar to the bubbles of this century in that new technologies and economic prosperity drove stock market valuations to extreme highs. The crash led to the great depression of the 1930s. |
| 1997 | The South East Asian Bubble | Significant foreign capital inflows in search of lucrative gains led to the South East Asian economies becoming overheated. When the bubble burst, the economies went with it. |
| 1995–2007 | The Celtic Tiger | The Irish economy grew sharply over this period until the global credit crisis in 2007. The economy subsequently contracted by more than 10 per cent in a year, and made the country one of the riskiest in the Eurozone. |
| 2006–present | The Property Bubble | Property prices are at historically extreme levels, with the majority of individuals being unable to comfortably afford mortgages. It is argued that property bubbles currently exist in China, France, Greece, India, Ireland, Italy, the Netherlands, Norway, Spain, the UK and the US. The bubble hasn't burst yet … |

**Table 19.1** Bubbles in history

**FIGURE 19.3**

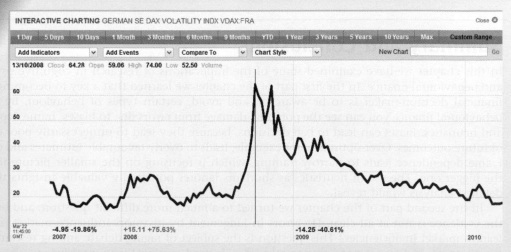

**Figure 19.3** German stock exchange volatility as represented by the VDAX index

reflect the true value of underlying equities, proponents of efficient markets will not see asset bubbles forming, and will therefore extend their duration and exacerbate the negative impact when the bubble inevitably bursts.

## In Their Own Words . . .

### Hersh Shefrin on Behavioural Finance

Most of the chief financial officers (CFOs) I know admit that there is a gap between what they learned about corporate finance in business schools and what they put into practice as executives. A major reason for this gap is the material you are studying in this chapter. It really is true that financial managers do not practise textbook corporate finance. In the 1990s I became convinced that this was the case after I joined the organization Financial Executives International (FEI), which gave me an opportunity to meet many CFOs on a regular basis and discuss with them how they practise corporate finance. In doing so, I gained a great deal of information that led me to conclude that behavioural finance was highly applicable to corporate life.

Behavioural corporate finance is important for at least three reasons. First, being human, financial managers are susceptible to the behavioural phenomena you are reading about in this chapter. Textbook corporate finance offers many valuable concepts, tools, and techniques. My point is not that the material in traditional corporate finance textbooks lacks value, but that psychological obstacles often stand in the way of this material being implemented correctly. Second, the people with whom financial managers interact are also susceptible to mistakes. Expecting other people to be immune to mistakes is itself an error that can lead managers to make bad decisions. Third, investors' mistakes can sometimes lead prices to be inefficient. In this respect, managers can make one of two different mistakes. They might believe that prices are efficient when they are actually inefficient. Or they might believe that prices are inefficient when they are actually efficient. Managers need to know how to think about the vulnerability to both types of errors, and how to deal with each.

The material in this chapter is a wonderful start to learning about behavioural finance. However, for this material to really make a difference, you need to integrate the material with what you are learning about traditional topics such as capital budgeting, capital structure, valuation, payout policy, market efficiency, corporate governance, and mergers and acquisition. You need to study behavioural cases about real people making real decisions and see how psychology impacts those decisions. You need to learn from their mistakes in an effort to make better decisions yourself. This is how behavioural corporate finance will generate value for you.

*Hersh Shefrin holds the Mario Belotti Chair in the Department of Finance at Santa Clara University's Leavey School of Business. Professor Shefrin is a pioneer of behavioural finance.*

## Summary and Conclusions

In this chapter we have examined some of the implications of research in cognitive psychology and behavioural finance. In the first part of the chapter we learned that a key to becoming a better financial decision-maker is to be aware of, and avoid, certain types of behaviour. By studying behavioural finance you can see the potential damage from errors due to biases, frame dependence, and heuristics. Biases can lead to bad decisions, because they lead to unnecessarily poor estimates of future outcomes. Over-optimism, for example, leads to overly favourable estimates and opinions. Frame dependence leads to narrow framing, which is focusing on the smaller picture instead of the bigger one. The use of heuristics as shortcuts ignores potentially valuable insights that more detailed analysis would reveal.

In the second part of the chapter we turned to a much more difficult question, and one where the evidence is not at all clear. Do errors in judgement by investors influence market prices and lead to market inefficiencies? This question is the subject of raging debate among researchers and practitioners, and we are not going to take sides. Instead, our goal is to introduce you to the ideas and issues. We saw that market inefficiencies can be difficult for arbitrageurs to exploit because of firm-specific risk, noise trader (or sentiment-based) risk, and implementation costs. We called these difficulties limits (or barriers) to arbitrage, and the implication is that some inefficiencies may only gradually disappear, and smaller inefficiencies can persist if they cannot be profitably exploited. Looking back at market history, we saw some examples of evident mispricing, such as Royal Dutch and Shell. We also saw that markets appear to be susceptible to bubbles and crashes, suggesting significant inefficiency.

# Concepts Review and Critical Thinking Questions

1  **Limits to Arbitrage [LO4]**  In the chapter we discussed the 3Com/Palm and Royal Dutch/Shell mispricings. Which of the limits to arbitrage is least likely to have been the main reason for these mispricings? Explain.

2  **Overconfidence [LO1]**  How could overconfidence affect the financial manager of the firm, and the firm's shareholders?

3  **Frame Dependence [LO4]**  How can frame dependence lead to irrational investment decisions?

4  **Noise Trader Risk [LO4]**  What is noise trader risk? How can noise trader risk lead to market inefficiencies?

5  **Probabilities [LO3]**  Suppose you are flipping a fair coin in a coin-flipping contest and have flipped eight heads in a row. What is the probability of flipping a head on your next coin flip? Suppose you flipped a head on your ninth toss. What is the probability of flipping a head on your tenth toss?

6  **Efficient Market Hypothesis [LO4]**  The efficient market hypothesis implies that all mutual funds should obtain the same expected risk-adjusted returns. Therefore we can simply pick mutual funds at random. Is this statement true or false? Explain.

7  **Behavioural Finance and Efficient Markets [LO4]**  Proponents of behavioural finance use three concepts to argue that markets are not efficient. What are these arguments?

8  **Frame Dependence [LO2]**  In the chapter we presented an example where you had lost €78 and were given the opportunity to make a wager in which your loss would increase to €100 for 80 per cent of the time and decrease to €0 for 20 per cent of the time. Using the stand-alone principal from capital budgeting, explain how your decision to accept or reject the proposal could have been affected by frame dependence. In other words, reframe the question in a way in which most people are likely to analyse the proposal correctly.

To help you grasp the key concepts of this chapter check out the extra resources posted on the Online Learning Centre at www.mcgraw-hill.co.uk/textbooks/hillier

Among other helpful resources there are mini-cases tailored to individual chapters.

# Financial Risk Management

## LEARNING OBJECTIVES

After studying this chapter, you should understand:

LO1 The exposures to risk in a company's business, and how a company could choose to hedge these risks.

LO2 The similarities and differences between futures and forward contracts, and how these contracts are used to hedge risk.

LO3 The basics of swap contracts, and how they are used to hedge interest rates.

LO4 The pay-offs of option contracts, and how they are used to hedge risk.

ANYONE STUDYING CORPORATE FINANCE must be familiar with the principles of financial risk management. Many students think that only financial institutions use derivatives such as futures and swaps. However, every company that does business overseas, sources raw materials from other countries, borrows or lends money, or buys commodities today for delivery in the future will use risk management techniques to manage risk and optimize its business.

For example, in 2008 BMW was faced with a very challenging problem. Its biggest growth area for X series cars was the United States. However, because the cars are made in Germany, the euro's strength against the dollar was making them too expensive in the US. Moreover, at the time, the euro was expected to strengthen further over the coming months. What could BMW do to ensure that its cars did not become too expensive in the United States? This chapter will review some of the financial methods open to BMW's management.

Since the early 1970s, prices for all types of goods and services have become increasingly volatile. This is a cause for concern, because sudden and unexpected shifts in prices can create expensive disruptions in operating activities, even for very well-run firms. As a result, firms are increasingly taking steps to shield themselves from price volatility through the use of new and innovative financial arrangements.

The purpose of this chapter is to introduce you to some of the basics of financial risk management. The activities we discuss here are on the frontier of modern, real-world financial management. By describing one of the rapidly developing areas in corporate finance, we hope to leave you with a sense of how the art and practice of corporate finance evolve in response to changes in the financial environment.

## 20.1 Hedging and Price Volatility

**hedging**
Reducing a firm's exposure to price or rate fluctuations. Also, *immunization*.

In broad terms, reducing a firm's exposure to price or rate fluctuations is called **hedging**. The term *immunization* is sometimes used as well. As we shall discuss, there are many different types of hedging, and many different techniques. Frequently, when a firm desires to hedge a particular risk, there will be no direct way of doing so. The financial manager's job in such cases is to create a way by using available financial instruments to create new ones. This process has come to be called *financial engineering*.

Corporate risk management often involves the buying and selling of **derivative securities**. A derivative security is a financial asset that represents a claim to another financial asset. For example, an equity option gives the owner the right to buy or sell equities, a financial asset: so equity options are derivative securities.

In a world where prices were very stable, and changed only slowly, there would be very little demand for financial risk management. Given the financial turmoil in the last five years, financial risk management has become central to the operations of every business.

> **derivative security**
> A financial asset that represents a claim to another financial asset.

## Price Volatility: A Historical Perspective

In trying to understand why we claim that the financial world has become more risky, you will find it useful to look back at the history of prices. Figure 20.1 provides a long-term view of price levels for the United Kingdom. The price level series shown begins in 1800 and runs through to 2009. The remarkable fact revealed by this series is that for the first 100 years prices changed very little (except in wartime). In contrast, in the last 40 years prices have increased dramatically. This price trend is not just confined to the UK, but applies to the whole of Europe.

Although the rate of change in prices has slowed in recent years, inflation is still a very big concern. The important lesson is that even though the inflation rate is now relatively low in Europe, the uncertainty about the future rate of inflation remains. Beyond the unexpected changes in overall price levels, there are three specific areas of particular importance to businesses in which volatility has also increased dramatically: interest rates, exchange rates, and commodity prices.

## Interest Rate Volatility

We know that debt is a vital source of financing for corporations, and interest rates are a key component of a firm's cost of capital. Over the last 30 years interest rates have been

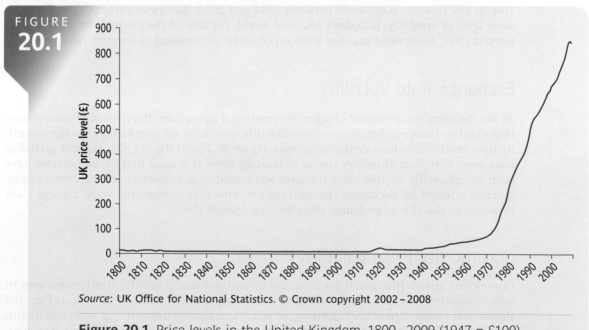

*Source*: UK Office for National Statistics. © Crown copyright 2002–2008

**Figure 20.1** Price levels in the United Kingdom, 1800–2009 (1947 = £100)

FIGURE
20.2

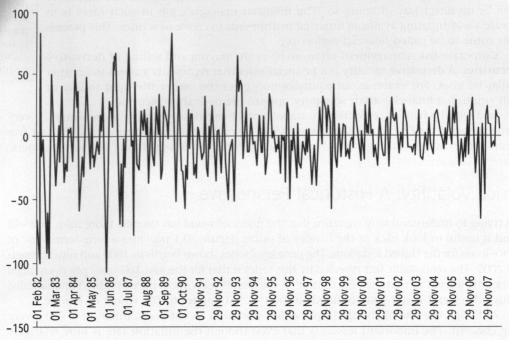

*Source*: Bank of England
The rate changes in this figure are changes in monthly nominal average yields on 10-year zero discount UK government bonds. They are measured in basis points, where one basis point is 1 per cent of 1 per cent – that is, 0.0001.

**Figure 20.2** Monthly changes in 10-year UK government bond yields, February 1982 to February 2010

fairly volatile in Europe. Figure 20.2 illustrates this volatility by plotting the changes in 10-year UK Treasury bond yield between 1982 and 2010. European interest rates have the same level of volatility. In today's financial world, because of the uncertainty surrounding interest rates, firms must manage their exposure to movements in interest rates.

## Exchange Rate Volatility

As we discussed in an earlier chapter, international operations have become increasingly important to European businesses. Consequently, exchange rates and exchange rate volatility have also become increasingly important. Figure 20.3 plots the £/$, £/€ and €/$ exchange rates since European Monetary Union in January 1999. It is clear that exchange rates have been exceptionally volatile since the euro was introduced. Importers and exporters can be severely affected by exchange rate movements, and it is crucial that they manage their exposure to the risk of exchange rates moving against them.

## Commodity Price Volatility

Commodity prices (the prices for basic goods and materials) are the third major area in which volatility has risen. Oil is one of the most important commodities; and, as Fig. 20.4 shows (and recent experience confirms), oil prices can change dramatically from one month to the next. The behaviour of oil prices is not unique; many other key commodities have experienced increased volatility over the past two decades.

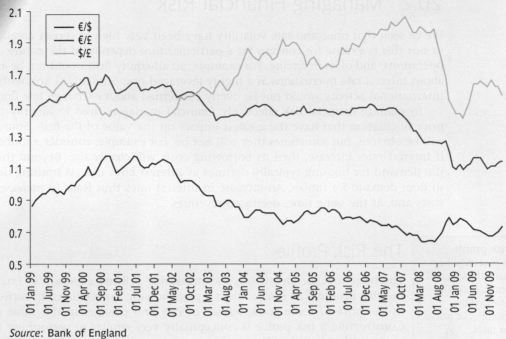

*Source*: Bank of England

**Figure 20.3** Average monthly exchange rates between the British pound, the euro and the US dollar, January 1999 to February 2010

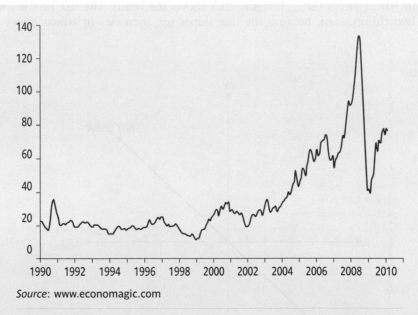

*Source*: www.economagic.com

**Figure 20.4** West Texas spot oil price ($/barrel), 1990–2010

| CONCEPT QUESTIONS | |
|---|---|
| 20.1a | What is hedging? |
| 20.1b | Why do firms place greater emphasis on hedging now than they did in the past? |

## 20.2 Managing Financial Risk

We've seen that price and rate volatility have been very high in recent decades. Whether or not this is a cause for concern for a particular firm depends on the nature of the firm's operations, and of its financing. For example, an all-equity firm would not be as concerned about interest rate fluctuations as a highly leveraged one. Similarly, a firm with little or no international activity would not be overly concerned about exchange rate fluctuations.

To manage financial risk effectively financial managers need to identify the types of price fluctuation that have the greatest impact on the value of the firm. Sometimes these will be obvious, but sometimes they will not be. For example, consider a timber company. If interest rates increase, then its borrowing costs will clearly rise. Beyond this, however, the demand for housing typically declines as interest rates rise. As housing demand falls, so does demand for timber. An increase in interest rates thus leads to increased financing costs and, at the same time, decreased revenues.

**risk profile**
A plot showing how the value of the firm is affected by changes in prices or rates.

### The Risk Profile

The basic tool for identifying and measuring a firm's exposure to financial risk is the **risk profile**. The risk profile is a plot showing the relationship between changes in the price of some good, service or rate and changes in the value of the firm. Constructing a risk profile is conceptually very similar to performing a sensitivity analysis (described in Chapter 10).

To illustrate, consider an agricultural products company that has a large-scale wheat-farming operation. Because wheat prices can be very volatile, we might wish to investigate the firm's exposure to wheat price fluctuations – that is, its risk profile with regard to wheat prices. To do this, we plot changes in the value of the firm ($\Delta V$) against unexpected changes in wheat prices ($\Delta P_{wheat}$). Figure 20.5 shows the result. The risk profile in Fig. 20.5 tells us two things. First, because the line slopes up, increases in wheat prices will increase the

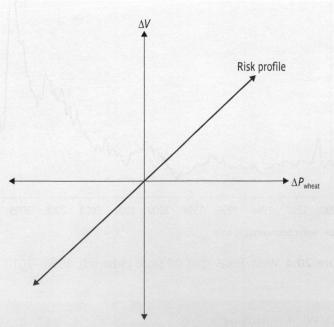

FIGURE
**20.5**

For a grower, unexpected increases in wheat prices increase the value of the firm.

**Figure 20.5** Risk profile for a wheat grower

value of the firm. Because wheat is an output, this comes as no surprise. Second, because the line has a fairly steep slope, this firm has a significant exposure to wheat price fluctuations, and it may wish to take steps to reduce that exposure.

## Reducing Risk Exposure

Fluctuations in the price of any particular good or service can have very different effects on different types of firm. Going back to wheat prices, we now consider the case of a food-processing operation. The food processor buys large quantities of wheat, and has a risk profile like that illustrated in Fig. 20.6. As with the agricultural products firm, the value of this firm is sensitive to wheat prices; but because wheat is an input, increases in wheat prices lead to decreases in firm value.

Both the agricultural products firm and the food processor are exposed to wheat price fluctuations, but such fluctuations have opposite effects for the two firms. If these two firms get together, then much of the risk can be eliminated. The grower and the processor can simply agree that, at set dates in the future, the grower will deliver a certain quantity of wheat, and the processor will pay a set price. Once the agreement is signed, both firms will have locked in the price of wheat for as long as the contract is in effect, and both of their risk profiles with regard to wheat prices will be completely flat during that time.

We should note that, in reality, a firm that hedges financial risk usually won't be able to create a completely flat risk profile. For example, our wheat grower doesn't actually know what the size of the crop will be ahead of time. If the crop is larger than expected, then some portion of the crop will be unhedged. If the crop is small, then the grower will have to buy more to fulfil the contract and will thereby be exposed to the risk of price changes. Either way, there is some exposure to wheat price fluctuations; but hedging sharply reduces that exposure.

There are a number of other reasons why perfect hedging is usually impossible, but this is not really a problem. With most financial risk management the goal is to reduce the risk to more bearable levels and thereby flatten out the risk profile, not necessarily to eliminate the risk altogether.

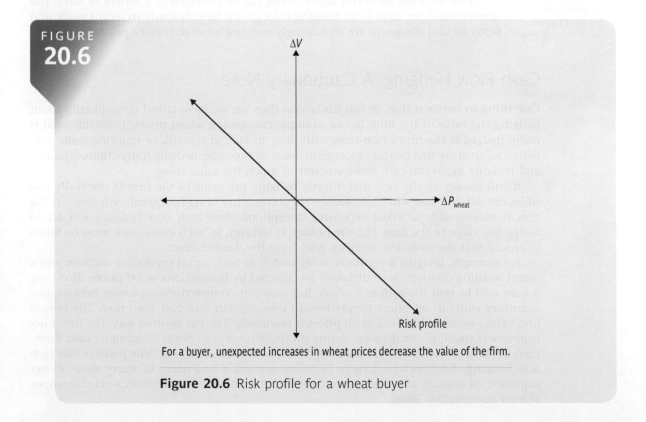

**FIGURE 20.6**

For a buyer, unexpected increases in wheat prices decrease the value of the firm.

**Figure 20.6** Risk profile for a wheat buyer

In thinking about financial risk, there is an important distinction to be made. Price fluctuations have two components. Short-run, essentially temporary changes are the first component. The second component has to do with more long-run, essentially permanent changes. As we discuss next, these two types of change have very different implications for the firm.

## Hedging Short-Run Exposure

Short-run, temporary changes in prices result from unforeseen events or shocks. Some examples are sudden increases in orange juice prices because of a late season freeze, increases in oil prices because of political turmoil, and increases in coffee prices because of a serious drought. Price fluctuations of this sort are often called *transitory* changes.

Short-run price changes can drive a business into financial distress even though, in the long run, the business is fundamentally sound. This happens when a firm finds itself with sudden cost increases that it cannot pass on to its customers immediately. A negative cash flow position is created, and the firm may be unable to meet its financial obligations.

For example, wheat crops might be much larger than expected in a particular year because of unusually good growing conditions. At harvest time, wheat prices will be unexpectedly low. By that time, a wheat farmer will have already incurred most of the costs of production. If prices drop too low, revenues from the crop will be insufficient to cover the costs, and financial distress may result.

**transactions exposure**
Short-run financial risk arising from the need to buy or sell at uncertain prices or rates in the near future.

Short-run financial risk is often called **transactions exposure**. This name stems from the fact that short-term financial exposure typically arises because a firm must make transactions in the near future at uncertain prices or rates. With our wheat farmer, for example, the crop must be sold at the end of the harvest, but the wheat price is uncertain. Alternatively, a firm may have a bond issue that will be maturing next year that it will need to replace, but the interest rate that the firm will have to pay is not known.

As we shall see, short-run financial risk can be managed in a variety of ways. The opportunities for short-term hedging have grown tremendously in recent years, and firms around the world are increasingly hedging away transitory price changes.

## Cash Flow Hedging: A Cautionary Note

One thing to notice is that, in our discussion thus far, we have talked conceptually about hedging the value of the firm. In our example concerning wheat prices, however, what is really hedged is the firm's near-term cash flow. In fact, at the risk of ignoring some subtleties, we shall say that hedging short-term financial exposure, hedging transactions exposure, and hedging near-term cash flows amount to much the same thing.

It will usually be the case that directly hedging the value of the firm is not really feasible; instead, the firm will try to reduce the uncertainty of its near-term cash flows. If the firm is thereby able to avoid expensive disruptions, then cash flow hedging will act to hedge the value of the firm, but the linkage is indirect. In such cases, care must be taken to ensure that the cash flow hedging does have the desired effect.

For example, imagine a vertically integrated firm with an oil-producing division and a petrol-retailing division. Both divisions are affected by fluctuations in oil prices. However, it may well be that the firm as a whole has very little transactions exposure, because any transitory shifts in oil prices simply benefit one division and cost the other. The overall firm's risk profile with regard to oil prices is essentially flat. Put another way, the firm's net exposure is small. If one division, acting on its own, were to begin hedging its cash flows, then the firm as a whole would suddenly be exposed to financial risk. The point is that cash flow hedging should not be done in isolation. Instead, a firm needs to worry about its net exposure. As a result, any hedging activities should probably be done on a centralized, or at least co-operative, basis.

## Hedging Long-Term Exposure

Price fluctuations can also be longer-run, more permanent changes. These result from fundamental shifts in the underlying economics of a business. If improvements in agricultural technology come about, for example, then wheat prices will permanently decline (in the absence of agricultural price subsidies!). If a firm is unable to adapt to the new technology, then it will not be economically viable over the long run.

A firm's exposure to long-run financial risks is often called its **economic exposure**. Because long-term exposure is rooted in fundamental economic forces, it is much more difficult, if not impossible, to hedge on a permanent basis. For example, is it possible that a wheat farmer and a food processor could permanently eliminate exposure to wheat price fluctuations by agreeing on a fixed price for ever?

The answer is no; in fact, the effect of such an agreement might even be the opposite of the one desired. The reason is that if, over the long run, wheat prices were to change on a permanent basis, one party to this agreement would ultimately be unable to honour it. Either the buyer would be paying too much, or the seller would be receiving too little. In either case the loser would become uncompetitive, and fail. Something of the sort happened in the 1970s when public utilities and other energy consumers entered into long-run contracts with natural gas producers. Natural gas prices plummeted in later years, and a great deal of turmoil followed.

> **economic exposure**
> Long-term financial risk arising from permanent changes in prices or other economic fundamentals.

## Conclusion

In the long run, either a business is economically viable or it will fail. No amount of hedging can change this simple fact. Nonetheless, by hedging over the near term, a firm gives itself time to adjust its operations and thereby adapt to new conditions without expensive disruptions. So, drawing our discussion in this section together, we can say that, by managing financial risks, the firm can accomplish two important things. The first is that the firm insulates itself from otherwise troublesome transitory price fluctuations. The second is that the firm gives itself a little breathing space to adapt to fundamental changes in market conditions.

| CONCEPT QUESTIONS | 20.2a | What is a risk profile? Describe the risk profiles with regard to oil prices for an oil producer and a petrol retailer. |
| | 20.2b | What can a firm accomplish by hedging financial risk? |

# 20.3  Hedging with Forward Contracts

Forward contracts are among the oldest and most basic tools for managing financial risk. Our goal in this section is to describe forward contracts, and discuss how they are used to hedge financial risk.

## Forward Contracts: The Basics

A **forward contract** is a legally binding agreement between two parties calling for the sale of an asset or product in the future at a price agreed on today. The terms of the contract call for one party to deliver the goods to the other on a certain date in the future, called the *settlement date*. The other party pays the previously agreed *forward price* and takes the goods. Looking back, note that the agreement we discussed between the wheat grower and the food processor was, in fact, a forward contract.

Forward contracts can be bought and sold. The *buyer* of a forward contract has the obligation to take delivery and pay for the goods; the *seller* has the obligation to make

> **forward contract**
> A legally binding agreement between two parties calling for the sale of an asset or product in the future at a price agreed on today.

delivery and accept payment. The buyer of a forward contract benefits if prices increase, because the buyer will have locked in a lower price. Similarly, the seller wins if prices fall, because a higher selling price has been locked in. Note that one party to a forward contract can win only at the expense of the other, so a forward contract is a zero-sum game.

## The Pay-Off Profile

**pay-off profile**
A plot showing the gains and losses that will occur on a contract as the result of unexpected price changes.

The **pay-off profile** is the key to understanding how forward contracts (and other contracts we discuss later) are used to hedge financial risks. In general, a pay-off profile is a plot showing the gains and losses on a contract that result from unexpected price changes. For example, suppose we were examining a forward contract on oil. Based on our discussion, the buyer of the forward contract is obligated to accept delivery of a specified quantity of oil at a future date and pay a set price. Part A of Fig. 20.7 shows the resulting pay-off profile on the forward contract from the buyer's perspective.

What Fig. 20.7 shows is that, as oil prices increase, the buyer of the forward contract benefits by having locked in a lower-than-market price. If oil prices decrease then the buyer loses, because that buyer ends up paying a higher-than-market price. For the seller of the forward contract things are simply reversed. The pay-off profile of the seller is illustrated in Part B of Fig. 20.7.

## Hedging with Forwards

To illustrate how forward contracts can be used to hedge, we consider the case of a public utility that uses oil to generate power. The prices that our utility can charge are regulated, and cannot be changed rapidly. As a result, sudden increases in oil prices are a source of financial risk. The utility's risk profile is illustrated in Fig. 20.8.

If we compare the risk profile in Fig. 20.8 with the buyer's pay-off profile on a forward contract shown in Fig. 20.7, we see what the utility needs to do. The pay-off profile for the buyer of a forward contract on oil is exactly the opposite of the utility's risk profile with respect to oil. If the utility buys a forward contract, its exposure to unexpected changes in oil prices will be eliminated. This result is shown in Fig. 20.9.

Our public utility example illustrates the fundamental approach to managing financial risk. We first identify the firm's exposure to financial risk using a risk profile. We then try to find a financial arrangement, such as a forward contract, that has an offsetting pay-off profile.

**FIGURE 20.7**

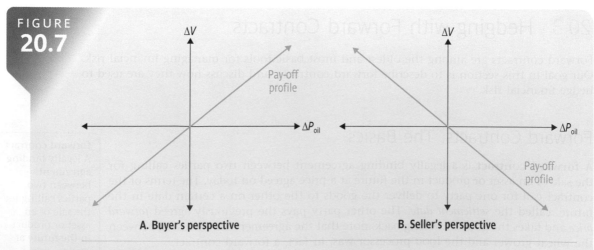

**Figure 20.7** Pay-off profiles of a forward contract

**A Caveat** Fig. 20.9 shows that the utility's net exposure to oil price fluctuations is zero. If oil prices rise, then the gains on the forward contract will offset the damage from increased costs. However, if oil prices decline, the benefit from lower costs will be offset by losses on the forward contract.

This illustrates an important thing to remember about hedging with forward contracts. Price fluctuations can be good or bad, depending on which way they go. If we hedge with

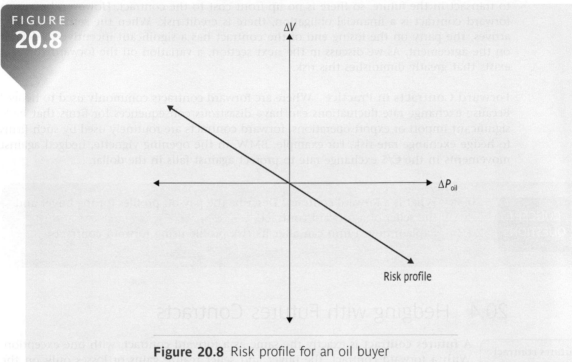

**Figure 20.8** Risk profile for an oil buyer

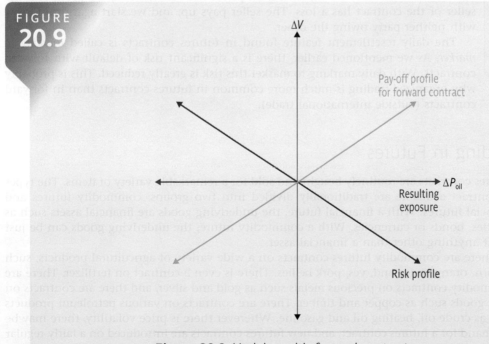

**Figure 20.9** Hedging with forward contracts

forward contracts, we eliminate the risk associated with an adverse price change. However, we also eliminate the potential gain from a favourable move. You might wonder whether we couldn't somehow just hedge against unfavourable moves. We can, and we describe how in a subsequent section.

**Credit Risk**   Another important thing to remember is that, with a forward contract, no money changes hands when the contract is initiated. The contract is simply an agreement to transact in the future, so there is no up-front cost to the contract. However, because a forward contract is a financial obligation, there is credit risk. When the settlement date arrives, the party on the losing end of the contract has a significant incentive to default on the agreement. As we discuss in the next section, a variation on the forward contract exists that greatly diminishes this risk.

**Forward Contracts in Practice**   Where are forward contracts commonly used to hedge? Because exchange rate fluctuations can have disastrous consequences for firms that have significant import or export operations, forward contracts are routinely used by such firms to hedge exchange rate risk. For example, BMW, in the opening vignette, hedged against movements in the €/$ exchange rate to protect against falls in the dollar.

| CONCEPT QUESTIONS | 20.3a   What is a forward contract? Describe the pay-off profiles for the buyer and the seller of a forward contract. |
|---|---|
| | 20.3b   Explain how a firm can alter its risk profile using forward contracts. |

## 20.4   Hedging with Futures Contracts

**futures contract**
A forward contract with the feature that gains and losses are realized each day rather than only on the settlement date.

A **futures contract** is exactly the same as a forward contract, with one exception. With a forward contract, the buyer and seller realize gains or losses only on the settlement date. With a futures contract, gains and losses are realized daily. If we buy a futures contract on oil, then if oil prices rise today, we have a profit and the seller of the contract has a loss. The seller pays up, and we start again tomorrow with neither party owing the other.

The daily resettlement feature found in futures contracts is called *marking to market*. As we mentioned earlier, there is a significant risk of default with forward contracts. With daily marking to market this risk is greatly reduced. This is probably why organized trading is much more common in futures contracts than in forward contracts (outside international trade).

### Trading in Futures

Futures contracts are routinely bought and sold for a remarkable variety of items. The types of contract available are traditionally divided into two groups: commodity futures and financial futures. With a financial future, the underlying goods are financial assets such as equities, bonds or currencies. With a commodity future, the underlying goods can be just about anything other than a financial asset.

There are commodity futures contracts on a wide variety of agricultural products, such as corn, orange juice and, yes, pork bellies. There is even a contract on fertilizer. There are commodity contracts on precious metals such as gold and silver, and there are contracts on basic goods such as copper and timber. There are contracts on various petroleum products such as crude oil, heating oil and gasoline. Wherever there is price volatility, there may be a demand for a futures contract, and new futures contracts are introduced on a fairly regular basis.

## Futures Exchanges

There are a number of futures exchanges around the world, and more are being established. The big three futures exchanges are Euronext Liffe, Eurex and the Chicago Mercantile Exchange. While trading on the exchanges spans whole geographic regions, there are many smaller exchanges, such as OMX (Nordic and Baltic markets), BELFOX (Belgium), IDEM (Italy), MEFF (Spain) and LME (London).

Figure 20.10 gives a partial *Financial Times* listing for selected futures contracts. Taking a look at the Liffe cocoa contracts, note that the contracts traded on Liffe are for delivery of 10 tonnes of cocoa, and are quoted in pounds per tonne. The price of cocoa for delivery in the future is expected to fall over 2010. For example, the price of a May 2010 cocoa futures contract is £2,218, falling to £2,184 for a September contract and £2,158 for a December 2010 contract.

For the Liffe cocoa contract with a May maturity, the first number in the row is the settlement price (£2,218), and is essentially the closing price for the day. For purposes of marking to market this is the figure used. The change, listed next, is the movement in the settlement price since the previous trading session (+£7). The highest price (£2,238) and lowest price (£2,207) over the life of the contract are shown next. Finally, there were 4,800 contracts traded, and open interest (58,800) – the number of contracts outstanding at the end of the day – is shown.

## Hedging With Futures

Hedging with futures contracts is conceptually identical to hedging with forward contracts, and the pay-off profile on a futures contract is drawn just like the profile for a forward contract. The only difference in hedging with futures is that the firm will have to maintain an account with a broker, so that gains and losses can be credited or debited each day as a part of the marking-to-market process.

Even though there are a large variety of futures contracts, it is unlikely that a particular firm will be able to find the precise hedging instrument it needs. For example, we might produce a particular grade or variety of oil, but find that no contract exists for exactly that grade. However, all oil prices tend to move together, so we could hedge our output using futures contracts on other grades of oil. Using a contract on a related, but not identical, asset as a means of hedging is called **cross-hedging**.

> **cross-hedging**
> Hedging an asset with contracts written on a closely related, but not identical, asset.

When a firm *does* cross-hedge, it does not actually want to buy or sell the underlying asset. This presents no problem, because the firm can reverse its futures position at some point before maturity. This simply means that if the firm sells a futures contract to hedge something, it will buy the same contract at a later date, thereby eliminating its futures position. In fact, futures contracts are rarely held to maturity by anyone (despite horror stories of individuals waking up to find mountains of soya beans in their front yards); as a result, actual physical delivery very rarely takes place.

A related issue has to do with contract maturity. A firm might wish to hedge over a relatively long period of time, but the available contracts might have shorter maturities. A firm could therefore decide to roll over short-term contracts, but this entails some risks. For example, Metallgesellschaft AG, a German firm, nearly went bankrupt in 1993 after losing more than $1 billion in the oil markets, mainly through derivatives. The trouble began in 1992 when MG Corp., a US subsidiary, began marketing gasoline, heating oil and diesel fuel. It entered into contracts to supply products for fixed prices for up to 10 years. Thus, if the price of oil rose, the firm stood to lose money. MG protected itself by, among other things, buying short-term oil futures that fluctuated with near-term energy prices. Under these contracts, if the price of oil rose, the derivatives gained in value. Unfortunately for MG, oil prices dropped, and the firm incurred huge losses on its short-term derivatives positions without an immediate, offsetting benefit on its long-term contracts. Thus its primary problem was that it was hedging a long-term contract with short-term contracts – a less than ideal approach.

FIGURE 20.10

# FT COMMODITIES & AGRICULTURE

## 23/03/2010

### BASIC METALS

#### LONDON METAL EXCHANGE

| $/tonne | Cash Official | 3 Mth Official | Kerb PM 3 Mthclose | Day's High/Low (3 Mth) | Open Interest (Lots) | Turnover (Lots) |
|---|---|---|---|---|---|---|
| Aluminium | 2230/2231 | 2257/2258 | 2258/2592 | 2279,25/2235,25 | 680,930 | 115,282 |
| Alum Alloy | 2050/2051 | 2075/2085 | 2100 | 2100/2085 | 4,742 | 390 |
| Amer Alloy | 2140/2150 | 2165/2175 | 2170/75 | 2170/2145 | 11,244 | 1,331 |
| Copper | 7404/7404.5 | 7435/7435 | 7435/40 | 7515/7407 | 279,958 | 90,862 |
| Lead | 2135.5/2136 | 2165/2170 | 2104/05 | 2195/2100 | 88,638 | 21,345 |
| Nickel | 22335/22340 | 22385/22390 | 22495/500 | 22630/22057 | 98,055 | 18,525 |
| Tin | 17545/17550 | 17600/17605 | 17575/600 | 17800/17567 | 19,802 | 3,220 |
| Zinc | 2235.5/2236 | 2269/2270 | 2240/40.5 | 2300/2240 | 218,420 | 56,697 |

Spot 1.5044  3 Mths:1.5036  6 Mths:1.5032  9 Mths:1.5026  Official £/$ rate: 1.5012
LME Closing £/$ rate: 1.5051  Kerb close 17:00.
Source: Amalgamated Metal Trading www.amt.co.uk  For further trading information see www.lme.co.uk

### ■ HIGH GRADE COPPER COMEX

| | Sett price | Day's chge | High | Low | Vol 000s | Open int 000s |
|---|---|---|---|---|---|---|
| Mar | 336.95 | -0.30 | 339.50 | 337.15 | 0.4 | 0.5 |
| Apr | 337.30 | -0.15 | 340.00 | 335.45 | 0.7 | 1.7 |
| May | 337.90 | -0.15 | 340.95 | 335.80 | 30.3 | 85.4 |
| Jun | 338.85 | -0.15 | 341.55 | 337.90 | 0.1 | 0.8 |
| Total | | | | | 35.1 | 130.8 |

### PRECIOUS METALS

### ■ GOLD COMEX (100 Troy oz: $/troy oz)

| | Sett price | Day's chge | High | Low | Vol 000s | O int 000s |
|---|---|---|---|---|---|---|

### ■ LME WAREHOUSE STOCKS (tonnes)

| Aluminium | -6,925 | to 4,596,350 |
|---|---|---|
| Aluminium Alloy | -260 | to 78,360 |
| Amer Alloy | -20 | to 175,200 |
| Copper | -1,400 | to 520,675 |
| Lead | +475 | to 171,850 |
| Nickel | -342 | to 157,368 |
| Zinc | -25 | to 540,825 |
| Tin | -150 | to 24,010 |

### ■ LONDON BULLION MARKET

| Gold (Troy oz) | $ equiv | £ equiv | € equiv |
|---|---|---|---|
| Close | 1,103.10-1,102.10 | | |
| Opening | 1,103.45-1,102.45 | | |
| Morning fix | 1,100.75 | 733.25 | 814.47 |

## SOFTS

### ■ COCOA NYSE LIFFE (10 tonnes: £/tonne)

| | Sett price | Day's chge | High | Low | Vol 000s | O int 000s |
|---|---|---|---|---|---|---|
| May | 2,218 | 7 | 2,238 | 2,207 | 4.8 | 58.8 |
| Jul | 2,227 | 9 | 2,244 | 2,214 | 4.6 | 36.8 |
| Sep | 2,184 | 14 | 2,192 | 2,167 | 0.7 | 21.6 |
| Dec | 2,158 | 10 | 2,163 | 2,140 | 1.0 | 15.8 |
| MAR1 | 2,125 | 9 | 2,135 | 2,122 | 0.6 | 15.3 |
| MAY1 | 2,120 | 8 | | | 0.3 | 3.1 |
| Total | | | | | 12.4 | 155.1 |

### ■ COCOA NYBOT (10 tonnes: $/tonne)

| | Sett price | Day's chge | High | Low | Vol 000s | O int 000s |
|---|---|---|---|---|---|---|
| May | 2,895 | 22 | 2,935 | 2,857 | 6.5 | 52.9 |
| Jul | 2,919 | 20 | 2,956 | 2,891 | 2.5 | 33.4 |
| Sep | 2,941 | 20 | 2,976 | 2,915 | 1.1 | 14.0 |
| Dec | 2,968 | 19 | 3,007 | 2,945 | 0.6 | 9.3 |
| MAR1 | 2,984 | 16 | 3,022 | 2,981 | 0.3 | 12.2 |
| MAY1 | 2,989 | 16 | 3,026 | 3,001 | 0.3 | 5.2 |
| Total | | | | | 11.2 | 131.3 |

### ■ COCOA ICCO (SDR's/Tonne)

| | Price | Prev.day |
|---|---|---|
| Mar 22 | 2,038.40 | |
| Daily | 2,038.40 | 2,007.34 |

### ■ COFFEE NYSE LIFFE (10 tonnes: $/tonne)

| | Sett price | Day's chge | High | Low | Vol 000s | O int 000s |
|---|---|---|---|---|---|---|
| Mar | 1,255 | 14 | 1,262 | 1,251 | 0.0 | 0.1 |
| May | 1,287 | 14 | 1,297 | 1,265 | 5.9 | 55.1 |
| Total | | | | | 8.2 | 93.1 |

### ■ COFFEE 'C' NYBOT (37,500lbs: cents/lbs)

| May | 134.75 | 1.75 | 135.00 | 132.40 | 10.5 | 72.2 |
|---|---|---|---|---|---|---|
| Jul | 136.35 | 1.65 | 136.45 | 134.10 | 3.7 | 23.5 |

## MEAT & LIVESTOCK

### ■ LIVE CATTLE CME (40,000lbs: cents/lbs)

| | Sett price | Day's chge | High | Low | Vol 000s | O int 000s |
|---|---|---|---|---|---|---|
| Apr | 95.700 | -1.400 | 97.300 | 95.250 | 14.4 | 64.4 |
| Jun | 92.375 | -1.700 | 94.675 | 92.325 | 22.3 | 163.4 |
| Aug | 89.875 | -1.425 | 91.825 | 89.725 | 7.2 | 70.5 |
| Oct | 91.950 | -1.125 | 93.475 | 91.700 | 3.3 | 33.4 |
| Total | | | | | 50.0 | 361.6 |

### ■ LEAN HOGS CME (40,000lbs: cents/lbs)

| Apr | 71.925 | -1.175 | 73.350 | 71.600 | 6.3 | 31.0 |
|---|---|---|---|---|---|---|
| Jun | 79.225 | -0.625 | 80.150 | 78.675 | 7.4 | 6.1 |
| Jun | 82.050 | -0.800 | 83.200 | 81.775 | 7.4 | 78.3 |
| Jul | 82.700 | -0.450 | 83.550 | 82.300 | 2.8 | 27.7 |
| Total | | | | | 19.6 | 203.0 |

### ■ PORK BELLIES CME (40,000lbs: cents/lbs)

| Mar | 94.500 | 3.000 | 94.500 | 93.250 | 0.0 | 0.0 |
|---|---|---|---|---|---|---|
| May | 96.150 | 3.000 | 96.150 | 93.000 | 0.0 | 0.2 |
| Jul | 96.950 | 1.050 | 96.950 | 95.300 | 0.0 | 0.1 |
| Aug | 88.000 | 0.000 | 91.000 | 0.000 | 0.0 | 0.3 |
| Total | | | | | 0.0 | 0.3 |

### ■ FEEDER CATTLE CME (40,000lbs: cents/lbs)

| Mar | 105.375 | 0.675 | 105.550 | 104.550 | 0.7 | 2.8 |
|---|---|---|---|---|---|---|
| Apr | 107.050 | -0.400 | 108.275 | 106.650 | 1.2 | 8.3 |
| May | 108.750 | -0.550 | 109.875 | 108.275 | 2.4 | 16.9 |
| Aug | 109.550 | -0.850 | 110.750 | 109.200 | 1.0 | 10.9 |
| Total | | | | | 5.5 | 41.6 |

## SPOT MARKETS

### ■ CRUDE OIL FOB (per barrel) + or -

| Dubai | $78.52-78.54 | $78.52-78.54 | +0.3 |
|---|---|---|---|

Source: *Financial Times*. © The Financial Times Limited 2010.

**Figure 20.10** Data on futures contracts, Tuesday 23 March 2010

## 20.5 Hedging with Swap Contracts

As the name suggests, a **swap contract** is an agreement by two parties to exchange, or swap, specified cash flows at specified intervals. Swaps are a recent innovation; they were first introduced to the public in 1981 when IBM and the World Bank entered into a swap agreement. The market for swaps has grown tremendously since that time.

> **swap contract**
> An agreement by two parties to exchange, or swap, specified cash flows at specified intervals in the future.

A swap contract is really just a portfolio, or series, of forward contracts. Recall that, with a forward contract, one party promises to exchange an asset (such as bushels of wheat) for another asset (cash) on a specific future date. With a swap, the only difference is that there are multiple exchanges instead of just one. In principle, a swap contract could be tailored to exchange just about anything. In practice, most swap contracts fall into one of three basic categories: currency swaps, interest rate swaps, and commodity swaps. Other types will surely develop, but we shall concentrate on just these three.

### Currency Swaps

With a *currency swap*, two parties agree to exchange a specific amount of one currency for a specific amount of another at specific dates in the future. For example, suppose a US firm has a German subsidiary and wishes to obtain debt financing for an expansion of the subsidiary's operations. Because most of the subsidiary's cash flows are in euros, the company would like the subsidiary to borrow and make payments in euros, thereby hedging against changes in the euro–dollar exchange rate. Unfortunately, the company has good access to US debt markets but not to German debt markets.

At the same time, a German firm would like to obtain US dollar financing. It can borrow cheaply in euros, but not in dollars. Both firms face a similar problem. They can borrow at favourable rates – but not in the desired currency. A currency swap is a solution. These two firms simply agree to exchange dollars for euros at a fixed rate at specific future dates (the payment dates on the loans). Each firm thus obtains the best possible rate, and then arranges to eliminate exposure to exchange rate changes by agreeing to exchange currencies – a neat solution.

### Interest Rate Swaps

Imagine a firm that wishes to obtain a fixed-rate loan, but can get a good deal on only a floating-rate loan – that is, a loan for which the payments are adjusted periodically to reflect changes in interest rates. Another firm can obtain a fixed-rate loan, but wishes to obtain the lowest possible interest rate: it is therefore willing to take a floating-rate loan. (Rates on floating-rate loans are generally lower than rates on fixed-rate loans. Why?) Both firms could accomplish their objectives by agreeing to exchange loan payments: in other words, the two firms would make each other's loan payments. This is an example of an *interest rate swap*; what is really being exchanged is a floating interest rate for a fixed one.

Interest rate swaps and currency swaps are often combined. One firm obtains floating-rate financing in a particular currency and swaps it for fixed-rate financing in another currency. Also, note that payments on floating-rate loans are always based on some index, such as the one-year Treasury rate. An interest rate swap might involve exchanging one floating-rate loan for another as a way of changing the underlying index.

## Commodity Swaps

As the name suggests, a *commodity swap* is an agreement to exchange a fixed quantity of a commodity at fixed times in the future. For example, airlines hedge fuel costs using jet fuel swaps. Commodity swaps are the newest type of swap, and the market for them is small relative to that for other types. The potential for growth is enormous, however.

Swap contracts for oil have been engineered. For example, say that an oil user has a need for 20,000 barrels every quarter. The oil user could enter into a swap contract with an oil producer to supply the needed oil. What price would they agree on? As we mentioned previously, they can't fix a price for ever. Instead, they could agree that the price would be equal to the *average* daily oil price from the previous 90 days. As a result of their using an average price, the impact of the relatively large daily price fluctuations in the oil market would be reduced, and both firms would benefit from a reduction in transactions exposure.

## The Swap Dealer

Unlike futures contracts, swap contracts are not traded on organized exchanges. The main reason is that they are not sufficiently standardized. Instead, the *swap dealer* plays a key role in the swaps market. In the absence of a swap dealer, a firm that wished to enter into a swap would have to track down another firm that wanted the opposite end of the deal. This search would probably be expensive and time-consuming.

Instead, a firm wishing to enter into a swap agreement contacts a swap dealer, and the swap dealer takes the other side of the agreement. The swap dealer will then try to find an offsetting transaction with some other party or parties (perhaps another firm or another dealer). Failing this, a swap dealer will hedge its exposure using futures contracts.

Banks are the dominant swap dealers in Europe. As a large swap dealer, a bank would be involved in a variety of contracts. It would be swapping fixed-rate loans for floating-rate loans with some parties, and doing just the opposite with other participants. The total collection of contracts in which a dealer is involved is called the swap *book*. The dealer will try to keep a balanced book to limit its net exposure. A balanced book is often called a *matched* book.

## Interest Rate Swaps: An Example

To get a better understanding of swap contracts and the role of the swap dealer, we consider a floating-for-fixed interest rate swap. Suppose Company A can borrow at a floating rate equal to EURIBOR plus 1 per cent, or at a fixed rate of 10 per cent. Company B can borrow at a floating rate of EURIBOR plus 2 per cent, or at a fixed rate of 9.5 per cent. Company A desires a fixed-rate loan, whereas Company B desires a floating-rate loan. Clearly, a swap is in order.

Company A contacts a swap dealer, and a deal is struck. Company A borrows the money at a rate of EURIBOR plus 1 per cent. The swap dealer agrees to cover the loan payments; in exchange, the company agrees to make fixed-rate payments to the swap dealer at a rate of, say, 9.75 per cent. Notice that the swap dealer is making floating-rate payments and receiving fixed-rate payments. The company is making fixed-rate payments, so it has swapped a floating payment for a fixed one.

Company B also contacts a swap dealer. The deal here calls for Company B to borrow the money at a fixed rate of 9.5 per cent. The swap dealer agrees to cover the fixed loan payments, and the company agrees to make floating-rate payments to the swap dealer at a rate of EURIBOR plus, say, 1.5 per cent. In this second arrangement the swap dealer is making fixed-rate payments and receiving floating-rate payments.

What's the net effect of these machinations? First, Company A gets a fixed-rate loan at a rate of 9.75 per cent, which is cheaper than the 10 per cent rate it can obtain on its own. Second, Company B gets a floating-rate loan at EURIBOR plus 1.5 instead of EURIBOR plus 2. The swap benefits both companies.

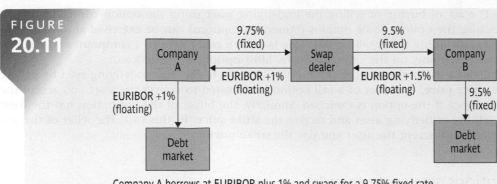

Company A borrows at EURIBOR plus 1% and swaps for a 9.75% fixed rate.
Company B borrows at 9.5% fixed and swaps for a EURIBOR plus 1.5% floating rate.

**Figure 20.11** Illustration of an interest rate swap

The swap dealer also wins. When all the dust settles, the swap dealer receives (from Company A) fixed-rate payments at a rate of 9.75 per cent and makes fixed-rate payments (for Company B) at a rate of 9.5 per cent. At the same time, it makes floating-rate payments (for Company A) at a rate of EURIBOR plus 1 per cent and receives floating-rate payments at a rate of EURIBOR plus 1.5 per cent (from Company B). Notice that the swap dealer's book is perfectly balanced in terms of risk, and it has no exposure to interest rate volatility.

Figure 20.11 illustrates the transactions in our interest rate swap. Note that the essence of the swap transactions is that one company swaps a fixed payment for a floating payment, while the other exchanges a floating payment for a fixed one. The swap dealer acts as an intermediary, and profits from the spread between the rates it charges and the rates it receives.

| CONCEPT QUESTIONS | 20.5a | What is a swap contract? Describe three types. |
| | 20.5b | Describe the role of the swap dealer. |
| | 20.5c | Explain the cash flows in Fig. 20.11. |

# 20.6 Hedging with Option Contracts

The contracts we have discussed thus far – forwards, futures, and swaps – are conceptually similar. In each case, two parties agree to transact on a future date or dates. The key is that both parties are obligated to complete the transaction.

In contrast, an **option contract** is an agreement that gives the owner the right, but not the obligation, to buy or sell (depending on the option type) some asset at a specified price for a specified time. Options are covered in detail elsewhere in our book. Here we shall only quickly discuss some option basics, and then focus on using options to hedge volatility in commodity prices, interest rates and exchange rates. In doing so we shall sidestep a wealth of detail concerning option terminology, option trading strategies and option valuation.

## Option Terminology

Options come in two flavours: puts and calls. The owner of a **call option** has the right, but not the obligation, to *buy* an underlying asset at a fixed price, called the *strike price* or *exercise price*, for a specified time. The owner of a **put option** has the right, but not the obligation, to *sell* an underlying asset at a fixed price for a specified time.

**option contract**
An agreement that gives the owner the right, but not the obligation, to buy or sell a specific asset at a specific price for a set period of time.

**call option**
An option that gives the owner the right, but not the obligation, to buy an asset.

**put option**
An option that gives the owner the right, but not the obligation, to sell an asset.

The act of buying or selling the underlying asset using the option contract is called *exercising* the option. Some options ('American' options) can be exercised at any time up to and including the *expiration date* (the last day); other options ('European' options) can be exercised only on the expiration date. Most options are American.

Because the buyer of a call option has the right to buy the underlying asset by paying the strike price, the seller of a call option is obligated to deliver the asset and accept the strike price if the option is exercised. Similarly, the buyer of the put option has the right to sell the underlying asset and receive the strike price. In this case, the seller of the put option must accept the asset and pay the strike price.

## Options versus Forwards

There are two key differences between an option contract and a forward contract. The first is obvious. With a forward contract, both parties are obligated to transact; one party delivers the asset, and the other party pays for it. With an option, the transaction occurs only if the owner of the option chooses to exercise it.

The second difference between an option and a forward contract is that no money changes hands when a forward contract is created, but the buyer of an option contract gains a valuable right and must pay the seller for that right. The price of the option is frequently called the *option premium*.

## Option Pay-Off Profiles

Figure 20.12 shows the general pay-off profile for a call option from the owner's viewpoint. The horizontal axis shows the difference between the asset's value and the strike price on the option ($\Delta P$). As illustrated, if the price of the underlying asset rises above the strike price, then the owner of the option will exercise the option and enjoy a profit ($\Delta V$). If the value

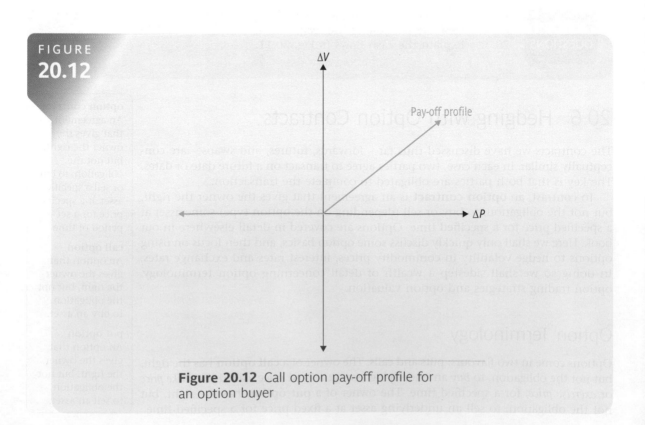

**FIGURE 20.12**

**Figure 20.12** Call option pay-off profile for an option buyer

of the asset falls below the strike price, the owner of the option will not exercise it. Notice that this pay-off profile does not consider the premium that the buyer paid for the option.

The pay-off profile that results from buying a call is repeated in Part A of Fig. 20.13. Part B shows the pay-off profile on a call option from the seller's side. A call option is a zero-sum game, so the seller's pay-off profile is exactly the opposite of the buyer's.

Part C of Fig. 20.13 shows the pay-off profile for the buyer of a put option. In this case, if the asset's value falls below the strike price, then the buyer profits because the seller of the put must pay the strike price. Part D shows that the seller of the put option loses out when the price falls below the strike price.

## Option Hedging

Suppose a firm has a risk profile that looks like the one in Part A of Fig. 20.14. If the firm wishes to hedge against adverse price movements using options, what should it do? Examining the different pay-off profiles in Fig. 20.13, we see that the one that has the desirable shape is C, buying a put. If the firm buys a put, then its net exposure is as illustrated in Part B of Fig. 20.14.

In this case, by buying a put option, the firm has eliminated the downside risk – that is, the risk of an adverse price movement. However, the firm has retained the upside

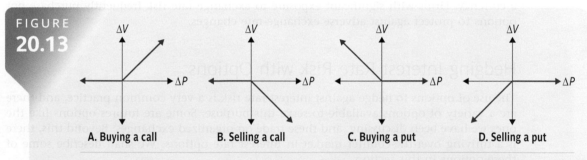

**FIGURE 20.13**

A. Buying a call    B. Selling a call    C. Buying a put    D. Selling a put

**Figure 20.13** Option pay-off profiles

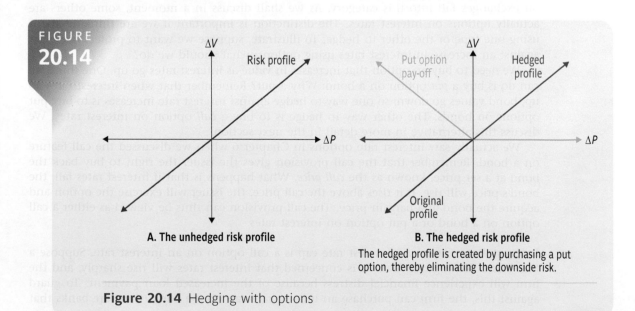

**FIGURE 20.14**

Risk profile    Put option pay-off    Hedged profile

Original profile

A. The unhedged risk profile    B. The hedged risk profile

The hedged profile is created by purchasing a put option, thereby eliminating the downside risk.

**Figure 20.14** Hedging with options

potential. In other words, the put option acts as a kind of insurance policy. Remember that this desirable insurance is not free: the firm pays for it when it buys the put option.

## Hedging Commodity Price Risk with Options

We saw earlier that futures contracts are available for a variety of basic commodities. In addition, an increasing number of options are available on these same commodities. In fact, the options that are typically traded on commodities are actually options on futures contracts: for this reason, they are called *futures options*.

These work as follows. When a futures call option on, for example, wheat is exercised, the owner of the option receives two things. The first is a futures contract on wheat at the current futures price. This contract can be immediately closed at no cost. The second thing the owner of the option receives is the difference between the strike price on the option and the current futures price. The difference is simply paid in cash.

## Hedging Exchange Rate Risk with Options

Futures options are available on foreign currencies as well as on commodities. These work in exactly the same way as commodities futures options. In addition, there are other traded options for which the underlying asset is just currency rather than a futures contract on a currency. Firms with significant exposure to exchange rate risk frequently purchase put options to protect against adverse exchange rate changes.

## Hedging Interest Rate Risk with Options

The use of options to hedge against interest rate risk is a very common practice, and there are a variety of options available to serve this purpose. Some are futures options like the ones we have been discussing, and these trade on organized exchanges. Beyond this, there is a thriving over-the-counter market in interest rate options. We shall describe some of these options in this section.

**A Preliminary Note**   Some interest rate options are actually options on interest-bearing assets such as bonds (or on futures contracts for bonds). Most of the options that are traded on exchanges fall into this category. As we shall discuss in a moment, some others are actually options on interest rates. The distinction is important if we are thinking about using one type or the other to hedge. To illustrate, suppose we want to protect ourselves against an increase in interest rates using options: what should we do?

We need to buy an option that increases in value as interest rates go up. One thing we can do is buy a *put* option on a bond. Why a put? Remember that when interest rates go up, bond values go down; so one way to hedge against interest rate increases is to buy put options on bonds. The other way to hedge is to buy a *call* option on interest rates. We discuss this alternative in more detail in the next section.

We actually saw interest rate options in Chapter 6 when we discussed the call feature on a bond. Remember that the call provision gives the issuer the right to buy back the bond at a set price, known as the *call price*. What happens is that if interest rates fall, the bond's price will rise. If it rises above the call price, the issuer will exercise the option and acquire the bond at a bargain price. The call provision can thus be viewed as either a call option on a bond or a put option on interest rates.

**Interest Rate Caps**   An interest rate cap is a call option on an interest rate. Suppose a firm has a floating-rate loan. It is concerned that interest rates will rise sharply, and the firm will experience financial distress because of the increased loan payment. To guard against this, the firm can purchase an interest rate cap from a bank (there are banks that specialize in such products). What will happen is that if the loan payment ever rises above an agreed-upon limit (the 'ceiling'), the bank will pay the difference between the actual payment and the ceiling to the firm in cash.

A *floor* is a put option on an interest rate. If a firm buys a cap and sells a floor, the result is a *collar*. By selling the put and buying the call, the firm protects itself against increases in interest rates beyond the ceiling by the cap. However, if interest rates drop below the floor, the put will be exercised against the firm. The result is that the rate the firm pays will not drop below the floor rate. In other words, the rate the firm pays will always be between the floor and the ceiling.

**Other Interest Rate Options**    We shall close our chapter by briefly mentioning two relatively new types of interest rate option. Suppose a firm has a floating-rate loan. The firm is comfortable with its floating-rate loan, but it would like to have the right to convert it to a fixed-rate loan in the future.

What can the firm do? What it wants is the right, but not the obligation, to swap its floating-rate loan for a fixed-rate loan. In other words, the firm needs to buy an option on a swap. Swap options exist, and they have the charming name *swaptions*.

We've seen that there are options on futures contracts and options on swap contracts, but what about options on options? Such options are called *compound* options. As we have just discussed, a cap is a call option on interest rates. Suppose a firm thinks that, depending on interest rates, it might like to buy a cap in the future. As you can probably guess, in this case what the firm might want to do today is buy an option on a cap. Inevitably, it seems, an option on a cap is called a *caption*, and there is a large market for these instruments.

## Financial Risk Management in Practice

Because the true extent of derivatives does not usually appear in financial statements, it is much more difficult to observe the use of derivatives by firms compared with, say, bank debt. Much of our knowledge of corporate derivative use comes from academic surveys. Most surveys report that the use of derivatives appears to vary widely among large, publicly traded firms. Large firms are far more likely to use derivatives than are small firms. Table 20.1 shows that for firms that use derivatives, foreign currency and interest rate derivatives are the most frequently used.

The prevailing view is that derivatives can be very helpful in reducing the variability of corporate cash flows, which in turn reduces the various costs associated with financial distress. Therefore it is somewhat puzzling that large firms use derivatives more often than small firms – because large firms tend to have less cash flow variability than small firms. Also, some surveys report that firms occasionally use derivatives when they want to speculate about future prices and not just to hedge risks. However, most of the evidence is consistent with the theory that derivatives are most frequently used by firms where financial distress costs are high and access to the capital markets is constrained.

By far the most common tool used by firms to manage risk is the forward contract, customized to the specific requirements of the business. Table 20.2 presents the main concerns of companies in using derivatives to manage risk. The most important issue is their effectiveness in managing risk, followed by the additional risks associated with derivative use. Transaction costs are also regarded as important.

| | |
|---|---|
| **CONCEPT QUESTIONS** | 20.6a  Suppose that the unhedged risk profile in Fig. 20.14 sloped down instead of up. What option-based hedging strategy would be suitable in this case? |
| | 20.6b  What is a futures option? |
| | 20.6c  What is a caption? Who might want to buy one? |

TABLE
20.1

| Companies that use derivatives (%) | | | |
| --- | --- | --- | --- |
| | Overall | Under $1 billion | Over $1 billion |
| December 2005 | 68 | 53 | 83 |
| December 2004 | 74 | 67 | 83 |

| Do you use derivatives to manage ...? (%) | | | |
| --- | --- | --- | --- |
| | Overall | Under $1 billion | Over $1 billion |
| Short-term assets | 55 | 35 | 68 |
| Long-term assets | 29 | 17 | 37 |
| Short-term liabilities | 59 | 54 | 63 |
| Long-term liabilities | 61 | 67 | 57 |

| In which asset classes do you use derivatives? (%) | | | | |
| --- | --- | --- | --- | --- |
| | Overall | | Over $1 billion | |
| | 2005 | 2004 | 2005 | 2004 |
| Interest rates | 70 | 73 | 77 | 76 |
| Currencies | 67 | 54 | 80 | 68 |
| Credit | 9 | 7 | 12 | 13 |
| Energy | 17 | 10 | 21 | 11 |
| Commodities | 20 | 11 | 30 | 13 |
| Equities | 7 | 12 | 10 | 16 |

*Source*: Adapted from *Treasury & Risk Management* (December/January 2006). Results are based on a survey of 190 financial executives. In the sample, 30 per cent of the companies had revenues under $500 million, 18 per cent were between $500 million and $1 billion, 33 per cent were between $1 billion and $5 billion, and 19 per cent had revenues over $5 billion.

**Table 20.1** Derivative usage: survey results

TABLE
20.2

| Issues of concern to risk managers | UK (%) | US (%) | Asia (%) |
| --- | --- | --- | --- |
| Board approval | 16 | 9 | 18 |
| Compliance with accounting and disclosure requirements | 17 | 21 | 10 |
| Associated risks of derivative use | 17 | 15 | 17 |
| Effectiveness in managing risk | 24 | 26 | 22 |
| Ease of use | 10 | 11 | 13 |
| Transaction costs | 14 | 17 | 18 |
| Other issues | 2 | 1 | 2 |
| Total | 100 | 100 | 100 |

*Source*: F. M. Lee, A. Marshall, Y. K. Sztoo, and J. Tang (2001), 'The practice of financial risk management: an international comparison', *Thunderbird International Business Review*, vol. 43, no. 3, pp. 365–375.

**Table 20.2** Main concerns in using derivatives to manage risk

# Summary and Conclusions

This chapter has introduced some of the basic principles of financial risk management. The motivation for risk management stems from the fact that a firm will frequently have an undesirable exposure to some type of risk. This is particularly true today because of the increased volatility in key financial variables such as interest rates, exchange rates and commodity prices. We describe a firm's exposure to a particular risk with a risk profile. The goal of financial risk management is to alter the firm's risk profile through buying and selling derivative assets such as futures contracts, swap contracts and options contracts. By finding instruments with appropriate pay-off profiles, a firm can reduce or even eliminate its exposure to many types of risk.

Hedging cannot change the fundamental economic reality of a business. What it can do is allow a firm to avoid expensive and troublesome disruptions that might otherwise result from short-run, temporary price fluctuations. Hedging also gives a firm time to react and adapt to changing market conditions. Because of the price volatility and rapid economic change that characterize modern business, dealing intelligently with volatility has become an increasingly important task for financial managers.

Many other option types are available in addition to those we have discussed, and more are created every day. One very important aspect of financial risk management that we have not discussed is that options, forwards, futures and swaps can be combined in a wide variety of ways to create new instruments. These basic contract types are really just the building blocks used by financial engineers to create new and innovative products for corporate risk management.

# Chapter Review and Self-Test Problems

**20.1** **Futures Contracts** Suppose Golden Grain Farms (GGF) expects to harvest 50,000 bushels of wheat in September. GGF is concerned about the possibility of price fluctuations between now and September. The futures price for September wheat is £2 per bushel, and the relevant contract calls for 5,000 bushels. What action should GGF take to lock in the £2 price? Suppose the price of wheat actually turns out to be £3. Evaluate GGF's gains and losses. Do the same for a price of £1. Ignore marking to market.

**20.2** **Options Contracts** In the previous question, suppose that September futures put options with a strike price of £2 per bushel cost £0.15 per bushel. Assuming that GGF hedges using put options, evaluate its gains and losses for wheat prices of £1, £2 and £3.

# Answers to Chapter Review and Self-Test Problems

**20.1** GGF wants to deliver wheat and receive a fixed price, so it needs to sell futures contracts. Each contract calls for delivery of 5,000 bushels, so GGF needs to sell 10 contracts. No money changes hands today.

If wheat prices actually turn out to be £3, then GGF will receive £150,000 for its crop; but it will have a loss of £50,000 on its futures position when it closes that position, because the contracts require it to sell 50,000 bushels of wheat at £2, when the going price is £3. It thus nets £100,000 overall.

If wheat prices turn out to be £1 per bushel, then the crop will be worth only £50,000. However, GGF will have a profit of £50,000 on its futures position, so GGF again nets £100,000.

20.2  If GGF wants to insure against a price decline only, it can buy 10 put contracts. Each contract is for 5,000 bushels, so the cost per contract is $5,000 \times £0.15 = £750$. For 10 contracts, the cost will be £7,500.

   If wheat prices turn out to be £3, then GGF will not exercise the put options (why not?). Its crop is worth £150,000, but the £7,500 cost of the options has already been incurred, so it nets £142,500.

   If wheat prices fall to £1, the crop is worth £50,000. GGF will exercise its puts (why?) and thereby force the seller of the puts to pay £2 per bushel. GGF receives a total of £100,000. If we subtract the cost of the puts, we see that GGF's net is £92,500. In fact, verify that its net at any price of £2 or lower is £92,500.

# Concepts Review and Critical Thinking Questions

1  **Hedging Strategies [LO1]**  If a firm is selling futures contracts on timber as a hedging strategy, what must be true about the firm's exposure to timber prices?

2  **Hedging Strategies [LO1]**  If a firm is buying call options on pork belly futures as a hedging strategy, what must be true about the firm's exposure to pork belly prices?

3  **Forwards and Futures [LO2]**  What is the difference between a forward contract and a futures contract? Why do you think that futures contracts are much more common? Are there any circumstances under which you might prefer to use forwards instead of futures? Explain.

4  **Hedging Commodities [LO1]**  Bubbling Crude plc, a large oil producer based in Aberdeen, would like to hedge against adverse movements in the price of oil, because this is the firm's primary source of revenue. What should the firm do? Provide at least two reasons why it probably will not be possible to achieve a completely flat risk profile with respect to oil prices.

5  **Sources of Risk [LO1]**  A company produces an energy-intensive product, and uses natural gas as the energy source. The competition uses primarily oil. Explain why this company is exposed to fluctuations in both oil and natural gas prices.

6  **Hedging Commodities [LO1]**  If a textile manufacturer wanted to hedge against adverse movements in cotton prices, it could buy cotton futures contracts or buy call options on cotton futures contracts. What would be the pros and cons of the two approaches?

7  **Options [LO4]**  Explain why a put option on a bond is conceptually the same as a call option on interest rates.

8  **Hedging Interest Rates [LO1]**  A company has a large bond issue maturing in one year. When it matures, the company will float a new issue. Current interest rates are attractive, and the company is concerned that rates next year will be higher. What are some hedging strategies that the company might use in this case?

9  **Swaps [LO3]**  Explain why a swap is effectively a series of forward contracts. Suppose a firm enters into a swap agreement with a swap dealer. Describe the nature of the default risk faced by both parties.

10  **Swaps [LO3]**  Suppose a firm enters into a fixed-for-floating interest rate swap with a swap dealer. Describe the cash flows that will occur as a result of the swap.

11  **Transaction versus Economic Exposure [LO1]**  What is the difference between transactions and economic exposure? Which can be hedged more easily? Why?

12  **Hedging Exchange Rate Risk [LO2]**  If a Dutch company exports its goods to the UK, how would it use a futures contract on sterling to hedge its exchange rate risk? Would it buy or sell sterling futures? Does the way the exchange rate is quoted in the futures contract matter?

13 **Hedging Strategies [LO1]** For the following scenarios, describe a hedging strategy using futures contracts that might be considered. If you think that a cross-hedge would be appropriate, discuss the reasons for your choice of contract.

(a) A public utility is concerned about rising costs.

(b) A chocolate manufacturer is concerned about rising costs.

(c) A corn farmer fears that this year's harvest will be at record high levels across the country.

(d) A manufacturer of photographic film is concerned about rising costs.

(e) A natural gas producer believes there will be excess supply in the market this year.

(f) A bank derives all its income from long-term, fixed-rate residential mortgages.

(g) An equity mutual fund invests in large, blue-chip equities and is concerned about a decline in the stock market.

(h) A Spanish importer of Swiss army knives will pay for its order in six months in Swiss francs.

(i) A Norwegian exporter of construction equipment has agreed to sell some cranes to a German construction firm. The Norwegian firm will be paid in euros in three months.

14 **Swaps [LO3]** Syco SA, a distributor of food and food-related products, has announced it has signed an interest rate swap. The interest rate swap effectively converts the company's €100 million, 4.6 per cent interest rate bonds for a variable rate payment, which is the six-month EURIBOR minus 0.52 per cent. Why would Syco use a swap agreement? In other words, why didn't Syco just go ahead and issue floating-rate bonds, because the net effect of issuing fixed-rate bonds and then doing a swap is to create a variable-rate bond?

# connect Questions and Problems

**BASIC**

**1 – 3**

1 **Futures Quotes [LO2]** Refer to Fig. 20.10 in the text to answer this question. Suppose you purchase a June 2010 Live Cattle futures contract on 24 March 2010, at the last price of the day. What will your profit or loss be if Live Cattle prices turn out to be $0.80 per lb at expiration?

2 **Futures Quotes [LO2]** Refer to Figure 20.10 in the text to answer this question. Suppose you sell five April 2010 copper futures contracts on 24 March 2010 at the last price of the day. What will your profit or loss be if copper prices turn out to be $350 at expiration? What if copper prices are $300 at expiration?

3 **Put and Call Pay-offs [LO4]** Suppose a financial manager buys call options on 50,000 barrels of oil with an exercise price of $140 per barrel. She simultaneously sells a put option on 50,000 barrels of oil with the same exercise price of $140 per barrel. Consider her gains and losses if oil prices are $135, $137, $140, $143 and $145. What do you notice about the pay-off profile?

**INTERMEDIATE**

**4 – 5**

4 **Hedging with Futures [LO2]** Refer to Fig. 20.10 in the text to answer this question. Suppose today is 24 March 2010, and your firm produces chocolate and needs 75,000 tonnes of cocoa in July 2010 for an upcoming promotion. You would like to lock in your costs today, because you are concerned that cocoa prices might go up between now and July.

(a) How could you use cocoa futures contracts to hedge your risk exposure? What price would you effectively be locking in, based on the closing price of the day?

(b) Suppose cocoa prices are £1,764 per contract in July. What is the profit or loss on your futures position? Explain how your futures position has eliminated your exposure to price risk in the cocoa market.

5 **Interest Rate Swaps [LO3]** ABC Company and XYZ Company need to raise funds to pay for capital improvements at their manufacturing plants. ABC Company is a well-established firm with an excellent credit rating in the debt market; it can borrow funds either at 11 per cent fixed rate or at EURIBOR +1 per cent floating rate. XYZ Company is a fledgling start-up firm without a strong credit history. It can borrow funds either at 10 per cent fixed rate or at EURIBOR +3 per cent floating rate.

(a) Is there an opportunity here for ABC and XYZ to benefit by means of an interest rate swap?

(b) Suppose you've just been hired at a bank that acts as a dealer in the swaps market, and your boss has shown you the borrowing rate information for your clients ABC and XYZ. Describe how you could bring these two companies together in an interest rate swap that would make both firms better off while netting your bank a 2.0 per cent profit.

**CHALLENGE 6**

6 **Financial Engineering [LO2, LO4]** Suppose there were call options and forward contracts available on coal, but no put options. Show how a financial engineer could synthesize a put option using the available contracts. What does your answer tell you about the general relationship between puts, calls and forwards?

## MINI CASE McAfee Mortgages Ltd

Jennifer McAfee recently received her university Masters degree, and has decided to enter the mortgage brokerage business. Rather than work for someone else, she has decided to open her own shop. Her cousin Finn has approached her about a mortgage for a house he is building. The house will be completed in three months, and he will need the mortgage at that time. Finn wants a 25-year, fixed-rate mortgage for the amount of £500,000 with monthly payments.

Jennifer has agreed to lend Finn the money in three months at the current market rate of 8 per cent. Because Jennifer is just starting out, she does not have £500,000 available for the loan, so she approaches Ian MacDuff, the president of IM Insurance, about purchasing the mortgage from her in three months. Ian has agreed to purchase the mortgage in three months, but he is unwilling to set a price on the mortgage. Instead, he has agreed in writing to purchase the mortgage at the market rate in three months. There are Treasury bond futures contracts available for delivery in three months. A Treasury bond contract is for £100,000 in face value of Treasury bonds.

1 What is the monthly mortgage payment on Finn's mortgage?

2 What is the most significant risk Jennifer faces in this deal?

3 How can Jennifer hedge this risk?

4 Suppose that in the next three months the market rate of interest rises to 9 per cent.

(a) How much will Ian be willing to pay for the mortgage?

(b) What will happen to the value of Treasury bond futures contracts? Will the long or short position increase in value?

5 Suppose that in the next three months the market rate of interest falls to 7 per cent.

(a) How much will Ian be willing to pay for the mortgage?

(b) What will happen to the value of T-bond futures contracts? Will the long or short position increase in value?

6 Are there any possible risks Jennifer faces in using Treasury bond futures contracts to hedge her interest rate risk?

# HAPTER

# 21

# Options and Corporate Finance

## KEY NOTATIONS

| | |
|---|---|
| C | Call price |
| N(d) | Probability that a standardized, normally distributed, random variable will be less than or equal to d |
| P | Put price |
| PV(E) | Present value of exercise price |
| $R_f$ | Risk-free rate of return |
| S | Equity or share price |
| t | Time (in years) to expiration date |
| $\sigma^2$ | Variance (per year) of the continuous share price return |

## LEARNING OBJECTIVES

After studying this chapter, you should understand:

LO1 The basics of call and put options, and how to calculate their pay-offs and profits.

LO2 The factors that affect option values, and how to price call and put options using no arbitrage conditions.

LO3 The relationship between stock prices, call prices and put prices using put–call parity.

LO4 The famous Black–Scholes option pricing model and its uses.

LO5 The basics of employee stock options, and their benefits and disadvantages.

LO6 How to value a firm's equity as an option on the firm's assets.

LO7 How option valuation can be used to evaluate capital budgeting projects, including timing options, the option to expand, the option to abandon, and the option to contract.

---

IN 2009, MANY COMPANIES ANNOUNCED that they would exchange their employee share options for restricted stock units (RSUs). An RSU is a share of equity that can't be sold or exchanged until it is vested. The vesting period can vary, but is usually between three and five years. When an RSU vests, the employee receives a full share of equity. The biggest advantage of RSUs for employees is that they receive the equity no matter what the share price. With employee share options, on the other hand, the employee may receive nothing.

Employee share options are just one kind of option. This chapter introduces you to options, and explains their features and what determines their value. The chapter also shows you that options show up in many places in corporate finance. In fact, once you know what to look for, they show up just about everywhere, so understanding how they work is essential.

**option**
A contract that gives its owner the right to buy or sell some asset at a fixed price on or before a given date.

**exercising the option**
The act of buying or selling the underlying asset via the option contract.

**strike price**
The fixed price in the option contract at which the holder can buy or sell the underlying asset. Also, the *exercise price* or *striking price*.

**expiration date**
The last day on which an option may be exercised.

**American option**
An option that may be exercised at any time until its expiration date.

**European option**
An option that may be exercised only on the expiration date.

**call option**
The right to buy an asset at a fixed price during a particular period.

**put option**
The right to sell an asset at a fixed price during a particular period of time. The opposite of a call option.

Options are a part of everyday life. 'Keep your options open' is sound business advice, and 'We're out of options' is a sure sign of trouble. In Chapter 20 we showed that an **option** is an arrangement that gives its owner the right to buy or sell an asset at a fixed price any time on or before a given date. The most familiar options are equity options. These are options to buy and sell shares of equity, and we shall discuss them in some detail in the following pages.

Of course, equity options are not the only options. In fact, at the root of it, many different kinds of financial decision amount to the evaluation of options. For example, we shall show how understanding options adds several important details to the NPV analysis we have discussed in earlier chapters.

Also, virtually all corporate securities have implicit or explicit option features, and the use of such features is growing. As a result, understanding securities that possess option features requires a general knowledge of the factors that determine an option's value.

This chapter starts with a description of different types of option. We identify and discuss the general factors that determine option values, and show how ordinary debt and equity have option-like characteristics. We then examine employee share options, and the important role of options in capital budgeting. We conclude by illustrating how option features are incorporated into corporate securities by discussing warrants, convertible bonds, and other option-like securities.

# 21.1 Options: The Basics

An option is a contract giving its owner the right to buy or sell an asset at a fixed price on or before a given date. For example, an option on a building might give the buyer the right to buy the building for €1 million on or any time before the Saturday prior to the third Wednesday in January 2015. Options are a unique type of financial contract, because they give the buyer the right, but not the obligation, to do something. The buyer uses the option only if it is advantageous to do so; otherwise the option can be thrown away.

There is a special vocabulary associated with options. Here are some important definitions:

1　**Exercising the option**: The act of buying or selling the underlying asset via the option contract.

2　**Strike or exercise price**: The fixed price in the option contract at which the holder can buy or sell the underlying asset.

3　**Expiration date**: The maturity date of the option; after this date the option is dead.

4　**American** and **European options**: An American option may be exercised at any time up to the expiration date. A European option differs from an American option in that it can be exercised only on the expiration date.

## Puts and Calls

Options come in two basic types: puts and calls. A **call option** gives the owner the right to *buy* an asset at a fixed price during a particular time period. It may help you to remember that a call option gives you the right to 'call in' an asset.

A **put option** is essentially the opposite of a call option. Instead of giving the holder the right to buy some asset, it gives the holder the right to *sell* that asset for a fixed exercise price. If you buy a put option, you can force the seller of the option to buy the asset from you for a fixed price and thereby 'put it to them'.

What about an investor who *sells* a call option? The seller receives money up front and has the *obligation* to sell the asset at the exercise price if the option holder wants it. Similarly, an investor who *sells* a put option receives cash up front and is then obligated to buy the asset at the exercise price if the option holder demands it.

The asset involved in an option can be anything. The options that are most widely bought and sold, however, are equity options. These are options to buy and sell shares of equity. Because these are the best-known types of option, we shall study them first. As we discuss equity options, keep in mind that the general principles apply to options involving any asset, not just shares of equity.

## Option Quotations

Now that we understand the definitions for calls and puts, let's see how these options are quoted. Figure 21.1 presents information, obtained from the NYSE Euronext website (www.euronext.com), about Air France-KLM options expiring in June 2010. At the time of these quotes Air France-KLM was selling for €10.09.

There are three boxes in Figure 21.1. The first relates to the option contract, and it can be seen that Air France-KLM's option ticker is AFA, is denominated in euros, and is of American type (that is, it can be exercised before the expiration date). Each option contract relates to purchasing 100 shares. On 24 March 2010 the last transaction involved 84 contracts, and the total number of contracts outstanding on 23 March 2010 was 7,918.

The second box relates to the underlying asset, which is Air France-KLM equity. This is traded on Euronext Amsterdam and is denominated in euros. There were 332,171 shares traded in the equity on 24 March 2010 and the closing price was €10.09. Other price information, such as high and low price, is also presented.

The final box provides information on individual call and put contracts. The June 2010 €11.00, €11.50 and €12.00 call contracts were traded on 24 March 2010. Good news about the future expectations of Air France-KLM shares!

**FIGURE 21.1**

**Codes and classification**

| Code | AFA | Market | NYSE Liffe Amsterdam | Vol. | 84 | 24/03/10 |
|------|-----|--------|----------------------|------|-----|----------|
| Exercise type | American | Currency€ | | O.I. | 7,918 | 23/03/10 |

**Underlying**

| Name | AIR FRANCE -KLM | ISIN | FR0000031122 | | Market | Euronext Amsterdam |
|------|-----------------|------|--------------|---|--------|--------------------|
| Currency | € | | | | | |
| Time | CET | Last | 10.09 | 13/01/09 17:35 | Last change % | 2.44 |
| Volume | 332,171 | High | 10.19 | | Low | 10.00 |

**June 2010 Prices - 24/03/10**

| | | | | Calls | | | | Strike | | | | | | Puts | | | |
|---|---|---|---|---|---|---|---|---|---|---|---|---|---|---|---|---|---|
| Settl. | Day volume | Vol | Time (CET) | Last | Bid | Ask | C | | P | Bid | Ask | Last | Time (CET) | Vol | Day volume | Settl. |
| 1.70 | - | - | - | - | 1.55 | 1.65 | C | 10 | P | 0.20 | 0.30 | - | - | - | - | 0.23 |
| 0.98 | 5 | 5 | 09:18 | 0.90 | 0.85 | 0.95 | C | 11 | P | 0.50 | 0.60 | - | - | - | - | 0.53 |
| 0.70 | 12 | 12 | 09:23 | 0.70 | 0.60 | 0.65 | C | 11.5 | P | 0.75 | 0.85 | - | - | - | - | 0.73 |
| 0.48 | 58 | 58 | 13:18 | 0.40 | 0.40 | 0.50 | C | 12 | P | 1.05 | 1.15 | - | - | - | - | 1.03 |
| 0.22 | - | - | - | - | 0.17 | 0.20 | C | 13 | P | 1.80 | 1.90 | - | - | - | - | 1.75 |

*Note*: Settlement price is for the trading day 23/03/2010

**Figure 21.1** Information about the options of Air France-KLM Corporation

## Option Pay-Offs

Looking at Figure 21.1, suppose you buy 50 June €11.50 call contracts. The option is quoted to buy at €0.65 (the ask price) and to sell at €0.60 (the bid price). You wish to buy, so the contracts cost €65 each (a call contract is for 100 shares). You spend a total of 50 × €65 = €3,250. You wait a while, and the expiration date rolls around.

Now what? You have the right to buy Air France-KLM shares for €11.50 each. If Air France-KLM is selling for less than €11.50 a share, then this option isn't worth anything, and you throw it away. In this case we say that the option has expired 'out of the money', because the share price is less than the exercise price. Your €3,250 is, alas, a complete loss.

If Air France-KLM is selling for more than €11.50 per share, then you need to exercise your option. In this case the option is 'in the money', because the share price exceeds the exercise price.

Suppose Air France-KLM has risen to, say, €14.50 per share. Because you have the right to buy Air France-KLM at €11.50, you make a €3 profit on each share upon exercise. Each contract involves 100 shares, so you make €3 per share × 100 shares per contract = €300 per contract. Finally, you own 50 contracts, so the value of your options is a handsome €15,000. Notice that because you invested €3,250, your net profit is €11,750.

As our example indicates, the gains and losses from buying call options can be quite large. To illustrate further, suppose you simply purchase the equity with the €3,250 instead of buying call options. In this case, you will have about €3,250/€10.09 = 322.10 shares. We can now compare what you have when the option expires for different share prices:

| Ending share price (€) | Option value (50 contracts) (€) | Net profit or loss (50 contracts) (€) | Share value (322.10 shares) (€) | Net profit or loss (322.10 shares) (€) |
|---|---|---|---|---|
| 6 | 0 | −3,250 | 1,932.60 | −1,317.39 |
| 8 | 0 | −3,250 | 2,576.80 | −673.19 |
| 10 | 0 | −3,250 | 3,221.00 | −28.99 |
| 10.09 | 0 | −3,250 | 3,250.00 | 0.00 |
| 12 | 2,500 | −750 | 3,865.20 | 615.21 |
| 14 | 12,500 | 9,250 | 4,509.40 | 1,259.41 |
| 14.50 | 15,000 | 11,750 | 4,670.45 | 1,420.46 |

The option position clearly magnifies the gains and losses on the equity by a substantial amount. The reason is that the pay-off on your 50 option contracts is based on 50 × 100 = 5,000 shares of equity instead of just 322.10.

In our example, notice that, if the share price ends up below the exercise price, then you lose all €3,250 with the option. With the equity, you still have about what you started with. Also notice that the option can never be worth less than zero, because you can always just throw it away. As a result, you can never lose more than your original investment (the €3,250 in our example).

It is important to recognize that equity options are a zero-sum game. By this we mean that whatever the buyer of an equity option makes, the seller loses, and vice versa. To illustrate, suppose, in our example just preceding, you *sell* 50 option contracts. You receive €3,250 up front, and you will be obligated to sell the equity for €11.50 if the buyer of the option wishes to exercise it. In this situation, if the share price ends up below €11.50, you will be €3,250 ahead. If the share price ends up above €11.50, you will have to sell something for less than it is worth, so you will lose the difference. For example, if the share price is €14.50, you will have to sell 50 × 100 = 5,000 shares at €14.50 per share, so you will be out €14.50 − 11.50 = €3 per share, or €15,000 total. Because you received €3,250 up front, your net loss is €11,750. We can summarize some other possibilities as follows:

| Ending share price (€) | Net profit to option seller (€) |
|---|---|
| 6 | 3,250 |
| 8 | 3,250 |
| 10 | 3,250 |
| 10 | 3,250 |
| 12 | 750 |
| 14 | −9,250 |
| 15 | −11,750 |

Notice that the net profits to the option buyer (calculated previously) are just the opposites of these amounts.

## EXAMPLE 21.1

## Put Pay-offs

Looking at Figure 21.1, suppose you buy 10 Air France-KLM June €12 put contracts. How much does this cost (ignoring commissions)? Just before the option expires, Air France-KLM is selling for €10 per share. Is this good news or bad news? What is your net profit?

The option is quoted at €1.15, so one contract costs $100 \times €1.15 = €115$. Your 10 contracts total €1,150. You now have the right to sell 1,000 shares of Air France-KLM for €12 per share. If the share price is currently €10, then this is most definitely good news. You can buy 1,000 shares at €10 and sell them for €12. Your puts are thus worth $€12 - €10 = €2$ per share, or $€2 \times 1,000 = €2,000$ in all. Because you paid €1,150 your net profit is $€2,000 - €1,150 = €500$.

---

| CONCEPT QUESTIONS | 21.1a | What is a call option? A put option? |
|---|---|---|
| | 21.1b | If you thought that an equity was going to drop sharply in value, how might you use equity options to profit from the decline? |

# 21.2 Put–Call Parity

Recall that the purchaser of a call option pays for the right, but not the obligation, to buy an asset for a fixed time at a fixed price. The purchaser of a put option pays for the right to sell an asset for a fixed time at a fixed price. The fixed price is called the *exercise* or *strike* price.

## Protective Puts

Consider the following investment strategy. Today, you buy one share of Vodafone for £110. At the same time you also buy one put option with a £105 strike price. The put option has a life of one year, and the premium is £5. Your total investment is £115, and your plan is to hold this investment for one year and then sell out.

What have you accomplished here? To answer, we created Table 21.1, which shows your gains and losses one year from now for different share prices. In the table, notice that the worst thing that ever happens is that the value of your investment falls to £105. The reason is that if Vodafone's share price is below £105 per share one year from now, you will exercise your put option and sell your equity for the strike price of £105: so that is the least you can possibly receive.

TABLE
21.1

| Share price in one year (£) | Value of put option (strike price = £105) (£) | Combined value (£) | Total gain or loss (combined value less £115) (£) |
|---|---|---|---|
| 125 | 0 | 125 | 10 |
| 120 | 0 | 120 | 5 |
| 115 | 0 | 115 | 0 |
| 110 | 0 | 110 | −5 |
| 105 | 0 | 105 | −10 |
| 100 | 5 | 105 | −10 |
| 95 | 10 | 105 | −10 |
| 80 | 25 | 105 | −10 |

Original investment: purchase one share at £110 plus a one-year put option with a strike price of £105 for £5. Total cost is £115.

**Table 21.1** Gains and losses in one year

Thus, by purchasing the put option, you have limited your downside risk to a maximum potential loss of £10 (= £115 – £105). This particular strategy of buying an equity and also buying a put on the equity is called a **protective put** strategy, because it protects you against losses beyond a certain point. Notice that the put option acts as a kind of insurance policy that pays off in the event that an asset you own (the equity) declines in value.

> **protective put**
> The purchase of equity and a put option on the equity to limit the downside risk associated with the equity.

In our example we picked a strike price of £105. You could have picked a higher strike price and limited your downside risk to even less. Of course, a higher strike price would mean that you would have to pay more for the put option, so there is a trade-off between the amount of protection and the cost of that protection.

## An Alternative Strategy

Now consider a different strategy. You take your £115 and purchase a one-year call option on Vodafone with a strike price of £105. The premium is £15. That leaves you with £100, which you decide to invest in a riskless asset such as a T-bill. The risk-free rate is 5 per cent.

What does this strategy accomplish? Once again, we shall create a table to illustrate your gains and losses. Notice that in Table 21.2 your £100 grows to £105 based on a 5 per cent interest rate. If you compare Table 21.2 with Table 21.1, you will make an interesting discovery. No matter what the share price is one year from now, the two strategies *always* have the same value in one year!

The fact that the two strategies always have exactly the same value in one year explains why they have the same cost today. If one of these strategies were cheaper than the other today, there would be an arbitrage opportunity involving buying the one that's cheaper and simultaneously selling the one that's more expensive.

## The Result

Our example illustrates a very important pricing relationship. What it shows is that a protective put strategy can be exactly duplicated by a combination of a call option

TABLE 21.2

| Share price in one year (£) | Value of call option (strike price = £105) (£) | Value of risk-free asset (£) | Combined value (£) | Total gain or loss (combined value less £115) (£) |
|---|---|---|---|---|
| 125 | 20 | 105 | 125 | 10 |
| 120 | 15 | 105 | 120 | 5 |
| 115 | 10 | 105 | 115 | 0 |
| 110 | 5 | 105 | 110 | −5 |
| 105 | 0 | 105 | 105 | −10 |
| 100 | 0 | 105 | 105 | −10 |
| 95 | 0 | 105 | 105 | −10 |
| 80 | 0 | 105 | 105 | −10 |

Original investment: purchase a one-year call option with a strike price of £105 for £15. Invest £100 in a risk-free asset paying 5 per cent. Total cost is £115.

**Table 21.2** Gains and losses in one year

(with the same strike price as the put option) and a riskless investment. In our example, notice that the investment in the riskless asset, £100, is exactly equal to the present value of the strike price on the option calculated at the risk-free rate: £105/1.05 = £100.

Putting it all together, what we have discovered is the *put–call parity (PCP) condition*. It says that

$$\begin{array}{c} \text{Price of underlying} \\ \text{equity} \end{array} + \begin{array}{c} \text{Price of} \\ \text{put} \end{array} = \begin{array}{c} \text{Price of} \\ \text{call} \end{array} + \begin{array}{c} \text{Present value of} \\ \text{strike price} \end{array} \qquad (21.1)$$

In symbols, we can write

$$S + P = \text{PV}(E) + C \qquad (21.1a)$$

where $S$ is the share price and P is the put value, and PV($E$) and C are the present value of the exercise price and the value of the call option.

Because the present value of the exercise price is calculated using the risk-free rate, you can think of it as the price of a risk-free, pure discount instrument (such as a T-bill) with a face value equal to the strike price. In our experience, the easiest way to remember the PCP condition is to remember that 'share plus put equals T-bill plus call'.

The PCP condition is an algebraic expression, meaning that it can be rearranged. For example, suppose we know that the risk-free rate is 0.5 per cent per month. A call with a strike price of €40 sells for €4, and a put with the same strike price sells for €3. Both have a three-month maturity. What's the share price?

To answer, we just use the PCP condition to solve for the share price:

$$\begin{aligned} S &= \text{PV}(E) + C - P \\ &= €40/1.005^3 + 4 - 3 \\ &= €40.41 \end{aligned}$$

The PCP condition really says that between a riskless asset (such as a T-bill), a call option, a put option and a share of equity, we can always figure out the price of any one of the four given the prices of the other three.

## Put–call parity

**EXAMPLE 21.2**

Suppose a share of equity sells for £60. A six-month call option with a £70 strike price sells for £2. The risk-free rate is 0.4 per cent per month. What's the price of a six-month put option with a £70 strike?

If we just use the PCP condition to solve for the put price, we get

$$P = PV(E) + C - S$$
$$= £70/1.004^6 + £2 - £60$$
$$= £10.34$$

Notice that in this example the put option is worth a lot more than the call. Why?

## More Parity

**EXAMPLE 21.3**

Suppose a share of equity sells for €110. A one-year, at-the-money call option sells for €15. An at-the-money put with the same maturity sells for €5. Can you create a risk-free investment by combining these three instruments? How? What's the risk-free rate?

Here, we can use the PCP condition to solve for the present value of the strike price:

$$PV(E) = S + P - C$$
$$= €110 + €5 - €15$$
$$= €100$$

The present value of the strike price is thus €100. Notice that because the options are at the money, the strike is the same as the share price, €110. So, if you put €100 in a riskless investment today and receive €110 in one year, the implied risk-free rate is obviously 10 per cent.

**CONCEPT QUESTIONS**

21.2a  What is a protective put strategy?

21.2b  What strategy exactly duplicates a protective put?

## 21.3  Fundamentals of Option Valuation

Now that we understand the basics of puts and calls, we can discuss what determines their values. We shall focus on call options in the discussion that follows, but the same type of analysis can be applied to put options.

### Valuation of a Call at Expiration

We have already described the pay-offs from call options for different share prices. In continuing this discussion, the following notation will be useful:

$S_1$ = Share price at expiration (in one period)

$S_0$ = Share price today

$C_1$ = Value of the call option on the expiration date (in one period)

$C_0$ = Value of the call option today

$E$ = Exercise price on the option

From our previous discussion, remember that if the share price ($S_1$) ends up below the exercise price ($E$) on the expiration date, then the call option ($C_1$) is worth zero. In other words:

$$C_1 = 0 \text{ if } S_1 \leq E$$

Or, equivalently:

$$C_1 = 0 \text{ if } S_1 - E \leq 0 \tag{21.2}$$

This is the case in which the option is out of the money when it expires.

If the option finishes in the money, then $S_1 > E$, and the value of the option at expiration is equal to the difference:

$$C_1 = S_1 - E \text{ if } S_1 > E$$

Or, equivalently:

$$C_1 = S_1 - E \text{ if } S_1 - E > 0 \tag{21.3}$$

For example, suppose we have a call option with an exercise price of £10. The option is about to expire. If the equity is selling for £8, then we have the right to pay £10 for something worth only £8. Our option is thus worth exactly zero, because the share price is less than the exercise price on the option ($S_1 \leq E$). If the equity is selling for £12, then the option has value. Because we can buy the equity for £10, the option is worth $S_1 - E = £12 - £10 = £2$.

Figure 21.2 plots the value of a call option at expiration against the share price. The result looks something like a hockey stick. Notice that for every share price less than $E$ the

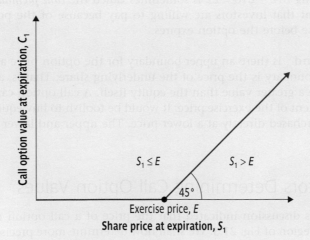

FIGURE
21.2

As shown, the value of a call option at expiration is equal to zero if the share price is less than or equal to the exercise price. The value of the call is equal to the share price minus the exercise price ($S_1 - E$) if the share price exceeds the exercise price. The resulting 'hockey stick' shape is highlighted.

**Figure 21.2** Value of a call option at expiration for different share prices

value of the option is zero. For every share price greater than $E$ the value of the call option is $S_1 - E$. Also, once the share price exceeds the exercise price, the option's value goes up in step with the share price.

## Bounding the Value of a Call

Now that we know how to determine $C_1$, the value of the call at expiration, we turn to a somewhat more challenging question: how can we determine $C_0$, the value some time *before* expiration? We shall be discussing this in the next several sections. For now, we shall establish the lower and upper for the value of a call option.

**Lower Bound** Consider an American call that is in the money prior to expiration. For example, assume that the share price is £60 and the exercise price is £50. In this case, the option cannot sell below £10. To see this, note the following simple strategy if the option sells at, say, £9:

| Date | Transaction | (£) |
|---|---|---|
| Today | 1 Buy call. | −9 |
| Today | 2 Exercise call – that is, buy underlying share at exercise price. | −50 |
| Today | 3 Sell share at current market price. | +60 |
| Arbitrage profit | | +1 |

The type of profit that is described in this transaction is an arbitrage profit. Arbitrage profits come from transactions that have no risk or cost, and cannot occur regularly in normal, well-functioning financial markets. The excess demand for these options would quickly force the option price up to at least £10 (= £60 − £50).

Of course, the price of the option is likely to be above £10. Investors will rationally pay more than £10, because of the possibility that the equity will rise above £60 before expiration. For example, suppose the call actually sells for £12. In this case we say that the intrinsic value of the option is £10, meaning it must always be worth at least this much. The remaining £12 − £10 = £2 is sometimes called the *time premium*, and it represents the extra amount that investors are willing to pay because of the possibility that the share price will rise before the option expires.

**Upper Bound** Is there an upper boundary for the option price as well? It turns out that the upper boundary is the price of the underlying share. That is, an option to buy equity cannot have a greater value than the equity itself. A call option can be used to buy equity with a payment of the exercise price. It would be foolish to buy equity this way if the shares could be purchased directly at a lower price. The upper and lower bounds are represented in Fig. 21.3.

## The Factors Determining Call Option Values

The previous discussion indicated that the price of a call option must fall somewhere in the shaded region of Fig. 21.3. We shall now determine more precisely where in the shaded region it should be. The factors that determine a call's value can be broken into two sets. The first set contains the features of the option contract. The two basic contractual features are the exercise price and the expiration date. The second set of factors affecting the call price concerns characteristics of the equity and the market.

**Exercise Price** An increase in the exercise price reduces the value of the call. For example, imagine that there are two calls on an equity selling at £60. The first call has an exercise price of £50 and the second one has an exercise price of £40. Which call would you rather have? Clearly, you would rather have the call with an exercise price of £40, because that

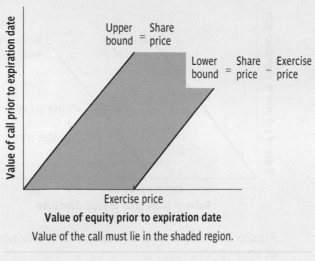

Figure 21.3 The upper and lower boundaries of call option values

one is £20 (= £60 – £40) in the money. In other words, the call with an exercise price of £40 should sell for more than an otherwise identical call with an exercise price of £50.

**Expiration Date**   The value of an American call option must be at least as great as the value of an otherwise identical option with a shorter term to expiration. Consider two American calls: one has a maturity of nine months, and the other expires in six months. Obviously, the nine-month call has the same rights as the six-month call, and it also has an additional three months within which these rights can be exercised. It cannot be worth less, and will generally be more valuable.

**The Risk-Free Rate**   The higher the risk-free rate ($R_f$) is, the more the call is worth. This result is a little less obvious. Normally, we think of asset values as going down as rates rise. In this case, the exercise price is a *cash outflow*, a liability. The current value of that liability goes down as the discount rate goes up.

**Share Price**   Other things being equal, the higher the share price, the more valuable the call option will be. For example, if an equity is worth £80, a call with an exercise price of £100 isn't worth very much. If the share price soars to £120, the call becomes much more valuable.

Now consider Fig. 21.4, which shows the relationship between the call price and the share price prior to expiration. The curve indicates that the call price increases as the share price increases. Furthermore, it can be shown that the relationship is represented not by a straight line, but by a convex curve. That is, the increase in the call price for a given change in the share price is greater when the share price is high than when the share price is low.

**The Key Factor: The Variability of the Underlying Asset**   The greater the variability of the underlying asset, the more valuable the call option will be. Consider the following example. Suppose that, just before the call expires, the share price will be either £100 with probability 0.5 or £80 with probability 0.5. What will be the value of a call with an exercise price of £110? Clearly, it will be worthless, because no matter what happens to the equity, the share price will always be below the exercise price.

What happens if the share price is more variable? Suppose we add £20 to the best case and take £20 away from the worst case. Now the equity has a one-half chance of being worth £60 and a one-half chance of being worth £120. We have spread the equity returns, but of course the expected value of the share has stayed the same:

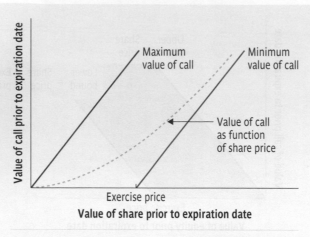

**Figure 21.4** Value of a call option as a function of share price

$$(1/2 \times £80) + (1/2 \times £100) = £90 = (1/2 \times £60) + (1/2 \times £120)$$

Notice that the call option has value now, because there is a one-half chance that the share price will be £120, or £10 above the exercise price of £110. This illustrates an important point. There is a fundamental distinction between holding an option on an underlying asset and holding the underlying asset. If investors in the marketplace are risk-averse, a rise in the variability of the equity will decrease its market value.

More generally, increasing the variance of the possible future prices on the underlying asset doesn't affect the option's value when the option finishes out of the money. The value is always zero in this case. On the other hand, increasing the variance increases the possible pay-offs when the option is in the money, so the net effect is to increase the option's value. Put another way, because the downside risk is always limited, the only effect is to increase the upside potential. In a later discussion we shall use the usual symbol, $\sigma^2$, to stand for the variance of the return on the underlying asset.

## Summary

The most important thing to remember is that the value of an option depends on five factors. Table 21.3 summarizes these factors, and the direction of their influence for both puts and calls. In Table 21.3 the sign in parentheses indicates the direction of the influence.

| Factor | Direction of influence | |
|---|---|---|
| | Calls | Puts |
| Current value of the underlying asset | (+) | (−) |
| Exercise price on the option | (−) | (+) |
| Time to expiration on the option | (+) | (+) |
| Risk-free rate | (+) | (−) |
| Variance of return on the underlying asset | (+) | (+) |

**Table 21.3** Five factors that determine option values

In other words, the sign tells us whether the value of the option goes up or down when the value of a factor increases. For example, notice that increasing the exercise price reduces the value of a call option. Increasing any of the other four factors increases the value of the call. Notice also that the time to expiration and the variance of return act the same for puts and calls. The other three factors have opposite signs in the two cases.

| CONCEPT QUESTIONS | |
|---|---|
| 21.3a | What is the value of a call option at expiration? |
| 21.3b | What are the upper and lower bounds on the value of a call option any time before expiration? |
| 21.3c | Assuming that the share price is certain to be greater than the exercise price on a call option, what is the value of the call? Why? |

## 21.4 An Option Pricing Model

Option pricing can be a complex subject. Fortunately, as is often the case, many of the key insights can be illustrated with a simple example. Suppose we are looking at a call option with one year to expiration and an exercise price of £105. The equity currently sells for £100, and the risk-free rate, $R_f$, is 20 per cent. The value of the equity in one year is uncertain, of course. To keep things simple, suppose we know that the share price will be either £110 or £130. It is important to note that we *don't* know the odds associated with these two prices. In other words, we know the possible values for the equity, but not the probabilities associated with those values.

Because the exercise price on the option is £105, we know that the option will be worth either £110 – 105 = £5 or £130 – 105 = £25; but, once again, we don't know which. We do know one thing, however: our call option is certain to finish in the money.

**The Basic Approach**  Here is the crucial observation: it is possible to duplicate the pay-offs on the equity exactly, using a combination of the option and the risk-free asset. How? Do the following: buy one call option and invest £87.50 in a risk-free asset (such as a T-bill).

What will you have in a year? Your risk-free asset will earn 20 per cent, so it will be worth £87.50 × 1.20 = £105. Your option will be worth £5 or £25, so the total value will be either £110 or £130, just like the value of the equity:

| Share price (£) | vs. | Risk-free asset value (£) | + | Call value (£) | = | Total value (£) |
|---|---|---|---|---|---|---|
| 110 | | 105 | | 5 | | 110 |
| 130 | | 105 | | 25 | | 130 |

As illustrated, these two strategies – buying a share of equity or buying a call and investing in the risk-free asset – have exactly the same pay-offs in the future.

Because these two strategies have the same future pay-offs, they must have the same value today, or else there would be an arbitrage opportunity. The equity sells for £100 today, so the value of the call option today, $C_0$, is given by

$$£100 = £87.50 + C_0$$
$$C_0 = £12.50$$

Where did we get the £87.50? This is just the present value of the exercise price on the option, calculated at the risk-free rate:

$$E/(1 + R_f) = £105/1.20 = £87.50$$

Given this, our example shows that the value of a call option in this simple case is given by

$$S_0 = C_0 + \frac{E}{1 + R_\text{f}}$$

(21.4)

$$C_0 = S_0 - \frac{E}{1 + R_\text{f}}$$

In words, the value of the call option is equal to the share price minus the present value of the exercise price.

**A More Complicated Example** From our previous example, we have an equity that currently sells for £100. It will be worth either £110 or £130 in a year, and we don't know which. The risk-free rate is 20 per cent. We are now looking at a different call option, however. This one has an exercise price of £120 instead of £105. What is the value of this call option?

This case is a little harder. If the equity ends up at £110, the option is out of the money and worth nothing. If the equity ends up at £130, the option is worth £130 − 120 = £10.

Our basic approach to determining the value of the call option will be the same. We shall show once again that it is possible to combine the call option and a risk-free investment in a way that exactly duplicates the pay-off from holding the equity. The only complication is that it's a little harder to determine how to do it.

For example, suppose we bought one call and invested the present value of the exercise price in a riskless asset as we did before. In one year we would have £120 from the riskless investment, plus an option worth either zero or £10. The total value would be either £120 or £130. This is not the same as the value of the equity (£110 or £130), so the two strategies are not comparable.

Instead, consider investing the present value of £110 (the lower share price) in a riskless asset. This guarantees us a £110 pay-off. If the share price is £110, then any call options we own are worthless, and we have exactly £110 as desired.

When the equity is worth £130, the call option is worth £10. Our risk-free investment is worth £110, so we are £130 − 110 = £20 short. Because each call option is worth £10, we need to buy two of them to replicate the value of the equity.

Thus, in this case, investing the present value of the lower share price in a riskless asset and buying two call options exactly duplicates owning the equity. When the equity is worth £110, we have £110 from our risk-free investment. When the equity is worth £130, we have £110 from the risk-free investment plus two call options worth £10 each.

Because these two strategies have exactly the same value in the future, they must have the same value today, or arbitrage would be possible:

$$S_0 = £100 = 2 \times C_0 + £110/(1 + R_\text{f})$$
$$2 \times C_0 = £100 - 110/1.2$$
$$C_0 = £4.17$$

Each call option is thus worth £4.17.

### EXAMPLE 21.4

# Don't Call Us, We'll Call You

We are looking at two call options on the same equity, one with an exercise price of €20 and one with an exercise price of €30. The equity currently sells for €35. Its future price will be either €25 or €50. If the risk-free rate is 10 per cent, what are the values of these call options?

The first case (with the €20 exercise price) is not difficult, because the option is sure to finish in the money. We know that the value is equal to the share price less the present value of the exercise price:

$$C_0 = S_0 - E/(1 + R_f)$$
$$= £35 - 20/1.1$$
$$= £16.82$$

In the second case the exercise price is €30, so the option can finish out of the money. At expiration, the option is worth €0 if the equity is worth €25. The option is worth €50 – 30 = €20 if it finishes in the money. As before, we start by investing the present value of the lowest share price in the risk-free asset. This costs €25/1.1 = €22.73. At expiration, we have €25 from this investment. If the share price is €50, then we need an additional €25 to duplicate the equity pay-off. Because each option is worth €20 in this case, we need €25/20 = 1.25 options. So, to prevent arbitrage, investing the present value of €25 in a risk-free asset and buying 1.25 call options must have the same value as the equity:

$$S_0 = 1.25 \times C_0 + €25/(1 + R_f)$$
$$€35 = 1.25 \times C_0 + €25/(1 + 0.1)$$
$$C_0 = €9.82$$

Notice that this second option had to be worth less, because it has the higher exercise price.

## A Closer Look

Before moving on, it will be useful to consider one last example. Suppose the share price is £100, and it will move either up or down by 20 per cent. The risk-free rate is 5 per cent. What is the value of a call option with a £90 exercise price?

The share price will be either £80 or £120. The option is worth zero when the equity is worth £80, and it's worth £120 – 90 = £30 when the equity is worth £120. We shall therefore invest the present value of £80 in the risk-free asset and buy some call options.

When the equity finishes at £120, our risk-free asset pays £80, leaving us £40 short. Each option is worth £30 in this case, so we need £40/30 = 4/3 options to match the pay-off on the equity. The option's value must thus be given by

$$S_0 = £100 = 4/3 \times C_0 + £80/1.05$$
$$C_0 = (3/4) \times (£100 - 76.19)$$
$$= £17.86$$

To make our result a little bit more general, notice that the number of options that you need to buy to replicate the value of the equity is always equal to $\Delta S/\Delta C$, where $\Delta S$ is the difference in the possible share prices, and $\Delta C$ is the difference in the possible option values. In our current case, for example, $\Delta S$ would be £120 – 80 = £40 and $\Delta C$ would be £30 – 0 = £30, so $\Delta S/\Delta C$ would be £40/30 = 4/3, as we calculated.

Notice also that when the equity is certain to finish in the money, $\Delta S/\Delta C$ is always exactly equal to 1, so one call option is always needed. Otherwise, $\Delta S/\Delta C$ is greater than 1, so more than one call option is needed.

## 21.5  The Black–Scholes Option Pricing Model

We're now in a position to discuss one of the most celebrated results in modern finance, the Black–Scholes Option Pricing Model (OPM). The OPM is a sufficiently important discovery that it was the basis for the Nobel Prize in Economics in 1997. The underlying development of the Black–Scholes OPM is fairly complex, so we shall focus only on the main result and how to use it.

**Black–Scholes Model**

$$C = SN(d_1) - Ee^{-Rt}N(d_2)$$

where

$$d_1 = \frac{\ln(S/E) + (R + \sigma^2/2)t}{\sqrt{\sigma^2 t}}$$

$$d_2 = d_1 - \sqrt{\sigma^2 t}$$

This formula for the value of a call, $C$, is one of the most complex in finance. However, it involves only five parameters:

1   $S$ = Current share price

2   $E$ = Exercise price of call

3   $R$ = Annual risk-free rate of return, continuously compounded

4   $\sigma^2$ = Variance (per year) of the continuous share price return

5   $t$ = Time (in years) to expiration date

In addition, there is this statistical concept:

$N(d)$ = Probability that a standardized, normally distributed, random variable will
          be less than or equal to $d$.

Rather than discuss the formula in its algebraic state, we illustrate the formula with an example.

---

**EXAMPLE 21.5**

# Black–Scholes Option Pricing Model

Consider Private Equipment plc (PEP). On 4 October of year 0, the PEP 21 April call option (exercise price = £49) had a closing value of £4. The equity itself was selling at £50. On 4 October the option had 199 days to expiration (maturity date = 21 April, year 1). The annual risk-free interest rate, continuously compounded, was 7 per cent. This information determines three variables directly:

1   The share price, $S$, is £50.

2   The exercise price, $E$, is £49.

3   The risk-free rate, $R$, is 0.07.

In addition, the time to maturity, $t$, can be calculated quickly: the formula calls for $t$ to be expressed in years.

4   We express the 199-day interval in years as $t = 199/365$.

In the real world an option trader would know $S$ and $E$ exactly. Traders generally view government Treasury bills as riskless, so a current quote from newspapers, such as the *Financial Times* or a similar source, would be obtained for the interest rate. The trader would also know (or could count) the number of days to expiration exactly. Thus the fraction of a year to expiration, $t$, could be calculated quickly.

The problem comes in determining the variance of the underlying equity's return. The formula calls for the variance between the purchase date of 4 October and the expiration date. Unfortunately, this represents the future, so the correct value for variance is not available. Instead, traders frequently estimate variance from past data, and they may also use intuition to adjust their estimate. For example, if anticipation of an upcoming event is likely to increase the volatility of the share price, the trader might adjust her estimate of variance upwards to reflect this.

The preceding discussion was intended merely to mention the difficulties in variance estimation, not to present a solution. For our purposes, we assume that a trader has come up with an estimate of variance:

5   The variance of Private Equipment plc has been estimated to be 0.09 per year.

Using these five parameters, we calculate the Black–Scholes value of the PEP option in three steps, as follows.

### Step 1: Calculate $d_1$ and $d_2$

These values can be determined by a straightforward, albeit tedious, insertion of our parameters into the basic formula. We have

$$d_1 = \left[ \ln\left(\frac{S}{E}\right) + (R + \sigma^2/2)t \right] \Big/ \sqrt{\sigma^2 t}$$

$$= \left[ \ln\left(\frac{50}{49}\right) + (0.07 + 0.09/2) \times \frac{199}{365} \right] \Big/ \sqrt{0.09 \times \frac{199}{365}}$$

$$= (0.0202 + 0.0627)/0.2215 = 0.3742$$

$$d_2 = d_1 - \sqrt{\sigma^2 t}$$

$$= 0.1527$$

### Step 2: Calculate N($d_1$) and N($d_2$)

Perhaps the easiest way to determine N($d_1$) and N($d_2$) is from the Microsoft Excel function NORMSDIST. In our example NORMSDIST(0.3742) and NORMSDIST(0.1527) are 0.6459 and 0.5607, respectively.

We can also determine the cumulative probability from Table 21.4. For example, consider $d = 0.37$. This can be found in the table as 0.3 on the vertical and 0.07 on the horizontal. The value in the table for $d = 0.37$ is 0.1443. This value is not the cumulative probability of 0.37. We must first make an adjustment to determine cumulative probability. That is:

$$N(0.37) = 0.50 + 0.1443 = 0.6443$$
$$N(-0.37) = 0.50 - 0.1443 = 0.3557$$

N($d$) represents areas under the standard normal distribution function. Suppose that $d_1 = 0.24$. The table implies a cumulative probability of $0.5000 + 0.0948 = 0.5948$. If $d_1$ is equal to 0.2452, we must estimate the probability by interpolating between N(0.25) and N(0.24).

Unfortunately, our table handles only two significant digits, whereas our value of 0.3742 has four significant digits. Hence we must interpolate to find N(0.3742). Because N(0.37) = 0.6443 and

| $d$ | 0.00 | 0.01 | 0.02 | 0.03 | 0.04 | 0.05 | 0.06 | 0.07 | 0.08 | 0.09 |
|-----|------|------|------|------|------|------|------|------|------|------|
| 0.0 | 0.0000 | 0.0040 | 0.0080 | 0.0120 | 0.0160 | 0.0199 | 0.0239 | 0.0279 | 0.0319 | 0.0359 |
| 0.1 | 0.0398 | 0.0438 | 0.0478 | 0.0517 | 0.0557 | 0.0596 | 0.0636 | 0.0675 | 0.0714 | 0.0753 |
| 0.2 | 0.0793 | 0.0832 | 0.0871 | 0.0910 | 0.0948 | 0.0987 | 0.1026 | 0.1064 | 0.1103 | 0.1141 |
| 0.3 | 0.1179 | 0.1217 | 0.1255 | 0.1293 | 0.1331 | 0.1368 | 0.1406 | 0.1443 | 0.1480 | 0.1517 |
| 0.4 | 0.1554 | 0.1591 | 0.1628 | 0.1664 | 0.1700 | 0.1736 | 0.1772 | 0.1808 | 0.1844 | 0.1879 |
| 0.5 | 0.1915 | 0.1950 | 0.1985 | 0.2019 | 0.2054 | 0.2088 | 0.2123 | 0.2157 | 0.2190 | 0.2224 |

**Table 21.4** Cumulative probabilities of the standard normal distribution function

N(0.38) = 0.6480, the difference between the two values is 0.0037 (= 0.6480 − 0.6443). Since 0.3742 is 42 per cent of the way between 0.37 and 0.38, we interpolate as:

$$N(0.3742) = 0.6443 + 0.42 \times 0.0037 = 0.6459$$

**Step 3: Calculate C**

We have:

$$
\begin{aligned}
C &= S \times [N(d_1)] - Ee^{-Rt} \times [N(d_2)] \\
&= \pounds 50 \times [N(d_1)] - \pounds 49 \times e^{-0.07 \times (199/365)} \times N(d_2) \\
&= (\pounds 50 \times 0.6459) - (\pounds 49 \times 0.9626 \times 0.5607) \\
&= \pounds 32.295 - \pounds 26.447 \\
&= \pounds 5.85
\end{aligned}
$$

The estimated price of £5.85 is greater than the £4 actual price, implying that the call option is underpriced. A trader believing in the Black–Scholes model would buy a call. Of course, the Black–Scholes model is fallible. Perhaps the disparity between the model's estimate and the market price reflects error in the trader's estimate of variance.

It is no exaggeration to say that the Black–Scholes formula is among the most important contributions in finance. It allows anyone to calculate the value of an option, given a few parameters. The attraction of the formula is that four of the parameters are observable: the current share price, $S$; the exercise price, $E$; the interest rate, $R$; and the time to expiration date, $t$. Only one of the parameters must be estimated: the variance of return, $\sigma^2$.

## Put Option Valuation

Our examples thus far have focused only on call options. Just a little extra work is needed to value put options. Basically, we pretend that a put option is a call option, and use the Black–Scholes formula to value it. We then use the continuously compounded version of the put–call parity (PCP) condition to solve for the put value. To see how this works, suppose we have the following:

$S = \pounds 40$

$E = \pounds 40$

$R = 4\%$ per year, continuously compounded

$\sigma = 80\%$ per year

$t = 4$ months

What's the value of a *put* option on the equity?

For practice, calculate the Black–Scholes call option price and see if you agree that a call option would be worth about £7.52. Now, recall the PCP condition:

$$S + P = PV(E) + C$$

The continuously compounded version of the above equation is

$$S + P = Ee^{-Rt} + C$$

which we can rearrange to solve for the put price:

$$P = Ee^{-Rt} + C - S$$

Plugging in the relevant numbers, we get:

$$P = £40 \times e^{-0.04(1/3)} + 7.52 - 40$$
$$= £6.99$$

Thus the value of a put option is £6.99. So, once we know how to value call options, we also know how to value put options.

## A Cautionary Note

For practice, let's consider another put option value. Suppose we have the following:

$S = €70$

$E = €90$

$R = 8\%$ per year, continuously compounded

$\sigma = 20\%$ per year

$t = 12$ months

What's the value of a put option on the equity? For practice, calculate the call option's value and see if you get €1.65. Once again, we use PCP to solve for the put price:

$$P = Ee^{-Rt} + C - S$$

The put value we get is

$$P = €90 \times e^{-0.08(1)} + 1.65 - 70$$
$$= €14.73$$

Does something about our put option value seem odd? The answer is yes. Because the share price is €70 and the strike price is €90, you could get €20 by exercising the put immediately; so it looks as though we have an arbitrage possibility. Unfortunately, we don't.

This example illustrates that we have to be careful with assumptions. The Black–Scholes formula is for European-style options (remember that European-style options can be exercised only on the final day, whereas American-style options can be exercised at any time). In fact, our PCP condition holds only for European-style options.

What our example shows is that an American-style put option is worth more than a European-style put. The reason is not hard to understand. Suppose you buy a put with a strike price of €80. The very best thing that can happen is for the share price to fall to zero. If the share price did fall to zero, no further gain on your option would be possible, so you would want to exercise it immediately rather than wait. If the option is American style you can, but not if it is European style. More generally, it often pays to exercise a put option once it is well into the money, because any additional potential gains are limited, so American-style exercise is valuable.

What about call options? Here the answer is a little more encouraging. As long as we stick to non-dividend-paying equities, it will never be optimal to exercise a call option early. Again, the reason is not complicated. A call option is worth more alive than dead, meaning you would always be better off selling the option than exercising it. In other words, for a call option, the exercise style is irrelevant.

Here is a challenge for the more mathematically inclined among you. We have a formula for a European-style put option. What about for an American-style put? Despite a great deal of effort, this problem has never been solved, so no formula is known. Just to be clear, we have numerical procedures for valuing put options, but no explicit formula. Call us if you figure one out.

Now that we have shown how to value call and put options, we now consider their use in corporate finance.

# Spreadsheet Strategies

The easiest way to find the value of an option is to use a spreadsheet. Consider an equity that has a share price of £65 and an annual return standard deviation of 50 per cent. The riskless interest rate is 5 per cent. Calculate the call and put option values with a strike of £60 and a 3-month period to expiration.

| | A | B | C | D | E |
|---|---|---|---|---|---|
| 1 | Share Price = | 65 | | d1 = | 0.495171 |
| 2 | Strike Price = | 60 | | d2 = | 0.245171 |
| 3 | Sigma = | 0.5 | | N(d1) = | 0.68976 |
| 4 | Time = | 0.25 | | N(d2) = | 0.596838 |
| 5 | Rate = | 0.05 | | | |
| 6 | | | | | |
| 7 | Call = | 9.468982 | | Put = | 3.72365 |

Formula entered in E1 is =(LN(B1/B2)+(B5+0.5*B3^2)*B4)/(B3*SQRT(B4))

Formula entered in E2 is =E1-B3*SQRT(B4)

Formula entered in E3 is =NORMSDIST(E1)

Formula entered in E4 is =NORMSDIST(E2)

Formula entered in B7 is =B1*E3-B2*EXP(-B5*B4)*E4

Formula entered in E7 is =B2*EXP(-B5*B4)+B7-B1

**CONCEPT QUESTIONS**

21.5a  What are the five factors that determine an option's value?

21.5b  Which is worth more, an American-style put or a European-style put? Why?

## 21.6  Employee Share Options

Options are important in corporate finance in a lot of different ways. In this section we begin to examine some of these by taking a look at executive (employee) share options, or ESOs. An ESO is, in essence, a call option that a firm gives to employees, giving them the right to buy shares of equity in the company. The practice of granting options to employees has become widespread. It is almost universal for upper management, and sometimes given to other employees. Although ESOs have become a controversial topic of late (see opening vignette), an understanding of ESOs is important.

### ESO Features

Because ESOs are basically call options, we have already covered most of the important aspects. However, ESOs have a few features that make them different from regular share options. The details differ from company to company, but a typical ESO has a 10-year life, which is much longer than most ordinary options. Unlike traded options, ESOs cannot be sold. They also have what is known as a 'vesting' period. Often, for up to three years or so, an ESO cannot be exercised and also must be forfeited if an employee leaves the company. After this period the options 'vest', which means they can be exercised. Sometimes, employees who resign with vested options are given a limited time to exercise their options.

Why are ESOs granted? There are basically two reasons. First, going back to Chapter 2, the owners of a corporation (the shareholders) face the basic problem of aligning share-holder and management interests and also of providing incentives for employees to focus on corporate goals. ESOs are a powerful motivator because, as we have seen, the pay-offs on options can be very large. High-level executives in particular stand to gain enormous wealth if they are successful in creating value for shareholders.

The second reason why some companies rely heavily on ESOs is that an ESO has no immediate, up-front, out-of-pocket cost to the corporation. In smaller, possibly cash-strapped companies, ESOs are simply a substitute for ordinary wages. Employees are willing to accept them instead of cash, hoping for big pay-offs in the future. In fact, ESOs are a major recruiting tool, allowing businesses to attract talent that they otherwise could not afford.

At the same time there are a number of significant criticisms of executive share options. The most notable criticism is that share options encourage managers to take on more risky projects so as to increase the size of their personal remuneration. Given the role of executive compensation in the banking sector, and the perverse incentives to maximize bank share price at the expense of bank risk, regulators across the world have moved to limit top executive pay. However, this does not seem to have reduced the extremely high remuneration deals for executives.

## Valuing Executive Compensation

In this section we value executive share options. Not surprisingly, the complexity of the total compensation package often makes valuation a difficult task. The economic value of the options depends on factors such as the volatility of the underlying equity and the exact terms of the option grant.

Only a few countries fully disclose the details of executive pay, and in Example 21.6 we shall estimate the economic value of the options held by the chief executive of a hypo-thetical company. Example 21.6 is necessarily simplistic, but it serves to illustrate the way we can value executive share options. Simple matters such as requiring the executive to hold the option during the vesting period can significantly diminish the value of a standard option.

Equally important, the Black–Scholes formula has to be modified if the equity pays dividends, and it is no longer applicable if the volatility of the equity is changing randomly over time. These are not issues with the standard short-term equity options, but are very important for long-term options such as ESOs. Intuitively, a call option on a dividend-paying equity is worth less than a call on an equity that pays no dividends: all other things being equal, the dividends will lower the share price. Nevertheless, let us see what we can do.

---

**EXAMPLE 21.6**

## Options at Sunshine Rain Ltd

Consider Ian Brown, the chief executive officer (CEO) of Sunshine Rain, who has been granted 2 million executive share options. The average share price at the time of the options grant was €39.71. We shall assume that his options are at the money. The risk-free rate is 5 per cent, and the options expire in five years. The preceding information implies that:

1   The share price ($S$) of €39.71 equals the exercise price ($E$).

2   The risk-free rate, $R = 0.05$.

3   The time interval, $t = 5$.

In addition, the variance of Sunshine Rain is estimated to be $(0.2168)^2 = 0.0470$.

This information allows us to value Ian Brown's options using the Black–Scholes model:

$$C = SN(d_1) - Ee^{-Rt}N(d_2)$$
$$d_1 = [(R + \sigma^2/2)t]/\sqrt{\sigma^2 t} = 0.758$$
$$d_2 = d_1 - \sqrt{\sigma^2 t} = 0.273$$
$$N(d_1) = 0.776$$
$$N(d_2) = 0.608$$
$$e^{-0.05 \times 5} = 0.7788$$
$$C = €39.71 \times 0.776 - €39.71 \times (0.778 \times 0.608) = €12.03$$

Thus the value of a call option on one share of Sunshine Rain equity is €12.03. Because Mr Brown was granted options on 2 million shares, the market value of his options, as estimated by the Black–Scholes formula, is about €24 million (= 2 million × €12.03).

The value of the options we computed in Example 21.6 is the economic value of the options if they were to trade in the market. The real question is this: whose value are we talking about? Are these the costs of the options to the company? Are they the values of the options to the executives?

The total value of €24 million for Ian Brown's options in Example 21.6 is the amount that the options would trade at in the financial markets, and which traders and investors would be willing to pay for them. If Sunshine Rain was very large, it would not be unreasonable to view this as the cost of granting the options to the CEO, Ian Brown. Of course, in return, the company would expect Mr Brown to improve the value of the company to its shareholders by more than this amount. As we have seen, perhaps the main purpose of options is to align the interests of management with those of the shareholders of the firm. Under no circumstances, though, is the €24 million necessarily a fair measure of what the options are worth to Mr Brown.

As an illustration, suppose that the CEO of London Conversation plc has options on 1 million shares with an exercise price of €30 per share, and the current share price of London Conversation is €50. If the options were exercised today, they would be worth €20 million (an underestimation of their market value). Suppose, in addition, that the CEO owns €5 million in company equity and has €5 million in other assets. The CEO clearly has a very undiversified personal portfolio. By the standards of modern finance, having 25/30 or about 83 per cent of your personal wealth in one equity and its options is unnecessarily risky.

Although the CEO is wealthy by most standards, shifts in share price impact on the CEO's economic well-being. If the price drops from €50 per share to €30 per share, the current exercise value of the options on 1 million shares drops from €20 million down to zero. Ignoring the fact that if the options had more time to mature they might not lose all of this value, we nevertheless have a rather startling decline in the CEO's net worth from about €30 million to €8 million (€5 million in other assets plus equity that is now worth €3 million). But that is the purpose of giving the options and the equity holdings to the CEO – namely, to make the CEO's fortunes rise and fall with those of the company. It is why the company requires the executive to hold the options for at least a vesting period rather than letting the executive sell them to realize their value.

The implication is that when options are a large portion of an executive's net worth, the total value of the position to the executive is less than market value. As a purely financial matter, an executive might be happier with €5 million in cash rather than €20 million in options. At least the executive could then diversify his personal portfolio. The shift in recent years from executive share options to restricted stock units suggests that, in practice, the effective minimum value of executive share options is not zero. If companies systematically respond to deep out-of-the-money options by converting them to RSUs, the firms are exercising another option to exchange the share option for an RSU. As with any option, this has value to the holder, in this case the senior executive.

## 21.7  Equity as a Call Option on the Firm's Assets

One of the most important insights we gain from studying options is that the equity in a leveraged firm (one that has issued debt) is effectively a call option on the assets of the firm. This is a remarkable observation, and we explore it next.

Looking at an example is the easiest way to get started. Suppose a firm has a single debt issue outstanding. The face value is £1,000, and the debt is coming due in a year. There are no coupon payments between now and then, so the debt is effectively a pure discount bond. In addition, the current market value of the firm's assets is £980, and the risk-free rate is 12.5 per cent.

In a year, the shareholders will have a choice. They can pay off the debt for £1,000 and thereby acquire the assets of the firm free and clear, or they can default on the debt. If they default, the bondholders will own the assets of the firm.

In this situation the shareholders essentially have a call option on the assets of the firm, with an exercise price of £1,000. They can exercise the option by paying the £1,000, or they can choose not to exercise the option by defaulting. Whether or not they will choose to exercise obviously depends on the value of the firm's assets when the debt becomes due.

If the value of the firm's assets exceeds £1,000, then the option is in the money, and the shareholders will exercise by paying off the debt. If the value of the firm's assets is less than £1,000, then the option is out of the money, and the shareholders will optimally choose to default. What we now illustrate is that we can determine the values of the debt and equity using our option pricing results.

### Case I: The Debt Is Risk-Free

Suppose that in one year the firm's assets will be worth either £1,100 or £1,200. What is the value today of the equity in the firm? The value of the debt? What is the interest rate on the debt?

To answer these questions, we first recognize that the option (the equity in the firm) is certain to finish in the money, because the value of the firm's assets (£1,100 or £1,200) will always exceed the face value of the debt. In this case, from our discussion in previous sections, we know that the option value is simply the difference between the value of the underlying asset and the present value of the exercise price (calculated at the risk-free rate). The present value of £1,000 in one year at 12.5 per cent is £888.89. The current value of the firm is £980, so the option (the firm's equity) is worth £980 − 888.89 = £91.11.

What we see is that the equity, which is effectively an option to purchase the firm's assets, must be worth £91.11. The debt must therefore actually be worth £888.89. In fact, we didn't really need to know about options to handle this example, because the debt is risk-free. The reason is that the bondholders are certain to receive £1,000. Because the debt is risk-free, the appropriate discount rate (and the interest rate on the debt) is the risk-free rate, and we therefore know immediately that the current value of the debt is £1,000/1.125 = £888.89. The equity is thus worth £980 − 888.89 = £91.11, as we calculated.

### Case II: The Debt Is Risky

Suppose now that the value of the firm's assets in one year will be either £800 or £1,200. This case is a little more difficult, because the debt is no longer risk-free. If the value of the assets turns out to be £800, then the shareholders will not exercise their option and will thereby default. The equity is worth nothing in this case. If the assets are worth £1,200, then the shareholders will exercise their option to pay off the debt and will enjoy a profit of £1,200 − 1,000 = £200.

What we see is that the option (the equity in the firm) will be worth either zero or £200. The assets will be worth either £1,200 or £800. Based on our discussion in previous sections, a portfolio that has the present value of £800 invested in a risk-free asset and (£1,200 − 800)/(200 − 0) = 2 call options exactly replicates the value of the assets of the firm.

The present value of £800 at the risk-free rate of 12.5 per cent is £800/1.125 = £711.11. This amount, plus the value of the two call options, is equal to £980, the current value of the firm:

$$£980 = 2 \times C_0 + £711.11$$
$$C_0 = £134.44$$

Because the call option in this case is actually the firm's equity, the value of the equity is £134.44. The value of the debt is thus £980 − 134.44 = £845.56. Finally, because the debt has a £1,000 face value and a current value of £845.56, the interest rate is (£1,000/845.56) − 1 = 18.27%. This exceeds the risk-free rate, of course, because the debt is now risky.

---

**EXAMPLE 21.7**

## Equity as a Call Option

Swenson Software has a pure discount debt issue with a face value of €100. The issue is due in a year. At that time the assets of the firm will be worth either €55 or €160, depending on the sales success of Swenson's latest product. The assets of the firm are currently worth €110. If the risk-free rate is 10 per cent, what is the value of the equity in Swenson? The value of the debt? The interest rate on the debt?

To replicate the value of the assets of the firm, we first need to invest the present value of €55 in the risk-free asset. This costs €55/1.10 = €50. If the assets turn out to be worth €160, then the option is worth €160 − 100 = €60. Our risk-free asset will be worth €55, so we need (€160 − 55)/60 = 1.75 call options.

Because the firm is currently worth £110, we have:

$$€110 = 1.75 \times C_0 + €50$$
$$C_0 = €34.29$$

The equity is thus worth €34.29; the debt is worth €110 − 34.29 = €75.71. The interest rate on the debt is about (€100/75.71) − 1 = 32.1%.

---

**CONCEPT QUESTIONS**

21.7a Why do we say that the equity in a leveraged firm is effectively a call option on the firm's assets?

21.7b All other things being the same, would the shareholders of a firm prefer to increase or decrease the volatility of the firm's return on assets? Why? What about the bondholders? Give an intuitive explanation.

---

**real option**
An option that involves real assets as opposed to financial assets such as shares of equity.

## 21.8 Options and Capital Budgeting

Most of the options we have discussed so far are financial options, because they involve the right to buy or sell financial assets such as shares of equity. In contrast, **real options** involve real assets. As we shall discuss in this section, our understanding of capital budgeting can be greatly enhanced by recognizing that many corporate investment decisions really amount to the evaluation of real options.

To give a simple example of a real option, imagine that you are shopping for a used car. You find one that you like for £4,000, but you are not completely sure. So you give the owner of the car £150 to hold the car for you for one week, meaning that you have one week to buy the car, or else you forfeit your £150. As you probably recognize, what you have done here is purchase a call option, giving you the right to buy the car at a fixed price for a fixed time. It's a real option, because the underlying asset (the car) is a real asset.

The use of options such as the one in our car example is common in the business world. For example, property developers frequently need to purchase several smaller tracts of land from different owners to assemble a single larger tract. The development can't go forward unless all the smaller properties are obtained. In this case the developer will often buy options on the individual properties, but will exercise those options only if all the necessary pieces can be obtained.

These examples involve explicit options. As it turns out, almost all capital budgeting decisions contain numerous *implicit* options. We discuss the most important types of these next.

## The Investment Timing Decision

Consider a business that is examining a new project of some sort. What this normally means is that management must decide whether to make an investment outlay to acquire the new assets needed for the project. If you think about it, what management has is the right, but not the obligation, to pay some fixed amount (the initial investment) and thereby acquire a real asset (the project). In other words, essentially all proposed projects are real options!

Based on our discussion in previous chapters, you already know how to analyse proposed business investments. You would identify and analyse the relevant cash flows and assess the net present value (NPV) of the proposal. If the NPV is positive, you would recommend taking the project, where taking the project amounts to exercising the option.

There is a very important qualification to this discussion that involves mutually exclusive investments. Remember that two (or more) investments are said to be mutually exclusive if we can take only one of them. A standard example is a situation in which we own a piece of land that we wish to build on. We are considering building either a petrol station or an apartment building. We further think that both projects have positive NPVs, but of course we can take only one. Which one do we take? The obvious answer is that we take the one with the larger NPV.

Here is the key point. Just because an investment has a positive NPV doesn't mean we should take it today. That sounds like a complete contradiction of what we have said all along, but it isn't. The reason is that if we take a project today, we can't take it later. Put differently, almost all projects compete with themselves in time. We can take a project now, a month from now, a year from now, and so on. We therefore have to compare the NPV of taking the project now with the NPV of taking it later. Deciding when to take a project is called the *investment timing decision*.

A simple example is useful to illustrate the investment timing decision. A project costs €100 and has a single future cash flow. If we take it today, the cash flow will be €120 in one year. If we wait one year, the project will still cost €100, but the cash flow the following year (two years from now) will be €130, because the potential market is bigger. If these are the only two options, and the relevant discount rate is 10 per cent, what should we do?

To answer this question, we need to compute the two NPVs. If we take it today, the NPV is

$$\text{NPV} = -€100 + 120/1.1 = €9.09$$

If we wait one year, the NPV at that time would be

$$\text{NPV} = -€100 + 130/1.1 = €18.18$$

This €18.18 is the NPV one year from now. We need the value today, so we discount back one period:

$$NPV = €18.18/1.1 = €16.53$$

So the choice is clear. If we wait, the NPV is €16.53 today compared with €9.09 if we start immediately, so the optimal time to begin the project is one year from now.

The fact that we do not have to take a project immediately is often called the *option to wait*. In our simple example, the value of the option to wait is the difference in NPVs: €16.53 − 9.09 = €7.44. This €7.44 is the extra value created by deferring the start of the project as opposed to taking it today.

As our example illustrates, the option to wait can be valuable. Just how valuable depends on the type of project. If we were thinking about a consumer product intended to capitalize on a current fashion or trend, then the option to wait is probably not very valuable, because the window of opportunity is probably short. In contrast, suppose the project in question is a proposal to replace an existing production facility with a new, higher-efficiency one. This type of investment can be made now or later. In this case, the option to wait may be valuable.

---

**EXAMPLE 21.8**

## The Investment Timing Decision

A project costs £200 and has a future cash flow of £42 per year for ever. If we wait one year, the project will cost £240 because of inflation, but the cash flows will be £48 per year for ever. If these are the only two options, and the relevant discount rate is 12 per cent, what should we do? What is the value of the option to wait? In this case the project is a simple perpetuity. If we take it today, the NPV is

$$NPV = −£200 + 42/0.12 = £150$$

If we wait one year, the NPV at that time would be

$$NPV = −£240 + 48/0.12 = £160$$

So £160 is the NPV one year from now, but we need to know the value today. Discounting back one period, we get

$$NPV = £160/1.12 = £142.86.$$

If we wait, the NPV is £142.86 today compared with £150 if we start immediately, so the optimal time to begin the project is now.

What's the value of the option to wait? It is tempting to say that it is £142.86 − £150 = −£7.14, but that's wrong. Why? Because, as we discussed earlier, an option can never have a negative value. In this case the option to wait has a zero value.

---

There is another important aspect regarding the option to wait. Just because a project has a negative NPV today doesn't mean that we should permanently reject it. For example, suppose an investment costs £120 and has a perpetual cash flow of £10 per year. If the discount rate is 10 per cent, then the NPV is £10/0.10 − 120 = −£20, so the project should not be taken now.

We should not just forget about this project for ever, though. Suppose that next year, for some reason, the relevant discount rate fell to 5 per cent. Then the NPV would be £10/0.05 − 120 = £80, and we would take the project (assuming that further waiting wasn't even more valuable). More generally, as long as there is some possible future scenario under which a project has a positive NPV, then the option to wait is valuable, and we should just shelve the project proposal for now.

# Managerial Options

Once we decide the optimal time to launch a project, other real options come into play. In our capital budgeting analysis thus far we have more or less ignored the impact of managerial actions that might take place *after* a project is launched. In effect, we assumed that, once a project is launched, its basic features cannot be changed.

In reality, depending on what actually happens in the future, there will always be opportunities to modify a project. These opportunities, which are an important type of real option, are often called *managerial options*. There are a great number of these options. The ways in which a product is priced, manufactured, advertised or produced can all be changed, and these are just a few of the possibilities.

**Contingency Planning**   The various what-if procedures, particularly the break-even measures we discussed in an earlier chapter, have a use beyond that of simply evaluating cash flow and NPV estimates. We can also view these procedures and measures as primitive ways of exploring the dynamics of a project and investigating managerial options. What we think about in this case are some of the possible futures that could come about, and what actions we might take if they do.

For example, we might find that a project fails to break even when sales drop below 10,000 units. This is a fact that is interesting to know, but the more important thing is to then go on and ask: what actions are we going to take if this actually occurs? This is called *contingency planning*, and it amounts to an investigation of some of the managerial options implicit in a project.

There is no limit to the number of possible futures or contingencies we could investigate. However, there are some broad classes, and we consider these next.

**The Option to Expand**   One particularly important option we have not explicitly addressed is the option to expand. If we truly find a positive-NPV project, then there is an obvious consideration. Can we expand the project or repeat it to get an even larger NPV? Our static analysis implicitly assumes that the scale of the project is fixed.

For example, if the sales demand for a particular product were to greatly exceed expectations, we might investigate increasing production. If this is not feasible for some reason, then we could always increase cash flow by raising the price. Either way, the potential cash flow is higher than we have indicated, because we have implicitly assumed that no expansion or price increase is possible. Overall, because we ignore the option to expand in our analysis, we underestimate NPV (all other things being equal).

**The Option to Abandon**   At the other extreme, the option to scale back or even abandon a project is also quite valuable. For example, if a project does not break even on a cash flow basis, then it can't even cover its own expenses. We would be better off if we just abandoned it. Our DCF analysis implicitly assumes that we would keep operating even in this case.

If sales demand were significantly below expectations, we might be able to sell off some capacity or put it to another use. Maybe the product or service could be redesigned or otherwise improved. Regardless of the specifics, we once again *underestimate* NPV if we assume that the project must last for some fixed number of years, no matter what happens in the future.

**The Option to Suspend or Contract Operations**   An option that is closely related to the option to abandon is the option to suspend operations. Frequently we see companies choosing to temporarily shut down an activity of some sort. For example, car manufacturers sometimes find themselves with too many vehicles of a particular type. In this case production is often halted until the excess supply is worked off. At some point in the future, production resumes.

The option to suspend operations is particularly valuable in natural resource extraction. Suppose you own a gold mine. If gold prices fall dramatically, then your analysis might show that it costs more to extract an ounce of gold than you can sell the gold for, so you cease mining. The gold just stays in the ground, however, and you can always resume operations if the price rises sufficiently. In fact, operations might be suspended and restarted many times over the life of the mine.

Companies also sometimes choose to scale back an activity permanently. If a new product does not sell as well as planned, production might be cut back and the excess capacity put to some other use. This case is really just the opposite of the option to expand, so we shall label it the option to contract.

**Options in Capital Budgeting: An Example** Suppose we are examining a new project. To keep things relatively simple, let's say that we expect to sell 100 units per year at €1 net cash flow apiece into perpetuity. We thus expect that the cash flow will be €100 per year.

In one year we shall know more about the project. In particular, we shall have a better idea of whether it is successful. If it looks like a long-term success, the expected sales will be revised upwards to 150 units per year. If it does not, the expected sales will be revised downwards to 50 units per year. Success and failure are equally likely. Notice that because there is an even chance of selling 50 or 150 units, the expected sales are still 100 units, as we originally projected. The cost is €550, and the discount rate is 20 per cent. The project can be dismantled and sold in one year for €400 if we decide to abandon it. Should we take it?

A standard DCF analysis is not difficult. The expected cash flow is €100 per year for ever, and the discount rate is 20 per cent. The PV of the cash flows is €100/0.20 = €500, so the NPV is €500 − 550 = −€50. We shouldn't take the project.

This analysis ignores valuable options, however. In one year we can sell out for €400. How can we account for this? What we have to do is to decide what we are going to do one year from now. In this simple case we need to evaluate only two contingencies – an upward revision and a downward revision – so the extra work is not great.

In one year, if the expected cash flows are revised to €50, then the PV of the cash flows is revised downwards to €50/0.20 = €250. We get €400 by abandoning the project, so that is what we shall do (the NPV of keeping the project in one year is €250 − 400 = −€150).

If the demand is revised upwards, then the PV of the future cash flows at year 1 is €150/0.20 = €750. This exceeds the €400 abandonment value, so we shall keep the project.

We now have a project that costs €550 today. In one year we expect a cash flow of €100 from the project. In addition, this project will be worth either €400 (if we abandon it because it is a failure) or €750 (if we keep it because it succeeds). These outcomes are equally likely, so we expect the project to be worth (€400 + 750)/2, or €575.

Summing up, in one year we expect to have €100 in cash plus a project worth €575, or €675 total. At a 20 per cent discount rate this €675 is worth €562.50 today, so the NPV is €562.50 − 550 = €12.50. We should take the project.

The NPV of our project has increased by €62.50. Where did this come from? Our original analysis implicitly assumed we would keep the project, even if it was a failure. At year 1, however, we saw that we were €150 better off (€400 versus €250) if we abandoned. There was a 50 per cent chance of this happening, so the expected gain from abandoning is €75. The PV of this amount is the value of the option to abandon: €75/1.20 = €62.50.

**Strategic Options** Companies sometimes undertake new projects just to explore possibilities and evaluate potential future business strategies. This is a little like testing the water by sticking a toe in before diving. Such projects are difficult to analyse using conventional DCF methods, because most of the benefits come in the form of *strategic options* – that is, options for future, related business moves. Projects that create such options may be very valuable, but that value is difficult to measure. Research and development, for example, is an important and valuable activity for many firms, precisely because it creates options for new products and procedures.

To give another example, a large manufacturer might decide to open a retail outlet as a pilot study. The primary goal is to gain some market insight. Because of the high start-up costs, this one operation won't break even. However, using the sales experience gained from the pilot, the firm can then evaluate whether to open more outlets, to change the product mix, to enter new markets, and so on. The information gained and the resulting options for actions are all valuable, but coming up with a reliable cash figure is probably not feasible.

**Conclusion** We have seen that incorporating options into capital budgeting analysis is not easy. What can we do about them in practice? The answer is that we need to keep them in mind as we work with the projected cash flows. We shall tend to underestimate NPV by ignoring options. The damage might be small for a highly structured, very specific proposal, but it might be great for an exploratory one.

| CONCEPT QUESTIONS | 21.8a | Why do we say that almost every capital budgeting proposal involves mutually exclusive alternatives? |
| | 21.8b | What are the options to expand, abandon, and suspend operations? |
| | 21.8c | What are strategic options? |

# Summary and Conclusions

This chapter has described the basics of option valuation and discussed option-like corporate securities:

1 Options are contracts giving the right, but not the obligation, to buy and sell underlying assets at a fixed price during a specified period. The most familiar options are puts and calls involving shares of equity. These options give the holder the right, but not the obligation, to sell (the put option) or buy (the call option) shares of equity at a given price.

   As we discussed, the value of any option depends on only five factors:

   (a) The price of the underlying asset.

   (b) The exercise price.

   (c) The expiration date.

   (d) The interest rate on risk-free bonds.

   (e) The volatility of the underlying asset's value.

2 The put–call parity (PCP) condition tells us that among a call option, a put option, a risk-free investment such as a T-bill, and an underlying asset such as shares of equity, we can replicate any one using the other three.

3 The Black–Scholes Option Pricing Model (OPM) lets us explicitly value call options given values for the five relevant inputs, which are the price of the underlying asset, the strike price, the time to expiration, the risk-free rate, and the standard deviation of the return on the underlying asset.

4 Many companies use executive share options (ESOs). Such options are similar to call options, and serve to motivate employees to boost share prices. ESOs are also an important form of compensation for many workers, particularly at more senior management levels.

5 Almost all capital budgeting proposals can be viewed as real options. Also, projects and operations contain implicit options, such as the option to expand, the option to abandon, and the option to suspend or contract operations.

# Chapter Review and Self-Test Problems

**21.1** **Value of a Call Option** Equity in REM plc is currently selling for £25 per share. In one year the price will be either £20 or £30. T-bills with one year to maturity are paying 10 per cent. What is the value of a call option with a £20 exercise price? A £6 exercise price?

**21.2** **Put–Call Parity** An equity sells for €40 per share. The continuously compounded risk-free rate is 8 per cent per year. A call option with one month to expiration and a strike price of €45 sells for €1. What is the value of a put option with the same expiration and strike?

**21.3** **Black–Scholes** An equity sells for €40 per share. The continuously compounded risk-free rate is 4 per cent. The standard deviation of the return on the equity is 80 per cent. What is the value of a put option with a strike of €45 and a three-month expiration?

# Answers to Chapter Review and Self-Test Problems

**21.1** With a £20 exercise price, the option can't finish out of the money (it can finish 'at the money' if the share price is £20). We can replicate the value of the equity by investing the present value of £20 in T-bills and buying one call option. Buying the T-bill will cost £20/1.1 = £18.18.

If the share price ends up at £20, the call option will be worth zero and the T-bill will pay £20. If the share price ends up at £30, the T-bill will again pay £20, and the option will be worth £30 – 20 = £10, so the package will be worth £30. Because the T-bill-call option combination exactly duplicates the pay-off on the equity, it has to be worth £25 or arbitrage is possible. Using the notation from the chapter, we can calculate the value of the call option:

$$S_0 = C_0 + E/(1 + R_f)$$
$$£25 = C_0 + £18.18$$
$$C_0 = £6.82$$

With the £26 exercise price we start by investing the present value of the lower share price in T-bills. This guarantees us £20 when the share price is £20. If the share price is £30, then the option is worth £30 – 26 = £4. We have £20 from our T-bill, so we need £10 from the options to match the equity. Because each option is worth £4 in this case, we need to buy £10/4 = 2.5 call options. Notice that the difference in the possible share prices ($\Delta S$) is £10 and the difference in the possible option prices ($\Delta C$) is £4, so $S/C = 2.5$.

To complete the calculation, we note that the present value of the £20 plus 2.5 call options has to be £25 to prevent arbitrage, so:

$$£25 = 2.5 \times C_0 + £20/1.1$$
$$C_0 = £6.82/2.5$$
$$= £2.73$$

**21.2** The PCP condition says that

$$S + P = E \times e^{-Rt} + C$$

Filling in the relevant numbers and rearranging to solve for $P$, the put price, we get:

$$P = €45 \times e^{-0.08(1/12)} + 1 - 40$$
$$= €5.70$$

**21.3** We shall do this one the long way, and then check our answer using our options spreadsheet. We shall calculate the value of a call option and then convert it to a put using PCP. We first need $d_1$ and $d_2$.

$$d_1 = \left[ \ln\left(\frac{S}{E}\right) + (R + \sigma^2/2)t \right] / \sqrt{\sigma^2 t}$$

$$= \left[ \ln\left(\frac{40}{45}\right) + (0.04 + 0.8^2/2) \times \frac{1}{4} \right] / \sqrt{0.8^2 \times \frac{1}{4}}$$

$$= -0.07$$

$$d_2 = d_1 - \sqrt{\sigma^2 t}$$
$$= -0.47$$

Referring to Table 21.4, the values of $N(d_1)$ and $N(d_2)$ are 0.4721 and 0.3192, respectively. Notice that in both cases we average two values. Plugging all the numbers in:

$$C = S \times [N(d_1)] - Ee^{-Rt} \times [N(d_2)]$$
$$= €40 \times 0.4721 - €45 \times e^{-0.04 \times (1/4)} \times 0.3192$$
$$= €4.66$$

Converting to a put as in our previous question:

$$P = Ee^{-Rt} + C - S$$

Plugging in the relevant numbers, we get

$$P = €45e^{-0.04(1/4)} + 4.66 - 40$$
$$= €9.21$$

Using our spreadsheet, we get the following:

| | A | B | C | D | E |
|---|---|---|---|---|---|
| 1 | Share Price = | 40 | | d1 = | -0.06946 |
| 2 | Strike Price = | 45 | | d2 = | -0.46946 |
| 3 | Sigma = | 0.8 | | N(d1) = | 0.472313 |
| 4 | Time = | 0.25 | | N(d2) = | 0.319371 |
| 5 | Rate = | 0.04 | | | |
| 6 | | | | | |
| 7 | Call = | 4.6638 | | Put = | 9.216043 |

Our 'by hand' approach was pretty accurate in this case.

# Concepts Review and Critical Thinking Questions

1  **Options [LO1]**   What is a call option? A put option? Under what circumstances might you want to buy each? Which one has greater *potential* profit? Why?

2  **Options [LO1]**   Complete the following sentence for each of these investors:

   **(a)**   A buyer of call options.

   **(b)**   A buyer of put options.

   **(c)**   A seller (writer) of call options.

   **(d)**   A seller (writer) of put options.

   'The (buyer/seller) of a (put/call) option (pays/receives) money for the (right/obligation) to (buy/sell) a specified asset at a fixed price for a fixed length of time.'

3 **Intrinsic Value [LO2]** What is the intrinsic value of a call option? How do we interpret this value?

4 **Put Options [LO2]** What is the value of a put option at maturity? Based on your answer, what is the intrinsic value of a put option?

5 **Option Pricing [LO2]** You notice that the share price of Patel Corporation is £50 per share. Call options with an exercise price of £35 per share are selling for £10. What's wrong here? Describe how you can take advantage of this mispricing if the option expires today.

6 **Options and Stock Risk [LO2]** If the risk of an equity increases, what is likely to happen to the price of call options on the equity? To the price of put options? Why?

7 **Option Rise [LO2]** The unsystematic risk of a share of equity is irrelevant in valuing the equity because it can be diversified away; therefore, it is also irrelevant for valuing a call option on the equity. True or false? Explain.

8 **Option Pricing [LO2]** Suppose a certain equity currently sells for €30 per share. If a put option and a call option are available with €30 exercise prices, which do you think will sell for more, the put or the call? Explain.

9 **Option Price and Interest Rates [LO2]** Suppose the interest rate on T-bills suddenly and unexpectedly rises. All other things being the same, what is the impact on call option values? On put option values?

10 **Option to Abandon [LO7]** What is the option to abandon? Explain why we underestimate NPV if we ignore this option.

11 **Option to Expand [LO7]** What is the option to expand? Explain why we underestimate NPV if we ignore this option.

12 **Capital Budgeting Options [LO7]** In Chapter 9 we discussed Porsche's launch of its new Cayenne. Suppose sales of the Cayenne go extremely well, and Porsche is forced to expand output to meet demand. Porsche's action in this case would be an example of exploiting what kind of option?

13 **Option to Suspend [LO7]** Natural resource extraction facilities (such as oil wells or gold mines) provide a good example of the value of the option to suspend operations. Why?

14 **Executive Share Options [LO5]** You own equity in the Hendrix Guitar Company. The company has implemented a plan to award executive share options. As a shareholder, does the plan benefit you? If so, what are the benefits?

15 **Options and Expiration Dates [LO2]** What is the impact of lengthening the time to expiration on an option's value? Explain.

16 **Options and Share Price Volatility [LO2]** What is the impact of an increase in the volatility of the underlying equity's return on an option's value? Explain.

17 **Protective Puts [LO3]** The protective put strategy we discussed in the chapter is sometimes referred to as *share price insurance* . Why?

18 **Option Valuation and NPV [LO5]** You are CEO of Titan Industries and have just been awarded a large number of executive share options. The company has two mutually exclusive projects available. The first project has a large NPV and will reduce the total risk of the company. The second project has a small NPV and will increase the total risk of the company. You have decided to accept the first project, when you remember your executive share options. How might this affect your decision?

19 **Put–Call Parity [LO3]** You find a put and a call with the same exercise price and maturity. What do you know about the relative prices of the put and call? Prove your answer, and provide an intuitive explanation.

20  **Put–Call Parity [LO3]**   A put and a call have the same maturity and strike price. If they have the same price, which one is in the money? Prove your answer, and provide an intuitive explanation.

21  **Put–Call Parity [LO3]**   One thing put–call parity tells us is that, given any three of an equity, a call, a put and a T-bill, the fourth can be synthesized or replicated using the other three. For example, how can we replicate a share of equity using a call, a put and a T-bill?

# connect Questions and Problems

**BASIC**
**1–9**

1  **Calculating Option Values [LO2]**   T-bills currently yield 5.5 per cent. Equity in Nina Manufacturing is currently selling for 55 Swedish krona (SKr) per share. There is no possibility that the equity will be worth less than SKr50 per share in one year.

(a)  What is the value of a call option with a SKr45 exercise price? What is the intrinsic value?

(b)  What is the value of a call option with a SKr35 exercise price? What is the intrinsic value?

(c)  What is the value of a put option with a SKr45 exercise price? What is the intrinsic value?

2  **Calculating Pay-offs [LO1]**   Use the option quote information on Fortis from Euronext Liffe shown here to answer the questions that follow.

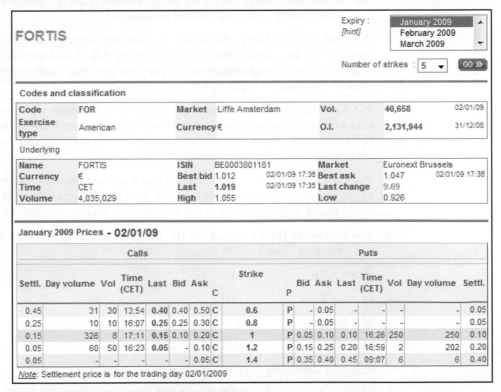

(a)  Suppose you buy 10 contracts of the January €1.20 call option. How much will you pay, ignoring commissions?

(b)  In part (a), suppose that Fortis equity is selling for €1.40 per share on the expiration date. How much is your options investment worth? What if the terminal share price is €1.05? Explain.

(c) Suppose you buy 10 contracts of the January €0.80 put option. What is your maximum gain? On the expiration date, Fortis is selling for €0.64 per share. How much is your options investment worth? What is your net gain?

(d) In part (c), suppose you *sell* 10 of the January €0.80 put contracts. What is your net gain or loss if Fortis is selling for €0.64 at expiration? For €1.32? What is the break-even price – that is, the terminal share price that results in a zero profit?

3 **Calculating Option Values [LO2]** The price of Ervin plc share will be either £75 or £95 at the end of the year. Call options are available with one year to expiration. T-bills currently yield 6 per cent.

(a) Suppose the current price of Ervin equity is £80. What is the value of the call option if the exercise price is £70 per share?

(b) Suppose the exercise price is £90 in part (a). What is the value of the call option now?

4 **Equity as an Option [LO6]** Rackin Pinion NV's assets are currently worth €1,050. In one year they will be worth either €1,000 or €1,270. The risk-free interest rate is 7 per cent. Suppose Rackin Pinion has an outstanding debt issue with a face value of €1,000.

(a) What is the value of the equity?

(b) What is the value of the debt? The interest rate on the debt?

(c) Would the value of the equity go up or down if the risk-free rate were 20 per cent? Why? What does your answer illustrate?

5 **Put–Call Parity [LO3]** An equity is currently selling for €61 per share. A call option with an exercise price of €65 sells for €4.12 and expires in three months. If the risk-free rate of interest is 2.6 per cent per year, compounded continuously, what is the price of a put option with the same exercise price?

6 **Put–Call Parity [LO3]** A put option and a call option with an exercise price of €70 and three months to expiration sell for €2.87 and €4.68, respectively. If the risk-free rate is 4.8 per cent per year, compounded continuously, what is the current share price?

7 **Put–Call Parity [LO3]** A put option and a call option with an exercise price of £65 expire in two months and sell for £2.86 and £4.08, respectively. If the equity is currently priced at £65.80, what is the annual continuously compounded rate of interest?

8 **Black–Scholes [LO2]** What are the prices of a call option and a put option with the following characteristics?

| | |
|---|---|
| Share price | = £86 |
| Exercise price | = £90 |
| Risk-free rate | = 4% per year, compounded continuously |
| Maturity | = 8 months |
| Standard deviation | = 62% per year |

9 **Black–Scholes and Asset Value [LO2]** You own a plot of land in Ardnamurchin, Scotland, that is currently unused. Similar plots have recently sold for £1.6 million. Over the past five years the price of land in the area has increased 12 per cent per year, with an annual standard deviation of 20 per cent. A buyer has recently approached you and wants an option to buy the land in the next 12 months for £1.75 million. The risk-free rate of interest is 5 per cent per year, compounded continuously. How much should you charge for the option?

10  **Abandonment Value [LO7]**  We are examining a new project. We expect to sell 7,500 units per year at £68 net cash flow apiece for the next 10 years. In other words, the annual operating cash flow is projected to be £68 × 7,500 = £510,000. The relevant discount rate is 14 per cent, and the initial investment required is £2,300,000.

(a)  What is the base-case NPV?

(b)  After the first year, the project can be dismantled and sold for £1,500,000. If expected sales are revised, based on the first year's performance, when would it make sense to abandon the investment? In other words, at what level of expected sales would it make sense to abandon the project?

(c)  Explain how the £1,500,000 abandonment value can be viewed as the opportunity cost of keeping the project in one year.

11  **Abandonment [LO7]**  In the previous problem, suppose you think it is likely that expected sales will be revised upwards to 9,500 units if the first year is a success, and revised downwards to 4,000 units if the first year is not a success.

(a)  If success and failure are equally likely, what is the NPV of the project? Consider the possibility of abandonment in answering.

(b)  What is the value of the option to abandon?

12  **Abandonment and Expansion [LO7]**  In the previous problem, suppose the scale of the project can be doubled in one year, in the sense that twice as many units can be produced and sold. Naturally, expansion will be desirable only if the project is a success. This implies that if the project is a success, projected sales after expansion will be 19,000. Again assuming that success and failure are equally likely, what is the NPV of the project? Note that abandonment is still an option if the project is a failure. What is the value of the option to expand?

13  **Abandonment Decisions [LO7]**  Allied Products is considering a new product launch. The firm expects to have annual operating cash flow of €18 million for the next 8 years. Allied Products uses a discount rate of 14 per cent for new product launches. The initial investment is €75 million. Assume that the project has no salvage value at the end of its economic life.

(a)  What is the NPV of the new product?

(b)  After the first year, the project can be dismantled and sold for €30 million. If the estimates of remaining cash flows are revised, based on the first year's experience, at what level of expected cash flows does it make sense to abandon the project?

14  **Black–Scholes [LO4]**  A call option matures in six months. The underlying share price is £85, and the share's return has a standard deviation of 20 per cent per year. The risk-free rate is 4 per cent per year, compounded continuously. If the exercise price is £0, what is the price of the call option?

15  **Black–Scholes [LO4]**  An equity is currently priced at £35. A call option with an expiration of one year has an exercise price of £50. The risk-free rate is 12 per cent per year, compounded continuously, and the standard deviation of the equity's return is infinitely large. What is the price of the call option?

16  **Abandonment Decisions [LO7]**  Consider the following project of Hand Clapper SA. The company is considering a four-year project to manufacture clap-command garage door openers. This project requires an initial investment of €12 million, which will be depreciated straight-line to zero over the project's life. An initial investment in net working capital of €900,000 is required to support spare parts inventory: this cost is fully recoverable whenever the project ends. The company believes it can generate €9.1 million in pre-tax revenues with €3.7 million in total pre-tax operating

costs. The tax rate is 38 per cent and the discount rate is 13 per cent. The market value of the equipment over the life of the project is as follows:

| Year | Market value (€ millions) |
|------|---------------------------|
| 1    | 8.20                      |
| 2    | 6.10                      |
| 3    | 4.70                      |
| 4    | 0.00                      |

(a) Assuming Hand Clapper operates this project for four years, what is the NPV?

(b) Now compute the project NPV assuming the project is abandoned after only one year, after two years, and after three years. What economic life for this project maximizes its value to the firm? What does this problem tell you about not considering abandonment possibilities when evaluating projects?

17 **Black–Scholes and Dividends [LO4]** In addition to the five factors discussed in the chapter, dividends also affect the price of an option. The Black–Scholes option pricing model with dividends is

$$C = S \times e^{-dt} \times N(d_1) - E \times e^{-Rt} \times N(d_2)$$
$$d_1 = [\ln(S/E) + (R - d + \sigma^2/2) \times t]/(\sigma \times \sqrt{t})$$
$$d_2 = d_1 - \sigma \times \sqrt{t}$$

All of the variables are the same as in the Black–Scholes model without dividends except for the variable $d$, which is the continuously compounded dividend yield on the share.

(a) What effect do you think the dividend yield will have on the price of a call option? Explain.

(b) Genmab A/S is currently priced at 2.26 Danish kroner (DKr) per share, the standard deviation of its return is 50 per cent per year, and the risk-free rate is 5 per cent per year, compounded continuously. What is the price of a call option with a strike price of DKr2.00 and a maturity of six months if the share has a dividend yield of 2 per cent per year?

18 **Put–Call Parity and Dividends [LO3]** The put–call parity condition is altered when dividends are paid. The dividend adjusted put–call parity formula is

$$S \times e^{-dt} + P = E \times e^{-Rt} + C$$

where $d$ is again the continuously compounded dividend yield.

(a) What effect do you think the dividend yield will have on the price of a put option? Explain.

(b) From the previous question, what is the price of a put option with the same strike price and time to expiration as the call option?

19 **Black–Scholes [LO4]** An equity is currently priced at £50. The share will never pay a dividend. The risk-free rate is 12 per cent per year, compounded continuously, and the standard deviation of the share's return is 60 per cent. A European call option on the share has a strike price of £100 and no expiration date, meaning that it has an infinite life. Based on Black–Scholes, what is the value of the call option? Do you see a paradox here? Do you see a way out of the paradox?

# Exotic Cuisines Employee Share Options

As a new university graduate, you've taken a management position with Exotic Cuisines plc, a restaurant chain that just went public last year. The company's restaurants specialize in exotic main dishes, using ingredients such as wild boar, crocodile and pheasant. A concern you had going in was that the restaurant business is very risky. However, after some due diligence, you discovered a common misperception about the restaurant industry. It is widely thought that 90 per cent of new restaurants close within three years; however, recent evidence suggests the failure rate is closer to 60 per cent over three years. So it is a risky business, although not as risky as you originally thought.

During your interview process, one of the benefits mentioned was employee share options. Upon signing your employment contract, you received options with a strike price of £50 for 10,000 shares of company equity. As is fairly common, your share options have a three-year vesting period and a 10-year expiration, meaning that you cannot exercise the options for three years, and you lose them if you leave before they vest. After the three-year vesting period you can exercise the options at any time. Thus the employee share options are European (and subject to forfeit) for the first three years and American afterwards. Of course, you cannot sell the options, nor can you enter into any sort of hedging agreement. If you leave the company after the options vest, you must exercise within 90 days or forfeit.

Exotic Cuisines equity is currently trading at £24.38 per share, a slight increase from the initial offering price last year. There are no market-traded options on the company's equity. Because the company has been traded for only about a year, you are reluctant to use the historical returns to estimate the standard deviation of the equity's return. However, you have estimated that the average annual standard deviation for restaurant company shares is about 55 per cent. Because Exotic Cuisines is a newer restaurant chain, you decide to use a 60 per cent standard deviation in your calculations. The company is relatively young, and you expect that all earnings will be reinvested back into the company for the near future. Therefore you expect no dividends will be paid for at least the next 10 years. A three-year Treasury note currently has a yield of 3.8 per cent, and a 10-year Treasury note has a yield of 4.4 per cent.

## QUESTIONS

1  You're trying to value your options. What minimum value would you assign? What is the maximum value you would assign?

2  Suppose that in three years the company's equity is trading at £60. At that time, should you keep the options or exercise them immediately? What are some of the important determinants in making such a decision?

3  Your options, like most employee share options, are not transferable or tradable. Does this have a significant effect on the value of the options? Why?

4  Why do you suppose employee share options usually have a vesting provision? Why must they be exercised shortly after you depart the company even after they vest?

5  As we have seen, much of the volatility in a company's share price is due to systematic or market-wide risks. Such risks are beyond the control of a company and its employees. What are the implications for employee share options? In the light of your answer, can you recommend an improvement over traditional employee share options?

# Mergers and Acquisitions

## KEY NOTATIONS

| | |
|---|---|
| EPS | Earnings per share |
| NPV | Net present value |
| $V$ | Value of firm |

## LEARNING OBJECTIVES

After studying this chapter, you should understand:

LO1 The different types of merger and acquisition, why they should (or shouldn't) take place, and the terminology associated with them.

LO2 How accountants construct the combined balance sheet of the new company.

LO3 The gains from a merger or acquisition, and how to value the transaction.

THE 2009 CONSOLIDATION OF TWO BRITISH BANKS, Halifax Bank of Scotland (HBOS) plc and Lloyds TSB plc, was just one of many corporate restructurings that took place as a result of the major downturn in developed economies. To understand the importance of the HBOS–Lloyds TSB consolidation, it is necessary to consider both banks in the context of the larger British banking sector. HBOS was Britain's largest mortgage lender, with a market share of 20 per cent. Lloyds TSB was in a similar position, but slightly smaller, having a market share of 9 per cent. Combining both companies resulted in the largest bank in the UK.

The consolidation also led to the British government owning 43.4 per cent of the shares of the new entity, Lloyds Banking Group plc. This was later increased to 65 per cent because of the disastrous state of HBOS's bad debts. So why did Lloyds TSB merge with HBOS? HBOS was in serious difficulty resulting from significant exposures to short-term funding requirements and bad loan portfolios. Hindsight has shown that Lloyds would have been far better off without the 'toxic assets' they inherited from the consolidation.

The main reason given by both firms for the merger was cost savings, which were estimated to be £1.5 billion per annum. Of course, the cost savings were only an estimate, and often such estimates are incorrect. Unfortunately for the new Lloyds Banking Group, the markets did not respond well, and in the first week of trading the share price collapsed. How do companies like Lloyds and HBOS determine whether an acquisition or merger is a good idea? This chapter explores the reasons why corporate restructurings, such as mergers, should take place – and, just as important, reasons why they should not.

There is no more dramatic or controversial activity in corporate finance than the acquisition of one firm by another, or the merger of two firms. It is the stuff of headlines in the financial press, and it is occasionally an embarrassing source of scandal.

The acquisition of one firm by another is, of course, an investment made under uncertainty, and the basic principles of valuation apply. One firm should acquire another only if doing so generates a positive net present value for the shareholders of the acquiring firm. However, because the NPV of an acquisition candidate can be difficult to determine, mergers and acquisitions, or M&A activities, are interesting topics in their own right.

Some of the special problems that come up in this area of finance include the following:

- The benefits from acquisitions can depend on such things as strategic fits. Strategic fits are difficult to define precisely, and it is not easy to estimate the value of strategic fits using discounted cash flow techniques.

- There can be complex accounting, tax and legal effects that must be taken into account when one firm is acquired by another.

- Acquisitions are an important control device for shareholders. Some acquisitions are a consequence of an underlying conflict between the interests of existing managers and those of shareholders. Agreeing to be acquired by another firm is one way in which shareholders can remove existing managers.

- Mergers and acquisitions sometimes involve 'unfriendly' transactions. In such cases, when one firm attempts to acquire another, the activity does not always confine itself to quiet, genteel negotiations. The sought-after firm often resists takeover, and may resort to defensive tactics with exotic names such as poison pills, greenmail and white knights.

We discuss these and other issues associated with mergers in the sections that follow. We begin by introducing the basic legal, accounting and tax aspects of acquisitions.

## 22.1 The Legal Forms of Acquisition

There are three basic legal procedures that one firm can use to acquire another firm:

1 Merger or consolidation

2 Acquisition of shares

3 Acquisition of assets

Although these forms are different from a legal standpoint, the financial press frequently does not distinguish between them. The term *merger* is often used regardless of the actual form of the acquisition.

In our discussion we shall frequently refer to the acquiring firm as the bidder. This is the company that offers to distribute cash or securities to obtain the equity or assets of another company. The firm that is sought (and perhaps acquired) is often called the *target* firm. The cash or securities offered to the target firm are the *consideration* in the acquisition.

### Merger or Consolidation

A **merger** is the complete absorption of one firm by another. The acquiring firm retains its name and its identity, and it acquires all the assets and liabilities of the acquired firm. After a merger, the acquired firm ceases to exist as a separate business entity.

A **consolidation** is the same as a merger except that an entirely new firm is created. In a consolidation both the acquiring firm and the acquired firm terminate their previous legal existence and become part of a new firm. For this reason, the distinction between the acquiring and the acquired firm is not as important in a consolidation as it is in a merger.

The rules for mergers and consolidations are basically the same. Acquisition by merger or consolidation results in a combination of the assets and liabilities of

> **merger**
> The complete absorption of one company by another, wherein the acquiring firm retains its identity and the acquired firm ceases to exist as a separate entity.
>
> **consolidation**
> A merger in which an entirely new firm is created, and both the acquired and acquiring firms cease to exist.

acquired and acquiring firms; the only difference lies in whether or not a new firm is created. We shall henceforth use the term *merger* to refer generically to both mergers and consolidations.

There are some advantages and some disadvantages of using a merger to acquire a firm:

- A primary advantage is that a merger is legally simple, and does not cost as much as other forms of acquisition. The reason is that the firms simply agree to combine their entire operations. Thus, for example, there is no need to transfer title in individual assets of the acquired firm to the acquiring firm.

- A primary disadvantage is that a merger must be approved by a vote of the shareholders of each firm.

Typically, two-thirds (or even more) of the share votes are required for approval. Obtaining the necessary votes can be time-consuming and difficult. Furthermore, as we discuss in greater detail a bit later, the co-operation of the target firm's existing management is almost a necessity for a merger. This co-operation may not be easily or cheaply obtained.

## Acquisition of Shares

**tender offer**
A public offer by one firm to directly buy the shares of another firm.

A second way to acquire another firm is simply to purchase the firm's voting shares with an exchange of cash, shares of equity, or other securities. This process will often start as a private offer from the management of one firm to that of another.

Regardless of how it starts, at some point the offer is taken directly to the target firm's shareholders. This can be accomplished by a **tender offer**. A tender offer is a public offer to buy shares. It is made by one firm directly to the shareholders of another firm.

Those shareholders who choose to accept the offer tender their shares by exchanging them for cash or securities (or both), depending on the offer. A tender offer is frequently contingent on the bidder's obtaining some percentage of the total voting shares. If not enough shares are tendered, then the offer might be withdrawn or reformulated.

The tender offer is communicated to the target firm's shareholders by public announcements such as those made in newspaper advertisements. Sometimes, a general mailing is used in a tender offer. This is not common, however, because a general mailing requires the names and addresses of the shareholders of record. Obtaining such a list without the target firm's co-operation is not easy.

The following are some factors involved in choosing between an acquisition of shares and a merger:

- In an acquisition of shares no shareholder meetings have to be held, and no vote is required. If the shareholders of the target firm don't like the offer, they are not required to accept it, and need not tender their shares.

- In an acquisition of shares the bidding firm can deal directly with the shareholders of the target firm by using a tender offer. The target firm's management and board of directors can be bypassed.

- Acquisition is occasionally unfriendly. In such cases an acquisition of shares is used in an effort to circumvent the target firm's management, which is usually actively resisting acquisition. Resistance by the target firm's management often makes the cost of acquisition of shares higher than the cost of a merger.

- Frequently, a significant minority of shareholders will hold out in a tender offer. The target firm cannot be completely absorbed when this happens, and this may delay realization of the merger benefits, or may be costly in some other way.

- Complete absorption of one firm by another requires a merger. Many acquisitions by shares are followed up with a formal merger later.

## Acquisition of Assets

A firm can effectively acquire another firm by buying most or all of its assets. This accomplishes the same thing as buying the company. In this case, however, the target firm will not necessarily cease to exist; it will have just sold off its assets. The 'shell' will still exist unless its shareholders choose to dissolve it.

This type of acquisition requires a formal vote of the shareholders of the selling firm. One advantage of this approach is that there is no problem with minority shareholders holding out. However, acquisition of assets may involve transferring titles in individual assets. The legal process of transferring assets can be costly.

## Acquisition Classification

Financial analysts typically classify acquisitions into three types:

1   *Horizontal acquisition*: This is an acquisition of a firm in the same industry as the bidder. The firms compete with each other in their product markets. Lloyds TSB's merger with HBOS in 2009 is an example of a horizontal merger in the banking industry.

2   *Vertical acquisition*: A vertical acquisition involves firms at different steps of the production process. The acquisition by an airline company of a travel agency would be a vertical acquisition.

3   *Conglomerate acquisition*: When the bidder and the target firm are in unrelated lines of business, the merger is called a conglomerate acquisition. The acquisition of a food products firm by a computer firm would be considered a conglomerate acquisition.

## A Note about Takeovers

*Takeover* is a general and imprecise term referring to the transfer of control of a firm from one group of shareholders to another. A takeover thus occurs whenever one group takes control from another.

This can occur through any one of three means: acquisitions, proxy contests, or going-private transactions. Thus takeovers encompass a broader set of activities than just acquisitions. These activities can be depicted as shown in Fig. 22.1.

As we have already mentioned, a takeover achieved by acquisition will occur by merger, tender offer, or purchase of assets. In mergers and tender offers, the bidder buys the voting equity of the target firm.

Takeovers can also occur with **proxy contests**. These occur when a group attempts to gain controlling seats on the board of directors by voting in new directors. A proxy is the right to cast someone else's votes. In a proxy contest, proxies are solicited by an unhappy group of shareholders from the rest of the shareholders.

> **proxy contest**
> An attempt to gain control of a firm by soliciting a sufficient number of shareholder votes to replace existing management.

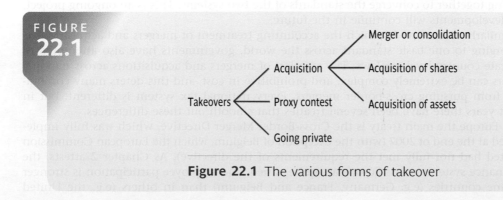

**Figure 22.1** The various forms of takeover

**going-private transactions** Transactions in which all publicly owned equity in a firm is replaced with complete equity ownership by a private group.

In **going-private transactions** all the equity shares of a public firm are purchased by a small group of investors. Usually, the group includes members of incumbent management and some outside investors. Such transactions have come to be known generically as **leveraged buyouts (LBOs)**, because a large percentage of the money needed to buy up the equity is usually borrowed. Such transactions are also termed *management buyouts* (MBOs) when existing management is heavily involved. The shares of the firm are delisted from stock exchanges, and can no longer be purchased in the open market.

**leveraged buyouts (LBOs)** Going-private transactions in which a large percentage of the money used to buy the equity is borrowed. Often incumbent management is involved.

## Alternatives to Merger

Firms don't have to merge to combine their efforts. At a minimum, two (or more) firms can simply agree to work together. They can sell each other's products, perhaps under different brand names, or jointly develop a new product or technology. Firms will frequently establish a **strategic alliance**, which is usually a formal agreement to co-operate in pursuit of a joint goal. An even more formal arrangement is a **joint venture**, which commonly involves two firms putting up the money to establish a new firm. For example, Verizon Wireless is a joint venture between Verizon Communications and Vodafone.

**strategic alliance** Agreement between firms to co-operate in pursuit of a joint goal.

**joint venture** Typically an agreement between firms to create a separate, co-owned entity established to pursue a joint goal.

| CONCEPT QUESTIONS | 22.1a | What is a merger? How does a merger differ from other acquisition forms? |
| | 22.1b | What is a takeover? |

## 22.2 Accounting and Tax Considerations

Many mergers involve companies in two different countries, which presents many difficulties in assessing the value of acquisitions. This is because accounting and tax rules can be very different across countries. In recent years there has been a concerted effort by accounting standard setters and regulatory authorities to streamline the administrative and bureaucratic challenges that face merging firms. In the subsequent discussion we shall try to be as generic as possible about the accounting and tax considerations, without losing the necessary important detail. However, given the heterogeneity of regulations across countries, it is impossible to be specific about every regulation in place regarding mergers.

In Europe and many other countries (but not the US), International Financial Reporting Standards govern the way that companies account for transactions. To improve the efficiency of the accounting treatment of cross-border mergers, the International Accounting Standards Board (IASB) and the US Financial Accounting Standards Board (FASB) have been working together to converge the standards of the two systems. This is an ongoing project, and developments will continue in the future.

Similarly to the way in which the accounting treatment of mergers and acquisitions is converging to one basic standard across the world, governments have also attempted to integrate country-level tax laws. The taxation of mergers and acquisitions across national borders can be extremely complex, and prohibitive in cost, and this deters many corporations from pursuing cross-border mergers. Every national tax system is different, but in recent years there have been several treaties that smooth out these differences.

In Europe the main treaty is the Cross-Border Merger Directive, which was fully implemented at the end of 2007 (with the exception of Belgium, which the European Commission reported had not fully met the requirements of the directive). As Chapter 2 attests, the governance systems across Europe are quite varied, and employee participation is stronger in some countries (e.g. Germany, France and Belgium) than in others (e.g. the United

Kingdom). Amalgamating the operations of corporations that are based in countries with different governance cultures and taxation systems presents some difficulty. The EU Merger Directive presents a cohesive framework that allows European national taxation systems to operate fully within a broader international context.

## 22.3 Gains from Acquisitions

To determine the gains from an acquisition, we first need to identify the relevant incremental cash flows or, more generally, the source of value. In the broadest sense, acquiring another firm makes sense only if there is some concrete reason to believe that the target firm will somehow be worth more in our hands than it is worth now. As we shall see, there are a number of reasons why this might be so.

### Synergy

Suppose Firm A is contemplating acquiring Firm B. The acquisition will be beneficial if the combined firm will have greater value than the sum of the values of the separate firms. If we let $V$ stand for the value of the merged firm, then the merger makes sense only if

$$V_{AB} > V_A + V_B$$

where $V_A$ and $V_B$ are the separate values. A successful merger thus requires that the value of the whole exceed the sum of the parts.

The difference between the value of the combined firm and the sum of the values of the firms as separate entities is the incremental net gain from the acquisition:

$$\Delta V = V_{AB} - (V_A + V_B) \tag{22.1}$$

When $\Delta V$ is positive, the acquisition is said to generate **synergy**.

If Firm A buys Firm B, it gets a company worth $V_B$ plus the incremental gain, $\Delta V$. The value of Firm B to Firm A ($V_B^*$) is thus

$$\text{Value of Firm B to Firm A} = V_B^*$$
$$= \Delta V + V_B$$

> **synergy**
> The positive incremental net gain associated with the combination of two firms through a merger or acquisition.

We place an asterisk (*) on $V_B^*$ to emphasize that we are referring to the value of Firm B to Firm A, not the value of Firm B as a separate entity.

$V_B^*$ can be determined in two steps: (1) estimating $V_B$; and (2) estimating $\Delta V$. If B is a public company, then its market value as an independent firm under existing management ($V_B$) can be observed directly. If Firm B is not publicly owned, then its value will have to be estimated, based on similar companies that *are* publicly owned. Either way, the problem of determining a value for $V_B^*$ requires the determination of a value for $\Delta V$.

To determine the incremental value of an acquisition, we need to know the incremental cash flows. These are the cash flows for the combined firm, less what A and B could generate separately. In other words, the incremental cash flow for evaluating a merger is the difference between the cash flow of the combined company and the sum of the cash flows for the two companies considered separately. We shall label this incremental cash flow $\Delta CF$.

# Synergy

Firms A and B are competitors with very similar assets and business risks. Both are all-equity firms with after-tax cash flows of £10 per year for ever, and both have an overall cost of capital of 10 per cent. Firm A is thinking of buying Firm B. The after-tax cash flow from the merged firm would be £21 per year. Does the merger generate synergy? What is $V_B^*$? What is $\Delta V$?

The merger does generate synergy, because the cash flow from the merged firm is $\Delta CF = £1$ greater than the sum of the individual cash flows (£21 versus £20). Assuming the risks stay the same, the value of the merged firm is £21/0.10 = £210. Firms A and B are each worth £10/0.10 = £100, for a total of £200. The incremental gain from the merger, $\Delta V$, is thus £210 − 200 = £10. The total value of Firm B to Firm A, $V_B^*$, is £100 (the value of B as a separate company) plus £10 (the incremental gain), or £110.

From our discussions in earlier chapters we know that the incremental cash flow, $\Delta CF$, can be broken down into four parts:

$$\Delta CF = \Delta EBIT + \Delta Depreciation - \Delta Tax - \Delta Capital\ requirements$$
$$= \Delta Revenue - \Delta Cost - \Delta Tax - \Delta Capital\ requirements$$

where $\Delta Revenue$ is the difference in revenues, $\Delta Cost$ is the difference in costs, $\Delta Tax$ is the difference in taxes, and $\Delta Capital$ requirements is the change in new non-current assets and net working capital.

Based on this breakdown, the merger will make sense only if one or more of these cash flow components are beneficially affected by the merger. The possible cash flow benefits of mergers and acquisitions thus fall into four basic categories: revenue enhancement, cost reductions, lower taxes, and reductions in capital needs.

## Revenue Enhancement

One important reason for an acquisition is that the combined firm may generate greater revenues than two separate firms. Increases in revenue may come from marketing gains, strategic benefits, or increases in market power.

**Marketing Gains**   It is frequently claimed that mergers and acquisitions can produce greater operating revenues from improved marketing. For example, improvements might be made in the following areas:

1   Previously ineffective media programming and advertising efforts

2   A weak existing distribution network

3   An unbalanced product mix

**Strategic Benefits**   Some acquisitions promise a strategic advantage. This is an opportunity to take advantage of the competitive environment if certain things occur or, more generally, to enhance management flexibility with regard to the company's future operations. In this latter sense, a strategic benefit is more like an option than a standard investment opportunity.

For example, suppose a computer manufacturer can use its technology to enter other businesses. The electronics and software technology from the original business can provide opportunities to begin manufacturing consumer electronics (think Apple).

One example is Procter & Gamble's initial acquisition of the Charmin Paper Company as a strategic investment, which allowed Procter & Gamble to develop a highly interrelated cluster of paper products – disposable nappies, paper towels, feminine hygiene products, and bathroom tissue.

**Market Power**   One firm may acquire another to increase its market share and market power. In such mergers, profits can be enhanced through higher prices and reduced competition for customers. Of course, mergers that substantially reduce competition in the market may be challenged by the governments, to avoid a monopoly situation that is too powerful.

## Cost Reductions

One of the most basic reasons to merge is that a combined firm may operate more efficiently than two separate firms. A firm can achieve greater operating efficiency in several different ways through a merger or an acquisition.

**Economies of Scale**   Economies of scale relate to the average cost per unit of producing goods and services. If the per-unit cost of production falls as the level of production increases, then an economy of scale exists (see Fig. 22.2).

Frequently, the phrase *spreading overhead* is used in connection with economies of scale. This expression refers to the sharing of central facilities such as corporate headquarters, top management and computer services. For example, in 2009, when Lloyds TSB and HBOS announced a merger agreement, this was one of the main reasons given for the action.

**Economies of Vertical Integration**   Operating economies can be gained from vertical combinations as well as from horizontal combinations. The main purpose of vertical acquisitions is to make it easier to co-ordinate closely related operating activities. Benefits from vertical integration are probably the reason why most forest product firms that cut timber also own sawmills and hauling equipment. Economies of vertical integration may explain why some airline companies have purchased hotels and car rental companies.

Technology transfers are another reason for vertical integration. Very frequently, a company will decide that the cheapest – and fastest – way to acquire another firm's technological skills is simply to buy the firm. For obvious reasons, this rationale is particularly common in high-tech industries.

**Complementary Resources**   Some firms acquire others to make better use of existing resources, or to provide the missing ingredient for success. Think of a ski equipment shop that could merge with a tennis equipment shop to produce more even sales over the winter and summer seasons, thereby making better use of shop capacity.

**FIGURE 22.2**

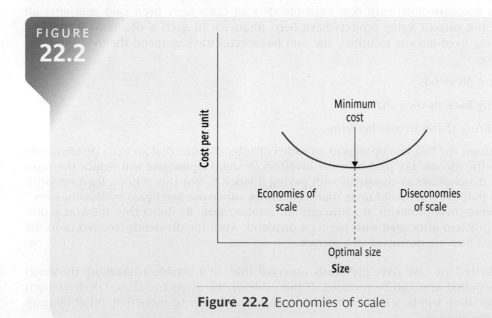

**Figure 22.2** Economies of scale

## Lower Taxes

Tax gains are a powerful incentive for some acquisitions. The possible tax gains from an acquisition include the following:

1  The use of tax losses

2  The use of unused debt capacity

3  The use of surplus funds

4  The ability to write up the value of depreciable assets

**Net Operating Losses**   Firms that lose money on a pre-tax basis will not pay taxes. Such firms can end up with tax losses they cannot use. These tax losses are referred to as *net operating losses* (NOL).

A firm with net operating losses may be an attractive merger partner for a firm with significant tax liabilities. In the absence of any other effects, the combined firm will have a lower tax bill than the two firms considered separately. This is a good example of how a firm can be more valuable merged than standing alone.

There are two qualifications to our NOL discussion:

1  Many countries' tax laws permit firms that experience periods of profit and loss to even things out through loss carry-back and carry-forward provisions. For example, a firm that has been profitable in the past but has a loss in the current year may get refunds of income taxes paid in the past three years. After that, losses could, for example, be carried forward for up to 20 years. Thus a merger to exploit unused tax shields must offer tax savings over and above what can be accomplished by firms via carry-overs.

2  Tax authorities may disallow an acquisition if the principal purpose of the acquisition is to avoid paying tax by acquiring a deduction or credit that would not otherwise be available.

**Unused Debt Capacity**   Some firms do not use as much debt as they are able to. This makes them potential acquisition candidates. Adding debt can provide important tax savings, and many acquisitions are financed with debt. The acquiring company can deduct interest payments on the newly created debt, and reduce taxes.

**Surplus Funds**   Another quirk in the tax laws involves surplus funds. Consider a firm that has free cash flow: cash flow available after all taxes have been paid, and after all positive net present value projects have been financed. In such a situation, aside from purchasing fixed-income securities, the firm has several ways to spend the free cash flow, including:

1  Paying dividends

2  Buying back its own shares

3  Acquiring shares in another firm

We discussed the first two options in an earlier chapter. We saw that an extra dividend will increase the income tax paid by some investors. A share repurchase will reduce the taxes paid by shareholders as compared with paying dividends, but this is not a legal option if the sole purpose is to avoid taxes that would have otherwise been paid by shareholders.

To avoid these problems, the firm can buy another firm. By doing this, the firm avoids the tax problem associated with paying a dividend. Also, the dividends received from the purchased firm are not taxed in a merger.

**Asset Write-Ups**   We have previously observed that, in a taxable acquisition, the assets of the acquired firm can be revalued. If the value of the assets increases, tax deductions for depreciation will be a benefit; but this benefit will usually be more than offset by taxes due on the write-up.

## Reductions in Capital Needs

All firms must invest in working capital and fixed assets to sustain an efficient level of operating activity. A merger may reduce the combined investments needed by the two firms. For example, Firm A may need to expand its manufacturing facilities, whereas Firm B may have significant excess capacity. It may be much cheaper for Firm A to buy Firm B than to build from scratch.

In addition, acquiring firms may see ways of managing existing assets more effectively. This can occur with a reduction in working capital resulting from more efficient handling of cash, trade receivables, or inventory. Finally, the acquiring firm may also sell off certain assets that are not needed in the combined firm.

Firms will often cite many reasons for merging. Typically, when firms agree to merge, they generate a list of the economic benefits that shareholders can expect from the merger.

## Avoiding Mistakes

Evaluating the benefit of a potential acquisition is more difficult than a standard capital budgeting analysis, because so much of the value can come from benefits that are intangible, or otherwise difficult to quantify. Consequently, there is a great deal of room for error. Here are some general rules that should be remembered:

1   *Do not ignore market values*: There is no point to, and little gain from, estimating the value of a publicly traded firm when that value can be directly observed. The current market value represents a consensus opinion of investors concerning the firm's value (under existing management). Use this value as a starting point. If the firm is not publicly held, then the place to start is with similar firms that are publicly held.

2   *Estimate only incremental cash flows*: It is important to estimate the incremental cash flows that will result from the acquisition. Only incremental cash flows from an acquisition will add value to the acquiring firm. Acquisition analysis should thus focus only on the newly created, incremental cash flows from the proposed acquisition.

3   *Use the correct discount rate*: The discount rate should be the required rate of return for the incremental cash flows associated with the acquisition. It should reflect the risk associated with the use of funds, not the source. In particular, if Firm A is acquiring Firm B, then Firm A's cost of capital is not particularly relevant. Firm B's cost of capital is a much more appropriate discount rate, because it reflects the risk of Firm B's cash flows.

4   *Be aware of transaction costs*: An acquisition may involve substantial (and sometimes astounding) transaction costs. These will include fees to investment bankers, legal fees, and disclosure requirements.

## A Note about Inefficient Management

There are firms whose value could be increased with a change in management. These are firms that are poorly run or otherwise do not efficiently use their assets to create shareholder value. Mergers are a means of replacing management in such cases.

The fact that a firm might benefit from a change in management does not necessarily mean that existing management is dishonest, incompetent, or negligent. Instead, just as some athletes are better than others, so might some management teams be better at running a business. This can be particularly true during times of technological change, or other periods when innovations in business practice are occurring. In any case, to the extent that corporate 'raiders' can identify poorly run firms or firms that, for other reasons, will benefit from a change in management, these raiders provide a valuable service to target firm shareholders and society in general.

**22.3a** What are the relevant incremental cash flows for evaluating a merger candidate?

**22.3b** What are some different sources of gain from acquisitions?

## 22.4 Some Financial Side Effects of Acquisitions

In addition to the various possibilities we have discussed thus far, mergers can have some purely financial side effects – that is, things that occur regardless of whether the merger makes economic sense or not. Two such effects are particularly worth mentioning: EPS growth and diversification.

### EPS Growth

An acquisition can create the appearance of growth in earnings per share, or EPS. This may fool investors into thinking that the firm is doing better than it really is. What happens is easiest to see with an example.

Suppose Global Resources Ltd acquires Regional Enterprises. The financial positions of Global and Regional before the acquisition are shown in Table 22.1. We assume that the merger creates no additional value, so the combined firm (Global Resources after acquiring Regional) has a value that is equal to the sum of the values of the two firms before the merger.

Before the merger, both Global and Regional have 100 shares outstanding. However, Global sells for £25 per share, compared with a price of £10 per share for Regional. Global therefore acquires Regional by exchanging 1 of its shares for every 2.5 Regional shares. Because there are 100 shares in Regional, this will take $100/2.5 = 40$ shares in all.

After the merger, Global will have 140 shares outstanding, and several things will happen (see the third column of Table 22.1):

1  The market value of the combined firm is £3,500. This is equal to the sum of the values of the separate firms before the merger. If the market is 'smart', it will realize that the combined firm is worth the sum of the values of the separate firms.

2  The earnings per share of the merged firm are £1.43. The acquisition enables Global to increase its earnings per share from £1 to £1.43, an increase of 43 per cent.

3  Because the share price of Global after the merger is the same as that before the merger, the price–earnings ratio must fall. This is true as long as the market is smart, and recognizes that the total market value has not been altered by the merger.

**TABLE 22.1**

|  | GR before merger | RE before merger | GR after merger: market is Smart | GR after merger: market is Fooled |
|---|---|---|---|---|
| Earnings per share (£) | 1 | 1 | 1.43 | 1.43 |
| Share price (£) | 25 | 10 | 25 | 35.71 |
| Price–earnings ratio | 25 | 10 | 17.5 | 25 |
| Number of shares | 100 | 100 | 140 | 140 |
| Total earnings (£) | 100 | 100 | 200 | 200 |
| Total value (£) | 2,500 | 1,000 | 3,500 | 5,000 |

**Table 22.1** Financial positions of Global Resources (GR) and Regional Enterprises (RE). Exchange ratio: 1 share in GR for 2.5 shares in RE

If the market is 'fooled', it might mistake the 43 per cent increase in earnings per share for true growth. In this case, the price–earnings ratio of Global may not fall after the merger. Suppose the price–earnings ratio of Global remains equal to 25. Because the combined firm has earnings of £200, the total value of the combined firm will increase to £5,000 (= 25 × £200). The per-share value for Global will increase to £35.71 (£5,000/140).

This is earnings growth magic. Like all good magic, it is just illusion. For it to work, the shareholders of Global and Regional must receive something for nothing. This, of course, is unlikely with so simple a trick.

## Diversification

Diversification is commonly mentioned as a benefit of a merger. The problem is that diversification *per se* probably does not create value. Going back to Chapter 12, recall that diversification reduces unsystematic risk. We also saw that the value of an asset depends on its systematic risk, and systematic risk is not directly affected by diversification. Because the unsystematic risk is not especially important, there is no particular benefit from reducing it.

Shareholders can get all the diversification they want by buying equities in different companies. As a result, they won't pay a premium for a merged company just for the benefit of diversification.

> **CONCEPT QUESTIONS**
>
> 22.4a Why can a merger create the appearance of earnings growth?
> 22.4b Why is diversification by itself not a good reason for a merger?

## 22.5 The Cost of An Acquisition

We've discussed some of the benefits of acquisition. We now need to discuss the cost of a merger. We learned earlier that the net incremental gain from a merger is

$$\Delta V = V_{AB} - (V_A + V_B) \tag{22.1}$$

Also, the total value of Firm B to Firm A, $V_B^*$, is

$$V_B^* = V_B + \Delta V \tag{22.2}$$

The NPV of the merger is therefore:

$$NPV = V_B^* - \text{Cost to Firm A of acquisition} \tag{22.3}$$

To illustrate, suppose we have the following pre-merger information for Firm A and Firm B:

|  | Firm A | Firm B |
|---|---|---|
| Share price (€) | 20 | 10 |
| Number of shares | 25 | 10 |
| Total market value (€) | 500 | 100 |

Both of these firms are 100 per cent equity. You estimate that the incremental value of the acquisition, $\Delta V$, is €100.

The board of Firm B has indicated that it will agree to a sale if the price is €150, payable in cash or shares. This price for Firm B has two parts. Firm B is worth €100 as a stand-alone, so this is the minimum value that we could assign to Firm B. The second part, €50, is called the *merger premium*, and it represents the amount paid above the stand-alone value.

Should Firm A acquire Firm B? Should it pay in cash or shares? To answer, we need to determine the NPV of the acquisition under both alternatives. We can start by noting that the value of Firm B to Firm A is

$$V_B^* = \Delta V + V_B$$
$$= €100 + 100$$
$$= €200$$

The total value received by A as a result of buying Firm B is thus €200. The question then is: how much does Firm A have to give up? The answer depends on whether cash or equity is used as the means of payment.

## Case I: Cash Acquisition

The cost of an acquisition when cash is used is just the cash itself. So, if Firm A pays €150 in cash to purchase all of the shares of Firm B, the cost of acquiring Firm B is €150.

The NPV of a cash acquisition is

$$NPV = V_B^* - \text{Cost}$$
$$= €200 - 150$$
$$= €50$$

The acquisition is therefore profitable.

After the merger, Firm AB will still have 25 shares outstanding. The value of Firm A after the merger is

$$V_{AB} = V_A + (V_B^* - \text{Cost})$$
$$= €500 + 200 - 150$$
$$= €550$$

This is just the pre-merger value of €500 plus the €50 NPV. The price per share after the merger is €550/25 = €22, representing a gain of €2 per share.

## Case II: Equity Acquisition

Things are somewhat more complicated when shares are the means of payment. In a cash merger, the shareholders in B receive cash for their equity. The cost of the acquisition in this case is the amount of cash needed to pay off B's shareholders. In a share merger no cash actually changes hands. Instead, the shareholders of Firm B come in as new shareholders in the merged firm. The value of the merged firm in this case will be equal to the pre-merger values of Firms A and B plus the incremental gain from the merger, $V$:

$$V_{AB} = V_A + V_B + \Delta V$$
$$= €500 + 100 + 100$$
$$= €700$$

To give €150 worth of shares for Firm B, Firm A will have to give up €150/20 = 7.5 shares. After the merger there will be 25 + 7.5 = 32.5 shares outstanding, and the per-share value will be €700/32.5 = €21.54.

Notice that the per-share price after the merger is lower under the share purchase option. The reason has to do with the fact that B's shareholders own equity in the new firm.

It appears that Firm A paid €150 for Firm B. However, it actually paid more than that. When all is said and done, B's shareholders own 7.5 shares of equity in the merged firm.

After the merger, each of these shares is worth €21.54. The total value of the consideration received by B's shareholders is thus $7.5 \times €21.54 = €161.55$.

This €161.55 is the true cost of the acquisition, because it is what the sellers actually end up receiving. The NPV of the merger to Firm A is

$$
\begin{aligned}
\text{NPV} &= V_B^* - \text{Cost} \\
&= €200 - 161.55 \\
&= €38.45
\end{aligned}
$$

We can check this by noting that A started with 25 shares worth €20 each. The gain to A of €38.45 works out to be $€38.45/25 = €1.54$ per share. The value of the equity has increased to €21.54, as we calculated.

When we compare the cash acquisition with the stock acquisition, we see that the cash acquisition is better in this case, because Firm A gets to keep all the NPV if it pays in cash. If it pays in equity, Firm B's shareholders share in the NPV by becoming new shareholders in A.

## Cash versus Shares

The distinction between cash and equity financing in a merger is an important one. If cash is used, the cost of an acquisition is not dependent on the acquisition gains. All other things being the same, if equity is used the cost is higher, because Firm A's shareholders must share the acquisition gains with the shareholders of Firm B. However, if the NPV of the acquisition is negative, then the loss will be shared between the two firms.

Whether a firm should finance an acquisition with cash or with shares of equity depends on several factors, including the following:

1 *Sharing gains*: If cash is used to finance the acquisition, the selling firm's shareholders will not participate in the potential gains from the merger. Of course, if the acquisition is not a success, the losses will not be shared, and shareholders of the acquiring firm will be worse off than if equity had been used.

2 *Taxes*: Acquisition by paying cash usually results in a taxable transaction. Acquisition by exchanging equity is generally tax-free.

3 *Control*: Acquisition by paying cash does not affect the control of the acquiring firm. Acquisition with voting shares may have implications for control of the merged firm.

In a typical year, in terms of the total number of deals, cash financing is much more common than equity financing. The same is usually true based on the total cash values, although the difference is smaller. The reason is that equity financing becomes more common if we look at very large deals.

| | | |
|---|---|---|
| **CONCEPT QUESTIONS** | 22.5a | Why does the true cost of a stock acquisition depend on the gain from the merger? |
| | 22.5b | What are some important factors in deciding whether to use equity or cash in an acquisition? |

## 22.6 Defensive Tactics

Target firm managers frequently resist takeover attempts. Resistance usually starts with press releases and mailings to shareholders that present management's viewpoint. It can eventually lead to legal action and solicitation of competing bids. Managerial action to defeat a takeover attempt may make target firm shareholders better off if it elicits a higher offer premium from the bidding firm or another firm.

Of course, management resistance may simply reflect pursuit of self-interest at the expense of shareholders. This is a controversial subject. At times, management resistance has greatly increased the amount ultimately received by shareholders. At other times, management resistance appears to have defeated all takeover attempts, to the detriment of shareholders.

In this section we describe various defensive tactics that have been used by target firms' management to resist unfriendly attempts. The law surrounding these defences is not settled, and some of these manoeuvres may ultimately be deemed illegal or otherwise unsuitable.

## The Corporate Charter

The corporate charter consists of the articles of incorporation and corporate by-laws that establish the governance rules of the firm. The corporate charter establishes the conditions that allow for a takeover. Firms frequently amend corporate charters to make acquisitions more difficult. For example, usually two-thirds (67 per cent) of the shareholders of record must approve a merger. Firms can make it more difficult to be acquired by changing this required percentage to 80 per cent or so. Such a change is called a *supermajority amendment*.

Another device is to stagger the election of the board members. This makes it more difficult to elect a new board of directors quickly. Such a board is sometimes called a *classified board*.

## Repurchase and Standstill Agreements

Managers of target firms may attempt to negotiate *standstill agreements*. These are contracts wherein the bidding firm agrees to limit its holdings in the target firm. These agreements usually lead to the end of a takeover attempt.

Standstill agreements often occur at the same time that a *targeted repurchase* is arranged. In a targeted repurchase a firm buys a certain amount of its own equity from an individual investor, usually at a substantial premium. These premiums can be thought of as payments to potential bidders to eliminate unfriendly takeover attempts. Critics of such payments view them as bribes, and label them *greenmail*.

## Poison Pills and Share Rights Plans

Illegal in Europe but common in the US, a *poison pill* is a tactic designed to repel would-be suitors. The term comes from the world of espionage. Agents are supposed to bite a pill of cyanide rather than permit capture. Presumably, this prevents enemy interrogators from learning important secrets.

In the equally colourful world of corporate finance, a poison pill is a financial device designed to make it impossible for a firm to be acquired without management's consent – unless the buyer is willing to commit financial suicide.

Poison pill provisions of one form or another are often called *share rights plans* (SRPs) or something similar. SRPs differ quite a bit in detail from company to company; we shall describe a kind of generic approach here. In general, when a company adopts an SRP, it distributes equity rights to its existing shareholders.

These rights allow shareholders to buy shares of equity (or preference shares) at some fixed price. The rights issued with an SRP have a number of unusual features. First, the exercise, or subscription, price on the right is usually set high enough that the rights are well out of the money, meaning that the purchase price is much higher than the current share price. The rights will often be good for 10 years, and the purchase, or exercise, price is usually a reasonable estimate of what the equity will be worth at the end of that time.

In addition, unlike ordinary equity rights, these rights can't be exercised immediately, and they can't be bought or sold separately from the ordinary shares. Also, they can essentially be cancelled by management at any time; often, they can be redeemed (bought back) for a penny apiece, or some similarly trivial amount.

Things get interesting when, under certain circumstances, the rights are 'triggered'. This means that the rights become exercisable, they can be bought and sold separately from the equity, and they are not easily cancelled or redeemed. Typically, the rights will be triggered when someone acquires 20 per cent of the ordinary equity, or announces a tender offer.

When the rights are triggered, they can be exercised. Because they are out of the money, this fact is not especially important. Certain other features come into play, however. The most important is the *flip-in provision*.

The flip-in provision is the 'poison' in the pill. In the event of an unfriendly takeover attempt, the holder of a right can pay the exercise price and receive equity in the target firm worth twice the exercise price. In other words, holders of the rights can buy shares in the target firm at half price. Simultaneously, the rights owned by the raider (the acquirer) are voided. The goal of the flip-in provision is to massively dilute the raider's ownership position.

The rights issued in connection with an SRP are poison pills, because anyone trying to force a merger will trigger the rights. When this happens, all the target firm's shareholders can effectively buy shares in the merged firm at half price. This greatly increases the cost of the merger to the bidder, because the target firm's shareholders end up with a much larger percentage of the merged firm.

Notice that the flip-in provision doesn't prevent someone from acquiring control of a firm by purchasing a majority interest. It just acts to vastly increase the cost of doing so.

The intention of a poison pill is to force a bidder to negotiate with management. Frequently, merger offers are made with the contingency that the rights will be cancelled by the target firm.

Some new varieties of poison pill have appeared on the scene in recent years. For example, a 'chewable' pill, common in Canada but not in the United States, is a pill that is installed by shareholder vote and can be redeemed by shareholder vote. Then there's the 'deadhand pill', which explicitly gives the directors who installed the pill, or their handpicked successors, the authority to remove the pill. This type of pill is controversial, because it makes it virtually impossible for new directors elected by shareholders to remove an existing poison pill.

Recently, a method of circumventing poison pills has grown in popularity. Hedge funds or other large investors, all of whom have the same agenda, such as removing the company's management or changing the way the company operates, band together and purchase a large block of equity. They then vote to remove the board of directors and company management without triggering the poison pill provision.

Since poison pills are illegal in many countries, including all of Europe, this has led to a higher frequency of hostile takeovers, especially by hedge funds looking to take over a company quickly and sell it on at a profit. Outlawing poison pills has also led to some criticism, because acquiring firms can quickly take control of a target firm before other, possibly better, bids are being prepared by other firms.

## Going Private and Leveraged Buyouts

As we have previously discussed, going private is what happens when the publicly owned shares in a firm are replaced by complete equity ownership by a private group, which may include elements of existing management. As a consequence, the firm's equity is taken off the market (if it is an exchange-traded equity, it is delisted) and is no longer traded.

One result of going private is that takeovers via tender offer can no longer occur, because there are no publicly held shares. In this sense, an LBO (or, more specifically, an MBO) can be a takeover defence. However, it's a defence only for management. From the shareholders' point of view an LBO is a takeover, because they are bought out.

## Other Devices and Jargon of Corporate Takeovers

As corporate takeovers have become more common, a new vocabulary has developed. The terms are colourful, and, in no particular order, some of them are listed here:

- *Golden parachute*: Some target firms provide compensation to top-level managers if a takeover occurs. Golden parachutes are very controversial in economic downturns, as there is nothing the media like more than to splash an incredibly generous severance package all over the front pages when the company is in financial distress. A good example concerns the chief executives of the Royal Bank of Scotland and HBOS, the big British banks that succumbed to the credit crisis in 2009. Fred Goodwin (RBS) and Andy Hornby (HBOS) gave up their golden parachutes of £1.2 million and £1 million respectively when they left their banks, after intense political and public criticism. The opposite of a golden parachute is a 'golden handcuff', which is an incentive package designed to get executives to stay on board once the acquisition is completed. Depending on your perspective and the amounts involved, golden parachutes can be viewed as a payment to management to make it less concerned for its own welfare and more interested in shareholders when considering a takeover bid.

- *Poison put*: A poison put is a variation on the poison pill we described earlier. A poison put forces the firm to buy securities back at some set price.

- *Crown jewel*: Firms often sell or threaten to sell major assets – crown jewels – when faced with a takeover threat. This is sometimes referred to as the *scorched earth strategy*. This tactic often involves a lock-up, which we discuss shortly.

- *White knight*: A firm facing an unfriendly merger offer might arrange to be acquired by a different, friendly firm. The firm is thereby rescued by a white knight. Alternatively, the firm may arrange for a friendly entity to acquire a large block of equity. So-called *white squires* or *big brothers* are individuals, firms, or even mutual funds involved in friendly transactions of these types. Sometimes white knights or others are granted exceptional terms or otherwise compensated. Inevitably, it seems, this has been called *whitemail*.

- *Lock-up*: A lock-up is an option granted to a friendly suitor (a white knight, perhaps), giving it the right to purchase equity or some of the assets (the crown jewels, possibly) of a target firm at a fixed price in the event of an unfriendly takeover.

- *Shark repellent*: A shark repellent is any tactic (a poison pill, for example) designed to discourage unwanted merger offers.

- *Bear hug*: A bear hug is an unfriendly takeover offer designed to be so attractive that the target firm's management has little choice but to accept it. For example, in 2008 Microsoft's $44 billion offer for Yahoo! was considered a bear hug by most observers, though Yahoo! was able to fend off the offer.

- *Fair price provision*: A fair price provision is a requirement that all selling shareholders receive the same price from a bidder. The provision prevents a 'two-tier' offer. In such a deal a bidder offers a premium price only for a percentage of the shares large enough to gain control. It offers a lower price for the remaining shares. Such an offer can set off a stampede among shareholders as they rush to get the better price.

- *Dual-class capitalization*: In an earlier chapter we noted that some firms, such as Google, have more than one class of equity, and that voting power is typically concentrated in a class of shares not held by the public. Such a capital structure means that an unfriendly bidder will not succeed in gaining control.

- *Countertender offer*: Better known as the 'Pac-man' defence, the target responds to an unfriendly overture by offering to buy the bidder! This tactic is rarely used, in part because target firms are usually too small to realistically purchase the bidder.

# Case Study: Ryanair's Attempt to Acquire Aer Lingus

Now that we have discussed the various strategies that an acquirer and target may use, it is insightful to examine a case study of what actually happens in a merger or acquisition.

At the end of 2008 the budget airline Ryanair plc announced a cash offer for its rival, Aer Lingus Group plc. This was the second time that Ryanair had tried to acquire its competitor, having been unsuccessful two years before. The legacy of this failed attempt was that Ryanair now owned 29.82 per cent of Aer Lingus shares, and was thus a major shareholder in its rival. On the date of the announcement, 1 December 2008, Ryanair's share price was €2.95 and Aer Lingus' share price was €1.105. The following is a timeline of events in the takeover bid.

**Announcement of Cash Offer and Initial Gambit**   On 1 December 2008 Ryanair announced a cash offer of €1.40/share for 100 per cent of Aer Lingus shares. Its proposal was to form one airline group, but with both companies operating separate brands in a similar way to Air France-KLM.

In its opening gambit Ryanair gave several reasons why the offer would benefit Aer Lingus shareholders:

1   The offer was a cash offer and not shares.

2   The bid premium was approximately 28 per cent over the Aer Lingus share price (€1.09).

The benefits to Aer Lingus employees were given as follows:

1   The Aer Lingus executive share option scheme would receive €137 million in cash.

2   The size of the fleet would double within five years, and 1,000 jobs would be created.

3   The growth prospects of the combined firm would improve promotion prospects and increase job security. The size of the new firm would be comparable to Europe's big three airlines: Air France-KLM, British Airways Group, and Lufthansa-Swiss.

Ryanair also criticized the performance of Aer Lingus management:

- The Aer Lingus share price had collapsed from €3.00 in December 2006 to less than €1.00 in November 2008.

- Aer Lingus long-haul customers had fallen by 7 per cent and short-haul customers had fallen by 2 per cent in 2008.

- Ryanair forecast that Aer Lingus would have operating losses of €20 million for 2008 and 2009.

- The firm had wasted €24 million on its defence against Ryanair's previous offer of €2.80 in December 2006.

- The basic directors' fee in Aer Lingus had tripled in three years from €17,500 to €45,000, and the non-executive chairman's fee had increased fivefold from €35,000 to €175,000.

- Short-haul fares had increased by 7 per cent and fuel surcharges were increased five times to an average of €75 per sector.

- Aer Lingus had suffered repeated strike threats, closed its Shannon base and opened a poorly performing Belfast base in 2007. It also ordered new A330 aircraft in 2007 when they were most expensive, and then deferred delivery of these to November 2008.

In response to the offer, the Aer Lingus board released a statement on the same day, arguing that Ryanair's 2006 offer for its shares was blocked by the European Commission on competition grounds, and, as a result, the new offer was not possible. It also stated that Aer

Lingus had a strong business, with significant cash reserves, and the Ryanair offer of €1.40 per share significantly undervalued the company.

The share price of Aer Lingus jumped 16.7 per cent to €1.29 from €1.105, and Ryanair's share price fell nearly 5 per cent from €2.9225 to €2.7825 on the day of the announcement.

**Aer Lingus fights back**    Ten days later the Aer Lingus board announced that it had met with the Irish Minister of Transport, Noel Dempsey, and made it clear that they had unanimously rejected the offer, because it would lead to a monopoly in Ireland and contravene competition laws. The Irish government held 25 per cent of Aer Lingus shares, and was the second largest shareholder in Aer Lingus.

The chief executive of Aer Lingus, Dermot Mannion, said in a statement afterwards:

> *Ryanair cannot spin away the fact that Aer Lingus is and will continue to be its fiercest competitor into and out of Ireland. It is offering other Aer Lingus shareholders a mere €525 million, a pathetic sum in the context of the €1.3 billion in cash on the Group's balance sheet, the substantial value of our fleet, and the value of the Heathrow slots. Aer Lingus remains a strong business with significant cash reserves and a robust long-term future. Despite all of Ryanair's insincere promises, this offer, if accepted, would be bad for Irish consumers, for Aer Lingus' shareholders, and for everyone who works in the airline.*

The share price of Aer Lingus at close of day on 11 December was €1.4975, and the Ryanair share price was €2.925. Why would the Aer Lingus share price be above the bid amount of €1.40? It could have been that the market expected that Ryanair would have to make an increased bid for the company if it was to be successful in the takeover attempt.

**Counterattack**    On 15 December Ryanair issued a 184-page formal offer document for Aer Lingus shares. The formal offer document contained essentially the same information as the original announcement. However, Ryanair also personally attacked the management of Aer Lingus. As the offer became increasingly hostile, the chairman of Aer Lingus, Colm Barrington, released the following statement:

> *This document contains nothing new. It is the usual stream of invective, spin and misrepresentation that we expect from the people at Ryanair. It also fails to address the recent EU prohibition decision which found emphatically that Ryanair wants to destroy consumer choice. It is a desperate last effort to create an airline monopoly in Ireland, and is clearly not in the interests of Aer Lingus shareholders and the travelling public. Aer Lingus is and will continue to be a strong independent airline. Ryanair clearly needs Aer Lingus but we do not need Ryanair.*

The Aer Lingus share price at close of day was now €1.4725 and the Ryanair share price was €2.77, a further fall from its starting value of €2.95.

**Robust Defence**    Exactly seven days later Aer Lingus released a 64-page document that presented a vigorous argument as to why the €1.40 cash offer from Ryanair was not good for Aer Lingus shareholders. The points it made were as follows:

1   The Aer Lingus business model was successful. Short-haul business had low prices, high return on capital, and a growing business base. Moreover, its expansion into Gatwick airport provided significant growth opportunities in short haul.

2   Aer Lingus was profitable, and would be in the future. In contrast to Ryanair's predictions, the Aer Lingus management argued that they would make a profit for 2008.

3   The balance sheet of Aer Lingus was one of the strongest in the industry. The company had €1.3 billion of cash reserves and €803 million of net cash. They argued that Ryanair wanted to spend €525 million to acquire Aer Lingus in order to gain access to the €1.3 billion cash.

4   Ryanair was opportunistically using the dreadful market conditions of late 2008 to profit from the Aer Lingus business model and access its cash resources and assets at a discounted price.

5   The Ryanair offer was flawed, because the previous offer in 2006 fell foul of European competition laws, and the current offer was no different.

The Aer Lingus share price was now €1.50 and Ryanair's had grown to €3.085!

**Flanking Strategy**   With the Christmas and New Year break on the horizon, nothing much happened. However, on 6 January 2009 Ryanair used its position as major shareholder of Aer Lingus to request an extraordinary shareholder meeting to block changes in the employment contract of the Aer Lingus chairman, Colm Barrington. The management had changed his contract at the turn of the year so that, in the event that Aer Lingus was bought over, he would be due a €2.8 million golden parachute payment if he resigned.

Ryanair also announced that only 0.01 per cent of Aer Lingus shareholders (excluding Ryanair itself, which owned 29.82 per cent of Aer Lingus shares) had accepted the cash offer of €1.40 per share. As a result of the extraordinary meeting call, the offer period was extended to 13 February 2009. Aer Lingus's share price now closed at €1.49, and Ryanair closed even higher at €3.20!

**Death of an Offer**   As the acquisition attempt became more hostile and more personal, on 22 January, the Irish government stepped in as both regulator and major shareholder of Aer Lingus to say that it would not support the Ryanair bid. It made a statement that the Ryanair offer

> . . . greatly undervalues Aer Lingus, and a merger on the basis proposed would be likely to have a significant negative impact on competition in the market. Because we live on an island, Irish consumers depend heavily on air transport. A monopoly in this area would not be in the best interests of Irish consumers. The offer by Ryanair did not include any proposed remedies for the virtual monopoly that would result if the offer was accepted.

Reluctantly, the chief executive of Ryanair, Michael Dempsey, conceded that the offer was no longer feasible:

> We respect that decision. It means our offer won't be successful since our 90 per cent acceptance condition can't be satisfied. Sadly it means the government won't receive €200m, and there won't be 1,000 new jobs created in Aer Lingus over the next five years.

The closing share price of Aer Lingus on 23 January 2009 was €1.15, and that of Ryanair was €3.11. Clearly, the market felt that the proposed takeover was bad for Ryanair's shareholders and good for Aer Lingus shareholders. As the probability of the proposed merger became zero, the price of Aer Lingus fell back to its pre-announcement value.

The Ryanair–Aer Lingus takeover bid provides many insights into the process of a hostile takeover. First, the bidder will criticize the company in terms of its performance, value, or management. Second, the target firm's management, if it does not wish to be taken over, will respond in a negative manner and defend its business model and performance. Third, the market will have its own view on the viability and likelihood of a merger. Finally, it is clear that much effort on the part of both management teams was expended over the period. This time could have been spent elsewhere improving the value of each firm's business operations.

| **CONCEPT QUESTIONS** | | |
|---|---|---|
| | 22.6a | What can a firm do to make a takeover less likely? |
| | 22.6b | What is a share rights plan? Explain how the rights work. |

## 22.7 Some Evidence on Restructurings: Do M&A Pay?

One of the most controversial issues surrounding our subject is whether mergers and acquisitions benefit shareholders. A very large number of studies have attempted to estimate the effect of mergers and takeovers on share prices of the bidding and target firms. These studies have examined the gains and losses in equity value around the time of merger announcements.

One conclusion that clearly emerges is that M&A pay for target firm shareholders. There is no mystery here. The premium typically paid by bidders represents an immediate, relatively large gain, often of the order of 20 per cent or more.

Matters become much more murky when we look at bidders, and different studies reach different conclusions. One thing is clear, however. Shareholders in bidder firms seem to neither win nor lose very much, at least on average. This finding is a bit of a puzzle, and there are a variety of explanations:

1 Anticipated merger gains may not be completely achieved, and shareholders thus experience losses. This can happen if managers of bidding firms tend to overestimate the gains from acquisition.

2 The bidding firms are usually much larger than the target firms. Thus, even though the cash gains to the bidder may be similar to the cash gains earned by shareholders of the target firm, the percentage gains will be much lower.

3 Another possible explanation for the low returns to the shareholders of bidding firms in takeovers is simply that management may not be acting in the interest of shareholders when it attempts to acquire other firms. Perhaps it is attempting to increase the size of the firm, even if this reduces its value per share.

4 The market for takeovers may be sufficiently competitive that the NPV of acquiring is zero, because the prices paid in acquisitions fully reflect the value of the acquired firms. In other words, the sellers capture all of the gain.

5 Finally, the announcement of a takeover may not convey much new information to the market about the bidding firm. This can occur because firms frequently announce intentions to engage in merger 'programmes' long before they announce specific acquisitions. In this case the share price for the bidding firm may already reflect anticipated gains from mergers.

| **CONCEPT QUESTIONS** | 22.7a | What does the evidence say about the benefits of mergers and acquisitions to target company shareholders? |
| | 22.7b | What does the evidence say about the benefits of mergers and acquisitions to acquiring company shareholders? |

## 22.8 Divestitures and Restructurings

**divestiture**
The sale of assets, operations, divisions and/or segments of a business to a third party.

In contrast to a merger or acquisition, a **divestiture** occurs when a firm sells assets, operations, divisions and/or segments to a third party. Note that divestitures are an important part of M&A activity. After all, one company's acquisition is usually another's divestiture. Also, following a merger, it is very common for certain assets or divisions to be sold. Such sales may be required by monopolies or competition regulations; they may be needed to raise cash to help pay for a deal; or the divested units may simply be unwanted by the acquirer.

Divestitures also occur when a company decides to sell off a part of itself for reasons unrelated to mergers and acquisitions. This can happen when a particular unit is unprofitable, or not a good strategic fit. Or a firm may decide to cash out of a very profitable operation. Finally, a cash-strapped firm may have to sell assets just to raise capital (this commonly occurs in bankruptcy).

A divestiture usually occurs like any other sale. A company lets it be known that it has assets for sale, and seeks offers. If a suitable offer is forthcoming, a sale occurs.

In some cases, particularly when the desired divestiture is a relatively large operating unit, companies will elect to do an **equity carve-out**. To do a carve-out, a parent company first creates a completely separate company, of which the parent is the sole shareholder. Next, the parent company arranges an initial public offering (IPO) in which a fraction, perhaps 20 per cent or so, of the parent's equity is sold to the public, thus creating a publicly held company.

Instead of a carve-out, a company can elect to do a **spin-off**. In a spin-off, the company simply distributes shares in the subsidiary to its existing shareholders on a *pro rata* basis. Shareholders can either keep the shares or sell them, as they see fit. Very commonly, a company will first do an equity carve-out to create an active market for the shares, and then subsequently do a spin-off of the remaining shares at a later date.

In a less common, but more drastic, move a company can elect to do (or be forced to do) a **split-up**. A split-up is just what the name suggests: a company splits itself into two or more new companies. Shareholders have their shares in the old company swapped for shares in the new companies.

**equity carve-out**
The sale of equity in a wholly owned subsidiary via an IPO.

**spin-off**
The distribution of shares in a subsidiary to existing parent company shareholders.

**split-up**
The splitting up of a company into two or more companies.

**CONCEPT QUESTIONS**

22.8a  What is an equity carve-out? Why might a firm wish to do one?
22.8b  What is a split-up? Why might a firm choose to do one?

## Summary and Conclusions

This chapter has introduced you to the field of mergers and acquisitions. We mentioned a number of issues:

1 *Forms of merger*: One firm can acquire another in several different ways. The three legal forms of acquisition are merger or consolidation, acquisition of shares, and acquisition of assets.

2 *Tax issues*: Mergers and acquisitions can be taxable or tax-free transactions. The primary issue is whether the target firm's shareholders sell or exchange their shares. Generally, a cash purchase will be a taxable merger, whereas an exchange of shares will not be taxable. In a taxable merger there are capital gains effects and asset write-up effects to consider. In an exchange of shares the target firm's shareholders become shareholders in the merged firm.

3 *Merger valuation*: If Firm A is acquiring Firm B, the benefits ($\Delta V$) from the acquisition are defined as the value of the combined firm ($V_{AB}$) less the value of the firms as separate entities ($V_A$ and $V_B$):

$$\Delta V = V_{AB} - (V_A + V_B)$$

The gain to Firm A from acquiring Firm B is the increased value of the acquired firm, $\Delta V$, plus the value of B as a separate firm, $V_B$. The total value of Firm B to Firm A, $V_B^*$, is thus:

$$V_B^* = \Delta V + V_B$$

An acquisition will benefit the shareholders of the acquiring firm if this value is greater than the cost of the acquisition. The cost of an acquisition can be defined in general terms as the price paid to the shareholders of the acquired firm. The cost frequently includes a merger premium paid to the shareholders of the acquired firm. Moreover, the cost depends on the form of payment – that is, the choice between paying with cash or paying with equity.

4   *Benefits*: The possible benefits of an acquisition come from several sources, including the following:

   (a)   Revenue enhancement.

   (b)   Cost reductions.

   (c)   Lower taxes.

   (d)   Reductions in capital needs.

5   *Defensive tactics*: Some of the most colourful language of finance comes from defensive tactics used in acquisition battles. Poison pills, golden parachutes, crown jewels and greenmail are some of the terms that describe various anti-takeover tactics.

6   *Effect on shareholders*: Mergers and acquisitions have been extensively studied. The basic conclusions are that, on average, the shareholders of target firms do well, whereas the shareholders of bidding firms do not appear to gain much.

7   *Divestitures*: For a variety of reasons, companies often wish to sell assets or operating units. For relatively large divestitures involving operating units, firms sometimes elect to do carve-outs, spin-offs, or split-ups.

# Chapter Review and Self-Test Problems

**22.1   Merger Value and Cost**   Consider the following information for two all-equity firms, A and B:

|                     | Firm A | Firm B |
|---------------------|-------:|-------:|
| Shares outstanding  |  2,000 |  6,000 |
| Share price (£)     |     40 |     30 |

Firm A estimates that the value of the synergistic benefit from acquiring Firm B is £6,000. Firm B has indicated that it would accept a cash purchase offer of £35 per share. Should Firm A proceed?

**22.2   Mergers and EPS**   Consider the following information for two all-equity firms, A and B:

|                     | Firm A | Firm B |
|---------------------|-------:|-------:|
| Total earnings (€)  |  3,000 |  1,000 |
| Shares outstanding  |    600 |    400 |
| Share price (€)     |     70 |     15 |

Firm A is acquiring Firm B by exchanging 100 of its shares for all the shares in B. What is the cost of the merger if the merged firm is worth €63,000? What will happen to Firm A's EPS? To its P/E ratio?

# Answers to Chapter Review and Self-Test Problems

**22.1** The total value of Firm B to Firm A is the pre-merger value of B plus the £6,000 gain from the merger. The pre-merger value of B is £30 × 6,000 = £180,000, so the total value is £186,000. At £35 per share, A is paying £35 × 6,000 = £210,000: the merger therefore has a negative NPV of £186,000 − 210,000 = −£24,000. At £35 per share, B is not an attractive merger partner.

**22.2** After the merger the firm will have 700 shares outstanding. Because the total value is €63,000, the share price is €63,000/700 = €90, up from €70. Because Firm B's shareholders end up with 100 shares in the merged firm, the cost of the merger is 100 × €90 = €9,000, not 100 × €70 = €7,000.

Also, the combined firm will have €3,000 + 1,100 = €4,100 in earnings, so EPS will be €4,100/700 = €5.86, up from €3,000/600 = €5. The old P/E ratio was €70/5 = 14.00. The new one is €90/5.86 = 15.36.

# Concepts Review and Critical Thinking Questions

1   **Merger Terms [LO1]**   Define each of the following terms:

  (a)   Greenmail.

  (b)   White knight.

  (c)   Golden parachute.

  (d)   Crown jewels.

  (e)   Shark repellent.

  (f)   Corporate raider.

  (g)   Poison pill.

  (h)   Tender offer.

  (i)   Leveraged buyout or LBO.

2   **Merger Rationale [LO1]**   Explain why diversification per se is probably not a good reason for merger.

3   **Corporate Split [LO3]**   During 2008 Time Warner was in the middle of a proposed corporate split that it expected to complete by the end of the year . The company, which had grown largely because of acquisitions, was discussing a plan to separate into three divisions. Time Warner would spin off both AOL and its cable TV business and retain its cable network, entertainment and publishing operations. Why might a company do this? Is there a possibility of reverse synergy?

4   **Poison Pills [LO1]**   Are poison pills good or bad for shareholders? How do you think acquiring firms are able to get around poison pills?

5   **Mergers and Taxes [LO2]**   Describe the advantages and disadvantages of a taxable merger as opposed to a tax-free exchange. What is the basic determinant of tax status in a merger? Would an LBO be taxable or non-taxable? Explain.

6   **Economies of Scale [LO3]**   What does it mean to say that a proposed merger will take advantage of available economies of scale? Suppose Eastern Power and Western Power are located in different time zones. Both of them operate at 60 per cent of capacity except for peak periods, when they operate at 100 per cent of capacity. The peak periods begin at 9:00 a.m. and 5:00 p.m. local time and last about 45 minutes. Explain why a merger between Eastern and Western might make sense.

7 **Hostile Takeovers [LO1]** What types of action might the management of a firm take to fight a hostile acquisition bid from an unwanted suitor? How do the target firm shareholders benefit from the defensive tactics of their management team? How are the target firm shareholders harmed by such actions? Explain.

8 **Merger Offers [LO1]** Suppose a company in which you own equity has attracted two takeover offers. Would it ever make sense for your company's management to favour the lower offer? Does the form of payment affect your answer at all?

9 **Merger Profit [LO2]** Acquiring firm shareholders seem to benefit very little from take-overs. Why is this finding a puzzle? What are some of the reasons offered for it?

# connect Questions and Problems

**BASIC**

**1 – 7**

1 **Calculating Synergy [LO3]** Evan plc has offered £740 million cash for all of the equity in Tanner plc. Based on recent market information, Tanner is worth £650 million as an independent operation. If the merger makes economic sense for Evan, what is the minimum estimated value of the synergistic benefits from the merger?

2 **Balance Sheets for Mergers [LO2]** Consider the following pre-merger information about firm X and firm Y:

|  | Firm X | Firm Y |
|---|---|---|
| Total earnings (£) | 40,000 | 15,000 |
| Shares outstanding | 20,000 | 20,000 |
| Per-share values: |  |  |
| Market (£) | 49 | 18 |
| Book (£) | 20 | 7 |

Assume that firm X acquires firm Y by paying cash for all the shares outstanding at a merger premium of £5 per share. Assuming that neither firm has any debt before or after the merger, construct the post-merger balance sheet for firm X.

3 **Balance Sheets for Mergers [LO2]** Assume that the following balance sheets are stated at book value. Construct a post-merger balance sheet assuming that Jurion SE purchases Johan GmbH, and that both sets of accounts are presented according to International Financial Reporting Standards.

| Jurion SE | | | |
|---|---|---|---|
| | € | | € |
| Current assets | 10,000 | Current liabilities | 3,100 |
| Non-current assets | 14,000 | Non-current liabilities | 1,900 |
| | | Equity | 19,000 |
| Total | 24,000 | Total | 24,000 |

| Johan GmbH | | | |
|---|---|---|---|
| | € | | € |
| Current assets | 3,400 | Current liabilities | 1,600 |
| Non-current assets | 5,600 | Non-current liabilities | 900 |
| | | Equity | 6,500 |
| Total | 9,000 | Total | 9,000 |

The fair market value of Johan's non-current assets is €12,000, compared with the €5,600 book value shown. Jurion pays €17,000 for Johan, and raises the needed funds through an issue of long-term debt.

4 **Balance Sheets for Mergers [LO2]** Silver Enterprises has acquired All Gold Mining in a merger transaction. Construct the balance sheet for the new corporation. The following balance sheets represent the pre-merger book values for both firms:

| Silver Enterprises | | | |
|---|---|---|---|
| | € | | € |
| Current assets | 2,600 | Current liabilities | 1,800 |
| Goodwill | 800 | Non-current liabilities | 900 |
| Net non-current assets | 3,900 | Equity | 4,600 |
| Total | 7,300 | Total | 7,300 |
| **All Gold Mining** | | | |
| | € | | € |
| Current assets | 1,100 | Current liabilities | 900 |
| Goodwill | 350 | Non-current liabilities | 0 |
| Non-current assets | 2,800 | Equity | 3,350 |
| Total | €4,250 | Total | €4,250 |

The market value of All Gold Mining's non-current assets (excluding goodwill) is €2,800; the market values for current assets and goodwill are the same as the book values. Assume that Silver Enterprises issues €8,400 in new long-term debt to finance the acquisition.

5 **Cash versus Equity Payment [LO3]** Penn NV is analysing the possible acquisition of Teller NV. Both firms have no debt. Penn believes the acquisition will increase its total after-tax annual cash flows by €3.1 million indefinitely. The current market value of Teller is €78 million, and that of Penn is €135 million. The appropriate discount rate for the incremental cash flows is 12 per cent. Penn is trying to decide whether it should offer 40 per cent of its equity or €94 million in cash to Teller's shareholders.

(a) What is the cost of each alternative?

(b) What is the NPV of each alternative?

(c) Which alternative should Penn choose?

6 **EPS, P/E and Mergers [LO3]** The shareholders of Flannery SA have voted in favour of a buyout offer from Stultz Corporation. Information about each firm is given here:

| | Flannery | Stultz |
|---|---|---|
| Price – earnings ratio | 5.25 | 21 |
| Shares outstanding | 60,000 | 180,000 |
| Earnings (€) | 300,000 | 675,000 |

Flannery's shareholders will receive one share of Stultz equity for every three shares they hold in Flannery.

(a) What will the EPS of Stultz be after the merger? What will the P/E ratio be if the NPV of the acquisition is zero?

(b) What must Stultz feel is the value of the synergy between these two firms? Explain how your answer can be reconciled with the decision to go ahead with the takeover.

7 **Cash versus Equity as Payment [LO3]** Consider the following pre-merger information about a bidding firm (firm B) and a target firm (firm T). Assume that both firms have no debt outstanding.

|  | Firm B | Firm T |
|---|---|---|
| Shares outstanding | 1,500 | 900 |
| Price per share (£) | 34 | 24 |

Firm B has estimated that the value of the synergistic benefits from acquiring firm T is £3,000.

(a) If firm T is willing to be acquired for £27 per share in cash, what is the NPV of the merger?

(b) What will the price per share of the merged firm be, assuming the conditions in (a)?

(c) In part (a), what is the merger premium?

(d) Suppose firm T is agreeable to a merger by an exchange of equity. If B offers three of its shares for every one of T's shares, what will the price per share of the merged firm be?

(e) What is the NPV of the merger assuming the conditions in (d)?

INTERMEDIATE

8–12

8 **Cash versus Equity as Payment [LO3]** In Problem 7, are the shareholders of firm T better off with the cash offer or the equity offer? At what exchange ratio of B shares to T shares would the shareholders in T be indifferent between the two offers?

9 **Effects of a Share Exchange [LO3]** Consider the following pre-merger information about firm A and firm B:

|  | Firm A | Firm B |
|---|---|---|
| Total earnings (DKr) | 900 | 600 |
| Shares outstanding | 550 | 220 |
| Price per share (DKr) | 40 | 15 |

Assume that firm A acquires firm B via an exchange of equity at a price of DKr20 for each share of B's equity. Neither A nor B has any debt outstanding.

(a) What will the earnings per share, EPS, of firm A be after the merger?

(b) What will firm A's price per share be after the merger if the market incorrectly analyses this reported earnings growth (that is, the price–earnings ratio does not change)?

(c) What will the price–earnings ratio of the post-merger firm be if the market analyses the transaction correctly?

(d) If there are no synergy gains, what will the share price of A be after the merger? What will the price–earnings ratio be? What does your answer for the share price tell you about the amount A bid for B? Was it too high? Too low? Explain.

10 **Merger NPV [LO3]** Show that the NPV of a merger can be expressed as the value of the synergistic benefits, $\Delta V$, less the merger premium.

11 **Merger NPV [LO3]** Fly-By-Night Couriers is analysing the possible acquisition of Flash-in-the-Pan Restaurants. Neither firm has debt. The forecasts of Fly-By-Night show that the purchase would increase its annual after-tax cash flow by £600,000 indefinitely. The current market value of Flash-in-the-Pan is £20 million. The

current market value of Fly-By-Night is £35 million. The appropriate discount rate for the incremental cash flows is 8 per cent. Fly-By-Night is trying to decide whether it would offer 25 per cent of its equity or £25 million in cash to Flash-in-the-Pan.

(a)    What is the synergy from the merger?

(b)    What is the value of Flash-in-the-Pan to Fly-By-Night?

(c)    What is the cost to Fly-By-Night of each alternative?

(d)    What is the NPV to Fly-By-Night of each alternative?

(e)    Which alternative should Fly-By-Night use?

12   **Merger NPV [LO3]**   Harrods plc has a market value of £600 million and 30 million shares outstanding. Selfridge Department Store has a market value of £200 million and 20 million shares outstanding. Harrods is contemplating acquiring Selfridge. Harrods's CFO concludes that the combined firm with synergy will be worth £1 billion, and Selfridge can be acquired at a premium of £100 million.

(a)    If Harrods offers 15 million shares of its equity in exchange for the 20 million shares of Selfridge, what will the equity price of Harrods be after the acquisition?

(b)    What exchange ratio between the two equities would make the value of equity offer equivalent to a cash offer of £300 million?

**CHALLENGE**

**13**

13   **Calculating NPV [LO3]**   Foxy News is considering making an offer to purchase Pulitzer Publications. The chief financial officer has collected the following information:

|                        | Foxy      | Pulitzer |
|------------------------|-----------|----------|
| Price–earnings ratio   | 15.5      | 11.5     |
| Shares outstanding     | 1,200,000 | 500,000  |
| Earnings (£)           | 3,600,000 | 680,000  |
| Dividend (£)           | 810,000   | 310,000  |

Foxy also knows that securities analysts expect the earnings and dividends of Pulitzer to grow at a constant rate of 5 per cent each year. Foxy management believes that the acquisition of Pulitzer will provide the firm with some economies of scale that will increase this growth rate to 7 per cent per year.

(a)    What is the value of Pulitzer to Foxy?

(b)    What would Foxy's gain be from this acquisition?

(c)    If Foxy were to offer £18 in cash for each share of Pulitzer, what would the NPV of the acquisition be?

(d)    What's the most Foxy should be willing to pay in cash per share for the equity of Pulitzer?

(e)    If Foxy were to offer 200,000 of its shares in exchange for the outstanding equity of Pulitzer, what would the NPV be?

(f)    Should the acquisition be attempted? If so, should it be as in (c) or as in (e)?

(g)    Foxy's outside financial consultants think that the 7 per cent growth rate is too optimistic, and that a 6 per cent rate is more realistic. How does this change your previous answers?

# The Birdie Golf – Hybrid Golf Merger

Birdie Golf has been in merger talks with Hybrid Golf Company for the past six months. After several rounds of negotiations, the offer under discussion is a cash offer of €550 million for Hybrid Golf. Both companies have niche markets in the golf club industry, and the companies believe a merger will result in significant synergies, as a result of economies of scale in manufacturing and marketing, as well as significant savings in general and administrative expenses.

Bryce Bichon, the financial officer for Birdie, has been instrumental in the merger negotiations. Bryce has prepared the following pro forma financial statements for Hybrid Golf, assuming the merger takes place. The financial statements include all synergistic benefits from the merger:

|  | 2010 | 2011 | 2012 | 2013 | 2014 |
|---|---|---|---|---|---|
| Sales (€) | 800,000,000 | 900,000,000 | 1,000,000,000 | 1,125,000,000 | 1,250,000,000 |
| Production costs (€) | 562,000,000 | 630,000,000 | 700,000,000 | 790,000,000 | 875,000,000 |
| Depreciation (€) | 75,000,000 | 80,000,000 | 82,000,000 | 83,000,000 | 83,000,000 |
| Other expenses (€) | 80,000,000 | 90,000,000 | 100,000,000 | 113,000,000 | 125,000,000 |
| EBIT (€) | 83,000,000 | 100,000,000 | 118,000,000 | 139,000,000 | 167,000,000 |
| Interest (€) | 19,000,000 | 22,000,000 | 24,000,000 | 25,000,000 | 27,000,000 |
| Taxable income (€) | 64,000,000 | 78,000,000 | 94,000,000 | 114,000,000 | 140,000,000 |
| Taxes (40%) (€) | 25,600,000 | 31,200,000 | 37,600,000 | 45,600,000 | 56,000,000 |
| Net income (€) | 38,400,000 | 46,800,000 | 56,400,000 | 68,400,000 | 84,000,000 |

Bryce is also aware that the Hybrid Golf division will require investments each year for continuing operations, along with sources of financing. The following table outlines the required investments and sources of financing:

|  | 2010 | 2011 | 2012 | 2013 | 2014 |
|---|---|---|---|---|---|
| **Investments:** | | | | | |
| Net working capital (€) | 20,000,000 | 25,000,000 | 25,000,000 | 30,000,000 | 30,000,000 |
| Non-current assets (€) | 15,000,000 | 25,000,000 | 18,000,000 | 12,000,000 | 7,000,000 |
| Total (€) | 35,000,000 | 50,000,000 | 43,000,000 | 42,000,000 | 37,000,000 |
| **Sources of financing:** | | | | | |
| New debt (€) | 35,000,000 | 16,000,000 | 16,000,000 | 15,000,000 | 12,000,000 |
| Profit retention (€) | 0 | 34,000,000 | 27,000,000 | 27,000,000 | 25,000,000 |
| Total (€) | 35,000,000 | 50,000,000 | 43,000,000 | 42,000,000 | 37,000,000 |

The management of Birdie Golf feels that the capital structure at Hybrid Golf is not optimal. If the merger take place, Hybrid Golf will immediately increase its leverage with a €110 million debt issue, which would be followed by a €150 million dividend payment to Birdie Golf. This will increase Hybrid's debt-to-equity ratio from 0.50 to 1.00. Birdie Golf will also be able to use a €25 million tax loss carry-forward in 2011 and 2012 from Hybrid Golf's previous operations. The total value of Hybrid Golf is expected to be €900 million in five years, and the company will have €300 million in debt at that time.

Equity in Birdie Golf currently sells for €94 per share, and the company has 18 million shares of equity outstanding. Hybrid Golf has 8 million shares of equity outstanding. Both companies can borrow at an 8 per cent interest rate. The risk-free rate is 6 per cent, and the expected return on the market is 13 per cent. Bryce believes the current cost of capital for Birdie Golf is 11 per cent. The beta for Hybrid Golf equity at its current capital structure is 1.30.

Bryce has asked you to analyse the financial aspects of the potential merger. Specifically, he has asked you to answer the following questions:

1  Suppose Hybrid shareholders will agree to a merger price of €68.75 per share. Should Birdie proceed with the merger?

2  What is the highest price per share that Birdie should be willing to pay for Hybrid?

3  Suppose Birdie is unwilling to pay cash for the merger, but will consider an equity exchange. What exchange ratio would make the merger terms equivalent to the original merger price of €68.75 per share?

4  What is the highest exchange ratio Birdie would be willing to pay and still undertake the merger?

To help you grasp the key concepts of this chapter check out the extra resources posted on the Online Learning Centre at **www.mcgraw-hill.co.uk/textbooks/hillier**

Among other helpful resources there are mini-cases tailored to individual chapters.

# APPENDIX A
# MATHEMATICAL TABLES

**Table A.1** Future value of £1 at the end of $t$ periods $= (1 + r)^t$

**Table A.2** Present value of £1 to be received after $t$ periods $= 1/(1 + r)^t$

**Table A.3** Present value of an annuity of £1 per period for $t$ periods $= [1 - 1/(1 + r)^t]/r$

**Table A.4** Future value of an annuity of £1 per period for $t$ periods $= [(1 + r)^t - 1]/r$

**Table A.5** Cumulative normal distribution

TABLE
**A.1**

| Period | | | | | | | | | | | Interest Rate | | | | | | | | | |
|---|---|---|---|---|---|---|---|---|---|---|---|---|---|---|---|---|---|---|---|---|
| | 1% | 2% | 3% | 4% | 5% | 6% | 7% | 8% | 9% | 10% | 12% | 14% | 15% | 16% | 18% | 20% | 24% | 28% | 32% | 36% |
| 1 | 1.0100 | 1.0200 | 1.0300 | 1.0400 | 1.0500 | 1.0600 | 1.0700 | 1.0800 | 1.0900 | 1.1000 | 1.1200 | 1.1400 | 1.1500 | 1.1600 | 1.1800 | 1.2000 | 1.2400 | 1.2800 | 1.3200 | 1.3600 |
| 2 | 1.0201 | 1.0404 | 1.0609 | 1.0816 | 1.1025 | 1.1236 | 1.1449 | 1.1664 | 1.1881 | 1.2100 | 1.2544 | 1.2996 | 1.3225 | 1.3456 | 1.3924 | 1.4400 | 1.5376 | 1.6384 | 1.7424 | 1.8496 |
| 3 | 1.0303 | 1.0612 | 1.0927 | 1.1249 | 1.1576 | 1.1910 | 1.2250 | 1.2597 | 1.2950 | 1.3310 | 1.4049 | 1.4815 | 1.5209 | 1.5609 | 1.6430 | 1.7280 | 1.9066 | 2.0972 | 2.3000 | 2.5155 |
| 4 | 1.0406 | 1.0824 | 1.1255 | 1.1699 | 1.2155 | 1.2625 | 1.3108 | 1.3605 | 1.4116 | 1.4641 | 1.5735 | 1.6890 | 1.7490 | 1.8106 | 1.9388 | 2.0736 | 2.3642 | 2.6844 | 3.0360 | 3.4210 |
| 5 | 1.0510 | 1.1041 | 1.1593 | 1.2167 | 1.2763 | 1.3382 | 1.4026 | 1.4693 | 1.5386 | 1.6105 | 1.7623 | 1.9254 | 2.0114 | 2.1003 | 2.2878 | 2.4883 | 2.9316 | 3.4360 | 4.0075 | 4.6526 |
| 6 | 1.0615 | 1.1262 | 1.1941 | 1.2653 | 1.3401 | 1.4185 | 1.5007 | 1.5869 | 1.6771 | 1.7716 | 1.9738 | 2.1950 | 2.3131 | 2.4364 | 2.6996 | 2.9860 | 3.6352 | 4.3980 | 5.2899 | 6.3275 |
| 7 | 1.0721 | 1.1487 | 1.2299 | 1.3159 | 1.4071 | 1.5036 | 1.6058 | 1.7138 | 1.8280 | 1.9487 | 2.2107 | 2.5023 | 2.6600 | 2.8262 | 3.1855 | 3.5832 | 4.5077 | 5.6295 | 6.9826 | 8.6054 |
| 8 | 1.0829 | 1.1717 | 1.2668 | 1.3686 | 1.4775 | 1.5938 | 1.7182 | 1.8509 | 1.9926 | 2.1436 | 2.4760 | 2.8526 | 3.0590 | 3.2784 | 3.7589 | 4.2998 | 5.5895 | 7.2058 | 9.2170 | 11.703 |
| 9 | 1.0937 | 1.1951 | 1.3048 | 1.4233 | 1.5513 | 1.6895 | 1.8385 | 1.9990 | 2.1719 | 2.3579 | 2.7731 | 3.2519 | 3.5179 | 3.8030 | 4.4355 | 5.1598 | 6.9310 | 9.2234 | 12.166 | 15.917 |
| 10 | 1.1046 | 1.2190 | 1.3439 | 1.4802 | 1.6289 | 1.7908 | 1.9672 | 2.1589 | 2.3674 | 2.5937 | 3.1058 | 3.7072 | 4.0456 | 4.4114 | 5.2338 | 6.1917 | 8.5944 | 11.806 | 16.060 | 21.647 |
| 11 | 1.1157 | 1.2434 | 1.3842 | 1.5395 | 1.7103 | 1.8983 | 2.1049 | 2.3316 | 2.5804 | 2.8531 | 3.4785 | 4.2262 | 4.6524 | 5.1173 | 6.1759 | 7.4301 | 10.657 | 15.112 | 21.199 | 29.439 |
| 12 | 1.1268 | 1.2682 | 1.4258 | 1.6010 | 1.7959 | 2.0122 | 2.2522 | 2.5182 | 2.8127 | 3.1384 | 3.8960 | 4.8179 | 5.3503 | 5.9360 | 7.2876 | 8.9161 | 13.215 | 19.343 | 27.983 | 40.037 |
| 13 | 1.1381 | 1.2936 | 1.4685 | 1.6651 | 1.8856 | 2.1329 | 2.4098 | 2.7196 | 3.0658 | 3.4523 | 4.3635 | 5.4924 | 6.1528 | 6.8858 | 8.5994 | 10.699 | 16.386 | 24.759 | 36.937 | 54.451 |
| 14 | 1.1495 | 1.3195 | 1.5126 | 1.7317 | 1.9799 | 2.2609 | 2.5785 | 2.9372 | 3.3417 | 3.7975 | 4.8871 | 6.2613 | 7.0757 | 7.9875 | 10.147 | 12.839 | 20.319 | 31.691 | 48.757 | 74.053 |
| 15 | 1.1610 | 1.3459 | 1.5580 | 1.8009 | 2.0789 | 2.3966 | 2.7590 | 3.1722 | 3.6425 | 4.1772 | 5.4736 | 7.1379 | 8.1371 | 9.2655 | 11.974 | 15.407 | 25.196 | 40.565 | 64.359 | 100.71 |
| 16 | 1.1726 | 1.3728 | 1.6047 | 1.8730 | 2.1829 | 2.5404 | 2.9522 | 3.4259 | 3.9703 | 4.5950 | 6.1304 | 8.1372 | 9.3576 | 10.748 | 14.129 | 18.488 | 31.243 | 51.923 | 84.954 | 136.97 |
| 17 | 1.1843 | 1.4002 | 1.6528 | 1.9479 | 2.2920 | 2.6928 | 3.1588 | 3.7000 | 4.3276 | 5.0545 | 6.8660 | 9.2765 | 10.761 | 12.468 | 16.672 | 22.186 | 38.741 | 66.461 | 112.14 | 186.28 |
| 18 | 1.1961 | 1.4282 | 1.7024 | 2.0258 | 2.4066 | 2.8543 | 3.3799 | 3.9960 | 4.7171 | 5.5599 | 7.6900 | 10.575 | 12.375 | 14.463 | 19.673 | 26.623 | 48.039 | 85.071 | 148.02 | 253.34 |
| 19 | 1.2081 | 1.4568 | 1.7535 | 2.1068 | 2.5270 | 3.0256 | 3.6165 | 4.3157 | 5.1417 | 6.1159 | 8.6128 | 12.056 | 14.232 | 16.777 | 23.214 | 31.948 | 59.568 | 108.89 | 195.39 | 344.54 |
| 20 | 1.2202 | 1.4859 | 1.8061 | 2.1911 | 2.6533 | 3.2071 | 3.8697 | 4.6610 | 5.6044 | 6.7275 | 9.6463 | 13.743 | 16.367 | 19.461 | 27.393 | 38.338 | 73.864 | 139.38 | 257.92 | 468.57 |
| 21 | 1.2324 | 1.5157 | 1.8603 | 2.2788 | 2.7860 | 3.3996 | 4.1406 | 5.0338 | 6.1088 | 7.4002 | 10.804 | 15.668 | 18.822 | 22.574 | 32.324 | 46.005 | 91.592 | 178.41 | 340.45 | 637.26 |
| 22 | 1.2447 | 1.5460 | 1.9161 | 2.3699 | 2.9253 | 3.6035 | 4.4304 | 5.4365 | 6.6586 | 8.1403 | 12.100 | 17.861 | 21.645 | 26.186 | 38.142 | 55.206 | 113.57 | 228.36 | 449.39 | 866.67 |
| 23 | 1.2572 | 1.5769 | 1.9736 | 2.4647 | 3.0715 | 3.8197 | 4.7405 | 5.8715 | 7.2579 | 8.9543 | 13.552 | 20.362 | 24.891 | 30.376 | 45.008 | 66.247 | 140.83 | 292.30 | 593.20 | 1178.7 |
| 24 | 1.2697 | 1.6084 | 2.0328 | 2.5633 | 3.2251 | 4.0489 | 5.0724 | 6.3412 | 7.9111 | 9.8497 | 15.179 | 23.212 | 28.625 | 35.236 | 53.109 | 79.497 | 174.63 | 374.14 | 783.02 | 1603.0 |
| 25 | 1.2824 | 1.6406 | 2.0938 | 2.6658 | 3.3864 | 4.2919 | 5.4274 | 6.8485 | 8.6231 | 10.835 | 17.000 | 26.462 | 32.919 | 40.874 | 62.669 | 95.396 | 216.54 | 478.90 | 1033.6 | 2180.1 |
| 30 | 1.3478 | 1.8114 | 2.4273 | 3.2434 | 4.3219 | 5.7435 | 7.6123 | 10.063 | 13.268 | 17.449 | 29.960 | 50.950 | 66.212 | 85.850 | 143.37 | 237.38 | 634.82 | 1645.5 | 4142.1 | 10143. |
| 40 | 1.4889 | 2.2080 | 3.2620 | 4.8010 | 7.0400 | 10.286 | 14.974 | 21.725 | 31.409 | 45.259 | 93.051 | 188.88 | 267.86 | 378.72 | 750.38 | 1469.8 | 5455.9 | 19427. | * | * |
| 50 | 1.6446 | 2.6916 | 4.3839 | 7.1067 | 11.467 | 18.420 | 29.457 | 46.902 | 74.358 | 117.39 | 289.00 | 700.23 | 1083.7 | 1670.7 | 3927.4 | 91C0.4 | 46890. | * | * | * |
| 60 | 1.8167 | 3.2810 | 5.8916 | 10.520 | 18.679 | 32.988 | 57.946 | 101.26 | 176.03 | 304.48 | 897.60 | 2595.9 | 4384.0 | 7370.2 | 20555. | 56348. | * | * | * | * |

*The factor is greater than 99,999.

**Table A.1** Future value of £1 at the end of $t$ periods $= (1 + r)^t$

|  |  |  |  |  |  |  |  |  |  |  | Interest Rate |  |  |  |  |  |  |  |  |  |
|---|---|---|---|---|---|---|---|---|---|---|---|---|---|---|---|---|---|---|---|---|
| Period | 1% | 2% | 3% | 4% | 5% | 6% | 7% | 8% | 9% | 10% | 12% | 14% | 15% | 16% | 18% | 20% | 24% | 28% | 32% | 36% |
| 1 | .9901 | .9804 | .9709 | .9615 | .9524 | .9434 | .9346 | .9259 | .9174 | .9091 | .8929 | .8772 | .8696 | .8621 | .8475 | .8333 | .8065 | .7813 | .7575 | .7353 |
| 2 | .9803 | .9612 | .9426 | .9246 | .9070 | .8900 | .8734 | .8573 | .8417 | .8264 | .7972 | .7695 | .7561 | .7432 | .7182 | .6944 | .6504 | .6104 | .5739 | .5407 |
| 3 | .9706 | .9423 | .9151 | .8890 | .8638 | .8396 | .8163 | .7938 | .7722 | .7513 | .7118 | .6750 | .6575 | .6407 | .6086 | .5787 | .5245 | .4768 | .4348 | .3975 |
| 4 | .9610 | .9238 | .8885 | .8548 | .8227 | .7921 | .7629 | .7350 | .7084 | .6830 | .6355 | .5921 | .5718 | .5523 | .5158 | .4823 | .4230 | .3725 | .3294 | .2923 |
| 5 | .9515 | .9057 | .8626 | .8219 | .7835 | .7473 | .7130 | .6806 | .6499 | .6209 | .5674 | .5194 | .4972 | .4761 | .4371 | .4019 | .3411 | .2910 | .2495 | .2149 |
| 6 | .9420 | .8880 | .8375 | .7903 | .7462 | .7050 | .6663 | .6302 | .5963 | .5645 | .5066 | .4556 | .4323 | .4104 | .3704 | .3349 | .2751 | .2274 | .1890 | .1580 |
| 7 | .9327 | .8706 | .8131 | .7599 | .7107 | .6651 | .6227 | .5835 | .5470 | .5132 | .4523 | .3996 | .3759 | .3538 | .3139 | .2791 | .2218 | .1776 | .1432 | .1162 |
| 8 | .9235 | .8535 | .7894 | .7307 | .6768 | .6274 | .5820 | .5403 | .5019 | .4665 | .4039 | .3506 | .3269 | .3050 | .2660 | .2326 | .1789 | .1388 | .1085 | .0854 |
| 9 | .9143 | .8368 | .7664 | .7026 | .6446 | .5919 | .5439 | .5002 | .4604 | .4241 | .3606 | .3075 | .2843 | .2630 | .2255 | .1938 | .1443 | .1084 | .0822 | .0628 |
| 10 | .9053 | .8203 | .7441 | .6756 | .6139 | .5584 | .5083 | .4632 | .4224 | .3855 | .3220 | .2697 | .2472 | .2267 | .1911 | .1615 | .1164 | .0847 | .0623 | .0462 |
| 11 | .8963 | .8043 | .7224 | .6496 | .5847 | .5268 | .4751 | .4289 | .3875 | .3505 | .2875 | .2366 | .2149 | .1954 | .1619 | .1346 | .0938 | .0662 | .0472 | .0340 |
| 12 | .8874 | .7885 | .7014 | .6246 | .5568 | .4970 | .4440 | .3971 | .3555 | .3186 | .2567 | .2076 | .1869 | .1685 | .1372 | .1122 | .0757 | .0517 | .0357 | .0250 |
| 13 | .8787 | .7730 | .6810 | .6006 | .5303 | .4688 | .4150 | .3677 | .3262 | .2897 | .2292 | .1821 | .1625 | .1452 | .1163 | .0935 | .0610 | .0404 | .0271 | .0184 |
| 14 | .8700 | .7579 | .6611 | .5775 | .5051 | .4423 | .3878 | .3405 | .2992 | .2633 | .2046 | .1597 | .1413 | .1252 | .0985 | .0779 | .0492 | .0316 | .0205 | .0135 |
| 15 | .8613 | .7430 | .6419 | .5553 | .4810 | .4173 | .3624 | .3152 | .2745 | .2394 | .1827 | .1401 | .1229 | .1079 | .0835 | .0649 | .0397 | .0247 | .0155 | .0099 |
| 16 | .8528 | .7284 | .6232 | .5339 | .4581 | .3936 | .3387 | .2919 | .2519 | .2176 | .1631 | .1229 | .1069 | .0930 | .0708 | .0541 | .0320 | .0193 | .0118 | .0073 |
| 17 | .8444 | .7142 | .6050 | .5134 | .4363 | .3714 | .3166 | .2703 | .2311 | .1978 | .1456 | .1078 | .0929 | .0802 | .0600 | .0451 | .0258 | .0150 | .0089 | .0054 |
| 18 | .8360 | .7002 | .5874 | .4936 | .4155 | .3503 | .2959 | .2502 | .2120 | .1799 | .1300 | .0946 | .0808 | .0691 | .0508 | .0376 | .0208 | .0118 | .0068 | .0039 |
| 19 | .8277 | .6864 | .5703 | .4746 | .3957 | .3305 | .2765 | .2317 | .1945 | .1635 | .1161 | .0829 | .0703 | .0596 | .0431 | .0313 | .0168 | .0092 | .0051 | .0029 |
| 20 | .8195 | .6730 | .5537 | .4564 | .3769 | .3118 | .2584 | .2145 | .1784 | .1486 | .1037 | .0728 | .0611 | .0514 | .0365 | .0261 | .0135 | .0072 | .0039 | .0021 |
| 21 | .8114 | .6598 | .5375 | .4388 | .3589 | .2942 | .2415 | .1987 | .1637 | .1351 | .0926 | .0638 | .0531 | .0443 | .0309 | .0217 | .0109 | .0056 | .0029 | .0016 |
| 22 | .8034 | .6468 | .5219 | .4220 | .3418 | .2775 | .2257 | .1839 | .1502 | .1228 | .0826 | .0560 | .0462 | .0382 | .0262 | .0181 | .0088 | .0044 | .0022 | .0012 |
| 23 | .7954 | .6342 | .5067 | .4057 | .3256 | .2618 | .2109 | .1703 | .1378 | .1117 | .0738 | .0491 | .0402 | .0329 | .0222 | .0151 | .0071 | .0034 | .0017 | .0008 |
| 24 | .7876 | .6217 | .4919 | .3901 | .3101 | .2470 | .1971 | .1577 | .1264 | .1015 | .0659 | .0431 | .0349 | .0284 | .0188 | .0126 | .0057 | .0027 | .0013 | .0006 |
| 25 | .7798 | .6095 | .4776 | .3751 | .2953 | .2330 | .1842 | .1460 | .1160 | .0923 | .0588 | .0378 | .0304 | .0245 | .0160 | .0105 | .0046 | .0021 | .0010 | .0005 |
| 30 | .7419 | .5521 | .4120 | .3083 | .2314 | .1741 | .1314 | .0994 | .0754 | .0573 | .0334 | .0196 | .0151 | .0116 | .0070 | .0042 | .0016 | .0006 | .0002 | .0001 |
| 40 | .6717 | .4529 | .3066 | .2083 | .1420 | .0972 | .0668 | .0460 | .0318 | .0221 | .0107 | .0053 | .0037 | .0026 | .0013 | .0007 | .0002 | .0001 | * | * |
| 50 | .6080 | .3715 | .2281 | .1407 | .0872 | .0543 | .0339 | .0213 | .0134 | .0085 | .0035 | .0014 | .0009 | .0006 | .0003 | .0001 | * | * | * | * |

*The factor is zero to four decimal places.

**Table A.2** Present value of £1 to be received after $t$ periods $= 1/(1 + r)^t$

TABLE **A.3**

| Number of Periods | 1% | 2% | 3% | 4% | 5% | 6% | 7% | 8% | 9% | 10% | 12% | 14% | 15% | 16% | 18% | 20% | 24% | 28% | 32% | 36% |
|---|---|---|---|---|---|---|---|---|---|---|---|---|---|---|---|---|---|---|---|---|
| 1 | .9901 | .9804 | .9709 | .9615 | .9524 | .9434 | .9346 | .9259 | .9174 | .9091 | .8929 | .8772 | .8696 | .8621 | .8475 | .8333 | .8065 | .7813 | .7576 | .7353 |
| 2 | 1.9704 | 1.9416 | 1.9135 | 1.8861 | 1.8594 | 1.8334 | 1.8080 | 1.7833 | 1.7591 | 1.7355 | 1.6901 | 1.6467 | 1.6257 | 1.6052 | 1.5656 | 1.5278 | 1.4568 | 1.3916 | 1.3315 | 1.2760 |
| 3 | 2.9410 | 2.8839 | 2.8286 | 2.7751 | 2.7232 | 2.6730 | 2.6243 | 2.5771 | 2.5313 | 2.4869 | 2.4018 | 2.3216 | 2.2832 | 2.2459 | 2.1743 | 2.1065 | 1.9813 | 1.8684 | 1.7663 | 1.6735 |
| 4 | 3.9020 | 3.8077 | 3.7171 | 3.6299 | 3.5460 | 3.4651 | 3.3872 | 3.3121 | 3.2397 | 3.1699 | 3.0373 | 2.9137 | 2.8550 | 2.7982 | 2.6901 | 2.5887 | 2.4043 | 2.2410 | 2.0957 | 1.9658 |
| 5 | 4.8534 | 4.7135 | 4.5797 | 4.4518 | 4.3295 | 4.2124 | 4.1002 | 3.9927 | 3.8897 | 3.7908 | 3.6048 | 3.4331 | 3.3522 | 3.2743 | 3.1272 | 2.9906 | 2.7454 | 2.5320 | 2.3452 | 2.1807 |
| 6 | 5.7955 | 5.6014 | 5.4172 | 5.2421 | 5.0757 | 4.9173 | 4.7665 | 4.6229 | 4.4859 | 4.3553 | 4.1114 | 3.8887 | 3.7845 | 3.6847 | 3.4976 | 3.3255 | 3.0205 | 2.7594 | 2.5342 | 2.3388 |
| 7 | 6.7282 | 6.4720 | 6.2303 | 6.0021 | 5.7864 | 5.5824 | 5.3893 | 5.2064 | 5.0330 | 4.8684 | 4.5638 | 4.2883 | 4.1604 | 4.0386 | 3.8115 | 3.6046 | 3.2423 | 2.9370 | 2.6775 | 2.4550 |
| 8 | 7.6517 | 7.3255 | 7.0197 | 6.7327 | 6.4632 | 6.2098 | 5.9713 | 5.7466 | 5.5348 | 5.3349 | 4.9676 | 4.6389 | 4.4873 | 4.3436 | 4.0776 | 3.8372 | 3.4212 | 3.0758 | 2.7860 | 2.5404 |
| 9 | 8.5660 | 8.1622 | 7.7861 | 7.4353 | 7.1078 | 6.8017 | 6.5152 | 6.2469 | 5.9952 | 5.7590 | 5.3282 | 4.9464 | 4.7716 | 4.6065 | 4.3030 | 4.0310 | 3.5655 | 3.1842 | 2.8681 | 2.6033 |
| 10 | 9.4713 | 8.9826 | 8.5302 | 8.1109 | 7.7217 | 7.3601 | 7.0236 | 6.7101 | 6.4177 | 6.1446 | 5.6502 | 5.2161 | 5.0188 | 4.8332 | 4.4941 | 4.1925 | 3.6819 | 3.2689 | 2.9304 | 2.6495 |
| 11 | 10.3676 | 9.7868 | 9.2526 | 8.7605 | 8.3064 | 7.8869 | 7.4987 | 7.1390 | 6.8052 | 6.4951 | 5.9377 | 5.4527 | 5.2337 | 5.0286 | 4.6560 | 4.3271 | 3.7757 | 3.3351 | 2.9776 | 2.6834 |
| 12 | 11.2551 | 10.5753 | 9.9540 | 9.3851 | 8.8633 | 8.3838 | 7.9427 | 7.5361 | 7.1607 | 6.8137 | 6.1944 | 5.6603 | 5.4206 | 5.1971 | 4.7932 | 4.4392 | 3.8514 | 3.3868 | 3.0133 | 2.7084 |
| 13 | 12.1337 | 11.3484 | 10.6350 | 9.9856 | 9.3936 | 8.8527 | 8.3577 | 7.9038 | 7.4869 | 7.1034 | 6.4235 | 5.8424 | 5.5831 | 5.3423 | 4.9095 | 4.5327 | 3.9124 | 3.4272 | 3.0404 | 2.7268 |
| 14 | 13.0037 | 12.1062 | 11.2961 | 10.5631 | 9.8986 | 9.2950 | 8.7455 | 8.2442 | 7.7862 | 7.3667 | 6.6282 | 6.0021 | 5.7245 | 5.4675 | 5.0081 | 4.6106 | 3.9616 | 3.4587 | 3.0609 | 2.7403 |
| 15 | 13.8651 | 12.8493 | 11.9379 | 11.1184 | 10.3797 | 9.7122 | 9.1079 | 8.5595 | 8.0607 | 7.6061 | 6.8109 | 6.1422 | 5.8474 | 5.5755 | 5.0916 | 4.6755 | 4.0013 | 3.4834 | 3.0764 | 2.7502 |
| 16 | 14.7179 | 13.5777 | 12.5611 | 11.6523 | 10.8378 | 10.1059 | 9.4466 | 8.8514 | 8.3126 | 7.8237 | 6.9740 | 6.2651 | 5.9542 | 5.6685 | 5.1624 | 4.7296 | 4.0333 | 3.5026 | 3.0882 | 2.7575 |
| 17 | 15.5623 | 14.2919 | 13.1661 | 12.1657 | 11.2741 | 10.4773 | 9.7632 | 9.1216 | 8.5436 | 8.0216 | 7.1196 | 6.3729 | 6.0472 | 5.7487 | 5.2223 | 4.7746 | 4.0591 | 3.5177 | 3.0971 | 2.7629 |
| 18 | 16.3983 | 14.9920 | 13.7535 | 12.6593 | 11.6896 | 10.8276 | 10.0591 | 9.3719 | 8.7556 | 8.2014 | 7.2497 | 6.4674 | 6.1280 | 5.8178 | 5.2732 | 4.8122 | 4.0799 | 3.5294 | 3.1039 | 2.7668 |
| 19 | 17.2260 | 15.6785 | 14.3238 | 13.1339 | 12.0853 | 11.1581 | 10.3356 | 9.6036 | 8.9501 | 8.3649 | 7.3658 | 6.5504 | 6.1982 | 5.8775 | 5.3162 | 4.8435 | 4.0967 | 3.5386 | 3.1090 | 2.7697 |
| 20 | 18.0456 | 16.3514 | 14.8775 | 13.5903 | 12.4622 | 11.4699 | 10.5940 | 9.8181 | 9.1285 | 8.5136 | 7.4694 | 6.6231 | 6.2593 | 5.9288 | 5.3527 | 4.8696 | 4.1103 | 3.5458 | 3.1129 | 2.7718 |
| 21 | 18.8570 | 17.0112 | 15.4150 | 14.0292 | 12.8212 | 11.7641 | 10.8355 | 10.0168 | 9.2922 | 8.6487 | 7.5620 | 6.6870 | 6.3125 | 5.9731 | 5.3837 | 4.8913 | 4.1212 | 3.5514 | 3.1158 | 2.7734 |
| 22 | 19.6604 | 17.6580 | 15.9369 | 14.4511 | 13.1630 | 12.0416 | 11.0612 | 10.2007 | 9.4424 | 8.7715 | 7.6446 | 6.7429 | 6.3587 | 6.0113 | 5.4099 | 4.9094 | 4.1300 | 3.5558 | 3.1180 | 2.7746 |
| 23 | 20.4558 | 18.2922 | 16.4436 | 14.8568 | 13.4886 | 12.3034 | 11.2722 | 10.3741 | 9.5802 | 8.8832 | 7.7184 | 6.7921 | 6.3988 | 6.0442 | 5.4321 | 4.9245 | 4.1371 | 3.5592 | 3.1197 | 2.7754 |
| 24 | 21.2434 | 18.9139 | 16.9355 | 15.2470 | 13.7986 | 12.5504 | 11.4693 | 10.5288 | 9.7066 | 8.9847 | 7.7843 | 6.8351 | 6.4338 | 6.0726 | 5.4509 | 4.9371 | 4.1428 | 3.5619 | 3.1210 | 2.7760 |
| 25 | 22.0232 | 19.5235 | 17.4131 | 15.6221 | 14.0939 | 12.7834 | 11.6536 | 10.6748 | 9.8226 | 9.0770 | 7.8431 | 6.8729 | 6.4641 | 6.0971 | 5.4669 | 4.9476 | 4.1474 | 3.5640 | 3.1220 | 2.7765 |
| 30 | 25.8077 | 22.3965 | 19.6004 | 17.2920 | 15.3725 | 13.7648 | 12.4090 | 11.2578 | 10.2737 | 9.4269 | 8.0552 | 7.0027 | 6.5660 | 6.1772 | 5.5168 | 4.9789 | 4.1601 | 3.5693 | 3.1242 | 2.7775 |
| 40 | 32.8347 | 27.3555 | 23.1148 | 19.7928 | 17.1591 | 15.0463 | 13.3317 | 11.9246 | 10.7574 | 9.7791 | 8.2438 | 7.1050 | 6.6418 | 6.2335 | 5.5482 | 4.9966 | 4.1659 | 3.5712 | 3.1250 | 2.7778 |
| 50 | 39.1961 | 31.4236 | 25.7298 | 21.4822 | 18.2559 | 15.7619 | 13.8007 | 12.2335 | 10.9617 | 9.9148 | 8.3045 | 7.1327 | 6.6605 | 6.2463 | 5.5541 | 4.9995 | 4.1666 | 3.5714 | 3.1250 | 2.7778 |

Interest Rate

**Table A.3** Present value of an annuity of £1 per period for $t$ periods $= [1 - 1/(1 + r)^t]/r$

**TABLE A.4**

| Number of Periods | Interest Rate | | | | | | | | | | | | | | | | | | | |
|---|---|---|---|---|---|---|---|---|---|---|---|---|---|---|---|---|---|---|---|---|
| | 1% | 2% | 3% | 4% | 5% | 6% | 7% | 8% | 9% | 10% | 12% | 14% | 15% | 16% | 18% | 20% | 24% | 28% | 32% | 36% |
| 1 | 1.0000 | 1.0000 | 1.0000 | 1.0000 | 1.0000 | 1.0000 | 1.0000 | 1.0000 | 1.0000 | 1.0000 | 1.0000 | 1.0000 | 1.0000 | 1.0000 | 1.0000 | 1.0000 | 1.0000 | 1.0000 | 1.0000 | 1.0000 |
| 2 | 2.0100 | 2.0200 | 2.0300 | 2.0400 | 2.0500 | 2.0600 | 2.0700 | 2.0800 | 2.0900 | 2.1000 | 2.1200 | 2.1400 | 2.1500 | 2.1600 | 2.1800 | 2.2000 | 2.2400 | 2.2800 | 2.3200 | 2.3600 |
| 3 | 3.0301 | 3.0604 | 3.0909 | 3.1216 | 3.1525 | 3.1836 | 3.2149 | 3.2464 | 3.2781 | 3.3100 | 3.3744 | 3.4396 | 3.4725 | 3.5056 | 3.5724 | 3.6400 | 3.7776 | 3.9184 | 4.0624 | 4.2096 |
| 4 | 4.0604 | 4.1216 | 4.1836 | 4.2465 | 4.3101 | 4.3746 | 4.4399 | 4.5061 | 4.5731 | 4.6410 | 4.7793 | 4.9211 | 4.9934 | 5.0665 | 5.2154 | 5.3680 | 5.6842 | 6.0156 | 6.3624 | 6.7251 |
| 5 | 5.1010 | 5.2040 | 5.3091 | 5.4163 | 5.5256 | 5.6371 | 5.7507 | 5.8666 | 5.9847 | 6.1051 | 6.3528 | 6.6101 | 6.7424 | 6.8771 | 7.1542 | 7.4416 | 8.0484 | 8.6999 | 9.3983 | 10.146 |
| 6 | 6.1520 | 6.3081 | 6.4684 | 6.6330 | 6.8019 | 6.9753 | 7.1533 | 7.3359 | 7.5233 | 7.7156 | 8.1152 | 8.5355 | 8.7537 | 8.9775 | 9.4420 | 9.9299 | 10.980 | 12.136 | 13.406 | 14.799 |
| 7 | 7.2135 | 7.4343 | 7.6625 | 7.8983 | 8.1420 | 8.3938 | 8.6540 | 8.9228 | 9.2004 | 9.4872 | 10.089 | 10.730 | 11.067 | 11.414 | 12.142 | 12.916 | 14.615 | 16.534 | 18.696 | 21.126 |
| 8 | 8.2857 | 8.5830 | 8.8932 | 9.2142 | 9.5491 | 9.8975 | 10.260 | 10.637 | 11.028 | 11.436 | 12.300 | 13.233 | 13.727 | 14.240 | 15.327 | 16.499 | 19.123 | 22.163 | 25.678 | 29.732 |
| 9 | 9.3685 | 9.7546 | 10.159 | 10.583 | 11.027 | 11.491 | 11.978 | 12.488 | 13.021 | 13.579 | 14.776 | 16.085 | 16.786 | 17.519 | 19.086 | 20.799 | 24.712 | 29.369 | 34.895 | 41.435 |
| 10 | 10.462 | 10.950 | 11.464 | 12.006 | 12.578 | 13.181 | 13.816 | 14.487 | 15.193 | 15.937 | 17.549 | 19.337 | 20.304 | 21.321 | 23.521 | 25.959 | 31.643 | 38.593 | 47.062 | 57.352 |
| 11 | 11.567 | 12.169 | 12.808 | 13.486 | 14.207 | 14.972 | 15.784 | 16.645 | 17.560 | 18.531 | 20.655 | 23.045 | 24.349 | 25.733 | 28.755 | 32.150 | 40.238 | 50.398 | 63.122 | 78.998 |
| 12 | 12.683 | 13.412 | 14.192 | 15.026 | 15.917 | 16.870 | 17.888 | 18.977 | 20.141 | 21.384 | 24.133 | 27.271 | 29.002 | 30.850 | 34.931 | 39.581 | 50.895 | 65.510 | 84.320 | 108.44 |
| 13 | 13.809 | 14.680 | 15.618 | 16.627 | 17.713 | 18.882 | 20.141 | 21.495 | 22.953 | 24.523 | 28.029 | 32.089 | 34.352 | 36.786 | 42.219 | 48.497 | 64.110 | 84.853 | 112.30 | 148.47 |
| 14 | 14.947 | 15.974 | 17.086 | 18.292 | 19.599 | 21.015 | 22.550 | 24.215 | 26.019 | 27.975 | 32.393 | 37.581 | 40.505 | 43.672 | 50.818 | 59.196 | 80.496 | 109.61 | 149.24 | 202.93 |
| 15 | 16.097 | 17.293 | 18.599 | 20.024 | 21.579 | 23.276 | 25.129 | 27.152 | 29.361 | 31.772 | 37.280 | 43.842 | 47.580 | 51.660 | 60.965 | 72.035 | 100.82 | 141.30 | 198.00 | 276.98 |
| 16 | 17.258 | 18.639 | 20.157 | 21.825 | 23.657 | 25.673 | 27.888 | 30.324 | 33.003 | 35.950 | 42.753 | 50.980 | 55.717 | 60.925 | 72.939 | 87.442 | 126.01 | 181.87 | 262.36 | 377.69 |
| 17 | 18.430 | 20.012 | 21.762 | 23.698 | 25.840 | 28.213 | 30.840 | 33.750 | 36.974 | 40.545 | 48.884 | 59.118 | 65.075 | 71.673 | 87.068 | 105.93 | 157.25 | 233.79 | 347.31 | 514.66 |
| 18 | 19.615 | 21.412 | 23.414 | 25.645 | 28.132 | 30.906 | 33.999 | 37.450 | 41.301 | 45.599 | 55.750 | 68.394 | 75.836 | 84.141 | 103.74 | 128.12 | 195.99 | 300.25 | 459.45 | 700.94 |
| 19 | 20.811 | 22.841 | 25.117 | 27.671 | 30.539 | 33.760 | 37.379 | 41.446 | 46.018 | 51.159 | 63.440 | 78.969 | 88.212 | 98.603 | 123.41 | 154.74 | 244.03 | 385.32 | 607.47 | 954.28 |
| 20 | 22.019 | 24.297 | 26.870 | 29.778 | 33.066 | 36.786 | 40.995 | 45.762 | 51.160 | 57.275 | 72.052 | 91.025 | 102.44 | 115.38 | 146.63 | 186.69 | 303.60 | 494.21 | 802.86 | 1298.8 |
| 21 | 23.239 | 25.783 | 28.676 | 31.969 | 35.719 | 39.993 | 44.865 | 50.423 | 56.765 | 64.002 | 81.699 | 104.77 | 118.81 | 134.84 | 174.02 | 225.03 | 377.46 | 633.59 | 1060.8 | 1767.4 |
| 22 | 24.472 | 27.299 | 30.537 | 34.248 | 38.505 | 43.392 | 49.006 | 55.457 | 62.873 | 71.403 | 92.503 | 120.44 | 137.63 | 157.41 | 206.34 | 271.03 | 469.06 | 812.00 | 1401.2 | 2404.7 |
| 23 | 25.716 | 28.845 | 32.453 | 36.618 | 41.430 | 46.996 | 53.436 | 60.893 | 69.532 | 79.543 | 104.60 | 138.30 | 159.28 | 183.60 | 244.49 | 326.24 | 582.63 | 1040.4 | 1850.6 | 3271.3 |
| 24 | 26.973 | 30.422 | 34.426 | 39.083 | 44.502 | 50.816 | 58.177 | 66.765 | 76.790 | 88.497 | 118.16 | 158.66 | 184.17 | 213.98 | 289.49 | 392.48 | 723.46 | 1332.7 | 2443.8 | 4450.0 |
| 25 | 28.243 | 32.030 | 36.459 | 41.646 | 47.727 | 54.865 | 63.249 | 73.106 | 84.701 | 98.347 | 133.33 | 181.87 | 212.79 | 249.21 | 342.60 | 471.98 | 898.09 | 1706.8 | 3226.8 | 6053.0 |
| 30 | 34.785 | 40.568 | 47.575 | 56.085 | 66.439 | 79.058 | 94.461 | 113.28 | 136.31 | 164.49 | 241.33 | 356.79 | 434.75 | 530.31 | 790.95 | 1181.9 | 2640.9 | 5873.2 | 12941. | 28172. |
| 40 | 48.886 | 60.402 | 75.401 | 95.026 | 120.80 | 154.76 | 199.64 | 259.06 | 337.88 | 442.59 | 767.09 | 1342.0 | 1779.1 | 2360.8 | 4163.2 | 7343.9 | 22729. | * | * | * |
| 50 | 64.463 | 84.579 | 112.80 | 152.67 | 209.35 | 290.34 | 406.53 | 573.77 | 815.08 | 1163.9 | 2400.0 | 4994.5 | 7217.7 | 10436. | 21813. | 45497. | * | * | * | * |
| 60 | 81.670 | 114.05 | 163.05 | 237.99 | 353.58 | 533.13 | 813.52 | 1253.2 | 1944.8 | 3043.8 | 7471.6 | 18535. | 29220. | 46058. | * | * | * | * | * | * |

*The factor is greater than 99,999.

**Table A.4** Future value of an annuity of £1 per period for $t$ periods $= [(1 + r)^t - 1]/r$

TABLE
A.5

| d | N(d) | d | N(d) | d | N(d) | d | N(d) | d | N(d) | d | N(d) |
|---|---|---|---|---|---|---|---|---|---|---|---|
| −3.00 | .0013 | −1.58 | .0571 | −.76 | .2236 | .06 | .5239 | .86 | .8051 | 1.66 | .9515 |
| −2.95 | .0016 | −1.56 | .0594 | −.74 | .2297 | .08 | .5319 | .88 | .8106 | 1.68 | .9535 |
| −2.90 | .0019 | −1.54 | .0618 | −.72 | .2358 | .10 | .5398 | .90 | .8159 | 1.70 | .9554 |
| −2.85 | .0022 | −1.52 | .0643 | −.70 | .2420 | .12 | .5478 | .92 | .8212 | 1.72 | .9573 |
| −2.80 | .0026 | −1.50 | .0668 | −.68 | .2483 | .14 | .5557 | .94 | .8264 | 1.74 | .9591 |
| −2.75 | .0030 | −1.48 | .0694 | −.66 | .2546 | .16 | .5636 | .96 | .8315 | 1.76 | .9608 |
| −2.70 | .0035 | −1.46 | .0721 | −.64 | .2611 | .18 | .5714 | .98 | .8365 | 1.78 | .9625 |
| −2.65 | .0040 | −1.44 | .0749 | −.62 | .2676 | .20 | .5793 | 1.00 | 8413 | 1.80 | .9641 |
| −2.60 | .0047 | −1.42 | .0778 | −.60 | .2743 | .22 | .5871 | 1.02 | .8461 | 1.82 | .9656 |
| −2.55 | .0054 | −1.40 | .0808 | −.58 | .2810 | .24 | .5948 | 1.04 | .8508 | 1.84 | .9671 |
| −2.50 | .0062 | −1.38 | .0838 | −.56 | .2877 | .26 | .6026 | 1.06 | .8554 | 1.86 | .9686 |
| −2.45 | .0071 | −1.36 | .0869 | −.54 | .2946 | .28 | .6103 | 1.08 | .8599 | 1.88 | .9699 |
| −2.40 | .0082 | −1.34 | .0901 | −.52 | .3015 | .30 | .6179 | 1.10 | .8643 | 1.90 | .9713 |
| −2.35 | .0094 | −1.32 | .0934 | −.50 | .3085 | .32 | .6255 | 1.12 | .8686 | 1.92 | .9726 |
| −2.30 | .0107 | −1.30 | .0968 | −.48 | .3156 | .34 | .6331 | 1.14 | .8729 | 1.94 | .9738 |
| −2.25 | .0122 | −1.28 | .1003 | −.46 | .3228 | .36 | .6406 | 1.16 | .8770 | 1.96 | .9750 |
| −2.20 | .0139 | −1.26 | .1038 | −.44 | .3300 | .38 | .6480 | 1.18 | .8810 | 1.98 | .9761 |
| −2.15 | .0158 | −1.24 | .1075 | −.42 | .3372 | .40 | .6554 | 1.20 | .8849 | 2.00 | .9772 |
| −2.10 | .0179 | −1.22 | .1112 | −.40 | .3446 | .42 | .6628 | 1.22 | .8888 | 2.05 | .9798 |
| −2.05 | .0202 | −1.20 | .1151 | −.38 | .3520 | .44 | .6700 | 1.24 | .8925 | 2.10 | .9821 |
| −2.00 | .0228 | −1.18 | .1190 | −.36 | .3594 | .46 | .6772 | 1.26 | .8962 | 2.15 | .9842 |
| −1.98 | .0239 | −1.16 | .1230 | −.34 | .3669 | .48 | .6844 | 1.28 | .8997 | 2.20 | .9861 |
| −1.96 | .0250 | −1.14 | .1271 | −.32 | .3745 | .50 | .6915 | 1.30 | .9032 | 2.25 | .9878 |
| −1.94 | .0262 | −1.12 | .1314 | −.30 | .3821 | .52 | .6985 | 1.32 | .9066 | 2.30 | .9893 |
| −1.92 | .0274 | −1.10 | .1357 | −.28 | .3897 | .54 | .7054 | 1.34 | .9099 | 2.35 | .9906 |
| −1.90 | .0287 | −1.08 | .1401 | −.26 | .3974 | .56 | .7123 | 1.36 | .9131 | 2.40 | .9918 |
| −1.88 | .0301 | −1.06 | .1446 | −.24 | .4052 | .58 | .7190 | 1.38 | .9162 | 2.45 | .9929 |
| −1.86 | .0314 | −1.04 | .1492 | −.22 | .4129 | .60 | .7257 | 1.40 | .9192 | 2.50 | .9938 |
| −1.84 | .0329 | −1.02 | .1539 | −.20 | .4207 | .62 | .7324 | 1.42 | .9222 | 2.55 | .9946 |
| −1.82 | .0344 | −1.00 | .1587 | −.18 | .4286 | .64 | .7389 | 1.44 | .9251 | 2.60 | .9953 |
| −1.80 | .0359 | −.98 | .1635 | −.16 | .4364 | .66 | .7454 | 1.46 | .9279 | 2.65 | .9960 |
| −1.78 | .0375 | −.96 | .1685 | −.14 | .4443 | .68 | .7518 | 1.48 | .9306 | 2.70 | .9965 |
| −1.76 | .0392 | −.94 | .1736 | −.12 | .4522 | .70 | .7580 | 1.50 | .9332 | 2.75 | .9970 |
| −1.74 | .0409 | −.92 | .1788 | −.10 | .4602 | .72 | .7642 | 1.52 | .9357 | 2.80 | .9974 |
| −1.72 | .0427 | −.90 | .1841 | −.08 | .4681 | .74 | .7704 | 1.54 | .9382 | 2.85 | .9978 |
| −1.70 | .0446 | −.88 | .1894 | −.06 | .4761 | .76 | .7764 | 1.56 | .9406 | 2.90 | .9981 |
| −1.68 | .0465 | −.86 | .1949 | −.04 | .4840 | .78 | .7823 | 1.58 | .9429 | 2.95 | .9984 |
| −1.66 | .0485 | −.84 | .2005 | −.02 | .4920 | .80 | .7881 | 1.60 | .9452 | 3.00 | .9987 |
| −1.64 | .0505 | −.82 | .2061 | .00 | .5000 | .82 | .7939 | 1.62 | .9474 | 3.05 | .9989 |
| −1.62 | .0526 | −.80 | .2119 | .02 | .5080 | .84 | .7995 | 1.64 | .9495 | | |
| −1.60 | .0548 | −.78 | .2177 | .04 | .5160 | | | | | | |

This table shows the probability [N(d)] of observing a value less than or equal to d. For example, as illustrated, if d is −.24, then N(d) is .4052.

**Table A.5** Cumulative normal distribution

# INDEX